With this provocative and deeply researched work, Aravindan Neelakandan makes a case for Hindutva, not only as a political movement, but also as a cultural movement, and in his words, 'a very relevant stream of consciousness...on this planet.' Whether one is a supporter or a critic of Hindutva, Neelakandan's work is essential for understanding its worldview and its historical and philosophical underpinnings.

—Dr. Jeffery D. Long
Carl W. Zeigler Professor of Religion, Philosophy, & Asian Studies
Dr Long is the author of *A Vision for Hinduism: Beyond Hindu Nationalism* (2007), *Historical Dictionary of Hinduism* (2011) and *Hinduism in America: A Convergence of Worlds* (2020)

This book by Shri Aravindan Neelakandan lives up to what one has come to expect from him: probably the most comprehensive and erudite book on *Hindutva* specifically, perhaps since the one written by Veer Savarkar himself a hundred years ago. It goes into the psycho-social origins of Dharmic traditions in India, how they differ from homogenising world views, and how both interact with modernity. Finally, it covers all the important personalities, especially from the Sangh, who have contributed to this cause and also hints at a way forward. The void left behind by Ram Swarup has partially been filled by the author. May he write many more books!

—Harsh Gupta Madhusudan
Investor, Coauthor, '*A New Idea of India*' (2020)

If there is one term that evokes extreme reactions in contemporary times and across nations, though largely detrimental ones, it is undoubtedly 'Hindutva'. The familiar modus operandi has been to locate and evaluate Hindutva alongside extremist, violent right-wing ideologies from other nations and to force-fit similarities and thereby draw false equivalences. Globally, violent calls to dismantle it and view it as one of the biggest dangers that humanity seems to face have become only too stereotypical and commonplace. In the wake of this motivated cacophony, an academic and scholarly work that lays out the contours of the term, its history & origins, its features, its evolution through the march of time and what the future portends has been conspicuously and deliberately missing by its absence. It is here that Aravindan Neelakandan's masterful book that is meticulously researched and referenced, fills a major gap in our understanding of what Hindutva is, how it came about and where it is headed. Going beyond the usual penchant to peg the term to politician, revolutionary and ideologue Vinayak Damodar Savarkar, Neelakandan traces a large arc of Hindutva's past—from being the 'essence of Hinduism' to Hinduism that resists predatory forces and also one that is modern and reformist in its outlook, driven by the desire to unify Hindu society from all ills and rigid divisions. His analysis punctures the claim of Hindutva being a rigid, orthodox, casteist, misogynist and xenophobic worldview—tags and slurs that are so easily and loosely associated with it the world-over by motivated people who have made little effort to scratch beneath the surface. As Neelakandan rightly points out, Hindutva is not an ideology, but a historical and civilizational process that belies all straightjackets of an ideological framework. From the hoary past to the contemporary times, Neelakandan's fascinating narrative marches through time periods in a racy and lucid manner, holding together the reader's attention and interest. Vexatious issues such as Hindutva's treatment of minorities of all kinds too has been dealt with in an objective and critical manner. The book needs to be universally welcomed as possibly the first-ever comprehensive and well-documented effort to strip away all the motivated campaigns that have been heaped on this term and to resurrect it in its pristine glory. If you want to understand what Hindutva actually is and stands for, then this magisterial work of Anand Neelakandan is a must-read.

—Dr. Vikram Sampath
Author, Historian, & Fellow of the Royal Historical Society

In this important, even pathbreaking book, Aravindan Neelakandan proceeds with the assumption that Hindutva is not an ideology, but a historical-civilizational process. This initial epistemic precaution saves him from turning into either a fervent defender of Hindutva or its apologist in the face of the mounting criticism. Instead, Neelakandan shows how Hindu culture and civilization has found the wherewithal to defend itself not just militarily, but intellectually whenever it faced life-threatening attacks. Seeing Hindutva as part of this age-old upsurge, Neelakandan also argues against its ownership or control by any one political or cultural group. Hindutva belongs to—and is an expression of—Sanatana Dharma. As such it must flourish not in any one trajectory, predetermined by any one dominant form of advocacy or other. Rather, its multiple paths and flights into the future already show a global Hindu reassertion and renaissance after such a long and dark interregnum."

—Makarand R. Paranjape
PhD., Author, Professor of English, Jawaharlal Nehru University

---

Aravindan's *Hindutva: Origin, Evolution and Future* is a grand journey of core Hindu ideas as they have evolved, expanded and endured over thousands of years. It is a story of seers, thinkers and activists who have shaped the cultural and intellectual discourse in India. Hindutva, in this journey, comes out not as a monolithic identity seeking to crush dissent and diversity, but as a dynamic and organic process that rests on the solid foundations of spiritual pluralism (*Shashtra*), open exploration and constructive dialogues (*Shashtrartha*). This is a work of profound scholarship and deep sensitivity that removes various distortions around 'the last pagan tradition' of the world and therefore helps in its revival for benefit of humankind.

—Dr Ram Sharma
Director, Indus Institute of Special Studies, & HOD
Centre for Indic Studies

There have been many books on the history of Hinduism and Hindutva, but this one is different, and significant, because it (correctly) takes a step back and identifies that our current situation is part of a global bio-psycho-sociological churn, something playing out over millennia, far beyond the lifespans of any one individual or organization or state. Aravindan, at his core, is a nature-lover and science-spirited, and it is this perspective that suffuses this book and makes it special. While there is plenty of ground-breaking content within this expansive, encyclopedic book, I believe the sections on the neurobiological connections of Hindu meditative and ritual practice, which tie the history of Hinduism to the broader evolutionary inheritance of the human species, are going to be very impactful in the years to come.

—Dr. Anand Venkatraman
Neuroscientist and Consciousness Researcher

HINDUTVA

Origin, Evolution and Future

HINDUTVA
Origin, Evolution and Future

Aravindan Neelakandan

Title: Hindutva: Origin, Evolution and Future
Author: Aravindan Neelakandan

ISBN: 978-93-92209-06-2
Edition: 1

Published by:
BluOne Ink LLP

Publisher's Address:
306, Tower-I, Assotech Business Cresterra,
Plot No. 22, Sector 135, Noida.

Website: www.bluone.ink
Email: publisher@bluone.ink

Printed in India at Thomson Press (India) Ltd.

Dedicated to

Srimat Swami Madhurananda Guru Maharaj (1922–1999)
Founder, Hindu Dharma Vidya Peedam,
Sri Vivekananda Ashram, Vellimalai, Kanyakumari District

Contents

Preface *xi*

Acknowledgements *xiii*

1. The Origins: Hindutva 1

2. Bharat Mata, Vande Mataram and Akhand Bharat 46

3. Cow Worship, Cow Slaughter and Beef 108

4. Racism, Casteism, Social Emancipation and Hindutva 144

5. Hindu Sanghatanists before the Sangh: Lives, Controversies, Values and Visions 211

6. Rashtriya Swayamsevak Sangh 298

7. Science and Hindutva 410

8. The Harmonizing Samanvaya and Protection of Theo-diversity 470

Conclusion *657*

Endnotes *659*

Glossary *713*

Index *728*

Preface

Hindutva: Origin, Evolution and Future studies *Hindutva* in both critical and holistic terms—an approach that is oft found missing in most studies on Hindutva, where a lot of critical knowledge has been left out either intentionally or out of ignorance. This omission has led to characterize Hindutva as a dangerous exclusivist majoritarian supremacist ideology. Hindutva is often studied similar to other extreme right-wing ideologies. However, the thesis presented in this book is built on the strong foundation that Hindutva is not an ideology but a process—a historical-civilizational process. As such, it does not fit the expectations of any ideological framework.

As a process, Hindutva predates Savarkar. There have been many contributors to it beyond Savarkar and even the Rashtriya Swayamsevak Sangh (RSS), the organization most prominently associated with Hindutva. Further, Hindutva is not monolith. It cannot be a monolith by its very nature. As a very fluid process, it is more a river than an ideology or dogma. There are many streams feeding into this river. From Vedic rishis to Veer Shivaji, Sri Aurobindo to Mahatma Gandhi, Veer Savarkar to Pandit Nehru, Acharya J. C. Bose to Bodhisattva Ambedkar, Pandit Deendayal Upadhyaya to Narendra Modi—the contributors and influencers as well as the manifestations of the flow of Hindutva are varied and even may look contradictory to each other. At another level, Hindutva has many streams flowing into it—Vedic, Buddhist, Jain, atheistic streams. Christianity, Islam and Marxism also interact with and influence Hindutva.

This really necessitates that one must jettison the usual academic and political frameworks to study Hindutva and Hindutva organizations. This book is an attempt at that.

This book is an answer to another fundamental question: Is Hindutva different from, and perhaps even opposed to, Hinduism?

The answer is in a Buddhist story that is known to every Indian child.

> It was a bright day, and a majestic swan was flying across the clear sky of Kapilavastu. Devadatta of the royal family, the cousin of crown prince Siddhartha, aimed his arrow at the bird, and the arrow found its mark.
>
> The wounded swan, though not dead, fell to the ground. The graceful Siddhartha, ever filled with compassion, embraced the wounded swan. He removed the arrow and healed it with great care. In a few weeks, the swan was well and healthy.
>
> Now Devadatta came and demanded that the swan be returned to him. After all, had it not been for his arrow, Siddhartha would not have found the swan. Siddhartha realized what would happen if the swan was given to Devadatta. He refused and took extra care of the bird. The dispute finally went to the court of the king.
>
> As the wise men of the court and the king contemplated over the situation, an old man appeared. The aura of righteousness around him was unmistakable and commanding. He declared that life does not belong to the one who has hurt it but to the one who rescued it from a near-painful death experience, healed its wounds and nursed it back to a rejuvenated life. Everyone agreed, and Indra, who had come disguised as an old man, disappeared.
>
> However, Siddhartha said that while the swan definitely did not belong to the one who intended to kill, hurt and injure it, it did not even belong to him who had cared for, nursed and protected it. He set free the majestic swan, Raja Hamsa, into the vast expanse of blue sky.

What is true for that *hamsa* is also true for Hindu Dharma, which includes its society, its history and its civilization.

> Hindu Dharma is the wounded swan. Hindutva is the healing care of Siddhartha.

Naturally, the Devadattas, who shot the arrows, are angry and frustrated. They demand that the swan belongs to none and that it must be set free. But their aim is not to set the swan free but to kill the wounded swan. This book explains both the wound of the swan and the healing care of Tathagata.

Acknowledgements

This book is in a way the result of a lifelong pursuit. My gratitude at the feet of my parents, both of whom I lost in 2020. They set me on this odyssey. My wife, Fontia Daniel Neelakandan, my son, Shukoh Neelakandan, and my daughters, Shuptah and Shubruh, have been my greatest supporters in writing this book, giving me the freedom and taking on the responsibilities of the house at some very crucial junctures. I can only say that they have been a blessing.

Swarajya, where I work as contributing editor, is a great place that befits an eternal misfit like me. They have been understanding and hugely supportive of me. The whole team has been like an extended family—Amar, Prasanna, Arush, Harsha and the entire team, who have supported me both institutionally and individually. It is hard to thank them; they are family.

When I first proposed this book that has always been in my mind, I thought I could finish it in a week, but it took two-and-a-half years. Two people who catalysed my writing and were extraordinarily patient were Ruchi Sood of Atharva Forum, and Praveen Tiwari—two friends to whom I owe the realization of this book. Thank you for the patience and faith you have shown in me.

I thank *Vijaya Bharatam* for allowing me to make use of their office and take digital copies of old issues. I thank the scholars for their valuable feedback despite a busy schedule: Dr Anand Venkatraman, Sri Harsh Madhusudan, Dr Jeffery D. Long, Dr Makarand R. Paranjape, Dr Ram Sharma and Dr Vikram Sampath—thank you all for your time, patience and good will.

Working with the BluOne Ink team has been a smooth sail. Particularly for a book like this, such a smooth sail is a rare thing. But the BluOne Ink team has gone beyond being a mere publisher; as a team, they have understood the spirit of the book, working in resonance with that spirit. Right from the beginning till the very end, Partho and Geetanjali, as well as the editing team, have put their heart and soul into the book, and I am ever thankful to them.

1

The Origins: Hindutva

The term 'Hindutva' appears in the writings of nineteenth century Bengali Hindu thinkers. Vinayak Damodar 'Veer' Savarkar (1883–1966) famously explained the term in his cryptic work *Essentials of Hindutva* (1923). Today a significant section of Indian polity, academia and media consider it a supremacist ideology, similar to fascism and Nazism of the West. Many Hindutva sympathizers also perceive it as a political ideology, distinct from Hindu Dharma, meant to protect Hindus or a movement to establish a theocratic state.

This chapter argues that 'Hindutva' translated as 'Hinduness' is inseparable from the word 'Hindu' historically.

Numerous debates rage on about the term 'Hindu'. Is it a colonial artificial construct, merely two hundred years old? Or is 'Hinduism' five thousand years old or more, as most of its adherents instinctively feel? Is it a religion? Is it a geographical description, which later came to be identified with a religion? The terms 'Hindu', 'Hinduism' and 'Hindutva' are thus perceived differently. Each perception has its own worldview, values and motives.

Savarkar himself made an enigmatic statement: Hinduism is 'only a derivative, a fraction, a part of Hindutva'. A holistic understanding of Hindutva can emanate from expanding the real significance of this statement. Hindutva becomes a universal set, of which Hinduism becomes a subset. This is a process understanding of Hindutva. The term 'Hindu' itself arises from the process that is Hindutva. This chapter explores this process relation between 'Hindutva', 'Hinduism' and 'Hindu'. It further aims to show how delinking any of these elements is fundamentally flawed.

Prehistoric to Historic Times: The Possibility of Neuro-cultural Emergence

In 1976 a psychologist from Princeton University Julian Jaynes (1920–1997) published a book *The Origin of Consciousness in the Breakdown of the Bicameral Mind*. Since then it has been hailed, debated, challenged and also dismissed with ridicule. Today, studies into the neurobiological basis of religious experiences as well as evolutionary approach to the phenomenon of religion have rekindled and have even validated some of the core concepts put forth by Jaynes. Neuroscientist Michael Persinger who invented the famous 'God Helmet' goes to the extent of comparing the thesis of Jaynes to the Copernican and Darwinian revolutions.[1]

The book suffers from the usual Eurocentric approach. Jaynes based his hypothesis exclusively on Homeric literature and the Bible. Yet, what it puts forth is refreshing and astonishing. Jaynes argues that from the prehistoric to the end of the ancient urban civilizations, humans possessed what he calls a 'bicameral mind'. In this phase, humanity had not successfully integrated the two hemispheres of the brain. The intuitive right hemisphere was the master and the analytical left hemisphere simply executed, subordinate to the intuitive flashes that happened in the right hemisphere. These right-hemisphere-based intuitions were received as auditory hallucinations which in turn were accepted as the voice of gods. In other words, there was a time in human civilization when gods (and goddesses) literally 'spoke'. However, with the emergence of urban civilization, the bicameral mind could not support the increasing complexity and related stress of everyday life. The development of writing too was a factor in undermining the 'gods' of the bicameral mind. Soon a void developed. Bicameral-mind-based civilizations collapsed or got transformed into civilizations in which the expression of the individual selves came to the fore. It was with the breakdown of the bicameral mind that consciousness emerged. Jaynes dismisses India with a single line and zeroes in on the Hebrew Bible:

> India hurtles from the bicameral Veda into the ultra-subjective Upanishads, neither of which are as authentic to their times…While the Old Testament, even as it is hedged with great historical problems of accuracy, still remains the richest source for our knowledge of what the transition period was like. It is essentially the story of the loss of the bicameral mind, the slow retreat into silence of the remaining elohim, the confusion and tragic violence which ensue, and the search for them again in vain among its prophets until a substitute is found in right action.[2]

And this painful transition from the bicameral mind was achieved in the monotheistic model in a very ruthless manner:

> Groups of bicameral men certainly persisted until the downfall of the Judean monarchy, but whether in association with other tribes or with any organization to their hallucinated voices in the form of gods, we don't know...What happened to them? From time to time, they were hunted down and exterminated like unwanted animals. Such a massacre in the ninth century BC seems to be referred to in I Kings 18:4, where out of some unknown, much larger number, Obadiah took a hundred nabiim and hid them in caves and brought them bread and water until the massacre was over. Another such massacre is organized by Elijah a few years later (I Kings 18:40).[3]

Despite the extremely sweeping statements, oversimplification of the problem of consciousness and a definitely flawed later day approach to the rise of self-awareness about consciousness as well as inner processes in humans and its monotheism-centric approach, Jaynes's approach is important. Justin E. H. Smith, author and professor of history and philosophy of science at the University of Paris, finds that 'Jaynes's approach is in principle promising', though he thinks that Jaynes was 'severely compromised by his hasty hermeneutical method'.[4] Darwinian philosopher of consciousness Daniel Dennett considers the hypothesized breakdown of the bicameral mind a 'software revolution' in the history of human species which was discovered by Jaynes. It is an 'absolutely wonderful idea', even if Jaynes got the details wrong.[5]

Since then, many discoveries in archaeology and neuroscience have revealed the hitherto unsuspected power and role of religious impulses in shaping human civilization. For decades, anthropologists believed that religion appeared after the hunter-gatherers started organizing human settlements. However, the archaeological finds at Göbekli Tepe, (Turkey, circa 9600 BCE) strongly suggest 'a reversal of that scenario...evidence that organized religion could have come before the rise of agriculture and other aspects of civilization'.[6] Psychologist Matt J. Rossano takes the roots of religion even further back. According to him, 500,000 years before present, hominids could have engaged in group rituals like singing and dancing that in turn could induce altered states of consciousness which in turn could enhance social bonding.[7]

All these facts point out that religious experiences with strong neurological basis and religion as a biocultural phenomenon have played a very significant role in shaping human evolution. Clearly Jaynes stands vindicated to a very significant extent. For a significant number of anthropologists today, the period from the middle of first millennium BCE called the 'Axial Age' is associated with the birth of radical new shift in the religious history of humanity. Though the term 'Axial Age' was coined by Karl Jaspers (1883–1969) as early as 1949, Jaynes opened up independently the possibility of complete complex neuropsychological developments associated with that age. Sidarta Ribeiro, a Brazilian neuroscientist, considers the hypothesis of Jaynes as one whose time to be tested has arrived at last for science through what he calls 'data-driven mental archaeology' and the initial results seem to validate what Jaynes had speculated:

> For many years, this shrewd hypothesis seemed untestable. Corollaries such as the right lateralization of auditory hallucinations were dismissed as too simplistic—although schizophrenic patients present less language lateralization. Yet, the investigation by Diuk et al. (2012) represents a pioneering successful attempt to test Jaynes' theory in a quantitative manner.... Diuk et al. show that the evolution of mental life can be quantified from the cultural record, opening a whole new avenue of hypothesis testing for Jaynes' theory.... As Jaynes would have predicted, the rise and fall of entire societies seems to be paralleled by increases and decreases in introspection, respectively.[8]

In 2015 a team of inter-disciplinary scholars, philosopher Nicolas Baumard, psychologists Alexander Hyafil and Pascal Boyer along with classicist Ian Morris published a study which considered the 'increased affluence' as an important factor in explaining the emergence of 'ascetic wisdom and moralizing religions' 'in three places in Eurasia (the Yellow and Yangzi rivers, the Ganga Valley, and the eastern part of the Mediterranean)' which resulted in 'old "ritual" religions emphasizing short term strategies would have been supplanted by new "spiritual" religions that emphasized long-term strategies through asceticism and self-control techniques.'[9] Unlike Jaynes, however, this work looks into what happened in Indic religious evolution and has this to say:

> In the Ganges Valley, Buddhism, Samkhya, Ajivikism and Jainism appeared in the Magadha and Kosama kingdoms in the late fifth century BCE, although ascetic movements were probably present already. These movements spread rapidly to the rest of India under the Mauryan Empire (ca. 320–185 BCE). Vedism, in turn influenced by these spiritual movements, underwent a massive transformation, integrating asceticism and karma in the new Brahmanic orthodoxy.[10]

Though a welcome development in the direction of studying the evolution of religion and its role in civilization as well as its own evolution through complex social realities, the papers usually show a deficiency when it comes to

Indic religions. For example, the above passage has four references, of which three are Buddhist and one (probably for the ascetic traditions being already there) Upanishadic.

In reality, thinking of a transitional phase, or emergence of the 'spiritual' after the 'ritual', itself may be fallacious.

In his critical evaluation of the hypothesis of Jaynes, Professor Justin Smith considers 'a change of practices', particularly writing as crucial to the emergence of a rational individual awareness and that this rational emergence 'required no genetic mutation, no internal transformation in the brain causing the voices to go silent and a new, more ordered and logical regime to take over.'[11] Whatever we call the transition, 'emergence of ascetic religious worldviews' or 'Axial Age' or 'breakdown of bicameral mind', etc., the completeness of the psyche demanded rituals to be present along with the transition. Justin Smith converges with the conclusion of Vedicist Frits Staal (1930–2012) who for decades studied the Vedic fire rituals and states:

> It may be that the shift in modern philosophy, and modern thought in general, to language as the locus of significance in human life has in turn caused repetition to appear... as "mere repetition." The philosopher Frits Staal, who immersed himself in Brahminic rituals for many decades, developed a theory of ritual as a system of "rules without meaning," which, he came to believe, is in fact more primordial than language in giving order and orientation, if not conceptual tools, to human existence....Thus, for Staal ritual is not simply the superstitious chaff we might hope to remove from the wheat of rationalized religion; it is the reason of religion itself, although in a deeper sense of "reason" than we ordinarily understand it, as order rather than conceptual articulation. It is ritual, some have felt, that holds the world together.[12]

As will be seen soon, the 'ritual' and the 'spiritual' co-evolved in India with organic linkages, no doubt necessitated by factors that were socio ecological, cultural and what can be deemed spiritual. The Vedic concept of *ṛta* that formed the basis of the ritual universe of Vedic society created a seamless transition by mapping itself with the developments of the notion of Brahman and Atman. Dr William K. Mohanty, author and professor of religion, explains how the ritualistic and introspective continuity has been achieved in Vedic religion through the concept of ṛta which in turn is central to Vedic rituals.

> Poetry, ritual and contemplative vision are closely connected to each other in Vedic religion; what pertains to one therefore pertains to the others as well....Because the later Vedic understanding of Brahman and thus of Atman is closely associated with the early Vedic concept of ṛta, we can say that Vedic sensibilities as a whole revolved

> around the cultivated awareness and energetic expression of the universal artfulness of being.[13]

In other words, with the centrality of impersonal ṛta to the ritual universe, the transition was not only seamless but also set in India earlier than in, say, Greek or Roman cultures. Given the fact that the studies seen so far into this important problem that connects our past, present and future have been centred around Western scholars studying the phenomena of the 'Axial Age' problem, it becomes essential to look into Indic literature to see how Hindu scholars themselves viewed these developments in their spiritual traditions, if they did observe them at all.

Indic Integration of 'Axial Age' Developments

The development of the inner transformation and its guiding of the very course of civilization, as can be seen in the evolution of the Indic civilization, provides interesting insights and even a better framework for understanding the evolution of that inner phenomenon which Jaynes had labelled as the emergence of consciousness.

Decades before Jaynes, Sri Aurobindo (1872–1950), the poet-seer whose system was defined as 'integral psychology' by eminent Indian psychologist Dr Indra Sen and who 'is now coming to be regarded as one of the pioneers of transpersonal psychology'[14], saw Vedic deities as 'higher powers' of the human mind. In a series of articles written between December 1918 and January 1921, Sri Aurobindo proposed that 'the poets of the Veda had another mentality than ours', particularly with respect to the way they viewed the outer and inner worlds. According to him, 'these godheads were at once masters of physical Nature and its principles and forms their godheads and their bodies and inward divine powers with their corresponding states and energies born in our psychic being … living and powerful suggestions and counterparts of inner things.'[15]

What one finds in the Indic context is then this: the bicameral mind, rather than 'breaking down', gets integrated into a thorough, holistic self through a systematic cultivation of inner disciplines. This is well attested in Harappan iconography as well as in the Vedic literature. In Harappan iconography, we find horned animals and deities on many seals. Most of these seals can be definitely categorized as belonging to the bicameral era if viewed from the Jaynesian perspective. However, the horned deity systematically evolves into an introspective deity. We find him sitting in a yogic posture surrounded by dwarfed animals. One famous seal of a horned deity in a yogic posture shows the male deity with three faces seated on a throne in the yogic position with what appears to be an erect phallus. According to Harappan archaeologist Jonathan Mark Kenoyer, 'the yogic posture and erect phallus have tantric overtones, representing the use of meditation and sexual powers to control or maintain balance in nature'.[16]

In other words, contrary to Baumard et al., the 'ascetic' 'introspective' traditions and techniques had already established themselves well in Indian society and we can only say that the so-called 'Axial Age' churn should have set in earlier in India. If in 'later Hinduism', both yoga and tantra were considered to have developed into well entrenched traditions of inner exploration, then 'later Hinduism' should have been there in place in medieval and late Harappan civilization already.

The same is true of Vedic literature. Many of the later metaphors for contemplating the self in Indian tradition have their origin in the imagery of the Vedas. The famous metaphor of the two birds is one example. Attributed to the seer Dīrghatamas, the *Rig Veda* hymn (1.164.20) speaks of two birds in the same tree united by bonds of friendship—one eats the fruit and the other merely observes. The imagery is again employed in the *Mundaka Upanishad* (3:1:1) and repeated in the *Svetashvatara Upanishad* (4:6). This is perhaps one of the clearest expressions of the integration of the bicameral mind which then gets developed in the later Upanishads. *Atharva Veda*, in a striking premonition of Jaynes, even hints that all gods abide within man as cows in the cow pen (2.8.37).[17] This is only one aspect of the integration.

The process also had other causes and ramifications which indicate that it was not a very serene and calm spiritual process cut off from the harsh realities of life. Both the transition and the integration of the bicameral mind in ancient India, as it happened elsewhere in the other cultures around the world, was definitely triggered by social tensions and/or also by natural calamities upon the organized human ecosystems. These in turn initiated their own sociocultural changes and dynamics. There is a strong possibility that the changes in monsoon should have played a crucial role. Harappan civilization had to face a nine-hundred-year-long drought because of an abrupt cold and dry climate in the northwest Himalaya, which in turn reduced the summer monsoon as well as the discharge of the life feeding rivers to the Harappan people.[18] This negatively impacted agriculture which in turn should have extremely disturbed the Harappan social fabric. The transition was definitely a churning that deeply impacted the psychological and physical existence of ancient Indians.

It was at this time that the Vedic rituals, which were already an integral part of the society and culture, should have started playing a very important psychological and socio-ecological role in helping society to tide over without massive violence. The strong pan-Indian association of the Vedic sacrifice as the ritual harbingers of the monsoon might have been imprinted in Indian psyche during this prolonged drought period. The change was also accompanied by the change in the social power structures and the purpose of the Vedic hymns. Eminent Indian philosopher Sarvepalli Radhakrishnan (1888–1975) noted the 'change in the atmosphere' in the transition period from the *Rig Veda* to the *Yajur* and *Sama Vedas* as well as *Brahmanas* in the following words:

> The freshness and simplicity of the former give place to the coldness and artificiality of the latter. The spirit of the religion is in the background while its forms assume great importance...The hymns are taken out of the *Rig Veda* and arranged to suit sacrificial necessities. The priest becomes the lord....The religion of the *Yajur Veda* is a mechanical sacerdotalism....The truly religious spirit could not survive in the stifling atmosphere of ritual and sacrifice.[19]

Despite the philosopher-statesman passing such a harsh hindsight judgment on the observed transition from the *Rig Veda* to *Yajur Veda*, the Jaynesian model suggests that the 'mechanical sacerdotalism' might have served yet another important function. It could have provided the psychosocial buffer zone for the natural evolution and integration of the inner seeds in the Rig Vedic literature. Dr Radhakrishnan himself, seemed to have taken this idea from Indologist Maurice Bloomfield. According to Bloomfield, the *Yajur Veda* 'presents the exceeding growth of ritualism and sacerdotalism as time went on'. Yet in his not-so-flattering account of the *Yajur Veda*, there is an important hint to the function that the Vedic ritual system played in the transition period. In his 1908 book *The Religion of the Veda*, Bloomfield observes:

> We notice that the main object of the ceremony, namely, the worship of the gods, is lost sight of. Solemn, pompous performance, garnished with lip service, now occupies the stage. The performance is supposed to have a magic or mystic power of its own, so that every detail of it is all-important. Mechanically, by its own intrinsic power, it regulates the relation of man to the divine powers.[20]

As Vedic deities became silent, the concept of the ritual became symbolic of a cosmic order. As against this, when the gods cease to speak in Babylonia, the cuneiform texts inform how 'the headache envelopes him like a garment'—the one who has no god. The buffering transitional role of the Vedic ritual is explicitly stated in early Tamil literature. *Paripādal*, which belongs to the

Sangham literature (though millennia later), explains how the Vedic ritual as performed makes even those who deny the gods exclaim in affirmation because of its sheer aesthetics.[21]

The chanted word of the Vedic ritual played an important role in this transition and integration to unity. Perhaps almost like a delicate operation were the Vedicists moving the sounds inside into audible chants and creating a harmonizing bridge. What Professor Antonio T. de Nicolas in his study of Vedas says throws some light in this context:

> The Ṛg *Veda's* song-poems were not only oral creations but also chanted creations. While the other sensory media provided discontinuity, sound alone, in spite of its evanescence, gave the Ṛg Vedic man the instance of eternal presence and unity he so well used to further develop the world of ṛta, the ability to be bodily at home with any god, any human personality, any perspective.[22]

Further, while Julian Jaynes considered the process to have taken place as a historical event, modern research indicates that this may recur continuously in our species. The chanted words along with the mathematics of music which in turn was highly integrated with the geometry of the ritual altar could have aided the Vedic civilization to respond to the transition in a different way. And more importantly this transition became an archetype in the inner exploration of the Hindus—the gods cultivated through inner practices merging into a vast all connecting unity—outwardly displayed in the immersion celebrations of the deities in the ocean.

Deeper Historical Analysis of Ram Swarup

While Jaynes dismissed Indic transition from the bicameral mind with a single line, Hindu scholar Ram Swarup (1920–1998) traced the evolution in a more detailed way in Indian historical context:

> ...During Vedic days while they lasted, Gods were a living presence. The worshippers established a sense of deep intimacy, trust and affinity with them. Everything around was astir with divinity, instinct with life. The Fire was no ordinary fire, just to cook one's food and warm one's cold nights. He was a messenger between the worshipper and his Gods...The Earth was not just sand, clod and mud. She was a veritable Mother on whose breast we all fed. She was a psychic reality...But this kind of approach is possible only when man is in a state of innocence as it seems he was during the ancient Vedic days.... The Gods are still in their handiwork and have not

> withdrawn...But something snaps, and that stage passes away...Vedic Gods suffer deflation. And strangely enough, it is first at the hands of the Upanishadic sages through the teachings of *brahmavāda* and *ātmavāda*.[23]

So far, the sequence that Ram Swarup develops, though completely independent of Jaynesian idea of the bicameral mind breakdown, gels with the latter. But there is one important difference. For Ram Swarup, the gods are not mere auditory or visual hallucinations arising out of the right hemisphere to a clueless infantile humanity. Rather, the gods and goddesses are inner luminous phenomena who co-create a healthy reality. Now Ram Swarup departs from Jaynes, and here comes the unique Indic feature in the post-bicameral mind evolution of humanity:

> But in reality, it was not real deflation. Rather it was an attempt to bring out the unity of spiritual life which in the Vedas was being expressed in a different way, but the sense of which was getting lost...The old Vedic approach was possible so long as the soul did not lose its primeval innocence, its childlike quality, its intuitive way of feeling and living the world. But when the soul put on another attribute, when the intuitive heart receded and the thinking mind came to the fore, the old approach was bound to lose its effectiveness.
>
> ...Upanishadic ātmavāda was an attempt to recover the old sense of intimacy with gods but under new conditions when they had withdrawn from before the eyes of man behind a veil...Later on, yoga came. It was an attempt to discover methods and processes by which to enter the depths of the heart where Gods had retired under increasingly more difficult conditions. In the Mahabharata, we have a great inner balance between all these forces. All aspects are equally and fully stressed and brought out. We have here the Vedic intimacy with gods; we have the highest form of ātmavāda without gods being interiorized; we have Brahmavāda with gods retaining their fullest status.
>
> ...But in the course of time, the spirit of the Mahabharata was lost. Brahmavāda of the *Upanishads* gave way to *mayavāda* and their ātmavāda to *anātmavāda*...The new doctrines were perhaps attempts at new adjustment with the new mentality of the age and new powers of the soul, which were strong in analysis and intellection but weak in synthesis and intuition...Whatever their fall from an original pedestal, gods in Buddhism were still great merit-forms and not desire-forms or ego-forms as they tend to become in different religions.[24]

Thus, instead of the complete breakdown and subduing of the right hemisphere to the left with a theological iron cage, a flexible harmony was achieved. Vedic deities, as they transformed, changed and evolved into the main gods and goddesses of later Hinduism, retained both the playful intuitive qualities of the bicameral phase while integrating themselves with further exploration of other dimensions of the inner self.

Persian Schism and Emergence of 'Hindu' Consciousness

Even as this mode of churning was happening in Vedic India, there has been another stream of development where there was complete breakdown and elimination of the bicameral mind with stiff opposition to its integration with the former state. The ancient Persian text *Vendidad* speaks of 16 holy lands which were created by Ahura Mazda and then made unfit for the ancestors of ancient Iranians by Angra Mainyu. Of these 16 lands, one was Hapta Hindu—which is the praised Sapta Sindhu of Vedic civilization.[25] The very name *Vendidad* is the contraction of the Avestan language *Vî-Daêvô-Data*—given against the *daevas* (demons).

It is significant the way the term 'Hindu' had been used in this context. It is used to differentiate the land which has become 'unfit' for the worshippers of Ahura Mazda—the one God who had emerged after the complete breakdown of the bicameral mind in the framework of Jaynes. It was the term used by a post-bicameral civilization which had sought monotheism (along with the innovation of proto-Satan as antagonist in the package), and it was used to denote the civilization that went for the integration of bicameral mind and thus refused to abandon the old gods as demons but sought to unite them with further evolution. The Soma/Haoma tradition of the undivided Indo-Iranian people was banned by the cult of Zoroaster. His *gathas* alluded to the 'filthiness of the intoxicant', which was also the 'averter of death'.[26]

The political use of Zoroastrian monotheism catalysed the evolution of a centralized king-state. It also meant a sustained depletion of theo-diversity.[27] Darayavaush or Darius I (522–486 BCE) declared very emphatically a monotheist-deity-centralized king correlation:

> A great God is Ahura Mazda, who created this earth, who created yonder sky, who created man, who created happiness for man, who made Darius king, one king over many, one lord over many ... Ahura Mazda when he saw this earth in commotion, thereafter he bestowed it upon me, he made me king. I am king. By the grace of Ahura Mazda, I set it in its place. ...This which has been done, all that by the will of Ahura Mazda I did. Ahura Mazda bore me aid, until I did the work.[28]

Incidentally, he also clashed with a section of Magi. Here is an interesting paradox. In his Behistun inscription there are hints of the destruction of temples of the devas by one Guamata. Now Guamata was for the politics of Darius in the opposite camp—opposing Darius and hence was considered a usurper. Darius I himself had restored the demolished temples.[29] Like Constantine, centuries after him, Darius I, a monotheist Zoroastrian with a binary worldview, had attempted a syncretism while officially favouring the Zoroastrian religion but advocating at best the tolerance for the older religions while also emphasizing their inferior status with reference to the one true religion.

It was his Hamadan inscription which mentions Hindus as a people—the inhabitants of lower Indus valley. Darius I was followed by his son Khshayarsha or Xerxes (486–465 BCE). He boasts openly about the destruction of the temples of the devas. There is an uncanny resemblance to similar boasting of Islamic invaders destroying Hindu temples centuries later. He mentions in his inscriptions his hold on the regions of Gadara and Hidu (Hindu). According to historian Upinder Singh, the destruction of temples 'may allude to goings-on in Gandhara'.[30] The inscription is indeed revealing:

> When I became king, there was among the provinces (a land where there was) confusion. Then Ahura Mazda brought me aid: by the favour of Ahura Mazda, I smote that land and put it down in its place. And among the countries there was (one) where previously the daevas were worshipped. Then by the favour of Ahura Mazda, I destroyed that temple of the daevas and proclaimed: 'The daevas shall not be revered.' Where the daevas were previously revered, I piously worshipped Ahura Mazda and the Arta.[31]

Expansionist Monotheism, Divine Feminine and Hindu Genesis

The transition of the 'Axial Age' was dealt with by the Hindus and the Iranians in fundamentally different ways. While Iranians opted for one God, Hindus opted for one Unity. The unity which the Upanishadic seers formulated had its roots in Vedic hymns, chants and rituals.

Though Brahman itself was impersonal and gender-neutral in Upanishadic thought, the Vedic Goddess Aditi, 'that which is not divided and that which is not bound or limited', and the 'divine continuum',[32] provided the prototype for this Brahman. The *Rig Veda* speaks of her as 'the sky; the air; the mother, and father and son; all the gods and the five tribes; whatever has been born and whatever shall be born' (1.89.10). Sure enough, Aditi appears in *Brhadaranyaka*

Upanishad in her own name.[33] We can construe that while the Iranian and monotheist resolution of bicameral mind breakdown was centred on the masculine creator God, the Indic solution of Unity had the Divine Feminine as its substratum.

Wherever such monotheism arose, it was not very monolithic as later Christianity and Islam tend to project it. Just as how Hindus moved away from Iranian monotheism, there were also multiple voices which wanted a higher integration in place of complete breakdown and tearing away from the bicameral roots.

Elaine Pagels, eminent historian of ancient Christianity, notes three such protest voices from the Nag Hammadi texts (manuscripts from perhaps 300–400 CE discovered in 1945 near the Egyptian town of Nag Hammadi) in her seminal book *The Gnostic Gospels*. A text titled *On the Origin of the World* speaks of how the monotheist God boasted:

> 'I am God and no other one exists except me.' Then the text informs the reader that when he said that, he 'sinned against all of the immortal ones' and 'when Faith saw the impiety of the chief ruler, she was angry...She said, "You err, Samael (i.e. blind god). An enlightened, immortal humanity (anthropos) exists before you!"'

When the 'creator' God made the statement that there was no other god before him, another text *Hypostasis of the Archons* states that he sinned against (the Entirety) and that a voice came forth from above the realm of absolute power, saying, 'You are mistaken, Samael.' Even the fundamental monotheistic proclamation, 'I am a jealous God, and there is no other God beside me' is questioned by *The Secret Book of John*, which states that by announcing this, he indicated to the angels that another God does exist; for if there were no other one, of whom would he be jealous?[34]

The gods who became emanations within Judaism, died out as monopolistic religions took over. Nevertheless, the Jewish mystic school of Kabala is an excellent instance of a unity in the monotheistic milieu as distinct from expansionist or monopolistic monotheist religions. Why was there such resistance to the replacement of all old deities with the new creator-God of monotheism? Ram Swarup explains the fundamental problem of such monotheist solutions:

> One God is an outer sense of the idea of One Reality. In this sense God is a unit, not a unity, a unit superior to and truer than other units. Unfortunately, it is in this sense that the doctrine has been accepted by its votaries. And in this sense, it has been a fertile source of religious fanaticism and bigotry.[35]

There was also the issue of power and control. Elaine Pagels calls this the 'politics of monotheism'. She explains:

> As the doctrine of Christ's bodily resurrection establishes the initial framework for clerical authority, so the doctrine of the 'One God' confirms, for orthodox Christians, the emerging institution of the 'one bishop' as monarch ('sole ruler') of the church.[36]

Roman emperor Constantine would use this to consolidate his own power. He was actually repeating what Darius had declared in Persia almost 600 years before. But the power structures that Constantine forged proved more successful and enduring than the one attempted by Darius.

There was yet another crucial dimension in the Iranian breakdown of the bicameral mind. Unlike the ethnic monotheism of Judaism, Iranian monotheism had an adversary to Ahura Mazda—the evil Ahriman who would contribute substantially in both Islamic and Christian theologies to the evolution of the Satan. In what she calls 'the social history of Satan', Pagels shows how the fight between God and Satan in Christian gospels has led Christians to identify 'their opponents, whether Jews, pagans, or heretics, with forces of evil, and so with Satan'.[37] Later, this Christian concept of Satan would move on to Islam as well.

The divide had become well-defined. Hindus, as a people, opted for a holistic and a pluralistic alternative in dealing with the transition from the bicameral mind. To Ram Swarup, the distinct nature of the Hindu approach comes out well in the epic Mahabharata:

> The Mahabharata develops a different viewpoint. There the sages and gods meet in great mutual welcome. They offer each other seats and homage. They do it because they see in each other the reflections of the same truth, power of Yoga and Dharma.[38]

Thus, the word 'Hindu' when it is used almost 3,000 years earlier has a very strong religious-spiritual significance and is not a mere geographical term. Was it a term given to Indians by the Persians and just a Persian distortion of the term 'Sindhu'?

A Ritual Connecting Inner Unity and the Sacred Geography

The inner developments naturally manifested themselves in external symbols. In the Harappan civilization, we come across one such symbol which shows synchronizing a central Vedic ritual with the sacred geography of India. It should be noted that the Rig Vedic hymns and rituals already had in them structures which gravitate towards the unique inner unity and a cosmic harmony.

According to Prof. Ernest G. McClain who studies musical mathematical commonalities across the ancient civilizations, particularly Vedic, says that as the five Vedic tribes spread over the 'Land of Seven Rivers', the barriers between the inner and the outer seem to have blurred, the Vedic chant-hymns are 'immersed in a symbolism which revelled in its power to express a cosmic unity, invented by men whose mathematical rigor matched their musical and poetic feeling, and in whom reverence was mated with humor'.[39]

Among the seals of the Harappan civilization, the highest frequency seal is that of the unicorn. Iravatham Mahadevan (1930–2018), an Indologist from Tamil Nadu, was the first one to point out the Vedic link while studying the Harappan unicorn and the cult object before it. Being a student of Sanskrit, he was familiar with the Vedic ceremony of the Soma filtering ritual. He says he was 'reminded of the two most powerful images in thc Soma chapter of the *Rig Veda*, *Pavamana* and *Indu*'. Pavamana means the flowing Soma, and Indu, the Soma drops collected at the bottom of the filter.[40]

The word Indu in the authoritative Monier-Williams Sanskrit dictionary represents not only the Soma drop but also the Soma itself. In the *Brahmanas,* Indu is used for moon. Monier-Williams also points out that 'the connection between the sense "Soma juice" and "moon" in the word Indu has led to the same two ideas being transferred in classical Sanskrit to the word Soma'. He also adds that it is the name of a river.[41] In the famous river hymns of *Rig Veda* (*Nadistuti Sukta* X.75), the River Indus is named as 'Good Soma' (Su-Soma). So, we have the droplets of Indu and the flowing Su-Soma, Sindhu. Both Indu and Sindhu thus refer to the central Vedic religious ritual—Soma.

In 1935 archaeologist C. L. Fabri brought out 'odd parallels' between depictions of animal motifs in punch-marked coins and Harappan seals. Fabri compared the depictions of 'the most frequent ones' which included 'the humped Indian bull, the elephant, the tiger, the crocodile and hare'.[42] Of course, the horse was left out as it was not depicted in the Harappan seals. Interestingly, in most of the coins belonging to the Sangham Age (300 BCE to 300 CE) wherever the horse is shown an object was depicted similar to the cult-object seen in Harappan unicorn seals.[43] This leads one to wonder if the Indu or the Soma was then a connecting strand across the regional principalities ruled by local chieftains.

While Indu and Sindhu are both related to the Soma ritual, the words Soma and Indu are usually related to the moon.

Hieun Tsang, the famous Buddhist scholar-monk pilgrim to India in the seventh century CE, makes an explicit connection to this term and associates it to the name of the nation in a spiritual sense. He says that India was 'anciently called Shin-tu, also Hien-tau'. However, 'according to the right pronunciation, it is called *In-tu*' says the Buddhist monk from China. And then he proceeds to point out that in Chinese the term also refers to the moon. 'This is appropriate,' says the seventh-century pilgrim because 'the bright connected light of holy men and sages, guiding the world as the shining of the moon, have made this country eminent, and so it is called In-tu'.[44]

These connections provide us another way of looking at the name 'Hindu', not as a Persian pronunciation of Sindhu or Indus but as a name that has direct roots in the Vedic-Harappan ritual as well as with connection to the sacred geography of India. That this Soma cult-object had become an accepted symbol of temporal power in South India by third century BCE shows the connections had started creating a unitary cultural matrix that encompassed the entire land mass from the Vedic Sapta Sindhu to South India.

Samanvaya to Cultural Matrix

The inner transition through integration by discovering a holistic 'higher' self becomes the hallmark of Indic culture and spirituality. This gives rise to a pluralistic society that has, as its core functional component, the movement of *samanvaya* or *samavaya*, a term which comes from the Ashokan pillar edicts but antedates him by centuries. It was popularized by Sri Ramakrishna Mission seer-thinker Swami Ranganathananda (1908–2005), who summarizes its working through centuries in an accurate yet bird's-eye view of Indian history:

> Our age-old tradition is samanvaya or samavaya...That is the unique glory of India, Hinduism, and of the Hindu spirit and attitude, the pulse of its mother-heart, with an impressive continuity of nearly 5,000 years. But, alas, this is not only not understood or appreciated by other religions, but even considered as a weakness to be exploited! The welcome that the Hindus gave to the Jews, who came to settle in Kerala when their temple in Jerusalem was shattered by Roman tyranny in 70 AD, is well known; so also the welcome given to Zoroastrians, or the Parsis from Iran, who had a glorious history and civilization for over 1,000 years, and who came as refugees in the eighth century AD when their home country was conquered by aggressive Arab Muslim armies and their religion destroyed and people massacred.[45]

That the samanvaya has been at work in shaping the psyche of a Hindu nation can be seen in the Gupta emperors adhering to the Vedic traditions, patronizing two of the greatest achievements of so-called heterodox Buddhism—the Ajanta Caves and the Nalanda University reached their pinnacle under the non-Buddhist Gupta kings.

The white Hun Mihiragula, despite his embracing the worship of Vedic deity Rudra, was defeated by a confederacy of Hindus under Narasimha Gupta (Baladitya) and Yasodharma about 528 CE.[46] This event is highly glorified in ancient Indian history and has crucial import: though India had assimilated invading clans into her social fabric, Mihiragula was marked as an alien and driven out of India. This is mainly because of his continued massacre of Buddhist monks and destruction of their monasteries. India's core historical movement identifies anything that threatens the samanvaya and unity as alien and fights to remove invaders from its organism or detoxifies the invader of the expansionist tendencies of monocultures and assimilate them.

This process of debates and dialogues with a common cultural matrix despite diversity of worldviews, some of which even looked antagonistic to each other, had been observed even during the Mughal period to define who the Hindus were. Even Marxist historian Irfan Habib, known for his prejudice against Hindu movement and subtly favouring a colonial constructionist school of Hinduism, writes:

> The author of *Dabistan-i-Mazahib* is hard put to describe what the beliefs of a Hindu are, and ultimately, he takes shelter in a very convenient position—Hindus are those who have been arguing with each other within the same framework of argument over the centuries. If they recognise each other as persons whom we can either support or oppose in a religious argument, then both parties are Hindus. The Jains, although they rejected Brahmanism, were still Hindus because they were arguing and polemicising with Brahmins. Such arguments were not taking place between Hindus and Muslims. The Muslims did not share any basic terminology with the others. Muslims had their own framework, an ideological framework, the semitic framework.[47]

The resurfacing of the word Hindu again in a prominent way of defining the national and spiritual self-identity is seen during the Islamist incursions. Here again it was not the invasions per se but the accompanying religious aggression and proselytizing zeal that stirred the national conscience to make the term Hindu a rallying focus point for indigenous communities.

The Resurfacing of 'Hinduness'

The 'Hinduness' or the Hindu awareness as a process more than just a geographical category is attested clearly in the fourteenth century inscriptions which appear in South India. Prof. Arvind Sharma, the Birks Professor of

Comparative Religion at McGill University, in his critical paper on Hinduism, Hindustan and Hindutva points out that the term 'Hindu-Raya-Suratrana' was used by Vijayanagara emperors in 'one form or another ... continued in use by Bukka's successors for at least ... 250 years, through three changes in dynasty'.[48] Could this simply mean 'Indic' without any religious connotations and only a geographical term? Studying the evolution of 'Hinduism', Indologist David Lorenzen, concludes:

> One interesting earlier reference comes from Andhra Pradesh. Cynthia Talbot has analysed how the military expansion of Muslim dynasties into the Andhra region in AD 1323 led to a sharper sense of regional, political and religious identity among the Hindu population in the region. She notes that the title 'Sultan among Hindu kings (*hindu-raya-suratrana*)', perhaps the earliest use of the term 'Hindu' in an Indian language, 'begins to figure in Andhra inscriptions from C.E. 1352 onward'. Talbot suggests that these references to Hindu kings possibly implied more a geographical than a religious identity. Negating this is the fact that Muslim dynasties had already been in control of most of the Ganges valley since the end of the twelfth century, for about 150 years before the first appearance of the phrase 'Sultan among the Hindu kings' in the Andhra inscriptions. In the circumstances, how could the Andhra kings consider their Muslim opponents to be non-Hindu in a merely geographical sense, i.e., non-Indians?[49]

Lorenzen also refers to an earlier Hindu source *Prithviraj Rasa*, a historical romance attributed to a Chand Bardai. Traditionally thought to be written not long after the 1192 CE defeat of Prithviraj Chauhan by invader Muhammad Ghori, scholars consider that all, or all but one of the versions of the text are more recent, but they have not reached a consensus about which was written when. Here too in all versions, 'Hindus' and Turks are mentioned, and in one version the religious nature of the term Hindu is well-defined.[50]

From the inscription of the Persian emperor Darius in the fourth century BCE to the Andhra inscription of fourteenth century CE, the term Hindu has had a consistent inner meaning of a cultural, spiritual and geographical nature. It has defined the one constant defining genome sequence in the ever-evolving national organism of the Hindu nation. The term 'Hinduness' or 'Hindutva' thus defines this ongoing process more appropriately rather than the term 'Hinduism'. Within the next two centuries during the Maratha ascendancy, the term '*Hindavi Swaraj*' was used by the legendary Shivaji (1630–1680) in a letter written in 1645 to Dadaji Naras Prabhu. By this term, Shivaji meant 'Hindu religious autonomy' for entire India. Sambhaji in his Danapatra calls Shivaji as 'Haindava-dharma-Uddharaka'.[51]

The fact that the modern Indian nation-state owes its conception to this stream of 'Hinduness' was explicitly acknowledged by Bengali poet Rabindranath Tagore (1861–1941) in his essay 'Shivaji O Guru Govind':

> The first and great leader of Maratha history had formed in his mind a clear concept of the establishment of a Hindu kingdom before launching a movement in the historical state for the rise of Maratha power. Whatever he did, conquest of territories, annihilation of the enemy, expansion of the kingdom, all this was a part of his All-India project.[52]

Bankim Chandra considers the Sikh Khalsa as the next Indic attempt at the second nation-state formation after Shivaji.[53] In both the cases, it was not religion in the narrow sense or ethnicity or language which formed the basis of this nationhood, but a Hinduness which included religion in the broadest sense and also a related geo-cultural matrix. So, by the end of seventeenth century, the term 'Hindu' had come to mean the national character of India, more identified with its core historical process of Hinduness than any specific set of religious beliefs but with the definite religious spirit of theo-diversity and an underlying spiritual unity. After centuries of unrelenting fight, it had tired the Islamic invaders and rulers and had made them accept the Indic cultural and spiritual superiority.

Under Colonialism

With the arrival of European colonialism, the dynamics of Hindutva entered a new phase. Even the word 'Hinduism', which is often claimed to have been coined by the British, actually came from a Hindu. The Brahmo social reformer Raja Rammohan Roy coined the term in 1816–1817. As Lorenzen rightly observes, the fact that it was an Indian-born Hindu who coined the very term Hinduism embarrasses the proponents of the British construction of Hinduism. It is interesting to note here that Roy was speaking of the Unity of God as true Hinduism in 1817. In 1821 he claimed:

> No people on earth are more tolerant than the Hindoos, who believe all men to be equally within the reach of Divine beneficence, which embraces the good of every religious sect and denomination.[54]

Rammohan Roy was against the evangelical attack on Hinduism. Missionaries who first eagerly promoted him as a possible leading intellectual

Hindu convert to Christianity, later even refused to publish his articles. Roy, on his part, created a Hindu framework for an encounter with Christianity. Even while accepting Jesus as an ethical—even a divine—personality, he rejected as gross absurdity the central theme of evangelical Christianity—Jesus dying on the cross as the substitutionary death for the sins of humanity.[55]

By the nineteenth century, in the southernmost part of India, at the princely state of Travancore, which was then under the protection of the British East India Company, both the forces of social stagnation and proselytizing were working complementarily to affect a complete destruction of local spiritual traditions. The Iyya Vazhi movement by Iyya Vaikundar (1810–1851) countered this situation in the most organized form. Though Iyya Vaikundar did not use the word 'Hindu' as such, he developed a remarkable critique of colonialism in Puranic language. The Asuric forces which came as Ravana, Duryodhana and Sura-Padman (subdued by Skanda-Muruga) in previous yugas and Puranic times, came in this yuga in two forms: the Kali-Neesa, which was social stagnation in the form of untouchability, and White-Neesa, or colonial disruption of Dharmic society and proselytizing. In condemning the proselytizing of both Islam and Christianity, he brought in the cosmic unity of Chithakasa against the mutually exclusive monopolistic gods:

> Those with vain scriptures competing for mutual supremacy
> Ultimately end up in mutual destruction;
> One such wants to put the cap over all the people;
> The other one wants to bring all under the cross and cloak;
> Such people of tyrannical scriptures always want to fault others.[56]

The movement manifested every feature that would characterize it as a Hindutva movement—including the saffron flag. Opposition to Christian and Islamic proselytizing, integration of Shaiva-Vaishnava streams, the avatar concept, use of Puranic metaphors for empowerment, visualizing a united India, uniting society under the saffron flag—are some of the salient features of this movement, which effectively halted the proselytizing while simultaneously empowering a depressed section of the society into a vibrant community. The Iyya Vazhi movement saved Hinduism in South Travancore from being annihilated by the missionary crusade. During the early period of British colonial stranglehold over South India, the seer-reformer Ramalinga Vallalar (1823–1874) used the term 'Hindu' in 1872 and defined Hindu scriptures as 'providing inner traditions for immortal wisdom' which he says 'if present in other religions are approximations of Hindu scripture'.[57]

Hinduness Redefines the Hindu

Meanwhile, the colonial-missionary-machine was set on defining who were and were not Hindus from the point of view of a superior ruling race. It used racial and other colonial frameworks towards this end. The Hindutva response was to redefine the term delving into deeper unity from which Indian culture draws its sustenance. Throughout the beginning of the colonial missionary onslaught, Hindutva manifested in the form of resistance to proselytizing and emphasizing the unity of humanity at the fundamental level.

The thought leaders of Bengali renaissance, Rajnarayan Basu (1826–1899), Bankim Chandra Chatterjee (1838–1894) and Chandramohan Basu (1844–1910) contributed mightily to the explicit redefining of Hindutva. Of these three, both the usage of the term by Bankim Chandra and the worldview of Rajnarayan Basu, in the context of their social milieu remarkably prefigures the Savarkarite usage of the term later. Chandramohan Basu who wrote a tract titled *Hindutva* veered more towards obscurantism in his social views. Historically, the works of Rajnarayan Basu and Bankim Chandra were the ones who played a decisive role in shaping how Hindutva was conceptualized in the modern context.

Rajnarayan Basu, who was called by historian Jadunath Sarkar as the 'grand old man of Indian nationalism', was also a strong social reformer. He emphasized the Hindu nature of Indian nationhood. In his lecture 'Hindu Dharmera Śreṣṭhatā' (Greatness of Hindu Dharma, 1879), Basu gives an organic simile for the nature of Hindu national life—that of 'an ancient banyan tree, each of whose branches has become a new tree'. At the same time, it 'has an internal substantiality (ābhyantarika sārabattā) such that it can regenerate itself, like the banyan'.[58]

In his work *Dharmatattva* ('Dharmic Principles', 1888), Bankim Chandra Chatterjee used the term 'Hindutva' in the context of universal love being the defining criterion of one's Hinduness:

> The divine is present in all human beings, so that if I love the divine reality, I love all humanity as well, and if I do not love all humanity, I cannot love the divine reality. As long as I have not understood that I and the world are not different, I have not gained either knowledge, dharma, devotion, or love. This universal love (prīti) lies at the root (mūla) of the Hindu dharma, and there can be no *Hindutva* without this inalienable and indivisible love.[59]

As the nation moved into the modern age under colonial rule, Swami Vivekananda (1863–1902) provided the next important definition of the term

'Hindu', in his paper on Hinduism (1893). He emphasized the authority of the Vedas as the basis of Hinduism:

> Now this word 'Hindu' as applied to the inhabitants of the other side of the Indus, whatever might have been its meaning in ancient times has lost all its force in modern times; for all the people that live on this side of the Indus no longer belong to one religion. There are the Hindus proper, the Mohammedans, the Parsees, the Christians, the Buddhists, and Jains. The word 'Hindu' in its literal sense ought to include all these; but as signifying the religion, it would not be proper to call all these Hindus. It is very hard, therefore, to find any common name for our religion, seeing that this religion is a collection, so to speak, of various religions, of various ideas, of various ceremonials and forms, all gathered together almost without a name, and without a church, and without an organisation. The only point where, perhaps, all our sects agree is that we all believe in the scriptures—the Vedas. This perhaps is certain that no man can have a right to be called a Hindu who does not admit the supreme authority of the Vedas.[60]

Though Swami Vivekananda emphasized the 'supreme authority of the Vedas', he also conceded the possibility of the inclusion of the heterodox Indic streams of Jainism and Buddhism within the Hindu family: 'Perhaps we may even take in parts of Buddhism, and of Jainism too, if they would come in—for our hearts are sufficiently large.'[61] Vivekananda consistently distinguished the meaning of the term 'Vedas' from the usual meaning of a specific scripture:

> The Hindus have received their religion through revelation, the Vedas...But by the Vedas no books are meant. They mean the accumulated treasury of spiritual laws discovered by different persons in different times.[62]

Thus, despite the apparent narrowing down of the definition to the Vedic authority, Swami Vivekananda kept the definition open-ended for further inclusion and evolution. According to Dr Anantanand Rambachan, an academician on Hinduism, Vivekananda crucially differs from Adi Sankara (seventh century CE) as Vivekananda placed personal experience above the scriptural authority (sruti) whereas, Adi Sankara considers scripture as the authoritative way to obtain the true knowledge of Brahman.[63] Rambachan considers this as result of Vivekananda being influenced by the nineteenth century challenge of science and European rationalism. But there is a tradition in Indic religions—particularly in Shaktic (Goddess) tradition—which consider scriptures as being subordinate to the divine experience presented by the imagery of the essence of the scriptures as the dust at Goddess's feet or the platform on which the Divine Feminine stands. In the celebrated work on the Goddess attributed to Adi Sankara titled *Soundarya Lahari*, the same imagery is used. That the image predates Adi Sankara but was prevalent even inside the deep forests of South India is attested by *Chilapathikaram*—the Tamil epic in which tribals are depicted as worshipping the Goddess standing on the scriptures as all permeating flame of consciousness.[64] Hence, despite Vivekananda making the authority of Vedas central to the definition of 'who is a Hindu', the definition is still open-ended and far more flexible than it seems at first glance. Swami Vivekananda is well in sync with the pan-Hindu tradition when he makes Vedas and realization an integral part in his definition of a Hindu.

The next important definition of the word 'Hindu' was given by the Indian freedom fighter Bal Gangadhar Tilak (1856–1920). Given in the form of a Sanskrit verse, the definition provides three criteria to call oneself a Hindu. They are: (i) Belief in the authority of the Vedas, (ii) Variety of means (of approaching the Divine), (iii) No insistence on single deity and form.[65] Here again, one finds that two out of the three criteria emphasize theo-diversity and flexibility. Another important aspect must be noted here. Despite the charges of Tilak being an orthodox supporter of caste, (which he was, to some extent, but he was also, to some extent, a radical social reformer), he did not bring in the *Varna* system as fundamental in his definition of the term 'Hindu'.

A significant definition of not the word Hindu but 'Hindutva' comes from Rabindranath Tagore (1861–1941) in his essay titled *Hindutva* (1901). This was almost a decade and a half before Savarkar would use the term. Tagore engages with the French thinker Renan's idea of 'national soul' and tries to adapt it to India. While Renan actually breaks the national soul into 'one … the wealth of public memories of the past, the other the mutual consent, the desire to dwell in the same place—the desire to preserve in a suitable way the whole of the inheritance one has received', Tagore finds Hindutvas being beyond the physically and tangibly unifying features that are present in Western nationhood. He explains Hinduness as a civilizational process that is extraordinarily inclusive:

> In the most astonishing, gigantic society that Hindu culture has created, there is not a race (*jat*) that has not found a place in it. The ancient Shakas, the Jaths and Rajputs; those of mixed origin like the Nepalis, the Assamese, the Rajvanshis; the Dravidians, Tailangis, the Nayars—in spite of their different languages, class (Varna), religion and customs (*acar*), they are all living together keeping up a great harmony within the wide Hindu society. By giving shelter to so many different people, Hindu culture in various ways has deprived itself, and still it has not abandoned anyone. High and low, homogeneous (savarna) and not homogeneous (asavarna), all of them it has drawn close, to all of them it has given the shelter of religion.

> Renan has shown that it is difficult to bring out the basic traits of a nation. Nationalness does not only rest on unity of people/race (*jati*), unity of language, unity of religion and geographical circumstances. Similarly, it is difficult to ascertain where lies the root of Hindu-ness (Hindutva). Various races (*jati*), various languages, various religions, many contrary customs and habits have found a place within Hindu society. The circumference is as large as it is difficult to find its centre. The field of unity of Hindu society is extremely wide, therefore it is not easy to bring out its original basis in the midst of such wide expansion and variegatedness.[66]

Tagore goes on to explain how to serve and carry on this 'Hinduness' into the present age—through service to all humanity. The passage presented here prefigures Savarkar's Hindutva as a historical and civilizational process subsuming in its grand flow the different religious streams. That Hinduness can harmonize in it 'various races, various languages, various religions, many contrary customs and habits', differentiates it from Western notion of religion, and according to Tagore it is precisely this that defines Hinduness. In 1902 when talking about the 'justification of India' he wrote:

> The sole effort of India has always been to establish unity in diversity, to direct many paths to the same end, and to perceive the one in the many profoundly and unambiguously.

This usage of the word 'unity and diversity' would later enter the Nehruvian vocabulary and be highly popularized in post-independent India as Nehru's own coinage. Though Tagore in his 1917 essay asserted that he had 'outgrown' the 'idolatry of the Nation ... almost better than reverence for God and humanity' and condemned the 'extremists' for bringing in nationalism similar to the Western notions into India, in 1923 he spoke of Indian history. Though he had accepted unquestioningly the Aryan-non-Aryan theory of the British, which made him take a completely crude binary of Aryan and non-Aryan elements in Indian culture, he still made the mingling of the Aryan and non-Aryan as setting the basis for India's unique ability to absorb diverse elements unlike the Western model which exterminated the other.[67]

Sri Aurobindo, the revolutionary-politician turned mystic seer-poet, in his now famous Uttarpara speech delivered on May 30, 1909, gave the following definition of Hinduism:

> But what is the Hindu religion? ... That which we call the Hindu religion is really the eternal religion, because it is the universal religion which embraces all others.... This is the one religion that can triumph over materialism by including and anticipating

> the discoveries of science and the speculations of philosophy. It is the one religion which impresses on mankind the closeness of God to us and embraces in its compass all the possible means by which man can approach God. It is the one religion which insists every moment on the truth which all religions acknowledge that He is in all men and all things and that in Him we move and have our being. It is the one religion which enables us not only to understand and believe this truth but to realise it with every part of our being. It is the one religion which shows the world what the world is, that it is the Lila of Vasudeva. It is the one religion which shows us how we can best play our part in that Lila, its subtlest laws and its noblest rules. It is the one religion which does not separate life in any smallest detail from religion, which knows what immortality is and has utterly removed from us the reality of death.[68]

In this definition, Sri Aurobindo explicitly states that Hinduism is defined so because of the geographical locality in which it was preserved and nurtured in 'the Hindu nation … in this Peninsula it grew up in the seclusion of the sea and the Himalayas, because in this sacred and ancient land it was given as a charge to the Aryan race to preserve through the ages'. Here it is to be noted that the use of the term 'Aryan race' is not the same as the term was used in the European context, where it means a biological race. In fact, Sri Aurobindo was one of the earliest critics of the concept of race as a pseudo-scientific category. A decade after his Uttarpara speech Sri Aurobindo again defined Hinduism:

> And if we are asked … what is Hinduism… we can answer that Indian religion is founded upon three basic ideas or rather three fundamentals …. First comes the idea of the One Existence of the Veda to whom sages give different names, the One without a second of the Upanishads who is all that is and beyond all that is, the Permanent of the Buddhists, the Absolute of the Illusionists, the supreme God or Purusha of the Theists who holds in his power the soul and Nature—in a word the Eternal, the Infinite. This is the first common foundation; ...For its second basic idea is the manifold way of man's approach to the Eternal and Infinite....The third idea… is that while the Supreme or the Divine can be approached through a universal consciousness and by piercing through all inner and outer Nature, That or He can be met by each individual soul in itself, in its own spiritual part, because there is something in it that is intimately one or at least intimately related with the one divine Existence.[69]

This definition has a strong affinity to that of Tilak. Both definitions emphasize pluralism and flexibility. It should be noted that the definition of Sri Aurobindo elaborates on the affirmative criterion of Tilak, namely the acceptance of Vedas as the Vedic 'idea of One Existence' and associates with it the Buddhist concept, though Buddhism rejects the scriptural authority of

Vedas. Once again, here the simplistic reading of the term 'Vedas' as similar to a scriptural authority as in a faith-based religion is rejected in favour of a deeper and larger understanding of the term.

Hindu Cultural Identity

In 1921 when Mahatma Gandhi was questioned by a section of traditionalists as to how a Hindu could oppose caste system, Gandhi gave a reply which contained his own definition of a Hindu:

> I call myself a sanatani Hindu, because, 1. I believe in the Vedas, the Upanishads, the Puranas and all that goes by the name of Hindu scriptures, and therefore in avatars and rebirth, 2. I believe in the varnashrama dharma in a sense in my opinion strictly Vedic but not in its present popular and crude sense, 3. I believe in the protection of the cow in its much larger sense than the popular, 4. I do not disbelieve in idol worship…The reader will note that I have purposely refrained from using the word divine origin in reference to the Vedas or any other scriptures…My belief in the Hindu scriptures does not require me to accept every word and every verse as divinely inspired…But that which distinguishes Hinduism from every other religion is its cow protection, more than its varnashrama.[70]

By making cow protection (in a 'much larger sense than the popular') as the distinguishing feature of Hinduness, Gandhi again reinforced, in a more concrete context, an ecologically relevant definition of Hinduness. It was already expressed by Bankim Chandra and implicit in the Vedanta as expounded by Swami Vivekananda and in the writings of Sri Aurobindo. In his book *Hind Swaraj* (1909), Gandhi also put forth an important view which would later play a major role in shaping the Hindutva emphasis on cultural nationalism and the primacy of the cultural unity defining India as a nation, than it being a colonial construct:

> (Our ancestors) saw that India was one undivided land so made by nature. They, therefore, argued that it must be one nation. Arguing thus, they established holy places in various parts of India, and fired the people with an idea of nationality in a manner unknown in other parts of the world. And we Indians are one as no two Englishmen are.[71]

Gandhi was also partially answering the emerging view that India was never a unitary entity but a dark land of warring clans and unrelated linguistic groups, led together by Pax Britannica into civilization and progress. Sri Aurobindo had stated in his Uttarpara lecture that the Hindu 'religion' had been nurtured by the Hindu nation geographically and historically. Now Gandhi considers the very nation unity of India as a modern nation-state predicated on its Hindu cultural unity.

Sri Aurobindo-Gandhi Influence on Later Day Hindutva

Earlier, Sri Aurobindo had stated in his Uttarpara lecture that Hindu 'religion' had been nurtured by the Hindu nation geographically and historically. Later, Gandhi considered the very nationhood of India coming out as part of the Hinduness. The later day Hindutvaites took in both these aspects. To them territorial as well as cultural nationhood and Hinduness organically co-create each other in an almost indistinguishable way—a concept also developed in the writings of Madhav Sadashiv ('Guruji') Golwalkar (1906–1973), the second all India leader of Hindutva movement Rashtriya Swayamsevak Sangh (National Volunteer Organization, RSS). Denying the north-south divide, M. S. Golwalkar used the same argument as Gandhi for the unity of India based on sacred geography:

> The part which is geographically called north is as dear to us as the one called south. Ganga is as holy to us as Cauvery. The great Shivalinga formed out of ice in the Himalayan cave at Amarnath claims the same devotion from all of us as the Linga at Rameshwaram. We are intrinsically one, transcending all superficial barriers of distance, creed or sect.[72]

Later, H. V. Sheshadri (1926–2005), then General Secretary of the RSS, elaborated on this and linked this cultural unity to Hindutva or Hinduness:

> Even Sri Achyut Menon, the former Communist Chief Minister of Kerala felt convinced that the essence of our national entity lies in "Hinduness". A few years back he wrote that he had now come to realize the fallacy of the Communist interpretation of Bharat's history of considering Bharat as a conglomeration of eighteen nationalities. Sri Menon specially pointed to the fact that Adi Shankara had, even as far back as 1200 years ago, travelled to all the four corners of the land and established four Mutts covering the entire length and breadth of the country which shows that our country has been a single national entity since hoary times. Finally, he said that at the root of this national unity lies the Hindu "faith". Sri Menon also clarified that Hindu "faith" is different from mere "religion".[73]

'This is exactly our concept of Hindu nation,' concluded the RSS General Secretary. The prominent identification of this dimension of Hinduness/ Hindutva, namely the reinforcement of the nationhood through sacred geography was brought to the fore prominently by Gandhi. There is yet another aspect of Hindutva that needs to be taken into consideration. The Hindutva discourse never speaks of a Hindu state (*rajya*) but a Hindu nation (*rashtra*). In fact, one of the major axiomatic statements that Hindutvaites learn early in the RSS *shakhas* is that India can never be a theocratic state including a Hindu rajya, precisely because it is a Hindu nation or a Hindu rashtra. And that India will remain a secular state only until it remains a Hindu rashtra. In 1989 K. Suryanarayana Rao (1924–2016), senior RSS worker then in charge of South India, explained in a symposium:

> Hindu Rashtra is generally misrepresented, as a theocratic state or a religious Hindu state. Nation (rashtra) and State (rajya) are entirely different and should never be mixed up. State is purely a political concept. It is political authority with sanction concerned with the governance of the people laying down and directing the policies of the government. The State changes as the political authority shifts from person to person or party to party. But the people and the Nation remain the same. ... That clearly explains the difference between a Rashtra and a Rajya, i.e., Nation and State. Rashtra is eternal and State is transitory. It is like the body and the Soul–Atma. According to Hindu conviction, the Atma is eternal and only the bodies and their forms are changed.[74]

Dr Arvind Sharma points out this aspect of the Hindutva movement which distinguishes itself from other religious or ideological movements which want to establish a theological or ideological state:

> It is significant that the Hindutva rhetoric to this day has largely and centrally been that of a nation (Hindu Rashtra) rather than of a state (Hindu Raj) (even Shivaji spoke of 'Hindu Svaraj,' not Hindu Raj). The key category is not Hindu statism but Hindu nationalism.

However, Dr Sharma is of the opinion that 'the internal contradictions of the word Hindu, however, imperil these exercises, whether one turns to religion or culture'. So, in his paper dealing with Hinduism, Hindutva and Hindustan he concludes:

> Because of the complex nature of the Indian reality, each approach runs into its own limitations; each generates its own dilemma. The regional approach

> generates the dilemma: does India belong to the Hindus or do Hindus belong to India? The religious approach generates the dilemma: Is Hinduism a religion like any other religion or does it itself include other religions, denominationally or universalistically? The cultural approach generates the dilemma: Is Hindu culture constitutive of Indian culture or expressive of it? And finally, the national approach generates the dilemma: Should India opt for the secularism of Hinduism or the Hinduism of secularism? At the heart of each lies the question central to all issues of identity: does the other belong to me or do I belong to the other?[75]

The dynamic process nature of samanvaya discussed above when included woven into the body fabric of Hindutva actually answers this core question by Dr Sharma. Hindutva or Hinduness is in realizing the other as yet another manifestation of the self while at same time inhibiting the expansionist monocultural drives that may be present in the 'other'.

This factor should be taken into consideration even as one looks into how the definition of the term 'Hindu' itself has been predicated upon the above-described features, which have historically acted as the core of Hindutva. Hindutva is the functional manifestation of these core elements of Indian civilization. Naturally, the term Hindu is umbilically linked to Hindutva. Hindutva is the nourisher that makes Hindu become universal human without being expansionist. If cut off from Hindutva, the Hindu lingers and then dies. So, the definition of Hindu is anchored to the nourishing substratum of Hindutva, and this is implicitly acknowledged in the definition of the term as accepted by the Constitution of India itself.

Savarkar-Ambedkar Definition

When in 1923 Vinayak Damodar ('Veer') Savarkar was writing his concise treatise (*Hindutva,* also *Essentials of Hindutva*), he was in an unenviable position. On the one hand, the traditionalists as well as the colonialists, were trying to insist that the caste system was the distinguishing feature of Hinduness. This view had the tactful British support. The Congress leadership was fast gravitating from cultural nationalism towards territorial nationalism in order to facilitate the inclusion of pan-Islamic forces through the Khilafat movement into the national liberation movement. The idea that Hindus are merely another religious community was gaining currency. Even those who recognized the unique nature of Hinduness paid lip service to it in the form of ethereal utopian dreams, seldom worrying about the dangers Hindus as a people faced in pockets of India where their numerical strength was going down.

Religion as a category predominantly meant religion in an Islamo-Christian sense. The term 'nation' was construed mainly as the nation in the nation-state as Europe understood it. Above all, there was the idea of race as a biological entity. In fact, at that time the Aryan invasion theory was axiomatic and was accepted as factual. (Only Swami Vivekananda, Dr B. R. Ambedkar and Sri Aurobindo had questioned the validity of this theory.) It was in such circumstances that Savarkar set out to define Hindutva as a means to salvage the holistic and unique legacy of Hindus and make them aware of their place in the world community. Savarkar rejected the Aryan race as the basis of Hinduness. He strongly rejected the idea of pure races. He rejected the orthodox stand of the Vedas and/or Varna as the common basis of Hinduness:

> All institution is meant for the society, not the society or its ideal for an institution. The system of four varnas may disappear when it has served its end or ceases to serve it, but will that make our land a Mlechchadesha—a land of foreigners? The sanyasis, the Arya Samajis, the Sikhs and many others do not recognize the system of the four castes and yet are they foreigners? God forbid! They are ours by blood, by race, by country, by God. 'Its name is Bharat and the people are Bharati' is a definition 10 times better because truer than that. We, Hindus, are all one and a nation, because chiefly of our common blood—Bharati Santati.[76]

Ultimately, his definition of a Hindu finds as its cornerstone the allegiance to the sacred geography of India. This definition was given by Savarkar in 1939 (based on his earlier work in 1923). In this he states:

> Every person is a Hindu who regards and owns this Bharat Bhumi, this land from the Indus to the Seas, as his Fatherland as well as his Holyland; i.e. the land of the origin of his religion, the cradle of his Faith. The followers therefore of Vaidicism, Sanatanism, Jainism, Buddhism, Lingaitism, Sikhism, the Arya Samaji, the Brahmasamaj, the Devasamaj, the Prarthana Samaji and such other religions of Indian origin are Hindus and constitute Hindudom, the Hindu people as a whole. Consequently, the so-called aboriginal or hill tribes also are Hindus: because India is their Fatherland as well as their Holyland of whatever form of religion or worship they follow. This definition, therefore, should be recognized by the Government and made the test of *Hindutva* in enumerating the population of Hindus in the Government census to come.[77]

In 1941 Dr Bhimrao Ramji Ambedkar, who would later become the chief architect of the Indian Constitution, in his book on the proposal of partition critically examined the alternative Savarkar proposed for Pakistan. While he was critical of the alternative Savarkar put forth for, he was very much impressed by Savarkar's definition of a Hindu:

> This definition of the term Hindu has been framed with great care and caution. It is designed to serve two purposes which Mr Savarkar has in view, firstly, to exclude from it Muslims, Christians, Parsis and Jews by producing the recognition of India as a holy land in the qualifications required for being a Hindu. Secondly to include Buddhists, Jains, Sikhs, etc., by not insisting upon belief in the sanctity of the Vedas as an element in the qualifications.[78]

Perhaps it was this influence which later made Dr Ambedkar adopt a similar legal definition of the term 'Hindu' in his celebrated and controversial Hindu Code Bill:

> to all persons professing the Hindu religion in any of its forms or developments, including Virashaivas or Lingayatas and members of the Brahmo, the Prarthana or the Arya Samaj; (b) to any person who is a Buddhist, Jaina or Sikh by religion.[79]

The definition is both Indic-centred and accommodative of pluralism with an inherent check towards creation of monocultures. The definitions eschew the colonial-traditionalist emphasis on the Vedas as authoritative scriptures and on birth-based caste system in defining who is a Hindu. Thus 'Hinduness' or Hindutva and the word 'Hindu' are organically inseparably related. The term Hindutva has come to mean emphatically the holistic historical, social, cultural and spiritual processes of Indian people. Collectively these processes have preserved a very unique and essential feature in the evolution of human consciousness. While Hindutva or Hinduness definitely has a federation of Indic-religious systems in it, it is much more than any of these religions, including the Vedic. Referring to the common confusion of Hinduism with the Vedic stream of Hinduness alone, Savarkar had pointed out the folly:

> if you identify the religion of the Hindus with the religion of the majority only and call it orthodox Hinduism, then the different heterodox communities being Hindus themselves rightly resent this usurpation of Hindutva by the majority as well as their unjustifiable re-exclusion...The religion of the majority of the Hindus could be best denoted by the ancient accepted appellation, the Sanatan Dharma or the Shruti-Smriti-Puranokta Dharma or the Vaidik Dharma; while the religion of the remaining Hindus would continue to be denoted by their respective and accepted names,

> Sikha Dharma or Arya Dharma or Jain Dharma or Buddha Dharma. Whenever the necessity of denoting these Dharmas as a whole arises then alone we may be justified in denoting them by the generic term Hindu Dharma or Hinduism.[80]

The same organic theo-diversity has been time and again recognized and reinforced as the defining unique feature of Hinduism by Indian Supreme Court. Though the term theo-diversity has been introduced earlier, it is apt here to define the term in the context of the present international milieu, particularly with respect to globalization. Prof. Lokesh Chandra, the Buddhist scholar who used the term extensively, explains it as the endorsement of the universality of human civilization:

> "True universality" will be rich diversity, with no single meaning. The various lines, the many realities will be lived in everyone's deepest feelings....Universality of civilization than a universal civilization will seek civil behaviour in the affirmation of diversity. Such a civilization will be multiple and the centre will be everywhere. Bio-diversity is the supreme law of nature.... Likewise, faith has to divine the several meanings of spiritual life, the fuzzy wisdom of nature, the light of the Many, and to image the sacrament that enshrines the Multiple, the Changing, the Silent.... The One has to become the Many. Theo-diversity is an inescapable corollary to the astounding discoveries in science and their universal application in technology. Theo-diversity alone will ensure the ascension of humanity to light and nobility that makes Joy (sac-cid-ananda) not an attribute of the spirit but its essential nature.[81]

Its judgment on Hindutva and Hinduism delivered on 11 December 1995, based on earlier observations by the constitution benches, stated:

> These Constitution Bench decisions, after a detailed discussion, indicate that no precise meaning can be ascribed to the terms 'Hindu', 'Hindutva' and 'Hinduism'; and no meaning in the abstract can confine it to the narrow limits of religion alone, excluding the content of Indian culture and heritage...the word 'Hindutva' is used and understood as a synonym of 'Indianization', i.e., development of uniform culture by obliterating the differences between all the cultures co-existing in the country.[82]

The 1995 judgment also quotes approvingly from the verdict delivered by a constitution bench in 1966 on how the architects of the Constitution were well aware of this unique nature of Hinduness, and made it the basis for including the heterogeneous Indic groups under the term 'Hindu'—again a constitutional reinforcement of the Savarkarian Hindutva:

> The Constitution-makers were fully conscious of this broad and comprehensive character of Hindu religion; and so, while guaranteeing the fundamental right to freedom of religion, Explanation II to Art. 25 has made it clear that in sub-clause (b) of clause (2), the reference to Hindus shall be construed as including a reference to persons professing the Sikh, Jaina or Buddhist religion, and the reference to Hindu religious institutions shall be construed accordingly.[83]

This is the constitutional reinforcement of Savarkarite definition that the heterogeneous nature of Hinduism from the very conception of Indian civilization makes the term larger than any religious sect and that it encompasses the entire process of Hindu existence.

Post-independence Stereotype: 'Syndicated Hinduism'

In the post-independent India, the Marxist–Nehruvian school of thought with a strong state-sponsored stranglehold on the national discourse has an inbuilt aversion for the term 'Hindu'. In this respect, the Marxist–Nehruvian school of thought is the continuation of the colonialist stereotype that identifies with Hinduism the caste structure—the so-called 'Brahminism'—which in turn has racial connotation (usually the Aryan race) and then sees 'Hinduism' itself as a product of British colonialism.

Though inherent in the Marxist and leftist Nehruvian discourse, this conception of Hinduism as Brahminism consolidated by British colonialism to serve India's own dominant castes and classes, was condensed and expressed by Prof. Romila Thapar in the context of the Hindu revival of 1990s. She called it 'Syndicated Hinduism'. Prof. Thapar, a Marxist historian promoted by the Nehruvian school, argues that modern Hinduism is essentially a colonial upper caste construct of a bygone period which ought to become extinct, having outlived whatsoever purpose for which it was created. The article contains passages which seem to project 'pre-modern Hinduism' as more pluralistic than the so-called 'Syndicated Hinduism', but the author demonizes the former too as discriminatory:

> Dharma now became the key concept. But, the significance of dharma was that it demarcated sharply between the upper castes—the dvija or twice born—for whom it was the core of the religion and the rest of society who were regarded as neither requiring nor practicing any dharma; they were adharma in every sense of the word…The attempt today in trying to redefine Hinduism is the implicit attempt

> to hold up dharma of the Dharmashastras as essential to...even those traditionally regarded as adharma.[84]

According to her, 'Hindu' was 'a term of administrative convenience, when the rulers of Arab, Turkish, Afghan and Mughal origin—all Muslims, had to differentiate between "the believers" and the rest'.[85] Then she goes on to trace the development of the term during the colonial era thus:

> The European adoption of the term "Hindu" gave it further currency as also the attempts of Catholic and Protestant Christian missionaries to convert the Hindu/ Gentoo to Christianity...Added to this was the contribution of Orientalist scholars who interpreted the religious texts from their own viewpoint which furthered the notion of 'Hinduism'...The 'Hindu' institutions...came largely to cater to the upper castes and legislated (on the occasions when they did) were not concerned with the beliefs, rituals and practices of such castes so long as they remained in a subordinate status...Of the social groups most closely associated with power the upper caste were the genitors of the new middle class and among them, initially, Brahmans were significant. Inevitably, the Brahminical base of what was seen as the new Hinduism was no unavoidable. But merged into it were various bits and pieces from upper caste belief and ritual with one eye on the Christian and Islamic models. Its close links with certain nationalist opinion gave to many of these neo-Hindu movements a political edge which remains recognizable even today.
>
> It is this development which was the parent to the present-day Syndicated Hinduism which is being pushed forward as the sole claimant to the inheritance of indigenous Indian religions...Social and economic inequality was a given fundamental of Brahmanism and whether one approves or disapproves of it. It was an established point of view...Whatever political justification there might have been for this development, as a form of nationalist assertion under British rule, no longer exists.[86]

Apart from the empirically wrong assertion that the so-called 'non-upper caste' populations in India were categorized as *adharma*, the author obsessively identifies 'Hindu' with 'upper caste' ethos and axiomatic inequality of society supposedly at the core of the phenomenon of Hinduism, both 'syndicated' and 'pre-modern', an ambiguous distinction with blurred edges invented by the author herself.

While both ancient and medieval India had many communities outside the Varna system, the Indic scriptures show a consistency towards respect for these communities and recognize the inherent values of their spiritual traditions. Not that there were no *Smriti* or *Dharmashastra*-based injunctions which were used by forces of social-stagnation against those outside the Varna system. But counteracting such forces of social stagnation were equally strong egalitarian movements which can be seen well placed within the corpus of the scriptures of Hinduism, with their roots in Vedanta and the Upanishads. And whether it was Vivekananda or Sri Aurobindo or Vallalar, they appealed not to the socially stagnant interpretations but to the socially emancipating injunctions of Vedantic humanism and Bhakti egalitarianism.

Hinduness: A Resistance Term against Social Stagnation and Racism

What Prof. Thapar fabricates as the 'Syndicated Hinduism' has since then become axiomatic in defining and caricaturing Hinduism in academia as well as media. 'However, a look into the process dynamics of Hinduness during historical, colonial and postcolonial periods show otherwise.' Please change this to 'However, a look into the process dynamics of Hinduness during historical, colonial and postcolonial periods shows otherwise.' The stereotyping put forward by Prof. Thapar is empirically and perhaps intentionally incorrect. Despite vested interests of social stagnation in India and the colonial masters trying to use birth-based discriminations as essentializing features of Hinduism, the national movement of Hinduness clearly aligned itself with egalitarianism and social emancipation.

With the Islamic conquest of Persia, the word 'Hindu' became a theo-racial stereotype. The word came to be attributed with meanings like 'thief', 'slave', 'black' and so on in Persian. During the colonial period, this was used by propagandists of other religions to shame Hindus. However, the Hindu reaction was to defiantly embrace the term—asserting that they refused to be cowed down by such racial demeaning. Swami Vivekananda hinted at the way 'Hindu' was being used as a humiliating name, and in response, said:

> We are Hindus. I do not use the word Hindu in any bad sense at all, nor do I agree with those that think there is any bad meaning in it....Upon us depends whether the name Hindu will stand for everything that is glorious, everything that is spiritual, or whether it will remain a name of opprobrium, one designating the downtrodden, the worthless, the heathen. If at present the word Hindu means anything bad, never mind; by our action let us be ready to show that this is the highest word that any language can invent.[87]

In the 1910s the propaganda against Hindus was again taken up by Islamic communal organizations. In the very first issue of a Hindi monthly titled *Gyan*

Shakti published from Gorakhpur in Uttar Pradesh in 1916, its editor Shiv Kumar Shastri wrote:

> One who really desires the welfare (hit) of Bharatvarsha or Hindustan, one who considers its gain to be his own gain, and who regards himself a Hindustani or Bharatiya, he is to be called Hindu. 'Hindu' does not signify 'kafir' or 'ghulam'. The Persian lexicons might have given this word whatever meaning they wished, but what has that got to do with us?[88]

In adapting the term 'Hindu' for themselves, the Hindus have actually made the word a symbol of protest of subjugated people against racial and religious stereotyping by the aggressors and colonizers. Yet this aspect of the term 'Hindu' is intentionally overlooked by Prof. Thapar. To her it has to mean only a colonial construct that chiefly dealt with the vested interests in the upper-sections of the colonized society which were also collaborators with the colonial forces. This characterization of Hinduism is a colonial-Marxist construct which would become axiomatic in the social science institutions of Nehruvian Indian State.

Social Justice and 'Subtle Indestructible Unity'

The earlier mentioned 1966 verdict throws light on yet another dimension of Hinduness. While the colonial-Marxist Nehruvian narrative claims the 'Hindu' definition as being 'artificial' or 'colonial' and based on the alleged axiomatic inequality of 'Brahminism', the legal definition of the term 'Hindu', with its roots undeniably in Savarkarite Hindutva, has been highly instrumental in making progressive reforms in the Hindu society.

In 1948 Muldas Vaishya, a Scheduled Community (SC) leader had launched both a popular struggle and a legal battle for the rights of the SC to enter the Swaminarayan temple at Ahmedabad. The Swaminarayan sect members (called *Satsangis*) who were predominantly upper caste, under the leadership of one Shastri Yagnapurushdas, went to court asking it to pass an injunction barring non-Satsangi SCs from entering the sect's temples.[89] The case ultimately ended up in the Supreme Court. The final verdict, on 14 January 1966, was in favour of temple entry for SCs and the judgment by then Chief Justice of India P. B. Gajendragadkar affirmed that the Swaminarayan sect was an integral part of Hinduism. The judgment also provided a panoramic sweep of the evolution of the Hindu identity and underlined a 'subtle indescribable unity' that runs through history:

> The development of Hindu religion and philosophy shows that from time to time saints and religious reformers attempted to remove from the Hindu thought and practices elements of corruption and superstition and that led to the formation of different sects. Buddha started Buddhism; Mahavir founded Jainism; Basava became the founder of the Lingayat religion, Dnyaneshwar and Tukaram initiated the Varakari cult; Guru Nanak inspired Sikhism; Dayananda founded Arya Samaj, and Chaitanya began the Bhakti cult; and as a result of the teachings of Ramakrishna and Vivekananda, Hindu religion flowered into its most attractive, progressive and dynamic form. If we study the teachings of these saints and religious reformers, we would notice an amount of divergence in their respective views; but underneath that divergence, there is a kind of subtle indescribable unity which keeps them within the sweep of the broad and progressive Hindu religion.[90]

The term 'Hindu' has been pivotal in democratizing Hindu society and organizing it on the broadest egalitarian foundations while at the same time preserving the inherent pluralism. The 'subtle indescribable unity' identified by Justice Gajendragadkar is what Hindutva essentially is. Indian nation is its geo-cultural incubator. This indescribable unity was also identified by Savarkar as 'subtle bonds that, like nerve threads, bind Hindus in One Organic Social Being.'

Despite the strong emphasis on the sacred geography, Hindutva is not nationalism in the conventional sense of the term—particularly as understood in the context of Western nationalism. Hindutva is rooted in deep psychological processes. One can say that these psychological processes and the culture that facilitates the selection of these processes and which in turn is made by the very processes, have been evolving in this geographical realm. Hence, Hindutva while having the semblance of nationalism, is not nationalism. In fact, this is what underlies the embedded universal non-expansionist mission of Hindutva.

Universal Mission

Sri Aurobindo, in his famous Uttarpara speech of 1909, spoke about such a universal mission for Hindu religion:

> But it is not circumscribed by the confines of a single country, it does not belong peculiarly and forever to a bounded part of the world. That which we call the Hindu religion is really the eternal religion, because it is the universal religion which embraces all others. If a religion is not universal, it cannot be eternal. A narrow religion, a sectarian religion, an exclusive religion, can live only for a limited time and a limited purpose.[91]

Earlier, in his famous address to the World Parliament of Religions in Chicago in 1893, Swami Vivekananda had spoken in detail about the Hindu mission of a universal religion. This he characterized as the sociocultural and spiritual aim of Hindu society. He unveiled the vision of this mission thus:

> The Hindu may have failed to carry out all his plans, but if there is ever to be a universal religion, it must be one which will have no location in place or time; which will be infinite like the God it will preach, and whose sun will shine upon the followers of Krishna and of Christ, on saints and sinners alike; which will not be Brahminic or Buddhistic, Christian or Mohammedan, but the sum total of all these, and still have infinite space for development; which in its catholicity will embrace in its infinite arms, and find a place for, every human being.[92]

Swami Vivekananda zeroed in on the phenomenon of religion as an inherent universal trait of human species both collectively and individually.

> There never was my religion or yours, my national religion or your national religion; there never existed many religions, there is only the one. One infinite religion existed all through eternity and will ever exist, and this religion is expressing itself in various countries in various ways. Therefore, we must respect all religions and we must try to accept them all as far as we can. Religions manifest themselves not only according to race and geographical position, but according to individual powers.[93]

This identification of religion as a universal human phenomenon rooted in the individual psyche, as well as a manifestation of the collective sociocultural activity, is important. Religion as an integral part of the human organism is a vision rooted in Upanishadic thought. Modern scientific attempts to link religious phenomena with neural correlates, including the evolutionary roots and consequences, seem to essentially reinforce the Indic vision of religion. In *Principles of Neurotheology*, his textbook on this emerging inter-disciplinary science, Andrew Newberg points out the Upanishadic roots of this new understanding of religion:

> The relationship between the mind and human spirituality has been considered for at least several thousand years. For example, this intersection was described in the ancient Hindu scriptures of the Upanishads in which it was realized that something within us, particularly within the head, enables us to explore and experience the universe via our cognitive and sensory processes and also to discover our own sense of spirituality.[94]

After quoting a long passage from the *Taittiriya Upanishad*, Newberg points out that just as the 'Upanishads reveal the importance of the body and the brain in achieving spiritual enlightenment', neurotheology is 'a more recent attempt at discerning how the study of the human mind and brain relate to the pursuit of religions and religious experience'.

Almost echoing the 'one infinite religion' of Swami Vivekananda, which in turn is derived from the Indic unitary model of consciousness, science exploring the neural basis of religious experiences identifies an almost universal experience of an 'Absolute Unitary Being' (AUB). The experience of AUB may or may not involve a deity. It is essentially an expansion of the self. In their book *The Neuropsychology of Aesthetic Spiritual and Mystical States*, Newberg and Eugene G. d'Aquili explain:

> As one moves into AUB, the Self seems to expand to become the totality of reality without individualized content. This is compatible with the Hindu interpretation and probably underlies Shankara's observation that the Atman (or soul) and the Brahman (or God) are one. The Christian Unio Mystica is phenomenologically the same, although care is taken by Christian theologians who reflect on this state to preserve the ontological independence of the soul. They would agree that in this state, the union of God and the individual soul is so perfect and so complete that an observer, if such were possible, could not perceive where one ended and the other began. Nevertheless, for theological reasons, Christian mystical theologians maintain the ontological integrity of the individual, although they would concede that the individual has, as it were, expanded to a perfect and a simple union with God... When Europeans first came into contact with certain Hindu sects, they were shocked and scandalized when they learned that part of ritual worship required the repeated assertion 'I am God, I am God, I am God.' What confused the Europeans was that the 'I' in the statement did not refer to the individual conscious ego with all its evil proclivities but rather to the Self or Atman, the deepest unconscious core reality of an individual. It is in this sense that every individual can truly state 'I am God,' because each individual can potentially expand into a state of AUB. A Hindu who states 'I am God" is all the while perfectly aware of the shortcomings and failings of his conscious ego in day-to-day life.[95]

However, in the West, there has been a strong inhibition to openly attribute the discovery of this experience and invention of systematic disciplines for the cultivation of this experience to Hindu traditions directly. This reluctance to identify openly with Hindu Dharma was observed by philosopher Alan Watts (1915–1973), who experimented with LSD-induced altered states of consciousness. In his autobiography titled *In My Own Way*, he concedes this fact based on his own experiences:

> Hindu philosophy was a local form of a sort of undercover wisdom, inconceivably ancient, which everyone knows in the back of his mind but will not admit.[96]

Neural Basis of Universal Ethics

The expansion of the Self also has strong ethical implications. In his lecture 'The Spirit and Influence of Vedanta', delivered at the Twentieth Century Club, Boston on March 28, 1896, Swami Vivekananda explained the ethical implications of the expanding Self experience:

> There are moments when every man feels that he is one with the universe, and he rushes forth to express it, whether he knows it or not. This expression of oneness is what we call love and sympathy, and it is the basis of all our ethics and morality. This is summed up in the Vedantic philosophy by the celebrated aphorism, Tat Tvam Asi (Thou art That).[97]

The experience of 'the Self being one with the universe', which is the basis of the 'Brahman', actually has a strong neurobiological basis. In 1995 the brain researcher Iaccomo Rizzolati of the University of Parma discovered what are today popularly known as 'mirror neurons' or 'empathy neurons'. Neurobiologist Dr V. S. Ramachandran explains:

> The mirror neurons, it would seem, dissolve the barrier between the Self and others. I call them 'empathy neurons' or 'Dalai Lama neurons'...Dissolving the 'Self vs other' barrier is the basis of many ethical systems, especially eastern philosophical and mystical traditions...The question of whether 'you' would continue in multiple parallel brain vats raises issues that come perilously close to the theological notion of souls, but I see no simple way out of the conundrum. Perhaps we need to remain open to the Upanishadic doctrine that the ordinary rules of numerosity and arithmetic, of 'one vs many', or indeed of two-valued, binary yes/no logic, simply doesn't apply to minds—the very notion of a separate 'you' or 'I' is an illusion, like the passage of time itself. We are all merely many reflections in a hall of mirrors of a single cosmic reality (Brahman or 'paramatman').[98]

The Serpent in the Flag

The recognition of this experience of the expanding Self as a universal right of the human being in maximizing his or her genomic potential has been one of the greatest unique and sustained features of Indian culture. The kundalini or the coiled serpent with the chakras is representative of this recognition and the development of allied inner disciplines for the recognition of the Self. In a paper published in 1997 in the *Indian Journal of the History of Science*, Prof. Subash Kak, a computer scientist and historian of science of ancient India, explains:

> In the tantras, seven, eight, or nine points of primary focus which are called chakras are described. It has been argued by some that the beginnings of this system go right back to the Vedic times, as in Atharvaveda 10.2.31–2, which describes the body as being eight-wheeled and nine-doored. Their positions appear to be areas in the brain which map different points on the spinal cord...It may be assumed that the stimulation of these chakras in a proper way leads to the development of certain neural structures that allow the I-ness to experience the Self. In other words, the chakras are points of basic focus inside the brain that lead to the explication of the cognitive process.[99]

Hindutva recognizes this aspect as a phenomenon universal to all humanity. It is this that sets Hindutva apart from narrow nationalism and makes it a validating vanguard of global spiritual pluralism and infinite variety. Savarkar explicitly recognized the kundalini and the chakras as the most important universal aspect of Indic civilization. Hence, in the flag of the Hindu Mahasabha, he introduced the spinal serpentine path of the chakras. He explained:

> Hindus have perfected a science based on experiment which can be termed as the highest blessing on human life. This shastra is called the Yoga. It is the highest means of the full development of man's internal powers. It is therefore very necessary that a clear symbol of Yoga which indicates the way to the highest bliss should be fixed on the flag of the Hindu Nation. The symbol is that of the Kundalini. It is not the characteristic of any particular Jati or Varna. It exists in all human beings...To acquire this supreme joy or bliss is the highest ideal of man, be he a Hindu or a non-Hindu (Muslim, Christian or Jew), i.e, believer or non-believer, citizen or foreigner. ...Therefore, the Kundalini which is the Muladhar Shakti of man's highest progress and eternally blissful state of superconsciousness which can alone be the symbol of the great ideal which the Abhyudaya (worldly prosperity) of the Hindu Nation aims for. Thus, the Kundalini which represents all the ultimate aspirations, feelings, and powers of mankind.[100]

Hindutva incorporates another important feature of Indic spirituality and culture. The symbols and forms are just instruments to achieve a goal, after which, clinging to the instruments, however lofty, is not encouraged. Hindutva recognizes that this is true even for the very term 'Hindu'. Making an appeal to the then colonized Hindus to unite and make their voice heard amidst the community of nations, Savarkar said in 1923:

> Oh Hindus! Whether Jain or Samaji or Sanatani or Sikh or any other subsection, afford to cut yourselves off or fall out and destroy the ancient, the natural and organic combination that already exists?
> ...Let the minorities remember they would be cutting the very branch on which they stand. Strengthen every tie that binds you to the main organism, whether of blood or language or common festivals and feasts or culture...Thirty crores of people, with India for their basis of operation, for their Fatherland and for their Holyland with such a history behind them, bound together by ties of a common blood and common culture, can dictate their terms to the whole world. A day will come when mankind will have to face the force.

After making this appeal, which is definitely nation-based, Savarkar declares:

> Equally certain it is that whenever the Hindus come to hold such a position whence they could dictate terms to the whole world—those terms cannot be very different from the terms which Gita dictates or the Buddha lays down. A Hindu is most intensely so, when he ceases to be a Hindu; and with a Kabir who claims the whole earth for a Benares...or with a Tukaram who exclaims: 'My country? Oh brothers, the limits of the Universe—there the frontiers of my country lie.'[101]

Thus, from the seven rivers (Sapta Sindhu) of Vedic lore to the seven chakras of the Hindu flag, Hindutva has been one of the most unique conceptions of nationhood in the history of the human species. Unlike the expansionist monocultural global dominance pursued by Christianity, Islam, Western colonialism and Marxism, Hindutva does not seek a global empire but instead seeks a global family of nations, cultures and spiritual disciplines— without one imposing itself on the other. This non-expansionist universality through the complete realization of national individuality is the unique nature of Hindutva.

So, for Rajnarayan Basu, Hindus should become strong so that they as a nation 'could participate in the universal progress', for Bankim Chandra there could be 'no Hindutva' without 'the inalienable and indivisible love', and for Savarkar, 'a Hindu at his most intense ceases to be a Hindu'.

C. L. Fabri's comparison of punch-marked coins and Harappan seals (1935)

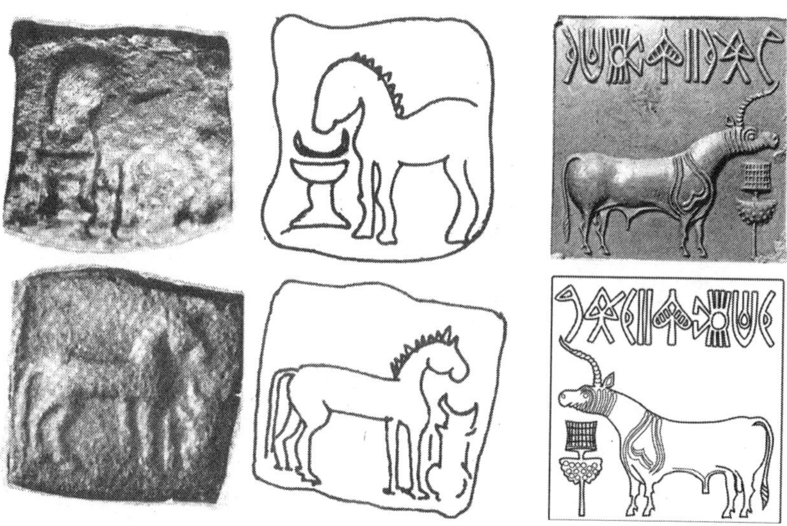

A comparison of the 'cult-object' in Harappan seal and punch-marked coins depicting a horse

The horned 'Yogi' ('Pasupati Yogi') seal in Harappa, showing early emergence of unitary consciousness in India

Sri Aurobindo and Ram Swarup, the two seers who gave a holistic narrative of the evolution of Indian culture from the perspective of inner dynamics

Swami Vivekananda (1863–1902)

'Bodhisattva' Dr B. R. Ambedkar and 'Veer' Vinayak Savarkar converged in defining the term 'Hindu'

2

Bharat Mata, Vande Mataram and Akhand Bharat

There are two images central to any discussion on *Hindutva*. One is that of Bharat Mata or Mother India, the other one is Akhand Bharat or undivided India. In the narratives of establishment media as well as discourses of the academia, these two are shown as disturbing images. In the Hindutva movement itself, Mother India is shown as a Goddess mounted atop a lion, with either a trident, a saffron or a tricolour flag in her hand—very similar to the Hindu Goddess Durga. This image is superimposed on the map of undivided India—whose political boundaries are almost non-existent as the undivided larger Indian landmass forms a flaming background. Are these images venerated by millions of Hindutvaites in their functions and meetings symbols of aggressive nationalism? Is the image of Akhand Bharat expansionist fantasy, and is the image of Bharat Mata actually the reworked image of Britannia and thus a colonial import in itself? Is Akhand Bharat equally an indication of fantasy in the minds of Hindutvaites for a military expansionist agenda against India's neighbours—particularly Pakistan?

> For what is a nation? What is our mother-country? It is not a piece of earth, nor a fiction of the mind. It is a mighty Shakti, composed of the Shaktis of all the millions of units that make up the nation, just as Bhawani Mahisha Mardini sprang into being from the Shaktis of all the millions of gods assembled in one mass of force and welded into unity. The Shakti we call India, Bhawani Bharati, is the living unity of the Shaktis of three hundred million people …
>
> —Sri Aurobindo, 1905[1]

> Bharat Mata has nothing to do with India's ancient or medieval past. It is a European import. Notions of motherland and fatherland were talked about in Europe…Bharat is mentioned in ancient India. It was first used in an inscription of king Kharvela in Prakrit. But representation of the country in human form as a mother or father was unknown in ancient India or medieval India. This was an idea that emerged in Europe with the rise of nationalism, and it was found in Britain, Russia, etc.
>
> —Prof. Irfan Habib, 2016[2]

> I am happy to say 'Bharat Mata ki jai' in the same way that I am also happy to say 'Deepika Padukone ki jai' or even 'Sunny Leone ki jai'.
>
> —Swaminathan S. Anklesaria Iyer, 2016[3]

During the Bengal revolutionary movement that flourished following the Bengal partition, the cry '*Bande Mataram*' (Sanskrit: *Vande Mataram*, 'I bow to the Mother') as well as the song composed by Bankim Chandra Chatterjee became very popular. Soon the cry '*Bharat Mata ki Jai*' (Victory to Mother India) emerged on the scene. All Indian freedom fighters, including Mahatma Gandhi (1869–1948), used the image of Bharat Mata to arouse people in the freedom struggle of India. Naturally, the image of Bharat Mata was detested by colonialists who always associated her with Kali and then Kali with the 'thugee' cult and thus projected the revolutionaries of Bengal as somehow related to a blood-thirsty pagan criminal barbarism. After Independence, this mantle of aversion to the image of Bharat Mata and Vande Mataram, was inherited initially in a milder form by Nehruvian ideology. As we will see, Nehru himself oscillated between diluting the imagery to being emotionally moved by it. However, as Nehruvian polity became more and more appropriated by Marxists, the Bharat Mata imagery was trivialized or seen as a passing fantasy in the evolution of the Indian State.

The song 'Vande Mataram', despite being recognized by the Parliament, consisting of the founding fathers of the modern Indian State as being at par with the National Anthem in status[4], has been systematically sidelined. For example, when in September 2006 the centenary of the adoption of Vande

Mataram as the national song by Indian National Congress during freedom struggle was celebrated, both the then Prime Minister of India Dr Manmohan Singh and party supremo Sonia Gandhi (born Edvige Antonia Albina Maino) decided to skip the celebrations, thus clearly signalling her party men and government to keep the celebrations a low key affair.[5] Both from the economic-colonialist right wing and the Marxist-Nehruvian left wing, those who see India as a colonial construct reject the image of Bharat Mata. Economist Swaminathan S. Anklesaria Iyer, popular for his column 'Swaminomics' wrote:

> In my youth, I did not hear of *Bharat Mata*. The concept began in Bengali literature, but the BJP later made it an aggressive Hindu symbol. As a Tamilian, I see it as one more example of north Indian imperialism.[6]

As we will see, this claim of being a Tamil and not having heard of Bharat Mata is totally contradictory to the actual sociopolitical climate then prevalent in Tamil Nadu. Nevertheless, this shows a typical perception of the culturally neutral economic right wing. Prof. Irfan Habib, the famous Marxist historian, announced in his Bipan Chandra Memorial Lecture (2016) at Jawaharlal Nehru University (JNU) that 'the idea of Bharat Mata was an import from Europe and there was no evidence of any such imagination in either ancient or medieval India'. Elaborating further on the same theme, Prof. Habib writes two years later that the 'rich Sanskrit literature of ancient India' lacked 'any text or poem, setting India as an object of love and admiration or as different from, or superior to, other countries'. On the other hand, he traces the appearance of a unified national conscience in India itself to Amir Khusrau:

> The first truly patriotic text came from the pen of the poet Amir Khusrau of Delhi in Persian. He knew all about Arab-Iranian and Turkic cultures and something about the Greek as well and so could, with some substance, make claims of India's superiority over them. He does so at great length in his *Nuh Sipihr* composed in 1318.

However, he concludes the imagery of India as a mother having come from European colonial sources:

> Dictionaries tell us that the word "fatherland" for one's country is traceable back in Old English to the twelfth century and "motherland", in the same sense, to 1711. Britannia is always portrayed as a woman. The country as "mother" in Bankim Chandra Chatterji's Vande Mataram, and the current "Bharat Mata" in Hindi are thus phrases of impeccable Western ancestry and not products of any ancient cultural tradition of India.[7]

At another level, Sumathi Ramaswamy, James B. Duke Distinguished Professor of History at Duke University, considers the imagery of Bharat Mata as the undoing of the European enlightenment through 'the recuperation of old myths and the return of fancy'. She also claims that 'modern secular and scientific mapped knowledge is hijacked' to assist that 'unravelling'.[8] Here also Bharat Mata is a regressive image constructed out of borrowed elements. So, in this context let us see if the image of Bharat Mata is really of Western origin—and if so, then a central image of the Hindutva movement becomes a colonial import. On the other hand, if there are indigenous historic and deeply Indic streams contributing to the emergence of the image of Bharat Mata, then her centrality in the visual culture of Hindutva movement is more related to the dynamics of India's own historical processes than to colonial influence.

Emergence of the Goddess during Early Indian Resistance to British Colonization

To understand this, we need to explore if the Goddess tradition played any role in the early resistance movement against the British colonization. The Goddess tradition started spreading throughout Bengal, coinciding with its coming first under the Mughal and then British rule. In the Bengal province by the end of sixteenth century, Krishnanada Agambagish, author of the famous *Brihat Tantrasara,* stayed and worked in Navadvipa—a major cultural centre of the region, spreading the Tantric Goddess traditions. When Bengal came under complete British control and started experiencing famines, the famous Sannyasi rebellion took place. Subsequent increase in dacoity after the Sannyasi rebellion saw the emergence of Kali as the syncretic Goddess, bridging the religious divide between Hindus and Muslims. Prof. Jati Sankar Mondal explains:

> The dacoits used to undertake their operations on moonless nights so as to take advantage of the darkness with its auspicious association with Kali. Still there are places in Bengal with temples named dakatia Kali or thangadiya Kali....Firstly, every gang of dacoits, whether they are Hindu or Muslim, used to follow the ritual. The reason is probably the amalgamation of sannyasi and fakir with the peasantry turned into dacoits. These sannyasis and fakirs like Majnu Shah of Birbhum along with others tried to resolve Hindu-Muslim bifurcation in their approach to religion and life.[9]

From these dacoity activities, the British soon 'discovered' the secret network of stranglers—the thugs. The thuggees and thugs were used by the British to justify their colonial project in India. Colonial narratives in the form of tales of brave British officers saving Hindus deluded by thugs filled the English press. According to the British, the thugs were worshippers of Kali who were motivated by their evil religion to waylay and strangulate people. As many postcolonial studies have shown, most of the excesses of thugs were colonial fabrications which enabled officials to fuel their campaigns and usurp authority. Decapitated 'thug' heads were sent to Edinburgh. Based on pseudo-scientific phrenology studies, the British doctors talked about the thug skulls showing 'representative examples of normal Hindoo type', of the 'apathetic, weak and lazy Hindoo' with 'natural inclination for the work of death'. It was Captain William Sleeman who led this profitable campaign against the 'thugs', a nineteenth-century 'war against terror' in nineteenth-century India. His close relative, Henry Harpur Spry of the Bengal Medical Mission, meanwhile developed a fascination and fetish for collecting the decapitated heads of the 'thugs' and 'studying' them. Sending to Edinburgh, seven decapitated heads of the 29 Hindus executed as 'thugs', he also sent a description of thugee in which he noted that the 'their presiding goddess' was *Bhowanee.*[10]

Historian Kim Wagner at the University of Edinburgh points out that established Hindu text *Bhagavat Purana* shows Kali as the patron of a band of thieves. Wagner points out that *Bhavani* was the patron Goddess of Marathas and family deity of many Rajput lineages. Marathas were prominent among the Indic forces offering resistance to the British and earlier to the Mughals. Wagner writes that the invocation of Bhavani by the thugs prior to their execution, which was interpreted by Sleeman as an admission of guilt, was in fact the war cry of Marathas and Rajputs. Further, unlike the monsters they were made out to be, in reality they had rules that forbade them from killing women and the poor, whom they considered as the descendants of the Goddess. Most of the 'thugs' captured, prosecuted and ultimately executed by the British, most often referred to Bhavani as their Goddess. D. F. McLeod, the officer in charge of operations against the thugs in Rajasthan in his report pointed out 'a notable fact' that not only among the so-called thugs 'but in an especial manner amongst all lawless fraternities, and to a certain extent throughout the uneducated population of Central India, the Mussulmans vie with the Hindoos in a devotion of this sanguinary deity [Devi or Bhavani] far exceeding that they pay to any other'.'[11]

The consolidation of political power by the British East India Company resulted ultimately in the Great Rebellion of 1857. The Goddess again played a role here—particularly in creating a liaison among the local communities. British accounts record the execution of one Shunker, a small Raja of the Gonds. He was charged along with his son for conspiring with the sepoys against the

British. He was 'blown away from the cannon's mouth'. British found with him a 'poetical invocation to Devi or Kali, the goddess of all cut-throats'. The verses invoked Goddess addressing her as 'Mata Chandi' and 'Mata Kali' and asked her to 'listen to the calling of the poor' and requested her 'not to delay' her actions, 'devour the English quickly' and 'protect Shankar and her disciples'.[12] Perhaps it is in this Ghond poetry against the British that we find the first prototype of Bankim Chandra Chatterjee's later 'Vande Mataram'.

If one is to look back into the centuries just preceding the arrival of the British, then one can discern a pattern. When the Mughal rule entered a particularly more oppressive phase, the Goddess tradition appeared both in Maharashtra in the form of Bhavani worship and in Sikh tradition, though subsumed to the impersonal supreme Ek Onkar principle, in the form of Guru Gobind Singh's *Chandi di Var*. In other words, the Goddess has appeared as a socio-spiritual node each time the nation faced a crisis. This is a uniquely Indic phenomenon. It is not just the principal people movements that take centre stage, for whom the Goddess provides inspiration but also the initially expelled marginalized sections of the population under any oppressive structure in Indian history, resort to dacoity as a show of resistance and they invariably worship the Goddess. So, was the emergence of Goddess precipitated by heightened social anxiety? Or is the Goddess a mythologized embodiment of the physical body as well as the natural resources of India and the human relations to them? Or is she something higher?

Answer from the 'Ankle Bracelet'?

Chilapathikaram (epic of the ankle bracelet), a Tamil epic variously dated between second century to fifth century CE, written by prince-turned-monk Ilango, may contain the answer to this pan-Indic phenomenon. The Sangham literature (300 BCE to 300 CE) classifies the land into five eco-cultural categories. These categories were originally intended as literary techniques. Yet they had clearly helped the rulers and administrators manage the natural resources of the land. Each of these categories have their names and deities:

Land	Name	Worshipped Deity	Activity
Hills and forests	Kurunchi	Skanda (Murugan)	Hunting, collection of honey and other forest-based products
Grasslands	Mullai	Vishnu (Mayon)	Cattle rearing
Farmlands	Marutham	Indra	Farming

Coastal areas and ocean	Neithal	Varuna	Fishing
Desertified zone	Palai	Kottravai – Goddess	Dacoity

Thus, the forest-based Kurunchi has as its deity, *Murugan*, whose consort is Valli, the daughter of tribal chieftain. The grassland Mullai has as its deity, *Vishnu*, as His most popular avatar is that of a cowherd, which is the human-resource interlink for the grassland ecosystem. The farms depend on rain and *Indra*, the Vedic deity of rain becomes naturally associated with the land that is interestingly named as *Marutham* after *Maruts*—the wind gods that accompany Indra. For Neithal, the coastal zone, it is the Vedic deity *Varuna*, the God of the waters. How then does the Goddess fit into the picture for the deserts? Ilango gives an extraordinarily insightful answer to this question. He points out that Palai is not a separate category:

> Chaotic and low the nation becomes,
> when a king and council of ministers do not deliver.
> The same, when climate does not deliver
> the Kurunchi and Mullai get degraded;
> painfully deteriorate and become Pālai.[13]

The parallel between the vagaries of climate and the non-deliverance of proper rule by the state, and subsequently people of the degraded lands resorting to dacoity, make it abundantly clear that the dacoity, clearly a punishable crime, was also understood as a symbol of protest or an indicator of the mismanagement of natural resources. It was also considered an indicator that the people associated with such affected natural zones had been pushed into robbery, whose ultimate responsibility came upon the head of the state. So, when such groups took to dacoity, the Goddess whose body is the natural resources, is worshipped in her fierce form. The subtle hint is that it is not the failing climate alone that must be blamed but also the human agency of the state, whose attitude did not mitigate the suffering of the people. They should share the blame for the people of hills and grasslands becoming dacoits.

The epic itself is the celebration of fierce nature of the Divine Feminine and explores through a forest chant invocation of tribal people, the various dimensions of the Goddess. The lines show how much the various streams of the Goddess tradition have seamlessly intermingled and emerged as a powerful symbol in an organic way. Shalini—the priestess of the tribes, who enters into an altered state of consciousness, manifesting the Goddess, blesses the heroine—an urban lady who is soon going to seek justice in a fierce way. The verses speak of the Goddess thus:

> Cloaked in the hide of the elephant and wearing the skin of the tiger
> Stands She on the black head of the wild buffalo;
> She stands at the end of the Scripture of the Scriptures,
> the all-permeating discontinuous Flame of wisdoms, worshipped by the celestials.[14]

While the first two lines show a fierce tribal Goddess, the next two lines indicate the Goddess whom the celestials meet, as narrated in *Chandogya Upanishad*. In Tamizh tradition, the phrase 'scripture of the scriptures' is used to denote the Upanishads. In the ensuing lines of the epic, the Goddess is given both the attributes of Siva and Vishnu. Their deeds are Her deeds. She drank the poison that emanated from the oceans. Hence, She has a blue throat. She destroyed the three flying towns of the demons with her bow, which was Meru or Axis Munda (which also alternates with Himalayas), and the bow string was the cosmic serpent. Traditionally, these are the deeds of Siva. But *Chilapathikaram* attributes them to Siva. Her wearing the hide of the elephant and the skin of the tiger are also very much the deeds of Siva. She is the one who destroyed with a kick the demonic wheel sent by the evil Kamsa, a childhood adventure of Krishna.

Thus, we have here a literary painting of a pan-Indic Goddess portrayed in all Her glory who includes in Her the male deities as well as the Upanishadic Goddess of wisdom as well as the fierce tribal goddess as an organic whole. And this Goddess is depicted by a South Indian Tamizh poet almost 1700 to 1500 years ago as being worshipped by forest communities in her fierce form when the harmony (social as well as ecological) was lost. In short, the Goddess, who emerges when the land and people suffer, is already right there with the tribal communities deep in South India. What is even more important is that this Goddess has her roots still deeper in Indian history, and in terms of literary evidence she is very much present in the Vedic literature and has an abiding presence in historical times as well.

The Vedic Roots

According to Gandhian scholar K. Gopinath Menon, Bharat Mata was an explicit 'transformation' of a national consciousness that can be traced back to the *bhoomi sukta* of *Atharva Veda*, veneration of rivers in Vedic literature, the concept and functional culture of Tirthas which was already in vogue during the composition of Mahabharata, reinforced through various Puranas. It was this 'national consciousness' which was transformed into Bharat Mata by the poet Bankim Chandra.[15]

Subsequently, many scholars of religion too have pointed out that the imagery of Bharat Mata has roots in Vedic Goddess tradition. Prof. David Kinsley (1939–2000), a scholar of religious studies, relates Vedic Prithvi to Bharat Mata:

> An important aspect of the reverence for the divine feminine in the Hindu tradition is an awe for the sacrality of the land itself and for the Indian subcontinent as a whole. The most ancient expression of this in the Hindu tradition is found in the *Rg Veda* and its several hymns that praise the goddess *Prthivi*.... The fundamental conviction that the earth, or the Indian subcontinent itself, is a goddess, indeed, that she is one's mother, pervades the modern cult of *Bhārat Mātā* (Mother India}, in which all Indians are called sons or children of India and are expected to protect their mother without regard for personal hardship and sacrifice.[16]

Echoing Gopinath Menon, Kinsley too credits Bankim Chandra for 'providing through "Bande Mataram", one of the earliest and probably still the most popular literary expressions of this theme'.[17] Another scholar who traced the roots of Bharat Mata to Vedic literature was Anwar Shaikh (1928–2006). This Pakistan-born British author and secular humanist, also traced the concept of Bharat Mata to 'bhoomi sukta' of *Atharva Veda*. According to him, while the hymn pays respect to entire earth, deifying it as *Prithivi*, it was specifically Bharat Mata whom it addresses as 'queen of all'. 'Prithivi, as I understand, is the deified earth' Anwar Sheikh opines and to him 'it refers to Bharat'. He associates 'bhoomi sukta' of *Atharva Veda* with the sacred geography of India:

> Here, it should be noted that the hymn shows respect to the entire earth but refers to the land of Bharat as the "Queen or all..." ...That this hymn is about Bhārat Mātā (the undivided India), is borne out by the facts especially connected with this country. Verse no. 3 states: "In whom the sea, and Sindhu, and the waters, in whom our food and corn-lands had their being, In whom this all that breathes and moves is active, this Earth assign us foremost rank and station." It must be remembered that Bhārat Mātā is originally associated with the areas of the Indus river (Sindhu). One should also note love and respect of the Vedic man for Bhārat Mātā because he believed that the mere fact of belonging to this country brought him "the foremost rank and station" in the world.[18]

Art historian Vidya Dehejia also asserts this continuity that Bharat Mata has with Prithivi:

> Since the land itself is spoken of in Sanskrit as Prithvi or goddess earth, it is perhaps not surprising that kingdoms, cities, districts, and boroughs roughs are gendered feminine. India is *Bhārat Mātā* or Mother India.[19]

While it is easy to associate Vedic Prithivi with the benign smiling Goddess of prosperity and fertility, it is hard to associate her with the ferocious form of the Goddess, which is very much an important aspect of Bharat Mata—who is pictured in the calendar art of Hindutva as simultaneously both the Goddess of fertility and the Goddess of war.

Nirṛti is another Vedic Goddess. Often considered a negative Goddess by the Western Indologists, she is black in form and golden haired. She is also the Goddess of the South. It is true the Vedic hymns ask her not to bind humans. They ask her to leave. There are bad omens associated with her. However, she was not despised. This is clear from the fact people were named after her and she was considered as motherly as any Goddess. Thus, we have a Rig Vedic seer Nirrti-Putra Kapota (dove). Nirrti is associated with the dove. Clay figurines of doves have been found at the Harappan sites of Mohenjodaro and Chanhudaro. C. L. Fabri had emphasized the dove symbolism with the Goddess tradition. Historian Bhairabi Prasad Sahu thinks that this may be a shared Goddess symbolism that ancient Harappans had with Crete and Sumer.[20] So Nirrti may have been known to India right from the Harappan times. Vedic scholar Ramachandra Narayan Dandekar considers Nirrti as the antonym or absence of ṛta in the cosmic and ethical context. In human realm it is *anṛta*.[21]

A detailed study on Nirrti was done by Sanskritist Sukumari Bhattacharji (1921–2014). Born in a Christian family, she belonged to the early phases of increasingly Hinduphobic Marxist camp. Despite her tendency to view Hindu spirituality through Western categories, her study of Nirrti is quite comprehensive. *Shatapatha Brahmana* (SB) identifies Nirrti with the Earth. Yama is Agni and Nirrti is Yami and 'this earth'. Being united in mind with Yama and Nirrti (being of one mind) liberates one. Nirrti not only binds humans but can also unloose the bonds. 'People rejoice in calling her the Earth' as stated in *Shatapatha Brahmana*. It also shows both her generative and destructive powers: 'Whoever comes into being, comes into being on her.' And those who become corrupted, this earth makes him decay' (SB 7:2:1:10–11). So here we have the Goddess, who is the Goddess of the Earth and who is black and fierce.

She punishes those who disrupt ṛta—the natural order. Sukumari Bhattacharji rightly identifies this aspect of Nirrti:

> In Indian language, should ṛta be disregarded, Nirrti is there. She is nature's revenge on the offender against ṛta. The Indian picture of Nirrti is one of a dread goddess; she binds the offender with a strong rope around his neck; freedom from this knot means long life, strength and vigour (AV VI: 63: 1, 2).[22]

Nirrti is the archetype from which the Goddess-warrior groups emerge from the communities of eco-degraded and oppressed lands in India. In Vedic ritual the land where nothing grows, she manifests. So, this explains why the Goddess in fierce form emerges in Tamizh eco-cultural zone of land degraded into deserts, or why the Goddess tradition is adapted by warriors fighting against invasion and communities suffering from ecological disturbances and social upheavals. From the Gond chieftain invoking *Chandi* to Bankim Chandra invoking *Durga* in Bande Mataram, there is a deeper continuity of this Vedic Goddess.

Other Streams of Goddess Traditions

There are also other mighty streams of goddesses who have merged into the body of Bharat Mata. One such is Saraswati. Originally a riverine Goddess, her description in Rig Veda has been a problem for the colonial claim of the 'Aryan' invasion/migration hypothesis. How could the 'Aryans' entering India in 1500–1200 BCE describe a river that had gone dry centuries before that? Some scholars have tried to circumvent the problem by suggesting the description of the mighty river to be poetic hyperbole. However, the geologists who studied the paleo-river channels discovered 'a perennial monsoonal-fed *Saraswati* river system with benign floods along its course' which to them was 'a testament to the acuity of the Rig Veda composers who transmitted to us across millennia such an incredibly accurate description of a grand river!'[23] There are also other studies which dispute the existence of a river during the Harappan times but point to a river that existed thousands of years before the very beginning of civilization in that area. But the importance of Saraswati in this context is beyond her physical reality.

Saraswati is not the only flowing riverine Goddess. The three goddesses who are invoked together in Vedas are Saraswati, Ila and Bharati. They are called the three goddesses in the *Rig Veda* ("*tisro devih*" RV 1:13:9). In the *Atharva Veda* all three are given the name Saraswati ('*tisrah Sarasvatih*'). Another Vedic Goddess of interest is Vac. In the *Vajasaneyi Samhita* (VS) of the *Yajur Veda,* Saraswati bestows Vac on Indra; she is the controller of Vac and she herself is the Vac. In *Shatapatha Brahmana,* the Goddesses Vac and Saraswati are declared as one. The Goddess Bharati is also identified with Vac. In the text *Brhad-Devata,* first compiled in 400 BCE and revised during early Puranic period, Vac united with Bharati, becomes the language of the Bharatas. Interestingly, both Vac and Saraswati are also warrior goddesses. Saraswati is compared to Indra and her assistance is requested in the battlefields. She is the only Goddess addressed as the slayer of Virtra-Virtragni. The epithet in its masculine form to address Indra 106 times is used only once in feminine form to address Saraswati. In the *Yajur Veda*, Saraswati is invoked with Rudras to help the people.[24]

In the Rig Veda's famous hymn 'Vac Sukta', she reveals herself as the Goddess. 'Vac Sukta' is interesting because this hymn is attributed to the human daughter Vac of sage Ambruna. Seized with an altered state of consciousness in which she merged with the archetypal Divine Feminine, she identifies herself with the Goddess. She declares her to be roaming the land with the Rudras (invoked with Saraswati in Vajasaneyi Samhita), Adityas (invoked with Bharati) and Vasus (invoked with Ila). Thus, she embodies in her all the three goddesses. Then she says that she fights for the people. She reveals herself as rashtri—embodiment of the nation. She says that she strings the bow of the Rudras and fights for the people. A comparable poetic manifestation of this Vedic hymn would arise centuries later in the worship of Goddess by tribes in the forest described in Chilapathikaram in South India. Again, we have here the primordial connectivity to the Goddess—both benign and a warrior Goddess that one finds in imagery which would later emerge during freedom struggle.

An Eight-armed Buddhist Battle Goddess with Vedic Roots

Dr Catherine Ludvik, Professor of Religion at Kyoto Sangyo University, points out that in *Suvarnaprabha Sutra* or the 'Sutra of Golden Light', Saraswati becomes a multi-armed fighting Goddess for Dharma and then asks:

> Would the Sutra of Golden Light, in the extant Sanskrit and in the versions represented by the Chinese translations of Yasogupta/Jnanagupta and Yijing—over two thousand years removed in time from the Rg Veda—have drawn on an aspect of the goddess that amongst the Hindus had been left behind, seemingly forgotten? Would the Buddhists have been studying the Rg Veda and its complex language so closely?[25]

She answers her own question in the negative and proceeds to establish that the sutra which first shows the original wisdom attribute of Goddess Saraswati later brings in the images of multi-armed battle goddesses which to her are mostly unrelated and then merges them with Saraswati. So, the Goddess becomes 'an eight-armed, weapon-bearing warrior' in the sutra. So, to Prof. Ludvik, Saraswati who takes the form of an eight-armed battle Goddess for dharma in the sutra and reaches Japan through China, is not Saraswati but more related to *Kausiki-Vindhyavasini* and *Mahishasuramardini*. This approach overlooks a strong connection that exists between Vac and Mahishasuramardini. In sixth and seventh century iconography of Mahishasuramardhini, the bow of the Goddess is emphasized. *Devi Mahatmiya*, which describes in detail the weapons of the Goddess and the deities who provided her weapons, states that it was the Maruts or the Rudras (sons of Rudra) who gave her the bow. In *Vac Sukta*, it is the bow of Rudra that she strings for the people. The organic interconnectivity of the imagery of these goddesses is indeed a very unique Indic phenomenon.

There is also another abiding continuity between Saraswati and Parvati, the consort of Siva who is more popularly identified with both Kali and Durga than Saraswati. Saraswati is not only a terrestrial riverine Goddess, but she is also a celestial Goddess. She is identified with Milky Way, the river of heaven. She is also associated with the cosmic tree which connects the celestial worlds and earth. Vedic scholar David Frawley sees in her cosmic symbolism, her higher status. He considers her the stream of consciousness.[26]

Aitareya Brahmana of the Rig Veda reveals a very interesting dimension of Saraswati. She is not only the celestial river, the river of this earth and the flow of consciousness; with all these aspects, she is also the stream of justice borne out of motherly love. Seers conducted a Soma ritual on the banks of *Saraswati*. Puranic scholar Sadashiv Ambadas Dange opines that they 'were trying assiduously, in a probable drought, for the gain of water'. They expelled Kavasha because he was the 'son of a dasi, a non-Brahmin and a gambler'. Humiliated and driven to the desert, there he was inspired and saw the famous 'Aponaptriya', 'the child of the waters'. He abided in her affection, says the text and *Saraswati* started flowing all around him. The dramatic contrast between the arrogant ritualists calling him 'dasiputra' and their shaming by Kavasha becoming the seer of 'the child of the waters', as well as the significance of the anecdote in rejecting the socially stagnant abuse of a person with a slur against his maternal lineage, pitting such slur against the Divine Feminine, cannot be lost on any careful student of Hindu history.

The *Rig Veda* speaks of the rivers as mothers of *Saraswati*, the seventh river. *Saraswati* herself is said to be *Sudughdh* or "yielding good milk". And this sacred geography gets mapped into the inner realms as well. In the *Rig Veda* (1.164.49), the seer asks Saraswati to allow him to suckle her breasts. Dr Ludvik insightfully observes:

> Her milk, in this stanza, represents all valuable things, which she gives in full from her abundant breast (*yena visva pusyasi varyani*), wealth in the widest sense. For the poet, as a poet, however, there is one treasure above all inspired thought (Dhi). Thus if one were to apply this stanza directly to the poet, one might say that he wishes to suck 'Dhi' directly from its source so that inspired thoughts might flow from him in the form of words.[27]

Dr Muhammad Israil Khan in his study of the evolution of *Saraswati* in Sanskrit literature points out that she is called 'Sindhumata'. This would mean she is the mother of the rivers and waters. So, here we have *Saraswati* who would also be associated with Bharati being the mother of Sindhu—from which the word 'India' is conventionally derived. Dr Israil Khan also points out another significant aspect—there is an inner significance to the outer geography of the river goddesses. The imagery of seven streams has an inner significance:

> Saptasvasa, saptadhatuh, saptathi, trisadhastha, svarranya rtavari delineate the social aspect of Sarasvati as a sister. The epithet saptasvasa assigns her to be one of the seven sister rivers namely Ganga, Yamuna, Sarasvati, Sutudri, Parusni, Marudvrdha and Arjikiya. The seven sisters also symbolise the stream of bliss the stream of existence, the stream of consciousness, the stream of truth, the stream of Manu, the stream of breath and the stream of gross body. ... Deities of the various regions reside in our body in their subtler form, while outside the body, they live in their gross form. But man does not realise this divine power in his own body, unless the vei1 of ignorance is cast away. In a mantra, Sarasvati has, therefore, been asked to provide a man with mind, intellect, thought, purpose, intelligence, hearing, sight, etc.[28]

So, the Goddess Saraswati also catalyses the internalizing of divine geography. The internalization of India's divine geography would later resurface in the discourse of Indian patriotism. Swami Rama Tirtha, a poet-seer and Vedantic patriot, envisioned his own body as India. Here he did not internalize in the spiritual sense but in a sense of empathizing with entire India as his own body and hence the sufferings and happiness of all Indian people as his own. Despite the conceptual difference, one can see the connection between the Vedic internalization of the sacred geography and the later identification of one's own body with India's geography in Swami Rama Tirtha:

> Do you wish to be a patriot? Tune yourself in love with your country and the people. Feel your unity with them.... Let me feel I am India the whole of India. The land of India is my own body. The Comorin is my feet, the Himalayas my head. From my hair flows the Ganges, from my head come the Brahmaputra and the Indus. The Vindhyachals are girt round my loins. The Coromandel is my right and the Malabar my left leg. I am the whole of India, and its east and west are my arms, and I spread them in a straight line to embrace humanity. I am universal in my love. Ah! Such is the posture of my body. It is standing and gazing at infinite space; but my inner spirit is the Soul of all. When I walk, I feel it is India walking. When I breathe, I feel it is India speaking. When I speak, I feel it is India breathing. I am India, I am Shankara, I am Siva. This is the highest realization of patriotism, and this is Practical Vedanta.[29]

Getting back to Saraswati, in the developing pan-Indian context, two of the greatest poet-seers from South India would get and seek the same milk of inspiration from the Goddess, though not from Saraswati but from Parvati, who is also the daughter of the mountains. According to Tamizh Saivaite tradition, Thiru Gnana Sambandar, the child prodigy and Saivaite saint of seventh century CE who revived Saivism in South India, was given the milk of wisdom by Goddess Parvati, when he cried as an infant. In *Saundarya Lahari,* a work conventionally attributed to Adi Sankara, arguably in early eighth century CE, the *Vedic Sarasvati* connection can be seen explicitly. Here a verse describes the milk from the breast of the Goddess as 'an ocean of milk flowing like the waters of Sarasvatam'. 'Sarasvatam' here represents the high poetic ability. Having drunk this milk, says Sankara, 'the Dravida Sisu (Dravidian infant) became poet-laureate among all great poets'. It is interesting that the Vedic imagery of the flowing river becomes linked to the poetic greatness of the South Indian seer. There have been discussions as to who is this Dravida child that Sankara speaks about—whether it is himself or Thiru Gnana Sambandar. The scholarly evidence points to the latter.[30]

In the context of Tamil Saivism, the distinction between Saraswati and Parvati does not matter at all, at least in the early philosophical realms. *Thirumanthiram* is a fifth century CE canonical Saivaite text written by the Tamil mystic seer Thirumoolar. He defines all the attributes of Saraswati clearly and then very emphatically identifies them with Parvati:

> *She that holds the Book of Knowledge in her hand divine*
> *She our mother, of eyes three,*
> *She of crystal form, She of comely white lotus,*
> *She chants the Vedas, She is Pārvati. (Thirumanthiram: Tantra 4:5:22, 1067)*

So, the mother Goddess, dread Goddess, warrior Goddess, Goddess of wisdom, Goddess of justice—all these Goddess streams unite through the history of Hindus, and she surfaces again in the collective consciousness of Hindus during the times of crisis, prompting them to act against the forces of disharmony.

Invoking the Goddess before a battle is a tradition we find in the Mahabharata. Arjuna, the Pandava hero, invokes Durga before the final battle of Kurukshetra. Though many consider it as material added in later centuries, it is consistent with the warrior Goddess stream already seen. The *stuti* by Arjuna also prefigures in it certain crucial aspects of Bharat Mata. Here is a partial rendering of the hymn:

> She is the head of the army of *Siddhas*; She lives in the forest of *Mandara*; She is *Kumāri*, *Kāli*, *Kāpāli* and She is of black and tawny hue; She is Mahākāli, Bhadra Kāli and *Chandi*; She is the bearer of a banner of peacock plumes; She holds the weapons, sword, spear and shield; She is dressed in yellow; She is also of white hue; She is the younger sister of Krishna; She is the killer of buffalo; She is ever present in the sacred abodes erected to you in the cities of *Jambvudwipa* (India); She is the science of *Brahman* among sciences; She is the great sleep (*Mahanidra*); She is *Savitri*; She is *Saraswathi*; She is the mother of Vedas; She is the unconsciousness, sleep, the illusion, the modesty, the beauty of (all life forms); The Siddhas and the Charanas behold Her in contemplation.[31]

In the hymns one can see that the Goddess is both white and black; she is associated with peacock (which is now the national flag of India). She is of varied races and the hymn also makes clear her association with the sacred geography of India—she dwells in the abodes for her in the holy cities of Jambvudwipa, and she also dwells in the forest. She is also the consciousness in all its dimensions.

In the post-Alexander period, the non-Indian powers who had learnt of India also felt India to be a feminine entity. The famous one is the depiction of India in the 'great hunt 'mosaic of Sicily with the characteristic fauna of India. Done around fourth century CE, it represents India as a woman in the right-side border of the Roman empire as conceived by the artist while on the other side it shows Africa or Mauretania. India personified as a woman is shown holding an elephant tusk in her hand, surrounded by tiger, elephant and a phoenix.[32]

More pertinent to the current discussion is the carved silver dish discovered at Lampsacus, Asia Minor which is now in the museum of antiquities at Istanbul. It was Eric Herbert Warmington (1898–1987), a professor of Latin, who in his book on the trade between India and Roman empire identified this serendipitous discovery in 1900 as 'an artistic representation of India as a woman surrounded by mammals and birds which were supposed to be typical of that region'.[33] The female-like figurine on an elephant-like Indian seat of royalty was surrounded 'by a parrot, a guinea-fowl, a tiger, a leopard, and hanuman monkeys though the guinea fowl was certainly African, the others were Indian".[34] While Warmington had described the 'India' depicted thus in purely the commercial fauna supposedly exported from India, later Indian scholars have seen in this 'India' the Divine Feminine. Archaeologist and art historian specializing in ancient Indian art Dr Prithvi K. Agrawala of Banaras Hindu University calls this figure 'Bharata Lakshmi' of probably Bactrian origin[35] while Prof. Saifurraḥman Ḍar considers her 'Lakshmi or Personification of Mother India'.[36] Umakant Premanand Shah, an expert on Jain iconography, considers the same figure as representing 'Indian Ardhanārīśvara'.[37] The three Indian (including Pakistani) identifications of the personification of India with Lakshmi and Ardhanarishwara show that India as a feminine personification was also associated with divinity. The two horn-like structures emanating in her crown may also suggest a continuity with the horn-seated yogic figure in the Harappan seal. India as a Goddess or a mother figure has thus entered the general human conscience at least 1800 years ago and the roots go to the Vedic conception of rashtri.

Resurfacing of the Sword-bearing Goddess

The Goddess resurfaces in the history of India at the time of historic crises, which synchronize with heightened psychological crises of communities and leaders. This manifestation of the Goddess phenomenon has been described in poetic and mystic terms, but one can understand that this is also the surfacing of the deeper historical process of Goddess based Indic resistance to aggressions that go against the national values of India.

Kumara Kampana and Meenakshi

When the Sultanate was established in Madurai, South India descended into a period of anarchy. The invaders ravaged the land and people suffered. In 1334 Tughluq general Jalal ud-Din Ahsan Shah rebelled against Delhi Sultanate and established an independent Sultanate at Ma'bar (which is the Madurai Sultanate). This sultanate was marked by 'dynastic violence, slaughter of Hindus, and war over trading stations'.[38] The period from 1335–1342 also saw famines ravage South India. It was during such a tumultuous time that Vijayanagar was established. The prince and army commander of Vijayanagar Kumara Kampana, through his brilliant attacks on Madurai Sultanate, decimated the Islamic State and killed the Sultan. His wife Gangadevi composed a poetic work in Sanskrit titled *Madhura Vijayam* describing the valorous deeds of Kampana. She describes how after an initial victory, the king becomes indulgent and relaxed, enjoying fine arts. At that time, a strange maiden arrives in his court who provides a pathetic picture of the Southern land ravaged by invaders. Gangadevi writes:

> A woman of extraordinary presence, whose identity no one in the region knew, arrived one day at the capital, and stood before Kampana raya, describing how the Southland was harassed by 'Turuksha' (Muslim or 'Turkish') invaders. At first the king and his court did not realize she was a Goddess. O Raja, Vyaghrapuri has reverted to its namesake! Yes, now it's literally a 'town' where 'tigers' roam! And Chidambaram and Perumparrapuliya! The whole region is truly becoming a wilderness again. Long ago, people civilized that land, but wild beasts run free again there now. The main shrine of the Shrirangam temple, including the superstructure, has pathetically fallen apart, so much that the only roof which covers the image of Sriranganatha, Lord Vishnu reclining on the world stage, sheltering him from the tumbling debris and crumbling masonary, is the hood of Adisesha, the cosmic serpent with coiled energy under whose protective presence the Lord always rests.... Even the womanly river Kaveri, once channelled with sturdy dams and bunds, flowing with life-sustaining order, now has begun to lose her discipline, randomly breaching her banks and sprawling anywhichway, as chaos of all sorts caused by the invaders, spreads....The graceful coconut trees, which used to flourish in garden scattered all around Madurai, have been felled by the invaders; instead, iron spears stand in their place, decorated with hideous garlands of decapitated heads. The river *Tamraparni*, which used to run bright with sandalwood paste rinsed from the breasts of young women bathing there, now flows red with cow blood as the invaders slaughter herds of cattle.

After explaining to Kampana the destruction of dharma and *rita* the woman then presents him with a sword:

> Thus did the strange lady decribe to Kampana, the fate that had overtaken the fair south, and drawing out from her girdle a resplendent sword, addressed the king once again as follows: "O Sovereign! Once upon a time the divine Visvakarma, gathering the splinters from the weapons of all the Devas and smelting them together, shaped

> this strange sword and presented it to Paramesvara for gaining victory over the daityas. By performing a severe penance, one of the Pandya kings obtained it from Lord Paramesvara. With the help of this divine weapon the descendants of this race continued to rule the kingdom prosperously for a very long period; ...Agastya, having secured this sword, presents this now to you. Just as Krishna slew Kamsa in Mathura in olden times, O King! do you also proceed now to the Southern Madhura and slaughter the Mussalman king, the enemy of the world and set up pillars of victory on the bridge of Rama. During your Administration of the south, you should also build a strong dam across the Kaveri and make her flow in a manner useful to the agricultural population."[39]

Dr William Jackson, a professor of religious studies and a pro-Gandhian, points out that Ganga Devi used the imagery that was already in the collective religious memory. Pointing out that 'the Goddess with the sword gives the right and responsibility, the power to prevail, entrusting the king with the means to undertake the righting of vast wrongs', Jackson underlines the fact that 'this fight for survival, not aggression for colonization' would reopen both the Meenakshi temple and Sri Rangam temple and change the destiny of South India. He calls this 'an archetypal event with divine paradigm'. He elaborates with an insight rare in most but not all Western scholars of Hindu history and symbolism:

> History may be full of delusive clashes, as poet Allen Ginsberg suggests: 'Fighting phantoms Egyptians mummied pharoahs ... Fighting phantoms David picked up his sling ... Fighting phantoms Siddhartha meditated under a Bo tr'ee' and so on. Fighting phantoms, poets wrote satires, people committed suicide, planned excesses and spent the wealth of nations, no doubt; but at Vijayanagara the fighting was against "phantoms" who were quite real. The Hindu king had a dharmic obligation to reclaim provinces lost to the Muslim invaders, and, through this action, Vijayanagara developed into a great empire governing much of South India in provincial segments for the next 250 years. The sword and the boar emblem impressed its meaning: power and rescue, the strength of protection, fighting non-phantom occupiers of a traditionally Hindu land.[40]

He traces this association of the divine sword and archetypal Divine Feminine to even the Harappan times, speculating that the so-called 'dancing girl' could have been originally a fencer and also pointing out that *Bharata Natya Sastra* includes sword fencing as one of the 64 arts a dancing girl should study.[41] So here we have a pan-Hindu Goddess related to India's sacred geography—the princess of the South married to Siva of the Himalayas—presenting the sword to a king to fight against aggression, which is against the values of Indic spirituality and culture. The poetess points out clearly the Goddess transcending the linguistic barriers—she makes the Kannada prince to continue the lineage of Tamizh Pandyas and Chozhas. Thus, she points to a common culture and values beyond linguistic pluralism while respecting it. In fact, Vijayanagara itself became a model multilingual state with patronage for all South Indian languages of that time. She also points to the harmony of nature and society through references to the rivers *Kaveri* and *Tamrabaruni*.

Shivaji and Bhavani

The Goddess giving the sword to fight oppression and the invaders again reappears in the traditions of Shivaji (1630–1680), the Maratha resistance leader who fought not only against Islamist intrusions in Deccan but also with a vision of installing 'Hindavi Swaraj'. The emergence of national consciousness in the Maratha movement would become pivotal in the emergence of the Indian nation-state.

If Shivaji appeared on the scene at a time of national crisis, Bhavani, the Goddess appeared to Shivaji at a critical hour during his own crisis. Historian Jadunath Sarkar, an authority on both Shivaji and his archrival Aurangzeb, the Hindu-hating Mughal dictator, describes this specific course of events:

> This was the most critical moment in the career of Shivaji. If he capitulated to Afzal Khan, all his hopes of independence and future greatness would be gone forever and he would have to end his days as a tame vassal of Bijapur, even if he escaped his sovereign's vengeance for his later rebellion. Yet, the open defiance of Bijapur authority now would forever close the door to reconciliation with that State, and he must be prepared ever afterwards to defend his life and independence against the power of that kingdom and of the Mughals and other enemies, without a single friend or protector to turn to in the wide world. His ministers and generals advocated the more ignoble policy. Shiva himself was in a terrible dilemma. For a night he pondered on his life's choice and then chose the manlier part. A legend, dating from his lifetime tells us that the care-worn chieftain's sleep was broken by a vision of the Goddess Bhavani who urged him to confront Afzal boldly and promised him victory and her full protection. (Sabh. 11.) His mind was made up. Next morning the council met again. Moved by Shiva's manly words, appeal to their sense of honour, and report of the Goddess's blessings, they resolved on war.[42]

The sword of Shivaji was also associated with the Goddess. While traditions and calendar art depictions show Shivaji receiving this sword from the

Goddess, historian H. S. Sardesai provides an account of the relation between the sword and the Goddess tradition:

> It was in this campaign that Shivaji obtained his famous sword "Bhavani", which he named after his tutelary deity Bhavani, and this historic weapon seldom left his side afterwards....After its acquisition, he never knew defeat in any campaign. While returning from the temple of Harihareshwar, Shivaji was told about a famous long sword, worth 300 hons, with a chief, Golwalkar Sawant by name. It was suggested to Shivaji that he should wrest this sword by force. But Shivaji replied, "A brave man should never covet what belongs to another. You will remember the Puranic legend about Syamantamani. The feuds that arose from the loss of that diamond required all the energies of Lord Krishna to settle." ...It seems that either Sawant received this news or on the advice of his ministers, presented Shivaji with the sword....It is true that Shivaji simply adored this sword. During the nine days preceding the Dasahara dedicated to the worship of the goddess Bhavani, he placed the sword on the consecrated altar next to the image of the goddess and worshipped it. On the tenth day he used to take it up devoutly from the altar and with this sacred weapon in his hand set out upon his campaigns.[43]

Guru Gobind Singh and Bhagavati

One can see here a continuity of the Goddess tradition related to the Indian resistance to the civilizational values held by the nation. Guru Gobind Singh (1667–1708), the tenth and the last living Guru of Sikhs, formed the institution of Khalsa in 1699. The organization fought against the religious persecution unleashed by the Mughals. Like the 'Hindavi Swaraj' of Shivaji, Khalsa also visualized India as a whole and put forth a vision of theo-diversity. In his fight against the expansionist monopolistic aggression Guru Gobind Singh employed in a very energetic and poetic manner the image of the Goddess. Prof. Surjit Singh Gandhi—an authority on Sikh history and tradition explains:

> In 1686, Guru Gobind Singh is said to have completed the composition of *Shastra Nam Mala* in the conventional literary style of the time having its model the emblematical verses of the great Masters. The true import of the composition lies in personifying the weapons and for the Guru they were the medium of worship.... Almost at the same time, the Guru composed *Var Sri Bhagauti ji ki*, popularly known as *Chandi Di Var*....Though the source of the composition as in *Chandi Charitra* was also the tenth Skanda of *Markand Puran*, he related in his composition only the battle of *Chandi* and *Durga*....*Chandi*'s battles were in the eyes of Guru Gobind

> Singh, fought on the side of righteousness....He pictured *Durga* as the one clad in armour from head to foot while serpents coiled around her neck hissing dreadfully at the foe. Her hand-drum makes the sound of roaring tigress. She is riding a lion and fights valorously against the Rakhshasas—tyrants and slays *Mahikhasur* among others....The gods themselves revere Durga as 'Mother' and they look up to her for help in overcoming and destroying their enemy. She in fact is represented as a moral power to challenge an oppressive system and to establish harmony, morality and justice. Her aggression is, therefore healthy as her anger is purifying.[44]

What is striking is the association of the Divine Feminine that Guru Gobind Sing gives to the sword which resonates with the entire pan-Indic tradition of the surfacing of the Goddess during the rising of resistance in India to civilizational aggression against the core values of the nation. Prof. Gandhi writes:

> The Guru's militarism had two things implicit in it, viz. Shakti and Divine Power. The Guru adopted two symbols for the propagation of his militarism: the Goddess Chandi and the Sword, Chandi being symbol of divine power and sword that of power and dignity....In Sikh religious parlance the sword conveys two-dimensional meaning. One, sword (Bhagauti) is an attributive name of the Real one in the compositions of Guru Gobind Singh. Thus, the wearer feels that he/she is ever under the protection of Bhagauti. Second, and which is in fact a derivative of the first, it symbolises manifestation of Shakti or Divine Power which is to be used in favour of the saints against the demonic powers as a last resort when all other means fail to impact.[45]

The sword of the Goddess is bathed in the blood of the demons, and Guru Gobind Singh here in his poetry employs the Vedic geography—'Drenched in blood, the naked swords appear like goddesses bathing together in the Sarasvati'. Nikky-Guninder Kaur Singh in her study of the birth of the Khalsa explains the Divine Feminine manifesting in the poetry of Guru Gobind Singh at the crucial period of history, which also saw the installing and spread of Khalsa movement:

> In (Guru Gobind Singh's) *Durga* compositions, the sword is personified as a female figure who appears in a variety of forms, combining princess, goddess, and lioness. Divisions and verticalities between the human, divine, and animal realms are erased as figures from each of the three unite to personify her....Though the setting of his story is primarily a battlefield, the guru imaginatively presents his heroine in different psychic and geographical landscapes....With the analogies to princesses and goddesses, the sword emerges as a fluid character, endowed with a

> status that is both secular and divine. Blood and water also come together to reveal the coexistence of her procreative and destructive dimensions. Her royal blood red sari turns into the transparent waters of Sarasvati, the goddess of knowledge and learning....She gets rid of all that is dead and dull within the self, stirring up our innermost senses and emotions....Durga and her sword are interchangeable. She is the matrix that biologically generates the universe, and the inspiration that motivates poets, philosophers, and artists....Together they artistically fuse many of the goddess's functions with that of her weapon. She is *mamta* (maternal love)—the source of emotional and mental cultivation. She is *namta* (humility)—the requisite for spiritual development. She avita*ita* (poetry)—the artistic surplus vital to our moral and spiritual sensibility.[46]

While Nikky-Singh identifies this Durga with the global Goddess tradition including the Buddhist, Shinto, Pagan and even Marian tradition (in which Goddess is actually subdued to the male Christian deity as a saint), the clear pre-figuring of Bharat Mata is clearest in the verses of Guru Gobind Singh. In fact, Bharat Mata herself in the Hindutva worldview, merges with the Earth Goddess and Cosmic Goddess. One can say that it is in the verses of Guru Gobind Singh that the Vedic Goddess tradition at last found Her fulfilment as the Goddess personifying India's core national values and the sum total of organic historical processes that make India a Nation. Later it was taken up by Bankim Chandra Chatterjee.

Sacred Geography and Divine Feminine

Prof. Diana Eck who is not at all an admirer of 'Hindu nationalism' (which she finds disturbing) accepts that Bharat Mata is more ancient than the colonial period of eighteenth or nineteenth century:

> Some historians, political scientists, and interpreters of the modern period in India have traced the popularization of the idea of Bhārat Mātā, or "Mother India," to the rise of Indian nationalism in the late nineteenth century, and to Bankim Chandra Chatterjee's "Vande Mātaram," ... But such a view lacks a longer historical perspective, for clearly the identification of devīs with the land has much older roots in the symbolization of the body-cosmos as inscribed in the system of devī shrines.[47]

Prof. Eck adds that what happened during the colonial period was the 'the cartographic surveying of India' which yielded 'a map of imperial mastery' and 'that familiar triangular shape also became a powerful icon of territorial India, especially when joined with the image of the Goddess Bhārat Mātā.'[48]

However, evidence suggests that even before the 'imperial cartography' what Prof. Eck calls as 'that familiar triangular shape' has been associated with both the physical and sacred geography of India. Sir Alexander Cunningham (1814–1893), military engineer-turned-archaeologist, in his work *Ancient Geography of India* (1871) points out that Mahabharata sees India as an equilateral triangle with Kanyakumari as the apex and Himalayas as the base:

> At a somewhat later date (which is 1st century CE which is the time of Mahabharata composition according to Cunningham) the shape of India is described in the "Mahabharata" as an equilateral triangle which was divided into four smaller equal triangles. The apex of the triangle is Cape Comorin, and the base is formed by the line of Himalaya mountains....The shape corresponds very well with the general form of the country, if we extend the limits of India to Ghazni on the north-west, and fix the other two points of the triangle at Cape Comorin and Sadiya in Assam.[49]

This triangle of India is also related with the triangle Yantras which in turn symbolize the Divine Feminine. Prof. Madhu Khanna, a historian of religion and scholar of Hindu Tantric tradition, sees the inverted triangle as 'the primal triangle, emblem of cosmic energy as Sakti, the female principle supporting the archetypal shapes of a Devi Yantra.'[50] This Yantra in turn is also associated with the sacred geography of India through the body of the Goddess. Prof. Khanna explains:

> Yantras have been described as symbolic extensions of the sacred pilgrim centres (pitha-sthana)—the most holy temples of the Supreme Goddess which are scattered throughout India—and as "spatial digits" of the divine....Thus yantras should be seen, not as "artworks" isolated from the religious tradition in which they developed and which sustains them, but as two-dimensional pitha-sthana or pilgrim temples in which the movement from the profane to the sacred takes place.[51]

According to archaeologist and historian of science Dr D. P. Agrawal, the use of human movement through such symbolic geoscape dates to third millennium BCE. The use of 'the location of their main metropolitan towns in a peculiar network of intersecting circles" by Harappans could have 'provided impetus for travel to these far-flung areas of the state' making it one of the factors in achieving 'this unification of a society with so much diversity'. He says that 'in later times, it was achieved by locating the main pilgrimage centres at the farthest points of the country, from Amarnath and Badrinath in the north, Dwaraka in the west, Puri in the east to Rameshwaram in the south.'[52]

In this context, it should be noted that Hindutva or Hinduness in Indian polity, whether it is Gandhi or Savarkar, has always zeroed in on the pilgrim networks to assert the oneness of India. For example, Gandhi wrote in his *Hind Swaraj*:

> What do you think could have been the intention of those farseeing ancestors of ours who established Setubandha (Rameshwar) in the South, Jagannath in the East and Hardwar in the North as places of pilgrimage?...They knew that worship of God could have been performed just as well at home....But they saw that India was one undivided land so made by nature. They, therefore, argued that it must be one nation. Arguing thus, they established holy places in various parts of India, and fired the people with an idea of nationality in a manner unknown in other parts of the world. And we Indians are one as no two Englishmen are.[53]

Prof. Phyllis K. Herman who teaches Religious Studies at California State University in her study of *Sita Rasois* (Kitchens of Sita) a series of pilgrimage centres connected to the places where Sita was said to have cooked, comparing them to *Sakta Pithas* states:

> The whole of the Indian subcontinent can be seen, I would argue, as the body of a goddess/pativratā: Sītā reenters the earth at the end of the Rāmāyana, Satī's body parts are scattered all over India, such that their diffused bodies both "fertilize" the subcontinent and unite it as a whole. Their shrines are local manifestations that connect and are connected to the larger "faithscape" of the subcontinent, nourishing the nation as a whole while expressing the ritual power of individual women.[54]

Prof. Eck rightly points out that India is thus 'a sacred geography enlivened by the presence of the gods and interlinked through the circulation of pilgrims... clearly one not of religious exclusivity, but rather of complexity, mobility, and plurality' and that this 'way of articulating a land and landscape is far older than the modern nation-state'. But given the fact that she was 'discouraged about the writing of it, fearing that somehow the image of a sacred geography... would further feed the fervour of an exclusive new Hindu nationalism', she tries to distance it from an imagined 'strident new form of Hindu nationalism', in reality the opposition to Bharat Mata and Vande Mataram comes not because these imageries are exclusive but precisely because they are pluralistic and inclusive. The politics of expansionism of monopolistic monocultures, naturally want to eliminate such emotionally surcharged imageries rooted in the tradition from the social and cultural life of India or weaken and sideline them as much as possible. Naturally, the colonial and Marxist dominated academia pays little heed to this aspect.

During the National Movement

Around 1905 in Baroda College, a young student hesitatingly approached an English professor about whom there was an aura of mystery. It had been rumoured that he had revolutionary links and that he was even connected with Russian anarchists. The boy with trepidation asked the professor with a typical Indian turban the question that was burning in the minds of many young Indian students, 'How can one develop nationalism?' The student was Kanhaiyalal Maneklal Munshi (1887–1971). The professor was Sri Aurobindo. Sri Aurobindo pointed to the student a wall-map of India and gave an answer. Years later, K. M. Munshi recollected it thus:

> Look at that map. Learn to find in it the portrait of Bharat mata. The cities, mountains, rivers and forests are the materials which go to make up Her body. The people inhabiting the country are the cells which go to make up Her living tissues. Our literature is Her memory and speech. The spirit of Her culture is Her soul. The happiness and freedom of Her children is Her salvation. Behold Bharat as a living Mother, meditate upon Her and worship Her in the nine-fold way of Bhakti.[55]

The words of Sri Aurobindo show a continuity of the Goddess tradition of the sacred geography. She is also a Goddess of national historical processes.

So, did Vande Mataram bring back at the appropriate time of national crisis the underlying waiting national consciousness of India? The answer is in the affirmative. According to historian Radhakumud Mukherjee (1884–1964), the basis of Bankim Chandra Chatterjee's 'Bande Mataram' was inspired by Vedic Democracy. It was 'the last Sukta of the last Mandala of the *Rig Veda*, the prayer offered by Rishi Angirasa to his chosen Deity, who from his name, may be taken as the Deity of Democracy' whose name 'is a most singular and abstract name ever given to a Deity of worship'. Mukherjee explained the meaning of the name of the deity called 'Saminana or Samajnana, a name which, according to Sayanacharya, symbolizes the national, collective, political consciousness evenly spread (*sama*) among a whole people, what may be called the National Mind whom individual minds are to invoke as the source of their own vitality'. But interestingly though Mukherjee sees it manifesting as the national consciousness, it is also 'visvachmtanya, cosmic consciousness, oversoul, in which the individual soul is to be merged in Yoga'. 'The *Rig Veda* describes the mantra with which this Deity of Democracy is to be worshipped by its votaries, the mantra of complete inner union of their hearts (*hridaya*) and mind (*manah*), their hopes and aspirations and in national policy (*mantra*)' And it was this deity that was expressing itself in Bande Mataram.[56]

So, her symbolism is dynamic and is responsive to the challenges of the milieu. This report by James Ker, ICS, a personal assistant to the Director of Criminal Intelligence, Shimla from 1907 to 1913 on the image of the demon slaying Goddess, named *Rashtriya Jagruti* (National Awakening) states:

> Her lion or tiger is labeled "Bahiskar" (Boycott) and is attacking the bovine monster labeled "Pardeshi Vyapar" (Foreign Trade), on whose back the goddess has placed her foot after, apparently, cutting off its head. The demon near the severed head of the monster is labelled "Vilayati Mal" (English Goods) and is being bitten in the arm by a snake called "Swabhiman" (Pride of Self), which is held in one of the hands of the heroine, while the same demon's head has been injured by the knife labeled "Svavalamban" (Self-Independence). The demon being held by the hair [by the goddess] is labeled "Desha Droha" (Disloyalty loyalty to Country)...the hand which holds his hair is labeled "Desh Seva"" (Service of Country).[57]

On 11 August 1910, the image of the Goddess would cost its painter Shridar Waman Nagarkar three years of rigorous imprisonment.

The Goddess Pan-Indic

Bharat Mata seized the rhythm of the national heart as Vande Mataram. Kazi Abdul Gaffar, an Urdu poet from Hyderabad, was 'greatly impressed by Vande Mataram song'. He warned the Muslim community that if they did not spread the message of patriotism through their work, it would spell defeat for the Muslims in the literary field. To this end, he also translated Vande Mataram and published in *Payama* popular Urdu paper on 7 October 1937: '*Madare Watan! Hum tujhe salaam karte hain. ... Tu hamari khahargiri karnewali hai, hum tujhe salaam karte hain*'.[58]

Linguistic sub-nationalisms emerged during the colonial period with the support of the colonial anthropology. Strategically encouraged by British administration, the proponents often based their narratives on the framework of Aryan/non-Aryan divide. One of the earliest Indian proponents who insisted on separate Tamizh identity was Maraimalai Adigal (1876–1950). Despite his fondness for separate Tamizh identity, he had composed a hymn on Mother India which is very similar to *Anandamath's* depiction of a glorious and fallen Mother:

> *...Oh Mother India who gave the world many riches,*
> *Thou art the lamp of light to the entire world!*

Thou art dear to me as very life of my life!
How can I with my little knowledge
elaborate upon the multi-splendored greatness of Thee!
Thou with wealth that can never be lost,
stand today Thee impoverished by plundering aliens!
That shame shall be wiped out by Thy children!
Enlightened they toil to revive Thy glory in fields diverse!
May they flourish and succeed in their efforts and
May our minds cease suffering![59]

In Tamil Nadu, Bharat Mata was celebrated in the famous lyrics of Subramania Bharathi (1882–1921). The poetry of Bharathi is so profound in meaning while being melodious and simple, that they were understood by all sections of the society and changed the literary course of Tamizh, launching the age-old language into the uncharted ocean of modernity. Bharathi's loadstone was the Vedanta of Swami Vivekananda and Sri Aurobindo. In fact, he was a very close friend of Sri Aurobindo during his stay in Pondicherry. He had met Sister Nivedita (born Margaret Elizabeth Noble, 1867–1911), Irish disciple of Swami Vivekananda and had accepted her as his Guru. Bharathi also wrote two long poems—one on Shivaji and the other on Guru Gobind Singh forming Khalsa. He related this to the present condition of India.

In the year 1908 in Chennai, the daily paper *Vijaya* was founded with Bharathi as its editor. He was later forced to move to the French-governed Pondicherry because of the troubles created by British authorities. The evening newspaper came from Pondicherry for eight months, between September of 1909 and April of 1910. Bharat Mata was featured on the front page of the newspaper, shown as a Mother Goddess with four hands—of which two hold to her bosom all communities depicted as infants suckling at her breasts while her body looks identical to the map of India. There are two banners showing 'Bharat Mata' and the slogan 'Vande Mataram' written in Devanagari and Urdu. Poet Bharathi is also incidentally the one who identified Bharat Mata with the consort of Siva in a definite manner:

Demonic Our Mother can be;
Great Madness carries She.
She loves dearly the Mad One
He who carries the Fire scorching.[60]

So, what does one make of this Hindu imagery? One persistent criticism of Bharat Mata is that being an image derived from Bankim Chandra's

Anandamath, a novel supposedly anti-Muslim in character, the image is inherently exclusive of Muslims. However, the analysis of the novel itself shows that the song does not have any anti-Muslim bias to it. Sabyasachi Bhattacharya in his systematic analysis of how the song appears in the novel points out that the battle scene in which the song plays out is against the East India Company:

> On the last two occasions when Vande Mataram is sung again, it is a battle song of the sanyasis in the thick of their fight with the East Indian Company's forces (Part III, Chapter IX; Part IV, Chapter VI). Among those who "willingly embraced" death in a hopeless battle was Jeebananda. The sanyasis give their lives singing *Vande Mataram*.[61]

Unless one construes the collaboration of Nawab with the East India Company that very much increased the human misery in 1770 famine as Islamic, there is nothing anti-Islamic in the song. As to the question of how Muslims, whose religion forbids idol worship, would accept the nation depicted in the form of a Goddess, the answer perhaps comes from Sikh dharma where Guru Gobind Singh showed that Sikhs who do not worship idols can use the Goddess as a poetic-spiritual symbol of the *Shakti* to fight against oppression even while remaining uncompromising in worshipping the formless Divine.

In a remarkable convergence, colonial authorities, Islamists and leftists meet at a focal point where they accuse the Bengali freedom fighters of Sri Aurobindo's time and Sri Aurobindo himself of promoting a Hindu religious form of nationalism associated with the Goddess worship. Evangelist, Indologist and a promoter of fulfilment theology (that Christianity fulfils Hinduism) J. N. Farquhar wrote in 1912 that the religious aspect of anarchism in India 'was merely an extension of that revival of Hinduism' that started in the nineteenth century. M. N. Roy, who was one of the founders of Communist Party of India, criticized Sri Aurobindo for 'adapting Vedantic teachings of Vivekananda to political purposes'.[62] But Bengali revolutionaries including Sri Aurobindo insisted on the non-sectarian vision of Bharat Mata. *Jugantor Patrika*, the revolutionary organ wrote:

> Each man has his own Dharma, and it is by the cultivation of this Dharma that he becomes fit for the path of emancipation. Therefore, the kingdom of righteousness is as indispensable to the Muslims or Christians as it is to the Hindu.[63]

Exhibit 1226 in Alipore Bomb trail—a document of the Bengali revolutionaries—not only called Hindus and Muslims to come together for the service of a common motherland without having to relinquish their individual religious identity, but also warns anyone trying to create trouble with dire consequences:

> Brother Hindus, in the name of Kali, Durga, Mohadeb, Srikrishna; brother Mohammedans, in the name of your Khodatala, circulate from village to village that we Hindus and Mohammedans jointly worship the feel of the mother native country. Any one of the priests who visit the village under the pretence of religion, but really with a view to create a disturbance will lose his head.[64]

Meanwhile, Hindu-Muslim riots had started erupting in Bengal. In 1906 Muslim League came into being. The red circular ('*Lal Ishtahar*') was circulated among the Muslims, asking them to economically boycott Hindus. Following Hindu-Muslim riots in Jamalpur, Sri Aurobindo wrote in *Bande Mataram*:

> The true policy of the Congress movement should have been from the beginning to gather together under its flag all the elements of strength that exists in this huge country. The Brahman Pandit and the Mahomedan Maulavi, the caste organizations and the trade unions, the labourer and the artisan, the coolie at his work and the peasant in his field, none of them should have been left out of the sphere of our activity.[65]

Yet he was well aware of how Islamist politics and British colonialism were finding a common cause to discredit the Swadeshi movement. In many of his articles in *Bande Mataram*, he pointed out how sections of Muslim aristocracy, particularly the Nawab of Dacca, the British administration and Anglo-Indian press were colluding actively against Swadeshi movement, and this was given the colour of Hindu-Muslim antagonism. Sri Aurobindo warned nationalists to be wary of this British strategy of 'Divide and Rule'. Even in its warning to the Muslims not to be left behind in partaking the 'nectar' of independence, *Jugantor* addressed Muslims as 'favoured sons of independence'. In all the Bengali revolutionary literature we find a strong tendency not to exclude the Muslims but requesting them not to fall prey to divisive tactics of the British colonialism and Islamist communal forces.

On 30 December 1939 when Sri Aurobindo was informed about the Islamist opposition to Vande Mataram and Congress support for the removal of some portions of the song, he responded by saying, that 'in that case Hindus should give up their culture.' Then he said:

> It is not a religious song. It is a national song and the Durga spoken of is India as the Mother. Why should not the Muslims accept it? It is an image used in the poetry. In the Indian conception of nationality Hindu view would naturally be there. If it cannot find a place there, the Hindus may as well be asked to give up their culture.[66]

One can see the same streams continue into modern India. The Hindutvaites celebrate the Muslims who venerate Mother India. To the leftists of modern India who continue the colonial legacy of pro-Islamism, such inclusive attitude is anathema. For example, Sadanand Menon, a radical leftist and art critic, shows his disdain for Hindutvaites when he writes (along with Romila Thapar and A. G. Noorani) about 'the sheer ecstasy and rapture into which Hindutva hacks went when A. R. Rahman performed in a virtuoso track of *Vande Mataram* nearly a decade ago'.[67] However, to understand the contempt that India's modern left has for Vande Mataram, which is very similar to the one harboured by the colonialists during freedom struggle, one needs only to compare how different and contemptuous the above statement is when compared with the one made by Dr A. P. J. Abdul Kalam (1931–2015), a scientist who was also the President of India (2002–2007), regarding the same Vande Mataram performed by music director A. R. Rahman: 'A. R. Rahman may be a Muslim but his voice echoes in the soul of all Indians, of whatever faith, when he sings Vande Mataram.'[68] One can contrast the 'ecstasy and rapture' of 'Hindutva hacks' described by Sadanand Menon with Dr Kalam speaking about Vande Mataram echoing 'in the soul of all Indians, of whatever faith'. The continuity of colonial collusion with pan-Islamist opposition to Vande Mataram and Bharat Mata can be seen in Menon very clearly. To the leftists, Muslim national icons like Dr Kalam who defy the stereotypes and leftist-assigned roles become enemies.

The passages by both Sadanand Menon and Dr Kalam presented here refer to the popular music album titled Vande Mataram released by Bharat Bala productions in 1997. In the second Vande Mataram album from Bharat Bala executed by Ranjit Barot, featured the rendering of Vande Mataram by Lata Mangeshkar. The video accompanying the song was interspersed with the faces of women from diverse village and tribal communities of India. The album also featured another rendering of Vande Mataram by famous singer Saddiq Khan Langa along with the recital of English translation of the verses by Sri Aurobindo. These emerging trends in purely non-political cultural activities are then the process of the Goddess nature of Bharat Mata inherently, steadily and spontaneously working towards inclusiveness rather than excluding Muslims. Depiction of her as nurturing all the children of territorial India without any religious, gender or ethnic discrimination while being rooted in the Goddess tradition of Hindu spirituality by Tamizh poet Bharathi shows the real nature of this Goddess. She is not a colonial import. She represents the unique and basic civilizational nature of India as a nation.

Bharat Mata Temples

The Bengali revolutionaries saw their movement as a temple of the Goddess, 'Bhavani Mandir'. There were others who wanted to build a very physical temple for Mother India. In an emotionally surcharged way, after his return from the World Parliament of Religions, Swami Vivekananda had given a clarion call to worship Mother India:

> For the next fifty years this alone shall be our keynote—this, our great Mother India. Let all other vain gods disappear for the time from our minds. This is the only god that is awake, our own race— "everywhere his hands, everywhere his feet, everywhere his ears, he covers everything." All other gods are sleeping. What vain gods shall we go after and yet cannot worship the god that we see all round us, the Virât? When we have worshipped this, we shall be able to worship all other gods.[69]

One finds an echo of this in Swami Shraddhanand (1856–1926). In his work on Hindu *sanghatan* or Hindu unity, he considered creation of 'Hindu rashtra temples' as the first step towards Hindu unity.

> The first step which I propose is to build one Hindu Rashtra Mandir at least in every city and important town, with a compound which could contain an audience of 25 thousands, and a hall in which Katha from Bhagavad Gita, the Upanishads and the great epics of Ramayana and Mahabharat could be daily recited....While the sectarian Hindu temples are dominated by their own individual deities, the Catholic Hindu Mandir should be devoted to the worship of the three mother-spirits the Gau-mata, the Saraswati-mata and the Bhumi-mata. Let some living cows be there to represent plenty, let "Savitri" be inscribed over the gate of the hall to remind every Hindu of his duty to expel all ignorance and let a life-like map of Mother— Bharat be constructed in a prominent place, giving all its characteristics in vivid colours so that every child of the Matri-Bhumi may daily bow before the Mother and renew his pledge to restore her to the ancient pinnacle of glory from which she has fallen!

Here Swami Shraddhanand is not concerned about non-Hindus particularly Muslims. He wants Hindus to accept Bharat Mata as a chief deity to create a social unity. The famous Lakshminarayan Mandir or Birla Mandir was built on the advice of Swami Shraddhanand, but before it was completed, Swami had been assassinated. The temple was opened by Mahatma Gandhi in 1938. It has a Gita Bhavan which serves as a lecture hall. The temple also has a pan-Hindu nature by having a shrine of Buddha.

In 1936, a Bharat Mata temple was inaugurated by Mahatma Gandhi in Banaras. Speaking after the inauguration, Gandhi observed:

> The temple contains no image of any God or Goddess. It has only a relief map of India made of marble stone in it. I hope this temple, which will serve as a cosmopolitan platform for people of all religions, castes and creeds including Harijans, will go a great way in promoting religious unity, peace and love in the country....As I was asked to perform the opening ceremony in the morning, and as I listened to the chanting of the Vedic mantras, I thought of a verse in our morning prayer which we have been repeating now for 20 years: "Mother Earth, Spouse of Vishnu, ocean clad and mountain-breasted, I bow to Thee. Forgive me the touch of my feet." It is this Mother Earth to the service and devotion of which we are dedicating ourselves today.[70]

There are two things which stand out here. One is that he explicitly wants everyone irrespective of religion to worship or venerate her. The second and most important aspect is that he ties the concept to Vedic veneration of Mother Earth. This attains significance because Gandhi had distinguished the Indian concept of *Purna Swarajya* from the western political notion of independence, seeing it as 'a sacred word, Vedic word'.[71] So Mahatma Gandhi, while identifying Bharat Mata herself to the Earth Goddess in the Vedic hymns, desired her temple to be 'a cosmopolitan platform for people of all religions, castes and creed'. Superficially, this may look different from the conception of Hindu rashtra mandir of Swami Shraddhanand, but in reality, it is not so. Both Swami Shraddhanand and Mahatma Gandhi looked at Bharat Mata as being associated with Vedic vision (Vedic Savitri and Bhumi Mata in the case of Shraddhanand, Mother Earth in the famous *Samudra Vasane Devi*... hymn in the case of Mahatma Gandhi.)

Incidentally, the Hindutva ideologue and leader of Bharatiya Jana Sangh (BJS, which later became the Bharatiya Janata Party), Pandit Deendayal Upadhyaya (1916–1968) uses the same hymn used by Gandhi, when he speaks about Mother India:

> In day-to-day routine also, this feeling of one nationhood should be imbibed. For this, *Sanskars* strengthening the feeling of patriotism have been prescribed. A Hindu, as soon as he gets up from his bed and places his feet on the ground prays to the motherland: "*Samudra-vasane devi parvatastanamandale Vishunipatni namastubhyam padasparsham kshamasva me*!" (O goddess with the seas as your cloths and the mountains as breasts, Lakshmi consort of Vishnu, please pardon my touching you with my feet.) This is the picture of the Akhand Bharat and is the fountain of intense love for motherland, expressing itself as first prayer in the morning.[72]

This striking similarity between the views of Gandhi and Upadhyaya shows the so-called religious aspect of Bharat Mata never really mattered for the soul of India and using the Divine Feminine sustained by Hindu nation in this part of the planet, India gave an expression to her nationhood, in the widest sense of the term, in the form of Bharat Mata.

Nehru, Nehruvians and Bharat Mata

Jawaharlal Nehru, India's first Prime Minister, was a man who had to 'discover India', having alienated himself with colonial education initially and with Marxist bias later. In 1937 Jawaharlal Nehru had complained that he needed a dictionary to understand Vande Mataram[73] while Tamizh poet Bharathi had translated the song into lyrical and simple Tamizh verses as early as 1905. However, the cries of 'Bharat Mata ki Jai' and Vande Mataram were the energizers of the masses.

According to historian Sita Ram Goel (1921–2003), Nehru tried to replace Vande Mataram with *Jai Hind* using the popularity of Netaji Subhash Chandra Bose despite the fact that Nehru was one of the most bitter critics of Bose.[74] Actually Bose himself had staunchly defended Vande Mataram when there was communal opposition to it. And he was not satisfied with the compromise solution worked out by Congress working committee under Nehru.[75] Later in 1943, the official programmes of the Provincial Government of Azad Hind (PGAH) always commenced with the singing of Vande Mataram.[76]

Nehru tried to project himself as an enlightened leader who was giving a rational explanation to the uneducated superstitious masses. After writing about how he 'seldom spoke of Hindustan or of Bharata, the old Sanskrit name derived from the mythical founder of the race' to his urban audiences who were 'more sophisticated', he explains in detail how he enlightened the ignorant masses raising the cry of 'Bharat Mata':

> Sometimes as I reached a gathering, a great roar of welcome would greet me: Bharat Mata ki Jai—"Victory to Mother India". I would ask them unexpectedly what they meant by that cry, who was this Bharat Mata, Mother India, whose victory cry they wanted? My question would amuse them and surprise them, and then not knowing exactly what to answer, they would look at each other, and at me. I persisted in my questioning. At last, a vigorous Jat, wedded to the soil from immemorial generations, would say that it was the *dharti*, the good earth of India, that they meant. What earth? Their particular village patch, or all the patches in the district or province or in the whole of India? And so, question and answer went on, till they would ask me impatiently to tell them all about it. I would endeavor to do so and explain that

> India was all this that they had thought, but it was much more. The mountains and the rivers of India, and the forests and the broad fields, which gave us food, were all dear to us, but what counted ultimately were the people of India, people like them and me, who were spread out all over this vast land. Bharat Mata, Mother India was essentially these people. You are parts of this Bharat Mata, I told them, you are in a manner yourselves Bharat Mata, and as this idea slowly soaked into their brains, their eyes would light up as if they had made a great discovery.[77]

The same story is repeated by Jawaharlal Nehru in 1957. Here he speaks of his talking to 'stout Jats' raising the cry 'Bharat Mata ki Jai' and here he says:

> I said is it some old lady, long haired lady you see in pictures etc., or sitting somewhere in a cave and they said no. I asked, what is it? Well, they were sons of the soil, a Jat is wedded to his soil, more to the mother earth, than his son or daughter or wife. So, he said, Bharat Mata is dharti, mother earth....[78]

Then he continues the same anecdote which he had stated in *Discovery of India*. Apart from the disturbing stereotyping of Jats ('stout Jats', 'slowly soaked into their brains'), here Nehru presents himself as the suave enlightening brown saheb liberating the ignorant masses from seeing Bharat Mata as more a symbolism of people collective than anything mystical or attachment to the soil of their land. Yet one can see this as a weak echo of the emotional imagery that Swami Vivekananda employed in his 1897 lectures—in which he asked his audience to see Mother India as the only deity worthy of worship through service in all Indians—who are collectively part of Mother India. Still Nehru could not dissociate himself from the cultural nationalist basis of the nation. He conceded that India has always been 'a geographical and economic entity, a cultural unity amidst diversity, a bundle of contradictions held together by strong but invisible threads'. Then he approvingly quoted poet Rabindranath Tagore, who had stated that adoring India was neither geographical idolatry nor mere patriotism of being attached to the land of one's birth but 'because she has saved through tumultuous ages the living words that have issued from the illuminated consciousness of her great ones'.[79]

This realization might have been because, after his initial flirting with the Marxist idea of India being a federation of linguistic nationalities, he had realized what Marxist ideologues actually had schemed for India. In 1942, influenced by the Soviet model, Nehru had approved a resolution, speaking of Indian Constitution as 'a federal one...with the residuary powers vesting in the units' which was immediately appreciated by the Communist Party leader G. Adhikari as one coming 'very near to recognizing the right of self-determination'.[80] Writing in his family-owned newspaper *National Herald*, both under his original name and nom de plume Kautilya, Nehru started exposing the Marxist strategy of dismantling India. The Communist plan was to 'let India be divided into bits so that the Indian National Congress may end... leaving the Communists free to make a revolutionary conquest of India part by part' and thus establish an 'Indian Soviet Republic'.[81] Writing as Kautilya, he actually anticipated what are today called 'Breaking India forces':

> In fact, Soviet and Communist policy...has opted in favor of splitting the country into many autonomous units. They deny that there is any such thing as an Indian nation. The Communist plan appears to be for a Balkanization of India.[82]

Though Nehru would later move towards a pro-Soviet, even a pro-Stalinist stand and show strong Hinduphobic tendencies, he would always return to the uniqueness of India and even strong cultural nationalism—particularly as he realized that Maoist China was not a civilizational ally as he had romanticized it to be but an aggressor. He rejected the comparison of the Soviet model of it being a union of multinational republics. On 7 July 1952, answering a question making such a comparison he said that 'because India has much more...of a unity than Soviet Union' and hence 'India cannot function on that (Soviet model) basis'.[83]

In the memoirs of sociologist and a staunch admirer of Nehru, Zarina Bhatty, Nehru's behaviour in London, probably during his visit in late 1950s or 1960s, showed an emotional attachment to the very soil of India, something which he had talked in quasi-ridiculing tone earlier:

> When (Nehru) finished talking, a woman raised her hand and shouted, "Pandit Nehru ki Jai!" Panditji became furious and said, "Why Panditji ki jai, you should say Bharat Mata ki Jai". On another occasion, Panditji was scheduled to speak at the Indian club in Osterly, London. A huge crowd of Indians and non-Indians had gathered there. He started speaking and then remembered the previous occasion when that Indian lady had said "Panditji ki jai" and recounted the incident. He then bent down, picked up a little mud from the lawn, and with tears in his eyes said in an emotionally charged voice, "You should all say Bharat Mata ki Jai, Bharat is mahan, her mitti is mahan, not me." He then wiped his tears and continued his speech.[84]

However, over the decades Nehruvians progressively neglected the unique unity of India that Nehru talked about which he traced to the very early ages of India. They either considered it a recent phenomenon—a colonial construct, a position that gels with the Marxist as well as colonial view of India, or they wanted to deny national consciousness to India before the Islamic times. This is seen in Marxist historian Prof. Irfan Habib who boldly asserts that no Sanskrit text has spoken of India as an object of adoration and that real patriotism towards India actually starts with Amir Khusrau.

On the contrary, Nehru government itself appealed to the authority of ancient Sanskrit sacred texts of Hindus, to assert the Himalayan boundaries of India when it was challenged by Maoist China as it claimed substantial portions of Himalayan India for the People's Republic of China. The Ministry of External Affairs during Nehru's government issued a white paper in 1959 in which it said the following:

> The Himalayas have always dominated Indian life, just as they have dominated the Indian landscape. One of the earliest Sanskrit texts, though its exact date is uncertain—the Vishnu Purana—makes it clear that the Himalayas formed the frontier of India. It states that the country south of the Himalayas and north of ocean is called Bharat, and all born in it are called Bharatiyas or Indians.
>
> *uttaram yat samudrasya himadrescaiva daksinam*
> *varsham tad (tam) bharatam naharatiati yatra santatih.*

The entire document approved by Nehru, which was sent to the Chinese authorities to prove the Indian historical presence in the Himalayan regions, quotes Vedas, Ramayana, Mahabharata, wades through tribal-Hindu resistance of Asom rulers to Mughal onslaught, continuance of cultural traditions even during the colonial period and ends with the assertion that 'few, if any, land frontiers in the world can claim as strong a sanction of long and unbroken tradition'.[85]

Thus, we see in Nehru a gradual transition towards the roots of cultural nationalist definition of India. And he moves from an elitist view explaining Bharat Mata to 'ignorant' villagers who considered the soil as Bharat Mata to embracing the very same concept emotionally. Perhaps, this transition was at the base of the willingness of Nehru to call the Rashtriya Swayamsevak Sangh (RSS) to the Republic Day parade of 1963.

M. F. Hussain and Bharat Mata

The painter Maqbool Fida Husain (1915–2011) had a love-hate relationship with Hindu culture. The artist in him could feel and enjoy the freedom and variety that the Hindu cultural milieu provided him. But there was deep in him a love for authoritarianism. Venkat Swaminathan (1933–2015), the veteran art critic from

Tamil Nadu, had pointed out that Husain praised and gloriously painted the Congress Supremo Indira Gandhi (1917–1984) when she brought emergency in 1975, the nearest fall of India to a real fascist regime, while showing his hatred for the democratic resistance leader of emergency and the first non-Congress Prime Minister of India, Morarji Desai, by painting him as a monkey. Swaminathan also points out that young Husain refused to go to Pakistan when most of his relatives went there because he would not get the artistic freedom in an Islamic State like Pakistan. He painted Siva and Parvati in the marriage invitation of his son which he claimed invited the fury of Islamic clergy.[86]

When the opposition of some fringe Hindu groups to his old paintings brought him extreme media attention, (and being a person who loved basking in media attention) M. F. Husain knew that this would catapult himself to further fame without getting into any real danger. His inherent bias towards authoritarianism might have also cultivated a deep hatred for Hinduism while at the same time paradoxically cherishing the freedom of the Hindu atmosphere. Hindu groups in the UK protesting the display of his paintings had pointed out that he used nudity on negative characters like Hitler and also used it on Hindus and Hindu deities. Indologist Dr Koenraad Elst is of the opinion that Husain gave 'a new expression to the old Islamic contempt for Hinduism.'[87]

These two opposing tendencies with his own love for publicity and fame would play into the way he developed the image of Bharat Mata during his painting career. During the fiftieth anniversary of Independence, M. F. Husain brought out the association of Bharat Mata and the consort of Siva, very forcefully in the visual medium. In his painting *Bharat Mata* (1997), he shows Her playing with Ganesha. And there is the uncompromising sacred geography of Himalayas depicted as the very head of Lord Siva—symbolized by the crescent. In 2006 Husain redid the painting. In the 1997 painting one can see the 'secular' dimensions of the state being both harmonized and subsumed to the sacred nature of the nation. In the 2006 painting, which relies more on the riot of colours than on innate dynamics of aesthetics and symbolism, one can see all dimensions of the sacred being erased. Despite the fall, the fact remains that the 1997 painting by M. F. Hussain who was despised by many in the Hindutva camp, remains as one of the boldest visual statements created to identify Bharat Mata with Goddess Parvati.

Jana Gana Mana: Secular Exorcism of the Goddess?

With continued opposition to 'Vande Mataram', another poem composed by Bengali poet Rabindranath Tagore was increasingly getting mooted as the national anthem of India. In the Azad Hind Government of Subhash Chandra Bose, the functions began with Vande Mataram and closed with *Jana Gana Mana* as the national anthem.

Mahatma Gandhi himself vacillated in the issue. In 1911 Gandhiji wrote a small note in Tamil to one of his compatriots. He signed it as 'Vandemataram M. K. Gandhi'. By 1930s, for the sake of communal unity, he accepted that the song could be truncated. He went even a step further and wrote, 'If at any mixed gathering any person objected to the singing of "Bande Mataram" even with the Congress expurgations, the singing should be dropped'. However, in 1940 in response to a students' strike in a missionary college in Calcutta for being stopped from singing Vande Mataram, he wrote, 'Whether the song is in fact national or not is not for the missionaries to determine. For them it is surely enough to know that their students recognize the song as national.'[88]

After Independence, with the shock of the heinous crime of the assassination of Mahatma Gandhi by a Hindutvaite in the background, on 24 August 1948 at the Constituent Assembly, it was announced that Jana Gana Mana composed by Tagore would be accepted as the national anthem. Making this announcement on the floor of the Parliament, the first President of India Rajendra Prasad ended the statement thus:

> The song Vande Mataram, which has played a historic part in the struggle for Indian freedom, shall be honoured equally with *Jana Gana Mana* and shall have equal status with it.[89]

Most of the Hindutvaites including the RSS go through an urban legend that gets circulated in their circles that Jana Gana Mana was actually written to greet King George V during his Indian visit. Many Swayamsevaks grew up listening to this urban legend and quite a few RSS pamphleteers have put this in print with all rhetorical flourish. However, the origin of this urban legend is not in Hindutva circles. Nor is its acceptance confined to the Hindutvaites. For example, Markandey Katju, a former Judge retired from the Supreme Court of India, known for his eccentric views, wrote a blog post whose title addressed Tagore as a 'British stooge'. After recycling the usual allegations against the national anthem, he stated that those 'facts almost conclusively prove that *Jana Gana Mana* was composed and sung as an act of sycophancy to the British King'.[90]

The critics of Hindutva on the other hand have seized upon this misinformed campaign in some quarters of Hindutva to drive a wedge between the spirit and values of Jana Gana Mana and Vande Mataram. Prof. Martha Nussbaum provides a good sample for this kind of approach. She writes:

> The conception of the nation's unity expressed in "Jana Gana Mana" is moral and political, not based on soil and ethnic belonging....Supporters of a more aggressive and romantic brand of nationalism keep returning to Chatterjee (whether they interpret him rightly or wrongly) for a tough-minded conception of the nation and its pride....This struggle between two anthems is essentially a struggle between two visions of patriotism, two visions of the nation, and indeed two visions of masculinity.[91]

She speaks of 'a stern challenge to the young nation in which it has two choices: "ethnic conflict and an idolatrous conception of the nation as mother", singing Chatterjee's "Bande Mataram"' or 'the fantasy embodied in Tagore's "Jana Gana Mana", that of a nation rich and joyful precisely because of its diversity, pursuing noble ethical goals with joy'.[92] As we shall see, such fabricated binaries are incorrect. In fact, one of the earliest post-Independence factual rebuttal to the canard against the anthem was written by Marathi writer P. L. Deshpande, an ardent admirer of Savarkar.[93] This response by P. L. Deshpande was well-researched and looked at the issue in a very holistic manner.

The rumours against the song arose even during the time of Tagore, and the poet himself had categorically rejected such claims. Later serious historians have also exposed the hollowness of such claims. Prof. Sabyasachi Bhattacharya refutes this myth sufficiently in his work on Tagore:

> Incidentally a myth regarding this song needs to be refuted and laid to rest. It is on record that the song was written on 11 December 1911. On December 12, 1911, the Delhi Durbar met to honour King Emperor George V. Obviously a poem written on 11 December could not be intended for an event the following day. The song was actually sung at the twenty-seventh session of the Indian National Congress, Calcutta on 28 December 1911 as the opening song at the beginning of the day's proceedings. Thereafter it was also sung at the foundation day anniversary of *Adi Brahma Samaj* in February 1912 and included in their collection of psalms, *Brahma Sangit*.[94]

Here it should be noted that Adi Brahma Samaj itself was a body formed after a schism between Keshub Chandra Sen, who wanted to cut off Brahmo movement totally from Hinduism and Indian roots to make it universal, and Debendranath Tagore, father of Rabindranath, who wanted to adhere to the Hindu roots while pressing for reformation.

> Keshub's letter to Debendranath of July 2, 1865, is a document typically reflecting a new generation's angry denunciation of its elders, whom it accused of Indianizing Brahmoism to the point where it had become another Hindu sect. (fn: As one

> historian aptly puts it, The Adi Brahmo Samaj cry was "Brahmoism is Hinduism"...)... Debendranath had already answered Keshub a year earlier when he defended the sacred thread and other attachments to Hinduism as symbols which if rejected, would lead to complete denationalization.[95]

The Anglo-India press, which in many ways anticipated India's post-Independent Nehruvian media, spread the fake news about the song being sung to welcome George V. In December 1911, the British loyalist *Statesman* was the one which seemed to have started the canard.[96] In a letter written to his friend P. B. Sen on 10 November 1937, Tagore refuted these allegations. He also explained the terms '*Bharata Bhagya Vidhata*', which his critics had taken to mean the visiting George V:

> I was stunned to hear of the request by a high ranking government officer. I was furious. In the song Jana Gana Mana, I have praised the God Bharat Bhagya Vidhata who is the constant charioteer of travellers through the ages, he who guides through all the difficult circumstances, he who is born in many ages. He can never be King George V or VI or any other George. That truth dawned on my "Loyal friend", because however strong his loyalty to the foreign rulers was, he was not devoid of intelligence. I also did not compose this song especially for the Congress.[97]

Turning to the song, which comprises five stanzas, it is not hard to find the identity of this 'dispenser of India's destiny'. The third stanza talks of Him as the 'Eternal Charioteer' (*chirosharothi*) and goes on to say that in the midst of revolution or chaos, this Eternal Charioteer's 'conch shell sounds' (*shongkhodhoni*). If the identity of this eternal charioteer with the conch shell is still ambiguous, then the poet himself makes the identity abundantly clear. So here we have the identity of '*Bharoto bhaggo bidhata*': Eternal charioteer, the one who blows his conch shell, He who guides us through different circumstances and who is born in many ages. Further, even the stanzas of Jana Gana Mana too can be construed to show a war-like situation with the imageries like thunder of the chariot wheel, the sound of the conch shell, etc. Is this deity of India's destiny male? Tagore gives a feminine description of this 'dispenser of the destiny of India': 'You protected us on your lap, Oh Affectionate Mother (*Snehomoyi tumi mata*).'

This shows the deep resonance Tagore's lines have with the very subtle yet deep identity transformations in the tradition of Indian divine forms. In South Indian traditions, Siva is not only shown as androgynous *Ardhanarishwara* (deity in half-woman form) where the Goddess takes the left side of Siva, but He is also shown in the Sankara-Narayana form—where Vishnu forms the left half of Siva. This creates an identity with Vishnu and Shakti. Karaikal Ammayaar, a mystic-poetess of Saivaite tradition from Tamil Nadu belonging to sixth century CE, sang of Siva as one part of him being Vishnu, who measured the worlds and as another part being Goddess Uma.[98] Bengali Shaktic traditions too have been well aware of this identity. The phenomenon is thus pan-Indic. Thus, contrary to the claims, one finds the same Hindu imagery pervading both Vande Mataram and Jana Gana Mana which sees Divine Feminine and looks to India as a place of special divine dispensation.

Goddess of the Tribes

Another criticism of Bharat Mata is that she only represents the 'Brahminical' Goddess tradition. So, recently the left radicals came out with an alternative version showing a tribal woman with the buffalo in the background, positioning this image as the alternative version. However, the supposedly 'Brahminical' Bharat Mata associated with the nationalist discourse in India even from the beginning have not shied away from the tribal cultural matrix of the nation.

Nivedita Louis, a Chennai-based journalist and part-time historian had pointed out that a calendar art Bharat Mata (printed originally by Nagpur City Press) was carved in the *Dhwajarohana Mandapam* of Kapaleeswarar Temple by a sculptor in 1939. The *Mandapam* itself was financed by Kaatupalli, Paiyur K. N. Shanmuga Mudaliar. The connection between tribal Bharat Mata and this pillar sculpture comes in the *Suthai* or painted terracotta sculptures that decorate the Gopuram of the Mandapam. She is shown again, along with Siva and Parvati taking the form of tribal chieftain and his wife. The motif of Siva and Parvati coming in the form of tribal chieftain and his wife is very popular in Tamil Nadu and Kerala. Dramas based on this aspect of Siva-Parvati as tribals like the *Kakkarishi Natakam*, were part and parcel of the cultural movement that Scheduled Tribes and Communities launched for social justice in South India. Mahatma Ayyankali, a Scheduled Community leader from Kerala who fought for the educational rights of the SC children who were denied entry into schools, economic freedom including freedom from forced labour as well as whipping, cultural rights including the temple entry and religious freedom including the resistance to proselytizing, in his *Sadhu Jana Paripalana Sangham* (SJPS) used the *Kakkarishi Natakam* along with other Hindu Puranic plays for spreading the message of social justice. Ayyankali himself would compose the songs and dialogues for these plays.[99] The morphing sculpturally Bharat Mata with Goddess inside the temple and then placing the Goddess in the tribal context at the top of the tower of the

Mandapam offers proof that she was in the popular nationalist imagination not an exclusive or limited to so-called 'Brahminical' imagery. In other words, decades before the 'progressives' started their discourse, mainstream Indian nationalism has placed her in the tribal context.

This ability is dynamic and has the capacity for self-regeneration based on the specific context. In Nagaland, during the British colonial rule and evangelical onslaught on local spiritual traditions, a resistance movement evolved—the Heraka movement was founded by Haipou Jadonang (1905–1931), a spiritual leader, freedom fighter and ultimately a martyr. After his execution by the British, his mission was carried on by Naga Rani Gaidinliu (1915–1993). Rani was a healer, spiritual and political leader who effectively led the resistance against the British. Her authority was established through a goddess-vision. In his academic informant thesis on the movement for school of Divinity at the University of Edinburg, Dr Arkotong Longkumer narrates the life-changing experience of Ranima as Gaidinliu, as called by her followers:

> On the third religious journey, 26 January 1930, Gaidinliu's birthday, Gaidinliu and her followers reach the cave. Other people from around the area have also come to the cave for prayers. But Gaidinliu's followers could hear only her voice as she prayed; the other voices were muffled. It was quiet, when suddenly a lightning like effect flashed near the entrance of the cave. A strange light illuminated the cave. There in front of them, the goddess suddenly appeared; she was visible only to those whose faith in the goddess was strong. Elated by the incident they started singing praise songs.

The Goddess tells her to search for a hidden gun. There is a shooting competition with that gun at a tree. Gaidinliu fell the tree with a single bullet. She was then accepted by the elders. It was then that she begins her mission:

> Her name spreads around the region and she is celebrated as their leader and even referred to as Goddess. She starts healing, prophesising, and preaching about the new religious teachings received from Tingwang in the cave. Her activities are also legitimised by the curious arrival of Goddess Namginai who comes riding on a lion pushed by the wind of God. The Goddess arrives at Gaidinliu's house and drinks water from the pond and rides away to Nsimbutlua Mountain. The people were surprised and somewhat frightened of these powers and regarded Gaidinliu as the incarnation of the Goddess.[100]

Dr Longkumer points out a natural parallel between Durga and Namaginai:

> I would also like to suggest that *Ranima* saw herself as a symbol of empowerment in the image of Durga. This can be related to Goddess *Namginai* who comes to Ranima's house riding on a lion and then retreats to Nsimbutlua Mountain (*Durga* also is depicted as riding on a lion and residing in Mount *Meru*). People there are reportedly amazed and view Ranima as the incarnation of the Goddess. Is Ranima seeing *Durga* as herself, or as a model for expressing her "supreme female divinity"?[101]

In his critical study Dr Longkumer observes that the autobiographical narrative of Ranima positions her as 'the great unifier—selfless, humane, compassionate and above all divinely chosen for her people' and that in the process she had adapted 'powerful symbols like Durga, indigenized within the tribal system' which in turn is 'also associated with Bharat Mata'.[102] After Independence, the plight of her people made her again take up arms. But she was never for separatism which was being fuelled by Naga rebels with foreign funding. The Heraka movement believed that the 'loss of religion is loss of culture and loss of culture is loss of identity'. The fight of Rani, for the protection of the freedom of religion of the indigenous traditions made her associate closely with Sangh Parivar organizations—particularly Vanvasi Kalyan Ashram and Viswa Hindu Parishad (VHP).[103] In his conclusion Dr Longkumer points out:

> The pan-Hindu idea of "Bharat Mata" (Mother India) as a territorial deity correlated with the image of a "mother" in Heraka contexts, and "Goddess" in Gaidinliu's biography. It portrays an imagery as uniting and including disparate groups in India, such as the Heraka, under the wings of "Bharat Mata".[104]

So, in conclusion, probably from the Harappan times and Vedic roots to the independence movement, Bharat Mata has been a symbolic representation of a uniquely Indic Hindu phenomenon—not in the sectarian sense. She is rooted in Hinduness and it is her Hinduness that inherently makes her embrace pluralism—a harmony and also the defence of that harmony of biodiversity and theo-diversity in the greater Indian landmass.

Akhand Bharat: An Expansionist Fantasy?

Closely associated with the image of Bharat Mata is the image of Akhand Bharat. When India was partitioned in 1947, Hindutvaites, mostly represented by Hindu Mahasabha and the RSS, were not able to accept it and strongly opposed the political vivisection of India. During the heat of partition and the trauma of the refugee crisis, hot and harsh words were spoken by certain Hindu nationalist leaders. These statements often helped the academic, media and political critics of Hindutva to frame an essentializing of Hindutva and Akhand Bharat. For instance, Hinduphobic academic and Hindutva observer Christophe Jaffrelot writes:

> The most extreme of the Hindu Mahasabha's article of faith concerned the annulment of Partition. The party called, in effect, and consistently, for the restoration of a united India—Akhand Bharat—if necessary, by force. Here it confirmed the central place which the notion of territory occupied in its ideology.[105]

Prof. Aditya Nigam associated with the Centre for the Study of Developing Societies (CSDS) characterizes Akhand Bharat as upper-caste imperialism:

> Sanghism…has always dreamed of achieving its ideal of *Akhand Bharat*—one that reveals its militaristic and imperialist ambitions of "uniting" every bit of land from Afghanistan to Myanmar under this rubric. "Uniting" in this lexicon has a very special meaning—that of uniting under North Indian Hindu upper caste hegemony.[106]

Do the Hindutvaites view Akhand Bharat as a territorial expansionist goal to be achieved through force? Or have their views from the initial trauma of partition to the present-day scenario of cross-border terrorism from Pakistan and illegal migrants from Bangladesh something qualitatively different?

Influence of Sri Aurobindo: Mukherjee to Upadhyaya

The first general elections in India were held five years after Partition in 1952. The newly formed BJS was contesting the polls and its manifesto had declared its unassailable conviction about Akhand Bharat' (undivided India), despite the historical and political reality of Partition. The brainchild behind the manifesto was a young full-time worker, who had been 'loaned' out from the RSS to the newly formed political party which would later become the present day Bharatiya Janata Party (BJP) —Pandit Deendayal Upadhyaya. Was he, his organization and party thinking in terms of a military expansion and undoing of partition through invasion?

In the vision of Akhand Bharat of both the RSS and the BJS (and later BJP), the real influence is that of Sri Aurobindo. So, what he said with respect to Partition needs to be quoted here exhaustively as it set the frame for the Hindutva vision of Akhand Bharat and the functional approach of Hindutva to the problem. In his Independence Day message broadcast at the All India Radio (AIR) station of Tiruchirapalli, Tamil Nadu, he said:

> India today is free, but she has not achieved unity. At one moment it almost seemed as if in the very act of liberation, she would fall back into the chaos of separate States which preceded the British conquest. But fortunately, it now seems probable that this danger will be averted and a large and powerful, though not yet a complete union will be established. Also, the wisely drastic policy of the Constituent Assembly has made it probable that the problem of the depressed classes will be solved without schism or fissure. But the old communal division into Hindus and Muslims seems now to have hardened into a permanent political division of the country. It is to be hoped that this settled fact will not be accepted as settled for ever or as anything more than a temporary expedient. For if it lasts, India may be seriously weakened, even crippled: civil strife may remain always possible, possible even a new invasion and foreign conquest. India's internal development and prosperity may be impeded, her position among the nations weakened, her destiny impaired or even frustrated. This must not be; the partition must go. Let us hope that that may come about naturally, by an increasing recognition of the necessity not only of peace and concord but of common action, by the practice of common action and the creation of means for that purpose. In this way unity may finally come about under whatever form—the exact form may have a pragmatic but not a fundamental importance. But by whatever means, in whatever way, the division must go; unity must and will be achieved, for it is necessary for the greatness of India's future.[107]

Dr Shyama Prasad Mukherjee (1901–1953) the founder of BJS, had visited Sri Aurobindo in 1951. On 7 June 1967, Mirra Alfassa—the 'Mother' (1878–1973) and spiritual collaborator of Sri Aurobindo was talking to her disciples about Sri Aurobindo's vision of 'a federation of all human nations of the world'. In that context she said:

> There is a group in the new Indian parliament, a group of people dissatisfied with the position taken by India, who have declared their wish to act according to Sri Aurobindo's ideal and instructions. And they've asked if we could send someone from here to hold conferences in Delhi.... It's a "group" —naturally not the whole parliament....There was a man who would have done—not fully well, not with enough breadth of mind to fully understand Sri Aurobindo, but very straight and strong—he was assassinated in Kashmir.[108]

Prof. Michel Danino adds that the conference she refers to happened on 24 April 1951.[109] So even in the 1952 manifesto when the BJS-RSS mentioned Akhand Bharat, it was very clear that they had no interest in a military or territorial expansionism but an appeal to common cultural links to facilitate a federation.

By 1964 Upadhyaya had found an ally for his stand on Akhand Bharat from the socialist camp. Veteran socialist leader Dr Ram Manohar Lohia together with Upadhyaya proclaimed an appeal to end the 'artificial situation' of Partition. They envisioned creating a 'Hind-Pak Mahasangha'—an 'India-Pakistan Confederation' as a first step towards that process. What necessitated this was large scale communal disturbances in Pakistan. Jawaharlal Nehru was still the Prime Minister of India. India was recuperating from the humiliation imposed by Maoist China in 1963. Upadhyaya and Lohia decided to take a proactive step of issuing a joint declaration that would bring both nations to the negotiating table to discuss communal violence in East Pakistan and also to stop it from spilling over into India. The statement, parts of which proved to be prophetic, read:

> As a result of extensive disturbances in East Pakistan, more than 2 lakhs Hindus and other minorities have been forced to migrate to Bharat. In Bharat there is severe anger about the events in East Bengal and it has expressed itself in some parts....We definitely feel that it is a duty of the Bharat government to protect and get protected the lives and properties of Hindus other minorities in Pakistan. To shirk this responsibility by giving the false excuse that they are Pakistan citizens is an invitation to genocide in both the countries. So far as the question of Indian Muslims is concerned it is our firm opinion that their life and property should be protected and safeguarded in all circumstances. This is basic truth, and no incidence or logic should /can set aside or override it. The state and the citizens who cannot guarantee the right of life to its people are barbaric. We believe that the division of our country into India and Pakistan is absolutely artificial. The reason for their bad relations is the wrong attitude of both. The two governments instead of thinking of just one problem at a time, should jointly consider all the problems and circumstances together. This would result in a far better mutual understanding and may initiate the process of forming a federation of the two countries. [110]

Two years later, Upadhyaya recorded in his 'political diary' a conversation with a *New York Times* columnist. Interestingly, in his conversation with this columnist, Pandit Upadhyaya criticizes him because 'he would not write India without the appellative Hindu'. He opposed the positioning of a 'Hindu India' against a 'Muslim Pakistan' by the US media. Upadhyaya pointed out to the columnist that it was Justice Muhammad Chagla, who was the ambassador of India to the United States. The columnist retorted saying that it proved nothing: 'By keeping Mountbatten as your Governor General for some time, India did not become a country of Englishmen as well'. Upadhyaya pointed out the fallacy in the argument and said that the 'Muslims in India were not exogenous'. The columnist nevertheless remained adamant and said that till India and Pakistan were reunited, they would be perceived only as Hindu and Muslim countries. And Upadhyaya terminates his political diary entry with the comment, 'Partition and secularism go ill together'.[111]

The stand Upadhyaya took, which is obviously secular, is also consistent with the deeper Hindutva conception of the term Hindu as an expression that combines the cultural, spiritual and geographical dimensions in which the religious label becomes a subset. The religious identity, in the narrow sense, is subsumed by the Hindu identity which is geo-spiritual.

M. D. Deoras Predicts SAARC

After the 1977 general elections, Janata Party came to power, with Jan Sangh becoming a vital part of the democratic experiment. A dominant section of the press, which had sided with the anti-democratic emergency of Indira Gandhi now raised the bogey of Akhand Bharat. With the Sangh-Parivar body namely BJS now part of the political power, would it not instigate the government to achieve its goal of Akhand Bharat? The then RSS Sarsanghachalak (chief guide) Madhukar Dattatreya Deoras (1915–1996) was asked about the RSS's conception of Akhand Bharat. In a detailed reply he gave to journalists at the Press Club of India on 12 March 1979, Deoras explained the Sangh's view on the matter:

> I believe that this country should be united. I have never made a secret of it because I have said that the partition of this country was wrong and unnatural in every sense—culturally, geographically, economically and strategically. So, these three parts, Bangladesh, Pakistan and India must come together. But at the same time, I have explained that I am aware of the fact that it is not going to happen by simply declaring war. Because if we go in for war, there will be interference from other nations. So, war is absolutely ruled out.... The other way is that the sober and saner elements in Pakistan and Bangladesh will realize the futility of the partition. A desire may develop in the minds of these elements, in the not too distant future that we should come together in some form or other. For example, they can form an economic unity.... So, I have said that Bangladesh, Pakistan and India may come together for economic reasons to begin with and then it may develop into some sort of a loose

> confederation. That is my idea of Akhand Bharat. I am stressing again that it is not possible by war and the whole structure of India before 1947 is not going to return.[112]

One of the important achievements of the short-lived Janata experiment was that the relation between India and its neighbours improved. J. N. Dixit (1936–2005) who served as Foreign Secretary in the Ministry of External Affairs and who was also National Security Adviser for Prime Minister Manmohan Singh, points out how India took natural proactive friendly steps towards Pakistan during the Janata rule:

> Without any intention of assuming a friendlier-than thou posture, it cannot be denied that India made a genuine attempt to normalise relations with Pakistan. The initiatives taken for high-level visits, for bringing about normality in economic and commercial relations, for improving people-to-people contacts, all came from India.... Pakistan's response to these endeavours was not totally negative, but it was selective.[113]

It is not a coincidence that the foreign ministry was then with Atal Bihari Vajpayee, an RSS man. In the case of neighbouring Bangladesh, after an initial warming, the relations between the two countries under the Congress regime had stagnated. This stagnation was broken by the efforts of Vajpayee. Thus, under Janata government, during 1979–1980, India's exports to Bangladesh touched $115 million, which was then a record for 20 years, from 1974–1994. India's imports from Bangladesh, which were also declining rose from $1 million to $6 million in the same period.

In a precise fulfilment of the prediction of RSS chief Deoras, the requisition and a design for a regional cooperation among South Asian countries came in 1980 from the then President of Bangladesh, Zia-ur-Rahman, who curiously enough was an anti-Indian politician. In 1985 the paper now called *Bangladesh Working Paper*, materialized into the South Asian Association for Regional Cooperation (SAARC) through a summit conference in Dhaka. Between 1980 and 1985, much had changed in India. Indira Gandhi had returned to power and had been assassinated, and her son Rajiv Gandhi had become the prime minister. India, under Rajiv Gandhi, became part of SAARC. In a subsequent press conference, Deoras applauded the formation of SAARC.

Pan-Islamic Radicalism versus Akhand Bharat

In the same year as SAARC was formed, Pakistan along with Iran and Turkey created another network—Economic Cooperation Organisation (ECO). With the breaking up of the Union of Soviet Socialist Republics (USSR) in 1991, nation-states with high Islamic populations (Azerbaijan, Kazakhstan, Tajikistan, Kyrgyz Republic, Turkmenistan and Uzbekistan) became independent and joined ECO. Interestingly, Pakistan had thus created an effective geo-Islamic network spanning the entire former Soviet region extending up to Turkey. In the coming years, Pakistan increasingly started throwing spokes into the wheel of constructive regional integration attempts of SAARC. This created a stagnation and a limit to what SAARC could achieve.

Similarly, when Vajpayee was Prime Minister, before the Kargil conflict in 1999, he again took proactive steps of friendship towards Pakistan. The 'bus diplomacy' and simultaneous as well as subsequent betrayal by both civil and military establishments in Pakistan happened with considerable support from the Pakistan Islamists. Husain Haqqani, former Pakistan ambassador to the United States and Sri Lanka, explains:

> The public mood in both India and Pakistan seemed to favor the peace process. Pakistan's Islamists and the military did not. The *Jamaat-e-Islami* threatened to block Vajpayee's bus route, described the Indian leader as Pakistan's "national enemy" and held street demonstrations against India to highlight the Kashmir problem. The Islamists also called for a general strike in Lahore on the day of the summit meeting. Several ambassadors invited to a state dinner for Vajpayee "were turned back after demonstrators banged on their vehicles and blocked the road." Sharif had planned to arrest *Jamaat-e-Islami* leader Qazi Hussain Ahmed ahead of the demonstrations. Ahmed, however, could not be found as he stayed at the homes of military intelligence officials to avoid arrest.[114]

Most studies of 'Hindu nationalists' try to portray them as ideological mirror images of Islamic radicals in Pakistan as well as India. So, the RSS in India gets compared to Jamaat-e-Islami, an Islamic fundamentalist outfit that operates in India, Pakistan and Bangladesh. Here then is the clear difference between the Hindutvaites and Islamists. The mainstream Hindutva organizations including the RSS welcome confidence building measures with Pakistan. Vajpayee's bus visit to Lahore was in synch with the Sangh vision of Akhand Bharat. For Hindutvaites, it is axiomatic that building people-to-people relation between the political states within the larger Indian landscape would make them realise their cultural oneness over their sectarian differences. At the same time, they also insist on not compromising on the territorial integrity and security of India, as for them India is the base on which this vision is built.

Naturally this was followed by the Kargil aggression involving the Pakistan army, which ultimately resulted in the defeat of Pakistan, loss of its face in the international arena and overthrow of Nawaz Sharif government by army establishment under Pervez Musharraf. In 2001 the Vajpayee-Musharraf Agra Summit meeting was being planned. Even after Kargil, the RSS resolution of 2001 on this summit does not sound either hawkish or of jingoism. The resolution welcomes the summit meet while cautioning the government:

> Despite doubts about the legitimacy of the present military government in Pakistan, ABKM welcomes the Vajpayee-Musharruf talks in the hope that Pakistan will positively respond to one another opportunity for ensuring peace between the two countries.[115]

The 2001 resolution further repudiates the two-nation theory by stating that Pakistan does not have a right to talk about Kashmir just because it has 'a few lakh Muslims' as the rest of India has 'a few crore Muslims'.

Afghanistan to Become Gandhara?

In this context of the Hindutva vision of Akhand Bharat, Afghanistan needs a special mention. A typical academic informant work on Hindutva for the Western audience explains in a seemingly neutral but subtly negative way, the inclusion of Afghanistan into the vision of Akhand Bharat:

> I once asked a male member of the movement what akhand Bharat included. He informed me that India, Pakistan, Bangladesh, and Afghanistan were all part of akhand Bharat. When I expressed surprise at the inclusion of Afghanistan, he responded by saying: Yes, Afghanistan—for after all Gandhari from the Mahabharata is from Gandhar or Kandahar, which is in Afghanistan. Many in the movement believe that all those countries are part of the sacred soil of Hindu nation, resonating with a common claim of nationalism and culture, blood and nation are not imagined but instead firmly rooted in territory. This territory is included in the landscape of the nation through imagined networks forged through folklore—in this case the ancient Hindu epic, the Mahabharata.[116]

As we will see, there are two contesting larger geo-cultural and geo-strategic contexts of Afghanistan, namely that of Akhand Bharat and that of Pan-Islamism. And whether one likes it or not, both have relevance for and impact on India and Afghanistan.

After the Soviet collapse, Afghanistan also became increasingly isolated from India and a hotbed of Islamic fundamentalist terrorism. Raja Chandran, now the director of Carnegie India, Delhi, pointed out in a report in 2003, that 'ever since the Partition in 1947, Pakistan had blocked India's access to Afghanistan and beyond'. India under the Congress rule of both Indira and Rajiv had aligned itself with the Soviet-backed regime, which had placed India at a disadvantage in the popular perception. After the Soviet occupation of Afghanistan and CIA started funding Afghan jihad against Soviets through Pakistan, Pakistan utilized the opportunity and turned Afghanistan into a base for intensifying jihad against India in Kashmir. Prof. Owen L. Sirrs points out:

> When Osama Bin Laden was expelled from Sudan in 1996, he returned to familiar turf in eastern Afghanistan, where ISI facilitated a meeting for him with the local Nangrarhar Shura....It was Bin Laden and the Taliban together who took over Gulbuddin Hekmatyar's militant training camps in eastern Afghanistan so that ISI's Kashmir Jihad would not be disrupted. Indeed, Bin Laden helped ISI train militants from various groups ostensibly formed to fight India in Kashmir such as Harakatul Mujahidin, Lashkar-e-Taiba, and Jaish-e-Mohammad.[117]

It was only after 9/11 that the West started seriously questioning the Pakistan's support to jihadist groups in Afghanistan. Bruce Riedel, a senior fellow at the Foreign Policy programme of Brookings Institution, explains the relation between Pakistan and Islamist terror network within Afghanistan from a Western security point of view:

> By 2001, Pakistan was providing the Taliban regime in Kabul with hundreds of advisers and experts to run its tanks, aircraft and artillery, thousands of Pakistani Pashtuns to man its infantry and small units of its Special Services Group commandoes to help in combat with the Northern Alliance. Pakistan provided the oil needed to run the Taliban's war machine. All of this despite a half dozen United Nations Security Council resolutions calling on all countries to cease aid to the Taliban because it was hosting al-Qaeda and Osama bin Laden. According to the 9/11 Commission, the ISI had mid-wifed the alliance between Mullah Omar and bin Laden, so it was no surprise that Pakistan ignored the UN.[118]

So, when 9/11 happened, the Vajpayee government took full advantage of the developing scenario to improve India's relations with Afghanistan. As the events unfolded, Vajpayee had said as early as November 2001 that India needed to play 'maximum role in Afghanistan'.[119] Under Vajpayee India broke the Pakistan-barrier and shook hands with Afghanistan—participating specifically in infrastructural projects to rebuild Afghanistan, which helped India open a new front. All these efforts paved the way for Afghanistan to enter SAARC in 2008. And it has been a shot in the arm for India in achieving regional cooperation for development.

Modi and 'SAARC minus One'

In 2014 when Modi became the Prime Minister, he found the SAARC progress being held hostage by hurdles created by Pakistan. According to C. Raja Mohan, Director, Institute of South Asian Studies, National University of Singapore, the Modi government proactively broke this Pakistan-imposed impasse in SAARC:

> In the past, Delhi simply shrugged its shoulders. Although it was clear that the SAARC caravan was going nowhere with Pakistan, it seemed there was little that India could do. PM Modi, however, took a different track. At the Kathmandu Summit, he called for a two-speed SAARC. Rather than let one country take the entire region hostage, Modi suggested, those who are ready for integration should move ahead.[120]

Taking forward SAARC with clearly no big-brother attitude but with mutually beneficial actions that were quite evident, Modi was able to isolate Pakistan. What emerged as 'Bangladesh, Bhutan, India and Nepal' (BBIN) framework, has today become BBINAM with the inclusion of Afghanistan and Maldives. With both Delhi and Kabul desiring to open connectivity and boost economic ties and catalyse development, Pakistan adamantly refused any help—particularly in creating link roads between India and Afghanistan. If already Pakistan's attempt to proxy-rule and almost colonize Afghanistan through Taliban had made Afghans develop an aversion for Pakistan's games, this attitude only further increased the divide. Today, India has opened a direct air route to Afghanistan, bypassing Pakistan and is also developing Chabahar port in Iran, which will provide India another direct route to Afghanistan bypassing Pakistan.

The use of BBINAM framework has already been effectively used by Modi in the SAARC context, which has left Pakistan embarrassed and isolated.

SAARC Satellite

After a month of his swearing-in as Prime Minister, Narendra Modi asked the Indian Space Research Organisation (ISRO) to work on creating a satellite for the South Asian nations which they can use collectively to enhance development. It was to be launched in December 2016, coinciding with, and commemorating the first SAARC summit in December 1985.

Initially, Pakistan showed enthusiasm, only to later raise questions, doubts and suspicions. It tried its best to either delay or stall the project. The result was that the December launch became impossible. Even the Indian observers thought that the idea of India gifting a common communication satellite to the South Asian countries, if realized an unprecedented event of constructive and cooperative space diplomacy, would be only a concept that had to be eventually dropped. One commentator wrote, quoting an anonymous ISRO scientist that the SAARC satellite was 'a bad dream' and that Indians should forget it. Pakistan made the ludicrous charge that India would steal the sensitive data of other countries through the satellite as it would have the control. Interestingly, other countries did not accept such paranoid accusations. So, ignoring protests from Pakistan, other countries signed the MoU for sharing and using the GSAT-9, or the SAARC satellite.

At last, on 5 May 2017, the geostationary communication satellite took off from the Satish Dhawan Space Centre at Sriharikota. The South Asian satellite with 12 Kurtz-under band transponders provides at least one transponder to every South Asian country, which they can utilize for a variety of services from DTH to telemedicine, education and disaster management. Now it is also possible to launch a common South Asian channel for all the countries.

The leaders of all South Asian countries minus one congratulated the dawn of space age regional cooperation in a coordinated video call. Perhaps, the richest tribute came from Afghan President Ashraf Ghani. 'The gap between talk and action is bridged today', he said. He added that 'the imperative of regional cooperation is changed to reality. If cooperation through land is not possible, it is certainly possible through sky, and we are confident that we will integrate.' In a veiled reference to the obstacles that Pakistan created in the India-Afghanistan connectivity, and through that inhibiting Afghan connectivity with other SAARC nations, he said, 'If we can't cooperate on land, we surely can cooperate in space'. Maldives President Abdullah Yameen, who ended his congratulatory video on the launch with the popular slogan that Modi had used in his 2014 campaign—'*sabka saath, sabka vikas*'—also made an indirect appeal to Pakistan to be more cooperative. 'I call upon all South Asian friends to seize this opportunity', he added. With SAARC movement literally having been taken to the skies, perhaps Modi delivered his mentor's message to Pakistan: 'With you if you come; without you if you do not; despite you if you oppose.'

A question may now arise. Are the Sangh and the BJP doing all these with a sinister motive of territorial expansionism? The answer is 'No'. There is no diabolical conspiracy here. The Sangh trained politicians and statesmen simply are more sensitive and aware to the bonding they have with the neighbouring countries. So those years in which BJP has been in power, which are fewer in the seven decades since 1947, the relations with the neighbouring countries have visibly turned upbeat, Pakistan no exception, though the anti-Indian vested interests then had to go to elaborate lengths to sabotage the budding goodwill.

Akhand Bharat: Imperialist Fantasy or Integrating Vision?

The idea of Akhand Bharat has often been caricatured as a nation-state expansionist fantasy of Hindu nationalists. The academic critics and political pamphleteers portrayed it as the militaristic expansion of the Indian nation-state. It has been used as a stick to beat the Hindutva proponents. However, a study of how the concept of Akhand Bharat has shaped the actions of these proponents says they have been in political power for fewer years of the last seven decades since Partition, and which taken together with the presentation of the concept by leading Hindutva ideologues, show a completely different picture.

The vision of Akhand Bharat is not centred on India as a nation-state in the modern sense of the term. It is definitely not a concept associated with territorial expansionism. On the other hand, it takes the cooperation among the modern young nation-states in the region, which share a very ancient, common yet pluralist culture, to weave organic networks, using that cultural unity as the basis for regional ties essential for development. For this it develops an emotional love for the unifying culture which in turn is a culture that celebrates diversity. So even at the cost of repetition it should be stated that the opposition to Bharat Mata and Vande Mataram is not because these imageries are exclusive but precisely because they are not exclusive and precisely because they are inclusive.

'Chilapathikaram', attributed to Illango Adigal, is the epic of the fierce Divine Feminine manifesting in the human realm

Mahishasuramardini at Mamallapuram (seventh century CE) shows a dynamic continuity with the bow-wielding Rashtri of Vedic Vak Sukta and weapon-wielding Goddess fighting for Dharma in Buddhism

Hindu calendar art showing Goddess Bhavani giving the sword to Shivaji (left)
1978 Souvenir from Kalika temple, Chennai for his 351st birthday celebrations because Shivaji worshipped in this temple on 3 October 1677 (right)

Striking visual similarity between the Trishul (with Goddess) tenth century CE, Tamil Nadu (Madras Museum) and Khanda insignia that emerged in modern form in the early part of twentieth century during the Indian freedom struggle

Kot Diji Phase Button Seal, which archaeologist Parveen Talpur identifies with the eye of Varuna; Goddess with three eyes; Popular worship combines Krishna and Kali in Bengal

Bankim Chandra Chatterjee (1838–1894) and Rabindranath Tagore (1861–1941) sang praises of the Divine Feminine in their anthems to India

Karaikal Ammaiyar (fifth century CE), Tamil Nadu sang of the combined form of Goddess and Vishnu as the complete feminine form of Siva

Bharat Mata as depicted in a children's magazine during the Chinese invasion. Bharat Mata was clearly depicted as Goddess Parvati with India's sacred geography identified with Siva. A painting by M. F. Hussain for the 50th Independence Day anniversary (right)

Bharat Mata depicted in a 1930s temple in Madras within Kapaleeswarar temple (identified by author Nivedita Louis) Bharat Mata and tribal form of Goddess Parvati share features here (centre and extreme right)

Subramaniya Bharati shows people from all communities as children clinging to Bharat Mata, just how all four Vedas cling to the fish avatar of Vishnu

Nirrti is a Vedic goddess who manifests when rta is disturbed. Such a feminine Goddess emerging to protect a tree, as depicted in a village Goddess temple in Kanyakumari district

A board in Mahabalipuram (Mamallapuram) says 'Tamizh thai' (Mother Tamizh) and the picture of Bharat Mata. In the collective psyche of India, all languages are emanations of the Divine Feminine, which resonates with the sacred geography of Mother India

Lampsacos silver dish, second century CE: Horned Goddess identified as 'Bharata Lakshmi' by historian of ancient India Prithvi K. Agrawala in 'Early Indian Bronzes' (1977)

3

Cow Worship, Cow Slaughter and Beef

Each time the BJP comes to power in India, at once a strong propaganda is unleashed against the government that it is complicit in promoting cow slaughter or beef related violence. During the National Democratic Alliance (NDA)-I rule under Atal Bihari Vajpayee (1998–2004), the brutal killing of Scheduled Community (SC) members by villagers was highlighted, and a campaign was launched against the BJP and Hindutva. During NDA-II under Narendra Modi (2014–2019), 'lynching' incidents related to beef have been decried by the media as well as eminent citizens. Cow slaughter ban and beef have always been major controversies in India. Cow veneration has always been seen as central to Hindutva. It is also seen as 'food fascism' or imposing of 'Brahminical values' on others, particularly SCs and religious minorities.

On the night of Dussehra, the end of the nine nights of the Mother Goddess, in October 2002, five youths, all in their twenties, were skinning the carcasses of cattle in Jhajjar in the Indian state of Haryana. A mob thought they were slaughtering a cow. They were initially beaten and handed over to the police. Later a mob assembled. With the police as mere onlookers, the mob killed them in a gruesome manner. The local police force did not intervene, either intentionally or out of fear. All five youths belonged to the SC. Soon after the incident, one of the senior vice-presidents of Viswa Hindu Parishad (World Hindu Council), Acharya Girilal Kishore (1920–2014), was reported as quoting scriptures in a press conference to state that the life of the cow is as sacred, perhaps even more sacred than a human life. The VHP, however, denies that Kishore issued such a statement and has reasserted that it works towards an egalitarian Hinduism by crusading against untouchability and caste discrimination.[1] Also, Mayawati, leader of the Dalit party Bahujan Samaj Party (BSP), in a speech condemning the incident, denied any role of Sangh Parivar organizations in the incident.[2] But then Prime Minister Atal Bihari Vajpayee himself condemned the killing.[3] Nevertheless, the media and political forces went along with the narrative that the Dalits were lynched by upper caste Hindus supported by Hindutva forces. At last, when the judgment came in 2010, seven persons (six Jats and one SC) were given life imprisonment. The judgment called the act 'well planned and premeditated' while at the same time rejected the 'anti-Dalit' angle.[4] But the stereotyping of linking illegal and violent cow-vigilantism that is part of the rural landscape of North India, which transcended party affiliations and even caste identities, with the Hindutva and Sangh Parivar organizations has been done successfully in the academia as well as media.

The same was repeated in 2015, after Modi came to power. On 28 September 2015, a mob of villagers attacked the house of Mohammad Akhlaq, accusing him of stealing and slaughtering a cow calf in Bisara village near Dadri, Uttar Pradesh, which was then ruled by Akhilesh Yadav of Samajwadi Party (SP). In the mob attack, 52-year-old Mohammad Akhlaq was killed and his son, 22-year-old Danish, was seriously injured. After the Dadri incident, the politics of beef has taken a central stage in Indian politics like never before. Just like the 2002 Gujarat riots were made the first riots in the era of politicized TV channels, the Dadri lynching in 2015 has become the first beef controversy in the era of social media and digital networks. Media succeeded in making an isolated event, probably with localized causes including personal rivalry, into a national debate on beef and cow slaughter.

Setting the Stage

The stage had already been set for blowing up such an isolated event into a national controversy by a section of the media. A limited restriction on meat, in a localized area, during the festival time of Jains, an Indic minority, was debated in high decibels on certain TV channels, as 'food fascism'. This, even though the Supreme Court in a 2008 verdict upheld such a restriction, and observed in a detailed manner why such a restriction is reasonable:

> The Jains have a religious festival called Paryushan during which they do penance. Out of respect for their sentiments, surely the non-vegetarians can remain vegetarians for 9 days in a year. ... In the present case we have noticed that the closure of the slaughter house is only for 9 days and not for a considerable period of time. This decision indicates that the restriction is reasonable. A period of 9 days is a very short time and surely the non-vegetarians can become vegetarians during those 9 days out of respect for the feeling of the Jain community. Also, the dealers in meat can do their business for 356 days in a year, and they have to abstain from it for only 9 days in a year. Surely this is not an excessive restriction, particularly since such closure has been observed for many years. ... In a multicultural country like ours with such diversity, one should not be oversensitive and over touchy about a short restriction when it is being done out of respect for the sentiments of a particular section of society.[5]

As far as the Dadri incident is concerned, what happened was a crime. Facts such as whether the lynched man ate beef or mutton, or whether he stole a calf or not are immaterial and insignificant. A mob had taken law in its hand and had committed a crime in violation of the Indian Constitution and hence those who committed the crime should be punished. The family of the lynched man should get not just monetary compensation but also justice. The media and the op-ed propaganda used the Dadri lynching to target the Modi government instead of the state. There was an avalanche of returning of state awards. Arun Shourie, an erstwhile 'Hindutva intellectual' who had scores to settle with Modi on account of him being denied an important berth in the central cabinet, said that the NDA-II was 'Congress scaled up plus a cow'.[6]

However, there is another side to the entire media outrage on cow vigilantism and its links to Hindutva. Following the Dadri incident, the 'progressives' started organizing the so-called 'beef festivals' in public spaces across India. The rhetoric in all these 'beef festivals' was always extremely anti-Hindu and Hinduphobic. In Karnataka, the Popular Front of India (PFI), an Islamo-fascist outfit, killed a cattle protection activist. In 2016, a minor girl was critically injured in shooting by the cattle smugglers in Uttar Pradesh (UP). Earlier, 29 cows were killed when a vehicle illegally smuggling 30 cows derailed. This too happened in UP.[7]

After compiling no less than fifteen incidents where the cattle smugglers firing fatally at cattle owners (including an SC), an investigative report in *Swarajya* revealed:

> These are not stray incidents but a continuation of a series of deadly attacks carried out by cattle smugglers on farmers across India. Gangs of smugglers enter villages at night, armed with guns and pistols, to kidnap cattle before fleeing away in trucks which they sell for slaughter. ... Even as the country is campaigning against crimes committed by men in the name of cow protection, this is another issue that deserves attention. The menace doesn't find much space in mainstream media but is one that a civilised society must stand up against.[8]

On 19 July 2017, *India Today* brought out how ordinary citizens, cattle owners, government officials, tourists and animal welfare activists were being attacked by cattle smuggling mafia. The report also made an observation about the underreporting of the violence by the cow-smuggler mafia:

> Fortunately for the meat mafia, cases of genuine animal lovers being intimidated or attacked are seldom being reported these days, as the outrage is primarily against *gau rakshaks* (cow vigilantes) and mobs who have lynched cattle transporters merely on rumours of consumption of beef.[9]

In the second week of July 2017 facing high voltage campaign linking his party, ideology and cow vigilantism Prime Minister Narendra Modi made a statement against the vigilantes stating that they would face full severity of law if they took the law in their own hands. The very next week saw the cow smugglers in Bihar chopping the fingers of a railway gate guard for refusing to open the gate for the cow smuggling vehicle.[10] The cattle-smuggling mafia which comprises both Hindus and Muslims also have terror links. This has been out in the open as early as 2013. When Islamic State (IS) carried out a terror attack in Dhaka, Bangladesh, Dr Souvik Chatterji stated in his paper on its consequences for India, written for the Institute of Peace and Conflict Studies (IPCS):

> ... in the guise of cattle smuggling, huge groups of Bangladeshis also smuggle fake currency. A member of Harkat-ul-Jihad al-Islami (HuJI) who was arrested in Uttar Pradesh in 2008 said that in the disguise of a cattle-smuggler, he had managed

> to smuggle guns and bullets for terrorists in the country. In April 2013, India's National Investigation Agency (NIA) filed a chargesheet after investigating the cattle smuggling case of a cadre of Hizbul Mujahideen (HuM). These individuals were also smuggling fake currency into India across the India-Bangladesh border.[11]

This is further corroborated by advocate Shiraz Quraishi and his team who had pointed out to the Supreme Court recently that cutting across religious boundaries, there are many '*gorashaks*' (cow protectors) who are battling strictly through legislative means, the cattle smuggling mafia. Talking to *India Today*, he said:

> The meat trade is a hazard to our national security. As per a report conducted by the National Investigation Agency, one of the biggest fundraisers for the terrorist outfit Hizbul Mujahideen was a cattle smuggler from Bangladesh. Recently several thousand cartridges, carcasses of endangered and extinct animals and several hundred illegal firearms were recovered from an animal poacher's house in Meerut.[12]

While cow smugglers using firearms against both cattle owners and policemen seemed to have increased from 2010, the higher ups have been concerned about this as early as 2006. A high-level meeting was held on 2 May 2006 to discuss cattle smuggling across the Bangladesh border as a major concern. Chaired by B. S. Laali, Secretary of the Border Management Division, Ministry of Home Affairs, the meeting was also attended by Director General (DG) of Border Security Force (BSF) along with representatives from UP, Bihar, Jharkhand, Uttaranchal and West Bengal. According to the estimates of the West Bengal government, the magnitude of animal smuggling across the border was 50 to 60 lakh per annum. The presentation also revealed the existence of illegal factories which converted the smuggled and slaughtered cow carcasses into ghee. The link of cattle smugglers to Harkat-ul Jihad-e Islami (HUJI) was also brought forth. In 2008, Mayawati, then Chief Minister of UP and supremo of Bahujan Samaj Party (essentially a Dalit political party) while discussing the need to deal with terror issued a stern warning that 'cow slaughter was not possible without the connivance of senior officials and that she would personally monitor the matter in order to attain positive results'.[13]

After NDA-II came to power in 2014, there has been a drastic decrease in illegal cattle smuggling across Indian border into Bangladesh. According to the data revealed by India's BSF, 1,74,469 cattle were seized by its personnel in 2016 which decreased to 1,11,615 in 2017. As on 31 May 2018, it had seized 16,847 cattle getting smuggled across the 444-kilometre border between the Indian state of Meghalaya and Bangladesh. According to BSF personnel, this decline in cattle smuggling was mainly due to the pro-activeness of the Central government. The cow vigilantism in the Hindi heartland which was the major source of cows was another key factor that led to a drop in the illegal trade.[14]

Such multidimensional nature of the problem has been brushed aside or downplayed by the dominant media and anti-Hindutva polity. The pro-beef Hinduphobic ideology has also developed a narrative that is seemingly liberal, rationalist and historical: Vedic seers relished beef, and so did Vivekananda. For Gandhi, cow protection was not central to his discourse. During the British Raj, 'communal' elements forged the beef issue as an anti-Muslim tool. And it was only Nehruvian secularism that saved India from becoming a barbaric land where cows were venerated more than humans. Or that Hindu fundamentalists are trying to make India a land of cow loving Nazis. Such a narrative along with the understanding of how cow veneration has historically been associated and evolved with the Hindu-ness, needs to be studied to understand the real politics and ideology behind the politics of cow in India. Beyond political motives and media sensation, the cow continues to remain an important aspect of *Hindutva*. However, there are historical reasons and sociological consequences for the Hindutva stand on cow.

Vedic Beef to British Cartridges

It is a matter of speculation whether the alleged Vedic ritual killing of the cow is mutually exclusive with the so-called sacred animal status of the cow. However, Vedic literature had already started developing a value-based tension in which it became a virtuous act to set free a cow meant to be killed. The cow had become associated with ṛta. Dr Nandita Krishna points out that the case for Vedic beef eating rests more on shaky foundations while Vedic literature abounds with injunctions to protect cow:

> The case for beef eating rests on one word: *goghna*, which appears in the *Shatapatha Brahmana* and *Vashishtha Dharmasutra* and was translated by one Taranath in the early twentieth century as 'killer of the cow' or serving beef to the guests. However, this is at total variance with Panini, the ancient grammarian, who translates the word as 'receiver of the cow' or one who receives a cow as a gift. On the other hand, the *Rig*, *Sama*, *Yajur* and *Atharva Veda* say that the cow is "*Aghnya*", one that ought not to be killed; "*Ahi*", one that must not be slaughtered; "*Aditi*", one that ought not to be cut into pieces. (Nighantu 11.4 by Yaska, commentator on the Vedas) The terms *aghnya*, *ahi* and *aditi*, are synomyms for *gau*, meaning cow. The *Yajur Veda* is replete with instructions to protect the cow: "Do not kill the cow

which is the splendour of life and inviolable. (13,43). Yo men and women both of you together protect your cattle" (6.11). The *Atharva Veda* (VIII.3.25) adds, "A man who nourishes himself on the flesh of man, horse or other animals or birds or who having killed untorturable cows, debars them for their milk, O Agni, the King, award him the highest punishment or give him the sentence of death."[15]

The Vedic veneration of cow is so much so that Dr Koenraad Elst speculates that the most sacred syllable of the Indic religions, 'Aum', 'the syllable that encompasses all Vedic hymns, that is also used at the beginning of the opening hymn, Aum, is nothing but a human vocalization of the sound made by the cow'.[16]

For those who believe in Aryan invasion/migration theories (AIT/AMT), the Vedic period was around 1500–1200 BCE. Those who question the AIT/AMT posit the Vedic age variedly, ranging from 4000 BCE to 2500 BCE. In the Harappan versus Vedic scenario, a binary has been set according to which the native Indus Valley people venerated only the bull while the Aryans worshipped the cow. Here is typically how the Western 'authoritative' work on Hinduism depicted the subject:

The cult of the bull was one of the chief religions of Indus Valley India, and representations of the bull are found among the steatite seals and terracotta statuettes of that period. ... But for the Vedic Aryans, an essentially pastoral people, it was the cow that was held in special esteem, for she gave milk and produced more bulls for the labour of the fields.[17]

This is basically based on the 'absence' of the depiction of cow in Harappan seals. This view has been falsified by archaeological finds. Cow figurines have been found at the Hakra Ware sites, and Lothal cow figurines have been discovered by archaeologists. The skeletons discovered in a ceremonial burial in Rajasthan, dated around 2000 BCE, are now considered the oldest case of leprosy. The burial can be considered as belonging to Vedic or proto/pre-Vedic Indian culture, depending upon the stand one takes on AIT/AMT. According to archaeologists, the 'second-millennium burial practice is suggestive of Vedic tradition' which had the burial pit filled with 'vitrified ash from burned cow dung', which clearly indicates a ritual veneration for the cow.[18]

Clearly, the Indic tradition of using cow-based products in rituals has a continuity spanning more than 4000 years in the least. In classical Indian medical treatises like *Sushruta Samhita* and *Ashtanga Sangraha*, cow-product-based medicines have become an integral part. *Panchagavya* has a long history both in medicine and agriculture. Irrespective of the ideology of the party in power, Indian institutions of science and technology have regularly published papers on the role of this cow product-based formulation in both medicine and sustainable agriculture.[19]

In 2012 Ghulam Nabi Azad, then Union Minister of Health & Family Welfare, informed Parliament that a study titled 'Evaluation of the Immunomodulatory Activity and Safety/Toxicity of Panchagavya Ghrita' had been conducted by the Central Council for Research in Ayurvedic Sciences (CCRAS). He also mentioned that the Council of Scientific and Industrial Research (CSIR) had conducted research in cow urine and secured the intellectual property generated through patents on the 'Use of Cow Urine Distillate (Go-mutra) as Bioenhancer of Anti-Infective and Anti-Cancer Agents' and also on the 'Pharmaceutical Composition Containing Cow Urine Distillate as an Antioxidant'. [20]

During Islamic invasions, cows were slaughtered by invaders as well as fanatical chieftains who wanted to humiliate and convert Hindus. The *samanvaya* process of Indian civilization had its impact on India's Islamic rulers, and some of them had banned and restricted cow slaughter. It was not a linear evolution. The Mughal emperor Akbar banned cow slaughter and made it punishable by death. However, his son Salim recorded with glee how he desecrated a Hindu temple by slaughtering a cow in it. In 1645, while Aurangzeb was the Governor of Gujarat, he converted the Chintaman temple into a mosque, called the Quwwat-ul-Islam. But before that, he ordered a cow to be slaughtered in the shrine. In 1757 Ahmed Shah Abdali desecrated the Golden Temple of Sikhs by filling the sacred tank with slaughtered cows.

With the British, cow slaughter was set to become a widespread economic offence and a theo-cultural onslaught. The 1857 uprising had its trigger in the beef-pork controversy. The last Mughal emperor promptly banned cow slaughter and made it punishable by death. According to historian Mahdi Husain, Bahadur Shah considered the ban on cow slaughter 'a necessary step in cementing Hindu-Muslim concord'. After accepting the leadership of the rebellious soldiers on 12 May 1857, he agreed to enforce a ban on cow slaughter. On 28 July he confirmed it and announced that anyone slaughtering a cow would be shot dead. The announcement was repeated by the Mughal emperor on Bakar-'id on 2 August. Husain says that it enabled Bahadur Shah to 'maintain communal harmony in Delhi during the most crucial period of the war' (May to September 1857).[21]

When the British established their 'Raj' officially in India, they saw the Hindu tradition of cow veneration as a stumbling block to taking the animal to their dining tables. Science writer John Reader writing critically on the British attitude provides a benign tilt to the British attitude:

> Britain's colonial administrators inclined to salivate at the mere thought of a well-roasted joint, generously apportioned, regarded the sacred cow as the ultimate absurdity among a host of ritual customs and traditions that thwarted their attempts to bestow European civilization on India. People would be better fed and their land better used, if the Hindus would kill a cow and eat beef occasionally, they reasoned.[22]

Karl Marx also echoed the same colonial missionary view when he accused Hinduism of 'brutalising worship of nature' for making man the 'sovereign of nature' fall before '*sabala* the cow'. Thus, cow veneration was considered a downfall, superstition and abomination.[23] Making Indians eat beef was considered a civilizing mission. The British mission in spreading beef consumption in India may not have been actually 'civilizing' India but rather subjugating her in a thorough manner—had it succeeded, it could have set back by a couple of centuries the national movement for Independence.

Extermination of Another 'sacred animal'

A similar scenario developed in the plains of United States, where the colonizers were hunting another 'sacred animal'. For Native Americans, the buffalo was a sacred resource to be utilized according to human need. For many tribes, the animal is sacred because in their sacred lore, the buffalo and humans share a common mythological origin. The nomadic lives of the Native American tribes centred around the sacred bison. Though they did consume the meat of bison, they never slaughtered them wantonly and venerated it as a 'sacred animal'.

If cow veneration in India was deemed an uneconomical burden for the Indian farmer, in the United States, the extermination of the sacred bison was essential for the agricultural settling of native Indians. The United States Interior Secretary Columbus Delano wrote in 1872 that he would not be sad for the 'disappearance' of the bison as he regarded it as a means of 'hastening their (Native Americans') sense of dependence upon the products of the soil and their own labors'. But the real reason was not civilizational altruism but political subjugation, as revealed by US Representative James Throckmorton in 1876:

> There is no question that so long as there are millions of buffaloes in the West, the Indians cannot be controlled, even by the strong arm of the Government. I believe it would be a great step forward in the civilization of the Indians and the preservation of peace on the border if there was not a buffalo in existence.[24]

The extermination of sacred bison became a feverish military and economic activity. The nineteenth century American-ruling elite were well aware of the importance of conservation of wildlife and the threats of extinction. But there was a political equation behind the extermination of bison. It was only in 1886 with William T. Hornaday, the chief taxidermist of the National Museum, reporting only traces of about 600 wild buffaloes that Washington was shocked because 'now that Indian was no longer a threat, Washington could afford to be shocked'.[25] Daniel Brister, the executive director of 'Buffalo Field Campaign' points out the clash of worldviews behind the slaughter:

> At the root of the buffalo slaughter lies a clash of cultures. The dominant Euro-American worldview holds that nonhuman animals are not entitled to the same rights as humans. Human comfort comes before animal survival. To the Lakota and other plains tribes, the notion of "people" encompasses more than the human race. Buffalo are people. Agreements have been worked out since the earliest days when people and buffalo shared life inside the earth, and the buffalo made the original sacrifice for the humans. These agreements are renewed every year through seasonal re-enactments like the Sundance, a ceremony through which people sacrificed their bodies to the buffalo.[26]

After the holocaust of the sacred bison in the American plains, along with the bleached bones of the massacred bison also lay the shattered spine of the resistance of the Native American tribes against the atrocities and transgressions of the Euro-American colonizers. Interestingly, yet another American connection would emerge later in India with respect to cow in the form of elitist ecological argument.

South Indian Traditions: From Sangham Literature to Sri Narayana Guru

Sangham literature of ancient Tamil Nadu clearly speaks of the importance of cow and its veneration. A verse that lists the worst evil deed a human could commit places the harming of a cow first, followed by harming the human embryo and so on.[27] *Chilapathikaram* depicts Kannagi, the bereaved wife of Kovalan, while she burns Madurai, as instructing the fire to burn the city and the bad people in it while keeping away from 'the Brahmins, virtuous people, cows, women, children and the old aged'. This list also enumerates the categories not to be harmed during any invasion. Later, Chozha traditions speak highly of a Chozha king killing his own son under his chariot wheels for a calf. The incident which has become in Tamizh mind the symbol of just governance needs elaboration. The Chozha prince accidentally kills a calf when he goes around the city roads in his chariot. The king has a complaint bell at his doorstep which should be rung by the subjects when demanding justice from the king. The bereaved cow comes and pulls the bell rope. The king, on finding what has happened, asks his counsel what to do. Either he could perform ritual cleansing for the sin or he should make the prince suffer the same death and thus feel for himself the pain of the cow. The king prefers the second. He makes the prince lie down and runs the chariot on him. Of course, the entire episode was a means to test the king's sense of justice by the gods, which is revealed later. But the legend has become the symbol of justice in Tamil Nadu.

During the mid-nineteenth century, Ramalingam Vallalar (1823–1874), the famous spiritual seer and social reformer who particularly concentrated on alleviating food insecurity caused by frequent famines resulting from the East India Company's increased control of South India, made this episode famous through his prose and poetry. In his dramatizing of the entire episode, we find some peculiar features. The work titled *Manu Murai Kanda Vachagam* was first published in print at Chennai in 1854. In the work, the traditionalists argue that a human life should not be killed in exchange of that of the cow-calf. They say that according to *Manusmriti*, a person who has killed the cow should wear the hide of the cow and then serve the herd for a specific period; taking human life is not at all advocated. As against this, the protagonist, the Chozha king argues the greatness of the cow:

> Of all births being born as a cow is considered superior. Under its horns are Brahma and Vishnu. At the tip of its horns are the sacred water bodies like Kaveri. In its head resides Siva and in its forehead Shakti. Subrahmanya is in her nostrils. In her ears are the Asvini Devas. Her eyes are the sun and the moon and Varun resides in her tongue, Sarasvati in the sounds she makes and the Gandharvas reside in her chest. Indra resides in her neck and Rudras reside in her back. The Sapta-Matrika reside in her genitals. Lakshmi resides in her anus. Ganga abides in her urine. Earth goddess resides in her stomach. Yamuna is in her dung. The ocean of milk is in her udders and the fire of all sacrifices is in her vital organs of stomach, heart and face. Great of the women like Arundhati reside all over her body. So it is said. Further she gives us treasured milk with which we bathe Siva, and she is the basis for the production of holy ash. She is the mother of that bull of Siva which has the four Vedas as its legs, Karma and wisdom as its eyes, Scriptures as its horns, Dharma itself as its body and penance as its gait. Can we consider such a cow as just animal?[28]

Thus, cow protection forms the basis of ethical system in South India as much as it is so in North India. The emphasis on cow protection by Vallalar at a time when British colonialism was spreading in South India is in a way an expression of Indic resistance to the British policy of encouraging cow slaughter. Another non-Brahmin Saivaite Tamizh saint of the same period Vannasarabam Thandabani Swamigal (1839–1898), who was one of the earliest voices for female education and widow remarriage in Tamil Nadu, criticized the British rule: 'It is intolerable to see the Mother Earth cry, as She suffers under the lowly tyrants who kill and eat daily cows innumerable.'[29]

When Sri Narayana Guru, the eminent spiritual savant and social emancipator of Kerala, was asked what was wrong in eating the flesh of a cow as we anyway drink its milk, he replied, 'There is nothing wrong.' Then he asked the person if his old mother was alive. 'No,' said the devotee. The Guru said, 'You drank her milk as a child. What did you do to her? Did you eat her flesh or bury her body?'[30] The unusually harsh retort from a saint known for his gentle peace-loving nature shows the deep roots of cow veneration in the South.

Victorian Holocaust and Indic Resistance

The same scenario could have been reenacted in India, with the difference of India being mainly an agrarian rather than nomadic society. In India, forest-dwelling and agrarian communities had developed syncretic relations, in which Hinduism played a major role. Cow veneration giving way to respect for all life also played an important role in the evolution of these relations. The British systematically destroyed and distorted these bonds. The repeated famines which plagued India during the colonial regime had, as one of their causes, the robbing of the grazing land for Indian livestock by both the colonial forest department that prevented villages from getting fodder for their livestock and the railways that refused to haul fodder. Behind the myth of 'uneconomical cows exerting pressure on the meagre natural resources of India' lies the fact of the ruthless destruction of Indian pastoral communities by the British and the systematic destruction of grazing commons. Historian Mike Davis points out the cascading effect of the collapse of the Indic system, with a focus on the cattle population. This systemic collapse ultimately resulted in severe repeated famines:

> The traditional Deccan practices of extensive crop rotation and long fallow, which required large farm acreages and plentiful manuring, became difficult to maintain as the land became more congested and cattle less numerous. "More than any single asset, in the dry-crop regions of Bombay, the use of agricultural bullocks was vital

> to efficient farming operations." Between 1850 and 1930, the ratio of plough cattle to cultivated land in the Deccan steadily declined, making it almost impossible, according to Charlesworth, to raise per capita agricultural output. At the same time, the quality of bullocks also deteriorated as expert nomad cattle breeders were deliberately squeezed out of the economy. Similarly, the government did little to sponsor the planting of drought-resistant fodder crops. Kaiwar estimates that between 1843 and 1873, cattle numbers in the Deccan fell by almost 5 million. The 1876–1878 drought killed off several million more, with cattle populations plummeting by nearly 60 per cent in some districts.[31]

It is in this connection that one must see cow veneration as performing an important survival function during the raging colonial famines. What anthropologist Marvin Harris says about cow veneration as sustaining the agricultural system during prolonged drought-like conditions in India, applies even better to the repeated famine conditions of the colonial period:

> The prohibition against eating meat applies to the flesh of cows, bulls, and oxen, but the cow is the most sacred because it can produce the other two. The peasant whose cow dies is not only crying over a spiritual loss but over the loss of his farm as well. Religious laws that forbid the slaughter of cattle promote the recovery of the agricultural system from the dry Indian winter and from periods of drought ... During droughts, the cows often stop lactating and become barren. In some cases, the condition is permanent, but often it is only temporary. If barren animals were summarily eliminated, as Western experts in animal husbandry have suggested, cows capable of recovery would be lost along with those entirely debilitated. By keeping alive the cows that can later produce oxen, religious laws against cow slaughter assure the recovery of the agricultural system from the greatest challenge it faces—the failure of the monsoon.[32]

Unlike in the United States where the Euro-Americans succeeded in exterminating the sacred bison, the British in India could not popularize beef and destroy the sacred cow and thus make Indian agriculture completely collapse, because the political resistance to the British took the form of cow protection in a very virulent way. It is not an accident that the first economic boycott of British goods and advocacy of self-reliance (Swadeshi) was advocated by the Punjab-based cow protection movement of Namdhari Sikhs.

It is interesting to note here that while colonial historiography and its dialectical descendant, the Marxist historiography of today, have attributed cow protection as an anti-Dalit Brahminical reactionary movement, historical facts prove otherwise. Baba Ram Singh Kuka whose Kuka movement was the fiercest cow protection movement in Northwestern India was also a strong advocate for the abolition of untouchability. Their cow protection along with the economic boycott of the British resulted in a violent suppression of the movement with the execution of 69 Namdharis, including women and children, who were placed in front of canons and blown away. The macabre execution continued for three days in July 1872.[33]

It was in the 1870s that the bisons were getting exterminated on the other side of the planet. But in India, the physical extermination of the cows was stopped by the sacrifice and resistance of spiritual groups like the Namdharis and later Arya Samajists. However, British propaganda as well as their efforts to use cow veneration as a tool to drive a wedge between Hindus and Muslims took deep roots in the modern polity. As shall be seen, this aspect of the British legacy would later be inherited by the Nehruvian regime.

In South Africa, where a large number of Hindus, mostly South Indians, have gone as indentured labour, the decision of South African government to shoot down two cows on the grounds that they were tick-infested caused a lot of heartburn. The South African press reported:

> The indignation caused in consequence of the threatened shooting of the two cows, among the Hindoos is not likely to be forgotten by those who have been an eyewitness to the scene of their activity.... Women were crying and shedding torrents of tears as if their very children were being snatched away by the mighty hand of the messenger of death.[34]

A SC leader from Tamil Nadu, Rettamalai Sreenivasan, was visiting the housewarming ceremony of a friend settled in South Africa. He had recorded in his autobiography that his friend performed the Vedic ceremony of *go daan* or gifting of the cow. He chose Rettamalai Sreenivasan as the person befitting the ritual gift.[35]

Tilak, Gandhi, Savarkar and Ambedkar

Lokmanya Tilak clearly saw the British game plan and was cautious in respecting the civil rights of Muslims, and instead rightly targeted the British government for disrespecting Hindu sensitivity. In an article in the *Kesari* dated 22 August 1893, he wrote:

> Just as the Hindus have the right to celebrate their festivals so also the Muslims have theirs, and so long as neither group deliberately crosses the path of the other

or tries to hurt its sentiments, a government should give equal protection to both. We do not say that British, like Mahadaji Scindia, should secure from the Muslims a sanad of cow-protection for the sake of the Hindus and even if we were to say so the British government would not listen to it. But government should always bear in mind that it is tantamount to unnecessarily provoking the Hindus to allow the opening of cow-slaughter shops in predominantly Hindu localities where formerly there were no such shops.

Again, in *Kesari* dated 13 February 1894, he wrote:

If a Muslim slaughters a cow in a Hindu locality, he should be punished. In the same way if a Hindu in his religious zeal enters a Muslim locality to forcibly free a cow, he must also be punished.[36]

But when the British catalysed Islamist politics became increasingly aggressive, not without Gandhian support to the political pan-Islamist project of Khilafat movement, cow slaughter started becoming a way of asserting Islamist identity and to underscore the fundamental difference of Islam and Hinduism.

Yet in the case of cow veneration during the pre-British times, what historian and Bharatiya Jana Sangh leader Prof. Bal Raj Madhok (1920–2016) called 'imperceptible process of Indianisation of Islam'[37] was at work within the Muslim community as well. While the communal process of Pakistan movement during British struggle often emphasized the stereotype of 'Hindus cow-worshippers, Muslims cow-slaughterers', the Hindutva movement at large did not seek to stereotype Muslims as such. Instead, it appealed to Muslims to respect the Hindu sentiment, citing instances from history, as is the case of Akbar and Bahadur Shah Zafar, who banned cow-slaughter. Pakistani author Haroon Khalid visiting the shrine of Sufi saint Sher Shah at Kahna Nau, where cows are considered sacred, writes:

"The Hindus and Muslims are two separate nations. They worship cows and we slaughter them," resonated in my head while I drove to the shrine. This was one of the most popular lines justifying the need of Partition, I had heard. It used to come up in every discussion that I ever had on the differences between Hindus and Muslims, and hence the need for a separate country. Contradicting the statement here was a Muslim shrine where cows were regarded sacred. Here cows were deemed to be sacred and treated in a manner not very different from the way Hindus treat them.

After narrating how the cows presented to the saint, originally a few centuries ago from India, were considered sacred in the village, the shrine keeper had this to say to Khalid:

> There are, but they roam around. Only once during the year, on the 11th of Chaitar [month in indigenous calendar], they come to this shrine for the festival of the saint. There are about 70 to 80 cows. Earlier they used to be in thousands. But now people's religious views are changing. They no longer tolerate the cows of the saint walking through their fields. Earlier, they would welcome them. It is particularly the Wahhabi-like people who have an issue with the cows.[38]

For Gandhi, cow protection was not about simply Hindu sensibilities and religious feelings. He saw it as the greatest civilizational gift Hinduism should give to the world in general and fellow Indians of other faiths in particular:

> Cow protection to me is one of the most wonderful phenomena in human evolution. It takes the human being beyond this species. The cow to me means the entire sub-human world. Man through the cow is enjoined to realize his identity with all that lives....Cow protection is the gift of Hinduism to the world.[39]

Ambitious 'no less than to see the principle of cow protection established throughout the world'[40], Gandhi wanted to set his own house in order. Towards this end, he wanted no constitutional provision for cow protection but wanted Hindus to convert Muslims to the same Hindu mindset that venerates the cow:

> Cow slaughter can never be stopped by law. Knowledge, education and the spirit of kindliness towards her alone can put an end to it. It will not be possible to save those animals that are a burden on the land or, perhaps, even man if he is a burden.[41]

Norwegian eco-philosopher Arne Naess, who propounded the concept of 'deep ecology', had admiringly written the influence of Gandhi and his conception of 'essential unity of man and for that matter all that lives'.[42] And for Gandhi, cow protection was in a way symbolic of justice to all non-human lives.

Contrary to the popular view that Savarkar was for killing the cows, Savarkar had some convergence of thought with Gandhi on the issue of cow protection and veneration. In 1934 he considered cow protection a 'humanist act' and a 'personal, familial' and in the case of India, a 'national duty'. To him, the movement for cow protection had to be based and popularized on 'clear-cut and experimental economic and scientific principles' and then only it could be genuine. In his 1938 speech at Hindu Mahasabha, Savarkar reiterated the same:

> A worshipful attitude is necessary for protection. But it is improper to forget the

> duty of cow protection and indulging only in worship. The word 'only' used here is important. First protect the cow and then worship it if you so desire.[43]

Gandhi had also suggested that cow protection should incorporate scientific principles. For example, he wanted Hindus to learn the 'science of cattle breeding' and replace the cruel methods like castration by 'the humane treatments developed in the West'.

Dr B. R. Ambedkar, who had written elaborately about how beef-eating was used by dominant castes to perpetuate untouchability, had empathy for the cow veneration of Hindus. His approach to cow veneration anticipates Marvin Harris decades before:

> The love of the ancient Hindoo and for that matter of the modem for agriculture transcends that of the ancient Greek and is just manifested in the worship of the cow. The Hindoo devotion to the cow has been an enigma to most of the foreigners and above all has been an efficient lore in the hands of those half-baked theological failures, who go to India to conduct their missionary propaganda for blackmailing the Hindoo. The origin of cow worship is as much economic as that Roman practice of not offering wine to the Gods from unpruned vines. The cow and for that matter all draft animals, is the soul of the farmers. The cow gives birth to oxen which are absolutely necessary to the cultivation of the farm. If we kill the cow for meat, we jeopardize our agricultural prosperity. With full foresight, the ancient Hindoos tabooed cow-flesh and thus prevented cow killing. But man hardly pays any attention to dry rulings. It must have religious sanction; hence the grotesque mythology around the cow in old Hindoo religious literature.[44]

Naturally with Dr Ambedkar as the principal architect, the protection of cow and her progeny found a place in the Directive Principles of Indian Constitution.

Scenario in Post-Independent India

After Independence, the British legacy of viewing cow protection as a superstition and stumbling block to progress was inherited by the Nehruvian government and most of its technocrats. However, the Gandhian-Savarkarite thought of holistic cow protection was emphasized by India's first agriculture minister K. M. Munshi. In a view that was ecologically advanced for his own times, Munshi emphasized on the role of the cow in particular and livestock in general as transformers of the quality of soil and saw them as important nodal points in the matter-energy cycles of agroecosystem:

> Mother cow and the Nandi are not worshipped in vain; they are the primeval agents that enrich the soil—nature's great land transformers—that supply organic matter which, after treatment, becomes nutrient matter of the greatest importance. In India, tradition, religious sentiment and economic needs have tried to maintain a cattle population large enough to maintain the cycle, only if we know.[45]

Gandhian economist J. C. Kumarappa saw cow protection as symbolic of a cow-centred economy. He also pointed out that during the war, the British need to feed the army with beef had an adverse impact on the Indian cattle. Interestingly, some of the gentlemen who got rich through the supply of beef to the British were Hindus. When he was the chairperson of the Agrarian Reforms Committee of Indian National Congress, Kumarappa recommended optimum utilization of cow dung to achieve village self-sufficiency. He advocated the development of an entirely new package of cow-centred technology that included biogas plants and also use of biogas slurry as manure.[46]

Soon after Independence, cow protection assumed a communal colour. Nehru inheriting the British view on cow slaughter saw it through the prism of both communalism and communism. He considered the issue of cow 'unimportant and reactionary'.[47] So when the first President of the Indian republic, Rajendra Prasad pressed upon Nehru to bring a central legislation for banning cow slaughter, the Prime Minister refused. Later in April 1955, he threatened with resignation if the bill banning cow slaughter was passed in Parliament. However, the theatrics by Nehru were already made irrelevant by the attorney general who had declared in 1954 that cow slaughter was an 'exclusive sphere of the State Legislature', and by the end of 1947 many important districts in North India which included Allahabad, Varanasi, Mathura, Jhansi, Meerut, etc., had all banned cow slaughter.[48]

The legislation prohibiting cow slaughter in Bihar was challenged on the grounds that it violated the religious freedom of Muslims in the famous 1958 Mohd. Hanif Quareshi case. The Supreme Court rejected Quareshi's petition pointing out that the Quran does not make cow slaughter mandatory for Muslims. The verdict went through all aspects of the problem and also various state legislations. It rejected laws that imposed total ban on cattle but upheld the ban on cow slaughter. The verdict read:

> Total ban on the slaughter of cattle, useful or otherwise, is calculated to bring about a serious dislocation, though not a complete stoppage, of the business of a considerable section of the people who are by occupation butchers (*kasais*), hide merchants and so on. Such a ban will also deprive a large section of the people of what may be their staple food.... We now proceed to test each of the impugned

> Acts in the light of the aforesaid conclusions we have arrived at. The Bihar Act, in so far as it prohibits the slaughter of cows of all ages and calves of cows and calves of buffaloes, male and female, is valid.... In our view the ban on slaughter of she-buffaloes, breeding bulls and working bullocks (cattle and buffalo) which are useful is reasonable but of those which are not useful is not valid. ... As regards the Madhya Pradesh Act we likewise declare that it is constitutionally valid in so far as it prohibits the slaughter of cows of all ages and calves of cows, male and female, but that it is void in so far as it totally prohibits the slaughter of breeding bulls and working-bullocks without prescribing any test or requirement as to their age or usefulness.[49]

Islamic scholar Tahir Muhammad elaborates the stand of Islamic law concerning cow slaughter in India:

> It is undoubtedly true that to discharge the qurbani-liability on the Baqrid day, killing a cow is not *farz, wajib* or even *mandub*. On the contrary, though the Prophet did not prohibit the eating of the cow, he did warn his people of beef-borne diseases, in view of which eating the cow should be regarded as *makruh*. By no logic of interpretation can killing a cow be regarded as an essential religious practice of Muslims. On the contrary, abstaining from doing so conforms to the Islamic teaching that Muslims must respect the religious sentiments of others if this does not deprive them of their *faraiz* and *wajibat* (obligatory religious practices).[50]

Nehru's hagiographers had tried to present those who supported cow slaughter ban as biased conservatives, juxtaposing them against the supposedly 'scientific-tempered' Nehru. But a closer scrutiny proves otherwise. For example, despite the displeasure of Nehru, it was under the determined leadership of Dr S. Sampurnanand, the then Chief Minister of UP, that the state successfully adopted the cow slaughter ban legislation. Far from being a biased conservative Dr Sampurnanand was a radical reformer who advocated an open jail system. The adamant stand of Jawaharlal Nehru would however evolve into an even harsher stand under the dynastic and manipulative politician which was Indira Gandhi.

Golwalkar, Karpatri and Kurien

In 1966 the Rashtriya Swayamsevak Sangh (RSS) and Jan Sangh made the ban on cow slaughter a major issue and started a campaign that was received well by the rural populations of North India. The movement started with a conference by a body called Gosevak Samiti (Cow Protection Committee) in 1964. It was inaugurated by M. S. Golwalkar, and Deendayal Upadhyaya gave a talk. Prabhu Dutt Brahmachari, a freedom fighter turned monk who had contested against Nehru in 1951, also blessed the conference. A movement called Sarvadaliya Goraksha Maha-abhiyan Samiti (SGMS—All Party Cow Protection Committee) was formed on 25 September 1966.

In this movement, a prominent figure that emerged was Karpatri Maharaj. Swami Karpatri Maharaj (1907–1982) was a staunch orthodox leader who had founded the political party Ram Rajya Parishad (RRP) out of an Akhil Bharatiya Sanatana Dal he formed in 1950. A strong opponent of eradication of untouchability, he declared that Kasi Viswanath Mandir, the holiest of the Siva temples for Hindus, had become irreparably polluted by the entry of SC members following the constitutional abolition of untouchability in free India. Then he went to the extent of building a private temple for the deity.[51] He was bitterly opposed to the inclusion of SC members in the Jan Sangh. When in 1956 a merger was talked about between Jan Sangh and RRP, the Jan Sangh was uncompromising on the issues of social equality and abolition of untouchability. This led to the failure of the merger. Still, he was revered as a sanyasi by the Sangh. This created a lot of false propaganda in the establishment media, conflating the socially backward views of Karpatri with the limited support the RSS and Jan Sangh gave for the cow protection in which Karpatri was sincere. Maharaj suffered and underwent physical torture for cow protection. Later, attacking the RSS for its egalitarian views, particularly its opposition to untouchability and birth-based *Varna* system, Karpatri came out with a book in 1970 accusing the RSS in general and Golwalkar in particular of being 'blasphemous' and going 'against the fundamentals of Hindu religion'. By treating any portions of the *Smriti* part as outdated, Golwalkar 'was destroying the tenets of Hindu religion itself', alleged Karpatri.[52]

On 7 November that year, a rally of Hindu monks, North Indian rural masses and advocates marching towards Parliament was prevented by the police. In the ensuing violence, the police opened fire. Unruly mobs attacked the houses of Congress leaders including that of K. Kamaraj—a prominent Congress leader from Tamil Nadu. Indira Gandhi quickly capitalized on the issue and asked for her potential rival Gulzarilal Nanda's resignation; Nanda was then the home minister and also one of the heavyweight detractors of Indira. There were clearly other political dynamics and schemes at work. K. Kamaraj, the President of Congress Party, who had supported Indira Gandhi initially was beginning to regret his decision. He wanted a strong alternative to Indira Gandhi inside the cabinet. Kamaraj backed Gulzarilal Nanda for the important home affairs office, and he indeed became the home minister. The support of Kamaraj for Nanda is important in its own way because he was one of the openly pro-Hindu Congressmen. In 1956 Nanda had helped organize the Bharat Sadhu Samaj and had been active in Hindu Sanghathan work through creating social institutions and *goshalas*. Indira Gandhi decided to ensure that this very reason would cause the downfall of Nanda. The unexpected police firing at the unarmed but highly agitated sadhus demonstrating against the government demanding protection for cows led to the sacking of Nanda by Indira Gandhi. Historian Promilla Kalhan explains:

> Some people evidently allowed mischief-makers, even perhaps goonda elements to become part of the procession consisting mainly of sadhus. These elements forced their way into the precincts of Parliament House. The police naturally took action. Also, it appears, some of the mischievous elements even forced their way into the house of the Congress President. It was in the guise of sadhus that some mischief-makers were able to bring about violence, which ultimately created a problem for the Home Ministry which Nanda had to leave. The whole matter appears to have been engineered. Nanda's enemies won the day.[53]

However, following the violence, RSS had to cut a sorry figure and pass a resolution in their apex body that they had to condemn the acts of hooliganism and incendiarism causing damage to public and private property by anti-social elements during the anti-cow slaughter demonstration in front of Parliament House. The resolution called the 'attack by these elements' on Kamaraj's house as 'particularly reprehensible'.[54]

According to the official announcement, seven to eleven persons died, including a cop. Govindacharya, former BJP leader and Hindutva ideologue, puts the number at around 249 'according to some newspaper reports of that time'.[55] Manmohan Sharma, a journalist with the RSS-associated *Hindustan Samachar*, says in a video interview that he counted more than 300 dead bodies in one hospital alone on that day. He states that he saw quite a number of dead bodies of infants who did not have bullet wounds but would have been killed in the resulting stampede. According to Manmohan Sharma, a strict instruction was sent from the PM office to all the prominent journal houses that the number of victims should be put at 11.[56] Shankaracharya of Puri puts the number of victims of police firing at around 800.[57] So, the number of deaths in the shooting still remains controversial. If the number of those who were killed during that firing were even half the number claimed by the pro-Hindu journalist and the venerable traditional Hindu seer like Puri Shankaracharya (with whom even as one completely differs as this author from his social views, there is no reason to believe that he tells a lie, unless in the heat and chaos of the movement he mistook people falling for cane-beating and teargas firing for bullet victims), what had happened was almost a massacre not very dissimilar to the Amritsar massacre by General Dyer.

Prime Minister Indira Gandhi who was using the whole series of events to strengthen her own hold on the party and government saw in this a golden opportunity to attack the RSS as well. She threatened that as its activities seemed indistinguishable from political activities, the RSS members could be barred from the civil services. The RSS did not yield. The sadhus, including the Shankaracharya of Puri, had started a fast unto death campaign. On 1 December 1966, a sadhu undergoing fast-unto-death died. An establishment magazine from Delhi, *Statesman* wrote that the death of Puri Shankaracharya would move the votes from Congress (meaning it would politically benefit Hindutvaites, mainly Jan Sangh). However, Jan Sangh leader Deendayal Upadhyaya persuaded the Shankaracharya to stop his fast-unto-death campaign.

Still, the indefinite hunger strikes taken up by Hindu seers including the Shankaracharya of Puri compelled Indira Gandhi, who had famously declared that she would not 'cow before the cow worshippers', to reverse her stand. Apart from agreeing to implement a ban in all Union Territories, she also established a high-level committee of inquiry to investigate the possibility of bringing a central legislation to bring cow slaughter ban. It included among others RSS chief M. S. Golwalkar, Shankaracharya of Puri, Verghese Kurien, who was the chairman of the National Dairy Development Board, and Justice A. K. Sarkar, Chief Justice of the Supreme Court. The decision of the government to form this committee was communicated to Golwalkar by Babu Jagjivan Ram, the then Defence Minister. The former wrote back:

> But today itself one letter has been received by me from Tihar Central Jail. It is from a friend being punished in jail as a Satyagrahi of the cow protection movement. The letter described the agony of the Satyagrahi in prison and the way most venerable Shri Karpatri Swami and other saints are being tortured. On listening to such an incident, my soul has been engulfed in sorrow and grief. What will the *samiti* (the government committee) do about such kind of incidents? I feel that the constitution of the *samiti* is a show off; there is nothing factual, no truthfulness of heart. It is necessary to purify the atmosphere of such distrust.[58]

Kurien in his autobiography narrates how both he and Sarkar used to smoke cigarettes to the discomfiture of Shankaracharya. The committee was essentially a sham. For example, Kurien was briefed by the government to prevent any ban on cow slaughter. Ultimately after fruitless repeated meetings over twelve years, it was scrapped by the Janata government. But Golwalkar and Kurien developed a deep friendship, and Golwalkar explained his rationale for cow protection to Kurien in private. The RSS chief confessed that he started the movement 'actually to embarrass the government'. But seeing a housewife who after finishing her morning work took the petition from house to house 'to collect signatures in that blazing summer sun', he realized that the woman was actually doing it for her cow, which was her bread and butter. This made him realize the importance of the cow. Then he saw that 'the cow has potential to unify the country—she symbolizes the culture of Bharat'. And in a way echoing Kumarappa about the cow-centred life of India, Golwalkar said to Kurien:

> What I'm trying to tell you is that I'm not a fool, I'm not a fanatic. I'm just cold-blooded about this. I want to use the cow to bring out our Indianness. So please cooperate with me on this.[59]

The story narrated by Kurien also states how from his death bed, Golwalkar asked the Gujarat RSS chief to convey his blessing to Kurien after his death. The RSS head of Gujarat expressed his surprise to Kurien why Guruji chose only Kurien from Gujarat to give his blessings. Kurien passed away in 2012. Though a Syrian Christian, Kurien, '... keeping with his wish, was cremated as per Hindu ritual'.[60]] The entire cow protection movement thus for the first time in independent India brought all the Hindu political forces, both socially stagnant as well as Hindutva movement, together on a common platform. Perhaps, it also set the stage as a rehearsal for the later Ayodhya Sri Ram Janmabhoomi movement.

Ecological Campaign for Cow Slaughter

Michael Lewis, a historian studying the influence of US ecological concepts and institutions in the development of global narrative particularly with reference to India, gives quite a few details as to how the picture of India's religious veneration based on the population of cattle was a threat to ecological preserves of India. It was a cleverly designed campaign.[61] But as it turned out to be, it was not very much a good science.

The aim was to use a scientific study to reinforce the problem of overgrazing due to uncontrolled cattle population and related ecological degradation and its impact on biological sanctuaries and conservation of lions and tigers. In 1966, Bombay Natural History Society (BNHS) got an American graduate student Juan Spillett to write 'by far the most thorough critique of livestock in

Indian national park'. So, the US student who had come to India to do research on ungulates in Kanha National Park now asked by his funding sources (at Johns Hopkins University) to do the research on wharf rats in Calcutta, wrote an article titled 'General Wildlife Conservation Problems in India', which was published in the *Journal of the Bombay Natural History Society*. Spillett started his article identifying two major problems of India which were at the root of all other problems that were prominent then in the national conscience, 'such as the scarcity of food, lack of foreign exchange, poor living standards, and so forth'. These two problems were '(i) too many people, and (ii) too much domestic livestock'. Comparing overgrazing by the unlimited 'domestic livestock' (read cows) to 'cancer', he declared that the overgrazing in India had 'created the largest man-made desert in the world'.

The commentary of Michael Lewis is important here:

> Such arguments are questionable, but not unusual. Vasant Saberwal has traced debates blaming desertification and erosion on livestock grazing in India. He found that scientists and bureaucrats consistently make the (flawed) assumption that overgrazing causes deserts. In fact, Saberwal asserts there is not a direct correlation between grazing and desertification in India, and that this sort of monocausal analysis is misleading. It is a powerful environmental myth, though. We all have seen the photographs of a bare-ribbed cow standing in the midst of a sand dune, plucking the leaves off the only plant in the frame. Such presentations are often more effective in shaping the popular imagination than arguments that global climate change and weather patterns cause deserts, not overgrazing. To this point, grazing has completely destroyed no park in India; conservationists have feared that it will happen for nearly half a century now. Misidentifying the causes of deserts is a mild sin, at best. Far more severe is making policy recommendations based on those beliefs which result in, literally, human deaths.

In fact, Vasant Saberwal cited here, who had researched deeply on pastoral politics, livestock raising rural and nomadic communities as well as the restrictions imposed on them by forestry officials, states that this was more due to 'the politicization of forest conservation, necessitated by the continuing opposition to the Forest Department's restrictive policies, than a response to rigorous scientific enquiry on the relationship between grazing and environmental degradation'.[62] Taking the specific case of Bharatpur sanctuary, Spillett went rhetorical comparing cattle overgrazing in the forest area to terrorists bombing a public building and reminded that the State had the right to shoot down the terrorist before he did the act of bombing. The editors of *Journal of the Bombay Natural History Society* praised his paper in their editorial. Extrapolating from the specific sanctuary they pointed out 'the disastrous effect of overgrazing by domestic livestock all over the country' and were 'grateful to the author of the report for the facts which had uncovered the disastrous effect of overgrazing by domestic livestock all over the country'. Prof. Lewis comments:

> Spillett was not working on his own when he wrote these words. He was a US graduate student writing on behalf of the BNHS, lending his US citizenship and training to their crusade. Obviously, on his whirlwind tour with his BNHS hosts, he saw what they showed him, and they published his article because his views coincided with their own.

Essentially, Zafar Futehally, then secretary of BNHS and nephew of Salim Ali, was also an ornithologist like Ali. But both Ali and Futehally were close to Nehru-Gandhi family and wielded power in their domain. Lewis points out that because of this proximity, they 'consistently relied upon non-democratic politics to effect' what they considered as their environmentalist goals. So, unconsciously the cow protection movement had in a way become the voice of the muted herding communities by making grazing in wild areas an important option for fodder if there was ban on cattle slaughter. Perhaps, this would also explain the tremendous reception the movement gained. The religion and a holistic ecology that included human-cattle-wildlife interaction seemed to have been at play in the cow protection movement of the sixties.

As the Parliamentary Committee 'to investigate the implications of a total ban on the slaughter of the cow and its progeny' got framed, the establishment naturalists went into action. Zafar Futehally wrote an editorial in the *Times of India* in which he quoted Spillett and warned the educated Indians of the dangers of livestock population and the resultant overgrazing doing 'much harm ... to wildlife and to the habitat in such unique areas as Kanha, Kaziranga, Sariska, and Bharatpur'.

> Futehally was serving as the Indian chair of the International Biological Programme Terrestrial Conservation subgroup, and he moved to get the International Biological Programme (IBP) to fund a study in India on cattle and wild herbivores. He approached the Smithsonian, to check on the availability of PL 480-rupee funds. The Smithsonian was amenable but would be too slow.

In their own way, the establishment naturalists were taking the war-against-Hindutva cause of the cow protection movement to another level in the perception and propaganda battle. But there were some unforeseen hurdles—Jairam Ramesh, a Congress politician, points out in his hagiography of Marxist bureaucrat and Nehru-Gandhi family friend P. N. Haksar:

> After the committee had been announced, leading Indian naturalists like Salim Lai and Zafar Futehally, who had unfettered access to Indira Gandhi, got into the act. They proposed that the Bombay Natural History Society (BNHS) collaborate with the Washington-based Smithsonian Institution to carry out studies on the ecological consequences of India's large cattle population....[63]

A staunch Marxist and complete pro-Soviet, Haksar advised Indira against the use of Smithsonian Institution. Indira Gandhi the politician also became non-responsive to this move by courtier naturalists. Then US ambassador Chester Bowles also gently rebuked the US intermediary (Ripley) who was trying to catalyse the BNHS proposal that it was 'better to leave the complexities of the cow problem to the Government of India'. George Beals Schaller, German-US biologist, conservationist and one of the important popular science writers of that time, particularly with respect to conserving gorilla and African lions, in his book on Indian wildlife *The Deer and the Tiger* (1967) took the typical stand of India's livestock being 'a great scourge of India's land'. He found them 'undernourished, diseased, and unproductive, yet ... permitted to exist for religious reasons'. But as Michael Lewis points out, that at the end of his book, though, he had become more moderate. His own observations forced him to conclude that livestock grazing within Kanha National Park actually helped to sustain an abnormally high density of tigers. Lewis quotes him as saying, 'From the standpoint of tiger conservation, it makes no difference whether the prey consists of cattle or wildlife.' But an overall objective had been achieved that the overpopulation of unproductive cattle, particularly cows, would degrade the forests and result in desertification became an established wisdom.

The initiatives made by Futehally did not go completely in vain. In 1969 a scientific study 'as a whole directly considered the role of cattle—domestic and feral—in this ecosystem ... exactly the sort of specific study that Futehally and Ripley had been pushing for' in 1967, was conducted with PL 480-rupee funds in the Gir Forest reserves of Asiatic lions. In 1969 at the International Union for the Conservation of Nature (IUCN) a paper from the study was presented which helped in the launch of tiger conservation projects. When the larger report based on which the paper at IUCN was presented, was accessed by Michael Lewis, he found some very interesting observations which contradicted the official wisdom connecting livestock grazing with wildlife sanctuary destruction.

First, it indicated that the cattle diet differed from that of the wild ungulates in the forest. Then, it suggested that even if all the cattle and buffalo were removed, it would not lead to a corresponding increase in deer and antelope. As the paper suggested, the wild ancestors of the buffalo and cattle perhaps once lived in this forest and played a similar role in its ecosystem. If the cattle were gone, the wild ungulates still would not eat the newly available grass. Then the paper concluded this chain of logic: 'removal of livestock will sharply reduce the capacity of the Gir to support lions and other large carnivores'.

The Smithsonian official overseeing the project was not amused. He wrote the young researcher a long letter. In that, among other things, he pointed out that while he 'would quite agree that the sudden removal of all domestic stock from the forest would be likely to be detrimental from several standpoints', nevertheless 'the authorities in India who have been working hard for the establishment of national parks as well as others … would be quite unhappy with the conclusion that can be drawn from a last census of your third paragraph of the discussion …'

In 1972 the Wildlife (Protection) Act was enacted by the Indira Gandhi government, which made livestock and livestock related human activities illegal in the national parks. In 1981 Bharatpur was declared a national park, but villagers and their livestock continued the age-old grazing in the area. In 1982 the environment-loving Indira Gandhi chaired a high-level meeting and ordered a strict ban on livestock grazing. In 1982 nine villagers protesting the ban on livestock grazing were shot dead by the police. Then came the surprise. By 1987 a mid-study report showed that bird diversity in Bharatpur was dropping since the ban on grazing and fodder collection had taken effect. In 1991 the final report pointed out with alarm that a few weeds which the wild ungulates do not eat had taken over the national park and the scientists were forced to conclude that the only solution was to allow the livestock of the local villagers again into the national park.

Incidentally, the relation between the livestock grazing in the forest and the predators like lion eating them had not been left out of Indian psyche. In the famous Raghuvamsa of Kalidasa, a lion attacks Nandini, the celestial cow, in the interiors of the Himalayan forest. When Dileepa, the ancestor of Rama tries to attack the lion, he gets into a state of suspended animation. The lion asserts its rights for the blood of the cow, which it likens to the moonlight being eclipsed by Rahu—the traditional Hindu name for the north lunar node incision point in the orbit of moon that causes eclipse. It is a stationary point in the orbit, and it is the moon that comes to it. So, the simile employed by Kalidasa through the lion points to the fact that it is the livestock that is trespassing into the forest territory of the predator and hence the latter has its rights over the animal, a logic that Dileepa agrees but offers himself in the place of the cow.[64] So, Indian tradition was definitely aware of the dynamics of livestock interaction with pristine forest ecosystem interactions. Unfortunately, the conservationists in India and rulers like Indira Gandhi paid scant regard to work and update that tradition, and the reality of the local models. Though unaware, the cow protection movement of 1960s was also indirectly fighting for the grazing rights of the local rural and nomadic communities of native Indian livestock, which included not only cows but also buffaloes.

Sangh Campaign for Cow Protection

For Golwalkar and the Sangh, cow protection had now become a part of positive Hindutva. He stated that Hindus should not indulge in cow protection merely because Muslims kill the cow, and he characterized such an attitude as 'negative' and 'reactionary'.[65] He also stated that it was wrong to blame the beef-eating tribals of the North-East and consider them non-Hindus. If at all they should cease to eat beef, it should be a gradual voluntary process and should not be implemented on them from an equal plane and not from a high pedestal. He also rejected the idea of not including tribals as Hindus if they have the custom of beef eating.[66]

Over the decades, the Sangh attitude towards cow protection has clearly undergone a transformation. Today, the Sangh runs a research institute on cow products and desi cow breed protection. A look into the activities of the Sangh affiliate Go Vigyan Anusandhan Kendra (GVAK) shows that they have mostly moved away from the legislation demanding mindset as well as an anti-Muslim narrative to a holistic cow protection mindset. Consider the following examples:

- In 2002 GVAK along with the Central Institute for Medicinal and Aromatic Plants (CIMAP) filed a patent for cow-urine distillate-based formulation as a 'bio-enhancer' of antibiotic drugs. In 2005 the patent was granted.[67]
- A Saraswati Vidya Mandir School in Bhopal has been working for the past 10 years to conserve non-renewable energy by using biogas plant from a *goshala*. The plant saves around 2 cylinders of LPG each day.[68]
- In 2010 a US patent was obtained on 'a composition (RCUD) for protecting and/or repairing DNA from oxidative damages' was obtained by National Environmental Engineering Research Institute (NEERI) and GVAK.[69]
- In 2013 GVAK developed a cow-urine based drug for crop protection

> in collaboration with National Botanical Research Institute (NBRI), a Lucknow-based laboratory of Council of Scientific and Industrial Research (CSIR).[70]

The point here is that the Sangh had come out of the old confrontational narrative of cow protection and is now ready to take the path of holistic cow protection, testing its validity in a scientific framework, which may validate or falsify its claims. Further, the Sangh affiliate has also taken up the protection of desi breeds of cow. The importance of livestock diversity is vital to the future food security and ecological health of the nation.

Progressive Time Warp: Tale of Two Books

However, the Marxist and Nehruvian historiographers and propagandists seem to have stuck in a time warp and still view cow protection through the colonial prism. Unfortunately, they also tap into a market of the mind which belongs to a bygone era of stereotypes. A classic example is the book *Myth of the Holy Cow* written by Marxist historian Dwijendra Narayan Jha in 2001. The book did not create any agitation or violent backlash in India. It was of course debated in the op-ed columns, 'letters to the editor' sections of English newspapers and in the internet circles —most probably with some intemperate email reactions from trolling internet Hindus.

Beyond that, there was no public property damaged or violent mobs baying for the blood of the author. The government of India under Vajpayee did not want to burn the book. Yet when the book was out in the international market, it went with the byline 'a book the government of India demands be ritually burned'. The author was projected by the Western press as one threatened next only to Salman Rushdie. Soon the academic cottage industry in the South Asian departments of US academic citadels had incorporated this urban legend into their discourse on Hindu nationalism. Wendy Doniger and Martha Nussbaum recycle the allegations in their new book published by Oxford University Press in 2015:

> To take another example: the only shocking thing about D. N. Jha's book...is the news that anyone has been shocked by the argument that people used to eat beef in ancient India....Yet the cover of the book proudly proclaims "A Book the Government of India Demands be Ritually Burned," and the flyleaf assures us that the book has been "banned by the Hyderabad Civil Court and the author's life has been threatened." The *Observer* likened the book's reception to that of Salman Rushdie's *Satanic Verses*...Jha was so violently attacked, physically as well as in

> the press, that he had to have a police escort 24 hours a day for several years after his book was published in India. The shocked resistance to the idea that Hindus ever ate beef inheres for some in the fact that it contradicts the party line of the Hindutvavadis, who argue that We Hindus have always been here in India and have Never Eaten Cows; Those Muslims have come in and Kill and Eat Cows and therefore must be banished or destroyed.[71]

Even *Frontline,* the Marxist Indian tabloid which attacked the Vajpayee government in a sustained way, had no such report of physical attack on Jha in the claimed period 2001–2003, though anyone in India can get police protection round the clock alleging a threat to life—a classical political trick of Indian politicians to raise their market value. The more amusing fact is that contrary to the stereotype of a scholar exposing the beef-eating verses from the Vedas shocking the 'fundamentalist' Hindus, these arguments have been answered as early as 1950s by the Supreme Court judgment quoted earlier. The judges had studied the so-called beef-eating attributed to the so-called 'Aryans' in Vedic times. The relevant portion of the judgment had explained the whole process in detail:

> 'It would appear that in Vedic times animal flesh formed the staple food of the people.... *Agni* is called the "eater of ox or cow" in *Rig Veda* (VIII. 43, 11). The slaying of a great ox (Mahoksa) or a great goat (Mahaja) for the entertainment of a distinguished guest has been enjoined in the *Satapatha Brahmana* (111.4.1–2).... Though the custom of slaughtering of cows and bulls prevailed during the Vedic period, nevertheless, even in the Rig Vedic times there seems to have grown up a revulsion of feeling against the custom. The cow gradually came to acquire a special sanctity and was called *Aghnya* (not to be slain). There was a school of thinkers amongst the Rsis, who set their face against the custom of killing such useful animals as the cow and the bull.
>
> High praise was bestowed on the cow as will appear from the following verses from *Rig Veda*, Book VI, Hymn XXVIII (Cows) attributed to the authorship of Sage Bhardvaja.... Kautilya's *Arthasastra* has a special chapter (Ch. XXIX) dealing with the "superintendent of cows" and the duties of the owner of cows are also referred to in Ch. XI of Hindu Law in its sources by Ganga Nath Jha. There can be no gainsaying the fact that the Hindus in general hold the cow in great reverence and the idea of the slaughter of cows for food is repugnant to their notions and this sentiment has in the past even led to communal riots.'[72]

So, while the fabricated fundamentalist and State violence against Jha was a great marketing technique for the book in the West, it hardly stands scrutiny.

Anti-Hindu academics in the West were more than eager to buy this line either intentionally or were bamboozled.

The only incident that can be construed as a response from the NDA government was the then Prime Minister of India Atal Bihari Vajpayee asking the eminent Gandhian historian Dharampal to write a historical work on the history of cow slaughter. Dharampal and his colleague T. M. Mukundan came out with a book that explained the historical origins of the present-day controversies surrounding the cow protection. Titled *The British Origin of Cow-Slaughter in India*, the book exploded the stereotype of Muslims as cow butchers. On the contrary, it showed how many prominent Muslims as well as the Parsis and Sikhs actively participated in the anti-cow slaughter movement and how the movement was originally aimed at the British. With data from Urdu press of the colonial times as well as correspondence of the British officials, Dharampal showed that the cow-slaughtering Indian Muslim was a colonial myth created by the British and that Indian Muslims were not beef consumers, as alleged by then colonial rulers, communal elements, and now Marxist scholars.[73] It was the initiative of a 'Hindu nationalist' Prime Minister that historically documented this fact that shattered a communal stereotype whereas the Marxist historians capitalized on the colonial stereotypes of irrational Indian cow worship.

Real Problems and Half Truths

The tendency of the Nehruvian press and Marxist propagandists to essentialize Hindutva through fringe elements has had a serious cascading effect. Basking in the media limelight, the fringe elements have become a serious threat to evolving genuine cow protection strategies and discourse. For example, organizations like Gau Raksha Dal stop trucks carrying (mostly smuggling) cattle, and taking the law in their own hands, beat the drivers of these vehicles in an inhuman way. These fringe groups can soon become a real headache for livestock farmers, who under the present system have no other way but to dispose of their 'unproductive' livestock. With the depletion of native livestock germplasm and the inability to sustain crossbreed livestock past their productivity, the farmers would really end in a fix with violent groups enforcing a mindless and heartless cow protection.

Today the beef taboo has actually positioned Indian beef in a better standing in the international beef market. An OECD-FAO study enumerates how Indian beef has a comparative advantage over other countries in the international beef market:

> First, commercial beef-ranching is not practised in India, and the male and unproductive female buffaloes are allowed to be slaughtered. Since these animals do not produce milk, they are rarely fed expensive nutritious feeds and therefore the cost of producing meat is much lower than other beef-exporting countries. Second, as the production is going up while the domestic market is limited, India will have surplus to export, which at present stands at around 30 per cent of its total production. Third, the beef produced in India is *halal* meat, which is preferred in a number of South Asian, African and the Middle Eastern markets.[74]

Thus, both the Hindu and Muslim syncretic environment has created a unique advantage for India. Beef-ranching is today considered one of the worst offenders of global climate change. If Indian meadows have not become the beef-ranches for the United States, it is mainly because of the beef-taboo that Indian culture has evolved and the flexibility in allowing the culling of animals which is also equally an integral part of Indian culture. Perhaps *Hindutvaites* can think in terms of creating legislations like the 'Humane Methods of Livestock Slaughter Act', a federal US law that has resulted in technological innovations which have helped reduce the cruelty and stress for the animals that are slaughtered.

However, those who want to destroy this unique niche created by a web of biocultural threads have often peddled half-truths to make beef a part of consumerist food culture in India. *India Today* in its cover story on the politics of beef stated that Indian cows are a major source of greenhouse gases (GHGs) causing global warming:

> Like buffaloes, sheep and goats, cows excrete high quantities of methane, a greenhouse gas (GHG) capable of trapping 21 times more heat than carbon dioxide that irretrievably escapes into the atmosphere. India's total livestock population of over half a billion, also including goats, camels, horses and other such animals, accounts for more than a sixth of the total GHGs from the world's livestock. Data published last year in the Asian-Australasian *Journal of Animal Sciences* shows that India's livestock annually produces 14.32 million tonnes of GHGs, which is 15 per cent of the global total.[75]

But it never bothered to tell its readers another basic ecological fact. The energy potential of cow and buffalo dung comes to 562.2 Peta Joules (PJ) and 336 PJ respectively. This potential can be used by 17 million biogas plants and 1,50,000 community biogas plants for reducing GHG emissions by 5 Tonnes of Carbon (TC)/year and 10.8 TC/year respectively. The climate change benefits in terms of carbon emission reductions are to the tune of 110 TC per year, provided the available potential of bio-energy technologies are utilized. Experts contend that optimum biogas production has the potential of reducing greenhouse gas emissions by 138.33 million tonnes of CO_2-e from manure management. Under the Clean Development Mechanism (CDM), by mid-2012, India had bio-energy projects with a carbon credit of 730.8 million tonnes worth ₹20,1730 million.[76] It is only discounting all these aspects that *India Today* makes cows an eco-liability and hence implies that they should be slaughtered.

From 2008 to 2014 every year the National Geographic Society has been taking a survey of Greendex—a measure of environmentally sustainable consumption, which includes vital areas such as food, habitat, transport, etc. And every year, Indians have come first in the survey. The report notes the following about India's sustainable food habits:

> India, which has ranked first in food sustainability in every Greendex, came out far ahead again, thanks to its culturally dictated eating habits. Nearly one in four Indians is a vegetarian, and those who aren't, tend to avoid beef, the most environmentally damaging meat.[77]

So, cow-protection is an Indic phenomenon that has evolved over the millennia with historical, social, cultural, ecological, political and spiritual dimensions. It is part of the web of Indian life and hence cannot be mechanically implemented in a ruthless manner through blunt legislation. It also cannot be used to stereotype Hindus or Muslims and negatively caricature the political enemies of Marxists and Nehruvian secularists. If positioned rightly, cow-protection can be, as Gandhi rightly envisaged, one of the greatest civilizational gifts from Hindus to an ailing planet. Hence it becomes important for those who stand by cow protection that they create the discourse holistically and devise the strategies scientifically and in an all-inclusive manner. From Golwalkar to GVAK, mainstream Hindutva has moved towards a holistic inclusive and tentatively scientific discourse. There are also maverick statements including 'cow-dung offering radiation protection', etc., which are unscientific and actually hurt the real deeper cause of cow protection.

At the same time, cow protection is organically connected with the food culture of India. In 2016 even as manufactured debates were raging with respect to cow protection, and beef-eating festivals were organized by anti-Hindu and anti-Hindutva elements across India, a paper was published in *Global Environmental Change*, an Elsevier peer-reviewed journal. It spoke of a new index called the HALF—Human Appropriation of Land for Food production. Considering various metrics, it pointed out that 'hypothetically, if the world were to adopt the average Indian diet, 55 per cent less agricultural land would be needed to satisfy demand, while global consumption of the average American diet would necessitate 178 per cent more land'. One may argue here that when Indian diet has the protein and carbohydrates of the US diet, the land requirement may increase. The lower land requirement may be because of the malnourished and impoverished nature of Indian diet. While there is definitely a possibility of increase in land needed for food production increasing with the nutritional quality of the food, still the land disparity is extreme. The paper points out:

> In 2011 the per capita land required to sustain a USA diet was 635 per cent of that required for an Indian diet, even though the energy content of the food was only 65 per cent greater (or 99 per cent greater in terms of protein). This disparity stems from the profile of commodities consumed, with 30 per cent of energy derived from animal products in the USA and 9 per cent in India (65 per cent and 19 per cent respectively for protein). This greater proportion of animal products increases the land requirements in comparison to a predominantly vegetarian diet, e.g., as in India.[78]

Yet another study on the environmental impacts of agricultural production systems, agricultural input efficiency and food choice of mainly highly industrialized system (read the West) states that 'ruminant meats', of which the primary one is beef, 'have impacts that are 3–10 times those of other animal-based foods and 20–100 times those of plant-based foods for all indicators examined.'[79] This indicates a worrying possibility. With the industrialized high-energy consuming West having to move away from the meat-based diet because of ecological compulsions, the breaking of beef-taboo in Indian food culture can easily make India another South America-like beef exporter to the West. But it will ultimately create ecological disaster for India.

At the same time, the mainstream Hindutva movement, led by the RSS, categorically states that cow protection cannot be handed over to lumpen elements. Democratic means should be used to further the cause of cow protection. This is in tune with the legacy of Tilak and Gandhi with respect to cow protection. Unfortunately, the colonial-Marxist worldview, which also dominates media propaganda on cow protection, is caught in a time warp—perhaps intentionally to serve vested political interests at the cost of national interests. All said, the media and global narrative of Hindu fanatics killing humans and demeaning humans to 'protect' the cows persist. The cow-lynch libel is the Hinduphobic equivalent of blood-libel of anti-Semitism.

Thiruvarur sculpture showing a Chozha prince executed under the chariot wheels because his chariot had killed a calf, and the cow had complained. Chidambaram Ramalingam 'Vallalar' (1823–1874) used this traditional account to propagate cow protection and food security, even as British-engineered famines loomed over the horizon

Ram Singh Kuka (1816–1885) led Namdharis into the first Swadesi movement against the British. The movement ended in the mass execution of Namdharis. Cow protection fuelled the movement

Mahatma Gandhi made cow protection a movement for the outreach of Hindu ecological ethos. According to Arne Næss, who advocated Deep Ecology, Gandhian ecological thinking was predicated on his Advaita

4

Racism, Casteism, Social Emancipation and Hindutva

The dominant sections of the academia, polity and establishment media have all claimed that *Hindutva* is an ideology that divides people on the basis of religion, asserting the supremacism of Hindus—in terms of ethnicity and religion—and that it naturally gravitates towards ethnic and religious hate politics, obscurantism and manifestations of social stagnation like caste, untouchability and the subjugation of women's rights. Is Hindutva a racist doctrine? Is it a doctrine that promotes social hierarchy? Beyond the academic stereotypes, political rhetoric and media constructs, let us look at some of the key historical contexts and contributions of Hindutva—from Savarkar to Sangh—to the social life of India.

Hindutva: Racist and Ethnic?

Most Western observers of Hindutva as well as a considerable section of left-dominated Indian academia have always tried to present Hindutva as an Indic variant of racism. The following passage by Prof. Chetan Bhatt, who teaches sociology at London School of Economics (LSE) and is also the director of LSE's Centre for Study of Human Rights, provides a good example:

> The Hindutva movement condenses numerous themes about ethnogenesis, religious authoritarianism, cultural absolutism, the nature of secular post-colonial citizenship, majority-minority relations, and "racial" and ethnic hatred that often appear separately in other examples of contemporary religious ethnic conflict. In this sense, Hindutva ideology can represent a universal example of the numerous directions that absolutist and totalitarian ideologies can travel in the late modern period. Similarly, in describing Hindutva ideology using conventional theoretical paradigms, none of the analytical concepts of race, racism, religion, ethnicity or culture on their own suffice, but all are deeply relevant in a combination that perhaps requires a new description, as perhaps do many other contemporary "absolutist ideologies of indigenism".

Though Bhatt accuses Hindutva of harbouring 'a powerful hereditarian "race concept"', he is aware of the fact that it has 'little to do with western scientific racism'. According to him, unlike in the West, where 'opposition between biology and culture' defines the position of racism, in Hindutva, the culture itself contains 'powerful epistemic resources' which provide 'sentimentalist racism'. He relates this, in turn, to 'primordial origin myth and tropes of breeding, cultivation, blood and lineage' and goes on to claim that 'this kind of "racism" is virtually definitive of a Hindutva discourse'.[1]

Shorn of the jargon, what the passage actually states is that though Hindutva cannot be considered racist in terms of what racism has been historically, by tying Hindutva with caste, and caste with the origin myth (as in *Purusha Sukta*) and endogamous marriage systems within communities in India, the sociologist invents a means to categorize Hindutva as 'racism'. Even when Hindutva does not fit into the category of racism, it has to be shown in a negative light. Such academic attempts, more often than not, lead to the construction of convoluted narratives, steeped in almost meaningless jargon-dropping, leading to paradoxical scenarios, not to mention censoring of significant and relevant data.

In reality, Hindutva does not cling either to the caste system (more correctly the *jati*) or even *Varna* as the basis or defining aspect of Hinduness. Vinayak

Savarkar makes it clear in his work *Hindutva*. The sociocultural history of India is also replete with instances where social stagnation is resisted through the 'spiritual' values considered essential to Hindu culture. Dr Ambedkar had rightly pointed out that the Upanishadic concept of *Brahman* has provided India with a strong spiritual basis for social democracy, while the *smriti*-based religious movement nurtured social stagnation.[2] It can be observed that while the social stagnation provides a literal interpretation of the myth of the primordial *Purusha*, symbolizing the organic unity of society through different sections of the society emanating from his body parts, the social emancipation movement which is an integral part of Indian culture and society has often worked against such an interpretation, and emphasized the divine equality of all humans.

The modern era commenced in India with the advent of the colonial regime. While the orthodoxy emphasized a socially fundamentalist interpretation of the origin myth, Hindutvaites or the so-called 'Hindu nationalists' mostly rejected such an interpretation. When Nehruvian prejudices against Hindutva, along with the Marxist model, became the dominating framework for Indian social studies, stereotyping of Hindutvaites as homegrown 'racists' began in earnest. Savarkar, in his work *Hindutva*, not only rejects the idea of caste as the defining feature of Hindu culture but also consistently argues for the abolition of the caste system.

Contrary to how academics like Bhatt try to portray Hindutva as a form of desi racism based on 'a powerful hereditarian "race concept"', Savarkar argues against the so-called scientific arguments put up by the orthodoxy in favour of the caste system. Sure enough, the justification of the caste system based on Western notions of eugenics had resulted in an argument not very dissimilar to the nature versus nurture debate, in which the notion of racism was placed in the Western realm. However, the arguments of Savarkar clearly show on which side of the fence he stands. In a hard-hitting statement too radical for the time it was written (and even for some of the orthodoxy of today), he said:

> Heredity is not the sole determinant of merit; rather it is one of its many determinants. Even if inbreeding occurs, change in other factors such as light, food, water, climate, mental makeup of ancestors, their upbringing, education, availability of opportunity and means, enhance or diminish or change the innate merit of children. Even where inbreeding occurs, like good qualities, bad qualities too may get enhanced or accentuated....Even if inbreeding occurs, the good qualities of ancestors may occasionally diminish or get distorted with passage of time. In such circumstances too, cross-breeding proves beneficial to animals. While it is possible to maintain blood purity by inbreeding in case of natural species, it is virtually impossible to

> maintain it if the same is ordained by scriptures or belief. And in those Hindu castes such as the Brahmins etc. too which have strict rules regarding inter-marriages, cross-breeding has been occurring for generations past as ordained by scriptures or secretly due to sexual attraction. This will undoubtedly continue in future too and hence even if inter-marriages are strictly prohibited, the very belief that the son of a Brahmin has the innate qualities of a Brahmin or that the son of a Kshatriya must be naturally imbued with the qualities of a Kshatriya needs to be discarded. This is because of the fact that due to cross-breeding between all our castes from time immemorial, no caste can claim monopoly over a specific merit.[3]

It is obvious that Savarkar totally rejected the argument that the caste system was based on notions of inherited characters that ancient Indians had. He was not apologetic about caste as part of the Indian heritage. It was a great experiment, but he observed that it was a failed experiment. And collective human knowledge has been enhanced by our failed experiment, he opined. Interestingly, Theodosius Dobzhansky, the Ukrainian-born American geneticist and one of the key figures in the synthesis of evolutionary biology and genetics, expressed the same sentiments: 'The caste system in India was the grandest genetic experiment ever performed on man.'[4]

For the academics and activists who accuse Hindutva of racism of any form, even more problematic are the views that Savarkar puts forth on the fundamental unity of humanity:

> After all there is throughout this world, so far as man is concerned, but a single race—the human race kept alive by one common blood, the human blood. All other talk is at best provisional, a makeshift and only relatively true. Nature is constantly trying to overthrow the artificial barriers you raise between race and race. To try to prevent the commingling of blood is to build on sand. Sexual attraction has proved more powerful than all the commands of all the prophets put together. Even as it is, not even the aborigines of the Andamans are without some sprinkling of the so-called Aryan blood in their veins and vice versa. Truly speaking all that anyone of us can claim, all that history entitles one to claim, is that one has the blood of all mankind in one's veins. The fundamental unity of man from pole to pole is true, all else only relatively so.[5]

If one compares the way Savarkar denies any 'pure blood' of any single race in the context of humanity with the way he denies 'purity' for even the so-called high-caste Brahmins with their strict rules for 'inbreeding' in the Indian context, then one important aspect of Savarkarite worldview comes out clearly. In both the cases, he points out that sexual attraction prevails in a defining and dominant way over the 'artificial barriers' put forth by 'all the prophets' (in the case of races and entire humanity) and how it is 'virtually impossible' for the scriptures to maintain 'inbreeding', particularly in the context of castes and hence for the entire Hindu society. Once again, Hindutva as presented by Savarkar, provides a far more radical anti-racist perspective than any of the social views prevalent then at the contemporary times. As an interesting aside, one can see that he even qualifies the term 'Aryan blood' with the adjective 'so-called'—clearly an expression of innate scepticism, though at that time 'Aryan race' was accepted as a proven category.

Even the definition of Savarkar which speaks of Hindus as a 'race' is not the same as the European racist concept of race. While discussing his notion that Hindus have a 'common blood', he explains:

> We are well aware of the not unoften interested objection that carpingly questions "but are you really a race? Can you be said to possess a common blood?" We can only answer by questioning in return, "Are the English a race? Is there anything as English blood, the French blood, the German blood or the Chinese blood in this world? Do they, who have been freely infusing foreign blood into their race by contracting marriages with other races and peoples possess a common blood and claim to be a race by themselves?" If they do, Hindus also can emphatically do so.[6]

Sometimes, critical academic observers of Savarkar's work *Hindutva*, including the academic informants for the Western academic world, provide empirically wrong data to show *Hindutva* as racist. Here is Prof. Chetan Bhatt on *Hindutva*:

> Parsees, for example, were not considered aversely by Savarkar, though ostensibly the "holyland" of the Avestans and Zoroastrians was Persia; the Aryan race factor was presumably the predominant one in their affiliation with Hindus. Conversely, Savarkar excluded both the Theosophist and Congress freedom fighter Annie Besant and Margaret Noble (Sister Nivedita) from Hindutva on strictly racial grounds.[7]

The same claim is repeated by Prof. Shamsul Islam in his study on Savarkar. The professor of political science at Delhi University claims that according to Savarkar, Sister Nivedita could not claim to be a Hindu as she was not married to a Hindu.[8] But what Savarkar wrote about Sister Nivedita and Annie Besant actually negates the charge of racism on Hindutva:

> Is, for example, Sister Nivedita a Hindu? If ever an exception proves the rule it does so here. Our patriotic and noble-minded sister had adopted our land from Sindhu

> to the seas as her Fatherland. She truly loved it as such, and had our nation been free, we would have been the first to bestow the right of citizenship on such loving souls. So the first essential may, to some extent, be said to hold good in her case. The second essential of common blood of Hindu parentage must, nevertheless and necessarily, be absent in such cases as these....But although this second essential failed, either way to hold good in her case, the third important qualification of Hindutva did entitle her to be recognized as a Hindu. For she had adopted our culture and come to adore our land as her Holy land. She felt, she was a Hindu and that is, apart from all technicalities, the real and the most important test.... But it must be understood that a religious or cultural convert possesses only one of the three essentials of Hindutva, and it is owing to this disqualification that people generally do not recognise as a Hindu anyone and everyone who subscribes to the religious beliefs of our race. So deep our feeling of gratitude is towards a Sister Nivedita or an Annie Besant for the services they rendered to the cause of our Motherland and our culture, so soft-hearted and sensitive to the touch of love as a race we Hindus are, that Sister Nivedita or a person like her who so completely identifies his or her being with the Being of our people, is almost unconsciously received in the Hindu fold. But it should be done as an exception to the rule. The rule itself must neither be too rigid nor too elastic.[9]

So, people dedicated to India like Annie Besant and Sister Nivedita are exceptions, and the third criterion carries more weight than the second. The second rule on parentage should not be by itself neither too rigid nor too elastic. Here, Savarkar speaks about how generally Hindus look at a convert from foreign land and says that their inability to accept them comes from the convert not fulfilling the second criterion. But that is only the general perception. As Savarkar himself clearly explains the third criterion, which 'is, apart from all technicalities, the real and the most important test' subsumes the second, as in the case of a person like Sister Nivedita, she naturally 'almost unconsciously' is accepted as a Hindu. Inside his treatise, Savarkar again defines the family as not one bound by blood but 'the practices and customs that are called a family'.[10]

Similarly, contrary to the assertion of Prof. Bhatt that Savarkar included Parsees not aversely because of their 'Aryan race factor', what Savarkar says about Parsees is entirely different. In his Presidential address at the 1937 Hindu Mahasabha, he had categorically stated that 'by the first constituent of Hindutva, the possession of a common Holyland—the Indian Mohammedans, Jews, Christians, Parsees, etc., are excluded from claiming themselves as Hindus which in reality also they do not...' Then he again specifically talked about the Parsees:

> The Parsees have ever been working shoulder to shoulder with the Hindus against the English domination. They are no fanatics. From the great Dadabhai Nowroji to the renowned revolutionary lady Madam Kama the Parsees have contributed their quota of true Indian patriots, nor have they ever displayed any but goodwill towards the Hindu Nation which to them had proved a veritable saviour of their race. Culturally too they are most closely akin to us. In a lesser degree the same thing could be said about the Indian Christians.[11]

Next year, at the Nagpur session of the Hindu Mahasabha, he mentioned Parsees in the context of Indian minorities:

> The Parsees are by race, religion, language and culture most akin to us. They have gratefully been loyal to India and have made her their only home. They have produced some of the best Indian patriots and revolutionists like Dada Bhai and Madam Cama. They will have to be and therefore, shall be incorporated into the common Indian State with perfectly equal rights and trust....The Christian minority is civil, has no extra-territorial political designs against India, is not linguistically and culturally averse to the Hindus and therefore, can be politically assimilated with us.... As to the Jews in India, they are too few, have given us no political or cultural troubles and are not in the main a proselytizing people, they will to be friendly towards Hindus who have sheltered them when homeless and can be easily assimilated in a common Indian State.[12]

(Interestingly, in the case of Jews, he is against the Congress proposal of creating a colony for non-Indian Jews in India instead of a Jewish State in Palestine.) The next year, at the annual session of Hindu Mahasabha in 1939, he again mentions and considers Parsees 'most eminently' because they are 'too allied to us in culture and too patriotic' but makes no mention of race. In all the instances, the 'race' of Parsees does not play any important role at all in viewing them positively. On the other hand, it is their contribution to the national life of India, particularly the freedom struggle that makes Savarkar speak highly of them. Further, he categorically says that there should be no discrimination based on race, parentage or religion by the Indian State. So actually, what we have here is an academician's sleight of hand trick to prove that Hindutva is predicated on 'Aryan blood', while for Savarkar, his favourite viewing of Parsees comes from his view of their patriotism.

In the annual session of the Hindu Mahasabha held at Ahmedabad (Karnavati) in 1937, he also unveiled the 'Hindu Sanghatanist' vision of the Indian State. He said:

> Hindudom cannot advance or fulfil its life mission unless and until our Motherland is set free and consolidated into an Indian State in which all our countrymen to whatever religion or sect or race they belong are treated with perfect equality and none allowed to dominate others or is deprived of his just and equal rights of free citizenship as long as everyone discharges the common obligations and duties which one owes to the Indian Nation as a whole....Let the Indian State be purely Indian. Let it not recognise any invidious distinctions whatsoever as regards the franchise, public services, offices, taxation on the grounds of religion and race. Let no cognizance be taken whatsoever of man's being Hindu or Mohammedan, Christian or Jew. Let all citizens of that Indian State be treated according to their individual worth, irrespective of their religious or racial percentage in the general population.[13]

To consider a person Hindu, Hindutva does not look to blood or ethnicity and least of all race, in the sense the term is being used in the Western political and anthropological discourse, is further proved by the example of Sister Nivedita being venerated in the ritual of the morning veneration hymn (*Pratah Smaran*) of the Rashtriya Swayamsevak Sangh (RSS). This morning veneration hymn by the RSS—sung throughout India in all the RSS offices by office bearers and cadre—is a litany of the names of all personalities the Sangh considers as the nation builders. It has the name of Sister Nivedita.

Aryans and Hindutva

Another negative portrayal of Hindutva in characterizing it as desi racism, is that it tries to make 'Aryans' indigenous to India and hence, it stridently opposes the Aryan invasion/migration theory. Here is one such characterization from Tony Joseph, a business magazine editor turned popular-science writer, who seems to specialize only in proving the 'Aryan invasion/migration' into India. He writes:

> For Hindu nationalists, there is a cost to admitting that the Aryans were not the first inhabitants of India and that the Harappan civilisation existed long before their arrival. It would mean acknowledging that Aryans or their Vedic culture were not the singular fountainhead of Indian civilisation and that its earliest sources lay elsewhere....The idea of the mixing of different population groups is also unappealing to Hindu nationalists as they put a premium on racial purity. There is also the additional issue of the migration theory putting Aryans on the same footing as latter-day Muslim conquerors of India—such as the Mughals.[14]

As shown by the passage by Savarkar on race quoted in the preceding section, racial purity is not at all emphasized by the Hindutvaites. In reality, the Aryan race theory has been, from the very beginning, used by the colonial and later a section of Nehruvian and dominantly Marxist schools, to argue that the Hindus too are 'outsiders'. While Hindutva has been progressively moving towards calling all Indians culturally Hindus and being celebrated as role models for all Indians, Muslims like Dr A. P. J. Abdul Kalam, Bismillah Khan and Ashfaqullah Khan, the anti-Hindutva camp has been trying to divide Hindus into binaries: Brahmin versus non-Brahmin, caste Hindus versus tribal communities and non-Dalit versus Dalit, ultimately mapping them to Aryan and non-Aryan. Hindutvaites have consistently decried this approach as both unscientific and against the historical spirit of the nation. However, of late, science—particularly molecular anthropology—has become a new tool in the hands of the proponents of the Aryan race theory.

Though Tony Joseph, the author of the above quoted article, characterizes himself as one who has 'ceased to be a believer of any religion in his early 20s, and considers himself an atheist with a liking for the original teachings of the Buddha', he made a spirited defence of the transnational proselytizing industry targeting Hindus in 2015.[15] Taking this into consideration, let us look at the way he characterizes the 'Aryan invasion' in one of his recent articles. Soon, he became a popular science writer with a specific focus on molecular genetics to prove various migrations—something actually no one has seriously contended. However, in his 2017 article that became viral in Dravidianist circles and first published in the pro-Chinese newspaper *The Hindu,* he did not just talk about different migrations, but ascribed specific characteristics to each of these migrations. When he weaves a grand picture of the waves of migrants, he gives a subtle racial interpretation and mapping. Such mapping of migrations with specific dimensions of a current society has a disturbing parallel, or perhaps roots in the recent past.[16]

In 1936 two Catholic anthropologists, both ordained clergy, Wilhelm Schmidt (1868–1954) and Wilhelm Koppers (1886–1961) came up with a new racial theory that countered the Nazi racial theory. Schmidt, the more important of these two, heard in a lecture in 1902, an anti-evolutionist concept of primitive proto monotheism. He was so touched by it that he made it the mission of his academic career to prove it. Schmidt envisioned ancient human societies as comprising of three cultural circles: The 'agrarian-matriarchal' cultural circle spreading from Indo-China to China, the Indus culture, Mesopotamia, Africa and Europe. This circle was neither rational nor irrational. The second cultural circle was the one he called 'the totemic cultural circle of the higher hunters'. To this circle, he assigned the Dravidians and the aboriginals as 'irrational'. He called the third primary cultural circle as 'the Central Asian herding culture' and to him this was the one that 'best preserved the better elements of the original culture's family culture and religion' which essentially meant patriarchy and a belief in a single creating God. Koppers now added the domestication of the horse to the Indo-European achievements. The horses were not only domesticated for food, but the Indo-Europeans also learnt to ride it. The horse sacrifice (*ashvamedha*) was addressed to the heavenly high god.

Wilhelm Schmidt was an authority in anthropology for the Catholic church. He had serious problems with the Nazi historiography which he considered as glorifying the pagan elements. However, his own position was not much different from that of the Nazis with respect to anti-Semitism. Schmidt saw Nazism as modernist and he himself saw the future of Europe as the restoration of a church-controlled 'medieval type of society with stable hierarchies and integrating corporations'. His anthropology was a means to promote this worldview. This vision of the medieval type Catholic society was also the favourable position of Austro-Fascists who supported the anthropological studies of Koppers and Schmidt. Fr. Schmidt had hatred for the Jews who were guilty of deicide and who were now also 'trying, along with the Freemasons, to make up the avant-garde of materialism, liberalism, republicanism, socialism and robber capitalism'.

Indo-Germans domesticated the horses in the steppes and forged the cavalry and war chariots drawn by horses. These Indo-Germans were joined by Hamito-Semites who were darker, while the Indo-Europeans were lighter and both were tall. These people were 'born rulers'. Historian Stefan Arvidsson explains Schmidt's view of ancient history:

> The totemic and agrarian-matriarchal cultural circles had already melted together at an early stage and formed city-states, with trade and crafts. But since 'there was still no vertical, hierarchical order,' these city-states could not yet be united into greater units, kingdoms and empires. It became the civilizing task of the Indo-Germans and the Semites, Schmidt writes in one of his books, to create hierarchies that could integrate the city-states. They themselves would become the highest caste, the endogamous aristocracy of the kingdoms. Those high cultures that were created were 'not simply the invention or work of one race or one cultural circle', since the totemic and agrarian-matriarchal conglomerate contributed agriculture, handicrafts, trade, writing, time systems, and so forth. The pastoral cultural circle, on its part, contributed animal husbandry and leather working-but above all, the crucial sense of order.

But even here India is a special case—a demonstration of what happens when the In-India Indo-Germanic arrogance led to the Brahmans 'who claim to present the Aryan racial purity, uphold a caste system that is completely destroying India'. So, the Hindu shows that the ruling castes have created 'a heavenly elevation where one no longer walks on earth and where every similarity with the people as a whole has been lost'. The Indo-Germans who were heroes everywhere creating social order, degenerated into villains in India. The above passage about the racial anthropology of Fr. Schmidt can be compared with the following passage from Tony Joseph:

> The Out of Africa immigrants, the pioneering, fearless explorers who discovered this land originally and settled in it and whose lineages still form the bedrock of our population; those who arrived later with a package of farming techniques and built the Indus Valley Civilization whose cultural ideas and practices perhaps enrich much of our traditions today; those who arrived from East Asia, probably bringing with them the practice of rice cultivation and all that goes with it; those who came later with a language called Sanskrit and its associated beliefs and practices and reshaped our society in fundamental ways; and those who came even later for trade or for conquest and chose to stay, all have mingled and contributed to this civilization we call Indian. We are all migrants.[17]

While in the last statement Joseph appears to be suggesting a multi-ethnic past for India, what is actually implied is the neat segregation, assignment and mapping of cultural and civilizational components to specific waves of migrations. In his grand picture of the waves of migrants, the migrants of Bronze Age created Indus Valley Civilization and the migrants who came next, brought agriculture. Then there were 'those who came with a language called Sanskrit and its associated beliefs and practices and reshaped our society in fundamental ways'. In fact, when discussing the stopping of the admixture of communities and emergence of endogamy, he gives a racial interpretation and calls it 'shifting attitudes towards mixing of the races in ancient texts'. So essentially, the Aryans brought with them Sanskrit, associated beliefs, rituals, a patriarchal social structure, and 'reshaped our society in fundamental ways'. That is very euphemistically saying that Aryans brought in the caste system and fitted themselves at the top of the pyramid—which is exactly what Fr. Schmidt had proposed in his Catholic racial anthropology in 1930s.

Here it should also be noted that the Aryan home theory is not central to the Hindutva discourse. While it is true that Hindutvaites would be really happy if the Aryan invasion/migration theory is proved wrong and, in fact, that particular aspect of the theory had been proved wrong, Hindutva does not predicate itself on the so-called racial purity. In fact, Hindutvaites claim that there is no such race called Aryans. To their credit, indeed, no anthropologist really talks of an Aryan race.

Of course, Hindutvaites will be happy if the origin of Indo-European (I-E) languages is found to be within the greater Indian landmass. That aspect is still contentious. Yet, this is not central to the core discourse of Hindutva. To them, Vedic culture is indigenous. The fact of the matter is Iravatham Mahadevan to Asko Parpola scholars averse to Hindutva who have studied Harappan culture and who subscribe to the notion of I-E speakers coming from outside, use the Vedic imagery to understand Harappan culture. Mahadevan characterized the Harappan culture as Vedic speaking a Dravidian language.

At the same time, contrary to the claims made by academic and political critics of Hindutva, the Hindutvaites do not claim that Aryans were the original inhabitants of India. Rather, they claim that there was not at all a race called Aryans. Historian Shriram Sathe, who was the divisional head of Bharatiya Ithihasa Sankalana Samiti—the official organization dealing with history in the Sangh Parivar, came with a book on the Aryan issue which described the official stand on the question of Aryan race. In this, Sathe explained:

> Did the mother tongue from which the sister Indo-European languages are said to have evolved, exist? Can the humanity be divided into a few races out of which one is an "Aryan" race? If the answers to these questions are in negative, i.e., if there is no possibility of the existence of the Aryans, either as a linguistic or a racial group, how can their original home be located?[18]

Sathe goes on to characterize the quest for Aryans as 'searching for a black cat in a dark room which was not there'. Similar views have been expressed by Shrikant Talageri, a bank-clerk who had been studying the Aryan race theory intently and in a scholarly manner, from the Hindutva point of view. Indologist Dr Edwin Bryant of Columbia University says that his book 'reveals a very keen mind examining the basis of the whole Aryan invasion theory'. According to Talageri, Hindutva which he calls Hindu nationalism, has nothing to do with the question of the so-called Aryan homeland:

> Hindu nationalism has nothing to do with any childish, petty and ridiculous idea of dividing Indians into "outsiders" and "insiders" on the basis of whether or not their ancestors, actually or supposedly, came from outside....Even if it is assumed that a group of people, called "Aryans", invaded, or immigrated into, India, ...they have left no trace, if ever there was any, of any link, much less the consciousness of any link, much less any loyalties associated with such a link, to any place outside India.[19]

Dr Edwin Bryant further observes how despite Golwalkar suggesting an Indian homeland for Aryans with Tilak's polar home being somewhere in Bihar long time ago, the Hindutva movement has not been an ideological monolith on the issue:

> The *Bharatiya Itihasa Sankalana Samiti* co-sponsored a conference on the Aryan problem in Poona, in 1994, which resulted in a publication. The conference was well attended, but by no means all the participants that I met were RSS or BJP (Bharatiya Janata Party) supporters. Indeed, several of the papers presented at the conference supported the theory of Aryan invasions. In 1993, the *Samiti* (its identity unbeknownst to at least one of its invitees) also organized a small function in honor of several new books that had been published by Indigenous Aryanists. After arriving at the function in good faith, but then subsequently becoming aware of the affiliation of the organizers, one of the authors made it a point to publicly declare that he had absolutely no connection with the political viewpoints of the organizers. Here, again, the point is underscored that whitewashing all Indigenous Aryanists as right-wing Hindu fundamentalists is not just erroneous, but unscholarly, dogmatic, and offensive.[20]

'Arya' in Traditional Indian Usage

Traditionally, the term *Arya* has meant for Hindus at least for the last three thousand years, if not more, not an ethnically superior person but a person of virtues. The teacher, the husband, the head of the family, and the Guru etc. were all called Arya. In Tamizh literature too, the term *Ariyan* was used to denote the deity and the Guru. Incidentally, what can be considered as one of the most important definitions of the term, occurs in the Ramayana; and Valmiki, who wrote the Ramayana, attributes it to Sita. After Rama had killed Ravana, Hanuman brings the news of liberation to Sita. Then he asks her permission to slay the guarding women who had tortured Sita, almost driving her to suicide. But Sita stops Hanuman from slaying them and then reminds him the 'dharmic' words of a bear in the presence of a tiger. This was an old Hindu fable of a tiger asking to throw back to it a treacherous human hunter who had taken asylum in a tree where the bear lived. Even after the human tried to push down the bear to the tiger so that he could escape, the bear refused to throw the man to the tiger, stating that good people do good deeds unconditionally. Then Sita says that it is the exhibition of such compassion towards all that defines a person as Arya, as there is none in the world without a blemish.[21] This statement of Sita is revered as a *mahavakya* (authoritative statement) by the Sri Vaishnavaites throughout India, defined the term Arya as used in the Indian context.

In South India, during the freedom struggle, Subramania Bharathi used the term Arya in many of his songs which stirred Indians against the British. He called Mother India 'Arya Rani'. He called the legendary sage Agastya as 'Arya son'. Soon, this was taken up by the Dravidianists. Congress had grown in Tamil Nadu using the songs of Bharathi. The women's liberation movement in Tamil Nadu had used the songs of Bharathi. However, after Indian National Congress came under Sonia Gandhi and forged an explicitly anti-Hindu ideological alliance with the Dravidian movement, it started jettisoning Bharathi. The Congress which had grown in Tamil Nadu because of the use of Subramania Bharathi's songs, simply stopped defending his songs against this new Dravidian onslaught. Dravidianist ideologues continued to mount their attacks on Bharathi.

Bharathi had categorically stated that the term Arya as he used it, referred to the collective heritage of all Indians:

> Our Vedas, our Shastras, our social fabric, our languages, our poetry, our sculpture, our music, our dance, our industries, our temple towers, our ornate halls, our simple huts—all these are collectively our Aryan heritage. *Shakuntala* of Kalidasa in Sanskrit, *Ramayana* of Tulsidas in Hindi, *Kamba Ramayanam, Chilapathikaram, Thirukural, Aandal Thirumozhi* in Tamizh —all these have a common name—our Aryan heritage. The grand temple of Thanjavur, the Mahal of Thirumalai Nayakar, the *keerthanas* of Thyagaraja, the cave temple of Ellora, Taj Mahal in Agra, the melodius flute of Saraba Shastri—all these have the common name—Aryan heritage.[22]

Dravidian ideologues interpret this passage as a cunning Brahminical conspiracy on the part of Bharathi to assign all these to Aryans. So, to them, Bharathi was doing an Aryan appropriation of non-Aryan genius and hard work. His usage of the term 'Arya Bhoomi' to characterize India was considered as the result of his Brahminical racial inclination. Today, Ve.Mathimaran, a rabid Dravidianist ideologue promoted by the Dravida Munnetra Kazhagam (DMK)—a valued and a consistent alliance partner of the United Progressive Alliance—calls Bharathi a pro-casteist and an Aryan supremacist. His book accusing Bharathi of being a hate-ranting supremacist poet is titled *Bharathi'ya Janata Party*.

However, for the use of the term Arya Bhoomi by Bharathi, who was from the penultimate southern district of Tirunelveli, Tamil Nadu, one need not look in the Western appropriation of the term at all. An eighteenth-century Tamizh literary work titled *Kutrala Kuravanji* written by Thirikooda Rasappa

Kavirayar, a poet with no European influence, but from the same Tirunelveli region as Bharathi. The *Kuravanji* speaks about the glory of Kutralam, a famous scenic pilgrimage centre known for the falls, through the words of a tribe woman (*Kurathi*):

This is the land of primacy among all southern lands;
This is the land where all Gods are loved;
This is the land hailed in all directions;
This is the land bereft of betrayal to Siva;
This is the land where the Three-eyed One frolics;
This is the land of Him who has as His inseparable half the beautiful eyed Goddess;
This land of ours is the ever spring seasoned Aryan land![23]

The glorification runs thus for nine such verses. The poet, through the tribal woman, ends each verse, hailing his land as the 'Aryan land'. So Bharathi, when he glorified India as 'Arya Bhoomi', was following a lineage that was more localized and totally non-racial and not the European appropriation and implications for that term.

With all these cultural, literary, ideological and historical contexts in mind, one has to see an important contribution Hindutva made to the global fight against racism.

Hindutva and Apartheid: Dr N. B. Khare

In July 1914, Mahatma Gandhi returned from South Africa to India, following his monumental moral and spiritual victory over General Jan Christian Smuts (1870–1950). However, the material conditions of Indians in South Africa did not improve much. In fact, South African Indians saw newer and newer laws take away their livelihood freedoms one by one. Thus, since 1919, the Asiatic private companies were not entitled to hold fixed properties. The Mines and Works Act debarred Indians from becoming skilled workers. In 1932 the Asiatic Land Tenure Act also debarred any Asiatics (read Indians) from even holding shares in minority, in any company. In 1939 General Smuts further introduced an 'Interim Asiatic Land and Tilling Act'. It restricted Indians economically well within the areas which were 'pegged' as their community area. The Act evolved even more menacingly by 1943. General Smuts, the friend of the Mahatma, was the Prime Minister of South Africa. The interim Act of 1939 was renamed the Pegging Act and was extended to both Transvaal and Natal.[24] The result was that 24,000 Indians were confined to 200 acres in Transvaal and

Natal, while 7,000 whites were given 5,000 acres at their disposal.[25] Ahmed M. Kathrada, a veteran of the South African liberation struggle, records the response of the Natal Indian Congress (NIC) to what Smuts did, and the counter-response of the apartheid regime to the NIC's appeal:

> In line with their established response, the leaders of the Natal Indian National Congress sent a deputation to convey to Smuts their dissatisfaction with the law, and to plead with him to repeal it. They did manage to secure an undertaking that the law would be repealed, but the quid pro quo was the humiliating and spineless suggestion by the Indian politicians that in place of the Pegging Act, the government should set up an Occupation Council Board to regulate Indian residence in white areas. The board would consist of two Indians and three white members, which meant, in effect, that it could do exactly what the Pegging Act was designed to do, except that Indians would themselves be complicit.[26]

With this timid capitulation by the NIC, the fate of Indians in South Africa seemed sealed. At this point, a fierce Hindutvaite came to the rescue of the people of Indian origin in South Africa, and through the process, opened up a new strategy for the fight against the apartheid regime in the future. Dr Narayan Bhaskar Khare (1884–1970) is better known as the Hindu Mahasabha leader who made that caustic remark about Nehru being 'an Englishman by education, Muslim by culture and a Hindu only by the accident of birth'.[27] Less known is the fact that he earned the displeasure of the Congress high command when he made a Scheduled Community member one of his cabinet ministers.[28] When he refused to yield ground, he had to pay with his dismissal by the Congress high command. His parting with the Congress was bitter. Decades later, none other than Rajaji conceded to Dr Khare that he was 'treated badly by a powerful organization which did not suffer from any lack of arrogance'.[29]

As a member of the Viceroy's executive committee, Dr Khare was also in-charge of the department of Indians overseas. But the Viceroy had overriding powers. Despite such a disadvantaged condition, Dr Khare strongly advocated retaliatory measures for safeguarding the welfare of the people of Indian origin in South Africa. There was one such law he learnt of, but it had legal and technical difficulties in actually getting implemented. So, he quickly made amendments to the law and within the same July month of Smut's law damning Indians, on 26 July 1943, he had succeeded in placing on the Statute book the Indian Reciprocity Act Amendment Bill. Then he started demanding that it be implemented against South Africa.[30] That in itself was a great accomplishment, but now the real challenge was to make the British Viceroy implement this against South Africa. He also cautioned the British that war cannot be made an excuse for South Africa to humiliate its citizens of Indian origin. He made himself bluntly clear in the Council:

> Same means must be found for maintaining the dignity and prestige of Indians and the Government of India, even in wartime....Had India been independent, she would have considered this a casus belli against South Africa.[31]

In October 1943, the new Viceroy, Archibald Percival Wavell had arrived in Delhi. When Dr Khare met him and raised the issue of South Africa, he discovered that the Viceroy, like Mahatma Gandhi, considered Smuts 'a good friend and a thorough gentleman' and hence 'would not allow enforcing the decisions against South Africa' and 'would not allow anyone to do anything against Smuts'. Dr Khare, in his own words, was totally dejected.[32] Yet he carried on. His repeated and harsh interventions in every executive council meeting forced Wavell to act. Though today this Hindutvaite's role in the history of fight against discrimination in South Africa is almost forgotten, even biased British historians are forced to acknowledge it. For example, one historian writes that it was the 'sharp words from Dr Khare' which made Wavell telegraph his 'very good friend' that 'unless he can give satisfactory answer now', the doctor would press for drastic action against South Africa.[33]

On 15 April 1944, the Indian High Commissioner in South Africa was made to give a note to Smuts, threatening countermeasures. Three days later, the Pretoria regime came out with the so-called Pretoria Agreement, partly in consultation with the NIC. This too, was racially biased against the Indians. It essentially meant that Indians would agree to residential restrictions, but the Pegging Act would be withdrawn only after an ordinance had been passed by Natal legislature (where even the Indians would be represented only by white men). Even this was too much for the whites. Sensing the dissatisfaction of the white population, Smuts quickly announced that his government would extend the Pegging Act for all time to the whole of Natal.[34]

Indians in South Africa were shocked by this abject betrayal. Back in India, at a meeting of the Central Legislative Assembly, Dr Khare echoed the sense of betrayal and minced no words and declared: 'I wish India was in a position to declare war against South Africa, here and now'. Sir Ramaswamy Mudaliar, the Member for Industry and Civil Supplies, announced that if a force was raised to attack South Africa, he would enlist.[35]

Dr Khare telegraphed the British government about the mounting displeasure in India. This led Viceroy Wavell to personally caution Smuts about the increased Indian pressure that might force the British government to take action against

South Africa. Finally, Dr Khare's efforts made history of sorts when a not-yet independent India implemented the Reciprocity Act against South Africa, an independent state. This was essentially symbolic, but he was not satisfied with such symbolic gestures and moral victories. Meanwhile, the Second World War had come to an end, and by June 1945, the League of Nations was being reconstituted and established as the United Nations. Dr Khare now came up with a radical new plan that completely transformed the terrain of the fight for justice in South Africa. He decided to submit a memorandum to the United Nations against South Africa and announced this to the media—the Associated Press of America in Delhi. This created shock and uproar in many circles—from the Viceroy to the bureaucratic establishment. Dr Khare describes the response of the establishment to his announcement of going to the UN:

> The Associated Press of India took very pointed notice of my interview with the Associated Press of America in Delhi and of my speeches made in Nagpur. On account of this, the bureaucratic atmosphere of the Government of India in Delhi became hostile to me, and I was accused of making irresponsible speeches and giving irresponsible interviews without making any reference to the Government of India. One of my colleagues said to my face that an ICS would never have behaved irresponsibly like that...Viceroy also charged me with irresponsibility...and there was great bitterness between me and the Viceroy...Lord Wavell the Viceroy did not at all like my attempt to lodge a complaint against South Africa before the UNO. He tried his level best to dissuade me from this attempt.[36]

But Dr Khare stood his ground. He forced the Viceroy to consider going to UNO by bringing an adjournment motion in the legislative assembly. The Viceroy, who considered the proposal 'irresponsible', had asked the secretary of India's external affairs department Hugh Weightman to see if there was any substance to Dr Khare's announcement. Weightman, who also thought India going to UNO was an 'ill-considered action' which would have 'grave repercussions', asked his undersecretary to see if there was anything to it. To the shock of both Wavell and Weightman, the undersecretary came back with the finding that India 'would have every right to raise the question' at the General Assembly (and not at the Security Council, as originally intended by Dr Khare) of the United Nations.[37]

Things were becoming somewhat favourable for the cause of Indians in South Africa. Winston Churchill, who harboured an intense hatred for India and Indians, had been defeated in the UK general elections of 1945. By January 1946, Ramaswamy Mudaliar, one of the sympathetic cabinet colleagues of Dr Khare, had been appointed as the head of the United Nations Economic and Social Council. He had informed the legislative council that the efforts of Dr Khare would be put into action as soon as South Africa made the bill a permanent law. In April 1946, Dr Khare succeeded in making the Indian government withdraw the high commissioner to South Africa. But there was still pressure from British bureaucratic circles to dissuade Dr Khare from raising the issue in the UNO. Arrogant and oblivious to such protests, General Smuts went ahead and made the Asiatic Land Tenure and Representation Act a permanent law on June 1946. Suddenly, time was running out for Dr Khare. There were efforts to install a caretaker government by September which would be a Congress government under Jawaharlal Nehru. He had to hurry and make sure that the issue would be submitted to the UNO, so that the Congress government with the Nehru-Gandhi high command would not be able to reverse or dilute it. Through the services of his secretary R. N. Banerjee, a lengthy memorandum was prepared that studied the various aspects of the racial discrimination of the South African regime and drew a parallel to 'the Nazi principles and practice of race superiority'.[38] Perhaps, Dr Khare was the first person to compare the policies of the Pretoria regime to those of the Nazis in an international forum, which would later evolve to have its own dynamics.

The draft of the memorandum running to 18 pages was sent by an air telegram to Mudaliar who on 22 June 1946 submitted it to Trygve Lie, Secretary-General of the United Nations. Satisfied that he had achieved his primary goal for South African Indians, Dr Khare quit his office in September 1946. Soon a caretaker Congress government came into effect. Pandit Jawaharlal Nehru presided over with the blessings of Mahatma Gandhi. Pandit Nehru immediately appointed his own sister Vijayalakshmi Pandit as the head of the delegation to the United Nations Organization. Mahatma Gandhi, with his characteristic spiritual magnanimity, had summoned Vijayalakshmi Pandit before her departure to UN and had instructed her, she revealed to Smuts, 'that I should shake your hand and ask your blessing for my cause'. As she received the media limelight and showed the world how her brother's government championed the cause of the rights of South African Indians, the perseverance with which Dr Khare fought to arrive at that point, was relegated to the footnote in history and eventually his contribution would be forgotten. No academic work on Hindu nationalism would care to reveal this contribution of a Hindutvaite. The work he had done against a racist regime, the first pioneering seed so painstakingly planted, eventually became the international sanctions against South Africa decades later. Thus, from Vinayak Damodar Savarkar to Narayan Bhaskar Khare, the contribution of Hindutva, both in principle and action, has stood against racism of all sorts. Yet, it is a strange paradox that Hindutva itself gets discussed today in international academia and media as if it is a desi version of racism.

Hindutva, Obscurantism and Social Emancipation

Often, both in the world of Western observers of Hindutva as well as in the dominant academic discourse on Hindutva in India, it is presented as an upper-caste-oriented conservative ideology that often finds resonance with white supremacist ideologies in the West. In fact, this follows from the assumption that Hindutva is an imitation of the one race/one blood-based nation, states that rose in Europe with the beginning of the modern era. To this notion of race, caste is also combined—the Indian upper caste wanting to imitate the European race-based nation-building ended up with Hindutva. Often, Indian nationalism itself is construed as an upper-caste Aryan race construct. The subtle point to be noted is that while it is crudely argued that the Aryan upper castes created Indian nationalism, in more suave academic circles the argument is that the upper castes, believing themselves to be Aryans—linked racially to their European rulers—constructed Indian nationalism and its more virulent form, Hindutva.

A Flawed Narrative

A striking instance of this narrative-building can be seen in the work of Prof. Romila Thapar, one of the most prominent Marxist historians of our times. In her lecture titled *The Aryan Question Revisited*, delivered on 11 October 1999 at the Academic Staff College, Jawaharlal Nehru University, she stated:

> On the Indian nationalist side, it could be argued that the upper-caste Indian who has always been regarded as "the" Indian, that was the creator of the Indian civilization, is Aryan, and is related in fact to the colonizer, the British. And there is one statement which I am very fond of quoting. I quote it in everything that I write, which is Keshub Chandra Sen talking about the coming of the British to India being the coming together of "parted cousins" which in a sense gives you an idea of part of the reason why there is the interest in this theory.[39]

The historian presents Keshub Chandra Sen as an ideal sample of Indian nationalists of the time—an upper-caste person who rationalized caste hegemony by linking his caste status to the Aryan race theory. However, Sen turns out to be more a social reformer than a nationalist. He was no supporter of caste hegemony. Originally a Brahmo Samaj member, Sen even organized inter-caste marriages. In fact, he virulently fought against 'nationalist' tendencies as we saw in the previous chapter. He was a universal Brahmo-

Samajist. So, the question arises as to why Prof. Thapar did not talk about two of the most influential personalities who are associated with Indian nationalism of that period and even to this day: Swami Vivekananda and Sri Aurobindo. Though Prof. Thapar did not mention them, elsewhere in a similar context, she refers to 'upper castes like Brahmanas and Kayasthas'. So, the implication is clear. The process of Indian nationalism was an upper-caste imitation of European race theory of the nineteenth century. According to her, 'the Aryan race theory has not only served cultural nationalism in India but continues to serve Hindu revivalism and, inversely, anti-Brahmin movements.'

Therefore, one needs to explore the writings of Swami Vivekananda and Sri Aurobindo and see if they supported the Aryan race theory and the caste hegemony. There is ample documentary evidence to show that a section of Indians, an educated, powerful and wealthy class, did want to identify themselves with the colonial administrators, copying their manners and dissociating themselves with anything Indian. Most of these people belonged to Indian 'upper castes'. Not only were they not nationalists, the emerging nationalist school of thought strongly criticized them.

Swami Vivekananda harshly criticized Indians for identifying with the British and distancing themselves from the downtrodden masses on the basis of race:

> When I see Indians dressed in European apparel and costumes, the thought comes to my mind, perhaps they feel ashamed to own their nationality and kinship with the ignorant, poor, illiterate, downtrodden people of India! ... Again the Westerners have now taught us that those stupid, ignorant, low-caste millions of India, clad only in loin-cloths, are non-Aryans. They are therefore no more our kith and kin![40]

Swami Vivekananda called such a distancing of oneself from the masses of India as 'slavish weakness' and 'vile detestable cruelty'. Sri Aurobindo, during his vigorously nationalist period of life, had written about caste prejudices existing in the Hindu community. From Prof. Thapar's point of view, he is expected to rationalize the caste discriminations on the basis of race. On the other hand, his stand differs even from the opinion of Lokmanya Tilak. In his essay 'The Unhindu Spirit of Caste Rigidity', published in the journal *Bande Mataram* on 20 September 1907, he wrote:

> The Nationalist does not quarrel with the past, but he insists on its transformation, the transformation of individual or class autocracy into the autocracy, self-rule or Swaraj, of the nation and of the fixed hereditary anti-democratic caste organization into the pliable self-adapting, democratic distribution of function at which socialism aims.[41]

In the same article, Sri Aurobindo further points out that Indian nationalism must, by its inherent tendencies, move towards the removal of unreasoning and arbitrary distinctions and inequalities. In a subsequent article, Aurobindo further pointed out that caste was originally a division of labour and that the caste of a person depended on his dharma—'his spiritual, moral and practical duties'—which, in turn, 'depended on his *svabhava*, his temperament and inborn nature'. In none of this, race or even clan or tribe was brought in. Then Sri Aurobindo spoke about historical instances where the caste arrogance was held in check by spiritual tradition in India: 'Chokha Mela, the Maratha Pariah, became the Guru of Brahmins proud of their caste purity; Chandala taught Shankaracharya.' Then he writes about heredity entering the institution of caste:

> Heredity entered into caste divisions and in the light of the conclusions of modern knowledge who can say erroneously? But it entered into it as a subordinate element. For Hindu civilization, being spiritual, based its institutions on spiritual and moral foundations and subordinated the material elements and material considerations.

This insight by Sri Aurobindo, made as early as 1907, is important for many reasons. It not only rejects the racial interpretation of caste system but also rejects the eugenics emphasis on birth-based selections within the society, which was found at least by sections of English-educated Indian orthodoxy to be attractive and provided justification for caste. So, while demanding that caste system as the history of an institution should be protected from cheap attacks, Aurobindo was clear that its present version should not be shielded from harsh criticism:

> [The caste system] ceased to be determined by spiritual qualifications which, once essential, have now come to be subordinate and even immaterial and is determined by the purely material tests of occupation and birth. By this change it has set itself against the fundamental tendency of Hinduism which is to insist on the spiritual and subordinate the material and thus lost most of its meaning. The spirit of caste arrogance, exclusiveness and superiority came to dominate it instead of the spirit of duty, and the change weakened the nation and helped to reduce us to our present condition. It is these perversions that we wish to see set right.[42]

It is also well known that Sri Aurobindo in his *The Secret of the Veda* criticized the Aryan race theory as 'falsehood' and 'hazardous speculations', and warned about its 'most far-reaching political, social or pseudo-scientific conclusions'. Free of this flawed framework that associates upper-casteism, the Aryan race theory and Hindu nationalism, one needs to evaluate the Hindutva process in issues related to social emancipation—particularly in matters such as of fighting racism, caste discrimination—including untouchability— and gender-related issues.

Social Emancipation Movement and Hindutva

In the modern times, the social emancipation movement started with the Arya Samaj which was founded by Swami Dayananda. Extreme Hindu-phobic Hindutva observer Christophe Jaffrelot characterizes Arya Samaj as one of 'the socio-religious movements initiated by high caste Hindus' from which 'Hindu nationalism' derives its ideology.[43] Arya Samaj was not a high-caste movement as characterized by Jaffrelot. Many of its members directly faced excommunications, death threats and violent attacks from the traditionalists. They initiated most of the anti-caste movements in many parts of India during the nineteenth and early twentieth century. So, it was essentially a social reform movement and a Hindu-revival movement—in the sense that it has the slogan 'Back to the Vedas' as its kernel. The British recognized the danger that social emancipation in the proto-Hindutva process represented by the Arya Samaj posed to the colonial regime. The movement (though with its own conditionings of the period), with its anti-caste and pro-woman empowerment credo, played a very important role in the emergence of what would be later called the Hindu Sanghatan (Hindu Unity) movement. The movement was instrumental in creating an effective chain of schools and service institutions.

As the web of its activities increased, Sir Harcourt Butler, the Lieutenant Governor of Oudh and Northwest Provinces, wrote to Sir James Dunlop Smith, private secretary to the Viceroy Lord Minto, words which may explain the bitterness felt by Western scholars like Jaffrelot:

> What will be the end of the Arya Somaj? What will be the upshot of female education? If the Government is not quick, it will find the women of India educated by Arya Somajists. Now is the time, it seems to me, to get out ladies from England in numbers as Inspectresses and teachers to guide female education. There are many objections to this, I know, but it seems to me that our position in the country will be almost hopeless, if the women are trained up in hostility to us. The Arya Somaj is a dangerous movement because it combines an appeal to national feeling with a tendency to elevate the low castes. Shivaji did this. So has every great Hindu leader.... They swept in new forces by promoting low castes to be Rajputs and Brahmans. The eddies in Hindu society show that there are strong currents at work now.[44]

Swami Shraddhanand: The Greatest and Sincerest Champion of the Untouchables

Swami Shraddhanand was one of the tallest leaders of the Hindu Sanghatan movement who came from the Arya Samaj stream. When Swami Shraddhanand was forced through party-bureaucracy hurdles to resign from the committee meant for 'Harijan' welfare in the Congress, Babasaheb Ambedkar called him 'the greatest and sincerest champion' of Scheduled Communities:

> The Swami was the greatest and the most sincere champion of the Untouchables. There is not the slightest doubt that if he had worked on the Committee (for the Untouchables created by the Congress), he would have produced a very big scheme.[45]

He was also the first person to use the term 'Dalit'. The letters of the Swami to the then high command of Congress and its lieutenants reveal an interesting fact. Here, we see the Hindu nationalist pursuing vigorously a radical programme for the emancipation of the Scheduled Community and the Nehru-Gandhi high command backtracking. In a letter written to Mahatma Gandhi in September 1921, Swami Shraddhanand drew the attention of the Mahatma to the fact that in Delhi and Agra, all that the Scheduled Castes (SCs) were demanding was that they be allowed to draw water from the wells used both by Hindus and Muslims, and that water be not served to them through bamboos or leaves. 'Even this appears impossible for the Congress Committee to accomplish,' the Swami pointed out in his letter, with a heavy heart. He was precise and categorical in his assessment of what he perceived as Gandhi's failure to accomplish his promises to the SCs:

> The Delhi and Agra Chamars simply demand that they be allowed to draw water from wells used both by the Hindus and Mohammedans and that water be not served to them (from Hindu water booths) through bamboos or leaves. Even that appears impossible for the Congress Committee to accomplish. Not only this; a Musulman trader of Sadr went to the length of saying that even if Hindus allowed (these men) to draw water from common wells, the Musulmans would forcibly restrain them from drawing water because they ate carrion.... At Nagpur you laid down that one of the conditions for obtaining Swarajya within 12 months was to give their rights to the depressed classes and without waiting for the accomplishment of their uplift, you have decreed that if there is a complete boycott of foreign cloth up till the 30th September, Swarajya will be an accomplished fact on the 1st of October...I now want to engage my limited energy in the uplift of the depressed classes. I do

> not understand whether the Swarajya obtained without the so-called Untouchable brethren of ours joining us will prove salutary for the Indian nation.[46]

With regard to the taboo of eating carrion the Swami, who himself, advocated abstaining from meat for all sections of Hindus, answered with a rhetorical question: 'I ask—do Hindu and Muslim meat-eaters devour flesh of living cattle? Do they not eat the flesh of the cattle when they are dead?' In 1922 he wrote to Congress leader Vithalbhai Patel, describing how Gandhi had relegated to an obscure corner the emancipation of SCs.[47]

It should be noted that Swami Shraddhanand was the one who strongly propagated both Hindu Sanghatan and Hindu-Muslim unity. His concept of Hindu-Muslim unity was based on the concept of mutual respect borne from the unity of Hindu society. In 1923 Swami decided to overtly move away from politics and dedicate himself to Sanghatan work. With the centenary celebrations of Swami Dayananda approaching, Shraddhanand made use of the occasion to form Dalitoddhar Mandal. He appealed for the help of the organization to remove the problem of untouchability:

> Noticing even the Congress powerless to absorb the so-called untouchables, I have made it the sole mission of my remaining life. I appeal to all Hindu Aryans irrespective of religious or political differences, who do not like their six crore brethren to be out away from their community to help me with money and men.[48]

In his most important work titled *Hindu Sanghatan—Saviour of the Dying Race*, Swami stated that the whole humanity was one race which, for him, of course, belonged to the Vedic civilization and the only division between the Arya and Dasyu was based on presence or absence of virtues.[49] And later, 'Varna' was based on 'attributes and works, qualities and action, character and conduct' and 'mere birth had no standing in determining the position a man was to hold in the society'.[50] His most scathing attack was reserved for untouchability which he saw as the sin of Hindu society:

> The curse of untouchability among the Hindus is a blot upon their reputation and the whole Indian nation is suffering for their sin. Whenever a plea is put forward by our political leaders for Swarajya their mouth is shut by flaunting before them their own sin. Those who enslave and trample under their feet almost one third of their own kith and kin, have no right to complain of the tyranny of the foreigner.[51]

The most interesting part of his account is how, from being a mere religious organization, All India Hindu Sabha became Hindu Mahasabha, a Hindutva movement. After the establishment of the Muslim League, some Hindu leaders desiring a similar communal organization for themselves, formed a Punjab Hindu Sabha. Soon, some leaders wanted to have an all-India organization. So, during the Kumbh festival of 1915, they formed an association and named it the Sarvadeshik (or All India) Hindu Sabha. Swami narrates with disdain how the organization was originally a mere organization for religion-based activities:

> With the Maharajah of Kasimbazar as President, with 13 Vice Presidents including three Shankarachayas, with the Hon'ble Lala Sukhbir Singh as General Secretary assisted by four Secretaries and 50 Councillors hailing from all Provinces, the Sarvadeshik Hindu Sabha appeared to be a body which was expected to transform the Hindu Samaj in no time. The Sabha went on holding Annual General and Special Meetings, at intervals, for the purpose of passing resolutions on subjects of general Hindu interests, but as to ameliorating and improving the condition of all classes of the Hindu community it did practically nothing.

Three things marked the Sabha negatively in the perception of Swami Shraddhanand—loyalty to the British, uncaring attitude towards all sections, particularly the downtrodden sections of Hindu society, and appeasement with Muslim communal elements. These characteristics marked the Hindu Sabha up till its 1918 annual session. Swami writes:

> This was the last Annual Meeting of the All-India Hindu Sabha which was run by those Hindus in whose estimation every invader who snatched the Government of a country from its people was God personified.

He was happy that the Hindu Mahasabha was formed at last and the foundation for Hindu Sanghatan was laid by the work of Pandit Madan Mohan Malaviya. Once revitalized as Hindu Mahasabha, the stand of Mahasabha became clearly anti-British. It moved from loyalty to the British to non-cooperation and boycott of the Prince of Wales visit. For the first time, it started considering social issues seriously. Even as it started taking tentative steps, with the orthodox elements inside still retaining their power, the Swami himself made it clear that Hindu society needs serious and radical social reforms in the coming turbulent ages. Here is the resolution passed by the Hindu Mahasabha with the traditionalists still exercising complete control of the organization and Swami Shraddhanand criticizing the resolution from the Hindu Sanghatan point of view:

> The Hindu Mahasabha has passed a lengthy resolution purporting to deal with the problem of untouchability, but it has resulted in confounding confusion worse....As regards allowing admission to the children of the so-called untouchables in public schools and colleges, the less said the better. But the climax is reached when, after allowing all the above-mentioned ambiguous privileges, the Hindu Mahasabha lays down the authoritative dogma that "initiating the untouchables with sacred thread, teaching them the Vedas and to interdine with them is against the Shastras and custom according to Sanatan Dharma". To get rid of all this rigmarole and to root out the curse of unseeability, unapproachability, untouchability and exclusiveness, there is only one sovereign remedy and that is the resuscitation of the Ancient Aryan "Varnadharma".[52]

Similarly, while the Hindu Mahasabha resolution recommended 16 and 12 as the ages for the marriage of boys and girls respectively, the Swami recommended 25 and 16 as the marriage age for boys and girls. He also wanted all child marriages declared void if the girls so wanted. In discussing the initial confused steps of the Hindu Mahasabha, one should remember that even Mahatma Gandhi was uncomfortable with temple entry of Scheduled Communities as late as 1932. Hindu Mahasabha was fast turning into a platform where the reformist and social emancipation schools in Hindu society were bringing the democratic churn to the traditionalists. The Sanghatan movement shunned racial categorization-based interpretations of the Hindu social structure and sought to change it by call to unity.

The fight of Hindu Sanghatanists of the Arya Samaj was filled with mortal dangers. In 1923 Arya Samaj worker, Lala Ram Chandra of Akhnoor, was beaten to death by casteists for fighting for the equal rights of Scheduled Communities. In Indore, Meghraj, another Arya Samaj leader, was murdered for organizing temple entry agitation. The most important contribution of Swami Shraddhanand was that he made Hindu Sanghatan philosophy the basis for social emancipation and made the abolition of untouchability, the removal of disabilities of Scheduled Communities and the upliftment of women the basis of the Hindu Sanghatan. He considered these as the major objectives. Later, the Hindu Sanghatan-Hindutva movement would take it over from these stands of Swami but not without opposition from a section of the traditionalists.

One of the greatest achievements of the Sanghatan movement was *shuddhi* (or purification ceremony) which was revived. Swami had founded the Bhartiya Hindu Shuddhi Sabha and was also its President. One of the most remarkable milestones under Swami Shraddhanand was the reconversion to the Hindu fold, of the Malkana Rajputs in some districts of the United Provinces and also in Bharatpur State. The desire of the Malkana Muslims to return to their ancestral religion and the ability of the Swami to create the conducive social milieu, as well as to provide them the organizational infrastructure to realize their ambition, came as a great surprise. Soon, it became a major national issue. A body of political leaders consisting of C. R. Das, Motilal Nehru, Sarojini Naidu and Maulana Abul Kalam Azad, joined Swami Shraddhanand and toured the provinces to ascertain the reality of the desire of the Malkanas to return to Hinduism. The leaders' team including Maulana Azad had to concede that the aspirations of the people were genuine. But they wanted Swami Shraddhanand, who was the President of the Bhartiya Shuddhi Sabha, to dissociate himself from the movement. Swami Shraddhanand, supported by another Sanghatan leader Lala Hansraj (hailed in Arya Samaj circles as 'Mahatma'), refused to dissociate himself from the Shuddhi movement, as long as the Muslim political leaders continued their proselytizing work. Then, a compromise was presented by the team that both Hindu and Muslim workers would put a self-moratorium on their activities for a year among the Malkanas. This was rejected by the Islamists. So, the team of national leaders failed to get a compromise, and to his credit, Maulana Abul Kalam Azad declared that Muslims should have to accept the right of Malkanas to return to their ancestral religion, as their lifestyles even before their formal return was already Hindu anyway.[53]

But for this achievement, Swami Shraddhanand had to pay with his life. He was assassinated by an Islamist Abdul Rashid on 23 December 1926.

Bhagat Phool Singh: The Satyagrahi of Haryana

Famously revered as 'Bhagatji', Bhagat Phool Singh (1885–1942) was another Hindu Sanghatanist who was inspired by Swami Shraddhanand. His father wanted him to become a *patwari*—a local government official considered powerful in the village. He did become a patwari, but soon he joined Arya Samaj. As a government official, he was used to vices and corruption, but the Arya Samaj connection transformed all that. Further, it also ended his government job, as Arya Samaj was highly monitored and an almost proscribed organization. The real transformation for Phool Singh came when he met Swami Shraddhanand. From 1917 onwards, he went from village to village preaching Hindu Sanghatanist ideology of social egalitarianism, Vedic education for all and women's education. His work was viewed with suspicion by the government and earned the hostility of Muslims. Even though, at the end, Islamists of the Ranghar community would murder him, he had helped them during the famine when their crops were destroyed. He is today known mainly for spearheading the female education movement, and he also contributed to social justice and harmony. A staunch Hindu Sanghatanist, he felt that he should be born in his next birth as a poor Hindu in a Scheduled Community like the Chamar.[54] This had led him to his confrontation with his own Jat community and the Ranghars, when they refused to allow a well to be dug from which all Hindus including the Scheduled Communities could draw water. So, on 2 September 1940, Bhagat Phool Singh started a fast unto death. His health rapidly deteriorated as the fast entered the second week. On September 21, Mahatma Gandhi was informed of the fast, and he was so concerned for his life that he sent the following telegram to Ghanshyam Das Birla:

> Fulsinghji fasting regarding well for Harijans in village Moth your estate Hissar. Am told your interference alone can save life precious worker. Muslim and Hindu Jats opposing any well for Harijans. This well almost built from public donations and would have been finished but for said opposition.[55]

As the fast completed a fortnight, the opponents to the well yielded and the well was completed and made functional. Describing his fast unto death as 'sacred', Mahatma Gandhi belittled his own fast at Rajkot as 'lacking in faith' compared to the one by Bhagatji. He wrote in *Harijan Sevak* (26 October 1940) thus:

> Bhagatji was very unhappy for the grave injustice done to the Harijans. He had good feelings for both the parties (non-Harijans and Harijans). The Harijans had great difficulty in getting drinking water and to get over this difficulty Bhagatji resorted to fast. He wanted to show the correct and truthful path to the Muslim Ranghars and the Jats by his fast. His fast was inspired by Dharma and faith in God. Many a times the clouds of failure hovered around during the time of his fast. But Bhagatji's patience and faith in God were very powerful. He saw his success in the light of God. There came the time and he became successful in his fast.[56]

He participated vigorously in Hyderabad Satyagraha organized by Arya Samaj and Hindu Mahasabha. He strongly supported the cause of shuddhi. When he was attacked physically by Muslims during the sending of a team to Hyderabad Satyagraha, he in the true spirit of a Gandhian Satyagrahi, requested both Hindus and Muslims to realize their respective mistakes rather than finger-pointing at each other.

Barrister Jayakar: '... Same Hope and Zeal as That of Dr Ambedkar'

If Swami Shraddhanand provided the vision for social emancipation rooted in Hindu Sanghatan, the stalwart of the Hindutva movement who gave legal shape and pushed these reforms practically was Barrister Mukund Ramrao Jayakar (1873–1959). He fought for the reservation of SCs not only in education but also, and more crucially, in administration, particularly in the police force. Though the legislative bodies were established in India as early as 1861 by the British, only on two occasions were SCs mentioned. The first was in 1916 when a Parsee member moved the resolution for 'a small representative committee of officials and non-officials for an amelioration in the moral, material and educational condition of what are known as the Depressed Classes'. The next and more forceful voice for SC empowerment was raised by Jayakar in 1928. The resolution he moved was that the assembly should recommend to the Governor-General-in-Council to issue directions to all Local Governments to provide special facilities for the education of the 'untouchables' and other depressed classes, and also for opening all public services to them, especially the police.[57]

The year 1917 was important for Jayakar. On 12 May 1917, a political conference was held at Nasik which was presided by Srinivas Shastri and attended by Lokmanya Tilak, where Jayakar spoke on an important resolution on self-government. He said:

> There can be no parleying, no compromise, one people cannot rule another people permanently except for their own gain and spoliation. This is an absurd claim and ought to be repudiated. Whether we have become fit for Self-Government or not should be decided by the enlightened political opinion of the country. Liberty alone could prepare a people for the enjoyment of liberty. In the interest of England herself, the bureaucracy should be removed from India. The time is ripe when India should ask for Self-Government, finding that the feeling in England, consequent on the participation of India in the war, has become favourable to such a claim.[58]

One can note that for Jayakar, the demand for freedom and self-government was based on the universal application of democratic principles—a feature that one notices with almost all Hindu Sanghatan leaders. Lokmanya Tilak supported this resolution. After this, a social conference was held in which Tilak was also present and it was presided over by Jayakar. The presence of Tilak for the social conference was not an accident, but a calculated move on the part of Jayakar. He explains:

> I made a personal request to Tilak to be present at the Social Conference. I was anxious that by his presence he should remove the wrong impression that he was against Social Reform and I am very happy to record that he attended the Social Conference and was present to hear my speech along with some other Nationalist friends....Tilak's presence at the Social Conference was regarded as a great event not only at Nasik but in Western India and many journals commented on that fact.[59]

In his speech, Jayakar made very important points with regard to the removal of caste distinctions in the Hindu society. He criticized those schools of reformers who desired social reforms only as 'a defence or a reform of Brahmanism so as to make it acceptable to its Christian critics' and 'not even a revival or a restoration of the ancient ideals of the Vedic period'. But he wanted social change for 'organising the entire Hindu society, in all its component parts, as to furnish a social environment wherein the children of the community will grow in the full development of the social virtues', which the country demands. Condemning the 'perception of fictitious differences between men and men, due to heredity and birth' as an evil from which arises 'the existing family arrangements, where woman is entirely subordinated to man, the lower castes to the higher, to the length of depriving men of their natural respect for humanity'. As per him, unless these changes happened in the minds, no amount of change in the external institutions and outward social reforms would help change the society. He compared a Hindu religious head who considers a fellow Hindu as an untouchable, as a person having a Hindu body but the soul of the British autocrat:

> They are both, to our mind, manifestations of the same vice, with varying degrees of pigment in the skin. We expect, if we may boldly say so, that same mischief from the rule of each. The same heart beats in each, under different forms of clothing and heredity. As Hindus are accustomed to the doctrine that a person in one life can have the body of a man and the heart of a hyena and, with this traditional belief, we find nothing difficult to understand that the body may be Indian with the heart of an alien autocrat....We cannot understand the phenomenon, which we observe in the present age, of advanced political thinkers rebelling against the misuse of political powers by the British bureaucrat remaining dumb and acquiescent before the irrational tyranny of religious autocrats.[60]

Dr Annie Besant, who was very much in synch with the Hindutvaites, appreciated this talk of Jayakar and wrote to him that having 'read with interest his admirable address to the Social Conference', she found herself 'in accord with it', and she was glad that he had 'spoken out so clearly and bravely'.

In the 1920s Barrister Jayakar headed the Hindu Rashtriya Samajik Parishad (HRSP). His speech, made as the president of HRSP, was considered quite scintillating and radical. According to A. K. Vakil, an Ambedkarite-scholar, Jayakar 'had the same hope and zeal as that of Ambedkar'. According to Jayakar, beyond the superficial reforms there needed to be a fundamental change. To this end, he demanded drastic changes in the Hindu legal system and social attitudes. The marriage acts were to be suitably amended along with a sanction for inter-caste marriages. The Presidential speech of Jayakar was published by Dr Ambedkar in his *Bahishkrit Bharat*.[61]

Jayakar was working with Bombay Hindu Mahasabha which in 1929 adapted the Savarkarite definition of Hindu in its constitution that 'Hindu means any person professing any religion of Indian origin'.[62] It includes 'Sanatanists, Arya Samajists, Jains, Sikhs, Buddhists, Brahmos, etc.' However, even in October 1925, issuing an appeal for the provincial session of the Hindu Mahasabha, Jayakar and another Mahasabha leader Govindlal Shivlal had announced that its sessions and committees were open to 'every Hindu, whether a Sanatanist, Vaishnava, Arya Samajist, Jain, Sikh, Brahmo or Buddhist'. In the social reform movement of the Mahasabha, the Arya Samaj influence was quite dominant: this disturbed the traditionalists. With respect to this 1925 appeal of the Hindu Mahasabha for its provincial session, Mahadev Rajaram Bodas, a lawyer from Bombay High Court wrote to Jayakar, warning him that the 'Arya Samajist connection' prevented many traditionalists sympathetic to the Mahasabha from joining it. So, he proposed to Jayakar the solution for handing over the Mahasabha leadership to the orthodoxy and that 'the subsidiary questions of shuddhi and untouchability' be 'subordinated to the main aim for the present'. The Bombay Hindu Mahasabha Conference was held on 3–4 December 1925. Jayakar was the chairman of the Reception Committee and declared that the twin objectives of the conference were to promote friendship among all communities and reform in the Hindu society. Jayakar also passed a set of resolutions that had come from Poona which was then considered the seat of orthodoxy:

1. That the several castes and communities of Hindus gain equal status, dignity and importance.
2. Nobody, by reason of mere birth, can be inferior and superior but only his personal merit and action can make him so.
3. Amongst Hindus, nobody, by reason merely of birth, can be deemed an untouchable and all Hindus should have equal right to use all public places, watering places and places of worship.
4. Every Hindu has the right to perform ceremonies according to Vedic rituals.

5. Every Hindu has the right to get his ceremonials and rituals performed at the hands of another Hindu and in consequence thereof, no Hindu has the right to impose restrictions on another.

The session was also attended by Swami Shraddhanand, who stated that Hindus need to establish an institution for destitute Hindu women. He had seen the plight of Hindu women ravished by Moplah rioters. Most of the time, the abducted Hindu women could not return to their houses because of social stigma, so he wanted the Hindu Mahasabha to create an institution to support such affected women, widows and children, till they could settle in life.[63]

The following year, a true believer in democracy and pluralism, Jayakar was of firm belief that the consolidation of Hindus and their social organism being free of social ills, was the precondition for a healthy and secular India. He explained:

> Religion and politics, I observed, are often intermixed in India, not without far-reaching consequences on either of these domains of human activity. If this interaction is desirable which many people doubt, it could only be made successful when our religion becomes more human and affiliated to our daily life. Our religion, therefore in the present age, must necessarily take the form of a gospel of vigorous work set in contrast, not necessarily in conflict, with that of our neighbours professing rival forms of faith. Peace and harmony very often come out of an equal contest between contending forces if the contest is fair and equal and if it invariably leads to mutual respect and mutual toleration. The next few years in India would in my opinion, see such a contest between some of the important forms of faith.[64]

In fighting against untouchability, Jayakar was highly influenced by an incident in the life Adi Sankaracharya in which a Chandala or outcaste in Kasi made the Acharya to follow the Advaita (non-dual spiritual tradition) practically eschewing social divisions and exclusion. The traditional biography of the Sankaracharya, written in the fourteenth century, puts the following words into the mouth of the Chandala who questions the notion of social exclusion thus:

> You are always going about preaching that the Vedas teach the non-dual Brahman to be the only reality and that He is immutable and unpollutable. If this is so, how has this sense of difference overtaken you? There are hundreds of Sannyasins going about, indulging in high-sounding philosophical talk, donning the ochre robe and exhibiting other insignias of holy life like the water pot and the staff. But not even a ray of knowledge having found entrance into their hearts, their holy exterior serves

> only to dupe house-holders. You asked me to move aside and make way for you. To whom were your words addressed, O learned Sir? To the body which comes from the same source and performs the same functions in the case of both a Brahman and an outcaste? Or to the Atman, the witnessing Consciousness, which too is the same in all unaffected by anything that is of the body? How does such differences as "This is a Brahmana, this is an outcaste" arise in non-dual experience?[65]

Based on this approach, Jayakar told his co-religionists:

> These are not the days when gods come down on earth incognito to chastise the erring humanity. But it is certain that they send down their agents to regulate things so that erring races may suffer humiliation for their sins.[66]

In 1930 it was Jayakar who introduced the Hindu Untouchable Castes Disabilities Removal Bill in the Central Legislature. It aimed to remove the obstacles created by British courts in India which viewed temple entry as against the religious unity of Hindu society. More importantly, it also demanded the removal of disabilities created in the name of caste against any person to enjoy the rights of entry into public institutions. In the bill, Jayakar had proposed thus:

> No person belonging to the Hindu community shall be deemed to be incapable by reason of this caste, of sharing the benefit of a religious or charitable trust created for the general benefit of persons professing the Hindu religion, or for sharing the benefit of a convenience, utility or service, dedicated to or maintained or licensed for the use of the general public, any custom or interpretation of the law to the contrary notwithstanding....The Bill also provides for the removal of disabilities from which the untouchable classes suffer in the use of conveniences like public wells or services like tram cars, buses, etc., which are maintained or licensed for the use of the public.[67]

Later, while talking about the bill, Jayakar minced no words when he stated that the bill 'was intended to remove the obstacles created by the British Indian courts giving legal recognition to customs and usages regarded as unjust, anti-social and irreligious by a section of the Hindu community'.[68] By 1933 there were four bills. Jayakar could not move the bill as he was no more the member of the house. Apart from the bill brought by Jayakar, there were bills by Subbaroyan, Ranga Iyer and Harbilas Sarda. Mahatma Gandhi wanted the bill by Subbaroyan to be approved by the Viceroy. He sought the help of Jayakar and Jayakar worked with him and pointed out to him that 'if the Government wished it could make it possible to pass at least one of the Bills during the ensuing session of the Assembly'.[69] This helped Gandhi take up the matter with the British government as well. What strikingly marks the social emancipation views of Jayakar is the absolute absence of fissiparous tendencies. As one of the tallest leaders of the national non-Brahmin movement, Jayakar repeatedly cautioned against the movement becoming a tool in the hands of the British. So, to him the non-Brahmin should 'believe in his struggle as an enlightened patriot refusing to allow himself to be made a tool by the British official in the game of perpetuating his rule'. He further made it clear that the non-Brahmin movement should not add to 'further divisions in the ranks of the Hindu community'.[70]

The legacy of Hindutvaites has been more crucial than their ideological adversaries in effecting the empowerment of the marginalized sections of society. In many instances, it has been the pioneering guiding light for future affirmative action programmes of the 'free democratic sovereign state' of India—incidentally, these were the words introduced by Jayakar through an amendment at the Constituent Assembly in 1946. It should also be mentioned that despite being bitterly opposed to the Muslim League, the democratic Hindu nationalist Jayakar thwarted an undemocratic plot by the Congress to exclude the Muslim members from attending this session.

Another very important aspect of Jayakar's political life is also symptomatic of the Hindutva relation to the legacy of Mahatma Gandhi. The biographer of Jayakar, V. B. Kulkarni brings forth this aspect very well in the following words:

> Jayakar did not accept as sacrosanct everything that Gandhi said or did.... Nevertheless he was drawn irresistibly towards the great leader for his high moral qualities. ... During his visit to the Sabarmati Ashram at Ahmedabad in 1920, Jayakar had the most convincing demonstration of Gandhi's freedom from caste prejudices. He saw Mahatma ready to eat a boiled potato with a Harijan girl although it had been half-bitten by her. "I have", writes Jayakar, "never found a man so free from caste aversion as Gandhi".[71]

But such a great admiration for Mahatma Gandhi in his fight against casteism and untouchability did not prevent Jayakar from criticizing the Khilafat movement for what it was:

> Jayakar had no illusions about the true implications of the Khilafat movement and Gandhi's association with it. Writing to C.R. Das on January 6, 1923 he doubted the wisdom of including Khilafat issue in the non-cooperation programme. He wrote: 'It is widely felt that the party should not be dragged at the heels of Mahomedan fanaticism, which will be swayed by every political change in Turkey, apart from the religious

> significance.' He pointed out that, despite Gandhi's 'smiling placidity and habitual moderation', the country had embraced the philosophy of 'unbelief and destruction.'[72]

This attains significance because often the critics of Hindutva bundle the opposition of orthodoxy to Mahatma Gandhi's reform movements with the Hindutva opposition to his appeasement policies. It was not only Jayakar but also Savarkar and the leaders of the latter dominant RSS who take the same stand with respect to social emancipation and opposition to the appeasement of monopolistic expansionist religious politics of Christianity and Islam in India.

Yet another prominent Hindu nationalist who was way ahead of his Congress counterparts in empowering SCs was Dr Khare, whom we have met already. He was the elected head of the Central Provinces and was dismissed by Nehru, following the assassination of Mahatma Gandhi. In the 1930s he appointed a Dalit minister in his cabinet, for which he was taken to task by the then Congress high command and sacked. Dr Ambedkar made a scathing attack on the Mahatma for what he considered as the abject betrayal of the cause of the SC community. Dr Khare was also instrumental in securing the Arya Marriage Validation Bill on the Statute Book, which allowed large-scale widow remarriages and marriages breaking caste boundaries. This was also the forerunner in legally liberating marriages from the ritual sanctioning of birth-based priesthood.

Savarkar and Social Emancipation

Savarkar was always consistent and forthright in his condemnation of the caste system and untouchability. In his letters to his family members from the Andamans, written mostly in the period 1912-1920, he repeatedly condemned caste and untouchability. On 9 March 1915, he wrote to his brother thus:

> One thing more—the social institutions—the greatest curse of India is the system of castes. The mighty current of Hindu life is being threatened to perish in bogs and sands. It is no good saying "we will reduce it to four caste system first." That would and should not be. It must be swept away, root and branch. The best means to that effect is crusade against it, in all forms of literature, especially drama and novel. Every true patriot should cease to have double dealing and speak out his mind clearly and act up to it.[73]

In his letter dated 6 July 1916, Savarkar again wrote of caste and creed as 'the artificial and harmful barriers' impeding the flow of the 'great river of life' of the Hindus. He wanted that the Hindu authorities should 'come in to sanctify but not to silence love altogether'.[74]

During Savarkar's confinement in Ratnagiri, he immersed himself in a series of activities against untouchability. The first challenge he took upon himself was the fight for the continuation of all caste students studying in the same classrooms in government schools. He got into a direct confrontation with the stagnant sections of society. Savarkar wrote to the District Magistrate (DM) to file charges against the 'upper caste' ruffians who disrupted the schools: 'I wish, sir, to enlist not only your legal protection as a Magistrate, but also your human sympathies as a gentleman, in the cause'. Later, when the DM himself inspected the schools, he observed that it was because of the forceful appeal of 'Mr. Savarkar's lectures that the untouchable boys had been allowed to sit mixed and get their education without any invidious distinction being made in their case.'[75]

While the Congress was taking tentative steps even in inter-dining feasts, the events organized by Savarkar, and his fellow Sanghatanists in Ratnagiri went quite radical in tackling the caste issue. Dhananjay Keer quotes a report from the *Times of India* dated 9 December 1930, which details the difference between the events organized by Savarkar and Gandhi-led Congress:

> This all-caste dinner was celebrated in a unique manner—a manner that has given deep offence to Nationalist Congressmen, who are mostly believers along with Mr Gandhi in four watertight castes by birth. For, at Ratnagiri some enthusiastic reformers, who regarded caste system as the bane of Hinduism, held an all-caste dinner which was attended by Brahmins, Banias, Chambhars, Mahars and Bhangis!... What is still more interesting, the spirit of this splendid essay in practical reform, Mr. V. D. Savarkar, delivered a speech in which he flung into the teeth of orthodoxy the daring credo of his party. "From today I shall not believe in highness or lowness of caste. I shall not oppose the intermarriage between the highest and lowest castes. I shall eat with any Hindu irrespective of caste. I shall not believe in caste by birth or by profession and henceforth I shall call myself a Hindu only—not Brahmin, Vaishya, etc."[76]

During the Mahad Satyagraha of Dr Ambedkar (1927), Savarkar was among the very few leaders who unreservedly supported him. But Savarkar was still under restrictions, and he could not come out of Ratnagiri. Yet, he issued a strong statement of support:

> Untouchability must be condemned and abolished not only as the need of the hour but also as the command of true religion; not only as a policy or as an act of

expediency but also as a matter of justice, not only as a matter of obligation but also as a service-to humanity.[77]

On 30 November 1927, Hindu Sanghatanists called a meeting of the citizens of Mahad and communicated the support of the Hindu Mahasabha for Satyagraha.[78]The influence of Savarkar on the Mahasabha was such that while even as orthodox leaders were trying for various options of compromise, the general direction of the Mahasabha became pro-Satyagraha. Dr Ambedkar, who came to Ratnagiri for a lawsuit, met Savarkar, who planned a public meeting with him. But a telegraphic message from Bombay demanded that Dr Ambedkar return urgently.[79] Dr Ambedkar was becoming more and more frustrated with the attitude of the orthodoxy. His last Satyagraha was the famous Kalaram temple at Nasik. Savarkar issued a statement supporting the Satyagraha and appealed to the orthodoxy to open the temple to their Scheduled Community brethren. The statement was circulated by Bhaurao Gaikwad, one of the leaders of the Kalaram movement. Savarkar also declared that had he been free, he would have been the first man to court jail in the Nasik Satyagraha.[80]

In 1933 when Savarkar opened the pan-Hindu temple in Ratnagiri, he again invited Dr Ambedkar. The latter could not come because of previous engagements, but he took that 'opportunity to convey to him his appreciation for the work Savarkar was doing in the field of social reform'. He further stated that to make the Scheduled Communities a part and parcel of Hindu society, the very jargon of *Chaturvarna* should be dropped and Savarkar was one of the very few leaders who understood this. Though Savarkar used the Chaturvarna which he 'qualified by basing it on merit' even that was 'unfortunate' and wanted him to drop the term. Ambedkar ended his letter expressing his desire to meet Savarkar.[81]

Savarkar's Philosophy of Social Emancipation

Even as Dr Ambedkar had faulted Savarkar with using the term Chaturvarna as jargon, despite the fact that the latter did 'qualify by basing it on merit', Dr Ambedkar himself had said that Varna was based on worth initially and later it became rigid, based on birth.

> The original system seems to have in contemplation the determination of the Varna of adults. It was not based on prior training or close scrutiny of bias and aptitude.... The determination of the Varna was done in a rough and tumble manner. This

> system seems to have gone into abeyance. A new system grew up in its place. It was known as the Gurukul system....The new method was undoubtedly superior to the old method. It retained the true feature of the old method namely that the Varna should be determined by a disinterested and independent body....On the ground that training alone develops an individual in the makeup of a person and the only safe way to determine the Varna of a person is to know his individuality, the addition of this new feature was undoubtedly a great improvement....Varna instead of being Varna for a period became Varna for life. But it was not hereditary.[82]

Then Ambedkar alleges that this system was intentionally made into a birth-based system by the conspiracy of Brahminism—'Brahminism changed Varna to Caste'. Savarkar too considers a similar idealistic Varna system degenerating into a birth-based system that is found in the present times. However, he did not blame it on the so-called Brahmins and Kshatriyas alone. In his 1930 article on the caste system, Savarkar wrote:

> This craze of caste is not limited to the Brahmin alone; it pervades the non-Brahmin, out-caste, indeed the whole of Hindustan is imbued with it! The societal body has become wasted with this disease of caste arrogance, caste hatred and caste conflict....The Varnas represent the four human tendencies of learning, fighting, trading and serving). These four Varnas were determined by merit and actions and not by birth....Both chaturvarna and caste divisions are but practices. They are not coterminous with Sanatana Dharma. The practice of caste division arose from a tectonic change in the practice of chaturvarna. As the Sanatana Dharma did not die due to this tectonic change, so too it will not die if the present-day distortion that is caste division is destroyed....Caste division is not the conspiracy of a handful of Brahmins...it is not the joint conspiracy of the Brahmins and Kshatriyas.... No one should ever think that a certain Hindu caste is high or that another is low. The notion of high and low will be determined by overt merit of individuals. Every Hindu child has but one caste at birth—Hindu. Other than that, consider no other sub-caste. "*Janmanaa jaayate Hinduhu*" ("every one is a Hindu by birth")! In truth, every man has but one caste at birth—human. [83]

Here, we can see a striking parallel between Ambedkar and Savarkar. Both considered Charturvarna to be initially worth-based and later to have devolved into castes. It is quite interesting to note that Savarkar had tweaked the famous *Smriti* injunction that all are born Shudras—'*janmanaa jaayate shudraha*'. Smritis originally mean that it was through rites which are allowed strictly based on birth that, they become twice-born. But Savarkar interprets that as 'all are born Hindus' and simply leaves out the twice-born part with which he disagrees. So, at least three years before Dr Ambedkar's letter to him, Savarkar had repudiated the concept of Varna as the term was used and understood commonly in the society. But Savarkar also thought of the areas in which the caste system should be attacked so that it could be abolished. In 1937 he diagnosed a 'scripture-based caste division' as a 'mental illness'. He identified the 'seven shackles' which should be broken to liberate the Hindu society from the stranglehold of caste. These seven shackles were:

1. Prevention of Vedic chanting;
2. Prevention of entering into certain occupations;
3. Untouchability;
4. Forbidding the crossing of sea;
5. Denial of reconversion or *shuddhi*;
6. Absence of inter-dining; and
7. Prohibition of inter-caste marriages.[84]

According to Savarkar, if these seven obstacles were to be broken, then caste system would cease to exist as a force of social stagnation.

Hindu Mahasabha and Social Reforms

The Hindu Mahasabha itself became the platform where the social reform forces debated with traditionalists and pushed forward the reforms in Hindu society. Going through the various resolutions and Presidential addresses made at the annual sessions of the Hindu Mahasabha, one can clearly see the attitude of Hindu Sanghatanists with respect to social egalitarianism and the eradication of untouchability. Far from being a patronizing approach (though such attitudes were sometimes present) or a mere gesture for numerical strength, the criticism of untouchability was based on democratic and humanistic principles which they construed as the basis of Hindu Dharma.

In the 1926 Presidential address of the Hindu Mahasabha session held at Delhi, 'the sanction given by Hindu society to untouchability and to the treatment meted out to the depressed classes' was termed as 'a negation of democracy and democratic principles' and said that a more illogical position was difficult to conceive.[85] In the same session, the following resolution was passed:

1. The Hindu Mahasabha requests all Hindus to remove such restraints as may be existing at present in the way of the so-called untouchable Hindus using public schools, public wells and public roads and attending

public meetings.

2. The Mahasabha further requests the authorities of Hindu temples to provide facilities to the so-called untouchable Hindus for Deva-Darshan.[86]

The 1936 Annual Session of the Hindu Mahasabha was held in Poona under the chairmanship of Pandit Madan Mohan Malaviya, where the following resolution was passed:

> The Hindu Maha Sabha further affirms its faith that untouchability must not be regarded as a part of Hindu religion or social system. The Mahasabha recommends to the Hindus the abolition of all distinctions in the Hindu Society based on birth or caste in the spheres of public, social and political life in which such distinctions ought to have no application and are out of place in the present age.[87]

There is a historically significant event associated with this. Indrani Jagjivan Ram, wife of late Babu Jagjivan Ram (1908–1986), described in her memory how her husband won a significant victory for the Scheduled Communities against the orthodoxy with the support of Hindu Sanghatanists:

> At the seventeenth session of the Hindu Mahasabha held in Poona from 29 to 31 December 1935, the chairman Pandit Madan Mohan Malaviya appealed to the Dalits not to separate from the Hindus. 'We shall bow before you', he said. It was recommended that the discriminations that existed among Hindus due to birth or caste should be removed from social, public and political life. A resolution was passed that said all public conveniences and institutions like schools, wells, bathing ghats, drinking water providers, eateries, roads, parks, dharmashalas, temples and other public places of worship should be open to all Hindus irrespective of caste or religion. Jagjivan Ram had to argue a good deal with the Shankaracharya of Nasik (Puri) to get this proposal passed....Jagjivan Ram pressed his proposal with the backing of thirty Dalit members. His amendment stated that there should be no discrimination against Harijans. It was a stiff fight. The Shankaracharya had a strong support base - people looked up to him with respect and faith. My husband opposed him vehemently and threatened a walkout. Pandit Madan Mohan Malaviya gave a strong speech in support of Jagjivan Ram. Leaders like Munje and Jayakar also supported him and the amendment he put forth was passed late at night after strong tussle.[88]

The 'who's who' of Hindu Sanghatanists or Hindutvaites of the time, Malaviya, Moonje and Jayakar, sided clearly with the nationalist Hindu SC leader Jagjivan Ram and opposed their own revered religious head for the rights of the Scheduled Community.

In Berar municipality, the Hindu Mahasabha was able to get a SC candidate elected to the Municipal Council from a non-reserved constituency, defeating the so-called upper caste Hindu.[89] In Ratnagiri, which was then the seat of orthodoxy, Savarkar was working for the eradication of social evils in the Hindu society through the Hindu Mahasabha. The famous Patitpawan Mandir which he created also had a well in which all Hindus, the Brahmins, the SCs and other non-Brahmin communities were made to draw water. This was indeed a very important step, as usually it was the access to water bodies which was being denied by dominant castes to the SCs. In Bengal, Hindu Mahasabha had two preachers tour the districts, taking the 'constructive programme' which was defined as pursuing:

> ...removal of untouchability, abolition of child marriage and dowry systems, amelioration of the condition of the Hindu widows, protection of women, widow-remarriage, uplift of the backward classes, organisation of Sarbajanin Pujas for the benefit of Hindus of all castes, establishment of Akharas, Clubs and Gymnasiums for the physical regeneration of the Hindu youths and similar other social uplift works.[90]

Bole Resolution to Bhagwa Recommendation

One cardinal problem of Hindu Mahasabha was the conflict of interest between the so-called upper castes and affluent sections of the Hindu society and the working classes as well as marginalized communities. This was not something peculiar to Hindu Mahasabha. One could see this in all national movements. Colonialists and those subscribing to colonized ideologies like Marxism used this division effectively. In the case of Hindu society, frozen caste dynamics, stagnated community relations and consequently magnified social evils like untouchability played even a further deepening role. Historian Vikram Sampath points this out in his work on Savarkar:

> The Swarajists who represented the HIndu Mahasabha ideology in the legislative council opposed many legislative measures that could have ushered in social reforms....Between 1921 and 1929, council members such as A. N. Surve and C. K. Bole raised the complaints of the agricultural classes (kulas) against the oppression of the landlords (khotis) in the Ratnagiri and Kulaba districts of Konkan. Many khots were from the upper castes and belonged to the Swaraj Party and the Congress.... Similarly, the bills that sought to strip off the hereditary special privileges to village priests (Joshis) and accountants (Kulkarnis) were opposed by the Swaraj Party and HIndu Mahasabha leaders, given the obvious conflicts of interest. Though in this

> case, despite their opposition, the bills...were eventually introduced and passed in the legislative council. But the stand taken by the Hindu Mahasabha on such crucial reforms impacted its image badly.[91]

It was because of the progressive stands (often bitterly criticized within the institution) taken by stalwart Sanghatanists like Jayakar and Savarkar that this feudal obscurantist components of Hindu Mahasabha began to change.

This was not an easy change. It was a battle within.

On 4 August 1923, Rao Bahadur Sitaram Keshav Bole (1868–1961), one of the fiercest social reformers of India, passed a resolution in the Bombay Legislative Council to the effect that 'the untouchable classes be allowed to use all public watering places, wells and dharmashalas which are built and maintained by Government or created by statutes as well as public schools, courts, offices and dispensaries'. In 1926 the Mahad City Council also endorsed this resolution.[92] Yet, the Scheduled Community members were not allowed by the upper castes to drink water from the public water body. This would soon lead to the famous Mahad Satyagraha led by Dr Ambedkar on 20 March 1927. It was supported by Vinayak Savarkar.

The Hindu Mahasabha, generally considered to be an orthodox body, came in support of the Scheduled Communities for opening the Mahad water body to all Hindus irrespective of caste. Dr Ambedkar was quite happy with this stand of Mahasabha, which was often identified with the interests of the so-called upper castes. Dr Ambedkar wrote:

> The Brahman leaders from Pune, Mr Baburao Gokhale and the sub-editor of Kesari, Mr J. S. Karandikar had purposefully gone to Mahad from Pune a few days ago. On 30 November, they organized a meeting of the people from Mahad and conveyed the message of the Hindu Mahasabha that they should not oppose the Satyagraha of the Untouchables. It will surely have a good impact on the Brahmans of Mahad. At least they would be able to say that the Brahmans had made efforts to discharge their responsibility. The non-Brahman leaders however have done nothing in this respect. We hear that the Marathas from the surrounding villages are preparing for a strong opposition to the Untouchables' Satyagraha.[93]

The Satyagraha also ushered in a legal battle. Nothing brings out the faultlines within the Hindu Sanghatan movement as represented by Hindu Mahasabha then as the stand taken by its leaders during this battle. Pandurang Bhaskar Shastri Palaye, a learned Brahmin with Sanghatan connections, had filed an affidavit in support of Dr Ambedkar on 30 January 1928. Dr

Ambedkar stayed in the house of Shastri Palaye in the heart of orthodoxy, and none dared to protest this stay. With regard to the case, Shastri advised Dr Ambedkar to contact two important Mahasabha leaders namely N. C. Kelkar and Dr Kurtkoti Sankaracharya. Kelkar staunchly supported Dr Ambedkar and supplied him with strong material to back the claims of the Scheduled Community to enter the tank. However, during the legal proceedings, he was not interested to be a witness and thus did not accompany him. Such was the condition of Sanghtanists then when it comes to walking the talk. It was a mixed bag of some bravely doing that and some standing against progress. One prominent Sanghtanist to stand as witness in the proceedings supporting the case of Dr Ambedkar was Dr Narayan Damodara Savarkar, the younger brother of Vinayak Damodar Savarkar.

Though Vinayak Savarkar had legal restrictions on movement, that he supported the proceedings clearly showed the stand taken by the Sanghatan movement under the leadership of Savarkar and team. Thus, the works of dedicated leaders and magnificent personalities in the Sanghatan movement—Savarkar brothers, Barrister Jayakar and Swami Shraddhanand slowly and steadily changed the view that Hindu Mahasabha was a pro-upper caste/class organization.

While on the outside the Sanghatan movement opposed orthodoxy and paved way for Hindu Sanghatan, at another level it was, perhaps without even being aware, fighting a deep battle against colonialism, as is revealed in the case of Sitaram Keshav Bole, who was at the heart of initiations of many revolutionary social reforms of the period.

In the late 1930s, Bole, a very strong warrior for the cause of social justice, joined Hindu Mahasabha. In 1938 he became the chairman of Prantik Hindu Mahasabha .

In the end of May 1941, the British CID intercepted a draft resolution of Calcutta Session Hindu Mahasabha, a draft circulated by S. K. Bole and a letter of S. K. Bole to P. C. Joglekar, another Mahasabha leader. The letter was with the Central Intelligence Office (CIO) by 21 May 1941. Another letter written by S. K. Bole to N. C. Chatterjee of Bengal Hindu Mahasabha dated 16 May 1941 was also intercepted by the intelligence. All these letters were written and sent from Savarkar Sadan of Vinayak Savarkar.

The draft was about the way the 'Direct Action' being planned by the all India Hindu Mahasabha should take shape. Abhorring the Congress way of going to jails, the Sanghatanists planned an all India British boycott. S. K. Bole was the first signatory and others included Narayan Savarkar, Ganesh Savarkar, D. G. Abhyankar and B. N. Bhagwat. The letters conveyed that as this was a draft which would be put for vote, Vinayak Savarkar himself being the President of Mahasabha did not sign it, but he clearly stated his endorsement and support of the move.

R. M. Maxwell, one of the most powerful officers of home department at the time, fumingly recorded his shock and displeasure:

> I am surprised at Rao Bahadur S. K. Bole having a hand in this resolution. He and the depressed classes whom he represented (as a Govt. nominee, I think) in the Bombay Legislative Council owe every consideration they have received to the British Govt., which has stood between them and the Hindu Mahasabhaites with whom he has now apparently allied himself. His change of attitude is so remarkable that it would be interesting to have the comments of the CIO Bombay on Bole's real part in this affair.[94]

On 18 July 1941, the CIO from Bombay sent a reply.

'After having secured a place of honour among men of his own community through Government favour', S. K. Bole now wanted to enter politics. While there were depressed class leaders in other parties, he had 'ventured to enter the Hindu Mahasabha as no depressed class leader had so far entered that field'. The CIO report also observed:

> Savarkar has always been sympathetic towards the depressed classes and he must have encouraged Bole to enter the organisation, thinking that the presence of a depressed class leader in the Hindu Mahasabha would greatly strengthen its position. In course of time, Bole was made the President of Bombay Hindu Mahasabha, which was undoubtedly a high honour for a depressed class leader.

Finally, the CIO report concludes:

> Bole honestly believes that if the Hindu Mahasabha succeeds in securing all its demands, the depressed classes would be benefitted immensely thereby. He is therefore genuinely interested in the direct-action scheme, as he believes that their demand cannot be achieved except through a struggle.[95]

The communication between the colonial authorities also shows how much they had invested in deepening the faultlines among the various Indian communities and how the so-called upper castes fell into this ditch because of their vested interests in the malaises of social stagnation.

On 10 July 1947, Rao Bahadur Sitaram Keshav Bole along with the delegation of Hindu Sanghatan activists met Dr Ambedkar at the Bombay airport. Their demand was that the saffron flag be made the national flag of India. Dr Ambedkar accepted their demand and asked them to organize and conduct a people's movement for the same.

Earning the respect and, more importantly, the faith of a leader of S. K. Bole's stature was not a small achievement. Hindu Sanghatanists like Savarkar and Bole had to fight against this social stagnant mindset while also fighting the colonial aggression and theo-colonial evangelism.

Yet, the dominant establishment historiography in India and the South Asian observers in the Western academia and media always characterize Hindutva as a pro-upper caste, anti-Muslim, anti-Christian ideology. Towards this end, they need to be extremely selective with their data and have to ignore intentionally or otherwise, a significant quantum of data. Two cases usually presented in sections of academia and media with respect to Hindutva illustrate this point. One is that of Swami Satyananda and the other, Dr Moonje.

Upper Caste Nazi or Forgotten Fighter for SC Rights?

The only context in which the name of Swami Satyananda is mentioned in academic treatises is in connection with Maximiani Portas alias Savitri Devi—a Nazi writer who worked for some time in India. She worked with the Hindu Mission of Swami Satyananda for a while. This is how historian Nicholas Goodrick-Clarke presents her association with Hindutva movements:

> Savitri Devi regarded Hinduism as the only living Aryan heritage in the modern world. In her eyes, Hinduism was a powerful ally in her campaign to confront and oppose the Judaeo-Christian tradition. But her Aryan-Nazi championship of Hinduism also interacted with domestic political movements in India between the wars. These movements were concerned with varieties of Hindu nationalism, conceived as an upper-caste strategy to unify and strengthen Indian society against the threat of other cultures (Islam and Christianity), while seeking to emulate the confidence and authority of the British. These movements were strongest in northern India, where the Muslim threat was more acutely perceived, and originated in Maharashtra, where Brahmin prestige had been challenged by backward caste movements from the 1870s onward. When Savitri Devi became politically active in the later 1930s, such Hindu national movements as the Hindu Mahasabha and the Rashtriya Swayamsevak Sangh were growing rapidly in an urgent response to Muslim ascendancy.[96]

Then he describes her meeting with Swami Satyananda of the Hindu Mission in Bengal. Here Goodrick-Clarke completely reproduces claims of Maximiani Portas as facts:

> When Satyananda asked about her own religious beliefs, Savitri Devi declared she was an Aryan pagan and regretted the conversion of Europe to Christianity. She wanted to prevent the sole remaining country honoring Aryan gods from falling under the spiritual influence of the Jews. She also added that she was a devotee of Adolf Hitler, who was leading the only movement in this Aryan pagan spirit against the Judaeo-Christian civilization of the West. Satyananda was impressed by the young Greek woman with intense eyes and an outspoken manner. The Hindu Mission could certainly use such an ardent and educated fighter fluent in both Bengali and Hindi. In fact, Satyananda shared many Hindus' admiration for Hitler on account of his Aryan mythology and use of the swastika, the traditional sign of fortune and health. He told her that he considered Hitler an incarnation of Vishnu, an expression of the force preserving cosmic order. In his eyes the disciples of Hitler were the Hindus' spiritual brothers. With this meeting of minds, Satyananda engaged Savitri Devi as a Hindu Mission lecturer.... When she asked Srimat Swami Satyananda, the president of the Hindu Mission in Calcutta, if she might make reference to Hitler and Mein Kampf in her official lectures, he replied that Hitler was for them an incarnation of Vishnu, the god who keeps things from rushing to destruction, who keeps things back and goes against time. She was welcome to say what she liked in her lectures, provided that she said it from a Hindu point of view. Satyananda repeated this view of Hitler in 1942, adding that they needed National Socialism in India. She encountered similar pro-Hitler attitudes among many other educated Brahmins besides Asit Krishna Mukherji, and even among illiterate Sudras. Satyananda's references to Hitler as an "incarnation of God" and the "Saviour of the world" were in fact commonplace among high-caste Hindus. Writing of his impressions of university life in India during the 1950s, Agehananda Bharati declared that the active Hindu loves all dictators due to incurable hero worship.[97]

The passage is an excellent example of the Western 'scholarship' generating negative stereotypes against Hindus. One can note how the concept of avatarhood is brought in to make Hindus inherently tyrannophiles and make anti-democracy an inherent value system of Hindus. It is noteworthy here to remember that Narsimha, the fiercest avatar of Vishnu, has been presented in Indian mass tradition as a response to the fight of Prahlad against his father and often described in devotional literature as a 'satyagraha'. Mahatma Gandhi himself refers to Prahlad as the foremost Satyagrahi in his 1919 pamphlet.[98] And Prahlad is associated with the memory of an avatar in India through countless devotional hymns and folk traditions transcending language barriers. So, to say that Hindus gravitate towards dictatorship because of their belief in avatarhood is to say the least.

Belgian Indologist Dr Koenraad Elst has pointed out that the relation between the 'Hindu nationalist movement' and the Nazi ideologue was not as smooth as Nicholas Goodrick-Clarke paints it out to be. Elst writes:

> There was a sharp contradiction between her own racist and anti-egalitarian convictions and the reformist and egalitarian programme of the Hindu Mission. To the Hindu Mission, Hinduism was a value in itself; to Savitri Devi, it was but an instrument of her imagined Aryan race. In her years as a preacher, she kept her non-Hindu preoccupations to herself, but in her memoirs (Memories and Reflections of an Aryan Lady), she declared that she conceived of her reconversion mission as an exercise in deception: "From the racist Aryan viewpoint, it was necessary to give the most backward and degenerate aborigines a (false) Hindu consciousness."

Further, Dr Elst points out that according to her, the Hindu Mission's leader, Swami Satyananda, had seen through her insincerity and told her to preach from the Hindu viewpoint and keep her private opinions to herself.[99]

There are many factors which indicate that the Hitler-Vishnu equivalence attributed to Swami Satyananda was more an invention of Ms Portas herself than factual.

Let us consider first if Hitler was actually viewed within Hindutva or Hindu Nationalist circles as a benevolent leader, leave alone a leader worthy of being identified as an avatar of Vishnu. In 1939 M. S. Golwalkar published his work titled *We or Our Nationhood Defined*. In all academic works on Hindutva, a passage from this book gets quoted as proof for Hindutva's love for Nazism. But what goes unnoticed often is that he characterized the 'Race Spirit' of Germany as not benevolent but as 'depredatory', contrasting this with the Hindu 'Race Spirit' which produced only spiritual savants who moved around the world with 'serene majesty'.[100]

Similarly, Savarkar, the President of the Hindu Mahasabha, grouped Nazis along with Fascists and Bolsheviks and wanted Hindus to choose between these forces and those which called themselves democratic—pointing out that both were aggressors. So, he asked Hindus to make their own national interest the independence of India as the criterion for supporting them. He explained:

> Under whatever label their principles are trotted out whether as Bolshevism or Nazism or Fascism or Republicanism or Parliamentarianism their armed domination over other peoples they have conquered or wish to conquer does not

> and cannot saviour of anything else but autocratic tyranny....The sanest policy for us which practical politics demand is to befriend those who are likely to serve our country's interests in spite of any "ism" they follow for themselves and to befriend only so long as it serves our purpose.[101]

At the same time, Savarkar also revealed that he was aware of Islamic-Nazi collaboration, as in the case of an Iranian Shah who was 'hand in glove with Nazis' whom he thought a section of Islamists were looking to as saviour.[102] Even this neutral attitude of Savarkar towards both Nazis and British in terms of practical politics, was not without absolute positions in terms of values. Nirmal Chandra Chatterjee, the vice-President of the Hindu Mahasabha during the war and subsequently the all-India President, stated categorically:

> In the conflict of ideologies, the Hindus have made their position perfectly clear. We hate Nazism and Fascism. We are the enemies of Hitler and Mussolini. We are longing and struggling for our own emancipation, and we want to repel any dictator who would try to reduce sections of humanity to slavery to serve the whims of his own megalomania.

Later, he explained in detail:

> We recognized that Fascism was a supreme menace to what is good and noble in our civilization. It is the subtle scheme of political propaganda to describe, the Hindu as a pro-Fascist. It is a cruel calumny (sic) which has been spread in America and other countries; the Hindu Mahasabha stood for Veer Savarkar's policy of militarization and industrialization.

Interestingly, Swami Satyananda's approach to the caste problems in India had been recorded elsewhere and provides one an opportunity to see if the Hindu nationalist movement was really an upper-caste one that rose in reaction to the assertion of the so-called lower castes.

The Munshiganj Satyagraha, which was the temple entry movement organized by Swami Satyananda for the Scheduled Community of Namashudras of Bengal is a historically important episode. Yet, no study of Hindutva mentions this important role of the 'Hindu Sanghatan' (Unity) movement in the struggle for Dalit rights.[103]

In 1929 Swami Satyananda was approached by the SC community members of Bengal for their right to enter the Kali temple at Munshiganj in Bengal province (now in Bangladesh). The Swami made a public speech demanding an end to the discrimination:

> 'If the depressed classes get the right of free access to all places of public worship and can sit side by side with the high-class Hindus, the caste prejudice will be mitigated to a great degree. I think this is the most elementary right of every member of a religious community. So, I have begun with the assertion of this right by the depressed classes and temple entry is the first step towards its realization.'

Following the adamant stand of upper caste Hindus, on 12 September 1929, the President of the Hindu Mission, Calcutta, wrote to Jamnalal Bajaj, the convener of the Anti-Untouchability Committee of the AICC, informing the latter of the satyagraha being launched. Bajaj wrote that the existing conditions did not warrant starting a satyagraha. However, the satyagraha was launched and at one point, the upper castes abused and threatened Swami Satyananda with violence. He was even attacked with bamboo sticks. The Swami again pointed out, in spite of the attacks and abuses, that this was not a Brahmin vs. non-Brahmin fight, but part of an all-India movement that had the blessings of leaders like Mahatma Gandhi, Madan Mohan Malaviya, Dr B. S. Moonje and N. C. Kelkar. On 16 May, the movement took a new turn with local upper-caste Hindu youths joining the satyagraha. Six Brahmin boys started an indefinite fast in support of Dalit temple entry. The Swami and one of his celibate disciples also joined the hunger strike. The ladies of the households of the six boys joined them.

The next morning, about 200 ladies removed all the barriers and threw open the doors of the temple to all Hindus, irrespective of caste, amidst shouts of *Vande Mataram.* The 261-day-long Satyagraha conducted by the Hindu Mission of Swami Satyananda triumphed without Congress support. It was a complete victory, unlike satyagrahas conducted by the Congress which often ended in compromises and partial victories. Thus, the Hindutva movement, despite the abject indifference to facts shown by the academic researchers of the movement, did contribute immensely to social emancipation.

Dr Balakrishna Shivarama Moonje (1872–1948) is another Hindutvaite leader shown negatively in the academia-media critique of Hindutva. He is often projected as a fascist who admired Mussolini and modelled Hindu Sanghatan youth bodies, particularly the RSS, after fascist youth organizations.

Moonje, Mussolini and Military Education: Hindutva's Fascist Connection?

In 2015, *Frontline,* the Chennai-based Marxist fortnightly of a pro-Chinese publication house, ironically named *The Hindu*, published excerpts from an article by Marzia Casolari on the supposedly Italian fascist connection of the Hindutva movement, particularly during World War II. The article was originally published in 2000 in the *Economic and Political Weekly*. The essence of the thesis is that Moonje was impressed by Mussolini's fascist cadre and that was the inspiration for the RSS. Towards this end, Casolari quotes extensively from Moonje's diary—from the 13 pages that describe the meeting of Moonje with Mussolini. A. G. Noorani, a self-styled 'secular Muslim' but who clearly and cleverly weaves an Islamist historiography with Marxist media support, adds the following observation to Casolari's article:

> The intimate friendship between Moonje and Hedgewar and the former's declared intention to strengthen the RSS and to extend it as a nationwide organisation prove a strict connection between Moonje and the RSS. Moreover, it makes sense to think that the entire circle of militant Hinduism must have been influenced by Moonje's Italian experience.[104]

Dr Moonje was originally an ophthalmologist, who became one of the prominent ideologues of modern Hindutva. As an ophthalmologist, he invented a new method of extracting cataract without removing the capsule. Dr Moonje had carried out research in the field of ophthalmology and discovered a new technique in the cataract operation of removing the shell along with the cataract. Though it is called the Smith Theory, Moonje had practiced it prior to Smith as early as 1903 and had submitted a research paper to the Medical Association of Grant Medical College Bombay long before Dr Smith.[105]

In 1931 when Dr Moonje went to England for the Second Round Table Conference, he visited military training academies throughout Europe. He did not single out Mussolini or fascist Italy for this purpose, as the diary entry clearly states:

> I said I am interested in the military training of boys and have been visiting the Military Schools of **England, France and Germany.** I have now come to Italy for the same purpose, and I am very grateful to say that the Foreign Office and the War Office have made good arrangements for my visiting these schools.[106] (Emphasis not in the original)

So, it was not fascist Italy alone that provided the only inspiration for Dr Moonje. There was nothing ideological about it. While the papers critical of Hindutva which want to establish the 'Italian fascist' connection to Hindutva, highlight his admiration for Italian society—they seldom speak of his observations about other European nations.

By highlighting military training for all youths in European nations, whether it is Italy, England, Germany or France, Moonje had another intention which flew in the face of racist discourse. The racist idea of classifying certain ethnic groups or races as 'martial' and others as 'non-martial', was generally accepted in the European common psyche, and even by the English educated Indians. In Nazi Germany, such a racial taxonomy was taken to its logical, ludicrous and inhuman conclusions. In colonial British India, such a racial taxonomy of dividing society into 'martial' and 'non-martial' races was used to justify British imperialism. For example, Sir Reginald Craddock opposed 'rapid Indianization' as 'futile' and opined that the Indian Army itself would disintegrate without British leadership, as the 'officers from martial races would not follow Congress politicians, and that men in their turn would not follow 'the non-martial intellectual officers'. As against this, Dr Moonje not only rejected the racial division but wanted a pan-Indian army with all regional representation. According to him, a quota system by provinces was required and that the distinction between the martial and non-martial classes perpetuated a mercenary army and propagated communalism.[107] Dr Moonje not only spoke about Italian society but also of France, which is even more relevant here. The magazine Modern Review reports: 'In the course of his inquiries in France, Dr B. S. Moonje found that many French military officers were sons of grocers, bank clerks, etc. and that the parentage of some was unknown'.[108]

In 1931 the Chetwood Committee which submitted 'dissertations' of 'dissent summarising the Indian position on Indianisation', had documented Dr Moonje accusing the British Government as having forgotten that Indians 'wanted to be the architects of their own destiny'. It further noted that he was critical of the policies based on 'martial-race' concepts. He denounced 'the myth of artificial distinction of martial and non-martial races' which introduced 'the poison of communalism in the body politics of India'.[109]

So, Dr Moonje was using the study of military training to civilians in European societies including Italy and France, to reject the theory of racial categories—something that was central to Nazi ideology.

Dr Moonje's idea of military education to all Indians was also shared by Dr Ambedkar. He wanted to create a similar military science establishment in India. He had written about this to G. M. Jadhav of Baroda and wrote to Chitre that a college teaching military science would be doing 'a great national service and also service to Scheduled Castes'.[110] One should remember again that the Moonje-Mussolini meeting was much flaunted in the academic and media criticism of Hindutva in March 1931. At that time, not many Indian leaders knew nor cared much about the real face of fascism.

More importantly, Mussolini supported the Indian claim for dominion status, while Churchill was opposed to it. Almost nine months after Dr Moonje visited Mussolini, another Indian leader visited the fascist dictator. Unlike Moonje, this leader had well-informed international friends who could warn him about the real nature of fascism. Yet, this leader decided against such strong advice and still visited Mussolini. When Romain Rolland tried to persuade Gandhi not to visit fascist Italy, the Mahatma had opined 'that the Europeans should suspend judgment on Mussolini's 'reforms' until an impartial study could be carried out'. After visiting the fascist state, Gandhi recommended every Indian visiting Europe to make it a point to go to Italy and meet Mussolini. Ironically, another person he recommended was anti-fascist pro-Vedantist Romain Rolland.[111]

Women Empowerment

For anyone studying women's empowerment in a society that is in transition from pre-modernity to modernity, one of the vital indicators would be the marriage age of girls. It is obvious that the legal prohibition of marrying off girl children in the name of custom and tradition plays an important role in women achieving education and empowerment. Social reformers in India fought a very tough battle for this. Among the important pioneers who paved the way for stopping child marriage was Hari Singh Gour, who, through his repeated appeals to recognize the standards of modern clinical psychology, was able to get the law passed that raised the age of consent in marriage for girl children from 12 to 14 years. This war for raising the marriage age of women and the prohibition of child marriage was carried on further by Harbilas Sarda. Many great men like Dr Ambedkar stood with Sarda shoulder to shoulder. Due to their efforts, the Child Marriage Restraint Act, also known as the Sarda Act, was passed on 1 October 1929. Setting the minimum age for marriage for girls at 14 and boys at 18 years, it was a crowning glory for the social reform movement in India.

While the abolition of sati was a great victory for social reform, it was actually dealing with an essentially localized and colonially exaggerated phenomenon. But the Sarda Act had and still has strong implications for the nation as a whole, and made women participate in large numbers in the coming Gandhian movement. Women's empowerment became possible, thanks to the Sarda Act. The implication of these acts for the participation of large numbers of women in the struggle for Indian Independence is brought out by Dr Muthulakshmi Reddy, medical practitioner, social reformer and one of the earliest woman legislators in India:

> Sir Hari Singh Gour was responsible for raising the age of consent for girls.... Sir Harbilas Sarda worked for the act which restrains child marriages. So, we have much for which we must thank our men. It is not strange that now, when they want political freedom, we women are willing to stand beside them in their effort to attain it.[112]

Gour was the member of the Legal Advisory Committee of the Hindu Mahasabha, while Sarda was one of the strongest proponents of pan-Hindutva. In his book titled *Hindu Superiority: An Attempt to Determine the Position of the Hindu Race in the Scale of Nations* (Rajputana Printing Works, Ajmer, 1906), Sarda envisaged a common Indic alliance for Buddhism and the Vedic religion, and groups all religions of Indic origin together. Such a broad categorization of Hindu cultural unity, based on Hindu-Buddhist-Jain-Sikh unity rather than the scriptural authority of the Vedas, is the hallmark of the thoughts of both Veer Savarkar and Dr Ambedkar. One should remember that Sarda also came from the Arya Samaj stream which was not well-disposed towards Buddhism. Yet Sarda was able to enlarge the definition of 'Hindu' by seeing Buddhism as not differing 'materially from the Vedic religion in its scientific aspects'—a classic instance of *samanvaya* (equanimity) in action. The fight against child marriage and the triumph in increasing the legal marriage age of women were definitely the greatest achievements on the path towards gender equality and were ideologically, integral parts of the larger social emancipation movement created by the Arya Samaj.

As seen earlier in 1925, Swami Shraddhanand in the Bombay provincial Hindu Mahasabha session held under Lala Lajpat Rai wanted a home for helpless women and children. In 1926 he was assassinated by Rashid, an Islamist. M. R. Jayakar decided to make the women's house a reality. Dr Neela Dabir had elaborately studied this Ashram for her thesis which was later published as a book.[113] The Hindu Women's Rescue Home Society was registered on 22 December 1927 under Act XXI of 1860 with Jayakar as its founder-president. Getting even a rental accommodation for the Mahila Ashram was difficult. When a rental building was found and the Ashram was started with four women and four children, the locals started opposing it. When they found a place near Wadala Vitthal Mandir and started negotiating with Municipal authorities, the local Hindus and Parsees residents opposed it. Finally, they found a rather isolated place and started the Ashram. While initially they wanted Lala Lajpat Rai to inaugurate the home, Jayakar changed his mind and avoided any public function. So, in his letter dated 23 March 1928 to Dr Navare, he wrote:

> I do not believe in any showy efforts and would prefer that we justified ourselves by our quiet work before obtruding on public attention. At last when the Ashram started functioning it was in March 1929 and the inaugural function happened on 29 July 1929.

While important Hindu Sanghatanists of Bombay, Dr Navare and Dr Udgaonkar became honourable secretaries, generally most were reluctant to become members of the committee. All the members of the committee were from the Hindu Mahasabha, including V. D. Savarkar and Yashodabai Bhatt. One remarkable aspect of the Ashram was that it served as a shelter for women with children born out of wedlock, along with their children. In fact, during the first decade of the Ashram (1927–1936), 56 per cent of the women admitted with pregnancy out of wedlock were widows. While, with the passing of years, the proportion of widows decreased in the category of women with pregnancy out of wedlock, the proportion of unmarried women increased. Even married women with pregnancy out of wedlock were admitted to the Ashram, though their percentage was small. Definitely speaking, the Ashram had operated radically for the period in which it was established.

Originally, the Ashram was run by the Hindu Women's Rescue Home Society. After Independence, it was renamed the Hindu Women's Welfare Society. The original document specified Hindu women and their children as beneficiaries and in 1955, the word 'Hindu' was changed into 'India'. The objective originally was 'to impart to such women as part of their education, moral and religious instructions of the Hindu faith' and here too, the word 'Hindu' was dropped and so now it read: 'To provide for such women and children as a part of the assistance, suitable academic, vocational and moral education.' This de-Hinduization of an institution meant for Hindu women had its effect. Dr Dabir notes:

> During the period between 1966 and 1984, the Ashram promoted the placement of its infants and children in intercountry adoption regardless of the fact that such adoptions often involved the conversion of the babies to other religions generally Christianity. One wonders whether the influence of Hindu Mahasabha and other Hindu organisations on the policies of the Ashram declined around this period.[114]

But this also suggests another ominous dimension. In 1986, it was revealed that the Catholic church in Kerala had networks that indulged in what was called 'nun running'. *India Today* reported:

> Fr. Cyriac Puthenpurakal of Ettumanoor had earned notoriety for 'exporting' about

> 5,000 Christian girls from Kerala to the convents in Europe. The women were lured with jobs and whisked away to nunneries where they were initiated as nuns.... The Catholic Church seems immune to his covert activities and the church authorities refuse to talk about him.[115]

However, it was not an isolated case. Earlier in the 1970s, a huge network had been discovered and reported in the Western press. The same Fr. Cyriac was involved then also. On 23 August 1970, *The New York Times (NYT)* reported the suspension by Vatican of 'a system that enabled Roman Catholic convents to pay high fees to bring poor and often unqualified peasant girls from the Indian state of Kerala to under staffed institutions in Europe'. From a 'trustworthy Vatican source...who asked to remain anonymous' informed the *NYT*, that 'the Rev Cyriac Puthenpurakal, a Keralan priest, was the main but not the exclusive supplier of the Indian novices'.[116]

That was in 1970. Under international adverse media light, the Catholic church denied any wrongdoing and outwardly announced the suspension of operations. But that the racket actually continued unabated at least for the next 16 years came out when similar operations surfaced in 1986. Equally important was the fact that Christian centres often catalysed the adoption of children from the orphanages to countries like the United States which involved the conversion of the children. Taking all these together with the discovery by Dr Dabir that after the de-Hinduization of the institution almost forcibly by the state government, 'the Ashram promoted the placement of its infants and children in intercountry adoption' which involve 'the conversion of the babies to other religions generally Christianity', shows how a Hindutva institution for women's emancipation, instead of allowing it to evolve and adapt itself to the changing scenarios and milieu, was forcefully made to change its very purpose and then get involved in processes which the founders of the institution wanted to halt.

Coming back to the work of the pre-1947 Hindu Mahasabha on women's empowerment, the Hindu Mahasabha decided to start Vidhwa Ashram and Vidhwa Viwah Samsthah (Widows Remarriage Association) in Berar. Apart from this, they also worked against the taboos of Hindu families in taking back the women abducted by Muslims during riots, whom the Sabha often rescued through courts. During the great flood of 1934 in Assam, in the flood-affected districts, the Hindu Sabha Relief Committee took special care for women in its relief operations. The Sabha took 'special care of 200 widows, rescued 7 helpless girls from starvation and shame'. Even during the floods, the abduction of women was reported. The Sabha secured the release of 233 girls, 58 adult females and 34 children, in most of the cases through courts, and then had to persuade the families to get the abducted girls resettled in their families. The relief committee also arranged the marriage of 44 girls. Though most marriages were within their own castes, marriages across castes were also conducted by the Sabha. The Sanghatanists also took care of nine babies between the ages of 2 to 10 months, of which they could arrange families for seven children. Mahasabha worked for abducted and rescued Hindu women to be given a respectable position in society.[117]

Hindu Sanghatanist and Arya Samaj leader Bhagat Phool Singh ji of Haryana, about whom we have already read, had contributed a lot for women empowerment in the state.[118] Started in the forest near Khanpur village as a *pathshala* in 1928, it was named Kanya Gurukul in 1936. The preparation of the syllabus and teaching methods for a Kanya Gurukul had, however, started as early as 1919 by an eminent educationist Acharya Ramdev to whom the All-India Arya Pratinidhi Sabha had entrusted the responsibility. A main consideration was 'to establish equality between the male and the female' which was deemed 'possible only through female education'. Bhagatji had to face a lot of hurdles, from the resistance of local population to financial obstacles. Sometimes the hostels were even hard-pressed for food grains. The education was mostly common for boys and girls, though in the case of science, there were differences. He wanted the initial batches of the Kanya Gurukul to dedicate themselves to the cause of female education through the Gurukul. He wanted his own children to set an example. So, he compelled his elder daughter Subhashini to dedicate herself to the Kanya Gurukul. But she was then working as a teacher in a school in Jind. To persuade her, he even started a fast. However, it was his assassination that made Subhashini resign her job and dedicate herself to the Kanya Gurukul. By 1947, 150 girls were studying in the Gurukul.

An important aspect of this Sanghatan's female education initiative was that the Kanya Gurukul became a strong movement in Haryana, improving literacy among women. In 1945 a Kanya Gurukul was started by Mansa Ji Tyagi in Panchgaon village of Dadri district, which ran till 1955. It was then restarted in 1978. Acharyakul Arsh Kanya Gurukul at Lovakalan (Jhajjar) was established in 1965 by Swami Manacharya Saraswati. The girl students can get an 'Acharya' degree in Sanskrit (affiliated to Sampuranand Sanskriti Vishvavidyalaya of Varanasi). Of the 234 students studying here right now, 70 per cent are from a rural background, 60 per cent are from uneducated families and 90 per cent are from the middle and lower classes. Arya Kanya Gurukul with Sanskrit Vidyalaya at Padha village in Karnal was established in 1973 by Dr Ganesh Das Aneja. Currently, it is supporting 251 students. Kanya Gurukul Mahavidyalaya of Kharkhoda (Sonipat) was started by Bhagat Daryav Singh in 1974. He was a *pauranik* turned Gandhian turned Arya

Samajist. He also took active interest in the cow protection movement. He opened the Gurukul on 15 August 1974. These are all just a few examples of how Bhagatji's Kanya Gurukul had become a movement in female education in a socially conservative state like Haryana. The hostels of Kanya Gurukuls have strict rules. These Gurukuls make the girls perform all the Vedic rituals including fire sacrifices which, in traditional Hinduism, are performed only by male Brahmins. There are no caste distinctions in these Gurukuls. Most of the girls are from middle and lower classes and rural areas, 'because here education is cheaper and better' and 'also from security point of view villagers prefer to send their ward to the Hostels'.

Social Views and Values of a South Indian Hindu-Sanghatan Magazine in the 1940s

Hindu Sanghatan had played an important role in social emancipation movements of South India and their role has received only little attention. The social justice agenda had already been hijacked by Dravidianists who prescribed to the Aryan-Dravidian race theory and through that lens, called themselves non-Hindus. At the same time, on the other end was the orthodoxy which resisted temple entry movement in a big way and was not uncomfortable with inhuman social evils like untouchability. Hindu Sanghatanists, particularly in what is today Tamil Nadu (then Madras Presidency as well as South Travancore), had to work against the force while they also had to fight the proselytizing forces which had the tactical support of the colonial empire.

All these tensions can be perceived in a Tamil magazine that came from the very end of the Indian mainland, what is today called Kanyakumari district. The magazine was named *Thondan*, meaning 'volunteer'. In the Tamil context, it meant one who provides services to people voluntarily. The name of the founder-editor was Arumuga Navalar, not to be confused with Arumuga Navalar of Eezham. Though in a way, it was a magazine published from a remote corner of India, the contributors to the magazine were the who's who of the Tamil intellectual world of that period. The list of the names of those who had wished well for the magazine, was the cream of Tamil society of the time—the famous poet Kavimani Desigavinayagam Pillai, the eminent trade unionist Thiru V. Kalyanasundaranar, and scholar of varied domains, C. P. Ramaswami Iyer, Marai Thirunavukkarasu, the son of Maraimalai Adigal, the originator of the pure Tamil movement, Shuddhananda Bharati, Ki Va Jagannathan, Namakkal poet Venkatarama Ramalingam Pillai, a Gandhian freedom fighter, and so on. The messages sent went beyond the customary ones. For example, poet and author Shuddhananda Bharati (1897–1990) in his lyrical message, defines Hindu as one who removes the misery of others and the Hindu Dharma as the ocean of bliss. He wished the magazine would make Hindu Dharma flourish all over the world. The Namakkal poet Ramalingam Pillai (1888–1972), the famous freedom fighter, wished the magazine to revive the valorous tradition of Tamil Nadu and remove the 'mental sickness of so-called atheists'.

In the magazine, a debate was initiated as to whether the revenue from Hindu temples could be used for public education. The editor of the magazine *Navalar* and his colleague Ramanathan Chettiar, wrote:

> In the name of public schools, public hospitals and public student hostels, other religions are proselytizing Hindus in large numbers. Despite knowing the intention of proselytizers, the government which is supposed to take a neutral stand, is giving them financial assistance from the exchequer. From the surplus revenue of Hindu temples, we too can run public educational institutions and nurture Hindu Dharma. Towards this end we need a Hindu reformist union under the government supervision to run such schools. Government should in a non-partial way provide the Hindu schools the same financial assistance it is offering to non-Hindu schools. Whatever services the other religions are providing, Hindus are more qualified to provide such services. Without doing this if the government continues its partiality while using the revenue from Hindu temples simply for public education, it will lead to the gradual destruction of Hinduism.

In the same magazine, another article written by Alladi Krishnaswamy Iyer, who would later become one of the members of the Constituent Assembly of free India, argued that the revenue from Hindu temples should not be used by the government for public education. The magazine has a separate column titled 'Appreciations'. The temple entry proclamations made by Travancore, Ettaiyapuram, Malabar, and Kochi administrations are appreciated prominently.

On 12 October 1946, the Panchayat board of Thiruchendur (a famous Murugan pilgrimage centre), under Sri Kanagasabapathy Pillai passed a resolution to open the Thiruchendur Subramanya Swamy temple for all Hindus. The 'king' of Sivagangai made a proclamation for temple entry at all famous temples, namely Thirukoshtiyur-Kallaiyar temple, as well as temples in Manamadurai province. All these proclamations are highlighted and appreciated. The magazine was clearly at the forefront of mobilizing public opinion and the views of all sections of Hindu society in favour of temple entry. The magazine had published a statement made by Malaviya on the Noakhali riots. Malaviya had cautioned Hindu society against the complacency of feeling that they were the majority. 'Such a feeling could be the death knell of Hindu society,' he had warned. The magazine also published this announcement by Mukerjee in the background of the Noakhali massacre and the great Calcutta killings:

> Today the very survival of Hindus in this nation is under threat. There is a need today to protect the welfare of Hindus, their rights and the self-respect of Hindu women. We need an organization of well-trained fearless Hindu youths for this purpose—a national army of Hindustan.

The second issue of the magazine carries an important opinion editorial. It is titled 'We are all Hindus!' This article should be considered an important document in the history of Hindutva in Tamil Nadu. Here is an excerpt:

> The sufferings and problems heaped on us Hindus come not only from fanatics of other religions, but also from our own people. We know this from history. It was Jaichand whose tracery (sic) led to Islamist invasion....Not only then, even now same is the case. If we are to live, we need to remove all the discrimination we have among us in the name of castes. In this regard it is not only untouchability but the feeling of separate castes, should also go. There is a tendency among a group of political leaders to blame only one community for the caste discrimination. How can such leaders create any unity in the society? These leaders also spew venom on Hindu religion and temples because of their hatred for one community. This only shows that these leaders suffer from inferiority complex and cowardice who lack self-confidence. Such people are claiming that they are Dravidians and not Hindus, for they have nothing but suicidal hatred towards Hinduism. Actually they are not interested in removing the discrimination but only interested in destroying Hinduism.... Such people also go and talk in the Muslim League platforms....Why not these people actually fight against orthodoxy and work for reforms within Hinduism? That is what real reform movements in this nation do. Organizations like Saiva Siddhanta Maha Samajam, Saiva Siddhanta Publishing house, Arya Samajam, Vaishnava Samajam, Sri Ramakrishna Mission are doing such constructive work. Leaders like Mahatma Gandhi, Malaviya, Maraimalai Adigal, Sachidanandam Pillai, Venkitaswamy Naidu, Thiru Vi Ka—are all toiling for the same. And when we say orthodoxy do not think it means a particular community. All communities have orthodoxies and reformists. But the real paradox is that the Dravidianists because of defeatist mentality they suffer from had become real obscurantists and are supporting Muslim League. They oppose the nationalist parties and support the British. Let these Jaichands of today leave Hinduism and become Muslims. We care not for them. But we who toil to reform our society and raise our civilization, we say with pride that we are Hindus!

This forceful proclamation against the Dravidianists of the day was made by Marai Thirunavukarasu, the son of Maraimalai Adigal, the progenitor of the chaste Tamil movement. One of the foremost Hindutva voices against Dravidian racism was raised by the scholar son of Adigal!

The next issue of the magazine is quite stormy. It took the orthodoxy opposing the temple entry movement head on. The editorial likened those sections of orthodoxy opposing temple entry to the old lady who thinks that by brandishing her broom she could stop the ocean waves. Navalar further wrote that those who considered themselves authorities of dharma should come forward and voluntarily proclaim their support for temple entry without waiting for a legislation to impose it. A suggestion was also made in the magazine to give relief and financial assistance to Noakhali riot victims from the Tirupati temple funds. *Thondan* also published an article by Babu Jagjivan Ram titled 'Ever Renewing Eternal Hinduism'. Ram brought out both the agony of Scheduled Communities and their self-respect as Hindus:

> We Harijans do not want to leave it to the so-called caste Hindus to decide whether we are Hindus or not. We have already taken a decision. We are Hindus and we are determined to remain as Hindus. I do not even like it that we are agitating for temple entry. I have great faith and love for the Hindu Gods, and it pains me to think that Harijan entering the temples can pollute the Deities. Our Gods are not that weak. All I want to ask our orthodox friends is this: Has Hinduism come to such a low position that it does not allow its own followers inside the temple? You do not have to take the decision for the welfare of Harijans. You have to take a decision for the welfare of Hindu religion – for the complete goodness of the entire Hindu society. If we stand by temple entry, then we show to the world that we are a religion that has vitality to renew itself. Otherwise, we will be considered a dead religion. By standing by temple entry, we can frustrate the British who are using every division in our society to further their rule.

Women too wrote in *Thondan* and very bold articles for their time appeared in that magazine. For example, one Rama Seethabhai from the port town of Tuticorin wrote an article on the 'Love of Gothai' (Aandal). The boldness is striking even for today:

> Music arises from the organs of inner cognition. When these organs attach themselves to an object and become harmonized to that object, music emerges. He came with shining jewels on His blue coloured body. And in His lips, He placed the conch shell and sounded His victory. And for Aandal at that very moment arrows of love come in torrents and make her feel agonized. That very moment she compares

> with the conch. How lucky that conch is! Will you not tell me dear conch! How great and sweet is the ambrosia from His lips!

Even as early as 1947, a Hindu Sanghatanist magazine discussed the so-called body-based poetry of Aandal—without compromising on both its sensual dimension and spiritual core—and a woman wrote it!

A series on Indian science mentioned Satyendra Nath Bose, clearly keeping itself updated with the latest science developments. There was also the fallacy about ancient technology, but then, given the textual availability of the period, it could be understood and excused in hindsight. This pre-Independence magazine even assured the readers that when India would become independent, leaders like Jawaharlal Nehru would assure that India achieve her glory in science once again.

February 1947 saw in Madras a Hindu conference inaugurated by Govardhan Sankaracharya. The head of the conference was Sri V. V. Srinivasa Iyengar. The conference passed a resolution demanding the cessation of temple entry. The conference demands that at least four temples—Bhadrachalam Rama temple, Tirupati Venkatachala temple, Kanchi Varadaraja temple, and Triplicane Parthasarathy temple should be exempted from temple entry. Thondan harshly criticized this stand: 'Are these four temples going to be the Pakistan of orthodoxy?' it taunted.

There was also activism at ground zero. *Thondan* reported in April 1947 about proselytization attempts by evangelists of the Scheduled Caste community families near Thirukazhukundram. *Thondan* used the term '*aadhi Hindu*' (aboriginal Hindu) instead of *Harijan*. A primary school teacher of the area who was also an evangelist, had told families there that if they converted to Christianity, he would be able to get for them land from the British government and ₹ 200 per person. As a first step to prove their conversion, he had asked the families to demolish the Gangai Amman Goddess temple and build a church there. However, a youth, one Gothandaraman, told Marai Thirunavukkarasu about this. So, the latter went there and held talks with the families which were planning to convert. They told him about the problems they faced at the hands of certain so-called caste Hindus. After the talks with all sections of society, they tore the agreement they had made with the evangelist. Further, they made it clear that they would live their lives as Hindus. A committee consisting of Kothandaraman and some eminent citizens was made to take care of the problems of the people in the area.

The old pages of the magazine, now fast getting discoloured, reveal that there was even a programme to train Tamil Hindu youths as *pracharaks* for dharma. There is a question-answer section and there are cartoon-like illustrations. *Thondan* published a cartoon supporting temple entry, depicting the gods and acharyas blessing temple entry from the sky, while a small group of orthodox people are opposing it. Unfortunately, that page is too damaged to be scanned. Another cartoon depicted the contrast of a government temple board affluent with revenue, while temples are in a dilapidated condition—that was in 1947 and conditions of the temples today under Hindu Religious and Charities Endowment Board (HR & CE) of the government have only deteriorated more.

Another cartoon shows Hinduism as a sleeping saint and *Thondan* as a boy volunteer awakening him, blessed by gods and acharyas. This cartoon is titled *Thirupalliyezhuchi* or *Suprabatham*. On the whole, the magazine is another testimony to the fact that Hindu Sanghatan movement was not limited to North India alone and that it extended to South India as well, particularly South Travancore, where the society faced the onslaught of proselytization and social stagnation. In the case of social stagnation, the stand taken by the South Indian Sangthanists was clearly pro-reform.

Swami Dayananda Saraswati and his 1861 letter to Pandit Gauri Shankar to teach Vedas to Kayasthas and the artisans as all castes have equal right to the Vedas

Barrister Mukund Ramrao Jayakar (1873–1959), the first Vice-Chancellor of the University of Poona . He was a strong social reformer and a staunch Hindu Sanghatanist

Har Bilas Sarda (1867–1955), Hindu Sanghatanist and advocate of women's rights. He fought against child marriages and brought the legislation to ban it

Swami Shraddhanand—the greatest champion of the oppressed, according to Dr Ambedkar

'தொண்டன்'
இந்துமத சீர்திருத்த
மாத வெளியீடு.
விய கார்த்திகை முதல்
வெளிவருவது.

தற்கால நிலையில் ஒவ்வொரு இந்துவும் புத்துயிர் பெற்று இந்து மதத்திற் குழைக்கவேண்டுமென்பது பேரறிஞர் கண்ட முடிபு. அவ்வாறுழைக்க இந்து உலகைத் தட்டியுணர்த்த இதோ 'தொண்டன்' வெளிவந்திருக்கிறான். வாங்கிப் படித்து இந்து மதத்திற் குழைக்க ஒவ்வொரு இந்து ஆண், பெண் மக்களையும் ஆர்வத்தோடு வேண்டிக் கொள்கிறோம்.

ஆசிரியர்:
கெ. ஆறுமுக நாவலர்,
நாகர்கோவில்.

சந்தா.

ஆயுட் சந்தா	ரூ.	100-0-0
வருடத்திற்கு	ரூ.	5-0-0
6 மாதத்திற்கு	ரூ.	3-0-0
தனிப்பிரதி	ரூ.	0-8-0

விளம்பரம்.

அட்டை வெளிப்புறம்	ரூ.	100
,, உட்புறம்	ரூ.	75
முழுப்பக்கத்திற்கு	ரூ.	60
½ பக்கத்திற்கு	ரூ.	30
¼ பக்கத்திற்கு	ரூ	15

ஏஜெண்டுகள் இல்லாத இடங்கட்கு ஏஜெண்டுகள் தேவை
விளம்பரங்கள் தேவை.
சந்தா சேர்ப்பவர்க்கு 10% கமிஷன்.
விளம்பரம் சேர்ப்பவர்க்கு 25% கமிஷன்.
ஏஜெண்டுகளுக்கு 18¾% கமிஷன்.
100 பிரதிகட்கு மேல் விற்பனை செய்பவர்க்கு 25%

தொண்டன் காரியாலயம், நாகர்கோவில்.

Edited, Printed & Published by K. Arumuga Navalar at the M. S. M. Press, Nagercoil,

Thondan magazine was run by Arumuga Navalar of present day Kanyakumari district. His Hindutva magazine strongly advocated temple entry for Scheduled Communities and condemned the orthodoxy

Babu Jag Jjivan Ram (1908-1986) (right) was supported by Pandit Madan Mohan Malaviya in his fight against untouchability and orthodoxy. Similarly later RSS leader and Chairperson of SC & ST National Commission Suraj Bhan (1928-2006) (left) was supported by VHP leader Ashok Singhal (1926-2015) in his demand that passages of social degradation in Smritis be denounced by Hindu religious leaders

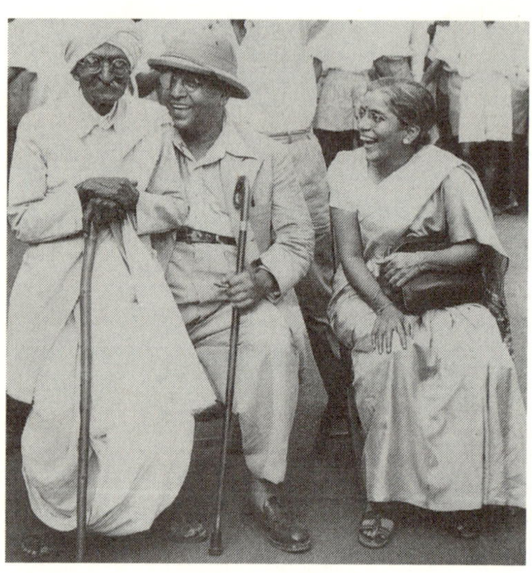

Sitaram Keshav Bole(1869-1961) started a new chapter in India's social revolution with his resolution in 1923 declaring the rights of SC and ST to use all public spaces equally. Here he is seen sharing a lighter moment with Dr. Ambedkar. Rao Bahadur S.K.Bole was a Hindutvaite and wanted the saffron flag to be India's National flag

5

Hindu Sanghatanists before the Sangh: Lives, Controversies, Values and Visions

A look into the worldviews, contributions and controversies related to the Hindu Sanghatanist leaders prior to the formation of the Rashtriya Swayamsevak Sangh (RSS) reveals how the *Hindutva* worldview of Sangh today has been shaped through the struggle against colonialism and social stagnation. In this chapter, we look into the lives and worldviews of four Hindu Sanghatanist leaders, namely Vinayak Damodar Savarkar, Lala Lajpat Rai, Lala Hardayal and Bhai Parmanand, whose contributions have shaped the Hindutva worldview of today's RSS. It also shows the historical roots that lead up to the space for the presence of Hindutva's own left wing within the Hindutva universe which makes it difficult to classify Hindutva as 'right-wing' proper.

Vinayak Damodar Savarkar (1883–1966): The Person and his Mission beyond the Clemency Petitions

Indian critics of Hindutva in the media and academia have a strange ritual. Every year, on the birth anniversary of Vinayak Damodar Savarkar, columnists, politicians and editors dig up the clemency petitions written by him. Their line is that Savarkar capitulated to the British and hence cannot be considered as brave or 'Veer'. Though this routine propaganda about the clemency petitions of Savarkar has been exposed many times equally by the admirers of Savarkar, it needs to be called out every year after the Vajpayee government decided to honour Savarkar with renaming an airport in the Andaman Islands where Savarkar was jailed mostly in subhuman conditions. When in 2004 the Vajpayee-led National Democratic Alliance (NDA) suffered reverses in the elections, Mani Shankar Aiyar, a self-styled 'secular fundamentalist' and Petroleum Minister in the UPA government, ordered that a plaque with a poem penned by Savarkar be removed from the Cellular Jail memorial in Andaman and Nicobar Islands. Later, the then Parliamentary Affairs Minister Ghulam Nabi Azad reiterated that the UPA government had decided not to restore the original plaque containing the quotation of Savarkar.[1] Though Indira Gandhi had praised Savarkar calling him 'a by-word for daring and patriotism'[2], her grandson and present Indian National Congress (INC) supremo and dynast, Rahul Gandhi had repeatedly called Savarkar a coward. In November 2018, Rahul had said that Savarkar had pleaded to the British to secure his freedom after he was sent to the Cellular Jail in the Andamans in 1911. Then again in 2019 at a New Delhi rally, he called Savarkar '*a coward*'.[3]

Savarkar in Andamans

Savarkar was awarded double life imprisonment—one on 24 December 1910 and the next on 31 January 1911. He entered the Cellular Jail in Andamans on 4 July 1911 with a badge marked 'D' for dangerous. There he was specially targeted and subjected to cruelties. Every time there was a disturbance, Savarkar was punished. It was clear that the British government did not want him to leave the prison alive. Yet Savarkar endured all that. But he never believed in rotting in the cell either, while he could do valuable work for the freedom struggle by getting himself free.

The critics of Savarkar chose to be economical with truth. A case in point is an article in the pro-Chinese propaganda magazine *Frontline*, written by one Ra. Ravishankar who was then 'a doctoral student at the University of Illinois at Urbana-Champaign, United States'. The 'doctoral student' confidently claims that Savarkar, 'in his petition pleaded only for himself', with respect to his 1913 clemency petition. To prove this, the writer quotes from the 1913 clemency petition thus:

> In a letter dated November 14, 1913, Savarkar said: "...if the government in their manifold beneficence and mercy release me, I for one cannot but be the staunchest advocate of constitutional progress and loyalty to the English government which is the foremost condition of that progress... Moreover, my conversion to the constitutional line would bring back all those misled young men in India and abroad who were once looking up to me as their guide....The Mighty alone can afford to be merciful and therefore where else can the prodigal son return but to the parental doors of the government?"[4]

But what the writer strategically leaves out falsifies the claim that Savarkar was 'pleading only for himself' in his petition. Here is the actual passage with the specific sentence that was removed by the essayist of *Frontline*:

> if the government in their manifold beneficence and mercy release me, I for one cannot but be the staunchest advocate of constitutional progress and loyalty to the English government which is the foremost condition of that progress. As long as ***we*** are in jails there cannot be real happiness and joy in ***hundreds of thousands of homes*** of His Majesty's loyal subjects in India, for blood is thicker than water: but if ***we be released*** the people will instinctly (sic) raise a shout of joy and gratitude to the Government, who knows how to forgive and correct, more than how to chastise and avenge.[5] (Emphasis added, not in the original)

Here Savarkar clearly speaks for the release of all political convicts. The writer, by removing this crucial portion from the petition, simply paints Savarkar as selfish by means which cannot be considered ethical even by the academic standards of the West. But what clearly counteracts the claim of Savarkar being broken by the Cellular Jail is the next petition he sent in 1914. Despite having faced one of the worst inhuman treatments in the hands of the authorities including six months of solitary confinement, canning and work in the oil mill, he was able to write after three years of suffering that his name could be omitted from amnesty and all other political prisoners should be freed.

This clemency petition written from jail on 3 October 1914 and dated by authorities as 5 November 1914—almost three years into imprisonment—makes for a very important read.[6] This is because an analysis of this letter reveals a veritable map into the way his mind worked. In the first paragraph, he speaks about the First World War providing an opportunity for Indian youths to get arms practice—a theme he would always stress and stress again strongly during the Second World War:

> Ever since this world-shaking war that is now being fought in Europe broke out, nothing has sent such a thrill of hope and enthusiasm in the heart of every true Indian patriot as the fact that Indians including the youth of India have been allowed to wear arms of fight against the common foe in defence of this country and the Empire. A thing which one has the right to protect is a thing in which one feels a sense of ownership; and fighting side by side with the other citizens of the Empire, the rising generations of India is sure to feel a sense of equality and therefore of a sincere loyalty to the same.

In the next part, he speaks of a human commonwealth and seeks to stress on the equality of all races and peoples in such a universal state. He hints that the British need to make their Empire such a State, but there is a conditional clause:

> Believing that the ideal of all political science and practice is or ought to be one Universal State; that therefore humanity is higher patriotism; and therefore any empire that succeeds in welding a number of conflicting races and nations in one harmonious whole without letting the growth of any one be staunched by the overshadowing domination of another, is a distinct step to the realization of the Ideal; I rejoice to see the volunteering movement succeed and felt confident in the ultimate triumph of the far sighted and truly Imperial policy of conciliation and confidence inaugurated by Lord Hardinge's administration. If the Government will but continue it, the manhood of the nation be allowed to share the glories and responsibilities of the empire with perfect equality with other citizens of it, then Indian patriots of all shades and opinions can conscientiously feel that burning sense of loyalty that one feels for one's motherland....I also beg to submit that nothing can contribute so much to the widening and deepening of the sentiment of loyalty as a general release of all those prisoners who had been convicted for committing political offences in India....and moreover when the Royal road of Constitutional success is thrown so wide open as Lord Hardinge has done, who is so depraved and fanatical as to hang to the thorny paths of blood and crime?

One can note here that Savarkar makes it a condition that the Government should follow the policies of Viceroy Lord Hardinge. He clearly wants the British Empire to identify its own stand with that of Lord Hardinge. And what was that 'Royal road of Constitutional success thrown so wide open' by Hardinge and what was the 'Imperial policy of conciliation and confidence inaugurated' by him? The answer comes from none other than Mahatma Gandhi who wrote the following about Hardinge:

> It was then (December 1913) that Lord Hardinge in Madras made his famous speech which created a stir in South Africa as well as in England. The Viceroy may not publicly criticize other members of the Union Government, but he also wholeheartedly defended the action of the satyagrahis and supported their civil disobedience of unjust and invidious legislation.[7]

Savarkar, after suggesting to the British to make the liberal policy of Lord Hardinge as that of their own, makes a veiled threat:

> Above all it is but a frank truth that there cannot be a real and wholehearted sympathy felt in a thousand homes in India—however they may hate the Germans--to that power which had kept a husband or a son or a father or a friend rotting in the jail; for blood is thicker than water.

And in the end, he makes a plea:

> If the Government suspects that my real intention in writing all this is only to secure my own release, then I beg to submit let me not be released at all, with my exception, let all the rest be released. Let the volunteer movement go on and I will rejoin in that as if myself was allowed to play an active part.

There is a pattern in all his petitions. He states repeatedly that he had relinquished all his 'revolutionary activities' and he also repeatedly spoke of returning to the Constitutional path. In his last petition, he also spoke about the danger of India being invaded by Turkish-Afghan-German axis. In his next petition dated 5 October 1917, Savarkar again requests the government that his name could be left out and other prisoners be released:

> If the Government thinks that it is only to effect my own release that I pen this; or if my name constitutes the chief obstacle in the granting of such an amnesty; then let the Government omit my name in their amnesty and release all the rest; that would give me as great a satisfaction as my own release would do.

This repeated request to keep him under arrest while releasing all the other political prisoners while putting moral pressure on the British would also definitely evoke the suspicions of the authorities as to Savarkar being still in sympathy with the revolutionaries and could lead to the rejection of the petitions. None should be knowing this better than Savarkar himself and yet he *chose* to put these lines in the petitions.

Dhananjay Keer, the official biographer of both Veer Savarkar and Dr B. R. Ambedkar, points out that 'during the war period Savarkar made vigorous attempts to effect his release'. Having studied the petitions of Savarkar to the government, Keer says that the petitions were indirect pressures on the British to run a responsible government in India. However, 'the authorities knew his intentions and were not at all willing to do so.' What Keer suggests is reinforced by the observation of the British authorities who saw no change of heart in the 'clemency' petitions of Savarkar. Reginald Craddock, a home member of the Governor General's Council, was the one to whom Savarkar presented his petition. Craddock saw that the petition of Savarkar was 'one for mercy. He cannot be said to express any regret or repentance'. As Craddock explains, Savarkar justified his action by saying that his sending of 20 Browning pistols to Nasik was not for murder 'but in furtherance of a revolutionary movement'. Craddock makes an astonishingly prophetic note in which he recorded that 'the degree to which Savarkar was dangerous or not depended quite as much upon circumstance outside as upon his own conduct in prison, and that no one could say what those circumstances would be 10, 15 or 20 years hence'.

Thus, the question that needs to be asked is, what did Savarkar do after he came out of the Andamans prison? Did he collaborate with the British or did he contribute to the freedom movement? Savarkar was released with harsh warnings from the British that he could, at any time, be jailed again and that his Andamans exile could be restarted. With this threat eternally hanging over his head like the sword of Damocles, he had to be careful, and careful he was. Nevertheless, he penned books under pseudonyms which became an inspiration for young revolutionaries.

Yet another criticism made against Savarkar is that he wrote a eulogizing account of himself under the nom de plume 'Chitragupta'—the accountant who keeps the Karma details of Yama, the divine in-charge of death in Hindu Puranas.

If it was indeed he who penned down the biographical book, it stands justified in hindsight. Savarkar the historian had seen how the memories of great heroes could be erased by State power. Had he doubted if his own contributions would suffer the same fate, the behaviour of the establishment of post-Independent India justifies that. Savarkar would also be justified if he thought his life would serve as an inspiration for revolutionaries of the future. The book under question, namely *Life of Barrister Savarkar* did serve the purpose. Durga Das Khanna, an associate of Bhagat Singh, said in an interview in 1976 that when he joined the revolutionary movement, Bhagat Singh and Sukhdev made *Life of Barrister Savarkar* a necessary reading. The book was clearly inspirational to anti-British next-generation revolutionaries, thus serving more the cause of the independence movement than of self-fame.

Author Harish Srivastava makes the claim that 'Chitragupta' was a pen name used by Chakravarti Rajagopalachari to hide his identity.[8] Historian Vikram Sampath considers two others possible authors—Rajagopalachari (also Rajaji) and V. V. S. Aiyar.[9] Rajaji has openly stated that his initial inspiration came from Savarkar and later he became a staunch Gandhian leader. At the time of the publication of the book, Rajaji was a committed Gandhian. Aiyar was a London colleague of Savarkar who had translated Savarkar's earlier works in 1857. He too became hyper-attracted to the Gandhian movement, though the British harboured doubts that he was a motivational cause to the assassination of the Tirunelveli collector Ashe in 1911. What gives credence to the claim of Rajaji being the author is in the condolence message he sent at the event of Savarkar's death: he had stated that Savarkar was 'his first revolutionary idol' and that when he plunged himself into the revolutionary movement from law studies, he had 'caught the imagination' of the then young Rajaji.[10] In later politics, however, their relationship soured. When Rajaji endorsed the acceptance of the demand for Pakistan, Savarkar stated him as behaving like a 'mad mullah'. Naturally, if Rajaji wrote a biography of Savarkar in his very young days under a pseudonym, there was no great reason to own it in the later days—and that too, when Savarkar was also caught up in the Gandhi murder controversy. Aiyar too, should be considered as a potential source for this book. As Sampath points out, the book speaks sparsely of Savarkar's early childhood, while gives in-depth details about his London activities and is titled as one written by 'a close friend'—also, the book came out from Madras. In addition, Dr Tiruvengimalai Sesha Sundara Rajan (1880–1953), and another associate of Savarkar during his London days, too, was living in the same region and was actively involved in the Gandhian movement. He too was a writer. So, there is a possibility that the book could have been brought out through the collaboration of these ex-associates of Savarkar or by an admirer from South India with inputs from these ex-colleagues.

The Role of Savarkar in the INA Episode

As the Second World War broke out, Savarkar also worked to influence the world opinion in favour of India's Independence. When the then US President Franklin Roosevelt sent an appeal to Adolf Hitler to ward off the colossal danger to civilization, Savarkar cabled the President that if the latter's appeal to Hitler was 'actuated by disinterested human anxiety for safeguarding freedom and democracy from military aggression' then he should also ask 'Britain too to withdraw armed domination over Hindustan'. Again, when Roosevelt and Winston Churchill announced the Atlantic Charter on 14 August 1941, Savarkar cabled President Roosevelt on 20 August 1941, asking whether the Charter also covered the case of India and whether the US supported the case for complete political independence of India within a year of the end of the War. The comparison Savarkar had consistently drawn between Nazi occupations of countries in Europe with the occupation of India under Churchill, can be appreciated even today, in the light of historians uncovering the Nazi-like racist hatred that Churchill had for Indians in general, and Hindus in particular.

Even with the risk of being monitored by the British intelligence, Savarkar established contacts with revolutionaries overseas, particularly Rash Behari Bose. The correspondence is the start of a parallel attempt to liberate India. Rash Behari Bose wrote to Savarkar:

> Every attempt should be made to create a Hindu bloc extending from the Indian Ocean up to the Pacific Ocean. For the purpose the Hindu Sabha should take immediate steps for establishing branches of Mahasabha in Japan, China, Siam and other countries of the Pacific and sending their representatives for creating solidarity among the Eastern races.[11]

On Savarkar's advice, Rash Behari Bose wrote a letter to Subhas Chandra Bose on 25 January 1938, informing him of the activities of Indian revolutionaries under the banner of India Independence League in Southeast Asia. Savarkar was the one whom Subhas Chandra Bose met before he left India in disguise. Earlier, on 22 June 1940, Savarkar had informed Subhas Chandra Bose about the activities of Rash Behari Bose.

In 1939 Subhas Bose had to resign as Congress President. He founded the Forward Bloc, a new radical non-Marxist left-wing party. In 1940 he was arrested and put in prison. When he came out of the prison the same year, he was a dejected man. Historian Uma Mukherjee in her biography of two Indian revolutionaries (Rash Behari Bose and Jatindranath Mukherjee) explains in detail the role played by Savarkar in the life of Bose subsequently:

> A feeling of frustration seemed to overwhelm Subhas at this stage, and he saw no way out for India's deliverance from slavery so long as he remained in this country. His conversation with V.D. Savarkar at Bombay and his talk with Sri Hem Ghose in the Presidency Jail in 1940 toned up his drooping spirit and gave a definite direction to his wandering mind.

In a closed-door meeting, Savarkar suggested to Bose that he leave the country, touch base with revolutionaries abroad and use the Asiatic part of World War II to liberate India. To impress upon Subhas Bose, he showed him a letter from Rash Behari:

> The letter of Rash Behari referred to here was sent to Veer Savarkar about April, 1940 through a Buddhist monk, emphasising the urgency of preparation on behalf of Indian revolutionaries, as Japan's entry into the World War II seemed already in sight.... Thus, it is clear that it was Savarkar who impressed upon Subhas the urgent need for going out of the country and joining hands with Rash Behari Bose for organizing an armed attack against British India at the suitable opportunity. It is pertinent to observe that Savarkar was perhaps the only Indian leader who on the eve of the Second World War persistently pleaded in his speeches and writings the supreme importance of learning the act of modern warfare by Indian youths by joining the Armed Forces either in India or outside. Under his direct inspiration many a young man of India left the country at that time with this end in view.'[12]

Savarkar's strategy seems to be two-fold. He tried to help India gain all the advantages the British government offered through any constitutional means. Consequently, Hindu Sanghatanists (Dr N. B. Khare) became a part of the Viceroy's Executive Council. And it was this participation that would ultimately ensure that the United Nations addressed the discrimination against the Indians and ultimately apartheid in South Africa. It was Savarkar who cabled the viceroy to include Dr Ambedkar in the executive council. In 1942 when Savarkar met Sir Stafford Cripps, who headed the infamous Cripps Mission and spoke about the integral nature of India, none other than Jawaharlal Nehru's *National Herald* wrote:

> Profoundly as we disagree with his politics...Savarkar showed the old fire in him, when he took up the thoughtless challenge, thrown to Hindu Maha Sabha by the Government of Bihar and obtained a resounding victory at Bhagalpur. With Sir Stafford Cripps he crossed swords which the former will never forget.[13]

At the same time, Savarkar too, was totally in sympathy with the national motives of the INC as far as it did not involve what he considered as the appeasement of Muslims. So, when Nehru was arrested and sentenced to four years imprisonment, Savarkar called it as 'a painful shock to every Indian patriot':

> In spite of differences as to principles and policy which compel both of us to work under different colours, I shall be failing in my duty as a Hindu Sabhaite if I do not

> express my deep appreciation of the patriotic and even the humanitarian motives which had actuated Pandit Jawaharlalji throughout his public career and my sympathy for the sufferings which he consequently had to face.[14]

Both Dr Ambedkar and Savarkar understood the urgent need to completely Indianize the British-Indian army, failing which it would become disastrous for the nation in the event of Partition. Savarkar also envisioned an army with Indian domination rebelling against the British. Later, Subhas Bose would appreciate this vision of Savarkar. Azad Hind Radio broadcast from Singapore on 25 June 1944, praised Savarkar by saying:

> When due to misguided political whims and lack of vision almost all the leaders of Congress Party are decrying all the soldiers of Indian Army as mercenaries, it is heartening to know that Veer Savarkar is fearlessly exhorting the youth to enlist in the armed forces. Those enlisted youths themselves provide us with trained men from which we draw the soldiers of our Indian National Army.[15]

The Indian National Army (INA) played a decisive role in forcing the British to quit India. And Savarkar, despite the looming threats of his incarceration in the Andamans again, made a decisive contribution to ensure coordination between the INA founder, the elder Bose and its last leader, the younger Bose—so Bose and Bose were both influenced by Savarkar in a practical way. Rash Behari Bose was a Hindu Mahasabhaite who made a decisive contribution to the formation of the INA. The contributions of Savarkarite thoughts, more specifically his Hindutva, have also gone into another stream of the Indian political movement–the Gandhian concept of the nation.

Hind Swaraj, Hindutva, 'Bully' Savarkar and 'Sissy' Gandhi?

It is often stated in certain academic circles and media that the 'Hindutva of Savarkar' and the 'Hind Swaraj' of Gandhi are diametrically opposite. While the former was masculine, more modelled on the Western conception of nation-state, particularly akin to Italian and German nationalist models, the Gandhian concept was considered more feminine, accommodative of diversity and rooted to Indian tradition.

The famous Kannada writer U. R. Ananthamurthy (1932–2014) was a bitter critic of Hindutva. Like the pop-social psychologist Ashis Nandy, he also pits Savarkar's Hindutva against Gandhi's Hind Swaraj. To these critics of Hindutva, Gandhi represents the best essence of Hindu civilization, while the

Hindutva of Savarkar represents the Western militaristic, mechanical, nation-state influence. Thus, Hindutva is to them an artificial construct and a hybrid monstrosity which is embraced by an aggressive middle class. How much truth is there in this argument?

The support for the above argument often stems from a particular version of the Gandhi-Savarkar encounter in London which is often cited. For pop-social psychologists like Ashis Nandy, the event shows the Indianness of a gentle vegetarian Gandhi as against the meat-eating rude Savarkar imitating the Westerners. The event has been narrated with a great flourish in many academic papers as well as media articles. Just a few months after Narendra Modi became the Prime Minister of India, *The Economist* in its Christmas special print edition, ran a story titled 'Savarkar: Modi's Mentor—The Man who Thought Gandhi a Sissy'. Here is the narration of the incident:

> In 1906, in a lodging house for Indian students in Highgate, a pleasant area of north London, a young lawyer called Mohandas Karamchand Gandhi dropped in on a law student called Vinayak Damodar Savarkar, who happened to be frying prawns at the time. Savarkar offered Gandhi some of his meal; Gandhi, a vegetarian, refused. Savarkar allegedly retorted that only a fool would attempt to resist the British without being fortified by animal protein.[16]

The event is also told by known Hindutva-baiters like Jyotirmaya Sharma and a host of others. The event is told for a single reason—to differentiate between a Western-influenced meat-eating Savarkar bullying a tender Indic vegetarian Gandhi. So, it starts with frying prawns and ends with Savarkar 'taunting' Gandhi. The source for this event comes from the well-researched work of Dr Harindra Srivastava. In this, the real nature of the encounter was more jovial than a taunting one:

> Gandhi in his usual nervous manner, regretted that he was a vegetarian. Savarkar retorted though jocularly, "Well, if you cannot eat with us, how on earth are you going to work with us? Moreover... this is just boiled fish... while we want people who are ready to eat the British alive..." [17] (Ellipses in the original)

A jocular retort becomes a taunt and then is transformed into Savarkar calling Gandhi a sissy. To achieve this, the narration has to leave out a more significant sequel to this episode.

The occasion was the Vijayadashami-Dussehra celebrations organized by Savarkar and his band of radical students from India House, London in 1909. The year 1909 was a particularly stormy one for the inmates of India House.

Madan Lal Dhingra (1883–1909) had assassinated Curzon Wiley. It was well known that Dhingra's inspiration was Savarkar. It was the first political murder of the British by Indian resistance outside of India. Savarkar openly supported Dhingra's act and visited him in jail. Dhingra was executed in August 1909.

In October the same year, the students at India House whose leader was Savarkar, had decided to celebrate Dussehra. They invited Bipin Chandra Pal to the event. To the shock of Pal, they informed him that there would be no toast to the British emperor, rather they would offer floral tributes to Sri Rama and 'Bharat Mata' or Mother India. With the British intelligence already monitoring India House activities, Pal decided it would be prudent on his part to decline the invitation. The same year, between 10 July and 13 November, Gandhi, not yet very popular, was in London, trying to garner support for his movement in South Africa.

Savarkar's Lieutenant Aiyar (1881–1925) set out to search for Gandhi. Fortunately for posterity, both Aiyar and Dr Rajan, another Tamil associate of Savarkar, had documented what happened. Aiyar initially looked at all the prominent hotels, where eminent Indian leaders used to come and stay in London. After much search, he discovered where Gandhi was living—it was in the house of an Indian, who was running a small restaurant. It was located in a lane that was too narrow for cabs to enter. He was living in a room, which had a few old chairs, a torn carpet and a bed. He had come to London to sensitize the general public as well as leaders about his new form of fighting in South Africa.[18]

The next day, Aiyar came with Savarkar. In the three days that followed, Savarkar, Aiyar and Gandhi spent hours discussing strategies to achieve freedom. Savarkar and Gandhi had one major difference—Gandhi insisted on unconditional and absolute ahimsa (non-violence). Both Aiyar and Dr Rajan founded the *Hind Swaraj* of Gandhi which was published later as a result of these intense interactions. Despite this cardinal difference, Savarkar and Aiyar insisted that Gandhi should preside over the Dussehra celebrations. Gandhi accepted on one condition. He was not interested in gathering together in some hotel and pay for their meals, talk and disperse. Instead, he felt that this was an Indian festival and should be celebrated in an Indian way—therefore, vegetarian Indian food should be prepared. Savarkar and Aiyar agreed to this condition.

On Dussehra day, the preparations for food which now had to be made by volunteers, had started by 1 p.m. at the venue of the event. A team of six volunteers under Dr Rajan was preparing the food. Dr Rajan found that a middle-aged person, who looked not so strong, came and volunteered with others. But he turned out to be the most enthusiastic one. Aiyar, who happened to visit the venue, saw the new volunteer and was shocked. It was none other than Gandhi himself. Aiyar reprimanded Dr Rajan and asked Gandhi to forgive them. Gandhi laughed and said it was he who should be forgiven for he was the first culprit. Gandhi explained:

> What have I to excuse and whom? I am the first culprit. I have put you all to strain. It is I who should apologise for suggesting this vegetarian dinner and its preparation by yourself. But the fact that young men like you have all come forward for this sort of work fills me with pleasure.

Gandhi also took it upon himself to serve the food to all the guests and insisted that he would be the last to eat.

Gandhian author and publisher Pramod Kapoor, who through years of painstaking research, produced *Gandhi: An Illustrated Biography* (2016), points out an important aspect of the speech made by Savarkar during the event. Here, Savarkar had expressed his conceptualization of India which would later become the kernel of Hindutva as espoused by him. Savarkar said, 'Hindus are the heart of Hindustan.' He further added that 'just as the beauty of the rainbow is enhanced by its varied hues, Hindustan will appear more beautiful if it assimilated all that was best in Muslim, Parsi, Jewish and other communities'. According to Kapoor, 'Gandhi agreed with his views.'[19]

Savarkar continued with his oration, but little did he know that both his Tamil colleagues had been transformed by Gandhi, and would later join Gandhi.

Gandhi himself seemed to have been influenced by the views of Savarkar, particularly on the nature of the Indian nation. At the same time, he also differed vitally from Savarkar with respect to the road to freedom, how the assimilation should happen and also industrialization. The biographer of Aiyar points out the fact that *Hind Swaraj* was written by Gandhi (originally in Gujarati) soon after this event when Gandhi was returning to South Africa through sea voyage. Perhaps *Hind Swaraj* should be re-read taking into consideration this historical context. Gandhi enters the conversation with two strands of thought there. One is that of a person who had accepted the idea that India itself was the creation of a benign British rule. Here, Gandhi stands with Savarkar, perhaps also influenced by Savarkar, and points to the thousands of years of cultural unity that makes India a nation—'we Indians are one as no two Englishmen are'. Then in his dialogue with the nationalist radicals, he rejects their idea of using violence as a means and their aim of making India an industrialized nation by aping the then imperial West. So, the event that was supposed to display the westernized and negative nature of Savarkar, juxtaposed with the Indic-rooted gentle Gandhi. When taken as a whole, it actually shows a Savarkar who had formulated his positive concept of Hindu nationhood and a strong democratic leader, who respects and values the perspective of the other person.

In 1915 Aiyar met Gandhi again and declared his full faith in Gandhian ahimsa. But the relation between them and Savarkar always remained warm, so much so that when the news of the tragic death of Aiyar reached Savarkar, though he knew Aiyar had become a Gandhian, Savarkar became unusually emotional: 'Heavy griefs have often embittered our life, but none heavier than what thy sudden death caused, oh friend, ever taxed our capacity to endure....' Savarkar called Aiyar, a 'Hindu of Hindus'. That Aiyar, his closest comrade during the revolutionary times had moved on to the Gandhian side had caused in Savarkar not a trace of animosity. Thus, in Savarkar, one sees a personality that values human relations and values beyond political affinities.

Savarkarite Criticism of Gandhi

Savarkar would, in later years, attack Gandhi bitterly because of his appeasement of Muslim separatists. In this, Savarkar was not alone. Dr Ambedkar also expressed views which echoed those of Savarkar's. Dr Ambedkar, who was also critical of Savarkar's alternative to Pakistan, reserved an elaborate and the most trenchant criticism as well as a warning, with regard to the approach of Gandhi, which he characterized as 'giving blank cheque' to Islamist aggressors. Dr Ambedkar observed that 'the policy of concession' practised by Gandhi had only 'increased Muslim aggressiveness' and that it was interpreted not as a large-hearted action but 'as a sign of defeatism on the part of the Hindus and the absence of the will to resist'. Then he warned the Hindus:

> This policy of appeasement will involve the Hindus in the same fearful situation in which the Allies found themselves as a result of the policy of appeasement which they adopted towards Hitler.

To Dr Ambedkar, it was just 'another malaise, no less acute than the malaise of social stagnation'. In 1939 Savarkar and Ambedkar, along with five other leaders, would declare that Gandhi's claim of the Congress representing all Indians was fascist. Those intemperate utterances as well as the harsh criticisms of Gandhi's politics were the result of political rivalry.

Savarkar's attitude towards Gandhi can be brought out by one incident that happened during the later years when both were political rivals. Gandhi had started a hunger strike on 10 February 1943 against his incarceration in Aga Khan Palace. The British did not relent and nor did Gandhi. On 19 February, extremely worried about the life of Gandhi, Savarkar wired liberal leader Tej

Bahadur Sapru 'to issue a national appeal to Gandhi himself to break his fast in the interest of the nation'. What he wrote shows what he really thought of Gandhi:

> We must all turn our faces from the alien and unsympathetic doors of the Viceregal Lodge to the bedside of Gandhi, and entreat him to break his fast in the national interest to serve which he must have undertaken it....His life, Gandhi himself may realize by such a national appeal, is not so much his own as it is a national asset, a national property.

At the same time, Savarkar rejected the proposal to single out the release of Gandhi on account of his fast. He demanded that all leaders, including Sarat Chandra Bose should be released. Savarkar was not a man to lose sight of what he considered as the larger interests of the nation, over his own personal admiration, however great the latter might be. Yet, we see Savarkar and Gandhi in harmony with regard to the fundamental nature of India's cultural unity, on the question of religious conversion, etc. In fact, for all the acknowledged founding fathers of the modern Indian state, the cultural nationalism that united the people of India has always been axiomatic. It is this aspect that unites more fundamentally than all their differences, Gandhi's Hind Swaraj and Savarkar's Hindutva.

Historiography of Vinayak Damodar Savarkar

When one looks at history, one finds that all great social leaders have taken a keen interest in history in the past. It is how they have viewed history that shaped their own actions. A good example of that is Jawaharlal Nehru. His romantic view of Indian history, his parroting of the colonial history handed down by the British, his extension of the same with his own Marxist spicing and his one-dimensional linear view of progress which essentially imitated the USSR, shaped his politics. It distorted his perceptions of geo-political realities and, to this day, a rather dominant class of the elite of the nation finds it profitable to thrust those outdated frameworks to understand Indian history and society. Of course, with his ornately worded, left-oriented, romantic view of international politics, Nehru could earn for himself personal accolades, even as the nation had to meet disastrous defeat at the frontiers. For decades, the influx of Hindu refugees from East Pakistan continued unabated. In the case of Dr Ambedkar, we find a much better, scholarly, original thinker. He questioned the Aryan race theory and foresaw its demise. He constructed his own view of the social history of the downtrodden masses of India that showed that they had a rightful claim to the glories of India's past magnificence and thus had an equally rightful share in the future of the nation. His strongly worded, merciless criticism of Hinduism, sometimes borrowing colonial frameworks, was essentially animated by his intense feeling of the need for the consolidation of Hindus as a nation. He oscillated between pointing to the Vedic period as a kind of uncivilized barbarism, to depicting the Vedic and Upanishadic periods as egalitarian and rooted in spiritual democratic values later corrupted by the vested interests of the forces of social stagnation, which he identified with so-called 'Brahminism'.

Savarkar was also a historian, though not an academic one. Yet, paradoxically, it was primarily as a historian that he contributed to the national movement. He was also a revolutionary and later a politician of penetrating foresight which often alienated him rather than making him a mass leader. How he viewed history and learnt lessons from the past to understand the present as well as prepare for the future, is an interesting dimension of this remarkable personality. At a very early stage, Savarkar the historian understood that the way history is constructed, the very terms of narrative are loaded with their own politics and power. For a nation to survive, it has to reclaim its past. Savarkar, the utilitarian historian wrote:

> The nation that has no consciousness of its past has no future. Equally true it is that a nation must develop its capacity not only of claiming a past, but also of knowing how to use it for the furtherance of its future.[20]

When the British historians and their Indian followers repeatedly termed the 1857 uprising as a 'mutiny', Savarkar contested this by calling 1857 a revolution, lamenting that 'the history of the tremendous Revolution that was enacted in the year 1857' has never been studied in 'scientific spirit by an author, Indian or foreign'.[21] It is important to note here that Savarkar uses the term 'scientific spirit' and not nationalistic or patriotic spirit. What Savarkar the historian wanted was history as it happened and not eulogy. The rationale of Savarkar is that only if the past is understood rationally and objectively can it be used for understanding the present and preparing the society for surviving the future. Otherwise, the society ends up living in a self-woven time warp, losing its ability to face challenges. Nevertheless, Savarkar was not a dry historian piling facts with no emotions. As a historian, he was brutally objective and the objective historian in him fed the emotional revolutionary. The research he did with the 'scientific spirit' of the 1857 rebellion, convinced the patriot in Savarkar that what happened in 1857 was indeed a national revolution. Armed with the facts of history, he made the study into an emotional call to his fellow countrymen, to carry on the unfinished tasks of the revolutionaries of 1857:

> We take up your cry, we revere your flag; we are determined to continue that fiery mission of 'away with the foreigner', which you uttered, amidst the prophetic thundering of the revolutionary war.[22]

Savarkar chose 1907 to release his book, which was the fiftieth anniversary of the great uprising. Consequently, the book was banned by the British and became a must-read for all Indian revolutionaries such as Madame Cama, Lala Har Dayal, Bhagat Singh, and Netaji Subhas Chandra Bose. When Savarkar brought out the work, British intelligence could lay their hand on only one chapter of the book. And what they found, shocked them. A report about this first chapter from an official with the Home Department of the Government of Bombay states with visible alarm:

> The [chapter] is only a small fragment of a book containing nearly 470 pages, each page redolent of the most inflammatory language with quotations from English authors describing most pathetic and pitiably tragic scenes and so forth.[23]

Savarkar had proved himself to be a historian of a different class altogether and definitely not an idle armchair one. And the work itself remained banned by the government for the next 40 years. Savarkar the historian made Savarkar the pragmatist a patriot to understand one bitter truth from the history of 1857: Indians have been intentionally and systematically demilitarized by the colonial regime. Unless that condition was reversed, another uprising was almost impossible. So, he waited. When the opportunity came in the form of the Second World War, he urged Indian youths to join the army. It was not just national independence that Savarkar envisaged. He saw military recruitment as an opportunity for the caste-ridden Hindu society to remove the ills of caste divisions. So he actively supported Dr Ambedkar's call for the Mahar youths to join the British army. Dhananjay Keer, the official biographer of Dr Ambedkar, states:

> Savarkar, who wished the Hindus to be reborn into a martial race, expressed his hope that under the able guidance of Ambedkar the Mahar brethren would be re-animated with the military qualities and their military uplift would contribute to the consolidation of Hindus.[24]

This move later helped Subhas Chandra Bose in his organizing of INA. Bose openly acknowledged this in his Azad Hind Radio broadcast, as noted earlier. Another important work that sets Savarkar as a historian of Hindutva was *Six Glorious Epochs of Indian History*. Any history textbook of India that a student studies today, shows India as being repeatedly overrun by invading foreigners. This is only natural because such a historical narrative helped the British to inculcate in the minds of Indians the idea that they are a society born to be slaves of another foreign power or culture. The success of this approach is that even today, we perceive ourselves as slaves of the mind and culture of the West. On the other hand, Savarkar concentrated on the various freedom struggles and peoples' movements against foreign invasions. He chronicled how Indian resistance to foreign invasions and the imposition of foreign ways of life on Indian people happened. The six epochs present Indian history as a long epic narrative of Indians facing the onslaughts of the enemies, sometimes being overcome, and how they formed resistance and overthrew the enemies or assimilated them or made them subservient to Indic might.

Savarkar, the social historian, was remarkably advanced for his times and not given to fantasies of casteism as well as social stagnation. Rather, he understood the social dynamics and presented the fact that only a society that regards talent and not birth-based ritualism as its civilizational ethos, can successfully face and conquer aggressive enemies. He decried the fabrication of fashionable genealogies constructed for great achievers. The social commentary Savarkar makes here remains relevant even today:

> Was Chandragupta a social outcaste? Was he not a Kshatriya? What matters though! Chandragupta could have said with justifiable pride, "More than any of you, nominal caste-born Kshatriyas, who bowed your heads to the Mlechhas, the Greek emperor and his commanders, I, a 'peerless' Chandragupta, have a greater claim to being a Kshatriya in as much as with my sword I have completely vanquished those very Mlechhas in every battlefield." With the same haughty affront of Karna, he could have flung in the face of those railing enemies the following words: "Whether a charioteer or a charioteer's son. Or whoever (else) I may be, (that is of no consequence!) Birth in a (noble) family depends on fate; but manliness depends on me I" (Bhatta Narayan, Act III, 37 91). The son of Mura is a Maurya! That is precisely why Chandragupta is called a Maurya. Proud of his maternal extraction Chandragupta designated his royal family as Maurya and immortalized the name of his mother, Muradevi in Indian history. The Maurya emperors accepted the same Moriya caste too, (one which traded in peacocks) that belonged to his mother.[25]

Perhaps the most important work on history written by Veer Savarkar was *Hindu Pad Padashahi*. Titled in English as *The Maratha Movement*, the book describes the Maratha struggle to re-establish the Hindu Empire in India. This was written in 1925, when Savarkar was still a political prisoner. Savarkar had no luxury of getting reference books from world libraries. Yet, when the book came, the whole thesis could be substantiated from varied research works and well-known authorities. The great Indian nationalist, Lala Lajpat Rai exclaimed that the book was 'full of facts congested in a small space arranged with skill and made to speak with tongues of force and love'. He endorsed the book, saying, 'In my opinion every Indian politician ought to read it.'[26] But then a question may arise as to whether such a historiography would lead to furthering of the bitterness between Hindu and Muslim communities. Savarkar, in his foreword to *Hindu Pad Padashahi*, answers this question both as a historian and as a humanistic nationalist:

> We ought to read history not with a view to finding out the best excuse to perpetuate the old strife and stress, bickering and bloodshed, whether in the name of our blessed motherland or of our Lord God, that divided man from man and race from race, but precisely for the contrary reason…far from standing in the way of any real and honourable unity between our Hindus and our Muslim countrymen, it makes a frank and lasting union far more feasible than it would have otherwise have been and deserves therefore to be especially recommended to the attention of all Indian patriots, Muslims as well as Hindus. It cannot fail to act as a sedative on blustering snobbery on the one hand and as a stimulant to mopping self-diffidence on the other.[27]

The Influence of Savarkar's Book on Bhagat Singh

Malwinder Jit Singh and Harish Jain, in their detailed study of Bhagat Singh's *Jail Notebook*, had pointed out how he had quoted Veer Savarkar from his *Hindu Pad Padshahi*.[28] The book clearly served as an important reading material for the revolutionaries. Singh and Jain point out that when Sukhdev Singh was arrested, he also had with him *Hindu Pad Padshahi*. Bhagat Singh had picked the following quotes of Savarkar:

> But what unresisting martyrdom fails (failed) to do, righteous and resisting force does (did) and (rendered) renders, tyranny impotent to do further harm.
> Rather get killed than converted... (was the cry prevalent amongst the Hindus then). But Ram Das rose and exclaimed: 'No: not thus: Better get killed than converted is good enough but it would be better so to strive as neither to get killed nor violently converted by killing the forces of violence itself. Get killed if that must be, but get killed while killing to conquer—conquer in the cause of Righteousness.
>
> —*Hindu Pad Padshahi*, 181–182

> Sacrifice was adorable only when it was, directly or remotely, but reasonably, felt to be indispensable for success. Sacrifice that leads not to ultimate success is suicidal had no place in the tactics of Maratha warfare.
>
> —*Hindu Pad Padshahi,* 257

> To fight with these Marathas is to battle with the wind, is to strike on the water.
>
> —*Hindu Pad Padshahi,* 258

> That remains the despair of our age which has to write history without making it, to sing of valorous deeds without the daring abilities and opportunities that can actualise them in life.
>
> —*Hindu Pad Padshahi,* 255–256

> Although fetters of political slavery can at times be shaken off and smashed, yet the fetters of cultural superstitions are often found far more difficult to knock off.
>
> —*Hindu Pad Padshahi,* 272–273

Singh and Jain write that those lines of Savarkar 'must have been energising to Bhagat Singh as he dug deep to find them embedded in a dense narrative bereft of paragraphs'. In fact, they also point out that the willing martyrdom of Bhagat Singh, Rajguru and Sukhdev was not an emotional act, but a well-executed sacrifice to communicate in a high-profile way, using all the media available to them, the message of the freedom struggle to all their countrymen to galvanize them into action. Interestingly, the police obtained a copy of *Hindu Pad Padshahi* from Sukhdev also during their raid. The Hindutva classic had been in the reading list of the Hindustan Socialist Republican Association (HSRA) revolutionaries.

The book brings out in great detail how the Maratha navy defeated the European forces and how complacency brought the curtains on the last Hindu empire. Based on this objective understanding of history, both the efforts that brought the nation successes and the complacency, as well as disunity that brought it failure, Savarkar asked Hindu youths to join the Indian army in large numbers. In his call given on 24 March 1942, he addressed the Hindu youths to join the army, particularly the navy in Konkan area. He reasoned:

> Ever since I was in Ratnagiri the District Hindusabha there along with some of my distinguished Bhandari friends in Konkan have been demanding entry into the Navy for the Konkan Hindus. Now that the Government has thrown open, under pressure of circumstances, the services in the navy to the Hindus we shall be only harming our own interests if we lose this long expected chance to revive the naval

> military spirit in our people in Konkan….
> It is these Hindu communities like the Dhandaris, Kharvis and others who once rendered the Maratha Navy a terror over the Portuguese and the English and had inflicted several crushing defeats in naval engagements on them as for example when in a sea-fight the well-known English war-ship 'Revenge' was captured by the Marathas. The children of Konkan, as it is said regarding the children of Britain, begin to play with the waves as soon as they begin to play with toys and have an inborn aptitude to make the best fighting material for the sea forces of our nation. Unfortunately these naval instincts were deliberately suppressed till today by the British Government….
> Remember again that the proportion of Hindus in the military, naval and aerial forces today is already dangerously low. If even now the Hindus, through folly or fear fail to enter these forces, others, unconcerned with Hindu interests and in cases even ready to endanger them will rush in and we Hindus shall find ourselves in a worse plight and weaker by far even than what we are today.[29]

Here, one sees how Savarkar the historian displays his ability to relate the history of the past with the challenges the nation faces in the present and intuit and shape the future with all the pregnant possibilities and challenges. History is witness to the genius of a historian in Savarkar when, during the Partition, thanks to his advice and efforts, Indian army was dominated by Hindus and Sikhs. Had the impractical romantic pacifism prevailed and prevented Indian youths from joining the army in early 1940s, the whole of Kashmir, large chunks of Punjab, Bengal and Assam would have become part of Pakistan, not to speak of the humiliating ethnic cleansing that would have taken place in these provinces.

Women in the Historiography of Savarkar

Closely associated with the historiography of Savarkar is the way he viewed the role of women in nation-building and in the national resistance movement. Before getting into how the historiography of Savarkar depicted women, it is interesting to see how Savarkar viewed women according to his official biographer. Dhananjay Keer writes:

> As for the role of women in life, Savarkar has definite views to offer. He believes that there is a fundamental and natural difference between man and woman. Their duties are different. So, their education, too, must necessarily differ. Reformer as he is, he does not like women to obey the dictates of old useless customs.

> Savarkar regards female education indispensable to the uplift of a nation; but by female education he does not necessarily mean university degrees, although he has no objection to their obtaining the degrees without disregarding their primary duty to the home, children, and the nation. He holds that a system of education must be drawn up on new lines, and women should be given some sort of specialized training congenial to the temperament of women. A woman should be a ministering angel rather than a masculine Amazon or a Virago. She should imbibe the quality of her proverbial modesty and grace rather than mere eloquence or proficiency in mathematics....The larger the number of good healthy mothers, he observes, the stronger and healthier will be the nation. Therefore, a woman's education should enable her to enrich the nation with a generation stronger, more beautiful, and more patriotic than the past. The Russian woman is on an equal footing with man. Yet, does it mean, he asks, that Stalin delivers a child instead of his wife?[30]

So Savarkar considered that women's education should take into consideration the gender-based differences. Perhaps based on today's feminist values and notions of women's liberation, the views of Savarkar are dated and clearly carry the gender-based stereotyping of his age.

Yet, throughout the historical works that he wrote, he presented women as fighting as equals with men. In his monumental work on the 1857 rebellion, the First War of Indian Independence, Savarkar spoke of the role of women in both igniting 1857 as well as participating in it. According to him, the revolutionaries of 1857 thought that the participation of women in the movement was so necessary that they took special efforts to reach out to them:

> These Tamashgars could not preach Revolution to the women, and so it would appear that the leaders of the Revolution sent out quack doctors and their wives—female gipsies—amongst the people, to move them with a new life for the war sacrifice.[31]

Particularly, it was his picture of Jhansi Rani Lakshmi Bai which set an ideal for Indian women patriots to fight the British. It should be remembered that in the nationalist discourse, the Rani was the ideal Indian woman. She is seen not as a mother fighting for her son but as a warrior queen fighting for the liberty of the nation. The picture of her emerging from Savarkar's work immortalized her for Indian revolutionaries:

> The men of Jhansi manned their guns, loaded the muskets; its women carried ammunition, built Top Khanas, supplied provisions....See how the goddess of war has taken the sword and see how she is making her way through the troops. She is moving about with lightning rapidity, presenting some with golden bracelets, some

> with dresses; some she is touching with her sacred touch to pat, to some she is offering her sweet smile; others she is encouraging with her heroic words.... Standing on the ramparts, the Ranee looked back for one moment at Jhansi. Before her rose the hideous picture of the terrible disaster that had happened near the south gate. The enemy had, after all, defiled her Jhansi! Her eyes were ablaze with anger; she was almost mad with rage....This rapid onslaught of the girl of twenty-one, her horse at full speed, her sword cutting men down to the right and to the left—seeing this who would not fight for her? Who would not be inspired by her? All the Revolutionaries were inspired by her strength; the battle raged bloody and hot.... She donned her usual military uniform, rode a noble steed, took out her gem-be studded sword from the sheath, and ordered the army under her to march on.... Even the insubordinate and hesitating felt heroic under her influence and, with them and her select band of horsemen, she charged hard the English army! Her two female friends, Mandar and Kashi, also fought bravely by her side. May the sweet memory of those two patriotic girls—beautiful in appearance, with male attire put on, taking pleasure in fight—live in history along with that of their mistress as long as history lives!... Oh Lakshmi, Lakshmi! The last drop of thy sacred blood is dripping and, therefore, now, Mother, take this last sacrifice for thee! Even at the point of death, she killed the British foe who had attacked her, and now the young Queen was breathing her last breath![32]

So here we have Savarkar who presents a woman who surpasses men in arms training, managing the armies and administration as the ideal of Indian womanhood before generations of Indian patriots. Whatever might have been his personal views on women, it was this picture which inspired and guided the participation of women in the freedom movement of India. Savarkar continued to honour and propagate the memory of the Rani among the public as on 18 June 1939 (the 80th anniversary of 1857), as part of the whirlwind propaganda tour of Savarkar, a big procession was held for remembering the fight of Jhansi Rani Lakshmi Bai.[33] This propagation of Jhansi Rani Lakshmi Bai as the warrior princess role model who became so embedded in the collective psyche of Indian freedom fighters actually goes contrary to the gender-based roles for women attributed to Savarkar, even though that was usually the dominant thinking then even among the most progressive thinkers of his time. According to Keer, when Subhas Chandra Bose founded the INA, the all-women regiment was named 'Regiment of Lakshmi Bai of Jhansi'. Freedom fighter Khurshed Framji Nariman, who was known to be close to Bose, wrote in *Free Hindustan Weekly* that 'the idea of the INA and particularly the Rani of Jhansi Regiment seems to have originated from Veer Savarkar's proscribed publication on the great 1857 Revolution and Mutiny'.[34] In Singapore, which was the field of action of INA, and where the government does not view it positively, associating it with Japanese occupation, the national museum exhibit on INA that it had 'notably for its time...an all-female regiment, the Rani of Jhansi Regiment'. So, irrespective of his personal views, the historiography of Savarkar and his subsequent popularizing of Jhansi Rani helped in the emancipation of women and in women emerging as equal partners in the freedom struggle and also in the armed revolution.

Jauhar Debate: When Savarkar and Gandhi Converged

When the movie about Padmavati directed by Sanjay Leela Bhansali was released in 2018, suddenly there erupted a media diatribe against *jauhar*—mass self-immolation by Hindu women, particularly in Rajasthan—the border state of India that mainly bore the brunt of Islamist invasions. Naturally, Savarkar was dragged too. Savarkar, in all his works, had constantly spoken in glorifying terms about jauhar. Whenever Hindus faced definite defeat in the battle against Islamist invaders, their women and children self-immolated themselves by jumping into burning pyres. A mixture of history and folk traditions carry forward the powerful imagery of the sacrifice of these women. Interestingly, throughout Indian history, up until the Islamist invasion (with the sole exception of an instance during the invasion of Alexander the terrible), such mass self-immolation was not done by Hindu women during intra-Hindu wars. History does not know of the phenomenon of mass women's self-immolation during the expansionist conquests of Samudra Gupta or Rajaraja Chozha.

The mass suicide of women has also been reported during the pre-Partition and Partition riots—particularly Hindu and Sikh women. It was again reported during the 1971 Bengal holocaust. The Yazidi women in Iraq committing suicide to escape sex slavery at the hands of Islamic State (ISIS) is also well-documented in recent years (2014–2017). There are two things which connect jauhar with these modern, well-documented cases of women killing themselves to escape religious conversion and sex slavery, particularly in the hands of Islamist outfits like ISIS. One is the insider version that views this as a sacrifice chosen by the women over degradation of self and their bodies. The other is the outsider view which sees women as victims of Hindu society who were compelled by patriarchal notions of body-based purity. Marxists and Euro-centric narrators of history often portray the self-immolation of Hindu and Sikh women as being the result of the ideas of body-based purity. Here is a typical view of a British historian, Patrick French, on the suicides of Hindu and Sikh women during the Partition riots:

> Many women did not wish to return to their original families, which would involve not only social humiliation but the abandonment of the babies they had had with their abductors. The Sikh and Hindu emphasis on ritual purity meant that a substantial number of women chose suicide or "sacrifice" rather than dishonour.[35]

Here is another similar view from Dr Bina D'Costa, a South Asian scholar from the Australian National University (ANU). Discussing Partition-related violence, she says:

> Women survivors recounted stories of carrying poison packets around their necks thinking that each day might be their last day. Notions of purity, shame and honour, deeply ingrained and internalized in both men and women, meant that they willingly embraced death.[36]

But to her credit, Dr D'Costa had recorded—perhaps unintentionally—how the abduction and distribution of Hindu and Sikh women was done in a systematic manner during the Partition. That will be seen in the next section. Both in colonial Indology and in the Marxist approach which decide the dominant view in the academia and the establishment media, there exists a strict self-imposed refusal to see how the Hindus have, through the centuries, reacted to a theo-political expansionist aggression spanning centuries that demanded the sexual slavery of women, belonging to what it considered as the false religion. The deep-seated Hindu phobia in the academia too, cannot be easily discounted.

In their point of view, Hindu women could not love their religion enough to sacrifice their lives for it and would rather prefer changing it. And somehow, the academicians believe the Hindu family structure to be something inherently diabolical and oppressive. So, if a woman prefers to die rather than being plucked away from her family, then she could only have been indoctrinated or brainwashed by patriarchy. After all, M. N. Roy, the founding father of Marxism in India, had viewed the Islamic jihad on Hinduism as a struggle of progressive forces versus the feudal reactionary ones. So, if a Hindu prefers death to either conversion or abduction by Islamists, then it should be because of patriarchal indoctrination.

Mahatma Gandhi repudiated this view with his simple yet precise observation regarding the mass suicides committed by Hindu women. Even as he was appealing for peace in Delhi, he did not whitewash the organized crimes of abduction done by Muslims in Pakistan against the Hindus and Sikhs. Writing a month after Partition became a reality and with massacres reaching a crescendo as never before, Gandhi specifically exclaimed about the mass suicides of Hindu-Sikh women during Partition riots. With excitement and anguish, he pointed out the real purpose of their action:

> I have heard that many women who did not want to lose their honour chose to die. Many men killed their own wives. I think that is really great, because I know that such things make India brave. After all, life and death is a transitory game. Whoever might have died are dead and gone; but at least they have gone with courage. They have not sold away their honour. Not that their lives were not dear to them, but they felt it was better to die with courage rather than be forcibly converted to Islam by the Muslims and allow them to assault their bodies. And so those women died. They were not just a handful, but quite a few. When I hear all these things, I dance with joy that there are such brave women in India.[37]

Savarkar also eulogized the self-immolation of Hindu and Sikh women, and it was always part of his historic narrative. To him it was the greatest act of self-sacrifice for motivating the coming generations to fight against oppression while also protecting themselves from degradation. But what about concepts of body-based purity? Of course, patriarchal tendencies develop in any society, and they tend to see the woman as a property or a possession. Hence, if she gets violated bodily, then there may be stigma associated with it in the society. Both as a Hindutva ideologue and historiographer, Savarkar provides a completely different approach to this mindset.

In his *Six Glorious Epochs of Indian History*, Savarkar provides a narrative of the events surrounding the life of Deval Devi, the fourteenth century princess of Gujarat. There are conflicting descriptions about her life. The facts are that her mother, Kamala Devi, the queen of Gujarat, was taken to Delhi by Allauddin Khilji, where he married her. However, her daughter Deval Devi had escaped capture by the Khiljis. Later, during a raid near Ellora, she too was captured in a chance encounter with Malik Kafur. At that time, her marriage had been fixed to Shankardev, a Yadav prince. Later, he would fight against the Islamist Sultanate and die. The princess was married off to Khijra Khan, one of Khilji's sons, who also happened to be her mother's stepson. However, it was Khilji's third son, Qutb ud din Mubarak Shah who became the Sultan. Soon, fearing a conspiracy, he killed many of his brothers including Khijra Khan and then took Deval Devi as his own wife. Later, he was also killed by Khusro Khan, one of his generals and a Hindu convert to Islam from Gujarat, who was abused by the Sultan. Khusro Khan married Deval Devi and then proclaimed himself to be the Sultan—only that he reconverted to Hinduism.

Muslim writers and court poets of Khilji had romanticized Deval Devi's relation with Khilji's first son. And subsequently, she had been described like an object of conquest, passing hands with no mind of her own. In the medieval historiography, she was depicted as one who got married to anyone who came to power. Savarkar, on the other hand, provides another view of the queen. He writes admiringly of her thus:

> Some writers vouch that Devaldevi and Khijrakhan greatly loved each other. But this seems to be the flattering way of the courtly writers. Her subsequent course of action makes it abundantly clear! But that shrewd Hindu princess seems to have affected her love for Islam and for her husband till she got the desired opportunity.[38]

That desired opportunity was, according to Savarkar, the coup by Khusro Khan against Mubarak, the last Khilji. Savarkar speculates that in this, 'his secret accomplice' was 'the former Hindu princess but now the Muslim empress, Devaldevi (who) must have been keeping him posted with every detail of the daily happenings at Delhi, even as Khusro Khan went for a southern expedition.' And while Muslim historians and others following them consistently and contemptuously called Khusro Khan as 'low born', Savarkar does not mention his community as 'low'. What is more, to him what the 'original Hindu Paria youth' and 'Devaldevi, originally a Hindu princess' had performed 'an unparallelled miracle not only in India but in the whole human history'.[39]

According to him, the proclamation said to have jointly made by Khusro Khan and Devaldevi on 15 April 1320 'thrilled everybody in India right from the Kings and Nawabs to the Parias and Pawars, Mahars and Mangs with a strange sensation'.[40]

The declaration of Khusro Khan presented by Savarkar in his book reads thus:

> Although till today I was forced to lead the most detestable life of a convert to Islam, I am originally a son of a Hindu. The mainspring of my life is Hinduism and the blood that throbs into my veins and arteries is that of a Hindu. Now that I have won independent and powerful status of a Sultan for myself I am hereby breaking off the shackles of conversion to a foreign religion, and I do hereby declare that I am a Hindu! I have now ascended publicly the throne of the vast and entire, undivided India as a Hindu Emperor! Similarly Sultana Devaldevi till very recently was originally a Hindu daughter. Her husband, the Raja of Devgiri, Shankardev Yadav, was most brutally murdered and she was treacherously captured from her father sneaking miserably through dense forest to avoid seizure by the enemy. She was brought to Delhi and put to shame and ignominious disgrace by being forced to marry Khijrakhan, in the first place, and secondly after his brutal murder, Sultan Mubarik who was killed in the coup d'etat last night. That Devaldevi is my queen, the empress of Hindustan of today! Being originally Hindu in flesh and blood and a Hindu royal princess,

> she also hereafter renounces disdainfully her shameful conversion to Islam and henceforth will lead her life strictly according to Hindu religion! May this solemn vow of ours absolve us both of our former sin of forceful conversion![41]

The emperor now renamed himself Nasir-ud-din, defender of *deen*. Only his deen was not Islam but Hindu Dharma. While every Islamic and British historian emphasized his 'low-caste' in a derisive manner, Savarkar writes:

> This Hindu Samrat converted with their willing consent the young wives, daughters and nieces of the earlier Sultans and other Muslim women to Hinduism and married them to his Hindu Paria followers.

The very idea of a Hindu caste as being low or superior does not appear at all in the discourse of Savarkar. The only epithets he uses for Nasir-ud-din are '*Dharmarakshak*' and '*Hindu Samrat*'. More relevant to the topic in question regarding Queen Deval Devi, Savarkar writes:

> (the) former Hindu royal princess and the Yadav Queen, Devaldevi, who was equally responsible for bringing about the unprecedented Hindu revolution of Shree Dharmarakshak Nasir-ud-din, and who was his important accomplice in the secret plot, and who became, after the successful accomplishment of the said revolution, the Hindu Empress of Shree Dharmarakshak, deserves even a greater place of honour, like that of Devi Padmini of Chitor, for the unimaginable mental agonies that she had to suffer in the most adverse circumstances! She deserves the honour of a brave warrior Rajput Princess burning herself on the pyre or in Johar![42]

So here again, one can observe that the Hindutva discourse has no special regard for bodily purity. To Veer Savarkar, if self-immolation and the memory of the martyrs associated with that deed is holy, then the strategic manoeuvring he perceives in the life of abducted and ravaged princess Deval Devi is also equally sacred. Here, the woman is not seen as a sexual property of high worth and with no mind of her own but as an equal intelligent and even independent partner in the preservation of Dharma, as she deems fit.

We also find the same attitude in Mahatma Gandhi when he repeatedly asked the Hindu society to overcome the social-stagnant prejudice of bodily pollution and accept the girls who were rescued from Islamic abduction:

> Even if a girl has been forced into marriage by a Muslim, even if she has been violated, I would still take her back with respect. I do not want that a single Hindu

or Sikh should take up the attitude that if a girl has been abducted by a Muslim she is no longer accepted to society.[43]

Here, we see both Savarkar and Gandhi converging in their view in distinguishing the respect for the choice of self-sacrifice of a woman from the concept of a rape victim being bodily polluted, which they both did not accept. Interestingly, this has its roots in traditional Hinduism itself.

The following traditional telling of events show that Hinduism catalysed people to rise above the notion of body-based pollution and honour. In the Kanchi Sankara Mutt tradition, Swami Atmabodha is considered as the 58th Acharya. According to tradition, he had a disciple by the name of Puroshotama, who was given the sannyasi name Bodhendra Saraswathi. Atmabodha ordered him to go to Puri Jagannatha Kshetra and get a text, the *Bhagwan Nama Gaumuthi* from a savant, Lakshmi Sridhara. The project was to compose one lakh verses based on this treatise. When Bodhendra reached Puri, he learnt from his son Jagannatha Pandita that the savant had died. At that time, Bodhendra witnessed an incident:

A South Indian couple had come to Jagannatha Pandita about a problem. When they were performing pilgrimage, the wife was abducted by Muslims. The husband became depressed and dejected and became a wanderer. After a few months, he by chance went near a river bank. There, some Muslim women were collecting water. One of those women, upon seeing him, came running. She was his abducted wife—she had been forced to marry a Muslim and live with him. She, however, decided to return with her husband and they made their way to Jagannatha Pandita to ask what the scriptural injunction would be to make her his wife again, as she had lived as the wife of a Muslim after her abduction. Jagannatha Pandita simply suggested that they both hold hands and get into the temple pond and say *Rama nama* three times, immersing themselves in water. Bodhendra, witnessing this event, asked Pandita if what he was doing was in accordance with the shastras. As an answer, Pandita gave Bodhendra the book written by his father. In another version, when Pandita mentioned the above prescription to the couple, the widowed mother of Pandita heard it and got angry. She condemned her son for suggesting the repetition of Rama Nama three times. According to her, there was no pollution which could not be removed by a single utterance of Rama Nama.

So, the criticism that the glorification of jauhar is similar to the glorification of Sati or female genital mutilation, or that it reduces the woman to her body alone, is because of the ignorance of Hindu tradition and history. In reality, in remembering the martyrs of jauhar, we remember how we have survived as a nation through such sacrifices. And we resolve that we will not allow such a fate to descend on our posterity. And that is the best tribute we can pay to their sacred memories. Padmavati is thus a living expression of the spirit of Dharma that still burns—from medieval Rajasthan under the Sultanate's siege to today's Yazidi villages under the siege of an Islamic state.

Did Savarkar Advocate Sexual Assault on Muslim Women?

On 28 May 2016, the 133rd birth anniversary of Savarkar, Ajaz Ashraf, a freelance journalist, wrote an article titled 'Reading Savarkar: How a Hindutva Icon Justified the Idea of Rape as a Political Tool' in a leftist webzine.[44] The article went viral. The gist of the article is that in his book *Six Glorious Epochs of Indian History* (finished in 1963, but started years earlier), Savarkar had criticized the chivalrous attitude of Shivaji towards the captured Muslim women during his victorious expeditions against the Mughals. The passages in question are these:

> Even now we proudly refer to the noble acts of Chhatrapati Shivaji and Chimaji Appa, when they honourably sent back the daughter-in-law of the Muslim Governor of Kalyan and the wife of the Portuguese governor of Bassein respectively. But is it not strange that, when they did so neither Shivaji Maharaj nor Chimaji Appa should ever remember, the atrocities and the rapes and the molestation, perpetrated by Mahmud of Ghazni, Muhammad Ghori, Alla-ud-din Khilji and others, on thousands of Hindu ladies and girls…Did not the plaintive screams and pitiful lamentations of the millions of molested Hindu women, which reverberated throughout the length and breadth of the country, reach the ears of Shivaji Maharaj and Chimaji Appa?

Then Savarkar observes:

> If they had taken such a fright in the first two or three centuries, millions and millions of luckless Hindu ladies would have been saved all their indignities, loss of their own religion, rapes, ravages and other unimaginable persecutions.

One should note here that Savarkar clearly talks about such a retaliatory violence in the context of bygone historical times—'in the first two or three centuries' of the Islamist incursions. Unfortunately, there is another aspect to his writings. He had been a witness to the communal riots that happened before Partition and which reached their zenith during the Partition. Till his last days, the systematic persecution of Hindus, particularly through violence against women, was happening in East Pakistan. Five years after his death, it would result in the 1971 genocide. In all these, there was definitely a theological asymmetry.

Let it be stated clearly that during the Partition, Hindus and Sikhs also committed shameful, inhuman and unforgivable crimes against helpless Muslim women, which included murder, rape and abduction. But in the case of Muslims and Pakistan, the crimes against women were committed in a more systematic manner with a clear theological goal. While the former, unforgivable as it is, was a spontaneous mob violence, the latter was well-planned, systematic and had theological as well as demographic goals.

The abduction and forced marriages through the Islamist nikah marriages and then repeated sales of the women were already getting systematized as weapons against Hindus in pre-Partition riots that would ultimately lead to Partition. Savarkar was one of the earliest historians and a political leader to bring out this connection in a blunt way. But by no means was he the only one who noticed. For example, J. M. Dutta, an eminent and a rigorous mathematician, pointed out that in 1941 the abduction of Hindu women in Bengal alone had reached on an average 700 per annum. In his paper titled 'Continued Abduction of Hindu Women: Its Effect on the Bengali Hindus', he concluded that 'in any view, abduction of Hindu women by the Muslims and their continued loss to the Hindu community, so far as it affects the growth of the Hindus is a matter which cannot be neglected any longer without serious consequences'.[45]

While it is easy to form a Hindu-Muslim symmetric narrative of violence on women by the rioting mobs, including pathological perverts on both sides taking advantage of the situation, not to mention the usual clichés of patriarchy and body-based shame and ingrained notions of pollution, etc., today it is hard for anyone to see the distinct way in which the abducted Hindu women shared their destiny with Yazidi women later. We find in the report of the Liaison Officer the remark that '... at *Man sera* and some other places (N. W. F. P.) there are regular camps where Hindu girls are being sold'.[46]

The Hindu and Sikh girls were not just distributed among rioters but were also married to Muslims and then sold in markets inside Pakistan. No such equivalent of markets for abducted women seemed to have existed anywhere in India. And even if it had existed, if at all, in the rarest of rare circumstances, Hindus themselves would not have tolerated it. But in Pakistan, such markets always came up whenever there was access to Hindu women by rioters during Partition in 1947, or marauders in Kashmir or the Pakistan army in East Pakistan in 1971. Here are a few memories of the events gathered by Dr D'Costa:[47]

> At the height of the riots, during August and September, when the majority of rapes and abductions occurred, there was almost no limit to the vehemence of the mobs. Throughout the chaos, both planned and random abductions of women and girls were carried out, particularly in situations in which large numbers of refugees—disoriented and inadequately protected—had assembled or were on the move. For example, Kirpal Singh records that two trains crossed on the Kamoke railway line, one carrying 260 refugees and the other carrying Pakistan Army soldiers. After the latter realized that the former was carrying Hindu refugees, it was attacked. Most of the men were killed and 50 women and girls were forcibly taken by the soldiers. Similarly, in East Bengal, the Ansars, a paramilitary force responsible for the safety of the citizens also perpetrated attacks and abducted Hindu women. One of my respondents was on one of the trains leaving Pakistan and recalled how she hid in a toilet....In the confusion that followed, while she was fortunate enough to avoid being abducted, she witnessed many girls and women being taken from the trains.... Describing the massacres of refugees in Kamoke, Gujranwala district, an Indian official wrote, the most ignoble feature of the tragedy was the distribution of young girls amongst the members of the Police Force, the National Guards (an Islamo-fascist organization-AN) and the local goondas. The Station House Officer Dilder Hussain collected the victims in an open space near Kamoke Railway Station and gave a free hands to the mob. After the massacre was over, the girls were distributed like sweets...Later on as a result of the efforts of the Liaison Agency and the East Punjab Police some girls were recovered from Kamoke, Eminabad and some surrounding villages ... A list of at least 70 untraced girls abducted from the Kamoke train was handed over the Police by District Liaison Officer...It is feared that most of these girls had been sold or taken underground.

A 13-year-old girl named Shrimati Chander Kanta recalled before Dr D'Costa, how the Muslim military surrounded the people of Mirpur and she was captured by one Abdur Rahman and was forced into marrying him. She remained with him for one month. She was rescued along with 48 other girls. She recounted how when she was in the camp, the Muslims who had married them, came there and tried to lure them back:

> The Muslims who visited the camp to meet the girls to whom they are married usually threatened them that if they go to India they would be killed by the Sikhs and Hindus and thus warned them that they should not express their willingness to be evacuated.

Similarly, when the jihadist tribal mujahideen raided Kashmir in 1947, the girls abducted by the jihadists 'were exhibited in the bazaars of Peshawar and

Bannu, thereby enticing Pathans towards Kashmir. Many were subjected to unmentionable indignities.'[48] Reports of Hindu women from Kashmir being auctioned at '150 rupees a piece' had reached Nehru himself.[49]

In 1971 when the West Pakistan army started indulging in the systematic abduction and rape of Bengali women, the abduction was justified because they still were Hindus, while being Muslim only in their names. Governor and Martial Law Administrator Tikka Khan considered this as a legitimate strategy: the rape of Bengali Muslim women which to him, was impregnation by proper Muslim men—meaning West Pakistani men—to elevate the genetic nature of East Pakistan and bring it under Pakistan's control. The unconverted Hindu women were mostly raped and killed. After the liberation of Bangladesh, even the new government was not very enthusiastic about the recovery of the abducted Hindu women. Hindu activists were complaining about this attitude. Contrary to the popular picture of Muslims and Hindus fighting together in Mukti Bahini on the ground, particularly in rural districts, the Muslims did not hesitate to plunder the deserted houses of Hindus. It was not just greed. They 'also tracked them to their hiding places in the jungle for blackmail, robbery and rape'.[50]

Whether it was 1947 or 1971, academics and media people have studied these abductions, mainly through the secular sociological lenses with ingrained anti-Hindu attitudes. The striking similarities of the modus operandi of the emerging Islamic State (ISIS), with respect to Yazidi women and their abduction, sexual slavery, selling in the market and forcible conversion, as well as marriages on the one hand, and the systematic abduction, rape, forcible conversion and marriage during pre-Partition and Partition riots, the 1950 East Bengal anti-Hindu riots and the 1971 genocide, shows that for radical Islamists from pre-Partition Muslim League to jihadist outfits, abduction, rape and forceful marriage of non-Muslim women seem to be a sanctioned means to achieve their goal of Islamic supremacy in the larger Indian mass.

So, when Savarkar was writing those lines, even as he was not prescribing the same horrendous treatment in the present conditions, he definitely should have been deeply affected by the abduction of Hindu and Sikh women during the riots, and it should have agonized him.

Again, Savarkar was not alone in that agony. The systematic abduction and conversion of Hindu women had reached such phenomenal proportions that Gandhi linked a demand from Indian Muslims of the return of abducted Hindu women by Pakistan Islamists with the former's loyalty to India. In his speech made to Indian Muslims in New Delhi on 18 September 1947, he told them that Patel had informed of his reasons to suspect that the vast majority of Muslims in India were not loyal to India. For Gandhi himself, the Muslims who wished to be citizens of the Indian Union, their loyalty to the Union must come before everything else. Muslims in Delhi had assured through their written declaration that they were loyal to the Indian Union. Then in the concluding part of his speech Gandhi 'advised them that, as a token of their loyalty to the Indian Union, they should issue a public statement that all Hindu women abducted by the Muslims in Pakistan should be restored to their families'.[51] In other words, Gandhi tied the loyalty of Muslims in India to their public denouncement of abduction and forcible conversion of Hindu women done by their co-religionists in Pakistan.

Coming back to Savarkar, a careful reading of Savarkar also shows that more important than his 'what-if' scenario of the bygone centuries, he was concentrating more on battling the social taboos that Hindus had in accepting the abducted women who returned. Savarkar gives the example of Ravana, the rakshasa king of Sri Lanka, who pooh-poohed the suggestion of his well-wishers to return Sita. Ravana considered the abduction not as irreligious but as 'the greatest duty'. He then draws a parallel to this attitude and that of 'Muslims of those times':

> With this same shameless religious fanaticism, the aggressive Muslims of those times considered it their highly religious duty to carry away forcibly the women of the enemy side, as if they were commonplace property to ravish them, to pollute them and to distribute them to all and sundry, from the Sultan to the common soldier and to absorb them completely in their fold. This was considered a noble act which increased their number.[52]

Then Savarkar moves on to the *Puranic* example of Sri Krishna fighting against Narakasura. Savarkar gives historicity to the episode. So Narakasura becomes an Assyrian war lord of ancient times who had raided and carried away 'Aryan women' of India. Krishna defeated Narakasura and killed him. But he did not stop with the military victory:

> Shree Krishna's army did not forsake their kinswomen, simply because they were forcibly polluted and violated—a dastardly thought which he never entertained for a minute. On the contrary Shree Krishna as the Bhoopati, the Lord of the whole Earth, brought all those sixteen thousand or more women to his kingdom, rehabilitated them honourably and took upon himself the responsibility of feeding and protecting them. This very act of Krishna, as the Bhoopati, has been fantastically construed by the writers of the Puranas as to describe him the husband of those thousands of women. He was later thought to have married all of them.[53]

With respect to the present context, the only things he advocates are very clearly the rehabilitation of abducted women by Islamists and the willingness to convert those Muslim women ready to embrace Hinduism. In this discourse, Savarkar considers jauhar—though an inspiring unparalleled sacrifice—the result of the restrictions which made it impossible for the violated, abducted and converted men and women to return to Hindu Dharma:

> Under the illusion of preserving the purity of their own caste and religion, the Hindu Society of the Islamic era began to enforce as their religious duty, the bans on exchange of food, on inter-caste marriage and other bans, even when they were harmful to the society.... Neither any single Hindu who was converted under coercion, nor even his progeny could ever come back to Hinduism: their sin had no redemption, no salvation. For generations together the Hindus believed this to be their inviolable religious injunction; ... On account of these very bans, thousands of our Hindu ladies kindled the fires of johar, century after century, in order to avoid violation at the hands of the Muslims. To save themselves from this humiliation of violation by enemies millions others leapt into rivers, lakes and wells, all over the country and destroyed themselves along with their small children at their breasts.

So, for Savarkar, the conversion of captured Muslim women and their distribution to Hindus was only a 'what-if' scenario of a bygone era. His insistence was more on the absorption and rehabilitation of abducted and abused women back into Hindu society against the then prevalent patriarchal social stagnation. While the despicable inhuman violence against women either to Hindu or Muslim women during the riots in India had happened long before Savarkar had written and published his book, the systematic abduction, sexual slavery, auctioning and conversion of women has been part of the pan-Islamist movement against Hindus in India, as it has been used against Yazidis in Iraq.

Even the criticism of Shivaji by Savarkar was not accepted by the Hindutvaites at large. This is attested in a letter written by Hindutva intellectual Sita Ram Goel. When a fellow Hindu activist was disturbed by the criticism on Shivaji's chivalrous behaviour towards Muslim women that he was not ready to believe Savarkar could have made it, a disturbed Goel wrote to him:

> Savarkar's statement about Shivaji's failure to distribute captured Muslim women among Hindu soldiers has been read by me with my own eyes in one of the chapters in Six Periods, published by an RSS set-up in Lucknow with a footnote, "We do not agree with this". ... But a single statement does not undo his vision on India's history. (12 March 1997)[54]

That an RSS publication found it important to say that it differed with Savarkar himself is important. Clearly, there are stands in the mainstream Hindutva process which can defy and differ with even a Savarkar. Clearly, there are forces operating in the larger Indian land mass which use abduction and conversion of women to further the religious war they are waging against theo-diversity of this region. But Hindutvaites are clearly not among them. And the historiography of Savarkar does not support such a view.

Lakshmi Bai and Yamuna Bai: A Revisit

In the book *The RSS: The icons of the Indian Right* (2019), written by Nilanjan Mukhopadhyay, an anti-Hindutva journalist-writer, it is alleged that Savarkar never allowed public participation of his own wife:

> For the significant part of the forty years that Vinayak and Yamunabai lived together after his jail term, the man spent most of his time fulfilling his life's mission. He had little time for his wife, and hardly made any effort to help her come into her own.... After his release from detention, Savarkar completely "excluded his wife from public life", but "attracted women followers to the cause of militant Hindu nationalism".[55]

For this, Mukhopadhyay gives as reference Lise McKean who, in her 1996 essentially Hinduphobic book on Gurus and 'Hindu Nationalist Movement' claims that on the authority of Dhananjay Keer, the biographer of Savarkar, that 'he excluded his wife from his public life and reports that when she was ill and departing for the hospital Savarkar was "not in the mood" to say farewell'.[56] However, the relevant portion that she had cited actually does not say that Savarkar 'excluded' his wife from his public life. The relevant portion reads:

> He returned home (from hospital after a thigh fracture) on June 24, 1963. When after three months he could walk a little with the help of nurse and staff, his wife was taken seriously ill. He got her removed on October 16, to Dr Talwalkar's clinic at Dadar, but he was not in a mood to see her even when she so much devotionally insisted on her bidding him farewell....The news of her death fell heavily on him.... He said that after his release from the Andaman she led a happy life with him for over forty years.[57]

Keer informs us that Savarkar asked for her body to be taken to the electric crematorium and then told his son that in a year or two, his body too should be taken to the same crematorium. It is from this passage that the picture of

Savarkar 'excluding' his wife from public life is construed by McKean and then repeated by Mukhopadhyay. However, this so-called 'exclusion' of his wife from Savarkar's public life, gets falsified by facts. History enthusiast Ratnakar Sadasyula points out there exists a small biography of Yamuna Bai Savarkar (affectionately called Mai Savarkar) by M. S. Dixit. In his article on Yamuna Bai Savarkar, he places the following facts:

> In 1930, Mai chaired a public meeting of women at the Vithal Mandir in Ratnagiri to propagate Swadeshi, that was attended by Dalit women too. Mai also took part in the inter community dining of women organized in 1932, at Ratnagiri, on the occasion of the visit of the Satyashodak leader Madhavrao Bagal. She along with Savarkar organized an Akhil Hindu Yagna, and in 1936 a holy palanquin, was taken out on occasion of Akhil Hindu Nama Saptah consecrated by Mai. One of the largest inter community dinner was organized for women of all castes at the Patit Pavan Mandir in Ratnagiri, and Mai along with Ms. Mundkur, the wife of the Dy Collector attended it. She was felicitated by ladies of the Chitpavan Brahmin Sangh in 1941 and she later attended an Akhil Hindu Tilgul function, saying "The nation is my home".[58]

When informed about the death of his wife 'Savarkar almost swooned' and 'had to be held to prevent him from falling'. Similarly, Mukhopadhyay tries to cast a negative slant to the way Savarkar had glorified the women who took part in the 1857 uprising:

> On the one hand, he praised women like Rani Lakshmibai, because of her valour and indomitable spirit. Yet, he blamed her and other women who participated in the First War of Independence for acting prematurely in Meerut, resulting in the failure of 1857.[59]

Though he does not mention it, this too is taken from the book by McKean rather than from primary sources. McKean writes:

> Foremost among courageous women is the Rani of Jhansi. Savarkar commemorated her as a fearless military leader, who on the battlefield was "found everywhere inspiriting heroism even in the coldest hearts". In his foreword to the 1970 edition of the Indian War of Independence, G. M. Joshi praises Savarkar's "gifted intuitions" for reviving the memory of this heroic Hindu warrior-queen and adds that "humble I and a thousand other Indians have named our dear daughters after Laximibai, Rani of Jhansi" (1970, xxiii).... In some circumstances, however, women can be impediments to the efforts of strategists and warriors. Savarkar blames women for the premature and failed Sepoy rising in Meerut.[60]

Note that while McKean presents Savarkar as blaming 'women for the premature and failed Sepoy rising in Meerut', Mukhopadhyay adds his own creative flourish by including Rani Lakshmi Bai as well: 'he blamed her and other women who participated in the First War of Independence for acting prematurely in Meerut'.

Going through what Savarkar actually wrote about these specific events shows that McKean had done the initial distortion and Mukhopadhyay simply once again recycled her distortion, adding the historically untenable expansion of the distortion as his original contribution. The sequence of events in Meerut happened on 9 May 1857 when 85 Indian soldiers were punished for refusing to use the new cartridges by handcuffing them and then sentencing them to ten years rigorous imprisonment. The remaining Sepoys already knew that there was a coordinated attack being planned for 31 May. However, the scene of their compatriots being handcuffed and humiliated, infuriated them. Along with that came the taunting of women and children and of their own for not reacting.

> It is true that the spirited and patriotic women of the Meerut bazaars, who taunted the soldiers and goaded them on to release their comrades, have added one more honourable episode to our history. But the Meerut Sepoys, by their rising, unconsciously put their brethren in unforeseen confusion by warning the enemy beforehand!

Rani of Jhansi was not the only woman warrior of 1857 that Savarkar praises, though he reserves the highest praise for her. He points out that both in Delhi and Lucknow, the affairs of the state were looked after by women: in the former on account of the old age of Emperor Bahadur Shah by Begum Zinat Mahal and in the case of the latter, by Begum Hazrat Mahal because the heir to the throne Birjis Kadar was a minor. Begum Hazrat Mahal of Oudh, 'though not quite another Lakshmi Bai was undoubtedly a great organiser, full of love of liberty and the spirit of daring.' Here he blames the lack of unity among 'the Revolutionaries, Rajas, and Maharajas' as well as the 'internal disorganisation and carelessness' and also the 'characterless Sepoys' who 'demanded pay before fighting' as reasons for the failure. At the same time, with regard to the Begum, he praises 'her able efforts' to bring unity and admires 'the resolute, daring, and capable Begum still maintained, in spite of all these disorders, the whole administration intact is a sure indication of her unequalled grit'.[61]

In the case of Lakshmi Bai, he points out that it was the unheeding of the advice of Lakshmi Bai and the indulgence of the chieftains after their initial success over the British that resulted in their failure:

> So far so good; but once having shocked Sir Hugh Rose and disheartened him, woe betide him who listened not to the words of Ranee Lakshmi Bai! All other functions but the one great function of war must be stopped. But it seemed that, as ill-luck would have it, the intoxication of the Revolutionaries would make them blind to the necessity of keeping the army in complete readiness. They were all immersed in luxury, good dinners, and fatal dilatoriness—they thought, perhaps, that this was the sole end of Swaraj.[62]

Once again, it is a tested modus operandi. A calumny gets created against Savarkar, that too by distorting a primary source by a Western Hinduphobic author in 1996. This distortion then gets recycled by a Hindutva-averse journalist in 2019. In reality, instead of providing a true picture of the Hindutva worldview, this provides a classic example of how the narrative against Hindutva is manufactured by establishment media and academics. Facts and contextual understanding of Hindutva itself, along with the personalities who propounded it, can alone show the fallacy of such a colossal and sustained campaign by a Hinduphobic campaign against Hindutva. But such a fact checking is never done either by Indian academia, or by mainstream media.

Savarkar was not the only exponent of the Hindutva-Hindu Sanghatan movement. There were others equally illustrious as him. Perhaps the only movement in India today which can claim the contribution of personalities who had literally sacrificed the best parts of their own lives for the sake of Indian freedom movement in the most inhuman and subhuman conditions of the cellular jails of Andamans, it may be the Hindutva movement. Let us look at another such leader of Hindu Sanghatan movement—Bhai Parmanand (1876–1947).

Bhai Parmanand: Lesser-known Hindu Mahasabha Leader's Saga of Sacrifice

> The room was of the smallest dimension—cold and dark. It seemed to be her only home. It was indescribably poor, and she herself was nursing on her lap her sick child, while the elder child was sitting by the mother, wan, listless and pale. The child in the mother's lap had fever, and the mother herself told me how her eldest child had died of this only six months ago. It was easy to see from the dark ill-ventilated room and the poverty-stricken condition of the family, how the eldest daughter had caught the disease.[63]

Those were the words of Reverend Charles Andrews (1871–1940), a church of England missionary and a close friend of Mahatma Gandhi, describing the condition of Bhai Parmanand's family. At that time, Bhai Parmanand was in the Andamans jail, suffering 'transportation with forfeiture'. The 'forfeiture' had deprived his family of even the cooking utensils and now his wife was supporting the family with a 'scanty pay', as Andrews put it, from her work as a primary school teacher in an Arya Samaj school.

Earlier, Bhai Parmanand worked as a lecturer of history and political economics. As a life-member of Arya Samaj with a vow to teach at a fixed allowance of ₹ 75, he had declined a higher career from Panjab University, as it would have raised his salary above the limit of his vow. He had worked as a Vedic missionary in South Africa. He had later gone to the United States to coordinate the overseas attempts by Indians to achieve Independence, where he was active in the Ghadar movement. His cousin Bhai Balmukund came in the line of Bhai Matidas, the disciple of Guru Tegh Bahadur, who was martyred by Aurangzeb. When the British hanged Bhai Balmukund to death, his young and beautiful wife, Ram Rakhi, married only for a year, ended her life.

Bhai Parmanand was deported to Andaman. Here he, along with other convicts, had to extract fine coconut fibre from the bundle of coconut fibre given to them. They had to grind oil in the mill tied to the yoke like draught animals. British used *tandeels*—black uniforms given to convicts to harass the convicts who beat up and abused them, particularly the political prisoners. Rev Andrews, learning about the plight of Bhai Parmanand, wrote:

> The thought has come home to me again and again... how futile, how stupid, how insensate it is to keep one of the brightest and keenest intellects in modern India, a man with such noble qualities of mind and heart, imprisoned along with the lowest criminals for the rest of his life and engaged in the useless, senseless and meaningless occupation of grinding hour after hour at the mill.[64]

Solitary confinement, restriction of movement by having an iron-stake between the legs, handcuffs on the wrists and handcuffing behind the back, and whipping with a maximum of 30 lashes....the prisoners had to endure all these tortures. Often the prisoners became suicidal. Bhai Parmanand records:

> For the future-blank despair, for the present, the severity of punishment and of hard labour; under such conditions many prisoners become indifferent to life and resolve to destroy themselves. Though there is a search every evening and the warder keeps going round the lines at night with lamp in hand, they manage to conceal a piece of rope or improvise one by tearing to pieces their shirt or breeches and hang themselves

> to death.... Several such cases occurred during my stay there and these served to impress firmly on our minds how near the life and death was our place of residence.[65]

Suicidal thoughts and a complete sense of purposelessness in rotting away his entire life in the subhuman conditions in the prison started taking its toll on him.

> My own mind was kept agitated by the thought, 'Why should I live longer?' A sort of special feeling of uneasiness occupied my heart. Every moment I was debating within myself whether I should cut shot my life or continue to live.[66]

As Bhai Parmanand toiled in prison, the First World War was coming to a close. His observations regarding the war show a very humanistic and Indic vision. He saw the war rooted in 'the very essence of European civilization, whose one ideal has been self-aggrandizement, by whatever means, at the expense of others'. Unlike some other nationalists, he did not harbour the notion that had Germany won the war, India would have become liberated. He observed with cold and remarkable objectivity thus:

> As regards the English nation, although it has kept us down and trampled on our rights, I had little hope that the atrocities would be less if the Germans came. No doubt, if both powers should fight in India, there might be a chance of improving our position.[67]

If Indian political prisoners had any hope that with the end of the War the government would release them, they were smashed with the behaviour of the government which enacted the Rowlatt Committee. Meanwhile, the Chief Commissioner of Andamans at that time was one Col. Douglas who happened to be a great friend of Sir Michael O'Dwyer. One day he came to Bhai Parmanand and informed him that O'Dwyer still remembered him and asked if he was still alive. Meanwhile, some of the letters of Bhai Parmanand which described the sordid conditions of the Andamans, got published in the *Punjab Tribune*. This led to the solitary confinement of Bhai Parmanand. At this point, Bhai Parmanand started a fast unto death. After a week, the authorities started force-feeding him. The doctor who came to see the prisoners came with a tube for forcing the milk into the stomach through the nose. Bhai Parmanand writes:

> Hands and feet were held tight, and a long rubber tube was introduced through the nose into the stomach through which the milk was passed down. The process was painful, but this is the usual thing in jail and was done by force.[68]

The struggle went on for eight weeks. And after much persuasion by a new Superintendent who took an admiration for him, Bhai Parmanand gave up the hunger strike which nearly killed him. In 1920, he was released after five years of incarceration. Upon returning home, he found it hard to get a job and made peace with the idea that his wife would work in the school and he would look after the house. Some friends sent him to Kashmir in 1930 to regain his health. There he observed, 'Yes, great injustice had everywhere been done to Hindus in respect to their religion, but such treatment had exceeded all the limits in Kashmir.' The sight of Kashmiri Hindu women and children with the vermillion on their forehead and religious marks, made him 'unconsciously bow' his head remembering the 'great sacrifice made by Guru Tegh Bahadur'.

Soon, he took up the work that was dearer to his heart—teaching. He wanted to create an educational system that was completely Indic. Therefore, when Gandhi started his national educational programme, 'Bhaiji' as he was called, gave his full cooperation. When he started teaching again in the college, one of the students who had enrolled received his particular attention. His name was Bhagat Singh.

Bhai Parmanand had a great respect for Gandhi, but he was highly critical of the Khilafat movement which he rightly recognized as having 'fanned bigotry and fanaticism in the minds of the Muslims'. Attacks on Hindus had already started taking place throughout the country: Malabar, Multan, Kohat, Calcutta, etc. At Saharanpur, where he went personally for relief work, he saw the utterly helpless plight of Hindus and discovered that the local Khilafat committee leaders were the ones indulging in the riots. When eminent Hindu leaders of the Congress like Swami Shraddhanand, Pandit Madan Mohan Malviya and Lala Lajpat Rai realized the danger the Hindu society was facing and started a movement for Hindu Sanghatan, Bhai Parmanand also joined the movement. The communal award system with which the British were playing havoc with social harmony and to which the Congress had largely compromised, pained the visionary in him. He stated that 'if the communal award remains the way to Swaraj would be closed for Hindus forever and that they would be subjected to double slavery'.

When Congress leaders started attacking him that he was being fearful, he remarked caustically that he knew no fear even when imprisonment was dreadful, so why he should be afraid 'of going to jail now when even such persons as have passed all their lives in wine and women could court two- or three-months' imprisonment and come to be known as fearless or brave patriots'. For the Congressmen, it would not have been lost upon them as to whom he targeted this rebuke. Though a great admirer of Gandhi, he never lost sight of what he considered as the truth, in the awe of the Mahatma. He rejected the idea that it was Gandhi who made Congress and national struggle a people's movement. Given the fact that even today, this idea that Gandhi made the independence movement a mass movement prevails, the observations of Bhai Parmanand need to be quoted at length:

> Very often I am told that the Congress, in spite of all its defects, has at least done one great good to India. It has brought awakening in the land.... If Mahatma Gandhi and the Congress did anything it was this: they harnessed that universal sentiment to the service of their own movement.

Bhai Parmanand was also a caste abolitionist and started the Caste-Elimination movement within Arya Samaj. He also adopted a child from another community as his own son and brought him up. Like M. C. Rajah of Tamil Nadu, he also held that before Hindu-Muslim unity, first Hindu unity should be achieved. In 1932 a tragedy struck him in the form of the death of his wife who had given him constant support in all his struggles. In 1939 his youngest daughter died too.

When at last in 1947, freedom came with the vivisection of India, Bhai Parmanand saw Hindus becoming refugees in their own land over a single night. He had long ago proposed a phased regrouping of people. In hindsight, one can say that had his words been listened to, much human tragedy and suffering could have been averted. Yet he saw an independent India before he died on 8 December 1947.

His Sanghatan Views

Bhai Parmanand wrote *Hindu Sanghatan* in Hindi. The book was translated into English by Prof. Lal Chand Dhawan and was published in 1936 by the Central Hindu Yuvak Sabha of Lahore. At the very beginning of the book Bhai Parmanand distinguishes between dogmatic religion and the Hindu spiritual traditions. He underscores freedom from dogmas as the unique positive feature of Hindu Dharma:

> What is the foundation of religion? Religion lays down a few dogmas and teaches us that these and these alone are true, and everything against them is untruth. It also teaches that salvation for man lies in having faith in those dogmas alone. These two things, however, will put an end to all freedom of opinion in the world. How can an intelligent man be ever compelled to believe against his reason that there is only one God, that he possesses certain characteristics and reveals His will in different ways?

> ... Religion presupposes the truth of a few postulates, and thus lays the foundations of narrow-mindedness and bigotry. And what if these postulates themselves happen to be wrong? The Hindu Shastras do not proceed on any such suppositions or hypotheses. They take note of the universe around us, and in trying to solve the mystery of the existence of the universe, they infer the existence of the power that controls the universe. Beyond this, they confess everything is unknowable. No one can ever say that he knows Him; even he who says that he does not know Him is wrong. The following verse of the Gita shows how important and venerable freedom of opinion is: 'All roads lead to me. He who seeks me, whatever way he may follow, shall surely find me'. The author of the Gita, too, had many postulates at his disposal. He could lay down one or two of these as obligatory and kill all freedom of thought. But he preferred that freedom to everything else; for therein lay the welfare of mankind.[69]

Then he proceeds to define who is a Hindu. While admiringly accepting the Savarkarite definition as 'the only correct and complete definition', he himself desires a much simpler definition and states that anyone who calls and considers himself a Hindu is a Hindu. A non-historian Parmanand does not delve into the truth of the Aryan race theory and he seems to have no problem in accepting the Aryans as a race, but it does not matter much to him. He approvingly quotes a scholar saying that Hindu as a name of the country might date back to pre-Aryan times.[70]

His analysis of the phenomenon of religion shaping the human mindscape anticipates the modern neuro-psychological approach to the phenomenon of religion. In his view, the religion becomes the carrier of values and is a motivating force for humans to sacrifice themselves for a cause greater than individual interests. However, as religions claim ownership to competing and at times mutually exclusive 'truths', one needs to apply to reason rather than to dogma and belief. In this, he criticized even his fellow Arya Samajists as well as proselytizing religions. Again, this is an approach that one finds in almost all Hindu Sanghatanist worldviews. The passage needs to be quoted here in a detailed manner, for it expresses one important aspect of Hindutva and the Hindu Sanghatan movement:

> In spite of the fact that the countless wrongs and atrocities have been perpetrated on account of the spread of religions and creeds, the world has got the same respect for them as before, and people are still prepared to sacrifice their everything for their respective religions....Man begins to love the religion or thoughts of his birth as much as his native soil and society. Belief in religious dogmas has a special advantage also. Piety and Devotion born of faith are not to be found in reason and argumentation. The principles in which we have faith fix certain ideas on our minds

> in which a form that we believe them alone to be true and become prepared to sacrifice our all for their sake. It is a noble aspect of man's nature that he is prepared to make any and every sacrifice for the sake of what he thinks and believes to be true. But for religions this side of human nature would have remained undeveloped. To keep alive this spirit in man is a good thing and this has been made possible by religion. But it should not be inferred from this that what the followers (of) different religions regard as true is in reality true....An idea of the mentality of such men can be gathered from this alone that in the teeth of reason and proofs, they still persist in believing the earth to be flat and are ready to break the head of any one who differs with them.... Is there no true religion in the whole wide world? The fact that religion is really true, though in a sense, all religions are true; for a religion is true tor him who believes in it. The common saying that Truth always triumphs means nothing more than that the truth in which more men or more powerful men have faith, triumphs. In reality what is Truth? To know and to judge this, man's reason alone is the means. According as a man's intellect is his understanding of truth will be. Hence, the prayer contained in the Gaitri mantra is that our reason and intellect may be sound....In the Punjab the Arya Samaj is considered to be the most active and powerful religious body among the Hindus. Now consider the case of the Arya Samaj. If anyone has the courage to say today that he doubts if the Vedas are revealed, plans will be made at once to turn him out of the Samaj. Such statements make for weakness of belief in doctrines; and it is feared that the weakening of belief in its doctrines will weaken Arya Samaj itself. If this is really so, then the Arya Samaj is nothing but a creed.[71]

One can see here that Bhai Parmanand points out how the religion serves an important role in human evolution, particularly how it makes individual members of human species sacrifice their own genetic survival for the group, and the genetic survival of those belonging to the same memetic clan (which usually also may have ethnic supremacist underpinning, like Islam enhances ultimately Arabic supremacism and Maoism Han-racism). However, he points out that while the kindling of martyrdom is an important achievement of religion, the other side of it is the fanaticism which rejects reason and breeds intolerance. With 'truth' being a construct, ultimately the appeal has to be reason. This is an important conceptual evolution in the Arya Samaj thought process which has been ignored by many Western observers of Hindutva and also 'South Asian' academic informants for the Western knowledge production. Arya Samaj in their narratives is merely shown as a monotheist projection of Vedic religion, a kind of 'return to Vedic purity' influenced by colonial encounters. However, the clear placing of reason over dogma and even belief in Vedas by an Arya Samajist leader makes such a characterization of the Arya Samaj movement.

Though Bhai Parmanand tends to accept the dominant narrative that Buddhism abolished 'caste system', a term he (or the translator) seems to confound with *Varna*, he considers that as a negative feature of Buddhism.

> Buddhism abolished the caste system and laid emphasis merely on the duties of the individual. The consequence was that the nation lost all sense of national and patriotic duties. It must be borne in mind that the distinction of castes was based on differences of work and worth and not, as in the present times, on birth.[72]

He further emphasizes that one of the important reasons for the fall of Hindus is because the basis of the Varna system shifted from worth to birth:

> As birth came into greater and greater prominence, worth and character sank into greater and greater oblivion, till at last all castes Brahmanas, Kshatriyas, Vaishyas and Shudras alike fell from their ideals and lost sight of their duties altogether. In my opinion the greatest and most harmful consequence of the importation of birth into the caste system was that as Brahmanas, Kshatriyas, etc. began to be regarded as such by birth, no one paid any heed to his duties nor was any one under the necessity of doing so....Only this slight change from worth to birth in the caste system dragged the nation from the summit of glory down into the bottomless pit of degradation. The Brahmanas' spiritual greatness and knowledge yielded place to ignorance and selfishness....The Kshatriyas lost their bravery and spirit of sacrifice and instead became cowards and ever ready to sell their country to its enemies. The Vaishyas, instead of earning wealth by honest means and giving charity for the welfare of the nation, grew greedy of gold and ready to sacrifice their country and even their religion at the altar of wealth. Even the Shudras gave up serving the community and took to serving him who paid them better.[73]

So according to him, the Hindu nation had become old and weak and it needed rejuvenation. Towards this end, Bhai Parmanand strongly advocates inter-caste marriages:

> The four Varnas or divisions of society date back to the very remote past. The sub-castes came into being much later, and are unnatural. These have split up our society into countless small sub-divisions so that the coming into being of the national sentiment is out of the question. The scope for marriages has become very restricted.... Castes have also restricted the mingling of blood a great deal. For instance, certain sections of society are growing more and more cowardly on account of confining their blood to their own castes. The low are becoming lower

still. It is a law of nature that the more distant the bloods that mingle the better will be the offspring....There is but one remedy for decay, namely, that new blood should be infused into the community. I think, therefore, that it is necessary to permit free inter-marriages with those castes among the Hindus which have got fresh blood in them so that a new life and spirit may be born in the community.[74]

There is a striking aspect of Hindu Sanghatan worldview here which sees endogamy as the reason for the physical fall of the Hindus. While world over the racists and racism-motivated eugenics stood for disallowing the racial mix-up, the Hindu Sanghatanists stood for the mixing of 'blood' and lifting the prohibitions of intermarriages. The narrative that Bhai Parmanand constructs where the Varnas were originally occupation-based and not birth-based and later, as they became birth-based, the coming up of the proliferation of 'sub-castes' and along with that, the restrictions of marriages between the castes, has a striking similarity to the narrative developed by Dr Ambedkar. In both narratives, the restriction on marriages did not transform Varna to caste, but there were other processes. According to Bhai Parmanand, this was the gradual emphasis on birth which became more and more central to the identification of one's Varna, while Dr Ambedkar puts the blame entirely on the process which he terms as 'Brahminism'. Dr Ambedkar based his speculation on:

Varna is not hereditary either in status or occupation. On the other hand, caste implies a system in which status and occupation are hereditary and descend from father to son....The change was accomplished by stages. In the transformation of Varna into Caste three stages are quite well marked. The first stage was the stage in which the duration of Varna i.e., of status and occupation of a person was for a prescribed period of time only. The second stage was a stage in which the status and occupation involved the Varna of a person ensured during lifetime only. The third stage was a stage in which the status and occupation of the Varna became hereditary.... According to ancient tradition as embodied in the Puranas the period for which the Varna of a person was fixed by Manu and Saptarshi was a period of four years and was called Yug. At the end of the period of four years there occurred the Manwantar whereby every fourth year the list was revised. Under the revision some changed their old Varna, some retained it, some lost it and some gained it. The original system seems to have in contemplation the determination of the Varna of adults. It was not based on prior training or close scrutiny of bias and aptitude.... The determination of the Varna was done in a rough and tumble manner. This system seems to have gone into abeyance. A new system grew up in its place. It was known as the Gurukul system. The Gurukul was a school maintained by a Guru (teacher) also called Acharya (learned man). All children went to this Gurukul for their education.

> The period of education extended for twelve years....Upanayan by the Acharyas was the new method of determining Varna which came into vogue in place of method of determination by Manu and Saptarshi. The new method was undoubtedly superior to the old method....The principal change made by Brahmanism was the transfer of authority from the Guru to the father in the matter of performing Upanayan. The result was that the father having the right to perform the Upanayan of his child gave his own Varna to the child and thus made it hereditary. It is by divesting the Guru of his authority to determine the Varna and vesting it in the father that Brahmanism ultimately converted Varna into Caste.[75]

One can note that both in Dr Ambedkar and Bhai Parmanand's views, the narrative core is the same which is that the original Varna system was not birth-based but worth-based. Both consider the fall from Varna to caste (which Bhai Parmanand—or his translator—calls sub-caste), as a great national misfortune. Thus, in a way one can say that though Dr Ambedkar positioned himself as against the Arya Samaj or even Hindu revivalists, he agreed that during the Vedic period, the original system was not one of oppression and was not unjust. On the other hand, the point of departure between most Hindu Sanghatanists and Dr Ambedkar is of the view that the latter puts the blame on 'Brahminism' and thinks of a motivated, almost a conspiratorial process, which intentionally changed the right of *upanayan* from the Guru to the father.

Another important element of Bhai Parmanand's worldview that comes out in his *Hindu Sanghatan* is the process of *samanvaya.* Though he did not name it in the book it comes out forcefully with respect to two issues. One is in the accommodation of so-called idol worship, and another was the cooperation between the traditionalists and the reformers' factions in the Hindu Sanghatan movement itself. As an Arya Samajist, he was required to be against idol worship. But his own experience in the Andamans Cellular Jail reduced his aversion for the worship of the Divine in forms:

> The greatest doctrine of the Arya Samaj is the refutation of idol-worship. Perhaps even the Sanatanists will admit that no image of God can be ever made; but where lies the harm in making idols of Rama, Krishna, etc., and raising temples to them. I was in the Andamans jail. I have no faith (in) idol-worship. But a deep study of the Gita produced in me a special reverence and devotion for Krishna. At that time my one grief was that I had not seen Brindaban, one of my greatest desires then was that in case I was set at liberty I must go on a sort of pilgrimage to the holy land of Brindhaban. Late when I had the good fortune to visit that place thoughts that welled up in my mind were too deep, for words. Every particle of dust there seemed to me to be worthy of worship. Who knows but Krishna might have touched that particle

with his feet? This line of Iqbal recurred to my memory again and again:..."Every particle of the dust of my mother land is like a god to me". Have we left off keeping with us pictures of great men? Admitted that they were of God, but they did reveal in their life and actions the power (of) God the greatest. If, therefore, Krishna or Rama was called an incarnation of that power, where lay the harm or sin?[76]

The second samanvaya process that he discerned was with respect to the two factions within Hindu society which were bitterly opposed to each other with respect to social reforms. Hence, this is even more important with respect to the Hindu Sanghatan movement. He pointed out that the radical Arya Samajists then spearheading social reforms in Hindu society, by themselves alone, would not be able to effect changes. On the contrary, the social reforms proved to be more effective when the reformers while initiating the reforms, also had the orthodoxy convinced and got them roped in as well in integrating the reforms in the society. He explained:

The Sanatan Dharm Sabhas, which had been brought into being with the sole object of offering opposition to the Arya Samaj, opposed all these things, even though it was not part of the Sanatanists' religion or doctrines to do so. Many years have since elapsed, and that opposition and the differences between these two religious bodies have grown much less, so much so that the Sanatan Dharm Sabhas themselves are now prepared to undertake all those reforms. Although the Arya Samaj preached the necessity of these reforms, yet it did not meet with any considerable success in the absence of support from the Hindus in general. Now there can be, owing to the Sanatanists joining hands with Arya Samajists, hope of real success in this direction, provided we all co-operate heart and soul and be determined to effect those reforms. Another effect of this has been that the work of social reform is no longer confined to the Arya Samaj.[77]

The next frequent common strand, also found in Bhai Parmanand is the oneness of humanity. This is a common theme in both Savarkar and Parmanand, in that they both saw the entire humanity as essentially one. While for Savarkar this was the ultimate reality, all distinctions man-made temporary, and would ultimately yield to the oneness of human species, for Bhai Parmanand this was an ideal vision towards which humanity—now selfish and fragmented—should strive for:

It is but a natural and ordinary thing for men to emerge from the individual or wild state of existence and found a family or clan. Their relationship by blood makes them friends and helpers to another and companions in weal and woe. On the other hand, mankind as a whole may be regarded as a big family and all men as brothers. But it is the gods alone who can do so. The human race will reach that stage only if and when there is a fundamental change in human nature, and man rises above all petty self-interests and imbibes some god-like characteristics. Maybe mankind is marching towards that goal, but there is no visible sign of it as yet. The stage which mankind has reached so far lies midway between these two: it is the stage of nationalism....But so far, the wish or thought of marching towards the final stage is hardly in evidence anywhere.[78]

Bhai Parmanand, Hindu Sanghatan and Crossing the Genders

Summing up, Bhai Parmanand wanted the Sanghatan to be one made of love—a love similar to one Radha had for Krishna. He compares the Sanghatanist to Radha and Krishna to the soul of India.

> Sabhas and Sewak Dals are all useful and necessary, but so long as the flame of love does not fire your soul, Sangathan is out of question. This is the true cement.... Krishna is the soul of this nation. Have that deep and boundless love for it as Radha had for Krishna. Like a devotee of Krishna bearing lotus flowers in his hands as offering, offer your life and soul to this Krishna of yours. This is the true worship of your Krishna; this, true devotion to Him.[79]

This passage filled with emotions, particularly coming from a patriot who lost his own daughter who had died in the arms of her mother, because of the self-imposed poverty and the cellular jail imprisonment of the father, is also significant for another reason. Hindu Sanghatan movement has often been portrayed by the Western academics as well as their Indian academic informants, as an exclusive call to masculinity. Here is a typical such academic portrayal of Hindutva as a masculine call for making 'men' out of Hindus:

> Masculine Hinduism anchored the image of strength within the Hindu nationalist discourse. While the discourse that centred on masculine Hinduism constituted a form of resistance to colonial British hierarchy, which itself was founded upon ideas of hegemonic masculinity, Indian masculine Hinduism was not a mechanical incorporation of British ideas dressed in Hindu cultural garb, nor was it monolithic. Rather the Indian construct essentially was a creative response to British disparagement of Indian men. Savarkar clearly perceived masculine Hinduism in terms of virile Aryan warriors riding onwards from a legacy of Indian (i.e., Hindu) imperialism; Vivekananda's image of masculine Hinduism—reflecting

purity and stance of a warrior-monk and derived from notions of a mythic ascetic warriorhood—was delineated most eloquently in Chatterjee's Anandamath. In Vivekananda's vision of masculine Hinduism, spiritual strength sat in the foreground; Savarkar's vision emphasized martial prowess. Both viewed physical strength as an important condition for expressing images of masculinity. Madam Cama, Sister Nivedita, and Sarala Debi drew on a figure of manhood that was closer to Savarkar's Aryan soldier than Vivekananda's fighting monk.[80]

The following passage which was written by an Indian academic informant in the *Berkeley Political Review* provides a typical example of how, after such an academic analysis, the kind of negative stereotyping that emerges in the academia and the media. Here, all social ills in Hindu society get essentialized and both Hindu culture and Hindutva get depicted as imbued with 'toxic masculinity' and then somehow gets related to Hitler and Mussolini:

> Throughout history, nationalist forces have justified the use of force, whether it be during war or conquest, by invoking a sense of threatened masculinity. Aggressive language displays of physical strength, and the pursuit of glory has been used by leaders from Mussolini to Hitler to create a need for violence....The combination of a militarised youth groups and the diet of toxic masculinity that is fed to men growing up in Hindutva led India is key to the maintenance of this 'culture'.[81]

What the above academic portrayal and its percolation in popular academic-media space as negative stereotypes hide, is the historical background and the inner dynamics of the call of Hindu nationalism to so-called 'masculinity'. What Sikata Banerjee calls in passing the 'British disparagement of Indian men', actually went beyond just the British. There was a definite element of religious stereotyping in this 'disparagement'. Christian theologian and academic in Hindu Studies at the University of Birmingham, Dr Sharadha Sugirtharajah explains this particular context vividly:

> Most missionaries portrayed Hinduism as an effeminate religion. They associated idolatry with effeminacy, and effeminacy with all possible vices, such as lying, dishonesty, perjury, and immorality. For Orientalists, by contrast, Hindu effeminacy was a mark of infancy rather than depravity. Most missionaries saw Hindu gods and goddesses as embodiments of vice, lacking in moral virtues and qualities, and thought therefore that those who worshipped them imbibed the immoral qualities of their deities. The missionary concept of Hinduism as an effeminate religion formed part of the larger colonial construction of India as an effeminate nation and as lacking any sense of order, progress, rationality, or the history that characterized Protestant

> Christianity and Western civilization. The implication was that India and Indian women could not be protected by effeminate men but only manly British men. Colonialists and missionaries justified their continued presence and intervention by constructing an effeminate India which was incapable of uplifting itself.[82]

Contrary to Dr Sugirtharajah saying that the missionary portrayal of the Hindu nation was effeminate as part of a colonial project, now it is clear that it is the other way round. In India today, Christian evangelism, Catholic liberation theology, Islamism and Marxism have inherited, nurtured and propagated this missionary view of Hinduism and Hindu society in academia, media and polity with not a less significant success.

It is in this context that one needs to view the 'make me a man' call of Vivekananda. Swami Vivekananda inverted the missionary and colonial caricature of Hindu effeminacy on its head. He accused the rootlessness caused by British education to the perceived effeminacy in Indian upper classes. And even his pure ascetic warrior-monk came from a tradition that has strong roots in the Divine Feminine. Vivekananda himself explained in 1896, in two lectures he delivered to the Western audience on Sri Ramakrishna on this aspect:

> Soul has no sex; it is neither male nor female. It is only in the body that sex exists, and the man who desires to reach the spirit cannot at the same time hold to sex distinctions. Having been born in a masculine body, this man wanted to bring the feminine idea into everything. He began to think that he was a woman, he dressed like a woman, spoke like a woman, gave up the occupations of men, and lived in the household among the women of a good family, until, after years of this discipline, his mind became changed, and he entirely forgot the idea of sex; thus the whole view of life became changed to him. We hear in the West about worshipping woman, but this is usually for her youth and beauty. This man meant by worshipping woman, that to him every woman's face was that of the Blissful Mother, and nothing but that. I myself have seen this man standing before those women whom society would not touch, and falling at their feet bathed in tears, saying, "Mother, in one form Thou art in the street, and in another form Thou art the universe. I salute Thee, Mother, I salute Thee".[83]

This passage of Swami Vivekananda shows how remarkably the 'make me a man' call of Hinduness was rooted in the Divine Feminine rather than on a masculinity that downgraded or marginalized the feminine. In another letter written in 1897 to his Gurubhai Brahmananda, Swami Vivekananda explained how seeing Shashi Babu—probably Shashipada Banerjee, founder of the Widows' Home of Baranagore—'with his feminine retiringness, stirred to work' his own courage had 'gone up by leaps and bounds.'[84] So, if for the evangelists and colonialists the feminine in Indian men was an evil, Vivekananda saw the ability to feel and animate the feminine in men a must for becoming pure and service-minded towards the society. When seen in this context, the passage of Bhai Parmanand represents a continuity in the Hindu Sanghatan thought process, if it can be called that. In his passage, we have a characterization where the Sanghatanist or the patriot is seen as a counterpart of the feminine Radha rather than a masculine virile warrior out to destroy the enemies or worse, spearhead an expansionist imperialism.

As the modern age, through colonialism and evangelism, encountered Hindutva, the resultant churn brought out a wide variety of magnificent thought processes. Internalizing Darwin, Freud and Marx on the one hand, struggling for the independence of their own nation and looking into their own history, tradition and fighting incursive expansionist theologies along with colonialism, the Hindutva Sanghatan movement enriched the Indian mindscape with quite a rich diversity. The life and thoughts of Lala Har Dayal (1884–1939) demonstrate the inherent plasticity and universal nature in Hindutva which came out when it interacted with the Western modern age.

Lala Har Dayal: Revolutionary, Sanghatanist and Free Thinker Extraordinaire

An Arya Samajist like Bhai Parmanand, Lala Har Dayal was closely associated with him in organizing overseas revolutionary activities, particularly during the First World War.

A brilliant student at Oxford University with a government scholarship, and even as everyone in his family and faculty expected him to start a brilliant career in the Indian Civil Services, Lala Har Dayal wrote to the British Secretary of State for India, renouncing his scholarship and leaving the university. This was because he had come to realize the British government in India as illegitimate and thus his conscience would not allow him to get scholarship from that government. Then to everyone's shock, he plunged himself into the national liberation movement.

After spending years in India, he left initially for Europe where he worked with Madam Cama and her friends, and then moved to the United States. During his stay in Europe, he started admiring its modernization and advocated radical modernization for India. It was almost at this time when living a self-imposed frugal meditative life, he also started giving thought to developing his own religious sect. Bhai Parmanand persuaded him to stop creating yet another creed and pointed out that his way of thinking was closer to the ancient Sankhya Darshan of Hinduism.

In the United States, he became a lecturer of Indian philosophy at Stanford University. Soon, he resigned and started giving freelance lectures. During this time, the articles he wrote in *Modern Review* created quite a debate as he seemed to discount almost all the ancient philosophies of India. His disdain was reserved mostly for religion. When Mahadev Govind Ranade, the great Indian philosopher, countered his attacks on Indian philosophy pointing out various inconsistencies, in his reply, Dayal called for 'renunciation combined with politics and economics', termed Aurobindo 'greater than Ramakrishna' and declared:

> There is more wisdom in one of Tilak's political speeches than in all the Upanishads. We do not want our young men to seek for Brahman (ultimate reality) just now. We want them to search for freedom and progress on Western lines.[85]

Emily Brown, who has written the most comprehensive and critical biography of Har Dayal, points out that in this aspect, he was ironically similar to Swami Vivekananda, the disciple of Ramakrishna:

> (Har Dayal) continued to emphasize the fact that society was undergoing a significant upheaval all over the world, that intellectual forces should be committed to serving the less articulate strata, and that dignity be accorded universally to women and laborers. In this he joined Vivekananda, the missionary of Vedantic Hinduism, who said at the turn of the century: "Whether the leadership of society be in the bands of those who monopolize learning, or wield the power of riches or arms, the source of its power is always the subject masses. By so much as the class in power severs itself from this source, by so much is it sure to become weak."

Yet for all his admiration of the West, the organization that he set up he called Yugantar Ashram, and he wrote of Marx as a 'rishi'. He condemned the use of the names of Varna and wrote that these terms should be thrown into the deepest wells of Rajasthan. But while warning against the control of the nationalist organization falling into the hands of the moneyed merchants and industrialists instead of serving the intellectuals, his cautioning was: 'The Brahman must be above the Vaishya.'

After the failure of the Ghadar revolution, Har Dayal started exploring the emerging schools of thought in modern society and in particular, political science. Har Dayal was a master of seven Indian languages—Hindi, Urdu, Punjabi, Marathi, Gujarati, Bengali and Tamil—and seven European languages—English, French, German, Italian, Turkish, Swedish and Portuguese.

He had deeply studied the latest research in Western sociology, their political science treatises, emerging ideologies and physical sciences. Impressed by the empirical approach to the deeper problems of existence, Dayal had developed a worshipful attitude towards the way science approaches the big questions. His admiration of science was not the marvelling at technology. He wanted to integrate science education with what Einstein would later call the cosmic religious experience.

In 1922 he wrote *Our Educational Problem*, a book on education in which he spoke of every member of the 'Hindu nation' learning two languages—Sanskrit and the provincial. True to his nature, he himself agonized over this perceived transgression he was making to the national cause for writing to his fellow countrymen in English:

> If I had followed nature, if our whole life had not been rendered ridiculous, artificial and miserable by this educational system, I should have written in Sanskrit to appeal to my countrymen in Bengal, Bombay or Madras (an aspiration which has not altogether been abandoned) and in Hindi to address the people of my province, I take this occasion to apologize to the Ancestors and to my countrymen of the present generation for thus dishonouring and weakening a national institution.[86]

A decade ago, the same man had written that there was more wisdom in one political speech of Tilak than in all the Upanishads. His major complaint against the 'British Educational Machine in India' was that it destroyed the patriotism and spirituality of the Hindus.

> Patriotism and spirituality—the two great character-making forces—are absent from this 'educational' system. The smaller virtues which are also inherited by Hindus, decay through the influence of ill-digested European ideas and the example of third-rate European professors. The Hindu character is ruined. The springs of the national moral life are poisoned. If a man gains the world, but loses his own soul, what shall it profit him? So said a teacher of old. And if a nation should acquire the learning of the whole world but lose its life, its institutions, and its character, how will it survive? We cannot give our life in exchange for a smattering of English literature and Science. We cannot consent to part with our nationhood for such paltry advantages. The British Educational System is the present of two great evils—denationalization and demoralization. It weakens Hindu social and religious institutions, and it undermines patriotism and moral courage.

He then identified as the corollary of this fundamental flaw, further important problems to the national life which he enumerated thus:

1. The Social Degradation of the Hindu race
2. The prestige of the bureaucracy
3. The Loss of Self-Government
4. The Extension of British Influence in Indian States
5. The Industrial Backwardness of the Nation

Here is a sample of his way of reasoning, associating the replacement of the indigenous educational system by British colonial education. Explaining how India lost her self-governance from the loss of a traditional decentralized educational system, he wrote:

> The old-world Pundit who opens an "indigenous" school on his own account practises self-government on a small scale. But enlightened public men who patronize Government Colleges, help the extension of bureaucratic influence in our social life....A public library established by Government only hinders the growth of popular civic life while it confers a temporary benefit on us. Even a *pathshala* or a temple which is established by Government for the promotion of Sanskrit learning is injurious to our national interests for it undermines the habits of self-help and self-reliance, which alone can save the Hindu race and its religion.[87]

One can see that in his thought process, he had anticipated or influenced the views of Gandhi about an indigenous education system which he expressed in London during his visit for the Round Table Conference in 1931. His interest in Buddhism, which he had stated to have waned during his stay in the United States, seemed to increase. He now wanted Pali, the ancient language of Buddhism, to be included as one of the national languages of India. He, like many Indian social reformers and later Dr Ambedkar, considered Buddha as a social rebel. He wanted Indians to learn Pali. He proto-figured some of the fundamental elements of Dr Ambedkar this way. His work on the Bodhisattva doctrine earned him a PhD.

Love for Science

In 1934 five years before his death at a not-so-old age, he had written *Hints for Self Culture,* published by Hy S. L. Polak and Co. London (UK). It is essential that every Indian educationist who desires a robust cultural and science education in India, should read this classic. Here, Har Dayal speaks of how studying zoology, cosmology and evolution, in particular, frees our mind from the tyranny of superstition and takes us forward into a vision of the universe and our own place in it, which is far magnificent than any presented by scriptural fantasies. Why should one study zoology? Har Dayal answers:

> Zoology leads you from the lowliest worms to the loftiest wisdom. Zoology will also provide you with a scientific theory of the Origin of Life, which excludes the dogma of Creation by a Deity. Man and the animals have been evolved from the protozoa, and the latter are either eternal or were evolved out of inorganic Matter at a remote period in the history of the earth.

So, what is the relation between life and matter? Is life a separate category?

> The question is, "Is living Matter an ultimate category by itself, like Energy and inorganic Matter, or is it derived from the latter?" There is no theoretical difficulty in admitting that there is a difference of kind, and not merely of degree, between living and inert Matter. [88]

Life has always come from life. Har Dayal refers to the famous experiment by Louis Pasteur that conclusively disproved spontaneous arising of life from inanimate matter. Do you think life cannot be reduced to matter and energy? It is okay, says Har Dayal. There is no compulsion for such reduction. But he at the same time, warns against using this as a backdoor to creationism. For him, seeing life as a special category in the universe can be a stimulant to do science, but finding solace in a creator-deity is detrimental to the health of the society and an obstacle to the progress of science. He writes:

> Spontaneous generation has been shown to be impossible through the research of Redi, Spallanzani, and Pasteur. You need not create such an avoidable difficulty for your own mind, if you find that it is impossible for you to conceive of Life as developing spontaneously out of lifeless Matter. Philosophy is under no obligation to refer all things to the one category—of Energy-Matter: such a factitious Monism is unscientific. So, if you are inclined to believe that living and non-living Matter cannot be reduced to a common denominator, you are free to postulate that Life is sui generis and has existed eternally, like Energy and Matter. Then you need not worry about the problem of the Origin of Life. The chief point is that you must not believe in the creation of Life by a Deity.

But he does not stop here. He explores the other side of the problem. Quoting Huxley and citing the experiments of J. C. Bose, he shows that there is indeed a case for a continuum.

> There is, however, another side to this thorny question. T.H. Huxley wrote "if It were given to me to [...] I should expect to be a witness of the evolution of

> living protoplasm from not-living Matter." Professor J. C. Bose's researches have demonstrated that inert and living bodies have much in common. He says: "Living response in all its diverse manifestations is found to be only a repetition of responses seen in the inorganic." Several organic compounds have been built up in chemical laboratories since Wohler first produced urea in 1828. The ultra-microscopic units called "bacteriophages" may be an intermediate form between living and non-living Matter (if they exist at all). It is conceivable that the simplest forms of Life, like the invisible viruses or even the micro-organisms, may have appeared on earth spontaneously about 1300 million years ago, when the temperature and the atmospheric conditions were favourable for such a radically new development. Of course, the process of the transformation of chemical matter into the first living cells will ever remain a mystery. But Science and Philosophy must at least attempt to unify and simplify Nature. The mind of Man loves the logic of Monism, and must ever strive to arrive at one ultimate category, if it is at all possible.[89]

The ability to present both diametrically opposite positions and, at the same time, argue against the pitfalls of pseudo-scientific creationism, makes this passage by Lala Har Dayal a guiding principle for a true scientific approach to a problem. After pointing out that matter and energy, considered two separate categories, have been found to be 'mutually convertible', he argues for a possibility of a monist view of life.

> How can we then be so sure that a living cell can never be produced from inert Matter under certain circumstances? Such dogmatism would be unworthy of a modem philosopher. If a monistic interpretation of Nature can be achieved without doing violence to facts, it must be appreciated and acclaimed as the crowning glory of Science and Philosophy.

The reader should note the words 'without doing violence to facts'. This is a very important caution. One should never allow one's love for a particular philosophical or ideological position to crowd one's mind's eye in observing the facts and yielding to their superiority. So, he concludes why one should study zoology. What he says may well have been written by a popular scientist decades after him, like Lewis Thomas or Richard Dawkins. He writes:

> Zoology will also teach you compassion towards animals. Study always evokes interest and sympathy. To a Zoologist, a sheep is not merely mutton and wool, a lobster is something more than a 'delicacy', and a spider is not just a horrid ugly creature. He has learned to look upon all worms and birds and beasts as struggling, scheming, suffering, food-hunting, mate-seeking, death-fearing individuals, born

> without their consent and compelled to complete their short life-cycles in an infinite Universe that they do not understand. A course in Zoology, will leave you a sadder and a wiser man. It will also help you to realize the essential unity of living beings, so that you will begin to feel that you owe a duty to them all.

One theme that runs consistently throughout the work of Lala Har Dayal is his insistence that the sciences should be studied for experiencing the greater mystery of existence, without giving in to the weakness of mysticism of any sort. When criticizing reductionism, Har Dayal takes a very careful line. While pointing out the fallacy of trying to reduce biology into chemistry and physics and imposing Darwinian principles erroneously on to the society as Herbert Spencer did (social Darwinism), he warns his readers that this should not make them fall into the trap of vitalism:

> Herbert Spencer applied the physical concept of "persistence of force" and the biological concepts of "organism" and "embryonic evolution" to the human phenomena of History and Sociology, and the result was disastrous. Such methods lead only to confusion and error....The attempt to foist all the physical and chemical laws upon Zoology or zoological laws upon Psychology and Sociology must be abandoned. Each branch of Science deals with its own phenomena and discovers its special laws, besides those universal laws that apply to all phenomena. ...You should also beware of the fallacy of "Vitalism". You should admit that the phenomena of plant-life, animal-life, and human life are not always physico-chemical processes; but it is not necessary to go further and postulate a "life-force" in order to "explain" them....You should thus recognize the existence of fundamentally diverse orders of phenomena, with their special laws; but you need not take refuge in the obscure and misleading terminology of "Vitalism".[90]

The clarity and depth of thought is amazing, to say the least. He attacks all aspects of religion as delusional. But he is not non-spiritual. He completely dismisses the theistic religions of all sorts as not only incompatible with science but injurious to human development and social morality. In this, Har Dayal anticipates what British evolutionist Richard Dawkins presents in *The God Delusion*:

> All the theoretical arguments for Theism are very bad indeed, but its practical and social consequences are infinitely worse. Superstition is never harmless, and this dogma is a veritable Pandora's Box of calamities and sufferings for mankind.... Science emphasizes the idea of impersonal, invariable Law in Nature, while Theism postulates a living Person's Thought and Will behind or above or in Nature....Theism

> leads to stagnation and decay in society, as it regards the laws and ideals of a certain religious system as divinely ordained for all nations and epochs....Theism robs mankind of all the advantages and benefits that Science confers upon us. It also blocks the forward-moving traffic on the highway of History....Study the biography of Gautama Buddha, and note how he treated the members and leaders of other sects. Read the edicts of Asoka, and imbibe the spirit of religious toleration. The literature and history of Buddhism and Hinduism provide the best antidote to the ingrained and ineradicable intolerance of Islam and Christianity.[91]

One can see that in his criticism of theism, he completely reverses the colonial notion of monotheism being part of colonial progress brought to heathen land. He also rejects the argument that theism is needed for ethics. He was equally harsh on mystic notions, which separate the body and soul while demeaning the body.

> The metaphysical doctrine of the Summum Bonum has been developed chiefly by the Hindus, the Christian mystics, and the Platonists, who postulate a fundamental Dualism in human personality....We are taught to suppress the body and the mind, and to develop and unfold the "Spirit". The body is reviled and condemned as the 'prison-house of the soul'....The Body, which is the basis of Personality, is despised; the Mind, which is the light of Personality, is ignored. Society, which is the cradle of Personality, is neglected; while the imaginary 'Spirit' is considered to be the real essence of Man....The folly and futility of this disastrous doctrine are exhibited in the pathetic tragedy of the wasted lives of such ascetics as Simeon Stylites, the ravings maniacs of the Thebaid, immured Buddhist monks of Tibet who never leave their dark caves and cells, the Hindu fakirs who make long pilgrimages by measuring their lengths along the ground, the Trappists who never speak, the nuns who never go out of their convents etc. These are the earnest men and women condemned to slow suicide by "spiritual" Metaphysics.[92]

Another feature that is remarkable in the writings of Har Dayal is that while he was all praise for the success of Jews in the emerging modern society, he does not attribute it to any inherent superiority or the 'cunningness' of the Jews. To him, on the other hand, the communal investment the Jews make in education and the progressive mindset of the community, make the Jews a model to emulate for others. This was written at a time when Israel had not yet come into being and Jews would soon face the Holocaust and anti-Semitism was almost axiomatic in Christendom. Yet, we find a great admiration for Jews—from the point of view of humanity—in terms of the Jewish contribution to the human civilization:

> The Hebrews found a wise guide and legislator in Moses; this bond of union was valuable for social unity and moral training. They also secured the Ten Commandments, and a definite ethical code was thus accepted by the whole nation. They had a spirit of sturdy independence, which was reflected in their laws and their revolts. They cared more for happiness in this life than for felicity after death.... When almost all other peoples in Asia bowed to the Roman yoke, the Hebrews defied the tyrants again and again, and paid the penalty for their love of freedom. They produced the group of eloquent prophets, Isaiah, Amos, and others, whose writings may still be read with profit, though they are couched in theological terms. The ideas of a cosmopolitan society and universal peace were developed by the advanced Hebrew thinkers. But the Hebrews are also responsible for intolerant monotheism and its terrible consequences. They learned much from the Persians and the Babylonians, and passed it on to the Christian Church. We owe our Sunday rest, the achievements of Jesus and Paul, and the noble ethics of the Talmud to this people. Their religion teaches them charity and chastity. In spite of dispersion, proscription, isolation, and suffering, the Hebrews are still alive and active. Modern music, science, and socialism owe much to them. To Philosophy, they have contributed the supremely lovable figure of Spinoza. Maimonides, Mendelssohn, Marx, and Einstein are also the gift of this people to the world. The history of the Hebrews shows that good leaders, a well-defined ethical code, a worldly creed, a living historical tradition, and unity of fundamental ideas will enable a people to accomplish great things.[93]

It is quite interesting to see that a Hindu nationalist, an atheist, a person who condemned monotheism of Christianity and Islam, praise the Jews and even suggested that the 'terrible consequences' of 'intolerant monotheism' were more the result of certain ideas getting passed on to the Christian church. More importantly, Har Dayal finds the Jewish contribution to diverse fields including varied schools of thoughts as one that enriched human civilization. He does not attribute this to concepts like 'chosen people' or a 'different or superior race' but to social ethics which he wants all human communities to emulate. Perhaps, this secular-humanist love for Jews that he had was the reason why the committee formed in Germany in the late 1930s to engage in anti-British activities with German support, found him 'unreliable'.

Har Dayal criticizes capitalism and considers it unsustainable. But he also criticizes the dogmatic Marxist view of history which gives extreme importance to economic relations. A revolutionary in exile getting attracted to Marxism was something quite common in those times. However, what is remarkable again is that Har Dayal was able to see the problematic areas of

Marxism which would later blow up the Marxist States. In fact, Har Dayal was one of the earliest writers to 'bring' Marx to India. In 1912 he wrote a highly emotional hagiography of Marx titled 'Karl Marx: A Modern Rishi' in the popular Indian magazine *Modern Review*. Even then he had observed cardinal weaknesses in Marxist fundamentals. In this, one can see his roots in Indic wisdom of the ability to approach a problem in a multi-dimensional way:

> Class-struggle is only one part of the whole drama. And I repudiate the idea that society is divided into classes by any hard and fast line of demarcation. It is not class-selfishness, but social co-operation based on the appreciation of a higher ideal that has been the motive force of progress in all epochs.[94]

Har Dayal spoke of the need to study theoretical and practical Marxism. At the same time, he could see that the Marxist state was acquiring the characteristic of a theocratic state, so much so that while it allowed blasphemy of religious leaders, it prohibited the blasphemy of Marx and Lenin. To him, Marxism devalued and did not properly recognize the human personality and individuality. He criticized the Marxist approach, exhibiting a sense of humour:

> Capitalism produced the necessary external circumstances for the growth of Socialism, but Capitalism did not go every morning to the British Museum in London for many years, and write 'Das Kapital'. It was a particular individual, named Karl Marx, who did it. Capitalism did not enable Marx's parents to give birth biologically to that original brain.[95]

The book shows Har Dayal as a complete internationalist and a humanist par excellence. He wanted free thinkers to be pioneers of a world-state who should establish cosmopolitan centres and denounce the 'cruel institutions of capitalism and nationalism', as seen in the West.

> Do your duty within the nation-state to-day, but do it in the spirit of a world-citizen of the future. Eschew all hatred and contempt for other nations and races.... Establish a Cosmopolitan Club in your town. Join an inter-national correspondence society. Preach peace, when others howl in hate or rage for revenge. Welcome all to your home and your heart, whites and blacks, browns and yellows, creoles and mulattoes, gypsies and Hottentots—all men and women and children without distinction of race or colour. Eat and drink with all. Love and serve all. Do good to all....You may be born in the present nation-state, but you are not of it. Your heart is elsewhere. Waking and sleeping, you think of the World-State and long for its advent. When the Sun is still below the horizon in the early morning, he cannot be

seen; but he sends before him sister Dawn, holy Ushas, radiant Aurora, who has also been deemed worthy of adoration. Such a slow brightening Dawn, are ye privileged to witness in this age, though your eyes cannot behold the Sun.[96]

Though there is a romantic flourish in his utopian vision, he was not too much of a romanticist who would forget the harsh realities on the ground. His love for all humanity was as genuine and as sincere as his understanding of geo-political and demographic ground realities. He conceived five concentric circles which consisted of the family, the relatives, the municipality, the nation and ultimately the world-state. The concentric ever-widening circles again is a Hindu metaphor which was also used by Gandhi and is prevalent in various Hindu systems of thought.

A Hindu Nationalist and a Secular-humanist Internationalist

Did Lala Har Dayal undergo a transformation and change after the failure of the Ghadar movement? Is it right as some have alleged that while his revolutionary colleagues Bhai Parmanand and Savarkar went on to embrace religious nationalism, he embraced Western thought and culture that he despised?

In the statement after his arrest in the United States on 25 March 1914, Lala Har Dayal spoke about his success in 'Hindu nationalist revolutionary propaganda' as the 'immediate occasion' for his arrest. At the same time, he encouraged Muslim participation in the 'revolutionary' movement. In his lecture at the Hindu Association of the Pacific Coast in Sacramento on 31 December 1913, he spoke of 'Muslims who are now joining the party'. In his reports of the meeting, he 'kept pressing the point that there were many Muslims present' and that put forth 'strong arguments' for Hindu-Muslim unity.[97] But he was opposed to proselytization. When the Secretary of the Young Men's Christian Association, Lahore, once requested Har Dayal for discussion, he got the following blunt reply from Dayal: 'You want to convert Hindus to Christianity, whereas my mission of life is to check this onslaught. Therefore, what is the use of your meeting me?'[98]

This is a common denominator in almost all Hindutvaites. They are not against 'the other false religions' and consider them to have the only revealed Truth. They do not want proselytization and expansionist monocultures to destroy the diversity that has been preserved through generations in India. His advocacy of Hindu-Muslim unity received its first jolt at Constantinople.

While from the beginning he had been against the Christian conversions, the aftermath of Khilafat and the riots clearly made him see the Islamist politics as a danger rather than an ally against the British occupation. He considered as a very real scenario, the possibility of Islamist forces in India forging an extra-territorial alliance and enslaving entire India. This led to a very harsh statement which should be understood as more a reaction to his times than his actual intention.

> I declare that the future of the Hindu race, of Hindustan and of the Punjab rests on four pillars: (i) Hindu Sanghatan (ii) Hindu Raj, (iii) *Shuddhi* of Moslems (iv) Conquest and *Shuddhi* of Afghanistan and the frontiers. So long as the Hindu nation does not accomplish these four things the safety of our children and great grandchildren will ever be in danger and the safety of the Hindu race will be impossible. The Hindu race has but one history and its institutions are homogeneous. But the Muslims and Christians are to be removed from the confines of Hinduism for their religions are alien and they love Persian, Arab, and European Institutions. Thus, just as one removes foreign matter from the eye *Shuddhi* must be made of those two religions. Afghanistan and the hilly regions of the frontier very formerly part of India but are at present under the domination of Islam. Just as there is Hindu religion in Nepal so there must be Hindu institutions in Afghanistan and the frontier territory. Otherwise it is useless to win Swaraj for mountain tribes are always war like hungry. If they become your enemies the age of Nadirshah and Zamanshah will begin anew. At present English officers are protecting the frontiers; but it cannot always be. If Hindus want to protect themselves they must conquer Afghanistan and use from tiers and convert all the mountain tribes.... Some Hindus say that when the English leave India, the Indian Mussalmans and Afghan Pathans will read the fine speeches of the Congress-wallahs and sing "Bande Mataram". and embrace the Hindus like affectionate brothers!...As long as Islam survives in India and Afghanistan, so long will the mouth of these brothers water to see the wealth and belongings of the Hindus, and so long will their leaders wish to establish Moslem Raj in India and live in luxury. As long as the Afghans and Pathans remain Moslems, so long will the passion to loot India be strong in their veins....The thirteen centuries of Islam and the thousand years of war between Afghanistan and India cannot be swept away by the Mahatma's fast of 21 days. The magic of history is far more potent than that of a Mahatma's penance....Those who preach Hindu Sangathan on the one hand and on the other sing the tune of Hindu-Moslem unity are making a grave blunder. In this way neither will be achieved, nor will Hindu-Moslem unity be attained—even if such unity were possible.[99]

Unfortunately, his reference to the mountain tribes being used against Hindus and India by Islamists became true in 1947 when they were used in the jihad against India in Kashmir. He never hated Islam and Christianity as religions or Muslims and Christians as people, but was against the expansionist and proselytizing drives of these religions he perceived as being closely coupled with hidden or explicit political agenda. This is borne by the fact that in 1934, he recommended 'the literature and history of Buddhism and Hinduism' as 'the best antidote to the ingrained and ineradicable intolerance of Islam and Christianity'. This shows that his Hindutva elements are not exclusive to, but in tune with, his internationalist secular humanist elements.

When he was in the process of writing *Hints for Self Culture*, his former revolutionary colleague and Hindu Mahasabha leader, Bhai Parmanand, requested Har Dayal to write a book on nationalism. Har Dayal replied, saying he would write a pamphlet, instead. But he could not. The reason being his penetratingly uncompromising vision and value system. He said:

> I want to write in a scholarly manner; so that this pseudo-nationalism is washed off from the minds of Hindu youths and they begin to feel that what they term as Hindu communalism is, according to the tenets of political science, real nationalism.[100]

Taking all these into consideration, one has to doubt if Lala Har Dayal simply meant 'all Indians' when he used the term 'Hindu', as claimed by some of his family members during post-independence. Dharmavira, who had been privy to the interactions of Bhai Parmanand and Lala Har Dayal, explains how the 'inner spirit' of Har Dayal expressed itself through different manifestations or 'personalities'. Emily Brown explains the view of Dharmavira on Har Dayal thus:

> The first became evident when Har Dayal was still a student in India, and this was the spirit of love of humanity. The spirit then changed its form to one of love for Hindu nationalism, and finally it became one of 'the love of freedom for Hindustan...love of freedom, love of Hindustan equally.[101]

In the ultimate analysis, Lala Har Dayal represents an important dimension of the Hindutva movement. He showed its inherent plasticity. Whether one accepts his views or not, they are part of the heritage of Hindutva and Hindu Sanghatan movement. When academics portray him as 'a Hindu nationalist' usually they quote only his passage about his wanting to convert Afghan and Pakistan area tribes—which now lie in Pakistan—to Hinduism. Taken in isolation, it looks like a fanatical stand but taken together with his entire worldview, a churn and yet valuable, it was contextual. His concern was more about not losing the theo-diversity and openness that characterized Hinduism to 'ingrained and ineradicable intolerance' of monopolistic faiths. In his rationalism, he shares elements with Savarkar. Thus, the influence of this particular stream continues to this day in the Hindutva movement.

The parallels of thoughts in conceiving humanity as one and all divisions as temporary is shared by both Savarkar and Lala Har Dayal. In a passage that looks like a premonition of the passage and imagery employed by Carl Sagan in his book *Pale Blue Dot*, Har Dayal speaks of the oneness of humanity, quoting a passage from the Mahabharata:

> As an air-pilot rises far above the ground and sees the whole landscape at a glance, even so you should rise in spirit above the barriers of race, colour, language, and nationality, and embrace all men, women, and children in your love. Let no one be shut out from your loving heart. As the Earth nourishes all and the Sun shines on all, so let your fraternal sympathy extend to all men and women, excluding none. The ancient epic, "Mahabharata," teaches this ideal in Sanskrit verse:
>
> "Small souls inquire, 'Belongs this man
> To our own race or sect or clan?'
> But larger-hearted men embrace
> As brothers all the human race."
>
> The fundamental rule of social duty is this: Let all your thoughts and actions promote the development and happiness of all mankind, Look upon yourself as a very tiny part of the larger whole that is Humanity. At present, for instance, you represent about 1 in 2 billionth of Humanity. Never lose sight of the great Society, with reference to which all your ideas and deeds must be measured and judged. As a criterion of social duty, there is no smaller unit than Mankind in its entirety. For Mankind, we are born, live, think, and work; and for Mankind, we die.[102]

At the risk of repetition elsewhere in the book, just to bring out the striking similarity, here is a parallel passage from the Hindutva of Savarkar which, written a decade before *Hints of Self Culture*, speaks almost in the same vein:

> Truly speaking all that any one of us can claim, all that history entitles one to claim, is that one has the blood of all mankind in one's veins. The fundamental unity of man from pole to pole is true, all else only relatively so. And speaking relatively alone, no people in the world can more justly claim to get recognized as a racial unit than the Hindus and perhaps the Jews....Equally certain it is that whenever the Hindu come to hold such a position whence they could dictate terms to the whole world—those terms cannot be very different from the terms which Gita dictates or the Buddha lays down. A Hindu is most intensely so, when he ceases to be Hindu; and with a Shankar/Kabir claims the whole earth for a Benares "Waranasi Medini" or with a Tukaram exclaims: "my country! Oh brothers, the limits of the Universe—there the frontiers of my country lie."[103]

Hindutva also has to it the contribution of another important freedom fighter. To understand the present Hindutva movement in its entirety, it is essential that we understand this colossal personality as well. His life shows how Hindutva does not exclude proactive consideration of Hindu-Muslim unity while being practically cautious, and how it contributed to one of the most important sequence of events in the struggle for Indian Independence.

The Lion of Punjab: Lala Lajpat Rai

It was 30 October 1928. A large number of Indians had gathered on the streets of Lahore to protest against the Simon Commission in a silent, non-violent march. The British officers decided to use force against the peaceful demonstrators. And they had a special target—'the man holding the umbrella'. Frail and old, yet the turbaned man was the one who was restraining the crowd, making it orderly and absolutely non-violent against all sorts of police provocations. So, the Senior Superintendent of Police himself decided to assault him and in that he was assisted by Sanders, one of his sidekicks.

Historian Feroz Chand, a biographer of Lajpat Rai, describes the event with emotion, but without any exaggeration:

> A rather frail puny thing he looked, but his spirit was dauntless. He could receive the blows like a man. He did not flee. He did not flinch. He did not budge. He did not permit his people to hit back. His lieutenants tried to surround him and to share the blows aimed at him. He still received the lion's share so that one of his doctors—Gopi Chand Bhargava who gauged the force of the blows not as a mere eye-witness but more intimately and more exactly as one of those who took on themselves some of the blows meant for the Chief wondered how it was that he stood up to it without collapsing on the spot. Manfully he took the blows and shouted with a lion's roar at his assailant, asking for his name. More lathi blows were the only reply. Again, he shouted and challenged the assaulter's manhood demanding his name once again.…The brute automaton just delivered more blows.[104]

With all the blows raining on him, he still held the crowd under control and when the demonstration time was over 'he marched at the head of the procession on the way back'. In the evening, to the citizens of Lahore who had assembled after congratulating them for their splendid behaviour, he uttered those immortal words: 'Every blow that they hurled at us drove one more nail into the coffin of the Empire.' Though indomitable in spirit, his fragile body had actually been wrecked by the blows. He would succumb to the injuries on 17 November 1928.

And his life—as his death was—had been one extraordinary battle against British colonization in India, both in the mind and in the State.

The year 1907 was a year that the British administrators wanted to pass quickly. It was the fiftieth anniversary of 1857. This led the British colonial machine into a fear psychosis overdrive. There was fear among the authorities that a hundred thousand soldiers were waiting for a word from Lajpat Rai to start another rebellion. The government report stated that the people in the province of Punjab were 'urged to combine to withhold payment of Government revenue, water rates and other dues; to refuse supplies, carriages and other help to Government officers on tour and Native soldiers. Police were pilloried as "traitors" and adjured to quit the service of the Government'. The government assumed that the Arya Samaj, the organization to which Lajpat Rai belonged, had a secret Committee and was organizing the propaganda. The cipher telegram informed the authorities:

> The head and center of the entire movement is Lala Lajpat Rai, a Khatri pleader who has visited England as the Congress representative of the Punjab. He is a revolutionary and a political enthusiast who is inspired by the most intense hatred of the British Government.[105]

Lajpat Rai was not a Khatri but then, being an Arya Samajist, he was against caste and untouchability. So in 1907, he had been deported to Mandalay without any trial. Viceroy Minto eagerly gave his consent. As he was being spirited away, he wrote to his father that 'whatever comes should be manfully borne.' Eventually Lajpat Rai was arrested and deported to Mandalay on 9 May 1907 without a hearing and trial. After being shut in the former fort of the Burmese king with no permission to write letters or receive newspapers, Lajpat Rai was not even informed of the reason for his arrest. It was only months later that he learnt that he had been arrested according to an 1818 law for having created 'commotion' in the British Empire. Right during his arrest, the British administration started playing the Islamic card. While the loyalist Hindus accused the Arya Samaj of being fanatics fanning sentiments against the British, loyalist Muslims wrote letters to newspapers expressing their jubilation over his arrest. However, Lajpat Rai pointed out in his autobiographical account of his deportation: 'the Mohammedan merchants of Ahmedabad and Surat gave a crushing reply to the lie circulated by Anglo-Indian journalists that the Mohammedans were happy at' his deportation.[106]

In 1914 he was in the United States, where he was striving to network with the patriotic elements and strive for the freedom of India. However, unlike some of his compatriots who were carried away by the pro-German feeling when seeking their help for India's liberation, he stated clearly:

> I am an Indian patriot and I wish freedom for my country. I have no sympathy for the Germans nor have I anything against them....I had no faith in the Germans and did not believe in the deliverance of India with their help or through their agency. I have been always rather fanatically attached to the theory that liberty won with foreign help was not worth having.[107]

Yet, when such efforts, which he warned against, failed and the revolutionaries got into trouble, 'Lalaji' as he was called in the revolutionary circles, was always there to help. For example, when M. N. Roy had to flee to Mexico and was in dire straits, Lalaji was the one who came to his aid.

Lajpat Rai: Pan-Hindu Sanghatanist and Secularist

Many core elements of the Hindutva discourse and the process of today can be seen in the late nineteenth and twentieth century writings of Lajpat Rai. During the frequent famines of the colonial era that plagued Northwestern India, particularly in Punjab and Rajasthan in 1900, Lajpat Rai plunged himself in relief work through the Arya Samaj. In his book on Arya Samaj, he shows how these famines, during which the British were exporting large amounts of food grains from India, were also helping Christian evangelism through the colonial machine while administering relief work:

> In 1899–1900, when the country was suffering from one of the severest famines of the century, millions of hundredweights of wheat were exported to foreign countries; in 1877–78, when 5,220,000 persons died of hunger, 16,000,000 cwt. of rice were exported from the Calcutta port only....The Arya Samaj was the first non-Christian private agency which started a non-official movement for the relief of distress caused by famine....(The Hindu Orphan Relief Movement) was started in February 1897, for the relief of Hindu children left destitute in the famine of 1896–9.... Our agents again and again applied personally to the local officers in charge of the famine relief camps, but met with no success, although we have reason to believe that large numbers of Hindu children were, from time to time, handed over to Christian missionaries and by them sent to distant places in India....The reasons for our failure to get children from Government famine relief works need not be set forth in detail, the most important being that the missionaries were everywhere too strong for us....

> We carried on a successful campaign in Kathiawar, the Central Province, and parts of Bombay, and succeeded in rescuing altogether about 1,700 children....All classes of the Hindu community, without distinction of caste or creed, helped us in this undertaking, and the movement proved a blessing in more ways than one.[108]

Lajpat Rai was the organizing secretary of these relief services. The Arya Samaj famine relief work also evolved into other relief works during natural disasters. The Arya Samaj relief activities prefigures crucially the RSS relief work during such disasters later. Lajpat Rai writes:

> At the time of the great earthquake in the Kangra Valley in 1904 it organized relief on a large scale for the sufferers, and earned the thanks of the people and the Government. In this calamity the Arya Samajists were the first to reach the afflicted area.

During his famine relief work, he encountered the aggressive Christian proselytization which enjoyed tacit and overt colonial support. His analysis of Christian missionary work in the context of their proselytizing charity activities during the 1900 famine brings out the underlying ethical problems and also the deficiency of Hindu institutions and the advantage of missionaries under a colonial State which itself was subtly relegating its responsibilities to the missionaries. The passage quoted below exhaustively from his appeal for famine relief and orphan support shows how the colonial government favoured the missionaries in famine relief, giving Hindu children to missionary orphanages—thus facilitating conversions—how the Hindu service missions were disadvantaged at ground zero and how the English-educated Indian press was indifferent to this gross injustice. As will be seen later, though the appeal was made in 1900, nothing much had changed in the present postcolonial Indian rule:

> Now, although it is exceedingly good of the Christian missionary to take interest in the Hindu orphan, and to help the latter, in these days of starvation, still it must be remembered that the Hindu gets this help at the sacrifice of what is, and ought to be, dearer to him than life itself—his religion. It must be admitted that the charity of the missionary is not altogether disinterested charity. It is this charity (distributed in the days of famine) that swells the number of native Christian population in India and justifies the existence and the continuance of the various Christian Missions now working in India. But for the results obtained in these epochs of drought the returns of the different proselytizing agencies in India exhibit very meagre figures. So, although from the Christian point of view the work of the missionary in these days of famine is nothing but noble, it is from the Hindu point of view an elixir

mixed with a deadly poison which permeates through the system of those to whom it is administered and makes them non-Hindus forever. Practically, it amounts to this: That the Hindu community is so indifferent to its strength that it allows its people to leave its ranks, because in days of scarcity it cannot afford to render them that help which is so readily offered and supplied by the Christian missionary. Well, the resources of the missionary are so varied and vast that it is almost impossible to compete with him, still it cannot be denied that a Government like that of the British in India has a duty of their own in this respect which they must in no case neglect....No British officer can therefore assume an attitude of partiality towards the missionary without to some extent compromising the august Government which he represents. It is therefore of the utmost importance that the famine administration of the Government should be perfectly above suspicion in this respect. But we know that over and above the vast pecuniary resources of the padre, the latter has many other advantages over his Hindu and Mahomedan brother (working in the same line of charity) in the facilities of access to the official, in securing a hearing from him, in making him accept his statements and in gaining his sympathy....I would, therefore, earnestly appeal to the Hindus of all provinces to combine and make a joint representation to the Government in this matter. Hindu charity is proverbial and with a little better management it can be diverted, at least to some extent, to this direction. Even a portion of it should be quite enough to supplement the noble efforts of the Government towards the alleviation of the sufferings of the fatherless and the motherless.... Will not the Hindu press come to the rescue of the children of their community in this year of trial?...Will not the *Amrita Bazar Patrika*, the *Indian Mirror*, the *Bengalee*, the *Indian Nation*, the *Lucknow Advocate*, the *Mahratta* and *The Hindu* and a host of other Hindu papers, conducted in English and vernacular, listen to our humble prayer and wield their powerful pens for the protection of their own kith and kin? Our silence and indifference can only mean ruin and misery to a number of Hindu families, who will lose their hopefuls forever.[109]

There is an interesting instance of pan-Hindu conscience, embracing all religions born in India, in one of the early writings of Lajpat Rai. One Pundit Shiv Nath Shastri had taken exception to the Shuddhi movement taken up by Arya Samaj. Shastri himself belonged to the Brahmo Samaj. In his response, an important aspect of the Shuddhi movement which emerges is that the Shuddhi movement did not win converts to Arya Samaj. Rather, those who desired to return could return to the original religious sect from which they were converted.

The Arya Samaj does not preach or claim to establish and propagate a new religion. It simply aims at the reform of the prevailing religion and the social customs of the Hindus. For it an unreformed Hindu is nearer than one who renounces the Hindu

> religion and completely goes over to an antagonistic faith. So long as he is a Hindu he is as good a brother as a member of the Arya Samaj because it makes absolutely no difference to him so far as his social status is concerned. Pundit Siva Nath Shastri of course could not see this. To him every effort made to prevent the Hindus from falling a victim to the teachings of other faiths is fomenting discord amongst the people of different religions. He has nothing to say against the Christian Missionary who is making havoc in Hindu society and ruining families after families. He has nothing to say against the Mahomedan who is getting converts every day and abuses the Hindu religion in the most offensive language possible that can be used by man....The Arya Samaj does sympathise with the work of Shuddhi on the principles stated above, but it is sheer injustice to the leaders of the Shuddhi Sabha to give the credit of its work to the Arya Samaj. The leaders of the Shuddhi Sabha are Sikhs and the conversions made by the Sabha are towards Sikhism.[110]

Perhaps Pundit Shiv Nath Shastri provides us with an earlier version of modern Shashi Tharoor variety who want to differentiate between fashionable philosophical ornamental Hinduism that belongs only to the upper sections of the society and characterize as problematic, any ground level attempt to save and reclaim Hindu society from proselytizing religions. Further, the support of Arya Samaj to the Shuddhi movement by Sikhs documented here by Lajpat Rai anticipates in a crucial way the pan-Hindu definition of Savarkar.

It is interesting to note that Lajpat Rai was one of earliest Hindu Sanghatan leaders to express concern for non-monopolistic pagan co-religionists being persecuted and violently converted outside India.

In 1895 Amir Abdur Rahman Khan, made ruler of Afghanistan by the Durand treaty with the British, had embarked on a jihad against the remaining non-Islamic Kafir tribes of the area known as Kafiristan. In a campaign that ran for 40 days with well-equipped ammunition, the army of the Amir subjugated the Kafirs to tyranny. On 2 November 1895, the Amir had ordered that all above the age of seven who did not accept Islam would not be spared. Captured Kafir women were made to embrace Islam and then sent to the harem of the Amir. Captured women were put in jail and widows were registered to be married off to those who converted to Islam. In the Kafir villages, the village heads were made to pay extra taxes, and if they could not pay, then their women and children were seized and carried to Kabul. From the Waigal region alone, 80 Kafir women were seized and sent to Kabul. Documentary evidence shows that the campaign had continued till as late as 1899. For example, a report speaks of 100 captured Kafir men, women and children who were kept in confinement until they agreed to convert to Islam.[111] All adult Kafir women captured in the campaign were sold in markets.

All these created some noise in the Indian press. Only a few magazines wrote against the atrocities: 'One trembles to think of the fate of these Kafirs. They will now probably disappear from the face of the earth. It is hoped that the English government will repair its mistake and insist upon the restoration of Kafferistan as a condition upon which permission can be given to the Amir to keep an envoy in England,' wrote an India newspaper *Hitavadi* in its issue dated 24 January 1896. It also noted that their religion was similar to Hinduism. On 15 February 1896, *Mihir-o-Sudhakar*, another magazine, reported that many 'Kaffers' were killed in the Amir taking possession of 'Kafferistan. It reported Dr Leitner as having taken up the cause of the Kafirs, who he believed were the descendants of Greeks and asked Amir to stop their slave trade if he wanted Afghanistan to have its ambassador in the British court. Perhaps the harshest criticism in Indian media regarding this came from a magazine called *Sajivini* which in its magazine dated 25 January 1896 stated that '...the British government should be held responsible for the loss of the independence of the free people and for the destruction of their ancient monuments by the army of the Amir of Afghanistan'. It termed it 'an instance of treachery almost without a parallel in the history of humanity'. The Kafirs had 'with their wonted simplicity always depended upon the British government for protection, but the British government, in order to serve a selfish purpose, had betrayed them', it accused.[112] In the end, except for a handful of Kalash tribes who managed to find refuge in the then British Chitral province (now in Pakistan), all other Kafirs were either killed or dispersed or converted. Kafiristan was renamed as Nooristan.

About this genocidal campaign by the Amir of Afghanistan, Lajpat Rai was one Hindu politician who condemned unequivocally. Most probably from the political Hindus, his seemed to be the lonely voice raising concerns. The Kafirs were 'the descendants of the forefathers of the Indian Hindus' but they were 'manlier and more handsome than the Hindus'. He considers them as 'Aryan'. But his emphasis was more on their religion and culture rather than their ethnic stock. He explained that their religion had 'a close affinity to Hinduism' and they had always been a free people and they never invaded others. Then he made a brilliant analysis of how colonial politics, and the proselytizing religions work in tandem to effect the destruction of indigenous people:

> Is it not a crying shame that the political powers of the present day should dispose of men like cattle, and apportion the world among themselves as if it were of their own creation? Today Europe rules the whole of this terrestrial globe, and in Africa and Asia the European powers are casting lots for God's earth and His creatures. They tell the world that the Almighty has entrusted to the Missionaries (lit. shepherds of Christ) the task of enlightening mankind, and that the Christian Kingdom will

> hoist the flag of civilization by preaching Christianity throughout the world. It is terrible, however, to think that this object is being effected by depriving mankind of their freedom and trampling underfoot the religions followed by them. Kafiristan has come in for a share of this 'civilization', and, as a consequence, has lost its independence. The Amir has, with the permission of the people of England, overrun this country and reduced its inhabitants to a state of slavery. The Jihad led against them by the ruler of Kabul has accordingly ended in the extinction of this ancient people. The writer then goes on to say that although hundreds of Kafir villages were burnt down, innumerable places of worship levelled to the dust, thousands of people massacred and the survivors sold as slaves, the whole of Kafiristan could not be brought to embrace the Mahomedan religion. The Commander-in-Chief of the Amir's army then resorted to torture, threats and promises to induce the Kafirs to embrace Islam. This has been the end of Kafiristan, and the last independent Aryan race in Asia has been exterminated with weapons purchased with money realized from the Hindus.[113]

Then he advised Hindus to learn from the Muslims who agitate for the Muslims in distant lands and raise their voice for the Hindus being massacred in nearby Afghanistan.

Encounters with Islamist Balkanizing Strategies

A Hindu Sanghatanist and hence a strong Hindu secular at heart, Lajpat Rai believed that the Hindu-Muslim problem was the creation of the British.

While in jail during the non-cooperation/Khilafat movement, Lajpat Rai had a fellow prisoner Maulvi Habib-ur-Rahman. When Lajpat Rai asked him how long Muslims would be fellow travellers with Hindus in the fight for freedom, he answered clearly thus:

> Believers could certainly remain in partnership with Infidels in turning out the alien Christian rulers, but not beyond the achievement of that objective. To the credit of pan-Islamists of India it should be said that they were not secretive or deceptive about this stand of theirs.

It is not that the Islamists were deceptive about their goals. Had the Hindu leaders cared to go through the terminology and the theological implications of the same of the Khilafat leaders, they would have understood where both Hindus and Muslims stood with respect to Khilafat and the concept of Swaraj. But most of the Hindu leaders of the Congress were so carried away by the euphoria of Hindu-Muslim unity and viewed Muslim participation purely through Hindu lenses, that they misread the Islamists.

Let us take an example. There were questions from the believers who asked 'the learned in Theology (ulema-i-din) and the law-givers of the great shariat' with regard to the Non-Cooperation movement launched by Gandhi, obviously an idolater. Among these questions were the following:

1. Is it permissible by the 'shariat' to have social unity with a non- Muslim who is not inclined to be hostile and also to take help from him in any matter?
2. Is it permissible by the 'shariat' to accept sound advice tendered by a non-Muslim and to act upon it in order to attain a religious object, which is apparently considered adherence to and following the non-Muslim?

And the following were the answers as fatwas given to first question (fifth question in the original list):

> It is certainly permissible by the "shariat" to have political (mulki) and social unity with such non-Muslim who is not at war with the Mussalmans....But in the extreme enthusiasm of unity the Mussalman should not do anything which is not permissible by "shariat" as any such union which produces other evils is not permissible....The Prophet in the skirmishes of the Khyber took help from some Jews against the Jews. In the engagement at Hunain, the Prophet sought the help of one Safiwan-ibn-Umayya who was an idolater. Its details are given in *Fathul Qadir*, etc.

For the second question (sixth in the original), the answer fatwa stated:

> It is permissible to accept and to act upon the good advice tendered by a non-Muslim "which is not against the interest and expediency of religion. In fact, this is in accordance with the orders of God and his Prophet. The law-givers of Islam have considered it permissible to follow the leaders of idolaters at the time of attacking an enemy during Jehad....But it is not permissible and is forbidden to follow the aspirations of idolaters. God says, (Arabic verse) If thou followeth the aspirations of idolaters after having knowledge of it, verily thou act as a tyrant". But this should be remembered that it is not permissible for a Mussalman to be under the leadership of a non-Muslim whether wholly or partly....Allah knows the best.

The fatwas were signed by Abdul Mohasin Mohamed Sajjad of Nazim Jamiat Ulema along with 120 other ulemas, certifying the correctness of the fatwas.[114]

While the answer to the second question in the fatwa is straightforward, the examples given in the first answer have interesting consequences for Hindus and Sikhs. The wife of Safiwan-ibn-Umayya got converted to Islam and separated from him as he was still an 'idol-worshipper'. Later he embraced Islam. The extermination of Jews of Khaybar is a well-documented episode in the annals of early Islam. The theological implications are not hard to find.

Lajpat Rai was perplexed. In a letter to Deshbandhu C. R. Das, written in December 1922, he opened up about his innermost fears. He did not pretend to have answers. He sincerely wished that he should be wrong. The letter, now famous, reveals one of the abiding problems in Hindu-Muslim relations:

> I have devoted most of my time during the last six months to the study of Muslim history and Muslim Law, and I am inclined to think it (Hindu-Muslim Unity) is neither possible nor practicable. Assuming and admitting the sincerity of Mohammedan leaders in the non-cooperation movement, I think their religion provides an effective bar to anything of the kind....I can only hope that my reading of Islamic law is incorrect. And nothing would relieve me more than to be convinced that it is so. But if it is right, then it comes to this, that although we can unite against the British, we cannot do so to rule Hindustan on British lines. We cannot do so to rule Hindustan on democratic lines. What is the remedy? I am not afraid of the seven crores of Mussalmans. But I think the seven crores in Hindustan plus the armed hosts of Afghanistan, Central Asia, Arabia, Mesopotamia and Turkey will be irresistible. I do honestly and sincerely believe in the necessity and desirability of Hindu-Muslim unity. I am also fully prepared to trust the Muslim leaders. But what about the injunctions of the Quran and the Hadis? The leaders cannot override them. Are we then doomed?[115]

Yet he wanted to have faith in Hindu-Muslim unity. He wrote thus of the India of his vision, in a book published in 1924 (significantly, three years after the Moplah massacre in Kerala):

> The problem before us is not how to mix them or how to reconcile them, but how to integrate them. What we aim at is not the merging or the absorption of one into the other, but the integration of all into one whole, without in anyway injuring or lessening each group individually. Hindus, Muslims, Christians, Sikhs, Jains will not have to cease to be such in order to be Indians. Let them but recognize themselves to be Indians as well as Muslims, Christians etc., let them think themselves as Indian Muslims and Indians Christians, and then all will be well.[116]

The same year in August, he met Obeidullah, a Maulvi involved in the Khilafat movement in Istanbul. When Obeidullah handed Lajpat Rai a card stating that he was a functionary of the Kabul Congress Committee, Lajpat Rai was shocked, because it did not make any sense, nor did he have any knowledge of it. Later enquiries revealed that one such committee had indeed been formed in 1922 when Lajpat Rai was in jail and C. R. Das was the president of the Congress. But what shocked Lajpat Rai even more was the printed scheme that the Maulvi presented the former, a scheme of federated republics of the rest of India. At Istanbul he discovered of a scheme to subordinate a weakened Balkanized India to an evidently strong theocratic Islamist rule, presumably from Afghanistan. Called the Obeidullah plans, the methodology of this included creating an alliance with world Muslim powers and aligning themselves with Indian nationalists during the last part of World War I. The aim was to create a pan-Islamic caliphate and creating an Indo-Afghan Islamic empire as a step towards that end. At the same time, he also met Indian Muslim youths in Istanbul who were totally disillusioned with Khilafat and the concept of Darul Islam.

When Lajpat Rai returned to India in October 1924, he received the news of the cleansing of Hindus from Kohat and subsequent fasting by Gandhi. In a thirteen-part series on the Hindu-Muslim problem which was published in *The Tribune* November–December 1924, he analysed the Hindu-Muslim problem in a clinical and objective manner. In quite a critical assessment of Gandhi, Lajpat Rai wrote:

> As regards Mahatma Gandhi's fast, it is an open secret that the desecration of Hindu temples, one after another, at Amethi, Gulbarga, Kohat and other places, and the tragedy of Kohat gave him such a shock that he considered it his duty to undergo a penance for his misunderstanding and mishandling the Hindu-Muslim situation during the last three years. For the first time he felt miserable at the thought that he, who had striven his best to obtain Hindu co-operation for the saving of the Muhmmadan "temple" Khilafat, had to see desecration of Hindu temples by tens, in most cases without any provocation, at the hands of Muhammadans, The sense of helpless-ness and disappointment generated by this shock impelled him to impose a purificatory penance of twenty-one days' fast on him, in the hope that whilst he purified himself of any sin that he might have committed unconsciously he would be able to create an atmosphere which might give opportunities of improving Hindu-Muslim relations.[117]

To him, though Mahatma Gandhi meant well, he seldom went into the heart of the problem. This long essay should be considered as a critical Hindutva document studying Hindu-Muslim relations in India. But that criticism was tempered equally by the respect and awareness of Gandhi's contribution to the nation-building in India:

> Yet amidst all these disappointments and disconcerting events and circumstances and in the midst of resulting chaos, there is one fact which emerges boldly and which gives hope to all well-wishers of India. However divided Hindus and Muslims may be, however bitter their relations with each other, they are still united in their demand for Swarajya, in their opposition to the Government and in their hatred of the subjugation imposed upon them from without. It will stand to the eternal credit of Mahatma Gandhi that he has brought politics home to the masses of India, that he has created a wonderful and never to be effaced awakening in them and that he has produced a consciousness which marks the beginning of a real nationhood.

Lajpat Rai was of the view that all the religions and communities should subordinate their claim for 'absolute rights' for the welfare and progress of overall humanity. He observed that the Khilafat movement had the dangerous side-effect of strengthening the bigots within the religious communities. Gandhi himself was found paradoxical in this regard by Lajpat Rai and he noted that the British were efficiently manipulating the differences arising out of the bigotry, insisting upon their 'absolute rights' in public spaces:

> The sum total of my reasoning is this, that one of the causes of the present tension between Hindus and Muhammadans has been the unfortunate revival of the idea of absolute freedom in the matter of religious observances....In a country like India, to inculcate the idea that every religious practice so far observed or presumed to be sanctioned or, enjoined by one's faith, is holy and sacred and unchangeable, for, in my humble judgment, mischievous, and requires to be counteracted. At the present stage of its development India requires more of rationalism and toleration than orthodoxy and bigotry....Never before did I see educated Hindus, Mussalmans and Sikhs attaching so great an importance to insignificant and petty things in the name of religion as they do now. Shastras and shariats have been studied and requisitioned only to create an atmosphere of narrowness and bigotry.

He then explored how Hinduism and Islam differed—Hinduism being liberal and Islam being dogmatic. Yet he pointed out that there had been Hindu leaders who could break the social taboos of Hinduism such as untouchability, and have been accepted by Hindu masses. Similarly, there had been Muslim leaders who had challenged the notions of all non-Muslim (Hindus and Sikhs) being branded as kafirs. But still he noticed certain very disturbing facts in the Hindu-Muslim riots. Not only did these riots seem to follow certain Islamist fundamentalist axioms against kafirs during the war, later there was a propaganda to attribute to Islamist violence, an economic justification. Lajpat Rai observed and registered these tendencies:

> The fact that wherever there have been riots between Hindus and Mussulmans, the latter have looted the former, desecrated their temples and assaulted their women, betrays the widespread diffusion of the idea that the Hindus are Kafirs, that the Muslims are in a state of war with them, and that in fighting them, their property and women are "halal" for the Muslims. There are some persons who maintain that this has been the work of Goondas. I say, no! The riots have been inspired by cleverer brains than those of the Goondas, they have been encouraged and supported by influential people. It is only the actual outrages that have been committed by Goondas, fanatics and poor people. An esteemed Muslim leader has propounded the theory that the fact that the Hindus are rich and Muslims arc poor, explains these riots. Assuming the explanation to be correct, how does he explain the irrefutable fact that poor Mussulmans do not loot their rich fellow religionists? The real explanation is that the latter are Muslims and the Hindus are Kafirs. This notion has been rubbed into the mind of the Muslim masses and Muslim middle classes, by clever propagandists and influential leaders. It is the duty of the Muslim nationalist leaders to inaugurate and carry on an extensive propaganda to destroy this notion and to impress on the minds of their co-religionists the truth that Hindus are not Kafirs and that even on the occasion of fights and quarrels, their temples, their women and their property are inviolable and unassailable.

Then Lajpat Rai goes through the composition of the poet Dr Muhammad Iqbal. All his patriotic poems, filled with spiritual beauty and syncretic spirituality, were composed prior to 1905. After 1905 his poems reek of aggressive pan-Islamism. From 'Hindustan is the best of the nations in the world.... We are Indians and Hindustan is ours' (*Hindi hain hum,* waṭan *hai* Hindustan̠ *hamara*) he had moved to 'Muslims are we: All world is ours' (*Muslim hain hum,* waṭan *hai sara* jahan̠ *hamara*). This pan-Islamist transformation in Dr Iqbal was complete as early as 1910, Lajpat Rai noted.

The problem was the emerging Pan-Islamist propaganda and worldview among Indian Muslims. If the Khilafat movement gave a fresh breath of air to Hindu orthodoxy against the Sanghatanist reformers, in the case of Muslims, it not only emboldened the orthodoxy but also made pan-Islamism a part of Muslim political discourse. After explaining how wrong Indian Islamists were in their pan-Islamist ambitions by citing the experience of Muslims all over the world, he stated:

> I am afraid Indian Muslims are more Pan-Islamic and exclusive than the Muslims of any other country on the face of the globe, and that fact alone makes the creation of a united India more difficult than would otherwise be the case.

In the end, he appealed to the Muslims, the Hindus and to Gandhi:

For God's sake, don't threaten us with Jehad. We have seen many Jehads! For the last twelve hundred years we have heard that cry every day, of our national existence. Yet, Jehads have not succeeded in killing us, and God willing, no threat of Jehad will influence us by one hair's breadth in our determination to continue to live....It is true that Muslim distrust of Hindus can successfully block the avenues of Swarajya, but brother Muslims! Don't forget that active Hindu hostility may also be productive of some harm to the Islamic world. Away, then, with these threats and distrust. Let us live and struggle for freedom as brothers whose interests are one and indivisible. Let us live and die for each other, so that India may live and prosper as a Nation. India is neither Hindu nor Muslim. It is not even both. It is one. It is India.

To the Hindus, I will say, "If there are any among you who still dream of a Hindu Raj in this country, who think they can crush the Mussalmans and be the supreme power in this land, tell them that they are fools, or to be more accurate, that they are insane, and that their insanity will ruin their Hinduism along with their country...."

To leaders like Mahatma Gandhi, I would say in all humility. "Sirs, do not put the cart before the horse. Do not assume the existence of conditions which do not exist. Listen to the voice of experience and caution. It is better to proceed slowly than to run away with assumptions and presumptions which would not only do no good but might land your country into pits. Do not try to change human nature simply by resolutions and exhortations....The assumption that seven crores of Muslims had accepted Non-co-operation, was absolutely unwarranted. It was too much to expect educated Muslims to give up opportunities of preferment and promotion which they were just beginning to get, the Hindus being already much in advance."

In 1925 he delivered the Presidential Address at the convention of a provincial Hindu Mahasabha at Bombay. Here he pointed out how there was a concerted attempt to divide Indian communities by offering political sanction to communal differences:

The name of the country is Hindustan and all those who accept it as their home ought to be called or known as Hindus. But we know that is not so. There are large groups of humanity having their homes in this country who resent being called Hindus, and in its efforts to keep up these differences, the Government of the country has gone even so far as to divide the people of the country for all legislative and administrative purposes into Muslims and non-Muslims. The division, if any, should have been, into Hindus and non-Hindus....Recent developments, however, indicate that a time may come when every other community known by a separate distinctive name, may get special representation with separate electorates and the

> Hindus may be the only people in India left to be known as non-Muslims....Active efforts are being made by Government and non-Government agencies to divide the Hindus and split them into smaller groups so as to reduce their strength, their importance, and their influence. Unfortunately the prevailing social system of the Hindus lends support to these efforts. The existing caste distinctions are the weakest spot in the Hindu system and if the Hindu community and Hindu culture have to outlive these ridiculous and mischievous attacks, it is incumbent on the Hindus to take active steps to repel the attacks and to resist the attempts that are being made to destroy their unity and their communal existence.

In hindsight, the Presidential speech of Lajpat Rai looks prophetic. In post-independent India, there has been a race of many communities to announce themselves as non-Hindus and then hanker for concessions and minority rights. Then he drew parallels between the United States and India. He pointed out how though Jews and coloured people in the United States, despite having separate communal institutions, never have separate political representation. While in the US, he predicted that with time the communal distinctions and discriminations like Jews being not allowed in certain non-Jewish restaurants, etc. would slowly disappear, in the case of India, the political representation for communal groups would deepen divisions in the society. Thus, he pointed out how the British was deepening the fault lines in India, while in the US, the government policies are to remove the fissures in the society:

> In the United States there is a thick wall that separates the Jews and the Christians. In fact, the division is not between the Jews and the Christians but between Jews and non-Jews. Nor is the distinction of the making of the Jews alone. There are Jewish hotels where non-Jews are not admitted, and there are non-Jewish hotels where Jews and black men are not admitted. The Government of the country, however, recognises no such distinctions and a time is sure to come when these distinctions will altogether disappear even from the social field. This might have been the case in India as well, if the Government had not intervened and created communal compartments for political purposes and out of political motives....Personally, I would like my country to recognise no communal distinction in the political and the economic fields. In fact, I would go farther and recognise no communal distinction even in social life. I would like to see people professing different faiths intermingle in social life absolutely freely. But under the existing conditions that is not to be.

He emphasized the importance of Hindus organizing themselves. However, there is a difference between the Hindus organizing themselves and the Islamist communal organizations. In his address, he pointed out how once again, Jews could prosper in New York while keeping separate their communal identity, and at the same time without the need for a communal representation in the combined political interest of the society. So, the communal response, he pointed out, had been thrust upon the Hindus but they should not allow it to become communal wars:

> Under the circumstances it becomes absolutely essential for the Hindus to organise themselves in order to avert those consequences. If organizing for that purpose is anti-Muslim or anti-national, then I frankly confess that the Hindu Sabha movement is both. But I don't admit that such an organization is either anti-Muslim or anti-national. The desire for separate political existence and the move to secure that end has come from the Muslims. The Hindus are whole-heartedly opposed to that policy and are prepared to merge their separate communal entity into a common Indian nation. But they form the majority, and the Muslims are afraid of not receiving justice at their hands without the necessary guarantees for the protection and safeguarding of their communal or minority interests. These they believe can only be secured by communal electorates and by communal representation even in the services and on the local bodies. But this plea can only hold good if it be conceded that Hindus and Muslims have separate political and economic interests. So far as religious freedom is concerned one can appreciate the fear, but it may be safeguarded by the constitution. But so far as secular interests are considered, why should anyone claim any such rights as a Muslim or as a Hindu if the idea be to evolve a common nationhood? The whole idea of the existence of such separate interests is a negation of nationhood and it must be frankly confessed that those who desire a perpetuation of religious-communal distinctions in the secular line must be considered to be opposed to nationalism. New York is the biggest Jewish city in the world and even there the Jews are in a minority as against the Christians, yet they have never put forward a claim for communal representation....Communal organization has thus been thrust upon us. At the same time, it is our bounden duty to be perpetually vigilant so as to avoid its degeneration into a communal war.

The approach of Lajpat Rai to the Hindu Sanghatan movement as well as his appeal for Hindu-Muslim unity, are both based on facts and not on romantic conceptions or communal hatred. In the case of Muslims, he recognizes the genuine fears of a minority, for which he exhibits empathy. In the case of Hindu-Muslim riots, he does not invent a false symmetry but sees it as a theo-political war waged on Hindus—the kafirs—by Islamists of pan-Islamist fundamentalist variety. He did not compromise on the safety of Hindus which faced real threat against jihad and pan-Islamist mentality. At the same time, he cautioned Hindu Sanghatanists developing any hatred for Muslims. This stream of thought too, should be considered as an important part of the Hindutva movement in dealing with the problem of Hindu-Muslim relations. Ultimately, he rejects a theocratic State and promotes a secular State. In 1937, nine years after the death of Lajpat Rai, Savarkar was echoing the spirit of 'the Lion of Punjab' with respect to Hindu-Muslim unity, in his Presidential address to the Hindu Mahasabha:

> When will our unity-hankers understand that the real question at the root of this Moslem displeasure is not a word here or a song there! We would have sacrificed a dozen songs or a hundred words of our own free will if thereby we could really contribute to the unity and solidarity of Hindustan....Real Unity can only come when the Mohammedans need it!...The only threat that the Mohammedans always hold before the Hindus is to the effect that they would not join the Hindus in the struggle for Indian freedom unless their anti-national and fanatical demands are granted on the spot. Let the Hindus silence the threat once for all telling point blank: 'Friends! We wanted and do want only that kind of unity which will go to create an Indian state in which all citizens irrespective of caste and creed, race and religion are treated all alike on the principle of one man one vote. We, though we form the overwhelming majority in the land, do not want any special privileges for our Hindudom; any more, we are even willing to guarantee special protection for the language, culture and religion of the Mohammedans as a minority if they also promise not to infringe on the equal liberty of other communities in India to follow their own ways within their own respective houses and not to try to dominate and humiliate the Hindus.[118]

In other words, despite the harshness and heat of riots designed by the Muslim League and facilitated by the British administration, not to mention the wrong policies of appeasement taken by the Congress, which were dragging the nation towards Pakistan and definite annihilation of all Hindus in the region—Sanatanis, Arya Samajis, Sikhs and Buddhist tribes—the Hindutva discourse was even in that storm, primarily and predominantly, rooted in secular democracy. To them, the State must be secular even when the nation is Hindu, and they were 'communal' only with respect to defending the Hindus who were increasingly the victims of the jihad riots.

In their own way, each of these ideologues and activists of the pre-RSS/ non-RSS Hindu Sanghatan movement contributed to the worldview of Hindutva as we know it today. What is it that connects them all? They all felt the need of a Hindu Sanghatan. At the same time, they rejected theocracy of any kind. At least two of the leaders, namely Savarkar and Lala Har Dayal, were atheists in the conventional term of belief in a deity. They also believed in the fundamental oneness of global humanity and considered nationalism as a temporary phase in human evolution. All these ideological streams pouring into Hindutva make it quite a non-monolithic phenomenon. At the same time, most of the Sanghatan ideologues could not afford to be idle armchair ideologues. They were needed to constantly work in the ground also. They conducted social emancipation movements. They had to balance their way between a national freedom movement which they perceived to yield more and more to Islamist aggression, endangering the survival of Hindus and a colonial government that was strategically inflicting the maximum wounds to the society. Considering all the seemingly unsurpassable problems they faced, history bears witness to their endurance and significant successes.

Lala Har Dayal (1884–1939)

Bhai Parmanand (1876–1947)

Pandit Madan Mohan Malaviya (1861–1946)

Lala Lajpat Rai (1865–1928)

"But what unresisting martyrdom fails to do, righteous and resisting force does and renders tyranny impotent to do further harm."

: O :

"Rather get killed than converted" was the cry prevalent amongst the Hindus then. But Ramdas rose and exclaimed, "No: not thus, 'Better get killed than converted' is good enough: but it would be better so to thrive as neither to get killed nor violently converted by killing the forces of violence itself. Get killed if that must be, but get killed while killing to conquer – conquer in the cause of Righteousness

Hindu Pad Padshahi!

(184-85)

"Go Freedom, whose smiles we shall never resign,
Go tell the invaders, the Danes,
'Tis sweeter to bleed for an age at thy shrine
Than to sleep but a minute in chains." { Thomas Moore

Hindu Pad Padshahi ...

Quotes from Veer Savarkar's 'Hindu Pad Padshahi' in the handwriting of Bhagat Singh in his jail notes ('Bhagat Singh's Jail Notebook', Waraich & Harish Jain)

6

Rashtriya Swayamsevak Sangh

The *Hindutva* movement in the current Indian sociopolitical stream is explicitly represented by the Rashtriya Swayamsevak Sangh (RSS). It is an enigmatic organization in the sense that it does not have the many basic characteristics of any of the cadre-based movements in the world. It does not even have membership forms or a card holding system. It has a loose ground-based unit called the *shakha* which literally means 'branch'. It has a Western uniform, is manifest throughout India via its typically Western parades in different parts of the country and the band music it uses for that occasion, which too is Western. This quasi-military looking Western dressed nature has often led to the accusation that this organization is Nazi-like. Yet the other aspects of the Sangh, as the RSS is popularly called, defy such a characterization. It is still a mystery how this organization functions despite three bans against it.

Understanding Dr Hedgewar

Dr Hari Seldon, a mathematician, was born in the 11,988th year of the Galactic Era. As a mathematician, he specialized in a branch of science called psychohistory—a statistical science that studies human behaviour. He realized that the Galactic Empire in which he lived was slowly crumbling. So, he established at one end of the galaxy what came to be known as 'Foundation'. This was created to steer the Galactic humanity back into a vibrant civilization through the ensuing centuries of barbarism after the inevitable fall of the Galactic society.

It aimed to reduce the chaotic barbarism to a mere thousand years. For this, Seldon said that a group of scholars would sit in isolation and gather all human knowledge silently. They would then publish a series of Encyclopedia Galactic. Thus, 'Encyclopedia Foundation' came into being, which was later famously known only as 'Foundation' at the remote corner of the galaxy in an unnoticed small planet called Terminus. Fifty years after Seldon's death, a vault opens during a planetary crisis in Terminus. And the hologram of Seldon explains the real work of 'the Encyclopedia Foundation'. They are actually 'the seeds of Renaissance and the future founders of the Second Galactic Empire'.

Who could have thought that a bunch of isolated scholars working in a remote planet on encyclopedias would actually become the harbingers of Renaissance and builders of a new society on a galactic scale? That is science fiction—Hari Seldon was a fictional genius created by Dr Isaac Asimov.

And who could have thought a bunch of kabaddi playing youngsters would change the course of history of a nation of a billion people.

Dr Keshav Baliram Hedgewar actually lived.

He created the RSS in 1925. He wanted some boys in the neighbourhood to come together every day for one hour in a uniform—something one may find laughable today. These boys would do some physical exercises, sing patriotic songs, play kabaddi and then disperse. There was no membership form. There was no attendance. There was no need for much of an infrastructure. These youths, he predicted, would become the powerhouses of the nation in various sectors.

It should have been as laughable then as it is unbelievable today. They came, they played and then they dispersed. But they networked; they branched out; they grew—these kabaddi playing boys in half pants. And like Asimov's science fiction novel *Foundation*, the Sangh faced crisis after crisis. There was no physical hologram of Dr Hedgewar opening a vault in Nagpur. But there is a deeper vault within many Swayamsevaks—a resonance with the vision of the founder—that has guided the Sangh through the crisis.

It seems amazing that Dr Hedgewar could have involuted into the body of the Sangh, solutions for a crisis that would threaten the fabric of the Hindu society decades after his death. Take for instance the question of *jati* (caste). What should be the Hindu approach towards it? At the time that Dr Hedgewar formulated the Sangh, most of the dominant national leaders including Tilak and Gandhi were supporters of the caste system. Some of the greatest Hindu religious leaders including the Shankaracharyas of that time supported untouchability and opposed Scheduled Communities (SCs) entering Hindu temples. Dr Ambedkar opposed the system, but he was in minority at the time. Savarkar rejected the shastra-based (scripture-based) caste system as the disease of the mind. Between such stands, at the surface it seems, Dr Hedgewar never gave a clear stand on the problem. But the RSS ideologue Ramesh Patange explains:

> The precondition of unification of the Hindu society is to "decaste" the minds of the Hindus, and eliminate caste from their mental make-up. The Hindus total thinking in respect of caste needs reorientation. Dr Hedgewar initiated that process. The uniform of the Sangh Swayamsevaks, their band, drill in the Shakhas, were entirely modern devices, not traceable to the Indian tradition. It was Dr Hedgewar who introduced them in the Sangh. Dr Hedgewar never discussed or denounced religion in public. He never brought into the Sangh religious rituals based on inequality. Nor did he ever claim that the Sangh's objective is to revive the religion based on *Chaturvarnyashram*. He never brought such ideology to the Sangh. I have also not found in his writings any reference to the Manusmriti. "We are all brothers. We have to build up an integrated and united society. We have to become strong", he used to say, and he shaped the organisation of the Sangh accordingly. I had not realised the real meaning and essence of Dr Hedgewar's mantra of Hindu unification till I read Dr Ambedkar's biography.[1]

This is the genius of Dr Hedgewar. In 1935 Dr Ambedkar made his famous statement: 'Though, I was born a Hindu, I solemnly assure you that I will not die as a Hindu'. In 1939 Dr Hedgewar had called Dr Ambedkar to preside over the Makar Sankranti function at the RSS camp. A knee jerk reaction would be to brand Dr Ambedkar as an anti-Hindu and a colonial stooge. But Dr Hedgewar was able to see the real reason and pain behind the words of Dr Ambedkar. Gangadhar Bagul, one of the Swayamsevaks present in that training camp and a witness to the interaction between Dr Ambedkar and Dr Hedgewar, had given a complete description of the event in his autobiography. Dr Ambedkar asked Hedgewar if there were any Scheduled Community members in the Sangh camp. Dr Hedgewar replied that there were no touchables and untouchables in the camp but only Hindus. Dr Ambedkar, however, did go on to inquire the cadre in the camp and found that not only were there many Scheduled Community members but also there was an absolute sense of equality among them and no caste consciousness.

Dr Hedgewar then shines as the one Hindu leader who could peer into the dark future and see clearly how the faultlines would develop for the society with external forces trying to deepen them. Another important insight and direction Dr Hedgewar gave Hindutva movements is to never give in to the siege and imitate mentality. Once looking at the name of a locality named 'Hindu colony', he remarked how Hindus can have a colony for themselves in their own nation. It was an important insight. While Christians, Muslims and Parsis are communities in India, Hindus are the nation. They must remember this. They cannot behave in a way similar to other communities. So, each time a Hindutvaite, particularly of the neo-net variety, takes up the argument of 'why shouldn't we imitate the Islamist fundamentalist or a Christian fanatic' in securing a ban on a book or movie as a power statement, one needs to remember that Hindus in India are not a community but the nation.

Another interesting aspect of Dr Hedgewar's futuristic vision is his ability to tap into the traditional network ability of the Hindu society. He made *shakhas* the networking point for local Hindu cadre in a cost-effective manner. There was no building and thus no secrecy. All that was needed for the RSS to run a shakha was just an open ground available for one hour. This cost-effective networking strategy has made the Sangh the fastest rescuer of humans whenever there is a calamity anywhere in India. It does not matter whether RSS is 'strong' in an area. If there is an accident or a flood, the Sangh volunteers would be the first to reach the spot and start the rescue operations. For example, in Kerala when in 1988 more than 100 people lost their lives to the Trivandrum-bound Island Express as it plunged into a lake near Quilon, the RSS cadre were the first to reach the place and rescue many trapped in the derailed bogeys, reported Kerala's leading newspaper. The same story repeats in the Morvi dam disaster, Bhopal gas tragedy, Gujarat earthquake, tsunami of 2004 and so on.

What is amusing is the fact that there is not a single academic study of how the RSS has emerged as the only nationwide organization, reaching in rescue missions of all natural disasters without being capital intensive. The Sangh network and methodology is actually a boon for creating similar cost-effective voluntary organizations in other postcolonial developing societies. Today, there are Sangh affiliates working in various fields, Vigyan Bharati, Seva Bharati, Vidya Bharati and so on, not to mention Akhil Bharatiya Vidyarthi Parishad (ABVP) and the Bharatiya Mazdoor Sangh (BMS). India's two non-

Congress Prime Ministers who ran and run their office completely are from the Sangh. Some of the best administrative chief ministers of states are from the RSS. Sangh volunteers help the army even on battlefronts. All these came from the vision of Dr Hedgewar, who saw in those kabaddi playing young boys the power to regenerate India and make the nation realize its destiny.

In fact, what Dr Hedgewar did express was an age-old vision of India—as old as the Upanishads. When Uddalaka showed his son Svetaketu how the great banyan tree was involuted in the small seeds, he also showed that the principle can be repeated at all levels—from the biological to the spiritual and then to the socio-spiritual.

The RSS and the Freedom Movement

One of the oft-repeated charges against the RSS is that it had never participated in the freedom movement. Dr Hedgewar at the outset of creating the Sangh movement had made it clear that it would not involve itself with any of the then current political movements including the Indian National Congress (INC) and the Hindu Mahasabha (HMS). This created a serious conflict with the latter than the former. However, for Dr Hedgewar, organizing Hindus as a national body was a prerequisite for them to get involved in any national movement. This in turn stems from the fact that he considered the axiomatic Hindus as the nation of India. He was not too worried about political ideologies. In fact, his own ideological rhetoric, judging from his speeches and associations, often veered towards the left with talks about 'setting to fire the Ravana of Imperialism', etc. But as far as he was concerned, whether the ideology was leftist or rightist, the Hindus organized as a national body should have formed the substratum on which both should have functioned.

Rajguru Connection: 'Sarva Praharanayuddh'

The relation between Rajguru (one of the three revolutionaries hanged to death along with Bhagat Singh) and the Hindutva movement is important here in order to understand how Hindutva was actually perceived by the revolutionary movement in India, which is often depicted in establishment circles as completely pro-Marxist. While in terms of theory, the values of Savarkarite Hindutva historiography appears to be the single greatest Indian influence on revolutionaries, in terms of organizational support for Rajguru, it was the RSS that had helped him.

The three revolutionaries Bhagat Singh, Rajguru and Sukhdev were hung to death by the British government on 23 March 1930. Of them, Shivaram Rajguru is not as well-known as Bhagat Singh. Of all the three, including Sukhdev Thapar, Bhagat Singh had a charisma, and one could say that Rajguru had the least of it, at least in physical appearance. Yet this revolutionary was very distinct from the rest, and at many places, his life touches the high poetry of sacrifice and inner strength.[2]

But Rajguru was both a skilled wrestler and a Sanskrit scholar who had studied *Tarka Shastra*, and also knew by heart the *Lahu Siddhanta Koumudi*. Rajguru was to get Uttama degree in Sanskrit at Kasi, but he had been getting attracted to the revolutionary movement over a period of time. After meeting with Babu Rao Savarkar, the brother of Veer Savarkar, he decided to pursue the path of revolution. He joined Hanuman Prasarak Mandal—an organization to build physical strength and inculcate mental discipline among the youth. His jovial nature and immense physical strength got him many friends and it was here that he also came in contact with Keshav Baliram Hedgewar, the founder of RSS.

After meeting the firebrand revolutionary Chandrasekar Azad, Rajguru joined the Hindustan Revolutionary Army, which would later become the Hindustan Socialist Republican Army. The young revolutionaries despised sectarian violence that was stealthily fuelled by the British. It had among them a staunch nationalist, Ashfaqullah Khan, who himself became a martyr for Independence.

Swami Shraddhanand was assassinated in 1926. Swami had exposed a grand plan to convert Hindus by a Tabligh ideologue, Khawa Hassan Nizami (1873–1955). While he would try to flatter Hindus with his sweet words, he had also authored a book in Urdu titled *Dai-i-Islami* (*Missionary of Islam*) which in a detailed way spoke of how in every stratum of the society, every Muslim should engage in the conversion of Hindus. Making a departure from other radical Islamist movements which shunned Indian traditional religious dimensions, Nizami sought every aspect including music proscribed in Islam, to be used in conversion. He asked the rulers of Muslim princely states to set up Tablighs for Islam in their territories. He asked Muslim feudal lords to command conversions in their territories of influence. For he believed that 'whatever they (princes and feudal landowners) command the people under their influence to do, that will be followed by them (ordinary Hindus)'. In his book he had given elaborate plans for Muslims in every powerful section of the British empire namely police officers, village record keepers, postmasters, sepoys, etc., to do Tabligh.

So, in January 1928, Chandrasekar Azad recommended the name of Rajguru for the elimination of Hassan Nizami, the Delhi-based Sufi-faced strategist of

Tabligh activity. Rajguru was deadly and accurate in his shot; however, the target was wrong. He killed Somali, the father-in-law of Hassan Nizami.

On 17 December 1928, Rajguru would again pull the trigger. The shot would again be accurate and deadly. The bullet would pierce the chest of the target and finish him off. Only once again it would be a wrong target. It was not British police officer James Scott whom the revolutionaries had aimed to kill to avenge the death of Lala Lajpat Rai. Jai Gopal, one of the accomplices of the revolutionaries, had made a wrong signal to shoot. They had killed another police officer, Saunders. The very next day the revolutionaries in a public proclamation regretted that they had killed a man and yet he too was 'part of the cruel, despicable and unjust system'. Later while everyone appreciated the marksmanship of Rajguru, he jokingly said that he had actually aimed for the head, but the bullet hit the chest.

Rajguru might not have been endowed with the physical charisma of other revolutionaries. He himself was aware of that and instead of falling into any complex, he joked about it often. Once he had hung a wall calendar of a beautiful portrait of a girl. When he was away, Azad tore it into pieces, saying such things did not have a place in the life of a revolutionary. When Rajguru came and found the calendar torn into pieces, he was furious. A heated discussion ensued. When Azad said that beauty having no utility value could be destroyed, Rajguru asked him if he would also demolish Taj Mahal. Shaking in anger Azad replied, 'Yes, I will if I can.' Rajguru fell silent. Then he spoke softly, 'We want to make the world beautiful and that cannot be done by destroying and demolishing the beautiful things.' Now Azad also mellowed down. He too said that he did not actually mean what he said, but only that he was overemphasizing the need for the revolutionaries to be focused in their aim of getting freedom.

After avenging the death of Lala Lajpat Rai through the felling of British police officer John Saunders, Bhagat Singh escaped, posing as a 'saheb' with Durgavati, wife of another revolutionary who posed as a 'memsaheb'. Rajguru carried their luggage, acting as their servant. Rajguru would stick to his role, taking into account every minor detail so much that he would lie down by the side of the railway toilet—typically like a servant of the 'sahebs' of those times. No amount of persuasion from Bhagat Singh and Durgavati could change his mind. On 7 April 1929, Bhagat Singh was arrested after the Assembly bombing. Rajguru had actually fought with Bhagat Singh to accompany him, but Bhagat Singh did not allow that.

On 15 April, Sukhdev was arrested after a raid. Rajguru had meanwhile left Kasi and continued to move between Amravati, Nagpur and Wardha. During this time, he met Dr Hedgewar again, who helped him. He was kept safe by an RSS worker. He also used to visit his brother's house for meals. During one such visit, his mother saw a gun with Rajguru and asked him if it was befitting for a learned pandit like him to carry pistols. Rajguru explained to his ageing mother sincerely and patiently:

> When Dharma or the nation is in trouble, only arms are useful. The British are inflicting all sorts of injuries and insults on us, and I do not expect them to refrain from those acts merely because we are requesting them. If you remember even in Vishnu Sahasranama one of the names of the Lord is "Sarva Praharanayuddh"—one who is ever decorated with arms.

While Bhagat Singh was the most articulate of all the three revolutionaries, there is a strong possibility that the sleepy, simple looking and humorous Rajguru, though silent and almost invisible, was exerting a great influence on the thought processes of all of them. As noted in the earlier section dealing with the historiography of Savarkar, the book *Hindu Pad Padshahi* exerted a great influence on the revolutionary martyr-trio. Most probably, this was brought in by the silent impact of Rajguru to the organization.

Rajguru too was arrested on 30 September 1929 by DSP Syed Ahmed Shah. In the prison while awaiting death sentence which was quite certain, Rajguru was always his humorous self. During the end of the famous hunger strike within the prison, it was Bhagat Singh who took milk for Rajguru to end his hunger strike and jokingly said to him, 'Trying to overtake me, lad?' And Rajguru's reply made everyone laugh, 'I thought I would go early and book a room for you there. But it seems you require my services even during the journey!'

The life and martyrdom of Rajguru along with Bhagat Singh and Sukhdev show how Hindutva as a process was integrally intertwined with the freedom movement, no matter what political colour it took on the surface—left or otherwise. The help rendered by the RSS chief through RSS workers to hide Rajguru itself shows how the Sangh saw itself. It might not wish to be involved in politics, but it was clear with whom its sympathies stood.

The RSS and the Mass Freedom Movement

In December 1929, Congress had passed a resolution for complete independence. In 1930 it had announced that it would celebrate 26 January 1930, as the Independence Day. At that time, the Sangh was merely a five-year-old organization. Following the announcement, Dr Hedgewar wrote to all the Sangh officials in a circular dated 21 January 1930 thus:

> The Congress has declared "independence" to be its goal and the Congress Working Committee has announced that 26 January 1930 be celebrated as "independence day" throughout the country. It is but natural that all of us should feel heartened that this all-India national body has come close to its goal of independence. It is, therefore, our duty to cooperate with any organisation that works keeping this purpose foremost. Therefore, all shakhas of the RSS should organise the gathering of all the Swayam Sevaks at six 'o clock in the evening and salute the national flag which is the saffron flag. The true meaning of independence and how to present its goal must form the essence of the talk. Since we have accepted this goal of the Congress, the party must be congratulated for it. The report of this programme must be sent to us.[3]

For those who would like to criticize Dr Hedgewar for calling the saffron flag as the national flag, let us remember that a year later in April 1931, the Congress Working Committee would appoint a flag committee which would also include Maulana Abul Kalam Azad, and it would recommend the saffron flag as the national flag in its final report with the following words:

> We felt that the flag must be distinctive, artistic, rectangular and non-communal. Opinion has been unanimous that our national flag should be of a single colour except for the colour of the device. If there is one colour that is more acceptable to the Indians as a whole, even as it is more distinctive than another, one that is associated with this ancient country by long tradition, it is the Kesari or saffron colour.[4]

The Sangh as an organization nevertheless kept away from all agitation-based politics. Not only did it keep away from Congress agitations, it also never took part in the ones organized by Hindu Mahasabha. When the Mahasabha announced its agitation against the Nizam, the Bhaganagar Satyagraha, the RSS refrained from participating in it. A prominent former member of the RSS from Poona, who was with the Hindu Mahasabha then, was very angry with the RSS for this. His name was Nathuram Vinayak Godse. He openly accused the RSS of frittering away the Hindu energy. Despite great respect that the Sangh had for Vinayak D. Savarkar, on 8 April 1940, in Poona, the RSS head, Bhaurao Deshmukh (also known as Bhausaheb Deshmukh), gave a reply to the fringe elements in the Hindu Mahasabha:

> First of all, I wish to tell the malicious minds that the RSS is neither a military force for the Hindus nor the military wing of the Hindu Mahasabha. The Sangh's endeavor is to make the Hindus nationalists in the true sense

It is interesting to note that though individual leaders of the INC and Hindu Mahasabha praised the RSS for its discipline, the absence of untouchability and the services it rendered, both the organizations wanted the Sangh to be under their political control. When the RSS refused to play ball, scouts for both the parties, the INC and the Hindu Mahasabha accused the Sangh of being communal and anti-Hindu respectively.

Despite strict non-involvement of the RSS in political movements directly, the Sangh was ready to help any political movement indirectly by supplying its cadre and allowing it to give their faculties and facilities, provided it worked for the cause of India's welfare. Trailokyanath Chakravarty (1889–1970) was a Bengali revolutionary and freedom fighter. He met Dr Hedgewar, who promised him that the Sangh would provide him with the cadre for the future revolution he was planning.[5] Those in the Congress who could not rise above the pettiness of sectarian politics had passed the resolution in 1934 that their members could not join the RSS. Eminent historian Dr Kanchanmoy Mojumdar reveals that four years after the resolution of the Congress against the RSS, 'Bose reportedly sent emissaries to Hedgewar in 1939, perhaps seeking his help for an armed uprising'. *Modern Review* (March 1941) records about Hedgewar's death: 'Dr Hedgewar died in Nagpur of high blood pressure at the age of 51 only. Just one day before his death Subhas Chandra Bose went to see him.'[6]

Under Golwalkar

'Guruji' Golwalkar was different from Dr Hedgewar in his approach to politics. Unlike Dr Hedgewar who came from the background of the Calcutta-based revolutionary group Anuseelan Samiti, Golwalkar had taken spiritual initiation from Swami Akhandananda, a direct disciple of Sri Ramakrishna. Swami Akhandananda was known for his humanitarian services. Golwalkar shunned politics. He was dedicated to building a strong organization. This was the time when politics too had changed in the national arena. The threat of Partition had become very real. Along with the Quit India movement, the fate of Hindus and Sikhs in the provinces of Western Punjab and Eastern Bengal, was becoming worrisome. In the eventuality of Partition, towards which the events were fast gravitating despite the bravado and sentimental rhetoric of Congress leaders which was sounding more and more empty when seen with respect to ground reality, the Hindus and Sikhs in Western Punjab, as well as Hindus and Buddhist tribes in East Bengal needed to be protected and safeguarded. So, M. S. Golwalkar felt the need to spread and strengthen the organization. As the critics of the RSS never tire of repeating, 'Anderson and Damle point out that Golwalkar believed that the British should not be given any excuse to ban the RSS.'[7]

To substantiate the non-involvement of the RSS in national movement, Golwalkar's words are often quoted as stated below:

> In 1942, also there was a strong sentiment in the hearts of many. At that time too the royine work of the Sangh continued. Sangh vowed not to do anything directly. However, upheaval in the minds of the Sangh volunteers continued. Sangh is an organisation of inactive persons, their talks are useless, not only outsiders but also many of our volunteers did talk like this. They were greatly disgusted too.[8]

The operational term here is that the Sangh decided not to do anything directly. The British Intelligence reports indeed suggest that they could not find any evidence to connect RSS as an organization with the 1942 uprising. Nevertheless, the police did record many anti-British speeches made at the RSS training camps during the same period.

The file numbered 'D Home Pol (Int) Sec F No 28/8/42' in its page 20 provides the following report on the speeches of Golwalkar and other speeches made in the RSS camps over a period of moths:[9]

> On 27-4-1942 he (Golwalkar) denounced those persons who render every possible assistance to the present government for their own selfish ends. On 28-04-42 he declared that the Sangh had resolved to do its duty even though the whole world goes against it and Impressed on the volunteers that they must be ready to sacrifice their lives for the cause of country. On 28 April 1942, he declared that the Sangh has resolved to do its duty even if the whole world goes against it and impressed on the volunteers that they must be ready to sacrifice their lives for the cause of the country. On 3-5-1942 he made an important speech—"it was not possible to get Swaraj by begging it from foreigners and this could only be obtained by strength, it was therefore their duty to strengthen the Sangh. They would not waste their energy but would reserve it and would make use of it at the proper time. He said that they had nothing to do with what Japanese or the British were going to do but the question was what they should do. The opportunity for which they had been waiting so long had now come and they should utilise this to their advantage." On 5-5-42 he said that he was glad to see the war taking place as the time for their liberation was fast approaching. "They had to worship the goddess of war not by flowers but the sacrifice of their lives. They were not afraid of offering sacrifice to the goddess." In the same training camp of the Sangh Dada Paramarth of Nagpur on 6-5-42 said that the opportunity for which they had waited so long had now come and they should

> consider the slogan "Their difficulty is our opportunity." They should hope for a better future and prepare for the worst.

Another Home Department report [Pol F No 28/3/43 Pol(I)] has the following in its pages 8 and 9:

> Another speaker at Jubbalpore hinted that the aim of the Sangh was to drive the British out of India—a statement which is repeated by Gajjandhar of Nagpur at a private meeting in Amritsar on May 23rd. Recently an RSS organiser exhorted an audience in the Wardha district to prepare to die for India's liberation. At Gurudakshina meeting at Jubbalpore on September 12th Baba Sahib Apte (All India Prachar Pramukh) remarked that the behaviour of the British in India was becoming intolerable and he advised his audience to prepare to free their country.

The RSS workers and their communications too were constantly under the British surveillance. In his report (Int) on the RSS, E. J. Beveridge of the Home Department appended a note as to its real aim from a letter which was intercepted by the department in October 1942 which read:

> A Gwalior student member of the RSS to a friend gave some interesting facts about the policy of the Sangh. The writer who had learnt his facts a few days previously from the Lucknow organiser of the Sangh stated—our late leader (Dr Hedgewar) before his death asked all the organisers of the Sangh to make members 3 percent in the cities and 1 percent in the villages. They must be well trained. Before we do any work, we must think over it minutely. He (Dr Hedgewar) before his death declared that in 1942 there will be a good vast revolution in India, so we must be ready for it. And now when we will organise our fixed and limited organisation for this end we will put our stems forward for Swaraj.

Many freedom fighters received vital assistance from the RSS. Aruna Asaf Ali took asylum in the house of Lala Hans Raj Gupta, and Nana Patil was protected by Pandit Damodar Satavalekar and Sane Guruji stayed with Bhausaheb Deshmukh and Babasaheb Apte. On 16 August 1942, at Chimur in Maharashtra, many RSS workers participated directly in a Quit India agitation, which resulted in a brutal suppression by the British. Dada Naik, who was also the head of the Chimur RSS branch, was sentenced to death by the British. The Hindu Mahasabha leader Dr N. B. Khare took up his case with the authorities. Ramdas Rampure, another RSS cadre, was shot dead by the British.

Confidential reports blamed two persons for these uprisings. One was Dada Naik, who, the report said, 'was largely behind the recent disturbances' and the other was Sant Tukdoji Maharaj, who was closely associated with the RSS, and was suspected to have been involved in disturbances at Chimur. Later, Sant Tukdoji Maharaj became one of the co-founders of the Viswa Hindu Parishad (VHP), meaning the Global Hindu Federation.

Thus, contrary to the claims that the RSS did not participate in the national movement for freedom and that it did not stand with the spirit of freedom movement, it not only supported the freedom movement indirectly but also despite being a non-political movement within its first two-and-a-half decades, it substantially helped the movement for freedom despite a hostile political environment.

RSS and the National Flag

Another persistent accusation against the RSS in particular and Hindutva movement in general is the allegation that they never respected the national tricolour of India. This stems from the fact that the Hindutva movement sees the saffron flag as the expression of the spirit of the nation through the ages. In the case of the RSS the flag is said to symbolize the sum of all the preceptors or gurus of all the spiritual traditions of India throughout the ages. So often this distinction that the RSS makes between the saffron flag representing the ancient Hindu Nation and the national tricolour representing the State of India, has led to allegations that the RSS does not respect the national flag. For example, in an article written in 2004, historian Ramachandra Guha stated that 'during the thirties and forties, few, if any, RSS workers were seen saluting the national flag' which was because 'their allegiances were sectarian rather than national—indeed, they chose to elevate their own Bhagwa Dhwaj above the tiranga jhanda'.[10]

But the facts are otherwise.

Dr Hedgewar had explained to the organization the role of the saffron flag for the movement. To him the saffron flag became the symbol of impersonal national Guru. He said on the very first Guru Puja conducted by the Sangh, what the flag represented:

> The Rashtriya Swayamsevak Sangh does not recognize any individual as its Guru. The sacred Bhagawa Flag alone is our Guru. An individual, however great, is after all temporal and imperfect. The individual is conditioned by time; it is the principle alone which is timeless. The Bhagawa Flag symbolizes that timeless principle. The very sight of this Flag brings before our mind's eye the entire history, the glorious culture and tradition of our land; inspiration wells up in our mind. That is our true

> preceptor. The Rashtriya Swayamsevak Sangh therefore accords the place of Guru to none else, and has accepted the Bhagavd Flag as its Guru.[11]

So, the Sangh could recognize the distinction between the flag of the State or as it was then a party and the saffron flag or Bhagwa Dhwaj. While many Hindutvaites including 'Guruji' Golwalkar, the second Sarsanghachalak of the RSS, felt that the saffron flag should have been also made the official State flag for India, Dr Hedgewar himself did not seem to have worried much about what flag was accepted for the INC, which would ultimately be adopted as the national flag.

As already seen earlier, it was after nearly five years of founding the RSS on 2 April 1931, that the Karachi INC created a committee of seven persons to recommend a flag for the Congress and to examine the opposition people had for the flag it had then. Popularly known as the 'Flag Committee', it included among others, Sardar Patel, Abul Kalam Azad and Jawaharlal Nehru. After getting the opinions of the Provincial Committees and members of the All-India Congress Committee, the Flag Committee recommended the saffron flag with the emblem of the blue spinning wheel at the top corner. This flag was submitted to the party in August 1931. Of course, the Congress 'High Command' rejected it.

But Dr K. B. Hedgewar never allowed the rejection of the saffron flag by the Congress to cloud the vision of the RSS cadre. In December 1936, while the INC session was taking place at Faizpur, the Tricolour got stuck due to some mistake. It was RSS cadre Kishan Singh Rajput of Shirpur village who climbed the eighty-foot-high flagstaff and put the string back on the pulley and set the string right so the flag could fly high yet again. Dr Hedgewar conducted a special event and honoured the youth with a silver cup for the 'good deed without thinking about any party or organization'. This particular event has even been repeated in RSS literature. For example, one finds this episode described in *Organiser* (1978),[12] Malkani's *The RSS Story* (1980),[13] and the commemorative issue titled *How Others Look at RSS* brought out by the Deendayal Research Institute (1989).[14] It was also presented graphically in a comic book published in 1982 from the biography of Dr Hedgewar, an in-house Sangh publication.

During Independence, there was definitely a bitter acrimony between the Sanghathanists and the Congressites in what should be the national flag of India, with the former supporting the saffron flag naturally. In this connection it should be noted that Dr B. R. Ambedkar assured the Hindu Mahasabha leaders headed by S. K. Bole that if they initiate a popular movement to have the saffron flag as the national flag, he would support it.[15] As we have already seen, S. K. Bole was not only the Mahasabha leader but also an important leader of the backward classes and a prominent leader in the non-Brahmin movement of Maharashtra. Dhananjay Keer, the authoritative biographer of Dr Ambedkar (who had the draft, except the last chapter, approved by Dr Ambedkar himself) gives a detailed picture:

> Ambedkar returned to Bombay on July 3, 1947. As he was a Member of the Flag Committee of the Constituent Assembly, some Maratha leaders and leaders of the Bombay Provincial Hindu Sabha saw him at his residence. He promised that he would try to put in a word in favour of the Geruva flag if there was sufficient pressure and agitation from responsible quarters. On July 10 Ambedkar was given a send-off at the aerodrome by different leaders of the Marathas and the City Hindu Sabha leaders who handed over a Geruva flag to him when he was about to take his seat in the aeroplane. Ambedkar promised support if there was agitation for the establishment of that flag and with a hearty laugh asked S. K. Bole, Anantrao Gadre and others whether they expected the son of a Mahar to unfurl the Geruva flag on the Constituent Assembly.[16]

More important to the present discussion was the gesture displayed by Savarkar. When radical elements of the Mahasabha were hesitant to accept the national Tricolour, Vinayak Savarkar, the tallest of its leaders, made it a point to respect the national Tricolour. Dhananjay Keer, Savarkar's biographer explains:

> The Mahasabhaites hoisted only the Mahasabha Geruwa flag with the Kripan and Kundalini to display the asserting will of the Hindus. Savarkar hoisted the new tricolour flag of Free India with the Dharma Chakra of Buddhism as well as the Geruwa flag with Kripan and Kundalini; one State Flag and another a Symbol of Akhand Hindusthan....In saluting and flying the State Flag Savarkar showed his sense of and love for democracy. To his perturbed followers he said that they should hoist the Bhagwa flag with the Kripan and Kundalini as the State flag only after they could get it approved by the whole nation in a democratic way. Till then this new State Flag represented the Divided India and the Geruwa flag with the Kripan and Kundalini the Akhand Hindustan and so he had hoisted both.[17]

On 14–15 August 1947, the national Tricolour—the flag accepted as the State flag of India was hoisted at the national headquarters of the RSS at Nagpur. So, clearly the Sangh embraced the stand taken by Savarkar and not the other 'perturbed' Sanghatanists. Here one can note a commonality between the views of both Savarkar and Ambedkar on the National flag—that they were in fact in favour of the saffron flag as the national flag but they wanted it to become so through a popular movement. Further Keer points out another point of convergence between Dr Ambedkar and Savarkar here. In Savarkar's biography Keer writes:

> Savarkar's efforts to replace the Charkha by a Chakra were not fruitless. In a telegram to Dr Rajendra Prasad, the Chairman of the Constituent Assembly, who happened to be the chairman of the Flag Committee of the Constituent Assembly, Savarkar had requested them to have at least a strip of the saffron colour and a wheel-Chakra instead of the Charkha on the State Flag.[18]

This is further strengthened by what he writes in *Dr Ambedkar: Life and Mission* regarding the same subject:

> It is said that Ambedkar put in a word, but as there was no agitation from outside for the adoption of the Geruva flag, he threw his weight in favour of the Ashoka Chakra. Savarkar also had appealed to Dr Rajendra Prasad, the Chairman of the Flag Committee, to substitute Chakra for Charkha, the Gandhian emblem.[19]

Post-Independence Events: RSS & the National Flag

That the RSS accepted the Tricolour and was ready to defend its honour became very clear in its operations in Jammu and Kashmir, which was then a princely state ruled by a Hindu king with Muslim majority. The Hindu king was vacillating between India and Pakistan, while toying with the idea that it would remain an independent princely state. Though a Muslim majority state, it still had sizeable Hindu, Sikh and Buddhist populations. Pakistan had set its eyes on Kashmir and there were Islamist elements, which supported a takeover by Pakistan. According to RSS sources, the Sangh leadership explicitly took a pro-India stand and asked people to hoist the Indian Tricolour and not its own saffron flag. Here is an account of what happened on 14 and 15 August 1947 in Srinagar:

> On August 14, Pakistan Day, employees and officers of the postal department hoisted Pakistani flags on all post offices in the city on the ground that the Jammu-Kashmir postal division fell within the Sialkot postal circle, which had gone to Pakistan. The moment Sangh Swayamsevaks saw this they became active. In accordance with a plan prepared under Shri Balraj Madhok's guidance a large number of tricolour flags were made in the Sangh Karyalaya. Swayamsevaks set out with these flags in their hands, went to all post offices, took down the Pakistani flags, and hoisted the

> tricolour in their place. This operation was carried out simultaneously all over the city. The next day was August 15. That day, in response to the Sangh's appeal, all citizens hoisted the tricolour on their houses and shops. These flags too had been made in the Sangh Karyalaya overnight.[20]

Can one brush aside this as merely RSS propaganda?

The answer to this may exist in another event that involved the then RSS chief and Kashmir negotiations.

That RSS leader Golwalkar went and met the King of Kashmir as an unofficial emissary of the Indian government is a well-documented fact. On 17 October 1947, Golwalkar reached Kashmir and met the king the next day. As the meeting itself was confidential between the two, no one knew what exactly was discussed. A week after the meeting, the king signed the document of accession to India.[21] Many observers of RSS, including those sympathetic to it, naturally have concluded that it was Patel who should have decided to send Golwalkar to Kashmir. The view is also shared by the bureaucracy. For example, Arun Bhatnagar, an IAS officer of the 1966 batch is of the opinion that the idea of sending Golwalkar was at the insistence of Patel. It was Patel who had asked Golwalkar to go to Kashmir. But between August and October of 1947, it was Nehru who had been asking Sardar Patel to execute a series of operations for resolving the Kashmir problem. According to an article in the leftist magazine The *Economic and Political Weekly*, 'Sardar Patel did take action as Nehru desired. One of them was to solicit the help of RSS leader Golwalkar to persuade Maharaja to join India.'[22] One is made to wonder what made Nehru, a strong opponent of the RSS, ask Patel to seek help from a 'communal' organization. A probable answer is the way in which the RSS people hoisted the Tricolour in Srinagar on 15 August 1947, and the way they were able to sway the Hindu population of Jammu and Kashmir in favour of acceding to India, which in turn would leave the ruler with little choice.

There is of course the undeniable fact that the RSS cadre helped the Indian Army particularly the Indian Air Force after the King signed the Instrument of Accession of Kashmir to India; in fact, the IAF started operations against the raiders sent in by Pakistan. But the hoisting of the Tricolour in a Hindu princely state by the RSS on 15 August 1947, along with the hoisting of the flag in Nagpur show that RSS did honour the national flag. It also subsequently played a crucial role in making the king of Kashmir sign the accession of Kashmir to India.

The period between 1988 and 1990 saw the ethnic cleansing of Hindus from Kashmir valley. This was facilitated (intentionally or not) by Farooq Abdullah, the then Chief Minister of Kashmir, and Rajiv Gandhi, the supremo of INC, both of whom wanted the Governor, Jagmohan removed. Colonel Tej K. Tikoo, PhD, in his book on the ethnic cleansing of Hindus from Kashmir writes:

> Terrorist activity that began in earnest got an impetus during Farooq Abdullah's second term in the office. In fact, it was New Delhi's indulgence of Farooq Abdullah that served as a trigger to usher in full-scale insurgency in the state in early 1990's.... Some conscientious police officers took it as a challenge and succeeded in arresting quite a number of them, including some self-styled "Area Commanders" in the early days of militancy. "But in 1989, Farooq Abdullah released as many as 23 top militants on the plea that this would give them a chance to join the mainstream and claimed that this had the approval of Rajiv Gandhi." (*Kashmir: The Crisis in Perspective,* Indian Research Institute for Kashmir Affairs) This action of Farooq Abdullah dealt a severe blow to the morale of police officers who had carried out their responsibilities in arresting these militants, at great risk to their lives.... The militants, now emboldened by the government inaction, started burning the National Flag right under the nose of local police. They openly celebrated Pakistan's Independence Day on August 14, 1989, with great pomp and show. The next day, on August 15, 1989, they made a bonfire of Indian flags. They also observed a complete black-out in the evening, by burning transmission stations or by enforcing it by not letting the common people to switch on their lights." Indian flag could be unfurled only in Ganpathyar temple in the heart of Srinagar after Hindus had sought protection of the police. (*White Paper on Kashmir, Joint Human Rights Committee*)[23]

Once again, the Indian national flag in Kashmir became a symbol of the existence of Hindu aborigines of Jammu and Kashmir. The burning and insulting of the flag became the proto-symbolic event of the ethnic cleansing of Hindus that followed. These events were supported by the Indira Congress headed by Rajiv Gandhi who would soon lend tactical support to the ethnic cleansing itself by demanding the removal of the Governor of Kashmir, Shri Jagmohan, who was the last hope for Kashmiri Hindus to retain their ancestral land. So, the Sangh-BJP saw the entire process as a proof of pseudo-secularism and Islamism working in tandem to denationalize a province and create immense human tragedy. That was also the time when BJP had taken up the Ayodhya issue—the building of Ram temple in the Janmastan-Babri dome complex. Lal Krishna Advani the leader of BJP had launched a Rath yatra from Somnath in Gujarat to Ayodhya, from September to October 1990.

In 1991 when Dr Murali Manohar Joshi, an atomic spectroscopist turned politician became the president of the party, he announced an 'Ekta Yatra' or Unity Pilgrimage in 1991. It was a 15,000-kilometre journey from Kanyakumari, the southernmost end of Indian mainland, to Lal Chowk of Kashmir, lasting

47 days. Meanwhile, Rajiv Gandhi was killed by a Tamil suicide bomber to avenge the atrocities committed by the Indian Peace Keeping Force (IPKF) against the Tamils during the peacekeeping mission which proved to be India's Vietnam. In 1991 the central government was headed by P. V. Narasimha Rao, a statesman widely perceived to be sympathetic to the Hindu cause.

Though there had been a massacre of the volunteers at Ayodhya in 1990 and an ethnic cleansing of Hindus from Kashmir from 1988 onwards, the Sangh and BJP meticulously planned to show an inclusive symbolism in the Yatra. The day chosen for the commencement of the Yatra was 11 December 1991, which was also the birth anniversary of celebrated Tamil poet Bharati. Apart from that according to the Indian calendar that year, this day also marked the martyrdom of Guru Tegh Bahadur, the ninth Sikh guru, who had sacrificed himself against the Islamist attack on Kashmiri Hindus during the seventeenth century. The BJP, which was often known in Tamil Nadu as a 'North Indian' party, actually projected the image of Tamil poet Bharati. Also, an inclusive message had been sent to the Sikhs who were traumatized by the 1984 holocaust by the Congress. To emphasize that despite the Islamist nature of terrorism in Kashmir and the ethnic cleansing of Hindus, the Yatra was not against Muslims but to unite all Indians, the flag was handed over to Dr Joshi by Rajinder Singh and Devki Nandan Rajguru, the brothers of revolutionaries Bhagat Singh and Shivram Rajguru, who were hanged by the British, and also Junaid Alam and Ali Hassan, the two sons of the posthumous Param Vir Chakra awardee Abdul Hameed of the Indian Army, who was killed in the 1965 Indo-Pak war.[24]

Even as the Yatra reached New Delhi, the Kashmir jihadists intensified their attacks from 24 January 1992, onwards. A student jihadist reminisced that apart from attacks, the mujahideen outfits had divided tasks among themselves, of which the 'foremost thing' for them was to 'guard' the Jammu-Srinagar highway through which the BJP leader and the supporters had planned to come initially. The term 'guard' of course meant ambushing and thwarting the Yatra and killing the participants. But Dr Joshi persisted. The convenor of the Yatra was a young, bearded office bearer of BJP from Gujarat, a *pracharak* (life worker) of the RSS loaned to the BJP. His name was Narendra Modi. P. V. Narasimha Rao, widely considered as being sympathetic to Hindutva, arranged for airlifting Dr Joshi, Narendra Modi and the core group of workers to Srinagar's Lal Chowk—where the Islamists had challenged the hoisting of the tricolour. Dr Joshi hoisted the national Tricolour with Indian Army taking over entire Srinagar and killing ten jihadists on that day in separate incidents.[25]

Given all these facts, the assertion by historians like Ramchandra Guha that the 'RSS's acknowledgement of our national flag was very belated and totally opportunistic' is being economical with the truth, to say the least. The recognition and honour to the national Tricolour along with the values it stands for, come to the Hindutva movement through its anchorage in democracy exhibited by Savarkar himself and demonstrated by Dr Hedgewar. Golwalkar's emphasis on the national character of the saffron flag notwithstanding, the mainstream Hindutva movement in India has been able to use the difference between the saffron flag and the Tricolour, the distinction between the Nation and the Nation-State while using the respect and sacrifice for the Tricolour to emphasize the need for the integration of both.

Understanding RSS: Has There Been an Honest Academic Attempt?

In the history of academic study of Hindutva and its media representation, there is a strong lacuna. There are very few academic books which study the RSS with honest academic rigour. Western academic scholars like Christophe Jaffrelot who have made a career as 'Hindutva observers' and their Indian counterparts, most of whom come from strong Marxist and colonial backgrounds, exhibit a strong bias against the Hindutva movement. Christophe Jaffrelot personifies this kind of extremely biased Hinduphobic scholarship. He relies on a prism that combines strong Hinduphobic Euro-cultural supremacism and bases it in judging Hindu social reformers. Any movement within the Hindu culture for social emancipation gets analysed in a hair-splitting manner to prove that they are non-egalitarian. In the case of the RSS, there is an obsession to compare the Sangh with the fascist and Nazi organizations and ideologies, and when they obviously fail, there is heavy dependence on convoluted logic and the same hair-splitting argument to show that the RSS is authoritarian and anti-democratic. Here is a sample from Jaffrelot's initial work titled *Hindu Nationalism: A Reader* (late 1990s):

> To sum up: since a characteristic of the RSS's Hindu nationalism has been to downplay the role of the state, we cannot classify it straightforwardly as a fascist movement. As distinct from Nazism, the RSS's ideology treats society as an organism with a secular spirit, which is implanted not so much in the race as in a socio-cultural system and which will be regenerated over the course of time by patient work at the grassroots. Finally, in contrast to both Italian fascism and Nazism, the RSS does not rely on the central figure of the leader. Nonetheless, the RSS can be classed as authoritarian in its emphasis on discipline, in its refusal to recognise the specific character of minorities and in its intention of reforming the

> Hindu mentality absolutely to prepare the advent of a new man, implying the need to extend the sway of the organisation over the whole society.[26]

The academic obsession for comparing the RSS with fascists can be noted in the acknowledgement as: 'we cannot classify it straightforwardly as fascist'. So, if it cannot be 'straightforwardly' labelled as fascist and if the social vision of the Sangh is organismal with 'a secular spirit' which is also 'implanted not so much in the race', then simply one expects an academic to reject the charges of being Nazi or fascist. But still one finds in Jaffrelot a need to be classified as 'authoritarian' because of its discipline and 'refusal to recognize the specific character of minorities'. With respect to the latter charge, one needs to understand that the Sangh does not refuse to 'recognize' the minorities, but it is only very specifically against the expansionist tendencies of monopolistic expansionism. Nevertheless, Jaffrelot has been promoted by a significant section of the Indian academia and media as 'the' authority on the RSS and Dr Ambedkar.

That in such a prevailing condition it has taken two US academics to bring out an authoritative work without ideological blinkers on the RSS is a sad reflection on Indian academia and media. Except for a handful of scholars like Dr Rakesh Singha and Ratan Sharda, there are not many works which approach the RSS with an objective look. One work that stands distinct in this almost academic cottage industry of negative stereotyping of the RSS is the work by Walter K. Andersen and Shridhar D. Damle. Unlike the rest of the academic watchers of the Sangh, they have gone for the original sources, conducted field work, gathered empirical data without ideological filters and, of course, they do not seem to have any vested interests while presenting their study. This may be because they are driven by a need to understand the RSS and hence, they need to keep away from blinkers, both positive and negative. The picture that emerges of the RSS seems to be one radically different from the stereotypical 'Hindu nationalism' studies that have now become a veritable cottage industry and an easy passport into 'South Asian' departments of Western academia and media.

The RSS: A View to the Inside (2018) can be considered an upgrade to *The Brotherhood in Saffron* (1987) by the same authors. The earlier book itself provides some interesting insights into the nature of the RSS that most left-wing academics have intentionally left out. In their 'conclusion' of the 1987 study, Andersen and Damle made the following observation:

> Hedgewar incorporated into the RSS a training process which came to be called character building, stressing discipline, work and commitment. The process is based on the Hindu conception that disciplined training under an enlightened

> teacher results in an introspective recognition of truth. The truth was a secularized version of Advaita Vedanta; it took the metaphysical position that all men are basically one and applied it to Hindu society....In the face of orthodox resistance, he found justification in Indian history and culture for modern technology, scientific knowledge, and economic development. The RSS was conceived of as a school that would teach this new truth.[27]

This observation made three decades ago is still very relevant. Many of the criticisms of the RSS in traditional Hindu circles which have become more and more vociferous in the internet circles particularly among the 'traditional Vedanta' groups, arise because of the inability to grasp this fundamental truth about the Sangh. But the Sangh does not seek to eschew them. The situation is quite similar to the so-called traditionalists and Arya-Samajists in the pre-independent Sanghatan movement. Only here, the monotheistic Arya Samajist stands are replaced by more Vedantic non-dual traditions, though in no way does the Sangh worldview cling to the non-dual tradition in a dogmatic manner.

The increasingly vocal such neo-traditionalists or internet-traditionalists often ascribe the 'ignorance of shastras' to the Sangh, a point where they unconsciously and at times deliberately align themselves with the Shashi Tharoor-type critique of Hindutva. Often this criticism is confused as also camouflaged with the Sita Ram Goel-Koenraad Elst school of Sangh criticism, which in turn stems from some bitter experience that Sita Ram Goel had with the Sangh. In both these criticisms of the Sangh, there is a strong element of elitism and often a substantial inability to understand the ground social reality of India that Hindus are only a communal majority and not a political majority in India. Though the Sangh itself does not take a confrontationist position towards the Hindu traditionalists, except in extreme cases like the phenomenon of untouchability, it does try to change the worldview through dialogue. However, when there is gross injustice to the marginalized sections of the society the Sangh had taken the approach of confrontation.

An example of the Sangh approach to social reformation of traditionalist institutions is the case of the famous Kanchi Sankara Mutt. While the older and the most revered head of the Kanchi Sankara Mutt stridently opposed the entry of the SC and ST communities into major Hindu temples, his junior Sri Jayendra Saraswati, who more frequently interacted with the Sangh, was roped in by the Sangh-affiliated institutions to issue certificates for Hindus of all castes who had obtained training to become priests in temples. This was an impressive victory for the Sangh without taking a confrontational stand. We will look at this non-Brahmin priesthood movement in detail later in this chapter.

It is indeed impressive that Andersen and Damle have captured this fundamental core of the Sangh which has often eluded both its critics and peripheral supporters. Naturally, the 2018 book by the duo has excited every political and social observer of India who would be curious to know what the authors have to say this time—a time when the RSS has been afflicted with a lot of negative media and academic publicity, and especially with RSS men holding political power in both central and many state governments in India. In this study, the authors concentrate mainly on 'how the rapid expansion of the RSS and its affiliates over the past 25 years has affected the ways in which it operates and presents itself to the nation'. [28]

In their previous work, Andersen and Damle have studied the phenomenon of RSS 'loaning out' its full-time workers (pracharaks) to the affiliate organizations. They observed:

> Many of the pracharaks are loaned to the affiliates of the RSS . The pracharaks "on loan" have a dual loyalty—one to the RSS and the other to the affiliated organisation. Almost all pracharaks whom we interviewed stated that their primary loyalty was to the RSS, though they were careful to note that the RSS did not dictate policy to them. Should an affiliate develop on a separate path from the RSS, all insisted that they would immediately leave it. The pracharaks retain a close working relationship with the RSS organisation in whatever area they are assigned.[29]

Now three decades after and with the 'affiliate' or 'Parivar' organizations having become vast networks themselves with sometimes conflicting interests, they revisit the same phenomenon with another question.

> So what keeps the Sangh Parivar from disintegrating altogether, given the wide range of often-competing interests that it hosts? The key element, in our view, is the sanghathan mantri system: the 6,000 trained RSS pracharaks who occupy the top management positions (organizing secretary, general secretary, and joint general secretary) in the RSS proper as well as in virtually all the affiliates.... Besides the ideology binding the office-bearers of the 'family' together, there are several structural elements that also serve to unite these often-disparate factions.... Finally, and importantly, each of the affiliates operates autonomously, and the RSS usually asserts itself only when there is a power vacuum (as in the BJP after the 2009 Parliamentary losses) or to mediate differences within or among the affiliates. Even this is a relative rare occurrence—the Parivar operates by consensus precisely to avoid the kind of destructive factionalism that has ruined so many of its non-RSS peers and competitors.[30]

Studying the events after Narendra Modi became the Prime Minister of

India in 2014, Andersen and Damle point out that while the critics of the RSS use every opportunity (like twisting RSS Sarsanghachalak Dr Mohan Bhagwat's statement on reservation during the Bihar election), 'to demonstrate that the parivar is fundamentally controlled by high-caste Hindus unconcerned about the social and economic well-being of Dalits' and that 'at the ground level, the RSS has worked hard —and studies show it has had some success—to implement a wide range of social welfare activities among Dalits and tribals'.[31]

Hence, in this refreshing and comprehensive study, the fact that the characterization of the Sangh by Andersen and Damle is still inherently Western, can be overlooked. In their 1987 book, they conceived the Sangh as a pyramidal structure with the shakha at the bottom (p. 87). Here, after three decades, the book sees the Sangh more mechanically like 'organisational steel frame' and 'power vacuum' than in organic terms. The Sangh's organizing principles, which elude the Western frameworks, are essentially Indic and more ecological than mechanical. For example, one of the Sangh ideologues, K. R. Malkani, spoke as early as 1951 about 'biotechnic order'—showing an influence from the polymath and pioneering human ecologist Patrick Geddes,[32] who in turn was highly influenced by Indic principles of social and habitat organization as well as temple city planning.

The very term 'shakha' (branch) with the vast human networking suggests organizing principles of the RSS that are radically different from the Western social movements. Hence, seeing the Sangh approach as 'civic religion practised by the Lutheran leadership in Scandinavian states' though may be a good Western appropriation, it does not do full justice to the deeper dimensions of the Sangh worldview. The Sangh can be seen today as the grand meta-organism of Hinduness, adapting and reorganizing constantly towards the fast-changing milieu. Andersen and Damle themselves point out such adaptations like the view of the RSS towards women's issues. One should remember that not only is the woman affiliate of the RSS the first one to be formed, but it is the most independent of all the Sangh affiliates. It is not subordinate but a parallel organization. Further, it was founded by a widow—which in itself was a radical departure from orthodoxy those days in Maharashtra.

Now, the Sangh advocates gender equality in religious space (which even a substantial number of its own cadre are uncomfortable with) like, for instance, 'noting favourably that women are now officiating as priests'. These changes again should be seen as an organic evolution and adaptation, unlike the leftist slogan-borrowing from the West. Even Andersen and Damle are not immune to certain stereotypes despite their empirical studies, shattering many stereotypes about the Sangh. In the conclusion of the work, there is a passage where the authors quote Ashis Nandy and Donald Smith approvingly:

> In his analysis of the interaction of Hinduism and Hindutva, Ashis Nandy in the early 1990s wrote perceptively that, 'Hinduism and Hindutva now stand face to face, not yet ready to confront each other, but aware that the confrontation will have to come someday.... Golwalkar, the RSS sarsanghachalak at the time of Independence, also advised the founder of BJS to avoid a name that would give the party a sectarian orientation and favoured the more inclusive Bharatiya in its name. Thus, as Donald Smith has pointed out in his discussion of the RSS, the BJS adopted an inclusive view of nationhood covering all groups loyal to India that was incompatible with a Hindu rashtra (nation).[33]

Ashis Nandy is a Protestant by birth who became a social psychologist and Donald Smith was a theologian who turned out to be a political scientist. Their axioms are that Hinduism is fundamentally caste-based and that Hindu *rashtra* is an exclusive concept, respectively. It would have been better had Andersen and Damle taken a look at the way the RSS looks at Hinduism. In the RSS Hindu narrative reinforced every day by the *Ekatmata Stotra* or the morning prayer, they emphasize the social emancipation stream in Hindu Dharma and history. It has seers hailing from all sections of the Hindu society and two Islamic seers as well. The so-called inevitable war between Hindutva and Hinduism is only a myth, and like the fabled second coming or socialist utopia, shall always be in the imagined perpetual future, speculated by a section of academia and media, not to mention politicians out on bail.

This binary of Hindutva versus Hinduism, nevertheless, needs a deeper understanding of Hinduism. In this very book, Andersen and Damle make an important observation that the RSS camp rules require that all Swayamsevaks irrespective of their 'castes', 'to alternate between serving food to others and cleaning laterines (sic)—that aim to undermine notions of purity and pollution associated with various kinds of work in many layers of the Hindu caste hierarchy'.[34]

One finds this model in the educational institutions of Ramakrishna-Vivekananda order—particularly in the schools of Swami Chidbhavananda, where the residential school students are expected to work, alternating between toilet cleaning, and serving food in dining halls and in the altar services of temples attached to the schools. Chidbhavananda was one of the first saints in Tamil Nadu to welcome the RSS and give his own schools to conduct their training camps. Gandhi tried the same experiment, but it could not last long. One can trace these efforts to Sri Ramakrishna, who cleaned the nightsoil of the Scheduled Community members and carried it on his head. Had Andersen and Damle connected this particular Sangh exercise with their own wonderful insight that the principle underlying Sangh is the 'secularised version of Advaita

Vedanta', they could have seen that far from being at war with Hinduism, it is bringing to the social surface a deeper and more profound Hinduism.

All said, among the Western academic observers of the RSS, the work by Andersen and Damle with two works spanning a lifelong observation of the organization and the Hindutva movement demonstrates an objective approach to the workings of the Sangh and understanding what animates the Sangh despite all the negative propaganda and hostile state attitude against it for most part of its existence. The book explodes many myths built around the Sangh by the Hinduphobic academia-media sections with empirical evidence. The way the Sangh has diversified between 1987 and 2018, the period between the two studies, also dispels the myth of the Hindutva organization as being authoritarian and a monolith. The discipline of the Sangh is an entirely different type of discipline exhibited by the fascist, Nazi and Marxist youth organizations. Most probably this is based on the understanding of certain traditional unique aspects of the Hindu social life by Dr Hedgewar which he had put into a networked organizational mode.

RSS and its Unique Understudied Organizational Dynamics

Every time there has been a natural or man-made disaster, the Sangh has been at the forefront in extending assistance. It is a well-documented fact that has been consistently true. In 1979 M. V. Kamath, senior journalist and then acting editor of the *Illustrated Weekly of India* pointed out this aspect in his column:

> You can say a lot of things about the Rashtriya Swayamsevak Sangh (the RSS): that it is a fascist organisation; that it has been responsible for communal violence, that it is a Hindu revanchist society, that it is anti-Muslim, anti-Christian and anti-minorities in general, that it is dedicated to the establishment of Akhand Bharat or that it is exclusively setup with its own secret rituals and discipline....But look at the RSS this way: when the Andhra cyclone took its terrible toll, some of the first to arrive on the scene were the RSS volunteers and I have it from one of the highest officials in the Andhra Pradesh Government that they did a magnificent job without once asking the Government for assistance of any kind and not even looking for cheap publicity. It is also common knowledge now that, again, some of the first to go to Morvi to do the kind of dirty work that others were unwilling to undertake—like picking bloated and stinking dead bodies and giving them a decent cremation—were RSS volunteers....You might say anything about the RSS but, when it comes to serving their fellow countrymen, they seem willing and ready to roll up

> their sleeves and get to work and ask for nothing in return. Not even a picture in the *Weekly*. By all means damn them. But once in a while, stand back and thank them for what they have done.[35]

There are two noteworthy features of the above: one, the ability of the RSS to arrive at the scene of any disaster at the earliest in almost any part of India, and two, its willingness to shun publicity. The RSS till recently has followed the principle that its activities—particularly the *seva* (service) activities would not be publicized in the mainstream media. Of course, anecdotal events of the sacrifices made by individual Swayamsevaks during such calamities and limited number of photographs are used in the RSS camps and teaching sessions ('Boudhik') to inspire other RSS cadre. It is only recently and that too in a very measured manner that the RSS is opening itself to present its case of social service in the public sphere. On the other hand, the proselytizing charities operating in India have been popularizing their own activities with hyper aggression so much so that even questioning such personalities by the RSS at times has created very negative publicity in both the political arena as well as media.

Service Activities of the RSS

A good case in contrast is that of Teresa of Calcutta—a carefully cultivated icon of charity, which has today transcended all barriers of religion and has emerged as a national archetype for selfless service. Just as how the RSS has been the caricatured storm trooper of hatred in the media, in inverse proportion stands Teresa, the epitome of love and that is of course a monopolized Christian virtue. In February 2015, Mohan Bhagwat, the Sarsanghachalak of the RSS, who while inaugurating a *mahila sadan* (women's home) and a Bal Shishu Gopal Griha (children's home), stated that the services provided in these institutions would not be 'like that rendered by Mother Teresa'. Then he said:

> It is possible that her kind of work was good, but there was a motive behind that service. It was to convert those she served to Christianity. Someone wants to convert others to Christianity, that is another thing, but to do it under the garb of social service is to devalue that service. Here, nothing like that will happen. In our country, social service is done like this, selflessly, completely selflessly.[36]

This led to severe condemnation from political parties, which included even the allies of the BJP and the church. The Missionaries of Charity dubbed Bhagwat as being 'uninformed', asking him to see for himself their work. The

INC, whose supremo then was the Italian born Catholic Sonia Maino Gandhi, reacted very sharply on its Twitter handle, stating, 'Only a demented mind can say such a thing for a noble soul like Mother Teresa.'[37]

The general picture in the media was that a hardline right-wing Hindu fanatic had abused a humanitarian saint practising universal love. Such a media image is very carefully cultivated. In reality, it was the saintly Teresa who was right wing, and the RSS that was more secular in comparison to Teresa in rendering services to people during calamities.

Let us take just one important event in history for comparison. On the night of 2 December 1984 at Bhopal, methyl isocyanate leaked in the Union Carbide Plant and created the world's worst industrial disaster. One hears within the close circles of the RSS in the mid- and late-1980s frequently and now occasionally about how the Swayamsevaks managed to reach there along with the Indian Army and how they braved the gas leak and helped the victims. They toiled hard to restore the collapsing water and sanitation facilities. They repaired latrines. They removed the dead bodies and helped the bereaved identify the dead ones. The boys in half pants who were medical students came from Agra, camped at Bhopal and offered round-the-clock service to the affected people. All these one could hear in Sangh circles and read in Sangh literature. But are there any documents? Any photographs? The usual answer one gets in the Sangh circles is this: 'Serving our brothers in times of calamity is our duty. And one does not document what one does to one's own brother.'

Contrast this with what Teresa did soon after the Bhopal disaster. Her words and activities are well-documented. Let us leave out for a moment what her critics like Christopher Hitchens have accused her of—a sly empathy towards Warren Anderson, then Chairman of Union Carbide. What we have here are recordings from an admiring journalist, not a cub reporter but a veteran, Anees Chisti. His book *Dateline Bhopal* is, as the subtitle explains, 'A newsman's diary of the gas disaster' and is much acclaimed. The 'Mother of All', as the author-reporter calls her, was asked to spell out her message for the people of Bhopal reeling under the horrible effects of the disaster, to which she simply replied, 'Forgiveness.' 'Forgiveness gives one purity of heart and peace of heart,' she elaborated after a pause. 'Her answers to numberless and many of them child-like questions by reporters', Chisti states with obvious adoration, 'were short but thoughtful.' Here is an excerpt from the question-answer session Teresa had with the reporters which Chisti considers as 'thoughtful':

> Question: Where would you place the magnitude of the Bhopal tragedy among the many having experienced by you?
>
> Teresa: I never compare. Each one has its own dimension and effect.

Question: How has the tragedy affected you?

Teresa: We are so excited because it has affected us. No one thinks of millions of abortions taking place all over.

Question: Do you have any special feelings for pregnant mothers with whom their unborn kids also died?

Teresa: It was an accident; the mothers died, so, the children also died. [38]

Had any Hindu religious leader answered such questions in the above way, it would have been considered as crass, inhuman fundamentalism. It would have become part and parcel of every academic treatise on Hinduism and Hindutva. But not so with Teresa, the white-skinned Catholic saint exuding Christian love and charity for the indifferent, fatalist, karma-chained, dark-skinned heathens of India. She could get away with putting the onus of forgiveness on the victims and trivializing their sufferings by magnifying the pet-crusade cause of her church —battling abortions. She could get away with utter inhumanity towards fellow human beings who had been the victims of a colossal criminal negligence, particularly if that negligence is caused by someone sympathetic and fat in his chequebook towards the charity of Teresa. We now know that even as the Bhopal gas tragedy struck, Warren Anderson was engaged in negotiations with one Indira Ayengar, a rabid Christian fundamentalist activist, as to how they could avert the public relations fallout by donating to the Missionaries of Charity. That institution of Teresa, of course, being acutely aware of the negative publicity it would bring upon itself, refused to oblige. But Teresa, at once resorting to the next best strategy, started broadcasting the tune of forgiveness. One is left to wonder that if the Bhopal gas tragedy was indeed an 'accident' as Teresa claimed, whom should the victims of Bhopal disaster forgive? The Christian God?

The 'saint' could transform through media magic any inhumanity towards heathens into a Christian act of love. Imagine a Madhav Sadashiv Golwalkar or a Bhagwat or even a Mahatma Gandhi saying similar things during such a human tragedy and getting away with it! Gandhi's infamous statement on Bihar earthquake that it was divine punishment for practising untouchability is held against him even today, and was widely publicized and condemned at that time too. Compared with this media miracle that Saint Teresa could perform, the media miracle that the RSS achieves pales into insignificance. In the case of Bhopal, the RSS may be the only national organization in India that gets to the area of any natural calamity within a few hours and tirelessly dedicates itself to the rescue and care of the victims irrespective of their religion. Yet this organization is still studied in a minute manner for attributing to it any possible fascist nature and characterize them as storm troopers of hatred who can only perform the media miracle of becoming invisible to the cameras covering the disasters.

Decades later, one of Teresa's international spin doctors Dominique Lapierre would come out with a docudrama on Bhopal. Lapierre had earlier in his *City of Joy* alluded to the monks of Ramakrishna Mission as 'pimps' preying on the victims of natural disaster. A classic instance of how Hindu service organizations could be demonized, and Christian charities alone are glorified in the media is exhibited by Lapierre. Here is the relevant portion from *City of Joy*:

> Yet it took another three days for the Calcutta and New Delhi authorities to agree on the first rescue operations, three days of which certain individuals were quick to take advantage. The people in question wore the ochre robes of monks belonging to the mission of Ramakrishna, the Bengali saint who in the last century preached mutual aid and love between Hindus and other communities. As soon as the cataclysm was announced, they rushed from Madras, Delhi and even Bombay. The policemen cordoning off the area let them pass: barefoot angels of charity must not be intercepted. Going about in pairs, they mingled with the survivors and offered to take in as many orphans as they could. So much generosity did not fail to touch the hearts. Children abruptly deprived of their parents by the disaster were quickly rounded up. "Those men were generosity itself," one thirty-five-year-old widow was to testify....Like so many other victims of the tragedy, that poor woman would never see her child again. She did not know that these purported monks were pimps.[39]

In 2008 the United Progressive Alliance (UPA) government with Sonia Maino Gandhi, the Supremo of the Congress party, gave Lapierre Padma Vibushan, India's third highest civilian award. Now the same chronicler, with questionable credibility and even more questionable intentions and biases, would with media fanfare, make the Missionaries of Charity, particularly a young Scottish nun, probably a fictitious character, the crusader against the 'corrupt' Indian system that allowed thousands of Indians to die through crony capitalism.

Now that chronicle would become history and any role by the RSS in Bhopal disaster relief would be relegated to the whispering literature circulated within shakha circles. Yet strangely, something survived despite the RSS's constant urge to shun media limelight. Photographer Pablo Bartholomew can, by no stretch of imagination, be considered a friend or even a distant admirer of the Sangh. If anything, he seems to be more in awe of the Nehru-Gandhi family and its socialism. But in his online photo exhibition on the Bhopal gas tragedy, one finds those much-caricatured boys in khaki pants serving the victims, caring not for the photo flashes. Ironically, this may be the only media documentation of the RSS service to Bhopal victims outside Sangh circles.

In fact, while every English magazine and mainstream media today speaks about justice to the Bhopal gas tragedy victims, initially they simply went for the gory details and faithfully repeated the claims of the company. The role of 'Mother' Teresa in gaining this immediate and crucial media victory of the Union Carbide chief is still not fully revealed. But then at that time one magazine that constantly questioned the narrative put forth by the company was the *Organiser* of the RSS. Studying the media's role in the aftermath of the tragedy, Vidya Krishnan writes:

> The English media obediently repeated the company's claims about not compromising on safety standards (Hindustan Times, 4 December) and reports on "human failure" (*The Hindu*, 5 December). Barring the Rashtriya Swayamsevak Sangh's publication Organiser, which questioned the government's policies, the majority of the English-language media covered Bhopal with a myopic lens, repeating graphic images and eventually dropping the story altogether.[40]

Just as how the charity work of Teresa got hyped and her explicit fundamentalist worldview was underplayed behind the charity, scores of academic studies and media works on the RSS's relief and service works was not studied (and one can be sure that if at all it happens, it would be presented negatively through some convoluted argument).

Sangh, Seva and Worldview

But the RSS does have a worldview towards the relief and service works it does. It has been explained by the second Sarsanghachalak of the RSS, the much-maligned M. S. Golwalkar. In his lecture titled 'Serving the Neglected Brethren' (compiled in *Bunch of Thoughts*), he says:

> We have to serve all, be he a Christian or a Muslim or a human being of any other persuasion; for, calamities, distress and misfortunes make no such distinction but afflict all alike. And in serving to relieve the sufferings of man let it not be in a spirit of condescension or mere compassion but as devoted worship of the Lord abiding in the heart of all beings, in the true spirit of our dharma of surrendering our all in the humble service of Him who is Father, Mother, Brother, Friend and Everything to us all.[41]

This concept of serving and not charity, as a spiritual exercise recognizing the connecting common element in all humanity is then the basis of the RSS approach to mitigating human suffering. It does not use it or capitalize on it but sees it as an opportunity to venerate the human-divine in all. This concept of service could be traced back to the Sri Ramakrishna-Vivekananda Vedantic tradition.

M. S. Golwalkar had been initiated into *sanyasa* by Swami Akhandananda (1864–1937), a direct disciple of Sri Ramakrishna and a guru-bhai (brothers under the same Guru) of Swami Vivekananda. In the history of the Sri Ramakrishna order, Swami Akhandananda has a unique place. During the late 1897, an incident that happened in Daudpur completely changed the course of his life.[42] In his own words:

> Early one morning I washed my hands and feet in the Ganges and was approaching the bazar when I discovered a Muslim girl of about fourteen, clad in dirty rags and weeping bitterly. She held on her waist an earthen jar, the bottom of which had given way. On seeing me, she said, "Father, there is famine, we have nothing at home to eat. We had in our home only this earthen jar and two earthen pans. There is no second vessel at home to hold water. For fear lest mother should beat me, I am crying." I took her with me and bought her an earthen jar worth two paise and some fried rice of the same value.

The incident made him aware of the plight of the famine struck countryside and he resolved to serve them. When he went to see the Deputy Magistrate for getting help to the famine-ravaged peasants, he was politely informed that as 'Sahib was having his siesta', the Swami should come back later. There were certain other officials who were quite helpful. But he often got into skirmishes with officials for getting the people their food, proper wages and human dignity. With no money and just a firm resolve, the Swami opened a famine relief centre and started feeding people. Fellow *guru-bhais* in the central *mutt* were sceptical of the ability to feed thousands of people and thought the Swami should cease his operations and return. At this juncture, from Almora, Swami Vivekananda wrote on 15 June 1897, a strong letter of support to Swami Akhandananda:

> I am getting detailed reports of you and getting more and more delighted....Bravo! Accept a hundred thousand embraces and blessings from me. Work, work, work—I care for nothing else.... If in the attempt to carry morsels of food to starving mouths, name and possession and all be doomed even...—thrice blessed art thou! It is the heart, the heart that conquers, not the brain. Books and learning, Yoga and meditation and illumination—all are but dust compared with love. It is love that gives you the supernatural powers, love that gives you Bhakti, love that gives

> illumination, and love, again, that reads to emancipation. This indeed is worship, worship of the Lord in the human tabernacle.[43]

Madhav Golwalkar had gone to Swami Akhandananda and received initiation on 13 January 1937—the day of Makar Sankranti, celebrated in Tamil Nadu as Pongal. Clearly the service to humanity as worship of the Divine was imparted to him by Akhandananda. It was after the passing away of Akhandananda that Golwalkar returned to Sangh work. It would be natural to expect studies on the RSS and Golwalkar exploring this relation.[44]

Incidentally this concept of seva had been explained more completely by connecting it to Hinduness and a *yajna* (Vedic worldview of sacrifice as the functional archetype of the universe at all levels of existence) had been propounded by poet Rabindranath Tagore. In his 1901 essay 'Hindutva', which has been cited earlier in the book, he states:

> Let us install as a living reality in our hearts that ever-wakeful feeling of weal (*mangal*) [inherited] from our ancestors and apply it everywhere in society, only then will we again reach great Hindu civilization (*Hindu sabhyata*). To give education to society, health, food, wealth and riches, this is our own work; this alone is our weal; this should not not be regarded as trade, rather, not to hope for anything else in exchange for this [activity] but *Punya* and well-being (*kalyan*) is *Yajna*, is unification with Brahman through work (*karmayog*), to always remember this is Hindu-ness (*Hindutva)*....To bind society, from low to high, with the bonds of disinterested well-being (kalyan) is the object of the greatest of all our efforts. With this thread of unity, the religious connection in Hindu-tradition of the one with the other, and of the past with the present, has to be realized. This is our only means of achieving our humanness.[45]

Here one can see that just as Tagore had prefigured Savarkar's conception of Hindutva as a civilizational process, here he had prefigured the conception of seva as spiritual worship—a yajna.

But most of the leading academic and media observers on 'South Asia' who study the RSS are conspicuously silent about this crucial influence in the life and worldview of Golwalkar. There is at least one study where the Western anti-RSS academic gets a direct causal connection between the view of Golwalkar and the RSS service activities. But still with extraordinary convolutedness the academic enables herself to depict a negative picture of the service activities of Sangh Parivar:

> Like governmental agencies and other voluntary groups, the VHP involves itself

> in relief work among victims of natural disasters. In its discussion of "relief and rehabilitation" work, the VHP quotes "Guruji" Golwalkar, former head of the RSS: "In the field of human service, no distinction should be made between man and man. We have to serve all, be he a Christian or a Muslim or a human being of any other persuasion; for, calamities, distress and misfortunes make no such distinction but afflict all alike". Through such work, the VHP can establish or further contacts among disaster victim as well as local administration. Expansion of its influence into local affairs is also the means by whereby the VHP contributes to conditions leading to human-made calamities like communal riots.[46]

Lise McKean who wrote the above passage is a strong Hinduphobic writer—an independent anthropologist who considers all Hindu saints as 'anything but spiritual'.[47] At the same time she participates in events conducted by missionary religions like Islam (Indian Muslim Council-USA, 2005) and Christianity (PIFRAS symposium 2002).[48] One can see in the passage how she simply overlooks the relation between Golwalkar's vision of common humanity guiding the relief works of Sangh but obsessively connects the humanitarian service rendered by the Sangh Parivar (here VHP) with the hypothetical 'human-made calamities like communal riots', though in such riots proselytizing provocations and aggressions play a major role too. Yet one sees almost no academic work linking the proselytizing agenda of Teresa or missionaries leading to 'human-made calamities' including terrorism in the Northeast when studying their 'social service' work.

Analysis of an Academic Study of the RSS Relief Work

Even in the limited number of 'studies' by academics on the RSS's seva activities, though they are presented as 'neutral' academic authorities, most of them have deep prejudice not just against the RSS but also against the innate value of Indian culture itself. A recent work deviates significantly but not completely from this general trend. Malini Bhattacharjee, who teaches political science at Azim Premji University, has studied its work in times of disaster. The study exemplifies how the frameworks available in the Indian establishment academia are simply deficient in studying the seva phenomenon so basic to the RSS.

So, in early Hindu history, tracing the act of giving, on the authority of Romila Thapar, Dr Bhattacharjee states that while 'seva became popular mostly during the Bhakti movement in the medieval times, its closest predecessor may be traced to the ancient Hindu institution of "dana"' which in turn was 'giving gifts to priests and Brahmanas with elaborate itemization of the objects...' and hence 'dana was not made in the spirit of charity but as a symbol of success and investment for future returns'.[49]

Here, Thapar is demonstratedly wrong. *Rig Veda* itself makes it an obligation on the part of the rich to share their wealth with the needy. Hymn 117 in Mandala 10 of the *Rig Veda* named *Bhikshu Sukta* praises *dana* or liberality. It does not speak of any other-worldly pleasures as the motivation for sharing the wealth with the needy but provides very humane and empathy-based arguments.

Historian Radhakumud Mookerji explains paraphrasing through this hymn the Vedic attitude to what he roughly translates as 'charity' but which is more seva and sharing:

> It enjoins charity as more meritorious than Yajna, sacrifice. The gift of food is a gift of life, for hunger is a form of death. Friends forsake him who does not help them in need and leave him homeless, for home means friends. Fortune also is unstable like the wheels of a rolling chariot. So, one must not cling to it as a miser. Nor can it save him from death. Nor should one be proud of it, for a rich man finds another richer. Twins, looking alike, differ in mind (chit), strength (virya) and liberality. So, there is no religion higher than charity.[50]

Later, producing food in plenty and sharing it are decreed as vows binding humanity. Epics and Puranas again and again stress the importance of giving food to the needy. Jitendra Bajaj and M. D. Srinivas have shown how production and sharing of food for all or securing food security of the society through various institutional means had an unbroken continuity till the recent times.[51] The statement that 'the gift of food is a gift of life' is also found in the Tamizh Buddhist epic *Manimekalai* where the renunciate-heroine makes giving food to the needy her mission. The epic states that 'those who give food give life'. Thus, the Rig Vedic injunction of dana becomes the proto-Seva. Marxist historians such as Thapar always want to project the Vedic society as ethically deficient and hence the *suppressio veri suggestio falsi*. As the Marxist school became the dominant and subsequently the only halal way of doing social sciences, naturally it established itself as the only way of looking at any social phenomenon.

Hence, the perspective to look at the seva tradition of the RSS as the continuation of the long indigenous tradition does not occur to the author here. But the failure is not hers personally; it is the very academic ecosystem which is simply not equipped to study the Sangh's concept of seva. The author oscillates between 'the post-modernist' critique of the likes of Ashis Nandy and the questionable speculation of Meera Nanda that the 'decolonisation of Hindu mind' project of 'Hindutva ideologues' necessitates 'understanding science through Hindu categories'.

The reading of the author herself is more insightful and closer to reality than both Ashis Nandy and Meera Nanda, in that, she substitutes 'service' for 'science' in the RSS worldview and states:

> In arguing that seva is essentially an 'indigenous' institution, the RSS facilitates a huge ontological shift with regard to its perception as a superior form of ('selfless') giving, in the imagination of common people. It is an invocation of this capacious understanding of seva, which is set apart from 'modern', 'Western' ideas of philanthropy that contributes towards making it so attractive to contemporary donors and recipients.[52]

This study of the RSS seva is in one way very refreshing. One can see umpteen works churned out by the academic cottage industry, regurgitating the same quote of 'Guruji' Golwalkar from his 1939 book to establish the pro-Nazi nature of the Sangh, despite Belgian Indologist Dr Koenraad Elst exposing the fallacy of using that quote thoroughly. But what one does not see is the quote of the same Golwalkar on service. In a letter he wrote to a Sangh official, he strictly advocates never to discriminate based on religion, caste or any such sectarianism. This is perhaps the first academic book that presents this particular quote of Golwalkar of having to 'serve all, be he a Christian or a Muslim', which we have seen above without any prejudiced distortions.

The author gives the example highlighted in Sangh literature for such a non-discriminatory seva—the rescue work done in the case of 1996 mid-air collision of Saudi airliner with a Kazakhstan airliner in which the victims were mainly Muslims and the RSS were the first to reach the spot and rescue them as well as help with the identification of the dead bodies for the relatives. The author also quotes a stray incident of sectarianism exhibited by Swami Aseemanand in Andamans during the tsunami in 2004. In the calamity, this reviewer and his Ayurvedic doctor friend Dr S. Lenin (who comes from a pro-Marxist family) personally experienced the Sangh serving the Christian fishermen affected by the calamity. The medical unit of Seva Bharati headed by Dr Srinivasa Kannan, who was the head of the Nagerkovil RSS, was one of the first to reach the coastal villages.

She then draws her own conclusion that 'the provision of non-discriminatory seva is part of a strategic exercise' to display 'secular ethos' by the Sangh 'in order to gain popularity'. Had she stopped with that, this book would have been just another run-of-the-mill academic portrait of the RSS.

But she continues, and that changes everything:

> "However,…a deeper engagement with numerous swayamsevaks and volunteers of the RSS reveal that a large section of these people engage in Seva because they truly feel that they are doing good work to make a better society and a better nation." [53]

But just a few pages later, seva becomes, on the authority of Jaffrelot, 'a social welfare strategy of the RSS'.[54]

The question then is what does this strategy aim at? The Hindu rashtra, of course. Now we see Malini Bhattacharjee taking prejudiced opinions of select academics against the Sangh as objective facts:

> Hedgewar was, perhaps, the first leader during this period to seriously shape the idea of Seva as a means for constructing the Hindu Rashtra. For Gandhi and the Indian National Congress largely, nationalism was essentially a civic idea and transcended language, religion, caste and gender barriers. In this sense, as Ramachandra Guha (2007) has persuasively argued, India was indeed an "unnatural nation", as there was no similar counterpart in the Western Europe where people of such wide diversities have come together to claim a nation. For Hedgewar, the imagination of the nation was diametrically opposite. Deeply inspired by Moonje, who was an admirer of Mussolini's fascist military academies, Hedgewar was convinced that the physical and mental training of the swayamsevaks was the key to India's military regeneration. Seva played a key role in this imagination.[55]

The problem here is that Dr Hedgewar never thought of 'constructing the Hindu rashtra'. He considered India as a Hindu nation. In fact, to him, the nation itself had Hindu implied in it. Contrary to what Ramchandra Guha states, to both Gandhi and Dr Ambedkar, India was a very natural one nation—predicated on her deep cultural unity. And that B. S. Moonje was influenced by fascist ideology is an empirically falsified yet a living academic urban legend created by Marzia Casolari. However, the author makes this axiomatic in her study.

If there was one point where Gandhi, Savarkar and hence Dr Hedgewar, Dr Ambedkar and even Nehru to a significant extent converged, it was the oneness of the Indian nation through its deep cultural unity. Again, despite very serious differences, Gandhi and Savarkar converged with respect to fighting missionary conversion and they both agreed that tribal communities are Hindu. Further, the seva or humanitarian worship as the service of the *virat* as visualized and forcibly put forth by Swami Vivekananda and by Mahatma Gandhi.

The problem is even more compounded when she acknowledges that 'Hedgewar was attracted by Vivekananda's idea of creating a trained cadre of nationalist sanyasis who would be dedicated towards rendering service for the poor and underprivileged sections of the society' which 'eventually led him to establish Shakha...' on the very next page. Now fascism and the worldview of Vivekananda are mutually exclusive. Was the approach of Dr Hedgewar to seva predicated on the 'fascist' elements or Advaitic humanism of Swami Vivekananda? And both are mutually exclusive. Again, it is important here to emphasize that the author is honest. She does not present just select quotes and factoids and build a false stereotype, which is what usually most academics studying the Sangh indulge in. But the frameworks available to her are limited, and as she prefers to stay in the theoretical comfort zone and dares to venture into the real time data the paradoxes multiply.

Her detailed study of the Sangh seva following the natural disasters of Odisha Super Cyclone (1999) and during Gujarat earthquake (2001) provide the case in point. In the case of Odisha, she investigates if the Sangh seva discriminated or ignored non-Hindu communities through a 'field visit undertaken in a Muslim-dominated village named Chaulia in Erasama block which was completely ravaged by the cyclone':'

> Community members named UBSS (a Sangh Parivar organization) as one of the first agencies to have set up a community kitchen and also mentioned that it later undertook rehabilitation projects such as tilling the land and providing tools of livelihood to the villagers.[56]

Here again the source used by the author as authoritative, particularly with respect to Saraswati Shishu Vidya Mandirs (SVM) the schools run by the Sangh, is an article written by academic-activist Angana Chatterjee in 2003 in the magazine *Asian Age*. Here Chatterjee argues that the 'affordability and their emphasis on imparting cultural values to children provide a congenial space for mobilizing young and impressionable minds into the ideology of Hindutva'.[57] Then we see that the author herself concludes that 'expanding the educational apparatus after the Super Cyclone, keeping in mind future returns, therefore, was a political masterstroke on the part of the RSS'.[58] Finally, the interviews done with the teachers of SSVM by the Centre around *samskaras* reinforce the allegations made by Chatterjee. However, Dr Chatterjee is a highly problematic, if not totally unreliable, source with regard to any data related to the Hindu social phenomena in particular and India in general.

That Dr Chatterjee has an ideological vested interest in damning Hindu seva projects makes her far from a source with academic neutrality. She is part of an organization called the Campaign to Stop Funding Hate. This organization in turn is founded by members of Forum of Indian left , where she provided 'critical assistance' to an unsubstantiated report attacking a US-based charity organization called the India Development Relief Fund (IDRF). IDRF projects in India were linked to violence against religious minorities here. Communal bias was alleged against IDRF, which later proved to be wrong. But the real reason the IDRF was targeted was because through its service activities it provided resistance to proselytizing among the tribal and SC communities of Odisha.[59] The schools naturally became special targets because they provided direct stiff competition to the Christian missionary schools.

Even keeping aside the relevant fact of Angana Chatterjee's ideologically vested interest against the educational services provided by the Sangh seva activities and the support to these activities by non-resident Indians through the IDRF, not to mention her anti-India stand on the Kashmir issue as well, what is important is the way, the Sangh-run schools have delivered quality education in a very affordable manner through the dedication of teachers who work for far less salary than government school teachers.

In 2009 a report in the *Indian Express* pointed out that SSVMs had produced 44 of the top 102 students in the state in the high school exams, with seven of the top 10 ranks from SVMs. The report also spoke of 'over 11,000 Acharyas and Gurumas (male and female teachers) in 739 SVMs across the state who live a no-frills life to teach 1.8 lakh students from kindergarten to Class XII for a pittance'.[60]

A 2010 report by the *Times of India* (20 June) under the title 'Saraswati Vidya Mandir schools clean sweep toppers' list', mentions the maximum ranks in the top 10 list, including the top five in the state, going to students of SSVM. The report goes on to point out that as many as 55 students of SVM in the best 100 list show a pass percentage of 98.58 as against 71.41 of government schools.[61] In 2010 as many as 12,000 teachers were teaching across 793 SSVM schools.

In 2011 a total of 9,142 students belonging to 174 SSVM schools appeared in the Board examinations and came up with the pass percentage of 98.13, which was way higher than the overall pass percentage of the state at 66.75. Of the 174 SSVM schools, 94 schools had achieved cent per cent result. Out of 9,142 students who appeared in the examinations, 6,290 students passed first class. Even the state mass education minister, who is a non-BJP politician, admitted the better performance of SVM schools.

In 2018 in the Jharsuguda district of the state alone, of the top 12 rank holders, four belonged to SVM schools including the district topper.[62] In 2019 from Malkangiri considered 'a backward area of Odisha', Abhinash Behera, a class X student was among the top 20 winners of Young Astronomer Talent Search (YATS) 2019–2020 and earned a visit to the Indian Space Research Organization (ISRO). The boy participated in a talent search that involved

62,000 students from 300 schools across the state. He was from SSVM. He said that his science teachers in school had helped him a lot in his preparations.[63]

So, here is a school system that provides, for decades, one of the most affordable and good educational services in terms of even the 'secular' State board syllabus through dedicated teachers who work for lesser than their governmental counterparts. So, there is more to 'future returns' and a 'political masterstroke'—in the form of genuine service of the society in the field of education.

In the case of Gujarat earthquake relief too, she acknowledges that the Sangh provided immediate and exemplary relief services. But this time, she allows without scrutiny, the charges of sectarian discrimination against the Sangh. And the sources for these charges are clearly prejudiced against the Sangh—Kuldip Nayar (in an article in 2001), by a senior Congress party leader in 2012 and another report in the Islamist anti-Sangh magazine *Milli Gazette*.

At the same time, if one goes through the actual reports from mostly neutral sources, these allegations seem to be a well-calculated after-construction. For example, this is what a report in *India Today* said about the relief work by the RSS:

> On January 29, the residents of Nanireldi, a Muslim dominated village in Kutch virtually starving since the day of the quake were pleasantly surprised to see a batch of RSS and VHP workers land with foodgrain, clothes and medicines. Said Abha Ibrahimbhai: "I could never imagine that the RSS and VHP workers would come to our rescue".[64]

Dr Bhattacharjee also looks minutely into the Sangh disaster relief, searching for data-points that would reinforce the prejudices against the Sangh. Earlier she has stated that the work of Seva Bharati mostly focuses on 'the eradication of untouchability, imbuing people with the spirit of service and unity and serving the economically needy and socially backward sectors...'.[65] But pages later, it comes down 'to perpetuate religious and caste-based hierarchies' which in turn is claimed to be part of the 'traditionalist vision of Hindu nationalism'. Sangh seva workers distance themselves from the inter-community conflicts between the Other Backward Caste (OBC) Ahir and 'Dalit' community during disaster relief operations. This is seen as the 'strategy of non-interference in selective issues' and that is part of 'its conservative ideology of Hindutva'.[66] Now, this is more Christophe Jaffrelot than Malini Bhattacharjee.

Usually, the Sangh has its own organization that works on these issues of social conflicts. At a time of disaster relief work, the Sangh organization involved in that generally keeps its distance from such inter-community conflicts. At the same time, Bhattacharjee herself acknowledges that in the village where the Ahirs (the dominant OBC but pastoral community) owned land, they were allocated larger houses but where (as in Keshav Nagar) Seva Bharati had complete freedom, they built uniform houses for all[67], which shows the Sangh, in a very natural and spontaneous way, showing aversion to caste-based hierarchical distinctions.

Yet the prejudices take over here completely. That with respect to this, she has not talked to Samajik Samarasta Manch (SSM) and yet concludes that Sangh seva is aimed at 'conservative Hindutva'. This is despite the fact that Sangh organizations and the leadership have supported SC priests in major Hindu temples, inter-caste marriages and even in conservative Haryana, the BJP government increasing financial support for inter-caste marriage couples. Given all these facts, the conclusion of the author that because Seva Bharati initially kept a distance with respect to the Ahir-SC inter-community conflict during disaster relief means, keeping caste-hierarchies part of Hindutva is wrong both empirically and contextually.

With all these inner tensions running in the book, still the author must be congratulated for being honest in many of the pages. In a particularly telling passage, she does go beyond the lens of 'agenda of co-opting lower castes within Hindutva fold'[68] and 'strategies' and states:

> Despite these political dimensions however there is a certain materiality to seva that goes beyond its political ramifications. The most remarkable thing to acknowledge here is that the RSS's conceptualization of seva offers a resuscitation of an innate idiom, a common language, a common communicative structure, a common worldview that people (including performers and recipients of seva) instantly connect to because they recognize it as their own.[69]

Perhaps, this should have been the conclusion, or one can even say that this is the actual conclusion. Such originally Indic insights which come from her own groundwork are bogged down by the weight of the academic baggage of prejudices against the Indic in general and the Hindu in particular.

The book shows that after 75 years of Independence, we have not developed our own tools and framework to study a phenomenon that is rooted in our own national self. If academics realize this deficiency and start studying Ramakrishna-Vivekananda, Sri Aurobindo, Gandhi and Dharampal to develop their tools to study the Indic, then this book shall be a real pathfinder, serving to the need for a fresh and rooted framework to understand the seva phenomenon of the RSS. If not, there may be yet another academic book to conceive convoluted ways to explain away Sangh seva as mere 'strategy' and as agenda filled—a prejudiced, baseless fantasy of the academics.

Sangh and Social Emancipation

Whenever the Sangh is discussed, it is always projected as an organization that is pro-caste and more importantly pro-birth-based *Varna* system. The second Sarsanghachalak of the RSS is particularly singled out for the criticism that he often supported the status quo with respect to caste system and even glorified it. Quotes taken from his *Bunch of Thoughts*, mostly out of context and without any chronological order, become the favourite punching bag for the 'intellectuals'. With that, the Sangh gets essentialized too.

The RSS derives its vision on social emancipation and its template for the ground mission against stagnation from various value streams that flow into Hindutva. With its vast network of organizations and workers at the ground level, the Sangh has its own grasp of the dynamics of Hindu society—often better than the rhetoric-filled political-media grasp of the same. While the politicians of the identity vote bank politics have sought to invest in social faultlines even as they mouth slogans of social empowerment often predicating itself on binaries like Brahmin and non-Brahmin, Dalit and non-Dalit, Tribal and non-Tribal, often leading to violent conflict, the RSS tries to persevere for social emancipation of the marginalized and downtrodden while removing birth-based discriminations at various levels.

To understand the RSS view of social emancipation and how it differs from that of the anti-caste crusaders who identify Hinduism and/or Hindutva with it, one needs to also understand how the Varna-jati is seen in the historical and sociological context by Hindutva and the anti-Hindutva.

Essentialist versus Evolutionary Approaches

One can differentiate the Hindutva and the anti-Hindutva views of jati as essentialist and evolutionist approaches. The essentialist approach considers jati as a kind of a priestly imposed hierarchical system in which the masses have been exploited over the millennia by the elite caste of priests and rulers. The whole system is diabolical and a priest-ruler conspiracy for subjugation of the masses through religion. So here the entire Hinduism is essentialized as caste, or it is seen mainly as a system sustaining caste.

The evolutionist view on the other hand sees jati as a kind of a social phenomenon that has evolved out of various factors—the rigidity and flexibility of hierarchical nature being decided by various factors—sociopolitical, economic and ecological factors. In this view, two major drives are identified—one towards democratic social emancipation and another towards social stagnation, which is antagonistic to a democratic value system. This view sees jati as a specific form of more global human phenomenon and locates Hinduism not in the conventions supporting status quo, which are common in almost all pre-modern societies but in the voices which rose against such stratification process even in pre-modern times. Such voices are always conspicuous by their absence in most other societies while they are pronounced in India and Hinduism. Hence, it is the spiritual voices for social emancipation emerging from Hindu Dharma which define Hinduism.

The essentialist school is exemplified in the statement made by historian Ramchandra Guha at London School of Economics (LSE) in 2017. The historian declared, 'Caste system is the most rigorous, most diabolical system of social stratification ever invented by humans, and we, Hindus, invented it.'[70] This exemplifies the essentialist approach. Incidentally, traditional casteists also embrace the essentialist approach. They consider the system as the most perfect and just social system, unique to India. The evolutionist approach rejects the essentialist approach. It considers the system not as unique to India but as a stage in social development which should be discarded when it had run out of its use. If true, similar social discrimination, exclusion and divinely ordained birth-based hierarchies should be present in other societies.

Historian Kathy Stuart, who studies social stratification in pre-modern Europe, says that throughout the so-called Holy Roman Empire,

> dishonorable tradesmen suffered various forms of social, economic, legal, and political discrimination on a graduated scale of dishonor at the hands of "honorable" guild artisans and in "honorable" society at large. As a matter of course, dishonorable people were excluded from most guilds. In the case of the most extreme dishonor, that of executioners and skinners, Unehrlichkeit could lead to exclusion from virtually all normal sociability. Executioners and skinners might be pelted with stones by onlookers, they might be refused access to taverns, excluded from public baths, or denied an honorable burial. Dishonor was transmitted through heredity, often over several generations. The polluting quality of dishonor is one of its defining characteristics.[71]

While all pre-modern and even early modern societies had birth-based social hierarchies and social exclusion, Hindus, on the other hand, did invent the Varna system. It provided a worth-based counter matrix to the birth-based jati system. Perhaps when it originated, it would have been the only social system in the world that was more worth-based than birth-based. It served to check and control the ill effects of the birth-based system of privileges and disabilities. Even B. R. Ambedkar noted the diametrically opposite nature of Varna and jati:

> Varna is based on the principle of each according to his worth, while Caste is based on the principle of each according to his birth. The two are as distinct as chalk is from cheese. In fact, there is an antithesis between the two.[72]

Even this Varna system was not made as the basis of Sanatana Dharma, leave alone Hindutva according to both Hindu Sanghatanists as well as Hindu mystics.

The weakening of the caste system in India along with the upheavals as well as violent conflicts it brings about needs to be contrasted with apparent, almost complete disappearance of caste system in the West. The caste system in the West disappeared only with the colonial expansion of the West. With power over natural resources of three continents, namely Africa, Americas and Australia, and with inflow of slave labour, which was subsequently replaced by indentured labour mainly from India, the abolition of caste system was easier. Now untouchable communities like the Cogots and Cacoux are a distant memory for the West.

In the case of India, caste system became rigid in the same nineteenth century as drainage of resources started because of colonialism. One needs to add to this the colonial efforts to freeze castes through census and efforts to create as much division in the society as possible through essentializing of the communities. Thus, the British created out of Indian communities martial races and criminal tribes. Such fixed stereotyping of community characters was largely, though not entirely, absent in the Indian narrative.

So, for an anthropologist with a deeper vision, what is that which makes Indian caste system distinct? There is not a single instance of mass movement in Christendom that spoke for these voiceless people of 'dishonourable' trades. Martin Luther, the great Protestant reformer, took pride in saying he was instrumental in the massacre of peasants. There is not a single traditional Christian saint who spoke against the treatment meted out to European untouchable communities though they did exist. But what distinguishes India is the constant voice of spiritual emancipation which was raised for the marginal communities in society—and often helping communities break the shackles in the process.

Systems of hereditary social stratification can evolve anywhere in the presence of appropriate social conditions. In India it is called jati. But importantly it was tempered by Varna, which as the Bhagavad Gita points out, Arjuna, in his confusion, mixed it up with *kuladharma* and jati, while according to Krishna is based on *swadharma*, karma and guna.

Based on both religious knowledge and a more thorough understanding of society, the Sangh rejects the notoriety heaped on Hinduism by the essentialist view of caste-jati origin. Hindus neither invented the 'caste system' nor made it the most diabolical. Many such systems have thrived across the world in the past. That caste system and the inhuman practice of untouchability are not unique to Indian society cannot whitewash the fact that a great deal of injustice has been committed in the name of caste—and that it needs to be corrected. Simultaneously it should also be remembered that several reform movements have arisen from within the Hindu fold for social emancipation and the RSS considers itself the heir to this stream in Hindu history.

'Guruji' Golwalkar: Glorified Obscurantist or Ignored Reformer?

M. S. Golwalkar became famous in the academic studies of the RSS for only two quotes. Almost every academic studying the Sangh could almost recall verbatim these quotes to 'prove' the fascist and pro-Nazi inspiration of the RSS. As already briefly shown in the earlier chapter, the book in question *We or Our Nationhood Defined* (1939) calls the German race spirit that had arisen as 'depredatory'. Belgian Indologist Dr Koenraad Elst, himself a critic of the RSS, while discussing the RSS decision to openly denounce the book which was written before Golwalkar became the Sarsanghachalak, points out in conclusion:

> The image of M. S. Golwalkar (1906–1973) has posthumously been narrowed down to just two infelicitous and embarrassing quotations from his first book, one that he himself had repudiated early in his career as RSS leader. If read judiciously and within their context, they are by far not as incriminating as various anti-Hindu polemicists would like to have us believe. In particular, contrary to the common allegation, they do not prove that Golwalkar was a Nazi sympathizer, nor that he had mass murder in mind as the solution for the problems Hindu society experienced with its Muslim and Christian minorities.[73]

The academic world is slowly but increasingly realizing that the so-called pro-Hitler quotes of Golwalkar from the *We or Our Nationhood Defined* actually do not establish that he was pro-Hitlerian. In fact, there are quite a number of passages in his entire work which show that he was against the Nazi ideology. But more pertinent to the current Indian polity and society are the views that critics and opponents of the RSS attribute to Golwalkar with respect to caste.

Support of Racist Eugenics?

Prof. Shamsul Islam quotes Golwalkar's lecture at the School of Social Science, Gujarat University on 17 December 1960. He quotes verbatim the report made in none other than *Organiser* which reads thus:

> Today experiments in cross-breeding are made only on animals. But the courage to make such experiments on human beings is not shown even by the so-called modern scientist of today. If some human cross-breeding is seen today it is the result not of scientific experiments but of carnal lust. Now let us see the experiments our ancestors made in this sphere. In an effort to better the human species through cross-breeding the Namboodri Brahmans of the North were settled in Kerala and a rule was laid down that the eldest son of a Namboodri family could marry only the daughter of Vaishya, Kashtriya or Shudra communities of Kerala. Another still more courageous rule was that the first off-spring of a married woman of any class must be fathered by a Namboodri Brahman and then she could beget children by her husband. Today this experiment will be called adultery but it was not so, as it was limited to the first child.[74]

Prof. Islam points out the passage and states that the passage shows underlying his 'firm belief in the Race Theory'. Then he damns Golwalkar for having the following 'disturbing worldview':

> Firstly, it proves that Golwalkar believed that India had a superior Race or breed and also an inferior Race which needed to be improved through cross-breeding. Secondly, a more worrying aspect was his belief that Brahmans of the North (India) and specially Namboodri Brahmans, belonged to a superior Race. Due to this quality, Namboodri Brahmans were sent from the North to Kerala to improve the breed of inferior Hindus there. Interestingly, this was being argued by a person who claimed to uphold the unity of Hindus world over. Thirdly, Golwalkar as a male chauvinist believed that a Namboodri Brahman male belonging to a superior Race from the North only could improve the inferior human Race from South. For him wombs of Kerala's Hindu women enjoyed no sanctity and were simply objects of improving breed through intercourse with Namboodri Brahmans who in no way were related to them.[75]

At first look, the passage from the lecture of Golwalkar is indeed shocking and then along with the interpretation Prof. Islam gives, it indeed looks indefensible. It is indeed indefensible—had Golwalkar stated it as a model to be followed in modern society. He did not. In fact, all he did was to defend a particular local custom as a kind of brave sociological experiment. The custom was indeed a misconceived, totally erroneous not to mention inhuman attempt of a crude pre-modern eugenics. Golwalkar wants to see in that a daring scientific experiment. His emphasis is here more for the 'brave' and 'scientific' spirit of the ancestors and in doing so they did not do it out of 'carnal lust'. But nowhere does he state that this should be followed.

Incidentally, Golwalkar was not alone in considering the caste system an experiment. One of India's eminent anthropologists Nirmal Kumar Bose (1901–1972), a Gandhian and 'no partisan of the caste system' (as famous biologist Theodosius Dobzhansky called him), wrote:

> The careful way in which the tradition of close correspondence between caste and occupation was built up is clear indication of what the leaders of Hindu society had in mind. They believed in the hereditary transmissibility of character, and thought it best to fix a man's occupation, as well as his status in life, by means of the family in which he had been born.[76]

Quoting Bose in his important book *Genetic Diversity and Human Equality* (1973), Theodosius Dobzhansky clearly differentiates between what had happened in India and the same rationale being used by racists today, which is despicable. Dobzhansky states:

> The caste system in India was the grandest genetic experiment ever performed on man. The structure of the society endeavored for more than two millennia to induce what we would now call genetic specialization of the caste populations for performance of different kinds of work and functions. Such specialization has not been achieved. The evidence is as yet insufficient to rule out the possibility that some average differences between the caste populations may exist. This much is certain: although modern India has far to go to abolish inequalities of status and opportunity, all castes have produced persons of ample competence to acquire non-traditional education and to engage in non-traditional occupations.[77]

More relevant to this 'human experiment' angle to the 'caste' system, is how Savarkar, the foremost exponent of Hindutva whom Golwalkar venerated, had characterized the experiment. To Savarkar it was a temporarily failed experiment 'due to its extreme practice or distortion'. But according to him, by 'failing in this great experiment of the caste system, our Hindu race enriched human experience and has thereby succeeded in earning the gratitude of the human race; such was the scientific outlook and thought, sheer guts and amazing diligence at the root of this experiment'.[78] Hence, just because

Golwalkar described an obscurantist practice as being motivated by scientific spirit rather than patriarchal social stagnation, that could not be extrapolated to mean he condoned the practice as relevant in modern society.

Golwalkar did not hold the Varna system as sacrosanct to the Hindu society. To him the Varna system was only an arrangement, and it would wither away as society progresses and society could reorganize itself. So, he explained:

> As the older dried branches fall off a growing tree, to give place to the new ones, the society would shed Varna Vyavastha the existing social structure at one time and give place to a new necessary one. This is a natural process of the development of the society.[79]

Later, he elaborated:

> I have told you once that for the sake of construction of a new house, old house requires to be destroyed. Similarly perturbed social system must be put to an end here and now and should be destroyed root and branch. Going further we should proceed to establish a pure and harmonious society on the basis of pure Nationalism.[80]

One should note here that the 'pure and harmonious society' he sought to rebuild by destroying the old system was not based on genetic traits or racial superiority but 'pure Nationalism', and we should also remember that the concept of 'nationalism' that Hindus held, differed completely from the monolithic nation-state nationalism which had evolved in Europe. We also see that his views on caste had been evolving. Unfortunately, his critics, even those who position themselves as establishment historians try to define him through a few passages rather than document this more important evolutionary process.

Golwalkar's Evolving Views on Jati and its Culmination

A good instance of essentializing Golwalkar through frozen context-free quote is provided by Manu S. Pillai, an upcoming historian who worked in the office of controversial Congress Parliamentarian Shashi Tharoor. In 2017 he made a scathing criticism of Golwalkar, highlighting the parts where Golwalkar had stated that caste stopped conversions in medieval times and his criticism of the argument that India fell before invaders because of caste. Culling out quotes from *Bunch of Thoughts*, Pillai writes:

> To Golwalkar, the argument that caste weakened India is unadulterated nonsense. On the contrary, it was the absence of caste that invited calamity. "We know as a matter of history," he states, "that our north-western and north-eastern areas, where the influence of Buddhism had disrupted the caste system, fell an easy prey to the onslaught of Muslims.... But the areas of Delhi and Uttar Pradesh, which were considered to be very orthodox and rigid in caste restrictions, remained predominantly Hindu even after remaining the very citadels of Muslim power and fanaticism." So, Uttar Pradesh must be our model for national reinvigoration, as it is proof that "the so-called 'caste-ridden' Hindu Society has remained undying and inconquerable...(while) casteless societies crumbled to dust". And caste, which presumably B. R. Ambedkar got completely wrong, must be restored to its rightful dignity as an instrument of modern nation-building.[81]

The designed fallacy here is that Pillai leaves out carefully Golwalkar's criticism of caste which is also present in the same book where he speaks of caste as having 'degenerated beyond all recognition'. He had said that the caste system has 'perversity aggravated over the centuries' and that the present polity has further intensified this perversity of castes.[82]

The first edition of *Bunch of Thoughts* came out in 1966. This included mostly his speeches prior to that year, and in this we find Golwalkar mention untouchability just once. But when the final revised and enlarged editions came, which contained his other speeches from 1966 to 1973 (the year of his death), we find that he had become increasingly and even primarily more concerned about the problem of this social evil more than anything.

To him untouchability was a 'religious perversion' and many great savants of Hinduism like 'Guru Nanak, Acharya Ramanuja, Basaveshwara, Shankar Dev, Swami Dayananda, Narayana Guru, Gandhiji and Veer Savarkar, to name only a few' had fought against 'this pernicious practice', and he was pained that it still continued. Now it was not just the secular polity that he was finding fault with. Particularly in the case of untouchability he clearly found the response of the traditional religious heads wanting:

> At the root of the malady of "untouchability" lies the belief among the common mass of people that it is part of dharma, and transgressing it would be a grave sin.... Even now the so-called higher castes refuse to treat the so-called untouchables as their equals. Papers have reported that in a village in Rajasthan a Harijan youth was beaten to death because he grew moustaches, which was supposed to be the prerogative of only the Kshatriya! Nor did our dharma-gurus condemn such practices because even they mistook the custom for Dharma.[83]

But he was not rhetorically blaming the traditional heads like the modernist platform reformers. He set out to change them. The inspiration for this, interestingly, had come from none other than Dr Ambedkar himself. Dattopant Thengadi (1920–2004), an important RSS functionary then who would later become an important ideologue of the movement and founder of BMS, the labour union of the Sangh family, had worked closely with Dr Ambedkar. He was Dr Ambedkar's election agent.

Both Thengadi and Dr Ambedkar had discussed the RSS and a casteless Hindu society. Later, Thengadi reported this conversation with M. S. Golwalkar:

> Dattopant Thengadi: The members of RSS do not believe in untouchability.
> Ambedkar: Whether you handful of people believe it or not is not of much consequence in the context of solving the problem.
> Thengadi: You said this because of the smallness of their numbers.
> Ambedkar: Not necessarily because of that. There is an additional reason., which is of greater importance. Suppose on some critical social or religious issue your Golwalkar lays a particular line and the Shankaracharyas give a different verdict. Whose decision will carry weight with the ordinary orthodox caste Hindus?
> Thengadi: Of course, Shankaracharyas.[84]

When Thengadi reported this conversation to M. S. Golwalkar, to the former's surprise, Golwalkar completely concurred with Dr Ambedkar:

> It does not matter whether you or I recognize a Shankaracharya. The point is that the "touchables" whom we want to reform, accept their authority. They recognize neither you nor me. For them the Dharmacharyas' word is a religious commandment.[85]

Since then, it seemed to have fallen as a seed-thought inside the mind of 'Guruji' Golwalkar. He started working on it.

In 1964 'Guruji' Golwalkar and Shivram Shankar Apte (1907–1985) along with famous Vedantic exponent Swami Chinmayananda (1916–1993) founded the VHP. In 1966 at Prayag Kumbh Mela, which would have the largest confluence of Hindu traditional heads of its diverse streams, the VHP was launched in a big way. Here was Golwalkar's opportunity for policy conception and activism for the Hindu society, having all the traditional heads in one pan-Hindu platform. Ashok Singhal (1926–2015), who had worked as the international working president of VHP, described what happened when 'Guruji' Golwalkar brought up social issues and wanted the Dharmacharyas to come with positive solutions for the complete Hindu society:

> Sri Guruji attended the first conference of the Vishwa Hindu Parishad and remained there all the time when he severely condemned some social customs such as untouchability. Revered Sri Niranjandevji (then Shankaracharya of Govardhan Peeth) got infuriated and fulminated that religious scriptures and traditions cannot be tampered with. It seemed as if the conference will end up in a fiasco. At night Shri Guruji had a personal discussion with Poojya Sri Niranjandevji who got pleased by that.[86]

In other words, he had to convince the traditional heads educating them about the social situations and reminding them of their own duty towards the society. It was not an easy job. Nevertheless, 'Guruji' was able to achieve what then seemed utterly impossible.

'Guruji' Golwalkar planned to have the resolution condemning untouchability as having no shastric and dharmic sanction to be passed by all traditional Hindu religious leaders at 1969 Udupi conference of VHP.

The choice of Udupi itself was symbolic. It was here according to tradition, when the orthodoxy denied darshan of Sri Krishna, the presiding deity, to Kanakadasa, a mystic bard-devotee, the sacred idol or Vigraha itself turned and the enclosing walls cracked so that Kanakadasa could have darshan. To this day the deity stands turned west—'symbolically admonishing everyone not to practice the discrimination of high and low'.

The session of Dharmacharyas was presided by Sri R. Bharanaiah, an IAS officer, a veteran Gandhian and then sitting member of the State Public Service Commission. He was also one of the earliest members of the civil services from the Scheduled Community. Here is an eyewitness account of this historical moment:

> After a few persons spoke about the problem of untouchability and the signed directive of the Dharmagurus was read out to the assembly, the President Sri R. Bharanaiah moved a resolution that "In keeping with considered directions of the Revered Dharmagurus and Acharyas, this conference appeals to the Hindus to abandon any discriminatory feeling of high and low, touchable and untouchable and conduct all their religious and social affairs, on the basis of one single common Hindu brotherhood irrespective of caste, creed, birth, etc".
>
> As soon as the President completed reading the resolution, the entire assembly burst into cheers and claps in acclamation of the resolution. All the Dharmagurus seated on the dais heartily blessed the same. Indeed, this was a moment of history worthy to be carved in letters of Gold. It was a moment which proved once again that the Hindu Society is a dynamic race nourished with the nectar of immortality.
>
> All having dispersed, Sri Bharanaiah remained alone on the dais, immersed in emotions. He was reminded that the session was over. As he came down and saw

> Sri Guruji waiting, with joyous tears gushing from his eyes he firmly embraced Sri Guruji. There was silence all round for a few seconds. Then Sri Bharanaiah exclaimed in a voice choking with emotion, "Oh! How good of you that at last you have come to our rescue and taken up this mission for our sake!" Sri Guruji softly remarked, "What of me, the whole society is with you and has taken up the cause"[87]

Golwalkar did not stop with this resolution. He knew that a lot of work had to be done to convert this resolution into an integral part of the Hindu civil life. So immediately after the conference, on the occasion of Makar Sankranti (Pongal), he wrote a detailed letter to K. Suryanarayana Rao, who as a full-time worker was in charge of the Udupi conference. Here Golwalkar warns against complacency and reveals that tough task lays ahead of them:

> The success of the conference should not make us complacent....The resolution on untouchability blessed by all our Acharyas and Dharmagurus, Mathadhipathis and other holy men of all our sects—cannot be translated into actual life by mere pious expressions. Centuries old prejudices do not disappear by words or wishful thinking. Hard work, right propaganda have to be undertaken from town to town, village to village, house to house and people have to be educated to accept and practise what has been resolved, not merely as a concession to the pressure of modern times, but as an abiding principle and way of life, in an humble spirit of atonement for past mistakes. A change of heart, a moral and emotional change in the attitudes and behaviour has to be brought about....What we should desire and strive for is not, merely economic and political "equality"—we want a real change, a complete integration. This change is beyond the power of politics of Governmental plans. It is impossible to achieve it by a clever manipulation of political parties dealing in patch work in the name of integration. Strenuous work, springing from the heart and manifesting itself in day-to-day behaviour, work on a spiritual, moral and social plane is called for and all participants in the conference, as well as all who had extended sympathy and support, must come forward to put their shoulders to the wheel and with one mighty stroke, shatter to pieces the age long pernicious prejudices.[88]

Thus, what Dr Ambedkar sowed as a seed in the mind of Dattopant Thengadi got transplanted into the heart of Golwalkar which would ultimately result in a historically important moment in Hindu history, the importance which had been completely underplayed in most of the studies of the RSS.

A case in point is the study of RSS icons in Nilanjan Mukhopadhyay's *The RSS: Icons of the Indian Right* wherein he says that 'M. S. Golwalkar had remained unconcerned about it throughout his tenure as sarsanghachalak.'[89] Mukhopadhyay had used the biography of Golwalkar written by C. P. Bhishikar, making as many as 26 references to this book. The very same book contains the following response of Yadavarao Joshi (1914–1992), then the Joint General Secretary and chief full-time worker posted for the south in the Sangh, who when asked the happiest occasion for Golwalkar in his 33 years of being the RSS head, replied (as recorded by Bhishikar):

> During a conference of the Karnataka Pradesh Vishwa Hindu Parishad held at Udupi, the Dharmacharyas belonging to all various sects and sections of Hindu society passed a resolution unanimously and supported by all the four Jagadguru Shankaracharyas, declaring that there was no justification for untouchability or any kind of high or low in our shastras and all Hindus should be treated with equal respect and love....At that time his face was literally lit up with the joy of seeing the consummation of a long-awaited dream. I would say that for him this was the finest hour of his Sangh life.[90]

Further, the same book described how over the previous years, Golwalkar 'held discussions with Jain, Buddhist, Veerashaiva and Sikh religious leaders and the Dharmacharyas of all the other sects' and how all these efforts 'had culminated in that singular success at Udupi'. In any other society or in the history of any other religion, this conference and resolution would have been hailed as a decisive moment in the national life of the people. But as this defies the stereotype of the Sangh as a conservative status quo organization, we see a momentous truth being sacrificed at the altar of the convenience of ideologically vested interests—the Taj Mahal of real status quo.

The Udupi conference was held in the month of December 1969. Interestingly, in the same year in January, Golwalkar was asked in Kerala if people discriminated against due to their caste could be given the sacred thread, he answered in the affirmative:

> They should be given equal rights and footings in the matter of religious rites, in temple worship, in the study of Vedas, and in general in all our social and religious affairs. This is the only right solution for all the problems of casteism found nowadays in our Hindu society.[91]

As we will see later, this particular remark by Golwakar was not an empty statement. This would later become a major reform movement, silently bearing fruits but as usual unnoticed by the established old school academia-activist-media-polity axis. There are also views and opinions of Golwalkar with which the later Sangh leaders had differed. For example, he had said that the caste-based reservations should be discontinued after a stipulated period.

But Madhukar Dattatreya Deoras, his successor, declared that they should continue until the communities themselves feel that they do not need them.

'Balasaheb' Deoras (1915–1996)

There are quite a few recent studies of the Sangh which have tried to present the picture of Deoras the third Sarsanghachalak of the RSS as different and more radical in the social issues from his predecessor. This view is not correct.

Of course, 'Guruji' Golwalkar had a spiritual aura around him while Deoras presented himself as more rational. This author was in his early teens when he went to hear Deoras addressing a public meeting at Nagercoil, the capital town of Kanyakumari, which had witnessed quite a few communal riots because of aggressive Christian proselytizing. Going there expecting a Hindu communal lecture, the author was immensely surprised when Deoras stated that this was the age of science and that in this age when the existence of God itself is in question, how could anyone claim salvation through their own religion. That was the day this author (then a teenager) turned atheist (because of Darwin) was also convinced that the RSS was a truly secular movement than the political parties who were crypto-communalists for vote bank politics.

Even as a boy cadre of the Sangh Madhukar Deoras insisted that Swayamsevaks of all castes be treated the same way as he was when any of them visited. 'They should be served food in the same utensils which are used for other members of the family. I do not want any kind of discrimination on the basis of caste.' His mother agreed, and from then onwards, no questions were asked in the Deoras family about the caste of Swayamsevaks who visited and had food at their home. 'It was an uncommon practice in the country during that era when caste-based discrimination was rampant', points out journalist-author Arun Anand.[92]

In 1974 Deoras was invited to deliver the prestigious *Vasant Vyakhyanmala,* a lecture series organized at Pune during spring. He delivered it on 8 May 1974. Since then, the lecture has been accepted as a kind of policy document for the Sangh and its family organizations in the matters of social justice and harmony. Here Deoras asked the Hindu society to shun obscurantism. He asked them to emulate the Jewish principles of scriptural reinterpretation based on the modern context—something that Hindus had, but was unfortunately lost with stagnant times. He also pointed out how the Western society could still consider itself essentially Christian yet reconcile itself with Darwin. He was driving all these to point out that a tradition, if it does not suit the ethical compass of the society and individual, whatever the reason for its origins, could be jettisoned.

In the lecture, Deoras paraphrased Dr Ambedkar from a passage that Dr Ambedkar had put inside his most contemptuous attack on Hinduism. It is a passage that shows how much Dr Ambedkar was anxious to save and not destroy the Hindu society. Deoras said:

> Dr Ambedkar felt very much pained that in this society, which considers all human beings as children of God, nay, as part and parcel of that Divinity Itself, there should be found a sense of high and low. He also said that there could be no better basis for equality than the basic faith in the existence of a common spark of divinity in all human beings.

This is what the paraphrase read:

> Democracy demands that each individual shall have every opportunity for realizing his/her worth. It also requires that each individual shall know that he is as good as everybody else. Those who sneer at Aham Brahmasmi (I am Brahma) as an impudent utterance forget the other part of the Mahavakya namely Tat tvam asi (Thou art also Brahma). If Aham Brahmasmi has stood alone without the conjunct of Tat tvam asi it may have been possible to sneer at it. But with the conjunct of Tat tvam asi the charge of selfish arrogance cannot stand against Brahmaism....To support Democracy because we are all children of God is a very weak foundation for Democracy to rest on. That is why Democracy is so shaky wherever it was made to rest on such a foundation. But to recognize and realize that you and I are parts of the same cosmic principle leaves room for no other theory of associated life except democracy. It does not merely preach Democracy. It makes democracy an obligation of one and all. Western students of Democracy have spread the belief that Democracy has stemmed either from Christianity or from Plato and that there is no other source of inspiration for democracy. If they had known that India too had developed the doctrine of Brahmaism which furnishes a better foundation for Democracy they would not have been so dogmatic. India too must be admitted to have a contribution towards a theoretical foundation for Democracy....The result is that we have on the one hand the most democratic principle of Brahmaism and on the other hand a society infested with castes, sub-outcastes, primitive tribes and criminal tribes. Can there be a greater dilemma than this? [93]

If one goes through Ambedkarite literature, one will find that this is a particular quote that had not been noticed much or quoted by the conventional Ambedkarites. Only a handful of Hindutvaites (including the author) have been quoting this very crucial passage. But that as early as 1974, Deoras was able to paraphrase this passage of Dr Ambedkar shows how much he had deeply immersed himself in the Ambedkarite literature. In this incidentally, he was following his mentor and previous Sarsanghachalak Golwalkar, who had drawn a parallel between Dr Ambedkar and Swami Vivekananda, in his tribute to Dr Ambedkar:

> Swami Vivekananda...had declared that he saw God only in his poor, weak and down-trodden fellow-countrymen. Serving such suffering humanity, raising their levels of temporal life and elevating their spiritual vitality was indeed the true service to God. Vivekananda had also condemned the atrocious practices associated with untouchability and called for the building up of a harmonious society. These were the same sentiments that Dr Ambedkar had also expressed in different words, quite pungently though in the political and social context....Our nation is deeply indebted to Dr Ambedkar, and it is difficult to discharge this debt....Swami Vivekananda had said that the emancipation of Bharat needs the razor-like intelligence of a Shri Sankaracharya and the limitless compassion of a Bhagwan Buddha. By accepting and advocating Buddhism Dr Ambedkar, who himself reflected these qualities in an ample measure provided the inspiration to strive for the fulfillment of this guidance of Vivekananda. And he also felt that the inspiration to serve humanity by invoking the Buddhist tenets of equality and compassion was necessary for the good of the nation as also of mankind.[94]

In fact, that Dr Ambedkar himself had considered Swami Vivekananda as the greatest Indian of recent centuries shows that the Golwalkar's tribute was in sync with the spirit of Dr Ambedkar and that Deoras in pointing out the Advaitic basis of equality embedded in the thought of Dr Ambedkar was enlarging upon the vision of 'Guruji' Golwalkar.

In the lecture, Deoras further stated:

> Abraham Lincoln, who abolished slavery in America, said, "If slavery is not wrong, then nothing is wrong." Similarly, it is for all of us to declare, "If untouchability is not wrong, then nothing in the world is wrong!" Every one of us must therefore aim at eradicating social inequality in each and every form. We must clearly explain to the people at large how our society became weak and disorganized on account of social inequalities.

Deoras did not stop with lectures alone. He also made the Swayamsevaks understand their responsibility to rise above prejudices and against programmes like reservation. When anti-reservation riots were at its peak in Gujarat, Deoras made a historical move. Senior Sangh official and author Ramesh Patange gives a vivid picture:

> The problem of reservations had become a delicate and sensitive issue. Gujarat, a Western state of India witnessed a big agitation against the Reservation policy in 1981. A meeting of the All India Delegates of the RSS took place in March that year. The issue of agitations in Gujarat inevitably came up in the meeting. The workers from Gujarat had become high strung on the issue. When Resolution justifying reservations came up for discussion at the meeting, every word of it was subjected to minute scrutiny. Many representatives opined that the Resolution was hasty, and likely to evoke adverse reaction in a large section of the people. Swayamsevaks from Gujarat understandably were naturally were unhappy. I was intently listening to the discussions.
>
> In view of so much opposition from workers, I was worried and felt the resolution would not go through. Sarsanghachalak Balasaheb Deoras was calm but attentive at the meeting. After debate was over, the meeting broke for tea. When the meeting resumed, Balasaheb Deoras said, "I have heard the discussion in the meeting. I have understood that many amongst us are not in favour the of Resolution. I request you all to imagine yourself in the place of those for whom the Reservations are meant. Try to enter their minds and see the present condition of those of our brethren, who have been neglected for hundreds of years. Understand their feelings. Then only take your decision." After his speech, there was hardly any discussion, and the Resolution was passed. The Sangh had officially endorsed the Reservations.[95]

The social harmony predicated by social justice became the norm of the Sangh as it became a more powerful voice in the Hindu society. Ramesh Patange explains yet another such instance:

> In 1978 the Maharashtra Assembly passed a resolution approving the change in the name of the Marathwada University. The approval produced sharp and bitter reactions in Marathawada. Dalit localities were set on fire. The issue of the changing the name of the University soon turned into an issue about the very identity of dalits.... Later, I found that many Sangh activists in the Marathawada region wanted to support the change in the university's name. When I too became active in the change-of-name issue from the Samajik Samarasata Manch platform, Damu Anna told me a story. In 1978 Balasaheb Deoras was touring the Maharashtra Province. He had a programme in Sambhaji Nagar. In his discussion of the name issue, he said, "I think the change in the name should be endorsed. Those who oppose it are not right in their thinking." [96]

In 1980 Moreshwar Nilkanth Pingle, popularly known in Sangh circles as Moropant Pingle (after the famous seventeenth century Maratha strategist of Shivaji) took charge of the VHP. He had been in the Sangh under both Dr Hedgewar and 'Guruji' Golwalkar. He knew his fundamentals well. He had also faced emergency and seen the outcome of the Janata experiment. So, with Deoras as Sarsanghachalak and 'Moropant' Pingle as the organization head, VHP was entering into a new era of unexpected challenges.

The centuries old prejudices and inter-caste rivalries further deepened by vote bank politics were extracting their price from Hindu society. In 1981 a dusty village in southern South India, Meenakshipuram shot to fame when 180 families belonging to a Scheduled Community decided to convert to Islam. The immediate reason was to escape police harassment for this SC with respect to their conflict with the Backward Caste (BC) Thevar community and subsequent murder of two belonging to the BC community. Though the conflict and harassment emerged because of localized history of exploitation, atrocity and police harassment, the village SC families saw in converting to Islam a way out of police harassment. To this day, any financial inducements or charges by Hindutvaites are fiercely and indignantly rejected by the converts. More on this particular incident of conversion will be dealt with later in this chapter.

The conversions alarmed the nation in general. The stereotyping of Hinduism as the sole reason for caste-conflicts and caste-related oppression had resulted in a conversion that awakened the conscience of the nation, cutting across party lines. At the same time there was also delight in certain quarters of the polity at this apparently manifest failure of the Hindu society to resolve its problem thus leading to conversions. The Sangh took note of both these tendencies and also appealed to the Hindu society at large. In the year 1981 the annual all India functionaries meet of the RSS's Akhil Bharatiya Karyakari Mandal made the following resolution:

> It is also highly unfortunate that certain political leaders have sought to politicize the serious social problem and, in the process, provide moral justification for the conversion. Experience of past history amply bears out the fact that such conversions do not merely imply a simple change in way of worship, but destruction of national culture and sentiments, growth of separatist and secessionist tendencies and extraterritorial loyalties and communal animosities and flare-ups as well, which directly strike at the roots of our national integrity and security....The A.B.K.M welcomes the concern and disapproval expressed by the Prime Minister and Chief Minister of Tamil Nadu and a few other political leaders regarding such conversions....Finally, the A.B.K.M. calls upon the entire Hindu Society to bury deep the internal caste dissentions and the pernicious practice of untouchability

and stand up as one single homogenous family, so that the neglected and down-trodden sections will be assured of a place of equality, security and honor in the Hindu fold. And it heartily appreciates the initiative taken by several religious and social leaders and organizations in this direction and urges the people to whole-heartedly support their efforts.[97]

The organizations mentioned, apart from Arya Samaj were Tamil Nadu-based Sangh family organizations—Hindu Munnani (Hindu Front) and VHP. Based on the previous Udupi Conference model, they now contacted heads of traditional mutts in Tamil Nadu. A Hindu Unity Conference was organized on 14 July 1981. In this unity conference, prominent seers including Udupi Pejawar Mutt Swamil, Madurai Adheenam, Swami Anbukarasu of Tanjore, Swamy Guhananda of Sri Ramakrishna Tapovanam, etc., participated. The conference too proved to be historical. The *Indian Express* reported:

Unprecedented enthusiasm was witnessed in this sleepy hamlet nestling in the lush green Western Ghats valley as hundreds gathered here to watch the homa ritual conducted this morning to usher in a feeling of Hindu reawakening in this region. Later in the noon, the Swamijis participated in a mass bhojanam at the local Kali Amman temple. ***As many as 2000 Harijans partook of the lunch along with the religious heads, an event without precedence in the country.***[98] (emphasis not in the original)

A joint proclamation was made by the seers to the cheering public:

We, the religious leaders assembled today in Meenakshipuram, solemnly declare that our Vedas and Shastras have not mentioned untouchability in any form, anywhere but have propounded only complete brotherhood.... We therefore ardently appeal to all our Hindu brethren to individually and collectively throw out these evils lock, stock and barrel and strive to ensure equality and fraternity among all sections of our Hindu people. At the same time, we appeal to our Hindu-Harijan brothers to stand solidly in our Hindu Society as they have been doing so far, and remembering their forefathers and their noble examples join hands with us in wiping out the social perversions.[99]

This was followed by a mass contact programme called 'Gyana Rathams' (Wisdom Chariots) which carried the consecrated images of Goddess Amman and Skanda Murugan. These deities were taken inside the villages and people of all communities could worship them, thus breaking the caste barriers in a very explicit way. The programmes were quite a success in terms of creating social harmony and arresting conversions. From a Hindu Sanghatan point of view, this kind of unprecedented response by Hindu seers to such a serious proselytizing aggression which used the faultlines in the Hindu society was made possible by the efforts of Golwalkar in making the anti-untouchability resolution possible in 1969. Under the guidance of Deoras, the Sangh and its family organizations could chart the path forward and answer the related social challenges.

Subsequently in 1983 'Moropant' Pingle announced a mass contact programme called 'Ekatmata Yatra', which consisted of taking two uniting symbols of India in a van modified into a temple-like structure. The yatras launched were Mahadev Yatra (Haridwar to Kanyakumari), Pashupati Yatra (Kathmandu to Rameshwaram) and Kapil Rath Yatra (Gangasagar to Somnath). This massive programme contacted 1,50,000 villages and 60 million people.[100] Here too, social emancipation was an integral dimension.

Viswanathan Kakkan, the brother of the famous P. Kakkan—a freedom fighter who is to this day revered as the personification of honesty—was chosen for the prestigious task of carrying the sacred pots with Ganga water to the commencement of the Yatra. Two years later, reminiscing the event, Viswanathan Kakkan was visibly moved. Kakkan belonged to an SC and Viswanathan Kakkan had indeed felt transformed into a Bhagiratha who brought the Ganga to redeem his ancestors and benefit entire humanity.[101]

In 1983 the SSM had been launched on the birth anniversary of Dr Ambedkar. Dattopant Thengadi, who had worked closely with Dr Ambedkar as his election agent, inaugurated the Manch.

In 1987 the Maharashtra government published the collected works of Dr Ambedkar. It also contained the 'Riddles of Rama and Krishna' written by Dr Ambedkar. These writings were projected by certain elements as hurting the feeling of Hindus. The issue was initiated by one Madhav Gadkari, a close friend of Sharad Pawar. Soon the issue was fanned up as the Shiv Sena also took it up. They wanted a ban on 'riddles' because it hurt the Hindu sentiments. At this time, Ramesh Patange, who was in charge of the RSS front organization, SSM, had to deal with the issue of 'riddles'. His article took a stand that was not populist among the emotional Hindus who wanted to ban riddles. Both Patange and Sudhir Joglekar, the editor of the pro-Sangh *Tarun Bharat*, took the stand that it should not be banned. Later when asked about the official stand of the Sangh, Dattopant Thengdi answered that the stand expressed in Sri Patange's article was also the stand of the Sangh. The state secretary of the RSS for Maharashtra issued a press statement on 18 January 1988, in which he categorically stated that Hindus 'should not sentimentalize the Riddles issue and should look at it in the perspective of reason', adding that 'heavens are not going to fall if the chapter "Riddles of Rama and Krishna" remains in the fourth volume published by the State Government'.[102]

From Dr Hedgewar through Golwalkar to Deoras, an unitary process can be seen in the diverse works of the RSS.

Golwalkar had in his time as Sarsanghachalak achieved a grand renaissance event in Hindu history through the resolution against untouchability. He could achieve it through traditional Hindu heads.

For Deoras, a similar crowning achievement took place on 9 November 1989. It was the day the first stone was to be laid for the foundation of Sri Ram temple at Ayodhya. The person who had been chosen by the Sangh for this historical event was one of its full-time workers from Bihar—34-year-old Kameshwar Chaupal. Coming from a Scheduled Community, he was the one who would lay the first brick for the Ram temple. When Chaupal returned from Ayodhya to his village, the prominent Brahmin landlord invited Chaupal to his house. Chaupal was seated in the chair and all the members of the Brahmin family touched his feet. 'It was as if centuries of barriers had been broken. That day I cried like a child', he would later tell the press.[103]

The late 1980s and the early 1990s saw the Ram Janmabhoomi Ayodhya temple movement take the nation by storm. At the same time, SSM was organizing the rectification of another historical blunder in Hindu history. In 1992 a major campaign of the Manch started from Kalaram temple where Dr Ambedkar had held a satyagraha for temple entry in 1930. The priest then had opposed the temple entry. In 1992 the priest of the same temple, who also happened to be the grandson of the priest who denied temple entry, took the SC Hindus inside the temple and then apologized in the platform of the Manch for the sin his grandfather had committed.[104]

Post-Deoras Developments

In 1994 Deoras had handed over the responsibility of Sarsanghachalak to Sri Rajendra Singh—a physicist who had become a full-time Sangh worker. Meanwhile, the SSM process set in motion was transforming the nature of politics in the Hindi heartland.

In December 1992 the domes over the Ram Janmabhoomi at Ayodhya were demolished by Karsevaks. Following this event, an aggressive anti-Hindutva alliance between the pro-SC Bahujan Samaj Party (BSP) and largely feudal Samajwadi Party (SP) won the elections against the BJP in Uttar Pradesh. It was eulogized as the triumph of non-Brahminical secularism against Brahminical communism. But soon the alliance broke down because the SP did not want to make a 'Dalit woman' namely Mayawati the Chief Minister, though the parties had agreed for a rotational system. Then Mayawati was physically threatened and verbally abused. The BJP came to her rescue. She became the Chief Minister of Uttar Pradesh—the first SC woman to rule the largest state in the Hindi heartland as Chief Minister, and it was done with the support of the BJP. The alliance from the Hindutva point of view was not political opportunism. Rather it was a victory for the Hindutva way of social emancipation that went beyond narrow party boundaries.

Prof. Edmund Weber from the University of Frankfurt, a close observer of the Indian religious movements particularly with respect to Dalit questions, explains this aspect:

> That objective convergence of the Dalit and Hindutva interests will inevitably bring together both movements. Therefore, the newly (written in 1999) made political coalitions between the BJP and Dalit parties are very logical; they will continue even if the Dalit leaders influenced by the Congress ideology are very inconsistent in political affairs. Nevertheless, the egalisation of the Indian and particularly the Hindu society propagated by the Hindutvavadis and pre-formulated in Swami Vivekananda's socio-political programme of Brahmanisation including all castes and people is backed by the Dalit movement. [105]

Since then, Mayawati and her BSP had many fights with the BJP politically. What is significant from Sanghatan point of view is that the transformational nature of Hindutva is reflected in the slogan change of the BSP itself. '*Tilak, taraju aur talwar, inko maro joote char*', essentially meaning that the Brahmins, Vaishyas and Kshatriyas should be beaten with footwear by the Dalits.

But in 2007, the election slogan of BSP, referring to its symbol—the elephant, has changed and become '*Hathi nahin Ganesh hain, Brahma Vishnu Mahesh hain*', meaning 'Not just an elephant but it is Lord Ganesh, who is the embodiment of Brahma, Vishnu and Siva'—a clear transformation of positive Hindu assertion and a signal indicating the willingness for social harmony. In fact, it was with the latter slogan that the BSP came to power with absolute majority in 2007, defeating the BJP itself. But even in this defeat of the BJP, Hindutva won. In this connection one should attribute this transformational success to K. N. Govindacharya of the RSS, who was more an ideologue worker than a politician. He fell out with the BJP and was marginalized. But his so-called 'social engineering' and conscious enlargement of social base beyond the comfort of party politics changed the increasingly compartmentalized nature of identity politics that was conflict-oriented. In the largest historical perspective, he achieved a very important success for Hindutva as a nation building process.

In 2004 Dr Suraj Bhan, an RSS pracharak, became the chairperson of the

Scheduled Castes Commission. Even a Western RSS baiter such as Christophe Jaffrelot had no other way but to appreciate his work as the governor of Uttar Pradesh, where according to Jaffrelot, Bhan had shown 'great dynamism assessing the performance of schemes concerning Scheduled Castes such as reservations or the virtually unused SC/ST MLAs Forum in the state assembly'.[106]

In 2005 as chairperson of National Commission for Scheduled Castes, Suraj Bhan asked the religious authorities to remove all derogatory remarks against Dalits in the so-called scriptures like *Manusmriti*. He conveyed his wishes to the Shankaracharya of Sringeri himself that this detoxification of Hindu scriptures should be done. While orthodoxy expectedly claimed that there was not a single word of objection in the Hindu scripture, VHP President Ashok Singhal openly sided with Suraj Bhan and stated that *Manusmriti* did contain objectionable derogatory references towards Dalits.[107]

In 2006 noted Marathi poet and founder of Dalit Panthers, Namdeo Dhasal, shared the platform with K. S. Sudarshan, the fifth all-India leader of RSS. In the function Dhasal, a devoted follower of Dr Ambedkar stated: 'Nothing can be more wrong than any attempt to separate Buddhism, Jainism and Sikhism from the Hindu track.'[108]

In 2005 Milind Kamble had set up the Dalit Indian Chamber of Commerce and Industry (DICCI). He was an ABVP activist turned Dalit entrepreneur. DICCI came up with the slogan 'Be a job-giver and not a job-taker'. Kamble considers the MUDRA scheme of Prime Minister Narendra Modi as the best support system for this slogan and according to him the scheme had given Dalit entrepreneurs a great advantage. In 2018 after four years of Modi government, Kamble compared the way the anti-Hindutva UPA government and National Democratic Alliance (NDA) government under Modi, and made the following assessment:

> In the tenure of the Prime Minister Narendra Modi's government, maximum work has been done for the development of Dalits. From formulation of schemes in the the interest of the Dalits, and their effective implementation, the performance of the Narendra Modi government has been comparatively better than the government of former Prime Minister Manmohan Singh.[109]

Dr Mohan Bhagwat, the present Sarsanghachalak made the visit to Deekshabhumi and paying homage to Dr Ambedkar the first public event. Then he stated that 'the rebuilding of Bharat based on the ancient and lasting moral and spiritual values of this land was the dream of Dr Babasaheb Ambedkar and that he had come there to take inspiration from his work'.

Welcoming the RSS chief, the secretary of Dr Ambedkar Memorial Committee Shri Sadanand Phulzele, remembered the visit of the last Sarsanghachalak Shri K. S. Sudarshan and stated that such visits create a healthy goodwill amongst various sections of society.[110]

In September 2018 at a mega outreach programme, Dr Mohan Bhagwat further asserted that the Sangh was not only not against inter-caste marriages, but its voice was one of the earliest to support it. He said:

> First inter-caste marriage in Maharashtra took place in 1942, congratulatory messages poured in for them, including ones from Baba Saheb Ambedkar and Sri Guruji. Guruji had said "you aren't getting married only due to physical attraction. You want to convey that everyone is equal. If you do a survey of inter-caste marriages in India, maybe you will find the maximum percentage of those being swayamsevaks from Sangh".

The claim made by Dr Bhagwat is not an empty rhetoric.

Wherever in power, the Sanghatanist vision has been implemented by the state BJP governments as well. A good instance is provided by Haryana government under Manohar Lal Khattar, a former RSS pracharak. In a state where khap panchayats reign and where the problem of social stagnation seemed to weigh heavily against inter-caste marriages, the BJP has been silently bringing in a revolution which is consistent with the Hindu Sanghatan vision. In 2016 the BJP government increased its support grant for 'a Scheduled Caste boy or a girl of Haryana who marries a non-Scheduled Caste girl or boy' from ₹ 50,000 to ₹ 1,01,000.[111] In 2018 it was raised from ₹ 1,01,000 to ₹ 2,50,000. In an effort to further strengthen the inter-caste marriage in a gender-equal way, the incentive 'would be provided in the form of fixed deposits (FD) jointly in the name of the couple after getting the marriage registered with the competent authority.' [112]

In 2016–2017, 465 couples availed this government benefit, in which one of the spouses must belong to an SC or ST community. In 2017–2018 this number increased to 608. Of all the districts in Haryana, it was Karnal, the district of the Chief Minister which saw the highest number of such inter-caste marriages. Even the Communist Party affiliated 'All India Democratic Women's Association' (AIDWA) could not but praise the Chief Minister's scheme of increased financial assistance for inter-caste marriage couple, which is given the typical Sangh name, Chief Minister's 'Samajik Samrasta Antarjatiya Vivah Shagun Yojna.' [113] Thus, RSS could break important social barriers in the society with minimal or no violence and maximizing social harmony.

All Hindus to be Priests in Temples: Sangh Contribution

As far back as 1969, Golwalkar had stated during one of his interactions in Kerala that all Hindus, particularly those belonging to the marginalized sections of the society should not be discriminated against.

Kerala already has a non-Sangh pre-Sangh Hindutva heritage through Sri Chattampi Swami, Sri Narayana Guru and Sri Ayyan Kali. When in Kerala, Swami Vivekananda visited and interacted with Sri Chattampi Swami. Swami Vivekananda was a wandering monk then in 1892. Sri Chattampi Swami (1853–1924), a strong Advaitin of Sankara school, was also against institutionalized birth-based discriminations. He had written a book on the authority of Vedas rejecting the birth based jati authority on the sacred texts. He had also written a book on the rejection of Christianity. Swami Vivekananda and Sri Chattampi Swami had their entire conversation in Sanskrit. Sri Chattampi Swami had written a book titled *Vedadhikara Nirupanam* (*Proof on Vedic Authority*, 1893). In this he established through proof from Vedas and Upanishads how all communities have the right to study Vedas and practice rituals. He also rejected the claims of Vedas being *apourusheyam* or not man-made. He showed that the Vedic seers came not just from priestly clans but from all walks of life. In continuation of this Vedic social and spiritual reality, he wanted all communities to become temple priests and adept in Vedic literature. Sri Narayana Guru was guided by him in advanced Tantric systems of puja, and his other disciple Neelakanta wrote *Devarchana Paddhathi* (*Protocols for Worshipping the Divine*) and *Achara Paddhathi* (*Protocols for Ritual Purity*).[114] It should be remembered here that Sri Chattampi Swami was strongly against Christian proselytizing, and he also wrote a strong renunciation of Christianity titled *Christu Matha Chethanam* (1884).

The RSS through its work in Kerala became the natural inheritor of the legacy and vision of Sri Chattampi Swami. In 1983, the centenary year of Sri Narayana Guru, Vishal Hindu Sammelan was organized by the RSS in Ernakulam. The chief tantrik of the main puja conducted in the *sammelan* was an Ezhava (a non-Brahmin by birth) and his assistant was a Namboodri (Brahmin by birth). The same year saw the founding of the Thanthra Vidya Peedham (TVP) by senior pracharak of the RSS Madhavanji, along with eminent Vedic scholars. Since then, TVP has been an integral part of the sociocultural movement that has today culminated in appointment of priests from all Hindu communities without any discrimination. The Peetham trains youngsters in all traditional knowledge domains to become qualified priests in Kerala irrespective of their caste. In a public ceremony the certificates were given to the students trained in TVP by none other than then junior acharya of Kanchi Sri Jayendra Saraswati.[115] Roping in the head of an orthodox monastery in launching a programme that many would feel as radical, is a typical Sangh strategy that aims at harmony-oriented social reform rather than create conflict in the name of social reform.

When the NDA-I (1998/1999–2004) was in power, it tried to implement this 'Kerala model' of socio-spiritual unification all over India. The University Grants Commission (UGC) introduced 'Karma Kand' courses, which could be studied by any student irrespective of community, to become a certified priest. In the northern states, where social stagnation has resulted in caste atrocities and deep fractures, UGC-certified priests cutting across community lines would have been a phenomenal aid to social harmony. Interestingly, the move was opposed tooth and nail by Marxists and so-called progressives. Nevertheless, the *paurohitya* (priesthood) course launched by Sanskrit Sansthan in Uttar Pradesh did become a success. The priest training course was given a support grant of ₹ 14 lakh by the Human Resources Development ministry under Dr Murli Manohar Joshi. It is interesting to note that all these attempts to democratize priesthood had happened under the NDA rule and were not actively pursued by the succeeding governments belonging to the so-called 'progressive parties.

In 2006 RSS magazine *Panchajanya* announced in its editorial that trained priests from Scheduled Communities should be appointed as priests in all 'major temples in the country'. The editorial announced that 'the time has come to strengthen Hindu unity and ensure that along with those priests who are born Brahmins, Dalits and other backward classes are trained and made priests'.[116]

In 2008, RSS leader K. S. Sudarshan graced a historically important function in Gaya, Bihar of appointing a Dalit as the chief priest at the Jagannath temple of Gaya. The function was attended by Buddhist monks from the Mahabodhi temple.[117]

In 2013 when Nair Service Society (NSS) of Kerala made a call for Hindus of their own caste to be given opportunity to be trained for priesthood, the RSS outfit 'Hindu Aikya Vedi' supported the call and wanted it to be broadened to include all *jatis*. Well known veteran RSS leader of Kerala Kummanam Rajesekharan categorically stated that priesthood should not be determined by birth: 'Sound knowledge and proper training to conduct the rituals should be the criteria to become a priest and not the caste. The NSS calling for Nair priests should also welcome other sections into their temples.'[118] In 2017 the administration board for Kerala's state-controlled temples, Travancore Devaswom Board (TDB), recruited six priests from the Scheduled Communities and 36 others from OBC. Though typically hyped as leftist achievement in 2017, the phenomenon is neither new to Kerala nor does it depend on a particular political dispensation in power. In 2012 TDB had filled up 50 of the 100 posts for priests with non-Brahmins. What was common to both 2012 and 2017 is the presence of TVP in the interview board selecting the priests.

With remarkable consistency the Sangh family tries to adapt its 'Kerala model' in other states where it is in power. In North India where colonial impoverishment has resulted in rigidity of birth based social hierarchies and has increased social stagnation, the fragmented Hindu society has been used by Nehruvian polity as separate vote banks. Playing on the mutual fears and inevitable social conflicts the non-BJP parties have built what is called a vote-bank politics. The Sangh battles these division through harmonious implementation of the 'Kerala model'. At times it has limited success and even faces opposition from what is often traditionally considered as its own 'client base'. In April 2017 the BJP government in Madhya Pradesh announced commencement from July that years onward a 'Hindu Purohityam' course through the Government-run Maharshi Patanjali Sanskrit Sansthan. Press Trust of India (PTI) further reports of opposition from a section of orthodoxy 'who had staged a protest in May last year when the government had proposed to make priests from Scheduled Caste community'.[119] Such measures could even affect the BJP electorally. When the BJP lost in a very narrow manner in 2018 state elections in Madhya Pradesh, some 'upper caste' social media handles did flaunt the defeat as because of the 'upper castes' moving away from the BJP because of its pro-social justice policies.

Yet Modi government seems to be ready to take the next very important move for the social emancipation of Hindu society which Dr Ambedkar envisioned as necessary in order to 'succeed in saving Hinduism' in his undelivered address 'Annihilation of Caste', which was later published as a book in 1936:

> Every person who professes to be a Hindu must be eligible for being a priest. It should be provided by law that no Hindu shall be entitled to be a priest unless he has passed an examination prescribed by the state, and holds a *sanad* (order) from the state permitting him to practice....It should be welcomed even by the Arya Samajists, because this is merely an application of their own doctrine of *guna-karma*.[120]

In 2020 the Narendra Modi government in its second term has planned similar 'skill-based training programme for pandits and pujaris (Hindu priests)' under the Ministry of Skill Development and Entrepreneurship. An official working on this plan speaking to a news portal informed that 'the government will not only create more employment opportunities, but also formalise this unorganised sector'. The priest training course will be a format-based one 'designed to meet the standards of the National Skills Qualification Framework, a competency-based framework that organises all qualifications according to levels of knowledge, skill and aptitude'. The system is very similar to the one envisioned by Dr Ambedkar. In its present form the course had been designed by Rajaram Shukla, vice-chancellor of Varanasi's Sampurnanand Sanskrit Vishwavidyalaya, who proposed it to the ministry, and it has been well-received.[121] When this becomes a reality it would have become the natural and logical next major milestone in Hindu social emancipation history after the 1969 Udupi resolution against untouchability and birth-based discriminations.

The Challenge of Social Change: Devendrakula Vellalar and the RSS

The infamous 1981 Meenakshipuram conversion has been already seen before. The standard narrative since has been that in order to escape the oppression and humiliation by caste Hindus, Dalits embraced the egalitarian Islam or the lure of egalitarianism promised by Islamists. But what went unnoticed by almost all national newspapers and even the Hindu Sanghatanists was another event that happened later the same year for the SC community in another part of the same state, Tamil Nadu.

A few hundred kilometres away from Meenakshipuram in Perur of Coimbatore, invitations were sent out to all communities in the village and vicinity for the annual chariot festival for Siva Pateeswara. The invitation proudly proclaimed the centrality of the very same community (whose members got converted in Meenakshipuram), to the festival through its own traditional monastery. The chords of the grand ceremonial chariot carrying Siva and Parvati get first pulled by the community leaders of Devendrakula Vellalars and then the other communities follow their lead and the chariot is pulled.

That in an important Hindu Saivaite centre the very same community known by the press as 'Dalit' or 'broken community' was accorded the highest sacred adoration by Hinduism was completely missed by the media—both national and local. They went on to describe the conversion, which happened more because of alleged police harassment owing to strained Thevar and Devendrar community relations. The two communities were engaged in a conflict, vying for limited resources and power. Vote bank politics also played its part. The police harassed an SC youth in a murder case and to escape harassment, the villagers decided to use conversion as a shield.

There have been allegations of Islamists using petro-dollars, an allegation vehemently and indignantly rejected by the converts then as well as now. However, it was actually a London-based Islamic organization called the Islamic Cultural Centre which spilled the beans when it linked the SC conversion to an agricultural project worth $50,000 and it was then also reported by the *Arab Times* of Kuwait. Then Prime Minister Indira Gandhi, herself a Nehruvian, a pro-Soviet and self-declared secular quasi socialist, expressed concerns about foreign money playing a role in these conversions: 'Enormous amounts of Arab money are coming in. And they (the Arabs) made it a conscious effort to convert the very poor, mostly Harijans.'[122]

So, the real problem was the conflict between the SC and the specific backward caste Thevar community in that area. The conflict in a way goes back to the time of the British who played on inter-community conflicts, changing those conflicts into long lasting rivalry by cunningly increasing the number of monotheists in the police force in specific villages. The Dravida Munnetra Kazhagam or DMK, which ruled Tamil Nadu previously, had further announced such communal appointments, this time favouring the Thevar community members in the police force as one of its achievements.

This harassment and marginalization of the Devendrakula Vellalar in Meenakshipuram in the 1970s and 1981 were thus more localized. The police played a partisan role and the general narrative of associating caste problems with Hinduism made a section of the villagers opt for conversion to Islam, which was also used by pan-Islamist forces inside and outside India. Still the myth persists that the converted members did so because they were the oppressed Dalits—discriminated by the Hindu religion and society for millennia. In reality, the victim narrative was perpetuated by a combined vicious cycle of vote bank and reservation politics. Ultimately, it resulted in the community being lured by non-Hindu proselytizers, thus threatening to cut them off completely from their ancestral culture.

Today there has been a demand from a significant section of the society to take the community out of the SC list and change its name to its original traditional name—Devendrakula Vellalar has come as a great show of strength for Hindu unity. The enlightened Hindu society in Tamil Nadu, irrespective of caste affiliations, has welcomed this social renaissance. However, there are powerful 'Break the Hindu Society' forces also trying to scuttle his efforts. They have been opposing this demand saying the claim of the 'Vellalar' title by the Devendrakula Vellalars is 'inappropriate'.

Devendrakula Vellalars or Mallars were derisively called Pallar by the socially stagnant sections of society. It should be remembered that during the pre-colonial period in Tamil Nadu, the Devendrakula Vellalar community managed and administered one of the most precious resources needed for agriculture—water. The traditional literary genre of the community called 'Pallu' is known for its melody and poetic richness, not to mention the spiritual values and historical data embedded and enshrined in them. None other than Subramanya Bharati used this genre to declare the independence of India. The highly regarded social status of this community can be gauged by the fact that they were honoured during the temple tank festival in Madurai. Sri Ma. Thangaraj in his book *Thevendrakula Vellalar: Spiritual Heritage* notes the following:

> In Madurai, the temple city of Tamil Nadu, a pond was created by Thirumalai Naikkar at Anuppanadi. From that time every year during Thai Poosam (in January), pond festival is conducted. On the first day, Goddess Meenakshi comes there for the harvesting of the fields, which get irrigation from the first channel of the irrigation network of the Kirudumal river near Chinthamani. These first fields are given by the traditional authority of Meenakshi Amman temple to 'Madai Kudumar' clan of Thevendrakula Vellalar. The name means that they are the family managing the inlet and outlet of the irrigation network and hence masters in integrated water management. Next day during the sacred raft festival in the temple tank, Thevendrakula Vellalar community family of "Oor Kudumban" is ceremonially invited by traditional temple authorities. The Thevendrakula Vellalar family patriarch gets the traditional crowning with sacred silk-white yellow cloth—Parivattam.

Among the Vellalar communities of Tamil Nadu, there is a famous Purana detailing their Puranic history called *Marabala Purana* or *Vellala Purana*. Though written in 1907 by Mahavidwan Kandaswamy Kavirayar, it is considered to contain valuable historic information which has come down from previous centuries. In this literature, the poet narrates the story of the Puranic forefather of Vellalars or the farming communities in Tamil Nadu as having arisen from the *jada-makuda* or the matted hair-crown of Siva. This patriarch hero seeks the hand of the daughter of Devendra. However, to prove his Deva nature, Marabalan had to take a bath in the fire, which he does. Then Indra gives the title of 'Deva' to his heirs. The Purana says that Marabala married both the daughters of Devendra and Kubera.

One can decode the Puranic language here easily and map it to historical processes. Devendra controls the water through rain. Kubera is identified with accumulation of wealth. While there are many Vellalar subgroups with names like Kongu Vellalar, Nanchil Vellalar (identifying with the region), Saiva Vellalar (identifying with spiritual tradition), Karkatha Vellalar (in which community was born Meikandar the great Saiva Siddhanta seer), the word 'Deva' is used only by Devendrakula Vellalar. In terms of their occupation too Devendrakula Vellalar are related to water management and hence rains (associated with Indra), thus validating the Puranic information. In many of their 'Pallus', whenever there was a need for rain, the Devendrakula Vellalar could communicate with Devendra and bring rain.

The association of Mallar or Devendrakula Vellalar with agriculture is also expressed in the local Hindu religious narratives of Tamil Nadu. According to tradition, when Sundarar one of the four Nayanmars, came to Perur, Siva appeared in the form of a Mallar farmer and Parvati was transplanting a rice sapling helping Her husband, while Murugan and Ganesha were playing as Mallar children. To this day this vision given to Sundarar is reenacted in Perur Pateeswara temple. A Devendrakula Vellalar couple are venerated as Siva and Parvati, and they perform the ritual reenactment of the Sundarar episode.

Now, the question arises as to how then did they become suppressed and even branded as 'Dalits', etc. against which they are right now fighting? Prof. Mike Davis in his in-depth and exhaustive study of the colonial famines points out how the colonial administrators and policy makers systematically destroyed the irrigation infrastructure of Hindustan. Under British administration, the well-being of traditional water bodies and irrigation system was ignored, and they were progressively replaced by a canal system.

Prof. Davis writes:

> Finally, in most of India, water had always been a communally managed common resource. Generally, there was no notion of selling titles to land and its water resources. In British common law as witlessly applied to India, however, water rights went along with land titles as private property. "In effect," as David Hardiman emphasizes, "this meant that only those who owned land had a right to the water on it. In this way, all those who did not hold colonial land-deeds were excluded from access to water ... [leading to] the collapse of traditional water management structures."

On the authority of David Mosse and Ludden, Davis explains further:

> Likewise, in the districts of the Madras Deccan, the development of private property rights and the dissolution of landowning collectivities...destroyed the investment capacity of mirasidar assemblies altogether. British rule, in various ways, emancipated local political chiefs and big men from the obligation to invest in community resources and public institutions such as tank systems. The shortfall was not made good by the government's own public works.

The meteoric fall of Devendrakula Vellalars should be traced to this period. Along with their fall came the famines that killed millions of Indians. Traditional Dharmic system of reciprocal relations and responsibilities gave way to the rise of landowning castes who stood to gain not only social status as feudal landowners but also freedom from the responsibilities to fellow communities. Those communities who proudly call themselves 'Vellalar' today must look into this colonial baggage that their assumed and perceived privileged position in today's society carries.

It is indeed ironic if one looks at the way we have been taught history: A caste-ridden Hindu society dictated by Brahminical Hindu religion kept the SCs or Dalits oppressed. The enlightened British rule and those Indians enlightened by the British democratic value system started liberating the oppressed Dalits. It is this false narrative that has shaped many young minds of today.

In reality, what history really reveals is that the so-called 'Dalits' ('broken people') were not broken at all, but have been proud contributors to the material, cultural as well as spiritual prosperity and heritage of this nation. It was the colonial administration and our own narrow vested interests colluding with the colonial regime, which created the SCs, and the blame was unethically and comfortably shifted to Hinduism and the ever evasive 'Brahminism'. Today, these communities which had been deprived of their rightful place are rejecting the victim narrative imposed on them and reasserting their rights in our cultural, social and economic domains.

The voices from within this community to regain their position, which is also the sociocultural and hence naturally sociopolitical emancipation, has been taken up by Dr Krishnasamy, who is one of the most visible leaders of the community, particularly in northern Tamil Nadu. But his battle for landless labourers in the estates of southern Tamil Nadu had earned him a lot of respect. He was also a brilliant physician achieving some major successes in surgeries in Coimbatore district before he embarked upon social activism and politics. In June 2019, Dr Krishnasamy participated as a special invitee in the RSS function held at Nagpur.

Yet another important leader of the community is Sri John Pandiyan from southern Tamil Nadu, who also accepts the Hindutva stand of all Indians being culturally Hindus. He considers his being instrumental in securing to the community the lost 'Parivattam' respect in the Pazhani temples as an important achievement. Though both the leaders may have conflict of interests with respect to polity, they both are united in their voice of them being part and parcel of Hindu society and that their reclamation of their justified and harmonious place for their community is actually in the template of Sanatana Dharma.

That all these aspects of this community were hidden, and a localized conflict was conflated to essentialize Hinduism and justify a conversion in which money had definitely played a role is telling regarding the stereotypes perpetuated at various levels in Indian society. That today the RSS is seen by the very same community leaders as one of the major hopes in restoring the just place of the community is also a victory to the harmony-oriented approach of the Sangh workers in the ground.

Washing the Feet of Sanitary Workers

In February 2019, Narendra Damodardas Modi, the 14th and current Prime Minister of India, had the sanitary and hygiene workers place their feet on a tray and washed them with his hands. He called them 'Karma Yogis'. He in his characteristic way, sent a strong signal to the entire Indian society.[123] And that is no simple message.

The power of the image of the Prime Minister is bound to demolish domes of prejudices deep seated in the collective society colonized in its mind for a thousand years. And then he spoke about *sanskars*. In a response to a BJP corporator from Pune in Maharashtra during a video conference, Modi clarified that the act was not political but that it was sanskar.[124] The use of the term 'sanskar' is important here. This term is quite central to RSS psychology as we have seen earlier with respect to the teachers and students in the Sangh-run schools. In traditional Hinduism, it essentially means inculcating values at young ages mainly through rituals for the spiritual advancement of the child. In the Sangh worldview, sanskars take on its broadest meaning and involve inculcation of values considered positive, for national, cultural and individual advancement. So, when the PM talked about washing the feet of sanitary workers as his sanskar, he essentially meant his shakha-imbibed sanskar and it does have its own historical and cultural context.

The ugly prejudices not only exist against sanitary workers in India, but they are reinforced. For example, in a blockbuster comedy movie in Tamil Nadu when the hero comes to know that the original job of the comedian in Dubai was cleaning toilets, he asks him to move away as he could still smell the bad odour. Incidentally, this 'comedy' scene which encouraged untouchability and prejudice against sanitary workers was enjoyed by the entire state and is still popular on YouTube. Not a single film critic saw this 'comedy' through the eyes of the child of a sanitary worker, whom the film degraded. This is just one instance.

Modi has been systematically working to demolish this mindset. The values that the RSS promotes through its shakhas are quite contrary to such sanskars. This is because of the deep anchorage that the Sangh has with Sri Ramakrishna-Vivekananda Vedanta. In India, social stagnation, like in all pre-modern and colonized civilizations, had marginalized sections of fellow human beings and had assigned to them certain jobs generally considered defiled. Sanitary and hygiene workers were considered untouchable. When Hindu renaissance began in the modern age, it happened not through the British educated elite but through the so-called illiterate but spiritually rooted Gurus.

One such was Sri Ramakrishna Paramahansa born as Gadhadhara. This illiterate Kali temple priest took up, as part of his spiritual sadhana, cleaning with his head the night soil of a person considered as untouchable. He chose for this a sanitary worker who had been cleaning the toilets in and around the Kali temple complex where Sri Ramakrishna worked as the temple priest.[125] While doing this he prayed that the goddess remove all notions of superiority and inferiority both social as well as individual. 'Make me a servant of all' was his prayer when he did this sadhana.[126] Later, his illustrious disciple, Swami Vivekananda, spoke of a new India arising 'out of the peasants' cottage, grasping the plough; out of the huts of the fisherman, the cobbler and the sweeper'.[127]

In 1918 in the princely state of Indore, the prince honoured the polymath Patrick Geddes for battling the plague that was ravaging Indore. To improve the sanitary conditions of the city, Geddes decided to use the annual Deepavali pageantry to propagate values of hygiene. Ram killed the Ravana of unhygienic conditions. This was followed by the sanitary workers proceeding in richly decorated chariots, wearing turbans like the other high officials of Indore.

The Mayor of Indore was happy, and what he told Geddes, recorded by him, are words that would deeply shame us as Indians. He said that it was a marvellous idea but as a Brahmin he himself could not do it, but Geddes could, as he had no problem with the local taboos as a European. The mayor ended his words of gratitude to Geddes thus, '...you have treated them as men, as equals'.[128] It should be noted that the Indophilia of Geddes itself was triggered by the influence of Swami Vivekananda and Sister Nivedita. Yet the truth of the words he spoke surely makes us all cringe in shame.

Mahatma Gandhi, though initially wedded to the idea of caste by birth, was gradually transformed by his interactions with the seers of Ramakrishna-Vivekananda Vedanta. He came to accept Varna by worth rather than birth. Nevertheless, he was always against untouchability. He insisted that all his followers and companions clean their own toilets, a task which was then done manually by hygiene workers. When RSS was created by Dr Hedgewar, in its training camps, the approach to remove the notion of defilement and pollution was taken further. The Swayamsevaks in the camps are given tasks alternating between preparing food and cleaning of toilets. This aspect has already been discussed in the section dealing with the Andersen and Damle book on the RSS. So, here the Swayamsevak, who cleaned the toilets of everyone in the camp the previous day, would be preparing food for everyone the next day. Andersen and Damle have pointed out in both their books on the RSS that this was meant to 'undermine notions of purity and pollution associated with various kinds of works in the many layers of Hindu caste hierarchy'.

Swami Chidbhavananda (1898–1985), a Ramakrishna-Vivekananda Vedanta monk and an important educationist as well as institution builder in Tamil Nadu, was one of the earliest personalities to question Mahatma Gandhi's notion of birth-based Varna system. In his educational institutions, he emphasized that the worship hall, puja room, kitchen and toilets should be kept clean with the same dedication. Swami Chidbhavananda himself had got into the septic tank to clean it when there was shortage of people. Swami, who was initially apprehensive about the Sangh, later became a strong supporter and regularly allowed Sangh camps to be conducted in his institutions. He also used to address the RSS cadre.

Earlier it was the Jan Sangh, when it was in power in Udupi municipality, made manual scavenging illegal. Modi had been nurtured through the RSS shakhas and camps. Naturally, when he meant sanskars he meant these deep valued embedded in the shakhas.

In 2016 the Modi government appointed Dr Bindheswar Pathak, the founder of Sulabh Foundation, also called the 'toilet man of India', as the brand ambassador for Swachh Rail Mission. Dr Pathak had not only spearheaded the cost-effective toilet movement in India for the last four decades, but he had also fought against the untouchability associated with sanitary service providers. He had broken the caste taboo.

Sulabh International also employs Brahmin caste labourers as well in their Sulabh toilets. According to journalist Francois Gautier, all the 50 Sulabh public toilets in Delhi are cleaned and maintained by Brahmins with five to six of them working in each of these toilets. That the Modi government made Dr Pathak its brand ambassador for the Clean India mission speaks volumes about the value system embedded in this government.

In June 2017, the *mygov.in* portal asked the citizens to publish photographs of them with the manual workers around them, and in response, many published photos with sanitary workers. Thus, Modi has been fighting against perverted notions that certain occupations are demeaning. In Modi's words:

> I have been to Kumbh in Uttar Pradesh, which was widely appreciated for its cleanliness. Around 22 crore people visited the Kumbh. It led me to think about the efforts put in by the sanitation workers and I decided to express my gratitude towards them by cleaning their feet. When people from the administration asked me how I want to perform the house warming of my official residence, I had plainly asked them to get someone who works as a class four employee in the government. They found a Dalit person, and I placed the "kalash" in his daughter's hands. It is part of culture, my sanskar.[129]

And these words come from the shakha sanskar which Modi had inherited from the RSS.

Sangh Intellectualism: Oxymoron or Cinderella?

One of the persistent stereotypes and a strong negative caricature about the Sangh is that it is bereft of any intellectual activity. While Hindutva as a whole is considered as a movement incapable of producing any good intellectual activity leave alone a scholarly narrative by the left, there is a new brand of 'internet Kshatriyas' who though sympathetic to Hindutva cause in general, look down upon the Sangh as incapable any intellectual ability. Some important Hindutva thinkers like Sita Ram Goel and more vehemently Dr Koenraad Elst, both having made enormous contribution to Hindutva have also expressed this view. Dr Elst states this across decades with remarkable consistency:

> Dr Hedgewar's successor Madhav Sadashiv Golwalkar, *Sarsanghachalak* in 1940–73, though having worked as a university teacher in Biology, despised intellectual pursuits. When he saw RSS people reading books or newspapers, he would ask them if they had "useful to do for the Sangh?" (testified by K. R. Malkani, interview, December 1990). When I mention this to RSS activists , they protest that there are many doctors, engineers and scientists in the RSS, and some of them recount their personal experience that Golwalkar had encouraged them in their studies (interview with US-based child psychiatrist Dr Manohar Shinde, 1993)....Golwalkar's approach to academics was (and the RSS approach still is) status-oriented rather than thought-oriented.[130]

That was in 2001. Then again when defending Golwalkar against historian Ramachandra Guha, Dr Elst writes in 2016:

> Indeed, Golwalkar himself was emphatically anti-bookish and berated his volunteers when they were caught "idling" by reading a book. More than anyone else, he is responsible for the RSS's anti-intellectual orientation, which has been very consequential: (1) a complete absence from the public debate; (2) a propensity to make fools of themselves with fantastic claims, e.g. that "ancient Indians had airplanes", as if India's real contributions to science and technology weren't good enough; (3) a complete passivity when Nehruvians and Marxists moved in to monopolize the cultural and educational sphere; and (4) to really drive the negative implications home, an utter inability to give a credible defence of Golwalkar's own books.[131]

At the surface this looks quite objectively correct. Again, look inside the way the Sangh's cerebral heritage does not sustain this pet stereotype of Sangh-critics, both haters as well-wishers of a 'Sanghi' as nothing more than a non-English speaking riffraff in an outdated clownish military uniform of khaki shorts.

The Sangh as an organization and movement never had state patronage in most of the seven decades of independent India. With whatever resources it had, it needed to work at different levels—from tribal welfare to running medical and educational services to labour union to ground zero work throughout India. They had limited human resources as full-time workers and even more limited economic resources. Yet with all these they did succeed in creating an alternative vision for India's development rooted in Hind culture and history. And that cannot be easily discounted.

While one is not able to ascertain in what context M. S. Golwalkar's comment on reading a book as a waste of time was uttered, that singular incident could not be made to define the entire Sangh or even Golwalkar's attitude towards intellectual pursuits. Ashok Mitra, a Communist leader [Communist Party of India Marxist, CPI(M)] and former Finance Minister of West Bengal had recorded an incident of meeting Golwalkar during a train journey in 1966, and this is how he ends it:

> The train started. It was getting dark. I took a reading material from the bag and started to read. Golwalkar started reading too. I thought that RSS chief, the vanguard of Dharma, would pick up a religious text or a hardcore Vedanta text. But I got one more surprise: He was reading an American novel, the latest one by Henry Miller. I do not hide, that moment my respects to Golwalkar increased many-fold. Perhaps a die-hard swayamsevak might take me to killing field for revealing this.

In fact, the last line is the typical Sanghi-stereotyping. The truth is the same could be said about many of the Sangh leaders who were contemporaries and subordinates of Golwalkar. Dr Rajendra Singh, the fourth Sarsanghachalak of the RSS, in his reminiscence of Pandit Deendayal said this:

> He was a voracious reader. In spite of his busy programmes and crowded engagement, he found time to read the latest literature. He preferred to travel by passenger trains, so as to get more time for studying during journey.[132]

More interesting is another incident narrated by the senior RSS worker Laxman Rao Bhide regarding Deendayal Upadhyaya (referred here as Panditji):

> At Nagpur meeting, a topic was under discussion. There are always points of

> difference in discussions, so the then Sarkaryavah Bhaiyaji Dani and Panditji were on the opposite sides. Panditji produced one argument after another and contradicted the opposite side. All were happily convinced of Panditji's power of debate, even Bhaiyaji was so. But, all of a sudden Bhaiyaji had a brain wave. 'Panditji, you please now argue the other side of the picture too. "Everyone was swept by this clever move....Shri Guruji was also there, and he was also curious. Panditji accepted the challenge. He began, 'But the other side of the picture is ...'" and he argued the opposite case carrying equal conviction.[133]

The above incident explodes some of the stereotypes about the Sangh and also Golwalkar. Golwalkar was not a person who was averse to intellectual debates and discussions. In fact, he had encouraged such debates and dialogues inside the Sangh. He did not see them as futile or waste of time, as one would expect an anti-intellectual head of a highly disciplined cadre-based organization as Golwalkar and Sangh had been depicted.

Dattopant Thengadi too was also an avid reader. He was well aware of the various ideological streams within Marxism as well as how the modern physics was creating a paradigm shift. In fact, he was perhaps one of a very few social activists in India who understood and had referred to this aspect. Another RSS full-time worker of Golwalkar period whose love for books is well known in Sangh circles was H. V. Sheshadri (1926–2005). A study of their works shows that they were well versed in modern thoughts. But what distinguishes these Sangh veterans from the leftist intellectuals is that the Sangh intellectuals never stayed 'intellectuals' but were engaged in working at ground zero. They built human institutions with no State support—in fact despite State opposition and negative propaganda most of the times.

As already seen 'Balasaheb' Deoras too was well versed in political philosophies including the works of Dr Ambedkar so much so that he could zero in precisely the positive and holistic nature of his criticism of Hindu society rather than indulge in superficial use of Dr Ambedkar either to denigrate Hinduism or just to attack Islamist politics using his book, *Thoughts on Pakistan*.

So, to summarily dismiss both Golwalkar and the Sangh as anti-intellectual or as institutionally incapable of creating an intellectual narrative, based on a singular incident (whose context is unknown) is, to say the least, prejudiced. But with Dr Koenraad Elst this misconception was more because of concern for Hindutva movement (and because of the anti-Sangh bias he had inherited from him mentor Sita Ram Goel). With the most anti-Sangh 'intellectuals' it is often mere stereotyping with intentional prejudice.

Balraj Madhok (1920–2016) and Indianization

As seen earlier in the section on the national flag and the RSS, Balraj Madhok was a veteran soldier of the Sangh from one of its toughest battlegrounds, Jammu and Kashmir. He was one of the trio along with Pandit Deendayal Upadhyaya and Atal Bihari Vajpayee, who prepared the preliminary ideological documentary on the 'principles and policy' of the then budding Bharatiya Jan Sangh (BJS) in 1964 at the National Session of BJS conducted at Vijayawada, Andhra Pradesh. The year 1966–1967 saw the ascendancy of Madhok as the president of BJS. Political analyst and author Craig Baxter who wrote the 'biography' of BJS in 1969 noted that to that day 'the Madhok presidency was the most active and widely reported in the party up to that time' and that 'the president travelled extensively and expressed his views publicly on every issue' which in turn 'were given a prominence in the press unprecedented for a Jana Sangh leader'.[134] Even as the internal dynamics and developments within the BJS increasingly sidelined and embittered Madhok eventually leading to his expulsion and he himself resorting to a bizarre conspiracy theory, his 'Indianization' remains a seminal contribution in the political thought process of Indian polity. One can say that in its own way it became the seed thought for what Lal Krishna Advani (who would become the President of Bharatiya Janata Party) popularized later as 'cultural nationalism'.

Madhok traces the origin of the concept of 'Indianization' to the resolution passed under the Presidentship of late Dr Shyama Prasad Mukherjee at the Kanpur session of BJS in December 1952. The resolution spoke about the need to emphasize and propagate among Indian people 'the concept of the whole of India and all its people irrespective of their way of worship, sect or region being one nation with one culture'.[135]

According to Madhok, the 'Indianness of a man or a woman is something which is both acquired and inherited'. He explains this with instances from recent Indian history:

> It is not the birth in India but the Indianness of a man which makes him an Indian, This Indianness of a man is not determined by one's colour, caste, language, way of worship or political party. It is determined by the mental attitude towards India and all that is distinctive about her as a nation....People like Mrs. Annie Besant, Sister Nivedita and Mr. Stokes became better Indians and did more for India in our own times than most of those born in India did, even though they had been born and nurtured outside India....Indianness of a man or a woman is something which is both acquired and inherited.[136]

The work, though mere 120 pages, contained in it a framework that is uniquely Hindu in dealing with religious and linguistic diversity. The way Madhok deals with the Nehruvian establishment view of Indian culture as 'composite culture' is quite significant. While Prof. Madhok rejects the term 'composite culture', he does not argue for a 'pure culture'. He recognizes the fact that like pure race, pure culture is only a myth and in that way every culture in the world is a composite culture. Yet the term is used in India only to reject the unique Indian nature that underlies the culture of India and hence it has become, according to him, a meaningless sophistry meant to indulge in self-negation.

> Talk of pure culture is as much a myth as that of a pure race. In course of history, culture also grows through assimilation of various currents. In that sense every culture of the world is a composite culture.... But still no country calls its culture a composite culture because that militates against the unity of the nation. In India the word composite culture was first used by Mr. Jinnah in support of his two-nation theory. There is only one Indian culture which is common to all Indians....To call Indian culture a composite culture, or a mixture of Hindu and Muslim cultures is as nonsensical as to call Ganga water as Ganga-Jamuna water at Prayag and Ganga-Gandak water at Patna. This culture and tradition of India which has grown and got enriched in course of history and which has many hues and facets in keeping with the geographical and linguistic diversities, which are essential part of the Indian pattern, constitute the soul of India.[137]

That Jinnah first used the term composite culture is a questionable claim. As early as 1908 we find this in the nationalist magazine *Bande Mataram* founded by Bipin Chandra Pal then under the editorship of Aurobindo Ghosh (Sri Aurobindo):

> The groundwork of what may well be called the composite culture of India is undoubtedly Hindu. Though the present Indian nationality is composed of many races, and the present Indian culture of more than one world civilization, yet it must be admitted that the Hindu forms its based and center....The dominant note of Hindu culture, its sense of the spiritual and universal, will, therefore, be the peculiar feature of this composite Indian nationality....And the type of spirituality that it seeks to develop, is essentially Hindu.[138]

However, the criticism made by Madhok on the political use of the term 'composite culture' by Nehruvians brings out clearly how the post-Nehru Nehruvians differed crucially from the way Nehru himself saw Indian culture. In fact, in the book Madhok quotes Nehru to substantiate his thesis of Indianization.

Instead of blind Nehru-baiting, Prof. Madhok was able to identify the basic common elements in Nehru which brought out his Indianness and showed that Hindutva could raise itself above sectarian politics and view even its opponents in an inclusive context. His identification of the common ground between Hindutva and 'unity in diversity', a concept often officially projected as Nehruvian vision of India can be considered as a process of *samanvaya*—harmonization of the agreeable essences over the differences. He quotes at large almost one-and- a-half pages in the book, the Convocation Address Nehru gave at Aligarh Muslim University (AMU) in 1948. Here Nehru said to the AMU students that he was 'proud of our inheritance and our ancestors who gave an intellectual and cultural pre-eminence to India' and asked if they too felt as 'sharers in it and inheritors of it' and hence proud of that inheritance that belonged to them as much as to him. Or if they felt 'alien to it' and passed it by 'without understanding it'. Then he told the students that the fact he was a Hindu and them Muslims should not 'take away from that cultural inheritance that was as much theirs as it was his'.[139]

That he admits to Nehru having a better and holistic vision of the cultural oneness of India does not make Madhok dilute his criticism of Nehru whom he considers as 'more a politician than a statesman'. More acidic attack is but reserved for Indira Gandhi the daughter of Nehru and Supremo of the faction of INC which later destroyed all other factions. He characterizes her politics as 'an unprecedented example of political immorality and exploitation of communalism and casteism for political ends'.[140] In hindsight, the objective political observers, even those who may not agree with Madhok's worldview may tend to agree on this observation on Indira Gandhi as an accurate description of her politics.

Madhok wants Indianization to be encouraged consciously not only in polity and education. Here Madhok proves to be quite accurate in his diagnosis and prediction. He warns:

> In the name of secularism, historical facts are being distorted or whitewashed to suit the ideological or political convenience of the powers that be....This tampering with history and removal of references to India's traditional heroes and heroines from the textbooks in the name of secularism and eradication of communalism is most impolitic and may have the opposite effect. Historical memories cannot be effaced by whitewashing the history....the Indian secularists want the Indian people not to know the misdeeds of Aurangzeb and martyrdom of Guru Teg Bahadur and many other saints and patriots at liis hands. If they want to create respect for an Indianized Akbar, they must condemn the un-Indian and inhuman conduct of Aurangzeb.[141]

Madhok thus became one of the earliest leaders from the Hindutva movement to identify the distortions made in the History textbooks in the name of promoting communal harmony while the actual exercise was meant to promote the sympathizers of Islamist expansionism clothed in Marxist terms. Given the relatively justified obsession with the projection of Akbar as an enlightened ruler by establishment historians in India, he has also pointed out how that is inconsistent with whitewashing of the abject hatred Aurangzeb had for Hindus.

He then turns to Indianization of the places of worship:

> The same is true in regard to places of worship. Indianisation demands that places of worship of all creeds should be respected....Even a Muslim like Kamal Pasha found it difficult to reconcile himself to the use of the Church of Saint Sophia in Constantinople as a mosque. As a via media, he converted it into a museum. But here in India some of the holiest places of the country like the birthplaces of Shri Ram and Shri Krishna are still in the hands of Muslims. It is true they did not demolish these temples and built mosques in their places. That was the work of barbarians like Aurangzeb. But has the conscience of any so-called "nationalist" Muslim or their secularist patrons been ever pricked by such ghastly sights which continue to be the greatest barrier in the way of emotional integration of our people? Truly Indianized Muslims will offer these places to those whom they belonged voluntarily, and I am sure that this gesture will be reciprocated by construction of new mosques for them nearby.[142]

Madhok here comes out prophetic. He was perhaps the first leader in the BJS-BJP pantheon to talk about the liberation of Ayodhya and Mathura. He was also the one to envision a solution prototype, even if it was in the passing in his thesis of Indianisation. In the ruthless world of democratic real politics Madhok got sidelined, and eventually he turned bitter and his contribution to the national intellectual discourse, which is by any reckoning substantial, got underestimated and understudied. But the later much debated conceptions like cultural nationalism found a solid grounding in his work.

Pandit Deendayal Upadhyaya (1916-1968) and Integral Humanism

Vasant Annaji Vaidya was a dispatch clerk in the office of the RSS weekly magazine *Panchajanya* at Lucknow. The Rashtradharma press which printed the magazine had received a new printing machine, but no mechanic was ready to assemble it fearing subsequent police trouble. Vaidya reminisced how

Pandit Deendayal Upadhyaya, who was then in the office with Vaidya, took upon himself assembling the machine by reading the instruction manual. Due to Satyagraha going on, the editor Vajpayee was not there nor were the compositors. So Upadhyaya wrote the editorial himself and needed articles. He put the frame and then started working on the hand treadle lever himself. In short, he did all the works of the editor, composer, other writers, mechanic and brought out the magazine in time despite the RSS being banned.[143]

The incident exemplifies the Sangh 'intellectuals' work. For most part of post-independent Indian history, they had to work on ground, carry out mass outreach, do organizational work and update their intellectual frameworks rooted in ancient Indian thought.

Almost with no state or extra-territorial patronage which the leftist intellectuals enjoyed (and continue to enjoy), and added to that a widespread establishment hostility, what Deendayal Upadhyaya produced was quite remarkable and as always underevaluated sometimes even by pro-Hindutva intellectuals. His major contribution is the well-known 'Integral Humanism' (IH). The basic documents of IH consist of the document drafted by Upadhyaya, which was then adapted by the all-India representative body of the BJS held at Vijayawada from 23rd to 25th January 1965, and the text of four lectures delivered by him at Bombay from 22nd to 25th April the same year.

Before getting into IH in depth, let us look at the critical studies on IH made by various academic observers and informants on Hindutva. Belgian Indologist and Hindutva observer Dr Koenraad Elst alleges that the Western critics of Hindutva both in the academia and media do not talk about IH because it does not fit into the negative stereotype or caricature they want to make of the BJP-RSS:

> Official ideology of the RSS and BJP is Integral Humanism. If you read the secondary literature on the RSS or BJP, you will probably will not know that. Because ninety something of the publications about Hindu Nationalism do not mention the official ideology. That is bizarre. You cannot find any serious publication about the British Labour Party that does not mention socialism. But in the case of Hindu nationalist party that is the done thing....The reason is that Integral Humanism sounds too innocent. Practically everybody who writes about (Hindu nationalism) has one-point mission which is to spread hate against Hindu nationalists. And in that project the name 'Integral Humanism' does not fit very well.[144]

In reality, quite a number of critical and negative academic studies on Hindutva movement do mention IH. Bruce Desmond Graham of the University of Sussex in his 1990 study, *Hindu Nationalism and Indian Politics*, with more than 270 pages, just mentions IH as 'its central philosophy' and 'the term...to describe the ethical views which he ascribed to his party'.[145] In his 1996 study of the Hindutva movement, Christophe Jaffrelot, a Hinduphobic scholar who had established himself as an authority on 'Hindu nationalist' politics, does give a detailed study of IH. According to Jaffrelot, what Upadhyaya calls the 'national identity' of India 'was the Western one' and that he relied on 'the so-called "historical" varnas...to affirm the existence of a Hindu nation'. He accuses Upadhyaya of remaining 'within the framework that stigmatized and emulated the Other through a reinterpretation of tradition'.[146] Yet Jaffrelot who became increasingly overt with his anti-Hindu hatred here had to acknowledge one aspect:

> His reference to the schema of the four varnas should not be taken to mean that Upadhyaya favoured the restoration of this social system. Such a hierarchical organisation of society would have been regarded as illegitimate and hence rejected by RSS ideologues because they considered it to be divisive. When RSS writers refer to the Varna system, they are using it as a metaphor in the sense proposed by Schalanger, who shows that such metaphors can be used to promote a unitarian ideological project.[147]

Despite this acknowledgement, Jaffrelot ties the concept of National 'soul' or '*chiti*' developed by Deendayal Upadhyaya to 'the society of varnas'. Another book on Hindu nationalism that deals with IH is the 2001 work by sociology professor Chetan Bhatt, which had been seen in another context in the earlier chapter. Chetan Bhatt claims that his study offers a 'critical evaluation of Integral Humanism' and also as evaluating whether it 'emerged' as claimed 'from authentic Hindu advaita traditions'. The preamble to his approach is contained in the following statement he makes on the relation of distortion which he claims exists between 'Hindu nationalism' and 'the dense and sophisticated metaphysical content of Hindu and Buddhist philosophy':

> Indeed, a vivid characteristic of Hindu nationalism is its reduction of the dense and sophisticated metaphysical content of Hindu and Buddhist philosophy to bare Hindu nationalist political slogans and mottos that are incapable either of conveying the vast range of speculative metaphysics within the different schools of Indian philosophical thought or of challenging Western or Eurocentric philosophical hegemony, aspects of which they uncritically reproduce.[148]

To him this 'characteristic' is quite 'explicit' in IH. In his supposedly 'critical evaluation' of IH, he considers the traditional categorization of 'body, mind, intellect and soul' as used by Upadhyaya as 'hierarchically organized attributes'. The whole exercise of Chetan Bhatt is to contain IH into an Indic variant that is Western in style and an anti-democratic totalitarian supremacist ideological straitjacket as exemplified in this passage:

> In Upadhyaya's rather derivative and mechanically holistic 'third way' philosophy, there is also the continuation of a strand of 'religious' nationalism (similar to Ernest Renan's nineteenth century proclamation of 'national soul') that travelled from Aurobindo and Savarkar, and into Golwalkar's writings. Upadhyaya's 'dharma' was in all its essential aspects nationalism, though it should be noted that at its core is the idea of 'Man'. Upadhyaya's assertion that his 'dharma' was based on Hindu precepts is highly problematic. Leaving aside the caste and gender supremacist strictures of *varnashramadharma* or *stri-dharma*, for solemn devotees, the dharma within Hindu metaphysics is nothing less than the universal arrangement of the cosmos (!), whereas for Upadhyaya, dharma is redacted to the soul (chiti) of the densely parochial Hindu Rashtra.[149]

So even as Upadhyaya accepts democracy in IH, Bhatt states that 'he did not privilege the majority will of the people'. He provides a long passage from the Bombay speech of Upadhyaya to prove this point. Then he characterizes IH as exposing an inherent aversion in the Hindutva movement towards democracy:

> While Upadhyaya's philosophy employed a modernist conception of 'the people', he did not privilege the majority will of the people. He argued that dharma could not be guaranteed simply by the resolve, motivation or desires of the mass of people: ... Upadhyaya's drastically circular and tautological argument contained a revealing vagueness regarding democracy. ... If democracy is apparently necessary, but must depend on dharmic precepts, and if dharma necessarily oscillates between 'natural law', 'national soul' and 'Hindu Rashtra', then the democratic process must perpetually be subsidiary to whatever is decided to be the religious imperative.

This is clearly a distortion of what Deendayal implies. The example that Deendayal actually gives to illustrate his assertion 'Majority is not always right' makes that abundantly clear:

> During the Second World War, when Hitler attacked France, the French army could not stall the onward march of the Nazi troops. The then Prime Minister of France, Marshall Petain, decided to surrender. The French public supported the decision. But de Gaulle escaped to London where he declared that he did not accept the surrender. France is independent and will remain so....Now if the majority rule is

> to be considered supreme, then de Gaulle's action will have to be condemned. He had no right to fight in the name of Independence. De Gaulle derived his right from the fact that the French nation was above the majority public opinion. The national Dharma is above all. Independence is Dharma for every Nation.[150]

This illustration by Upadhyaya through a historical instance shows that what he means by Dharma of the nation making the majority opinion subsidiary to it is in no way related to any sectarian religion or religious dogmatism. In fact, in the very first lecture on Integral Humanism to highlight 'pursuance of the healthy principles of public conduct', Upadhyaya chose the example of Shri Hafiz Mohammed Ibrahim who resigned from his seat to which he was elected on the Muslim League ticket and sought re-election.[151] Thus, the Dharma that Upadhyaya emphasizes is not a sectarian dogmatic religion to which he wants to subdue the majority will.

While Chetan Bhatt sees Integral Humanism (as well as the entire Hindutva movement) as rejecting all social contract theories, Christiane Brosius of Ruprecht Karls University sees social contract being inherent in Integral Humanism in her study of Hindutva movement, particularly in the context of Ayodhya movement and globalization of economy started by Narasimha Rao's Congress government (1991–1996):

> BJP ideologues aimed at exploiting Ram rajya as a 'think-model' from which to present their ideas on the state's rights and obligations to society. Again, this goes back to Upadhyaya's Integral Humanism where despotic divine kingship (Ram rajya), people's rule (jana rajya) and moral rule (dharma rajya) are projected as prototypical forms of a mutual understanding and binding between state rule and Indian people. This "contract" could then be easily juxtaposed with so-called illegitimate, "bad rule" (goonda rajya)....The king's authority is based on his duty to provide the people with a sacred ethical doctrine and a source of social order and political stability as well as the protection of this sacred law from abuse. In return, the citizenry is indebted to the king and state and ask in return to express its respect and absolute loyalty to, if not worship of, the royal state. However, should a king or government ignore its duties, it is society's responsibility to remind them of their essential obligations and prove the sovereign power of dharma....This idealized reciprocal relationship between people and state, with the added emphasis on dharma as essentially independent of and superior to the state, demonstrates a radically different configuration of law and power to that of the European secular state.[152]

According to her, Upadhyaya 'politicized the idea of fraternity by providing a link between collective awakening and radical political action in the context of nation building'.[153]

Dr Koenraad Elst himself has made a detailed critical evaluation of Integral Humanism in his book *Decolonizing the Hindu Mind* (2001) wherein he makes a comparison with Christian Democracy:

> In its assumption that man liveth not by bread alone and its opting for the harmony model of society, Integral Humanism is most akin to the Christian-Democratic movement in Europe. ... Another point which Integral Humanism has in common with Christian-Democracy is that both have a progressive dimension, which is not based on an unbridled conflictual stance of one class hating another and trying to defeat it. As RSS general secretary H. V. Seshadri puts it: "Haters cannot reform". Social justice can be brought about only by assuming a collective responsibility for "the evils of Hindu society", not by imputing it to one particular class and posturing as a victim with only rights to be claimed from others....At any rate, while both Christian-Democracy and Integral Humanism have a harmony model of society in mind, they also try to incorporate the existing emancipatory movements....In general terms, Deendayal Upadhyaya's Integral Humanism amounted to a social-democratic programme combined with a non-materialistic philosophy.[154]

Dr Elst, who even while characterizing the civilizational essence of Hinduism itself as the 'Integral Humanism' of Deendayal Upadhyaya, concludes by considering Integral Humanism as 'a corrective and a return to the mainstream, in that it attempts to formulate a recognizably Hindu political vision in universalist terms', instead of the usual Hindutva emphasis on 'nationalism' which he considers as historical baggage, its 'excessive emphasis on nationalism, eclipsing larger and deeper civilizational concerns'.[155]

Looking into Integral Humanism itself, the oft repeated criticism is that the concept of chiti which is very central to IH's relation to the nation for Upadhyaya is derived (borrowed) from that of Renan. In reality, Hindu deep thinkers fighting colonialism posited a concept of nationhood to counter the concept of statist Nationhood of European powers, which to sustain themselves were creating immense human misery in colonized societies. This concept of nation, though having affinity to the concept of nation in Renan in the Western thought, was rooted in Indian reality as Tagore directly pointed out. This is seen in diverse Hindu thinkers of colonial times despite their mutually opposing political views like Tagore and Gandhi, Savarkar and Ambedkar. Deendayal's chiti then should be seen as the continuation of this legacy rather than that of Renan. In fact, it stands in stark contrast to the European concept of nation.

What political scientist Amartya Mukhopadhyay's analysis of Tagore's concept of Hinduness as the alternative to Western nationhood brings out (though unrelated to Deendayal) is also what Deendayal Upadhyaya considers as the chiti of the nation:

> While the kind of community Tagore discovers in *samajtantra*, or societalism of ancient India would be termed by modern-day communitarians like Sandel as "constitutive", different from community in a merely "cooperative" sense. inhabited by Rawlsian "unencumbered selves" and critiqued by communitarians, the methodological problems Tagore's communitarianism raises are more deep-rooted. Is he allowed to pit the ancient community in India, "constitutive" in its essential, against the modern nation? Tagore seems to agree.[156]

Then Mukhopadhyay quotes Tagore:

> Everyone in a 'nation' sacrifices his or her interests for the protection of 'national' interests. But when the Hindu community was living, all the parts of society considered the interests of the whole social body as their only interests.

According to Tagore, 'the primary glory' of 'the statist-political efforts... would consist in its success in supplementing the social unification of ours up to a point'. In a strikingly similar vein, Upadhyaya also emphasizes the limitation of State and subordinated it in the service of Nation:

> We had not considered the State to be the sole representative of the Nation. Our national life continued uninterruptedly even after the State went into the hands of foreigners....Those Nations whose life centred in the State were finished with the end of the State. One the other hand, where State was not believed central to its life, the Nation survived the transfer of political power....In our socio-political set up, the king and the State were never considered supreme....Although the various limbs of the body are not absolutely indispensable, yet each of them serves an important purpose. From the same standpoint, State too, should have been deemed important in the life of a Nation....However, to consider something important is different from saying that it is supreme. The State is not supreme.[157]

It is indeed a deep colonized thinking that because Renan's conceptualization of nation in certain basics concurred with the conceptualization of nation for the Hindu thinkers, the latter borrowed it from the former or were influenced by the former. However, unlike Tagore and Gandhiji, Pandit Upadhyaya could see how the Indian State could deviate from the soul of India. What he conceptualized as the soul of India has a remarkable similarity to the conceptualization of Gandhi, Tagore and Sri Aurobindo.

IH has an evolutionary view of humanity—from nature there is a transition to culture. But even in the case of nature, there is unity of life and mutual dependence. In this, Deendayal had been influenced by Hindu darshanas like Samkhya and also the works of modern Hindu seers—Swami Vivekananda and Sri Aurobindo. While rejecting social Darwinian 'survival of the fittest' as 'Western', he puts forth an alternative:

> But we, in this country, perceived the basic unity of all life. Even the dualists have believed nature and spirit to be complementary to each other rather than contradictory. The diversity in life is merely an expression of the internal unity. There is complementarity underlying the diversity. The unity in seed finds expression in various forms - the roots, the trunk, the branches, the leaves, the flowers and the fruits of the tree. All these have different forms and colours and even to some extent different properties. Still, we recognise their relation of unity with each other through the seed.[158]

It is very easy to recognize the continuity of the 'tree in all its glory contained in the seed' imagery, which goes back to the *Chandogya Upanishad* where seer Uddalaka enlightened his son Shvetaketu through the crushed banyan seeds the *Mahavakya*— '*tat tvam asi*' ('That Thou Art').[159]

Vasudev Nene (1919–1996), known in Sangh circles as Rajabhau Nene, was an authority on Integral Humanism and initiated the bringing out of multi-volume exposition of IH. He was also the editor of the Marathi magazine *Vivek*. With respect to the much controversial Varnashrama system, he makes it abundantly clear how Integral Humanism views it. He writes:

> The first thing that comes to the mind in this context is that at present this system is no more extant in the original form....And, secondly Varna has come to be closely associated with castes and perverted notions of superiority and inferiority. The extreme protagonists of Varna Vyavastha (Varna system) maintain that Varna Vyavastha is God-made and as such it is a part of the ancient Dharma. They further maintain that the Varna in which one happens to be born is decided by one's good or bad actions in previous births and so Varna is determined by birth. Most of the opposition to Varna Vyavastha is on this last-mentioned point. In the present age of science, individual freedom, and equality, it is repulsive to consider a social system which chains down a man to follow a certain profession on the grounds of the circumstances of his birth.[160]

Another important aspect of Integral Humanism is the awareness of environmental issues. It was only in the September of 1962 that Rachel Carson's

Silent Spring had been published. By 1965, the problems of chemical fertilizers had been recognized and Deendayal's Integral Humanism has the distinction of being one of the earliest political thoughts in post-Independent India to include environmental concerns as a moderating influence in socioeconomic development—a proto-vision for sustainable development. The following passage needs to be quoted at length. Given today's problem of climate change that threatens the very planetary fabric of life as we know it:

> Now this (Western) economic structure is not merely consumption-oriented but is clearly leading to destruction. Throw away the old one and buy a new one! Rather than satisfying the need and demand of the people, to create fresh demand has become the aim of modern economics. Supposing that we need not worry about the limited supply of natural resources, there is yet the question of balance in nature. There is a cyclic relationship in different parts of nature. If one of the three sticks, which stand with mutual support, is removed, the other two will automatically fall. The present economic system and system of production are fast disturbing this equilibrium of nature. As a result, on the one hand, new products are manufactured for satisfying ever increasing desires, and on the other hand, new problems arise every day, threatening the very existence of humanity and civilisation. It is essential, therefore, to use up that portion of the available natural resources which nature itself will be able to recoup easily. When the fruits are taken, the fruit tree is not injured; it may even be helpful to the tree. However, in the effort to take a greater harvest from the land, chemical fertilizers are used, which in a few years time, will render the land altogether infertile....This (Hindu-Integral Humanist) system will not think of merely a single aspect of human life, but of all its aspects, including the ultimate aim. This system will be constructive rather than destructive. This system will not thrive on the exploitation of nature, but will sustain nature, and will in turn itself be nourished. Milking, rather than exploitation, should be our aim. The system should be such that overflow from nature is used to sustain our lives. If such human angle inspires the economic system than our thinking on the economic question will undergo through transformation. [161]

Deendayal provided an important Hindu framework for green activism and politics in India long before they were discovered as politically fashionable by the leftist Indian establishment. More importantly, Deendayal associates such ecological values as transformative to the economic system. Nene differentiates between the Western worldview and that of the 'Bharatiya' worldview as put forth by Deendayal in the form of two diagrams — 'a series of concentric circles' and a spirally expanding open circle. Nene explains the spiral expansion thus:

> The spiral begins with the individual represented by the centre of the spiral. The individual consciousness of what 'I' is grows successively, travelling outward along the spiral. Of course, this sort of development is possible only for those individuals who work for the four Purusharthas (Objectives in life). This goes on till the whole universe is reached. And *Bharatiya* thought does not stop even at the universe. It ends in a big circle which represents the Universal Soul, who is all pervasive and is the heart of this philosophy of Integral Humanism.

Nene explains in his exposition of Integral Humanism the basic importance and relation of diversity and unity. According to him the dominant Western models—that of Christianity, Islam and Marxism—try to stamp out the diversity resulting in immense human misery while 'Bharatiya' model is verily based on recognizing the unity in diversity.

> Like individuals, each family (and nation) has its own personality. Thus, a family has its ancestral deity and customs and traditions. In the case of a nation, it has its history and geography, its traditions, its ideals, and out of those arises an identity of its own. Thus, every individual, family and nation has its domain, a peculiarity and a strength. This must be taken into account in attempts at unity. Real unity will come if we plan so that all these will be able to cooperate without giving up their separate personalities. The principle will be unity in diversity.

This understanding of the diversity and underlying unity has been propounded as the basis of national character of India and Deendayal extended or at least tried to extend this to other systems—both within and beyond the nation. Nene writes:

> Bharatiya culture has considered unity of men nay it has considered the unity of humans, the animal and plant world and even the inanimate world. But the basis of this consideration is not the superficial diversity but the underlying unity. Since there is a single principle—Atman—common to all, the diverse manifestations are naturally inclined to cooperate with each other. Culture consists in promoting this complementary nature.

Dattopant Thengadi (1920–2004)

On 10 November 2021, the Government of India released the postage stamp of Dattopant Thengadi. It was to mark the 101st anniversary of the Hindutva trade unionist and thinker in his own right. 'Vanar Sena' or monkey brigade was the organization of students that would become the 'prelude' to the All-India Students' Conference, which would participate in the agitations launched by the INC later.[162] Displaying political awareness and organizational skills even as a teenager, Thengadi, then 15, became its Taluk head. Soon he got attracted to the new organization RSS. In 1942 when Golwalkar sent the first batch of full-time workers to different parts of India for expanding the organization, Thengadi was one of them. He first went to Kerala and then worked in Bengal and Assam during the tumultuous period of partition between 1944–1948.

Among all the initial formative pracharaks, it was Thengadi who had exposure to the complete spectrum of political ideologies and activisms then existing in India. In independent India, the dominant trade unions were in the hands of the Communist Party, which in turn had strong extra-territorial loyalty. The ruling INC had launched its own trade union only in May 1947, a few months before Independence. It needed dedicated workers to strengthen the trade union movement. The INC then had the advantage of not having extra-territorial loyalty and was hence more interested in labour problems from a national point of view. So when in 1949 Dwaraka Prasad Mishra of INC, the Home Minister of Madhya Pradesh, approached the RSS for strengthening it, it loaned out Thengadi to work in INTUC.[163] Between 1950–1951, he was the organizing secretary of INTUC in the state of Madhya Pradesh. Between 1951–1953, he was the organizing secretary of BJS in Madhya Pradesh. Then till 1955, he also worked as the State Organising Secretary of the Communist ideology-oriented 'All India Bank Employees Association' (AIBEA).

Even as Thengadi worked in organizations with diverse ideological orientations, his guiding principle had been laid down clearly by Golwalkar. He had asked Thengadi to 'faithfully follow the discipline of the organization for which he was going to work'. While organizational discipline should be given first priority, should there be a conflict with conscience, Thengadi was expected to 'resign immediately'. He should always stay with labour colleagues during travels and experience first-hand the living condition of workers and should become 'mentally one of them'. In an advice that predates but emphatically foresees the uniting of what the modern academics and media call 'subaltern' into one national network subsuming other identity politics, Golwalkar advised Thengadi that giving prominence to the common economic problems of the SC organizations and all India landless labourer organizations should be brought together, which in turn 'would also help check mutual ill will and bitterness'. While concentrating on organizational work, Golwalkar also advised Thengadi to make a complete comparative study of the economic ideas of Marx and Mahatma Gandhi while studying the methodology of the Marxist trade unions. An advice that Golwalkar gave which seemed to have made a deep impact on Thengadi was this:

> You have been elected to the General Council of INTUC as a representative of 30,000 Manganese labourers. Now give me a straight and truthful answer to one question: Do you love these thirty thousand labourers as much as your mother loves you?[164]

On 23 July 1955, Thengadi launched the Bhartiya Mazdoor Sangh (BMS)—a trade union affiliated to no political party. It was also the 101st birth anniversary of Bal Gangadhara Tilak, the famous Indian freedom fighter. Golwalkar's insistence of being like a mother to the workers evolved in the thoughts of Thengadi into the concept of 'Industrial Family' which he considered as 'perhaps the most central one in the economic organization of the society'. He explained:

> All the persons working in any industry should be considered as constituting an industrial family. What should be the scope and content of common services or benefits that this industrial family makes available for itself should be largely left to its own choice. This need not exclude the law from making some compulsions in this regard.

Perhaps BMS founder was the only trade unionist ideologue-activist to conceptualize welfare of the proletariat, capitalist, state and society in terms of economic as well as psychological terms. And this was uttered decades before industrial psychology became fashionable. Thengadi states:

> An industrial establishment does not mean installed machines surrounded by large working-class colonies looking like an industrial empire. The industry is a world or family within another larger world and family viz. nation on one hand and a world of families living within it on the other. The family is, not a mere body, there is a family mind, a family soul. These psychological circles are not patterned as separate entities, so that a circle called industry or industrial family can think and plan independently without linking itself to the churning of another circle called individual family life or national family. If it is the need of a primary family living that life in the family or home must be full of *samskars* of good living, then the activities of industrial life cannot or should not be planned without any relations to these requirements of the family life. Rather the one must come out from the other in an organic manner just as from the seed comes out a plant, a trunk and leaves and flowers and fruits.

Thengadi created a new alternative to the left-wing trade union philosophy, without becoming an economic right wing. While BMS is nationalistic, it is neither pro-capitalism nor pro-socialism. BMS can actually be considered as a trade union movement founded on the Vedantic principles. It is anybody's guess how difficult it would be to formulate a Vedantic philosophy for trade union and then create such a trade union movement from scratch, with no party affiliation. That Thengadi succeeded in this mammoth task is attested by the growth of the BMS and it replacing Marxist and Congress party affiliated trade unions to become India's largest trade union.

In 1967 the BMS had its first All-India Conference at Delhi. With 541 affiliated unions, its membership was 2,46,000. In 1984 the central government, after verifying the membership of all major national trade unions, declared BMS as India's second largest trade union. Its membership then was at 1.2 million. In 1996 the labour ministry recorded that the BMS with 3.1 million members became India's largest trade union. In 2002 also the position remained the same with a membership of 6.2 million.[165]

Unlike the Marxist and party-affiliated trade unions which need to adapt a top-to-bottom approach, the BMS did not suffer from that feature. It could build its network from the ground and expanded the network. The conceptualization of the proletariat as regimented workers in the industrial sector and at the maximum agricultural sector where the small landowners create a conceptual problem was another problem for the conventional trade unions. This excluded many informal workers. But the traditional Hindu view of the BMS includes all occupational groups and hence helps in its expansion. Thengadi pointed out:

> BMS was the first trade union centre to recognize the special importance of 'self-employment sector', which it termed as 'Viswakarma Sector', in the national economy. It urged for a separate department under the Ministry of Labour and Employment to assist the self-employed persons.[166]

BMS rephrased the classic Marxist slogan 'workers of the world unite' into 'workers unite the world'. In 1978 Thengadi formed the Bharatiya Kisan Sangh (BKS). Another important concept that was put forth by the BMS borrowed from the Western system was Employee Share/Stock Ownership Plan (ESOP)—a concept originally floated by Louis Kelso, San Francisco lawyer and investment banker in 1967. From ESOP, BMS moved to the concept of labourization.

> The credit for introducing the term 'labourisation' goes to BMS only. It stressed that under all categories of 'employer' and under the various patterns of industrial

> ownership, the labour of workers must be evaluated in terms of shares and workers raised to the status of shareholders contributing labour as their share.[167]

BMS has a case study of the success of its innovative policy in the famous New Central Jute Mills Co. Ltd (NCJM). It was a sick industry employing about 13,000 workers.[168] Yet it restarted its functions since March 1987 because of the 'experiment' by the BMS. With the demands of the workers meeting a deadlock with neither the old management nor the government ready to invest any money, the BMS proposed that the workers come forward to participate in the equity share of the company, which caused the old owners to have some amount of faith. BMS achieved a bipartisan agreement between the mill and its workers. Then there was the problem of pressing creditors and finding working capital. BMS which had roped in the workers as shareholders now worked out an arrangement here as well:

- All the big creditors such as raw jute supplier, store supplier and others would continue to supply all the necessary inputs on a two-month credit basis at a simple interest of 2 per cent.
- Those who would be interested in trading finished goods could get the same on market price.
- The company would deduct the salary, wages and other necessary expenses for running the mill, and the balance would be paid to creditors on an instalment basis.

Thus, the BMS experiment reopened the mill in March 1987, and made it run fully operational by April. According to the BMS archives, though there were 12 unions, there has been constructive cooperation among these unions and the machinery had been modernized and products have been diversified. BMS literature states:

> The success of this venture shows that workers' initiatives can overcome the problems faced by traditional industries. While other jute mills are languishing, NCJM has improved its production and the quality of its products. NCJM stands as a model worker owned company and glorifies the achievements of BMS.

Again, the point here is that BMS deviates from the usual trade unionism and tries to charter a new course based on novel inputs from the West and then integrating it with its own indigenous visions and values. One need not point out how much of intellectual conceptualization, practical strategizing and organizing genius it takes. Though in this case the credit for the entire operation was that of Sri Baji Nath Rai, General Secretary of West Bengal BMS, the whole vision emanates from Thengadi. That this successful experiment happened at West Bengal, then the den of militant Marxist rule, shows the achievement of the organization.

Thengadi also worked with Dr Ambedkar and his experience as well as interaction with Dr Ambedkar helped him understand and stand with the depressed sections of the society in their fight for justice. He was instrumental in enacting the anti-untouchability resolution supported by traditional Hindu heads. This has been dealt with in the earlier section.

Thengadi as well as BMS, BKS and Swadeshi Jagran Manch—the organizations that Thengadi created—have emerged as the leftist and protectionist critic of the BJP government's economic policies which mostly follow the liberalization and globalization trend set by the 1991–1996 Congress government led by P. V. Narasimha Rao (1921–2004). The economic policies of both Vajpayee (1998–2004) and Narendra Modi have come under bitter criticism by Thengadi and later leaders of BMS and BKS. In a way Thengadi's thought process provides the left-wing criticism within the Hindutva ecosystem.

To understand the conceptual clarity Thengadi displayed, let us take the term 'Hindu nationalism'. The term is liberally used by the sympathizers and critics of Hindutva as well as Hindutvaites themselves as being synonymous with Hindutva. But with increasing global connectivity, the negative connotations of the term, particularly in the Western context, severely impact the perception of the Hindutva movement. Even among the sympathizers there have been strong critics who depreciate the term 'nationalism'. Dr Koenraad Elst wrote in 2017:

> The nationalism by which the Hindutva crowd swears, is a Western invention. Feelings for your home country are universal, and natives of India will need no prodding nor any foreign or native ideology to defend their country when necessary. Nationalism is just there, as a gut feeling, not in need of any promotion or defence. But as an ideology, it is the creation of the modern West, hardened in the fires of World War I. Of the secularists, we already knew that they always ape the West (or what they assume to be Western), but for champions of native civilization, it is worth noticing.[169]

When asked during the 2014 election campaign if he was a Hindu Nationalist, Narendra Modi, then Prime Ministerial candidate of the BJP, famously said that he was a Hindu and a nationalist and hence a Hindu nationalist. Though simple, the answer pointed out that the term Hindu nationalist may not mean the same for a westerner, or a westernized academic/

media person and an Indian Hindutvaite. Thengadi, as early as 1961, recognized the problematic nature of the term 'nationalism'. Though he himself used the term for convenience, he explained that the proper term was *rashtriyatva* which according to him differed from the Western notion of nationalism by being internationalist—which he called *vishva sanskriti* in its very nature.[170] This Hindu rashtriyatva rejected both expansionism and exclusivism. He pointed out that the term had its own historical context. It had the baggage of both expansionism and exclusivism. As against this, he proposed the term rashtriyatva which he pointed out, though used interchangeably with nationalism, was basically different from it:

> Hypnotised by Western education our intellectuals are tempted to gauge everything Eastern by the yardstick of the West. Hence, this general misunderstanding about the precise meaning or import of the terms 'Rashtriyatva' and 'Nationalism'. Interchangeability of these terms has been blindly taken for granted. But there is such a marked difference substantial as well as qualitative between the two that the one cannot be treated as an equivalent of the other. Our 'Rashtra' concept is unique in many respects.[171]

This is again an instance of how Thengadi could think deeper into the concepts which he formulated through rootedness in Indic thought.

Manthan: A Case Study of the Intellectual Churning Process of the RSS

The official magazine of Deendayal Research Institute (DRI) is *Manthan* (now defunct). A study of its issues in the late 1980s and early 1990s gives us a glimpse of how the 'intellectual activity' of RSS actually worked.

In 1987 K. R. Malkani was the editor of the magazine. The January issue was dedicated to the theme of 'Bhakti'. The editorial in the same issue speaks of Bhakti neither as reactionary nor as other-worldly. With 21 articles written on Bhakti by scholars in various Indic traditions including Vaishnavaite, Vedantic, Jain and Sikh traditions, the issue looks at Bhakti as a spiritual nation building force. Understanding it is also to evolve a similar process for national integration in modern times. While recognizing the spiritual core, the editorial introduction tried to show how Bhakti made Karma-Yogi nation builders out of Gurus and their followers drawn from all sections of the society. Some statements in it are quite bold, whether one accepts them or not.

> Since God is there in all men, service of man became service of God. Social service became a religious duty. All the saints came out for the poor and the oppressed. Kabir said that the poor had no access to justice. Surdas said: 'The Patwari is arrogant, the Amir is dishonest, the Kotwal is deceitful and the Vazier is sinful'. Tukaram said that 'Kings are butchers'. And Tulsi viewed poverty not as a virtue, but as a sorrow to be avoided....It will be no exaggeration to say that it was the Bhakti movement that transformed 'Brahminism' into 'Hinduism' and made Indian survival and revival possible....The challenges that face the country today are partly old and partly new. But the need to meet them is if anything even greater than before. What can be the twentieth century equivalent of Bhakti as People's Power—that is Question Number One before the country.

The issue is definitely a treasure chest for challenging the prevalent dominant narrative of history. For example, contrary to the popular dominant conception among historians about Bhakti as a 'Brahminical' reaction to Buddhism, a paper by Prof. Kewal Krishan Mittal who was then the head of the Department of Buddhist Studies at Delhi University, argues for the presence of Bhakti in Buddhist tradition as well.

> then the entire Buddhist tradition of Sila and Samadhi can be safely said to be "The Buddhist Bhakti Tradition."...Bhakti as a mental attitude (Bhavana) of admiration and adoration of "the Triple-Gem (Triratna)—the Buddha, Dharma and Sangha"—"numerous gods", "ancestors" and "good men and women" and as "silent meditation" till date but also has been strengthened, made elaborate and variegated through various phases and developments of the excellent religio-philosophic movement that Buddhism is. The external form of Bhakti started in Buddhism with the worship of the relic of the Buddha and some of his chief disciples enshrined in the specifically constructed structed called Stupas, passed into the worship of certain symbols and yielded place to the worship of the statues of the Buddha

Another important paper was by Dr Sharan Bihari Goswami, the Principal of the Institute of Oriental Philosophy at Vrindavan. In this long essay, the author traces a continuity of the Bhakti tradition from the Vedic-Upanishadic period right down to Mahatma Gandhi. Here he highlights the role Sant Pran Nath (1618–1694) and points out how Bhakti while acting as a force for resistance against Islamist aggression, uniting the masses for a people's revolution, also, at the same time, worked for Hindu-Muslim unity at the level of the common people:

> The struggles of Sant Pran Nath were very important in the history of armed resistance.... He was also a powerful centre of inspiration, backing Chhatrasal's movement of liberation in Central India. The rousing call of Pran Nath was the clarion call of history:
>
> > ... This land of Bharat is the best in the three worlds. The great Hindu Dharma is there. The Dharma is in danger. This is a matter of great shame for the rulers. Vishnu himself is in the battle-field. He is giving everyone a rousing call. Hardwar has been destroyed. Tapaswins have been expelled from the Tirthas, holy spots. The butchers are massacring the cows. The whole world now knoes the oppressions. But, Hindu kings have not united and they are ready for action. The tyrant with elephant's foot breaks the idols of the Lord, drags it, puts the pieces on the road for people to tread upon. The demons have imposed Jeziya tax on Hindus, who do not get food to ear. If anyone cannot pay Jeziya, he is beaten and converted to Islam.
>
> This saint for whom Hindus and Muslims were equal, had to give a clarion call for the masses to stand up. This is a historical truth and it shows the role played by the saints. No one should think that the saints remained indifferent to the society in critical times. The saints of the Brij exhorted the Jat chieftain Gokul to challenge Aurangzeb. The state of Bharatpur was the result of that resistance.

One should read these articles in the context of the building up of the Sri Ram Janmabhoomi movement. It is a clear pointer to the fact that the movement wanted to somehow make itself an extension of the Bhakti-movement resistance to Islamism which distinguished between Muslims, the common Hindu citizens of India and Islamist politics as well as politics of conversion which the RSS saw as using the appeasement policy of Nehruvian polity to further its expansionist aggression. Thus, the Babri structure would become the symbol not of Islam, the faith of Muslims, but Islamism, the expansionist politics furthered by Nehruvian appeasement.

In February, *Manthan* reported the proceedings of a National Intellectuals Convention held at DRI on 11–12 January sponsored by the Publications Division of the RSS Suruchi Sanstha. The convenor was Prof. M. M. Shankhdhar. Apart from K. S. Sudarshan who would later become the all-India RSS leader, the attendees included among others Devendra Swarup, Sita Ram Goel and Ram Swarup. Here is an excerpt from what *Manthan* reported as the contribution of Ram Swarup to the discussion:

> Dharma is fundamental. It is greater than the country. We have to take cosmic view of things. Today Hindus are not only ignorant of the true nature of Islam and

> Christianity, they are quite innocent even of Hinduism. They glibly talk of the unity of religions and think that only the mode of worship differs. This is not so. For example, Islam and Christianity are more in the nature of political ideologies than spiritual seekings. We have been face to face with Islam for over a thousand years. But there has been no Hindu study of Islam. Even Swami Dayanand's commentary on Islam is more polemical than informative and analytical.

When asked about Western rationalism and consumerism, Swarup answered:

> Consumerism is a menace. But rationalism is necessary and desirable. It was rationalism that exposed Christian orthodoxy and civilized the West. Hinduism should accept Rationalism as its ally in the search for Reason, Peace and Humanity.

This actually shows that contrary to the popular perception in the post-NDA-I period among Hindu activists mainly in the Internet that the RSS never cared for the intellectual Hindutvaites like Goel and Swarup, in reality the RSS was perhaps the only national organization that gave a platform to the views and discussions of these intellectually indomitable Dharmic duo. Here is another instance. Vasant Sathe (1925–2011), an Indira Congress ideologue and then Minister for Broadcasting and Communication, made a statement in the now defunct magazine *Illustrated Weekly of India* that the *abhisheka* (ceremonial bathing) of Sivalinga was actually symbolic of cleaning one's private parts, and that it was mass hygiene education of ancient times.

So, the 1987 December issue of *Manthan* roped in Sita Ram Goel, the distinguished scholar, to write a crisp rebuttal, in which Goel, after pointing out how all Hindu deities are given a bath, wrote with his characteristic penetrating insight this:

> Image worship is a vast subject to which Hindus have devoted many compendiums. Sri Aurobindo, Ananda Coomaraswamy, Alice Boner and V. S. Agarwal have written on it in modern times with a dee understanding. One need not go to pseudoscientists and petty politicians for knowing the meaning of a particular Puja....Superficial rationalism of this sort in the spheres spiritual, leads to Ucchedavada in the long run. Go to Mahatma Gandhi whom I have been re-reading with great profit.

Coming back, in the March issue is a paper by the renowned archaeologist Dr V. S. Wakankar titled 'Where is the Saraswati River?' Fourteen Historic Findings of Archaeological Survey'. According to this paper homo sapiens should have moved to *Saraswati* and other perennial water channels 'during the drier periods of Upper Palaeolithic period...and established the Mesolithic and early Neolithic settlements in those regions':

> The vast concentration of pre-Harappan sites in the districts of Karnal, Jind, Sonipat, ... and Hanumangarh leaves one in no doubt that some pre-Harappan agricultural settlements must have occupied these areas and there is no evidence that these cultural elements which form the core of pre-Harappan culture, have migrated from regions outside the territories of India.

Despite some impassioned statements attributing creationist motive to the dating of Mahabharata to 1500 BCE, the paper is overall academically robust. Wakankar further states that as Harappan and pre-Harappan civilizations developed along *Saraswati*, instead of Indus-Harappan, it should be called 'the Vedic Sindhu-*Saraswati* culture'. It is a matter of fact today that there is a growing number of mainstream scholars (even those still subscribing to Aryan or Indo-European migration theories[172]) who use the term '*Indus-Saraswati*' instead of merely stating Indus valley civilization. Most probably it was in this *Manthan* issue the call for such a change of term was voiced.

There was another National Thinkers Meet at Bangalore organized by another RSS affiliated organization called the Rashtrothana Parishat. Among the many speakers, Rama Gopalan (1926–2020), a Hindutva leader from Tamil Nadu, spoke about how August 14 was venerated as the 'Hindu Holocaust Day'. In the June issue there is an article on the ethnic conflict happening in Sri Lanka between Tamils and Singhalese which was slowly moving towards a civil war. The general tone of the article, it should be noted, is critical of Singhalese chauvinism.

There is a detailed review of Wali Khan's book *Facts are Facts: The Untold Story of India's Partition* (Vikas Publications, 182 pages). *Manthan* informs its readers how Islamism was used effectively by British imperialism. According to Wali Khan, while Muslim League was Jinnah's, 'keeping it together was the Viceroy's responsibility', and Jinnah thanked the Viceroy for keeping the party together in 1939. Details emerge from the book on how the British refused to recognize the voices of Nationalist Muslims who opposed partition while at the same time going out of the way to make sure the Muslim League emerged stronger. The book also brings out how Jinnah falsely asserted that in the frontier region in the Northwest, Hindi was being imposed as he was not able to differentiate between Hindi and Pashtun. Top British bureaucrats worked tirelessly to make Muslim League strong in the Northwestern provinces. For this, the support of mullahs had to be brought. According to Wali Khan, Sir George Cunningham persuaded Jamiat-ul-Ulema-e-Sarhad leaders to create a pro-British atmosphere. Mullahs were categorized into various levels and were bought for ₹ 10–15 a month!

In the September issue there are two important facts. One is that eminent freedom fighter and socialist Achyut Patwardhan (1905–1992), who was living as a recluse, when presented Lokmanya Tilak award by Lokmanya Tilak and Kesari-Maratha Trust, consisting of a citation and a cash prize of ₹ 35,000, gifted the entire amount to DRI rural reconstruction work in the Gonda and Beed area. Second is the report of the Independence Day celebration at DRI in which Prof. Rajendra Singh of RSS participated. One of the speakers was Ahmed Rashid Sherwani, an educationist. This is what *Manthan* reported of his speech:

> Geo-culturally India is one. Although Islam permits polygamy and easy divorce, the two things are not any commoner among Muslims than among Hindus. Indeed, the word "Talaq" is a taboo in all good Muslim homes....Also, Muslims regard Ganga-jal for its purity and sanctity. This our geo-cultural unity can promote political unity also, if we establish a healthier State-Central relationship, and give more powers to the state. Muslims cannot ask for a communal Pakistan and then demand a secular India. Hindus cannot treat Muslims as unclean, and then expect them to join the national mainstream.

Again, one need not agree with what Ahmed Rashid Sherwani stated. What is more important is that the RSS journal published his speech which was also critical of the Hindutva movement vis-à-vis RSS. One can see all these in hindsight as an intellectual build-up and preparation to a national Ayodhya movement in which the fight was against pseudo-secularism and monopolistic expansionism, not becoming a communal hatred against Muslims. While riots did happen, the ideological narrative was very clear—that it should be accommodating Muslims and not antagonizing them. But one should say the leftists beat the RSS ideologues here in projecting the Ayodhya movement as anti-Muslim movement. The entire *Manthan* approach to the Bhakti movement and Islam in India is dealt with in the chapter on theo-diversity and samanvaya.

Engagement with Indian Marxists and Response to the Collapse of USSR

The exceptionally impartial display of the accommodation exhibited by the RSS journal is noteworthy here. On 13 and 14 February 1988, the DRI held a seminar on the October Revolution to mark its anniversary. It included the then who's who of the Indian left. Veteran Marxist leader Elamkulam Manakkal Sankaran Namboodiripad (1909–1998), who was also the first head of a democratically elected Communist government in Kerala, which was a first anywhere in the world, was invited but could not attend the seminar in person. He sent a paper. When he read the paper by K. R. Malkani he felt compelled to write a rebuttal to it, and he wrote and sent it to Manthan. Thus, when in March 1988, *Manthan* came out with the proceedings of the seminar, it contained two papers by E. M. S. Namboodiripad, who was a bitter ideological enemy of the RSS.

The seminar shows the interest that the Hindutva movement has for Communism as a movement and ideology despite the strong political rivalry. At that time, Sailendra Nath Ghosh (1923–2013), one of the pioneering ecological thinkers of post-independent India, was with the DRI as research director. He was also a former Marxist. He made a detailed analysis of the systemic problems of the Marxist-Leninist state. His essay titled 'October Revolution's Lost Horizon: Roles of Marx's Ambiguities, Lenin's Errors, and Stalin's Distortions' is in its own way a classic in Hindu critique of Marxism where he brings out what he considers as the fundamental fallacies as well as humanist intentions of Marx and how they lead to the errors of Lenin and then the inhuman brutality of Stalin.

According to Ghosh, Marx's basic concern was humanism—'to see self-creative, self-directing man', who 'makes his life activity an object of his will and consciousness'. So, what held back the Soviet Union from realizing the vision of this man? He writes:

> First: there was nothing in Marx's voluminous writings to indicate what constituted the essence of socialism....Secondly, even though Marxism gave a sound analysis of the functioning of the capitalist society, it provides no clear theoretical concept of the future ordering of the socialist society. Acharya Vinoba Bhave was correct when he said that Marxist is merely a reactive ideology, not an active ideology....Thirdly, Marx's doctrine suffered from many inadequacies, ambiguities and omissions which gave rise to serious errors of direction.

Then as fourth and fifth points, he added the contributions of Lenin and Stalin. In the case of Stalin, the usual Marxist apologist's line is that the inhumanity of Stalin was his personal failing and paranoia. Marxism could not be made responsible for the personal perversion and power lust of Stalin. But Ghosh points out that the problem was deeper:

> Stalin plunged the Soviet Union into orgies of violence against peasants and also his former comrades in the revolution....But in fairness to him, the scope for misinterpretations and distortions often lay in the opacities and omissions in the

> Marxist theories and Leninist expositions themselves....To try to explain this in terms of personal paranoia or "personality cult" is to evade the issue.

Ghosh points out that Stalin's cruelty on the farmers could be traced ideologically to Marx himself:

> Stalin possibly inherited Marx's prejudice against peasants. (Marx had made an exception in the case of Indian ancient peasant community) Marx used to regard peasants as contemptibly backward, individualistic, self-centred and ignorant because of their isolation....Dr B. N. Ganguli correctly stated that the dichotomy between "civilised nations" and the "barbarian nations" in the Communist Manifesto reflected the Westerner's pride and prejudice against non-Western civilization....If Stalin's extortion of tribute from the peasants for industry-building and his "forced collectivization" programme were murderous, he could always utilise Marx's observations against peasantry to justify his actions.

The holistic approach makes the paper avoid the pitfalls of binary stereotyping, an empathy that Golwalkar never got from the Marxist academia. Ghosh points out how Marx and Engels also strove for a vision of a complete human renaissance but could not present it correctly. He quotes a letter written by Engels after the death of Marx, answering the criticism that they placed economic factor as the primary determinant:

> According to the material conception of history, the ultimately determining factor in history is the production and reproduction in real life. Neither Marx nor I have ever asserted more than this....Marx and I are ourselves partly to blame for the fact that the younger people lay more stress on the economic side than is due to it. We had to emphasise the main principle vis-a-vis adversaries, who denied it, and we had not always had the time, the place or the opportunity to give the other factors involved in this interaction their due.

It was this fundamental deficiency of Marxism which actually got amplified as its singular perspective and unique explaining power. Naturally, the Sangh argument considers Pandit Deendayal Upadhyaya's Integral Humanism as removing this fundamental deficiency of Marxism. Further, the Marxist concept of base and superstructure makes Marxists desist from accepting new ideas. This is a keen observation on Marxist psychology:

> Marx's influential followers devalued the role of ideas. Hence Marxists in general have been reluctant to explore ideas beyond the written text of Marxism. They

> have no use for new ideas which could aid the fulfilment of Marx's humanistic objectives....Marx's interpreters often read a kind of economic determinism into his statement, supposing him to have said that other elements in the historical process were determined uniquely by the economic one....Since socialism was "scientifically proved" to be inevitable, the Marxists could afford to be both dogmatic and arrogant and to lower the need for introspection.

The importance of this paper cannot be overemphasized. The hallmark of Hindu thinking, not to fall into binaries, exists throughout the paper like a non-interfering background drone. Ghosh gives a hint of an important possibility in the context of Marx's observation about the agrarian Hindu communities:

> If India now takes this pattern as the basis to build upon, and seeks to meet its present-day requirements by skipping both capitalism and industrialism, will it be impossible to build a civilised, highly satisfying, durable communitarian system? This would, of course, depend on a clearer concept of a satisfying lifestyle and also of an ecological union of agriculture and manufacture.

In the third issue dealing with the Soviet Union, Dr Murli Manohar Joshi, a physicist and who would later become the BJP's all-India leader, made the following observation in his long comment:

> Now the question is: How is it that while in the rest of the world, science and technology have attained tremendous progress and attained phenomenal heights, it has stagnated in Soviet Russia, specially in the case of pure sciences?... I trace the roots of the exploitative system to (Cartesian) dichotomy where the "mind" was allowed to manipulate, exploit and degrade "matter". What Marx has done, or what socialists have done, is that they have reversed the role of matter and mind. They have made matter superior to mind. But the problem of exploitation of mind by matter or of matter by mind has not been resolved....Therefore, in my opinion, the contribution of October Revolution to world economy is the same as that of Keynes, Adam Smith or of anybody else, because you have not deviated from Cartesian, Newtonian and Calvinist concepts of science and technology.

And then in three years, the Soviet Union ceased to be and India started moving in the path of 'liberalisation and globalisation'. In the aftermath of the collapse of the Soviet Union, *Manthan* brought out twin issues addressing this historical event. Poet, former Marxist and author of *Guru Gobind Geeta*, P. K. Nijhawan presented an in-depth paper on the 'Soviet Experiment—A Dream turned Nightmare'. In a detailed analysis spread over ten pages, he made the following important points:

> The first and foremost point of criticism against Marxism is that it could not concretize itself as an alternative civilizational paradigm—alternate to capitalist paradigm of civilization.…The second most important point of criticism is that Marx failed in the very laboratory where he fashioned his profound thesis.…The third main point of criticism is that an idealist philosophy cannot be really translated into action in the world of real politik.…And finally, just as the French revolution had petered out—dividing Europe vertically into contending nations—the Marxian internationalism also proved illusory.…Because as Sri Aurobindo has upheld, there is something objective, there is something psychological and spiritual in the growth and development of nations.

The *Manthan* issues dealing with the decline and fall of the Soviet Union do not indulge in gloating over the fall of what might perhaps be the most vicious of their enemies, who constantly labelled them as communalists, fascists, counter-revolutionary and the worse. They did not rejoice over the fall of the 'evil empire'. The perception of Hindutva movement was quite different from the way the Western right wing viewed the fall. For the Hindutvaites of the late 1980s and early 1990s, the Soviet Union was a great idealistic dream of the Western civilization, which got experimented on Eurasian people and turned into a nightmare of continuous human misery and tragedy because of some fundamental deficiencies including the absence of freedom, which the Hindutva ideologues thought could be removed by the freedom and Dharma that Hindu Dharma provided.

Another crucial aspect of the RSS intellectual churning vis-à-vis *Manthan* will be dealt in both the sections on science as well as samanvaya. However, all these should point out how the Hindutva in general and the RSS in particular have worked towards creating an intellectual discussion and interaction-based approach to the diverse thought processes in the nation. Unfortunately, even with the Hindutva sympathizers, the stereotype image of the Swayamsevak as a kind of muscular, non-cerebral automaton persists. A deeper look shows that with no State support or support from extra-territorial agencies, the thinkers from the Sangh, usually spending most of their times sleeping on railway platforms and working among some of the most marginalized sections of the society, evolved an intellectual tradition, unborrowed from Western academia and sociopolitical philosophies but rooted in Indian soil.

Dr Keshav Baliram Hedgewar (1889–1940), the founder of RSS

Hedgewar participating in the Forest Satyagraha of Congress (21 July 1930, seated third from left)

Madhav Sadashiv Golwalkar 'Guruji' (1906–1973)

Saint Tukdoji Maharaj (1909–1968), freedom fighter and social reformer, was one of the founders of Viswa Hindu Parishad in 1964

Balasaheb Comments

Sir—I thank you for reproducing my interview ("How Powerful Is The RSS?", March 12) faithfully, but a few corrections are necessary:

'Smriti Bhavan' where the interview took place is not the headquarters of RSS. We were using that building for our session of the Akhil Bharatiya Pratinidhi Sabha. The headquarters is situated in another building in the heart of the city.

About Mr Kanetkar, there is a sentence: "Now he is a bitter critic of RSS." Instead, it should be: "He has been a consistent critic of RSS from the beginning."

In one of the answers (page 27) there is a sentence: "We do not claim to have the solutions for the ills of this country." It should read: "We do not claim to have the solution for *all* the ills of the country."

In the reference to Bangladesh the last sentence is, "We have at least to advise the Government of India". I think I must have said: "We have to do something about it."

The headline "Our Critics Are Perverts" is not correct. I have not said that all critics are perverts. The word "perverts" has been used for the Sampradayikata Virodhi Samiti.

On the front cover page you have printed a photo of Swayamsevaks doing lathi drill. I think you could have as well printed a photo of Swayamsevaks doing relief work in cyclone-hit Andhra Pradesh.

New Delhi M. D. DEORAS

Madhukar Dattatreya Deoras (1915–1996) featured in the 'Illustrated Weekly of India'; his subsequent letter to the 'Illustrated Weekly', asking them to correct errors. His criticism of the cover image used to portray the RSS is important

Swami Chidbhavananda (1898–1985), a Vedantin sage who held revolutionary social reform ideas in the RSS platform. 'You are all blessed to be the servants of Mother India,' he had said to the RSS cadre

விஜய பாரதம்

வரலாறு புகட்டும் பாடம்

ராஷ்ட்ரீய ஸ்வயம்சேவக சங்கம்
தமிழ்நாடு

பௌத்திக் திட்டம்

அக்டோபர், நவம்பர், டிசம்பர்
1986

விஜயதசமி விழா :
அக்டோபர் 12-ம் தேதி (ஞாயிற்றுக்கிழமை)

...ர் மூவரின்
...தனைகளுநப்
...போதுமே
...ன்றுதான்

வீர சாவர்க்கர், ஆர் எஸ். எஸ் ஸ்தாபகர்டாக்டர் ஹெட்கேவார் ஆகியோரின் சிந்தனைகள் குறித்து நம்மில் பலருக்கு முன்னமே தெரிந்திருக்கும் இந்த இருவரின் சிந்தனைகளுடன் டாக்டர் அம்பேத்கர் அவர்களின் சிந்தனை எவ்வளவு அருமையாக இசைந்திருக்கிறது என்பது பின்வரும் எடுத்துக்காட்டுக்களிலிருந்து தெளிவாகும்; அத்துடன் ஆயிரக்கணக்கான ஆண்டுகளாக நாம் இழைத்த சமூகத் தவறுகள், அவற்றால் சமுதாயத்தில் ஏற்பட்ட பதட்டநிலை, ஆகியவற்றையும் பற்றி தக்கபடி நாம் அறிந்துகொள்ள இந்த எடுத்துக்காட்டுகள் உறு...

மூலமும் நீக்கிட வேண்டும் என்று நாம் கங்க... பூணுவது அவசியம்.

டாக்டர் அம்பேத்கர் பிறந்தது தீண்...

While most political parties and movements in India started using the name of Dr Ambedkar only after the 1990s, the RSS decades before that have been venerating the social revolutionary, as shown in the official 'intellectual' training manual of the RSS as well as in their official popular magazine

Ekatmata Yatra or the National Unity Pilgrimage organized by VHP in 1983

நான் சுமந்த கங்கை

பரமசிவன் தலையில் தாங்கிய அன்னை கங்கையை நாம் தலையில் சுமப்பது என்பது மிக சாதாரண செயலல்ல, அனைவருக்கும் கிடைக்கும் பாக்கியமும் அல்ல!

அந்த பாக்யம், எனக்குக் கிடைத்தது, கடந்த நவம்பர் மாதம்– ஆர். எஸ். எஸ். இயக்கத்தின் ஒத்துழைப்புடன் விஸ்வ ஹிந்து பரிஷத்தினரால்–லட்சக்கணக்கான ஹிந்து மக்களிடம் ஜாதி பேதமற்ற ஒற்றுமை உணர்வை உண்டாக்கிய கங்கை யாத்திரையில் பங்கு கொண்ட புனித கங்கையைத்தான் நான் சுமந்தேன்.

வெள்ளிப்பனி மலையின்மீது வசித்த அன்னை கங்கை நவம்பர் பத்தாம் தேதி சென்னையை வந்தடைந்தாள். சென்னையில் தொடங்கிய யாத்திரை நவம்பர் 16ம் தேதி ராமேஸ்வரத்தில் முடிவடைந்தது.

தமிழக மக்கள் லட்சக்கணக்கில் இனம், மொழி, பிராந்தியம், ஜாதி, மதம், வித்தியாசமின்றி ஆராதனை செய்தார்கள், ஆடிப்பாடினார்கள், தொட்டு வணங்கினார்கள்.

தமிழக மக்களின் பண்பாட்டினையே அழித்துக்கொண்டிருந்த நாத்திகவாதிகளை தமிழகத்தின் தெருக்களிலேயே காணமுடியாதவாறு பக்தி வெள்ளம், ஆன்மீகப்புரட்சி தமிழகத்தினையே பெருமைப்படச் செய்தது. சமுதாயத்தின் அடித்தளத்தில் நிலைத்து நின்று கொண்டிருந்த சகோதர உணர்வினை அனைவரையும் உணரச் செய்தது.

எடுத்துச் செல்லப்பட்டது. 'ஜய் காளி ஜெய்காளி, ஹரஹர சங்கர, ஜெய ஜெய சங்கர என்று பல கோஷங்கள் விண்ணதிர முழங்கின. ஊர்வலம் கோவிலின் வாசலை வந்தடைந்தது. யானையின் மீதிருந்து கங்கா தீர்த்த கலசங்கள் கீழே இறக்கப்படுகின்றன.

விஸ்வ ஹிந்து பரிஷத்தின் அகில பாரத பொறுப்பாளர்களான ஸ்ரீ ஹரிமோஹன் லால் ஜி, அசோக் சிங்கால்ஜி முதலியோரும் குவாலியர் ராஜமாதா சிந்தியா தேவி எம். பி அவர்களும் தமிழகத்தின் விஸ்வ ஹிந்து பரிஷத் கிளையின் பொறுப்பாளர்களான திரு. வேதாந்தம், திரு. சங்கரநாராயணா போன்றவர்களும் அங்கு அப்போது குழுமியிருந்தனர்.

இறக்கப்பட்ட கலசத்தை பெற்றுக்கொண்ட தலைமை அர்ச்சகர் ஒருவர் அதை ராஜமாதாவின் கையில் தருகிறார். பிரகாரத்தில் ஊர்வலம் துவங்குகிறது. கூடியிருந்த மக்கள் பக்தி கோஷங்களுடன் கங்கை தரிசனத்திற்கு முன்னேற முயற்சி செய்த வண்ணம் பாய்கின்றனர். நான் அனைவரையும் ஒழுங்குபடுத்தும் பணியில் ஈடுபட்டுக்கொண்டிருந்தேன்.

ஸ்ரீ அசோக்சிங்கால்ஜி திடீரென்று விஸ்வநாதனை கூப்பிடுங்கள் என்று குரல் கொடுக்கிறார். அனைவருடைய கவனமும் என்மேல் திரும்புகிறது. நான் கூட்டத்தை கலைத்துக்கொண்டு கங்கை கலசம் இருக்குமிடத்திற்கு அருகில் செல்கிறேன்.

தியாகி கக்கன்ஜி என்று தமிழக மக்களால் அழைக்கப்பட்டவரின் அன்புச் சகோதரர் திரு. பூ. விஸ்வநாதன் அவர்கள் தாழ்த்தப்பட்ட சமுதாயத்தின் முன்னேற்றத்திற்காக பலகாலமாக பணியாற்றி வருகிறார்.

மதுரை மாவட்டம் மேலூர் தாலுகா தும்பைப்பட்டி கிராமத்தில் உள்ள ஸ்ரீ வீரகாளியம்மன் ஆலயத்தில் பூசாரியாக பணியாற்றியவர் இவரின் தந்தை. திரு. கக்கன், திரு. விஸ்வநாதன் இருவரும் அக்கோவிலில் பலகாலம் தந்தையுடன் பணியாற்றியுள்ளார்.

அவருக்கு ஆர். எஸ். எஸ். தொடர்பு கிடைத்தவுடன் ஆர். எஸ். எஸ். ஸ்வயம் சேவகர்களால் நடத்தப்பட்ட நிகழ்ச்சி ஒன்றில் கலந்துகொண்டபோது தனக்கு ஏற்பட்ட அனுபவத்தை வாசகர்களுக்கு

Ekatmata Yatra also aimed at achieving social integration. Sri Viswanathan Kakkan (1943–2010), the younger brother of freedom fighter and social reformer P. Kakkan, carried the Ganga water for the Yatra

Prof. Rajendra Singh (1922–2003), the fourth all India RSS head in conversation with Nyiva Mwendwa, then Kenya's Minister for Culture and Social Service (1997)

Despite some sharp differences and misunderstandings Sita Ram Goel was a respected mentor for the RSS thinkers and activists. Here he is at a seminar organized by Deendayal Research Institute having tea with Dr. Rajendra Singh, Sri Sudarshan and Sri. Devendra Swaroop. Both Sitaram Goel and Sri Devendra Swarup worked as editors for the monumental volume on India's contribution to world thought and culture brought out by Vivekananda Rock Memorial Committee in 1970. It was under Sri Eknath Ranade who was the general secretary of the RSS (Manthan, 1984)

7

Science and Hindutva

Hindutva is considered as antiscience and pseudoscience by its critics. It is characterized as a fundamentalist movement that lacks the open nature very essential to science. The Indian Constitution makes it the duty of Indian citizens to nurture in them what is called 'scientific temper'—a term wrongly attributed to Jawaharlal Nehru. Is Hindutva like fundamentalist Christianity and Islam in its relation to science? Then there are criticisms which consider the very Hindu Dharma as being basically antagonistic to the spirit of science because the former is ideologically deficient to do good science. Here a study of relation between Hindutva, Hindu Dharma and science is made.

Cargo Cult Hindutva

The Hindutva worldview—though not at its dominantly Vedantic-Buddhist and Vivekananda-Savarkarite conceptions—but at the level of its adherents and also at several middle level functionaries and activists, does have the problems of pseudoscience and of late, antiscience. While Hindutva is not a religious movement completely, yet religion is also a substantial part of Hindutva. Even though religion in India is qualitatively different on the whole from the dogmatic and purely faith as well as scripture-based religion, such religious components cannot be completely ruled out from the Indic religious phenomenon. So, such trends can be considered inevitable even when unwanted and harmful to the process of nation building—the process with which Hindutva identifies itself.

The following instances illustrate this.

In 2009 the Tamil Nadu branch of the Viswa Hindu Parishad (VHP) launched its web TV. In one of its first webcasts, it claimed that a stone carving found at a village in Tamil Nadu which was claimed to be a 'yantra' dedicated to Shani, the deity of Saturn, resembles the design of the polar region of Saturn, the planet, that NASA's Cassini spacecraft had photographed.

Anyone who goes through Hindu forums on the internet would be struck by similar claims which are totally baseless, unscientific and pseudoscientific. These claims often go viral with the 'true believers' spreading them in the digital networks including social media. NASA satellites stopping over a famous Siva temple in a village named Thirunallar in Tamil Nadu is another such example. Then we have the completely fantasy-based narrative about why a statue of Nataraja was installed at the European Organization for Nuclear Research (also known as CERN), which operates the world's largest particle physics laboratory. This viral meme claims that the world faced the threat of apocalypse due to CERN's experiment to discover the till-then-theorized Higgs boson, popularly known as the God Particle. Scientists around the world were terrified. Dr A. P. J. Abdul Kalam then came to the rescue and proposed that invoking Lord Nataraja would avert the wrath of the gods. So, the two-metre-high bronze statue symbolizing Siva's cosmic dance of creation and destruction was installed. These memes get shared in thousands if not millions. The truth is that the statue was a 2004 gift from the Government of India four years before the experiment began. It was gifted to celebrate CERN's long association with India, with no connection to the divine thwarting the destruction of the planet because of CERN experiments.

Then there is the persistent obsession with ancient flying machines and atomic weapons supposedly used in the events and wars of Hindu epics. A treatise on aeronautics attributed to the ancient sage Bharadwaj was apparently downloaded through 'psychic channelling' during the years 1918–1923, and since then Bharadwaj has been projected in much of the Hindu propaganda literature as the father of aeronautics.

All these have given the critics of Hindutva valuable ammunition to brand it as pseudoscientific and justifiably so.

Superficially, the juvenile need to find all modern scientific and technological achievements in ancient Hindu civilization and scriptures look very much like the theo-politically motivated pseudoscience of Intelligent Design (ID)/ Creationism, which denies evolution, that is very much a part of the Western right-wing package. However, there is a crucial difference.

Molecular biologist Paul F. Lurquin and anthropologist Linda Stone, in their 2007 work studying the response of scientists as well as varied human cultures to the science of evolution, point out the important difference between the encounter with science of the Western right-wing kind and Hindu nationalist kind, particularly in the context of National Democratic Alliance (NDA)-I (1998–2004). A negative bias against the Bharatiya Janata Party (BJP) permeates their book, which is expected given the staunch global propaganda against Hindutva as 'Hindu fundamentalism'. Lurquin and Stone acknowledge that 'the *Rig Veda* does not present its version of the creation of the universe as fact', yet they point out that 'there is the potential for Hinduism also to generate its own fundamentalism'. And they quote the BJP to be proof of the existence of such Hindu fundamentalism.

> The BJP is an ultra-nationalist movement whose aim is to show and teach the ascendancy of all things Hindu, from history to science. In particular, the BJP advocates the development of 'Vedic Science' based on the posited scientific superiority of Hindu sacred traditions...Also, the BJP does not advocate ID or anything like it. The BJP has not singled out the theory of evolution as a threat to Hindu values. Hindu fundamentalism, then, is not interested in detracting science (including evolution) or proving it wrong but in integrating Vedic and Hindu traditions within the main body of science. This may reflect the enormous power of syncretism in Hinduism.[1]

This is a significant difference. And in this difference lie the possibilities for the Hindutva movement to forge positive and healthy relations for the dialogue between science and cultural and philosophical traditions of India. And exactly this is what makes that space of Hindutva mainly on the internet and social media, inhabited by what we can call 'cargo cult' memes replacing serious dialogue with grotesque invention of fantasies that belittle both science and the umbrella of Indic philosophical traditions—a tragedy and serious threat to Hindutva as a nation-building process. This alternate aspect of Hindutva has been evolving through such pseudoscientific memes and claims accelerated by the internet and social media.

The original 'cargo cults' are symptoms of a deeper longing. The term originates from New Guinea, where waiting for ships or planes to bring dead ancestors and cargo began as a religious tradition in the 1910. The natives mimic the entire operation of radio communication of the planes with wooden replicas and await the arrival of the cargo as well as their promised leader. At first sight, the whole phenomenon looks juvenile and superstitious. Cultural anthropologist Marvin Harris (1927–2001), in an insightful study, pointed out that the cult actually carried within it a deeper criticism of global unequal distribution of wealth:

> It is easy to dismiss cargo beliefs as the ravings of primitive minds: Prophet leaders are either consummate rogues preying upon the greed, ignorance, and gullibility of their brethren, or if sincere, they are psychopaths who spread their mad ideas about cargo through autohypnosis and mass hysteria. This would be a cogent theory if there were nothing mysterious about how industrial wealth gets manufactured and distributed. But in point of fact, it is not easy to explain why some countries are poor and others rich, nor is it easy to say why there are such sharp differences in the distribution of wealth within modern nations. What I'm suggesting is that there is really a cargo mystery, and that the natives are justified in trying to solve it.... Without the cheapness of native labor and the appropriation of native lands, the colonial powers would never have gotten so rich. In one sense, therefore, the natives were entitled to the products of the industrialized nations even though they couldn't pay for them. Cargo was their way of saying this. And that I believe, is its true secret.[2]

The invention of the fantasy-filled stories like why the Nataraja statue was installed at CERN, connecting it with God Particle and protecting the world from annihilation, or the NASA Saturn yantra discovery, or the stopping of satellites by a mysterious ray above a particular temple, etc. are equivalents of the cargo cult. And the remarkable insight of Marvin Harris must be applied to this fringe yet significant movement within Hindutva in its encounter with science.

There is unquestionably a Hindu contribution to the generation of knowledge, and there is space for the dialogue for Vedic-Buddhist-Jain philosophical systems with the core questions that move the finest human minds towards probing the mysteries of the universe. But in the last seven decades, the institutions of the State have consistently denied any such healthy dialogue in the name of secularism. Radical left-wing propaganda, the Dravidian pseudo-rational movement, and so on, have either reduced the Hindu philosophy to the determinism of production relations or worse, to racial interpretations of the lowest kind.

Cargo Cult Hindutva: The Case of the Cosmic Dance of Siva

This is well exemplified in how the famous Nataraja iconography is received and perceived in the knowledge domains of modern science (mostly in the West) and in the anti-Hindutva polity of India. This also explains the problem at the root of cargo cult Hindutva.

A typical WhatsApp forward of Nataraja in the famous Chidambaram temple goes like this:

> The scientists researching God Particle in CERN discovered that because of their experiments, the world was becoming unstable and was headed towards destruction. They wanted to stop it. Some scientists from NASA discovered that Chidambaram was the centre of the universe. They also discovered that the dancing Siva has been controlling and harmonizing all the destructive forces and keeping the earth and entire universe functioning without destruction. Having studied this secret, the NASA scientists advised the CERN scientists to install a Nataraja at CERN and when it was done, the danger to the earth and universe was averted.

One does not have to be a scientist to understand the layers of deception and delusion which exude through every word of such fantasies. The tragedy is even more telling because the dance of Siva has been quite a deepening and expanding metaphor connecting real science, art and creative human quest for an all-permeating unity.

The traditional interpretation of the dance of Siva was popularised by Dr Ananda Coomaraswamy, who wrote the now famous essay in the scholarly magazine *Siddhanta Deepika*, a magazine espousing *Saiva Siddhanta*.

> Now to summarize the whole interpretation we find that The Essential Significance of Siva's Dance is threefold: First, it is the image of his Rhythmic Play as the Source of alt Movement within the Cosmos, which is Represented by the Arch: Secondly the Purpose of his Dance is to Release the Countless souls of men from the Snare of Illusion: Thirdly the Place of the Dance, Chidambaram, the Centre of the Universe is within the Heart....How supremely great in power and grace this dancing image must appear to all those who have striven in plastic forms to give expression to their intuition of Life!...Every part of such an image as this is directly expressive, not of

> any mere superstition or dogma, but of evident facts. No artist of today, however great, could more exactly or more wisely create an image of that Energy which science must postulate behind all phenomena....In the night of Brahma, Nature is inert, and cannot dance till Siva wills it; He rises from His rapture, and dancing send through inert matter pulsing waves of awakening sound, and lo! matter also dances appearing as a glory round about Him. Dancing, He sustains its manifold phenomena. In the fulness of time, still dancing, he destroys all forms and names by fire and gives new rest. This is poetry; but none the less, science.[3]

It soon became very popular with some of the best minds of science and art. Fritjof Capra, a Particle Physicist who became famous through his best-selling book *The Tao of Physics* explains in the preface to the book a life-changing experience he had:

> I was sitting by the ocean one late summer afternoon, watching the waves rolling in and feeling the rhythm of my breathing, when I suddenly became aware of my whole environment as being engaged in a gigantic cosmic dance. Being a physicist, I knew that the sand, rocks, water and air around me were made of vibrating molecules and atoms, and that these consisted of particles which interacted with one another by creating and destroying other particles. I knew also that the Earth's atmosphere was continually bombarded by showers of "cosmic rays", particles of high energy undergoing multiple collisions as they penetrated the air. All this was familiar to me from my research in high-energy physics, but until that moment I had only experienced it through graphs, diagrams and mathematical theories. As I sat on that beach, my former experiences came to life; I "saw" cascades of energy coming down from outer space, in which particles were created and destroyed in rhythmic pulses; I "saw" the atoms of the elements and those of my body participating in this cosmic dance of energy; I felt its rhythm and I "heard" its sound, and at that moment I knew that this was the Dance of Shiva, the Lord of Dancers worshipped by the Hindus.[4]

The photomontage of dancing Siva superimposed on the subatomic particle tracks published in his book became quite a symbol of the synthesis of spirituality, art and science for significant sections of the intelligentsia in the West. Capra explains this further:

> The metaphor of the dance naturally comes to mind when one studies the dynamic web of relationships that constitutes the subatomic world. Since mystics have a dynamic world view similar to that of modern physicists, it is not surprising that they, too, have used the image of the dance to convey their intuition of nature. The metaphor of the cosmic dance has found its most beautiful expression in Hinduism

> in the image of Shiva Nataraja, the Lord of Dancers. For the modern physicist, the dance of Shiva is the dance of subatomic matter. As in Hindu mythology, it is a continual dance of creation and destruction involving the whole cosmos the basis of all existence and of all the natural phenomena.[5]

Nobel Laureate Ilya Prigogine saw in the dance of Siva a symbolism that explains the dual nature of irreversibility so fundamental to thermodynamics. In his 1986 Darwin lecture on the Origins of Complexity, he stated:

> Irreversibility generally has a dual aspect; it corresponds to dissipation (here the heat flow) and to the formation of order (the thermal diffusion). That is why I have put on the cover of one of my books a representation of a well-known Indian symbol, the dancing Shiva, who holds in one hand a fire which destroys, and in another a drum which creates![6]

Astrophysicist Carl Sagan in his famous serial-turned science popularizing book *Cosmos* had the following to say about the cosmic dance of Siva:

> The Chola bronzes, cast in the eleventh century, include several different incarnations of the god Shiva. The most elegant and sublime of these is a representation of the creation of the universe at the beginning of each cosmic cycle, a motif known as the cosmic dance of Shiva. The god, called in this manifestation Nataraja, the Dance King, has four hands. In the upper right hand is a drum whose sound is the sound of creation. In the upper left hand is a tongue of flame, a reminder that the universe, now newly created, will billions of years from now be utterly destroyed. These profound and lovely images are, I like to imagine, a kind of premonition of modern astronomical ideas....If there is more matter than we can see...then the universe will hold together gravitationally and partake of a very Indian succession of cycles, expansion followed by contraction, universe upon universe, Cosmos without end. If we live in such an oscillating universe, then the Big Bang is not the creation of the Cosmos but merely the end of the previous cycle, the destruction of the last incarnation of the Cosmos.[7]

Yet, in Tamil Nadu, the icon was crudely criticized by the so-called rationalists of the Dravidian movement. Ironically, this racist social movement which prided itself as rationalist was itself based on pseudoscientific colonial axioms of a separate Aryan and Dravidian race. In the name of pseudo-rationalism, it transformed the symbol of Nataraja into a literal rendering and made a cruel caricature of it, demeaning the dancing Siva into an emblem of primitive superstition. A Dravidian racist propaganda poster of 1970s shows an American astronaut descending on the crescent-wearing head of the dancing Siva.

There is a fundamental ironic paradox here. Throughout the world, it is usually fundamentalists who resort to literal interpretations of the scriptures. But in India, the so-called rationalists are the most eager to do the same, while the so-called believers often speak of their deities as symbolic rather than literal.

Unfortunately, the entire Indian educational system has a deeply inbuilt aversion to Indian symbols that have the capacity to harmonize science, philosophy, art and aesthetics. It is this rejection, the denial of a healthy dialogue between science and philosophical systems of India that is the reason for the cargo cult caricatures inventing such fabulously nonsensical narratives involving Siva, God Particle and world destruction.

The delusional digital contaminators spreading such message even forget to notice the obvious Indian connect to the so-called 'God Particle'—the Higgs boson. The boson, one of the two classes of subatomic particles, is named in honour of Indian scientist Satyendranath Bose, the prime creator of Bose-Einstein statistics, one of the foundations of particle physics. Incidentally, Bose was an ardent admirer of Swami Vivekananda. He drew a parallel between the words of Vivekananda and the works of Teilhard de Chardin [the Jesuit anthropologist who introduced the term 'noosphere' (more about him in the chapter on *samanvaya*). To Bose, 'the unprecedented synthesis of scientific temper and spirituality' that he finds in Swami Vivekananda was a need 'that persists even today' in the educational system of India.[8]

For the anti-Hindutva ideologues, academics and media, such pseudoscientific claims in the name of Hinduism, which find a receptive audience in most pro-Hindus on the internet, provide an opportunity to stigmatize and stereotype Hindutva. However, the dialogue and interaction of science and Hindu movement have been mostly fruitful and have helped the cause of science and humanity at large.

Hindu Science: Bankim Chandra to Prafulla Chandra Ray

The colonial conquest of the West as well as the introduction of Macaulay education created quite a lot of agonized churning in Indians. The Macaulay education was modern in the sense that it was universal education, while at the same time it was colonial in the sense that it aimed at creating obedient bureaucrats. Naturally, an educated elite was created—one who was well-versed in literature and law, economics and bookkeeping but divorced from science.

But it was evident to this elite that ultimately the power of the West derived itself from the power of institutional science. Hindus, both Macaulay-educated and traditionalist, reacted to this in different ways—from claiming superior knowledge encoded in the ancient literature to blaming Indian culture and tradition for India lagging in science and technology—the reactions varied through these two ends of the spectrum.

It should be noted that Bankim Chandra Chatterjee, the founding figure in the Hindutva revival movement, was quite sceptically cautious about the claims of Indians already having knowledge of modern science or interpreting every Hindu custom as having a scientific basis. For example, the traditionalist Sasadhar Tarkacudamani (1851–1925), a Sanskrit scholar and founder the 'Calcutta Dhanna Mandali' vociferously championed such views. Rabindranath Tagore provides a detailed account of Bankim Chandra's reaction to such claims:

> I first heard about him from Bankimbabu himself. I recall it was Bankimbabu who introduced me to him. At that time, the Hindus, in order to prove the superiority of their own religion, tried to make fantastic claims by citing evidence from Western science; and within a very short period this movement became all pervasive. For a long time before this, however, it was theosophy which created the background for such a movement. It was not the case, again, that Bankim babu was able to join this movement completely. No shadow of *Tarkacudamani* darkened the kind of explanation of religion that he was attempting at in the journal called *Prachär*; for this was altogether impossible.[9]

Incidentally in his 1873 essay on Hindu philosophy, Bankim Chandra makes an elaborate critique on what he considered was the impact of Hindu philosophy on the evolution of natural sciences in India that is worth quoting in detail and it is ironically a passage that might find resonance with today's leftist critique of the so-called other worldliness of Hindu philosophy being detrimental to the development of science:

> It must be borne in mind that Philosophy in India had never the restricted signification attached to it in modern Europe but was co-extensive in meaning with the knowledge of Nature. Philosophy therefore included Science. The Hindu laboured under the disadvantage of an erroneous method. An intense theological spirit rarely leads to anything but the deductive method, and the Hindu method was almost solely and purely deductive. Observation and Experiment were considered beneath the dignity of Philosophy and Science. Nor is even deduction as a rule pushed on its legitimate consequences....A Hindu philosopher in Torricelli's place would have contented himself with simply announcing in an aphoristic sutra that the air had weight.

> No measure of the quantity of its pressure would have been given; no experiment would have been made with the mercury; no Hindu Pascal would have ascended the Himalayas with a barometric column in hand. To take a parallel case. The diurnal rotation of the earth is shadowed forth in the *Aitareya Brahmana.* (Colebrooke's Essays, ii. p. 392.) Arya Bhatta distinctly affirms it. '*The starry firmament is fixed*,' says he, '*it is the earth which, continually revolving, produces the rising and the setting of the constellations and the planets*' (Dr Haug's Translation, ii. p. 142). In addition to this, the apparent annual motion of the sun and the periodical motion of the planets were well known. The only legitimate deduction from the combination of these three facts, viz., the diurnal rotation of the earth, the fixity of the heavenly bodies, and the apparent annual motion of the sun, was the heliocentric theory. But the heliocentric theory was never positively put forward—never sought to be proved—never accepted and never followed out to the establishment of the further laws of the universe. In modern Europe, the announcement of the Copernican theory rendered certain the future discovery of the laws of Kepler and of the great law of Universal Gravitation. In India, Arya Bhatta's remarkable announcement rendered certain that nothing further would come of it.[10]

The continuity of the dialogue between the Hindu movement and science reaches another high in Acharya Prafulla Chandra Ray's (1861–1944) voluminous *A History of Hindu Chemistry* (1903). Apart from about 200 original papers that he published in the *Journal of Chemical Society* (London), Acharya Ray was the first to synthesize mercurous nitrite. It was his work that established that nitrites were stable substances contrary to the dominant view that they were unstable. His demonstration that ammonium nitrite is indeed stable was highlighted by *Nature* (15 August 1912). Motivated by French chemist and politician Marcellin Berthelot, he wrote his monumental work on Hindu chemistry.

The work can rightly be considered the concretization of the Hindu civilizational tryst with the discourse of science that was initiated in the modern times by Swami Vivekananda. It was neither just a collection of facts nor vain glorification. It was a critical study taking into account the dynamics of social evolution and its role in shaping the way institutions of science emerge. Acharya Ray sharply criticizes the Euro-centric attitude in weaving the history of science that had a clear agenda of Western superiority. The tendency of colonial historiographers to impute Greek origins to many Indic scientific discoveries is carefully analysed by Ray:

> It is curious to reflect that the upholders of the 'Greek Culture' are often found ready, though unconsciously, to twist and torture facts and conclusions to serve

> their own purpose, and reserve to themselves the benefit of doubt as regards date: but whenever the priority of the Hindus is unquestionable, an appeal is made to the theory of common origin and independent parallelism of growth. These scholars seem to smart under a sense of injury if they have to confess that Europe owes an intellectual debt to India, hence many a futile attempt to explain away positive historical facts.[11]

Acharya Ray also analyses how social stagnation has led to the decline of science in ancient India. The remarkable passage that anticipates the later critique of caste by Dr Ambedkar is worth quoting in detail. Here the criticism and the judgement that he passes on India for not developing scientific enquiry and institutional science may not hold true with respect to a deeper postcolonial analysis and with larger set of data. But it shows that the 'nationalist' school was not all vain praise for ancient past and that they were trying to develop a self-critical all-encompassing social model with respect to science, sincerely and with an open mind. Acharya Ray states:

> In ancient India, the useful arts and sciences, as distinguished from mere handicrafts, were cultivated by the higher classes. In the White *Yajur Veda* and in the *Taittitriya Brahmana*, we meet with the names of various professions which throw light on the state of society of that period; unfortunately, the knowledge of these perished with the institution of the caste system in its most rigid form.... We also find that, among the companions of the poet Vāna were an assayer and a metallurgist. Such terms as '*lohavid*' and '*dhātuvid*' which occur repeatedly in Sanskrit literature show that the metallurgists were held in high esteem and expert knowledge sought....In the Vedic age the Rishis did not form an exclusive caste of their own but followed different professions according to their convenience or natural tastes...But all this was changed when the Brahmins reasserted their supremacy on the decline or the expulsion of Buddhism. The caste system was established de novo in a more rigid form. The drift of Manu and of the later Puranas is in the direction of glorifying the priestly class, set up most arrogant and outrageous pretensions. According to *Susruta*, the dissection of dead bodies is a sine qua non to the student of surgery and this higher authority lays particular stress on knowledge gained from experiment and observation. But Manu would have none of it. The very touch of a corpse, according to Manu, is enough to bring contamination to the sacred person of a Brahmin. Thus, we find that shortly after the time of *Vagbhata*, the handling of a lancet was discouraged and Anatomy and Surgery fell into disuse and became to all intents and purposes lost sciences to the Hindus.
>
> ...The arts being thus relegated to the low castes and the professions made hereditary...was done at a terrible cost. The intellectual portion of the community

> being thus withdrawn from active participation in the arts, the how and why of phenomena, the coordination of cause and effect were lost sight—the spirit of enquiry gradually died out among a nation naturally prone to speculation and metaphysical subtleties, and India for once bade adieu to experimental and inductive sciences. Her soil was rendered morally unfit for the birth of a Boyle, a Descartes or a Newton and her very name was all but expunged from the map of the scientific world. [12]

During the times of Acharya Ray too there were claims of ancient Hindus having what was then modern technology—missiles with chemical explosives. Today the same claims have evolved. The fertile scenarios created by Indian epic writers regarding the weapons of ancient wars are being projected as proofs of ancient nuclear technology. Here the Indian tendency to seek glory in the past alone is not to blame. The notorious documentary series *Ancient Aliens* aired on History Channel peddles such fantasies which simply get recycled by internet neo-Hindutvaites. Later, in academic studies on Hindutva, the movement gets strongly identified with such crackpot delusions. Yet as early as 1902–1903, Ray had dismissed any attempt made then to read any prevalent technologies of the times in the weaponry of the epics. He also rejected even certain Western scholars making claims for prior Indian knowledge of firearms. For example, When Dr G. Oppert standing up for the antiquity of *Sukraniti* that deals in a large passage with how fire powder was to be used for gun, etc., Acharya Roy wrote that it was 'more rational' to conclude that those verses 'were added some time after the introduction of gunpowder in Indian warfare during the Moslem period'.[13] Similarly, certain verses of Manu on the authority of Nathaniel Halhed's *A Code of Gentoo Laws* were proof of Hindu knowledge of firearms. He analysed the verses and concluded that it was only through 'a forced interpretation that anything in Manu might be taken to refer to a projectile discharged from a gun'. He writes:

> In Sanskrit literature, there are frequent but vague references to "agni astra" or firearms, but we have no reason to suppose that the combustible matter these firearms contained, supplied a motive power of the nature of the gunpowder. The fire missiles were probably of the same category as the "Greek fire" i.e., arrows or darts tipped with oiled flax, resin, regalar, naptha or other bituminous substances discharged from bows; sometimes elaborate machines being devised to hurl the weapons with more deadly effect. In the *Udyogaparava* of the Mahabharata, Yudhisthira is described as "collecting large quantities of resin, tow, and other inflammable articles for his great fratricidal war". But there is nothing to show that gunpowder of any sort was in use or any chemical which would act as a propelling agent.[14]

Acharya Ray is one of the first significant initiators in modern times, from the Hindu side, of a dialogue with science as a historical and human phenomenon. This is a legacy that has often been forgotten conveniently by the left-wing scholars studying the Hindutva movement and forgotten by Hindutvaites themselves. It is an area worth exploring further.

One can see in both Acharya Prafulla Chandra Roy and Bankim Chandra, a criticism of Indian society and culture as deficient in contributing factors to the development of science. But eminent Indian philosopher Bimal Krishna Matilal (1935–1991) in his analysis of Bankim Chandra's critique (which also applies to the criticism made by Acharya Prafulla Roy) makes the following observation:

> It is paradoxical to note that the lack of interest in deductive systems or formal science was compensated well enough by their avid interest in discovering the epistemic and empirical basis of logic, by their study of the theory of knowledge and the theory of evidence called pramänasästra (which was more akin to the inductive method based on observation and citation of supporting example). Thus, contrary to the general preconceived idea (and Bankim himself held such an idea also), I must say that the philosophical background (reinforced by the doctrine of the pramänas) was favourable towards the development of experimental science (though not for formal science). Unfortunately, other external factors intervened and stultified the growth of the natural sciences, for the spirit of experiment stopped at a certain level, and the technicians or proto-technicians lacked the basis of knowledge and the principles of logic to grasp and spell out for others the significance of any intuitively gained truths or any practical knowledge and skill they possessed.[15]

So, the divide between theory and practice which did exist in India could have been more due to the 'other external factors' like the invasions and later the colonial rule that aimed more at creating clerks than scientists. Again Prof. Matilal points out this aspect as well:

> When the Western-style education system was introduced in India through the efforts of people like Macaulay, we should note that the emphasis was liberal arts, literature and the humanities (the idea was to create a number of excellent and loyal bureaucrats). There was much less enthusiasm about experimental science and technological development. For the industrial West needed a ready market in the colonies, as well as supply of raw material to feed its industries, not any competition in technology or in the production of goods from the colonies. Thus, there remained for a considerable period of time a gap in the knowledge of experimental science and technology in colonial India.[16]

One can see that both colonialism and nationalist revivalism both placed the blame on the supposed other worldliness of Hindu view of life. In the case of the latter, there is at least the redeeming feature of reasserting an Indic or Hindu-Vedantic framework for scientific exploration.

But what must be looked at more seriously is the erroneous tendency that the above devaluing and decoupling of Indian culture has created in the way Hindu revivalism looks at modern science. With the rise of social media, it is *Tarakachironmani* recycled once again—this time through digital media—making the mental contagion even more severe.

One such worrying tendency is the attack on Newton in the digital Hindutva meme rhetoric. Before getting into the details of this disturbing phenomenon, we need to distinguish between an earlier type of critique of Newton's worldview and the recent attacks on him—the person and his science.

Of Newton, Gravity and Mathematics: Cargo Cult versus Hindutva Scientific Dialogue & Duty

As seen in the earlier chapter, Dattopant Thengadi (1920–2004) and H. V. Sheshadri (1926–2005) were two profound Hindutva ideologues coming from the Rashtriya Swayamsevak Sangh (RSS). They have criticized Newton's worldview. To them, the Newtonian universe offered a mechanical worldview and was the root cause of most problems at all levels that the individual, society and nature face today. They placed Hindutva as the organic alternative to this worldview.

Thengadi, in his lectures, had made the critique of Newton's worldview, integral to his critique of Marxism, which he considered 'an intellectual parasite on Newtonian science...' (*The Perspective*, 1971). He further considered it as a larger problem in the Western society:

> Except for a few modern scientists, the West, being still under the influence of Newtonian science, clings to the myth that mind is only a super-structure on matter and hence believes that socioeconomic structure is basic, deserving our exclusive attention. The religion, culture, ethics, literature, arts etc.—all these constitute a mere super-structure, which will automatically undergo appropriate corresponding changes, once the socio-economic order is altered...[17]

Based on the views of the Gandhian-Buddhist economist E. F. Schumacher, Seshadri made the following critique:

> In short, the overall dominance of the economic factor, of considering economic growth alone as the yardstick for measuring standard of life—to the exclusion of all other values of life, has verily led to the destruction of human personality. It has made man a mechanical part of the huge mechanical world he has created which has destroyed the natural rhythm of his life.[18]

The importance of the above Hindutva critique of Newton's worldview is that they contribute to the conceptual evolution of Hindutva by interacting with the deeper value system. It can be noted here that Newton's science was not questioned. The critique is on the worldview based on Newtonian physics, mainly in the context of society and the individual. In this, both Thengadi and Seshadri have not hesitated to align themselves with another Western tradition, though not dominant, which can be said to start from the critique of Newton by William Blake to the works on deep ecology and systems view of life by physicist-author Fritjof Capra.

That is not the case now.

What we have here is another instance of memes mediating on the 'cargo cult' Hindutva. Here, it is often claimed that Hindus discovered gravity, and Newton 'stole' from Hindus the idea of gravitational force. Such claims come from cultural illiteracy and an inferiority complex, and the ignorance of how global science evolves through contributions from various cultures. More importantly, such claims also deprive the Hindutva supporters of the important work of bringing to the fore the contributions that India really made to the evolution of scientific discourse.

Such claims have always been there though. However, when such claims were made, they were viewed with the scepticism and rejection they deserved and were critiqued. For example, even during the time of Lokmanya Bal Gangadhar Tilak (1856–1920), it was claimed that Vedic seers knew of the seven colours of the prism and that the horses of the sun were symbolic of that knowledge. But Tilak did not accept it. He wrote:

> The late Mr. S. P. Pandit goes so far as to assert that the seven rays here referred to may be the prismatic colors with which we are familiar in the Science of optics, or the seven colors of the rainbow. All this appears to be very satisfactory at the first sight, but our complacency is disturbed as soon as we are told that along with the seven rays and horses of the sun, the Rig-Veda speaks of ten horses or ten rays of the same luminary.[19]

Despite Tilak pointing out the ineffectiveness of drawing such parallels, this continues to be a part of the lore of 'Vedic science'. But the real twist in the tale comes from the fact that Newton's idea of seven colours itself emerges from a parallel he wanted to construct with the seven notes of the music scale. Peter Pesic, a physicist, a pianist and author of *Music and the Making of Modern Science* (MIT, 2014) says that there is 'no justification in experiment exactly' and that it represented 'something' that Newton was 'imposing upon the color spectrum by analogy with music'.[20] So much for Vedic rishis introducing the symbolism of Newton's discovery in the seven horses of the sun! There is a consolation though. The opening statement of the physicist-pianist-author reads:

> Music entered deeply into the making of modern science because it was already a central element of ancient philosophy. Greek concepts of number and cosmos were the foundations to which their successors looked, even when they turned toward new directions.[21]

And in the reference not given to this, he states:

> I will restrict myself to Greek developments, but the foundations of Chinese and Indian natural philosophy were also deeply involved with music. *Indeed, evidence suggests influence flowing from India to Greece*; though the interrelations with China need further study, the centrality of music in all three traditions is no accident, whatever may be the variety of historical influence and parallel invention.[22] (Emphasis not in the original)

So, there is indeed a Hindu connection but not as crude as the memes and its forefathers suggest.

With the dominance of social media, the problem escalated. In 2018 Satyapal Singh, who was then the Minister of State for Human Resources and Development, was reported to have claimed that 'there were mantras which codified "laws of motion" much before it was discovered by Newton'.[23] Even if one gives enough discount for the distortions that the mainstream media is capable of making in any BJP minister's statement, here the possibility is more that the minister could have made such a statement. A few months ago, in November 2017, another BJP leader, a bitter critic-turned-new-entrant to the party and now a Member of Parliament in the upper house (Rajya Sabha), Dr Subramanian Swamy tweeted that Manchester University had confirmed 'this how Newton stole the concept of gravity from a Hindu Gurukul'.[24]

The tweet is linked to an article with a meme which depicts Kanada—the seer associated with Vaisheshika Darshan as a 'Vedic nuclear scientist' and all three laws of motion by Newton get ascribed to the seer—which, of course, can only be obtained by Zakir Naik-like distortions.

This Kanada-Newton linkage provides an insight into the cultural illiteracy ailment that is inherent in cargo cult Hindutva. The connection comes from the fact that among the different qualities or gunas of Vaisheshika Darshana is *gurutva*. Earlier, colonial Indologists translated gurutva as gravity, and Vaisheshika sutras associate this quality with falling of the bodies. So, it is quite tempting to presume that Kanada indeed first discovered gravity. While Kanada's Vaisheshika system had in it some of the fundamental and crucial insights into the science of motion, it was still far from formulating the laws of motion and gravitation. Here is an insightful analysis by a physicist:

> While speculating on matter, the Vaisheshika realists did not fail to notice the fundamental importance of motion. In fact, one of their definitions of substance recognizes motion as an inherent quality of the substance (kriyaavattva). Moreover, motion (karma) is acknowledged as one of the six categories with which to comprehend the physical world.... The basic concepts of motion were introduced during the formulation of the Vaisheshika aphorisms (c 300 BC). Unfortunately, no further study of the nature of motion was undertaken by the later exponents of the school until *Prasastapada* (c AD 600) revived the idea in his *Padarthadharma-sangrha....Prasastapada* defines motion as the change of place of particles as "property of acting as independent cause of conjunctions and disjunctions". He regarded motion as instantaneous in its simplest form, distinguishing it from impressed motion, momentum, which is a persistent tendency and implies a series of motions. This concept does not readily correspond with Galileo's (1564–1642) concept of uniform motion in a straight line....Although Prasastapada was aware of the nature of vectors, he did not explore their properties. In any case, he may be considered to be the pioneer in vectorial concept.[25]

In the Vaisheshika system, the objects were qualitatively viewed, and motion was thus caused by a quality in the substance. And it did not bother itself with time. It was the Nyaya school which brought in the idea of a series of samskara (impressed motion). According to Dr Chatterjee, with this, the Nyaya-Vaisheshika school also brought in the concept of '*vega*':

> The power of samskara diminishes by doing work against counteracting forces and when the samskara is in this way exhausted, the moving body comes to rest. Thus, *vega* corresponds to inertia in some respects and to momentum in some others. This is the nearest approach to Newton's first law of motion.[26]

It is important here to understand the parallel evolution of science in the Western tradition.

Galileo Galilei (1564–1642) discovered that the speed at which a body falls is independent of the weight or size of the body. Galileo proved, with experiments, that the objects having different weights (varied gurutva) fall at the same time, if the air resistance is removed. Yet for all his pioneering efforts, Galileo was so wedded to the ideas of Plato that he rejected the Johannes Kepler's idea of elliptical orbits for planets. For Galileo, the planetary orbits had to be circular.

Newton's first two laws have contributions from Galileo. Newton himself acknowledged that he was standing on the shoulders of two giants—Galileo and Kepler.

So, if someone accuses Newton of 'stealing' the concept of gravity from a Hindu gurukul, then he should also blame Galileo of the same. But then, even for the cargo cult Hindutva brigade as it is for other rational Hindutva supporters, Galileo is clearly a symbol of resistance to the church. And to accuse him would be to undermine their own case. So, the accusation that Newton 'stole' the laws of motion and gravity from India simply falls flat. Far from a person who steals and publishes, Newton had lost all interest in mechanics until 1684. It was at the insistence of astronomer Edmond Halley that he published his magnum opus *Principia Mathematica*. That is not exactly the behaviour of a person who 'steals' and refuses to give credit.

However, there is indeed a Hindu connection to the Newton story. Mathematician C. K. Raju makes a passionate and plausible case for the transmission of what is called the 'Taylor-series' expansion, which is at the heart of the mathematical tool used by Newton. C. K. Raju argues that it came from India, and Jesuits were instrumental in bringing this knowledge.

> The English-speaking world has known for over one-and-a-half centuries that "Taylor" series expansions for sine, cosine and arc-tangent functions were found in Indian mathematics/astronomy/timekeeping (jyotisa) texts, and specifically in the works of Madhava, Nilakantha (Tantrasangraha, 1501 CE), Sankara Variyar (Tantrasangraha Vyakliya), Jyesthadeva (Yuktibhasa, ca 1530 CE), Kriydkrarnakan, etc.... Historically, to relate Madhava's sine, cosine, and arc-tan series expansion to the European use of the calculus, it is convenient to consider two stages: (i) the import of these infinite-series techniques into Europe, and (ii) the dissemination of those techniques within Europe....(T)he Jesuits were initially not sufficiently well-trained in mathematics and astronomy to understand how the panchanga was made. After about 1575, however, Jesuits, like Matteo Ricci, who trained in mathematics and astronomy under Clavius' new syllabus were sent to India. (Ricci also visited Coimbra and learnt navigation. He remained devoted to Clavius, and he later translated Clavius' books into Chinese.) In a 1581 letter to Petri Maff'ei, Ricci

> acknowledged that he was trying to understand local methods of timekeeping from "an intelligent Brahmin or an honest Moor"....by 1610, the Jesuits were confident enough about their knowledge of Indian mathematics and astronomy to write polemics against its older versions.[27]

Here it should be noted that the mainstream historians of mathematics, even while acknowledging that Hindu mathematicians arrived earlier than Newton and Leibniz, hesitate to acknowledge the knowledge transmission from East to West. For example, mathematics historian Kim Plofker of Princeton University, while accepting that the infinite series of Madhava 'predate by centuries Newton's and Leibniz's versions of them'[28] and that they 'did not appear in Latin mathematics until late in the seventeenth century' and wants it to be 'economically explained as cases of parallel evolution than as evidence of direct transmission'.[29] Acknowledging the earlier discovery by the Hindu mathematician, he even suggests a change of name to the series: 'Madhava-Leibniz series for $\pi/4$ and the Madhava-Newton power series for the Sine and Cosine'.[30]

Another economist from Kerala, George Gheverghese Joseph, had also written a book on the same subject titled *A Passage to Infinity* (Sage, 2009) when the author was with the University of Manchester. There was a bitter controversy with C. K. Raju alleging that Joseph had used most of Raju's work. In 2010 the university declared that 'Indians predated Newton's "discovery" by 250 years'. It also acknowledged that 'the significant body of work was conducted by Professor C. K. Raju in this area'.

Now this brings us to the question: If Hindutva or Hinduness is reasserting the scientific heritage of India, then what should be the unique civilizational element that Hindutva should take to the students, so that delusions and fallacies of cargo cult Hindutva could be avoided?

Almost a thousand years before Galileo and Kepler, Aryabhatta had declared the paths of the planets and the moon should be elliptical; he also declared that the diurnal changes happen because of earth's rotation—this was, however, not the dominant view then. The dominant view as reflected in *Surya Siddhanta* was geocentric and with circular orbits of planets. Thus, in comparison, Aryabhatta was a rebel far more complete than Galileo. But he was not persecuted. India never produced an index of forbidden books and placed in it. Instead, Aryabhatta was, and to this day, is hailed as an acharya. Of course, Aryabhatta had not arrived at a direct heliocentric theory. As seen earlier, even a nationalist like Bankim Chandra Chatterjee did not try to hide the fact. He faulted with Hindu philosophy for not taking forward the discovery of Aryabhatta, which would have logically led to the discovery of a heliocentric solar system. But as seen earlier, that criticism was more the result of a colonial stereotype of Hinduism and Hindus than it had to do with historic reality.

Even if Aryabhatta had explicitly arrived at a heliocentric theory, it would not have created an inquisitional persecution. Computational scientist and historian of science Subhash Kak explains:

> This was because the physical centrality of the Earth in the universe was a central belief in the dogma of the Christian Church, although it originated in the earlier Aristotelian ideas. This was in contrast to India where the Earth did not play a central role in cosmology. In the Puranas, there is mention of innumerable world systems beyond our own.[31]

This aspect of the non-confrontational, open and flexible nature of Puranic cosmology with respect to empirical astronomy fosters and facilitates a healthy scientific outlook in the society.

Also important in the tradition of Hinduness is the scientific spirit of Nilakantha Somayaji, who was an astronomer and mathematician of Kerala school. He died 20 years before the birth of Galileo. Nilakantha advocated what Plofker calls 'actual, gradual, process of creating a scientific tradition' over 'a naive view of scriptural authority'. In his work *Jyotirmeemamsa*, Nilakantha says:

> ...this [is what] some think. "Because of Brahman's omniscience, freedom from passion and hatred etc., and certainty of truth, how [can there be] criticism [or testing] of that?" Stupid! [It is] not thus. The favor of the deity is just the cause of mental clarity. Neither Brahman nor the Sun-god [but Aryabhatta] himself taught it

Such an approach that gives primacy to knowledge gained through observation over established authority resulted in the creation of some very impressive models:

> This bold approach to the construction and revision of mathematical models allowed Nilakantha to make some ingenious modifications to the Aryapaksha system. Most strikingly, he changed the arrangement of planetary orbital circles to something that was computationally equivalent to a quasi-heliocentric system similar to the later one of Tycho Brahe, where most of the planets orbit the sun, which in turn orbits the earth.[32]

India has never shown tendencies like inability in accepting the irrational numbers that the West had, because of its adherence to the concept of Platonic perfection as understood in a limited anthropomorphic way or later because of the West's overdependence on abacus-based mathematics. In the words of mathematician C. K. Raju (definitely a non-Hindutvaite):

> Unlike Greek tradition, no special mystical significance was attached to ratios (or the corresponding musical harmonies), and irrational numbers like \/2 are treated like other numbers from the days of the sulba sutra...Indian tradition had no problem with irrational numbers like \/2 or the so-called transcendental numbers like "pi" for which it long accepted the impossibility of stating an exact value. However, such irrational numbers arising from the solution of quadratic equations, or interest calculations, were viewed with suspicion in European tradition, since the abacus could not very well be used to solve quadratic equations, or to represent irrational numbers.[33]

Thus, Hinduness or Hindutva in the larger and deeper sense of the term has the duty not to indulge in cargo cult fantasies, but to fulfil its historical duty of taking the uniquely favourable civilizational aspects of Hindu culture and philosophy to the Indian public—including the educated elite who are under the impression that Indian culture in general and the so-called 'Brahminical' aspects in particular are responsible for the downfall of Indian science.

Cargo Cult of the Colonized Left

This line, blaming the uniquely Hindu 'Brahminical' for India not being 'scientific' is yet another kind of cargo cult pop socio-psychology. During the colonial rule, this was used as a response to the British line of thinking that Hindus by nature lacked the ability to practice science. So, this was the nationalist answer, saying the reason for Hindus not practising science was some kind of internal fall. But soon this very line of argument, which has been mostly and correctly countered by Prof. Bimal Krishna Matilal, as seen earlier in this chapter, started getting reused by anti-Hindu ideologues.

A quintessential instance of this line of argument can be understood from the writings of one such ideologue S. Anand. In his article on what ails science in India, he tows the same line. After speculating a historic grand fight between what he considers 'heterodox, atheistic credos such as Buddhism or the Lokayata of Charvak' and 'orthodox tendencies of Vedic Brahminism', he states 'what really triumphed over all else was the Advaita Vedanta of Sankara that deals almost entirely with metaphysical speculation based on the Upanishads'. This, he says, had disastrous consequences for the development of science in India:

> In the Brahminical universe, a dichotomy was constructed between the spiritual and physical realms, where the former was prioritised as clean and the latter as polluting. Knowledge systems that involved physical labour came to be inferiorised as menial. Hence, the celebration of the intellectual "science as logic, mathematics and astronomy-astrology (in ancient India, the two came under one head, jyothishya, and hence the persistent, Murli Manohar Joshi led confusion). In fact, one historian of science believes that philosophical formulations concerning shoonya (emptiness/void) could have led to the conceptualisation of zero. Abstruse intellectual jugglery and philosophical mumbo-jumbo passed for science. The rupture between the physical and intellectual meant Brahmins couldn't soil their hands with "impure" materials, while the working castes were denied access to logical and philosophical training of the gurukuls. There was thus never any ground for genuine people-centric science to take root.[34]

The problem in this kind of argument is multifold. Actually what S. Anand postulates is, in a way, the 'good proletariat science' versus the 'bad bourgeois science' framework of the Soviet era which bred Lysenkos and killed Vavilovs. Further, this line of argument also suffers from the fallacy pointed out by Hindutva thinker Sita Ram Goel, which is

> An intellectual inclination to compare Hindu ideals and institutions from the past not with their contemporaneous ideals and institutions in the West but with what the West has achieved in its recent history—the 19th and the 20th Centuries.[35]

The reason behind learning the theory but not doing the practical is a colonial system imposed upon India rather than a feature inherent to India. Applying Sita Ram Goel's principle to the argument of S. Anand brings out the latter's fallacy. As proof of his argument, he states that 'a brahmanised Ayurveda came to be privileged as a science to be practiced by "upper" caste vaids while surgery and midwifery became the domain of the "lower" castes'.

In reality, this divide between the surgeons and doctors was minimal in India.

Far from that, despite all the glorification of the 'Buddhist' era as being more scientific than 'Brahminical', in reality we see the Buddhist era as more authority-dependent than the Vedic.

The allegiance to the Vedas were never bounding like say the scriptural utterances of prophetic religions. The poetic nature of Vedic hymns and plural ways of interpreting and understanding them along with Upanishadic way of interiorizing the rituals—they all combined to create a system where the scientific pursuit of any individual was not hampered. Any new advancement could be accepted through a novel interpretation. But in the utterances of Buddha, what one finds is a definiteness which is closer to the dictates of the prophetic religions. Thus, while Ayurveda did continue to prosper thanks to the humanitarian expansion of the Buddhist monks and the state patronage to religious charities (mostly cutting across sects in ancient India), cadaver dissection to use of sharp instruments started rapidly decreasing in Buddhist and post-Buddhist India.

The physicians were looked down upon in pre-modern human societies. We do find this prejudice in pre-modern Indian society too. But Hindu value system worked against this prejudice.

Sangh and Science: Propaganda

> The building was buzzing too, with a human hum. I followed the sound and found most of the staff gathered in Professor Habib's office and his desk littered with placards: Unite and fight saffronization—Saffronization the main danger today! Don't cover up saffronization in the mock fight against 'globalization'. I wasn't enlightened. Another imperative, leaning against a cupboard, offered a clue: Say No to Vedic Astrology departments in universities. In a lull in the debate, one of the lecturers explained. A conference on higher education was taking place, and many of the faculty had been picketing it in protest at government plans to fund the teachings of astrology and other occult Hindu sciences in universities. It had even been suggested that the new course components should include palmistry and levitation.
>
> Hand-reading would be a devil to examine, at least in its applied form; but levitation?... Somebody had been reading too much of Harry Potter. "You're joking", I said.
>
> He wasn't. Serious money was being earmarked for the scheme and the inspiration behind it was not Hogwarts School for Witches and Wizards but the Rashtriya Swayamsevak Sangh or Organization of National Volunteers. In a sensible world, the RSS too would be a joke: with their uniform of forage caps and Boy Scout shorts, they look like some offshoot of P. G. Woodhouse's fictional foot-bagged fascists, the Black Shorts. But they too are deadly serious and with the Prime Minister and many of his party elite as members immensely powerful. Sartorially Stanley Matthews and ideologically Joseph Goebbels, the RSS are Brahminical supremacists who regard India's 140 million-odd Muslims—not to mention all other non-Hindu minorities—as at best aliens to be tolerated on sufferance, at worst insufferable parasites.[36]

The reader who has been with the book so far will probably identify the above passage as an excerpt from some left-wing propaganda pamphlet, or an academic tome by a 'South Asia scholar' from a Western University, most probably from the United States, studying the Hindu 'right-wing' politics in India. But this is from neither. This is from a travelogue written by Tim Mackintosh-Smith, British Yemen-based Oxford-educated Arabist, writer, traveller and lecturer. *The Hall of a Thousand Columns* is a travelogue in which Smith follows the footsteps of Ibn Batutta, the fourteenth century Muslim traveller in India. The above passage is when Smith comes to Aligarh Muslim University (AMU) and meets historian Prof. Irfan Habib.

The extract provides the kind of negative caricature of Hindutva that is indulged in by the Nehruvian establishment circles in India which the mainstream Western academia and media bought without scrutiny. The fact that even a travelogue contains such a biased critique and negative caricature of Dr Murli Manohar Joshi, Human Resource Development (HRD) Minister in the Atal Bihari Vajpayee-led NDA government (1998–2004), making the situation sound very similar to the Nazi fascination for the occult, should make one realize the quantum of propaganda that the anti-Hindutva forces assiduously carry out against the 'Hindu nationalists' in office.

Did Dr Joshi and his team try to turn the wheel backwards and introduce 'occult Hindu' pseudosciences funded by the taxpayers' money? What exactly is the legacy of Dr Joshi and broadly the Sangh Parivar with respect to science and technology when NDA ruled India for six years? The answers may start at least three years earlier than 1998 when the NDA came to power.

India saw a mass religious phenomenon across the country on 21 September. Kiran Bedi, then an IPS officer, offered milk to the statues of Hindu-Buddhist deities in her house, and they all accepted the milk. 'The milk just disappeared into thin air,' she stated. Vishnu Hari Dalmia, then President of the VHP, called it a 'divine miracle'. The Congress leaders like Vasanth Sathe and V. N. Gadgil charged the Sangh Parivar for starting a fake miracle 'to exploit religious feelings for political ends'. However, Gopinath Munde, then Deputy CM of the BJP-Shiv Sena government in Maharashtra, declared unequivocally that neither his government nor he believed this milk drinking by idols to be possible. Even more remarkable was the statement by Dr Joshi. A qualified nuclear physicist, Dr Joshi declared: 'As a physicist, I have to conclude that it's due to capillary action and surface tension. Nothing more'.[37]

It was the same Dr Joshi who, as HRD Minister in the NDA government, was targeted in a sustained way by leftists as well as anti-BJP media houses and repeatedly caricatured as an anti-scientific obscurantist trying to introduce Hindu mumbo-jumbo into the curriculum, taking modern scientific education thousands of years back into the Vedic dark age. The propaganda against Dr Joshi centred on the allegation that he was the brain behind the University

Grants Commission's (UGC's) decision to allow the introduction of 'Vedic astrology' in the university curriculum. In an article published in the pro-Chinese magazine *Frontline*, theoretical physicist Dr T. Jayaraman alleged that there was a 'high-profile and pro-active campaign' by Dr Joshi and the then Chairman of the UGC 'for the introduction of Vedic astrology as a "scientific discipline" to be pursued as a subject of study in universities in India.'[38]

Eminent citizens and scientists signed petitions and issued public statements against the pseudoscience of astrology and saffron propaganda. Far from indulging in any 'high profile pro-active' campaign in support for astrology, Dr Joshi distanced himself from the UGC decision. In an interview to the magazine *India Today*, he categorically stated: 'The astrology course isn't my policy. That's UGC's baby.' The former physics professor at Allahabad University clearly knows his physics well enough not to defend astrology as a 'science'. Hence, he spoke in the interview about the larger issues of what is science and invited a debate among scientists on the issues of reductionism and holism, etc. With regard to Vedic astrology, Dr Joshi was not so keen to defend the decision unequivocally, leave alone indulge in any 'high profile' campaign. But there was one strong defender of the decision of UGC to allow universities the introduction of Vedic astrology. Just as Dr Joshi denied his role in the introduction of astrology, this leader defended the decision categorically: 'Astrology is a science, so there is nothing wrong if some do research in astrology.' That was Digvijaya Singh, the arch-Nehruvian pro-dynasty politician and then the Chief Minister of Madhya Pradesh.[39]

Dr Joshi & TKDL

Nevertheless, the period under the NDA-I Government (1998–2004) saw some very important milestones with far reaching consequences not only for India, but also for the so-called 'Third World' in science and technology. On 13 August 2014, two days before India's celebration of her 68th Independence Day, the European Patent Office (EPO) withdrew patent application no. EP2419508. The application, 'Method for the induction of a reward response by modulation of dopaminergic systems in the central nervous system' had been filed by US-based Somalab. It proposed the use of lotus and cowage in the treatment of obesity and hunger control. However, there was a third-party intervention. The third party claimed that this formulation was already part of the traditional medical knowledge of India. Three ancient Indian medical texts were shown as evidence: *Vangasena*, *Kaiyadevanighantau* by *Kaiyadeva* and *Aryabhisaka* by *Smkaradajisatrapade*.[40]

That third-party intervention was made by 'Traditional Knowledge Digital Library' (TKDL).

TKDL was initiated in the year 2001. An interdisciplinary task force, it has been vigorously documenting traditional bio-cultural knowledge of Indic communities and has been at the forefront of fighting patents of these community knowledge bases by pharmaceutical companies—mainly based in the West. The concept of Traditional Knowledge Systems (TKS) was emphasized by Dr Murli Manohar Joshi in his inaugural speech at the 87th Indian Science Congress on 3 January 2000 at Pune. He explained:

> I would urge you to also think in totally new directions.... Also, our cultural and civilizational base is strong. But, in referring to "traditional knowledge systems", we refer to all those knowledge systems that have been developed in India and in other ancient societies of the world, based on long periods of empirical observation and experience. These knowledge systems have not yet been integrated into modern science and technology. It is important to recognise that these traditional knowledge systems may contain truths derived in a different way, often by processes that are very slow compared to those that man has developed in the last few centuries. That however does not make them invalid. I would call upon the scientists and technologists of our country to undertake a major exercise so that the areas where traditional knowledge systems appear to offer us new clues—for example, areas like herbal medicine, physical and mental health, environment and other related matters—are made the subject of serious investigation along modern scientific lines. I would envisage persons with knowledge of Sanskrit, other Indian languages, and Arabic, Persian, etc., and specialists in different areas of modern science and technology such as biotechnology, botany, geography, information, technology, computer simulation etc., as well as in social sciences like anthropology and archaeology, to come together and create new knowledge products based on traditional knowledge. Such 'knowledge mining' from ancient cultures and knowledge bases is today seen as a fruitful practice all over the world. The developed world is making a serious study of the traditional knowledge systems for this purpose. Let us make our national heritage a great national resource.[41]

TKDL is of course the result of sustained and innovative teamwork including regional TK experts, scientists and software professionals. Dr V. K. Gupta was particularly instrumental in the conceptualization of TKDL. One important member of the core team for this endeavour, starting from the recognition of the need for the creation of a traditional knowledge database to the presentation of the vision and concept was Dr Raghunath Anant Mashelkar, then Director General of the Council of Scientific and Industrial Research (CSIR), with an immense knowledge in the field of Intellectual Property Rights (IPR).[42] It was the Joshi-Mashelkar synergy that was instrumental in the spirited speeding up of things. India's renowned experimental and reverse pharmacologist Dr Ashok Vaidya pointed out in a 2011 interview how the in-depth knowledge of patent and IPR issues that Dr Mashelkar possessed immensely helped in infusing a new culture to the scientific establishment.[43]

Nehruvian McCarthyism

The anti-Hindutva forces almost immediately started a campaign against Dr Mashelkar. A staunch Nehruvian tabloid *Communalism Combat*, run by Javed Anand and Teesta Setalvad, in an article published in 2001 fired the first salvo:

> The director general of the CSIR, R. A. Mashelkar was felicitated by the RSS's Rashtriya Suraksha Mahashivir last month. This created some public discomfort for the ministry because it was more evidence (if any were needed) of the growing influence of Swayamsevak Joshi's influence over the orientation of the CSIR.[44]

In the general elections of 2004, the BJP-led NDA lost power. Still, in 2005 the CPI(M) mouthpiece *People's Democracy* targeted Dr Mashelkar:

> The Director, R. A. Mashelkar was busy attending the RSS shakhas and defending his actions. The HRD minister, who happened to be the vice-president of CSIR was busy implementing the agenda of saffronisation. The prime minister, the ex-officio president of CSIR was proclaiming himself to be a Swayamsevak![45]

In 2007 the Nehruvian historian Ramachandra Guha wrote:

> The report, submitted after Dr Mashelkar demitted office, was found by two eagle-eyed researchers to have lifted chunks, without attribution, from a report prepared by an Oxford researcher at the behest of multinational pharmaceutical companies. In the resultant furore Dr Mashelkar withdrew his report, while claiming that the error was accidental, and unprecedented. Soon it turned out that in a book on intellectual property that he co-authored with another Indian in 2004, Dr Mashelkar had based some of his findings, again without attribution, on a paper written by a British academic in 1996. In his time at the CSIR, Dr Mashelkar had a reputation for dynamism, for infusing life and energy into a somnolent organization. To be sure, he did things scientists were not supposed to do. For example, he was felicitated in a function hosted by the Rashtriya Swayamsewak Sangh.[46]

The facts of the case are that the so-called non-attributed original source mentioned in the first allegation was a report by Prof. Shamnad Basheer. Prof. Basheer himself made it abundantly clear that there was no case of plagiarism as alleged:

> Those with the patience to read the entire report including the Annexures would have gathered that some of the Committee's observations were borrowed from my report and not "plagiarized".[47]

Another expert Cara Bradley points out:

> In other words, the appendices to the Mashelkar report had included an overview of relevant practices in other countries, and had provided a brief summary of Basheer's work, although it did not give a complete citation and rather than mention Basheer himself, referred to the institute for which he was commissioned to produce the report.[48]

In the case of the other book Guha mentions titled *Intellectual Property and Competitive Strategies in the 21st Century*, the non-attribution was more an error than a case of intentional plagiarism. Incidentally, Mashelkar co-authored the book with Shahid Ali Khan, and it was Khan's name that appears as the first author. But Guha hides that name under the blanket 'another Indian'. But in the very next edition of the book (2006), the error was corrected, and the proper attribution was done.[49] Guha's piece appeared in the newspaper *The Telegraph* in March 2007.

Clearly the denigration has only one aim: a lesson to other scientists that they would face high voltage smear campaign even if a guilt by association is suspected on them by Nehruvian establishment—in other words, a Nehruvian McCarthyism and inquisition.

The Success of TKDL

All these cannot change the fact that TKDL went on to become quite a success. In 2003 Dr M. M. Joshi, releasing the TKDL CD-ROM related to Ayurveda, stated that efforts are also being made to link the traditional knowledge resource classification developed by India with the International Patent Classification (IPC). Further elaborating his vision, Dr Joshi stated that the TKDL database would be made available to patent examiners globally under a non-disclosure agreement and would be put on the web with secured access.

Pointing out the earlier battles like in Basmati and Turmeric patents where India had spent millions of dollars to get them back, TKDL would cut down the costs considerably in such battles. He also wanted an ambitious expansion of TKDL in other areas as well including folklore, art, etc. Smt. Sushma Swaraj (1952–2019) then the Minister for Health and Family Welfare, in the same function emphasized the fact that the TKDL CD-ROM would be submitted to the Director General of the 'World Intellectual Property Organisation' (WIPO), Geneva. [50]

Since then, TKDL has stopped many patents on herbal formulation of Indic origin in both US and European patent offices (even though, unfortunately, Indian immigrant techies have been instrumental in providing the West considerable leads). In the process, TKDL has taken on multinational giants like Johnson & Johnson, Nestle and Unilever.[51] A study on the impact of TKDL for more than a decade points out that in this period, TKDL has developed its own classification system—the 'Traditional Knowledge Resource Classification (TKRC)' and 2,92,662 transcriptions of traditional medicine formulation in TKDL have been completed, among them 97,203 from Ayurveda, 1,70,990 from Unani, 22,815 from Siddha and 1,654 from Yoga. TKDL has also crated substantial decrease in herbal-patents from India by transnational pharmaceutical companies. The paper then points out the global impact of TKDL:

> World Intellectual Property Organization, including the global community has acknowledged TKDL and India's leadership in the area of IPR and TK. Though India presently is not a member of the IPC union, the TKDL database has been chosen for a pilot study by 170 member states of World Intellectual Property Organization. Considering the novelty, importance, efficacy and success of TKDL in preventing the grant of wrong patents, several countries and organizations (like South Africa, African Regional Industrial Property Organization, Mongolia, Nigeria, Thailand, Malaysia) have expressed their eagerness in replicating the TKDL model in their own countries. [52]

In the 2001 Science Congress lecture by Dr M. M. Joshi, he had pointed out that the traditional knowledge systems are not unique to India but that all ancient civilizations throughout the world have them and that they need to be preserved. In 2014 more than a decade down the line, the system that his swadeshi science vision triggered has indeed become a model for global traditional knowledge preservation.

It would be expected that in an unbiased media and academia, it is this initiative that would have been considered, if not as the most important achievement of the Indian science establishment under the 'saffron' regime, at least for a proper mention while dealing with the so-called 'saffronization', etc. TKDL combines swadeshi, science and traditional wisdom as well as international IPR issues like never before. It is this aspect which Dr Joshi promoted vigorously that should have defined the swadeshi agenda, which under his regime concretized into a global fight against bio-piracy as well as verifying and validating traditional knowledge through modern science and conserving it for posterity through digital technology. Yet the questionable allegation on Dr Joshi promoting 'astrology and other occult Hindu pseudosciences' is what the media and anti-Hindutva propaganda, both in the media as well as academia, continuously disseminated, and they did it so effectively that the general educated psyche both in India and abroad bought it without questioning and without caring to see what Dr Joshi actually achieved for not just India but humanity at large.

Hindutva Science and Technology: Critical Study of Two Critiques

In this aspect, two books are important. One is about studying the Hindutva approach to science and another a general study of technology in independent India with a focus on how the BJP government under Modi approaches science. The former is *Holy Science: The Biopolitics of Hindu Nationalism* (University of Washington Press, 2019) written by Prof. Banu Subramaniam of the University of Massachusetts Amherst, where she heads research in Feminist Science Studies. The latter is *Midnight's Machines: A Political History of Technology in India* (Penguin Random House India, 2019) by Arun Mohan Sukumar. He is a PhD candidate at the Fletcher School, Tufts University and a junior fellow at the school's Centre for International Law and Governance, who also heads the Technology Initiative at the Observer Research Foundation, New Delhi.

'Holy Science': Academic Sleight of Hand Hindumisia

Holy Science by Banu Subramaniam is a liberal cocktail of postmodern and postcolonial jargon meshed with tortured narratives and assemblage of misinformation about 'Hindu nationalism' in particular and Hindu Dharma in general. The anti-Hindu bias is explicit.

Ultimately, it ends with the usual lament as to 'how many bodies and voices might never have been allowed into these Brahminic hallways through the inhuman dictates of caste and gender that relegated some bodies to exist outside the folds of Hinduism'—'the same bodies mobilized to build the temples were the same bodies turned away when in prayer'.[53] One should note here that the social history of Hindu Dharma has ample proof that negates this assertion. Both women and men of all *jatis* had access to temples at one time or another. While social stagnation, social hierarchy and social elimination did exist in India as it existed in almost all the pre-modern societies, Hindu spirituality asserted against social stagnation as a notion of spiritual democracy that had consequences in social value system.

Banu Subramaniam often resorts to her childhood memories of 'puritanical Brahminism'—a neat trick to emphasize her emancipated nature for the Western reader. But if only she had taken a moment's time to look at the temple tower of Mylapore, she would have found a proclamation made for all humanity to see—Siva appearing in the form of a defiled 'impure body' of an outcaste of that time—and the pious who shunned him getting cursed to social exclusion themselves. These are stories Hindu children grew up with. If one goes through the multiple titles of Amar Chitra Katha one would find repeated rejection of the concepts of bodily purity and social exclusion. There are reasons why social exclusion exists and persists—but it must be sought in the factors of power politics, colossal colonial impoverishment and other such reasons that cause social stagnation.

Central to Subramaniam's approach is the term 'bionationalism', which is actually a term she borrows from Herbert Gottweis and Byoungsoo Kim, academicians from the University of Vienna, who coined it in the wake of the fraud committed by the South Korean stem cell scientist Hwang Woo-Suk. She uses or rather misuses the term in a completely different context, 'where Hindu nationalist ideas and ideologies are scientized through biopolitical claims about gender, race, caste and sexuality'. She also charges contemporary India with bolstering 'essentializing claims of caste'.[54]

From the Indian Genome Variation Project (IGVP) to Ayurgenomics—all of them become 'agents' of bionationalism and genomic-nationalism. Of course, behind all these, there lurks ominously the spectre of Hindu nationalism—upper caste and patriarchal. Attempts to link caste with race in international forums get a positive flip, and any attempt to delink caste and race become suspect. 'Dalit' activists (who are actually connected with right-wing evangelical organizations in the United States) who used genetic studies to further their propaganda about caste and race become the good people in her narrative.

The 'upper-caste' scientists of India who challenge them are the antagonists. It is interesting that the author avoids mentioning Dr Ambedkar at all in this context. The reader may be reminded that Ambedkar had rejected the racial interpretation of caste system and social exclusion even as he uncompromisingly fought against both. Her ignorance of Indian culture, history and Indian social reality can be only matched by her ability to use every Western theorist to demonize Hindutva. For example, she confidently claims:

> Swami Vivekananda created a nationalist discourse that is central to Hindu nationalism in all its versions, including the RSS/BJP/VHP brand of Hindu nationalism. ...Vivekananda believed that women should not be educated in modern sciences but should achieve fulfilment within the family.

A reviewer in *India Today* is more than eager to accept this as gospel truth and states: 'Subramaniam nails the patriarchy, correctly tracing its roots to Vivekananda, who believed women should not be taught science....' Banu Subramaniam's own reference for this assertion on Vivekananda is Kumari Jayawardena's *Feminism and Nationalism in the Third World* (1988), in which she says thus:

> Ramakrishna's renowned disciple Vivekananda, however, a radical on many issues, believed that a woman should not be educated in the modern sciences but should be trained to achieve fulfilment within the family.

But what Swami Vivekananda has actually said is entirely different from the above depiction and subsequent distortion.

When asked about women's education he pointed out that 'we have not only to teach them but to teach ourselves also'. And the first thing he insisted on was 'chastity', which a woman shall maintain 'whether married, or single if they prefer to remain so'.[55] Lest the postmodern feminists zero in on chastity, it should also be remembered that Vivekananda did not see chastity as a bodily or gender-specific quality. He insisted on it for all genders. And it had more to do with strength of character than body. And then he stated that 'along with that they should be taught sciences and other things which would be of benefit, not only to them but to others as well, and knowing this they would easily learn these things and feel pleasure in doing so'.[56]

This was from a conversation in 1898, and Swami Vivekananda was all for gradual obliteration of marriages within the same caste and for increasing the age of marriage for girls. Regarding those who opposed the ban on child marriage, he was extremely harsh. Condemning them as 'religious hypocrites', Swami Vivekananda said, it was 'as if religion consisted in making a girl a mother at the age of twelve or thirteen'.[57] And not just increasing the age of women for marriage, he wanted that both boys and girls should be given education before that. He wanted education that would produce, 'great fearless women—women worthy to continue the traditions of Sanghamitra, Lila, Ahilya Bai, and Mira Bai—women fit to be mothers of heroes'.[58] As an aside it should be noted that Vivekananda's guru Sri Ramakrishna was instructed in Tantric practices by one 'Brahmini'—a Yogini who was well outside the family limits and who had chosen her own path of liberation.

Still would be possible that yet Vivekananda thought of women as being 'fit to be mothers of heroes' only—kind of biological machines to create male members of a super race?

If one looks at the examples he gives, only some in the list ever became biological mothers: Sanghamitra was a princess-turned-Buddhist monk; Lilavati was generally considered India's first female mathematician; Ahilya Bai was an eighteenth century widow-queen, who, instead of committing sati, grew into an extraordinary administrator and general; and Mira Bai was again a widow who explicitly refused sati and instead, rebelliously immersed herself in devotion. None of these women bore biological children. But they inspired many down the generations. So, them being 'women fit to be mother of heroes' has to be seen as a figure of speech and not as a comment meant specifically referring to women being biological wombs for heroes.

This long explanation is needed because Banu Subramaniam betrays an important process in action here. After making Swami Vivekananda 'central to Hindu nationalism in all its versions', the author asserts that Vivekananda did not want science to be taught to women—an empirically wrong assertion, but one that is central to her construction of the villainous Hindutva 'biopolitics'.

Similarly, she must acknowledge the fact that the Rashtriya Swayamsevak Sangh (RSS) is not homophobic, but then in the same sentence she rushes to remind her readers that it is a homosocial organization. She has to invent convoluted arguments to circumvent such uncomfortable facts as the RSS not being homophobic. So, she claims that '"the RSS" idea of the bond of "love" rests on Hindu male repression of homosexuality—drawing a distinction between friendship and its distinction with the erotic and the sexual'.[59]

This book came out in 2019. In September 2018, Mohan Bhagwat, the leader of the RSS had declared that 'the LGBTQ community is very much part of the society, and they should not be isolated'. Neither Jamaat-e-Islami nor the Catholic church can say that. Then the real questions Banu Subramaniam should have asked are: How can the Sangh take such a stand and so easily at that? What civilizational values went into it? How does this aspect distinguish the Sangh from other religious organizations?

To her credit, Subramaniam writes that 'several Hindu nationalists in the RSS and the Bharatiya Janata Party (BJP) spoke in favour of decriminalization', but at once adds 'for a variety of reasons'. She then singles out Baba

Ramdev as a 'prominent Hindu nationalist religious leader' who claimed homosexuality to be an unnatural addiction. As against this, she projects Sri Sri Ravishankar as 'one of the other religious leaders who strongly supported decriminalization' of homosexuality and who argued for 'an interpretation of divinity, consciousness, and love that supersedes genetics and allows for fluidity in gender and sexuality'.[60]

But the fact of the matter is that these two personalities—the modern Yoga-spiritual guru Sri Sri Ravi Shankar and Yoga teacher-cum-entrepreneur Baba Ramdev—have huge following, and both are considered close to the Hindutva movement. So, if Ramdev considers homosexuality a problem that needs to be cured and Sri Sri is all for LGBTQ rights, then neither of their views can be used to essentialize the Hindutva standpoint. But the stand of the RSS itself then becomes important. Though a scientist, she allows her need to stereotype Hindutva take precedence over what the facts convey.

Naturally her agenda does not make it important to inform her readers that it was Sri Sri Ravi Shankar who was the chief guest at one of the most important annual functions at the RSS headquarters—the concluding function of the third-year training camp in 2014. Now, the important aspect of this comes pages later, almost towards the end of the book when the author describes a newly emerging Hinduism where 'new gurus offer to cure illnesses, cancer, infertility and homosexuality with the age-old promises of religion'.[61]

This is what one calls academic sleight of hand. One should note how initially she mentions that 'several Hindu nationalists' supported decriminalization of homosexuality. She spoke of the RSS as a non-homophobic organization. She quoted exhaustively from Sri Sri Ravishankar, who supports the LGBTQ community. But then when she speaks of the emerging 'bionationalist' Hindu nationalism, she essentializes one Baba Ramdev to stereotype the entire Hindu movement as homophobic. Finally, what is a good book on Hindu nationalism if it does not talk about the 'designer baby project of the right-wing RSS'? The target here is the Garbhvigyan Anusandhan Kendra of Arogya Bharati, a Sangh Parivar organization.

This organization essentially provides what it calls 'services for preconception, antenatal and postnatal healthcare for best progeny'. Here, the author claims that 'the programs and the website make grandiose forecasts including a higher IQ, fairer skin, and tall stature for the baby and an easy labour for the mother ...'[62]

Her main sources for this information are Ashutosh Bhardwaj in *The Indian Express* (7 May 2017), and a report in the *Washington Post* (5 August 2017) by Annie Gowen titled 'Straight Out of the Nazi Playbook: Hindu Nationalists Try to Engineer "Genius" babies in India'. Subramaniam adds a part about the 'hopeful claims linking their projects to the successes of Nazi Germany'. The proof offered here again is an anecdote. In this, a senior RSS ideologue, was told 40 years ago by a German woman that the new generation in Germany was born through 'Garbh Sanskar'. Even assuming the anecdote to be true, which most probably was more apocryphal than real, that would make the woman talk not about Nazi Germany but the post-war rebuilding of Germany.

But what is interesting is that the actual principles of 'Garbh Sanskar', despite the question of their scientific validity, go against the principles of Nazi racism.

These practices clearly dissociate manifest traits from genetic influence. The 'Garbh Sanskar' does not care about the genes of the parents. Secondly, Arogya Bharati has rejected that they work for 'fair-skinned babies'. In its press release dated 17 May 2017, the organization categorically stated:

> What is so abhorrent is that these media campaigns are claiming that this program focuses on achieving a fair skin color child, showing the program something akin to the racial selection program run by Nazi Germany. Skin color prejudice has never been a narrative of Bharatiya culture. Arogya Bharati strongly condemns all these biased media campaigns.[63]

When a seminar for expectant parents was organized by the organization in Calcutta, a Public Interest Litigation (PIL) was filed to stop the event based on similar press reports. The High Court in its order accepted the arguments of Arogya Bharati and opined that 'the article which had led to filing of this Public Interest Litigation is prima facie misleading and it is necessary to question why such an article was published'.[64]

But such facts are deemed irrelevant to the negative stereotype that Banu Subramaniam builds up. Such demonization helps advance an academic career in the West. The book won the 2020 Michelle Kendrick Memorial Book Prize from the Society for Literature, Science & the Arts. Banu Subramaniam was one of the star speakers of 'Dismantling Global Hindutva' conference that was held online on 11 September 2021.

Malaviya-Modi Obsession of 'Midnight's Machines'

But the next book titled *Midnight's Machines* by Arun Mohan is different. It positions itself as a refreshing attempt to study the technology odyssey of the Indian state through the prism of Indian politics—including the values, visions, polity, and Prime Ministers that make up that politics. The author does achieve this to a significant extent, and yet, a binary narrative that he wants to see, where none exists, mars the objectivity of the book.

In the introduction itself, the author makes a not so convincing attempt to project Prime Minister Narendra Modi's approach to technology on the vision of Madan Mohan Malaviya, the famous Indian freedom fighter who was also a Hindu Sanghatan leader. This is unconvincing, because the political movement from which Modi comes has many more diverse and stronger streams of influence with respect to technology.

This problematic stand aside, the book does a decent job of presenting a coherent narrative with respect to the way politics, values, and technological development interacted with each other in India, particularly during the Nehru and Indira Gandhi regimes. It also provides significantly detailed view of what happened during the liberalization period of late 1980s and early 1990s—particularly with respect to telecom and IT.

Let us consider the Nehruvian era. The author points out one of the initial setbacks to the development of a solar cooker, which was a good technological initiative by the scientists of the National Physical Laboratory. Nehru eating vegetables cooked in the solar cooker became a headline. The Prime Minister, having alerted himself to the problem of patents by 'the long and ultimately aborted negotiations with Merck and other Western pharmaceutical companies over the manufacture of penicillin', gave 'permission to Egypt to adopt the solar cooker design at no cost'. According to the author, the failure of this solar cooker technology was instrumental in turning the 'gaze' of Nehru from 'niche' technologies to big industrial projects.'[65]

The author almost obsessively repeats the phrase 'the temples' of Nehru, which were the words Nehru had supposedly whispered to himself when he visited the Bhakra Nangal in 1956. They are nowhere in Nehru's official speeches, including the one he made at Bhakra Nangal, but the story perhaps has its source in a news report. In fact, during his speech at the inauguration of the dam in 1954, he had called the dam a place holier than any temple, mosque, church or gurdwara.

But more crucially, the author somehow has missed out on the scepticism that seemed to have crept inside Nehru towards such huge dams. This was shown in his speech to engineers and technocrats just two years later, wherein he referred to the 'diseases of gigantism'. Was Nehru trying to free himself in his later years from Soviet and Western influences—and that too in such an important domain as people-oriented technological development?

The author does indeed suggest something in that direction.

Ernst Schumacher, the cult economist who daringly explored a kind of Gandhian alternative to the dominant Western industrial economic model was invited by the Planning Commission in 1961. But Schumacher was not much in favour of the five-year plans and Nehru's fascination with the huge dams and other high-end technologies. Instead, he advocated that he wanted Nehru and his planners to abandon the five-year plans of industrialization, but make 'every Indian child, woman, man, everybody up to grandma—who could handle a seedling, to just (plant) one tree a year for five years running'. He argued that the ecological and economic benefits from such an endeavour 'would outweigh those of planned industrialization'. In other words, Schumacher advocated that India should focus on technology that is 'close to nature', is labour intensive and consumes little foreign exchange. But the author tells us that Nehru's advisers, already deeply committed to the 'temples of Nehru', rejected the suggestions, and the 'alternate technology' movement that Schumacher envisioned died as quickly in India as it started.[66]

But it was not over.

Indira Gandhi, the daughter of Nehru, when she was India's Prime Minister, tried to make political capital out of the 'appropriate technology' movement that was becoming quite a fad in the Western counter-culture movement. By 1973 Schumacher had published his cult classic *Small is Beautiful*. Arun Sukumar states that 'Schumacher's foolish romanticism, produced exactly the narrative Indira's government needed to cover up its failure to industrialize, and to keep the economy on a tight leash'. Here, he observes that while in the United States, where the counter-culture movement originated, it brought 'computing closer to the individual', in India it enabled the state to create a powerful bureaucratic stranglehold 'that effectively prevented "everyday" technologies from reaching people'.[67]

Meanwhile, the ideological opposition to the Indira Congress represented mainly by the Bharatiya Jan Sangh (BJS) that would later become the BJP, had developed its own approach to technology. Pandit Deendayal Upadhyaya (1916–1968), the main ideologue of BJS, in his criticism of Soviet style planning and technological imposition made the following observation:

> We should have our own concept about agriculture and industry. Instead of importing technology, we should invent a new technology which suits our situation. We need a technology which would provide for total employment and would remove disparity in incomes. By so doing, we shall be able to raise the standard of living of the people. Modern technology, in the West is also being developed along these lines. But the Second Five Year Plan here is based on pre-recession technology and economic concepts.

In 1977 the Hindu thinker Ram Swarup (1920–1998) gave a lecture sponsored by The Appropriate Technology Development Association of

Lucknow, in which he observed:

> In the last 200 years, a technology has come into being which favours centralization, large-scale operations and circular production....there are other technologies possible which work for decentralization, for individual and local production and yet are as productive and as efficient as the best that we know. If we cannot evolve this technology, Gandhian Economics will remain a dreamy stuff, soothing to the ear and warming to the heart but ineffective and irrelevant.

The above views of Deendayal and Ram Swarup might sound utopian—so were the views of Malaviya. And the streams to which these views of technology belong were closer to the ideological realm from which Modi came than the views of Malaviya. But these visions of technology are not taken into account. Even from the point of view of the author, Veer Savarkar, with his favourable view on the machine as a great benefactor of humanity, would have been more relevant than Malaviya. But again, we find him missing.

So, in a study which moves beyond stereotypes, their views would have become important. But when it comes to the BJP, Modi and technology, the book develops a stereotyped and blinkered view.

The author takes the Nehruvian view that 'Indians at the margins of society would be easily overwhelmed by technology' and thus get 'chained to it', and juxtapose it with the mission of Modi which seeks 'the application of technology to farming, fisheries, forest resource management, policing and even prison systems, with the idea that enhanced connectivity and the ready availability of data can help India address the needs of its most under-served communities'.[68]

Of course, Modi's period has occurred at 'a sweet spot in the arc of India's quest for machines', but for Arun Sukumar, that is not the only reason for the brazen embrace of technology by Modi. To him, somehow, the Congress has a more people-sympathetic approach to technology. And this is guided by concerns for the corruption of democratic values by technological growth.

As against this, the BJP is uninhibited about technology, and this nonchalance is rooted in its Hindutva worldview. He concludes that while the Congress is alive to the concerns of technology being great 'corruptor', the BJP uses technology as the great 'disruptor'. This binary stereotyping itself has glaring holes.

The author himself had pointed out earlier in the book how Sangh outfits like the Swadeshi Jagran Manch are uncomfortable and find with Modi's technology thrust, a 'frustrating figure'. He states the Sangh 'has no particular affinity towards technology'.[69]

The author also sidelines how the Indira regime made India dependent on

Soviet technology and how Soviet aid arm-twisted India in accepting inferior technology. Such an import of technology went against the Swadeshi spirit of Constitution makers but fitted the 'socialist' political agenda of the Congress. The book has also ignored the way NDA-I initiated an innovative technological attempt to preserve India's indigenous knowledge system and made it a model for other developing countries.

Dr Murli Manohar Joshi, who is mentioned fleetingly in the context of the world genome project, had earlier given the slogan 'yes to computer chips, but no to potato chips' when globalization commenced. There is a link between this slogan and the 'Make in India' project of the present-day Modi government. An exploration of that link would have provided objective insights into the ideological orientation of BJP with respect to technology.

And Modi's own fondness for technology in accelerating India's inclusive growth comes from quite a number of streams—from Dr Shyama Prasad Mukherjee who contributed to the commencement of self-reliant nuclear technology in India to Dr A. P. J. Abdul Kalam. When Dr Meghnad Saha was striving to establish the Institute of Nuclear Physics in the newly born Indian state, Dr Shyama Prasad Mukherjee became a strong supporter of Saha in this effort. He also got the University senate to accept the Tata Trust seed grant for a cyclotron as early as 1941.[70]

Dr Kalam became famous with his popular handbook *India 2020* (co-authored by Y. S. Rajan) for using technology for national development in major domains in a people-oriented way. The book dominated the national bestseller charts for almost a decade. Its popularity was also partly because it rode on the wave of nationalism which followed the nuclear tests by the Vajpayee government.

Again, this should have been part of any narrative on India and technology. Then, the author does not seem to have bothered about it. In fact, the technological mission that Modi had made an integral part of his politics and action has stemmed largely from *India 2020*. It may not be a coincidence that Arun Mohan mentions Dr Kalam only fleetingly, here in the context of SLV and subsequent Agni missile development. But when the same book tries to sell the sub-mediocre oscillation of Rahul Gandhi over Aadhar card as a kind of high moral dilemma, then we do realize the politics that guides this study of the politics of technology.

Overall, one can see here a new front opened to attack Hindutva with the specific instance the BJP's pro-technology narrative with professional selective scholarship. So that makes one look into how exactly the Sangh views science and technology in its own realm.

Eco-Awareness in Hindutva Movement: Concept, Implementation and Technology

While Savarkar was all for industrialization and mechanization, Gandhi was against it. Gandhi considered mechanization of the European kind as inflicting grievous wounds on the colonized societies. Yet he was not a complete Luddite as he was very much for alternative technologies. One sees the post-Independence Hindutva movement as ideologically taking forward more Gandhian approach to technology than the Savarkarite approach. Deendayal Upadhyaya, K. R. Malkani, H. V. Sheshadri and Dattopant Thengadi were some of the thinker-activists who shaped the RSS worldview and their thinking was very much Gandhian with respect to technology. It is already seen how Deendayal Upadhyaya envisioned 'milking rather than exploiting nature' to be woven into the economic system, so that it could transform the economic processes. Thinking of Ram Swarup in terms of the technological need to fulfil the Gandhian concept of economics has also been seen already.

In the June 1988 issue of *Manthan*, Sailendra Nath Ghosh wrote an exhaustive paper on 'the Philosophy and Technology of Living in Tune with Nature'. Running into 32 pages in the magazine, the paper dealt with the scientific and philosophical dimensions of the then accelerating ecological crisis (which is today a full-blown global threat to human species).

> "Mankind is a part of Nature and has to live in harmony with Nature"—this great truth has been known to the people of India from the dawn of civilisation. That is why worship of Nature has been a part of Indian tradition. India's ancient culture emphasised that one can live only by letting others—including all other species of creation—live.[71]

While considering the philosophical basis of Western civilization as 'aggressive' with their high-consumption lifestyle along with 'industrial and military prowess', he also pointed out how 'outstanding poets and thinkers like William Blake, William Wordsworth, Percy Shelley, Mary Shelley, Henry Thoreau, John Ruskin, Leo Tolstoy, Edward Carpenter, Rabindranath Tagore and Mahatma Gandhi' had voiced their objection to this 'pattern of dehumanizing technological civilization'. He also pointed out an important ecological aspect of Indian culture in the context of Western criticism:

> Voluntary limitation of wants is not primitivism, pastoralism or "ruralism" as Westernisers (euphemistically called "modernists") seek to describe it....Wilful

> limitation of wants to the minimum of absolute needs, thus, enlarges the possibility of true happiness, true freedom and self-determination.

The paper actually drew upon some of the most scientific understanding of the basic biological processes and blended that with evolving a living philosophy:

> Man can enlarge his freedom by knowing Nature's way of working and by moving in step. Man's spirit can soar in sacrifice and love by imbibing reverence for life, which Nature evolved and has been sustaining by her multiple processes of mutualism, commensalism, amensalism and the like, in a co-evolutionary rhythm encompassing all forms of life and their environments. Conforming to Nature's laws is the way to utmost elevation of human spirit.

He goes on to distinguish between variety of environmentalisms and calls for a holistic environmentalism:

> One is the environmentalism of industrial and commercial interests which seek to continue the pollution-creating, concentrated-energy-based pattern of technology in production system:...Then there is another kind of environmentalism which is the favourite of the Establishment in countries like India. It wants to cleanse rivers of visible pollutants and to organise "forestry" by planting saplings of a dozen varieties, while allowing the destruction of natural forests of immense biodiversity in the name of "development";...The third kind of environmentalism fights consistently against anti-ecological projects such as big dams, nuclear power plants and the quarrying activities which dry up springs and choke rivers with debris but does not relate these struggles to any concept of alternative civilisational patterns.... Then there is a thorough-going environmentalism which views things holistically. It seeks to link the movement for ecological preservation with mankind's survival and liberation of the oppressed. It seeks an alternative lifestyle, alternative science and technology, alternative politico-economic concepts with its structuring and superior ethics based on universal love and harmony with the cosmos.

Ghosh ends the paper with the following words:

> Nature-harmonic pursuit of knowledge can save life from extinction, bring about a renaissance in science and open up common people's access to resources. This can make possible a five-tier federalism, embodying people's self-governance at village and block levels....This harmony of the local and the larger communities (as distinct from dominance by the so-called Centre), harmony of man and Nature, of individual

existence and cosmic consciousness-based recognition of organic relations with all creation, animate and inanimate—is the key to man's freedom and self-fulfilment.

Here is then a serious attempt to create an alternate politics of science, technology and natural resources based mainly on the thoughts of Gandhi and Deendayal while taking into account both the emerging need for green politics including the politics of green technology and the need to converse with the positive elements of Marxism. This is an indigenous thought process and the Deendayal Research Institute (DRI) provided the institutional support as well as platform though there was no big support for DRI itself when compared to the enormous financial and institutional support that the establishment left wing was getting in India. There is also a continuity of thought process. From 'biotechnic order' of Malkani with its indebtedness to Patrick Geddes who in turn was influenced by the non-dual Vedantic vision being translated into science tentatively but refreshingly by Jagadish Chandra Bose to 'Nature-harmonic' view of development advocated by Ghosh, one can see this consistency of vision.

While Ghosh himself is an ex-Marxist who belonged more to a truly leftist thinking, he could work with the RSS institution DRI as part of it. When DRI closed and he moved away in his characteristic reclusive style, he continued contributing to *Mainstream*, a magazine started by Nikhil Chakravarty (1913–1998), who too was a staunch leftist and shared platform with the RSS in its swadeshi opposition to multinational companies entering India. Apart from being part of DRI, he was also the member of the Governing Body of the Chitrakoot Gramodaya Vishwavidyalaya founded by Nanaji Deshmukh, the ideologue-activist of the RSS. That this paper, a milestone in ecological thinking and in the history of environmentalism in India, appeared in the RSS-affiliated journal is telling with respect to the kind of churning that the Sangh was undertaking despite no support from the Government or aid agencies.

Perhaps not all environmental idealism with a rigorous scientific framework may be possible to be adapted by the BJP as part of its political programme or implemented by the BJP government. Particularly given the monstrous and threatening growth of China with the aggressive Western style technology and industrialization, taken to the maximum with least care for human suffering, India feels vulnerable in any geopolitical confrontation with such a well-equipped emerging superpower. So, it has been forced to follow rapid industrialization with the checks and balances of a vibrant democracy. Further agitations against development projects in the garb of environmentalism but with the support of extra-territorial vested interests have only muddied the waters more. Yet the present BJP-headed NDA government under Narendra Modi has implemented some core people-oriented resource democratization.

In 1987 *Manthan* published a paper on evolving an all-party consensus on environment. It was written by senior civil servant B. B. Vohra, who was one of the earliest bureaucrats to study the land degradation and problems of natural resources utilization. Instrumental in establishing a department for environment, he enjoyed the confidence of Indira Gandhi. Yet his attempts at creating a detailed report on resource utilization did not bear fruits. At the time of writing, he was the chairman of the advisory board on energy in Rajiv Gandhi's government.

> Problems of rural immigration apart, it must be admitted that if insanitation and filth are so much part of the Indian scene, this is basically because we are not sufficiently intolerant of such conditions—in turn because most of us have known nothing better. In such a situation, "Project Ganga" needs to be urgently supplemented by a nation-wide cleanliness drive which should aim at the transformation in the first instance of all religious places and pilgrim centres into models of cleanliness and then go onto tackle railway stations, bus stands, government offices and shopping centres, etc.,—in brief all the places where people congregate for one purpose or other. [72]

It is not hard to see what Vohra wrote for *Manthan* was getting implemented in Modi's 'cleanliness drive', which at once attacks the problems of sanitation as well as cleanliness of public places with an emphasis on pilgrim centres and railway stations.

In the 1988 issue of *Manthan* regarding water policy, Ghosh wrote a detailed paper, where among other things he wrote:

> Drinking water, for both humans and cattle in quality and quantity, has to be our highest concern. Even though the Government's water policy gives primacy to drinking water, the emphasis on its quality is lacking. There is as yet little awareness that water contaminated by nitrate or pesticide residue or industrial chemicals does not deserve to be called drinking water.

The following is from a report on village Kagri of Jammu and Kashmir (with a population of 1500) on bringing tapped water to every house under the ambitious 'Jal Jeevan Mission' of Modi:

> During the rainy season while the quantum of water increases at these sources, but the water body gets polluted by surface water from the streams and rivulets, thereby increasing waterborne diseases. The water supply scheme Ambhkhori

> commissioned in March, 2020 was designed to bring an end to the drudgery caused by a lack of such basic service.... Provision of functional tap connections has to be achieved through community participation. The recent modification of the Jammu and Kashmir Panchayati Raj Act, 1989 strengthens the local bodies with a three-tier structure directly elected by the people – district development councils, Halqa panchayats, and block development councils.

While the article of Ghosh is against mega dam projects like Narmada, the present BJP government has embraced such projects. At the same time, there is a strong decentralization in creating access to fundamental natural resources for ordinary citizens in a highly efficient manner. In this 1988 article, Ghosh speaks of the importance of creating rainwater catchment areas and creation of natural forests for the purpose. Jal Jeevan Mission also speaks in the same way:

> In addition to providing functional tap water connections, the emphasis is laid on in-situ treatment of greywater and rainwater harvesting. Provisions are being made in water-stressed, drought-prone, hilly, forested, and desert areas to ensure overall water security.

While Ghosh's critique of mega irrigation project seems to have been ignored in BJP's onward march towards development that has been embraced by the polity across the ideological spectrum after liberalization, in the special mega initiatives taken by the BJP to empower people through access to resources, the modus operandi significantly differs from the usual socialistic-welfare state mode of implementation. The implementation is more goal and sustainability-oriented, and bureaucracy is answerable to the community feedback. The four cardinal principles of Jal Jeevan Mission could have well been taken from the worldview of Sailendra Ghosh himself:

- It is necessary that 100 per cent of households in a village are included at all stages. No household, irrespective of its social or economic condition should be left out ....
- Ensuring participation of every section and taking affirmative steps to ensure that women and poor people are included in management....
- Everyone has to share the costs. Insisting on a significant contribution to the initial capital cost and that people bear the cost of running and maintaining the facility helps build people's stakes.
- The insistence that people 'take responsibility' from an early stage to generate consensus, mobilize local contributions, manage construction,

and take charge of operations & maintenance is a sound way to ensure long term sustainability.

In August 1990 a round table conference between Europe and India was held in the field of solar energy technology. Smt. Maneka Gandhi, then Minister of State for Environment and Forest, highlighted the need for a Solar Energy Commission in India. Pointing out both these events, Ghosh wrote the following in *Manthan*:

> Vested interests in fossil fuels and nuclear power have been restraining R&D efforts in solar technology and also preventing the spread of whatever developments have already emerged. Within this country the resources are so pre-empted on non-renewable forms of energy that the talk of solar and solar-related energy use is almost ritualistic....One thing more. While cooperation between the Western countries and India on solar technology is desirable, it is necessary that solar energy is a diffuse form of energy and can best be harnessed in a decentralized manner.[73]

This kind of thinking embedded in the RSS worldview would later reflect in the actions of the then BJP Chief Minister of Gujarat, Narendra Modi, who inaugurated an innovate pilot project on a branch canal of Narmada in a village at Mehsana district on 24 August 2012. It covered the canal with solar panels aimed to generate 1 megawatt electricity while preventing the evaporation of 9 million litres of water from the canal. Eight years later, BBC reported this:

> A pilot 750m stretch in Gujarat in 2014 led to the first large-scale canal-top solar power plant in the Vadodara district of Gujarat in 2015, at a cost of $18.3 million.... Since this power is generated in a rural area, the transmission losses are reduced and the local grid is strengthened. Since the first solar canal project, a number of others have been commissioned in India, including a 100MW canal-top solar power project atop the branch canals off the Narmada River, stretching for a distance of 40km, at an estimated cost of 1bn Indian rupees ($13.9m/£9.3m). Overall, Gujarat has more than 80,000km of canals meandering through the state. According to Gujarat State Electricity Corporation, if 30% of this were converted to solar, 18,000MW of power could be produced, saving 90,000 acres of land....With their water-cooled efficiency, and mutual benefits for the canals that run beneath, it looks likely that these snaking, glittering solar canals will become a much more common sight in India.[74]

Later, Narendra Modi would launch the idea of International Solar Alliance to combat the global climate crisis. Dr Alyssa Ayres, the dean of Elliott School of International Affairs, in her book on the new India, points out how from being a combative developing country fighting against the green politics of the rich nations, India changed its strategy without compromising its rights by proposing a new international solar alliance that would curb carbon emissions naturally, thus changing the fundamental game of climate politics at the Paris summit of 2015:

> Indian negotiators arrived in Paris with a positive proposal that leveraged India's domestic emphasis on renewables as a major energy security focus. Prime Minister Modi and then French President François Hollande announced a new international solar alliance, the declaration of which focused on "sustainable development, universal energy access, and energy security," as well availability, making "clean and renewable energy...affordable for all." India has great solar energy generation potential, and intends to scale production to one hundred gigawatts by 2022—said to be a $100 billion solar ramp-up, the world's largest—so the solar alliance created a global leadership role for India building on its pre-existing national plans.[75]

Thus, one sees in the ideological field and intellectual churning of the Hindutva movement that there are both ecological thinking and scientifically oriented concerns in evolving solutions for ecological crisis. Further, this is rooted in the Indian thought tradition while getting inputs from around the world. Again, during November 2021 in the COP26 climate summit, the Indian stand was seen by many Western-centric environmental activists as 'weakening a move to end the use of coal'. But *New Scientist* writer Adam Vaughan pointed out the significant solar dimension that Modi brought to the table:

> Less widely recognised is that the country also started the Glasgow summit in a more positive fashion, with a plan to massively expand the reach of solar power by joining up the electricity grids of countries and even entire continents. Indian prime minister Narendra Modi has talked about the idea before, but the One Sun One World One Grid initiative launched in Glasgow now has the backing of more than 80 countries, including Australia, the UK and the US...."The Indian government is keen on links to the Middle East, to help India decarbonise using imported renewable energy," says Jim Watson at University College London. The UK, one of India's partners on the One Sun One World One Grid initiative, is also considering new long-distance cables.[76]

In all these what one sees is that Modi combines both national interest, national resource advantage and innovative use of renewable energy technology in changing the world discussions to India's advantage. One can rightly see this as the next step in the Hindutva green thinking.

Sangh Parivar and Science: 'Science India'

The words 'Sangh' and 'science' for any India observer often bring to mind obscurantist organizations selling cow products and the so-called 'Vedic mathematics'. However, the Sangh Parivar's approach to science, technology and society goes far beyond such media-academia stereotypes of 'Cow/Vedic Science' of peddling cow-urine based products.

Vijnana Bharati (VIBHA) is an organization associated with popularizing science in society and reviving what it considers the ancient traditional knowledge systems of India. Though VIBHA came into existence at a conceptual level as early as 1982, it was only in 1990 that it started functioning with organizational vigour. On 29 December 1990, a consultative meet was organized at Bangalore. It was attended by RSS leaders with a science background, and also Dharampal, the extraordinary Gandhian historian who had documented the status of traditional science and technology in India at the commencement of the colonial era. Dr Joshi was also present. One of the offshoots of the conference was the Swadeshi Science Movement. Its Kerala chapter started functioning energetically during the NDA rule, and launched a magazine, *Science India*.

A random skim through the issues of *Science India* provides a clue as to what kind of science popularization culture the Sangh Parivar attempts—a genuine popularization of science for a democratic society or peddling of religion-oriented pseudoscience promoting fundamentalism.

In the August 2004 issue, there is a moving tribute to American evolutionary biologist Stephen Jay Gould, calling him 'Darwin's worthy successor'. Here is an excerpt:

> Gould has studied the relationship between physical development of an organism and its evolution. Spandrels of spaces in corners above arches in the buildings are not an architectural necessity but exist by virtue of simply un-purported design. Likewise, he warned that all physical features which exist in an organism should not be taken to be adaptational in origin.[77]

The tribute also points out how Gould exposed the fallacious theory of intelligence quotients as 'based more on political witchcraft than on scientific knowledge'. In 2005 *Science India* ran a two-part paper by Arpita Subash titled 'Gender and Science'. Among other things, the paper states:

> The conservative society in India forces loneliness and professional exclusion of women scientists from informal groups, committees and science societies

> which impinges on their contribution and productivity....Bal (2002) opines that discrimination against women practitioners of science may not be due to conscious efforts from male colleagues. However, cultural upbringing and values do contribute to the discrimination observed....Various studies found that class, caste and religion play important role in women's representation in science.[78]

The Swadeshi Science Movement received the Jawaharlal Nehru Prize for the year 2005–2006 instituted by the Indian Science Congress Association for the popularization of science from then Prime Minister Dr Manmohan Singh. In 2007 it received the national award for 'Outstanding Efforts in Science and Technology Communication' from Ministry of Science and Technology.

There is no doubt that Sangh Parivar organizations have a fixation with cow-based formulations and Vedic mathematics. Some important unhealthy trends in Hindutva movement with respect to its approach towards science will be discussed in the coming sections of this chapter. However, the Hindutva movement, including the much-maligned Dr Joshi, has made a strong contribution to India's science landscape, and it goes definitely beyond cow and Vedic mathematics. What is truly unscientific, prejudiced and biased is the media-academia fixation that unquestioningly accepts left-wing propaganda of painting the entire Sangh as antiscience by highlighting only certain questionable aspects of the Sangh worldview rather than its unique as well as positive role in promoting science in India, and Indian science.

A study of *Science India* magazines of 2021 for the first six months shows an emphasis on technological self-reliance, particularly in biological sciences, artificial intelligence, space and defence, inclusive development and history of science with Indo-centric approach.

In the January 2021 issue, there is a feature on Lakshmikutty Amma, the famous poison healer from Kerala who is called 'Vana Muthassi' (forest grandmother). She hails from Kanni, a Scheduled Tribal community. She was awarded the Padma Shri in 2018— the fourth highest civilian award. The article in the magazine records:

> It is a matter of concern that no one from her next generation has come forward to learn and inherit these rare formulations from her which are nowhere recorded. It is saddening that all her precious knowledge will disappear with her if we do not take some action to preserve it for future generations. Tribal organisations, government and other NGOs must come forward to record the knowledge she had accumulated and to survey and record the medicinal properties of each plant, fish and animal she knows. She says she is willing to transfer the knowledge if someone takes interest and sets up an institution to teach young students.[79]

In dealing with ancient India's scientific legacy, there are no exaggerated claims like Vedic space shuttles—the kind with which the anti-Hindutvaites like to caricature Hindutva. Instead, as in the case of an article on the Hindu-Jain origins of what is known in the West as Fibonacci series, and which are today accepted as Hemachandra series (named after the Jain seer) the magazine ends as below:

> When we appreciate a tabla concert of Zakir Hussain the aesthetics generated is due to the time evolution of Hemachandra series converging to the golden ratio. In sculpture and in painting the beauty is frozen in space. In fact, one can think of music concert as a sculpture in time.

It is important here to note the inclusive tone of the above passage. VIBHA not only speaks of ancient and present traditional knowledge systems but also conducts workshops for the modern technology outreach for the society:

> To provide a common technology outreach platform and enable all stakeholders to work with the people of rural India in identifying development challenges and evolving appropriate solutions for accelerated sustainable growth in 2019 UBA (Unnat Bharat Abhyan Campaign for uplifting India—under the Ministry for Human Resources and Development) and Vijnana Bharti(VIBHA) jointly organised 3-day technology outreach workshop "Tech for Seva". The concept of this workshop is clear in its name where "Tech" refers to Technology and "Seva" means Selfless Service—both for the greater good of the society.

The workshop brought together scientists from prominent science institutions of India like ISRO, IITs, DRDO, ICAR, BARC, CSIR, etc., with community leaders from Panchayat institutions, and entrepreneurs. 'Tech for Seva' successfully connected 'the Need (people) and Solution (R&D Institutions) through Service Providers (CSRs Voluntary Organisations and NGOs)' through six major themes—Agriculture, Environment, Livelihood, School Education, Sustainable Energy Solutions for de-centralized applications and Hygienic and Clean India Campaign.

February comes with Science Day celebrations in India on 28th of the month, commemorating the discovery of the Raman effect on this very day in 1928. Eminent physicist Dr B. N. Jagatap in his article 'A Paradigm Shift in Indian Science' points out how with globalization in 1990s, Indian science has actually become less self-reliant with respect to manufacturing its own instrument. In a hard-hitting passage in the article, he writes:

> In the globalised economy, scientific research must connect to the society intellectually as well as economically. Research must be seen as an important instrument of economic growth; it can no longer be perceived as the sole prerogative of researchers but must include people as an important stakeholder. Research must translate into products, devices, processes and services. It must develop new skills and fuel the spirit of innovation and S&T driven entrepreneurship, thereby impacting socio-economic development. Instead, we defined good science only in terms of good papers, imported equipment, more funds and a few centres of excellence. This definition is not inclusive of its important stakeholder and therefore is unsustainable in the current times. The result of this mindset is there to see for everybody. Today we boast of the third rank internationally in research publications. While we take pride in this achievement, we need to ask—how does this third rank compares with India's rank in other socio-economic indicators?[80]

The point here is this article appears as one of the lead and commissioned articles in a magazine associated with Hindutva family of organizations by its critics, not without truth. But given the stereotype of Hindutva as Hindu supremacism, the passage and the tone of the article completely falsifies the academic-media stereotype of Hindutva.

The March issue of the magazine celebrates Indian women scientists. It forms the cover story and is written by Dr Ranjana Aggarwal, who heads the CSIR-Science, Technology and Development Studies (as of 2021) and CSIR-National Institute of Science Communication and Information Resources. She writes:

> It is high time we projected women scientists, who have dared to walk an untraversed path, who have had the courage to make new beginnings and created a niche for themselves, as role models for younger girls. Kadambini Ganguly, the first female graduate of the British Empire and also the first physician of South Asia to be trained in western medicine; Anandibai Joshi, the first Indian woman physician and the first woman to have graduated with a two-year degree in western medicine in the United States; Janaki Ammal the first Indian scientist to have received the Padma Shri Award; Kamala Sohonie, the first Indian woman to have bagged a PhD degree in any scientific discipline; Rajeshwari Chatterjee, the first woman engineer from the state of Karnataka are some of the legendary women who chose S&T as their career in pre-Independence period.

She points out that subsequent to Prime Minister Atal Bihari Vajpayee declaring 2001 as the year of empowerment of women, in 2002 the Department of Science and Technology brought out the Women Scientist Scheme with three main streams—(a) for core S&T research, (b) for S&T societal interventions and (c) for women to become IPR professionals. Designed specifically to overcome the hurdles and breaks of motherhood and family responsibilities to the career of women as scientists, the scheme then benefitted 6,000 women who had chosen science as their career.[81] In 1999 the then BJP-led NDA government had instituted an award for women scientists in biosciences. In 2020 this award was renamed as Janaki Ammal award. Again, the article which calls for a women-friendly working environment and a harassment-free atmosphere for women scientists, who should be treated as equal partners in the institutions of science helps break stereotypes in more ways than one. It is also quite interesting to see that while the Sangh Parivar, including the BJP as the organizational movement and the Hindutva as an ideology, have been accused of being patriarchal and obscurantist in dominant sections of media and academia, they have played quite a significant role in advancing the cause of women in science and technology in recent times.

The April 2021 issue of *Science India* deals mainly with space. An article on Aryabhata, the most well-known ancient Hindu astronomer after whom India named its first satellite, cautiously deals only with his real achievements, and refrains from making any tall claims, which are usual in nationalist circles. While pointing out that the estimate of the circumference of earth as given by Aryabhata (39,968 kilometres) agrees closely with the modern estimate (40,074 kilometres), and that Aryabhata 'calculated an accurate table of sines, considered the first sine table constructed in the history of mathematics', it does not make the claim that Aryabhata discovered helio-centrism, but rather that he discovered the earth was rotating on its own axis, which makes the stars look revolving.[82] The magazine celebrates the life achievement of Jayant Vishnu Narlikar—an Indian cosmologist, who despite being a Sanskrit scholar places himself in the lineage of Galileo and Newton.

Dr Chaitanya Giri was the only Indian to be linked to the famous Rosetta Mission that aimed to land on a comet and then collect, bring back and study cometary dust particles. With a PhD in astrochemistry from the Max Planck Institute for Solar System Research and University of Nice, he is also a technology strategy analyst. He is a frequent contributor to *Science India*, and in this issue he deals with two topics—one on reorienting science ministries to reap dividends from 'the tremendous global churn of S&T' and another on how to use India's IT prowess to propel astrobiology. Here Dr Giri takes quite a novel approach and points out that India can also use search for extra-terrestrial intelligence (SETI) to create spin-off effects in various technological sectors and can also be an important player in a major planetary pursuit of a mystery of universal dimensions. He writes:

> Let us assume a scenario where an analytical instrument analyses the regolith (soil) samples on Mars searching for signatures of extinct or extant life and generates large volumes of data. Such a device will likely demand innovation in interplanetary daya communication networks to handle big data transmission over millions of kilometres. Let us also assume a mission is looking for life-forms in the cold and frigid lakes of methane on Saturn's moon Titan. This mission will demand novel robotics and instruments to operate in fluidic environments and temperatures as low as minus two hundred degrees Celsius. Due to its inherent interdisciplinarity, astrobiology can boost innovations in many such ongoing technology pursuits.... Astrobiology can help transform India from being an IT giant to a giant of the fourth industrial age. It now depends on our ability to derive short-term dividends from this Holy Grail.[83]

What one sees in this article is not just communicating science as usually the accomplished Western science communicators do. But here Dr Giri goes beyond mere communication and unveils to his readers a missionary vision—of transforming India into a global science player by innovating its indigenous S&T capabilities.

It is not only space science and technology that gets covered in *Science India*. There is also a two-page detailed report on a discovery by Kerala-based young engineers that would provide a solution to end the dehumanizing problem of manual scavenging. The article points out that despite enacting laws that make this dehumanizing practice illegal, the practice is still widely spread. GenRobotics, the company founded by these engineers, has developed 'Bandicoot' that cleans manholes remotely using robotic arms and computer vision.[84]

There are also articles which claim scientific basis for ancient Hindu traditions followed to this day like a scientific basis to Kumbh Mela—through the 12-year-cycle of Jupiter. Dr V. P. N. Nampoori, Emeritus Professor in the International School of Photonics, Cochin University of Science and Technology (CUST), has written in an article 'the 2016 Nobel prize in physiology and medicine recognized the immense health benefits of fasting or upavas, a practice observed by Hindus since time immemorial'. Yet the article makes no outlandish claims, but rather points out that the lifestyle tradition of India receives a boost from modern findings in science:

> Upavas or fasting along with Yoga and meditation have a central position in the Hindu way of life. This helps in rejuvenation and fight against diseases by strengthening immunity. This Indian knowledge system has received respect from the West when scientific research coined the term "intermittent fasting" for which

> the Japanese cell biologist Yoshiori Ohsumi won the Nobel Prize in Medicine in 2016. Ohusmi's work elucidated the method by which cells recycle and renew their content through a process called autophagy. His main finding was that during fasting, autophagy is activated which helps in slowing down the aging process, has positive impact on cell renewal, improves body immunity, and even helps in weight loss. Most of the religions in the world follow fasting of different styles. For example, Muslims and Christians follow fasting for one month during one year. However, in Hinduism, there are different types of fasting in a week, such as fasting on Mondays by women, fasting on Thursdays, Saturdays, on full moon days, etc., as prayer to particular Gods, in which regular meals are taken only once a day except a few snacks in between, and avoiding food at night. The duration of fasting varies from 12–20 hours, depending on the days' importance. Ohsumi termed the observance of fasting as intermittent fasting.[85]

One can note that the article not only refrains from drawing any outlandish conclusions, but also points out how fasting as a tradition exists in both Christianity and Islam while highlighting how it is an integral part in Hindu culture.

The May 2021 issue runs the cover story of *Atmanirbhar Bharat*—a mission that Prime Minister Narendra Modi announced, aiming to self-build India through nationally developed science and technology as well as entrepreneurial efforts. As India was battling the sudden eruption of the Covid-19 second wave, the international media saw in it an opportunity to attack the 'Hindu nationalist' government. The *Lancet*, in particular, came out with an article based more on rhetoric than actual facts. In its editorial published on 8 May, the magazine declared on the authority of the Institute for Health Metrics and Evaluation Estimates that India would see 'a staggering 1 million deaths by August 1', and that if such an outcome were to happen, 'Modi's Government would be responsible for presiding over a self-inflicted national catastrophe'.[86] Debobrat Ghose, the editor of *Science India*, gave a lengthy rebuttal to the magazine. Perhaps the most important approach to *Atmanirbhar Bharat* came from physicist Prof. Jagatap:

> The technology landscape of India does carry a historic baggage. After independence, public sector and national laboratories were bestowed with the responsibility of technology development and implementation. This resulted in a large focus on a few narrow areas which were considered strategic. Many of these entities got themselves trapped in the development of technologies which emerged as a fall out of Cold War; several of them, as per Schatzberg's classification, were instrumental. The situation started changing only after the mid '80s when information technology and

> biotechnology started growing outside the government laboratories....Expanding the technology development space is unleashing the true potential of India.... We also need to understand the modes of acquisition of technology....The most important mode is to develop an indigenous technology, which is done by an Indian entity through its own R&D or academia-industry collaboration....India needs to learn this if she aspires for the status of technologically empowered country. The success story of Covaxin, which Bharat Biotech and ICMR joined hands to produce an indigenous vaccine, is an example. Can hydrogen energy by the next one?...In 1924 Mahatma Gandhi said, "I am convinced that Swaraj cannot come so long as tens of millions of our brothers and sisters do not take to charkha, do not spin, do not make khadi and wear it." We need this spirit today to win independence in technology. Included in this spirit are two things: participation of all and being vocal for locals.[87]

The purpose of quoting in detail these passages is to make the reader realize how the Hindutva movement does not see science as merely a substratum for technological development, or a lopsided view of technology itself as merely a demonstration of national pride. The magazine shows a very mature and holistic approach to science and technology and strives to make a case for an all-inclusive, people-oriented technology. There are three women contributors to this issue of the magazine and its associate editor is also a woman—Sonam Singh Subhedar, who also regularly writes for the magazine.

The June issue of the magazine makes as its cover story the rekindled interest of the global scientific community in the possible lab-leak hypothesis of Covid-19 virus. There is an email interview of the editor of the magazine with the Twitter whistleblower handle 'The Seeker' who 'pried open the massive Chinese database of academic journals...to find missing links behind the death of three miners in Mojiang in Yunnan in 2012, due to an illness possibly caused by the closest relative of SARS-CoV-2 virus.' In the interview, the 'Seeker' rejects the claim that SARS-CoV-2 was developed as a bioweapon, and calls the claim 'scientifically unfounded.' If the lab-leak theory is right, then it should have been more 'an accident rather than anything malicious', he states. But he also points out to the non-transparent nature of the Wuhan institute:

> Yes. It is now more than obvious that Wuhan Institute of Virology did not disclose all the sequences they were studying, and it is very much possible that there are similar unpublished viruses or several—sitting in their database which mysteriously vanished.[88]

Then the magazine carried two more interviews. Dr Monali C. Rahalkar, a

Pune-Based microbiologist, who along with her husband Dr Rahul Bahulkar published a paper 'Lethal Pneumonia Cases in Mojiang Miners (2012) and the Mineshaft Could Provide Important Clues to the Origin of SARS-CoV-2' in *Frontiers in Public Health*. She expressed the possibility of lab manipulation of an original SARS-CoV-2-like virus:

> I suspect that the virus which infected the miners could have been similar to SARS-CoV-2 but not exactly as it might not be adapted enough to human beings and not transmissible. Therefore, it is possible that if the SARS-CoV-2 came from the mine or the miners, it was genetically manipulated in some sense.[89]

Then Dr Bahulkar was also interviewed. He stated:

> When the pandemic started, we were bombarded by TV channels, newspapers and scientific publications about the possible origin of SARS-CoV-2 from China's wet market. Scientific journals like The Lancet were also supporting the zoonotic origin of the virus....As days went by, we asked ourselves many questions, which forced us to dismiss the zoonotic origin and favour the lab leak hypothesis.[90]

Again, one needs to appreciate the restraint with which *Science India* reported the possibility of the lab leak of Covid-19. In most of their articles, the magazine refrained from calling it the Chinese or Wuhan virus.

Another important contributor to *Science India* is the physicist Dr Mrittunjoy Guha Majumdar, a senior postdoctoral researcher at the Centre for Excellence in Quantum Technology (CEQT) of Indian Institute of Science (IISc), Bangalore. Having worked with Nobel Laureate Prof. Brian Josephson, who was known for his love for Hindu Vedantic worldview, Dr Majumdar also shows a strong interest in Vedanta and the parallels between the non-dualist Hindu worldview and the metaphysical as well as ontological implications of the developments in 'New Physics'.

> In ancient India, we have had the logical argument of the Chatushkoti that is an individible quarternity, which has seen applications in various Dharmic and Buddhist traditions of logic and epistemology as well as in Pyrrhonism. In this four-cornered system of argumentation involving the systematic examination of each of the four possibilities of a proposition P:P, not P, P and not -P, neither P nor not -P....However, the key question here is: if the wave-particle duality is actually found to be a non-duality, can we associate a third conceptual element to explain it? ***One may feel that this negation can be done ad infinitem, as the Madhyamaka proponents or Buddhists or even Vedantin would do, so as to finally establish that***

> ***reality is beyond binaries and dualities. But since we talk of the physical sciences, one must rely on actual empirical findings and not just theorising.*** After all, even String theory, arguably the most complete and mathematically consistent "*Theory of Everything*", is not accepted as one conclusively since it still lacks experimental backing.[91] (Emphasis not in the original)

As one can see here Dr Majumdar does not stop with merely drawing parallels in a self-congratulatory way. Instead, he explores if the ancient Darshana worldviews including their argument tools and views of reality, can actually help students of modern physics in their exploration and understanding of the fundamental physical reality.

If *Science India* is taken as an indicator of the Hindutva approach to science, and there is no reason to doubt otherwise, then what we have is neither an antiscience or pseudoscience attitude. There is definitely a pro-Indic approach. There is pride in Indian achievements. There is also a consistent coverage of military technologies. A Hindu philosophical approach is seen in understanding the implications of scientific discoveries. But there is also inclusive approach to science and technology both in terms of the entire society and gender.

Typical pseudo-rationalist Dravidian propaganda where moon landing happens on the head of Siva. Apart from its spiritual nature, the image of Siva conveys to scientists including Nobel Laureate Ilya Prigogine, the dynamic process-centred nature of deep reality in their domains

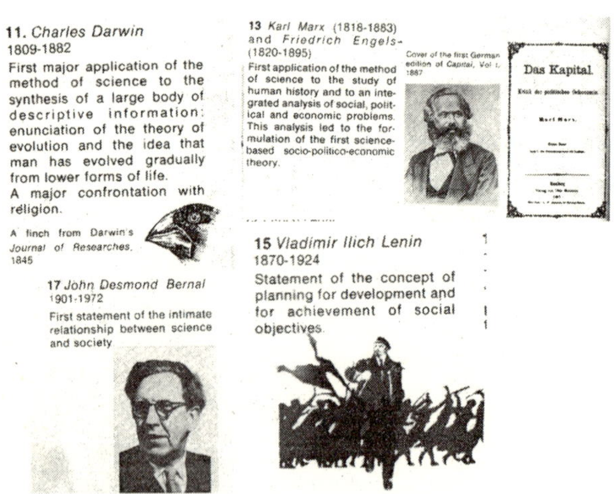

Here is an example of how Marxists abused the term scientific temper. In this 'Method of Science Exhibition' made with tax-payers' money, Karl Popper and Thomas Kuhn were ignored; Charles Darwin was just mentioned. But Karl Marx and Lenin were shown as in propaganda posters

Acharya Jagadish Chandra Bose with the team of science students, including Meghnad Saha and Satyendranath Bose

Dr Shyama Prasad Mukherjee as the Minister of Supplies and Industries in GoI, laying the foundation for the Institute of Nuclear Physics (INP). Mukherjee strove hard to fulfil Meghnad Saha's vision (21 April 1948)

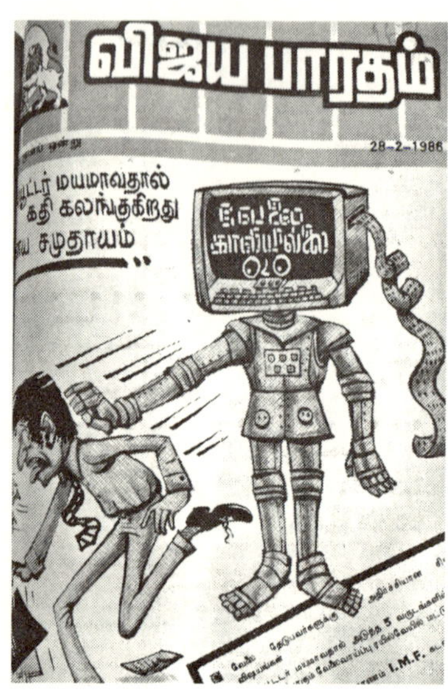

Cover illustration of the official popular magazine of the RSS, giving a strong message that computerization would increase unemployment. The Sangh's stand was proven wrong

'Science India', the official magazine of the RSS Vijnana Bharati—the science and technology wing of the RSS

75

THE LEGEND: **Dr Kadambini Ganguly (18 July 1861 – 3 October 1923)**

The Doctor Who Broke The Glass Ceiling in India

From active suppression to character assassination, Dr Kadambini Ganguly faced all to pave way for higher education for women in India before independence

• Sonam Singh Subhedar

Dr Kadambini Ganguly is not a household name and not many are aware of the fact that she was the very first female doctor who practiced with a degree in western medicine not just in India, but in the whole of South Asia. She was born on 18 July 1861 to headmaster Brajakishore Basu, who was a passionate follower of the Brahmo Samaj ideals.

The family of Dr Ganguly was from Chandsi, in Barisal which is now in Bangladesh. Her father was headmaster of Bhagalpur School. He started the movement for women's emancipation in Bhagalpur, establishing the women's organisation, Bhagalpur Mahila Samiti, in 1863, the first in India.

After completing her preliminary education, a young Kadambini wanted to appear for the entrance exam at the University of Calcutta (CU), and so did a Bengali girl from Dehradun — Chandramukhi Basu. But the university was still not admitting female students. This is when Kadambini met her future husband, Dwarkanath Ganguly, who played the biggest role in helping her realise her full potential.

According to the *Proceedings of the Indian History Congress Vol. (2005-06)*, Brahmo reformers like Durgamohan Das and Dwarkanath Ganguly were enthusiastic supporters of medical education for women. A number of newspapers and journals emphasised the need for women doctors trained in western medicine for women patients. *Brahmo Public Opinion* wrote in 1883: "If there be any one country where more than in another, the want of lady doctors is most keenly felt, it is no doubt, India". The *Bamabodhini Patrika* wrote: "Everyone with prudence will admit that as for men, medical education is equally necessary for women. There are certain types of female diseases which can only be appreciated by women and their treatment by males cannot be as effective as by females".

The article 'Kadambini and the Bhadralok' published in the *Economic and Political Weekly* in 1986, narrated how as a result of Dwarkanath Ganguly's efforts, Kadambini was deemed fit in 1877, to appear for the entrance examination for Calcutta University at a time when no leading British University had opened its doors to women. Kadambini passed her First Arts (FA) examination in 1880 leading to her dream to get admissions at the Calcutta Medical College (CMC). In 1882, Kadambini Ganguly and Chandramukhi Basu completed their BA from Bethune College. Kadambini now decided to study medicine at the university, where only a simple BA degree was adequate for admission. After much efforts by Dwarkanath Ganguly, Kadambini was given permission to try for the university examination. Though the examination paper and the books were the same as for male candidates, a separate examination centre was set up. She passed the entrance with second division.

In 1883, Kadambini married Dwarkanath Ganguly, a widower and 17 years older than her. They had eight children together. Dr Ganguly's work as a doctor slowed down due to household work and social obstacles. Many refused to acknowledge their marriage due to Dwarkanath Ganguly's status as a widower, though it was culturally permissible for widowers to get remarried.

The government offered Kadambini Rs 20 per month as scholarship for the medical college education, but the CMC professors didn't like her studying there. Explaining the episode, Dr Sankar Kumar Nath, a 73-year-old Consultant Oncologist and Researcher on History of Medicine, said, "She entered the medical college to get an MB degree but she failed in 1886 by the margin of only one mark. The rumour is that some professor, who was not happy with the admission of a woman in medical college, probably failed her intentionally. When the matter reached Dr JM Coates, the then Principal of Calcutta Medical College, he asked her to continue her degree. But again, she was failed by the same person. Kadambini got sure that her dream of passing the exam will always remain a dream. But then she approached the Calcutta University Senate and Dr Coates was entrusted to take any decision. So, finally Dr Coates awarded her GMCB (Graduate of Bengal Medical College) diploma, affiliated to London University that allowed her to start private practice as a doctor. This was before CMC came under the jurisdiction of Calcutta University."

An old, undated photograph of Calcutta Medical College and Hospital

When a young Kadambini was finally allowed to write her university exam for studying medicine, she was made to sit in a separate examination centre from male candidates even though the syllabus and paper were the same

In 1886, when Dr Ganguly got a Graduate of Bengal Medical College diploma, she became one of the two — Dr Anandi Gopal Joshi being the other — Indian women doctors who qualified to practice western medicine. Also, another Indian woman by the name of Abala Bose passed entrance in 1881 but was refused admission to the medical college and went to Madras to study medicine but never graduated. But there is a confusion regarding who was India's first female doctor to practice western medicine. Dr Anandi Gopal Joshi got her degree from Women's Medical College, Pennsylvania in 1886 and Dr Ganguly got her first medical degree in India. But sadly, Dr Joshi passed away in 1887 due to tuberculosis, before starting her medical practices. Thus, Dr Ganguly became the first female practitioner of western medicine in India while Dr Joshi was the first female to receive a medical degree in Western medicine from the west.

Dr Ganguly's achievements were so huge for the time that even Florence Nightingale heard about her. She wrote to a friend in February 1888: "(she) has already passed what is called the first licentiate in medicine and surgery examinations and is to go up for the final examination in March next. This young lady, Mrs. Ganguly, married! after she made up her mind to become a doctor! and has had one, if not two children since. But she was absent only thirteen days for her lying-in!! and did not miss, I believe, a single lecture!!"

But when Dr Ganguly's career started, discriminations stacked against her. "In 1888, she joined Lady Dufferin (medical college and hospital in Calcutta) at Rs 300 per month. These hospitals were

RSS emphasizes in general a larger role of women in the national science movement

8

The Harmonizing Samanvaya and Protection of Theo-diversity

One of the charges against *Hindutva* is that it is a homogenizing ideology that erases all pluralism, destroying all voices of dissent within Indian cultural and social history into one monolith, in which every voice of difference is subordinated to 'Brahminism', which in turn is nothing but a hierarchical social system with notions of Brahmin superiority and ritual pollution. Further Hindutva is also characterized as an anti-Muslim and anti-Christian hate ideology. Generally, Hindutva is portrayed as anti-pluralist and pro-homogenizing. Also relevant for the proponents of Hindutva, who consider it as a national process that predates its modern categorization, is the question whether this national process is nothing but violent persecution and destruction of ancient Buddhism and Jainism, which are considered both heterodox and more egalitarian. Then, there are allegations from those who consider Hindutva as opposing the core positive elements of Hindu Dharma while appropriating Hindu Dharma and so run the danger of destroying all things good, beautiful and positive in Hindu Dharma.

Samanvaya: An Integral Part of Hindutva

Through millennia, India has evolved her own organic processes to harmonize diversity and generate a ceaseless dialogue and exchange of ideas between diverse elements. At any point of time, one can see eddies of such evolutionary dialogues happening between seemingly diverse and even conflicting elements. This has been true from the Vedic to modern times.

Not that India has been bereft of conflicts. There have been many conflicts—ethnic, religious, political and so on. But the general subsuming meta-movement has always been towards harmonizing the diverse elements through placing them in an underlying matrix, where the diverse—even conflicting—elements become its complementary manifestations. We call the process *samanvaya*, and it goes way beyond the concept of tolerance.

One finds such harmonizing processes throughout Vedic literature. A popular one is seer Dirghatmas's verse: 'Truth is One and the wise call it differently'.[1] Vedic society should have known internal strife with various social groups, diverse spiritual traditions, etc. Yet the deities and traditions were harmonized through an elaborate system of ever-growing body of Puranas as well as rituals.

We see this evolution through the Upanishadic period as well. In the verses of *Ishavasya Upanishad*, we see the bringing together of the strongest binaries that the human mind has created. The knowledge of the temporal is made complementary with the knowledge of the absolute. This complementary pair of knowledge is then made mandatory for the attainment of the knowledge that liberates and gives immortality to the seeker. In the same way, the worship of the personal deity and the contemplative adoration of the impersonal Divine are integrated as complementary in obtaining liberation rather than pitting one as superior to the other.[2]

Vedic religious system was also harmonized with the supposedly non-Vedic Pancharatra doctrine. The latter forms the ground for temple worship, image worship, etc. Definitely, the temple as well as Vedic form of worship could have had a conflict. Hence, the Western Indological mind naturally thought of Pancharatra as non-Vedic or even anti-Vedic. However, Indian scholars with traditional roots differ significantly from the Western scholars. They do not see the Vedic and Pancharatra as opposing or unrelated entities. Rather, they are diverse elements in interaction, embedded in the substratum of a harmonizing cultural field. There are traditional scholars who even go to the extent of saying that 'the influence of the *agamas* or tantras as they are more familiarly known in Indian life has been profound', adding enigmatically that 'the living Hindu religion of today from Cape Comorin to remotest corners of

Tibet is essentially Tantric'.[3]

Pancharatra was internalized and harmonized rather than pitted against the Vedic as a distinct system. It speaks of the four *vyuhas* or emanations of Vishnu: Vasudeva, Sankarshana, Pradyumna and Aniruddha. When Pancharatra was internalized as a spiritual phenomenon, Vasudeva becomes the supreme Godhead and Sankarshana, his manifestation as the individual soul (*jiva*); Pradyumna the mind; and Aniruddha the ego-sense. Vaishnavaite scholar and Indologist Edwin Bryant points out that this internalization of the *Bhagavata* doctrine then finds resonance with the verses of the *Chandogya Upanishad* ('He becomes one then becomes threefold,' 7.24.2).[4]

What is true of the Vedic religion is also true of Buddhism.

In *Lalitavistara*, an early Buddhist work, we find the Buddha condemning tantra. However, Buddhism later developed its own tantra system. Similarly, despite the rejection of the Vedic authority, we find Buddhist architecture—particularly the stupa—incorporating the features of the Vedic fire altar (or according to some authorities 'Brahminical fire altar tumulus').[5] The six *darshanas* as well as the Jain and Buddhist approaches to reality have provided the Indian approach to knowledge with dynamic pluralism—both in terms of epistemology and ontology. The cognitive flexibility that these systems provide to the Indian mind is staggering. The *Satkarya-vadha* in the Vedic system where the effect is involuted in the cause in the non-linear way, along with *Sankhya*, resonates with the autopoietic (self-producing) view of life put forth by philosophers of modern biology. The *Syadvada* of the Jains seems to anticipate the mathematical formalism of quantum bits. The Buddhist doctrine of *Pratityasamutpada* can provide us epistemological tools to explore various ways in which evolution functions. One can contrast this with the almost strangling effect that the imposition of Aristotelian philosophy, along with Christian theology, had on the development of material and psychological sciences in the West. The extraordinary diversity also has a connecting dynamic matrix. The Jain seer Acharya Mahaprajna, on the authority of Jain text *Anyayogavyavacchedadvatrimsika* of Haribhadrasuri, shows how seemingly varied Indic systems of knowledge form a whole:

> The Vedantic monism is like the waveless ocean and the Buddhist phenomenonalism is like the state of ocean with strong waves. (Jain) Non-absolutism appropriates them both.[6]

Even where there were somewhat violent attitudes towards fellow Indic sects, samanvaya proved successful in the long run. A good example is the so-called impaling of 8,000 Jains by the Saivaite saint Gnana Sambandar—a seventh century Saivaite prodigy-poet-mystic.

This is often quoted by anti-Hindutva forces to show that ancient Indian history was that of violent persecution performed by a Brahminical religion against Jains and Buddhists. During the Ayodhya debate, Prof. Romila Thapar accused other Hindus (mainly Brahmins and rulers belonging to Vedic streams) as not only having destroyed Buddhist and Jain places of worship but also of massacring them:

> Evidence on the persecution of Jainas by Saiva sects comes from a variety of sources....The Shaivaite saint Jnana Sambandar is attributed with having converted the Pandya ruler from Jainism to Shaivism, whereupon it is said that 8,000 Jainas were impaled by the king.

Here is a typical rhetorical use of this narrative by the rabidly anti-Hindu Dalit leader Thol. Thirumaavalavan:

> Though the Pallavas were Jain kings, they listened to Brahmins, and they turned against Buddhist and Jains. They went on violent rampages killing Buddhist and Jaina monks and destroyed Buddhist and Jaina shrines. Do you know who secretly headed these violent rampages?... He is the Saivaite Nayanmar saint Thirugnana Sambandar who was born in Sirkali. He came to Madurai, turned Koon Pandiyan against Jains and was the cause for 8000 Jains to be impaled to death on a single day. This is history.[7]

However, a little look into this allegation of massacre reveals something different. Though Sambandar was against the Jains and Buddhists from his religious worldview, the internal evidence in his poetry also suggests that ultimately he considered both these sects as the working of Siva himself.[8] To him even the non-flattering tirade against Siva by Buddhists and Jains as acceptable because Siva himself considered them as 'principled'.[9] There is no evidence of the impaling story in the contemporary historical records, including those of Jains or in the Pandya inscriptions, under whose reign the event was said to have happened. So, scholars of South Indian history, including K. A. N. Sastri, had dismissed the episode of voluntary impalement of 8,000 Jains who were defeated by Sambandar in debate, as Saiva braggadocio without any basis in facts.[10] After almost 1300 years from the time of Sambandar, Tamil Hindu scholar U. Ve. Swaminatha Iyer (1855–1942), popularly known as 'Tamil Grandpa', set forth to discover and preserve ancient Tamil classics, some of which were of Jain and Buddhist origins. When he discovered *Jivakachintamani*, an ancient Tamil Jain classic, it was through the help of reputed Saiva mutt at Thiruvavaduthurai that he published the Jain work.[11]

Despite the colonial Indologist as well as postcolonial Marxist approaches to ancient Indian history viewing it as a conflict between the so-called upper caste Brahminical system oppressing and assimilating the 'non-Brahminical' systems, the Indic approach has always been harmony oriented. In fact, the finest achievements of Buddhism in India namely the Ajanta cave paintings and Nalanda University were patronized by the Vakataka king Harisena and the Gupta emperors respectively. Both royal lineages were rooted in Vedic religion. When Mihirahula, the Hun, massacred Buddhist monks, Indic kings Baladitya and Yasodharma came together and vanquished the oppressor, as will be seen later in this chapter in detail.

It is not only in the realms of high philosophy and royal history that the harmonization process worked. It equally worked in the folk traditions and popular culture of India throughout the ages. Thus, in the popular story of Adi Sankara, it is said that when Adi Sankara defeated the famous Jain scholar Amarasimha, the latter became so dejected that he started burning his own works. When he came to know of this, Adi Sankara went and prevented him from burning any further of his scholarly works, and thus we got the famous Sanskrit thesaurus *Amarakosha.*

A similar story is also told about the emperor Shalivahana. The emperor, originally hailing from a family of potters, was humiliated when the Naga princess he had married exclaimed playfully in Sanskrit and the king could not comprehend what she had said. So, when he set forth to study Sanskrit very quickly, his minister Gunadya told him that it would take him a minimum of 12 years while another minister, Sarvavarma, was confident of making the king an expert in six months. The infuriated Gunadya stated that he would cease speaking in Sanskrit if that happened. And that is exactly what happened. Gunadya left the emperor's court and vanished.

Later the emperor had tribal visitors who offered him a classic *Brihatkatha* written in their language Paishacha. Shalivahana considered Paishacha an uncivilized language and hence refused. Soon after this, the emperor fell ill from eating inferior meat, and inquiries revealed that the animals in the forest literally starved, captivated by the music of the guru of the tribals. So Shalivahana went to the forest himself to witness this phenomenon. There he saw that it was Gunadya singing his Paishachic *Brihatkatha* and burning the palm leaves with verses written on them one by one. Regretting his error, the emperor prevented further burning and returned to his capital with his minister and the Paishachic classic.

These traditions, both oral and classic, have layers of meaning and show how samanvaya works not just in the realms of religion and philosophy but also in the realm of linguistic diversity. One, it shows that contrary to the myth built around it, Sanskrit is not very hard to learn. Then it subtly criticizes the vanity that may come with the learning of Sanskrit, which was the cultural lingua franca of classical India. Further, it shows the beauty of a supposedly crude tribal language and elevates it to a sublime height. It underlines the duty of those in authority to nourish linguistic diversity. The result has been that Sanskrit itself has evolved more as a pervading matrix absorbing local linguistic substrata in its course rather than imposing itself as an annihilator of local linguistic diversity. Folk tales similar to the one about Shalivahana exist throughout India in almost all local languages.

The process of samanvaya has never ceased in Indian history.

In the seventeenth century, the ninth Sikh Guru Tegh Bahadur had campaigned against the tantric traditions in Assam and related regions. Probably they had degenerated. But within the next generation, the harmonization had brought together again the Shaktic and the core Vaishnavism of the Sikh Panth together when the 10th Sikh Guru Gobind Singh wrote *Chandi di Var* (a martial ballad of the Goddess battling the demons based on the *Markandeya Purana*) with the advent of the Khalsa movement.

The fierce Hindu resistance to Islamic invasions is just one side of Indian history.

Underneath, the Indic matrix was also working on Islam and harmonizing it. When Abul Fazal's *Akbar Nama* had Akbar confess regretfully that he had 'forced many Brahmins by fear of power to adopt Islam', it was indeed a significant moment for the process of samanvaya triumphing over the monocultural expansionist tendencies. Akbar went on to say that he had done such proselytization when his mind was not enlightened. Despite the regressive movement during Aurangzeb's reign, samanvaya reached its zenith in the immortal works of Dara Shukoh, the martyred elder brother of Aurangzeb.

The importance of Dara Shukoh in the process of samanvaya has not yet been studied and realized to its full potential. From the condescending admission of Amir Khusrau that Hindus did have some correct beliefs, which, in turn, stemmed from rigid Islamist theological framework, the point reached by Shukoh is amazingly universal.

In his introduction to the Persian translation of the Upanishads (*Sirr-i-Akbar*, *The Greatest Secret*), Shukoh reveals his religious philosophy. He compares the different world scriptures—the Vedas, the Upanishads, the Hebrew and Christian Bibles (*Taurat* and *Injil*) as well as the Psalms (*Zabur*). He declares that the degree of clarity and intelligibility in them is not uniform. He states that the content of the Koran is allegorical. Then he goes on to do the unthinkable. He contends that the Upanishads are the Koran in a protected book—*Kitab Maknun*—a reserved term in the Islamic theological world that refers to the original form of the Koran inscribed by Allah himself. Thus, for Dara Shukoh, the Upanishads stand as a holy text by themselves, but to understand the real meaning of the Koran, Muslims have to study the Upanishads. Elsewhere, the prince had also considered the idol worship of Hindus positively. According to him, a concrete representation of a deity was essential till one gets the inner meaning of religion.[12] This shall be dealt in detail under the section on Islam.

The martyrdom of Shukoh would not go waste as demonstrated by another martyr Ashfaqulla Khan, who when asked by the British why he was fighting for the freedom of Hindustan despite being a Muslim, he replied that he preferred his Hindu brothers over British colonialism. The spirit of Shukoh still lives vibrantly in India through the dialogues of the popular TV series Mahabharata, written by Rahi Mazoom Raza, which struck a chord with the entire nation in the late 1980s as they sat glued to their television screens every Sunday morning while the show was telecast. In the life of A. P. J. Abdul Kalam, this spirit of Dara Shukoh has become an inspiration for the entire nation.

In modern times, with respect to Abrahamic religions, the process of samanvaya was initiated by the Ramakrishna-Vivekananda tradition. Swami Brahmananda, the heir to the Vedanta mission in the United States, initiated the celebration of Christmas. Swami Ranganathananda, one of the highly respected monks of the Ramakrishna movement, gave a Christmas lecture—*The Christ We Adore*. The booklet shifts the importance from the historicity and exclusive salvation into an inner message of sadhana and experience of the Divine. The Ramakrishna-Vivekananda-initiated samanvaya has continued to bear fruit despite strong scepticism from some quarters of Internet-based Hindutva activists (who mostly are outside the Sangh and often antagonistic towards it).

However, even here there are a few significant milestones as well as formidable setbacks. A good instance of a milestone is Fr Anthony Elenjimittam (1915–2011), a Gandhian Christian priest from Kerala, who worked in Italy, bringing Indic values to Christianity. Incidentally, he was also the one who coined the term 'pseudo-secularism', and he was also perhaps the first person to write an appreciative book on the Rashtriya Swayamsevak Sangh (RSS) in English from a Gandhian perspective titled *Philosophy and Action of the RSS for the Hind Swaraj* (1951).

A detailed discussion of both the achievements and challenges that the Hindutva faces in this regard will also be discussed subsequently, mostly but not exclusively restricting to the pre-RSS time.

Equally important is the work of Anthony de Mello, S. J. (1931–1987), who, through his book *Sadhana—A Way to God* (1978), became a veritable phenomenon in Catholic monasteries throughout the world and among other religionists. Rejecting exclusivist claims, he placed his 'storytelling Master' as 'not a single person' but a 'Hindu guru, a Zen roshi, a Taoist sage, a Jewish rabbi, a Christian monk, a Sufi mystic'. The Master of Wisdom for Anthony de Mello was also 'Lao Tzu and Socrates, Buddha and Jesus, Zarathustra and Muhammed'. He sidelined the historic-centric approach to religion, emphasizing it as an inner journey: 'Do (the Master's) historical antecedents really matter? History, after all, is the record of appearances, not Reality; of doctrines, not of Silence.'[13] Eleven years after his death in 1998, the Congregation for the Doctrine of the Faith, previously known as Supreme Sacred Congregation of the Roman and Universal Inquisition, restricted the use of his work as some of his positions were found to be 'incompatible with the Catholic faith' with the potential of causing 'grave harm'.[14] The path of samanvaya is not a rosy one.

Tolerance at least, as has been brought up in Indian political parlance, is mostly a Cartesian concept of mechanistic tolerance of mutually competing worldviews, waiting for their time to come. So, the peace is a peace of strategic treaties with background processes in the form of political manoeuvre, and it is simply an interlude for the battle of gathering forces waiting to attain critical mass to subjugate or annihilate the other. What is needed for a real pluralist society is harmonization with mutual respect. In his work on the Brahma Sutra, Dr S. Radhakrishnan zoomed in on the word 'samanvaya' and pointed out its relevance in modern times:

> Today the *Samanvaya* or harmonization has to be extended to the living faiths of mankind. As the author of the Brahma Sutra tried to reconcile the different doctrines prevalent in his time, we have to take into account the present state of our knowledge and evolve a coherent picture.[15]

The very diverse nature of Hindu historic-cultural substratum makes it mandatory for Hindutva to harmonize the diverse Indic traditions—even ones with mutual conceptual oppositions—into an organic unity. It also makes it impossible for the emergence of a specific kind of theocratic fundamentalism, as is the case with a theocratic state that is typical of Islamist, Christian or Marxist.

Ancient India: Holy Wars or Samanvaya?

The picture of samanvaya does not paint a complete haven of passive acceptance with no conflicts. There were conflicts—sometimes even violent confrontation. There were efforts to use state power to suppress the other—

whoever that might be. However, these tendencies which in the histories of most monopolistic states have devolved into holy wars like crusade and jihad, inquisitions and Marxist State purges, samanvaya as an organic process saved India from such devolution.

Marxist historian Dwijendra Narayan Jha, whose work and politics have been discussed in Chapter 3, in his 2018 book, strategically titled *Against the Grain: Notes on Identity, Intolerance and History* (Manohar, 2018) questions this aspect of Indian history and society. In an uncritical appreciative review of the book published on a left-leaning portal, the reviewer provides a succinct and accurate portrayal of Jha's denial of samanvaya in ancient India—as he questions the 'oft-intoned self-adulatory declarations about India's rich culture of non-violence, religious harmony and tolerance of all communities'. The reviewer summarizes the 'counter evidence' provided by Jha 'to interrogate such an idea of India—India as a land of intrinsic religious tolerance':

> Jha disagrees with such a flattering image of ancient India and argues that even if it were to be accepted that Brahmanism gave space to other sects, there still exists enough counter evidence to interrogate such an idea of India—India as a land of intrinsic religious tolerance. "Not only did the different Brahmanical sects fight among themselves, of which we have plenty of evidence, they also bore huge animosity towards the two heterodox religions, Buddhism and Jainism, in early India," writes Jha.... Jha observes that the "invectives" against Buddhists and Jains were often channelled through violent and aggressive actions. For instance, the writer cites Hsuan Tsang (seventh century) who wrote about the Huna ruler Mihirakula, a devotee of Shiva, destroying 1,600 Buddhist stupas and monasteries, besides killing thousands of monks and laity. "Although there is evidence that the adherents of Shramainc retaliated against Brahmanism, it remains certain that the Brahmanical sects did not, as they are said to have done, practice tolerance towards non-Brahmanical faiths," he argues, going on to add: "on the contrary, they seemed to have played a leading role in fomenting religious conflicts and perpetrating sectarian violence during the early medieval period and later." No wonder, Alberuni (the 11th century Persian scholar who studied India) wrote, according to Jha, that Hindus are "haughty, foolishly vain and self-conceited". They "believe that there is no religion like theirs."[16]

As one moves through instances of 'intolerance and violence' given here case by case, one finds how they are not only distorted but actually proof of the opposite.

The Case of Mihirakula

Mihirakula was a Hun emperor who ruled the Hephthalite Empire in the northwestern part of India. In 520 CE he captured the Sindh province. He proclaimed himself a devotee of Rudra. He massacred Buddhist monks and destroyed Buddhist monasteries. But why did he do that?

Historian of ancient India Dr Upinder Singh explains the reason for Mihirakula's violence as narrated by the Buddhist pilgrim-monk Hsuan Tsang:

> Xuangzang (Hsuan Tsang) states that initially Mihirakula was interested in learning about Buddhism and asked the monks to send him a teacher; the monks insulted him by recommending a servant of his own householder for the purpose. This incident is said to have turned Mihirakula virulently anti-Buddhist. Xuangzang states that he destroyed 1,600 monasteries in Gandhara and had 9,000 men killed or sold into slavery on the banks of the Indus.[17]

What about the Brahmins of India? Were they happy that their religious rivals were being annihilated by an invader? Kalhana, the Sanskrit poet (twelfth century) who himself belonged to the so-called 'Brahminical' religion, records in his authoritative work on Kashmir's history titled *Rajatarangini* how the Kashmiri Brahmins refused to accept the donation of 1,000 *agraharas*—living quarters granted to them by Mihirakula. 'They refused to accept them from the hands of a brutal king', writes Kalhana.

While Mihirakula was a self-proclaimed worshipper of Rudra, that did not factor in Indic resistance to his invasion and the aversion towards his atrocities. Far from that, the Indian ruler who proudly proclaimed the formation of a coalition of Indic principalities to fight Mihirakula (any resemblance to election-necessitated modern Shiva-devotee impostor is pure coincidence), was himself a staunch devotee of Mahadeva—Yasodharma.

> May the long flying banner of Shulapani (Trident wielding Shiva) destroy the strength of your enemies; the banner with the Nandi (Shiva's bull), marked by the five fingers (dipped in Sandal and vermilion) of the daughter of the mountains (Parvati, the consort of Shiva), that bull whose bellowing causes all the quarters of the worlds shake and grips the demons with fear, whose horns shatter the rocks of the mountain Sumeru!

Eminent Indologist Hans Bakker quoting the above inscription finds in it 'the language of the war' and states that with it 'the Shaiva age had begun', meaning the tone and worldview of the inscription indicate the heralding of the Shaiva age.[18] But the enemy here was no heterodox religion or its followers, but the invader who also worshipped Shiva, but massacred the Buddhists and civilians. The inscription says:

> He whose head has never known humility save before Sthanu (Shiva), he whose expanding grabbing hands made the impregnable nature of Himalayas a false vanity, even that king Mihirakula, humbly offers worship at the feet of Yasodharma with the flowers fallen from his crest and with the arms of Yasodharma the head of the Huna king is bent painfully, compelled to pay obeisance.

Apart from Yasodharma, kings like Baladitya or Narasimha Gupta, who belonged to the Gupta dynasty, also offered resistance to Mihirakula. He not only defeated Mihirakula and rebuked him for the massacre of Buddhists, but eventually pardoned him and spared his life. This Gupta emperor, whose coins show him with a *garuda* standard and Goddess Lakshmi on the reverse, also built a brick temple for the Buddha at Nalanda University.

How has the traditional Hindu historiography outside the mainstream academia, including the modern Hindutva one viewed these events? The same grand narrative of traditional Hindu historiography that makes villains out of Ghazni and Ghori also makes a villain out of Mihirakula. The same tradition that makes Prithviraj Chauhan, Rana Pratap and Shivaji national heroes also makes Yasodharma and Baladitya or Narasimha Gupta national heroes.

While Jawaharlal Nehru could not ignore the victory of Yasodharma over Mihirakula, he reduced it to a few sentences. In his *Discovery of India*, he wrote:

> These were the White Huns, as they are called, who ravaged the land, as under Attila they were ravaging Europe. Their barbarous behaviour and fiendish cruelty at last roused the people, and a united attack by a confederacy under Yashovarman was made on them. The Hun power was broken and their chief, Mihiragula, was made a prisoner. But the descendant of the Guptas, Baladitya, in accordance with his country's customs, treated him with generosity and allowed him to leave India. Mihiragula responded to this treatment by returning later and making a treacherous attack on his benefactor.

However, subsequent history textbooks of free India rarely talked about this important Indic victory. Social science textbooks do not refer to him or say very little about Yasodharma. After thus erasing the memory of Yasodharma through seven decades of institutional strangulation comes the Marxist historian Jha, who inverses the narrative and wants the gullible, culturally illiterate English-reading Indians to believe that Mihirakula was a hero to ancient Hindus.

Brahminical Versus Heterodox

While there is no denying that there were and still are strong textual debates, dialogues, and even polemical attacks between sects, sometimes even violent conflicts, it was not a clear binary between Vedic-Brahminism and the so-called heterodox religions (by which he means Jainism and Buddhism). Far from being such opposing binaries, the Vedic, Buddhist and Jain religious systems show organic inter-linkages, conflicts and harmonizing relations between each other.

Indologist Yuvraj Kishan and Dr Kalpana K. Tadikonda, an expert in Buddhist iconography, explain:

> In fact, the Buddhist (and Jains) adopted the Vedic cultural features. In Vedic religion, the yajnasthana is treated as a caitya. It is a significant that the Buddhist stupa is called asthi or dhatu chaitya, mound containing the sacred relic.... In fact, the account of the Buddha's birth in the Buddhist text has considerable similarity with the story in the Rig Veda of the birth of Indra. (Dr P. Banerjee, *Birth of Buddha and its Vedic Parallel, Buddhist Iconography*, p. 1–6, 1984)[19]

Adrian Snodgrass, an authority in Buddhist art and philosophy, agrees with this idea. He points out that there is 'a continuity of symbolic content that runs from Vedic Brahmanism to Buddhism' and similar 'considerable overlap of the symbolic expressions of later Hinduism and Buddhism'.

> There is a common store of metaphysical symbols whence both traditions draw their spiritual sustenance. All that has been said of Brahman, Agni, Shiva and Vishnu as the skambha, the Cosmic Pillar, axis mundi and ontological foundation of the world, is equally true of the Buddha....Among the reliefs from Amaravati are to be seen many representations of the Buddha as a fiery pillar, comprising feet marked with the Wheel of the Dharma and a trident (trisul) head. The representation of the Buddha as a fiery pillar is a survival of the Vedic symbolism and more specifically that embodies in the God of Fire, Agni. The Buddha and Agni are ontologically equivalent persons.[20]

Even with respect to Vedic rituals, Buddha, as revealed in early Buddhist texts, had an approach that was consistent with the approach of pre-Buddhist

Upanishads, which in turn had their roots in Vedas themselves. For example, *Chandogya Upanishad*, a pre-Buddhist Upanishad, says that the real fire sacrifice—the highly exalted *agnihotra*—consists of oblations to the self. In this symbolism, the chest becomes the altar, the heart becomes the *garhapatya* fire, the mind, the *anvaharya* fire, and the mouth, the *ahavaniya* fire. If one does not understand this and does the ritual without intent, then it is depreciated as 'an oblation offered in dead ashes after removing the live coals.[21] Here the Vedic ritual is not only internalized, but transformed into an act of doing good to all beings—thus sharing of food, without the discrimination even unto a social outcaste also becomes a sacrifice.[22]

One finds the same methodology and symbolic interpretation of Vedic sacrifices in Buddha's discourses too. In *Kutadanta Sutta*, the three modes of Vedic sacrifice correlate to the states of mind. The 16 conditions (requirements concerning the altar, the priest's clothes, etc.) are re-conceived as the cooperation of the four varnas and so on. In *Aggi Sutta*, while Buddha repudiates the fire ritual in which animals are offered, he proceeds to reinterpret them—*ahavaniya* corresponds to parents, *garhapatya* to wife, children, and servants, and the *daksinagni* to Brahmins and mendicants.[23]

Professor Kristin Beise Kiblinger, in her book on Buddhist inclusivism, concludes that such Buddhist reinterpretations of Vedic sacrifices 'are not subordinating sacrificial ritual under higher level Buddhist practices; rather they are replacing metaphysics with ethics'.[24] But as seen earlier, this reinterpretation process has a continuity with the Upanishads. Mircea Eliade finds this type of reinterpretation, which he calls 'ritual interiorization', pan-Indian and traces it partly to Vedic hymns in the *Rig Veda* and *Brahmanas*. In *Sutta Nipata*, Buddha speaks of agnihotra as the best among the sacrifices and Savitri as the best among the hymns, and then he makes services rendered to the monks of the Sangha the best of the sacrifices.

While Buddhism shows an overall reverence to the Vedic sacred realm with suitable modifications of its own, there is also a bitter rivalry against Jainism revealed in Buddhist literature. Buddhist hagiography of Ashoka, *Ashokavadhana*, says that when a Buddhist devotee reported to Ashoka about a follower of Nirgrantha Jnatiputra, who drew a painting depicting the Buddha bowing down to Mahavira, Ashoka got enraged and ordered that 'all of the Ajivikas in the whole of Pundavardhana be put to death at once'. According to the hagiography, on that day alone, 'eighteen thousand of them were executed'. Similarly, later in Pataliputra, when another devotee of Nirgrantha drew a painting of Buddha bowing to his master, Ashoka burnt the man and his entire family.[25]

Jha also speaks of the 'retaliatory violence' of Vedic Hindus.

In fact, there were conflicts between Buddhism and Jainism which were more severe than the one between the so-called Vedic-Brahminism and Buddhism. Questionable instances like that of Pushyamitra Shunga are brought in to emphasize the binary conflict. But what about such violent conflicts recorded in ancient Indian history? Were they real persecutions? Do they in any way invalidate the picture of religious pluralism with mutual respect in ancient India, as alleged by Jha?

Even Dr Upinder Singh casts doubts on the nature of persecution of Buddhism under Pushyamitra. In her book on political violence in India, she points out that despite John Marshall linking 'great damage' that was 'wantonly inflicted' on Sanchi Stupa 'with the anti-Buddhist reputation acquired by Pushyamitra Shunga' and Pushyamitra 'sometimes been held responsible for the destruction of the Ghoshitarama monastery at Kaushambi and the Deur Kothar stupa in central India', 'Sanchi and other Buddhist monasteries in central India continued to exist and flourish during the Shunga period'. So, she asks:

> Was this in spite of Pushyamitra's persecution of the Buddhists? Was it because later Shunga kings discontinued his anti-Buddhist policy? Or should the Buddhist stories of Pushyamitra's persecution be considered exaggerated?[26]

While conceding that it is 'difficult to say for sure', she thinks there might be 'some historical basis', while the claims of the Buddhist tradition 'cannot be taken at face value'.

In the case of Sasanka, another king from East India, who was accused of persecuting Buddhists, again the evidence is wanting. As historian Sailendra Nath Sen points out, 'the Chinese pilgrim's description of the flourishing condition of Buddhism in Sasanka's capital cannot be reconciled with the active persecution of Buddhism' as alleged by the same Hsuan Tsang.[27]

Textual accounts of violence—either to boast the victory or play martyrs—mostly do not portray the social reality—unlike in the case of Islamic conquest, where the textual boasting and ground reality get corroborated with evidence. An example is provided by historical facts discovered about Ashoka and the traditional account found in *Ashokavadhana* of him massacring Ajivikas. However, the inscriptions found in the four caves on the Barabar Hill, north to Gaya, reveal that Ashoka donated these caves to the Ajivika ascetics.

Similarly, while Marxist historians like Jha and Romila Thapar insist on a confrontational model of conflict and replacement with the 'Brahminical' religions inflicting violence and persecution on the so-called heterodox religions, more and more detailed studies reveal that the movement of Indian culture was towards reconciliation and harmony. In fact, Tamil Nadu here provides a very good framework. The Shaivaite account about voluntary impaling of 8,000 Jains who were defeated by Thirugnana Sambandar had been often quoted by Marxist and colonial scholars as an example of elimination and violent persecution of 'heterodox' sects by 'Brahminical' Hinduism. As seen earlier, even Sambandar, who was quite harsh in repudiating Jainism, considered it as part of the divine play of Sivan and did not characterize it as pure evil to be purged.

This also leads us to another question—a question that has become almost axiomatic for the Marxist scholars —that similar to Islamic invaders, the Vedic sects also destroyed Buddhist and Jain places of worship and built their temples over them. This has been thrust through academia, media and political rhetoric in such a way that Dr Lisa Owen, a specialist in Jain history, studying the Jina images of Kalugumalai, Tamil Nadu, calls this 'standard narrative' which 'presents the history of interaction in this region solely in terms of dispute and conflict between bounded and monolithic communities of Shaivas and Jains'. She supports the view of another Indologist, Richard Davis, specializing in Shaiva-Jain encounters who too points out that 'if we cling to narratives such as the "standard narrative", we lose sight of the complex ways in which these traditions interact and the ways these interactions are themselves constitutive'. This perspective also questions the categorization of ancient Indian holy space in a linear manner as Vedic, Buddhist and Jain phases, which is part of the 'standard narrative' constructed by the dominant Marxist school historians:

> The evidence of work being produced simultaneously at Ellora is, however, often not recognized by scholars as the site continues today to be described as exhibiting three separate phases: Buddhist, Hindu and Jain. This is unfortunate, as many of India's ancient and medieval sites, particularly rock-cut monuments, clearly demonstrate multi-religious interests in their artistic expressions. This also seems to have been the case at Kalugumalai.[28]

What Owen and Davis point out in the context of Tamil Nadu is also true for most of India's cultural matrix, as has been pointed out by Susan Verma Mishra and Himanshu Prabha Ray in the context of Gujarat.

Again, the distortion through selective concealment of facts, exhibited by Jha shows Hemachandra, the twelfth century Jain scholar, as 'denouncing the ancient code of law *Manusmriti* on the grounds that it supported ritual violence'. But what he does not reveal entirely about Hemachandra is more relevant to the question in hand—the mutual respect and nurturing of pluralism—the defining nature of Indian culture and spirituality. Susan Mishra and Prabha Ray explain:

> Hemachandra's acceptance of (Shaivaite) Kumarapala's creed was reciprocated by the sovereign, who was an important patron of Jaina foundations and reportedly worshipped at Jaina temples. This mutual participation in the practices of the other hints at meanings of religion and community identification that are not always acknowledged in modern academic framework.[29]

So, what we witness in Indian civilization is that it never allows religious conflicts to become fully blown holy wars against any religious sect. The basic underlying dictum that has emerged from this understanding is enshrined in the Vedic statement that the one Truth is perceived in various ways.[30]

The Continuity

This inherent pluralist dimension of Hindutva is expressed by Savarkar in his rejection of any attempt to elevate a single Hindu sacred text as the sacred text of the Hindus. At a time when many English educated and British influenced intellectuals even on the nationalist side wanted a single text, particularly Bhagavad Gita, to be made the 'Bible' of Hindus, Savarkar considered Hindus having no single sacred text as a positive and defining feature of Hindutva. In July 1937, barely five months before he became the president of the All India Hindu Mahasabha, Savarkar delivered a speech: '*Ek hi dharm-pustak nahin, yeh achcha hai*!' ['There isn't one sacred text (for Hindus) and that is good.'] Historian Vinayak Chaturvedi, an anti-Hindutva Western academic informant-scholar, in his paper on the relation of Savarkar to Bhagavad Gita gives the essence of this speech:

> Savarkar's central argument was that the Bhagavad Gita should not be considered the singular or monolithic text for the creation of the Hindu nation. He explained that the Gita was a seminal work, but that it needed to be read alongside other books that constituted the diverse literary traditions within Hinduism. Savarkar's claim for textual pluralism was a direct response to contemporary arguments that Hindus needed to elevate the Gita to the status of the Bible in Christianity or the Koran in Islam as a way to strengthen the foundation of Hinduism in the making of modern India.[31]

This aspect of the acceptance of sacred diversity with mutual respect can be traced centuries before Savarkar in the tradition of Hinduness. For instance, the inscription of the Kesava temple at Belur, Mysore states:

> May Hari the Lord of the three worlds, worshipped by the Saivas as Siva, by the Vedantists as Brahman, venerated by the Buddhists as the Buddha, by the logicians as the chief agent, by the Jains as the emancipated being and by the ritualists as the principle of observance, grant our prayers.[32]

The verse in its original or the oldest form was from *Mahanataka* or *Hanuman Nataka* and was attributed to Hanuman—the fierce warrior associated with the protection of Dharma. Scholars attribute the date to tenth century and as having composed by Damodara Misra, a poet named in *Bhoja Prabandhu.*[33]

This is quite important because Udaipur inscription of the Paramaras of Malwa speaks of Bhoja, who corresponds to the above period of composition and whose reign was between 1015–1052, as having defeated 'Turuksas' (Islamic invaders), which probably refers to Mahmud Ghazni. Historian Dr Ram Gopal Misra considers the possibility of Bhoja being part of a pan-Hindu confederacy that was formed following the gruesome sacking of Somnath by Mahmud Ghazni and so the inscriptional verse may well refer 'to the defeat sustained by the forces of Yamini ruler of Ghazni in 1043 A.D.' which Dr Misra points out was also corroborated by Firishta, who had recorded that the 'Raja of Delhi in conjunction with other Rajas liberated Hanis, Thaneshwar and Nagarkote and pushed back the frontiers of the Ghaznavid kingdom across the Ravi'. The Paramara king Bhoja 'might have been a member of this confederacy'.[34]

It is well known to historians that Hanuman became a symbol of Hindu resistance to Islamic invaders in later centuries. Usually, this emergence of Hanuman as the symbol of Hindu resistance is traced to Vijayanagar or post-Vijayanagar development and seventeenth century Mughal period.[35] However, the verse emphasizing the unity of Hindu family of religions as well as various Vedic *sampradayas* composed in the name of Hanuman may point to the initial pan-Hindu consolidation and explicit awareness at least a few centuries before the formation of Vijayanagar where Hanuman worship fully assumed the status of martial tradition.

Prof. Arvind Sharma in his book on the history of religious tolerance points out that this has been modified in modern times to include Jesus and Allah:

> It has been proposed, in modern times, that another line be added to this invocation as follows: '*Kristvah kristuriti kriyaparaparata alleti mahammadah*' (Radhakrishnan, 1948. p. 159); that is to say whom the socially active Christians call Christ, and the Muslims Allah'. This would have the effect of making the invocation even more comprehensive in its eclectic embrace, as it would also bring Christianity and Islam within its catholic reach.[36]

The passage that Prof. Sharma cites from S. Radhakrishnan is this:

> Udayanacarya writes: 'Whom the Saivas worship as Siva, the Vedantins as Braliman, the Buddhists as Buddha, the Naiyayikas who specialize in canons of knowledge as the chief agent, the followers of the Jaina code as the ever free, the ritualists as the principle of law, may that Hari, the lord of the three worlds, grant our prayers.' If he had been writing in this age, he would have added 'whom the Christians devoted to work as Christ and the Mohammedans as Allah' ('*Kristvah kristuriti kriyaparaparata alleti mahammadah*').[37]

And this comes as part of Dr Radhakrishnan's commentary on Bhagavad Gita 4:11. This inclusion of Christ and Allah in a hymn form like the oldest possible version of the same *Maha Natak* predates even Radhakrishnan's mentioning it in his commentary of Bhagavad Gita. Dr Wendell Thomas, one of the earliest scholars to study Hindu religious movement in the United States records in his thesis a service in Vedanta Society of New York in the year 1928 in which Swami Jnaneshvarananda after a Sanskrit prayer recited the following in English:

> May that One who is called Siva by the Shivaites, Vishnu by the Visnuites, Brahman by the Vedantins, Allah by the Muslims and God the Heavenly Father by the Christians, inspire our hearts with love for all mankind. Peace! Peace! Peace![38]

The RSS, which is the most prominent (though not the only one) continuer of the Hindutva, continues the same tradition of *samanvaya*. The *Ekatma Mantra* (Unity Invocation) of the organization chanted every day before the *Ekatmata Stotra* (Unity Hymn) states:

> *Whom*
> *the Vedic traditionalists and the seers of Vedic-Mantras and Puranas call as Indra, Yama and Mātariśvā (Vedic Deities),*
> *the holders of Vedānta, experience of sacred knowledge at the end of all scriptures, indicate by the word the Brahman -the One that which cannot be explained,*
> *the Saivaites invoke as Śiva*
> *the Vaishnavas worship as Vishnu,*
> *the Buddhists venerate as the Buddha*
> *the Jains call as Arhant (without any end),*
> *the Sikh sages call Sat Śrī Akāl (Truth, Beauty and Eternal)*
> *yet some address as the Nature, Kumāra, Sāsta and*
> *the devoted call as the Mother, Father and Master*
> *It the only One (Eka Eva) and in non-dual*

Of course, the RSS hymn does not invoke Allah and Christ by name, but the salutations of the Divine as Father and Master do correspond to the way these Abrahamic religions relate to the Divine. This is a clear indication that the Hindutva as it manifests today consciously continues the traditional strand of samanvaya. The samanvaya happens both within what the Hindutva considers as the family of Hindu religions as well as outside in the present context.

Buddhism, Jainism and Sikh Panth are considered by the Hindutvaites as the Hindu family of spiritual traditions along with Vedic religions of Saivism, Shaktic, Kaumara, Ganapatya and Vaishnavism. Dr Ambedkar, the chief architect of Indian Constitution, too considered all the Indic religions as belonging to the same cultural-national matrix or family.

Samanvaya and Sikh Panth

From the Hindutva perspective, Sikhs have been part and parcel of Hindu society in the larger context of protecting the Dharma and *rashtra*. The RSS considers the Sikh heritage as not regional but pan-Indian. This is in sync with the views of the Sikh gurus themselves. In the Sikh tradition, Guru Tegh Bahadur spoke for the entire India when faced with the threat of Islamist proselytization.

Both during the British rule and after Independence, the Sikhs as a separate religious identity have been nurtured by a set of scholars and a dominant section of politicians. The visceral hatred the Islamists had for Sikhs came out in full cruelty during the 1947 partition riots, which also helped to cement the divide that had emerged during the colonial period.

After Independence, particularly under the tenure of Nehruvian dynast Indira Gandhi as Prime Minister, the Congress party started playing the same games of divide-and-rule. The Sikhs were particularly targeted. The divide between Sikhs and other Hindus started with the secular veneer of Hindi-Punjabi divide. The Sikh-dominated Akali Dal batted for Punjabi, while the Arya-Samaj-dominated Jan Sangh asked the Punjabi non-Sikh Hindus to register Hindi as their mother tongue. The Jan Sangh batted for Hindi over Punjabi at the Punjab provincial level. But the RSS took the opposite stand.

This is a classic instance of parochial superficial anchoring of Hindu identity politics versus Hindutva. K. R. Malkani, the veteran RSS leader wrote:

> Things nevertheless, began to settle down, but then the Arya Samaj made a Himalayan mistake. In the Punjab University Senate, Bhai Jodh Singh, Principal Khalsa College, Amritsar, and Principal Niranjan Singh, leading academician, long-

> time Congressman and brother of Akali leader Master Tara Singh, proposed that Punjabi in two scripts—Gurumukhi and Devnagari—be accepted as the language of instruction and examination upto matriculation. But the Arya Samaj friends, who dominated the Senate, in their excess of love for Hindi, refused. Shri Guruji Golwalkar was the only leader who urged Punjabi Hindus to accept Punjabi, their own language, with good grace, but to no avail. This soured the Hindu-Sikh relations.[39]

The nation would pay a heavy price for this 'Himalayan mistake' of non-Sikh Punjabi Hindus. Both the national leadership of the RSS and Jan Sangh had foreseen in the problems of Punjab the possibility of a national-disaster in the making.

Veteran Punjabi journalist Krishan Lal Dhall was present in the meeting addressed by Golwalkar at Jalandhar during his visit to Punjab in 1960. In 2015 he still remembered the then famous and important statement of Golwalkar over the Punjabi-Hindi language divide: 'Punjab is the mother tongue of every Punjabi.' Even the persuasion of Punjab Jan Sangh leader Krishan Lal Mai, who specifically met Golwalkar, to retract or at least change the statement was met with refusal from Guruji. The impact of Golwalkar's statement was that many non-Sikh Hindus changed their stance from registering Hindi as their mother tongue in the census to accepting Punjabi as their mother tongue.[40] In 1966 Balraj Madhok, the new in-charge of Jan Sangh, specifically warned of the dangerous consequences of the extreme stands taken by Akalis and Aryas and the harm of the social divide such stands begot.[41]

All these were very helpful in mellowing down the differences, so much so that the Jan Sangh and Akali Dal could form an electoral alliance for the municipality elections, which helped the Akali Dal in the urban areas and the BJS in the rural areas. Nevertheless, the Akali Dal had its fears that the identity politics, which was its basis, would be subsumed by the Hindutva of the RSS.

Though the initial demand for Punjabi Sabha was not having any overt secessionist tendencies or hatred towards non-Sikh Hindus, soon the divisive and radical elements began to take an upper hand, not without the support of Indira Gandhi. Political analyst Sunil K. Salu describes how Indira Gandhi's Machiavellian politics led to a national tragedy:

> The Sikh terrorism and violence which engulfed and paralyzed Punjab was India's most important political issue in the mid-1980s....Although the Akali Dal did not have majority support in this majority Sikh province, Indira Gandhi sought to minimize their political clout by encouraging a split in the group. She encouraged the extreme Sikh faction within the Akali Dal to break away from their party, and later she supported Bhindranwale, leader of the Sikh Student Federation and a

> popular militant preacher, to further weaken the Akali Dal. The Akali Dal responded by mobilizing the forces of religious nationalism through the chain of Sikh temples available to the party. in order to unite its power base. Thus, the Congress party's mobilization to split the Akali Dal and the latter's counter-mobilization led to the rise of Sikh militancy, violence and civil disorder ... increasingly out of control of both the Akalis and the national government.[42]

Later, Indira Gandhi did not hesitate to play the fear generated in the minds of non-Sikh Hindus by imposing humiliating restrictions on Sikhs, thus, posturing to be the sole and able protectors of Hindus. Sikhs were humiliated repeatedly, both by the Congress-ruled Haryana government and the central government. Particularly during the 1982 Asiad, which was held in New Delhi, when Akalis threatened to launch a demonstration at New Delhi, Indira Gandhi decided to create a situation that was reminiscent of the Mughal persecution periods. During the 1982 Asian Games, over 1,500 Sikhs were arrested and thousands more were humiliated by Congress-I Government of Haryana, headed by Bansi Lal. Even national war heroes like Air Chief Marshal Arjan Singh, Lieutenant General Jagjit Singh Aurora and Major General Shabeg Singh were subjected to humiliation by the Nehruvian State.[43]

The Congress under Indira had nurtured the terrorist leader Bhindranwale, with the then Home Minister himself getting involved in releasing him twice in cases connected with the killing of prominent Punjabi residents. Now Indira Gandhi and her 'think tank' on Punjab, which included her son Rajiv Gandhi as well, did not hesitate to seek political capital out of the fear among the non-Sikh Hindus who were being targeted and killed by Bhindranwale.

The Punjab of 1980s should be rightly considered the laboratory of Nehruvian divide-and-rule conducted by dynast Prime Minister Indira Gandhi. Both Sikhs and non-Sikh Hindus paid a huge human price for this experiment. The RSS, through its Hindutva prism, took an entirely and extraordinarily healing and conciliatory yet also pragmatic stand with respect to the Sikh-Hindu divide.

With terrorism becoming a serious menace, the RSS conducted a massive Vishal Hindu Dharma Sammelan on 3 March 1983 right at Amritsar. The Dharmacharyas from all over India had come to Amritsar, and Sikh spiritual leaders also participated in the conference. The conference saw a significant number of Mazhabi Sikhs participating in it. There was a 6-kilometre-long procession, and the langar service was provided by local gurdwaras. The conference impressively brought together various Sikh factions as well as Hindu traditions on one platform.

In Delhi, the RSS launched another programme called the Ekta Abhiyan in the same year as an outreach to non-Sikh Hindus to counter the deep psychological divide the Congress was creating. Various programmes were launched, including seminar and cultural events highlighting the sacrifices and contributions of Sikh Gurus to the nation building and protection of Dharma.

1984: The Holocaust and After [44]

This year was traumatic for Sikhs in particular and the nation in general. One of the most sacred shrines of India, Harmandir Saheb or the Golden Temple, was attacked by the Indian Army to kill the terrorists who had turned the temple into their operating headquarters. The Sikhs were extremely hurt by the military operations. This was followed by the assassination of Indira Gandhi by her Sikh bodyguards. The mobs mainly organized by Congress Party leaders went on a murderous rampage of innocent Sikhs.

It was then that the Sangh launched the 'Punjab Kalyan Forum', which organized programmes to counter divisiveness. Its president was Lieutenant Colonel Chanan Singh Dhillon (1920–2011), a legendary war hero of Punjab. In 1984 the Forum organized the conference 'Punjab Today'. Lieutenant General J. S. Aurora, the liberator of Bangladesh, openly declared in the conference that Khalistan was a futile fantasy. Dr Mann Singh, another prominent Sikh, and retired Principal of Amritsar Medical College, denounced the separation between Sikhs and other Hindus and categorically stated that the Sikhs were part of the Hindu community, and their duty was to protect India.

If these activities were an existential challenge to the core Khalistan-separatist ideology and terrorists and the divisive manoeuvring of Nehruvian dynast politics, the RSS also simultaneously launched Punjab Peedit Sahayata Samiti, which worked in the terrorism-hit rural Punjab. They carried out relief measures to the families of terror victims, making provisions for their livelihood and sponsored education of the children of the affected families. In the cities of Amritsar, Ferozepur, Batala, etc., Swayamsevaks donated 109 bottles of blood to 300 persons wounded by the Pakistan-sponsored Khalistan terrorists. They also provided hospitals for taking care of terror victims and life-saving medicines worth ₹ 70,000. While expressing 'its deep anguish at the sad course of events, making the Army action inevitable in Punjab to flush out the terrorists from the Golden Temple Complex', the RSS resolution identified in a clinical manner 'the low-level political rivalry indulged in by the ruling Congress (I) and the Akali Dal, and factional fighting within both the parties' for the spiralling down of the situation into murderous events. Expressing 'great distress to all our countrymen, more so to the devout Sikhs' because of Operation Blue Star, the RSS exhorted 'all our countrymen in general and Swayamsevaks in particular to come forward to restore the pristine glory of our Darbar Sahib through all possible means including Kar Seva'.[45]

That year, for the annual Guru Puja programme, an important function for the RSS which it conducts in every town in India, prominent Sikhs including those who had differences with the RSS were invited in most places. Khushwant Singh, a well-known RSS baiter, was invited to preside over the Guru Puja at Chennai, where Singh stated that none could doubt the patriotic fervour of the RSS. In Delhi, the veteran Sikh scholar Padma Shri Dr Attar Singh presided over the Guru Puja of the RSS. He said:

> It is here that I find the real Sangham (confluence) of various streams of national culture. The majority of the Sikhs are not for Khalistan. They want to live and die in India and for India. It is the medieval Sikh history of resistance against Muslim fanaticism to protect Hindu Dharma and culture that inspires most of the Sikhs even today. By underplaying this we have been helping the forces of separatism. It is this aspect that the RSS and people like me are pledged to emphasize and strengthen. Our ties are unbreakable. I am confident that Punjab will ever remain an integral part of India and Sikhism an inseparable limb of the great Hindu body.[46]

The RSS Guru Puja function at Delhi was held in September 1984. Then in October 1984, Indira Gandhi was assassinated. Goons belonging to Congress launched a genocidal attack on Sikhs. Rajiv Gandhi, who was coronated as the Prime Minister, justified the attacks. While Rajiv Gandhi made the statement 'earth shakes when a tree falls', all-India leader of the RSS Madhukar Dattareya Deoras sternly cautioned the Hindus to go beyond stereotypes:

> We should keep in mind that every Sikh is not an Akali, every Akali is not an extremist and every extremist is not a Khalistani.[47]

Today, it is well-documented though not well known that while perhaps the only genocidal pogroms of independent India happened following the assassination of Indira Gandhi, the chief architect of the Punjab tragedy, the RSS fought to save the Sikhs while the Congress methodologically facilitated the 'holocaust'. Khushwant Singh, a bitter critic of the RSS, wrote in 1989 that he should 'give due credit to RSS and the BJP for showing courage for protecting Sikhs during those difficult days'.[48] Then again in 2005, Singh acknowledged 'that some leaders of the Sangh Parivar and the RSS, including Atal Bihari Vajpayee, went out of their way to help the Sikhs'.[49]

Researcher and author Vinay Sitapati writes:

> As many as 2,733 Sikhs were killed while Congress leaders led angry mobs and the police looked on. One such mob surrounded the Sikh-run taxi stand outside Vajpayee's house. When a Sikh driver escaped and took shelter inside his bungalow, Vajpayee emerged and stood protectively at the gate until the police arrived. Vajpayee and Advani even visited Home Minister Narasimha Rao to ask him to activate the government machinery. What they did not know was that Rao had been bypassed by a direct order from the Prime Minister's Office.[50]

It was not only the prominent Swayamsevaks like Atal Bihari Vajpayee and L. K. Advani, who became concerned about protecting the Sikhs from Nehruvian rioters, in the wake of the anti-Sikh pogrom unleashed by the Congress using the tragedy of Indira Gandhi's assassination, one of the crucial steps that the RSS took was to organize protection squads to save the Sikhs in Delhi and parts of Haryana.

At Nanakpura, though the gurdwara itself could not be saved from the mob, the RSS cadre rescued at least some of the Sikhs. At Kalkaji, the RSS-organized patrol saved the Sikhs. It also made available the necessary supplies of food and clothes for the Sikh riot victims at Bala Saheb Gurdwara, Bhagwan Nagar, where 1,000 Sikhs including women and children had taken shelter.

Sardar Uttam Singh, chief of the Gurdwara Prabandhak Committee, Majlis Park, was overwhelmed by the gesture of the RSS workers. The gurdwaras of the area were saved from the rioters by the RSS. In Indira Nagar, the RSS cadre provided day and night vigil for three days to save the gurdwara from the stormtroopers of the Congress. Hans Raj Gupta of the Delhi RSS visited the camps of Sikh victims and made sure that they were provided essential relief material including food and medicine, and kept safe.

Post-1984

The Sangh continued its healing operations for the entire society in full earnestness. Lt Gen. J. S. Aurora, who had been humiliated by the Congress government earlier, was the chief guest at the 'Guru Puja' event of the RSS held on 22 October 1985. He told his audience:

> There have never been Hindu-Sikh riots at any time in the past history. Even to this day, even though the terrorists kill people, the common people live in amity in Punjab. In the same family one brother would be Hindu, another a Sikh. Inter-marriages are quite a common feature. Guru Granth Sahib is an eclectic book of religion for all.

The RSS had to face the murderous wrath of the terrorists who targeted the RSS *shakhas* and massacred the cadre. The Hindutva movement paid a heavy price for its resilient anchorage in samanvaya, as new political fly-by-night players entered the arena to reap the fear and hatred generated by the terrorists.

Prof. Atul Kohli, a political science scholar, who was not really an admirer of the Hindutva movement (and later joined Princeton University) observed:

> While there is considerable anger among the Hindu population in Punjab and the rest of the north against Sikh fundamentalists, the RSS and the BJP have actually exerted sobering influence. This is despite the fact that the Sikh fundamentalists have made a special target of RSS-BJP leaders and workers. On at least three occasions they have fired at the RSS shakhas (morning drills) in Punjab, killing people. Predictably, their sober attitude has not made them popular with the Hindus of Punjab, many of whom complain of having been let down by the BJP and RSS. The consequence is the rise of plethora of Shiv Senas in Punjab....So far, despite selective killings of Hindus by Sikh terrorists in Punjab, there have been few incidents of retaliation by Hindu mobs against Sikhs in major towns...which have a Hindu majority. But whenever clashes have taken place, the new Shiv Senas have been involved.[51]

During this crucial time, RSS publications countered the terror and hate campaign with a concern for Sikh unity and integrity within the society, which overrode even its ideological opposition for the Marxists. In June 1986, RSS published a compilation '*My Dear Fellow Sikhs...*', which contained an article written by Harkishan Singh Surjeet (1916–2008) of CPI(M) for the *Statesman*. The publication also had an 'open letter' to the Sikh youths by Dr Gopal Singh, the eminent Sikh scholar, originally published in *Hindustan Times* wherein the former and first regular governor of Nagaland brought out the deep unity of the Sikh Panth with Sanatana Dharma. 'You are now-a-days being fed on anti-Hindu fables and canards', he warned the Sikh youths and went on to explain:

> But just read your holy scriptures and see how much you are part of the Hindu ethos. Our belief in Karma, transmigration and moksha through yoga (bhakti, gyan and karma yoga) are the same as those of the Hindus....We worship at the same altar, listen to and recite the sacred Word of the same Gurus....The two words 'Ram' and 'Omkar'—most sacred words to Hindus—are repeated thousands of times in the Adi Granth (which we worship as the living embodiment of the Gurus). Read the 'Sahasranama' of Guru Arjan Dev, and you find a thousand sacred Hindu names of God enumerated therein—Murli Manohar, Sarangdhar, Bhagwan, Bital, Hari, Mohan, Madhav, Krishan, Murari and many more....Could you give me one instance of a Hindu-Sikh fight as such throughout your whole history? Must we

create a new history to shame all our glorious past and all our sacred heritage?[52]

The samanvaya of Hindutva, which expressed itself through the acts of the RSS, stood the most strenuous tests during the Punjab crisis which was created by the Nehruvian State.

Samanvaya and Non-Indic Religions

Dialogues with Judaism: Beyond 'Avoda Zara'

A remarkable quality of Hindu-Jewish dialogues is that they are largely free of any proselytizing agenda. Here are two religions, ancient cultural traditions, that appear entirely different and even mutually exclusive. Further, the Hindu society has a chequered past and a not-so-comfortable present with two expansionist monopolistic religions—Christianity and Islam—claiming to have originated from Judaism.

There is also the past experience of the Jewish in India, perhaps the longest, and remarkably free of anti-Semitism. Add to this the fascination most Hindus have for Israel, both for its incredible achievements of making ploughshares out of swords and successfully fighting a battle against all odds.

All these aspects make Hindu-Judaism dialogues a very important phenomenon. The dialogues and studies provide us with a model where the comparative analysis can be done largely free of any agenda, as often suspected by the Hindu side, with respect to evangelical, Islamist and even Marxist 'dialogues'. The suspicion, while need not always be right, is not without justification as often the dialogues by monopolistic faiths are usually camouflaged for proselytizing, having read many of the comparative studies of religions by evangelical strategists from colonial ages to Clooney and Witzel, which are essentially scouting expeditions for studying the faultlines and strategies for appropriation and conversion.

The Hindu-Jewish dialogues serve as a model where the similarities and dissimilarities of religions are observed largely free of any agenda, and with what the late Swami Dayananda Saraswati (1930–2015), head of a traditionalist Vedanta school, called 'mutual respect' accommodating mutual differences.

The dialogue between Hindus and Jews must address a crucial problem—*Avoda Zara*, or the problem of foreign deity or idolatry. Jewish scholar Alon Goshen-Gottstein is also a theoretician and activist-scholar of interfaith dialogue and founder-director of the Elijah Interfaith Institute in 1997. In his book *The Same God, Other God: Judaism, Hinduism and the Problem of*

Idolatry, his approach to the problem is honest and respectful. His 'is not an argument for Hinduism not being Avoda Zara. Rather, it is an argument for applying a richer and more nuanced method and for rethinking the very category of Avoda Zara'. [53]

The 'mutual respect' espoused by Dayananda Saraswati is not an easy principle—at least among the academia of Western religious studies. It needs a great level of understanding of the other with the deepest level of empathy. The following conclusion that Goshen-Gottstein derives for the Jewish understanding of Hinduism from a deeper Jewish spiritual point of view shows the enormous strength and wisdom one needs for the exercise of 'mutual respect':

> The subject of idolatry can itself become the victim of an idolatrous attitude....The encounter with another religion is also one that requires an understanding of the heart, lest our approach to the other religion itself become a graven mental image.... We need to shift the idolatrous attitudes in us as a condition for discovering God in the other. Herzel Hefter has made us aware of the problem of idolatry within, as it relates to the Hindu concern with the dynamism of the image....To view the other primarily through the eyes of Avoda Zara is to make our own look deadly, cursed by the fixity of perspective that sees the Other as other. What we need is a different regard, one that removes the idolatry within the heart as a condition for engaging the other....We have moved from ruling to discernment, and with Rabbi Leiner we move from legal principles to the understanding of the heart, open to the Divine. Any encounter must be lived in this way. Hinduism makes it particularly easy for us to do so. In important ways, the encounter with Hinduism may force us to be less idolatrous in our own view of reality.[54]

If the so-called 'idol worship' of Hindus has been perceived by insightful Jews as not the idolatry abhorred in the Hebrew sacred texts, Hindus need to realize that the spiritual monotheism of Judaism is qualitatively and spiritually different from the expansionist monopolistic monotheism of Islam and Christianity.

The strong spiritual dimension that the centuries-old tradition of Kabbalah has imported to the monotheism of Judaism should reinforce this for Hindus. As author Ram Swarup pointed out in another context, Hindus need to understand monotheism as the expression of unity (as in the case of Judaism) and distinguish it from the political ideology of expansionism, as is the case of evangelical monotheism. Such an understanding may also immunize Hindus against the proselytizing attempts which have diminished and distorted the spiritual value of Hebrew Bible through the term 'Old Testament'.

In his next book *The Jewish Encounter with Hinduism*, Goshen-Gottstein explores the question of what the current students of dialogue can learn from the historic experience of the 'Jews of India'? He answers:

> Rather than highlighting the idolatry, strangeness, and otherness of their Hindu neighbors, Indian Jews seem to have reciprocated the acceptance and tolerance they enjoyed through an attitude of respect.... Surely the Jews must have realized how different the religious landscape of the Hindus is. How come, then, that this difference is not expressed in their writings?...If Jews came to view Hindus as monotheists, who worship different representations of One God, as Hindus could understand themselves, the level of tension in relation to Hindus would obviously be lower than if they showed concern about forbidden idolatrous worship. It is noteworthy that other travelers, even while they report on Hindu practices that constitute idolatry from the Jewish perspective, are silent on the attitudes of the local Jewish community. The tone is descriptive, and we do not hear of a criticism or rejection of Hindu practices, as part of the prevailing attitude of the Jewish community.[55]

This lack of uncomfortable feeling of being in a strange land is, again, the result of the general atmosphere created by samanvaya and usually it is the natural evolution of human culture which has no monopolistic-expansionist theological worldview.

Unfolding Dialogues: Sarmad to Brilliant

For Goshen-Gottstein and Prof. Nathan Katz, who retired as the Bhagwan Mahavir Professor of Jain Studies at Florida International University, Sarmad Kashani (1590–1661), a mystic of Jewish origin, who came to India and was killed in India by Aurangzeb provides a crucial link in the dialogue between Jewish mystic spirituality and Indic spiritual traditions. Goshen-Gottstein points out that 'the Jewish authors who wrote on Sarmad spoke of him approvingly, owning and embracing him, or at the very least appreciating his positive contribution from a Jewish perspective'.[56] Prof. Nathan Katz, who visited the samadhi of Sarmad as part of the Dharamshala dialogue, recited Kaddish on Sarmad's tomb, 'a recognition of his being the group's predecessor in dialogue, a culmination of the image of Sarmad the Jew, independently of the Muslim context within which it is offered'. Katz himself wrote, in the year 2000, an article discussing the religious identity of Sarmad, where he emphasized 'Sarmad's rejection of religious practice and piety, in favour of a higher spiritual principle' and by extension 'affirming his simultaneous identity as a Jew, a Hindu, and a Muslim'.[57]

Goshen-Gottstein positions Sarmad this way in the Hindu-Jewish dialogue process:

> The core attitude is not one of converting from one religion to another, leaving the former behind. For this reason, one should not speak of Sarmad in terms of "conversion" to another religion. Sarmad's path seems to have been one of deepening spirituality and love for God, based upon which he could return and own multiple religious identities, training others to follow such an interreligious spiritual path. Nathan Katz has listed for us various ways of considering Sarmad's identity— Jewish, Muslim, Mystic, atheist, and Hindu. We are now in a position to offer another formulation—Sarmad held a multireligious identity. This identity was indeed mystically grounded and was based on a recognition of a spiritual reality that both transcends and contains particular religious identities.[58]

This aspect is quite important because it is the natural bedrock of Hindutva. The multireligious identity with the spiritual quest and divine realization at its core is what that has been animating Indian civilization through the ages. This acceptance of theo-diversity as the hallmark of human spirituality is a cornerstone of Hindutva.

A detailed study of Sarmad was published by Hanuman Poddar Smarak Samiti authored by scholar Lakhpat Rai in 1975. He was then the editor of *Kalyana Kalpataru* magazine of Gita Press. Gita Press and Hanuman Poddar had been strongly criticized by the anti-Hindutva proponents as one of the chief architects of modern Hindutva movement.[59] In this book, Lakhpat Rai writes:

> (Sarmad)'s proficiency and early education in sacred Judaic scriptures is borne out by the statements of the author of the *Dabistan*....His curiosity spurred him on to the study of Islamic religious books and the "scientific works of the wise men of Iran, such as Mulla Sader and Mir Abul Kasem of Kazersak and many others....Says the author of *Dabistan* "at last, for the sake of commerce, he undertook by sea the voyage to Hindustan....It is stated in the *Dabistan* that when he arrived in the town *Tata*, he fell in love with a Hindu boy called Abhai Chand and abandoning all other things, like Sanyasi naked as he came from his mother, he sat down before the door of his beloved." This was no ordinary love but Divine love indeed which acted as an alchemy and completely transformed the personality of Sarmad....It goes without saying that Sarmad's love for Abhai Chand was not tainted in the least with any temporal motive. It is almost certain that he saw in the young boy his personal God—Lord Sri Rama Himself in the juvenescent state.[60]

What Rai writes, gleaning from various historical sources about Sarmad, gels with the observation of Goshen-Gottstein. That Sarmad did not actually convert, rejecting Judaism, is borne out by Rai:

> The father of the object of his love, after having found by investigation the purity of the attachment manifested for his son, admitted Sarmad into his house, and the young man too met him with equal affection, so that he could no more separate from him and he read the book of Moses, the psalms of David and other books with Sarmad. The following verses are the compilation of this young Hindu:
>
> I submit to Moses' Law; I am of thy religion, and the guardian of thy way;
> I am a Rabbi of the Yahuds, a Kafir and a Musalman.[61]

Rai implies the possibility of the influence of Sarmad in Dara Shukoh commissioning the translation of *Yoga Vasishta*. There was already a translation of *Yoga Vasishta* done by one Mulla Sufi, but Shukoh thought that it 'did not serve the purpose of the seekers of truth'. The immediate reason was that the prince had a dream vision of Rama and Vasishta in which Vasishta asked Sri Rama to offer a sweet to Dara Shukoh. This vision made Shukoh undertake the project. Rai writes:

> The vision of Sri Rama and His preceptor Vasishta forcefully recalls to mind saint Sarmad, who during this period used to wander about naked in the streets of Delhi and who, on his own admission, had become "a devotee of Lachhman and Rama".[62]

Apart from the stated official reason of Sarmad's nudity, which was offensive to the shariat, according to Rai, it was his devotion to Sri Rama that should have led to his execution by Aurangzeb.

Thus, we have in Sarmad a Hindu-Jewish encounter, which through its influence on Dara Shukoh, turns out be of pivotal importance to the samanvaya process involving Islam as well.

Later in the twentieth century, the dialogue between Hindu spirituality and Judaism continued through the Jews among the Western seekers, particularly during the counterculture. Important among the Hindu Jews or Jews influenced by the Hindu Dharma are Ram Dass (Richard Alpert, 1931–2019) and Dr Larry Brilliant. They both were disciples of Neem Karoli Baba (c. 1900–1973).

Ram Dass was a professor of psychology at Harvard University and was fired for his experiments with LSD, along with Timothy Leary. He came to India as a seeker and became the Baba's disciple. In 1974 he was one of the founders of Hanuman Foundation. It became one of the major engagers of Dharma with modern problems in the Western society in particular and humanity in general. Poet Rodger Kamenetz in his work that mainly focusses on what he calls 'the rediscovery of Jewish identity in Buddhist India' has this to write about Ram Dass:

> I saw Ram Dass in the hotel lobby, dressed in white pants and sandals....I'd lost track of his spiritual evolutions, so my first question was, "What religion do you follow these days?"
> "I worship a monkey."
> I laughed—though I was a little taken aback, as I suspect he wanted me to be. He explained that the monkey in question, Hanuman, is a servant to Ram, and that his devotees likewise stress service to others. Specifically, Ram Dass helped start the Seva Foundation, which funds charitable projects in South India. Now this Jewish Hindu was on his way to Dharamsala to meet with the Dalai Lama ...[63]

In the case of another Jewish seeker guided by Neem Karoli Baba, the tension of his Jewish identity with respect to Hindu spiritual atmosphere was more explicit and yet it gets resolved without any religious conversion. Larry Brilliant, a freshly minted medical graduate, and his wife Elaine, who had later taken a Hindu name, Girija, had come to India in their quest. As a Jew, Larry Brilliant was having his own struggle with the Hindu atmosphere. In his autobiography he explains:

> The first of the Ten Commandments is, "I am the Lord thy God and thou shalt have no other gods before me," and yet all over the ashram idols were being worshiped—not just respected or loved but worshiped. It's a big deal for Jews. While I had been looking for spirituality elsewhere—in Buddha and Jesus and all over India —I never worshipped stone idols and I was skeptical of anyone who wanted me to worship an idol, stone or human, or touch his feet.[64]

Dr Larry Brilliant became an important soldier and later commander in the fight against smallpox in India and in this he was inspired by his Guru Neem Karoli Baba, who also gave him the name 'Subrahmanya'—the Divine Commander-in-Chief of the Army of the Devas and to whom people prayed for removal of diseases afflicting children, at least right from the time of Mahabharata. After the last case of smallpox in larger Indian landmass, a Bangladeshi child called Rahima Banu, Dr Brilliant took a pilgrimage to the famous six Murugan temples of Tamil Nadu named 'Arupadai Veedu' (the six commanding posts of Murugan).[65] He also established SEVA—a global NGO that works on eradication of removable blindness—in which his major inspiration and collaborator is Aravind Eye Hospitals of South India, established by Dr Venkataswamy, who in turn was inspired by Sri Aurobindo and his spiritual collaborator—Mother, who was Mirra Alfassa (1878–1973), born to a Turkish Jewish father and an Egyptian Jewish mother. These engagements with Judaism are devoid of poaching agenda while the results have been positive in a universally humanistic way.

So, one can say that in the Hindu-Jewish religious dialogue, not only the two religions, but all human spiritual traditions have a model for two completely varied spiritual traditions to come together, engage in dialogue, involve in spiritual quest and, more importantly, for the secular realm, coordinate humanitarian works without any agenda of proselytization. That said, any Hindu-Jewish dialogue cannot overlook the relation between Israel and India and their relation to the Muslim world.

Dialogue: Spiritual to the Temporal

Hindu nationalists have consistently asked for normalizing relations with Israel. However, the Nehruvian foreign policy that had been dominant in India had always had an overt aversion for any association with Israel, while sympathizing with Palestinian issues.

Jews in Palestine: Muslim League and Gandhi-Nehru

The Palestinian issue itself has been used in the construction of the anti-Hindu rhetoric right from the pre-1947 Pakistan-partition movement. In 1937 the chief ideologue of Pakistan movement, Muhammad Iqbal, wanted the implementation of shariat and found it impossible in this country without a free Muslim state or states. In the absence of a free Muslim state or states for the implementation of shariat, the other alternative that Iqbal put forth was 'civil war'. To him the Hindu-Muslim riots were no riots, but an expression of a civil war that was already being fought. He wrote, 'I fear that in certain parts of the country, such as N.W. India, Palestine may be repeated'.[66] Palestine, then under British control, had seen increased attacks on Jews—most of them were wholesale massacres of Jewish villages. Iqbal again wrote a confidential letter to Jinnah pointing out to him that in 'the Palestine question', which had agitated Indian Islamists, existed a 'very fine opportunity for mass contact for the purposes of the League'[67] —which would be the partition of India.

In the years 1937 and 1938, Muhammad Ali Jinnah gave speeches on Palestine from the Muslim League's platform. In 1938 a resolution was passed on the Palestine issue. Jinnah invoked the anti-Semitic imagery of Jewish moneybags. After the resolution, Muslim League delegates on the dais drew fierce rhetoric parallel between Hindus and Jews.

> One delegate "pointed to the need for taking practical steps to carry out the intention of the resolution. He said that both the British and the Hindus were Jews to Muslims, that is, their enemies. In India, Mr Gandhi was the leader of the Hindu Jews". Another delegate "described British policy in Palestine as being pursued only for preserving the integrity of the Empire under the cloak of the white man's burden. The real Jews of the West were the British, and those of the east were the Hindus, and both were the sons of Shylock."[68]

Prof. P. R. Kumaraswamy (Centre for West Asian Studies), from whose book the above passage is taken on the authority of the chronicler of Muslim League Pirzada, states that the statement, 'Jews of the East and West are sons of Shylock' was considered objectionable and was withdrawn. However, the statement that the Hindus were Jews to the Muslims and Gandhi being the leader of Hindu Jews was not withdrawn.

Congress leaders themselves were mostly divided on the question of the emergence of a Jewish homeland in Palestine. Nehru had secularized the Jewish-Muslim conflict in Palestine as a conflict between imperialistic designs of the British through the Jews and the nationalist uprising of the Arabs.

In 1936 a German linguist Dr Immanuel Olsvanger came to India to meet Indian leaders. His diary entries show that the poetess Sarojini Naidu of the Congress was sympathetic to the Jewish cause. Rajendra Prasad was against Nehru's anti-Zionist stand and wanted Congress to remain neutral. But the dominant leaders or the 'high command' had embraced the pan-Islamist stand.

The diary entry of Dr Olsvanger on Nehru reads: 'A slim beautiful man but not very clever....He does not know anything about Zionism; has seen Palestine once as he flew over the country. Maintains, though, to know Zionism and its connection with the "affairs of the world" very well.' In the first meeting, Nehru excused himself soon. Within a short time, Dr Olsvanger could understand the real reason for the vehement opposition Nehru had for a Jewish homeland in Palestine:

> There are about 200,000 villages in India. Of course, Jawahar needs the sympathy of the Muslims here at the moment as the country is preparing for new elections to the Legislative Assembly....He will surely try to please the Muslims in order to get their votes.[69]

In the next long meeting, Nehru's only argument was 'imperialism'. He even called Zionism 'a movement of Jewish high finance'[70]—a typically anti-Semitic perception. Incidentally a year after Nehru uttered these words in the quasi-informal dialogue with the Jewish emissary, the Muslim League resolution in its 1937 conference headed by Jinnah would speak 'of British Imperialism backed by Jewish finance'.[71] As the conversation progressed, Nehru said that 'he was opposed to any imperialism whether British or Hitlerite'. Dr Olsvanger seized that and pointed out the Nazi support for Arabs. In his retaliation: 'Our sympathies cannot be diminished by the fact that the nationalist Arab movement coincided with Hitler's interests'.[72]

When Dr Olsvanger met the aged poet Rabindranath Tagore at Shantiniketan, the latter expressed his sympathy with the Zionist cause and expressed hope that 'the Arabs one day would appreciate the influx of the Jews'. Dr Olsvanger writes in his diary: '(Tagore) was sorry about Nehru's tactics based on internal Indian interests, which are also rather bad for India itself.'[73] At the same time, Tagore was reluctant to make his sympathy for Zionist cause public.

Gandhiji, who even went to the extent of considering himself 'half-Jewish', was totally against Jewish presence in Palestine under British mandate. He was aware of Jews getting mass-murdered, women raped and even children not spared by Arab mobs in a series of riots in Palestine. In 1937 in a statement given to his South African Jewish colleague Hermann Kallenbach specifically on Zionism, Gandhiji wrote:

> Assuming that Zionism is not a material movement, but represents the spiritual aspirations of the Jews, the introduction of Jews in Palestine under the protection of British and other arms, is wholly inconsistent with spirituality....In my opinion the Jews should disclaim any intention of realizing their aspiration under the protection of arms and should rely wholly on the goodwill of Arabs. No exception can possibly be taken to the natural desire of the Jews to found a home in Palestine. But they must wait for its fulfilment, till Arab opinion is ripe for it. And the best way to enlist that opinion, is to rely wholly upon the moral justice of the desire and therefore the moral sense of the Arabs and the Islamic world.[74]

What is important about the statement is that Gandhi was offering to Jews almost the same advice he was offering Hindus, his own religionists, in the context of anti-Hindu riots after the implosion of Khilafat movement in India, despite his recognition of the Jewish homeland in Palestine as 'the natural desire of the Jews'. However, this stand would drastically change the very next year. Perhaps this was because of Nehru's insistence or influence.

While the Congress resolutions would compete with those of Muslim League in offering support to the Arab insurrection in Palestine as well as their opposition to Jewish settlements, Gandhi came out with an article titled 'The Jews' in his magazine *Harijan* dated 26 November 1938. Subsequently this would become widely quoted as 'the' stand of Gandhi on the Palestine issue. In this Gandhi wrote:

> My sympathies are all with the Jews...But my sympathy does not blind me to the requirements of justice. The cry for the national home for the Jews does not make much appeal to me....Why should they not, like other peoples of the earth, make that country their home where they are born and where they earn their livelihood? Palestine belongs to the Arabs in the same sense that England belongs to the English or France to the French. It is wrong and inhuman to impose the Jews on the Arabs.

So, from 'no exception can possibly be taken to the natural desire of the Jews to found a home in Palestine' stand taken in July 1937, Gandhiji had moved to 'the cry for the national home for the Jews does not make much appeal to me' in November 1938. Then Gandhi went on to advice the Jews of Germany to offer satyagraha to Hitler though he made it clear that 'the German persecution of the Jews seems to have no parallel in history'. The strangest part of the statement was his views on the Arab violence on Jews.

> I am not defending the Arab excesses. I wish they had chosen the way of non-violence in resisting what they rightly regarded as an unwarrantable encroachment upon their country. But according to the accepted canons of right and wrong, nothing can be said against the Arab resistance in the face of overwhelming odds.

Interestingly, while he was asking the Jews to resort to satyagraha before Hitler and try their best to change peacefully the minds of Arabs, he never appealed to the Arabs to do the same to the Jews. But these efforts on the appeasement of Islamists, both at the domestic and international level, at the expense of the Jewish cause came to a naught. Simone Panter-Brick in her seminal work on Gandhi and the Middle East explains:

> However soft a line Gandhi adopted with them, however strongly the Indian National Congress gave support in their favour, no thanks were received in return, no reward. Pleasing the Arabs was a thankless task. ... Another more attractive, blue-eyed suitor, of Aryan demeanour was courting Arab nationalism, namely the extremist and pro-Nazi leader enthroned as Grand Mufti by the Mandatory Power....

> Gandhi excused their violence on the ground that it was a justifiable response to the Jewish immigrants' invasion of their land.[75]

While being devoid of sympathy to the Jewish cause in Palestine, Nehru wanted technically educated Jewish talent for India but was against an Israeli homeland in Palestine under British mandate. Much has been made out of Nehru helping persecuted Jews escape Germany and take asylum in India. Nehru even spoke of a completely untenable idea of providing a Jewish homeland in India.

Hindu Mahasabha on Savarkar

In his 1923 book on Hindutva, Savarkar had envisaged certain unique qualities binding Hindus and Jews. While rejecting the concept of pure race as myth and the unity of human race from pole to pole as the only reality, 'speaking relatively alone', Savarkar considered only Hindus and Jews to form one coherent racial unit.[76] Again to Savarkar, 'the ideal conditions, therefore, under which a nation can attain perfect solidarity and cohesion' could be seen only in Hindus, 'other things being equal' and then 'if ever the Jews could succeed in founding their state there (Palestine), could be said to possess this unique advantage'.[77] In the same book written from Ratnagiri jail just six years after the Balfour declaration, Savarkar observed:

> If the Zionists' dreams are ever realized—if Palestine becomes a Jewish State and it will gladden us almost as much as our Jewish friends.[78]

In 1938 Vinayak Damodar Savarkar, as President of Hindu Mahasabha, strongly opposed Nehru's idea that non-Indian Jews be brought to India and permanent homeland be made for them in Cochin and other Indian provinces. The statement in this regard made by Savarkar is totally free of anti-Semitism as it recognizes the value of Indian Jewish population to the Hindu nation throughout history.[79]

> While cherishing nothing but good will towards the Indian Jews who have been citizens of India for centuries in the past and who have already developed an intimate linguistic, cultural and civic affinities with the Hindus in India, I denounce most emphatically the proposal now and then discussed in the Congress quarters of inviting the non-Indian Jews from Europe to colonise Cochin and some other parts of India.

He explained his stand by stating that allowing such foreign colonies within India would pave the way for unnecessary and almost sure confrontation later, as Indian population would increase in the future. He goes on to point out that this Congress alternative of creating a Jewish homeland within India was actually a Congress way of denying the Jewish right to carve out their cultural and spiritual homeland in Palestine while at the same time posturing a moral high ground:

> Nevertheless, I have every sympathy with the Jewish community in Europe and elsewhere in their distress and assert that the best solution of the Jewish question can only be found in an unrestricted recolonization of Palestine by the Jewish people to whom alone it belongs of right as their Mother and as well as their Holy Land, the land of Moses and David and Soloman (sic) from time immemorial.

The statement of Gandhiji and others, that the Palestine belonged to Arabs while the Jews were aliens, was according to Savarkar, 'an amazing ignorance of history or to a deliberate and cowardly misrepresentation of facts with a view to placate the Indian Moslem'. Savarkar appealed to the British to continue their policy of re-establishing, the European Jews and enabling them to raise a strong Jewish Nation once again in Palestine—their real Mother Land and Holy Land.

Savarkar's statement that the inability of Indian National Congress (INC) leadership to support a Jewish homeland in Palestine was more because of the fear of Muslim reaction than based on principle would be proved right in 1946.

1946: Gandhi Returns to a Hindutva Understanding of Jewish Homeland

In 1946 Sydney Silverman, President of the World Jewish Congress, met Mahatma Gandhi and asked for his support for Israel, a national home for the Jews. Gandhi told him while he himself was sympathetic to the Jews, to get the support of the INC, they would have to convince the Muslim leadership in India. Then Gandhi asked Silverman why he insisted that the Jewish homeland be in Palestine. Were there 'not waste spaces enough in the world to receive the Jews'? Gandhiji promised the delegates nothing but asked them to meet the then President of Congress Party and significantly Muhammad Ali Jinnah to gain their sympathy, adding that without getting 'the active support of the Muslims, nothing is possible in a substantial way in India'.[80]

In 1946 Jawaharlal Nehru was the Congress President, whom the Jewish delegates had met a decade ago. However, three months after his interview with Silverman, Gandhi made a statement that actually resonates with the statement of Savarkar:

> The Jews have a good case. I told Sidney Silverman, the British MP, that the Jews have a good case. If the Arabs have a claim to Palestine the Jews have a prior claim, because they were there first.[81]

This statement of Gandhi published by Louis Fischer created a minor stir. On 18 May 1947, he made a statement in *Harijan*:

> It has become a problem which is almost insoluble. If I were a Jew, I would tell them: 'Don't be so silly as to resort to terrorism, because you simply damage your own case which otherwise would be a proper case. If it is just political hankering then I think there is no value in it. Why should they hanker after Palestine? ... If it is a religious longing then surely terrorism has no place. They should meet the Arabs, make friends with them, and not depend on British aid or any aid, save what descends from Jehovah.'

On 2 June 1947, *The Bombay Chronicle* recorded what would become the last words of Mahatma on the Jewish-Arab conflict in Palestine: 'The abandonment wholly by the Jews of terrorism and other forms of violence.'

What one sees in all these statements of Gandhi is a slow evolution from a politically strategic stand totally negating the Jewish rights to Palestine in 1937–1938 to a gradual understanding of Palestine being both the ancestral and sacred land of the Jews—a principle that was first recognized by Savarkar in Indian political landscape. So, setting up the Jewish homeland in Palestine became for Gandhi not only a 'prior' right of the Jews but also, he understood its religious-spiritual significance—in other words, he recognized the Punya Bhumi and Pitru Bhumi definition of Savarkar. This was also exactly the stand Mahatma had for India's Independence from the British that it should be *Swarajya*, which he described as a Vedic sacred concept. And hence his asking Jews to eschew violence, who were then indulging in 'terrorist' activities against the British, was very similar to his stand with respect to obtaining Swarajya for India.

On 4 November 1995, Yitzhak Rabin was shot dead by a militant Jew opposed to peace process. Israel thus had its own 30 January 1948.

Hindutva Raja who Saved the Jews

Even Savarkar's rejection of Nehru's offer to create a homeland or colony for non-Indian Jews in India does not complete the entire range of Hindutva response to the persecution of Jews in Europe. With respect to getting Jewish refugees into India and providing them with living quarters, educational and medical services, Maharaja Digvijaysinhji Ranjitsinhji Jadeja (1893–1966), also known as 'Jam Sahib' is a name that makes Hindutvaites proud. A thousand Polish children who had been suffering under totalitarian regimes—mostly Jews, who would have otherwise perished—were saved by this Hindu king.

On 23 August 1939, the infamous Molotov-Ribbentrop Pact was signed between the regimes of the world's two cruellest mass murderer-dictators—Joseph Stalin and Adolf Hitler. Both Soviet Union and Nazi Germany invaded Poland silently. Soon, about 1,000 Polish children, mostly Jews and Catholic, found themselves in Siberia. General Władysław Sikorski—the first prime minister of the Polish government in exile and Commander-in-Chief of the Polish Armed Forces appealed to Winston Churchill to protect these children. In 1942 Soviet Union no longer wanted to hold these children and just deported them out of Siberia. With no land to go, these child refugees from Soviet Gulags arrived at Bombay port, only to be denied entry by the British. The Maharaja, who was then a member of the Viceroy's War Council, came to know of the plight of these children, and he used his power and influence to get these children into his own territory, creating a comfortable living and learning quarter for them at Balachadi, about 25 kilometres from his capital, Jamnagar. Later by 1946, the children were taken to another accommodation with facilities in Kolhapur.[82]

While in recent days a lot has been written about this king and his humanitarian efforts to save the children, not much has been stated about his core Hindutva worldview.

The Maharaja was also a staunch Hindutvaite. As the Chancellor of the Chamber of Indian Princes, he warned of the dangers that Hinduism was facing in the coming years and exhorted the Hindu princes to be defenders of Dharma. At the reception given to him at Delhi by Hindu Mahasabha, he said:

> Whatever may have been their history, the Rajputs have always put their religion first. We are Hindus and whenever Hinduism is threatened neither I nor my brother Princes can remain behind to defend it to the last....Today Hinduism, like the Indian States is attacked from within and without but the princes will make sacrifices and stem the tide.[83]

In independent India, 'Jam Sahib' also became the Rajpramukh of Saurashtra government and the Chairman of the Somnath Temple Trust. The Trust was meant to help rebuild the demolished Somnath temple and consecrate it. Yale-based religious studies scholar Richard H. Davis narrates what 'Jam Sahib' did at the Somnath Sivalinga consecration:

> As board chairman, the Jam Sahib took on the royal role of Yajamana in the rituals of establishment necessary for construction of the new temple. He wrote letters to Indian diplomats serving as ambassadors of the new nation state around the world, asking that each send him soil, water and twigs from the countries in which they were stations to be used in the installation ceremony of the new Siva Linga....In this way Jam Sahib hoped the installation might symbolize, 'the unity of the world and the brotherhood of man'.

Dr Davis further explains the religious significance and upgrading of the significance to imply a universal symbolism:

> Jam Sahib's intention to make this major installation ceremony as encompassing as possible was nothing new in Hindu ritual practice....What was new was the post-World War II world order, with its worldwide networks of diplomatic missions, which enabled Jam Sahib to envision a consecration ceremony more comprehensive and international than ever before it. Siva Somanatha could become the most universal of all India's icons.[84]

However, certain diplomats, particularly K. M. Panikkar, ever anxious to please Nehru, were not amused. They complained to Nehru. And Nehru in turn wrote letters to K. M. Munshi, criticizing such a move. What 'Jam Sahib' envisioned for Somnath Sivalinga in 1951 would materialize in its own way in 1968. Mirra Alfassa of Jewish descent and spiritual collaborator of Sri Aurobindo would inaugurate Auroville, the futuristic city of her vision, belonging to all humanity, by placing an urn containing soil from 124 nations.

Israel & Judaism and Post-Independent India

In the post-Independent India, a continuity between the spiritual to the temporal could be traced in Mirra Alfassa, the Mother of Sri Aurobindo movement. Mother had a sympathetic mindset towards the nationalist Hindu polity of Dr Shyama Prasad Mukherjee. In 1951 Dr Mukherjee presided over the Sri Aurobindo convention in the presence of Mother. Later when talking to an inner circle of disciples, on 7 June 1967, as the conversation moved towards the Suez crisis, a disciple stated that three days earlier, Egyptian leader Nasser had declared that he wanted Israel wiped off the world map. To this Mother replied:

> Yes, that's it. But three years ago, they declared that Israel shouldn't exist. So that clearly puts them in the wrong....The whole world lives in falsehood, without a doubt, but one thing must be established in an absolute way: the right of each nation or country to individual existence, provided it doesn't interfere in another nation's right....There is a group in the new Indian parliament, a group of people dissatisfied with the position taken by India, who have declared their wish to act according to Sri Aurobindo's ideal and instructions....There was a man who would have done—not fully well, not with enough breadth of mind to fully understand Sri Aurobindo, but very straight and strong—he was assassinated in Kashmir.... He is the one who came here when we wanted to have a conference for the opening of the University, he presided over it. A rather tall man, and strong. I forget his name. But it was in Kashmir that he was assassinated (not officially, of course: he "fell ill.")

This reference was to Dr Shyama Prasad Mukherjee and it is a criticism towards the Nehruvian stand towards Israel. Mother went on to caution that this would go into the 'agenda' and would not be published immediately. Just then a disciple states the strong feeling for a prayer for Israel and Mother responded with an emphatic affirmation.[85]

Israel has also been a supporter of India in the international arena even when relations were not normalized by India. During the 1971 genocide, in what was East Pakistan then and the problem of refugees, Egypt, which used to be upheld as an example of secularism in the Arab world in Nehruvian discourse, displayed a 'studied indifference' to the crisis. Garry Bass in his *The Blood Telegram* points out how India's NAM pro-Arab diplomacy failed miserably during 1971. The Anwar-al-Sadat government 'was unsympathetic to India's refugee problem and seemed fixated on preventing East Pakistan's secession. And Egypt was considered the most Pro-India' nation in the Arab League. Bass writes:

> There was one surprising minor success: Israel. India did not have diplomatic relations with the Jewish State,...and many Indian leaders were frosty towards it. But in July, Golda Meir, Israel's Prime Minister, secretly got an Israeli arms manufacturer to provide India with some mortars and ammunition, along with a few instructors. When Haksar pressed Israel for support, Meir promised to continue helping out.[86]

It was in 1993 when the Pakistan-funded jihad in Kashmir was at its peak that Shimon Peres visited India as Israel's foreign minister. That he loved India dearly was obvious. But how far he was willing to go to help India amazed us all. He saw India essentially as a culture first. He wanted the nation to lead the world, as John Perry, a Mumbai-based Jew, remembered in a Facebook group. 'It was not surprising that Peres stood with India on the Kashmir issue,' remembered Perry. In fact, Peres had worked to change the US perspective on it.

> But what swept us off our feet was his observation that India should change the demography of Kashmir. He had suggested that at an official dinner, where among others, the then agriculture minister Balram Jakhar of Congress, and then leader of opposition L. K. Advani, were present. Then, he made the official statement that Israel supported 'fully and completely the territorial integrity of India'. He also warned against another partition.[87]

It is interesting to note that a statesman known for his peace efforts, and even criticized for the same in Israel, held the same premises about India, which are considered 'hawkish' in India.

Though the threat of terrorism can make 'right-wing' groups among Hindu and Jewish sections sympathize mutually, the vast canvas of history of interactions offer a more poignant possibility. On the whole, the Hindutva understanding of the Jewish religion, culture and polity by Hindutvaites and a Hindutva understanding of India by the Jewish students of India can help both in creating models for dialogue and growth, which can help not only Hindus and Hebrews, but also other diverse religious communities, nations and cultures to enter into dialogues without agendas.

Prof. Katz succinctly puts that the dialogue and relation between Hindus and Jews go beyond the obvious common problem they face—religious terrorism:

> Judaism and Hinduism have many parallels. Indigenous peoples develop a unique relationship to the home, unlike what is found in missionising religions. We share such deep connections to our homelands. We pray in an ancient sacred language, we follow our own dietary codes, we maintain our hereditary priesthoods, we honour family and learning. Yes, there are practical issues today—agricultural technology, IT, space exploration, counterterrorism and intelligence, trade, and much more. But because of our shared history, our contemporary relationship is deeply grounded and is not simply a matter of mutual interests.[88]

Samanvaya and Islam: Sufis vs Sufis, Akbar to Dara Shukoh, Jihad and Ayodhya

While the terms 'Hindutva' and 'Islam' might bring opposing binaries to one's mind, Hindutva has made serious attempts throughout history to bring Islam into the samanvaya process. Of course, 'Sufism' has become the dominant approach in any discussion on Indic or mystic Islam.

Right from the beginning, the persistent Hindu resistance to Islamist invaders prevented the invaders from adopting the strict Islamic implementation of complete annihilation of what would be considered as Kufr, totally incompatible with Koranic injunctions, unlike the Dhimmi-toleration extended to 'the people of the book' (Jews and Christians). Historian Dr Ram Gopal Misra points out that this happened because 'the political and cultural resistance encountered by the Arabs in Sindh stands out in sharp contrast to anything of its kind faced by them anywhere else in the world'.[89] He writes:

> In Sindh, Muhammad bin Kassimn started with fire and sword. The peoples of all the countries conquered by the Muslims had already been converted to Islam excepting Spain. An exception has been made only for "the people of the book" i.e., the Jews and Christians, who had been allowed to retain their cultural and religious identity after paying Jeziya. For the idolators of India there could be no choice except "Islam or death."...It did not take long for the Arabs to realize the utter folly of this policy which had succeeded in other lands. The matter was referred to Hajjaj and the latter had no hesitation in granting the exemption to Hindus....Thus, the first exception to the application of the Muslim law to non-Muslims was sanctioned.... When fire and sword failed, inducements were offered to the Sindhians to change their creed.... But Hinduism had not lost its earlier virility and ... most of the neo-converts took the earliest opportunity to go back to their original fold. Even as late as the 9th century AD an Arab geographer complains that "Islam has not made a single convert in India".[90]

That does not mean all was well. Dr Misra points out the massacres and massive enslavement of Hindus as well as the destruction of Hindu temples and their conversions to masjids. But overwhelming Hindu persistence to stick to their Dharma even in the face of death and hardships where territories were conquered and continued Hindu resistance around the conquered places always acted as checks to these violent acts. So eventually the Muslim rulers of pre-Mughal Delhi Sultanate had to come to terms with the Hindu reality of India:

> Later Muslim rulers of the Sultanate period, with a few exceptions, avoided taking extreme measures to eliminate the religious and cultural identity of the Hindus, much to the chagrin of the orthodox Ulemas. The advice of Wazir Junaidi to Iltumish, advising him against following a policy of "death or Islam" towards the Hindus is worth noting. "If the above orders are to be applied to the Hindus, it is possible they might combine, and a general confusion might ensue and the Muslims would be too few in number to suppress the general confusion".[91]

Such deviations from a fundamentalist standpoint of a theocratic empire is to be expected. Prof. Arvind Sharma in his book on the history of religious tolerance, in another context quotes affirmatively what Dr Vincent Cornell, a scholar of Islamic Studies states about such adjustments: 'the idea that either the "problem" or the "solution" of a particular faith may be found primarily in its scripture usually is "not a historical proposition".[92] Thus, the Hindu resistance made Islam compromise the stand on the worship of images and consider the Hindu Dharma and society differently. Consequently, the Sufi dimension of Islam in India thus, apart from being proselytizing, also brought forth more Hinduized streams, which were both accommodative of theo-diversity, hence, universal.

Of late, many historians have brought out facts to show that the Sufi Islam in itself had been not all positive and often became the precursor of a violent Islamist invasion or worse an accomplice in the persecution of Hindus. Dr Koenraad Elst, the pro-Hindu Belgian Indologist, and whose mentor was Hindutva thinker Sita Ram Goel, evaluates Sufism in the Islamic context thus:

> The central aim of Sufism, the self-extinction in the merger with God, is obviously borrowed from Buddhist and Vedantic sources. Initially the orthodox clergy persecuted outspoken Sufis who said blasphemous things like "*ana'l Haqq*" ("I am the True One", Arabic translation of the Upanishadic dictum "*Aham Brahmasmi*"), because they saw through its un-Islamic inspiration, but later they adapted and domesticated Sufism into an acceptable Islamic form of devotion for both the spiritual eccentrics and the sentimental illiterate masses.[93]

There is a general picture that the Sufi saints were against the orthodox Islamist dispensation and were liberal. In Indian context, the Sufis of North India and Deccan were more often, though not entirely combative, waging jihad and were 'cleansers of idol worship'. Dr Elst cites the work of Richard Eaton a scholar of Indian Islamic history from Princeton University to underline the Islamist nature of Sufis. Eaton states:

> The timing of the Warrior Sufis' arrival and disappearance in Deccan history provides further clues to the nature of their role They began to arrive around the time of the first invasions from Delhi and began to disappear around the time of the establishment of the Bahmani Kingdom (1347–1489). The fifty-year period encompassed by these two events, from 1296 to 1347, thus saw the passing of the Bijapur plateau from *Dar al-Harb* to *Dar al-Islam*. This suggests that these Sufis were not able to exist entirely independent of some kind of Muslim military presence in the Deccan. It also

> suggests that their existence was not necessary after Islam had achieved full political expression in a region that theretofore had been a Muslim frontier.[94]

Vedic scholar and Hindutva sympathizer David Frawley writes warningly of the continuing intolerant stream of Sufism, even as he recognizes elements in Sufism as important for a good Hindu-Muslim dialogue:

> One should not think, therefore, that Sufi militancy was an affair of the Middle Ages and has been entirely given up today. Militant Sufis have been active recently in the Middle East and there is a Sufi involvement in the Taliban in Afghanistan, a region that has long been a centre of their activity, not to mention their prominence in Pakistan.[95]

One of the many milestones in the history of Hindu-Muslim relations, the post-1670 transformation of Akbar from his jihadist Islamist stand towards Hindus to a more civilized stand was definitely a significant one. This was not unlike many typical Hindu emperors of India with a pre-Islamist presence. Many scholars discern a Sufi influence responsible for this transformation of Akbar. David Frawley writes:

> The Mughal Emperor Akbar advocated tolerance of all religions at least as a political policy, though overall he favoured Islam. He removed several anti-Hindu laws that prevented Hindus from publicly practicing their religion or building new temples, including the oppressive "dhimmis tax" or "jizya". Akbar was influenced by liberal Sufis and took a broader view of spirituality than previous rulers.[96]

Hindutva views have varied with regard to Akbar. Savarkar juxtaposes Akbar's later day compromise with Hindus with his earlier cruelty towards Hindus, which was in typical Islamist fashion.

Savarkar in his *Six Glorious Epochs of Indian History* gives a vivid picture of Akbar's sacking of 'Chitod' (Chittor) in which the 'heartless' Akbar behaved as any other fanatic inhuman Islamist invader. He castigates Hindu historians for calling Akbar a liberal monarch without taking into consideration his mass murder of civil Hindu population of Chittor numbering 30,000, along with the destruction of Hindu temples there. That this massacre of 30,000 Hindus, mostly peasants, was completely ignored when Akbar was glorified and the memory of the resistance and sacrifice of Chittor being gradually erased from the memories of history, not by the Mughals but by the modern historians of India, infuriated Savarkar.[97]

At the same time, Savarkar does not fail to see the transformation in Akbar, pointing out that Akbar 'is said to have bequeathed a large tract of land to' the fourth Sikh Guru Ramdas, who 'dug out a beautiful lake and built a temple on its bank, which is now known as "Amritsar"'. Savarkar also records the change in the policies of Akbar in the latter half of his rule, giving a separate subtitle to his book, but considers this as a strategy and 'certainly not because he did not consider the Hindus as kafirs!':

> On the contrary he knew quite well that whenever such atrocities were committed on the Hindus, in the name of religion, by the former Sultans, they were followed with disastrous revolts. Sometimes even the whole Sultanates were consumed in the conflagration of the Hindu wrath. In order to avoid this disastrous end for his empire and to establish a tranquil administration of his own did he treat all his subjects whether they were Hindus or Muslims, justly so far as their individual life was concerned and much more leniently and harmlessly than other emperors, like Allauddin or Aurangzeb.[98]

And ends his evaluation of Akbar thus:

> However, of the many great emperors that lived at the time in Europe or Africa or Asia, Akbar was the greatest in respect of his strategy, his wielding of the widest power, bravery, founding of a vast empire, his patronage of learning and arts and crafts....But with all that greatness he was, from our Hindu point of view, foreign, belonging to another religion and mean-minded and as such he should be decried by us, Hindus![99]

Where Savarkar sees only a strategy, Prof. Suhas Majumdar (1937–1995) in his work on jihad (with a foreword by Sita Ram Goel) sees a genuine change of heart and shunning of jihad. In an earlier record of Akbar's biography, Akbar beheaded with his own hand the Hindu king Hemu, who had been already captured and wounded. This act earned him the title of 'Ghazi' (killer of infidels). Yet in later biographies of Akbar, like the one written by Abdul Kadir Badayuni, Akbar is shown refusing to behead Hemu. Prof. Majumdar comments:

> Besides his contempt for jihad, Badauni's account contains an ideal of chivalry maturing in Akbar's mind which was little different from the Rajput ideal. That ideal again was the Hindu ideal of chivalry par excellence, harking back to the heroic exploits described in the Mahabharata. It has often been remarked that Akbar's brand of religious tolerance was more a matter of policy than conviction; but the above account indicates how, with advancing years, he inclined with his whole heart towards Hindu ideals and abhorred Islamic teachings in the secret recesses of his being.[100]

Here one should note that both Chishti and Naqshbandi Sufi orders had no problem with jihad against Hindus including the massacre of the infidel civilian population. After the massacre of the Hindu population of Chittor, Akbar made a thanksgiving visit to Chishti's Dargah and issued his victory decree from there:

> The text of his *Fathnama*, issued from Muinuddin Chishti's dargah at Ajmer in March 1568, was included in *Munshat-i-Namakîn* compiled in 1598 by Saiyid Abdul Qasim Khan, a prominent noble who served under Akbar as well as Jahangir. The *Fathnama* cites the jihadic verses from the Koran and refers to Hindus as accursed infidels. It has been translated into English by Ishtiaq Ahmed Zilli, and published in Proceedings of the Indian History Congress, 1972 (pp. 350–361).[101]

So, overall there seemed to have been a genuine change of heart more because of Hindu influence rather than the institutional Sufi influence. *Akbarnama* written by Abul Fazal, who was the most ardent supporter of the liberal policies of Akbar, more out of conviction than fear of the emperor, puts these words in the mouth of Akbar as a warning he issued to Islamists:

> I have forced many Brahmans by fear of my powers to adopt the religion of my ancestors; but now that mind has been enlightened with the beams of truth, I have become convinced that the dark clouds of conceit and the mist of self-opinion have gathered round you, and that not a step can be made in advance without the torch of proof....To repeat the words of the Creed (kalima), to perform circumcision, or to lie prostrate on the ground from the dread of kingly power, can avail nothing in the sight of God.[102]

What is to be noted here is the subtle reversing of theological imagery. In Islamic theology, the pre-Islamic period in a society is considered as the dark period and Islam brings light. So, the Islamic invasion and forced conversions are justified as a kind of process of enlightenment. Here the writer reverses this. Returning to a more Hindu-like universalism is related to being 'enlightened with the beams of truth' while adherence to monopolistic fanaticism as being blinded by 'dark clouds of conceit and the mist of self-opinion'. So, there is every reason to agree with Prof. Mazumdar that Akbar was more influenced by Hindu culture and spirituality even if he conducted his liberal policies as a form of strategy.

But Akbar's slow Hinduization moves, if they were that, got reversed soon after Akbar's death. Even those who had supported Akbar's ventures into 'universalism' like Abdul Qadir Badayuni (1540–1615) were closet Islamists.

Badayuni was a Sanskrit scholar who had translated the Ramayana and Mahabharata during Akbar's reign under his orders. But he published his uncensored work *Muntahb al-tawarikh,* wherein he attacked Akbar only after Jahangir had ascended the throne.[103]

Akbar was disappointed with Jahangir. His hope was instead pinned on Khur Khusrau Mirza, son of Jahangir and the Rajput Manbhawati Bai (who died by suicide the same year Akbar died). This grandson had been influenced by both Akbar and his Hindu mother, rebelled against his father trying to ascend the throne. The Islamist elements fanned the hatred Jahangir already had for his rebellious son and promised him their support, provided he became an Islamist and not a liberal like his father.[104]

This reversal of movement from Indic to Islamist is well exhibited in the fact that while Akbar had donated land to Sikh Guru Arjan Dev through Prince Salim (future Jahangir), Jahangir in his own memoirs had this to say about Guru Arjan:

> In Gobindwal, which is on the river Blyah (Beas), there was a Hindu named Arjun, in the garments of sainthood and sanctity, so much so that he had captured many of the simple-hearted of the Hindus, and even of the ignorant and foolish followers of Islam, by his ways and manners, and they had loudly sounded the drum of his holiness. They called him Guru, and from all sides stupid people crowded to worship and manifest complete faith in him. For three or four generations (of spiritual successors) they had kept this shop warm. Many times it occurred to me to put a stop to this vain affair or to bring him into the assembly of the people of Islam.... At last, when Khusrau passed along this road this insignificant fellow proposed to wait upon him....He behaved to Khusrau in certain special ways, and made on his forehead a fingermark in saffron, which the Indians (Hinduwan) call *qashqa* (tilak) and is considered propitious. When this came to my ears and I clearly understood his folly, I ordered them to produce him and handed over his houses, dwelling places, and children to Murtaza Khan, and having confiscated his property commanded that he should be put to death.[105]

The hatred that Jahangir had for Sikhs and other Hindus is evident in these lines. Thus, his descend into the Islamist state had started in the Mughal Empire and the role played by the Sufis was accelerating the descend. Dr Harry S. Neale, who specializes in 'Near Eastern Studies' from the University of California explains in detail how Sufi movement strongly suggested an uncompromising fundamentalist Islamist polity, which since then has influenced Islamic polity to this day:

> Many Indian Sunni Muslims considered Ahmad Sirhindi to be the renewer of Islam in the second Islamic millennium (mujaddid-i alf-i thani). Although Sirhindi wrote a number of treatises on Sufi themes, he is best known for his letters (maktubat) to various Sufi shaykhs and Mughal dignitaries, which have been regarded as a turning point in the development of Indo-Muslim religious thought....Sirhindi also wrote a number of letters concerning the martial jihad and relations with non-Muslims under Muslim rule. In these letters, Sirhindi consistently advocates a harsh and uncompromising stance toward the Hindus under Mughal rule. Concerning the martial aspect of jihad, Sirhindi's pronouncements are unequivocal: "Fighting the unbelievers and treating them harshly is one of the requirements of religion". Although his contempt for unbelievers is generally directed at Hindus, he also expresses the following opinion regarding Jews: "Whenever a Jew is killed it is to the benefit of Islam". Sirhindi repeatedly insists that the glory of Islam requires the humiliation of unbelievers: "The honor of Islam is in the degradation of unbelief and the people of unbelief". He considers the taxing of non-Muslims who have accepted Islamic rule as a means through which to further humiliate them and keep them in a constant state of fear: "The original aim of taking the jizya from (unbelievers) is for their degradation and this degradation (ought to be) to the extent that they cannot wear nice clothing for fear of the jizya…and that they are always fearful and trembling…." Sirhindi's harsh stance with regard to the martial jihad and the subjugation of those who refuse to embrace Islam is no less uncompromising than that of his Sufi spiritual predecessors al-Jilani, al-Ghazali, and Ibn 'Arabi.[106]

In Punjab where Hindu family of religions, particularly the Sikh Panth from sixteenth century onwards had an intense interaction with Islam, both in its invasionist and varied Sufi forms of proselytizing and dialogue, one can see two distinct but not unconnected streams in the development of Sufi movement in India.

One is Ijadist Sufism which was almost the Sufism in the beginning of its spread into India and makes for still a dominant school of Sufism in India and everywhere else. It has the following characteristic features: Lack of latitudinarianism, emphasis on shariat, transcendent and personal deity, obscurity of language and belief in the duality of man and God and obedience of servant to master as love. The influence of Hindu Vedantic movement in all its forms—particularly the bridal mysticism, Vaishnava devotional practices and also Yogas particularly of Nath-Yogis. For example, Farid Ganj-i-Shakar locked up a Hindu for three days and set him free only after he agreed to convert to Islam. Nizamuddin Auliya expressed concern that the Hindus were not prepared to renounce their faith under any circumstances and that for a man who did not follow shariat, there could be no refuge, and so on. As against the Ijadist Sufis, the Vedanta influenced Sufis exhibited the following characteristics: God-human unity, God as both transcendent and immanent, Grace, importance of guru, supremacy of love over all other aspects of religion and sadhana and wifely devotion.[107]

The transition from one of these streams to the other was a gradual process. One important Sufi saint who marked the transition was Farid Sani (1450–1554). Entry about Farid Sani in the detailed biographical encyclopedia of Sufi saints of South Asia states:

> His God is Transcendental as well as Immanent. His Transcendental God is Personal and of the concept of Ijadists....Like a true Vedantist, Farid Sani believes in the immanent aspect of God also. He seeks Him in everybody. He advises "not to speak sharp to anyone as God dwells in every creature"....However, it is interesting that unlike Ijadist Sufis or non-Indian Sufis, Farid describes the communion in the vocabulary of sugar or honey. It is purely Indian influence....The sway of the influence of the Indian Bhakti movement was so strong that Farid's compositions get hardly any chance to influence the Sufis of later period. The later Sufis like Shah Hussain and Bulleh Shah accepted influence direct from the Bhakti movement and its literature.[108]

The course Sufi mysticism took after the traumatic Taimur invasion and massacres, and also the fanatical reign of Aurangzeb, was decidedly the path of what can be called Vaishnavaite-Vedantic Sufism. One of the foremost scholars of Sufi poetry in Punjab writes:

> No doubt the Sufis during the reign of Shah Jahan, under the patronage of Prince Dara Shikoh, had absorbed a good deal of Hindu Vedantic thought, but they remained, save for a few rare exceptions, within the limits of their own religion. The intolerance of the orthodox people and of the Emperor Aurangzeb, however, later on compelled them to speak freely against Islamic dogmas, etc., and to turn more towards Hindu religion with real feeling than they had done before.[109]

Then there had also been persecution of Sufis by Islamic rulers at the instigation of the Islamist clergy. It is quite an interesting fact of history that most Hindu chieftains throughout India, despite their resistance to Islamist invasion and conversions, never had such track record of persecution of Sufis. Author and multilingual literary scholar Kartar Singh Duggal (1917–2012) points out this curious fact:

> Jalaluddin Khilji had Saidi Maula, an eminent Sufi of his time, crushed under the feet of an elephant. Similarly, Alauddin Khilji had almost got Hazrat Nizamuddin

> Auliya beheaded but for a miraculous escape. It is said that Mohammad Bin Tughlaq had Sheikh Shahabuddin Bin Ahmad murdered with his mouth filled with dung. A similar fate was meted out to Nasiruddin Chiragh Dehlvi who was tortured with holes bored in his cheeks. Firaz Shah had Ahmed Bihari executed since Bihari's disciples addressed him as God.[110]

All these diverse, conflicting and paradoxical dimensions of Sufism have to be taken into consideration before making use of the term 'Sufi' in a blanket way in the context of the samanvaya movement. It is not a monolith.

Dara Shukoh

Another spiritual height in the Hindu-Muslim interaction was reached by Dara Shukoh (1615–1659), the elder brother of Aurangzeb and the rightful heir to the Mughal throne.

Shukoh came under the spiritual influence of Mullah Shah who initiated him into the Qādiriyya silsila in 1639–1640 CE This Sufi sect too was not a monolith and had both mystic as well as strong orthodox masters. Mullah Shah was, however, a spiritual person not interested in the affairs of the state. Further, he also ran into considerable problem with the powerful ulema in the royal court who under their seal of authority had suggested death sentence to Mullah Shah for apostasy and what they considered as an insult to the prophet of Islam. The verse attributed to Mullah Shah stated that as he was now 'hand in hand with God' and hence 'why should he care for Mustafa!' The emperor at the time was Shah Jahan. It was the intervention of Dara Shukoh that saved Mullah Shah's life.[111] Later when Shah Jahan asked Mullah Shah if he wrote those lines, Mullah Shah dissociated himself from it stating:

> I feel a sense of heresy and dissimulation from this verse, because the composer has differentiated between him, God and the Prophet, and in my religion this discrimination is infidelity (kufr) and heresy (shirk).[112]

Yet for all such mysticism, when Aurangzeb became the emperor, Mullah Shah was quick to save himself from any possible capital punishment by sending the emperor verses praising him and which he suggested came to him through divine inspiration.[113]

In the Sufi influence that Shukoh had, it was more non-dualist (or what the Western philosophers may wrongly call pantheist) rather than monotheistic Sufism that influenced him. Mysticism of Ibn-al-Arabi was a decisive influence on Shukoh. He vigorously advocated the 'Oneness of Being' (*wahdat ak-wujud*). In the Indian context, the orthodox monotheistic Sufis, particularly powerful and influential Ahmad Sirhindi, who was against the abolition of jizya on Hindus, had strongly criticized wahdat ak-wujud.[114]

> Another possible source of inspiration, but one that has been little studied, is that of the various schools of Hinduism and perhaps, Buddhism. Both Hindu and Buddhist ideas must be assumed to have inflitrated into the Muslim world, and it is of particular interest to note that an Arabic version of a Persian translation of a Sanskrit work on Tantric Yoga has been attributed to Ibl al-Arabi. In this connection also, his important theory of the Creative Imagination bears a striking resemblance to the Hindu concept of maya. It is certainly true that a comparative study of Hindu and Sufi metaphysics often produces some surprising parallels.[115]

The journey of Shukoh into spiritual traditions then existing in India, is quite illuminating. He started as a Sufi follower of Hanafi law and through his journey he declared himself an idol-worshipper. Islamic scholar Prof. Perwaiz Hayat gives an overall view of the quest and inner journey of Shukoh:

> Dara's works on Sufism show a gradual development in his thought. He started his journey as a believer in a particular religion and a committed Sufi and reached the point where he understood that all religions lead to one Reality. Thus, in his work Safinat al-Awliya', like any Sufi, he introduces himself as a "ḥanafī al-mashrab" (follower of the Ḥanafī law) who belongs to the Qadiriyya silsila. In his second work his focus is on his Qadiriyya silsila and, even more so, on his broad-minded Sufi master Mulla Shah—who was an admirer of Ibn al-Arabi's philosophy of wahdat al-wujud (Unity of Being). The influence of Mulla Shah and the philosophy of wahdat al-wujud become more evident in Hasanat al-Arifīn, in his poetry (Diwan) and even more so in his letters to Muhibbullah Allahbadi and Shah Dilruba. In Hasanat, he describes Baba Lal Das—a Hindu Yogi—as one of the awliya. In his Diwan he uses the phrase hama ust (He is everything). In his letter to Shah Dilruba he introduces himself as but parast (idolator) and dayr nishin (a resident of the temple). He uses terms like majazi islam (superficial Islam) and kufr-i haqiqi (true unbelief).[116]

One of the most decisive influences on the understanding Dara Shukoh had on Hindu spiritual traditions was from Yogi Lal Das, also known as Lal Bhairagi. Shukoh through his copyist Momin Chand records the following answer by Lal Das on the Hindu worship of sacred forms:

> It (idol worship) is for strengthening the heart. One who knows what is behind

> the form does not need (any particular form to worship). However, one who does not know the meaning behind form retains one's attachment to the form. It is like those girls who play with forms (dolls). They do not play (with them) after getting married. This is what idol worship is. Those (people) who do not know the inner meaning (batin) of form (remain attached to the form), (but) after attaining the knowledge of the inner meaning, they go beyond the form.[117]

Shukoh himself considered the Hindu worship of sacred forms essential for a spiritual seeker so much so that he, in one of his letters to the famed Fakir Shah Muhammad Dilruba, whom the prince considered as the 'king of Fakirs', writes that he considers himself the worshipper of the Divine through forms, and after speaking about superficial Islam and real unbelief in the same letter, he states that 'were Muslims to know the significance of the idol, they would have realized that real faith is in idol worship'.[118] Dr Kalika-Ranjan Qanungo in his well-researched two-volume biography of the prince makes a detailed analysis of his spiritual sojourns and gives this divine-intoxicated verse:

> The externals of Islam have fallen off from the heart of this faqir, and the real infidelity has been revealed to me. "I have become the wearer of the sacred thread, I an idol-worshipper; Nay, I have become the worshipper of the self (*Khud-parast*), and a priest of the temple of Fire-worshippers (*dair-nashin*)....If the infidel is alienated from the external Islam, who has come to know the real nature of infidelity? Life lies concealed in every idol and Faith lies hidden beneath Infidelity."[119]

Dr Qanungo quotes from Dara's work *Risala-i-Haqnuma*:

> When thou shaft carry this stage to perfection, then there will remain no doubt that thou art the truth". This is the realization of "I am God; I am the Truth" (ana' al Haqq) or as the Vedantin says—"I am the Brahman (brahmosmi)".

Then the historian comments:

> This was the truth of truths which the Vedic rishis proclaimed from the forests of Aryavarta; and this was the truth which startled the Muslim world in the palmy days of Harun-al-Rashid, when every drop of the martyred blood of Hallaj—(as they say)—cried out from the dust of Baghdad, "Ana'al-Haqq". In fact, the externals of Islam, save Allah, Muhammad, and the Quran, perished in the mysticism of Dara.[120]

Shukoh also had visions of Hindu divinities which inspired him to undertake civilizational projects. One such was the publication of a Persian translation of

Yoga Vasishta. It was published in 1656, just three years before his execution by Aurangzeb. Dara wrote an introduction to this translation wherein he wrote:

> When I had gone through the Persian translation of this book (the Joga-Vashishta), which is attributed to Shaikh Sufi, I saw in a dream two dignified figures of calm appearance, one of them standing on a higher level than the other. I was drawn involuntarily to their presence and Vashishta with great affection and graciousness placed his hand on my back, and said: "Rama, here is an earnest seeker of knowledge, and a comrade* (lit., brother) of yours in true search of the Reality; embrace him." Ramchandra held me in his embrace with great warmth and love. Then Vashishta gave to Ramchandra some sweets which I ate out of his hand. After having seen this in dream my desire to have this book translated became greater than ever; and one man from among my servants was appointed to translate this work. This translation was completed under the supervision of the Pandits of Hindustan.[121]

According to Qanungo, 'the philosophical views of Dara were rapidly veering towards the Advaita Vedantism becomes quite apparent from his selection of Sanskrit works for translation' which included, apart from *Yoga Vasishta,* also *Prabodha-Chandrodaya*, an eleventh century work on Advaita Vedanta.[122]

Thus, the approach of Dara was quite radical and differed from even the usual accommodative stands made by liberal Sufis who considered Hindu sacred texts like the Upanishads as similar to Jewish Torah—divine but superseded by Koran. Shukoh on the other hand considered the Upanishads as supreme standalone books and Koran as a text that needs Upanishadic light for human understanding. Islamic scholar Padma Shri Dr Malik Muhammad, whose life was cut short by a brutal contract murder, dealt in detail this contribution of the martyred prince Shukoh:

> Dara Shukoh creates an intimate connection between the Quran and the Upanishads by saying that they are hinted at in Sura 56:77-80.... The crucial question with regard to this verse is the interpretation of *kiab maknum*. Classical Islamic commentators normally prefer to consider this phrase as a reference to the preserved tablet (al-lauh al mahfuz) in which original text of the Koran was inscribed by Allah. Less frequently they take it to mean the actual copy of the book or the Taurat and the Injil. Dara Shukoh does not accept any of these exegetical attempts.... Dara Shukoh's view of the relationship between the Hindu religious literature and the Quran seems to be his most significant contribution to Islamic thought. The idea that one must use the Hindu scripture in order to attain the real meaning of the Quran is hitting at the very core of the conviction that Islam is a self-sufficient system that is in no need of ideas extraneous to it. It seems to have been deviant enough to put Dara

> Shukoh beyond the pale of medieval Indian Islam. The 18th century Naqshbandi Sufi Mirza Mazhar Jan-i-Jahan (died in 1781) also expressed relatively conciliatory views of the Hindus, but he did not go as far as Dara Shukoh in recognizing the legitimacy and validity of the Hindu religion after the emergence of Islam.…Dara Shukoh ascribes to the Hindu scriptures a legitimacy not less than that of the Quran. In a certain sense the Upanishads are even superior to all other heavenly books, because the divine message is expressed in them in the most explicit fashion. They are therefore essential for understanding the less clear statements of the Quran. In saying this, Dara Shukoh abandons the cherished Islamic conviction that Islam is, in the eyes of Allah, the only true faith (Sura 3:19) and that the Quran is a clear readily understandable book.[123]

At the same time, did Shukoh reject Islam? He did not. K. R. Qanungo points out:

> The Prince introduces his treatise (*Majmua-ul-Baharain* or *Mingling of Two Oceans*) in the right orthodox style with a praise of God in whom Islam and Hinduism meet, followed by an invocation of peace and blessings upon Mustapha (the Prophet), his family and his chief companions. This is enough to prove that Dara had not renounced allegiance to God and his Prophet.[124]

This is what makes Dara Shukoh important. Had he converted to Hindu Dharma he would have chosen the easier path. But he actually created within Islam a space for the Muslims to understand Hinduism and enrich and deepen their own spirituality through that understanding. In this he made the non-dual unity of the Upanishads, which he strove to discover and did discover in diverse traditions, the basis. Thus, one can say Dara Shukoh represents an important civilizational peak for India. And in him there is a model for approaching theo-diversity for Abrahamic religions—particularly Christianity and Islam.

The letter which most historians accept as having issued by Shivaji, written to Rajput chieftain Jai Singh probably around May 1665, praises Dara Shukoh and states that had he been the ruler he would have treated his people 'with kindness and favour'.[125]

The establishment Indology and Nehruvian school of historiography try their level best to relegate Shukoh as much as possible to a sidelined space in Indian history. They also try to explain him away through a dominantly Islamic framework as in the case of the 2020 book on Shukoh from Harvard University Press in which the author consistently labels his spiritual view 'monotheistic', and through a convoluted logic of the number of Hindu nobles who supported Aurangzeb in his succession war tries to prove that the feud between both the princes had little to do with the differences in their worldviews.[126] A contemporary example would be that of Rajiv Gandhi, who claimed through Jawaharlal Nehru the Kashmiri Pandit lineage and was with considerable number of Hindu members of Parliament yet demanded the removal of then Governor of Jammu and Kashmir Jagmohan, thus facilitating the ethnic cleansing of Hindus in the valley. A future Harvard academic sepoy-informer might as well claim that the ethnic cleansing in Kashmir was not a Hindu-Muslim conflict because an overwhelmingly Hindu Congress under the leadership of a Hindu with a supposedly Pandit lineage facilitated it. Equally problematic is the monotheistic twist to the spiritual world of Shukoh. Apart from the later day Nehruvian historiographers and Indian academic sepoys to the West, even early Arya Samajists had contributed to this portrayal.[127] As the above discussion of the religious worldview of Dara Shukoh shows his understanding of the Divine, which came through the churning of Vedanta, the Hindu-Muslim religious traditions and wahdat ak-wujud as well as acceptance of the worship of the Divine in chosen sacred forms as an essential spiritual practice, cannot be reduced to 'monotheism'.

The ideologues of the Hindutva movement have always highlighted Dara Shukoh as a model for Hindu-Muslim dialogue and synthesis. In 1993 K. R. Malkani wrote in his book on Hindu-Muslim relations in the backdrop of Ayodhya that 'the tragedy of India today was that New Delhi had a road named after Aurangzeb who divided the Indian society and ruined the country, but none after Dara Shikoh, the finest product of Hindu-Muslim synthesis and national unity.'[128]

K. R. Malkani was the Rajya Sabha (Upper House) Member of the Parliament from 1994 to 2000. On 13 May 1994, he asked a question in the Parliament. Question number 5712 reads:

> Will the Minister of Home Affairs be pleased to state: (a) whether Government is aware that Aurangzeb was the most controversial and divisive emperor of India, whereas his elder brother, Dara Shikoh, was the finest example of national unity and integrity; and (b) if so, whether Government would consider renaming Aurangzeb Road, New Delhi, as Dara Shikoh Road, to promote national unity?[129]

The Minister of State for Home Affairs Sri P. M. Sayeed gave a crisp answer: 'The Government of National Capital Territory of Delhi has reported that there is no such proposal under their consideration at this stage.'

Two decades after this, on 29 August 2015, the Aurangzeb Road was renamed as Dr A. P. J. Abdul Kalam Road by the New Delhi Municipal Council

(NDMC). It was following the request of Maheish Girri, a BJP Member of Parliament from East Delhi constituency. Then in 2017, the NDMC renamed Dalhousie Road, named after East India Company administrator, to 'Dara Shikoh' Road. The proposal for renaming came from Meenakshi Lekhi, the BJP MP. Here it is worth remembering what historian R. C. Majumdar wrote in his foreword to the two-volume biography on Dara Shukoh authored by Prof. K. R. Qanungo:

> Judged by ordinary standards Aurangzeb was a great success, and Dara a hopeless failure; but to those whose visions transcend the ordinary limitations imposed by worldly conventions, and catch a glimpse of ultimate reality, the position may be exactly the reverse.[130]

Perhaps the shift from Nehruvianism towards Hindutva reflects the values Majumdar delineates above. In the Hindu-Muslim dialogue and the civilizational process of samanvaya, Dara Shukoh represents an important milestone proving that an open approach which is based on experience and harmony and without agenda of either proselytizing or constructing a theology of superseding is possible. It is telling that Shukoh who personalized this approach has been honoured neither by Nehruvians nor by other political and ideological dispensations but by Hindutvaites.

Along with Dara Shukoh one also must look at the way Shivaji perceived Islam despite having to face the severe most Islamist persecution of Aurangzeb. Here it is important to see how Nehru viewed what he called the 'emergence of Hindu nationalism' in the context of the Islamism of Aurangzeb and the resistance offered by Shivaji:

> All over the widespread domains of the Mughal Empire there was a ferment and a growth of revivalist sentiment, which was a mixture of religion and nationalism. That nationalism was certainly not of the modern secular type, nor did it, as a rule, embrace the whole of India in its scope. It was coloured by feudalism, by local sentiment and sectarian feeling. The Rajputs, more feudal than the rest, thought of their clan loyalties; the Sikhs, a comparatively small group in the Punjab, were absorbed in their own self-defence and could hardly look beyond the Punjab. Yet the religion itself had a strong national background and all its traditions were connected with India. "The Indians," writes Professor Macdonell, "are the only division of the Indo-European family which has created a great national religion—Brahmanism—and a great world religion—Buddhism; while all the rest far from displaying originality in this sphere have long since adopted a foreign faith." That combination of religion and nationalism gained strength and cohesiveness from

both elements, and yet its ultimate weakness and insufficiency were also derived from that mixture. For it could only be an exclusive and partial nationalism, not including the many elements in India that lay outside that religious sphere. Hindu nationalism was a natural growth from the soil of India, but inevitably it comes in the way of the larger nationalism which rises above differences of religion or creed.... Shivaji was the symbol of a resurgent Hindu nationalism, drawing inspiration from the old classics, courageous, and possessing high qualities of leadership. He built up the Marathas as a strong unified fighting group, gave them a nationalist background, and made them a formidable power which broke up the Mughal Empire.[131]

As one can see here, Nehru portrays what he calls 'Hindu nationalism' as a kind of pre-modern, non-secular, feudal, parochial and only unconsciously national phenomenon, which though 'a natural growth from the soil of India… comes in the way of the larger nationalism which rises above differences of religion or creed'. It is precisely Shivaji's approach to Islam despite the violent Islamist persecution that shows that what Nehru calls 'Hindu nationalism' was not an impediment in the way of 'the larger nationalism' but is the very basis and substratum of nationalism, which Nehru artificially uproots from its very source.

The letter of Shivaji to Aurangzeb shows neither 'an exclusive and partial nationalism' nor can it in the remotest sense be charged as 'not including the many elements in India that lay outside (Hindu) religious sphere' as alleged by Nehru. In the letter Shivaji decries jizya and argues that the true Islam would not allow discrimination based on religion, and in fact, he argues that Islam and Hinduism are both spiritual yearnings of humanity and should not be discriminated as such:

They are (diverse pigments) used by the true Divine Painter for blending the colours and filling in the outlines (of His picture of the entire human species.) If it be a mosque, the call to prayer is chanted in remembrance of Him. If it be a temple, the bell is rung in yearning for Him only. To show bigotry for any man's own creed and practices is equivalent to altering the words of the Holy Book. To draw new lines on a picture is equivalent to finding fault with the painter…

Economist and historian Dr Bal Krishna in his multi-volume work on Shivaji rightly points out the all-inclusive nature of Shivaji's polity:

Shivaji saw the tide of persecution and oppression advancing from Delhi to the Deccan in the reign of Aurangzeb. He would have been justified in retaliating the fanaticism of the Muslim rulers and paying them in their own coins. But he was

> not a product of his times. He rose far above the contemporary rulers of India and Europe in following a liberal policy of religious harmony, tolerance and equality. Herein lies his claim to greatness.[132]

Dr Bal Krishna cites this letter to Aurangzeb and also the way Shivaji treated his Islamic subjects. Even Aurangzeb could not find Shivaji's administration in anyway intolerant or non-inclusive, so much so that he even called Shivaji 'the Defender of the Muslim religion' in four of his letters covering a decade. Shivaji never stopped or discontinued the patronage an erstwhile Muslim ruler gave to Muslim places of worship when Shivaji annexed those provinces.[133] Islamist chronicler Khafi Khan, whose hatred for Shivaji was explicit in his writing, observed the following about Shivaji:

> "But he made it a rule that whenever his followers went plundering, they should do no harm to Muslims, the Book of God, or anyone's women. Whenever a copy of the Holy Kuran came into his hands, he treated it with respect and gave it to some of his Mahomedan followers. When the women of any Hindu or Mahomedan were taken prisoners by his men and they had no friend to protect them, he watched over their liberty." Further on, he remarks that he entirely abstained from other disgraceful acts and was careful to maintain the honour of the women and children of Mahomedans when they fell into his hands. His injunctions upon this point were very strict, and anyone who disobeyed them received punishment.[134]

The path was not an easy one. Sometimes, highly placed Islamic personnel like Qazi Hyder returned to Aurangzeb. But overall, this was the direction the religious policies of the Hindavi Swarajya of Shivaji took.

The principles enunciated by Shivaji in his letter as well as his inclusive administrative deeds give a national mission to the concept of true religion as understood by Dara Shukoh in his spiritual vision. Hindavi Swaraj envisioned by Shivaji and hence his Hindutva was not in any sense non-inclusive. Instead, it treated Islam at par with other religions. It is exactly this which had been accomplished by 'enlightenment' and rise of secularism in the West to Christianity in general. It compelled all religious doctrines to be treated equally and kept the state away from the church, though most European states also held to a national or state religion as an ornamental centripetal force of national identity. In India, Shivaji continuing the Vedic dictum of non-monopolistic non-expansionist theo-diversity provided resistance to monopolistic expansionism.

Thus, Hindutva, as it manifested itself through the Maratha confederacy, by providing an armed protection to theo-diversity, also proceeded in effecting samanvaya of Islam with the Hindu spiritual traditions. This would become the bedrock of true secularism in India—far more complete, organic and holistic than Nehru could ever comprehend in his superficial understanding of secularism, almost meaningless in Indian context—historically and socially—a fact hidden by his flowery language and cultivated charisma.

Moving into Modern Times

In the modern times, one of the important high points of interaction with Islamic spiritual traditions comes from the life of Sri Ramakrishna.

The Ram Swarup-Sita Ram Goel school has questioned the Islamic sadhana of Sri Ramakrishna as later day exaggerations. Following their line of argument, Dr Koenraad Elst has done the same. This was after the 1981 petition by Sri Ramakrishna Mission that they should be considered a minority religion. The Calcutta High Court agreed with the stand of the Mission, and it was in 1995 that Supreme Court of India rejected the claim. But it should be noted that while rejecting the claim of the Mission being a non-Hindu minority, the Supreme Court provided the Mission with the administrative concessions available to minority institutions in India. So, the purpose of the Mission in seeking a non-Hindu minority status was more to do with the institutional advantages the post-independent Indian state confers on non-Hindu religious minority institutions—an extension of the institutional apartheid against Hinduism that was inherent in the colonial Indian administration. However, the arguments of the Mission in the court used the so-called outwardly Islamic and Christian spiritual practices of Sri Ramakrishna as the proof of the non-Hindu nature of the Mission. Sri Ramakrishna practised Hindu spiritual traditions just like other spiritual traditions.

Naturally Ram Swarup, a spiritual master in his own right and a deep as well as sharp original thinker, rightly concerned about these developments, questioned these claims and brought out a scholarly monograph published by Sita Ram Goel's Voice of India. Ram Swarup made an incisive analysis of the Mission's stand thus:

> This is the pattern which the affidavit faithfully observes—when the inclusiveness of the Mission is to be shown, Islam and Christianity are mentioned; when its distinct character is to be shown, Hinduism is mentioned. The Mission is distinct from Hinduism in some respects and like Islam and Christianity in others. That makes it unique and universal—that is the line of argument.

Quite interestingly, the 1995 Supreme Court judgment turned the same argument of the Mission on inclusiveness to consider it as part of Hinduism:

Ram Swarup went further in his book, casting doubts on the very claims of 'Islamic form of sadhana' that Sri Ramakrishna practised:

> As regards Ramakrishna's "practice of Islam and Christianity" of which the Mission makes so much, it finds no mention in the Gospel, the earliest and most authentic account of Ramakrishna's thoughts and experiences in his own words. In this work we find that though Ramakrishna reminisces often about his experiences and God-filled states, there is hardly a word about his so-called practice of Islam and Christianity. It first finds place in Swami Saradananda's biography, "Sri Ramakrishna: The Great Master", a devout work alright but not "untarnished by the writer's mind", an eminent quality of the Gospel in the words of Vivekananda.[135]

However righteous his indignation was and however right his argument and stand were, he was wrong with respect to data. Sri Ramakrishna himself refers to Islamic sadhana in the very *Gospel of Sri Ramakrishna* compiled by Mahendranath Gupta ('M'):

> I received the Allah mantra from Govinda Rai. Rice with onions was cooked for me in the Bungalow; I ate some. I ate curry in Mani Mallick's garden house, but I felt a kind of repulsion to it.[136]

The adjoining footnote mentions that this food habit of eating onions forbidden to orthodox Brahmins was relished by Muslims. In the *Gospel of Sri Ramakrishna* itself, there are repeated references to the name Allah, placing it at par with other Hindu Divine names. In the *Gospel*, Sri Ramakrishna mentions, in a humorous manner, the case of a *sakta* who forcefully converted to Islam to emphasize the futility of sectarian highhandedness in the matters of spirituality. In the context of a pundit arguing with Mani Mallick, a Brahmo-Samajist, Sri Ramakrishna advised the pundit with this parable:

> You can't convert him to your views. Is it an easy thing to destroy old tendencies? Once there lived a very pious Hindu who always worshipped the Divine Mother and chanted Her name. When the Mussalmans conquered the country, they forced him to embrace Islam. They said to him: "You are now a Mussulman. Say 'Allah' From now on you must repeat only the name of Allah". With great difficulty he repeated the word Allah but every now and then blurted out "*Jagadamba*". At that the Mussalmans were about to beat him. There upon he said to them: "I beseech you!

> Please do not kill me. I have been trying my utmost to repeat the name of Allah, but our *Jagadamba* has filled me up to the throat. She pushes out your Allah."[137]

Thus, the *Gospel of Sri Ramakrishna* gives quite a view of the aspects of samanvaya with respect to Islam as held by Sri Ramakrishna. He accepted Allah. He respected the lifestyle differences that the Muslims have with respect to food, etc., by himself practising them, and despite the difficulty in adjusting, he had a mystic experience. He obliterated the usual forms of prejudice the 'otherness' could create by anchoring to a higher principle—the universal nature of his mystic experience.

The authoritative biography of Sri Ramakrishna of Swami Saradananda gives further details:

> Gradually it came to him that, since Mahomedanism was also a means to the realisation of God, he would see how the Lord blessed the devotees who worshipped that way. He made up his mind to be initiated by Govinda. Once the idea became fixed in his mind, there was no delaying its fulfilment. He intimated his desire to Govinda, who was glad to initiate him. To the practice of this new religion the Master applied himself with his characteristic thoroughness. Thus, did he describe his mentality at this period: "Then I used to repeat the name of Allah, wear my cloth in the fashion of the Mahomedans and incite the Namaz regularly. All Hindu ideas being wholly banished from the mind, not only did I not salute the Hindu gods, but I had no inclination even to visit them. After three days I realised the goal of that form of devotion." First of all he saw a radiant Person with a long beard and of grave appearance, and then his mind, passing through the realisation of the Brahman with attributes, was finally absorbed in the Brahman without attributes.[138]

For the publishers, the significance of this experience on the national life and the developing communal scenario was not lost. The following passage underlines this fact:

> Sri Ramakrishna's realisation in the Mahomedan form of practice appears to be fraught with far-reaching consequences for India. That he practised it after attaining perfection in the Advaita makes it clear that only through this, the underlying basis of all faiths, can the Hindus tind Mahomedans be united with each other. The Master was aware of the wide differences in views and temperament between these two rival faiths, but may we not infer from his successful practice of Mahomedanism that the existing barriers will one day be obliterated, and the two races clasp each other in amity and love? Time alone will prove the truth of our surmise.[139]

Almost during the corresponding years in Maharashtra, two Muslim saints—Sai Baba of Shirdi and Hazrat Babajan became quite famous. The former saint is nearly revered as a Hindu deity today, at par with Siva and Vishnu. Most calendar art of Sai Baba of Shirdi include symbols from all religions with the words—'*Sab ka Malik Ek Hai*' (There is only one master). While a section of orthodox Hindus, even to this day, object to the worship of the saint, the Hindu following of the saint outweighs the opposition hugely. On the other hand, the popularity of the saint among the Muslims seems to be the opposite. However, for the academic informers of the West with their deep-rooted self-hatred against anything Hindu, there is a great uncomfortable feeling about the so-called 'Hinduization' of the Sai Baba tradition.

Syncretic Mysticism of South Indian Muslims

In South India, Muslim spiritual experience has had a profound and deep interaction with indigenous mystic traditions like Suthaadvaita Saivaite tradition and bridal mysticism of Sri Vaishnavism. This has created a rich literature of mystic hymns—mostly of non-dual nature. It has also created a vibrant system of Yogic tradition where Yogis from Islamic traditions have launched many Yogic *paramparas*, which have been so flexible that most followers take the Muslim heritage as nothing alien.

The mystic hymns of Kunangudi Mastan Sahib (1792–1838) in Tamil Nadu, for example, show a strong influence of a Hindu mystic who preceded him—Dayumanavar (1705–1742). The works of both speak of a unitary mystic experience and combine it with a deep sense of devotion. Kunangudi Mastan freely employs Hindu spiritual terminology as he sings of Nandi, Shivam and Shakti. He sang of the attainment of the 'Siva Raja Yoga' state. The biography of Mastan Sahib based on oral traditions, written by his great grandson, speaks of an incident in which the Tanjore king of the time wanted to test the genuine nature of Mastan and arranged two beautiful damsels to perform for him. Everyone in the court saw Mastan completely immersed in the dance. When one of the courtiers (assembled sannyasins) went to ask if Mastan loved the dance, he saw the dancers from his perspective. In his field of vision, the dancers appeared as Mother Goddess 'Valai Manonmani' performing the cosmic dance. The king too witnessed this miracle and realized that Mastan was indeed a genuine mystic.[140] In the modern Saudi-funded Islamist propaganda, Kunangudi Mastan is singled out for attack. The Hindu dimensions in his poetry are negated and it is argued that they are only superficial and symbolic, that the seer employed mystic symbolism not just as a poetic technique but also a tool for his sadhana is often forgotten.

The tradition of Indic Islamic seers in South India continues well into the twentieth century and has influenced the spiritual landscape of all communities.

Mahan Muhammad Rahim (1887–1939) was well known among the spiritual seekers of Tamil provinces by his spiritual name Sri Karunaiyananda Jnana Bhupati. He published a magazine in the mid-1920s called *Jnana Suriyan* (*Sun of Gnosis*). His books *Vedanta Baskaran* (1918), *Jnana Kalanchiam* (*The Granary of Jnana*, 1928) and *Jnana Yoga Rahasyam* (*The Secret of the Yoga of Jnana*, 1930) represent a significant milestone in the way Vedantic tradition was encapsulated with both openly Hindu and also equally Islamic terminology. *Vedanta Baskaran* was published by Thiruvarur-based Brahma Vidya Press.

He profusely quotes the Koran, Thirukural, Thirumanthiram, Bhagavad Gita, Achara Kovai, Thiruvarutpa, Thayumanavar, etc., and places the Koran in the context of the Indic spiritual texts and provides a mystic interpretation to the verses. He also uses well-known Puranic anecdotes derived from both known Puranas like *Srimad Bhagavatam* and local traditions to explain the real nature of Yogi and the spiritual seeker. While emphasizing the need for compassion for all life forms or *Jeeva Karunya*, he cautions the ethnic vegetarians not to judge the ethnic non-vegetarians as inferior.

In his book *Vedanta Baskaran*, he takes a liberal stand with respect to women defying the social conventions in their quest for truth:

> In seeking Moksha (liberation) there is no difference between men and women. But in the society men have the ability to move freely and mix with anyone and befriend anyone they want. That way they are able to pursue their quest. However, women have to depend on their parents initially and are in the control of their husbands after that. This is the only difference. Yet if a woman is determined and pursues her spiritual quest without caring about what the society says then who can stop her? The social restrictions are only for those who have filled themselves with the trash of worldly notions of honour and shame. People can talk. When dogs bark at the full moon then ultimately their mouths are going to ache and it is not going to affect the moon....We have the history of Ammakkadevi who renounced all worldly life and went out nude seeking the Truth. Allammadevar proclaimed her as the most suitable soul then alive for receiving enlightenment. Prabhulingaleela also mentions Allamadevar initiating his sister Muthaayi. We also have the tradition of Avvaiyaar the saint poetess whose "Avvai Kural" shows how immersed she was in divine wisdom. Then we have the great Gyaneswari Karaikal Ammayaar. Is not Saraswati Herself a woman, the head of all knowledge? If I am to expand on all the great women seers who have contributed to our spiritual heritage it will go on and on. So let me limit myself saying seeking truth and liberation is common to all genders.[141]

In the next edition of the book, the endorsement for it was given by Maulana Syed Shah Muhammad Inayathullah Kalphatul Kathri of Madras. The Maulana considers this book as keeping with the spirit of Islamic wisdom and a treasure chest. According to him, the book contains truths which would 'destroy the inner darkness of humans and make the lotus bud of their heart (*qalp* – Arabic term with mystic connotation) flower, expanding its petals and make their intelligence shine...and thus truly understand the Kalima'.[142]

In his 1928 work, Karunaiyananda deals with wide range of topics. His critique of the prevailing notions of caste superiority and social exclusion is quite impressive and is totally drawn from Hindu sources. Citing the Puranic origins of maharishis who were born not only from various *jatis*, like Vasishta from the womb of a dancing woman, Narada from a washer-woman, Vyasa from the daughter of a fisher-man, etc., but also from various non-human species—like Rishyasringha born from the womb of an antelope, Gautama from cow, Jambuka born in the womb of a vixen and Gargeya from a jennet. Then he lists the saints in Tamizh tradition:

> Karuvoorar was born in the jati of barbers, Bhoga Muni was a potter, Thiruvalluvar, Auvaiyar and Kapilar were born to Aadhi—a woman of so-called lower caste, Idaikadar was of Yadav caste. Did all these Siddhas attain their greatness because of the birth? No.
>
> To Brahma Vasishta was born of a dancer woman and to that Vasishta was born Sati of an outcaste woman and to that Sati was born Parasara through a Pulaya woman and to that Parasara Vyasa was born through a fisher woman. Did not all these four attain greatness through the learning of the Vedas and through their penances?...It is through wisdom and by one's character and good deeds that one becomes great and not through birth.
>
> All these show that to attain the Bhakti-Marg one's jati and kula are in no way useful. It is one's state of mind alone that is important.[143]

This argument seems to be a very prevalent traditional argument against the emphasis of birth-based authority in spirituality, privileges in the society and its inevitable integral social phenomenon of social exclusion. Sri Malayala Swami (1885–1962), who was the disciple of Sri Siddha Shivalinga Guruswamy, who in turn was the disciple of Sri Narayana Guru, established Vyasa-Ashrama in Andhra Pradesh, and he in his book *Vedanta Established in Its Own Light* provides the same set of names and the same argument.[144]

He positions music as a sure way to spiritual state of *sayujya*—the union with the Brahman according to Saiva Siddhanta—while he lamented that the music was increasingly getting used for sensual purposes. What surprises one is the nuanced way in which he condemns the then prevalent decadency in the Devadasi institutions. At the same time, he did not fall into the colonial Protestant and what would later become the pseudo-rationalist Dravidianist narrative of essentializing the system by its evil degeneration. Instead, he points out that the system was meant for the higher purpose of attaining liberation through the contemplation of God through music and dance. At a time when the Devadasis were considered low and mean, while criticizing the reality of their degradation, he also puts forward the stellar example of Devadasis who had great spiritual merits, defied the sex-work imposed on them by the system and served Siva, contributing to the growth of Tamizh literature. Nevertheless, he wholeheartedly supported the legal measures taken by the government to stop sex-work being forced on girls born in a particular community in the name of tradition.[145]

With respect to Swarajya, he states that while Swarajya is a noble mission, what is more important than merely attaining Swarajya is removing the fissiparous tendencies among various sections of Indian people, including those among the Hindus and Muslims, among the Hindus, among the Brahmins, among the Brahmins and non-Brahmins, among the various Muslim sects, etc. His solution was spiritual harmony not conversion. He was also critical of Hindus who considered themselves superior to Muslims on account of their vegetarianism. He was convinced that unless the various sectarian conflicts were resolved, Swarajya for 'Hindu Desam' would not be possible. For that, one must realize the oneness of the Self, which is called by various names, and which can manifest in infinite variety within one's own self, without which harmony cannot be achieved. In other words, he wanted spirituality to be the basis of real national unity. In order to explain the kind of harmony that has to be achieved for National Swarajya as against spiritual Swarajya, Karunaiyananda gives an instance from the Hindu traditional lore that emphasizes the Saiva-Vaishnava oneness. When Dasaratha wanted to name his child, who was Vishnu Himself, Vasishta named him Rama by combining Ra from Hara and Ma from Uma because all existence is Shiva-Shakti. Then he ends it thus:

> In the fertile farmland that is our nation should be free of all the weeds of sectarian strife so that the crop of Swarajya can give good yield of welfare. The almighty should bless our land to have the full benefit of Swarajya crop, removing all the weeds of sectarianism.[146]

So, to him more important than the Swarajya of the nation was the Swarajya of the Self. Naturally, the former based itself on the latter.

Karunaiyananda also gave special importance to the culture of physical fitness. On 28 December 1927, Karunaiyananda Bhupathi presided over the 'All India Physical Fitness Improvement Conference' held at Chennai and spoke thus:

> Today many of our college educated youths have stopped doing physical work and exercises which in turn is leading to diseases at a very young age....Many people hold the wrong opinion that our ancestors knew not the modern forms of physical exercises. In reality, the Westerners are only re-introducing our old traditional exercises of our land with some modifications. …
>
> The modern military practices of Europeans are indebted to the practices in Mahabharata and are adapted for the convenience of the Europeans....Without teaching our children our national traditional physical exercises, the government physical instructors are teaching western physical exercises. These exercises similar to Hanuman Baski could be easily done by our dancing damsels of Thanjavur. They do not give the needed strength for our bodies. They are useless. They do not take into account the climatic condition of our nation and the body types of our youths. Because we follow blindly the Western physical exercises, we also pave way for the Westerners to talk ill of us. That this land which gave birth to Bhima and Arjuna should learn physical exercises from the West is the most humiliating thing that has befallen us. ...
>
> The present education system is biased toward improving the intellect but does not care about the physical improvement....This will lead us to become weaker and weaker. So, I am planning to create an 'Akhil Bharata Desiya Physical Improvement College'. These college networks created all over India would take traditional exercises of our land, which would improve both subtle and physical bodies. Our national methods being taught in educational institutions, will make the students practice complete Brahmacharya and be in control of their senses.
>
> … If we truly desire Swarajya then we should be in a position to protect our nation without the help of outsiders. We should be ready for military training. Among our youths how many would actually qualify for military recruitment? It is very little. Unless we develop a good physical exercise culture, we will not be fit for military recruitment. So, the needed training should be given to our youths by eminent citizens. Let us pray to Bhagwan that the society would come forward and do the needful so that our nation shall regain its old glory of being the nation of Bhimasenas and Arjunas.[147]

Another link in this chain of spiritual tradition was Paranjothi Mahan (1900–1981), who is said to be an important initiator of modern yogic practices in Tamil Nadu through Vethathri Maharishi (1911–2006). Born in a traditional Muslim family in Ramnad, he went on to establish the 'Universal Peace Temple'. He has to this day a large following both in Tamil Nadu and Malaysia. His famous tract was titled *I God*. He freely used Hindu spiritual terms to explain his Yogic practices which centred around Kundalini awakening.

In defining various modes of worship in relation to Dvaita to Advaita, Mahan Paranjothi considered the stage of the feeling of separateness between the self and Easwara as the point where that which is Advaita becoming Dvaita. Worshipping various forms and sacred icons as well as worship at Dargas he considers as 'Rupa Dvaita'. Then he speaks of a third category Arupa-Dvaita which involves just seeking the blessing without worshipping any form, concentration, yogic practices and contemplation. With full blossoming of Gnosis, those who understand their own true nature and need no further worship, are according to him, *Suddha-Advaitins* or pure non-dualists.[148]

The general psychology of the anti-Hindutva doctrine is perhaps an important factor we need to look into. The Dravidian, Nehruvian and Marxist thinking feel uncomfortable with deep diversity—the diversity of the worldviews. The multiplicity of Divine means multiplicity of worldviews. Dravidianism, Marxism and Nehruvianism are enamoured by monopolistic worldviews and see that as strength. They see the deep diversity as a weakness. Then they invent a 'Brahminical conspiracy' as the basis of this weakness. This is actually a throw-back to colonial protestant view of the so-called 'Brahminical Hinduism' as the result of 'priestcraft'.

Over the last five decades, the Dravidian and Nehruvian-Marxist political forces have encouraged the Salafi-Wahabi forms of political Islamism over these syncretic South Indian spiritual traditions, such that the samanvaya process with Islam has evolved in South India. In fact, these movements are quite unique to Indian soil and their destruction by fundamentalist forces of monoculture would be a great setback to the inner evolution of entire humanity. That today Hindutva is the only barrier protecting these traditions from the destructive onward marching army of monocultures is a telling commentary on theo-diversity protection dimension of Hindutva.

Ayodhya Movement and RSS Samanvaya

While often many in academia, polity and media become vulnerable to drawing false symmetry between Pan-Islamism and Hindutva, there is a crucial difference. Author-educationist Haroon Khalid writes:

> A few years ago, when I was working at an elite school in Lahore, one that has more than a hundred branches all over the country, I came across a poster in the corridor captioned "Muslim heroes". The poster had photographs of Muhammad bin Qasim, Mahmud Ghazni and Ahmad Shah Abdali. Walking back, I wondered why our heroes cannot be people like Baba Farid, Waris Shah and Bulleh Shah, who spread the message of peace and brought several religious communities together instead of shedding blood.[149]

But in the *Ekatmata Stotra* (*Unity Hymn*) of the RSS recited every morning in all RSS branches from Kashmir to Kanyakumari, they honour Kabir and Ibrahim Ras Khan. And as we shall see, the Hindutva movement does see in saints like Bulleh Shah their heroes.

The Hindutva movement makes heroes of every Muslim contributor to Indian culture: Ashfaqulla Khan, Muhammad Kareem Chagla, Bismillah Khan and of course A. P. J. Abdul Kalam. They are all honoured role models for the Hindutva movement—not just for Muslims but for all Indians. While the Islamist movement tries to exclude every Islamic sect as non-Muslim, the Hindutva movement accepts all Muslims who manifest the civilizational ethos of India as Hindus without them having to make any theological adjustments or compromises.

However, there are challenges. Islamist expansionism, the monopolistic component of Islamic theology and the aggressive proselytizing strategies facilitate gravitating towards militancy and terrorism because of the lure of jihad, Nehruvian-Marxist-Dravidian polity pampering the regressive, parochially radical elements of Islamic society with state power and political dividends resulting in ghettoization of Muslims—all these are serious problems that the samanvaya process faces with respect to Islam in India. Hindutva then emerges as the one voice in India that stands for dialogue with Islamic population.

The RSS took the Ayodhya issue to unite Hindus while at the same time opening up a dialogue with Muslims. This might look counterintuitive. But going through the series of events in the mid-1980s and the RSS mind-space through documents, this does seem to be the case.

Even before the Ayodhya issue took centre stage, the RSS was engaged in serious dialogue with the Indian Muslim thought leaders. It brought together in one platform some of the brightest Muslim minds and some of the sharpest Hindutva ideologues, the latter category being represented by personalities like Sita Ram Goel. In the November 1984 issue of *Manthan*—the official magazine of the Deendayal Research Institute (DRI), Sita Ram Goel came out with a 25-point answer to the question—how to forge unity without imposing uniformity. In that Goel stated bluntly:

> The Muslim community and culture have already partitioned the country by means of sustained violence. They are hostile to the national society and culture and reject all national norms in the name of a divinely ordained code of socio-political conduct. Foreign invaders and imperialists are their heroes and national freedom fighters are villains in their eyes.

And then he went on to give a solution:

> The Muslim community and culture can get integrated in an Indian nation only if Muslims concede that (i) Islam is only one of the many ways of worship and respects all other ways of worship; (ii) conversions to Islam except by conviction cause disruption and disharmony; (iii) Muslims in India should share the national version of Indian history and feel closer to their non-Muslim neighbours in India than to their distant co-religionists; (iv) Muslims should never mix religion with politics and stop demanding concessions in the name of cultural identity; and (v) accept that the destiny of India is to become a strong, secular and modern state rather than Islamic theocracy.

The person who was called to respond not only to Sita Ram Goel's paper but also to the paper by K. S. Sudarshan, who would become the future RSS Sarsanghachalak, and others, was Badruddin Tyabji, an illustrious bureaucrat who had served as Indian ambassador in Iran, Indonesia and Japan and retired as Secretary of External Affairs, Ministry of Government of India. He expressed openly that he did not agree with many of the Hindu panellists like K. S. Sudarshan. He stated that the note presented by K. S. Sudarshan (along with Dr Sujit Dhar) and 'their reading of history and of current events and thought seem to go completely counter to my own understanding of it' and that what he called their 'lyrical waxing' about 'age-old unity of India' as being 'their imagination and wishful thinking' outrunning their sense of reality. He characterized the note by Goel as 'venom', but with respect to the five points that Goel had made, he said:

> Curiously enough I find nothing in these five criteria with which any reasonable Muslim would disagree; I personally would certainly support them.

In 1986 crucial events drastically affected the Hindu-Muslim relations: Violent Islamist radicalism arising in Kashmir, the Shah Bano case and the Ayodhya temple issue. In all these, Islamic fundamentalism and Islamist expansionist politics were gaining popular ground among the Muslim masses in India, facilitated by the vote-bank-centric polity that was Nehruvianism.

In Kashmir, Islamist terrorism was taking shape as a very tangible entity with tactical support from the Pradesh Congress leader Mufti Mohammad Sayeed. But the factors which facilitated the Islamist takeover of Kashmir polity go back almost a decade. In 1975 there had been 125 Jamaat-e-Islami run schools with 550 teachers; then there were 1,000 evening schools. When the organization was proscribed by emergency brought by Indira Gandhi, the state government with the Centre's tactical silent approval made sure that the 'teachers were absorbed into government schools that offered them a new and wider platform to propagate their ideology'.[150] Navnita Chadha Behera who is the Assistant Director at Women in Security, Conflict Management and Peace (WISCOMP), New Delhi writes that Congress also attempted to foment religious extremism by propping up the Jamaat-e-Islami in the Kashmir valley in order to undercut the support base of the secular and moderate National Conference. But 'the secular and moderate National Conference' itself 'administered oaths to the common people on the holy *Koran* and a piece of rock salt, the symbol of Pakistan in Kashmir, to seek votes'.[151] So in 1986, every pretext was used by Islamists to strike terror in the heart of Hindus in Jammu and Kashmir. Defence analyst Praveen Swami writes:

> In office without a popular mandate, the successor-administration of Gul Mohammad Shah was compelled to turn to Islamists and opponents of India, notably Maulana Iftikhar Ansari, Mohammad Shafi Qureshi and Mohiuddin Salati, to win it legitimacy. In February 1986, Jammu and Kashmir saw its first post-Independence communal riots, in the form of attacks on Pandit-owned homes and on Hindu temples in the south Kashmir town of Anantnag. One investigation of the Anantnag riots revealed that members of secular parties—rather than the Jamaat-e-Islami—had played a key role in engineering the violence. In essence, the Islamists who had been decimated in the 1983 elections had been given political space again, this time by secular politicians who, without a popular mandate, sought to obtain legitimacy by tapping religious chauvinist sentiment.[152]

The Rajiv Gandhi government brought the Muslim Women (Protection of Rights on Divorce) Act, 1986 to overturn the Supreme Court judgment favouring monthly maintenance of ₹ 179.20 given to an aggrieved elderly divorced Muslim woman named Shah Bano. Initially, Rajiv Gandhi asked Arif Muhammad Khan, a minister in his cabinet, to defend the judgment in the court. But soon he made a U-turn. Later, Rajiv Gandhi yielded to the pressure. According to Arif Mohammad Khan, it was Najma Heptullah who pressurized Rajiv and made him change his mind.[153] But according to the biography of Ziaur Rahman Ansari, then Environmental Minister in Rajiv Gandhi's cabinet, written by his son, it was Z. R. Ansari who was instrumental in bringing the Act.[154]

The same year also saw the opening of the locks of the Sri Ram Janmabhoomi temple-Babri dome complex at Ayodhya by the order of the Faizabad sessions judge. The RSS decided to use the Ayodhya issue—with a non-functional mosque—to unite Hindus so that the aggressive Islamist agenda could be checked from re-emerging, through Hindu unity. The RSS thought that being a non-functional mosque for decades and a functional temple, the Muslim population in general would agree to hand over the domed structure and that would isolate the Islamist fundamentalist leadership with which the pseudo-secular polity was appeasing.

Towards this end, the RSS also sought to highlight what it considers as the common sacred civilizational space indigenous Islam has always had in India.

In 1987 *Manthan* published a detailed paper by Prof. Moazziz Ali Beg, a renowned humanistic psychologist from Aligarh Muslim University (AMU). Titled 'Proposals for the Creation of an Institute for Research on Sufi and Bhakti Tradition as Historico-Cultural and Psychological Basis for National Integration', this rather long article called for non-political transformation of national integration 'into psycho-social and cultural process' along with 'the need to gear our resources for advanced technology'. He wrote in the RSS magazine:

> Modern scientific psychology has definitely unveiled the possibility of spiritual understanding of truth and...it treats the subjective, the esoteric and the transcendental datum of our psyche as the proper filed of scientific inquiry. Sri Aurobindo had predicted long ago that the state of affairs existing in modern scientific psychology today was inevitable....To sum up the spirit of Sufi and Bhakti traditions, it may be said that they have tremendous resiliency to sustain the power of altruism and unselfish love by activating our inner resources of the self and through developing insight into those settled truths of human nature that unfailingly repel hatred, and purge those foul and morbid sentiments from within us that tend to alienate us from our fellow beings....If the Indian Nation can open the secret of unleashing this power, it would possibly attain virtual ideological supremacy in the world, and nations after nation would follow the lead in a total revolt against the insanity of nuclear competition.

In 1987 the New Year issue of *Manthan* was brought out as the 'Bhakti' special. The New Year issue the following year, in 1988, was brought out as a special on 'Our Sufi Heritage'. K. R. Malkani, the editor of *Manthan*, wrote the editorial, appreciating the Sufi heritage and highlighting it critically:

> Bhakti is as old as the Vedas; but it had its finest flowering in Chaitanya and Dnyaneshwar, Tulsi and Mira, Sur and Kabir. Sufism had its birth in Iran, but it had its fulfilment in India in the works of Farid and Lallan Faqir, Shah Abdul Latif and Bulleh Shah. Not all Sufis were alike, and Sufism ranged all the way from sugar-coated Islam to salted Vedanta. However, any abatement of fanaticism and ritualism was welcome; and all Sufis were humanist and liberal in varying degrees.[155]

The nine articles contained in the issue can serve as an indicator to the way Hindutva, as internalized by the RSS, approached dialogue with Muslims in India. The emphasis was on the national character of Indian Sufism. Islamic historian Muhammad Habib in his work on the Early Medieval Period has stated:

> India has added nothing to mystic thought, for no substantial addition to it was really possible. Her contributions have been primarily to the field of mystic practice, to the ways of mystic living.

In his paper on the interaction of India and Sufism as reflected in Indian literature, Prof. Attar Singh critiqued this statement of Habib and wrote:

> Such a total negation of the efflorescence of Islam in India may be acceptable if one confined oneself to writings mainly in Arabic and Persian inspired by the Indian environ which dealt with the doctrinal aspects of Islam and its institutionalisation in spite of a new sophistry and even casuistry such exercises acquired through contact with the Indian scholastic tradition. To this tremendous body of doctrinal literature which is attracting some critical attention may also be added the fantastic records, more imaginary than imaginative, relating to Indian Muslim saintology and hagiology revolving round the persons of the leading lights of various Sufi orders....Here one comes across the glimpses of inter-mingling of faiths, melting of the group boundaries and confluence of cultural strains in which Indian Sufism found its proper role and spiritual sanction.

The essay contains very insightful observations and analyses the innermost tensions present in the Muslim psyche in India in the most empathy filled way:

> If mysticism is the highest reach of human freedom in a closed world ordered by religion, the mystical poetry in Indian languages describes the still higher reaches of mystical universalism because it seeks to break loose from the conventions not only of religious orthodoxy but also from mystical identities as well. In this precisely

> lies the source of the vitality and also the greatest paradox of mystical poetry, the potential and power of mystical poetry in overwhelming the mystic's bondage to his order. There are countless examples of such tension in mystical poetry between the name-form identity on the one hand and the universal spirit on the other. This tension had a greater relevance in the case of Sufi poets or for that matter all Muslim poets of Indian languages because the Indian Muslim culture is animated by an anxiety complex widely shared by the community: The anxiety of a well-defined and distinctly organized community of getting lost in the ocean of conflicting, clashing and contradicting movements, ideas and ideologies that was India.

The paper on Sufi contribution to Punjabi poetry also brought out many insights and information which showed many facets of civilizational dynamics missed out or marginalized in conventional history telling. In this paper by Dr S. S. Kohli, the reader is told that Fardi-Addin Masud or Shaikh Farid (also known as Baba Farid) was the first Punjabi poet, and that the Adi Granth contains 112 shlokas of Baba Farid and four hymns. Baba Farid 'was a mystic of a very high order' and that his mysticism 'may be called Koranic mysticism'. At the same time, there were some key distinguishing elements:

> Muslim law prohibits the use of music, but in India, the Chishti order of Sufis, to which Baba Farid belonged, adopted it. The spiritual teacher of Baba Farid, Khwaja Qutb-ad-din, had held musical festivals.

Though the author quotes scholar S. R. Sharda, he does not bring in the Ijadist aspects here. The paper also provides a glimpse of a typical Hindu or Indian transformation of Sufi 'steps'—as a kind of inner spiritual steps:

> In a hymn of Guru Arjan Dev in Raga Maru, we find his interpretation of the spiritual states mentioned by the Sufis. The Guru says:... The *Shariat* religious conduct is the practice (of the Name of the Lord). The *Tariqar* (the Path) is to become detached and to search for the Lord (within). *Marifat* (spiritual wisdom), O seer is the conquest of the mind and then realise *Haqiqat* (Ultimate Reality), so that there is no death again.

This is a typical Hindu spiritual process of transforming an outer framework or ritual into a symbolism for inner spiritual process. Mircea Eliade categorized this as 'interiorization' for the academia and pointed out that it could be traced to Vedic literature and is a pan-Indian phenomenon that found its fullest expression in Tantric and Yogic literature.[156] Guru Arjan had extended to the Islamic structure another form of interiorization, thus bringing it into the inner cosmos of Bhakti sadhana. The paper also deals with subsequent developments of Sufi poetry—particularly the mystics Shah Hussain and Bulleh Shah.

> According to Dr S. R. Sharda, Shah Hussain's verse stands as a clear proof of almost complete victory of Indian Bhakti thought over the Islamic Sufism. But for the one point that Shah Hussain does not believe in the doctrine of transmigration of soul, his verse presents him as a Hindu Bhakt. His verse indicates that the influence of Hindu thought was at the highest peak at his time....The Sufi poetry is also rich in imagery and symbols. Whereas the images of Surahi and Piala, Tigris and Euphrates were popular in Persian Sufi Poetry, the popular images in Punjabi Sufi poetry are those of Trinjan (sisters of the spinning wheel) and Jhanan (Chenab the river of love). Whereas romance of Heer and Ranjha has attracted the Qissa poets, it has given the symbols of Heer (Ashiq, lover) and Ranjha (Maashuq-Beloved) to the Sufi poets. The seeker is symbolised as Heer, who pins to meet her beloved Ranjha.... Bulleh Shah has used the symbols of Krishna and Rama for God.[157]

Yet another paper by poetess Prabhjot Kaur brings out the influence of Bulleh Shah on subsequent Punjabi poets from Bhai Vir Singh to Smt. Amrita Pritam and the writer herself. The paper on the influence of Sufi poetry on the development of Hindi literature has this interesting passage:

> The reflexive Hinduization of Sufism of Central Asian type, led to the organic growth of Indianization, to the composite Hindu-Muslim or Hindustani Renaissance during the four centuries (10–14 c. A.D.) of medieval India. The Sufi poets adopted the Hindu Aakhyayikas (love tales) deeply embedded in the collective unconscious of the folk-psyche. They neither hurt the religious sentiments of the Hindus nor coerced their world view through distortions or deceptions. Rather they regained the human innocence and the restlessness in human life through spiritual development.[158]

The article by Keval Ram Malkani (1921–2003) then editor of *Manthan* tries to contextualize Sufi movement in India in the context of what he termed 'Perennial Philosophy':

> ...Islam was a great and powerful movement. But with its formalism and fixity, it did not satisfy many thinking and feeling Muslims. On the other hand, many of them were drawn to the pre-Islamic mystic though of Arabia, Iran, Greece and India. They tried to integrate the old Perennial Philosophy with the new faith. The result was Sufism. But in the process many Sufis including Mansur in Iran and Sarmad

> in India—had to pay with their life. Although all Sufis are different from orthodox Muslims, there are any number of Sufi orders, with a wide range of ideological differences....Sufis accept life. Physical love (Ishq Majazi or Vishay-ananda), they believe can, by gradual stages, grow into divine love (Ishq Haqiqi or Brahm-ananda.)...Not only in Turkey and Iran, but in India also, some Sufi saints stood up to the kings. Nizamuddin refused to see Allauddin Khilji. Sheikh Fakhruddin Zarradi told Mohammed Tughlaq to "control your anger of wild animals". And Shaikh Bayazid took Aurangzeb to task for not giving his daughters in marriage, when even the Prophet had married off his daughter Fatima. Mansur said "Anal Huq" (Aham Brahma Asmi). And many Sufis look upon his "Masnavi" as the quintessence of the Koran, the Koran itself in Pahlavi, old Persian....Shaikh Abdul Quddus of India once wrote that concealed polytheism (of Sufis) was breaking the back of (orthodox) Muslims; that the destruction of the external aspect of religion sometimes becomes essential and it was for this reason that some men of God had shaved their beards, put on the sacred thread and gone into temples....In India the Bhajans moved and influenced many Sufis.[159]

At the end of the paper, Malkani quotes Sarmad. The special issue of the RSS magazine on Sufi heritage of India also had a paper on the influence of Sufism on Sindhi literature and another on Bengali literature. In the latter, the paper brought out the influence the poetry of Hafiz had on Rabindranath Tagore. According to Tagore, for his father 'the verses of the Upanishads were the light of the morn and Hafiz's poetry was his morning sun'.[160]

Then in June 1988 Malkani drafted a concept paper titled 'Resolving Religio-Cultural Differences in the Service of the Indian People'. Then it was circulated to 'over a hundred' thought leaders. Even Asghar Ali Engineer, a harsh critic of Hindutva, was so impressed by the draft that he wrote: 'This draft document, I must say, is remarkably balanced and certainly can become the basis for a dialogue with the brothers of the majority community.'[161] The tone of Malkani's paper can be gauged from the passage given below:

> Many Muslims look upon invaders and tyrants, who happened to be Muslim as welcome carriers of Islam....But at the same time the average Hindu should shed the idea that there were no Muslims who could be accepted as national heroes. Some of them object even to Akbar....Apart from Akbar, there were saints like Kabir and Chishti, statesmen like Abdul Fazal and Safdarjang, savants like Dara and Khusrau, poets like Jayasi and Rahiman, Bulleh Shah and Abdul Latif, Lallan Faqir and Habba Khatun. School texts should glorify these men—and street names should consecrate their memory.

In its December 1988 issue, *Manthan* again came with responses of various thought leaders—both Hindus and Muslims—to this draft submitted by Malkani.

The issue of *Manthan* dated February 1989 featured as its cover story: 'A Long Chat with Some Bright Young Men of Aligarh Muslim University', which covered the interaction of its editor K. R. Malkani with students of AMU who actually belonged to the Student's Islamic Organisation of India. In the question-answer session between the sides, the last two questions and the answers that Sri Malkani gave are interesting and relevant even today. To the question if he believed in God, Malkani answered:

> I do not believe in any god living in seventh heaven or swimming in Kshir sagar. I would say that the whole Brahmanda or the cosmos, the principle informing it and the spirit animating it is God. The popular concept of God is the invention of man. For long ages man has lived in fear and terror....He needed to think of a higher beneficent power protecting him. Such a comforting was a source of great solace and reassurance in an uncertain world....God is a working hypothesis. Without the concept of an almighty, all-knowing, all-merciful God helping him along, Man would not have been able to stand up and advance. Civilization would not have been possible. The greatest invention of man is not the fire or the wheel or even zero but God.

Then the final question from a student was on the future of Islam and if Malkani saw a bright future for it. The answer Malkani gave, though sounding utopian, contained a vision that is consistent with the universal vision of Hindutva:

> The world is moving in the direction of a global village, a world government. Perhaps a new and higher humanism will become the new religion of mankind. One cannot say what contribution Hinduism, Islam, Christianity, Judaism, Taoism or Science will make to the emergence and evolution of this New Religion. It will depend upon the intrinsic worth and inherent strength of the various ideas and institutions.

The issue of *Manthan* dated March 1989 is quite important for two papers in it. One was written by AMU psychologists Dr Moazziz Ali Beg and Dr Muhammad Ilyas Khan. Another was a discussion between Sita Ram Goel and Maulana Wahiduddin Khan on the Rushdie-Khomeini issue. The meeting had been originally organized in February 1989. The Maulana, who was the director of the Islamic Centre, initiated the discussion. Here are excerpts from the report of *Manthan* on the entire discussion:

> (Maulana) said he was hundred percent opposed to Rushdie's book and also hundred percent opposed to Khomeini's fatwa. He had read the book and it was full of abuse,

insult and innuendo....This book is not readable. The best reply to a book like that would have been to ignore it. Muslims had made the mistake of reacting to it.... Khomeini is not Islam. His fatwa is hundred percent un-Islamic. Islamic laws apply to Muslim lands only. And there is no punishment without trial. It was unfortunate that Muslims had become a clamorous group.

Sita Ram Goel, the noted Hindutva thinker, author and historian in his own right, started by saying he agreed with Maulana. Rushdie's book was 'bad, trashy'. Then he went on to say:

But it would be wrong to condemn a book without reading it....However, it is a fact that Mohammed got his literary critics murdered. One of them was the poetess Asma bin Marwan while she was suckling her child. Another was Abu Afak, an aged poet. Anybody giving up Islam is considered fit for being stoned to death. These things go counter to all canons of ethics....If I understand Rushdie aright, he is writing from the angle of men who opposed Mohammed and his teachings. These people were violently put down and many of them resented it. Rushdie is voicing their feelings. Religion should not be viewed as a candle-stick which can melt away under the fire of criticism. At the centre of Islam is Mohammed and not Allah....Rushdie is writing as a "Kafir", giving expression to the feelings of the defeated non-Muslims of Mohammed's time. Persian and Urdu poetry has long taken such liberties. In this situation, Khomeini has behaved like a village autocrat....Muslims should abide by Gandhiji's advice and sheath their sword. They must accept universal ethics and accept Reason.

In May 1989, *Manthan* brought out a special issue on the RSS in which observations on the RSS by leading Muslim intellectuals were published.

These contained voices that strongly criticized and dismissed the RSS but those also were published without any content being edited out. For example, Prof. Mohammed Shafi Agwani, then Vice Chancellor of JNU, gave the magazine a two-lined message: 'From what I know about the RSS, I believe its role, in the context of national unity, has been negative.' Asghar Ali Engineer, while calling the RSS cadre 'highly patriotic and wants to see this country built on strong foundations', said that he found that 'the RSS indulges in self-righteousness rather too much', which, he observed, 'would not help in making India strong'. Prefiguring Shashi Tharoor's vociferous view of Hindutva being different from Hindu, he stated:

It is true that Hindu religion by and large is non-doctrinaire, but Hindus in practice are as dogmatic as any other people could be. The Hindu praxis is far from being

> non-doctrinaire. I have great respect for Hindu religion and Hindu thinkers and the philosophy of Vedanta. It is part of my heritage....Hinduism is most tolerant of other religious groups. The RSS on the other hand is reducing it to intolerant dogma....The RSS should learn from true Hinduism and set an example of real non-doctrinaire approach and bring others to that level.

Well-known film critic and pro-left intellectual Iqbal Masood wrote that though he had 'profound differences of ideology with the RSS and its founders', he 'must set this down for record' that he did 'respect the RSS as a disciplined force on the national scene today' and that while having differences with it, it was 'also possible to have dialogue with it'. He found Nanaji Deshmukh and K. R. Malkani 'good human beings with a deep concern for a resurrection of Indian polity and culture'.

A very penetrating observation was made by Dr K. S. Durrany, who had authored many books on Islam. He was then with the Delhi-based Indian Institute of Islamic Studies. He wrote:

> The RSS does not preach that Hinduism is the only true religion in the world. The concept of finality and paramountcy of a single shade of divine revelation has always been alien to Hinduism and it appears that the RSS wants to retain that religious diversity with a sense of cultural unity throughout the length and breadth of the country. The recent initiative...(vide *Manthan* June 1988) suggests that the RSS has a keen desire to keep friendly relations with different religious denominations of the country. Islamic scholars like Maulana Wahiduddin Khan and Asghar Ali Engineer have appreciated these efforts as a good beginning to resolve the Hindu-Muslim differences....My personal experiences as a Muslim do not find RSS as against the Muslim interest and their Islamic faith. The stalwarts of RSS like Sri Nanaji Deshmukh talk about humanism rather than Hinduism or Hindu culture and civilization. It is not correct to say that the RSS is Hinduizing India, but the fact remains that the sub-continent is a Hindu India.

Dr Durrany also cautioned the RSS. The RSS could serve the country better if it champions the cause of suffering humanity at the hands of exploiters—Hindus, Muslims or modernists. He referred to the 'model commune' in Gonda, Uttar Pradesh (where Nanaji Deshmukh worked) where Muslim inhabitants turned to the RSS rather than their own religious courts to settle family disputes. He ended his observations by asking the RSS to befriend 'the exploited people...in search of their existential identity for self-respect'.

More important than the correctness of the views or otherwise, is the fact that even as the RSS was taking the Sri Ram Janmabhoomi movement on a large scale for Hindu consolidation, it was also earnestly engaging with the Muslim community in an intense dialogue. However, the leftist historians, academicians and a dominant section of the media checkmated these efforts of the RSS to engage in a dialogue with the Muslim community. This effectively scuttled the possibility of a settlement between Hindus and Muslims on their three holiest sacred spots being returned and thus effectively ending the communal animosity between the two communities in India.

Eminent archaeologist K. K. Muhammed has pointed this out in his autobiography and later in his interview for *Swarajya* magazine:

> When excavation was undertaken at Ayodhya by Dr B. B. Lal, I was the only Muslim archaeologist in the team. At that time, these controversies were not there. When the controversy came up, the JNU historians suppressed some of our crucial discoveries....the left historians and a section of the media played with facts, suppressing them and spreading the false notion that there was nothing under the Babri. Had they acknowledged the truth then, a lot of unpleasant events would not have happened. In fact, I know that many Muslim groups were willing to accept the truth, honour the sentiments of the fraternal Hindu community and work out a compromise. But the left historians and a section of the media thwarted it. So I wrote right then to the media, stating the facts. As a government servant, one should have obtained the permission to write to the media. But the government would not give me permission. Anyhow, I wrote a letter to the editor of the Indian Express, disclosing the facts. Then, explanation was sought by the department about my action. Fortunately, I was not suspended, but I was transferred from the eastern coast to the western one. It was to Goa. Then, in 1997, I was transferred to Bihar.[162]

On 30 October and 2 November 1990, the police force under the direct command of then Chief Minister of Uttar Pradesh, Mulayam Singh Yadav had opened fire on unarmed Karsevaks. It was a massacre. In the next elections to the state, the Mulayam government was ousted, and in June 1991, the BJP government was sworn in. Kalyan Singh became the Chief Minister. In October 1991, the Kalyan Singh government acquired a total of 2.77 acres of land adjoining the Ayodhya site for tourism development. It was immediately contested in the Allahabad High Court.

The Government in its rejoinder said that the land was urgently required for developing facilities for tourists and pilgrims who visit Ayodhya for the six-week Kartik Mela starting on 18 November. After hearing the arguments, Justice Satish Chandra Mathur, Justice Brijesh Kumar and Justice Syed Haider

Abbas held that the government was authorised to acquire land for the stated purpose—the development of tourism and facilities for pilgrims. However, in the light of the objections raised by the Waqf Board lawyers, the judges passed the interim order, pending final judgment, prohibiting the transfer of the acquired land to any person or organization, or its use for any permanent construction.[163] The Supreme Court itself assured both the sides in its 15 November 1991 order that the disposal in the Kalyan Singh government's Land Acquisition Act would be given 'sometime in December of this year', i.e., 1991.

Meanwhile the levelling activities in the acquired area in the beginning of 1992 brought out significant archaeological discoveries. The structures which came to be revealed like 'a big hoard of beautifully carved buff sandstone pieces', 'a huge burnt brick wall of more than a dozen courses', etc., were studied by professional archaeologists Dr Y. D. Sharma (former Deputy Director General, Archaeological Survey of India), Dr K. M. Srivastava (former Director, ASI), Dr S. P. Gupta (former Director, Allahabad Museum) and a team of eminent historians. They concluded that there should have existed a temple of Nagara style.[164]

Even as evidence started piling up for the existence of a previous temple, far from triumphalism, Kalyan Singh himself was asking Muslims to agree to an amicable settlement. In an interview given to *Hindu Vishwa*, the official magazine of Visva Hindu Parishad (VHP), Kalyan Singh made the following emotional statement:

> And I Kalyan Singh will be the first to put bricks on my head and carry it to the site. History has given Hindus an opportunity to do kar seva for the mosque and Muslims for the Mandir. I will place the first bricks of the foundation. From such a Mandir and Masjid, will emerge the real unity between Hindus and Muslims.[165]

Then on 6 December 1992, the demolition happened. Since then, it has been used to negatively stereotype the Hindutva movement as anti-Muslim. The fact remains that the Karsevaks assembled at Ayodhya never touched a single functional mosque well within Ayodhya. They had been let down by the system in a way.

Despite the demolition, the Hindutva movement during Ayodhya has been the single largest and most honest moment of dialogue with Muslim community.

For the Islamic community led to believe that what was demolished was actually a mosque, the event proved to be traumatic. Since then, the INC, Dravidianist Dravidar Kazhagam, Dravida Munnetra Kazhagam (DMK) and Marxist political parties (CPI, CPI-M & CPI-ML) have made themselves ideological and political partners of radical and fundamentalist Islamist forces.

Jihad as it Unfolds in South India

The way jihad has been unleashed in a systematic manner on Hindu activists in South India is a classic model of how Islamist encounters with Hindutva turn murderous. The South Indian state of Tamil Nadu has always been showcased by its Dravidianist rulers as model of 'communal harmony'. But a closer look reveals an efficiently coordinated elimination of Hindu activists.

On the night of 19 September 2013, the watchman said that he saw three youths in their twenties calmly walk around. One held the watchman while the two others zeroed in on their target. Their target was Mr Ramesh—a leading auditor and state general secretary of the Tamil Nadu BJP. They twisted his hand at an impossible angle, breaking it. Then they slammed his head against the wall. Then they started to slit his throat even as they were raining cuts against the struggling body of the fifty-three-year-old man. And when it was all over, the lifeless body lay down in a pool of blood with 23 cuts and a disfigured head. The killers did not run away. They simply walked and dissolved into the night of Salem—a prominent city in Tamil Nadu. And the night was still young when the auditor was no more: 9.30 p.m. It happened on a Friday in the Islamic holy month of Ramadan.[166]

Just weeks before this gruesome murder, 45-year-old Vellaiappan—a Hindu Front functionary, who was active in combating proselytizing and reclaiming the occupied temple lands, was killed in Vellore on 1 July 2013. The murder happened at a public place and in full view of the public.[167] On an early April morning in 2013, at Nagercoil in Kanyakumari district, a veteran BJP leader, who was respected by all communities and known for his soft nature, was attacked by a gang. With the arrest of four youths, who were behind this incident, a network comprising Islamists not just from Kanyakumari but from the Melapalayam area of Thirunelveli district became evident.[168] In the late night of 6 November 2012, Mr Anand, an RSS functionary, was attacked by Islamists. Ten days later the police arrested Syyed Abu Tahir (19) near Coimbatore.[169]

The sustained attacks and elimination of Hindu activists in the state of Tamil Nadu provides a classic example of how the anti-Hindu forces use the complacency of a generally de-Hinduized polity like the one in Tamil Nadu to execute their expansionist monopolistic agendas. Dravidianist parties, Nehruvian Congress and Marxist forces joined hands to create the political infrastructure that played down such killings. The ultimate aim of the killing of such Hindutva forces, as shall be seen, is to eliminate theo-diversity. In a curious way, these victims of jihadist terror in South India have also become the human price that the indigenous resistance must pay for resisting the takeover of a diversity nurturing spiritual culture by the monopolistic monocultures.

The 2012–2013 violence that became sensational for some time in Tamil Nadu has a prequel. During the last cycle of engineered violence, pan-Islamic forces used a combination of Dravidian polity, communal politics and terrorism to entrench their grip on the Tamil society, and it climaxed with the Coimbatore bomb blast. The events which happened prior to the Coimbatore bomb blast on 1998 have an uncanny resemblance to the present acts of violence.

Targeted Killings to RDX Bomb Blasts

One of the cherished arguments of anti-Hindutva forces is that Islamist terrorist activities started only after the 1992 demolition of the disputed structure. But the Islamist attacks on Hindu activists started much before that. A full decade before the demolition, the murderous attempts on the life of Hindu activists had started in Tamil Nadu.

In 1982 Badsha, who would later become a powerful Islamist leader, attacked a group of Hindu leaders returning from a meeting at Coimbatore. Then two years later, on 18 July 1984, in full public view at the Madurai railway station, Rama Gopalan, a prominent Hindu leader of Hindu Front—a vocal Hindu organization that combated conversions and Dravidianist propaganda, was attacked by the same Badsha. Though he was caught red-handed, he could not be convicted. This gave the Islamist forces their first taste of victory over the judicial system in Tamil Nadu.[170]

Within two years, the radical elements were gathered by one extremist preacher Ahmed Ali alias Palani Baba. In 1986 the first Islamic terrorist organization was formed—the All India Jihad Council (AIJC). Then the attacks started becoming virulent and systematic. On 30 August 1989, Veera Ganesh, a prominent Hindu Front worker was killed. Then on 5 September 1991, Veera Shiva, another Hindu Front functionary, was killed. All these killings happened in and around Coimbatore—the commercial hub of Tamil Nadu. Along with AIJC, another organization had come into being namely, the Al-Ummah.

One of the cherished and oft-repeated myth is that it was the demolition that triggered the bomb explosions. The fact that even months before the demolition happened, the jihadists had started preparing for the bomb blasts falsifies this pseudo-secular contention. The Tamil Nadu police arrested the Al-Ummah members Hyder Ali (38), Abdul Mudalif (47), Mohammed Abdul Khader (50) and Zakir Hussain (38) in October 1998 when they were smuggling explosives from Kerala on a stolen car. And this happened on 29 October 1992, a month before the demolition.[171]

The Kerala connection surfacing would later evolve into an elaborate, coordinated network later. During these years in Kerala, Abdul Nasser Madani was the ideologue. He was the counterpart of Palani Baba in Kerala. His organization, the Islamic Sevak Sangh (ISS) was proscribed in 1993. He rechristened his organization as the People's Democratic Party (PDP). At the same time the National Development Front (NDF) was born. Though technically two different organizations, as observed by A. V. George, Assistant Commissioner of Police, Ernakulam, Kerala, the NDF and the PDP units had cooperated with each other to carry out extremist activities.[172]

Neera Rawat, who was the City Police Commissioner, Kozhikode from 22 March 1997 to 16 May 1999, had prepared a confidential dossier on NDF activities. According to the information gathered by her, the Islamic State of Iraq (ISI) and Iran were sponsoring the NDF.[173] She also revealed that the Special Branch had submitted reports regarding the transportation of arms in ambulance vans. The significance of this piece of information would become clear later. In August 1993, RDX was used to destroy the RSS state headquarters, killing 11 persons. Then in October 1994, the State President of Hindu Front Mr Rajagopalan was dragged out of his house and killed. In April 1995, the headquarters of Hindu Front at Chennai were blasted using RDX. Individual killings also continued. Then in July 1995, a parcel bomb killed the wife of the District President of Hindu Front. Jihadist activities in and around Coimbatore continued with a renewed vigour.

In an extraordinarily insightful study of the southern jihad, BJP noted the ideological blind spot in the Dravidianist ideology that made the parties in power irrespective of the party affiliation look over the jihad activities. In July 1995 the BJP's parliamentary delegation visited Tamil Nadu, and the then leader of the Opposition in the Rajya Sabha Sikander Bakht observed in his report how 'the political climate in TN…marked by the influence of separatist Dravidian movement, which is mostly based on anti-Hindu (views)' made 'the powerful Dravidian parties' frown upon 'any pro-Hindu, nationalist activities'. Bakht's report further noted how 'a section of the AIADMK was also reported to have a sort of allergy towards Hindu organizations' and that 'the Al-Ummah led by Syed Ahmed Batcha of Coimbatore' enjoys the support of various political parties 'including some ruling AIADMK leaders'. The 1995 report surprisingly revealed the globalization attempt of the South-based jihad forces, noting how no action was taken against the founder of the AIJC, who had written a 'letter appealing to the international Islamic community for funds to carry on his fight against Hindu organizations' which was 'widely distributed in Gulf countries'. The report pointed out that the Tamil Nadu-based jihadist elements were now 'working in collaboration with the Kerala ISS chief Madani'.[174]

Meanwhile, a quasi-political offshoot had emerged from the 'Tamil Nadu Muslim Munnetra Kazhagam' (TMMK), which stated that it eschewed the violent path of Al-Ummah. But as events later showed, it was more an effort for a division of labour to facilitate an atmosphere conducive to Islamist operations than for democratizing their community. The All India Anna Dravida Munnetra Kazhagam (AIADMK) regime then was perceived as notoriously corrupt and inept by the general public. So, when it started making tentative steps to curb jihadist terror, it was too late. The police had set security check posts in some strategic points in areas like Kottamedu at Coimbatore. The media persons in Tamil Nadu close to DMK charged the AIADMK of isolating the Muslims. The DMK made the removal of the check posts part of its poll deal, which it struck with the TMMK in exchange for Muslim votes. When the DMK came to power, a mob of Islamists was allowed to dismantle the check posts and then a fresh round of nightmare began for Coimbatore.

In the period of 1989–1997, 42 Hindus had been murdered in the Coimbatore region by Islamists, with random killing of Hindus somewhere to 'instill fear' like the killing of five Hindus in one day (2 September 1997)[175] and many were targeted executions of Hindu activists. The organization that was carrying out these murders was Al-Ummah. Resolutely ignoring all Intelligence Bureau (IB) warnings, on 28 January 1997, Badsha and four others from Coimbatore jail were released by the DMK regime following its decision to withdraw the TADA cases.[176] Interestingly the Madras film industry even tried to glorify the jihadist by making a blockbuster in his name—Badsha starring Tamil superstar Rajnikanth. But such little acts of appeasement by Kollywood did not prevent Al-Ummah from throwing pipe-bombs at director Mani Ratnam's house, as a warning against the films he directed such as *Roja* and *Bombay*, which spoke against terrorism in Kashmir and the need for communal harmony after the Mumbai riots. Meanwhile, Badsha grew mysteriously stronger, with funds flowing in and state power turning a blind eye. He was giving, in the 1990s, ₹ 5,000 per month for his 'boys' and 100 cc motorcycles were gifted for the 'higher ups'.[177]

An early morning of November 1997 saw an altercation between two bike riding Al-Ummah youths and a policeman. This was followed by the Al-Ummah youths declaring that they would extract revenge. Then the threat was made real by a public execution of a police constable, Mr Selvaraj. To the shocked media and public, the images of the wives of policemen demanding security for their husbands clearly showed the pathetic condition to which law and order had been reduced. Two days after the brutal execution of constable Selvaraj, the Tamil Nadu Chief Minister Karunanidhi came out with an extraordinarily callous statement that the policemen should not have harassed the youths just for the sake of statistics.[178] Riots broke out in Coimbatore following the murder of Selvaraj. And then on Valentine's Day in 1998, Coimbatore saw 76 deaths due to a meticulously planned serial bombing—a terror plot code named 'Allahu Akbar'.[179] It was not an attack out of the blue. There had been enough early warnings about the possibility of such an occurrence. In the 20 months prior to the 14 February 1998 bomb blast, there have been 21 bomb explosions—some accidental and some by local Tamil groups, but the most sophisticated and well-coordinated bomb blasts, like the one in the Express trains at Tiruchi and Erode on the same day in 1997 were carried out by Al-Ummah with logistics from Kerala.[180] Soon after this mega-terror attack, the jihadists struck again. In March 1998, Prof, Paramasivam, a soft-spoken gentleman who had helped all students irrespective of their community, was executed brutally in public. Three Islamist youths were arrested initially.[181]

After the 1998 bomb blasts, an embarrassed DMK which had severe electoral reverses in the Parliament elections, allowed the police to crack down on Islamist forces. Meanwhile the political changes with DMK entering and AIADMK exiting the National Democratic Alliance (NDA) reinforced the DMK government's drive against Islamic terror network in the state. A relative period of vigil followed, though not without a few targeted murders by Al-Ummah elements, now mostly on the run. The 2001 election reverses suffered by DMK in Tamil Nadu State Assembly elections, made the DMK again move towards the minority appeasement policy and the AIADMK, now in power, started warming up towards BJP.

Meanwhile, the Islamist forces had started working earnestly towards regrouping, realignment and restructuring their strategies. A massive outreach programme was launched. Former jihadists, who were now ageing, started becoming evangelists for Islam. On television, in print as well as digital media, the Islamists started a vigorous propaganda that Islam was a religion of peace and that Islamic youths were targeted by an anti-Islamic regime. Every social ill was magnified and presented through the theological prism of Islamic monotheism. It was a virulent form of Islam that was being propagated now.

Tamil Nadu BJP as well as Hindu outfits seemed to have left everything in the hands of state agencies. While Islamists worked overtime to remove the stigma of terror, create a positive image in public psyche even as making their terror infrastructure ever more robust, Hindu movements in Tamil Nadu started getting lethargic. Unlike the observant 1995 BJP team and later the Akhil Bharatiya Vidyarthi Parishad (ABVP), which produced the detailed study of jihad terrorism in the state, the BJP of early 2000 was more worried about the benefits of power than about getting justice to the victims of jihadist terror in Tamil Nadu. Or at least that is the scenario one perceives through the happenings. Throughout the years that the BJP was in power, Islamists toiled hard building networks in the so-called secular community.

In 2001 the DMK lost the state elections and AIADMK won. TMMK had supported AIADMK. Islamists across South India, in a significant move, founded two major organizations in Tamil Nadu and Karnataka. They were given deceptively secular names namely Manitha Neethi Pasarai (MNP) and Karnataka Forum for Dignity (KFD). They were coordinated by NDF of Kerala. In 2002 all the six persons accused of murdering the Madurai College Professor, K. R. Paramasivam, were acquitted by a Madurai court today. Of the six accused, one young person raised his hands and shouted in triumph an Islamist slogan. His name was 'Police' Fakruddin.[182] In 2013, 11 years later, Tamil Nadu police would announce him as a major suspect in the inhuman killing of auditor Ramesh. In 2003 all eight Al-Ummah men were acquitted in the Selvaraj murder case.[183] In February 2003 and again in March 2003, 16 Al-Ummah men were acquitted because the police 'had failed to prove the charges beyond reasonable doubt'.[184]

While the murder accused were rescued through professional legal assistance and even when jailed, their comforts and their families' economic security were taken care of, what about the plight of those killed by terrorists? Here is a sample. It was reported in 2010 that P. Sivanandi, Inspector General of Police, West Zone, after persistent personal efforts and toil, tracked down Selvaraj's wife and daughter, who were found living in an impoverished state. A Hindu father who had lost his only son in the Coimbatore bomb blast was offered the post of attendant at the Government Medical Hospital at Coimbatore. There he was entrusted the care of a person in a wheelchair. He was required to get the patient hot water and tiffin; take him in the wheelchair to the bathroom, and serve all his needs. And the person in the wheelchair was none other than Abdul Nasser Madani or Madani, the main accused in the bomb blast that killed his son.[185] Such insensitivity towards victims was matched by exuding compassion towards the terror-accused.

In 2002 Syed Munir Hoda, IAS, was made Home Secretary for the Chief Minister Jayalalithaa, who entered into a tactical alliance with the TMMK for elections.[186] Later, Hoda would stand accused for helping Abdul Nasser Madani by lifting the ban on Madani's movements, enabling the high-profile prisoner to seek medical treatment.[187]

As Madani was moved out of jail, his capabilities to communicate with Islamist elements outside increased. On 2 May 2003, at the coastal village of

Marad, Kerala, eight Hindu fishermen were massacred brutally by Islamists. Investigative officers revealed before the Thomas Commission appointed by the Kerala government that one of the master minds of the massacre, Mohammed Nafi had met Abdul Nazar Madani in the Coimbatore Central Prison, eight times before the massacre.[188] The Commission later discovered that another IAS officer, Sooraj was responsible for the failure of the civil administration in preventing the Marad massacre, and pointed out that 'the allegation of communalism' raised against him could not be ignored and required to be enquired into by the State government.[189]

Should the assistance provided to Madani by IAS Munir Hoda in 2002, which allowed him to communicate with one of the architects of Marad massacre, and the act of omission by another IAS officer, Sooraj, which allowed the massacre to happen be taken as mere coincidences? It shows that the new reach of Islamist activities in the higher corridors of power in South India which can, in turn, provide jihad more capacity to strike at will.

In 2004 the AIADMK moved closer to having an electoral alliance with the BJP. It was then that the CM discovered the transgression of Hoda and sacked him. While the Islamist organizations raised a hue and cry, in 2004 elections, the NDA was defeated in the Parliament polls, and in Tamil Nadu, the NDA got washed out in all 40 constituencies. In 2004 the police busted a camp of MNP at a village in Cuddalore in Tamil Nadu. According to the police sources, the MNP was said to have a nationwide network and was suspected to have links with the Jammu and Kashmir Liberation Front of Yasin Malik, acting as a recruiting agency to beef up the terrorist forces in Jammu and Kashmir.[190]

Incidentally, the original flag of MNP was that of the Jammu and Kashmir Liberation Front, which was later slightly modified with a single star. In 2005 a bus was burnt near Kalamassery, Kerala. One of the accused here was Thadiyantavide Nazeer. He was also involved in planting bombs in the Coimbatore Press Club and blasts in Kozhikode bus stand to secure Madani's arrest. A native of Kerala, he had become the southern operations commander of Lashkar-e-Toiba. When at last he was arrested in 2009 by the Bangalore police, the Ministry of Home Affairs (MHA) decided to acknowledge this fact only after a week.[191]

Though in jail, Madani was spreading the Islamist network effectively across states. His supporters in Tamil Nadu were simultaneously creating a huge pressure through the human rights industry to secure his release. Left-wing writers, human rights lobbyists and Islamists came together to sign petitions for the release of Madani. Though Nazeer had attempted to murder E. K. Nayanar, then Kerala Chief Minister, the electoral alignment made the Marxist Party bat for Madani's release. By March 2006, the Kerala Legislative

Assembly passed a resolution supported by both Congress and Marxists for the release of Madani, who was then in Coimbatore jail.[192]

In 2006 the AIADMK was defeated, and the DMK government came to power in the state.

Chastened already in 2001, the DMK government returned to its original pro-Islamist stand with a born-again vigour. It promptly reinstated Hoda as the Home Secretary. In the neighbouring Kerala, the Left Democratic Front (LDF) had joined hands with Madani's political outfit, now named PDP. By July 2006, the DMK government gave the green signal to Islamists by allowing a costly Ayurvedic treatment for Madani, which involved ten masseurs and four senior Ayurvedic doctors. The 35-day treatment cost ₹ 50,000 then, and no prizes for guessing who paid the bill.[193] In the early hours of 22 July 2006, the Coimbatore police arrested five suspected members of the MNP and seized IEDs and detonators besides surveillance notes and maps from them. The police said the five had planned to blow up the Coimbatore Government Hospital, the railway station, the collectorate and the district police office. In August 2006, the Assistant Commissioner of Police, Coimbatore, V. Ratnasabapathy, revealed a plot of terror attack on Coimbatore city. He was promptly transferred by the state government. According to the police sources, the TMMK came to the rescue of MNP and pressurized the DMK to transfer the Assistant Commissioner of Police (ACP). The cases were weakened, the policemen were harassed and the arrested terror-accused were released.[194]

This gesture sent a green signal to Islamists and a warning signal to the police. Police officials had anonymously started talking to the press about how 'barely two weeks after it was sworn in, Tamil Nadu's DMK government had ordered that cases be dropped against 12 Muslim fundamentalists, all followers of Kichaan Buhari, an Al Umma sympathizer and key accused in the Coimbatore serial blasts'. These accused were initially detained under the National Security Act (NSA) and yet had managed to obtain bail. Now the epicentre of jihadist activities was shifting to Melapalayam in the hot dusty district of Tirunelveli. Soon the senior policemen in Tirunelveli were shocked by what they saw as the DMK government's 'blatant sympathy' for the Muslim fundamentalists.[195]

The fears of the police personnel became prophetic. Soon there were attacks not only on Hindu leaders but liberal Muslims. In July 2006, a head constable who went to arrest a terror accused inside Melapalayam area was beaten and chased away.[196] In November 2006, violent attacks by jihadist prisoners on fellow Hindu prisoners and jail officials led to their transfer out of Madurai prison.[197] On 17 Dec. 2006, M. R. Gandhi, a BJP leader in Kanyakumari, on his way back from a meeting, was attacked at night by a mob of Islamists who threatened to burn him alive.[198] The same night the Islamists also made their presence felt at Thenkasi, where Kumara Pandiyan—a prominent Hindu Front leader was murdered by an Islamist. He was opposing a plan to build a mosque opposite the famous ancient temple at Thenkasi.[199] As seen earlier M. R. Gandhi, the BJP leader known for his good relations with members of all communities, was again attacked in 2013.

Taliban-style public execution of Muslim women who did not adhere to strict purdah or the dictates of shariat was the order of the day. The TMMK—which was one of the proscribed organizations by the internal ministry to receive funds from abroad—became the darling of the DMK government. In March 2007, a 35-year-old Muslim woman was ceremonially stoned and then stabbed to death by young fundamentalists for being 'immoral' in Tirunelveli district.[200] A district TMMK official went on record demanding the implementation of the Islamic law of stoning women to death in secular India.[201] May 2007 saw another Muslim woman tea vendor hacked to death because she was selling tea in public.[202] In neighbouring Kerala, by 2010, the 2006 electoral alliance of CPI (M)-PDP has evolved into a moral police. The Democratic Youth Federation of India (CPI[M]) and PDP cadre started barging into houses and beating people.[203]

Meanwhile, the TMMK utilized the patronage of the DMK regime and went for an enlarged capacity building. An ambulance network was created. Ambulance services have been a favoured as a means of trafficking arms. At a thanksgiving function in November 2007, Chief Minister Karunanidhi made a personal donation of two ambulances to the TMMK ambulance network.[204] Earlier in August 2007, the TMMK had used its ambulances in a deadly attack on Hindus at Thenkasi. The attacks and killings of Hindu youths, who were brothers of the earlier slain Hindu Front leader, were symbolically done on 14 August—the Independence Day of Pakistan.[205] In Coimbatore, by August 2007, the case against Madani was weakened by the DMK government to such an extent that it was a foregone conclusion that he would be released. However, in a curiously inexplicable judgment, the judge, while accepting that there was a conspiracy through serial bomb blast to kill L. K. Advani then visiting Coimbatore and take revenge on Hindus, found 'several factors outweighed the legal factors for giving death sentences'.[206] Madani was cleared of all charges while Badsha was safely saved from the hangman and returned to the comfort of his cell. Madani came out in 2007. Two years later, without much fanfare, in 2009 the DMK government released nine more members of Al-Ummah, 16 months before the completion of their sentence.[207]

In 2008 there were multiple bomb blasts in Bangalore. And on 17 August 2010, Madani was again arrested, in connection with the conspiracy for the

2008 Bangalore bomb blast.[208] The geography of Southern jihad now included Karnataka very well beyond the tentative steps. So much so that the then Congress government ruling Karnataka, adhering to a familiar pattern, was set to spend ₹ 5 lakh for Madani's treatment at an Ayurvedic Spa.[209] Even as the BJP was getting defeated in the Karnataka elections at that time, *Arab News* from Saudi declared that unlike the outgoing BJP government, the elected Congress government would not oppose the bail petition of Madani. The article declared: 'Congress win bodes well for Madani'.[210] The then Chief Justice of India P. Sathasivam, who headed the bench of judges in the Supreme Court, rejected the earlier bail application of Madani and declared that the Supreme Court was 'not inclined to enlarge him on bail'.[211]

AIADMK Again

In 2011 the AIADMK came to power. The TMMK had shifted its alliance to AIADMK. This time it had launched a political party and had got two seats as well. Islamist forces were now well-entrenched in the power politics in Tamil Nadu. This is despite the fact that the TMMK is still in the list of organizations prohibited from receiving foreign contribution by the MHA (as on 18 November 2011).[212] The Central Bureau of Investigation (CBI) on 5 October 2011 stated in its website that a case was registered against five people—M. H. Jawaharullah, the then State President (TMMK), S. Hyder Ali, the then state general secretary (TMMK), H. Sayed Nizar Ahmed, the then State Dy. President (TMMK), G. M. Shiek and Nalla Mohmed Kalanjim, the then Authorised Signatories of Coimbatore Muslim Relief Fund, and members of TMMK, alleging that during the period from 15 December 1997 to 20 June 2000, they were involved in a criminal conspiracy in Chennai and formed an association to accept foreign contributions without registering the association and without prior permission of Govt of India. They had received foreign contributions of ₹ 1,54,88,000 (approximately) from foreign sources. This was used for the relief of the Coimbatore bomb blast accused. Additional Chief Metropolitan Magistrate, Egmore, Chennai convicted M. H. Jawaharullah in the case and had sentenced him to one-year rigorous imprisonment. Yet M. H. Jawaharullah continues to be an MLA in the Tamil Nadu Assembly.[213]

Though the AIADMK had created an impression that its leader was tough with anti-national forces, in reality it had to yield to the well-entrenched Islamist lobby. The AIADMK government also gave the green signal to Islamist forces, who made both veiled as well as blatant threats of violence against the Kollywood movie *Thupakki*, a 2012 film which dealt with 'sleeper cells'. The Tamil Nadu Government, instead of offering protection, mediated a compromise between the Islamists and the filmmakers.[214] In the same year, when a 20,000-strong mob of Muslim agitators violently laid siege to the US Consulate at Chennai, the police were told to look the other way.[215]

In 2013 *Viswaroopam*, a film by Kamal Hassan was targeted. Islamic fundamentalist organizations demanded a ban on the film. Kamal Hassan, known for his obscene attacks on Hindu deities, in an extraordinary display of submission to the Islamists, organized a private premier show for the censor groups of radical Islamists. The act boomeranged as they demanded a complete ban, and the government was more than eager to oblige the fundamentalists. The Chief Minister announced that the actor could thrash out the differences with the protesting Muslim groups and then alone government would clear the decks for the film's release.[216]

While some rumours had rife that Ameer Sultan, a Kollywood director who was also a fundamentalist Islamist closer to a rabid Islamic preacher in Tamil Nadu, also helped in settling the deal, earlier Ameer had caused a ban on a TV talk show by alerting the Tamil Nadu Towheed Jamat (TNTJ)—an Islamist organization.[217]

Kollywood, as the Tamil film industry is called, is a very important business place. In 2012 as the Islamist control of Kollywood began, Ameer had become the president of the Film Employees Federation of South India (FEFSI), one of the influential bodies of Tamil cinema.[218]

An Islamist stranglehold on Kollywood would help raise funds for many of the Islamist operations in Tamil Nadu. After all, foreign money trail, on which the dissemination of Islamist ideas and subsequent radicalization are dependent, always allows the security agencies to keep track and monitor the activities. It was after these events that in full earnestness, the second round of attacks on Hindu activists started. Hindu activists are not a serious threat to Islamists in Tamil Nadu in direct combat. Nevertheless, these attacks and murders help the Islamists get an experience of how to deal with the law enforcing agencies, how to evade arrests, and when arrested how to use the prison terms. The execution of these murders also reinforces the theo-politics of Islamism. Even if a jihadist is jailed, the political ecosystem has been compromised enough to secure his release through the manipulation of political and other establishments.

Understanding Islamism

In the Indian context, it was the Hindutva ideologue and historian Sita Ram

Goel who popularized the term 'Islamism'. To him Islamism is the residue of Islamic invasions, and he sees Indian Muslims as victims of Islamism:

> Its basic tenets are ultimately derived from Islam which has so far succeeded in sealing itself off from every form of empiricism, rationalism, universalism, humanism and liberalism which are the hallmarks of Hindu as well as Western culture....Islamism is a self-righteous psychology and a closed cultural attitude which makes it impossible for its converts to co-exist peacefully and with dignity.[219]

In the South Indian context where the institutions of democracy are not as strongly homogenous as in the West, the Islamist strategy is a bit different and a liberal combination of jihadism and Islamism. Already India's Nehruvian polity has developed an intrinsically Hinduphobic political discourse, which has become a dominant stream with the INC under Sonia Gandhi and dynasty embracing a strident anti-Hindu stand. It is more pronounced in the South with the Dravidianist discourse, which has elements of racial hatred towards Hindus. Islamism has been consistently drawing upon these resources in India—using every faultline in Hindu polity, whether the Dravidian in Tamil Nadu or Marxist-Congress in Kerala to the maximum advantage of furthering the cause of Islamization of the state.

Ascendancy of Radical Islamism & Destruction of Harmony between Communities

The years 2006–2013 saw a marked increase in radical Islamist activities in South India. In Kerala the foreign Islamist forces were enlarging their network, in Bangalore the links were being created with North Indian as well as Kerala outfits. Soon, the South Indian radical Islamist organizations would create a common platform for coordination.

Here is a sample course of events:

- In August 2006, 18 Islamists belonging to proscribed Students Islamic Movement of India (SIMI) conducted an indoctrination-jihad camp in Binanipuram near Kochi. The seized materials included a book titled *Mass Resistance in Kashmir* published by the Institute of Policy Research in Islamabad, along with political maps of India with Kashmir left out and other documents with anti-national exhortations. The book was taken from the library of Jamaat-e-Islami (JeI), the organizational mother of radical Islamist forces. The organization made the usual customary protest.[220] It was not a coincidence that the absconding aeronautical engineer CAM Basheer, a former SIMI president, hailed from the same area. He was an accused in the 2003 bomb blasts at Mulund near Mumbai. Basher handles 50 fronts of SIMI and their funding through his network. Clearly the SIMI meeting was not only a camp but also regrouping for the launch of a new strategy for the rise of radical Islamization in South India. The SIMI activists who were arrested by the Kerala Police from Binanipuram were later let off without a proper perusal of the case, thanks to the political pressure.

- There were cases where the arrests showed inter-state linkages mainly between Karnataka, Tamil Nadu and Kerala. In November 2006, two Pakistani terrorists were arrested in Mysore. Mohammed Fahad, one of the two, had come to Chennai and had obtained a fake driver's license from a driving school, staying at his 'uncle's' house. His 'uncle' Mohammed Koya was from Kerala.[221]
- On 1 January 2007, two Lashkar-e-Taiba (LeT) terrorists were arrested in New Delhi. They were fleeing to Chennai after they had failed in their mission to plant bombs at overcrowded New Year party functions in the capital. The two LeT men revealed that they were going to Chennai to meet some LeT operatives, who were active in south India.[222] In a week, the Special Task Force (STF) from New Delhi was at Chennai, and their findings revealed that the LeT men had been to Chennai earlier too and had established contact bases in South India, far from the probing eyes of mainstream counter-terror with its centre in North India.[223]
- On 6 January 2007, Bilal Ahmed Kota alias Imran Jalal alias Salim was arrested in Bangalore. He had scouted the top IT establishments and observed their security arrangements for LeT. The grenades seized from him were similar to the ones used in the attack on Indian Institute of Science (IISc) earlier in 2005. [224]
- Meanwhile, in Bangalore on 20 January 2007, following the US hanging of Saddam Hussein, Reuters reported: 'Muslims protesting against the execution of Iraq's toppled president clashed with police on Friday, ransacking shops owned by Hindus and burning at least 15 cars'.[225] A more detailed account of the attack was given by the vernacular *Dina Tanthi*, a Tamil daily known for its neutrality: 'Many of the youths who participated in the march condemning the Saddam execution, entered the houses and shops in the Timmaiah road. They humiliated the women entering the houses. They also tried to desecrate a famous

local Goddess temple'.[226] The above incidents centred on Bangalore and Chennai. They were connected to the jihad which was being waged in North India. The foreign connection mostly came from Pakistan.

- On 9 January 2007, in a Karachi-bound ship originating from Dubai, the Customs officials at Cochin, Kerala, accidentally discovered that the ship containment meant for a Muslim businessman, one Koya at Tiruchur district in Kerala, contained along with furniture boxes, weapons. What was interesting was that copies of *Koran* were found with every box of ammunition.[227]

  This is a vital indicator that the jihad in South India is being handled by professional groups with international backing. In recruiting Uzbek Mujahedeen to fight the Afghan jihad, one of the psychological strategies perfected by the CIA was the shipment of *Koran* along with supply of weapons. The CIA and jihad planners discovered that shipment with copies of *Koran* worked better than the usual Western tactics of using atrocity stories in the case of recruitment for Afghan jihad.[228]

  Similar pattern of placing *Koran* as part of every ammunition package in 2007 shows that those behind planning these South Indian operations are jihad veterans with international expertise. A concerned Indian Naval Chief, Sureesh Mehta stated gravely on the closing session of an international seminar on maritime trade and security that the Cochin seizure might only be the tip of the iceberg of the nefarious activities.[229]

It is in the background of these incidents that one should see the formation of the Popular Front of India (PFI). It was officially formed in 2007 by merging many state-based Islamist bodies, most of them with secular names—from Kerala's NDF to Manipur's Lilong Social Forum. However, the main functional components of PFI are MNP of Tamil Nadu, NDF of Kerala and the KFD of Karnataka. And it was launched during a seminar and rally named again deceptively secular as 'Empower India'. Already the MNP was running a magazine in Tamil called *Vidiyal Velli* (*Dawn Friday*) and in Kerala called *Thejas* (*Radiance*). The articles in the magazines advocate a radical Islamist and pro-Kashmir separatist stand, often calling the jihad terrorists of Kashmir 'fighters'. The 'Q' branch officials did not miss the SIMI connection in the launch of PFI. They noticed that majority of the leaders belonged to banned SIMI.[230] From then onwards in Kerala, Tamil Nadu and Karnataka the jihadist networks have an Islamist cover-up exploiting every inherent weakness of the pseudo-secular nature and vote-bank politics of Indian polity.

2008: Kerala Exports Terror with Political Help

The aftermath of the arrest in the SIMI training-indoctrination camp (August 2006) is in many ways typical of what happens in most of the cases against jihad capacity building at the early stages. The FIR was filed under the Unlawful Activities Prevention Act. Five were arrested and the rest were released. Even these five—Ansar Moulavi, Shaduli, Nizamuddin, Abdul Rafeeq and Shamas—were set free on bail. Then on 13 May 2008, Jaipur, the capital of Rajasthan, became the target of a serial bombing similar to the Coimbatore bomb blast. Nine synchronized bomb blasts within a span of 15 minutes left 63 dead with 216 or more people injured. Among those arrested were Shaduli and Ansar Moulavi. During the investigations, it was found that the duo had also attended two more terror camps at Vagamon, in Kerala's Idukki district in December 2007 and January 2008.[231] In January 2008, a Kashmiri terrorist, Altaf was arrested in Kerala. He was given a false SIM card by an agency at Trivandrum, and the terrorist had also talked to his contacts in Chennai, Tamil Nadu.[232]

On 26 July 2008, serial bomb blasts at Ahmedabad killed 53 people and injured over 200. Once again the Kerala and Karnataka connections came up during investigation. The main accused was trained at the Wagamon SIMI training camp. Then Home Minister of Kerala, Kodiyeri Balakrishnan, openly admitted that the state government was under 'pressure' to set the SIMI men free. In a very blunt confession made by the state Home Minister before the press, the CPI(M) leader stated that the jihadists were operating in Kerala. But their main activities were outside the state. He stated that there was a hue and cry from human rights activists, accusing the government of targeting the minorities when police action against SIMI took place.[233] In October 2008, two Kerala youths were killed in an encounter by the Indian Army in Kashmir. SIMI had not only been rebuilding but also recruiting the youths for jihad, outsourcing them to various parts of India to execute terror projects. According to the IB, SIMI fronts had become the strongest in specific pockets of Kerala and had been providing modules for jihad not only in various parts of India but also abroad.[234]

'Popular Front of India' Takes Over from SIMI

In July 2009, the Social Democratic Party of India (SDPI) was formed as a political wing of PFI. It was headed by E. Abubacker, who was the Kerala Zone President of SIMI from 1982–1984. PFI has many frontal organizations for specific target groups like the Campus Front of India (CFI) for college students and the National Women Front. Though formed in 2007, the PFI came to prominence only with the chopping of the hand of a Christian professor in July 2010. However, that did not mean the PFI or its Kerala constituent NDF had been silent all those years. The then Kerala Home Minister, in his statement, proclaimed that the outfit had been involved in 22 murder cases and 73 attempted murder cases.[235] The chopping of hand attack prompted the Marxist government to undertake a state-wide raid on various offices of the PFI as well as SDPI. The raids revealed a stockpiling of arms and ammunitions at the offices of PFI/SDPI.[236] V. S. Achuthanandan, the then Kerala Chief Minister, talked in detail about the plans of the PFI for Kerala, which according to him included making Kerala a 'Muslim-dominated' state within 20 years. He stated that the outfit was investing money to radicalize the youths, give them weapon training.[237]

The India Fraternity Forum (IFF), which projects itself as an organization to help Indians in the Gulf countries, is based in Saudi. According to an intelligence report submitted to the PMO, this organization has been helping the funding of PFI activities.[238] The IFF has hosted a series of meetings by SDPI leaders at Gulf countries. In January 2011, Nasarudhin Elamaram, the National Committee Member of SDPI, addressed a gathering organized by the Kuwait India Fraternity Forum. In October 2011, the IFF hosted Abubacker, the National President of SDPI, at Emirates for his campaign to promote the 2011 rally of PFI at New Delhi. These are just a few instances of different chapters of IFF extending support to PFI and SDPI.[239]

Curiously, another source of steady income to PFI had been the government advertisements in their media. Though the Union Home Ministry had warned the government of the anti-Indian and communal nature of *Thejas* publications as early as 25 November 2009, in a confidential communication, in October 2010, N. P. Chekkutty, Executive Editor of *Thejas* boasted to *Tehelka*—a pro-Islamist magazine (which produced a half-empathetic and half-critical story on PFI) that in the past financial year, the PFI got more than ₹ 80 lakh as revenue from government advertisements alone. It was only on 14 May 2010, that the Kerala government briefly stopped the advertisements, only to be continued again in a few months.[240] It seemed that under the United Progressive Alliance, either due to negligence or by design, the government machinery itself had been compromised by Islamists at key places. A Home Ministry report had stated that a senior IPS officer had met some people with terrorist links in Qatar. Though the officer in question had been suspended when he was IG (Kannur) for allegedly making a foreign trip without government permission as prescribed by the service rules and was also suspended earlier in a case relating to amassing wealth disproportionate to known sources of income; he had been reinstated thanks to the dragging of the case by the vigilance.

PFI provides the vital link between the terror masterminds across the border and reaching out to the Muslim population and radicalizing them. The PFI also has a battery of human rights activists and lawyers at its command and pay who are pressed into service to secure the release of their arrested cadre. All these services provided by the PFI are used by jihadists effectively. It is a highly effective symbiotic approach to thwart or vitally delay any attempt by the police to stop the investigations, etc. This is demonstrated in the case of Himayat Baig, who was arrested as the mastermind behind the German Bakery blast in Pune, which was executed on 13 February 2010. He had joined the PFI and was trained in the methods of indoctrinating youth and the techniques to deal with police interrogation. His primary job was to recruit and send local Muslim youths for jihadist training to Pakistan.[241]

Even as evidence mounted on the PFI-LeT (Lashkar-e-Toiba) links, the Kerala police informed the High Court in September 2010 that they were investigating the possible links. Weeks before, the same police had revealed that the LeT militant Tadiyantavide Nasir had stayed at the PFI's district office in Ernakulam.[242] Yet, despite the statement of the Chief Minister, who was also the polit bureau member of CPI(M), the political equations including the vote-bank considerations made the left government soft pedal the issue of banning the outfit by neither seeking the ban nor opposing it. The responsibility was passed on to the Centre, while at the same time the Marxist state government opposed passing cases to the National Investigation Agency (NIA).[243] Even as this political buck passing with the terror-accused happened, the PFI through the SDPI demonstrated how to use the Indian democratic system to further the Islamist cause. In October 2010, one of the accused in the hand-chopping case was made to stand in the election to the block panchayat division in Ernakulam on an SDPI ticket, and the accused won.[244]

For all its high decibel pro-Dalit voices the PFI makes, it always is pro-Islamist in any confrontation between the Scheduled Community (SC) Hindus and Islamists. The PFI was also involved in a Taliban-like execution of a Dalit youth. On 27 April 2010, the body of a young Dalit worker was found hanging from the terrace of a lodge in Kannur in Kerala. He was tortured severely before death. No less than 22 brutal injury marks were found on the body. The veins in his hands and legs had been punctured, and a lot of blood had oozed out. It took six months for the Kerala police to admit in the court that the youth had been tortured to death and the Investigating Officer reported that the accused belonged to PFI.[245] In 2011, in a replay of Marad, the PFI and its student wing CFI stabbed three Hindu fishermen in Kerala.[246]

On July 2012, the Kerala government again submitted before the High

Court of Kerala that PFI was 'a resurrection of the banned outfit Students Islamic Movement of India (SIMI) in another form'. It also submitted that it was involved in 27 murders.[247] In July 2012, the PFI men stabbed two Hindu students Sachin Gopal (20) and Vishal Kumar (19) to death.[248]

The additional networking capacity of PFI was revealed in August 2012. Following the riots in Assam which were triggered by an attack by Bangladesh infiltrators on Bodos, the Islamist forces began a campaign of using terror rumours against the Northeast students in the state of Karnataka. According to sources in intelligence agencies, the bulk hate messages which originated from the servers in Pakistan were received by the cadres of PFI, who helped spread them along with the cadres of Bangladeshi jihad outfit Harkat-ul-Jihad-al-Islami (HuJI). The PFI has, as usual, denied it.[249]

The Assam connection to PFI comes from Badruddin Ajmal, whose Islamist party All India United Democratic Front (AIUDF) was the political partner of the then ruling Congress coalition and is strongly in favour of pro-Bangladeshi Muslim illegal immigrants. Badruddin had expressed solidarity with PFI/SDPI.[250] Such a political backing of an Islamist party from Assam and logistic network with HuJI can provide the PFI the Koranic power to 'strike terror into the heart' of the perceived enemies of Islam—like the student communities of Northeast in the southern states.

On 23 April 2013, the Kerala police stormed into the office of Thanal Charitable Trust, one of the many fronts of PFI, in Narath. Twenty-one PFI activists, all in their twenties were caught with human shooting targets, bombs, bomb making materials, gunpowder, eight swords, foreign currency notes, Iranian entry card in the name of Sadik Mangalodan to Kish Island free zone and leaflets of PFI and SDPI.[251] The police suspect that the PFI camp activists may have a hand in the Bangalore blast before the BJP office on 17 April 2013. Many times, Bangalore has been a favourite hiding spot for PFI jihadists in murder cases.[252]

The Bangalore blast could have been then a calculated risk by the PFI in showing their ability to strike at will. Given the assured defeat of BJP in the state polls then, the PFI knows that the Congress government would go soft on the Islamists and jihadists. Simultaneously, the coastal regions in Karnataka saw a sudden expansion of the SDPI. With SDPI becoming politically strong and the INC under Sonia at the helm of affairs, the PFI striking right at the office of BJP would prove how it could act daringly and yet escape any punishment with its political clout. As C. D. Souza, a political observer from Karnataka pointed out, the emergence of the SDPI in coastal Karnataka could very well have the same effect as the rise of the AIUDF in Assam, where the party helps the cause of illegal infiltrators from Bangladesh, leading to frequent clashes, which in turn can help radicalize Islamic society. The SDPI could have planned to do to Karnataka what the AIUDF was then doing for Assam.[253] At least one of the arrested PFI activists had his bank account connected with one Sanaulla Shabandri, who belonged to the Bhatkal family, which had been accused of having been involved in the founding of the dreaded Indian Mujahideen (IM). Sanaulla was also reportedly a close aide of Dawood Ibrahim.[254]

Another important aspect that emerged was the way the Gulf money got routed to fund the PFI's jihadist operations. One of the chief trainers of the Narath camp, Abdul Aziz was an accused in the murder of a Hindu activist. The other chief trainer, Kamaruddin had escaped from police. A raid at his house has revealed, apart from arms piled in a secret enclosure, some vital details about jihadist financing. Funds from the Emirates National Bank of Dubai had been transferred according to the documents (which include bank account numbers) seized during the raids. The probe has revealed that another PFI man had operated at least nine bank accounts in his name and other family members for receiving more than ₹ 80 lakh from a non-resident Indian in Dubai. The funds had been transferred through Western Union as deposits of ₹ 1 lakh to multiple accounts to deftly escape the surveillance of the Financial Intelligence Unit functioning under the Union Ministry of Finance. The pattern of fund transfer shows that repeated transfers were done to a few persons from banks in West Asia. A preliminary investigation shows the PFI's involvement in Real Estate.[255]

The IFF operating from the Gulf regions was active in hosting SDPI leaders campaigning for their mega-Indian events in Dubai and other Gulf countries. According to sources, the camp raid had also revealed a highly structured and multi-layered approach of the PFI. The training had a special 'Encounter Group' for combat training; a 'Legal Cell' to provide basic legal awareness to counter police interrogation at the starting phase, and a 'Harbouring Cell' for shifting and accommodating them safely, and a 'Media Cell' for propaganda.[256]

However, the decision to hand over the case to the NIA and taking decisive actions against PFI were mostly determined by political considerations. With the more PFI-sympathetic, Congress-led United Democratic Front (UDF) being in power during these events, the LDF then in opposition, through its former Home Minister, openly acknowledged the political pressure during their regime in taking action against the terror training camp, and oscillated between shelling out government advertisements to PFI media, which formed a significant revenue of the organization. The PFI too had used all Islamist political parties including the Indian Union Muslim League (IUML) to make the ruling coalition go soft on PFI. The radical Islamist organizations had lent their support to the IUML in the last assembly election, and the IUML had

20 MLAs and five ministers in the UDF government. This made the UDF government go soft on PFI/SDPI, despite the police revelations. The state government gave PRD and PSU advertisements of the Kerala government to the SDPI/PDI mouthpiece *Thejas*, ignoring all Central agency instructions.[257]

Here then is a textbook case of Islamist influence in the state machine. Even as the security agencies of the nation and states were fighting a pitched battle against the radical Islamist terror, mostly unseen by public eyes, the political leadership of the central and state level security agencies were compromised before the very same radical Islamist forces.

PFI in Tamil Nadu

In Tamil Nadu the situation has been even more comfortable for Islamist-jihadist elements. As early as 2007, the Tamil Nadu police sources have warned that the misleading calmness in Tamil Nadu was covering a 'deep undercurrent of Muslim extremism'. Former zonal presidents of SIMI in Tamil Nadu had started a number of fronts, all working with the objective 'to establish Islamic rule in India'. Ghulam Ahmed, former Zonal SIMI President (Tamil Nadu), was the founder of the MNP. Jawahirullah, the TMMK leader was a State SIMI President. Another Tamil Nadu SIMI President, S. M. Baucker was in the top leadership of the TNTJ.[258]

There were some initial conflicts between the TMMK and PFI (then as MNP) over cadre poaching. At that time, some detailed revelations were made regarding the way MNP radicalizes the Islamic youth through systematic brain washing. However, over the next five years, the Islamist organizations have bought their peace with PFI. The TMMK has joined the PFI-led national alliance of Muslim groups and parties. By 2011 a pro-PFI TMMK with its own political party, has now a presence in the Tamil Nadu Legislative Assembly.

In 2008 though the police declined permission, the High Court bench at Madurai granted permission to the PFI parade. In 2009 the annual parade, which PFI conducts as a show of strength and intimidation, led to conflicts between the Tamil Nadu police and PFI jihadists. In February 2010, the Executive Editor of *Tehelka* magazine, Ajit Sahi delivered a speech in Madurai at a PFI-held two-day camp and exhorted the PFI cadre to continue their fight. [44] In Tamil Nadu, the PFI could conduct camps similar to the ones in Kerala with far more ease. In June 2012, the Tamil Nadu police booked 30 PFI cadres who participated in the PFI camp held at Ramanathapuram district in Tamil Nadu, near the famous Hindu pilgrimage spot Rameshwaram. Later, they were released on bail. Incidentally the MLA of Rameshwaram was Jawahirullah of the TMMK. The agencies in Tamil Nadu alerted the state Special Branch after they found that cadres from Assam, Bihar and Kerala took part in the camp. [45] Since the Bangalore bomb blast, it has been found that the PFI had been running camps in several places in Tamil Nadu, from where the main accused in the case hailed.[46] According to the Karnataka police, the police suspect that the Bangalore blasts were masterminded in Kerala and were carried out by a chain of persons based in Coimbatore. Explosives were reportedly seized from raided houses in Coimbatore.[47]

In a classic coordinated move, a human rights organization namely, National Confederation of Human Rights Organisations (NCHRO) had started the campaign that their 'fact finding committee' had found that the Tamil Nadu and Karnataka police had fabricated evidence against 11 Muslims arrested in connection with the Bangalore bomb blast.[48] Such human rights fronts are part of the PFI operations. Seemingly secular and including many leftists and anti-Indian activists with Hindu names, these human rights organizations are actually part of the PFI's larger project of using democratic institutions to weaken democracy and create an Islamist state.

For example, in the case of NCHRO, the State Secretary N. M. Siddique was one of the two arrested PFI men by the Kerala police in 2010.[259] The PFI has also taken an active role in supporting the anti-nuclear movement in Tamil Nadu. This has helped the PFI to link itself with Tamil nationalist separatists.[260] This is in line with the Saudi Arabian lobby, which is said to be funding anti-nuclear movements in other countries.[261]

The SDPI has also started working closely with Viduthalai Chiruthaigal Party (VCK), a militant Dalit party, whose supremo Thirumavalavan endorsed the Mayoral candidate of SDPI in Chennai electoral elections.[262] Even as the PFI has been accused of involvement in the Taliban-style execution of Dalit youth in Kerala, in Tamil Nadu, the VCK has no hesitation in associating itself with the PFI/SDPI. During a recent state election the SDPI associated itself with a splinter group of AIADMK formed after the death of its supremo and former Tamil Nadu CM Jayalalithaa. But general strategy of the SDPI is to align with and provide platform for the virulent anti-Hindu elements irrespective of party boundaries. In 2018 the SDPI announced a conference in which not only the VCK supremo Thirumavalavan was one of the main speakers, it also included the State President of the Tamil Nadu Congress Committee.

After 2014, a lull in the overt violent activities of radical Islamist outfits was interrupted by two violent incidents. A Hindu front activist, Sasikumar of Coimbatore was hacked to death on 22 September 2016. The case was first handled by the rural police and then transferred to the special investigation division of CB-CID, who arrested Syed Abuthahir, Saddam Hussain, Subair and Mubarak. The case was, however, transferred to NIA in January 2018. By April 2018, the NIA in its charge sheet stated that Saddam, Subair, Mubarak and Syed, all PFI members, hacked the Hindu activist 'to strike terror' in their minds.[263] By this time, 16 months had passed, and one of the main accused had fled the country and settled in Oman. Again, on 5 February 2019, Ramalingam from Thanjavur district was killed by the activists of PFI and SDPI. He was not a Hindu activist. He had argued with Islamist proselytizers and had stated that he was ready to wear the Islamic cap, and they too should be ready to accept *vibhuti*—the sacred ash. He too was brutally murdered. The NIA named 18 persons belonging to the PFI-SDPI, of which 12 have been arrested.[264]

Samanvaya with Islam Now

It is taking all these factors into account that one must look at the way Hindutva enters into a samanvayic dialogue with Islam in India. While for the non-Hindutva polity the abandonment of indigenous Islamic traditions, ghettoization of Muslims and subsequent vicious cycle of radicalization and alienation and using these radical Islamization helping in vote-bank politics is a set equation, for Hindutva it must battle against hatred of the other as well as the expansionist radical forces of Islamism which are becoming dominant in an alienated community. It is to this end that Hindutva follows a multi-pronged approach.

In 2016 Narendra Modi inaugurated a global Sufi conference in New Delhi. The four-day conference was organized by All India Ulama and Mashaikh Board, the apex body of Sufi dargahs in India. The speech Narendra Modi gave at the inaugural session can also be considered as the definite statement of the way RSS looks at Hindu-Muslim interaction in India. Modi said:

> For the Sufis, therefore, service to God meant service to humanity.... And its humanism also upheld the place and status of women in society. Above all, Sufism is a celebration of diversity and pluralism, expressed in the words of Hazrat Nizamuddin Auliya, that every people has its own path of truth, beliefs and focus of reverence....And, it is in harmony with the soul of the Bhakti saint's saying in the Hindu tradition, 'Into the bosom of the one great sea, Flow streams that come from hills on every side'. And in the wisdom of Bulleh Shah, 'Lord is mixed in every heart'. These values are the need of our times. This is the reality of Nature. We learn this wisdom in the perfect balance and harmony that exists in the vast diversity of a forest....In Baba Farid's poetry or Guru Granth Sahib, we feel the same spiritual connection. We see compassion in the langars of Sufi shrines and the village tombs

> of local Pirs that attracted the poor and hungry; the words of Hindavi were spoken in the Sufi Khangahs. Sufism's contribution to poetry in India is huge. Its impact on the development of Indian music is profound....It is this spirit of Sufism, the love for their country and the pride in their nation that define the Muslims in India. They reflect the timeless culture of peace, diversity and equality of faith of our land; they are steeped in the democratic tradition of India, confident of their place in the country and invested in the future of their nation; and, above all, they are shaped by the values of the Islamic heritage of India. It upholds the highest ideals of Islam and has always rejected the forces of terrorism and extremism.[265]

One can see a conceptual continuity between the way DRI churned and presented the Sufi heritage of India continuously in its pages and the content of the speech of Modi. Though separated by almost three decades, the conceptual consistency is remarkable.

Indeed, the non-Ijadist Sufi heritage of India has been a great transforming force against Islamist terrorism, even in the highly radicalized Kashmir valley. Afghan American journalist Fariba Nawa records the following event.

> "Nasruddin" was an American-born Afghan boy who grew up as a "typical American teenager". He became an atheist after his parents died in a car accident. But sometime in the 1990s, he slowly became radicalised while living in Houston, Texas. The strain of Islam he acquired was Salafism—"the dominant form of Islam being preached in US mosqu'es, due in large part to funding from Saudi Arabia". Once he had become radicalised enough, Fawa writes that Nasruddin "was soon introduced to a recruiter for Lashkar-e-Taiba, a Pakistan-based Islamist militia fighting against India in Kashmir". He was given taped lectures, and when he was 18, he "flew to Pakistan and completed intense physical and weapons training before crossing over to Indian Kashmir, ready to become a martyr". And then the unexpected happened. "After four months in the freezing temperatures of the Himalayas, Nasruddin met a mystic, a Sufi sheikh from the United States, who told the impressionable young man that "fighting in Kashmir wasn't jihad".

Slowly he started questioning his Salafist conditioning even as he was being attracted to join the Taliban. The encounter with the Sufi mystic helped. Nasruddin returned to the United States, where he was rejected by the Salafists. After 9/11, he was being monitored by security agencies even as he himself had turned inwards. He started reading the holy texts of all religions and realized that he was not alone. There were other Salafists and even former jihadists who were abandoning hardline clerics, talking about mysticism, and praying at mosques that practised a different sort of Islam—Sufism.[266]

The RSS not only brings out the harmonious Sufi dimension of indigenous Islam, but it also helps in the educational betterment of Muslims. Within its own cadre, even while bitterly fighting proselytizing Islamists and political Islamist expansionism on ground, it tries to prevent hatred against Muslims. The way RSS's children's literature, mostly meant for the children of its cadre and educational institutions, portrays a Muslim freedom fighter and martyr, often ignored in mainstream history textbooks, serves as an example.

Bangalore-based RSS publishing house Rashtrotthana Sahitya brings out a children's book series *Bharata Bharati*. The book series brings out the lives of illustrious men and women from Indian history, Puranas and Ithihasas. Its book number 9 (first published in 1974 and reprinted in 1996) was written by N. P. Shankaranarayana Rao. The booklet introduces the hero as 'the Pathan patriot who kissed the hangman's noose with the name of Allah on his lips' and continues

> He stood six feet tall, with a broad chest; he was strong as steel and had the heart of a lion. His beard added a charm to his face. There was always a smile of firmness on his lips and it shone even now....He said 'My hands are not soiled with the murder of man. The charge against me is false. God will give me justice'. The he prayed in clear ringing tones: '*La illahi il Allah, Mohammed ur Rasool Allah*'. The hangman's noose came round his neck.[267]

The martyr thus described with his Islamic identity not only unhidden but highlighted is Ashfaqulla Khan. In the book the children were told of the famous incident between Tasadruk Khan Ashfaqulla. Tasadruk had risen from being a British agent in Arabia to the post of Superintendent of Police in India—one of the very few Indians to be given that post in British India. He was asked by the British to talk to Ashfaqulla in prison. He asked Ashfaqulla why he, a Muslim, was fighting with Hindus: 'Hindus are fighting for Hindu India. Why are you fighting?'

> But Ashfaq did not like his advice. He was tired of hearing the evil advice. In the end he told Tasadruk to his face 'Khan Sahib, I am sure that Hindu India will be much better than British India.[268]

At the same time, the children's book published by the RSS publication does not secularize or 'Hinduize' Ashfaqulla Khan:

> Life in prison had made Ashfaq very pious. He grew a beard. He said his prayers regularly. During Ramzan he fasted very strictly. Now and then the friends discussed religion. Sachindra Bakshi had no faith in God. But Ashfaq used to say, "I consider

the unseen power as supreme. It is above us and it is greater than the world. That is my faith. But you do not agree. Faith is entirely personal matter." He believed that religious faith is the greatest concept uniting God and man in a single principle. His considered opinion was that it was not a matter for discussion in the streets.[269]

The book informs children that Ashfaq was a poet. He used to write in Hindi and Urdu. It quotes the following poem:

> Did not Lord Krishna say to Arjuna in the battlefield that life and death are unreal? Alas! Where is that wisdom? A man is bound to die; so why should anyone be afraid of death? Let our motherland become free and shine through the ages. What matters whether we are alive or dead?[270]

The book also records how another revolutionary—Ram Prasad Bismil got over his prejudice against Muslims in his own words:

> Some friends warned me that I should not trust a Muslim or will get cheated. But success was yours. Nothing could stand between us now. We ate from the same plate almost always. I began to get over the feeling that there is difference between Hindus and Muslims.... You always supported Hindu Muslim unity. You were a true Muslim and a great patriot. If you were worried about anything it was about Hindu-Muslim unity. You wanted them to work for the betterment of the country.[271]

The book meant for children from the RSS book house clearly breaks stereotypes at two levels. One, it breaks the negative stereotype against Muslims through a revolutionary freedom fighter, and second, it disturbs the negative stereotype about the RSS itself.

In 2016, 16-year-old Sarfaraz Hussain of Assam hit the headlines for topping the High School Leaving Certificate (HSLC) examination in the state. Having scored an average of 98 per cent in all subjects, Hussain expressed his desire to become an engineer. His father was a waiter in a small restaurant. He attributed his success to his school—an RSS-run school. Shankardev Shishu Niketan in Betkuchi in Guwahati is one of the many schools run by Vidya Bharati—the education wing of the RSS. In a statement Hussain said, 'I am proud to have been a student of this school. It is because of my school that I have been able to secure the top position in the state'.[272]

This is not an isolated event. The RSS diversified into education services in 1977 with the formation of an exclusively educational wing—Vidya Bharati. However, the first RSS-affiliated school was opened as early as 1952. While by conservative estimates, more than 10 million students have benefitted from

RSS-run schools, more and more Christian and Muslim students have been found recruiting in these schools. In an exclusive report on Vidya Bharati, the *Daily News Analysis* wing of Zee TV states this about the schools: Today, 12,850 schools are being run in India under Vidya Bharati. A total of 30,000 educational institutions are functioning, including 49 colleges and schools. Around 80,000 Christian and Muslim children are also studying in these schools.

RSS not only runs its own schools but also helps other schools by sending its teachers. P. A. Inamdar, an educationist from Maharashtra, as the chairman of the Haji Gulam Md. Azam Educational Trust, Pune had produced Muslim student toppers in the State Secondary School Certificate in the district of Pune—the so-called Oxford of the east. In an interview to *The Hindu*, Inamdar acknowledged the contribution of the teachers from the RSS-schools:

> Indeed, none of these students would have made it to the top had it not been for the contribution of Hindus. Mr. Inamdar makes it a point to declare that teachers from RSS-run schools have not only come whenever invited as guest teachers for his special Merit List batch, but have also taught his students diligently.

Thus, the Hindutva engagement with the Muslims and Islam cannot be categorized as monolithic. It has varied frameworks: from that of Savarkar to Sita Ram Goel, Golwalkar to Balraj Madhok to Malkani to Narendra Modi. The approach cannot be negatively labelled as majoritarianism or as totally harmonious. In essence, Hindutva is not opposed to Islam as a different religion or Muslims as a different people. The opposition is mostly against what Hindutvaites perceive as expansionist proselytization and political agenda of Islamist transformation of India—a fear that becomes hatred during riots. Historical package has not been kind to the relations between Hindus and Muslims. Often the Marxist-Nehruvian-Dravidianist approach is to rationalize and even justify the Islamist excesses with not-so sound nor factual secular excuses. This in turn becomes ammunition in the hands of Islamists who make heroes out of Hindu-hating genocidal emperors like Aurangzeb or warlords like Tipu ('Sultan').

On the other hand, the Hindutva or the RSS type insists on handing over three masjids built by Mughals in the holiest sacred spots of Hindus—which have no religious significance for Muslims. This gesture of the RSS Hindutva means a symbolic sealing of past memories and healing of wounds. The Sita Ram Goel school of Hindutva on the other hand wants Islam itself to jettison Koranic verses, which in their view advocate violence against non-believers. While in the era of internet, the Hindutva school of Sita Ram Goel got traction, on ground the RSS school has more appeal and practical possibilities. In fact, the success of such an RSS appeal to Indian Muslims will also make the Sita Ram Goel school mellow down.

Without expansionism and Islamism, Hindutva has almost neutral or even positive relation to Muslims in India.

Christianity

Much has been written about the Hindu-Christian encounters and Christian networks working on deepening the faultlines within Hindu society for evangelical purposes in the book *Breaking India*, which this author co-authored with Rajiv Malhotra. The approaches that Christianity takes towards Hinduism in India should be regarded here before getting to the present Hindutva organization's dialogue with Christianity and its institutions.

One approach is sophisticated, theologically well designed and institutional. It is about appropriating Hindu symbols, spiritual traditions and Christianizing them while devaluing Hindu traditions. Another approach is to employ violence and use violent ethnic conflicts as well as leftist insurgency to destroy Hinduism, which is branded as oppressive. The third is using a political proxy war. Hindutva must encounter and deal with all these approaches and also keep room for dialogue open—which it has been able to do with significant success.

Unlike Indian Islam, which also has to an extent strong Indic roots and no centralized institutional control, Christianity is yet to develop genuine Indic roots. A major impediment may be the very institutionalized attempts at Indianization which have produced forms that are theological equivalents of Indianized coke advertisement using Indian film music than genuine Indianization. Yet there are certain key positive engagements which have happened outside the institutions which sometimes the church (particularly the Catholic church) does not really approve.

Here instances for each of these Christian approaches to Hinduism shall be seen in detail, and then we shall move towards the Hindutva responses.

Approach I: Appropriation through Institutional Inculturation

In 1950 Jules Monchanin, a forty-year-old French Catholic missionary—till then 'unexceptional'[273]—working in India, succeeded in persuading his church superiors to allow him to establish a Christian institution with a Hindu sounding name—the 'Saccidananda Ashram' at the village of Kulithalai near Trichy by the banks of the sacred river of the Hindus—Kaveri, in Tamil Nadu.

In establishing the institution, he had declared that his aim was 'nothing less than the assumption into the church of the age-old Indian sannyasa (life of total renunciation) itself'.[274] He further stated his mission plan:

> We would like to crystallize and transubstantiate the search of the Hindu sannyasi. Advaita and praise of the Trinity are our only aim...This means that we must grasp the authentic Hindu search for God in order to Christianize it.[275]

Despite the Hindu label, the institution was established strictly within the hierarchical structure of Roman Catholic church as a Benedictine monastery. For this, Monchanin sought help from a French Benedictine monk named Henri Le Saux, who was interested in the Catholic mission in India, and wrote him thus:

> We can begin together. I will initiate into life in India, and you will initiate me into Benedictine life, for I strongly agree with you, that [Saint Benedict,] the Patriarch of the West must also, in the plan of God, become the Patriarch of the East. [276]

Henri Le Saux defined the aim of the establishment as follows:

> The monastery will be in Indian style. We would like to crystallize and transubstantiate the search of the Hindu sannyasi...This means that we must grasp the authentic Hindu search for God in order to Christianize it, starting with ourselves first of all, from within.[277]

Monchanin and Henri Le Saux started wearing saffron and gave themselves Sanskrit Hindu sounding names: Monchanin donned the name Swami Parama Arubi Anandam (meaning ultimate formless happiness) and Henri Le Saux became Swami Abhishiktananda (meaning bliss of the anointed One). The official name of the institution, inaugurated on 21 March 1950, the feast day of Benedict, was Saccidananda Ashram, which they translated as 'Hermitages of the Most Holy Trinity'. James Stuart explains the strategy behind adopting the name thus: 'Saccidananda i.e. *sat* (being), *chit* (awareness), *ananda* (bliss)—one of the deepest Hindu insights concerning God, with Trinitarian overtones which are drawn out in Abhishiktananda's book of the same name'[278].

Despite the outwardly adaptation of Hindu symbols and forms, his contempt for Hinduism and his certainty about the error of Hinduism were overwhelmingly deep-rooted in him. He saw the Indian religion as being tainted with errors and making vain attempts; his aim was humbling of Hinduism before Christianity. Making a comparison between pagan Greece and present-day India he wrote:

> Unfortunately, Indian wisdom is tainted with the erroneous tendencies and looks as if it has not yet found its own equilibrium. So was the Greek wisdom before Greece humbly received the Paschal message of the Risen Christ...we hope that India, once baptized to the fullness of her body and soul, and to the depth of her age-long quest for Brahman will reject her pantheistic tendencies and discovering in the splendours of Holy Ghost, the true mysticism and finding a long last the vainly longed for philosophical and theological equilibrium...India has to receive humbly from the Church the sound and basic principles of true contemplation, to keep them faithfully, to stamp her own seal, and develop through them along with the other members of the Church.[279]

He further proclaimed, 'My sole desire is that one India may be totally Christian; if I did not desire this, I would not be a Christian myself.' It was neither through old-fashioned proselytization nor simply individual humans he aimed at. He explained, 'For the task at hand is the deification not just of individual Indians but of their entire civilization.'[280] Towards this end as early as 1948, Monchanin contemplated over creating 'Christian Yoga', enumerating ten points against the idea and five points in its favour. Nevertheless, he noted:

> If Yoga is not Christianized, the whole of an essential aspect of India—realization in the body—will escape Christ.[281]

Then he goes on to list the four perils of yoga—physiological, psychological, moral and spiritual. Catholic scholar Thomas Matus details Monchanin's view of yoga thus:

> The greatest dangers are of a moral and spiritual order; in both cases, an underlying 'Pelagianism' in the various Hindu and Buddhist schools (Monchanin allows very few exceptions to this blanket judgment) seems to subtract yogi from grace; under the illusion that the isolated ego is the Higher Self, the yogi falls prey to the seduction of a monism that allows no room for agapic love. [282]

Yet Christianizing yoga, he again and again stressed as vital for the mission as 'its non-Christianization would be tantamount to refusing to Christianize India itself'[283]. So, to achieve this, Monchanin made a tactful adjustment. Thomas Matus explains:

> At this point Monchanin makes an important distinction: Yoga does not pertain to the essence of Indian civilization but to its form....Yoga as a "method" not "doctrine" as "form-manifestation" not "essence" would seem to guarantee

> considerable freedom in a Christian theologian's assessment of the Yoga component in the various Indian schools, while also guaranteeing a Christian contemplative's use of yogic forms of meditation.[284]

According to him, yoga in its original form excluded grace. Yet Monchanin hoped:

> In spite of this accumulation of obstacles, the need remains urgent: if Yoga is not Christianized, an essential aspect of India...will forever remain outside the pleroma of the Mystical Body.[285]

As the years rolled by, differences arose between himself and his collaborator Henri Le Saux. The latter wanted to extend Christianizing to Advaitic experience too. Henri Le Saux took extensive tours to Hindu places of pilgrimages and started practising meditations. Monchanin disapproved of Henri Le Saux going on pilgrimages, for example to Rishikesh, about which he wrote 'a place where Sadhus, real or supposedly so (both kinds no doubt) devote themselves to delusive exercises verging on mirage'. [286] His phobia for Vedanta increased particularly as his life neared its end. He wrote:

> It seems to me more and more doubtful that the essence of Christianity can be found by going through Adavita (the non-dualism of Sankara). Advaita like yoga and more than yoga is an abyss. Whoever dizzily plunges into it cannot know what he will find in its depths. I fear it may be himself rather than the living triune God.[287]

According to him, it was for harbouring this Advaitic vision that Hinduism should die:

> In this mystery, Hinduism (and especially advaita) must die to rise up again Christian. Any theory which does not fully take into account this necessity constitutes a lack of loyalty both to Christianity—which we cannot mutilate from its essence—and to Hinduism—from which we cannot hide its fundamental error and its essential divergence from Christianity. Meanwhile our task is to keep all doors open, to wait with patience and theological hope for the hour of the advent of India into the Church...Hinduism must reject its atman-brahman equation, if it is to enter into Christ. [288]

Harry Oldmeadow narrates:

> In later years Abhishiktananda (Henri Le Saux's Indian alias) himself referred to

> Monchanin's skepticism about any reconciliation of Christianity and Vedanta and spoke of Monchanin's fear that his Christian faith might be overwhelmed by Vedanta as it had nearly been earlier by Greek rationalism. Some hard words on these subjects were exchanged at Shantivanam, but their mutual respect and deep affection withstood the strain imposed by these disagreements.[289]

In 1957 when Monchanin died, there came a time when at least as a public posturing, his views on Hinduism could not be accepted by the mission. When alert Hindus belonging to the Hindutva school of Sita Ram Goel, suspicious of the Catholic 'Ashram' inculturation movement, pointed out the explicitly demeaning quotes of Monchanin with respect to Hinduism, the successor of his successor, Bede Griffiths, responded by distancing himself from Monchanin with no qualms. To a Hindu sannyasin Devananda, who had questioned Bede Griffiths's motives vis-à-vis Monchanin, he wrote:

> Thank you for your letter and the enclosure about Father Monchanin. Of course, if I held the same view as Father Monchanin, you would be justified in suspecting me of deception. But you must remember that Father Monchanin was writing forty years ago and immense changes have taken place in the Church since then.[290]

However, that this was only a public posture whereas the mission of Monchanin is very much integral and at the heart of Shantivanam movement can be gleaned from the fact that the bulletin of Bede Griffiths's Trust, in an article published in its winter 1997–1998 issue, hailed Monchanin's quote to 'grasp the authentic Hindu search for God in order to Christianize it' as 'prophetic'.[291]

Monchanin was followed by Henri Le Saux. When Henri Le Saux first came to India, Monchanin took him to a neighbouring Ramakrishna Tapovan to give him a feel of the Hindu ashrams in order to enable him to imitate them. What impression the Ramakrishna monks made on his collaborator was observed keenly by Monchanin, who commented:

> (Henri Le Saux) senses quite independently of me, the human impossibility of the conversion of a Hindu who is truly a Hindu (...): the more spiritual a Hindu becomes, the further in a sense he distances himself from Christianity.[292]

Henri Le Saux, as part of the project, started visiting Hindu saints and places of pilgrimage. He visited Sri Ramana and stayed in Arunachala. He visited great Hindu temples of Chidambaram, Kumbakonam and Tanjore in the saffron garb, enjoying the hospitality of gullible Hindus who welcomed them into their temples. He recounts in a letter:

> (At Chidambaram) they were very liberal and showed us everything. They even wanted to give rice and cakes presented to the images. You can understand that all the same our devotion could not go as far as that![293]

At Sri Rangam, the famous Vishnu temple, he purportedly violated the explicit notice at the entrance that non-Hindus are not allowed inside the temple. He went into the inner corridor. Stuart narrates:

> clad in Kavi, he followed a group of children into the inner sanctuary of the temple at Srirangam (carefully averting his eyes from the notice which prohibits entry to all non-Hindus.[294]

And then standing right in front of the sacred statue of Vishnu, he refused to accept aarti and created a scene. In his own words:

> and the priest took up a tray containing camphor (...), set it alight, recounted the lories of Sri Rangam Nadar (i.e., Vishnu), and began to offer a puja in my honour...I have never had such good treatment but, all the same it was nothing doing, for I should have had to make the anjali, prostrate spread my hands over the flame and bring them to my eyes, put the ashes on my forehead etc....I protested—horror indignation![295]

With such field experiences of Hinduism, Henri Le Saux went further than his mentor Monchanin in the mission to Christianize Hinduism. He often found himself pondering about his stay and experience at Arunachala at the abode of Ramana Maharshi. In 1953 he expressed his desire about Arunachala in a letter to his family: 'When will Arunachala be inhabited by Christian monks?'[296] Despite his pretensions of becoming a Hindu sannyasin, he was always ready to throw away the saffron attire, abstain from taking meat and wine for such very mundane things like humouring his friends who otherwise would not finance his books.[297]

By 1954 he was planning of a Christian Advaita. He wrote to a fellow Catholic priest:

> We have to work out a Christian advaita, and you know what that means; we shall not come to that by exploding advaita at the outset on the ground of its incompatibility. We have to strive to be faithful to advaita to the end. Only a heroic fidelity will make it possible in God's own time to transcend it (...). Not mutilation but sublimation.[298]

By 1955 he was grooming a young Christian boy of 20 to become a Christian Ramana.[299] That year he also visited the elephant cave and declared that the Siva there was not pagan and conducted a Christian mass in front of that Siva.[300] Meanwhile, he was also working in Shantivanam, introducing Hindu elements into Christian mass and was not averse to appropriate the very Hindu elements, which in their original Hindu setting were declared by him as 'indignation and horror' into his Christian worship. In his own words:

> ...So we have been singing Mass and the Office (Lauds to Compline, omitting Prime) since last Sunday in our mandapam, with prostrations, anjali, light and incense.... And we begin our dinner with a psalm in Tamil and some Sanskrit texts...What will it all come to?...Am I right to allow myself to be caught up in this? Arunachala has dug depths in me which the Opus Dei [the Office] cannot touch...However, it is the way to lead our potential postulants to the heart of Arunachala(...).[301]

After taking over the responsibility of Shantivanam following the death of Monchanin, Henri Le Saux soon developed the 'fulfilment theology' to include Advaitic experience. Fulfilment theology was first introduced in India by a Scottish educational missionary named John Nicol Farquhar, who worked at YMCA (1902–1923). His book *The Crown of Hinduism* published by the prestigious Oxford University became popular with Protestant missionaries. Fulfilment theology in the Hindu context as put forth by Farquhar states:

> Christ provides the fulfilment of each of the highest aspirations and aims of Hinduism...In Him is focused every ray of light that shines in Hinduism. He is the crown of the faith of India. [302]

Like Monchanin would proclaim decades later, Farquhar also declared that Hinduism should die in Christianity: 'Hinduism must die in order to live. It must die into Christianity'.[303] Farquhar's Catholic counterpart, Pierre Johanns, a Jesuit missionary, claimed that 'almost all elements of Christian religion...are to be found among them (the Hindus) in a higher form than they were ever known among the Greeks'.[304] Both Johanns as well as Farquhar had paid special attention to Vedanta. Farquhar wrote:

> The Vedanta is not Christian and never will be—simply as Vedanta: but very definite preparation for it. ... It is our belief that the living Christ will sanctify and make complete the religious thought of India.[305]

In 1920s Johanns was publishing a periodical titled *The Light of the East,* where he serialized articles under the title 'To Christ through the Vedanta' over a period of 20 years. This fulfilment theology of Farquhar always had an abiding presence in the works of both Monchanin as well as Henri Le Saux according to the latter's biographer Harry Oldmeadow[306].

Henri Le Saux was now using this theology to Christianize Advaita through a work of his which would become one of the important texts of the inculturation movement in India in general and Shantivanam in particular. After finishing the 100-page draft in 1962, he named the book rather elaborately and revealingly as *The Experience of Saccidananda: Advaitin Experience and its Trinitarian Fulfilment.* Thus, he tried to solve the problem that was a heartache for his mentor-collaborator Monchanin. James Stuart says the book thus held 'together Advaitic experience and Christian faith…through the adoption of a 'theology of fulfilment'.[307] In the book, Henri Le Saux explained the need to Christianize Advaitic Vedanta:

> ...the integration of the advaitic experience into his own faith is for the Christian a necessary task. Christianity presents itself to the world as the supreme message from God to mankind, as possessing the definitive word in which God have revealed all that can be told of the divine life and love. If Church's claim is true, then it follows that whatever men have found that is true, beautiful and good, both can and should be integrated into Christian experience.[308]

He wrote that Hinduism belongs to the religions of the Cosmic Covenant, which means all religious traditions outside the Biblical revelation. Of these non-Biblical Cosmic revelations, he called Hinduism in general and Advaita in particular 'the acme of man's spiritual in the cosmic religions'[309]. He stressed that though 'the cosmic covenant and Christ's revelation are not opposed to one other', they are not the same. On the contrary, 'it is that the first prepares the way for the second'.[310] Later he would add another theological dimension here. It was the primeval evil that entered the Garden of Eden that is stopping this fulfilment of Hindu Advaita in Christian Divinity:

> In everything that has any positive content of truth Christianity recognizes itself as potentially present, for as Augustine says, Christ is already there. The Church too is already present everywhere, for the Church is simply Chris reaching out to all places at all times....There is nothing true, beautiful or good that does not bear the mark of the Spirit. Evil only emerges when what is true, beautiful or good stops short at itself claiming to be the All, the final plentitude, and refuses the role in the history

> of salvation which is the very purpose of its creation. This was the temptation of the cherub in the Garden of Eden...[311]

For all his Catholic zeal, Henri Le Saux harboured serious doubts regarding his own thesis, wondering whether through fulfilment theology he really Christianized Advaita. He dropped the subtitle 'Vedanta to Trinity' in the English edition. He confessed to Raimundo Panikkar, '...Whatever we do is it not a qualified visishta advaita?—and advaita is lost as soon as there is qualification?'[312] Yet he was doing all these for a purpose, which he never lost sight of. He explained in one of his letters: 'Without this recollection in (Jesus), the Indian church will never be capable of transforming Hindu India into Christian India.'[313] His efforts he always pointed out were aimed at one thing:

> The prayer "for the heathen" ought to turn into a prayer that the Christians may at last gather in the spiritual riches of the Gentiles, so that God might finally have no more need to conserve them outside the Church, precisely in order to prevent these riches from being lost.[314]

In 1964 Raimundo Panikkar had published his thesis *The Unknown Christ of Hinduism,* which was based on fulfilment theology. Henri Le Saux appreciated this as exceeding in boldness his own work[315]. He discussed the book extensively in ecumenical study groups.

Henri Le Saux always made it a point to go to the most venerated places of Hindus and conduct a Christian mass there taking advantage of the gullibility of unsuspecting Hindus who would take him clad in saffron dress for a western Hindu sannyasin. In January 1965, he climbed to the summit of Arunachala—the hill worshipped by Hindus as sacred, conducting a Christian mass there.[316] While at Uttarkashi, another highly esteemed place of Hindu pilgrimage, while enjoying the hospitality of a Hindu ashram, he went into 'the crypt of a small temple besides Ganges, 'sitting cross-legged, round the bread and wine after the order and rite of Melchizedech (…).' He then declared this act as 'a prophetic sign'.[317] At Uttarkashi he again started experimenting with creating an Indian liturgy with a Sanskrit base. He wrote:

> In the loft fitted up in my hut I offer Mass each morning seated like a brahmin priest, with ceremonies of offering water, incense, fire. I read the gospel in Sanskrit and also sing the Our father in Sanskrit….My Upanishadic rite takes shape day by day. [Details follow] But all that is very Hindu…[318]

He now started fashioning his masses based on fulfilment theology. For the Christmas eve celebration of 1965, he planned the event, starting with the reading of Hindu texts followed by the prophets and then Christian Gospel—thus Hindu texts becoming the preparation for the advent of Christianity.[319] He considered mantras as short prayer phrases which could be related to Christian devotion. In his work *Prayer*, he draws parallels between the Indian 'Om' and 'Saccidananda' and the Christian phrase 'abba', the prayer of Jesus. The mechanism for creating a Christian mantra, which Henri Le Saux calls as 'Mantra Sandwich' was later consolidated in Shantivanam. Here a traditional Indic mantra venerated for centuries or millennia like '*Om Namaha Sivaya*' or '*Om Namo Bhagavate Vasudevaya*' or '*Om Mani Padme Hung*' are taken. Then the Hindu or Buddhist spiritual principle (the deity's name or symbol) is removed, and a Christian name is slipped in between.[320] Thus, *Om Namaha Sivaya* or *Om Namo Narayana* becomes '*Om Namo Christaya*', '*Aum Sri Yesu Bhagavate Namaha*', and in the case of *Om Mani Padme* Hung, it becomes '*Om Yesu Christa Hung*'. This type of 'Sandwich Mantras' are justified by fulfilment theology thus: 'A strong connection between "*Om Mani Padme Hung*", as a universal expression into human heart and the spirit of Jesus has already been made in Buddhist circles'.[321]

In 1968 he left Shantivanam, handing over the charge to new occupants. On parting he gave a fourfold address to a Jesuit priest who had founded a Christian centre for dialogue with Hindus, where he suggested Christians to take up the celebration of Hindu festivals such as Deepavali as a joyful expression of their own faith and also use aarti or Deepa Puja in Christian churches, giving it their own Christian interpretation.[322]

Henri Le Saux has an interesting postscript after he left Shantivanam. By the banks of Ganges there seemed to have happened in him some genuine transformation. He disowned his own writings about 'fulfilment theology', considering only what he wrote about Swami Sri Gnanananda—Guru and Disciple as 'almost the only thing that remains afloat. All the rest consists of *nama-rupa*, amusing itself with 'the theology of fulfilment' '[323] He declared that it was the Advaitic experience and realization that is important, and everything else needs to be dropped:

> Jesus may be useful in awakening the soul–as is the guru–but is never essential and, like the guru, he himself must in the end lose all his personal characteristics. No one really needs him. (...) Whoever, in his personal experience (...) has discovered the Self, has no need of faith in Christ, of prayer, of the communion of the Church.[324]

He also got critical about the church, though he offered mass till his death.

He felt the church's insistence of Christ as an obstacle to final spiritual liberation:

> Christ's namarupa necessarily explodes, but the Church wants to keep us virtually at the level of the namarupa.[325]

Quoting the Upanishad, he again criticized the church:

> Christianity believes that salvation comes from the outside, through thoughts, rites, "sacraments". The level of namarupa. Nothing comes from the outside, nothing that is made, krita, leads to what is un-made, akrita! (MundU I,2,12)[326]

He died on 7 December 1973, and was buried at Shantivanam.

Did he have an Advaitic experience? Sita Ram Goel, who had studied the Catholic Ashram movement exhaustively and who had actually interacted with him, strongly denies that and expresses the following harsh verdict:

> The only thing that does become clear, as one plods through the pages, is that he never arrived anywhere near the "Hindu experience" which he often described as the "advaitic experience". In fact, it is highly doubtful whether, with all his study of the Upanishads, he ever understood what Advaita really means. His obstinate obsession with Jesus and the Church prevented him from breaking the barrier.... He remained chained to the Church to the end of his days. He never learnt the elementary truth that Advaita must remain a mere word for those who refuse to rise above their mental fixations....In the case of Henri Le Saux there was an added difficulty: he was a poet. The flow of mellifluous phrases, particularly in his native French, was mistaken by him for mystic experience. One has to read his writings in order to see how he became a victim of his own word-imageries and figures of speech....Small wonder that the man ended as a neurotic.[327]

Henri Le Saux was succeeded by Bede Griffiths. Till his death he worked in the mission. Even before coming to Shantivanam he had started visiting holy Hindu places and working with Hindus. Like Le Saux, he also visited Hindu temples, often even the inner corridors where he made his unsuspecting Hindu friends to take him. He was sure that Hinduism was dying, and the Christian church should preserve what Christian theology would deem worth preserving:

> I am gradually clarifying my views on Hinduism. I feel it is passing away. However strong it may be at the moment, it cannot survive the impact of modern thought which is undermining it on all sides. What is necessary is that its essential holiness should be preserved....Its mythology—however beautiful cannot stand. I must

> come to recognize Christ as the unique historic manifestation of God and only then can its essential values be preserved. [328]

He was also not above racially and culturally stereotyping people. When a Syrian Catholic inmate was found stealing and having affairs with women, Bede Griffiths blamed it on both Hinduism as well as general Indian nature:

> There was also, as I believe you would find in a typical Hindu, a vivid sense of the presence of God in nature and a spontaneous piety. But with all this there goes almost complete absence of moral principle, and I am afraid this is terribly typical of India. I have found that it is almost impossible to trust anyone's word. Lying, cheating, stealing swindling seems to be in the blood and in his case at least (I don't know how much of this is general) sexual promiscuity.[329]

In 1956 he wrote that India needed the 'moral force' of Christianity outlining how to present Jesus as the fulfilment of Bhagavad Gita: 'Christ must be seen as the fulfilment of Krishna in the *Bhagavad Gita*. Krishna is not sufficient to receive the devotion he asks for, he is not serious enough'.[330] As we would see later, he developed this into a full-blown theological stand and was remarkably consistent in that stand.

He also observed the inherent universalism of Hindus. But unlike both Monchanin and Henri Le Saux who despised it and found it an obstacle, he saw it as an opportunity and a stage prior to accepting Jesus as the only God. He wrote:

> My idea is that Hinduism is valid as far as it goes but it is incomplete and needs Christ to fulfill its true purpose. If a man goes far enough in Hinduism with a sincere desire for truth, he will eventually come to Christ…I find that most of these (Hindu) boys know something of Christ and no Hindu finds any difficulty in acknowledging him as a son of God, an avatar (like the Buddha). But to realise how Christ is the son of God, how he fulfils all religion, how he delivers from sin and incorporate all mankind in himself, how he introduces us into inner life of the Trinity—all this is beyond them at present, and can only come in time.[331]

However, when a Christian author advocates universalism, he scorned at it and vehemently rejected it:

> I have been reading Schuon's latest book *Sentier de Gnose* (*Footpaths of Gnosis – Knowledge*). I see more clearly than I have ever done how fundamentally false is his whole position.…Everything he writes of Christianity is false in this sense—

> it is fundamentally perverted. It is nothing but a form of Gnosticism, the ancient heresy...Schuon is more subtle, because he knows the whole oriental tradition and attempts to assimilate Christianity, a form of Gnosis—an esoteric wisdom which places it on a level with Hinduism, Buddhism and Islam.[332]

He was also studying Hindu saints, comparing them with each other and critically evaluating them from the point of view of his own missionary activity. Thus, Sri Ramakrishna, no more holy than Ramana Maharshi, could come only just nearer to a Christian saint. He wrote after coming across the Gospel of Sri Ramakrishna:

> By the way, Bernard Kelly sent me the gospel of Ramakrishna. It is the most wonderful book....I don't think he is more holy than Ramana Maharishi, but his character is much more rich. His was the way of bhakti and he was carried away in ecstasy of love....He is perhaps nearer to St. Francis of Assisi than anyone....I don't think that anything gives a better idea of the real heart of Hindu religion. One can also see what it lacks in comparison with Christianity.[333]

Bede Griffiths's belittling view of Godhead-realized Hindu saints, though clothed in seemingly admiring words, would be consistently part of his writings. Almost a decade after writing the above words, he would write again:

> I mentioned Ramakrishna and Ramana Maharishi with their triumph over pain and their capacity to live in God above the whole state of the body. But I don't honestly believe that this is the highest state. Christ accepted pain—he really suffered, physically and mentally, as they did not and through his suffering he came to the total surrender to God.[334]

Regarding the disciples of Swami Sivananda addressing him as 'Bhagawan', he remarked that as 'a weakness of Hinduism'. Though he thought Swami Sivananda as one with great powers and one having done much good, he found the atmosphere 'not pleasant'. Swami Sivananda was 'very fat and a rather sickly man', 'conducted to coach and laid out as if in bed with devout females', many of whom were 'Germans of a theosophical kind'. [335] Despite such lesser regard for the spiritual status of Ramana Maharshi and Sri Ramakrishna vis-à-vis Christian superiority which he held in his bosom, he did not hesitate to use their names with superficial adoration when debating with suspecting Hindus. For example, when a Hindu sannyasin questioned his right to appropriate 'Aum', he accused the Hindu of being 'a sectarian' and wrote:

> I am concerned with the universal essence of Hinduism, as found in the Vedas, the Upanishads, the Gita and in modern masters like Ramakrishna, Vivekananda, Aurobindo, Ramana Maharishi and Mahatma Gandhi. These have always been my guides.[336]

Meanwhile, he was also interacting with Raimundo Panikkar, an advocate of fulfilment theology, whom he found as 'the greatest intellectual stimulus he had ever known'.[337]

During the December of 1956, he was staying at Shantivanam. He had meanwhile visited the great Hindu temples of South India—particularly Chidambaram, Kumbakonam, Tanjore and Sri Rangam. He did not hesitate to mix with Hindus or hide his Christian identity and enter unethically into the inner sanctorum of the temples in which only Hindus are permitted.[338]He postulated that it was the darkness of the unconscious that the Hindu temples represented and that was its attraction. He described:

> The whole effect is very strange—the Brahmin priests, naked to the waist, wearing the sacred thread and with heads half-shaven, the weird primitive music with beating of drums and the scent of incense—the crowds of people. Yet I felt through it all, an intense appeal to the unconscious....this great world of unconscious which is the real Hindu temple—architecture, music, sculpture, the shrine, half-hidden in darkness—all belong to the world of unconscious, and it is this symbolism of the unconscious that draws the millions of India to the temples.[339]

He wrote in the same vein about the temple architectures of Tanjore and then ended with his visit to Sri Rangam —the greatest of the Vishnu temples in South India:

> I have never seen anything so sublime, not even in Romanesque church. But at the same time, one feels the limitation of his (Hindu) religion. It is a religion of nature and never rising above nature. I came away with the sense of oppression. I feel that this is essentially a primitive religion which must be transcended. A time must come when Christ takes the place of all the worship which is offered to these gods of nature. As education grows, people will not be content with the myths of Siva and Vishnu; they will want the truth, and only Christ can answer this need of the soul.[340]

After these observations in Hindu temples and desiring to replace Hindu gods from the worship of their devotees with a Christian deity, he participated in the mass conducted with Indian imitation at Shantivanam.

> The chapel is most remarkable. It is built in the form of a Hindu temple—a mandapam or entrance hall and a garbha griha or sanctuary where the altar is. Over the altar and sanctuary is the sacred sign OM with Sanskrit texts. We sing the office in Latin but have Sanskrit prayers before and after.[341]

In Kerala, he watched a Kathakali performance, enacting a scene from Bhagavad Gita. Bede Griffiths again interpreted it as symbols of the unconscious enacting the conflict of the unconscious:

> The world of gods, and everything there, the darkness and the night, the moon and the stars, the lights in the temple…the drums and the trumpets, the music and the dance and the play, were all symbols of the unconscious…..In other words, all the figures were symbols of the unconscious, and the play was a 'conflict' of the unconscious.[342]

To him all the gods and godheads are nothing but forms of the Christian deity. Even those who reject Jesus consciously, unconsciously search for the Christian deity and their gods are but the unconscious searching in its darkness for the light of Jesus:

> All grace comes from Christ and the Holy Spirit and is offered to all men without exception. Thus, a Hindu and a Buddhist is saved by the grace of Christ-Krishna and Buddha are types of Christ—and is invisibly a member of the church. So also, with all men and women of goodwill whom you mention. Even though they reject Christ and the church in their conscious mind, yet unconsciously they are seeking that truth and goodness which is actually found in Christ[343]

So 'all men and women of goodwill' who are non-Catholics are just those who make 'better use of lesser grace'. 'But' he wrote, 'it remains true that the fullness of grace and revelation is only to be found within the church and this is our privilege and our responsibility'.[344]

He also started practising yoga, stating that he was using Swami Vivekananda's 'raja yoga' as his guide. At the same time, he made it a point to record that 'yoga did not help him to pray', as according to him prayer came from above:

> It is a grace of God to prepare the body and the mind to receive this grace of God is all that yoga can do…The aim must be to reach a state of perfect equilibrium of mind and body, so that the Holy Spirit can penetrate all the charkas and take possession of our whole being.[345]

Soon he was also discovering the Hindu Divine symbols, not simply incomplete to be fulfilled by Jesus, but as developing evil and negative power without the presence of the Christian deity in them:

> I believe that these symbols, the Golden Flower for instance or the Hindu temple can be a genuine revelation of God. But in so far as they are not redeemed—in other words do not belong to Christ—they have a daemonic aspect which can have a devastating power.…I see more and more clearly that Hinduism must be redeemed in order that it may reveal all is hidden power and beauty, otherwise it can devour the soul.[346]

He also studied Bhagavad Gita in the context of fulfilment theology, making explicit comparison of Hinduism with the Hebrew Bible (called Old Testament by Christians):

> In the same way in so far as Krishna in the Bhagavad Gita reveals the way to the ultimate goal of the Atman, he may be said to be a type of Christ. What Christianity brings is the fulfilment of this cosmic revelation. Christ is infinitely more than Krishna and the kingdom of heaven is infinitely (more) than Nirvana. But just as St. Thomas holds that the knowledge of the Trinity and the Incarnation is implicit in primeval revelation, so I would say that the knowledge of Christ and kingdom of heaven is implicit in the experience of the Atman or of Nirvana.…They are the same supernatural reality, but it is only in Christ that the fullness of this supernatural mystery is revealed. There is a very close analogy with the Old Testament. Noah, Melchisedec and Job (who are pagans) Moses, David and Isaiah, all had true knowledge of God, but their knowledge was incomplete, and their experience therefore imperfect. Christ fulfils at once the Old Testament and the cosmic covenant. In this sense, both Hinduism and Buddhism await their fulfilment in Him.[347]

In his letters, Bede Griffiths stereotyped Indians as immoral, and often traced the reason for the lack of morality in Indians to Hinduism. Quoting his old teacher C. S. Lewis, who considered the Hebrew Bible as filled with holiness and morality, he contrasted Indic religion thus:

> The Infinite holy god of wonder and terror was also the God of infinite justice and moral goodness. In India idea of the holy is still overwhelmingly strong, but it is not particularly moral. Siva (with his lingam) is a holy God, at once terrible and lovely, but he is not particularly good! So also Krishna is holy—an object of worship and love and adoration. But he does not make any great demand on his devotees. I feel that this is what Hinduism lacks and why it needs Christ. He alone is absolutely holy and absolutely good.[348]

What is remarkable about Bede Griffiths is the way such ideas about Hinduism become so fixed and rigid in his thought process. Despite his claims of 'studying Hinduism' and being guided by its universal essence, etc., one finds the very same ideas expressed again in almost the very same words almost 17 years later. For example, he writes about Krishna:

> What is more, he (Krishna) is morally ambivalent. He is a symbol of highest divinity, yet as a man he is shown to be a trickster, a deceiver who brings disaster on his people and is finally ignominiously slain….(Siva) is the symbol of the purest love but this is in terms of gross sexuality. It is the same with Siva. He is the God of love, of infinite beauty and grace, whose nature is being, knowledge and bliss, the Father, the Saviour, the Friend. Yet his symbol is the lingam and like Krishna has many wives.[349]

This idea of Hinduism lacking moral sense, he would project to the entire Indian society. He explained in a letter in what sense he loved Indians:

> Of course, I love these Indians as my brothers. (…) But I assure you I have no illusions about them. I see the virtues of the British very clearly—they are honest, straightforward, just and reliable—while Indians are lacking in these qualities. Of course, India owes almost everything as a modern nation to the British…But the British had a fatal defect—they could not accept the Indians as their equals—they always imagined themselves to be a superior race. There is good reason for this—we are superior in certain ways —but the Indians have qualities of religion and virtue and affection…They need us and (we) can help them and they are deeply thankful for all we have given them—but they could not accept (us) as superiors—that is why we had to go.[350]

His colonial prejudice of Indians and his faith in the lack of morality in the Indian psyche was so deep rooted that he even treated the Indian Catholics close to him with suspicion. For example, a Gandhian Catholic named Stephen was attracted by this saffron-clad westerner. Griffiths writes about him:

> I have been trying to form a group of oblates here…two or three young Indian Catholics. One of these is called Stephen—he has become a very close friend of mine. He calls me his "guru" and I act as his director. He is working in Vinoba Bhave's Sarvodaya movement….Stephen is heart and soul in this movement and is doing wonderful work…[351]

But the colonial prejudices bordering racism remained strong in Bede Griffiths:

> I have seen good deal of Stephen lately—like all Indians he needs watching—you never quite know what they will do next! But he is very faithful to us and has taken a private vow of obedience.[352]

Soon when he had doubts about the above-said Stephen, whatever faults he found he blamed them all on Hinduism:

> But Stephen is a queer mixture. I am afraid that he is very unbalanced. He had wonderful ideas but was quite incapable of carrying them out...All these are of course problems of the unconscious, which I still find difficult to fathom....This gives wonderful spontaneity, but it leaves one terribly exposed to the forces of emotions and the imagination. That is why I find people here so unreliable—they are carried away by their feelings and imagination (Stephen is very much this type.), and you can never rely on them. They may also be exposed to the deeper forces of the unconscious—the gods and demons. This is evident in Hinduism generally ...[353]

He combined his view that Hinduism is nothing but a descent into the darkness of unconscious with all its attractions and dangers, and that to swim it unharmed and reach real spiritual liberation, one needed Jesus, as Hinduism was deficient:

> How I love Hinduism! Everything is there except Christ. I see more and more clearly that all we have to do is to place Christ in the centre of Hinduism. But how to do it?...I am sure that it is a question of coming to terms with the unconscious (the Hindu lives from the unconscious)...The unconscious is full of demons and demonic powers which seek to 'possess' us as you say....There is evil in Hinduism and in all Hindu society...I believe that it is Christ alone who can set us free from the unconscious. ...For me Hinduism seems to act as a means for regaining contact with the unconscious, but it must be Hinduism transformed by Christ. Hinduism by itself will not do[354]

Just like his other negative views on Hinduism and Hindu society, this perception also showed remarkable consistency throughout his writings—often concealed with seemingly adoring words. Lest one think that this view of Bede Griffiths that Hinduism is evil and essentially exists at the unconscious, belongs to his past view or just a passing formative stage, as recent as 2005. The Shantivanam movement published this letter of Bede Griffiths in the *Bede Griffiths Sangha Newsletter* under the title 'Sin, Repentance and Unconscious'.[355]

Despite his usage of seemingly adoring words to portray Hinduism, a small scratch on the surface—a gentle criticism over his Christian religion or church would bring out torrents of this hatred he harboured against Hinduism. Almost 30 years after he wrote the above lines, in 1990 he wrote scathingly to Sita Ram Goel when the latter criticized the ethics of his methods and validity of his theology thus:

> I suggested to Mr Goel that the Voice of India might well make a special study of the various aspects of Hinduism. I suggested as a beginning the history of human sacrifice and temple prostitution from the earliest times to the present day.... Another institution is the practice of sorcery and magic....Above all there is the problem of untouchability. Surely one of the greatest crimes in the history of religion...I love Hinduism, not only the Vedas and the Gita and Vedanta but popular Hindu piety and its cultured traditions but I try to get a balanced view of it.[356]

Despite the claims of his hagiographers that his stand and views on Hinduism evolved and changed over a period of time, what one finds is a remarkable consistency of stands and perspectives which contain absolute certainty regarding the inferiority and deficiency of Hinduism on the one hand and need for appropriating the symbols and institutions of Hinduism, which he claimed need to be relieved of the demonic presence of Hindu deities creating moral disorders and replacing them with the Christian deity.

The second part of Bede Griffiths' autobiography is titled *The Marriage of East and West*. In this he wrote:

> I wanted to experience in my life the marriage of these two dimensions of human existence, the rational and intuitive, the conscious and unconscious, the masculine and feminine. I wanted to find the way to the marriage of East and West.[357]

This notion of Bede Griffiths has often been lauded by his followers as some sort of a deeper spiritual synthesis. A reviewer of a hagiographic video on Bede Griffiths says:

> The persistent theme throughout is of the union of opposites: East and West, Christianity and Hinduism (and other religions), right brain/left brain, masculine/feminine, rational/intuitive.[358]

Yet a study of the origin of this theme in its formative stages reveals more colonial prejudice and personal pathos than any genuine spiritual need for the harmony of deeper opposites. To Bede Griffiths, though Hinduism has 'affection and natural grace', it was lacking in being 'honest, straightforward, just and reliable'. He identified these qualities with the feminine and found the

British element masculine. He wrote:

> I feel in a sense they are our opposites—it is male versus female—conscious versus unconscious, and it is not easy to marry them. Yet this is what we ought to have done for their own sakes and for theirs. They need us and can help them ...[359]

He later revealed in another letter that he was also resolving a personal crisis in seeking the feminine in India:

> I am sure that my problem is that of the anima. At school we were brought up in a totally masculine world. We scarcely even referred to a mother or sister and a mother was known as 'the mater'. We never saw girls or women (except for the matron)....Unfortunately, there were not many feminine contacts at home either, so altogether I was starved....That is why people like Cherian and Stephen attract me—and why India attracts me. People here all live from the anima...Hence all the lying and cheating and stealing, and a lack of moral integrity.[360]

Repressed sex also bothered him. After a stroke in the early 1990s, he explained:

> It is your flesh and your blood that this has to penetrate. It then moves down through the sex region. That is very important too, because that tends to be suppressed. In my own experience, it was very much repressed. I am rediscovering the whole sexual dimension of life at the age of eighty-six, really. And that also means discovering the feminine.[361]

Bede Griffiths was a strategist par excellence for Christian proselytization. He was looking at almost all religiously significant changes happening in the postcolonial world. The new developments that were happening in physics had an impact on popular culture in the West that seemed more advantageous to the 'Eastern' religious movements. This made Bede Griffiths anxious. He was aware of the profound parallels between the new vision emerging out of quantum physics and Indic traditions:

> David Bohm speaks, as a theoretical physicist, of unity and interconnectedness in what he calls the implicate order, prior to the world of separate entities which is our normal experience. The implicate order is constantly unfolding, giving rise to the explicate order of particular forms and structures. This is where the new scientific understanding of the universe meets with the non-dualist traditions of Hinduism, Buddhism and so on.[362]

He was acutely aware of the deficiency of Christianity in incorporating within it the holistic vision provided by New Physics and the parallels pointed out by physicists like Schrodinger, Capra, Bohm, etc., between the vision of New Physics and Indic systems of inner science. Quoting Teasdale, Everardo Pedraza writes:

> Yet there was still the question of where and how Christianity and its mystical tradition fit into this interdisciplinary and interreligious dialogue. Indeed, "Father Bede was aware of this deficiency and sought in numerous lectures to show how Christianity and its mystical tradition fit in, primarily through the intuitions of Trinity, Godhead, and the Incarnation".[363]

Towards this end he found a collaborator in Rupert Sheldrake—a British biologist advocating questionable vitalist theories. [364] Shantivanam continues to operate today strictly in consistency with the principles and visions of its founders. It has also been influenced by fellow travellers. For example, the entrance to Shantivanam depicts a three-headed Jesus. Its origin can be traced to both Henri Le Saux and Bede Griffiths. In 1955 Henri Le Saux visited the Cave Temple of Elephanta:

> Yesterday evening we came here to Elephanta. Here Hindu temples cut out of the rock, only one well preserved. I was thunderstruck! I am more Hindu than Buddhist. You know the Shiva with here heads, incorrectly called Trimurti…When I saw it, I simply had to hold on to a pillar for support…This morning we said our Mass immediately in front of it. There is nothing pagan here.[365]

Bede Griffiths also visited the Elephanta Cave and recorded in his book *Christ in India* thus:

> When I landed at Bombay, I went to see the Elephanta caves and the great statue of Siva there left a lasting impression on me. Here at the threshold of India I found graven in stone that profound spirit of contemplation which has given inner meaning…[366]

In fact, Harry Oldmeadow compares the reaction of Bede Griffiths on seeing the Elephanta Mahadeva to that of Rudolph Otto, a post-Kantian Protestant theologian from Germany who compared it with ancient Christian art:

> Here an image rises out of the rock which I can only compare with the great representations of Christ in early Byzantine churches. It is three headed form,

> carved only as far as the breast in threefold human size...Nowhere have I found the secret of the transcendent world of the other world, more grandly and perfectly expressed than in these three heads... [367]

In the same book he also makes it clear that Siva is nothing more than a 'shadow of the mystery of Christ'[368]. Today we see at the entrance of Shantivanam, a three-headed Jesus. Further forms of Siva, particularly as Yogi are Christianized in Shantivanam as a continuation to the mindset of the founders. Thus, we see the *Bede Griffiths Sangha Newsletter* of June 2004 exhibiting a three-headed Jesus in the yogic lotus posture.[369]

Both Henri Le Saux as well as Bede Griffiths made it a point to visit the Hindu temples and wherever possible offer Christian prayer in Hindu holy places in accordance with 'fulfilment theology'. Shantivanam continues this appropriation on an institutional basis. The *Bede Griffiths Sangha Newsletter* announced in July 1999 its plan to organize a tour of Catholic activists and missionaries to Hindu holy places, closely following the footsteps of Henri Le Saux and Bede Griffiths. The announcement said:

> We would also like to include the Hindu temple at Chidambaram where the New Year festivities are a wonderful opportunity to experience the most holy place in Hindu southern India. We would also like to include a visit to Tiruvanamallai and Ramana Maharshi's ashram at the foot of Arunachala (Shiva in the form of a mountain), and Mahaballipuram, with its famous sea shore rock temples....The trip will be organised in conjunction with Soul of India Tours, which specialises in tours to spiritual places in India. Soul of India Tours organised the recent pilgrimage for the World Community for Christian Meditation which included a visit to Shantivanam and to his Holiness the Dalai Lama. Often Hindu credulity is well utilized to perform a prayer to Christian deity in the Hindu holy place.[370]

Already, Bede Griffiths had outlined Catholic missionaries how to Christianize Nataraja—the presiding deity of Chidambaram. Kim Nataraja explains:

> When Fr Bede visited Sr. Pascaline, a member of the Benedictine Sisters of Perpetual Adoration at the Osage Monastery, Forest of Peace, in Oklahoma in 1978. He presented them with a statue of Nataraja, saying that Christians must begin to see Nataraja as the symbol of the risen Christ. It is easy to see why he felt this to be so.[371]

And nearly a quarter of century after that, the *Bede Griffiths Sangha Newsletter* announces in its editorial:

> There is a Tamil saying, "To see is salvation at Chidambaram, to meditate is salvation at Arunachala". Our visits to both of these places were both very powerful and moving experiences. Chidambaram is the most sacred temple of Shiva Nataraja, and here we were permitted a puja in the Chit Sabha, the holiest place in the temple.[372]

The 'pilgrimages' are also conducted to other temples of importance to Hindus in a very calculated manner. For example, *The Golden String*, the bulletin of the Bede Griffiths Trust, reports how Catholic activists of Shantivanam entered the Hindu temples and offered prayers in the same manner that Bede Griffiths and Henri Le Saux did decades before:

> One of the highlights of this particular trip was a climb up to the top of the holy mountain known as Tirueengkoil Malai, considered to be one of the most powerful places of pilgrimage in South India. This mountain is recognized as the first among the 50 seats of spiritual power in India known as "peetams"....Once inside the precincts, we stopped to meditate in front of the stone statues of Shiva and Parvati, personifications of the opposites on every level of being. We chanted and prayed with sacred movements in the temple of Parvati and later did the same in the temple of Shiva alongside it.[373]

By 2007, the plans had enlarged to include Mount Kailash. The newsletter announced in its 'Other Announcements' section:

> Pilgrimage to the sacred Mount Kailash in Tibet Dates to be finalised, but will fall between June and October 2007. This holy place is sacred to all traditions that have encountered it: Hindu, Buddhist and Jain.[374]

The words used have been carefully crafted to enhance Christian appropriation. It is not a holy Hindu place. It is simply a holy place—holy to any tradition that encounters it. So if Christians can arrange, and given the nature of Kailash (which is inaccessible to common Hindus), and government control in selecting and regulating pilgrims, the fear that Christians masquerading as Hindus are at an advantageous position with nothing to stop them from conducting a Christian mass first clandestinely as Henri Le Saux did at the top of Thiruvannamalai—a mountain venerated as Siva itself, then openly, by planting a cross when the time is ripe—as Catholic church tried Christianizing at Auschwitz, is totally justified. [375]

An important aspect of Shantivanam, which all the three missionaries nurtured with interest, was including sacred Hindu literature into its daily Mass as well as liturgy. The Shantivanam prayer book *Sandhya Vandana* explains:

> The three common acts of worship at Shantivanam, our Sandhya Vandana, corresponds to the monastic offices of Lauds, Sext, and Vespers. Hence, they are based primarily on songs and readings from the Bible, according to Syrian Catholic and Latin Benedictine traditions. But the Christian prayer is always preceded by chanting in Sanskrit, the ancient sacred language of India, and by readings from the scriptures of Hinduism and the other traditions of this land and the East in general.[376]

The prayers always start with Gayatri Mantra—the holiest of Hindu mantras and ends with Christian hymns or prayers. This is the enactment of fulfilment theology in the daily prayer routine of Shantivanam. The most sacred of the Hindu mantras are taken and they are translated in the Shantivanam prayer book in such a way as to remove Hindu elements from them. For example, the Maha Mrityunjaya Mantra (*Rig Veda*, Mandala VII, Hymn 59), which is one of the holiest mantras for Hindus, is included in the Monday and Tuesday afternoon prayers of Shantivanam. The translation given reads:

> We worship the true God who is the Supreme Being; who is fragrant and who nourishes all beings; may He liberate us from death, for the sake of immortality; even as a cucumber is severed in its bondage to the creeper.[377]

In comparison, Griffiths's translation states: 'Tryambaka we worship, sweet augmenter of prosperity. As from its stem the cucumber, so may I be released from death, not reft of immortality'.[378] *Tryambaka* is quintessentially Hindu in its meaning and imagery. Dr Rolf Sovik: explains

> The prefix tri (pronounced with a short "i") means "three". When it is joined to ambakam, the letter "i" becomes "y", and the word reads tryambakam. Ambaka means "eye". Tryambakam is "three-eyed", an epithet for Shiva...[379]

However, it is exactly this Hindu term that gets the Christian distortion being translated as 'the true God'. The popular Hindu bhajans in all major Indian languages are distorted to Christianize them. For example, the famous '*Ragupathi Ragava Raja Ram*'—used by Mahatma declares Hindu universalism and aims to promote communal harmony. Thus, the Hindi section of bhajans present in the ashram handbook twist the bhajan to proclaim the superiority of Jesus as given in the translation by them:

> Sab bole Prabhu Yesu nam Paita pavana Yesu nam....Sab se accha Yesu Nam Papa nivarana Yesu nam (The name of Jesus is better than other names.)[380]

Even the Vaishnavaite mahamantra is Christianized as:

Hare Yeshu Hare Yeshu , Yeshu Yeshu Hare Hare Hare Christa Hare Christa Christa Christa Hare Hare[381]

Thus, the Shantivanam prayer book shows both stages of U-turn, namely incorporating Hindu prayers—removing their Christian features as well as changing these Hindu prayers and sacred mantras into explicitly Christian ones. Another important continuity that one finds in Shantivanam activities is the devaluation of Hinduism—stereotyping it as incomplete, fatalistic, non-humanistic or uncaring about human suffering, etc. Even a few months before his death, Bede Griffiths stated in an interview:

> It's a very interesting point. In the Hindu tradition the name for the godhead as far as it can have a name is sat-chit-ananda being, consciousness, and bliss, and the Hindu aims at reaching that state where you become one with the supreme being through reality in pure consciousness, and that produces a state of absolute bliss, transcendence, but it is not exactly love, so there is no relationship in it. I feel the danger of Hindu mysticism is to retire into an inner reality of infinite riches and beauty and so on, but it doesn't relate you to others, and the danger of the sannyasi in India is he is not really concerned with other people. That's why you can meet people dying in the streets of Calcutta and not worry much about it. It's part of karma[382]

That this is not an isolated observation but part of the Shantivanam worldview is shown by Rupert Sheldrake—another product of Shantivanam, who expressed the same view:

> Furthermore, after living there a while, I also saw the shadow side of the Hindu tradition, which I hadn't seen in my earlier brief visit. There is a fatalistic lack of concern for other people that was alien to me. That view was at variance with my more optimistic, progressivist Christian culture....In India I came face to face with the realization that rooted in the Christian tradition is the sense that you can, and should, help other people; we can aim for some better state of affairs on Earth, for the whole of society. When I talked with my Indian friends and colleagues, it became very clear that I had this view deep within me. I realized that this sense didn't come from Hindu philosophy, nor from my atheistic outlook. Instead, I saw it came from a deeply embedded Christian view of the world that I carried with me unwittingly. In fact, I realized this partly because in conversation with my Indian friends they would frequently point out that so much of what I was expressing was a Christian view. The repeated revelation of this, even to an avowed atheist, was difficult to ignore. I spent some time living in Father Bede Griffiths's ashram, and I found that coming back to a Christian path made sense to me.[383]

John Martin 'Sahajananda'—the present in-charge of Shantivanam continues this legacy when he writes:

> The advaitic experience of the Upanishad sages is towards unity with the divine, which tends to neglect creation and human relationships. The advaitic experience of Jesus is towards God and also towards human beings. When it moves towards God it says, "I and God are one", when it moves towards human beings, it says "whatever you do to the least of my brothers and sisters that you do unto me". The uniqueness of the message of Jesus was this radical love of God and radical love of the neighbour.[384]

Martin in his book *Jesus Christ—A Bridge* further elaborates upon this and divides spiritual traditions into wisdom traditions and prophetic traditions. In not-so-obviously demeaning terms, he pictures the wisdom traditions (i.e. Hindu tradition) as fatalistic and oblivious to the sufferings of fellow human beings while prophetic traditions (Judaeo-Christian) are sensitive and moralistic. In fact, he traces the roots of alleged Indian social indifference stereotyped by his mentor Bede Griffiths to the uncaring impersonal nature of the Indic Godhead, which he contrasts with the supposedly loving and caring nature of the Christian personal deity:

> (In prophetic traditions) To be born in this world is not an effect of karma, not a sin, but is a gift of God. Life in this world is meant to experience the blessing of God. People have to take responsibility for their neighbours, particularly those who are marginalized in the society, the widows and the orphans...The wisdom traditions give much importance to karma, cause and effect and believes in many lives and theory of reincarnation. They tend o believe in the absolute nature of cause and effect and propose an impersonal God or no God at all. One who does not or cannot interfere in the wheel of cause and effect. The prophetic traditions believe in creator, personal, loving and merciful God.[385]

And he offers Jesus as the solution to overcome the alleged deficiency of Hinduism:

> The Vedic tradition has its own difficulties when it comes to a theory about the origin of creation....Jesus Christ is the union between non-dualism and monotheism. Christianity has to learn the non-dual experience of Christ from the Vedic tradition and the Vedic tradition has to learn from all the monotheistic traditions the importance of creation and the love of neighbour, specially love towards the needy: "whatever you do to the least of my brothers and sisters that you do unto me".[386]

Though he clothes the words with seeming symmetry of exchange between Vedic and Christian traditions, in reality, he uses his words carefully. Christianity has to only rediscover the Christ in Vedic tradition while it is the Vedic tradition that actually lacks the concern and love for fellow human beings—which it has to positively receive from Christianity through Jesus. Another constant theme of devaluation of Hinduism is the Shantivanam claim that the Christian Trinitarian experience is deeper and richer than the Advaitic experience. The Jesuit priest Chacko Valiaveetil, claims in *The Golden String*—the bulletin of the Bede Griffiths Trust (winter 1998–1999):

> The Indian Christology developed by the Shantivanam School is rooted in the deepest God-experience of the Hindu and Christian traditions. Both experiences are advaitic, but the Trinitarian experience is deeper as it is a communion in love. It also accounts for the reality of the world as it is: not a simple unity, but a unity in distinction; the Son/Word being the principle of distinction.[387]

Equally important is the constant striving to adapt Hindu sacred icons and sculpture. The Shantivanam chapel was itself built in the style of Hindu symbols. For example, generally Hindu temples of South India have on the four corners of the Gopuram, the animal which is the mount of the deity. In the case of the Goddess, it is lion and in the case of Siva, it is the bull. The Shantivanam chapel features very similar bull, lion, eagle, and they actually represent the evangelists Luke, Mark and John. Those recognized officially by the Catholic church as saints are shown in the base tier of the Gopuram—in Hindu saffron clothing—like mendicants or siddhas, and above them, Jesus is depicted in yogic postures. In Siva temples usually in the southern side of the Gopuram, Siva is depicted as Dakshina Murti—in the Shantivanam chapel, Jesus is depicted as Dakshina Murti.

The inculturation attempt to Christianize Hindu sculptural and temple architectural elements cannot be seen in isolation. Independent of Shantivanam, Christian missionaries are developing pseudo-historical crackpot theories that it was the revolution of ancient Christianity brought by St Thomas to India that became all the Saivaite and Vishnu temples in South India, which were later appropriated by Aryan Brahmins. Thus, a notorious Dravidianist-Christologist named Deivanayakam, and his daughter Devakala claim:

> Though Saivism and Vaishnavism have nothing to do with the Vedas, the Saivaite and Vaishnavaite figures came to be considered as Brahminical gods and goddesses. There is a vast difference between the Hinduism of the Vedic period and that of the later period. The pantheon of the Hindu gods were given anthropomorphic form

> only in the later period. Saivism and Vaishnavism are the offshoots of Early Indian Christianity, and the sculptures of Saivism and Vaishnavism are actually the visual aids for the doctrine of Trinity, and the doctrine of incarnation or Avatar. Since these figures are seen in the post-Christian era, it is misconsidered that they are of the Brahminical contribution. The Doctrine of Trinity in both Saivism and Vaishnavism is expressed through the icons...The figures of Siva, Vishnu and Brahma are seen in Ellora, Kailasanatha, Mahabalipuram. Though there are three names for each of the three personalities of God, the entity is one and only one. This triune God is depicted as "three-faced Siva" with one body. In Ellora and Elephanta the icons of Siva with three faces in one body are seen in large numbers. This shows that though God is represented in three different personalities as Siva, ShaktI and Kumarakkadavul, or, Siva, Vishnu and Brahma, he is not three but one God in three personalities.[388]

Though at present, the Shantivanam movement and the Dravidian-Christologist movement appear to be separate, that they can converge can be gauged from the writings of Bede Griffiths as well as from some of the recent writings published in the newsletter/bulletin of the Shantivanam movement.

Though Griffiths himself never dwelt much on the Aryan race theory or Aryan-Dravidian binary, nevertheless he used them, and where he used them, he tried to show Hinduism as an Aryan development that integrated into itself a positive element of non-Aryan tribal tradition. Thus, Krishna worship, tantra, Siva worship were all originally non-Hindu, tribal traditions (for he considers tribal as non-Hindu and Aryan as Hindu) integrated into Aryan Hinduism. When analysing the historical development of the Krishna worship and devotion in India, he suggested that 'Krishna had been a non-Aryan deity absorbed into the Hindu pantheon through his identification with Vishnu'.[389] With regard to tantra, Griffiths speculates:

> But in the third century C.E., this movement of Tantra came into Hinduism and Buddhism. It was a movement from below and must have come from pre-Aryan people. It's not Aryan which is patriarchal, but pre-Aryan—it comes from the earth from matter.[390]

In an article that was published in the winter 2004–2005 issue of *The Golden String*—the bulletin of the Bede Griffiths Trust, the writer appreciatively described Bede Griffiths's perspective of grouping Indic spiritual traditions into racial binaries:

> Bede marvelously traces how historically the Tantric texts, which first begin to appear in the third century CE, rise out of the indigenous Dravidian Shaivism of south India,

> where devotion to God as mother is very strong, so the tendency is to assert the values of nature and of the body, of the senses and of sex. Many things which tended to be suppressed in the Aryan Vishnu tradition came to be reverenced by Tantra.[391]

After assigning such non-Hindu roots to tribal spiritual traditions (which in reality are organically associated with Hindu Goddess traditions), Mary is introduced as the 'dark mother of the oppressed'. Another Shantivanam product, the Christian artist Jyoti Sahi elaborates upon this idea of Griffiths thus:

> Some years ago, I was asked to make an image of the "Dalit ki Mata", or the Mother of the Dalits. The word Dalit, coming from Dal, meaning the earth, or that which is broken, crushed, made me think of this image of the cave. Could the Mother of the Dalits, be this primodial figure of the woman in the cave? But then what would this woman look like? Traditionally she has been pictured as dark skinned, as in the figure of the "Black Madonna" who was definitely a representation of "Our Lady of the Rocks", who perhaps was in ancient times worshipped in dark caves, where she was associated with the chthonic forces of the underworld.[392]

At another level, one can find many icons of Mary clad in an Indian dress, placed in many areas at Shantivanam. The chapel entrance tower displays a Mary similar to the Hindu Goddess, with even vermilion mark and Abhaya Hasta seated below Jesus. Today we find in select areas of Tamil Nadu such promotion of Indianized forms of Mary—specifically to compete with and replace Maariamman—the traditional Tamil Nadu Mother Goddess in folk tradition who was popularized during freedom struggle by the Tamil poet Bharati. After strategically promoting such designed syncretism, the missionary scholars enter, conduct research and proclaim that there are similarities between Mary and Maariamman worship[393].

Already we have seen that each of the forerunners of Shantivanam had a different view of yoga. Nevertheless, they all agreed that yoga should be Christianized. Judson B. Trapnell explains how 'it is apparent from Bede Griffiths's later writings how thoroughly he assimilated the language and techniques of this Indian system into his own spiritual practice, especially his use of a Christian form of meditation—the Jesus prayer—that he began in 1940'.[394] This was taken to the practical level by one of the Shantivanam inmates under the tutelage of Griffiths, who wrote a book on yoga titled *Yoga and Contemplation*, with no explicit reference to Christianity. In the preface to the book, he acknowledged that he had referred the text of his different masters. This included yoga from *Yogasanas Simplified* by Sri Yogendraji and *Yoga for the Students* by Hansraj Yadav, a disciple of Yogendraji of Yoga Institute Bombay and pranayama from *The Correction of Breathing Difficulties by Pranayama* by Dr Swami Gitananda of Ananda Ashram, Pondicherry[395]. In his foreword, Bede Griffiths explained yoga not as a spiritual discipline but as a mere physical and psychological discipline to aid Christian prayer and contemplation:

> Though developed in the context of Indian thought, both Hindu and Buddhist, it can be used as a method of prayer by a Christian no less than by a Hindu or a Buddhist. In this book, Brahmachari Amaladas…shows how the physical and psychological discipline of Hatha Yoga can be used as basis for Christian prayer and contemplation. It is hoped that this book may serve as a simple introduction to the practices of Hatha Yoga and as an initiation into a way of Christian contemplation.[396]

The book starts with an invocation to Jesus as '*Om Sri Sat Guruve Yeshu Devaya Namah*'. The picture of Amaladas in Padmasana shows him with Hindu chain of beads with a cross dangling at its end. At the initial stages of the book, superficial and erroneous parallels are drawn between Hindu concepts and Christian ones. For example, 'Aham Brahmasmi' is shown as an equivalent of St Paul's statement: 'It is not I, but Christ lives in me'[397]. But as the book proceeds, it becomes completely Christian, with very rare mention of Hindu concepts. Aum or Pranava is Christianized by mistranslating the word '*sabda*' (sound) as 'word' to make it resonate with the Christian theological concept of Logos or Word.[398] Further he claims that when a Christian uses the 'Aum', it is in the Christian sense:

> I would mention the difference of a Christian from a Hindu. When a Christian says Aum, he means this "Aum" which is in the fullness of time was made flesh in the incarnation of the Word. A Christian means precisely Universal Man Jesus Christ, who is the incarnation of "Aum".[399]

For Nama Japa Meditation, he suggests '*Om Jesu Christa Jaya Jaya Nam*'.[400] He also suggests meditation on the trinity with incoming and outgoing breaths. In the M.Sc. Yoga course offered by Bharathidasan University, Tiruchi (35 kilometres from Shantivanam) in the third semester under one of the electives 'Traditions of Yoga and Meditations', there is a unit titled 'Christian Traditions of Yoga and Meditation—The Practices of Jesus Christ, Francis Assisi, Quakers, Leo Tolstoy and Bede Griffiths'.[401] The Hindu nature of yoga is obliterated under the secular terms 'Ancient Indian traditions of yoga' and 'Modern Indian traditions of Yoga' thus further facilitating sectarian monopolistic takeover of yoga through the universalism of Hindu psyche.

Inside Shantivanam one finds thus various forms of Jesus at the experimental stage. These forms imitate popular sacred Hindu icons. For example, there is a statue of Jesus in yoga under a five-headed serpent. Given the fact that in Tamil Nadu, the sides of the roads and the banks of village water bodies abound in the images of Hindu gods and goddesses seated under such a five-headed serpent, the eventual installation of such theo-plagiarized Christian statues can create considerable confusion in the minds of people while at the same time fulfilling the mission of the Shantivanam founders to replace the Hindu deities by the Christian deity at the centre of Hindu spiritual traditions. They are at the experimental stage—waiting for the right time of launch—for Christianizing Hindu institutions and spiritual traditions. The Shantivanam movement finds parallel for this kind of operation in the history of church—when it captured the pagan religious institutions—their celebrations and places of worship. A commemorative issue in honour of Monchanin, its founder published by 'Saccidananda Ashram' puts the Shantivanam project in this historical perspective:

> When St Gregory the Great sent the monk Augustine to the Angles, he directed him not to deprive them of their places of worship or customary festivities, but to transform their temples into Christian ones and to dedicate to the Saints their religious festivals. The Indian Church at least in the Tamil Nadu made at times wonderful use of these directives...In short Shantivanam was only an attempt amongst others an effort to recapture a spirit and to prepare this spirit to find in due time is right outcome and Christian expression, in matters of cult, art, etc.[402]

The post-Shantivanam transformation of Henri Le Saux had its effect on the esteem with which he was held at Shantivanam. His experience was devalued by Shantivanam authorities and influential theologians connected with it. For example, in the second issue of the newsletter of the Bede Griffiths Trust titled *The Golden String*, Wayne Teasdale, comparing the supposedly mystic experience of Bede Griffiths as superior to that of Henri Laux, states:

> Bede's experience was thoroughly advaitic, and he came to realize that all genuine mysticism is fundamentally advaitic. What distinguishes Christian advaita from a purely monistic Hindu form is its inner dynamic of love. Love is the energy of inner distinctions within the ground of the divine nature and identity. The Incarnation is a revelation of this love, this inner dynamic quality of nonduality. It is this experiential insistence of Bede that further distinguishes him from Abhishiktananda, who seemed to lapse into a purely monistic advaita.[403]

This approach shows how much of theological brainstorming, strategic planning and institutional logistics go into what can only be considered as a war waged against Hinduism. It is deceptive and even alluring. While masquerading as dialogue and even an open-minded synthesis, the aim is very clearly to destroy Hinduism by capturing and Christianizing its core spiritual elements. Though the process of Christianizing may destroy the soul of the spiritual components while retaining only the lifeless form the church and the other similar evangelical movements do not care. Creating an appropriate defence response to this form of attack on Hindu culture and spirituality is quite challenging.

There is one school of Hindutva, represented by Sita Ram Goel, which has been at the forefront in bringing to light these attempts and exposing the theological engine that drives the inculturation-appropriation crusade. Sita Ram Goel makes offence the best form of defence and goes for the very person, Jesus Christ; he makes the thesis that such aggressive strategies of Christianity flow from the faults of its founder.

Approach II: A Political Proxy War

Whenever St Joseph's College, Trichy is mentioned, most Indian minds, cutting across linguistic and religious barriers, associate the name with a great personality and his memoirs—Dr A. P. J. Abdul Kalam. In his autobiography, *Wings of Fire*, Dr Kalam recollected the fond memories of 'Rev. Father T. N. Sequeira' of St Joseph's:

> On Deepavali, on his instructions, the Brother in charge of the hostel and the mess volunteers would visit each room and distribute good gingelly oil for the ritual bath.[404]

However, that may soon change. The institution that produced some of the greatest personalities of Tamil Nadu may soon be identified as the epicentre for nurturing racist storm troopers of Tamil separatism.

Seeman, the founder leader of Naam Tamilar ('We Tamils') party is a curious combination of many strands. He not only propounds a separate racial and linguistic identity for Tamils but also a separate religious identity. He also wears his Luddite cap, so to speak, when he opposes the Neutrino project. Yet, he threatens eco-activists if they were to oppose the imaginary dams he would build in Tamil Nadu to deny water to Kerala—he would have them deported or worse. He also believes strongly in Illuminati conspiracies and asks his cadre to familiarize themselves with such conspiracies against Tamils. He degrades Hindu Puranas in the most vulgar language, while at the same time claiming that Hindu gods from Siva to Muruga are all his ancestors. He justifies the destruction of Bamiyan Buddha by the Taliban.

His party's public banner announces Adolf Hitler as one of the guides of his movement. He proclaimed in a recent speech on the authority of Alex Collier that Tamil was the original language of humanity. Alex Collier, he says, is a linguist when the reality is otherwise. Collier is not a linguist. He says he got the information from extra-terrestrials of Andromeda. Tony Joseph, a former Editor of *Businessworld* magazine, in Seeman's rhetoric, becomes an Oxford professor who has discovered that Tamil was the original language of all South Asian inhabitants.

A rabble-rousing Tamil chauvinist, he is one of the fringe elements in mainstream Tamil politics. Yet he has been vigorously promoted by one section of the media. And now, the Roman Catholic church seems to have embraced him and has started promoting him to the unsuspecting students in its academic institution. One such academic campus happens to be St Joseph's College, Trichy.

The All India Catholic University Federation had arranged a speech by Seeman in September 2017 at the college. A large number of impressionable students from the college were made to listen to his speech which was filled with wild charges against the BJP government. For example, on the Goods and Services Tax (GST), Seeman said to the students that 'for Braille paper and the wheelchair used by the differently abled, there is a GST of 5 and 15 per cent respectively, but there is no tax for the petrol of Ambani, electricity of Adani and the arrack of Vijay Mallya'.

The unsuspecting students exposed to these baseless innuendos erupted into thunderous applause. Even the personal life of Prime Minister Narendra Modi was not spared. 'He is roaming around the world while his wife is fighting for maintenance,' the chief guest Seeman remarked again to the thunderous applause of students. Interestingly, even the dignitaries on the dais laughed uncontrollably over these remarks. Then, for Aadhaar, he cursed those in charge, 'Just watch! All these guys would die of leprosy!' He also went into pseudoscientific claims of Tamil being the mother of all world languages. Then he called on the students to have 'racial pride' and 'racial conscience'. The speech was filled with quotes attributed to Mao, Lenin and Marx.

The rhetorical mixture of Tamil nationalism and Maoist socialism leads slowly but surely towards the national socialism version II in Tamil Nadu. The next month, Trichy saw St Joseph's College host the cultural conference of another fringe Tamil nationalist group, named Tamizhaga Penkal Seyal Kalam (Tamil Women Work Field). The organization had announced earlier on Facebook that for them, Indian Independence Day was a black day. They called it a black day for 'Kashmiris, Central Indian tribes, Punjabis, Nagaland, Manipuris and Mizos' as well. (When contacted by this writer telephonically, the person who attended the call feigned ignorance and denied that they were secessionists: 'We consider Tamils being suppressed by India culturally; India is exploiting our resources and destroying our language; we want to find a remedy for this.'

The exhibition hosted by the college showed the unscientific 'lemurian/ Kumari Kandam' Tamils as the original first humans (and hence Tamil the first language). Then, they went into a totally uncorroborated account of Tamils having a separate culture with separate religion of 'Maalism' and 'Sivanism', which the panels said were made into Saivism and Vaishnavism by the cunning Aryan Brahmins. Anti-Brahminism, very similar to the Nazi anti-Semitism, was shown all over the panels. Tamil kings were alleged to have become puppets in the hands of Brahmins, and Brahmins were shown to usurp the lands of Tamils. Interestingly, while this unadulterated Tamil utopia was presented, the historically great Tamil kings, including the Pallavas and imperial Cholas were shown as being bamboozled by the Brahmin priestcraft.

This is not the first time the church has been playing such a mischievous role in spreading hateful racist theories in the name of social justice. Almost five decades ago, the famous social reformer and educationist of Tamil Nadu, Chidbavananda in his paper on Christian-Hindu encounters, painfully pointed out the way church officials had called the Dravidian movement a 'time bomb placed in Tamil Nadu to destroy Hinduism'. The Dravidian movement was given a lot of tactical but not overt support by the church. However, the Dravidian movement could not achieve what it aimed to. In a way, it fizzled out. Today, television channels owned by Dravidian politicians and their families compete with each other for telecasting the *Ramayana* and *Mahabharata*. The only thing the Dravidian movement achieved from the point of view of the church was a disruptive cognitive dissonance.

The church, relentless in its evangelical agenda, has zeroed in on more virulent elements within the Dravidian movement as well as fringe Tamil nationalist-secessionist movements. Mathimaran, a vociferous Dravidian rhetorician claims that Bharati, the great Tamil poet, was only a Brahmin supremacist. He pits Dr B. R. Ambedkar against Gandhi, much like Kancha Illaiah. He is invited for the training programmes of Christian nuns and his books filled with anti-Hindu hatred are sold in these programmes.

So, clearly the church now aims to switch to the next level in its crusade against Hinduism in Tamil Nadu. It promotes Tamil secessionist-nationalist fringe groups. While the Dravidian movement considered all Tamil Hindu culture as an Aryan Brahminical imposition, these groups take a more nuanced step. They claim that the original Tamil religion and culture were different and were corrupted by 'Aryan Brahmins'. Seeman, on the other hand, claims Siva and Muruga to be his ancestors. This claim, where Hindu deities are posited as secular ethnic ancestors, plays well into the evangelical Christian agenda. While it gives a psychological comfort of an emotional attachment to the Tamil culture, it effectively reduces the spiritual aspects of the Tamil culture to a naught. So, Siva is no more the cosmic principle but an ethnic ancestral totem symbol. Similarly, Tamil music and dance forms, temple architecture and literature—can all be reduced to ethnic elements and secularized (only to be later Christianized).

In a way this attempt of using proxy war through political forces adhering to linguistic-ethnic identity politics gels well with the former. Taken together, the Shantivanam to Seeman are different movements of a deeper strategy at various domains—from spiritual to the political—but they are all connected.

Ultimately it all moves to violent persuasion and persecution of Hindus to abandon their religion and culture and embrace Christianity. Here weapons and terror outfits are used. Here we see a classic example.

Approach III: Violent Encounters

For seven-year-old Shreema, 13 January 2002 was a special Sunday. All through the year, the girl had awaited the dawn of this day—for that was the day one went out and purchased new clothes, toys and sweets for Makar Sankranti—the harvest festival celebrated throughout India—the following day. The Singicherra Bazar was bustling with activity. Like Shreema's family, there were many people looking forward to a happy celebration. But they didn't realize that they were violating a fatwa issued by the Baptist church-created Christian Al-Qaeda, the National Liberation Front of Tripura (NLFT). Nor did they know that they would pay with their lives for celebrating a heathen festival of their indigenous culture. Shreema would never again celebrate Makar Sankranti—her life was cut short, along with 16 others as 13 terrorists of the NLFT encircled the people shopping for the festival and fired indiscriminately.[405]

The NLFT is backed by the Baptist church. Nagmanlal Halam, secretary of the Noapara Baptist church in Tripura, was arrested by the Tripura police for possession of 50 gelatin sticks, 5 kilogram potassium, 2 kilogram sulphur and other ingredients for making explosives. Halam confessed that he was involved in buying and supplying explosives to the NLFT over the past two years. Another church official, Jatna Koloi, who was also arrested, admitted that he had received training in guerrilla warfare at an NLFT base.

The Baptist church of Tripura was initially set up by proselytizers from New Zealand in the late 1930s. Despite their efforts, even until 1980, only a few thousand people in Tripura had converted to Christianity. Then the church used one of its most efficient and time-tested weapons of evangelization—creating racial and ethnic divide among the people. In the aftermath of one of the worst ethnic riots, engineered by the church, the NLFT was born—but not without the midwife role of the Baptist church. From its very inception, the NLFT has been advancing the cause of Christianity through armed persuasion. Every trace of indigenous culture is being eliminated through violent means. Every resisting group has been made to bleed its way to extinction.

The case of Jamatia tribals is telling. This tribal community has strong spiritual leaders and a network of social service organizations headed by their religious leaders. These indigenous sects are neither exclusive nor expansionist. The Baptist church has always failed miserably in its conversion efforts with regard to this well-knit community. Hence, it is no wonder that the NLFT has made Jamatia institutions and their religious leaders the targets of their attacks.

In the August of 2000, religious leaders of the community like Jaulushmoni Jamatia and Shanti Kumar Tripura were killed by the NLFT, and Jamatia families were uprooted from their homelands and made refugees. The death threats issued by the NLFT to the inmates of these institutions have already forced the closure of 11 Jamatia institutions like schools and orphanages, set up by the slain religious leaders in various parts of Tripura.[406]

In a meticulous compilation of NLFT's violent attacks against indigenous religionists of the Hindu tribal community of Jamatias between April 1995 to August 2003, researcher and author Sandhya Jain documented as many as 250 violent incidents including severe beating and injuring with machine guns, threats and executions.[407]

Here are a few samples:

- 23 October 1999: Kamala Sadan Jamatia of Amarpur South Tripura was beaten by NLFT and was warned against performing Lakshmi Puja.
- 15 August 2000: Dilip Kumar Jamatia, Guru Bhakta Para is killed by NLFT
- 13 October 2000: Joy Kishore Jamatia, is severely beaten by NLFT for performing Lakshmi Puja
- 2000 (date unknown): Padma Manik Jamatia is killed by NLFT
- 2 September 2001: Six persons including women of the family, including Hirendra Jamatia and his wife, are shot dead in a raid by NLFT, and the cows of the household are also burnt to death.
- 4 March 2003: Indra Kishore Jamatia is shot dead by NLFT

The greatest challenge to the NLFT came from the Sangh Parivar's Vanvasi

Kalyan Ashram. The dedicated life workers of RSS worked with the tribals by running many educational institutions, which while empowering them through imparting secular technical education also retain their tribal cultural and spiritual identity. Rather than making them disown their roots, the Kendra made the tribals feel proud of their culture. It even conducts national level tribal sports festivals. If the NLFT is to carve out a kingdom for Christ out of the secular republic of India, it must make sure that the Kendra activities are stopped at all costs. In July 2000, armed NLFT militants torched a residential school and students' hostel run by the Seva Mission in the remote Ananda Bazar area of North Tripura.[408] They had also taken hostage four RSS life workers. These RSS workers were all in their sixties. The crime committed by these old men was that they had dared to run educational institutions for tribals while preserving the tribals' culture. Later, all four were killed by the NLFT.

The NLFT has been an active partner of the Baptist church in winning converts to the Christian creed. They have killed tribal priests to threaten communities and effect mass conversions. But those tactics have obviously backfired. In 2001 alone, the NLFT killed more than 20 Hindus who refused to 'accept the love of Christ'. They also torched to death a Hindu family sleeping in a hut.[409] In 2001 community chiefs and religious heads of 19 tribes formed the Tribal Culture Protection Committee to counter the threat posed by the NLFT. [410]

Despite the NLFT taking all possible steps to enforce conversions, the conversions were not as rapid as expected. Frustrated, the NLFT began an all-out war against Hindu tribal communities. They issued fatwas against infidel activities. These fatwas prohibit people from celebrating festivals like Durga Puja and Makar Sankranti, listening to Indian music, watching Indian TV channels and films, and women from wearing bangles or sporting bindis, etc. Just a year before the NLFT started all these atrocities in India, the Southern Baptist church of the United States of America had given a clarion call to bring the light of the gospel to 'millions of Hindus and Jews lost in the darkness' of their religions.[411]

Tripura thus provides a sample of the kind of encounter that Hindus are having with Christianity. The Hindu-Christian encounters cannot be complete without considering what happens in Gujarat and Odisha (formerly Orissa).

In the years 1998–1999 as the BJP-headed NDA was ruling at the Centre, the clashes between Christian proselytizers and Hindu resistance in the tribal districts of Gujarat were increasing alarmingly. Violent incidents against Christian evangelists were getting media attention and were becoming political ammunition.

The communal violence resulting out of conversions, particularly in the tightly knit tribal societies where the conversions literally tore apart families and community relations, had always been there. However, when the BJP came to power, the violent incidents assumed a new dimension. There was increased media spotlight, not only nationally but also internationally, for the local events and Hindutva organizations were blamed for hate crimes. This had been going on in the tribal districts too, and with the new millennia of the Christian calendar approaching, there was an increased frenzy of conversions using the impoverished conditions, and subsequently, there were backlashes. It was an eerie resemblance to the hate attacks on Jews during the Nazi rule. The backlashes alone were highlighted in the media, both nationally and internationally. Hate crimes against missionaries in a country where pagan nationalists had come to power was cliché sensationalist selling news and a good political stick to beat the BJP in power in India.

According to the Home Ministry in Dang in Gujarat where the violent incidents were reported, the Christian tribal population shot up by 416 per cent since 1981 to approximately 30,000. Subsequently, Hindu tribal communities had become more strident.[412]

Ghelubhai Naik (1924–2015) was a Gandhian and a social activist, who too had worked in the Dang district among tribals, establishing a secular Gandhian Dang Swaraj Ashram. He had been asked by Vallabhbhai Patel to work for the tribal welfare. With the eruption of violence in the Dang region, he sent a fax message to the National Minorities Commission in which he pointed out the one-sided report of the violence and highlighted Christian misdeeds:

> Sirs, myself and many of my Gandhian colleagues condemn the violence being perpetrated in south Gujarat, particularly the attacks on churches, in the name of religion. However, we are anguished to bring to your notice the ground realities behind the recent violent incidents in Dangs which haven't come to the fore or have been deliberately ignored by large sections of the media, which in turn has led to a one-sided reporting and press statements thus vitiating the atmosphere further....The violence in Dang began on the Christmas day after some Christian youths pelted stones on the rally of the Hindu Jagran Manch and burnt the jeep of a tribal participant in the rally. ...The ire against the Christians in the area has been rising for the past few years and has reached a boil now because of the provocative activities of the Christians under the influence of their preachers. There have been at least 15 instances in the past three years in Dang wherein the Christians, under the influence of their preachers, have desecrated the idols of Lord Hanuman, who is worshipped in this area by large section of tribals for ages. In one incident in Gaadhvi village three years ago, they urinated on an idol of Hanuman and later in Jharsod village they crushed Hanuman's idol to pieces and threw it away in the

> river....Social conflicts in tribal families have greatly increased on account of the terror tactics of the converted tribal at the behest of the preachers....[413]

Atal Bihari Vajpayee, then Prime Minister, while condemning the violence also called for a national debate on conversions.

Two weeks after the Gujarati Gandhian had brought out the other side of the conflicts, a gruesome shameful event took place. On the dense night of 22–23 January 1999, Australian-born Christian evangelist Graham Stewart Staines, aged 58, along with his two sons, Phillip, aged 10 and Timothy, aged 7, were burnt to death when a mob set fire to their vehicles. The boys and their father were sleeping in their vehicles. The entire nation was shocked and Hindu organizations faced guilt and shame. In one day, as *India Today* later noted, the words 'Bajrang Dal', from being a fringe Parivar outfit had become a national byword for inhuman and violent fundamentalism. The reason was that one of the eyewitnesses of the gruesome killings saw the group that burnt them down shout 'Jai Bajrang Bali!'—a slogan praising Hanuman. But then it was reported by eager news merchants as 'Jai Bajrang Dal'. The Hindu organizations went into defensive. But the damage had been done. More importantly three precious lives had been lost.

Even a year before the shameful hate crime happened, the tribal districts of Odisha had become an intense battleground between Christian proselytizers and local Hindu tribal resistance. While the proselytizers were from foreign countries and India's southern states, who were well-trained in dealing with Indian bureaucracy and law, the resistance from local communities which had suffered the trauma of their kith and kin getting converted were supported by Hindutva organizations. They mostly had a confrontational attitude towards the bureaucracy and officials. In 1998 *India Today* brought out a detailed assessment of the battle for souls in Odisha:

> It all began with the arrival of Christian missionaries, some 20 years ago, backed by foreign-funded NGOs with the promise of changing the face of the region. Schools and hospitals came up at certain places to help the poor, but so did churches. With Christianity spreading, the Hindu backlash has just started.... As conversions and churches multiply, protests by Hindus are getting shrill. In January, at a huge rally in Padampur, Hindu protesters armed with traditional weapons bade for the blood of the local sub-collector, who they say is patronising the church. Two months ago, the row over the desecration of a village temple at Serang in Gajapati district ended in violent clashes. Sanity prevailed only after the harried administration rebuilt the temple with police protection and resettled the Hindus. A month earlier, Christians

> in Sundergarh charged Hindus with poisoning the village wells. And in Bolangir, most Christians stopped visiting local hospitals fearing a sterilisation programme.... Overzealous missionaries, many say, have contributed to the consolidation of the Hindu vote.... The missionaries, no doubt, are on an overdrive, apparently following the call made at the state pastors' seminar in Cuttack in November 1996 to "win Orissa for Christ by 2000 AD". Churches of all shapes and sizes have sprung up in most areas of the state in recent years....With local Christians referring to Krishnapur as Krishtopur (after Christ) and Hindus maintaining an all-night vigil in Bhubaneswar in January to resist a possible conversion, fanatics are holding centre stage....Though it has the Orissa Freedom of Religion Act, 1967, to prohibit conversions by inducements, the Government has rarely cracked the whip. In 1993 for the first time, a superintendent of police booked 21 pastors in Nowrangpur for breaking the law. But he was transferred immediately as many, including a sizeable section within the administration, were outraged by his boldness....As missionaries seek to win over Orissa for Christ, Hindu organizations have begun to strike roots in many places. The RSS, the VHP, the Hindu Jagran and the Banabasi Kalyan Ashram together have chosen to help people rediscover Hindu traditions by starting over 3,000 schools in the state.[414]

The 'poisoning of the water wells', charges by the evangelists against the Hindus is an age-old Christian propaganda which had been used in pre-modern Christendom against the Jews—to justify violence against them. In the case of the inhuman crime of Staines's burning, *India Today* reported:

> Yet, contrary to what has been claimed, conversion was not the immediate provocation....In June last year, during the Raja festival—the earth is said to be menstruating then—the converts violated local custom by continuing to till the land. This led to heated exchanges between the converts and traditional Santhals.... Known for guarding their customs zealously, the Santhals were incensed by this cultural separation.[415]

Such traumatic destruction of traditional tribal society by his proselytizing activity was also corroborated by Staines's own triumphant admission in the dispatches back home. Reporting the evangelical field conditions, he wrote this:

> It is encouraging to hear of some improvement in the church at Manoharpur and that they are preparing for the jungle camp. Misayel, Paul and Nehemiah visited Patna in early December but as many were away rice harvesting, they could meet only with a few. They were able to encourage a new believer who had been a priest of the Sana Dhoram, an animist sect. The village people pleaded with him not to

become a Christian, saying, "How can we continue our worship if you leave us?" "You can do so you like, but I am following Christ," he said.

Clearly the forest night camps were not related to his work at the leprosy hospital but evangelical work, which still in no way justifies the murder. But the tribal community needed no outside instigation. They felt helpless before the coordinated evangelical onslaught. The *India Today* report continued as follows:

> Staines's arrival in the village gave them a chance to get even with those who dared to go against the traditional customs. Help came readily from Dara Singh, a Hindu fanatic from Etawah in Uttar Pradesh who was active along the Mayurbhanj-Keonjhar border since 1980.

The Vajpayee government immediately formed an inquiry commission into the violent incident. The Wadhwa commission submitted its report in July the same year, blaming the systemic failure of the police including the IB and state machinery under the Congress party for what it called an 'avoidable' tragedy. The Commission pointed out that the state police intelligence had a lot to answer. Despite Dara Singh being arrested for cow protection vigilantism several times, they did not even have a photograph of him. The media often sensationalized incidents. While the media and sections of politicians had stated that the attackers raised the slogan 'Jai Bajrang Dal', witness after witness including Christians stated that what they heard was 'Jai Bajrang Bali', a common Hindu slogan and not the name of any organization. The commission observed that the perception of Dara Singh being associated with Bajrang Dal was related to vigilantism in cow protection and high-handed, violent rescue of cows smuggled across the state, and he had nothing to do with conversions as such. Then it concluded:

> The Commission has scrutinized the evidence before it and especially the evidence of the associates of Dara Singh who were involved in the carnage at Manoharpur. There is no evidence to suggest that any of the persons involved in the crime, was in fact a member of either the Bajrang Dal or BJP or any organization. There is nothing to suggest in the evidence before the Commission or in the investigation conducted by the crime branch and the CBI thus far that there is involvement of any organization, even that of Bajrang Dal in the planning and the execution of the crime.[416]

The evangelical field in Odisha started having a transformation soon. With globalization and coming of more aggressive and sophisticated international players, the evangelism also started getting a secular or a more left-oriented facelift. While the Roman Catholic church with its liberation theology could flirt with Maoist and Marxist guerrillas in non-Catholic regimes in agrarian South American countries, in India the Protestant missions also started embracing the leftist radicals in their fight against Hinduism.

With globalization and liberalization of the economy inevitably bringing in radical left retaliation, the evangelists formed a strange alliance with Maoists. Maoists could help evangelists to reach out to tribal communities. The destruction of tribal spiritual traditions helped both the evangelical soul harvest and Maoist recruitment. On 23 August 2008, in the evening of the very holy Hindu festival of Janmashtami, the birth of Sri Krishna, Swami Lakshmanananda Saraswati (1926–2008) was visiting a residential school for the tribal and economically downtrodden girls in a remote tribal region. That night the Maoists entered the ashram and fired to kill the monk who was known for his service to tribal communities and also resisting conversions. Along with the monk, the principal of the residential school Mata Bhaktimayee too was killed by the Maoists.

If the media highlighted only the leprosy hospital-related work in the case of Staines, while downplaying his role in conversions, here Swami's role in education and tribal welfare were downplayed and his role in resisting conversions was highlighted by the mainstream media. Cutting across party lines, the dedicated service of Swami had been recognized by the people of the state.

For instance, Amar Prasad Satpathy of the anti-VHP Congress Party, while mourning Swami stated that the state had lost a monk who had 'dedicated his whole life serving in the jungles to guide society and serve humanity through his valuable efforts' and that 'his commitment towards the social, economic and spiritual development of the State is unparalleled'.[417] Veteran Odisha journalist Basudev Mahapatra pointed out in his article that the Swami 'was considered as a godly person by the tribals of Kandhamal' as he 'was running schools, medicals, and various other utility centres, apart from an ashram in the forests of Kandhamal' and 'working for the welfare of the tribals who are economically and socially much backward...'[418]

On 5 October 2008, the Maoist leader stated that they were being pressurized by Christians to eliminate the monk. The scheduled caste Pannas who had converted to Christianity under Indian Constitution lost their scheduled caste status. Many Pannas who had converted to Christianity because of allurements and other reasons were getting scheduled tribe certificate and were enjoying the affirmative action benefits due for the tribals, who were really more impoverished and marginalized. The staunch support of the Khanda tribal community of Odisha in many of the anti-British uprisings was one of the reasons for their marginalization. But the scheduled tribes considered themselves Hindus and strongly resisted the evangelical war waged on them by Christian zealots from South Indian states like Kerala and Tamil Nadu as well as foreign countries. In this the tribal community was not supported by the government of free India and the mostly corrupt state machinery also exploited them. It was in these adverse conditions that the Hindutva organizations came as great saviours of the tribal community. Particularly Swami Lakshmanananda Saraswati showed the tribal community that they were part of the greater Hindu family of diverse spiritual traditions, and he gave them hope and strength. This simultaneously affected the Maoist recruitment from the tribal youths as well as Christian evangelists from converting tribal community.

All these interactions—violent and passive, strategic and direct—provide a background for the reactions, responses and dialogue engagement from the Hindutva organizations.

Hindutva Responses: The Theoretical Frame

The encounters that Hindu society has had with Christianity span centuries. The most influential and defining format for Hindu interaction with Christianity was set emphatically in modern times by Sri Ramakrishna, the master of Swami Vivekananda. He demonstrated that a Hindu could have direct experience of Jesus without having to accept Christianity. Sri Ramakrishna's Christ experience came in 1874. His biography published in 1924 mentions about this experience:

> One day, the Master was in the parlour of the garden-house of Jadu Nath Mallik at Dakshineswar, on the walls of which were many beautiful portraits, one of them being Christ's. Sri Ramakrishna was looking attentively at the picture of the Madonna with the Divine Child and reflecting on the wonderful life of Christ, when he felt as though the picture had become animated, and that rays of light were emanating from the figures of Mary and Christ, and entering into him, altogether changing his mental outlook.

For three days, Sri Ramakrishna was held in the grip of his experience of Christian devotion. He could not bring himself to Hindu Divinities despite his appeal to the Divine Mother (Kali). Then, on the fourth day, he had an experience:

> On the fourth day, as he was walking in the Panchavati, he saw an extraordinary-looking person of serene aspect approaching him, with his gaze intently fixed on

> him. Sri Ramakrishna was charmed and wondered who he might be. Presently the figure drew near, and from the inmost recesses of Sri Ramakrishna's heart there went up the note, "There is the Christ who poured out his heart's blood for the redemption of mankind and suffered agonies for its sake. It is none else but that Master-Yogin Jesus, the embodiment of Love!"[419]

Theology scholar Daniel E. Bassuk in his study of 'Incarnation in Hinduism and Christianity' points out the significance of this experience of Sri Ramakrishna:

> Ramakrishna's mystical experience with Jesus in 1874 is highly significant, as it marks the beginning of the assimilation of Jesus Christ into the Hindu religion on a par with the Hindu avatars. From this time forward, the Hindu Godmen have a spiritual brother in Sri Isha, another Avatar to contend with, and a Western one at that.[420]

After this, in 1882 an American missionary Joseph Cook of 'Protestant orthodoxy' met Sri Ramakrishna in a cruise arranged by Brahmo leader Keshab Chandra Sen. The official organ of Brahmo Samaj, 'The New Dispensation' (26 February 1882) reported this about the meeting:

> The revered Paramahamsa of Dakshineswar (Sri Ramakrishna)... successively went through all the phases of spiritual excitement which characterizes him. Passing through a long interval of unconsciousness, he prayed, sang, and discoursed on spiritual subject. Mr Cook represented the extreme culture of Christian theology and thought. The Paramahamsa represented the extreme culture of Indian Yoga and Bhakti, in short, the traditional piety of the East.

In 1886 *Indian Mirror* in its obituary of Sri Ramakrishna mentioned that 'Mr Cook, the American evangelist, ...witnessed Ramakrishna's divine exercises and he expressed his great surprise at it and remarked that he was not aware before that a man could become so much immersed in divine spirit as to lose all perception of the external world'. [421]

While later, once Sri Ramakrishna enquired of 'M' about Cook giving lectures in Calcutta, Joseph Cook himself never mentioned Sri Ramakrishna. In 1893 he saw in Swami Vivekananda an enemy. Prof. Lola Williamson in her study of 'Hindu-inspired Meditation Movements in the US' writes:

> One of Vivekananda's critics was the Reverend Joseph Cook of Boston, who had met Ramakrishna, Vivekananda's guru, and Keshab Chunder Sen, a leader of the Brahmo Samaj, in India in 1882....Cook was unsuccessful in dampening the spirits

of those Americans who were eager to hear a new perspective, and after the World Parliament, Vivekananda spent many years lecturing to enthusiastic audiences in much the same way that Emerson had done—in fact, reiterating many of the themes about which Emerson had spoken.[422]

Even as the expression of Hindu Bhakti of Sri Ramakrishna, which also included a mystical experience of Christ, had no impact on the evangelist, the impact the Christian theology had on Sri Ramakrishna is also important. Seven months after Rev. Cook witnessing Sri Ramakrishna, on 27 October 1882, the following conversation of Sri Ramakrishna with Keshab Chandra Sen was recorded by 'M':

> Once someone gave me a book of the Christians. I asked him to read it to me. It talked about nothing but sin. (To Keshab) Sin is the only thing one hears of at your Brahmo Samaj, too. The wretch who constantly says, "I am bound, I am bound" only succeeds in being bound. He who says day and night, "I am a sinner, I am a sinner" verily becomes a sinner.[423]
>
> In the room of Sri Ramakrishna, along with the pictures of Hindu gods, goddesses and saints, there was also a picture of Jesus 'raising the drowning Peter'. When Sri Ramakrishna applied vermilion brought by a devotee to the pictures of Hindu Gods and Goddesses, he left out that of Jesus. So, he clearly respected the cultural context of Jesus while at the same time holding on to his own experiential conviction of the universal divinity manifesting through Jesus.[424]

One of the songs he often heard from his disciples including Naren (later Swami Vivekananda), which propelled him into samadhi, had the following lines:

> *O Mother, make me mad with Thy love!*
>
> ...
>
> *Jesus, Buddha, Moses, Gauranga,*
> *All are drunk with the Wine of Thy love.*
> *O 'Mother, when shall I be blessed*
> *By joining their blissful company.*[425]

This situating of Jesus in the company of other spiritual masters and then seeing as filled with the love for the immanent Goddess rather than the masculine transcendental Father, further enriches the space for engagement and dialogue with Christian tradition.

The *Gospel of Sri Ramakrishna* also records the visit of one Misra—who was born in 'a Christian family in northwestern India and belonged to the

Quaker sect'. He visited Sri Ramakrishna, and during their conversation, he said that he had a vision of Jesus. Misra said that 'it is Rama alone who dwells in all beings' and Sri Ramakrishna said looking at 'young Naren' that 'Rama is one but He has a thousand names' and that whom Christians call 'God' and 'is addressed by the Hindus as Rama, Krishna, Isvara, and by other names'. Misra told the devotees there that Jesus was not the son of Mary but God Himself and that Sri Ramakrishna too was God Himself and that he had seen Sri Ramakrishna too in his vision. Later, Sri Ramakrishna blessed Misra saying that he would obtain what he sought.[426]

Thus, with Sri Ramakrishna, Hinduism acquired a deeply spiritual framework to accept Christ and his teachings, and experience the spiritual possibilities within Christianity without acquiring the theological and institutional colonialism that comes with proselytizing. Most of the later Hindutva engagements and dialogues with Christianity are anchored on this, with Savarkar and Golwalkar being clear instances and Sita Ram Goel being a prominent exception.

Swami Vivekananda had taken the missionary propaganda head on. He even pointed out the subliminal racial aspects in the missionary propaganda against Hindus and Hinduism. In his reply to the congratulatory meeting held for his success in the United States World Parliament of Religions, he wrote to his fellow countrymen:

> It is not true that I am against any religion. It is equally untrue that I am hostile to the Christian missionaries in India. But I protest against certain of their methods of raising money in America. What is meant by those pictures in the school-books for children where the Hindu mother is painted as throwing her children to the crocodiles in the Ganga? The mother is black, but the baby is painted white, to arouse more sympathy, and get more money. What is meant by those pictures which paint a man burning his wife at a stake with his own hands, so that she may become a ghost and torment the husband's enemy? What is meant by the pictures of huge cars crushing over human beings? The other day a book was published for children in this country, where one of these gentlemen tells a narrative of his visit to Calcutta. He says he saw a car running over fanatics in the streets of Calcutta. I have heard one of these gentlemen preach in Memphis that in every village of India there is a pond full of the bones of little babies. What have the Hindus done to these disciples of Christ that every Christian child is taught to call the Hindus "vile", and "wretches", and the most horrible devils on earth?

This perhaps is the first Hindu observation of the anti-Hindu propaganda material published in the United States by the Christian missionaries and sensitizing Hindus back home about the hate propaganda being made against them. Sri Aurobindo in a letter to Dilip Kumar Roy observed:

> Though Christ and Krishna are the same, they are the same in difference, that is indeed the utility of so many manifestations instead of there being only one as these missionaries would have it. But is it really because the historical Christ has been made too much the foundation-stone of the faith that Christianity is failing? It may be something inadequate in the religion itself—perhaps in religion itself; for all religions are a little off-colour now....I don't know why so many Christian writers have a way of writing and preaching which gives a sense of unpleasant unctuousness, a very small dish of religious emotion swimming in a too fat oil of holiness—as if the Pharisees and Sadducees had not only crucified Christ but laid the grip of their ecclesiasticism and Pharisaism on the religion also.

In modern times, Mahatma Gandhi had already defined the contours of later Hindutva interaction with Christianity. In 1926 answering an American Christian leader Milton Newberry Frantz, who had sent him an article on Jesus, positioning him as God, Gandhi wrote back:

> I am afraid it is not possible for me to subscribe to the creed you have sent me. The subscriber is made to believe that the highest manifestation of the unseen reality was Jesus Christ. In spite of all my efforts, I have not been able to feel the truth of that statement. I have not been able to move beyond the belief that Jesus was one of the great teachers of mankind.[427]

Then in 1935 when he was talking to a group of missionaries, he told them bluntly:

> If I had power and could legislate, I should certainly stop all proselytizing. It is the cause of much avoidable conflict between classes and unnecessary heart-burning among missionaries. But I should welcome people of any nationality if they came to serve here for the sake of service. In Hindu households the advent of a missionary has meant the disruption of the family coming in the wake of change of dress, manners, language, food and drink.

When the missionaries argued that nowadays they had stopped vilification of Hinduism in their campaign, Gandhi countered them with facts:

> Vilification of Hindu religion, though subdued, is there. If there was a radical change in the missionaries' outlook, would Murdoch's books be allowed to be sold

> in mission depots? Are those books prohibited by missionary societies? There is nothing but vilification of Hinduism in those books. You talk of the conception being no longer there. Only the other day a missionary descended on a famine area with money in his pocket, distributed it among the famine-stricken, converted them to his fold, took charge of their temple and demolished it. This is outrageous.

Hindus per se do not have any criticism of Christianity as a false religion or have a compulsion to reject Jesus as a kind of false God or false messiah. However, centuries of attacks on Hindus directly and indirectly through academia and polemics through institutional means and cultural wars have made many Hindu ideologues study Christianity if only to defend themselves. Sita Ram Goel writes in the preface to his work *History of Hindu-Christian Encounters*:

> No Hindu thinker has had the least objection to Christians believing in and seeking salvation through Jesus. Nor do Hindus bother about the dogmas of the only sonship, the virgin birth, the atoning death, the resurrection and the rest, so long as Christians keep these to themselves. It is only when the Christian missionary apparatus tries doggedly to impose these dogmas on other people that Hindu thinkers are forced to register a protest and have a close look at the Jesus of history.

While the Hindu influence on Christianity has been positive with respect to inculcating it with yoga and diverse spirituality, the Christian-Hindu encounter in India has been similar to that of a battlefield. Christianity, from Catholic church to charismatic evangelists of Protestantism, wants to conquer Hinduism and sees it as a potential field of harvest for the current millennia.

The Hindu response in terms of religion and theology can be divided into two broad categories. One is represented by Sita Ram Goel—characterizing Jesus as 'an artifice of aggression'. In his book, Sita Ram Goel starts with his own experience:

> Jesus did say in so many words not only that he was the only God but also that those who did not accept his claim would burn forever in the infernal pit. I realized with painful surprise that Jesus was not all Sermon on the Mount as I had been led to believe by his Hindu votaries. Years passed, and I had no time to spare for Jesus. I turned to him again in the eighties when Ram Swarup made me wise about the character of monotheistic creeds. It was then that I turned to the gospels. I was horrified. Now I could see why the history of Christianity had been what it had been. The source of the poison was in the Jesus of the gospels. The rest of my studies followed.[428]

And at the end of the book, he concludes:

> It is high time for Hindus to learn that Jesus Christ symbolises no spiritual power, or moral uprightness. He is no more than an artifice for legitimizing wanton imperialist aggression. The aggressors have found him to be highly profitable so far. By the same token, Hindus should know that Jesus means nothing but mischief for their country and culture. The West where he flourished for long, has discarded him as junk. There is no reason why Hindus should buy him. He is the type of junk that cannot be recycled. He can only poison the environment.[429]

The other dominant Hindu attitude to Christianity is characterized by the highly popular lecture 'Christ We Adore' by Swami Ranganathananda of Sri Ramakrishna Mission. He gives a complete Vedantic gloss over the life and teachings of Jesus. Here is a typical sample passage:

> The "Sermon on the Mount" expounds moral and spiritual ideas which are universal; ... and will not sound strange to any spiritual seeker nourished on the ideas of the Upanishads and the Bhagavad-Gita...."Be ye therefore perfect, even as your Father which is in heaven is perfect." This exhortation sounds strangely Vedantic in significance. ... Here is a refreshing statement of the scope and goal of religion. The emphasis is on sadhana, the practice of religion, with a view to attaining anubhava, realization. "Religion is realization; it is being and becoming", in the words of Swami Vivekananda; it is character. It is not a cosy belief, but an adventure, something that sets the soul on fire, the carrying, as Jesus would say, of one's cross by oneself and not by proxy. It reminds us of Buddha's last words addressed to his dear disciple, Ananda.[430]

Most of the Hindu responses to Christian core belief system vary between these two approaches. And that provides quite a lot of middle ground. Ram Swarup, the guru and mentor of Sita Ram Goel, considers the Bible as the source that raised English language morally and spiritually. [431] Elsewhere, Ram Swarup elaborates:

> By the time of Jesus, many changes have taken place in the Jewish world. It was no longer small and insular. It was open to all kinds of influences both from the East as well as the West.... Jesus belonged to this environment.... But he was one of those who must experience spiritual truths in their person. He was invaded by a sense of holy presence that he simply called his Father. In the Gospel part of the New Testament, there is no controversy about one God and many Gods, between Theism and Polytheism, between True God and False Gods. Jesus had no relish for intellectual, theological controversies. His simple message to the is to love their God with all their heart and to do unto others what they would like others to do unto

> themselves. The attempt was to bring a measure of inwardness to their worship. But as we proceed from the Gospels to the Acts, we find a spiritual deterioration. There is less direct experience and more of faith, less simplicity and more rhetoric... With introduction and triumph of Pauline Christianity, a new element came into the religious culture, a passionate narrowness, a fanatic faith, a doctrinaire intellectuality, a sanctimonious piety.[432]

This is more in tune with the Gandhian approach. While accepting that Jesus did have spiritual passion, there is rejection of the exclusivist theology of Christianity and its evangelical actions derived from that theology.

Swami Ranganathananda also makes a detailed exposition of this problem even as he presents a Vedantic gloss over the life and teachings of Nazarene. In the end of his *The Christ We Adore*, Swami Ranganathananda states:

> The dogma of one man's sin affecting all humanity gave rise to its logical corollary of the dogma of one man's blood washing away the sins of all; such an approach led inevitably to a chain reaction of such tragedies involving the lives of Stephen and Joseph, Peter and Paul, immediately after, and of countless other good and noble and innocent souls, thereafter. The theory that the blood of the martyr is the seed of the Church developed out of this dogma; and, in place of calm reason and generous love, frensy, fanaticism, intolerance, and bigotry gripped the propagation of the life-giving message of Jesus down the centuries, destroying as many lives as it undoubtedly helped to build, with groups interchanging places as persecutor and victim....The history of Christianity, in its twin records of persecution, violence, and war, on the one side, and lofty mysticism, moral passion, and humanitarianism on the other, bears the impress of this inner division, which also explains its recurrent conflicts with science....It is against this background that we view with hope the future of Indian Christianity. Under the guidance of the philosophy of Vedanta, the Christian message in India can achieve that synthesis by which it will flow as an entirely constructive force with its universal elements functioning free in the spirit of the universal, and its dogmatic elements digested and retained to accord with the spirit of the universal and human.... To ask and seek and knock is our share, and to give and reveal and open is the Lord's. That is the mood and attitude in which we adore Christ. That is the Hindu way of acceptance and assimilation.

The 1990s Hindutva Response and Dialogue

The Hindutva response to the aggressive Christian proselytizing in the 1990s was not only the ground-zero resistance from the Hindu organizations which brought them negatively biased bad press. There was also strong organized intellectual Hindu response as well. The Sita Ram Goel-*Voice of India* school was at the forefront in organizing this.

Arun Shourie had just then become a strong pro-Hindu intellectual voice. Since January 1994, on the occasion of the celebration of the 50th anniversary of the establishment of Catholic Bishop Council of India (CBCI), the apex Catholic body in India, Arun Shourie had been invited to give the Hindu perspective of their work. This gave Shourie access to some church documents. In March 1994, he brought out the book *Missionaries in India: Continuities, Changes, Dilemmas*. Within the same year, the book saw three reprints and became a bestseller. With original documents from the colonial period to the latest data from the CBCI, Shourie showed remarkable consistency in negatively stereotyping Hinduism and the colonial values underlying the proselytizing enterprise in India. In the book, Shourie observed:

> The departure of the British, that is the transfer of political power to persons who could not be dependent upon to automatically shield it, impelled the Church to make adjustments of many kinds. Eventually, as we know, the possibility of salvation in each religion has of late been acknowledged by the Vatican....this position is exactly the one Gandhiji had been pleading for. In a sense therefore the traditional Hindu position and the position of the Church have come closer....The shift has accordingly caused the greatest unsettling within the Church in India.

Even the tentative, hesitating and ambiguous admission of the possibility of salvation outside the church led to a decline in conversions, as pointed out by the CBCI working group paper. It went on to elaborate a plan on which Shourie made the following observations:

> Again, what the paper is driving at is clear, it is exactly what the Church has been trying to do for hundreds of years : to "inculturate" itself in the "little traditions"—to go tribal among the tribals, to don the ways and practices of Harijans among Harijans—so as to "undermine, encircle, and finally storm" the "dominant culture"—Hinduism in this case.But to what extent these practices of the "marginalised", these things which are "genuinely human" in those belonging to the "little traditions" the Church should adopt is not clear : how much of the "Animism" should it don? And were it to merely don the Animism, would that not be mere subterfuge, would it not be what the paper itself calls a mere "strategy"? On the other hand, if the Church were to genuinely internalize the Animism of the "little traditions", what would be left of it?

That was in 1994. Today, down the line, we have the answer to the questions raised by Shourie. There have been institutional interactions between the leftists who already have a stranglehold on social sciences, academia, the church in particular and evangelical organizations in general. The result is that the tribal and Scheduled Community cultures have been presented in such a way to facilitate Christian takeover. Elements inimical to Christian appropriation have been termed as Brahminical impurities introduced into tribal culture for the subjugation of the people.

The book by Arun Shourie was countered by the then Secretary of CBCI Augustine Kanjamala, though initially the Catholic priest accused Shourie of going back on his words—that he would make Kanjamala a co-author of his book. He wrote to Shourie that Shourie had agreed to a chapter by Kanjamala in which he would explain 'the process of conversion of tribals, Dalits either to Hinduism or Christianity and their relative merits and demerits'. Shourie responded with a letter clearly stating the facts and refusing to make any changes to his own book by adding the article of the priest and instead advised that the church publish its own rebuttal. Sita Ram Goel, who was privy to the entire correspondence writes:

> Controllers of the Church seemed to have realized what they would be in for if they were to persist in the concoctions which they had put out through Fr Kanjamala.…a letter arrived from Fr Kanjamala in which the good Father attributed what he had written to a "misunderstanding". Shourie wrote back to him saying how happy he was that the cloud had blown over. But once again he had reckoned without the Church. A series of articles had been appearing in different newspapers, especially in publications of the Church itself in which Shourie's book was not just traduced but in which completely perverted accounts of it were published. Fr Kanjanmala was at the forefront of these traducers.

Prajna Bharati, a Hindutva think tank, a Sangh Parivar organization founded in 1991 in Hyderabad (now in the state of Telangana) organized 'several senior churchmen' to discuss the book with Arun Shourie. Fr Kanjamala agreed to present his criticism of Shourie's book and Shourie agreed to answer the criticisms. This would be followed by question-answer sessions. The entire interaction, both the lectures and the question-answers, were published as a book by Voice of India. One important aspect that Arun Shourie brought out in his rebuttal was the kind of faultline fabrications that the Christian theologians were attempting at in Hindu society and religion. In his earlier article, as a reply to Arun Shourie, Fr Kanjanmala had written this in the popular newspaper *Deccan Chronicle*:

> Harijans worshipped deities of lower rank while caste Hindus worshipped deities of higher rank. For instance, Hanuman (Monkey God) is worshipped by Harijans and Rama is worshipped by the upper castes in the same village.

In his reply, Shourie exclaimed in disbelief:

> *Wah Wah*! This is the knowledge of the Church about *Hanumanji*! Such scholarship! I cannot imagine that this is the knowledge. This is insinuation, it is deliberate distortion. And Fr Augustine continues: "Hanuman was the servant of Rama; Harijans are the servants of high caste Hindus. A close affinity (exists) between hierarchy of Gods and the hierarchy of society."... Given what you have been perverting, what you are insinuating about our society now, I am surprised at my own moderation. [433]

Overall, the interaction brought out certain projects on which the church has already been working. In hindsight, in 2021 one can say that the fabricated faultlines which the church envisioned are today part of a dominant section of the humanities academia and media. From the Protestant side the same lenses have been used through the racist anti-Hindu approach of Kancha Illaiah.

It was then that in January 1999 the gruesome heinous killing of Staines and his sons took place in Odisha. The hue and cry against Bajrang Dal, a Parivar organization then accused of killing the evangelist and sons, then snowballed to become a guilt of association for the entire Sangh as well as the BJP and Hindutva as a hate ideology. It was an act that not only brought international bad press to Hindutva but also led to the demonization of BJP.

Arun Shourie responded with the book *Harvesting Our Souls: Missionaries, their Design, their Claims* (ASA, 2000). In the book Shourie went into the details of the Staines murder. He pointed out that Staines was not only a worker in a medical team eradicating leprosy, but unknown to the medical team, he was being secretive about his 'forest camps', and in his dispatches home, he was writing about how successfully he was converting the tribal community members. Shourie then pointed out how every violent incident involving a victim who happened to be Christian was sensationalized as hate crime by the media. Though most of these crimes were later found out to be unrelated to communal strife, the damage against the Hindutva movement had been accomplished. He also cites the Justice Wadhwa Commission report. The 250-page document submitted in July 1999 had pointed out that the murders of Staines and his pre-teen sons were premediated by Dara Singh, the main accused, and the motivation was 'misplaced fundamentalism'. Arun Shourie in this book took the same approach that Sita Ram Goel had taken in his work *Jesus Christ: Artifice for Aggression* and elaborated upon it.

It should be noted that Sita Ram Goel's book first came out in 1995, followed by a reprint in 2001. Sita Ram Goel came out with the second edition of the book *History of Hindu-Christian Encounters* in 1996. In a way this response from largely non-Sangh Hindutva circles—but given support through public forums by Sangh—countered the evangelical onslaught that started its accelerated ascendancy in the 1990s.

Another important addition to the literature is the rejoinder that Ram Swarup wrote to Pope John Paul for his 1994 book *Crossing the Threshold of Hope*. Here Pope spoke of other religions—not condemning them outright but highlighting what he considered as their deficiencies. After the rebuttal, Ram Swarup observed:

> Today the Church does not pour venom on non-Christian religions as freely and in the same style as it did before; now its new official line is that 'the Catholic Church rejects nothing that is true and holy in those religions'—though it is another matter and a sad commentary on Christianity that in the last 1900 years it has found nothing true and holy in other religions....However, the concession is withdrawn as soon as it is made for in the very next sentence the Vatican Council says: "The Church proclaims and is duty bound to proclaim without fail, Christ who is the way , the truth and life" and that in him alone, "men find the fullness of their religious life"....Throughout his book, Pope John Paul speaks of the problems connected with evangelization and proselytizing. He is aware of the difficulties in this post-colonial period when Christianity does not enjoy the same old political power and prestige....All this shows that there is only a change of tactics, not of larger aims, that the so-called new Vatican line is not a serious thing, that the conciliatory words said about other religions are a pretence, that they do not mean the end of an old era but the beginning of a new onslaught under different slogans ad labels. The fine words are deceptive, and it is an ill sign to see a fox lick a lamb.

Then in a subsequent passage, Ram Swarup set out a moral evaluation of the relation that a Christian enters with his or her non-Christian neighbour:

> In the spiritual world there are two important categories: God and your neighbour. You could look at neighbour's God through his eyes or could look at neighbour through the eyes of your God. If you respect your neighbour and think that he is good as you, then you will also think that his God is as good as your own. But if you think that he is no good then you also conclude that his God is no good and you would like to replace his God by your good God. ... "Love Thy Neighbour" becomes "Watch thy

neighbour and convert him to the Sole Truth". Christian theology of conversion is based not only on an inadequate idea of God, but also on hatred of one's neighbour.

In 1994 Sita Ram Goel brought out the second and very enlarged edition of his 1988 book *Catholic Ashrams: Sannyasins or Swindlers*? In this, he, Ram Swarup and a Hindu sage named Swami Devanananda Saraswati entered into a detailed correspondence with Bede Griffiths and quite a number of Christian theologians attempting inculturation. This book is perhaps a path breaker in the sense that for the first time, a Christian evangelical movement, that too which appropriates Hindu spirituality and symbols through institutional and theological means at various levels was investigated thoroughly and exposed in an empirical way. In the preface, Sita Ram Goel revealed his own relationship with the missionary Henry Le Saux (Abhishiktananda):

> My Christian friends whom I had known for many years, expressed pain and resentment at what I had written, particularly about Swami Abhishiktananda, who had met me in 1958 and known me rather well for years till he died in 1973. In our very first meeting, I had told him in so many words that Jesus came nowhere near even the most minor Hindu saint, and that the missionary attempts to foist him on Hindus with the help of Western wealth, was nothing short of wickedness. He had never mentioned Jesus again, and our discussions had centred on Hindu philosophy of which he knew quite a bit, at least better than I did at that time. I had never suspected that he himself was a missionary and a part of the apparatus. It was only when I read his writings that I learnt the truth. I happened to be a Treasurer of the Abhishiktananda Society in Delhi at the time the first edition of this book appeared.... Having been a student of Christian doctrine and history, I should have known that the post-Vatican II talk about tolerance and dialogue was intended to be a one-way affair.

Thus, the 1990s represent the period when Hindutva started forming some quantum of organized response to Christianity—particularly scrutinizing the theology and methodology of proselytization and forming the responses. Along with this non-Sangh Hindutva force, the RSS was also fighting proselytizing on ground while simultaneously engaging in dialogue with the Christians.

Space for Genuine Hindu-Christian Dialogue: Global Scenario

Though Hinduism has no institutions like the Catholic and Protestant Christianity and no state support like Buddhism, Hinduism has in its own way interacted with Christianity and the West. The scientific revolutions which dethroned the centrality of human to the universe also facilitated the dialogue.

What should be the purpose of such a dialogue? From the point of view of benefits to Western society in general and Christendom in particular, British philosopher and author Alan Watts (1915–1973) made a detailed conceptual map. He deals with it in his 1964 book *Beyond Theology: The Art of Godmanship* as follows:

> Now, some of the great Catholic missionaries to India, such as the Jesuit Robert de Nobill, have suggested that the Hindu scriptures—notably the Upanishads and the Bhagavad Gita—should be regarded as a supplementary Old Testament. The notion is laudable, but will it work? Does Hinduism assert anything positively that cannot be included within Christianity? Alas, there is in Hinduism the crucial doctrine of tat tvam asi ("That art thou"), which asserts the ultimate identity of oneself and the Godhead. At the level of philosophical theology, we can probably iron this difference out....At the mythic level, Hinduism asserts that all experience whatsoever is God's, and that God is the one and only knower and seer. All multiplicity, all sensations of limited and separate individuality, of the duality of here and there, I and thou, are God's dream or maya—a word that signifies not only illusion but also art and miraculous power. The universe is therefore conceived as God's game (lila) of hide and seek with himself, such that all beings are simply the masks of the one divine Self (atman)....If, then, the Christian system cannot contain the Hindu, can the Hindu contain the Christian?...When the Hindu says that the universe is God's maya or dream, the word maya is not necessarily used in a bad sense, as if it were a mere dream....From the Hindu's point of view, then, the Christian's predicament is the extreme adventure of God into his own maya....The point is rather that the "Hindu" myth of the Lord's maya, and of all beings as existing by his atma-yajna or self-sacrifice, not only gives the Christian myth a new and peculiar profundity; it acts as a catalyst through which there can be a full expression of Christian materialism.... We have seen that if the Christian view of the world is true, the Hindu cannot be true. On the other hand, if the Hindu view is true, the Christian can also be true—in the sense that the situation of seeming to be a lonely soul other than God and in peril of damnation could be one of the most extreme and adventurous roles of the Self. Thus, the intense seriousness of Christianity represents that moment in the drama of existence at which we are persuaded that this is not drama at all but "the real thing". ...This "Chinese box" inclusion of the Christian myth within the Hindu seems to me more fruitful and suggestive than the alternative of taking the Christian myth to be true, to the exclusion of the Hindu. It is also more complimentary to the Christian position because it makes it a dramatic triumph instead of a feat of pure dogmatic stubbornness.

All major conscious-unconscious Hindu influences, interactions and engagements with Christianity and the West can be considered as mostly without a proselytizing agenda and with a positive healthier outcome for the Christian religion and culture.

Teilhard de Chardin (1881–1955), a Jesuit palaeontologist and philosopher should be seen as a prime example of how Hinduizing of Christianity happened albeit not in a formal manner. The French evolutionist and Jesuit worked on the synthesis of science of evolution and religion. From the very basic beginnings of life to what he called 'noosphere'—where thinking humanity has become a qualitatively different kind of evolutionary force on the planet. He combined this evolutionary vision with what can be categorized as a kind of pantheistic experience:

> Lord, once again I ask: which is he more precious of these two beatitudes, that all things are means through which I can touch you or you yourself are so "universal" that I can experience you and lay hold of you in every creature?

Published posthumously, his book *Phenomenon of Man* is a cult classic of sorts. Almost for a decade even after his death, his works were censured.

Teilhard de Chardin had read William James's *The Varieties of Religious Experience* (1902) in late 1917. But as theologian Ursula King points out, 'between 1916, when Teilhard was working on *Cosmic Life*, and early 1918, the time of completing *The Soul of the World*, his essays contain no reference to either Hindu or Buddhist terms'.

Teilhard de Chardin visited India in 1935. He had all the colonial prejudices of his time. Well aware of the freedom movement, he opined that India was not ready for self-rule. Despite his life-long suffering quest for a 'cosmic religion', his theological and colonial conditioning seemed to have introduced a veil between him and his Indic experience. King writes:

> Teilhard was neither impressed...nor did he appreciate the Hindu assertion "of a cosmic unity, which was in many ways analogous to his own ideas," at least he did not realize it then. Close comparisons reveal a certain affinity between Hindu sense of unity and some of Teilhard's ideas about oneness, as Beatrice Bruteau has shown in a detailed study comparing his thoughts with central aspects of the Hindu tradition.

Beatrice Bruteau indeed writes about the way de Chardin could have found a validation for his formulation in Hinduism:

> The position on man as the active factor in the evolutionary process was an

important part of his theory and in Hinduism, he could have found a parallel to his ideas as close as his own religious tradition.

Despite his harsh and unjustifiable judgement on Hindus, he had witnessed the Hindu veneration for what can today be identified as the autopoietic movement of nature, a fundamental spontaneous creative process which is considered as important for evolution.

> Apparently, the god had visited their fields a few days ago in the guise of a flood, leaving behind numerous symbols of his procreative power in the shape of some longish pebbles, which were regarded as an especial mark of divine favour. From the temple, where festivities were in full swing, came the sound of flutes and drums and the nasal incantations of the priest...The whole village seemed to be involved in the festival. In several houses we glimpsed old men seated by candle-light, holding their hands before their foreheads in prayer...and chanting continuously from books with such devotion that for a moment we felt ourselves carried back in time to the far-off days when the Vedic hymns still formed part of daily worship.[434]

Yet Teilhard either missed it all or could never consciously bring himself to acknowledge the Hindu influence in his thought. Ursula King even thinks that he might have become aware of the works of Sri Aurobindo (1872–1950) at least in his last days:

> Although Teilhard was unfamiliar with Sri Aurobindo's writings, he may have recognized at the end of his life that Sri Aurobindo's great book, *The Life Divine*, is marked by a similar thrust and orientation as his own work.

By 1950, he was even acknowledging the 'Universal Feminine' as an overarching and all penetrating principle—ever present both in his individual spiritual journey and also in the planetary evolutionary process:

> The living heart of the Tangible is the Flesh. And for Man the Flesh means Woman. Ever since my childhood I had been engaged in the search for the Heart of Matter, and so it was inevitable that sooner or later I should come up against the Feminine. The only curious thing is that in the event it was not until my thirtieth year that this happened: so powerful was the fascination that the Impersonal and the Generalized held for me.... As I tell the story in these pages of my inner vision,...from the critical moment when I rejected many of the old moulds in which my family life and my religion had formed me and began to wake up and express myself in terms that were really my own, I have experienced no form of self-development without some

> feminine eye turned on me, some feminine influence at work....First, we have the appearance of a reflective monad, and then, to complete it, the formation of an affective dyad. And, after that, and only after that (that is, starting from this first spark) all that we have described the follows in sequence—the gradual and majestic development of a Neo-cosmic, of an Ultrahuman, and of a Pan-Christic…All three not only illuminated in their very roots by intelligence, but also impregnated throughout their entire mass, as though bonded by a unifying cement, by the Universal Feminine.[435]

This passage from Teilhard opens another important space for engagement with Hinduism. Hans Torwestern in his study of Sri Ramakrishna phenomenon and Jesus points out, among his conclusion, the feminine and material aspect of the Divine in surprisingly similar words: By worshipping God as Mother, Sri Ramakrishna also compels us to think about whether the male element in Christianity are not overstressed. And is the gulf between matter and God really so great?[436]

Teilhard de Chardin's term 'noosphere' as the next stage of planetary evolution was popularized by Russian systems geologist, a genius pioneer in the field, Vladimir Ivanovitch Vernadsky, who was also attracted to Swami Vivekananda. There are quite a few resonances with the evolutionary spirituality of Vivekananda and that of Teilhard, though the most emphatic mutual reflection of thoughts and ideas is between him and Sri Aurobindo. This easy resonance with the evolutionary spirituality of this hindered Jesuit with the contemporary Hindu savants suggests a deeper connecting stream.

Sri Aurobindonian scholar K. D. Sethna (1904–2011) in his exhaustive analysis of Teilhard de Chardin comes to the following conclusion about the fundamental nature of his work and its resonance with deep Hindu tradition:

> A fusion of genuine pantheism with genuine personalism sub specie Christi is what we reach as the fundamental of fundamentals in the faith of Teilhard de Chardin through the analysis of the use to which he frequently puts the term 'physical'.… The Teilhardian pantheism-personalism is rather akin to the ancient comprehensive Vedanta of the early Upanishads which continued the esoteric side of the still older Rig Veda. And the Christ-aspect links up vitally with that Vedanta as revived in Bhagavad Gita, where a Divine Incarnation such as would come from age to age in many forms focuses the cosmic-cum-transcendent God in human history. Modernize this revived Vedanta by setting it in the context of Evolutionism, with many of its religious overtones, it will be in tune, and you have the prototype of the full worldview of Teilhard, to which the proper understanding of his favourite term "physical" can be the most suggestive line of approach.[437]

Cut to twenty-first century, as the Catholic church finds itself faced with the need to engage with science, particularly global ecological problems, it has to invoke Teilhard. Papal encyclical, 'Laudato Si', released by Pope Francis on 24 May 2015, which deals with climate change and biodiversity, at last mentions Teilhard in one of its 172 references and footnotes. That is quite a recognition given that in 1963 there was a papal reprimanding the works of de Chardin.

Teilhard de Chardin, the person, despite his greatness yet because of his predetermined mental blocs could not use the Hindu wisdom tradition which could have helped him in conveying his vision of 'Omega Point' in a far more universal language. However, by continually marginalizing the vision of Teilhard, which is the natural spiritual evolution of Christianity in a universal spiritual direction, the church is missing out a great common platform for entering a creative dialogue with human diversity and plurality of world religions.

Thomas Merton (1915–1968) is another important Christian seer in this regard. After having graduated from Columbia University in 1938, he was working on his master's thesis on William Blake. That summer he had a chance meeting with a Hindu monk of Vaishnavaite tradition—Mahanambrata Brahmachari. When Morton asked the Hindu monk what he should read to gain a better understanding of the spiritual and mystical life, instead of recommending a Hindu text, Brahmachari suggested that Merton read Augustine's *Confessions* and Thomas À Kempis's *The Imitation of Christ*. Merton, after deep study and prayer, converted to Catholicism consciously the very same year.[438] Thus, Catholic theology got a modern seer thanks to an intervention by a Hindu monk.

A thorough Catholic monk, he was so respected by Hindu traditions that it was Merton who wrote a preface to the 1968 US edition of *The Bhagavad Gita As It Is* with purport by A. C. Bhaktivedanta Swami Prabhupada. It is quite interesting that an eminent Catholic theologian should write the preface to the book that would come the closest to the Hindu equivalent of the way the Bible gets distributed by proselytizers. Yet the preface was deeply spiritual than in any way sectarian. Anticipating the possible Western criticism as well as misunderstanding of the Bhagavad Gita as a book promoting warfare, he wrote:

> The Gita is not a justification of war, nor does it propound a war-making mystique. War is accepted in the context of a particular kind of ancient culture in which it could be, and was, subject to all kinds of limitations.... Arjuna has an instinctive repugnance for war, and that is the chief reason why war is chosen as the example of the most repellent kind of duty. The Gita is saying that even in what appears to be most "unspiritual" one can act with pure intentions and thus be guided by Krishna

> consciousness. This consciousness itself will impose the most strict limitations on one's use of violence because that use will not be directed by one's own selfish interests, still less by cruelty, sadism, and blood-lust.[439]

Another important Catholic philosopher-theologian influenced by Hinduism and also other 'Eastern' traditions was Thomas Berry (1914–2009). An ordained Catholic monk and a historian of world religions, his work can be seen as taking forward the work of Teilhard de Chardin. He was the president of the American Teilhard Association from 1975 to 1987. He concentrated on how the world spiritual traditions could come together to heal the planet that was undergoing an ecological crisis. Eastern traditions, Hinduism, Zen Buddhism and Confucianism as well as native American spiritual traditions had a strong influence in his worldview. One can see in Thomas Berry at least partially the kind of direction Teilhard would have taken, had the latter been more open to Hinduism.

Dr Christopher Key Chapple, Professor of Indic and Comparative Theology at Loyola Marymount University in his paper on the 'Influence of Eastern Religions on Berry' states that two themes from 'the Hindu Vedic tradition', emerge in his later works which are 'the articulation of the correspondence between the microphase and macrophase aspects of reality, and the shift in Hindu history from elaborate, expensive, priest-driven sacrifices or yajnas to simpler, home-centred ceremonies or pujas, generally conducted by women'. The much-maligned *Purusha Sukta* of *Rig Veda* receives a proper eco-spiritual treatment in the hands of this Catholic philosopher:

> In the early Vedic literature, the Purusha Sukta proclaims an identity between the human body, the structure of society, and the vast zones that compromise the cosmos. The feet represent the labour of the worker class. The legs correlate to the mobility of the merchants, the arms to the strength of the ruling class, and the head to the intellectual elite: the priests, doctors, lawyers, and teachers. Every society needs the reciprocal contribution of each part. Further, the feet connect the individual to the earth, the chest and the abdomen to the fire and air, and the eyes to the sun and the moon. The entire cosmos is contained within the human body. A term that Berry often invoked, intimacy, captures the complex web of relationships spoken of in the Vedas and the Upanishads. In his later work, this intimate relation between earth and food, and food as constitutive of body, would call forth an ethical imperative. If our food, which arises from earth has been tainted by pollution, then our bodies and our very selves are placed in peril. As we recover our intimacy with the earth, we are brought to our senses and must take corrective action.

Even in the value of authenticity which came to Berry from Confucianism, which 'in addition to carrying the existential meaning as found in the work of French philosophers Albert Camus and Marcel Proust, denoted for Berry the Sat or the truth of the Vedic world which also anchored the thought of Mahatma Gandhi ....'

Both in Thomas Merton and Thomas Berry, one finds how the Hindu-Christian interaction without the agenda of proselytization and appropriation can creatively and spiritually benefit humanity. In the case of theologians like Raimundo Panikkar and the Shantivanam project heads, there is the danger of the dialogue turning into a strategic battle waged against Hinduism. The church which may tolerate to an extent the fertilizing of its spirituality with inputs from Hindu Dharma, will react rather sharply to similar approaches when they come from Indian Catholic seers. The case in point is discussed next.

Anthony de Mello (1931–1987): A Genuine Christian Engagement with Hinduism

Anthony de Mello was a Jesuit priest who founded the Sadhana Institute of Pastoral Counselling at Poona. After having worked as 'retreat master and spiritual director' for Christian retreats, in 1978 he published his book *Sadhana—A Way to God* with the subtitle 'Christian Exercises in Eastern Form'. The book though mainly meant for Christian clergy, became popular even outside Christian circles. At the outset, given the constant appropriation attempts and strategies designed by the church, the book may look suspiciously like another such attempt. But it was not so. Anthony de Mello openly acknowledged with gratitude the source and separate spiritual greatness of the resources he was using and he was using them for Christian seekers and those who wanted to recharge their inner batteries. He even wanted Christians to invent their own thousand names of Jesus not as an attempt of appropriation but as a form of their inner meditation. In his introduction to the book, he wrote:

> A Jesuit friend once told me that he approached a Hindu guru for initiation in the art of prayer. The guru said to him, "Concentrate on your breathing." My friend proceeded to do just that for about five minutes. Then the guru said, "The air you breathe is God. You are breathing God in and out. Become aware of that, and stay with that awareness." ...The exercises I propose in this book are very much in line with the approach of that Hindu guru, whom I have never met or heard of since.[440]

Inside the book, we find another important passage:

> To silence the mind is an extremely difficult task....Our Hindu masters in India have a saying: one thorn is removed by another. By this they mean that you will be wise to use one thought to rid yourself of all the other thoughts that crowd into your mind. One thought, one image, one phrase or sentence or word that your mind can be made to fasten on....The mind must have something to occupy it. Well, then, give it something with which to occupy itself but just one thing. An image of the Saviour that you gaze on lovingly and to which you return each time you are distracted; an ejaculation that you keep repeating ceaselessly to prevent the mind from wandering. A time will come, hopefully, when the image will disappear from consciousness, when the word will be taken out of your mouth and your discursive mind will be perfectly stilled and your Heart will be given free scope to gaze, unimpeded, into the Darkness! [441]

Soon de Mello became a master storyteller of Indian spiritual seekers in circles that often escaped the popularity radars. By the 1980s, almost every youthful Indian seeker with English education would have read a book by de Mello. The Dancing God became an important spiritual image for him. In his book *The Song of the Bird* (1984), he described:

> Hindu India developed a magnificent image to describe God's relationship with Creation. God "dances" Creation. He is the Dancer, Creation is his Dance. The dance is different from the dancer, yet it has no existence apart from him. You cannot take it home in a box, if it pleases you. The moment the dancer stops, the dance ceases to be.[442]

In his book *Wellsprings*, he conceived all manifestations of existence—spiritual and secular, good and bad, dharmic and adharmic, as movements of the great grand dancer. He wrote:

> *... I see Jesus Christ and Judas,*
> *I see victims and persecutors,*
> *the killers and the crucified;*
> *one melody in the contrasting notes.*
> *I think of the people who dislike me and attack me*
> *and I see them and me as different,*
> *yet not-two,*
> *engaged in one task,*
> *one dance,*
> *one work of art.*
> ...

Finally, I stand before the Lord.
I see him as the dancer
and all of this maddening,
senseless,
exhilarating,
agonizing,
splendorous thing
that we call life
as his dance.[443]

At the same time, he was clear about his identity and his faith. He communicated this to his readers in no uncertain term—particularly when he wrote for readers of all religions and no religion. The dedication he wrote for *The Song of the Bird* reveals his faith and dedication to the church as his spiritual nourishing mother:

> This book has been written for people of every persuasion, religious and nonreligious. I cannot, however, hide from my readers the fact that I am a priest of the Catholic Church. I have wandered freely in mystical traditions that are not Christian and not religious and I have been profoundly influenced by them. It is to my Church, however, that I keep returning, for she is my spiritual home; and while I am acutely, sometimes, embarrassingly, conscious of her limitations and narrowness, I also know that it is she who has formed me and made me what I am today. So, it is to her that I gratefully dedicate this book.[444]

In his *One Minute Wisdom* (1985), the Master he introduced is described this way:

> The Master in these tales is not a single person. He is a Hindu Guru, a Zen Roshi, a Taoist Sage, a Jewish Rabbi, a Christian Monk, a Sufi Mystic. He is Lao Tzu and Socrates. Buddha and Jesus, Zarathustra and Mohammed. His teaching is found in the 7th century B.C. and the 20th century A.D. His wisdom belongs to East and West alike. Do his historical antecedents really matter? History, after all, is the record of appearances, not Reality; of doctrines, not of Silence.[445]

One can see here two important aspects: one marginalization of historic-centricity that so characterizes and forms a significant basis of Christian theology and another, the placing of Jesus as not the only but one among the spiritual personalities of the world.

In 1987 he suffered a massive heart attack and died. But his legacy lives on.

And then the Empire struck back. On 24 June 1998, the day considered as the birth day of John the Baptist, the 'Congregation for the Doctrine of the Faith' (CDF), which was formerly known as the 'Supreme Sacred Congregation of the Roman and Universal Inquisition', issued a 'notification Concerning the Writings of Fr Anthony De Mello SJ'.

After pointing out the immense popularity of his books in various spiritual retreats, it says:

> But already in certain passages in these early works and to a greater degree in his later publications, one notices a progressive distancing from the essential contents of the Christian faith. In place of the revelation which has come in the person of Jesus Christ, he substitutes an intuition of God without form or image, to the point of speaking of God as a pure void....This radical apophaticism leads even to a denial that the Bible contains valid statements about God....Religions, including Christianity, are one of the major obstacles to the discovery of truth. This truth, however, is never defined by the author in its precise contents. For him, to think that the God of one's own religion is the only one is simply fanaticism. "God" is considered as a cosmic reality, vague and omnipresent; the personal nature of God is ignored and in practice denied. Father de Mello demonstrates an appreciation for Jesus, of whom he declares himself to be a "disciple". But he considers Jesus as a master alongside others. The only difference from other men is that Jesus is "awake" and fully free, while others are not. Jesus is not recognized as the Son of God, but simply as the one who teaches us that all people are children of God....With the present Notification, in order to protect the good of the Christian faithful, this Congregation declares that the above-mentioned positions are incompatible with the Catholic faith and can cause grave harm. The Sovereign Pontiff John Paul II, at the Audience granted to the undersigned Cardinal Prefect, approved the present Notification, adopted in the Ordinary Session of this Congregation, and ordered its publication.[446]

When a Catholic priest wants to publish a book concerning religion, the book should have the Imprimatur ('Let it be printed') of the authority from Catholic church (Bishop or in the case of Jesuits the Provincial of the Order or Congregation. All the nine books of Anthony de Mello were published after being granted the Imprimatur.[447]

The result of the 'notification', though not an official ban, was that Gujarat Sahitya Prakash, the Jesuit publishing house with a secular name was stopped from printing new editions of the books and they 'disappeared from the shelves of Catholic bookshops overnight until the controversy was cleared'. Today the books are allowed to be published with the following note:

> The books of Father Anthony de Mello were written in a multi-religious context to help the followers of other religions, agnostics and atheists in their spiritual search, and they were not intended by the author as manuals of instruction of the Catholic faithful in Christian doctrine or dogma.[448]

The phenomenon of Anthony de Mello and the subsequent reaction from the church showcase both the opportunities and problems in the Hindu-Christian encounter. The Anthony de Mello incident is only a syndrome; the causes are deeper.

Mark Tully, the former BBC 'South Asia' correspondent, speaks of a Catholic priest whom he was reminded of during his conversation with the Catholic scholar Ursula King as she spoke of the similarity between the religiousness of the Catholic and Hindu places of worship:

> I was reminded of a Catholic priest who once told me that although his family had been Christians for generations and he has been through the full rigours of a Jesuit training he still, in his heart of hearts felt closer to the God Krishna than to Jesus.[449]

The Indian Catholic Jesuit's closeness to Krishna may mainly be because of the non-rigidity of 'theology' and the accommodative space of theo-diversity Hindu culture has cultivated through and around Sri Krishna. The entire Anthony de Mello episode then can be considered as showing this speciality of Indian Christians. Though they might be Christians for generations even, the very fact of them being immersed in the Hindu ocean of theo-diversity with all its colours of festivals and celebrations, rituals and art forms, has created deeply a synthesis which the global Christian community can make use of, to adapt itself to the postcolonial world where the cosmic visions unveiled by science demand a universal religion which is qualitatively different from a monopolistic-expansionist religion and which should even include and recognize atheism as a spiritually valid way of life. In India, the church has tried to answer this challenge by creating a history-centric narrative with ethnic overtones—a Dravidian St Thomas Christianity being corrupted by Brahminical Aryan Hinduism. Such pseudoscientific and racially inclined narratives are dangerous and can only generate more conflicts. Adapting the ways of Teilhard de Chardin, Thomas Berry and Anthony de Mello on the other hand can benefit humanity at large beyond the religious boundaries on both sides.

This also shows why Indian Christians should increase their demand for their share of representation in the global church, both in numbers and in doctrinal influence—in short, recognition of the peculiarity and speciality of Indian

Christians. It is in all these contexts—some positive and others negative—that one has to look at the way RSS approaches the Hindu-Christian dialogue.

RSS Dialogue with Indian Christian-Christianity

Golwalkar's Views

Guruji Golwalkar of the RSS considered Jesus as a spiritual personality and attributed the success of early Christianity more to the idealism of the disciples than any political power.

> Even after understanding all this, there are some who feel that political power is essential even to spread our dharmic ideology....But on a closer study, we will find that ultimately political power will never solve the problem. For instance, the Government and most of the people were ranged against that single individual, Jesus Christ. After he was crucified on the cross, his disciples had no one to guide them. But their hearts were charged with idealism. Fired with the spirit of Christ, with the faith and zeal of their new realization, they spread far and wide in the world. And the world bowed at their feet. Then they had no political power. But when, in course of time, their successors fell prey to the lure of political power, corruption and degradation entered their ranks.[450]

In general, in Golwalkar one finds a respectful attitude towards Jesus, but he resents the missionaries for destroying the religion of India and thus destroying its social harmony. He even does not hesitate to cite the value of the heartful offering emphasized by Jesus when talking about how the Sangh sees '*dhan*':

> Any offering made with the object of procuring something in return—even a name—is not an offering but a bargain. In the Sangh, such a mercenary attitude is never allowed to develop. We deem the offering made with real devotion as the noblest and highest, just as Jesus considered the poor old woman's small coin a nobler offering than the treasures donated to the Temple by persons rolling in wealth.

Even as he condemned the conversions and the agenda of the missionaries, he also pointed out to his cadre the way they work with the tribal communities:

> See how the foreign missionaries are working in these areas. What a tremendous amount of effort and perseverance they display! What an amount of trouble they

> cheerfully undergo! They come from far-off lands and go and settle in the deep jungles. They live there in small houses just like the local people. They mix with them, learn their languages and become one with the local habits and customs. They behave with sweetness and sympathy. Can we not take a leaf out of their experience and do something?

But he wanted complete cultural and spiritual assimilation of non-Hindus with the Hindu culture and spirituality:

> There are some people who claim that they have achieved unity of Hindus, Muslims, Christians and all others on the political and economic plane. But why limit the oneness only there? Why not make it more wide and more comprehensive so as to fuse them all in the Hindu way of life, in our dharma and take them back as lost brothers? To those who speak of unity on the political and economic plane, we say that we stand not only for political and economic unity but also for cultural and religious unity. We have thrown open our homes, our sanctuaries and temples, our age-old culture and heritage. Undoubtedly, this is a broader outlook.

Interestingly, when Golwalkar talks about the homecoming of lost brothers, he explains in full the famous parable of Jesus—prodigal son. He had stated elsewhere that while a person has complete freedom to choose whatever as his sacred text and preferred form of worship, he should fulfil his duty to the nation and his community. Thus, one can deduce that when Golwalkar speaks about returning to the 'Hindu way of life', he allows for theo-diversity of including Christianity and Islam in it.

A Gandhian Catholic Priest on the RSS

Fr Anthony Elenjimittam (1915–2011), an ordained monk of the Dominican Order, was from Kerala. After completing his theological studies in Rome, he had returned to India and joined the National Movement under Gandhi.

A prolific writer, he had penned books which had already attracted good attention and accolades. In 1947 he had written a book on Subhas Chandra Bose titled *The Hero of Hindustan*. The foreword for his 1948 book *The Poet of Hindustan* was written by Dr Sarvepalli Radhakrishnan. In 1951, three years after the assassination of Mahatma Gandhi, he published *Philosophy and Action of the RSS for the Hind Swaraj*—probably this could have been the first English book studying the Hindutva movement.

The book dedicated to 'the caste-creed-sex-free, steel-nerved, iron-willed, all-renouncing Patriots of New Bharat…countless sages, seers, bards, prophets, rishis, missionaries and apostles of Hindu-Buddhist Dharma who built up Greater India in Asian Continent…who repudiate the liability of birth-religion-labels…for attaining Truth, God, Over-Soul, Reality Supreme, Paramatman according to the Vedic dictum...' bluntly states in the first page itself that the INC, 'the Mother of Indian Freedom' had 'got diseased'; Bose, Gandhi and Patel, 'the great minds that built the Congress …have gone from our midst…'[451]

He then cautions that the Hindu-Muslim problem is not over with the creation of Pakistan:

> Muslim communalism cannot be cured by merely creating Pakistan; on the contrary, it has made the communal cleavage between Muslims and Hindus more real, accentuated and intransigent. Pakistan has become a springboard for the communal Muslims to reach out to their wider scheme of re-constructing their old Mogul Empire in India and making it the centre of the entire Pan-Islamic confederation.[452]

He laments that Indian leftists, instead of exploring 'unfathomable depths of their own country, their nation, their national culture and the spirit and aspiration of Indian people' look to 'Moscow as their Mecca' and 'parrot-wise repeat some sayings of Marx'. So, what is the alternative? He categorically says it is not in creating a communal counterpart to Islamist forces. Fortunately, the author sees 'a new nationalistic force' arising in the Indian horizon which transcends the right-left binary. 'That new force is the Rashtriya Swayamsevak Sangh in its ideal character.'[453]

According to Fr Elenjimittam, India needs an Indic-rooted organization working for the common good of all humanity and sees the RSS as the potential candidate, particularly given the 'weak nature' of the Nehru government and extra-territorial preoccupation of Indian leftists. 'While rejecting what he considers as the 'communalism' of 'either the Muslim League, Christian church or Hindu Mahasabha', he considers the 'eternal philosophy of Vedanta, the psychology of Buddha and Buddhism, metaphysics of non-dualistic idealism of Sankara, the integrated ethics and psychological religion of *Bhagavad Gita*' as providing the alternative.[454]

Then comes the term 'Hindu'. Fr Elenjimittam combines the territorial meaning of the term with a cultural-spiritual nationalist dimension:

> The term "Hindu" today stands for the essential Indian spirit...The word Hindu stands for anyone who is born in the land of Ganges, who is conscious of his cultural heritage, specially of the Vedanta, Yoga, Buddha, Sankara, Indian art and literature,

> who struggles to realize those vital truths in his life, whose purpose of life is Self-Realization or God-consciousness for himself and the subsequent dynamic service of his fellow beings, in leading his people, his society, country, mankind to a better social, economic and political pattern. Birth is of little significance; quality life means everything.[455]

The society started forgetting such national ideals and out of that agony, the RSS was born. The founder Dr Keshav Baliram Hedgewar of Nagpur was 'a man whose breath was nationalism, patriotism, service, sacrifice'.[456] The Dominican monk draws a parallel between the founding of the RSS to the commune of Jesus and his disciples. Then he compares the birth of Sangh to the Sangha of the Buddha. The RSS is 'the crowning and fulfilment of all that is best in Hindu and Buddhist traditions'.[457] The book traces what the author considers as the continuity RSS has with Hindu-Buddhist thought and the non-communal, non-fundamentalist nature of the Sangh. M. S. Golwalkar, the then head of the RSS, is quoted as saying that the RSS was founded and working 'to revive all that is best in Hindu i.e. Bharatiya culture...(RSS) tries to destroy the fissiparous tendencies in the Hindu society'.[458]

Fr Elenjimittam has in-depth knowledge of Indian spirituality and philosophy, not merely as theological subjects but as a life experience. He places RSS in that context. Fr Elenjimittam touches a crucial point that plagues Indian academic establishments to this day:

> "Why should we look to a Max Muller, a Schopenhauer, Monier Williams and Estlin Carpenter to learn Indian philosophy or Indian philology? Is it not a disgrace? Does it not reflect a slave mentality?" Of course, the book does not deny that we are indebted to these Indologists but points out that, ultimately, it is for us "the children of the soil of India" to explore further, revitalize and make "what is lasting, true, eternal in Indian culture and philosophy" to be "preserved, defended, propagated and made a living reality in the lives and mental habits of our people and in every sphere of Indian life".[459]

In the subsequent chapters, he deals with the various criticism and charges levelled against the Sangh then. Earlier he had cautioned the critics of the RSS, who were then entrenched in the seats of power, that all their 'persecutions and calumnies, slandering and back-biting can only strengthen the RSS.'[460] He differentiates the 'neo-nationalistic gospel of the RSS', from the 'racial myth of Rosenberg' as propagated by the Nazis.[461] The RSS, though a disciplined force, is not fascist because the discipline of the RSS is devoid of 'fascist totalitarianism, imperialist dreams and militarist pride' but is 'born out of the culture or sanskriti of the land and not on the military might or myths of the twentieth century'.[462]

Fr Elenjimittam quotes elaborately from the then contemporary lectures of Golwalkar to reveal a mindset that is contrary to the words written during the heated circumstances of pre-Partition era

> The word Hindu state is nowadays unnecessarily misrepresented as a theocratic one, which would wipe out all other sects. On the contrary, I want to state today that this State of country which has been made over to us is a Hindu State and it is also a secular state and all those who are now non-Hindus have equal rights to live here as Hindus do. From the point of view of what is considered a democracy, i.e. the rule of the majority, when vast majority of the people are Hindu the state is democratically Hindu; but the State cannot exclude all those who live here to occupy any position of honour in the State.[463]

Though well aware of the Communist threat to freedom, Fr Elenjimittam was not the typical Christian anti-Communist of that age. He clearly understood the real factors which fanned the fire of Communism, particularly in the newly liberated countries under colonialism. He opts for an Indic solution:

> Indian philosophy, Indian social system and above all the new upsurge of creative and dynamic nationalism can teach that not class struggle, as the Marxist Communists uphold, but class-co-operation is the right method and the royal road to lasting peace. The RSS believes India to become the Jagatguru. The Communist challenge can be met through the cultural soul of Mother India when she could show practical methods of class-cooperation. [464]

Drawing cues from Golwalkar's speech on ideal society, Fr Elenjimittam envisions a 'cooperative economics of a really and truly free people, emancipated from the clutches of totalitarianism and monopoly capitalism'.[465] Here the author plays visionary—foreseeing the fall of the gross national product and an inclusion of values in gauging human progress. In the RSS he sees the potential for a radically different alternative system that is holistic and though, right now, nationalistic can later flower into a global movement—preserving the best in all native traditions and spirituality.

The book places this significant burden on the RSS, which was then just an infant organization, recovering from the ban imposed on it by Nehru government and the continuing sustained negative image and propaganda against it. He cites the yeomen service work the organization has been doing for the refugees pouring into West Bengal. The RSS is the only national organization serving all people in India, apart from the duty-bound government and concludes that 'Hindu nationalism is Bharatiyata or Indianism.'[466]

The book is historically important for introducing into the political vocabulary of India a term that would become famous with the 'Ayodhya movement'. Fr Elenjimittam was perhaps the first person to coin the term 'pseudo-secularism', which he used to denote the 'new fad' of Nehru and other Congress leaders and contrasts it with the civilizational secularism that is inherent in Indian culture.

> But the religious secularism and nationalistic patriotism of those bygone prophets and the architects of modern India have little, nothing in common with the protagonists of pseudo-secularism of the type which, unfortunately, such an eminent scholar like Sri Nehru who continues to repeat his pet secularism ad nauseam in and out of season.[467]

Thus, it is to a Christian priest that the Hindutva movement owes its crucial ideological term. Then, the author points out the responsibility of RSS in the context of the scheme of planetary evolution—almost echoing Catholic Jesuit anthropologist Teilhard de Chardin:

> Being tarred with the same brush, germinating from the same seed of the protoparents, evolving from amoeba to the highest species of homo sapiens, this Manava Dharma, anti-communal religion, has a lasting value. It is this the RSS in India represents; it is this the Indian patriots uphold.[468]

Mostly, this book provides the anticipation that RSS created in a generation of intellectuals who placed RSS in the broadest possible context, taking a sympathetic view to the Indic vision of RSS. This book by Fr Elenjimittam, a Catholic-Gandhian monk, shows a very deep understanding of Indian culture as the world was entering a postcolonial era and positions the RSS as an indigenous, postcolonial, socio-cultural-spiritual movement with a lot of potentials and promises. After almost 65 years, today, the RSS has become an organization that has gained the capacity to influence and lead the nation. From its ranks, many State chief ministers and at least two Prime Ministers have emerged.

Some Important RSS-Christian Dialogues

In 1983 Shripati Shastri, the RSS spokesperson, received a communication from Dr Mathew R. Lederie, a Pune-based Jesuit scholar, to participate in a seminar at Jnanadeepa Vidyapeeth (a Hindu sounding name for papal seminary). The seminar was held at De Nobili College, Pune—a Jesuit seminary. Later, his talk and question-answer session were published as a book by the RSS with the approval of the Seminar Organizing Committee. Jesuit Fr Felix Raj had expressed the hope that a 'cordial invitation to an active RSS man to share his views on Christianity with us' would be 'the first step towards an open and fraternal dialogue between Christians and RSS in India' and would enable both 'to work for the betterment of people and for promoting justice and peace in our country'. The RSS, on its part, had stated that it too reciprocated 'the fond hopes'.

On 20 August 2002, the Indian Institute of Christian Studies hosted the RSS-Christian Perspective Analysis Meet. The Honorary Director of the institute was Joseph Pulikunnel. Among those who attended it were K. S. Sudarshan, then the Sarsanghachalak or All India Head of the RSS, Sri Parameshwaran, a senior RSS ideologue and director of Bharatheeya Vichara Kendram, Justice K. T. Thomas, retired Supreme Court Judge, Rev. Mathew Varkey of CSI Synod and some leading theologians and eminent citizens of the Christian community. In his keynote address, Retd Judge K. T. Thomas made the following observations on the principles of secularism and the problem of conversions:

> I am a great believer in the preaching and teachings of Jesus Christ. I have tried to adhere to it all through my life. But that had at no time impaired or eroded my secularism, which is an article of faith in me throughout my career, not only as an advocate but as a long-time judge for 25 years. I have very strictly adhered to the secularistic principles enshrined in the Constitution of India.... The position is therefore this: Conversion is not contemplated in the Constitution but propagation is made a fundamental right. Does propagation involve a right to convert another person? In my considered view, when propagation is the right of a person in India, converting another person is not a right. It is true, if one converts himself into another religion nobody can prevent him for doing so.... The protagonists of the right to convert other persons rely on the assumption that his religion is the correct religion, whereas your religion is a wrong religion. This is basically erroneous.

He also dealt with the vexed question of extending to the SC converts to Christianity the same concessions given to SC Hindus:

> When we make the plea for maintaining the same benefits to Dalits who became Christians, what is our moral right to say as our fathers deliberately refused to treat the converted Dalits with equal status? It is equally untenable for forward Hindu communities to oppose granting the same benefits to Dalit Christians. What is their moral right to oppose such benefits being granted to a section of people who

> became sufferers on account of the treatment meted out to them on the strength of misinterpretation of Hindu scriptures? While it is a vexed question, I strongly feel that what could be granted to Dalits when they follow Hinduism or Buddhism or Jainism should be granted to those following Christian religion also.

While in the issue of conversion Retd Judge K. T. Thomas seemed to agree with the RSS on the issue of conferring affirmative action benefits to SC members converted to Christianity, he is against the popular Hindu stand. K. T. Thomas also expressed that a concept of a national church might not be a practical idea.

K. S. Sudarshan, in his speech, spoke against conversions and stated that he differed from K. T. Thomas on the possibility of a national church and that he was also against extending reservation benefits to Christian SC converts from Hindu society:

> When conversion is done with a motive to just segregate a portion of the society for their imperialistic purposes, that becomes the cause for concern, the cause of conflict. And therefore, we say that conversion is a major irritant....But many of the Churches and especially funded by foreign countries, have got a political motivation behind conversion. They are serving the interests of foreign powers. Therefore, we are deadly against them....Hindu society is an ancient society and it also has its own defects. We do not deny it. But it is ultimately for the Hindu society to rectify it, and the process has been going on.... But anyway, some of them do say that if you come to our fold, you will be emancipated from all the cruelties that are being perpetrated on you. So after being converted to Christianity, how can they remain Dalits?...It was in 1936 that the demand was raised that the Dalit Christians should be given some special benefits. The British government refused saying that after converting to Christianity they do not remain Dalits. So, if the social disability is removed, then only economic disparity remains. And that is there in other communities also.

This shows that in discussing what the dialogue organizers have considered as 'the irritant topics', the participants were honest and were not towing any particular ideological line and openly disagreeing and converging with each other's point of view.

Dr M. P. Mathai, a reader in the school of Gandhian Studies at the Mahatma Gandhi University also differed from Sudarshan on the question of extending reservation benefits to converted SC members while agreeing on conversions. He said:

> On the question of conversions, I can agree with most of what Sudarshanji said here.

> Conversion in the sense of proselytization is actually creating a lot of problems, particularly in the contemporary context. A research scholar of mine had made a detailed study of what happened in the states of Madhya Pradesh and Orissa. He had come to the conclusion that one of the main reasons for the present troubles in those parts of the country is the large-scale proselytizing that is being attempted by evangelical groups. But one of the interesting things to note is that the facts and figures that these evangelical groups publish are not true.... What is important is that we must address the question as to why the Dalits and weak sections are really attracted by these enticements that they change their religion.... What is mainstream Hindu society doing? What are organisations like RSS and VHP, which vow by Hindutva ideology doing to eliminate these social evils of segregation, untouchability etc.... There is untouchability in Christianity. Why is there untouchability in Christianity? Because it is there in Hinduism. Gandhiji had said that by converting Harijans to Christianity you are not going to save them from untouchability. He had said that conversion is not the solution to this problem of untouchability in India for if untouchability persisted in Hinduism, it will be automatically transferred to other religions into which the untouchables go.... So my question is what are the Hindu organizations doing to address this problem?

After the discussions as well as question-answer sessions, a joint declaration, which was unanimously accepted by RSS delegates and members of various churches who participated in the meet, was read out which urged the 'process of self-analysis and mutual appreciation of perspectives to continue among religious groups, so that the peace of Jesus and the wish of the Indian rishis of the past: "Loka Samasta Sukhino Bhavantu" might be realized'. Though one might say that the statement was a little bit theologically loaded in favour of Christianity (peace of Jesus as against the wish of rishis), the RSS delegates did not hesitate to engage in such dialogues and exercises.

In 2014 RSS writer Virag Pachpore, who was also involved in interfaith dialogue projects of the RSS, wrote a book on the creation of an indigenous Indian church. According to the author, the need for a national church for Indian Christians was necessitated by a new Canon Law from Vatican:

> In 1992, Rome promulgated a Canon Law for five churches in the Middle East .... Though the name of the Indian Church is not included in the list of the Churches, Roman curia declared that this Law is applicable to the ancient Indian Catholics. According to this Canon Law all temporal wealth of the Indian Catholics belongs to Pope which is the head of the State of Vatican. According to the Canon Law, the Bishops appointed by Pope in India, govern the Bishoprics with legislative, executive and judicial powers on the temporal and spiritual wealth of the Indian

> Christians. The temporal wealth of the Indian Church which comes to billions of Indian rupees, now belongs to the Pope of Rome and administered by him through the Bishops appointed by him.

After an exhaustive study of the history and theology of Christianity and also the various transnational networks of which the prominent Indian churches are part of, Pachpore wrote:

> The idea of a national church is entirely a Christian idea and it is time for Indian Christians to at least start a debate on this issue raising above the narrow political and communal affiliations and party lines. Through healthy debate and dialogue something positive, definite and concrete would emerge which would pave the way for establishment of a truly National Church in India.

So the Hindutva engagement with Christianity emphasizes pluralism. While it offers a strong resistance to movements emanating from the monopolistic and hence proselytizing components of Christianity, it does not brand Christianity as untrue and assumes a mission to remove it completely. It also expects Indian Christians to be more anchored to theo-diversity, which is natural to India, than monopolistic proselytizing emphasized by institutional Christianity.

This provides for Christianity a safe ground in India to explore some of its own spiritual greatness that has been denied proper exploration in institutionalized Catholicism and evangelical Protestantism. Perhaps it is in the evolution of an indigenous spirituality which can accept Teilhard de Chardin and Anthony de Mello, that Indian Christianity can help the global Christianity to evolve and become more pluralistic. The Hindutva movement though not always consciously but ultimately effectively facilitates that process. From all these, one can conclude that the space for dialogue and interaction with Christianity is increasing and forming fascinating engagement spaces. Hindutva has been engaging with Christianity, both with its institutional forms, its indigenous developments and its proselytizing agenda. There have been violent conflicts, intellectual debates and peaceful dialogues too.

The media, with its colonial and theo-colonial prejudices still deep, highlights only the negative and violent confrontations, that too in a one-sided way—barbaric pagan exploiters of general public persecuting liberating Christian missionaries, though in reality it is more a well-funded, well-organized and proselytizing war on indigenous spiritual traditions of the land resulting in pan-Indian resistance.

But beyond these conflict points the samanvaya transformation is getting catalysed on both sides with the role of Hindutva being markedly higher.

Biography of Ashfaqullah Khan published by the publishing wing of RSS as children's literature

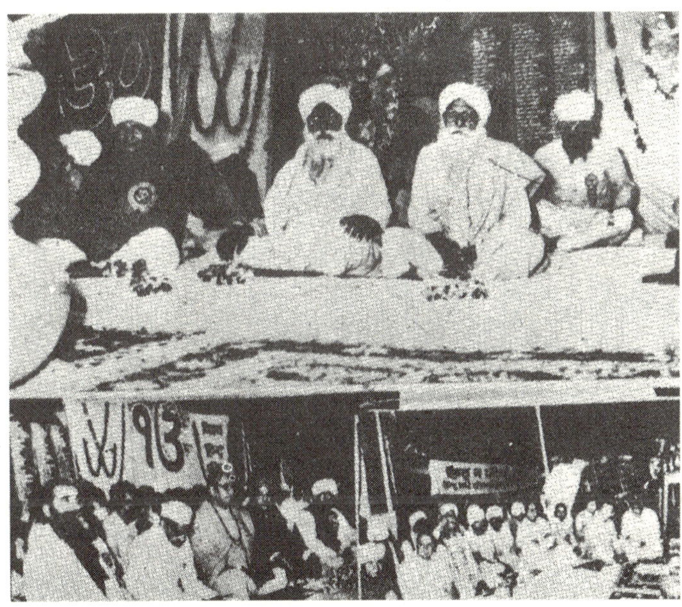

Various Sikh and other Hindu religious as well as social leaders brought together to emphasize the Sikhs and other Hindus at Amritsar in 1983

From 1981 to 1984, the official popular magazine of RSS in Tamil Nadu titled 'Vijaya Bharatam' carried out a relentless campaign against hatred towards Sikhs by bringing the essence of Sikh Dharma to non-Sikh Indians

His Holiness The Dalai Lama at the Second VHP conference in 1979

The fifth all India head of the RSS K. S. Sudarshan with Christian religious leaders (20 August 2002). Rev. Joseph Pulikunel (1932–2017), a very popular liberal theologian facilitated the dialogue

Sanskriti Sangam (International Conference and Gathering of Elders) 2003 was a Sangh initiative to bring together indigenous spiritual traditions from across the world to preserve and nurture theo-diversity

Maulana Wahiduddin Khan addressing the seminar addressed by RSS think-tank Deendayal Research Institute (Manthan, August,1988)

Conclusion

This book tries to look at Hindutva from a neutral as well as a Hindu perspective. The book argues that Hindutva is both a process and an existential reality, and contains many dimensions and currents. It represents an important and, perhaps, a very relevant stream of consciousness on the planet, and so it is worth preserving. Hindutva is, simultaneously, the stream to be preserved and the process of preservation. It operates in the political domain but is not a political ideology; it functions in the cultural sphere, but is not merely cultural. It is all encompassing. Paradoxically, it also includes the narratives of those who oppose it. The temple of Hindutva belongs as much to the Brahmin as it belongs to the Scheduled Communities and Tribes, as Dr Ambedkar said.

Finally, Hindutva represents theo-diversity. In that way, Hindutva is also the future of intelligent life on this planet.

Endnotes

Chapter- 1

1. Michael Persinger, 'Foreword' in *Reflections on the Dawn of Consciousness: Julian Jaynes's Bicameral Mind Theory Revisited* (Ed. Marcel Kuijsten), Julian Jaynes Society, 2006

2. Julian Jaynes, *The Origin of Consciousness in the Breakdown of the Bicameral Mind* , Mariner Books, 1976:2000, p. 313

3. Ibid., p. 311

4. Justin E. H. Smith, *Irrationality: A History of the Dark Side of Reason*, Princeton University Press, 2019, p. 91

5. Daniel Dennett, '*Julian Jaynes's Software Archaeology*', *Canadian Psychology*, 27, 1986, 149–154

6. Charles C. Mann, 'The Birth of Religion', *National Geographic*, June 2011

7. Matt J. Rossano, *Supernatural Selection: How Religion Evolved*, Oxford University Press, 2010, p. 197

8. Sidarto Ribeiro, 'The Onset of Data-driven Mental Archeology', *Frontiers in Neuroscience*, Vol. 8., August 2014

9. Nicolas Baumard et al., 'Increased Affluence Explains the Emergence of Ascetic Wisdoms and Moralizing Religions', *Current Biology*, 2015: http://dx.doi.org/10.1016/j.cub.2014.10.063

10. Ibid.

11. Justin E. H. Smith, 2019, p. 94

12. Ibid., pp. 284–285

13. William K. Mahony, *The Artful Universe: An Introduction to the Vedic Religious Imagination*, SUNY Press, 1998, pp. 200–201

14. Felicity Edwards in the entry for Sri Aurobindo in *Encyclopedia of Religion and Nature*, (Ed. Bron Taylor), A&C Black, 2008, p. 131

15. Sri Aurobindo, *Foundations of Indian Culture*, p. 265

16. Jonathan Mark Kenoyer, 'Master of Animals and Animal Masters in the Iconography of the Indus Tradition', in *The Master of Animals in Old World Iconography*, (Ed. Derek B. Counts and Bettina Arnold), Budapest, 2010, pp. 49–50.

17. Sahebrao Genu Nigal, *Axiological Approach to the Vedas*, Northern Book Centre, 1986, pp. 94–98

18. S. Dutt et al. 'A Long Arid Interlude in the Indian Summer Monsoon during ~4,350 to 3,450 cal. yr BP Contemporaneous to Displacement of the Indus Valley Civilization'. *Quaternary. International*, Vol. 482, 2018, pp. 83–92

19. Sarvepalli Radhakrishnan, *Indian Philosophy*, Vol. 1, Allen & Unwin, 1927:1948, p. 123

20. Maurice Bloomfield, *The Religion of the Veda, The Ancient Religion of India*, Putnam's Sons, 1908, pp. 31–32

21. *Paripadal* 2:60-62 quoted in M. Shanmugam Pillai, 'Religion and Rituals of Cankam Tamils' (Tamil), International Institute of Tamil Studies, 1996, p. 6

22. Antonio T. de Nicolas, *Meditations through the Ṛg Veda: Four Dimensional Man*, iUniverse, 1976:2003, p. 130

23. Ram Swarup, 'Meditations Yogas, Gods, Religions', *Voice of India*, 2000, pp. 143–144

24. Ibid., p. 144–149

25. P. L. Bhargava, 'The Comparative Antiquity of Mitra and Varuja', Ludwick Sternback Felicitation Volume, (ed. J. P. Sinha.), *Akhila Bharatiya Sanskrit Parishad*, 1979, pp. 59–61

26. Hervey De Witt Griswold, *The Religion of the* Ṛgveda, Motilal Banarsidass Publishers, 1971, p. 209

27. The term 'theo-diversity' was coined by Buddhist scholar Prof. Lokesh Chandra

28. Mary Boyce, *Zoroastrians: Their Religious Beliefs and Practices*, Routledge, 1979, p. 55

29. Muhammad A. Dandamaev and Vladimir G. Lukonin, *The Culture and Social Institutions of Ancient Iran*, Cambridge University Press, 2004, p. 352

30. Upinder Singh, *A History of Ancient and Early Medieval India: From the Stone Age to the 12th Century*, Pearson Education India, 2008, p. 274

31. Muhammad A. Dandamaev and Vladimir G. Lukonin, 2004, p. 353

32. Sahebrao Genu Nigal, 1986, p. 89

33. N. Ross Reat, *The Origins of Indian Psychology*, Jain Publishing Company, 1990, p. 11

34. Elaine Pagels, *The Gnostic Gospels*, Vintage Books, 1979:89, p. 29

35. Ram Swarup, 2000, p. 163

36. Elaine Pagels, 1979:89, p. 47

37. Elaine Pagels, *The Origin of Satan*, Vintage Books, 1996, p. xxiii

38. Ram Swarup, 2000, p. 149

39. Ernest G. McClain, *The Myth of Invariance: The Origin of the Gods, Mathematics and Music from the Ṛg Veda to Plato*, Nicolas-Hays, Inc., 1976:1984, p. 53

40. Iravatham Mahadevan, Interview: 'The Cult Object or "Filter" and Soma', Harappa.com, https://www.harappa.com/script/mahadevantext3.html accessed on 14 December 2018.

41. Monier-Williams, *A Sanskrit-English Dictionary*, Clarendon 1872, pp. 139–140

42. C. L. Fábri, 'The Punch-Marked Coins: A Survival of the Indus Civilization', *The Journal of the Royal Asiatic Society of Great Britain and Ireland*, No. 2 (April 1935), pp. 307–318

43. Ira Krishnamurthi, 'Sanghakala Malayaman Nanayangal' (Malayaman Coins of Sangham Era, Tamil), Madras, 1990

44. Hieun Tsang (629 CE), *Buddhist Records of the Western World*, Vol. 1, (Trans. Samuel

Beal), J. R. Osgood & Co, 1885, p. 69

45. Swami Ranganathananda, *Eternal Values for a Changing Society*, Vol. 2, Bharatiya Vidya Bhavan, 1985, p. 575

46. Vincent Smith, *History of India*, Vol. 2, 1906, p. 288

47. Irfan Habib quoted in Shashi Joshi and Bhagwan Josh, *Struggle for Hegemony in India 1920-47: The Colonial State, the Left and the National Movement Volume III: 1920-47*, SAGE Publications, 1992, p. 185 (cited in Arvind Sharma, 'On Hindu, Hindustān, Hinduism and Hindutva', *Numen*, Vol. 49, No. 1 [2002], pp. 9–10)

48. Arvind Sharma, 2002, p. 14

49. David N. Lorenzen, *Who Invented Hinduism? Essays on Religion in History*, Yoda Press, 2006, p. 32

50. Ibid., p. 33

51. Govind Sakharam Sardesai, *New History of the Marathas: Shivaji and his Line (1600-1707)*, Phoenix Publications, 1957, p. 277

52. Rabindranath Tagore quoted in A. K. Basu Majumdar, *Rabindranath Tagore: The Poet of India*, Indus Publishing, 1993, p. 60

53. Bankimchandra Chatterjee, 'Bharat-Kalanka: Bharatbarsha Paradhin Kena', *Bibidha Prabanda*, Vol. I–II, pp. 133–144

54. Rammohan Roy quoted in Arvind Sharma, *Hinduism as a Missionary Religion*, SUNY 2011, p. 112.

55. Cromwell Crawford, 'Raja Ram Mohan Roy's Attitude toward Christians and Christianity', in *Neo-Hindu Views of Christianity* (Ed. Arvind Sharma), BRILL, 1988, p. 27

56. Iyya Vaikundar, *Ahila Thirattu Ammanai (Tamil)*

57. Ramalinga Vallalar, Collection of Prose Works (Tamil), Vardhamanan Publications, 1997:2006, p. 513

58. Rajnarain Bose, *Hindu Dharmera* Śreṣṭhatā 1879: quoted in Ankur Barua, 'Vedantic Variations in the Presence of Europe: Establishing the Hindu Dharma in Late Nineteenth Century Bengal', *International Journal of Dharma Studies*, 2017

59. Bankim Chandra Chatterjee, Dharmatattva 1888: in Ankur Barua, 2017

60. Swami Vivekananda, *Vedanta in its Application to Indian Life: Complete Works of Swami Vivekananda* (CWSV), Vol. 3, pp. 248–268

61. Ibid.

62. Swami Vivekananda, *Paper on Hinduism*, 19 September 1893, CWSV, Vol. 1, p. 4 and again in *The Claims of Vedanta on the Modern World*, 25 February 1900 (CWSV, Vol. 8, p. 232).

63. Anantanand Rambachan, *The Limits of Scripture: Vivekananda's Reinterpretation of the Vedas*, University of Hawaii Press, 1994

64. Illango Adigal, *Vettuvavari* in *Chilapathikaram* (Tamizh: 4th century CE); Adi Sankara, *Soundarya Lahari* verse 84 (7th century CE); Abiramibhattar, *Abirami Anthathi* (Tamizh) verses 11 & 60 (18th century CE)

65. V. A. Naik, 'The Indian Renaissance and Lokamanya Tilak' in *Political Thought and Leadership of Lokmanya Tilak* (Ed. N. R. Inamdar), Concept Publishing Company, 1983, p. 50

66. Rabindranath Tagore, 'Hindutva'; later published as 'Bhāratbarṣer Samāj' in *Rabīndra Racanābalī*, Vol. 2, p. 623 quoted in Victor A. van Bijlert, 'Nationalism and Violence in Colonial India: 1880-1910', (Ed. Jan E. M. Houben, Karel Rijk van Kooij), BRILL,1999, pp. 330–331

67. Rabindranath Tagore, 'A Vison of India's History', orif *The Visva-Bharati Quarterly* Vol. 1:1 1923 in *The English Writings of Rabindranath Tagore: A Miscellany*, Sahitya Akademi, 1994, pp. 339–458. [orif??]

68. Sri Aurobindo, 'Uttarpara Speech (1909)' in *On Nationalism*, Sri Aurobindo Ashram, 1965:1996, pp. 375–376

69. Sri Aurobindo, 'Indian Spirituality and Life I', *Arya*, August 1919

70. Mohandas Karamchand ('Mahatma') Gandhi, *Young India*, 6 October 1921

71. M. K. Gandhi, *Hind Swaraj*, Rajpal & Sons, 1909:2010, p. 38

72. Madhav Sadashiv ('Guruji') Golwalkar, *Bunch of Thoughts*, Sahitya Sindhu Prakashan, 1966:2000, p. 104

73. H. V. Sheshadri, *Universal Spirit of Hindu Nationalism*, Vigil Publication, 1991, p. 3

74. K. Suryanarayana Rao, 'Hindu Rashtra: It is Not a Mere Slogan but a Vibrant Reality', Vigil Symposium, 24 October 1989, Vigil Publication, 1990

75. Arvind Sharma, 2002, pp. 1–36

76. Vinayak Damodar ('Veer') Savarkar,1923, p. 34

77. V. D. Savarkar, *Hindu Rashtra Darshan*, Maharashtra Prandik Hindu Mahasabha, downloaded pdf from www.savarkar.org, p. 43

78. Bhimrao Ramji ('Babasaheb') Ambedkar, *Thoughts on Pakistan*, Thacker & Co., 1941, p. 137

79. B. R. Ambedkar, *The Draft of the Hindu Code Bill* 1950: Part I preliminary: 2. Application of Code

80. V. D. Savarkar, 1923, pp. 94–95

81. Lokesh Chandra, 'Harmony through Theo-diversity', in *The Transition to a Global Consciousness* (Ed. Kishore Gandhi), Allied Publishers, 2007, p. 177

82. Judgment by J. S. Verma in the Supreme Court of India, Civil Appellate Jurisdiction, Civil Appeal No. 2836/1989, Judgment delivered on 11 December 1995

83. Judgment by P. B. Gajendragadkar in the Supreme Court of India, Civil Appeal No. 517 /1964, Judgment delivered on 14 January 1966: quoted in J. S. Verma, 1995

84. Romila Thapar, *'Syndicated Hinduism: A Dangerous New Fundamentalism'*, *Frontline*, 24 September 1993

85. Ibid.

86. Romila Thapar, *'Syndicated Hinduism: A Dangerous New Fundamentalism'*, *Frontline*, 8 October 1993 [pl check. Article with same title in No 85 above is dated 24 September]

87. Swami Vivekananda, *The Common Bases of Hinduism*, (CWSV), Vol. 3, p. 368
88. Shahid Amin, 'Representing the Musalman: Then and Now, Now and Then', in *Muslims, Dalits, and the Fabrications of History*, (Ed. Shail Mayaram, M. S. S. Pandian, Ajay Skaria), Subaltern Studies, Vol. 12, Orient Blackswan, 2005, p. 34
89. *Encyclopedia of Dalits in India: Leaders*, [Entry for Muldas Vaishya], (Ed. Sanjay Paswan, Pramanshi Jaideva), Gyan Publishing House, 2002, p. 207
90. Judgment by P. B. Gajendragadkar in the Supreme Court of India, Civil Appeal No. 517 /1964, Judgment delivered on 14 January 1966: quoted in J. S. Verma, 1995.
91. Sri Aurobindo (1909), 1965:1996, p. 375
92. Swami Vivekananda, *Paper on Hinduism*, 19 September 1893, CWSV, Vol. 1, p. 16
93. Swami Vivekananda, 'My Master', 1896, CWSV, Vol. 4, p. 180
94. Andrew B. Newberg, *Principles of Neurotheology*, Ashgate 2010, pp. 1–2
95. Eugene G. d'Aquili and Andrew B. Newberg, 'The Neuropsychology of Aesthetic, Spiritual and Mystical States', *Zygon Journal*, Vol. 35 No. 1 (March 2000), pp. 47–48
96. Alan Watts, *In My Own Way: An Autobiography*, New World Library, 1972:2011, p. 325 (emphasis not in the original)
97. Swami Vivekananda, 'The Spirit and Influence of Vedanta', (CWSV), Vol. I, p. 388
98. Vilayanur Ramachandran, 'Mirror Neurons and the Brain in the Vat', (1 September 2006), http://edge.org/conversation/mirror-neurons-and-the-brain-in-the-vat accessed on 30 March 2014
99. Subhash C. Kak, 'On the Science of Consciousness in Ancient India', *Indian Journal of History of Science*, Vol. 32, pp. 114–115, 1997
100. V. D. Savarkar, 'Abhinava Hindu Dhwaja' (Hindu National Flag), in *V. D. Savarkar* (Ed. Verinder Grover), Deep and Deep Publications, 1993, p. 187
101. V. D. Savarkar, 'Hindutva' (1923), in *Sources of Indian Tradition*, Vol. 2 (Ed. S. Hay), Columbia University Press, 1988, pp. 292–295 [In another Nagpur edition, 1923, instead of Kabir, one finds Sankara]

Chapter- 2

1. Sri Aurobindo, *Bhawani Mandir*, 1905 in '*On Nationalism*', Sri Aurobindo Ashram Trust, 1965, p. 69
2. Irfan Habib, 'Idea of Bhārat Mātā is European Import: Irfan Habib', Bipan Chandra Memorial Lecture – JNU 2016, *The Hindu*, 29 March 2016
3. S. A. Iyer, 'Why I'm Happy to Say Sunny Leone ki Jai', *The Economic Times*, 27 March 2016
4. Constituent Assembly Debates, Report Vol. 12, 24 January 1950, pp. 43–44
5. 'Congress Intended to Keep it a Low-key Affair: Explains about Vande Mataram Celebrations', *The Hindu*, 11 September 2006

6. S. A. Iyer, 'Why I'm happy to say Sunny Leone ki Jai', *The Economic Times*', 27 March 2016

7. Irfan Habib, 'From Amir Khusrau to Filthy Abuse', *Outlook*, 24 January 2018

8. Sumathi Ramaswamy, *The Goddess and the Nation*, Duke University Press, 2009, p. 9

9. Jati Sankar Mondal, 'The Spark of Rebellion: Dacoits and Bushrangers', in *Landscape, Place and Culture: Linkages between Australia and India* (Ed. Paul Brown, Deb Narayan Bandyopadhyay), Cambridge Scholars, 2011, p. 146

10. Ishita Pande, 'Medicine, Race and Liberalism in British Bengal: Symptoms of Empire', Routledge Studies in South Asian History, 2010, p. 54

11. Kim Wagner, 'Thuggee: Banditry and the British in Early Nineteenth-Century India', Springer, 2007, p. 138, 140, 141, 151

12. 'Crisis of the Sepoy Rebellion', *The London Quarterly Review*, Vol. 9, 1857–1858, pp. 534–535

13. Illango Adigal, *Chilapathikaram*: Puharkandam: *Kadukankathai* 60–66

14. Illango Adigal, *Chilapathikaram*: Puharkandam: *Vettuvavari:* song: 7

15. K. G. Menon, 'Spiritual Basis of Indian Nationalism', in *Gandhian Thought*, Vol. 4 (Ed. R. Achuthan), New Delhi, 1972, p. 31

16. David Kinsley, *Hindu Goddesses: Visions of the Divine Feminine in the Hindu Religious Tradition*, University of California Press, 1988, p. 178, 181

17. Ibid.

18. Anwar Sheikh, 'Bhārat Mātā' in *Liberty: The Humanist Quarterly*, Vol. 2, Issue 9, 1995

19. Vidya Dehejia, *Representing the Body: Gender Issues in Indian Art*, Kali for Women (Women Unlimited), 1997, p. 14

20. Bhairabi Prasad Sahu, *From Hunters to Breeders: Faunal Background of Early India*, Anamika Prakashan, New Delhi, 1988, p. 161

21. Ramchandra Narayan Dandekar, *Insights into Hinduism*, Ajanta Publications, 1979, p. 159

22. Sukumari Bhattacharji, *The Indian Theogony: A Comparative Study of Indian Mythology from the Vedas to the Puranas*, Cambridge University Press, 1970, p. 83

23. Liviu Giosan et al, 'Sarasvati – II', *Current Science*, Vol. 105 No. 7, 2013

24. Catherine Ludvik, *Sarasvati Riverine Goddess of Knowledge: From the Manuscript-carrying Vina-player to the Weapon wielding Defender of the Dharma*, Brill 2007 (The whole passage here is heavily based on the work of Prof. Catherine Ludvik.)

25. Catherine Ludvik, 2007, p. 199

26. David Frawley, *Gods, Sages and Kings*, Passage Press, 1991, p. 185

27. Catherine Ludvik, 2007, pp. 31–32

28. Mohammad Israil Khan, *Evolution of Sarasvati in Sanskrit Literature*, Aligarh Muslim University, 1969, p. 6 & pp. 13–14

29. Rama Tirtha, *Complete Works of Swami Rama Tirtha* Vol. VII: *India the Motherland*, The Rama Tirtha Pratisthan, 1930:1951, pp. 73–74

30. Pandit S. Subramaniya Sastri & Srinivasa Ayyangar, *Saundarya Lahari of Sri Samkara-Bhagavat-Pada*, The Theosophical Publishing House, Adyar, 1948, pp. 212–217

31. A partial and a free rendering of Arjuna's *Stuti* in the *Bhishma Parva*: based on the translation of Kisarimohan Ganguly: *The Mahabharata of Krishna-Dwaipayana Vyasa*, Vol.4, D. Bose & Co., 1925, p. 52
32. Valmik Thapar, *Tiger: The Ultimate Guide*, Hachette Books, 2004, p. 225
33. E. H. Warmington, *The Commerce between the Roman Empire and India*, Vikas Publishing House, 1974, p. 145
34. Ibid., p. 147
35. Prithvi K. Agrawala, *Early Indian Bronzes*, Prithvi Prakashan, 1977, p. 153
36. Saifurraḥmān Ḍār, *Historical Routes Through Gandhara (Pakistan) 200 B.C.–200 A.D.*, National College of Arts (Pakistan), 2006, p. 277
37. Umakant Premanand Shah, *Jaina-rūpa*-maṇḍana, Vol. 1, Abhinav Publications, 1987, p. 260
38. Pamela White, *Columbia Chronologies of Asian History and Culture* (Ed. John Stewart Bowman), Columbia University Press, 2000, p. 274
39. T. A. Gopinatha Rao, translated in his *Introduction* to *Madhura Vijaya or Virakamparaya Charita by Ganga Devi*' (Ed. G. Harihara Sastri & V. Srinivasa Sastri), Trivandrum, 1924, pp. 5–6
40. William J. Jackson, *Vijayanagara Voices: Exploring South Indian History and Hindu Literature*, Routledge, 2016, pp. 61–66, p.71
41. William J. Jackson, 2016, p.71
42. Jadunath Sarkar, *Shivaji and His Times*, Orient Blackswan,1919:1992, p. 49
43. H. S. Sardesai, *Shivaji, the Great Maratha*, Vol. I, Genesis Publishing 2002, pp. 292–293
44. Surjit Singh Gandhi, *History of Sikh Gurus Retold: 1606-1708 C.E.*, Atlantic Publishers, 2007, pp. 705–706
45. Surjit Singh Gandhi, 2007, p. 714, 787
46. Nikky-Guninder Kaur Singh, *The Birth of the Khalsa: a Feminist Re-Memory of Sikh Identity*, State University of New York Press, 2005, pp. 119–120
47. Diana Eck, *India: A Sacred Geography*, Three Rivers Press, 2012, pp. 27–28
48. Diana Eck, 2012, p. 27
49. Sir Alexander Cunningham, *The Ancient Geography of India: I. The Buddhist Period Including the Campaigns of Alexander and the Travels of Hwen-Thsang*, Trübner and Company, 1871, p. 5
50. Madhu Khanna, *Yantra: The Tantric Symbol of Cosmic Unity*, Thames and Hudson, 1979, p. 14
51. Madhu Khanna, 1979, p. 21
52. D. P. Agrawal and J. S. Kharakwal, *Bronze and Iron Ages in South Asia*, Aryan Books International, 2003, p. 138
53. M. K. Gandhi, *Hind Swaraj: Indian Home Rule*, Sarva Seva Sangh Prakashan, 2014, p. 41
54. Phyllis K. Herman, 'Sītā Rasoīs and Śākta Pīthas: A Feminine Reclamation of Mythic and Epic Proportions' in *Woman and Goddess in Hinduism: Reinterpretations and Re-*

envisionings (Ed. Tracy Pintchman & Rita D. Sherma), Palgrave Macmillan, 2011, p. 80

55. K. M. Munshi, *Bhavan's Journal*, 22 July 1962, Sri Aurobindo: Archives and Research, Vol. 2, Sri Aurobindo Ashram Trust, 1978, p. 218

56. R. K. Mookerji's Foreword in *Our National Insignia*, Ghoshti Book House, Amalapuram, 1954, p. xiii quoted in Thankappan Nair, *Indian National Songs and Symbols*, Firma KLM, 1959:1987, p. 42

57. Passage from the report of James Ker quoted in Sumathi Ramaswamy, 2009, p. 112

58. Aurobindo Mazumdar, *Vande Mataram and Islam*, Mittal Publications, 2007 p. 36

59. Maraimalai Adigal, *Viduthalai Poraatakala Padalkal* (*Songs of National Movement*) compiled by Aranthai Narayanan, National Book Trust, p. 18

60. Subrahmania Bharathi, *Collection of Desa Bhakthi songs: Our Furious Mother*

61. Sabyasachi Bhattacharya, 2003, p. 88

62. Peter Heehs, 'Religion and Revolt: Bengal under the Raj', *History Today*, Vol. 43, January 1993

63. Peter Heehs, 'The Maniktala Secret Society: An Early Bengali Terrorist Group', *The Indian Economic and Social History Review*, 29, 3, 1992

64. Amalendu De, *Raja Subodh Chandra Mallik and his Times*, National Council of Education, Bengal, 1996, p. 167

65. Sri Aurobindo, 'Lessons at Jamalpur', *Bande Mataram*, 1 September 1906 in *Early Political Writings*, Sri Aurobindo Ashram Society, 1973, p. 145

66. Sri Aurobindo quoted in *Sri Aurobindo and India's Rebirth* (Ed. Michael Danino), Rupa, 2018, p. 220

67. Sadanand Menon in *On Nationalism*, (Romila Thapar, A. G. Noorani & Sadanand Menon), Aleph Books, 2016

68. A. P. J. Abdul Kalam, *Ignited Minds: Unleashing the Power Within India*, Pearson Education India, 2010, p. 63

69. Swami Vivekananda, *The Future of India in Lectures from Colombo to Almora*, 1897 (*The Complete Works of Swami Vivekananda*, Vol. 3)

70. M. K. Gandhi, *Harijan*, 31 October 1936 in *The Collected Works of Mahatma Gandhi*: (21 October 1936–24 February 1937), Vol. 70, Publications Division, Ministry of Information and Broadcasting, Government of India, 2000, p. 7

71. M. K. Gandhi, Interview to Journalists, 6 March 1931, CWMG, Vol. 51, p. 220

72. Deendayal Upadhyaya, *The Sacred Flow of Nationality* (Introduction to the Biography of the Adya Shankaracharya) in V. N. Deodhar, '*Pt. Deendayal Upadhyay Ideology & Perception - Part 7: A Profile*', Suruchi Prakashan, 2014, pp. 56–57

73. Jawaharlal Nehru's letter dated 20 Oct. 1937 quoted in Sabyasachi Bhattacharya, *Vande Mataram: the Biography of a Song*, Penguin Books India, 2003, p. 32

74. Sita Ram Goel, Genesis and Growth of Nehruism, *Voice of India*, pp. 144–145

75. Sabyasachi Bhattacharya, 2003, p. 38

76. *The Selected Works of Subhas Chandra Bose, 1936–1946*, (Ed. Ravindra Kumar), Atlantic

Publishers, 1992, Vol. 2, pp. 16–17, 25–27

77. Jawaharlal Nehru, *Discovery of India*, Oxford University Press, 1944:1996, pp. 59–61

78. Jawaharlal Nehru, *Selected Works of Jawaharlal Nehru*, Vol. 39 (Edited Mushirul Hasan), Jawaharlal Nehru Memorial Fund, 2007, p. 39

79. Jawaharlal Nehru, 1944:1996, pp. 562–563

80. Selig S. Harrison, *India: The Most Dangerous Decades*, Princeton University Press, 2015, p. 151

81. *National Herald*, 6 January 1946, quoted in Selig Harrison, 2015, p. 151

82. Kautilya, 'Pakistan, Russia and the Communists', *National Herald*, 10 February 1946 quoted in Selig S. Harrison, 2015, p. 153

83. Jawaharlal Nehru, *Selected Works of Jawaharlal Nehru: 1 April–15 July 1952*, Jawaharlal Nehru Memorial Fund, 1996, p. 271

84. Zarina Bhatty, *Purdah to Piccadilly: A Muslim Woman's Struggle for Identity*, SAGE Publications India, 2016

85. Appendix-I: 'Historical Background of the Himalayan Frontier of India' in *White Paper II: Notes, Memoranda and Letters Exchanged and Agreements signed between the Governments of India and China*, September–November 1959

86. Venkat Swaminathan, *Kalai Ulakil Oru Sancharam* (An Exploration into the World of Art: Tamizh), Sandhya Publications, 2004, pp. 128–136

87. Koenraad Elst, 'M. F. Hussain – Bigotry vs Artistic Freedom', *Hindu Voice UK*, July 2009

88. M. K. Gandhi, *Harijan*, 6 October 1940

89. Constituent Assembly Debates: Official Report, Volumes 10–12, (Tuesday, 24 January 1950), Lok Sabha Secretariat, Reprint 1999, p. 1003

90. Markandey Katju, 'The British Stooge Tagore and the National Anthem', 20 April 2015: http://justicekatju.blogspot.com/2015/04/the-british-stooge-tagore-and-national.html

91. Martha C. Nussbaum, *The Clash Within*, Harvard University Press, 2008, pp. 14–15

92. Martha C. Nussbaum, 2008, p. 93

93. P. L. Deshpande, 'Jana Gana Mana—An Explanation', *Maharashtra Times*, 16 May 1980 (English translation: V. N. Godbole)

94. Sabyasachi Bhattacharya, *Rabindranath Tagore: An Interpretation*, Penguin Books India, 2011, p. [PAGE MISSING]

95. David Kopf, *British Orientalism and the Bengal Renaissance*, University of California Press, 1969, p. 203

96. Bal Jere, *Maharashtra Times*, 3 May 1980, quoted by P. L. Deshpande

97. Rabindranath Tagore, Letter quoted from *Ravindrajivani*, Vol. II, p. 339, in Deshpande letter, 1980

98. *Karaikal Ammaiyaar*, 41 *Arputha Thiruvanthaathi*

99. T. H. P. Chentharassery, *Ayyankali: the First Dalit leader*, Navdin Prakashan Kendra, 1996, p. 31

100. Arkotong Longkumer, 'Reform, Identity and Narratives of Belonging: The Heraka

Movement of Northeast India', *Continuum International*, 2010, pp. 175–176

101. Arkotong Longkumer, 2010, p. 181

102. Arkotong Longkumer, 2010, pp. 182–184

103. Dr Gangmumei Kamei, *Rani Gaidinliu (1915–1993): Freedom Fighter, Social and Religious Reformer*, Imphal Free Press, 1 November 2014

104. Arkotong Longkumer, 2010, p. 199

105. Christophe Jaffrelot, *The Hindu Nationalist Movement and Indian Politics: 1925 to the 1990s: Strategies of Identity Building, Implantation and Mobilisation (with Special Reference to Central India)*, Penguin Books India, 1999, p. 108

106. Aditya Nigam, '*The Nation's Orgiastic Fantasy and the Politics of "Nationalist" Anger*', 14 Mar. 2016, *Kafila Online*: https://kafila.online/2016/03/14/the-nations-orgiastic-fantasy-and-the-politics-of-nationalist-anger/

107.Sri Aurobdino, *Autobiographical Notes and Other Writings of Historical Interest, The Complete Works of Sri Aurobindo*, Vol. 36, Sri Aurobindo Ashram Trust 2006, pp. 478–479

108. Mirra Alfassa ('The Mother'), *Mother's Agenda*, Vol. VIII, 1967, Institute for Evolutionary Research, 1993, Vol. 8, p. 175

109. Michel Danino (Ed.), *India: The Mother*, Institute de Resecherches Evolutive & Mira Aditi, Mysore, 1998, p. 163

110. Joint appeal by Socialist leader R. M. Lohia and Jan Sangh Secretary Deen Dayal Upadhyaya calling upon for the formation of Indo-Pakistan confederation issued in New Delhi on 12 April 1964, *Organiser*, 20 April 1964

111. Deendayal Upadhyaya, *India, Pakistan and the United States*, 30 March 1964, *Political Diary*, Suruchi Prakashan, 2014, pp. 57–58

112. Madhukar Dattatreya Deoras, 'Balasaheb Deoras with Delhi Newsmen – in the Press Club of India', 12 March 1979, Suruchi Sahitya Publication, 1979. pp. 28–29

113. J. N. Dixit, *India-Pakistan in War & Peace*, Routledge, 2002, p. 237

114. Husain Haqqani, *Pakistan (Between Mosque and Military)*, Carnegie Endowment for International Peace, 2005, Kindle Edition, (Kindle Location 4487–4491).

115. *Caution about Vajpayee-Musharruf Talks, Akhil Bharatheeya Karyakari Mandal* (ABKM) *Resolution*, 2001, http://www.archivesofrss.org/Resolutions.aspx

116. Kalyani Devaki Menon, *Everyday Nationalism: Women of the Hindu Right in India*, University of Pennsylvania Press, 2011, p. 93

117. Owen L. Sirrs, *Pakistan's Inter-Services Intelligence Directorate: Covert Action and Internal Operations*, Routledge, 2016, p. 195

118. Bruce Riedel, 'Pakistan, Taliban and the Afghan Quagmire', 24 August 2013, https://www.brookings.edu/opinions/pakistan-taliban-and-the-afghan-quagmire/

119. 'India Seeks Larger Role', *Asia Times Online*, 28 November 2001

120. C. Raja Mohan, 'Raja Mandala: SAARC Minus One', *Indian Express*, 29 September 2016

Chapter- 3

1. Ranjit Bhushan, 'The Leap of Faith', *Outlook*, 11 November 2002

2. T. K. Rajalakshmi, 'Slaughter of the Dalits', *Frontline*, Vol. 19, Iss. 23, 09–22 November 2002

3. Atal Bihari Vajpayee, 'What Happened in Gujarat Cannot Be Forgotten', *Outlook*, 25 Oct. 2002

4. T. K. Rajalakshmi, 'Justice, at Last', *Frontline*, Vol. 27, Iss. 18, 28 August–10 September 2010

5. *Hinsa Virodhak Sangh vs Mirzapur Moti Kuresh Jamat & Ors* on 14 March 2008, http://indiankanoon.org/doc/560071/

6. 'NDA government is Congress Plus a Cow, says Arun Shourie', PTI, 18 January 2017.

7. Arvind Chauhan, 'Minor Girl Confronts Cattle Thieves, Shot At', Times News Network (TNN), 1 June 2016.

8. Swati Goel Sharma, 'Armed Smugglers are Killing Cattle Owners across India. Here's a List of Cases', scoopwhoop.com, 3 July 2017: https://www.scoopwhoop.com/cattle-smugglers-are-mercilessly-killing-farmers-the-issue-deserves-our-attention/

9. Shivan Chanana, 'The Other Side of Cow Protection: Attacks by Meat Mafia on Animal Activists, Common Citizens', *India Today*, 19 July 2017

10. Reena Martins, 'A dark trade', *New Indian Express*, 22 July 2017

11. Dr Souvik Chatterji, 'Terror Attacks in Dhaka: The Way Ahead for India', 11 July 2016, Institute of Peace and Conflict Studies, No. 5079: http://www.ipcs.org/comm_select.php?articleNo=5079

12. Shiraz Quraishi quoted in Shivan Chanana, 'Supreme Court Questions 6 States on "Gau Rakshaks": Band of Muslim Cow Protectors Respond', *India Today*, 2 May 2017

13. 'Cattle Smuggling & Terror Funding: A Concern', http://www.nja.nic.in/Concluded_Programmes/2016-17/SE-5_(25,26-03-2017)_PPTs/4.Cattle%20smuggling%20-%20Terror%20funding.pdf, accessed on 20 February 2019.

14. Rituraj Borthakur, 'Sharp Fall in Cattle Smuggling to Bangladesh', *Assam Tribune*, 24 August 2018

15. Nandita Krishna, 'Sacred Animals of India', Penguin India, 2010, pp. 77–78

16. Koenraad Elst, 'Origin of Aum', http://koenraadelst.blogspot.in/2013/05/the-origin-of-aum.html

17. Benjamin Walker, *Hindu World: An Encyclopedic Survey of Hinduism*, Vol. 1, Allen & Unwin, 1968, p. 255.

18. Gwen Robbins et al., 'Ancient Skeletal Evidence for Leprosy in India (2000 B.C.)', http://journals.plos.org/plosone/article?id=10.1371/journal.pone.0005669

19. M. N. Sreenivasa in *Microorganisms in Sustainable Agriculture and Biotechnology* (Ed. Tulasi Satyanarayana, Bhavdish Narain Johri, Anil Prakash), Springer Science & Business Media, 2012, pp. 62–65

20. 'Medicinal Use of Panchagavya', Press Information Bureau, Government of India, 31

August 2012

21. Mahadi Husain, *Bahadur Shah Zafar and the War of 1857 in Delhi*, Aakar Books, 2006, p. 38

22. John Reader, 'Human Ecology: How Land Shapes Society', *New Scientist*, 8 September 1988

23. Karl Marx, *The British Rule in India 1853, Selected Works of K. Marx and F. Engels*, Progress Publishers, Moscow, 1977, vol. 1., p. 493

24. Daniel Brister, *In the Presence of Buffalo: Working to Stop the Yellowstone Slaughter*, Graphic Arts Books, 2013

25. Peter Farb, *Ecology*, Time-Life Series, 1971, pp. 158–160

26. Daniel Brister, *In the Presence of Buffalo*, 2013

27. Alanthur Kizhar in *Puranaanuru*, 34: 1–4

28. Ramalinga Vallalar, *Manu Murai Kanda Vachagam* (Tamil), Chennai, 1854

29. Malayaman PhD, 'Vannasarabam Thandapani Swamigal', *Dinamani* (Tamil daily), 30 August 2009

30. Sri Narayana Guru quoted in A. M. Abraham, 'The State of Hinduism in 2000 A.D.: Some Emerging Trends' in *Religious Situation in the Present-day World* (Ed. Taran Singh), Guru Gobind Singh Department of Religious Studies, Punjabi University, 1980, p. 48

31. Mike Davis, *Late Victorian Holocausts: El Nino Famines and the Making of the Third World*, Verso Books, 2002, pp. 328–329

32. Marvin Harris, 'India's Sacred Cow', in *Anthropology: Contemporary Perspectives* (Ed. Phillip Whitten and David E.K. Hunter), 1990, p. 202

33. Anna Bigelow, 'Punjab's Muslims: The History and Significance of Malerkotla', *Journal of Punjab Studies*, Vol. 12, No. 1, 2005, p. 70

34. *African Chronicle*, 25 September 1909; Goolam Vahed, 'Institutional Hinduism: The Founding of the South African Hindu Maha Sabha, 1912', 2013.

35. Rettamalai Srinivasan, *Jeeva Saritham* (Tamil), 1939.

36. R. Inamdar, *Political Thought and Leadership of Lokmanya Tilak*, Concept Publishing Company, 1983, pp. 209-210

37. Balraj Madhok, *Indianisation*, Hind Pocket Books, 1970, p. 51

38. Haroon Khalid, *In Search of Shiva: A Study of Folk Religious Practices in Pakistan*, Rupa Publications, 2015, p. 130

39. M. K. Gandhi, *Young India*, 6 October 1921, p. 36, from *The Mind of Mahatma Gandhi*, (Ed. R. K. Prabhu & U. R. Rao), Navajivan Mudranalaya, 1966, p. 371

40. M. K. Gandhi, *Young India*, 29 January 1925, p. 38, R. K. Prabhu & U. R. Rao, 1966, p. 371

41. M. K. Gandhi, *Harijan*, 15 September 1946

42. Arne Naess, *The Ecology of Wisdom*, Counterpoint Press, 2010, p. 90

43. Vinayak D. Savarkar, 'Cow Protection and Cow Worship', English translation of Savarkar's assorted views on cow-protection and cow-worship: http://savarkar.org/en/

encyc/2017/5/23/Cow-protection-and-cow-worship.html, accessed on 20 August 2022

44. Bhimrao Ramji Ambedkar, *Writings and Speeches*, Vol. 12, Education Dept, Govt of Maharashtra, p. 7

45. K. M. Munshi, *Our Greatest Need and Other Addresses*, Hindustani Cellulose & Paper Company, 1953, p. 89

46. Joseph Cornelius Kumarappa, *The Cow in Our Economy*, Akhil Bharat Sarva Seva Sangh Prakashan, 1963.(For biogas and slurry see for example: *Industrial Economist,* p. 10.)

47. Attributed to Jawaharlal Nehru by Arthur Stratton, *One Man's India*, Norton, 1955. p. 68

48. Steven I. Wilkinson, *Votes and Violence: Electoral Competition and Ethnic Riots in India*, Cambridge University Press, 2006, p. 117

49. *Hanif Quareshi & Others vs The State of Bihar (And Connected)* ... on 23 April 1958, http://indiankanoon.org/doc/93885/

50. Tahir Muhammad, 'Interaction of Islam and Public Law in Independent India', in *Perspectives on Islamic Law, Justice, and Society*, (Ed. Ravindra S. Khare), Rowman & Littlefield, 1987, pp. 103–104

51. Bansi Dhar Tripathi, *Sadhus of India: The Sociological View*, Popular Prakashan, 1978, p. 225

52. Swami Karpatri, 'Rashtriya Swayamsevak Sangh aur Hindu Dharma', Mahanta Virbhadra Mishra, Varanaim 1970, p. 32, cited in Ritu Kohli, *Political Ideas of M. S. Golwalkar: Hindutva, Nationalism, Secularism*, Deep & Deep, 1993, p. 91

53. Promila Kalhan, *Gulzarilal Nanda: A Life in the Service of the People*, Allied Publishers, 1997, p. 58

54. Resolution No. 1 of Karya Kari Mandal, 1966, from *RSS Resolves 1950–2007*, Suruchi Prakashan, 2007, pp. 34–35

55. Govindacharya, 'We want to pay Respects to Gau Rakshaks who Faced Bullets', Rediff.com, 26 August 2016: https://www.rediff.com/news/interview/we-want-to-pay-respects-to-gau-rakshaks-who-faced-bullets/20160826.htm

56. 'Veteran Journalist on Shoot-at-Sight Order Given by Indira Gandhi on 07 Nov 1966': https://youtu.be/Xy-fjR266EQ

57. https://youtu.be/yVqQTYXGp2I

58. M. S. Golwalkar's letter to Jagjivan Ram dated 5 July 1967

59. Verghese Kurien, *I Too Had a Dream*, Roli Books, 2012, pp. 181–185

60. Piyush Patel, 'White Revolution Hero Dr Verghese Kurien Passes Away', *DNA*, 10 September 2012

61. This subsection is based on: Michael Lewis, 'Cattle and Conservation at Bharatpur: A Case Study in Science and Advocacy', Chapter 8 in *Inventing Global Ecology: Tracking the Biodiversity Ideal in India, 1947–1997*, Ohio University Press, 2004, pp. 199–232: all quotes unreferenced in this section are from this paper

62. Vasant K. Saberwal, *Pastoral Politics: Shepherds, Bureaucrats, and Conservation in the*

Western Himalayas, Oxford University Press, Delhi, 1999, pp. 7–8

63. Jairam Ramesh, *Intertwined Lives: P. N. Haksar & Indira Gandhi*, Simon and Schuster, 2018

64. Raghuvamsa, Canto 2, Verse 39: Moreshvar Ramachandra Kale, *The Raghuvamsa of Kalidasa: with the commentary (the Samjivani) of Mallinatha; Cantos I–X;* edited with a literal English translation, copious notes in Sanskrit and English, and various readings, Bombay 1922, p. 52

65. M. S. Golwalkar, *Bunch of Thoughts*, Jagarana Prakashana, 1966, p. 70

66. M. S. Golwalkar, *Spotlights*, Sahitya Sindhu, 1974, pp. 142–143

67. Sopan Joshi, 'Liquid Asset', *Down To Earth*, 15 August 2002 & 'US Stamp on Cow Urine Drug Booster', The *Telegraph*, 19 July 2005

68. Bhanvi Arora, 'School Makes 5000 Chapatis for 500 Students in a Day using Biogas', *DNA* (Bhopal), 18 June 2014

69. http://www.neeri.res.in/divisonal_patent.php?DIV=9

70. 'Nagpur Firm's Drug Developed for Crop Protection Gets US Patent', PTI, 16 September 2013

71. Wendy Doniger & Martha C. Nussbaum, *Pluralism and Democracy in India: Debating the Hindu Right*, Oxford University Press, 2015, p. 312

72. *Hanif Quareshi & Others vs The State of Bihar (And Connected)* ... on 23 April 1958, http://indiankanoon.org/doc/93885/

73. Dharampal & T. M. Mukundan, *The British Origin of Cow Slaughter in India with Some British Documents on the Anti-Kine-Killing Movement 1880–1894*, Society for the Integrated Development of Himalayas (SIDH), 2002

74. 'OECD-FAO Agricultural Outlook 2014', OECD Publishing, 11 July 2014, p. 184

75. 'Beef, Ban & Bloodshed', cover story, *India Today*, 19 October 2015

76. Mrinalini Goswami et al., 'Replacing Conventional Fuels through Biogas for Mitigating the Threats related to Climate Change in India: A State-wise Assessment for Emission Reduction', in *Management of Water, Energy and Bio-resources in the Era of Climate Change: Emerging Issues and Challenges* (Ed.N. Janardhana Raju, Wolfgang Gossel, AL. Ramanathan, M. Sudhakar) Springer, 2014, p. 197

77. Andrea Stone, 'Global Survey Says We're Eating Better, but Our Diet is Still Unsustainable', *National Geographic*, 29 September 2014

78. Ibid.

79. Michael Clark & David Tilman, 'Comparative Analysis of Environmental Impacts of Agricultural Production Systems, Agricultural Input Efficiency, and Food Choice', *Environmental Research Letters*, Vol. 12, No. 6, 2017

Chapter- 4

1. Chetan Bhatt, 'The Lore of a Homeland: Hindu Nationalism and Indigenist Neoracism', in *Theories of Race and Racism: A Reader* (Ed. Les Back, John Solomos), Psychology Press, 2000, p. 574
2. Dr Bhimrao Ramji Ambedkar, *Riddles in Hinduism*, pp. 216–217
3. Vinayak Damodar Savarkar, *Essays on Abolition of Caste*, 1931, Collected Works, Vol. 3, p. 472
4. Theodosius Dobzhansky, *Genetic Diversity and Human Equality*, 1973, p. 31
5. V. D. Savarkar, *Hindutva: Who is a Hindu?* Veer Savarkar Prakashan, 1923:1969, p. 90
6. V. D. Savarkar, *1923:1969*, p. 85
7. Chetan Bhatt, *Hindu Nationalism: Origins, Ideologies and Modern Myths*, Berg, 2001, p. 99.
8. Shamsul Islam, *Savarkar, Myths and Facts*, Media House, 2004, p. 113.
9. V. D. Savarkar, *Hindutva*, Veer Savarkar Prakashan, 1923:1969, pp. 129–131
10. V. D. Savarkar, 1923:1969., p. 88
11. V. D. Savarkar, *Hindu Rashtra Darshna*, Presidential Address at the 19th session of All India Hindu Mahasabha at Karnavati, 1937, p. 13.
12. V. D. Savarkar, 1938, ibid, p. 31. v
13. V. D. Savarkar, 1937, ibid., p. 3, 10
14. Tony Joseph, 'How Ancient DNA May Rewrite Prehistory in India', BBC-News, 30 December 2018, https://www.bbc.com/news/world-asia-india-46616574
15. Tony Joseph, 'Why Christianity Failed In India?' *Outlook*, 13 April 2015
16. The next two paragraphs are based on Stefan Arvidsson, *Aryan Idols: Indo-European Mythology as Ideology and Science*, University of Chicago Press, 2006
17. Tony Joseph, 'How Genetics is Settling the Aryan Migration Debate', *The Hindu*, 16 June 2017
18. Shriram Sathe, *Aryans: Who Were They?* Bharatiya Ithihasa Sankalana Samiti, 1991, p. 47
19. Shrikant Talageri, The *Aryan Invasion Theory and Indian Nationalism*, Voice of India, 1993, p. 47
20. Edwin Bryant, *The Quest for the Origins of Vedic Culture: The Indo-Aryan Migration Debate*, Oxford University Press, 2001, p. 277
21. *Valmiki Ramayana* (Yuddha Kanda:113:43-46)
22. Subramania Bharathi, *Bharathi Tamizh Vachana Thirattu* (Tamil) (Ed. Pe.Thooran), National Book Trust India, 1978, pp. 150–151
23. Thirikooda Rasappa Kavirayar, *Kutrala Kuravanji*, Rajam Chennai, 1960 (verse 78) p. 25
24. Ngwarsungu Chiwengo, *Understanding Cry, the Beloved Country: A Student Casebook to Issues, Sources, and Historical Documents*, Greenwood Publishing Group, 2007, pp. 92–93
25. Latha Varadarajan, *The Domestic Abroad: Diasporas in International Relations*, Oxford University Press, 2010, p. 62
26. Ahmad M. Kathrada, *Memoirs*, Zebra, 2004, p. 39

27. N. B. Khare, 'The Angry Aristocrat', in *A Study of Nehru* (Ed. Rafiq Zakaria), 1959; Rupa & Co.,1989, p. 231
28. Bhimrao Ramji Ambedkar, *What Congress and Gandhi Have Done to the Untouchables*, Gautam Book Centre, 1945:2009 p. 96–97
29. Rajmohan Gandhi, *Rajaji: A Life*, Penguin Books India, 1997, p. 413
30. Narayan Bhaskar Khare, *My Political Memoirs or Autobiography*, J. R. Joshi, 1959, p. 157
31. Hugh Tinker, *Separate and Unequal: India and the Indians in the British Commonwealth*, 1920–1950, C. Hurst, 1976, p. 226
32. N. B. Khare, *Memoirs*, 1959, p. 157
33. Lorna Lloyd, 'A Family Quarrel: The Development of the Dispute over Indians in South Africa', *The Historical Journal*, Vol. 34, Issue 3, September 1991, p. 711
34. Commonwealth Papers, Vol. 21, Athlone Press, 1974, p. 22
35. Hugh Tinker, 1976, p. 226
36. N. B. Khare, *Memoirs*, 1959, pp. 171–173, 177
37. Hugh Tinker, 1976, p. 226
38. Lorna Lloyd, 1991, p. 720
39. Romila Thapar, 'The Aryan Question Revisited', Transcript of lecture delivered on 11 October 1999, JNU
40. Swami Vivekananda, *The Complete Works of the Swami Vivekananda*, Vol. 4, 1948, p. 412
41. Sri Aurobindo, 'The Unhindu Spirit of Caste Rigidity', *Bande Mataram*, 20 September 1907 in *Early Political Writings*, Sri Aurobindo Ashram, 1973, pp. 533–535
42. Sri Aurobindo, 'Caste and Democracy', *Bande Mataram*, 22 September 1907, in *Early Political Writings*, pp. 537–539
43. Christophe Jaffrelot, *The Hindu Nationalist Movement in India*, Columbia University Press, 1996, p. 11
44. Sir James Robert Dunlop Smith & Martin Gilbert, *Servant of India: A Study of Imperial Rule from 1905 to 1910 as Told Through the Correspondence and Diaries of Sir James Dunlop Smith*, Longmans, 1966, p. 97
45. Bhimrao Ramji Ambedkar, *What Congress and Gandhi Have Done to the Untouchables*? Gautam Book Centre, 1945:2009, p. 23
46. Swami Shraddhanand, Letter to Gandhi dated 9 September 1921, in Swami Shraddhanand, *Inside the Congress: A Collection of 26 Articles*, Dayanand Sansthan, 1926: 1946: 1984, pp. 133–134
47. Swami Shraddhanand, *Inside the Congress*, pp. 179–180
48. Swami Shraddhanand in *Leader* dated 7 February 1923, in Gene R. Thursby, *Hindu-Muslim Relations in British India: A Study of Controversy, Conflict, and Communal Movements in Northern India 1923-1928*, BRILL, 1975, p. 150
49. Swami Shraddhanand, *Hindu Sangathan: Saviour of the Dying Race*, Arsh Sahitya Prachar Trust, 1926:2016, p. 59
50. Ibid. p. 61

51. Ibid. p. 69

52. Ibid. pp. 108–109

53. Prof. Shriram Sharma, *Mahatma Hansraj—Maker of Modern Punjab*, Arya Pradheshik Prathinithi Sabha, 1941, pp. 206–207

54. Nonica Datta, *Violence, Martyrdom and Partition: A Daughter's Testimony*, Oxford University Press, 2009. Though this section is based on this book, Datta is clearly biased in favour of the Islamist narrative in the whole presentation. She attributes the support of Bhagatji's support for the release of an accused in the honour killing of a Jat woman and her daughter who lived with a wealthy local Islamist. Incidentally, the funding for the release and financial aid of this accused was done by Jat philanthropist Chhotu Ram who was a Unionist opposing Hindu Mahasabha, Hindu Sanghatan and Shuddhi of Arya Samaj. It was Shuddhi activities of Bhagatji which ultimately cost him his life.

55. M. K. Gandhi, *Telegram to G. D. Birla*, CWMG Vol. 79, p. 244

56. M. K. Gandhi, *Harijan Sevak*, 26 October 1940, quoted in *Gandhiji and Haryana: A Collection of His Speeches and Writings Pertaining to Haryana*, (Ed. Jagadish Chandra), Usha Publications, 1977, p. 145

57. Bhimrao Ramji Ambedkar, *Writings and Speeches: Unpublished Writings, The Untouchables and the Pax Britannica*, Education Department, Government of Maharashtra, p. 139

58. M. R. Jayakar, *The Story of My Life Vol. I (1873–1922)*, Asia Publishing House, 1958, pp. 162–163.

59. Ibid., pp. 163–164

60. Ibid., p. 166

61. A. K. Vakil, *Gandhi-Ambedkar Dispute*, Ashish Publishing House, 1991, pp. 48–49

62. All the details with respect to 1925 Bombay Hindu Mahasabha provincial session taken from Namrata R. Ganneri, 'The Hindu Mahasabha in Bombay (1923–1947)', *Proceedings of the Indian History of Congress*, Vol. 75, Platinum Jubilee (2014), pp. 771–782

63. Neela Dabir, *A Study of a Shelter Home for Women in Distress* (PhD Thesis: SNDT Women's University), Chapter 8, 1994, p. 46

64. M. R. Jayakar, *The Story of My Life (1922–1925)*, Vol. 2, Bombay, 1959, p. 527

65. Madhava-Vidyaranya, *Sankara Digvijaya*: Canto 6 verses 20–32 (Trans. Swami Tapasyananda, Sri Ramakrishna Math, Chennai)

66. M. R. Jayakar, *The Story of My Life (1922–1925)*, Vol. 2, Bombay, 1959, pp. 9–10

67. M. R. Jayakar, 'Bill to Remove Disabilities Affecting Untouchable Castes of the Hindu Community': M. R. Jayakar's Bill of 1930.

68. *The Modern Review*, June 1933, Vol. 53, p. 648.

69. M. K. Gandhi, Letter to Private Secretary to the Viceroy, 1 February 1933.

70. V. B. Kulkarni, *M. R. Jayakar: Builders of Modern India Series*, Publications Division, Government of India, 1973, pp. 136–137.

71. Ibid., p. 84

72. Ibid., p. 117

73. V. D. Savarkar, *An Echo from Andamans*, Venus Book Stall, 1947, p. 24
74. Ibid., p. 33
75. Dhananjay Keer, *Veer Savarkar*, Popular Prakashan, 1966:2012, p. 178
76. Ibid., p. 186
77. Sanjyot Valsangkar, *The Hindu Mahasabha in Maharashtra*, Savitribai Phule Pune University, 1997, p. 88
78. A. K. Vakil, 1991, p. 70
79. Dhananjay Keer, *Savarkar and His Times*, A. V. Keer, 1950, p. 178
80. Dhananjay Keer, 1966:2012, p. 189
81. Bhimrao Ramji Ambedkar, Letter to Savarkar dated 18 February 1933 in *Letters of Ambedkar*, Bheem Patrika Publications, 1993, p. 86.
82. B. R. Ambedkar, 'The Triumph of Brahminism' in *Dr Babasaheb Ambedkar Writings and Speeches*: Vol. 3, Dr Ambedkar Foundation, Ministry of Justice & Empowerment, Govt. of India, 1987:2014, pp. 287–288
83. V. D. Savarkar, *On Abolition of Caste*, 1930 in *Samagra Savarkar Vangmaya*, Vol. 3, pp. 440–479 (Trans. Savarkar.org)
84. V. D. Savarkar, *Samagra Savarkar Vangmaya*, Vol. 3, pp. 497–499
85. Raja Narindra Nath address in Indra Prakash, *A Review of the History & Work of the Hindu Mahasabha and the Hindu Sanghatan Movement*, Akhil Bharatiya Hindu Mahasabha, 1938, p. 97
86. Indra Prakash, 1938, p. 171
87. Indra Prakash, 1938, pp. 72–73
88. Indrani Jagjivan Ram, *Milestones: A Memoir*, Penguin Books India, 2010, p. 52
89. Indra Prakash, 1938, p. 265
90. Indra Prakash, 1938, p. 270
91. Vikram Sampath, *Savarkar: A Contested Legacy 1924–1966*, Penguin/Viking, 2021, p. 62
92. Dhananjay Keer, *Dr Ambedkar: Life and Mission*, Popular Prakashan, 1954:1990, p. 79
93. Bhimrao Ramji Ambedkar, *Bahishkrut Bharat,* 23 December 1927, quoted in Anand Teltumbde, 2016
94. File No. 180/41-Political (Internal) 1941: Secret: Government of India: Sd/- R. M. Maxwell (30.5.41.)
95. Extract from a DO Letter No. B2/CA21 dated 18 July 1941 from GIO Bombay to AD(S)
96. Nicholas Goodrick-Clarke, *Hitler's Priestess: Savitri Devi, the Hindu-Aryan Myth and Neo-Nazism*, New York University Press, 1998, p. 43
97. Nicholas Goodrick-Clarke, 1998, p. 110
98. M. K. Gandhi, 'Sunday's Hartal: Its Religious Spirit', 6 May 1919
99. Koenraad Elst, 'Return of the Swastika: Hate and Hysteria versus Hindu Sanity', Voice of India, 2015, p. 119
100. M. S. Golwalkar, *We or Our Nationhood Defined*, 1939, pp. 82–83
101. V. D. Savarkar, 'Hindu Rashtra Darshna', Presidential Address at Bhagalpur Session of

Hindu Maha Sabha, 1941, p. 100

102. Ibid.

103. The following four passages are based on Buddhadeva Bhattacharyya et al, *Satyagrahas in Bengal 1921–1939* (1977)

104. A. G. Noorani, 'Moonje & Mussolini', *Frontline*, 23 January 2015

105. *Ophthalmic Review*, Volumes 25–26, p. 63

106. Marzia Casolari, 'Hindutva's Foreign Tie-up in the 1930s Archival Evidence', *Economic and Political Weekly*, 22 January 2000, p. 220

107. William Frank Gutterdige, *Military Institutions and Power in the New States*, Praeger, 1965, p. 93

108. *The Modern Review*, Vol. 65, 1939, p. 24

109. William Arthur, 'The Martial Episteme: Re-thinking Theories of Martial Race and the Modernisation of the British Indian Army during the Second World War' in *The British Indian Army: Virtue and Necessity* (Ed. Rob Johnson), Cambridge Scholars Publishing, 2014, p. 152

110. Dhananjay Keer, *Dr Babasaheb Ambedkar: Life and Mission*, Popular Prakashan, 1954:2009, pp. 405–406

111. David James Fisher, *Romain Rolland and the Politics of the Intellectual Engagement*, Transaction Publishers, 2004, p. 136

112. Muthulakshmi Reddy, 'Creative Citizenship' (1933) in *Documenting First Wave Feminisms*, Vol. 1 (Edited by Maureen Moynagh, Nancy Forestell), University of Toronto Press, 2012, p. 203

113. All the details about Shraddhanand Ananth Mahila Ashram taken from Neela Dabir, *A Study of a Shelter Home for Women in Distress*, (PhD Thesis submitted to SNDT Women's University), 1994

114. Neela Dabir, 1994, p. 327

115. Sreedhar Pillai, 'Kerala Catholic Priest Lures Girls with Jobs in Italy, but They End Up as Nuns in Rome', *India Today*, 31 August 1986

116. Alfred Friendly Jr, 'Vatican Halts Convent Payments for Recruiting of Girls in India', *The New York Times*, 24 August 1970

117. Indra Prakash, 1938, p. 116, pp. 283–284

118. The two paragraphs are based on Rukmesh Devi, *Women Education: Study of Gurukuls in Haryana (1900–1985)*, PhD Thesis submitted to Kurukshetra University, 2015, pp. 149–181

Chapter- 5

1. 'Savarkar Plaque will not Be Restored: Govt', PTI, 23 August 2004

2. Dhananjay Keer, *Veer Savarkar*, Popular Prakashan, 1966, p. 548

3. 'Complaint Lodged against Congress President Rahul Gandhi for Calling Veer Savarkar "Coward"', Times Now Bureau, 9 February 2019

4. Ra. Ravishankar, 'Reappraisal: The Real Savarkar', *Frontline*, Vol. 19, Iss. 15, 20 July–2 August 2002

5. R. C. Majumdar, *Penal Settlement in Andamans*, Gazetteer Unit, 1975, p. 213

6. All data of the petition taken from: Petition from jail (3 October 1914) by V. D. Savarkar to the chief commissioner, File No. 245 H (P) Part B, November 1914, National Archives of India

7. M. K. Gandhi, *Satyagraha in South Africa, Collected Works*, Vol. 29, Publications Division, Ministry of Information and Broadcasting, Govt. of India, 1968, p. 251

8. Harish Srivastava, *Five Stormy Years: Savarkar in London, June 1906–June 1911*, Allied Publishers, 1983, p. 11

9. Vikram Sampath, *Savarkar: A Contested Legacy 1924–1966*, Penguin Viking, 2021, p. 183

10. Dhananjay Keer, *Veer Savarkar*, Popular Prakashan, 1966:2012, p. 548

11. Rash Behari Bose letter to Savarkar dated 11 July 1938: Nehru Memorial Museum and Library: Savarkar Papers (NMML:SPP): 6450/23

12. Uma Mukherjee, *Two Great Indian Revolutionaries: Rash Behari Bose & Jyotindra Nath Mukherjee*, Firma K. L. Mukopadhyay, Calcutta, 1966:2012, pp. 159–160

13. Dhananjay Keer, p. 305

14. V. D. Savarkar, *Veer Savarkar's "Whirl-wind Propaganda": Statements, Messages & Extracts from the President's Diary of His Propagandistic Tours, Interviews from December 1937 to October 1941*, A. S. Bhide, 1941, p. 262

15. Dhananjay Keer, 1966:2012, p. 350

16. Adam Roberts, 'The Man Who Thought Gandhi a Sissy', *The Economist*, 19 December 2014

17. Harindra Srivastava, *Five Stormy Years: Savarkar In London, June 1906–June 1911*, Allied Publishers, 1983

18. The entire sequence of events here is based on the diary entries of V. V. S. Iyer and records of Dr Rajan–Tamizh comrades of Vinayak Savarkar: Ra. A. Padmanabhan, V.V.S. Aiyar (National Biography Series), National Book Trust, India, 1980, pp. 64–70

19. 'Mahatma Praised Ram, and Savarkar Praised Durga, When Two Shared Stage: Pramod Kapoor', PTI report dated 24 January 2016

20. Vinayak Damodar Savarkar, Author's Introduction to the original edition, *The Volcano*, English Edition: 1909

21. V. D. Savarkar, *The Volcano*, Chapter I, p. 19

22. V. D. Savarkar, circulated under the title 'Oh Martyrs' on 10 May 1908

23. Government of Bombay, Home (Special) Department, 60-C/1908-10: 'V. D. Savarkar: Indian War of Independence of 1857 by an Indian Nationalist', Maharashtra State Archives (MSA); cited in John Pincince, *V. D. Savarkar and the Indian War of Independence: Contrasting Perspectives of an Emergent Composite State*, University of Edinburgh, 2007

24. Dhananjay Keer, *Dr Baba Saheb Ambedkar*, Popular Prakashan, 1954:2011, p. 338

25. V. D. Savarkar, *Six Glorious Epochs of Indian History*, Bal Savarkar Sadhan, 1963:1971 (English), pp. 38–39

26. Lala Lajpat Rai, Endorsement in *The Maratha Movement*, Hindi Sahitya Sadan, 1925:2003

27. V. D. Savarkar, Author's Foreword, *The Maratha Movement*, 1925:2003, Hindi Sahitya Sadan, pp. 21–22

28. All data on the influence of *Hindu Pad Padshahi* on the revolutionary trio and Bhagat Singh's *Jail Notebook* based on Malwinder Jit Singh Waraich & Harish Jain, *Hanging of Bhagat Singh: Bhagat Singh's Jail Note Book: A Complete Notebook with additional Notes* Vol. V, Unistar Books, 2016

29. V. D. Savarkar, *Smart Hindu Youths Should Join the Navy*, Statement dated 23 April 1942

30. Dhananjay Keer, *Savarkar and His Times*, A. V. Keer, 1950, pp. 191–192

31. V. D. Savarkar, *Indian War of Independence 1857 by an Indian Nationalist*, London, 1909, p. 70

32. V. D. Savarkar, 1909, pp. 372–402

33. *Veer Savarkar's Whirl-wind Propaganda: Statements, Messages & Extracts from the President's Diary of His Propagandistic Tours, Interviews from December 1937 to October 1941*, Anant Sadashiv Bhide, 1941, p. 498

34. K. F. Nariman quoted in Dhananjay Keer, 1950, p. 61

35. Patrick French, *Liberty or Death: India's Journey to Independence and Division*, Penguin UK, 2011

36. Bina D'Costa, *Nationbuilding, Gender and War Crimes in South Asia*, Routledge, 2011, p. 57

37. M. K. Gandhi, *The Collected Works of Mahatma Gandhi*, Vol. 96, Publications Division, Ministry of Information and Broadcasting, Government of India, 2000 pp. 388–389

38. V. D. Savarkar, *Six Glorious Epochs of Indian History*, (Trans. S. T. Godbole), Savarkar Sadan: Rajdhani Granthagar, 1971 p. 297

39. V. D. Savarkar, 1963:1971, pp. 305–306

40. V. D. Savarkar, 1963:1971, p. 307

41. V. D. Savarkar, 1963:1971, pp. 307–308

42. V. D. Savarkar, 1963:1971, p. 322

43. M. K. Gandhi, *The Collected Works of Mahatma Gandhi*, Vol. 98, p. 117

44. Ajaz Ashraf, 'Reading Savarkar: How a Hindutva icon justified the idea of rape as a political tool', 28 May 2016 08:00 am, Scroll.in, https://scroll.in/article/808788/reading-savarkar-how-a-hindutva-icon-justified-the-idea-of-rape-as-a-political-tool

45. J. M. Dutta, 'Continued Abduction of Hindu Women-its Effect on the Bengali Hindus', *Modern Review*, 1941, pp. 358–359, (cited in Rakesh Batabyal, *Communalism in Bengal: From Famine To Noakhali*, 1943–1947, Sage, 2005, p. 287)

46. Kirpal Singh, *Select Documents on Partition of Punjab-1947: India and Pakistan, Punjab,*

Haryana, and Himachal – India and Punjab – Pakistan, National Book Shop, 1991, p. 639

47. Bina D'Costa, Routledge, 2011, pp. 57–60

48. Shanta Kumari, President, National Women's Conference of J&K, *Hindustan Times*, 30 December 1947

49. Diary of Lt Gen Roy Bucher dated 6 December 1947 in *Bucher Papers*, National Army Museum 7901–87

50. Christian Gerlach, *Extremely Violent Societies: Mass Violence in the Twentieth-Century World*, Cambridge University Press, 2010, pp. 155–61

51. M. K. Gandhi, 'Speech to Muslims' (*Harijan*, 28 September 1947), CWMG Vol. 96, pp. 385–386

52. V. D. Savarkar, 1963:1971, p. 176

53. V. D. Savarkar, 1963:1971, p. 182

54. Shreerang Godbole, 'Sita Ram Goel: Some Reminiscences' in *India's Only Communalist in Commemoration of Sita Ram Goel* (Ed. Dr Koenraad Elst), Voice of India, 2005, pp. 103–104

55. Nilanjan Mukhopadhyay, *The RSS: Icons of the Indian Right*, Tranquebar, 2019, p. 95

56. Lise McKean, *Divine Enterprise: Gurus and the Hindu Nationalist Movement*, University of Chicago Press, 1996, p. 87

57. Dhananjay Keer, 1966:2012, pp. 529–530

58. Ratnakar Sadasyula, *Veer Savarkar: The Woman in his life*, 13 February 2017, https://historyunderyourfeet.wordpress.com/2017/02/13/veer-savarkar-the-woman-behind/; http://www.savarkar.org/en/yamunabai-vinayak-mai-savarkar, accessed on 17 April 2019

59. Nilanjan Mukhopadhyay, 2019, p. 96

60. Lise McKean, 1996, p. 86

61. V. D. Savarkar, *The Indian War of Independence of 1857 by an Indian Nationalist*, London, 1909, p. 331

62. V. D. Savarkar, 1909, p. 397

63. Charles Andrews' letter quoted in 'Introduction' in Bhai Parmanand, *The Story of My Life* (*Atmakatha* – trans. N. Sundra Iyer and Lal Chand), Central Hindu Yuvak Sabha, Lahore, 1934, Ocean Books, 2003, p. 17

64. Charles Andrews in *Bhai Parmanand*, 1934:2003, p. 19

65. Bhai Parmanand, 1934:2003, pp. 126–127

66. Bhai Parmanand, 1934:2003, p. 137

67. Bhai Parmanand, 1934:2003, p. 136

68. Bhai Parmanand, 1934:2003, p. 140

69. Bhai Parmanand, *Hindu Sanghatan*, (Trans. Prof. Lal Chand Dhawan), The Central Hindu Yuvak Sabha,1936, pp. 6–8

70. Bhai Parmanand, 1936, p. 16

71. Bhai Parmanand, 1936, pp. 118–120

72. Bhai Parmanand, 1936, p. 145

73. Bhai Parmanand, 1936, pp. 143–144
74. Bhai Parmanand, 1936, pp. 151–152
75. B. R. Ambedkar, *The Triumph of Brahminism: Dr. Babasaheb Ambedkar: Writings and Speeches*, Vol. 3, Education Department, Govt. of Maharashtra, 1987, 2014, pp. 286–289
76. Bhai Parmanand, 1936, pp. 161–162
77. Bhai Parmanand, 1936, pp. 163–164
78. Bhai Parmanand, 1936, pp. 2–3
79. Bhai Parmanand, 1936, p. 236
80. Sikata Banerjee, *Make Me a Man! Masculinity, Hinduism, and Nationalism in India*, SUNY Press, 2012, p. 45
81. Meher Wadhawan, 'No Nation For Indian Women', *Berkeley Political Review*, 12 April 2018, https://bpr.berkeley.edu/2018/04/17/no-nation-for-indian-women/
82. Sharada Sugirtharajah, 'Colonialism' in *Studying Hinduism: Key Concepts and Methods* (ed. Sushil Mittal & Gene Thursby), Routledge, 2009, p. 81
83. Swami Vivekananda, *My Master* (1896), CWSV Vol. IV, 1948, p. 172
84. Swami Vivekananda, 'Letter to Swami Brahmananda', 10 October 1897, CWSV Vol. VI, 1948, p. 412
85. Har Dayal, 'Mr. Har Dayal's Rejoinder', *The Modern Review*, Vol. 12, 1912, p. 648
86. Har Dayal, *Our Educational Problem*, Hindustanbooks.com, 1922:2012, p. 75
87. Har Dayal, 1922:2012, pp. 81–88
88. Har Dayal, *Hints for Self Culture*, Watts & Co., London, 1934, p. 21
89. Har Dayal, 1934, pp. 21–22
90. Har Dayal, 1934, pp. 31–32
91. Har Dayal, 1934, p. 125
92. Har Dayal, 1934, pp. 185–187
93. Har Dayal, 1934, p. 73
94. Har Dayal, 'Karl Marx: A Modern Rishi', *The Modern Review*, 1912, Vol. 11, p. 283
95. Har Dayal, 1934, p. 64
96. Har Dayal, 1934, p. 363
97. Emily C. Brown, *Har Dayal: Hindu Revolutionary and Rationalist*, Manohar, 1975, p. 150
98. Har Dayal, *Letters of Lala Har Dayal*, Indian Book Agency, 1970, p. 21
99. Emily C. Brown, 1975, pp. 233–234
100. Emily C. Brown, 1975, pp. 254–255
101. Emily C. Brown, 1975, p. 7
102. Har Dayal, 1934, pp. 259–260
103. V. D. Savarkar, *Hindutva: Who is a Hindu?*, Veer Savarkar Prakashan, 1923:1969, p. 90 and p. 141 [In 1949 4th edition the passage reads 'A Hindu is most intensely so, when he ceases to be a Hindu; and with a Kabir claims the whole earth for a Banaran...': passage quoted in *Sources of Indian Tradition: Modern India, Pakistan, and Bangladesh*, Ed. Rachel Fell McDermott et al, Penguin UK, 2014

104. Feroz Chand, *Lajpat Rai: Life and Work*, Publications Division, Ministry of Information, Government of India, 1978, p. 540
105. Feroz Chand, 1978, p. 139
106. Lajpat Rai, *Story of My Deportation* (Punjabee Press, Lahore, 1908), pp. xvii–xviii
107. Lajpat Rai's Diary: *Recollections of His Life and Work for an Independent India while Living in the United States and Japan 1914, 1917*, National Archives, p. 5
108. Lajpat Rai, *The Arya Samaj: An Account of its Origin, Doctrines, and Activities: With a Biographical Sketch of the Founder*, Longmans, Green, 1915, pp. 212–219
109. Lajpat Rai, *'Call to Hindus to Excel Christian Missionaries in Relief Work'*, *The Tribune*, 22 March 1900 in *The Collected Works of Lala Lajpat Rai*: Vol. I, (CWLLR Ed. B. R. Nanda), Servants of the People Society, 2003, p. 130
110. Lajpat Rai, 'Insinuations against Arya Samaj', *The Tribune*, 2 November 1895: CWLLR Vol. I, 2003, p. 277–278
111. Schuyler Jones, *A Bibliography of Nuristan (Kafiristan) and the Kalash Kafirs of Chitral: Selected Documents and the Secret and Political Records 1885–1900*, The Royal Danish Academy of Sciences and Letters, København 1969
112. Amar Singh Chohan, *A History of Kafferistan: Socio-economic and Political Conditions of the Kaffers*, Atlantic Publishers, 1989, pp. 155–156
113. Lajpat Rai, *Arya Gazette* (Lahore), 27 May 1897: CWLLR Vol. I, 2003, pp. 279–280
114. P. C. Bamford, *Histories of the Non-Cooperation and Khilafat Movements*, Government of India Press, 1925, p. 254
115. Lajpat Rai letter cited in *The People*, 13 April 1929
116. Lajpat Rai, *Ideals of Non-co-operation*, Ganesan, Madras, 1924, p. 4
117. Lajpat Rai, 'The Hindu-Muslim Problem', in *Lala Lajpat Rai Writings and Speeches Vol. 2: 1920–1928* (Ed. Vijaya Chandra Joshi), University Publishers, 1966, p. 174
118. V. D. Savarkar, Presidential Address, Akhil Bharatiya Hindu Mahasabha, 1937, *Hindu Rashtra Darshan*, (https://www.savarkarsmarak.com/) p. 14

Chapter- 6

1. Ramesh Patange, *Me, Manu Ani Sangh* (*Manuvad and RSS*: Tamizh), Shakthi Publications, 1999, p. 45
2. The details on the life of Rajguru in this section are based on: Anil Verma, *Rajguru: The Invincible Revolutionary*, (Trans. Dr Yashwant Verma & Anil Verma), Publication Division, Govt of India, 2010
3. Rakesh Sinha, *Dr Keshav Baliram Hedgewar*, Publications Division, 2015, p. 95
4. Report of the Flag Committee, 1931
5. Satyavrata Ghosh, *Remembering Our Revolutionaries*, Marxist Study Forum, 1994, p. 57

6. *The Modern Review*, Vol. 69, March 1941, p. 352

7. Walter K. Andersen & Shridhar D. Damle, *The Brotherhood in Saffron: The Rashtriya Swayamsevak Sangh and Hindu Revivalism*, Avalon Publishing, 1987, p. 44: see it quoted in Abdul Gafoor Abdul Majeed Noorani in *The RSS and the BJP: A Division of Labour* (2000) and Ram Puniyani in *The Second Assassination of Gandhi* (2003)

8. M. S. Golwalkar, *Shri Guruji Samagra Darshan*, Bhartiya Vichar Sadhna, 1974, p. 40

9. This and the next three police reports taken from: Chitranjan, *Facts About RSS and Gandhi Murder, RSS and Freedom Movement, RSS and Communal Riots*, Suruchi Sahitya, New Delhi, 1979, quoted in D. R. Goyal, *Rashtriya Swayam Sevak Sangh*, Radha Krishna Prakashan, 1979, pp. 88–89

10. Ramachandra Guha, 'Truths about the Tricolour', *The Hindu*, 26 September 2004

11. K. B. Hedgewar quoted in H. V. Seshadri, 'Dr Hedgewar, The Epoch-maker: A Biography', Sahitya Sindhu, 1981, p. 105

12. *Organiser*, Vol. 30, p. 18, 1978

13. K. R. Malkani, *The RSS Story*, Impex India, 1980, p. 28

14. *How Others Look at the RSS*: Compilation of *Manthan* articles, Deendayal Research Institute, 1989, p. 16

15. Vasant Moon, *Dr. Baba Saheb Ambedkar: Biography*, National Book Trust, India, 1991:2002, p. 183

16.Dhananjay Keer, *Dr. Ambedkar: Life and Mission*, Popular Prakashan, 1954: 1971, pp. 394–395

17.Dhananjay Keer, *Veer Savarkar*, Popular Prakashan, 1950:1966:2012, p. 389

18. Dhananjay Keer, op. cit., p. 389

19. Dhananjay Keer, 1954: 1971, p. 395

20. Manikacandra Vajapeyi & Sridhara Paradakara, *Partition Days: The Fiery Saga of RSS*, Suruchi Prakashan, 2002, pp. 266–267

21. Ritu Kohli, *Political Ideas of M. S. Golwalkar: Hindutva, Nationalism, Secularism*, Deep and Deep Publications, 1993, p. 57

22. *Economic and Political Weekly*, Vol. 26, Sameeksha Trust, 1991, p. 2954

23. Col Tej K. Tikoo, *Kashmir: Its Aborigines and their Exodus* (Kindle Locations 5417–5483), Lancer Publishers LLC., 2013, Kindle Edition

24. Yegya Narayanan, 'Again on the Move: BJP Launches Ekta Yatra', *Frontline*, Vol. VIII, No. 26, 21 December 1991:3 January 1992

25. Wasim Khalid, 'Jan 26, 1992: When Joshi Hoisted Flag in Lal Chowk', *Greater Kashmir*, 23 January 2011

26. Christophe Jaffrelot, *The Hindu Nationalist Movement and Indian Politics: 1925 to the 1990s: Strategies of Identity-building, Implantation and Mobilisation (with Special Reference to Central India)*, Penguin Books India, 1999, pp. 63–64

27. Walter K. Andersen & Shridhar D. Damle, *The Brotherhood in Saffron: The Rashtriya Swayamsevak Sangh and Hindu Revivalism*, Avalon Publishing, 1987, p. 248

28. Walter Andersen & Shridhar Damle, *The RSS: A View to the Inside*, Penguin Random House India Pvt. Ltd., 2018, p. xxi
29. Andersen & Damle, 1987, p. 87
30. Andersen & Damle, 2018, pp. 40–41
31. Andersen & Damle, 2018, p. 90
32. Daniel Immerwhar, *Thinking Small: The United States and the Lure of Community Development*, Harvard University Press, 2015, p. 213
33. Andersen & Damle, 2018, pp. 247–248
34. Andersen & Damle, 2018, p. 81
35. Madhav Vittal Kamath, 'All things Considered', *Illustrated Weekly of India*, 30 September 1979
36. Mohan Bhagwat quoted in 'RSS Chief Mohan Bhagwat Targets Mother Teresa, says Conversion was Main Objective behind her Service', *The Indian Express*, 14 February 2015
37. https://twitter.com/incindia/status/570161856561565696
38. Anees Chishti, *Dateline Bhopal*, Concept Publishing Company, 1986, pp. 52–53
39. Dominique Lapierre, *The City of Joy*, Warner Books Edition, 1985, p. 498
40. Vidya Krishnan, 'Bhopal Gas Tragedy: The Media's Role in the Aftermath', *Livemint*, 3 December 2014: https://www.livemint.com/Politics/V5IUzapnU5nGE37EMeMCeJ/Bhopal-Gas-Tragedy--The-medias-role-in-the-aftermath.html
41. M. S. Golwalkar, *Bunch of Thoughts*, Sahitya Sindhu Prakashan,1966:2000, p. 364
42. Swami Annadananada, *Swami Akhandananda: An Apostle of Sri Ramakrishna*, (Trans. Narayan Chandra Bhattacharya), Advaita Ashram, 1993, pp. 130–145
43. Swami Vivekananda, *Epistels-Second Series/CXXVIII Akhandananda* (Trans. From Bengali), 15 June 1897, CWSV, Vol. 6, p. 361
44. C. P. Bhishikar, *Shri Guruji: Pioneer of a New Era*, (Trans. Sudhakar Raje), Sahitya Sindhu Prakashana, 1999, pp. 20–29
45. Rabindranath Tagore, 'Hindutva', later published as 'Bharatbarser Samaj' in *Rabindra Racanabali*, Vol. 2, p. 625, quoted in Victor A. van Bijlert, *Nationalism and Violence in Colonial India: 1880-1910*, (Ed. Jan E. M. Houben, Karel Rijk van Kooij), BRILL, 1999, p. 332
46. Lise McKean, *Divine Enterprise: Gurus and the Hindu Nationalist Movement*, University of Chicago Press, 1996, p. 109
47. Badrinath K. Rao, 'On Spiritual Entrepreneurs', *Frontline*, 29 November 1996: a Marxist Polemic Attack on Hindu Spirituality thoroughly based on McKean's work
48. For a detailed study of Lise McKean, see: Malhotra and Neelakandan, *Breaking India: Western Interventions in Dravidian and Dalit Faultlines*, Amaryllis, 2011, pp. 257–258
49. Malini Bhattacharjee, *Disaster Relief and the RSS*, Sage, 2019, p. 57, 58
50. Radhakumud Mookerji, *Ancient Indian Education: Brahmanical and Buddhis*t, Motilal Banarsidass Publications, 1989, p. 19
51. Jitendra Bajaj and M. D. Srinivas, *Annam Bahu Kurvita: Recollecting the Indian Discipline of Growing and Sharing Food in Plenty*, Centre for Policy Studies Madras, 1996

52. Malini Bhattacharjee, 2019, pp. 82–83
53. Ibid., pp. 84–85
54. Ibid., pp. 84–85
55. Ibid., p. 74
56. Ibid. p. 124
57. Ibid. p. 133
58. Ibid. pp. 133–134
59. Malhotra and Neelakandan, 2011, p. 264
60. Debabrata Mohanty, 'Sangh schools score high in Orissa', *The Indian Express*, 1 July 2009
61. Minati Singha, 'Saraswati Vidya Mandir Schools Clean Sweep Toppers' List', *Times News Network*, 20 June 2010
62. 'Omkar Sahi of SSVM Brajrjnagar Becomes Jharsuguda District Topper in Matriculation Exams', JSGlive.in, 7 May 2018, http://jsglive.in/2018/05/07/omkar-sahu-of-ssvm-becomes-jharsuguda-district-topper-in-matriculation-exams/
63. 'Space Science on His Mind: Malkangiri Boy Wins Talent Contest to Visit ISRO', *Odishabytes*, 16 December 2019, https://odishabytes.com/space-science-on-his-mind-malkangiri-boy-wins-talent-contest-to-visit-isro/
64. 'Gujarat Earthquake: Despite Delayed Government Action, Support of People Brings Hope', *India Today*, 12 February 2001
65. Malini Bhattacharjee, p. 94
66. Malini Bhattacharjee, p. 165
67. Ibid. p. 160
68. Ibid. p. 94
69.Ibid. p. 107
70. Meraj Bhat, 'Modi Set to Become India's Third Most Successful PM: Guha', 30 March 2017, Outlookindia.com (PTI report based)
71. Kathy Stuart, *Defiled Trades and Social Outcasts: Honor and Ritual Pollution in Early Modern Germany*, Cambridge University Press, 2006, pp. 1–2
72. Bhimarao Ramji Ambedkar, *Annihilation of Caste, Writings and Speeches: Castes in India and 11 Other Essays*, Vol. 1, Education Department, Government of Maharashtra, 1979, p. 93
73. Koenraad Elst, *Return of the Swastika: Hate and Hysteria versus Hindu Sanity*, Voice of India, 2007, pp. 247–248
74. M. S. Golwalkar, 'Students are not the Pillars of the Nation: They are its Servants', *Organiser*, 2 January 1961
75. Shamsul Islam, *Golwalkar: How the Breed of Kerala Hindus was Improved by Namboodiri Brahmins*, Countercurrents.org, 2 September 2015, https://www.countercurrents.org/islam020915.html THE LINK DOES NOT WORK
76. Nirmal Kumar Bose, *Caste in India. Man in India*: 31, 1951, pp. 107–123, quoted in Dobzhansky, 1973, p. 31

77. Theodosius Dobzhansky, *Genetic Diversity and Human Equality*, Basic Books Inc., 1973, pp. 31–32

78. Vinayak Damodar Savarkar, *Jatyuchchedak Nibandha* or Essays on Abolition of Caste, 1931, Samagra Savarkar Vangmaya, Vol. 3, p. 457

79. M. S. Golwalkar in *Samajika Darshan*, p. 24 quoted in M. Rama Jois, *Guruji and Social Harmony*, Sri Guruji Janmashatabdi Samiti, 2006, p. 13

80. M. S. Golwalkar in *Samajika Darshan*, p. 24, ibid., p. 14

81. Manu S. Pillai, *Decoding RSS Ideologue M. S. Golwalkar's Nationalism*, Livemint.com, 15 July 2017, https://www.livemint.com/Leisure/lqQhcXQ5MKFtDPpRtNAnmO/Decoding-RSS-ideologue-MS-Golwalkars-nationalism.html

82. Madhav Sadashiv Golwalkar, *Bunch of Thoughts*, Sahitya Sindhu Prakashana, 1996, p. 110

83. Ibid., p. 353

84. L. R. Balley, *India Needs a Cultural Revolution, Outcry*, 1984: *Untouchable!: Voices of the Dalit Liberation Movement*, Ed. Barbara Joshi, Zed Books, 1986, p. 147

85. Ibid.

86. Ashok Singhal, 'Some Reminiscences in Sri Guruji: A Living Example of Spiritual Nationalism' (Ed. P. Parameswaran), *Vivekananda Kendra Patrika*, Vol. 35, No. 2, August 2006–January 2007, p. 102

87. K. Suryanarayana Rao, 'Sri Guruji Golwalkar's Historical and Momentous Efforts for the Abolition of Untouchabilty', *Vivekananda Kendra Patrika*, Vol., 35 No. 2, pp. 143–144

88. M. S. Golwalkar, 'The Task Ahead', letter dated 14 January 1970 in K. Suryanarayana Rao, *Shri Guruji Reminiscences*, Vijaya Bharatham Publications, 2010, pp. 277–278

89. Nilanjan Mukhopadhyay, *The RSS: Icons of The Indian Right*, Tranquebar, 2019, p. 288

90. C. P. Bhishikar, (Trans. Sudhakar Raje), *Shri Guruji Pioneer of a New Era*, Sahitya Sindhu Prakashana, 1999, p. 207

91. M. S. Golwalkar, *Spotlights*, Sahitya Sindhu, 1974, p. 13

92. Arun Anand, *The Saffron Surge: Untold Story of RSS Leadership*, Prabhat Books, 2019 Kindle location:1609

93. Bhimrao Ramji Ambedkar, *Dr. Babasaheb Ambedkar Writings and Speeches* Vol. 4, Education Department, Govt. of Maharashtra, 1987, pp. 286–287

94. M. S. Golwalkar quoted in C. P. Bhishikar, 1999, p. 159

95. Ramesh Patange, *Manuvath and RSS (Manu Sangh and I)*, 1999, http://www.sanghparivar.org/blog/vikas/manu-sangh-and-i-the-book-by-ramesh-patange-ji

96. Ibid.

97. 1981 ABKM Resolution-1 *Meenakshipuram Conversion in RSS Resolves: 1950-2007* (Dharmendra Kaushal), Suruchi Prakashan, 2007, pp. 101–102

98. *Indian Express*, 16 July 1981, report cited in H. V. Sheshadri, *Warning of Meenakshipuram*, Jagarana Prakashana, 1981, p. 27

99. Ibid. pp. 27–28

100. Anil Kumar Mishra, *Vishwa Hindu Parishad: An Introduction*, Prabhat Prakashan,

2015, p. 27

101. Viswanathan Kakkan, 'Ganga I Carried', *Vijayabharatam* (Tamizh), 18 January 1985

102. Ibid.

103. Sumit Pande, 'Meet the Dalit Boy who Laid Foundation Stone of Ram Temple', News18.com, 5 December 2017, https://www.news18.com/news/immersive/25-years-of-babri-demolition/such-a-long-journey.html

104. Badri Narayan, *Fascinating Hindutva: Saffron Politics and Dalit Mobilisation*, SAGE, 2009, p. 32

105. Edmund Weber, *Ambedkar and the Hindu Culture, Journal of Religious Culture*, No. 18(b), 1999

106. Christophe Jaffrelot, *India's Silent Revolution: The Rise of the Lower Castes in North India*, C. Hurst & Co. Publishers, 2003, p. 487

107. 'VHP, Hindu Religious Leaders Differ on Suraj Bhan's Demand', PTI Report, 19 July 2005

108. 'Dalit Poet, RSS Chief Exchange Notes', *The Indian Express*, 31 August 2006

109. 'Modi Govt Doing Better Job than UPA: Dalit Body', PTI report dated, 24 June 2018

110. 'Sarsanghachalak Pays Respect to Dr Ambedkar Visits "Dikshabhumi"? of Nagpur', *Organiser*, 5 April 2009

111. 'Incentive for inter-caste marriage increased: Haryana govt', PTI report dated 27 March 2016

112. 'Hry Govt Doubles Incentive Amount for Inter-caste Marriage', PTI report dated 17 May 2018

113. 'Hry Incentive Boosts Inter-caste Marriages', *Times News Network*, 1 November 2018

114. R. Raman Nair & L. Sulochana Devi, *Chattampi Swami: An Intellectual Biography*, South Indian Studies, 2010, pp. 216–218

115. H. V. Sheshadri, *RSS: A Vision in Action*, Sahitya Sindhu Prakashana, 1988, p. 137

116. 'RSS for Dalit Head Priests in Temples', *Indiatimes News Network* (INN), 30 October 2006

117. 'Dalit Appointed the Chief Priest at Jagannath Temple', *Sahara Samay*, 15 February 2008

118. 'Call for Non-Brahmin Priests Sparks Debate in Kerala', PTI report, 20 January 2013

119. 'Madhya Pradesh Government to Launch Hindu Priesthood Course, Religion No Bar', PTI report, 6 April 2017

120. Bhimrao Ramji Ambedkar, *Writings and Speeches* Vol. I, Education Department, Government of Maharashtra, 1979, p. 77

121. Soniya Agrawal, *Modi Govt Wants to Train Pandits and Pujaris, Design Curriculum to Standardise Rituals*, ThePrint.in, 23 January 2020, https://theprint.in/india/governance/modi-govt-wants-to-train-pandits-and-pujaris-design-curriculum-to-standardise-rituals/353269/

122. Daniel Pipes, *In the Path of God: Islam and Political Power*, Routledge, 2017, p. 317

123. 'PM Modi Washes Sanitary Workers' Feet, Hails them as Karma Yogis', *Times News Network*, 25 February 2019

124. 'Sanskar Not Politics', PM on Washing Feet of Sanitation Workers, PTI report, 1 March 2019

125. Dr Krishna Verma, 'Sri Ramakrishna and the Caste System', *Prabuddha Bharata*, February 2005

126. Swami Ranganathananda, Lecture on Manisha Panchakam at Sri Ramakrishna Math, Hyderabad, 15 November 1992

127. Swami Vivekananda, *Memoirs of European Travel, The Complete Works of Swami Vivekananda,* Vol. 7, Advaita Ashrama, 1953, p. 309

128. Noah Hysler-Rubin, *Patrick Geddes and Town Planning: A Critical View*, Routledge, 2013, p. 90

129. 'Sanskar Not Politics', PM on Washing Feet of Sanitation Workers, PTI report dated 1 March 2019

130. Koenraad Elst, *Decolonizing the Hindu Mind: Ideological Development of Hindu Revivalism*, Rupa & Co., 2001, p. 233

131. Koenraad Elst, 'Guha's Golwalkar', *Pragyaya*, October 2016, http://koenraadelst.blogspot.com/2016/11/guhas-golwalkar.html

132. Rajendra Singh quoted in V. N. Deodhar, *Pt. Deendayal Upadhyay Ideology & Perception – Part 7: A Profile*, Suruchi Prakashan, 2014, p. 38

133. L. R. Bhide quoted in V. N. Deodhar, 2014, p. 40

134. Craig Baxter, *The Jana Sangh: A Biography of an Indian Political Party*, University of Pennsylvania Press, 1969, p. 258

135. Balraj Madhok, *Indianisation*, Hind Pocket Books, 1970, pp. 123–124

136. Ibid. p. 29

137. Ibid. p. 27

138. *Bande Mataram*, 14 June 1908: quoted in Girilal Jain, *The Hindu Phenomenon*, UBS Publishers, 1994, pp. 48–49

139. Madhok, 1970, pp. 69–70

140. Ibid., p. 77

141. Ibid., pp. 114–115

142. Ibid., pp. 115–116

143. Vasant Annaji Vaidya in 'Pandit Deendayal Upadhyaya: A Profile' (Ed. Nana Deshmukh) Deendayal Research Institute, 1972, pp. 108–109

144. Koenraad Elst, 'Integral Humanism', Indic Talk series at Centre for Indic Studies, Indus University, https://youtu.be/_Q6MtkG3UPo

145. Bruce Desmond Graham, *Hindu Nationalism and Indian Politics*, Cambridge University Press, 1990, p. 86, 215

146. Christophe Jaffrelot, *The Hindu Nationalist Movement and Indian Politics: 1925 to the 1990s: Strategies of Identity-building, Implantation and Mobilisation (with Special Reference to Central India)*, C. Hurst & Co. Publishers, 1996, p. 124

147. Ibid.

148. Chetan Bhatt, *Hindu Nationalism: Origins, Ideologies and Modern Myths*, Berg, 2001, p. 131

149. Ibid., p. 156

150. Deendayal Upadhyaya, 'Harmony Between the Individual and the Collectivity', 24 April 1965, in *Deendayal Upadhyaya's Integral Humanism: Documents, Interpretation, Comparisons* (Ed. Devendra Swarup), Deendayal Research Institute, 1992, p. 47

151. Deendayal Upadhyaya, *Integral Humanism*, 22 April 1965:1992, p. 19

152. Christiane Brosius, *Empowering Visions: The Politics of Representation in Hindu Nationalism*, Anthem Press, 2005, p. 79

153. Ibid, pp. 63–64

154. Koenraad Elst, *Decolonizing the Hindu Mind: Ideological Development of Hindu Revivalism*, Rupa & Co., 2001, p. 499

155. Koenraad Elst, 2001, p. 494, 504

156. Amartya Mukhopadhyay, '*Bhinnata*' *of Nations, in Tagore: At Home in the World*, (Ed. Sanjukta Dasgupta & Chinmoy Guha), SAGE Publications India, 2013, p. 141

157. Deendayal Upadhyaya, 1965:1992, p. 41

158. Deendayal Upadhyaya, 1965:1992, p. 27

159. *Chandogya Upanishad*: 6:12:1-3

160. V. V. Nene, *Pandit Deendayal Upadhyaya—Ideology and Perception-II: Integral Humanism* (Trans. M. K. Paranjape & D. R. Kulkarni), Suruchi Publications, 1991, pp. 74–75

161. Deendayal Upadhyaya, *Economic Structure Suited to National Genius*, 25 April 1965:1992, pp. 51–52

162. Anil Rajimwale, *History of Student Movement in India Origins and Development (1920–1947)*, Manak Publications, p. 122

163. Navin Kalingan and Anirban Ganguly, *Dattopant Thengadi: The Activist Parliamentarian* (p. 23), Prabhat Prakashan, 2020, Kindle Edition

164. Golwalkar quoted in C. P. Bhishikar, 1999, pp. 190–191

165. Arun Anand, *May Day vs Vishwakarma Day: How RSS-backed BMS displaced Left as Dominant Trade Union*, 1 May 2021, ThePrint.in, https://theprint.in/india/may-day-vs-vishwakarma-day-how-rss-backed-bms-displaced-left-as-dominant-trade-union/649800/

166. Dattopant Thengadi, *The Onward March of Bharatiya Mazdoor Sangh*, BMS Central Office, New Delhi, 1985, p. 8

167. Ibid., p. 10

168. Entire data for this case study taken from: Baij Nath Rai, *Story of New Central Jute Mill: A Workers Owned Company*, Bharatiya Shram-Shodh Mandal, Pune, 1992

169. Koenraad Elst, 'Down with "Nationalism"', *Bharat Bharati*, 28 September 2017, http://koenraadelst.blogspot.com/2017/10/down-with-nationalism.html, accessed on 11 January 2022

170. Dattopant Thengadi, 'Hindu Rashtra as old as the Vedas' (6 March 1961) in *The Perspective*, Sahitya Sindhu Prakashan, 1971, p. 38

171. Ibid., p. 39

172. For example, Sally Mallam of the 'Institute for the Study of Human Knowledge' in her 'Indus-Saraswati Civilization', https://humanjourney.us/ideas-that-shaped-our-modern-world-section/early-civilizations-harappa/; see also archaeologist Jane R. McIntosh in *The Ancient Indus Valley: New Perspectives*, ABC Clio, 2008, p. 3, pp. 85–86

Chapter- 7

1. Paul F. Lurquin and Linda Stone, *Evolution and Religious Creation Myths: How Scientists Respond*, Oxford University Press, 2007, pp. 25–26

2. Marvin Harris, *Cows, Pigs, Wars & Witches: The Riddle of Culture*, Random House, 1974, pp. 136–137, p. 152

3. Ananda Kentish Coomaraswamy, *Dance of Siva: Fourteen Indian essays*, The Sunwise Turn Inc., New York, 1924, pp. 65–66

4. Fritjof Capra, *The Tao of Physics*, Fontana, 1976, p. 11

5. Fritjof Capra, 'The New Vision of Reality: Toward a Synthesis of Eastern Wisdom and Western Science' in *Ancient Wisdom and Modern Science* (Ed. Stanislav Grof, Marjorie Livingston Valier), SUNY Press, 1984, pp. 138–139

6. Ilya Prigogine, *Origins of Complexity*, in *Origins: The Darwin College Lectures* (Ed. A. C. Fabian), Cambridge University Press, 1988, p. 72

7. Carl Sagan, *Cosmos*, Random House, 1980, pp. 258–259

8. Satyendranath Bose, *Rachana Sankalan*, 1963:1994, S. N. Bose National Centre for Basic Sciences

9. Rabindranath Tagore, *Rabindra Rachanavalī*, X, p. 115 quoted by Bimal Krishna Matilal, 'Bankimchandra, Hinduism and Nationalism' in *The Collected Essays of Bimal Krishna Matilal: Mind, Language and World*, (Ed. Jonardon Ganeri), Oxford University Press, 2002, p. 428

10. Bankim Chandra Chatterjee, 'The Study of Hindu Philosophy' (in *Mukherjee's Magazine*, May 1873) in *Bankim Rachanavali*, (Ed. Jogesh Chandra Bagal), Shishu Sahitya Samsad Pvt. Ltd., 1960, p. 147

11. Prafulla Chandra Ray, *A History of Hindu Chemistry: From the Earliest Times to the Middle of the Sixteenth Century A.D. Vol. 1*, The Bengal Chemicals & Pharmaceutical Works Limited, 1903, pp. xlii–xliii

12. Ibid., pp. 190–192, 195–196

13. Ibid., p. 178

14. Ibid., pp. 179–180

15. Bimal Krishna Matilal, 'Bankimchandra, Hinduism and Nationalism' in *The Collected Essays of Bimal Krishna Matilal: Mind, Language and World*, (Ed. Jonardon Ganeri), Oxford University Press, 2002, p. 430

16. Ibid., p. 429
17. Dattopant Thengadi, *Modernisation Without Westernisation* in *Third Way*, Sahitya Sindhu Prakashana, 1998, p. 201
18. H. V. Sheshadri, *Universal Spirit of Hindu Nationalism*, Vigil, Chennai, 1991
19. Bal Ganghadara Tilak, *Samagra, Lokmanya Tilak*, Vol. 7, p. 278
20. Peter Persic quoted in Ashley P. Taylor, 'Newton's Color Theory, ca. 1665', *The Scientist*, 1 March 2017, https://www.the-scientist.com/foundations/newtons-color-theory-ca-1665-31931
21. Peter Persic, *Music and the Making of the Modern Science*, MIT Press, 2014, p. 9
22. Ibid., p. 286
23. 'Mantras Codified Laws of Motion before Newton: Education Minister', PTI report dated 28 February 2018
24. https://twitter.com/Swamy39/status/933099418026311682
25. Dr S. D. Chatterjee, 'Physics and Mechanics in Ancient and Medieval India' in *The Cultural Heritage of India, Vol. VI: Science and Technology* (Ed. Priyadaranjan Ray and S. N. Sen), The Ramakrishna Mission Institute of Culture, 1986, pp. 102–103
26. Ibid., p. 104
27. C. K. Raju, 'Cultural Foundation of Mathematics: The Nature of Mathematical Proof and the Transmission of the Calculus from India to Europe in the 16th c. CE', Vol. X, Part 4, in *History of Science, Philosophy and Culture in Indian Civilization* (Gen. Ed. D. P. Chattopadhyaya), Pearson, 2007, pp. 326–333
28. Kim Plofker, *Mathematics in India*, Princeton University Press, 2009, p. 4
29. Ibid.
30. Ibid., p. 218
31. Subhash Kak, 'Terrestrial and Celestial Aspects of Natural Science – Ptolemy, Copernicus, Galielo, Kepler: A Historiographical Study', in *History of Science and Philosophy of Science: A Philosophical Perspective of the Logic of Ideas in Science*, Vol. XIII Part 6 (Gen. Ed. D. P. Chattophadhyaya), 2010, p. 83
32. Kim Plofker, 2009, p. 250
33. C. K. Raju, 2007, Ibid, p. 39, 124
34. S. Anand, 'Shoonya Sum Game', *Outlook*, 14 July 2003
35. Sita Ram Goel, *Hindu Society Under Siege*, Voice of India, 1993, p. 18
36. Tim Mackintosh-Smith, *The Hall of A Thousand Columns*, John Murray, 2006, p. 120
37. 'The Miracle of Ganesh?', *Sunday*, 1–7 October 1995
38. T. Jayaraman, 'Vedic Astrology and All That', *Frontline*, Vol. 18, Iss. 10, 12–25 May 2001
39. Sumit Mitra, 'Star Wars includes an Interview with Dr M. M. Joshi', *India Today*, 17 September 2001
40. 'Examiner(s) Comments in the Examination Report Dated 7 March 2014 on TKDL Submission Dated 20 March 2013 in the context of Patent Application No. 10765276.0 (EP2419508) at EPO', http://www.tkdl.res.in/tkdl/LangDefault/common/Examinarreport/

reports/EP2419508_1.asp, accessed on 25 October 2014)

41. Murli Manohar Joshi, *Science, Sustainability and Indian National Resurgence*, (Ed. J. K. Bajaj & M. D. Srinivas), Centre for Policy Studies, Chennai, 2008, p. 156

42. Caroline Ryan, *Patent to Protect Ancient Knowledge*, BBC News, 19 February 2002

43. Ravindra R. Pandharinath, 'Science Means Learning to Say—I Don't Know', an interview with Dr Ashok D. B. Vaidya, *Journal of Ayurveda and Integrative Medicine*, October–December 2011, pp. 211–216

44. Teesta Setalvad, 'Education with Values', *Communalism Combat*, January 2001

45. Santosh Das, 'Agenda of Desaffronisation a Casualty', *People's Democracy*, Vol. XXIX, No. 03, 16 January 2005

46. Ramachandra Guha, 'Public Office, Private Gain', *The Telegraph*, 31 March 2007

47. Shamnad Basheer, 'Empty Allegations', *DNA*, 25 February 2007

48. Cara Bradley, *Plagiarism Education and Prevention: A Subject-Driven Case-Based Approach*, Elsevier, 2011, pp. 59–60

49. Dr R. A. Mashelkar, Response to Queries by Society for Scientific Values, Communication dated 28 March 2007, http://www.scientificvalues.org/Mashelkar.htm

50. Communication dated 23 October 2003, Ministry of Science & Technology, Govt. of India, http://pibarchive.nic.in/archive/releases98/lyr2003/roct2003/23102003/r231020031 1.html

51. http://www.csir.res.in/csir/tkdl/TKDLOutcomes_MNCs.asp

52. Saikat Sen and Raja Chakraborty, 'Traditional Knowledge Digital Library: A Distinctive Approach to Protect and Promote Indian Indigenous Medicinal Treasure', *Current Science*, 106(10), May 2014, pp. 1340–1343

53. Banu Subramaniam, *Holy Science—The Biopolitics of Hindu Nationalism*, Orient Blackswan, 2019, p. 228

54. Ibid., p. 10

55. Swami Vivekananda, *The Complete Works of Swami Vivekananda* (CWSV) - Vol. 5, Advaita Ashrama, 1947, p. 258

56. Ibid.

57. Ibid., p. 341

58. Ibid., p. 161

59. Banu Subramaniam, 2019, pp. 93–94

60. Ibid., pp. 105–106

61. Ibid., p. 225

62. Ibid., p. 202

63. Press release by Arogya Bharati, 17 May 2017

64. Protection of Child Rights vs State Of West Bengal & Ors on 5 May 2017

65. Arun Mohan Sukumar, *Midnight's Machines: A Political History of Technology In India*, Penguin Random House India, 2019, pp. 27–28

66. Ibid., p. 69

67. Ibid., p. 71
68. Ibid., p. 186
69. Ibid., p. 188
70. Robert S. Anderson, *Nucleus and Nation Scientists, International Networks, and Power in India*, University of Chicago Press, 2010, pp. 136–137
71. Sailendra Nath Ghosh, 'The Philosophy and Technology of Living in Tune with Nature', *Manthan*, Vol. VIII, No. 6, June 1988, pp. 20–52 (All subsequent quotes till the next endnote are from this article.)
72. B. B. Vohra, 'Let there be All Party Consensus on Environment', *Manthan*, Vol. VIII, No. 9, September 1987, p. 14
73. Sailendra Nath Ghosh, 'Thoughts from the Grass Roots', *Manthan*, Vol. XI, No. 8, August 1990, p. 53
74. Kalpana Sunder, 'The "Solar Canals" Making Smart Use of India's Space', *BBC: Future Planet*, 4 August 2020, https://www.bbc.com/future/article/20200803-the-solar-canals-revolutionising-indias-renewable-energy
75. Alyssa Ayres, *Our Time Has Come: How India is Making its Place in the World*, Oxford University Press, 2018, pp. 167–168
76. Adam Vaughan, 'Renewable Energy: The Rise of Supergrids', *New Scientist*, 1 January 2022, p. 8
77. V. G. Rao, 'Stephen Jay Gould: Darwin's Worthy Successor', *Science India*, Vol. 7, No. 8, August 2004
78. Arpita Subhash, 'Gender and Science II', *Science India*, Vol. 8, No. 2, February 2005
79. Deva Kumar, 'Poison Healer in the Woods', *Science India*, Vol. 18, No. 59, January 2021
80. B. N. Jagatap, 'A Paradigm Shift in Indian Science', *Science India*, Vol. 18, No. 60, February 2021, pp. 12–16
81. Ranjana Aggarwal, 'Reclaiming their Place under the Sun', *Science India*, Vol. 19, No.61, March 2021, pp. 16–20
82. Science India Bureau, 'The Man We All Need to Know', *Science India*, Vol. 18, No. 62, April 2021, p. 15
83.Chaitanya Giri PhD, *India's IT Prowess Should Propel Astrobiology*, ibid., p. 33
84. Science India Bureau, 'Adding Dignity to the Life of Sanitation Workers', pp. 50–51
85. V. P. N. Nampoori, *India's Ancient Wisdom Repackaged for Modern Times*, ibid., p. 40
86. 'India's COVID-19 Emergency', *The Lancet*, Vol. 397, 8 May 2021
87. B. N. Jagatap, 'Technology and Atmanirbhar Bharat', *Science India*, Vol. 18, No.63, May 2021, pp. 22–26
88. Debobrat Ghose, Interview with 'The Seeker', *Science India*, Vol. 18, No. 64, June 2021, p. 7
89. Debobrat Ghose, Interview with Dr Monali C. Rahalkar, ibid., p. 9
90. Debobrat Ghose, Interview with Dr Rahul Bahulkar, ibid., p. 10
91. Mrittunjoy Guha Majumdar PhD, 'Can Reality be Represented in Dual Aspects?', *ibid.*, pp. 26–27

Chapter- 8

1. *Rig Veda*: 1.164.46

2. *Ishavasya Upanishad*, verses 11–14

3. P. T. Srinivasa Iyengar, quoted by Dr S. Rangachar, *Philosophy of Pancaratras*, Sridevi Prakashana, Mandya, 1991, p. 22

4. Edwin Bryant, *Krishna: A Sourcebook*, Oxford University Press, 2007, p. 318

5. Le Huu Phuoc, *Buddhist Architecture*, Grafikol, 2010, p. 142

6. Acharya Mahaprajña, *The Axioms of Non-absolutism, Facets of Jain Philosophy: Anekantavada and Syadvada* (Ed. Sreeland Rampuria), Jain Vishva Bharathi Institute, 1996, p. 2

7. Thirumaavalavan, *Uproot Hindutva: The Fiery Voice of the Liberation Panthers*, Popular Prakashan, 2004, p. 145

8. *Sambandar Thevaram*, 2.172.10

9. *Sambandar Thevaram*, 1.66.10

10. For a complete factual counter to this Marxist portrayal of ancient Indian past, see: Sita Ram Goel, *Hindu Temples: What Happened to Them,* Vol II, Appendix IV, *Questionnaire for the Marxist Professors*, Voice of India, 1991, pp. 409–422

11. Dr U. Ve. Saminathaiyer, *En Sarithram* (My history, Tamil), Dr U. Ve. Swaminatha Iyer Book Centre, 1950: 1997, pp. 575–577

12. Malik Mohamed, *The Foundations of the Composite Culture in India*, Aakar Books, 2007, pp. 53–55

13. Anthony de Mello SJ, *Note to One Minute Nonsense*, Gujarat Sahitya Prakash, 1992

14. Congregation for the Doctrine of Faith, Notification 'Concerning the Writings of Father Anthony De Mello SJ' (Joseph Card. Ratzinger): https://www.vatican.va/roman_curia/congregations/cfaith/documents/rc_con_cfaith_doc_19980624_demello_en.html

15. Dr S. Radhakrishnan, *The Brahma Sutra: The Philosophy of Spiritual Life*, George Allen & Unwin, 1960, p. 249

16. Monobina Gupta, '*Textual Evidence from Early India Tells Us the Ancients Weren't as Tolerant as We Think*', https://thewire.in/books/textual-evidence-from-early-india-reveals-hinduism-was-not-a-tolerant-religion (accessed on 6 June 2018)

17. Upinder Singh, *Political Violence in Ancient India*, Harvard University Press, 2017, p. 241

18. Hans Bekker, *The World of the Skandapurāṇa*, BRILL, 2014, p. 37

19. Yuvraj Krishan and Kalpana K. Tadikonda, *The Buddha Image: Its Origin and Development*, Munshiram Manoharlal Publishers, 1996, p. 16

20. Adrian Snodgrass, *The Symbolism of the Stupa*, Motilal Banarsidass Publisher, 1992, pp. 170–171

21. *Chandogya Upanishad*: 5.24.1

22. *Chandogya Upanishad*: 5.24.4

23. Kristin Beise Kiblinger, *Buddhist Inclusivism Attitudes Towards Religious Others*, Taylor

& Francis, 2005:2017, p. 42

24. Ibid.

25. John S. Strong, *The Legend of King Aśoka: A Study and Translation of the Aśokāvadāna*, Motilal Banarsidass, 1989, p. 232

26. Upinder Singh, 2017, p. 174

27. Sailendra Nath Sen, *Ancient Indian History and Civilization*, New Age International, 1987:1999, p. 276

28. Lisa N. Owen, *Demarcating Sacred Space: The Jina Images at Kalugumalai, International Journal of Jaina Studies* (Online), Vol. 6 No. 4 (2010) 1–28: https://www.soas.ac.uk/ijjs/file60307.pdf

29. Susan Verma Mishra & Himanshu Prabha Ray, *The Archaeology of Sacred Spaces: The Temple in Western India, 2nd Century BCE–8th Century CE*, Routledge, 2016, p. 159

30. *RV* 1.164.46 & *AV* 9.10.28

31. Vinayak Chaturvedi, 'Rethinking Knowledge with Action: V. D. Savarkar, the Bhagavad Gita and Histories of Warfare in Political Thought' in *Action: The Bhagavad Gita and Modern India* (Ed. Shruti Kapila & Faisal Devji), Cambridge University Press, 2013, pp. 155–156

32. *Cultural Study of Hoysala Inscriptions*, Directorate of Archaeology and Museums in Karnataka, 2000, p. 105

33. Horace Hilson in John Garrett, *Mythology Philosophy Literature Antiquities Arts Manners Customs & c. of the Hindus*, Higginbotham and Co., Madras, 1873, pp. 49–50

34. Ram Gopal Misra, *Indian Resistance to Early Muslim Invaders upto 1206 AD*, Anu Books, 1983:2018, pp. 91–92

35. For example: Kamil Zvelebil, *Two Tamil Folktales*, Motilal Banarsidass, 1987, p. xli

36. Arvind Sharma, *Religious Tolerance: A History*, Harper Collins India, 2019, p. 264

37. S. Radhakrishnan, *The Bhagavad Gita*, George Allen & Unwin, 1948, p. 159

38. Wendell Thomas, *Hinduism invades America*, The Beacon Press Inc, 1930, p. 97

39. K. R. Malkani, *Political Mysteries*, Prabhat Prakashan, 2009, p. 101

40. I. P. Singh, *'No Punjabi versus Hindi divide now'*, Times News Network, 17 May 2015, https://timesofindia.indiatimes.com/india/No-Punjabi-versus-Hindi-divide-now/articleshow/47313787.cms

41. Balraj Madhok, Presidential Address, Bharatiya Jan Sangh, 1966

42. Sunil K. Salu, 'Religion and Politics in India' in *Religion and Politics in Comparative Perspective: The One, The Few, and The Many* (Ed. Ted G. Jelen & Clyde Wilcox), Cambridge University Press, 2002, p. 249

43. Apurba Kundu, 'The Indian Armed Forces' Sikh and Non-Sikh Officers' Opinions of Operation Blue Star', *Pacific Affairs*, Spring, 1994, Vol. 67 No. 1 (Spring, 1994), pp. 46–69

44. Most data here unless otherwise mentioned are taken from: Kanwar Chander Deep Singh, *The Study of Hindu Right Wing in Punjab: A Case Study of Rashtriya Swayamsevak Sangh from 1935–1984*, Panjab University, 2008

45. Akhil Bharatiya Karyakari Mandal Resolution, 1984

46. 'RSS Spearheading National Renaissance', Prakashan Vibhag, Bangalore, 1985, p. 42
47. Kanwar Chander Deep Singh, 2008, p. 411
48. Khushwant Singh, 'Congress (I) is the Most Communal Party', *Publik Asia*, 16 November 1989
49. Khushwant Singh, 'Victory to The Mob', *Outlook,* 22 August 2005
50. Vinay Sitapati, *Jugalbandi: BJP before Modi*, Penguin:Viking, 2020, p. 132
51. Atul Kohli, 'From Majority to Minority Rule: Making Sense of the "New" Indian Politics' in *India Briefing, 1990* (Ed. Marshall M. Bouton & Philip Oldenburg). Westview Press 1990: Routledge 2018
52. Dr Gopal Singh, *The Hindustan Times*, 15 August 1985 in 'My Dear Fellow-Sikhs ...', Jagarana Prakashana, Bangalore, 1986, p. 18
53. Alon Goshen-Gottstein, *Same God, Other God: Judaism, Hinduism and the Problem of Idolatry*, Palgrave Macmillan, 2016, p. 2
54. Ibid., p. 206
55. Alon Goshen-Gottstein, *The Jewish Encounter with Hinduism*, Palgrave Macmillan, 2016, pp. 29–30
56. Alon Goshen-Gottstein, 2016, p. 31
57. Ibid., p. 36
58. Ibid., p. 37
59. For example, see: Akshaya Mukul, *Gita Press and the Making of Hindu India*, Harper Collins, 2015
60. Lakhpat Rai, *Sarmad His Life and Rubais*, Hanumanprasad Poddar Smarak Samiti, Gorakhpura, 1978, pp. 19–29
61. Ibid., pp. 25–26
62. Ibid., p. 12
63. Rodger Kamenetz, *Jew in the Lotus: A Poet's Rediscovery of Jewish Identity in Buddhist India*, Harper Collins, 1994:2007 p. 244
64. Larry Brilliant, *Sometimes Brilliant,* HarperOne:2016, Kindle Edition, p. 378
65. Ibid., p. 378
66. Letter of Muhammad Iqbal to Muhammad Ali Jinnah dated 28 May 1937: marked confidential
67. Letter of Muhammad Iqbal to Muhammad Ali Jinnah dated 7 October 1937: marked private and confidential
68. P. R. Kumaraswamy, *Squaring the Circle: Mahatma Gandhi and the Jewish National Home*, KW Publishers Pvt Ltd. 2018, Kindle Edition. Location 2245
69. Immanuel Olsvanger in his 1936 India Diary quoted in Yonathan ben David, *Indo-Judaic Studies*, Northern Book Centres, 2002, p. 22
70. Ibid., p.34
71. Simone Panter-Brick, *Gandhi and the Middle East: Jews, Arabs and Imperial Interests*, I. B. Tauris & Co., 2008, p. 106

72. Immanuel Olsvanger in Yonathan ben David, 2002, p. 22
73.Ibid., p. 37
74. Simone Panter-Brick, 2008, pp. 62–63
75. Ibid., pp. 152–153
76. Vinayak Damodar Savarkar, *Hindutva: Who is a Hindu?*, Veer Savarkar Prakashan, 1923:1969, p. 90
77. Ibid., pp. 136–137
78. Ibid., pp. 136
79. Vinayak Damodar Savarkar, *'A Statement on the Jewish International Question'* in *Veer Savarkar's Whirlwind Propaganda: Statements, Messages & Extracts from the President's Diary of his Propagandistic Tours, Interviews from December 1937 to October 1941*, A. S. Bhide, 1941, pp. 71–72: All subsequent quotes on the Jewish issue by Savarkar in this section are from this statement.
80. Simone Panter-Brick, 2008
81. Mohandas Karamchand Gandhi quoted in Louis Fischer, *Mahatma Gandhi—His Life & Times*, Bharatiya Vidya Bhavan, 2003, p. 479
82. Manik Mehta, 'How the "Indian Oskar Schindler" took in 1,000 Polish children during WW-II', *The Times of Israel*, 17 July 2017: https://www.timesofisrael.com/how-the-indian-oskar-schindler-took-in-1000-polish-children-during-wwii/
83. 'Hindu Princes and the Hindu Cause', *The Modern Review* (April, 1940), Vol. 67, 1940, p. 380
84. Richard H. Davis, *Lives of Indian Images*, Motilal Banarsidass, 1997:2015, pp. 216–217
85. *The Mother's Agenda*, Vol. 8, pp. 173–176
86. Garry J. Bass, *The Blood Telegram: India's Secret War in East Pakistan*, Random House India, 2013, p. 140
87. Aravindan Neelakandan: 'In Peres' Passing Away, Israel Grieves For A Leader; India, For A Friend', https://swarajyamag.com/world/in-peres-passing-away-israel-grieves-for-a-leader-india-for-a-friend, 28 September 2016, John-Perry's Facebook page: https://www.facebook.com/perryjohn7
88. Nathan Katz in 'The One-Man Bridge Between Indic and Jewish Traditions: An Interview with Prof Nathan Katz' (Interview by Aravindan Neelakandan), *Swarajya*, 4 October 2016
89. Ram Gopal Misra, 1983:2018, p. 33
90. Ibid., pp. 136–137
91. Ibid., p. 141
92. Arvind Sharma, 2019, p. 168
93. Koenraad Elst, 'Wahi: The Supernatural Basis of Islam-VII', *Kashmir Herald*, Vol. 2 No. 11, April 2003
94. Richard M. Eaton, *The Sufis of Bijapur, 1300-1700: Social Roles of Sufis in Medieval India*, Princeton University, 1978, p. 33
95. David Frawley, *Awaken Bharata*, Bloomsbury Publishing, Kindle Edition, 2019, p. 152

96. Ibid., p. 148

97. Vinayak Damodar Savarkar, *Six Glorious Epochs of Indian History*, (Trans & Edit: S. T. Godbole), Savarkar Sadan, 1971, pp. 382–383

98. Ibid., p. 400

99. Ibid., p. 402

100. Suhas Majumdar, *Jihād: the Islamic Doctrine of Permanent War*, Voice of India, p. 95

101. Ibid.

102. H. M. Elliot and John Dowson, *The History of India as told by Its own Historians: The Muhammadan Period*, Vol. VI, Trubner and Co., 1875, pp. 60–61

103. Burjor Avari, *Islamic Civilization in South Asia A History of Muslim Power and Presence in the Indian Subcontinent*, Taylor & Francis, 2012, p. 123

104. Saiyid Athar Abbas Rizvi, *Religious and Intellectual History of Muslims in Akbar's Reign*, Munshiram Manoharlal Publishers, 1975, p. 439

105. *The Tuzuk-i-Jahangiri* or *Memoirs of Jahangir*, (Trans. Alexander Rogers: Edit. Henry Beveridge), Royal Asiatic Society, 1914, pp. 72–73

106. Harry S. Neale, *Jihad in Pre-Modern Sufi Writing*, Palgrave Macmillan, 2017, p. 68

107. Sadhu Ram Sharda, *Sufi Thought: Its Development in Panjab and Its Impact on Panjabi Literature from Baba Farid to 1850 A.D.*, Munshiram Manoharlal Publishers, 1974, pp. 83–87, 100–102

108. N. Haif, *Biographical Encyclopaedia of Sufis (South Asia)*, Sarup & Sons, 2000, pp. 102–107

109. Lajwanti Rama Krishna, *Panjabi Sufi Poets AD 1460–1900*, Oxford University Press, 1938, p. xvii

110. Kartar Singh Duggal, *Sain Bulleh Shah: The Mystic Muse*, Abinav Publications, 1996, p. 12

111. Fatima Zehra Bilgrami, *History of the Qadiri Order in India*, Aligarh Muslim University, 1982, pp. 364–365

112. Ibid., p. 366

113. Supriya Gandhi, *The Emperor who Never Was: Dara Shukoh in Mughal India*, Harvard University Press, 2020, p. 246

114. Perwaiz Hayat, *The Conversation between Dārā Shukōh and Lāl Dās: A Ṣūfī-Yogī Dialogue of the 17th Century Indian Subcontinent*, PhD thesis submitted to McGill University Montreal, 2016, p. 148

115. R. W. J. Austin (Trans. & Introduction), *Ibn Al' Arabi: The Bezels of Wisdom*, Paulist Press, 1980 (in 'Introduction'), p. 23

116. Perwaiz Hayat, 2016, p. 33

117. Ibid., p. 71

118. Ibid. p. 44

119. Kalika-Ranjan Qanungo, *Dara Shukoh*, Vol. I, M. C. Sarkar & Sons. Ltd., 1935, pp. 119–120

120. Ibid., p. 121

121. Ibid., pp. 159–160

122. Ibid., p. 160

123. Malik Muhammad, PhD, *Foundations of India's Composite Culture*, Aakar Books, 2007, pp. 54–57

124. Kalika-Ranjan Qanungo, 1935, p. 144

125. Trans. N. H. Pandia, Ed. Govinda Sakarama Sardesai, *Shivaji Souvenir*, p. 174: While some historians doubt the authenticity of the letter, historians considered as authorities on Shivaji, Dr Bal Krishna and Dr Govinda S. Sardesai. The letter is also included in the first volume comprising of 62 of the 250 letters issued by Shivaji, published by historian Dr Anuradha Kulkarni in 2011. (Shiv Chhatrapatinchi Patre: Vol. I)

126. Supriya Gandhi, 2020

127. Ibid., p. 255

128. K. R. Malkani , *The Politics of Ayodhya & Hindu-Muslim Relations*, Har-Anand Publications, 1993, pp. 82–83

129. Parliamentary Debates Rajya Sabha Official Report: 'Renaming the Aurangzeb Road: http://164.100.47.5/Official_Debate_Nhindi/Floor/170/F04.05.1994.pdf, accessed in 16-5-2021, pp. 208–209

130. R. C. Majumdar in 'Foreword': K. R. Qanungo, p. viii

131. Jawaharlal Nehru, *The Discovery of India*, Signet (1946): Oxford University Press, 1985, pp. 271–272 & p. 273

132. Bal Krishna, PhD, *Shivaji, The Man and His Work* Vol. IV (of *Shivaji the Great*), The Arya Book Depot., 1940, pp. 173–174

133. Ibid., p. 175

134. Ibid., p. 176

135. Ram Swarup, *Ramakrishna Mission: In Search of a New Identity*, Voice of India, 1986, p. 9

136. Mahendranath Gupta, *The Gospel of Sri Ramakrishna*, (Trans. Swami Nikhilananda), Sri Ramakrishna Math, 1944:1974, p. 526

137. Ibid., pp. 441–442

138. *Life of Sri Ramakrishna: Compiled from Various Authentic Sources*, mainly based on Swami Saradananada 'Sri Sri Ramakrishna Lilaprasanga', Advaita Ashrama, Mayavati, 1924:1943, pp. 207–208

139. Ibid., pp. 208–209

140. 'Bala Yogi' V. M. Jamal Muhammad, *Jnana Kalanchiyam Kunangudi Masthan Varlaru* (Tamil), Poomakal Company, 1967, pp. 58–60

141. Guru Karunaiyananda Jnana Bhupathi, *Vedanta Baskaran* (Tamizh), 1918, Brahma Vidya Press, pp. 161–162

142. Maulana Syed Shah Muhammad Inayathullah Kalphatul Kathri in his endorsement to *Vedanta Baskaran* 1928 edition

143. Karunaiyananda Jnana Bhupathi, *Jnana Kalanchiyam* (Tamizh), Karunanidhi Publishers, 1930, pp. 286–288

144. Sri Malayala Swamulavaru, *Vedanta Established in Its Own Light*, Sri Vyasa Ashramam, 1980, p. 74
145. Karunaiyananda Jnana Bhupathi, 1930, pp. 303–365
146. Ibid., p. 382
147. Karunaiyananda Jnana Bhupathi, *Jnana Yoga Rahasyam* (Tamizh), Karunanidhi: Pari Nilayam, 1930:2008, pp. 27–30
148. Paranjothi Mahan, *Nan Kadavul* (I God) Tamizh, Universal Peace Sanctuary, 1954, p. 10
149. Haroon Khalid, *In Search of Shiva: A Study of Folk Religious Practices in Pakistan* (Kindle Locations 2119–2120), Rupa Publications, Kindle Edition
150. Navnita Chadha Behera, *State, Identity & Violence Jammu, Kashmir, and Ladakh*, Manohar Publishers & Distributors, 2000, p. 143
151. Navnita Chadha Behera, *Demystifying Kashmir*, Brookings Institution Press, 2006, pp. 45–46
152. Praveen Swami, *India, Pakistan and the Secret Jihad: The Covert War in Kashmir*, Routledge, 2007, p. 158
153. Ajaz Ashraf, '*Arif Mohammad Khan on Shah Bano Case: "Najma Heptullah was key influence on Rajiv Gandhi"*', Scroll.in, 30 May 2015, https://scroll.in/article/730642/arif-mohammad-khan-on-shah-bano-case-najma-heptullah-was-key-influence-on-rajiv-gandhi
154. Rasheed Kidwai, 'Who Really Influenced Rajiv Gandhi to Act Against Shah Bano Judgment?', *ThePrint.in*, 24 July 2018: https://theprint.in/opinion/who-really-influenced-rajiv-gandhi-to-act-against-shah-bano-judgment/87263/
155. K. R. Malkani, 'Our Sufi Heritage', *Manthan*, Vol. IX No.1, January 1988, p. 1
156. Mircea Eliade, *Yoga: Immortality and Freedom* (Trans. Willard R. Trask), Routledge & Kegan, 1958, pp. 111–112
157. S. S. Kohli, 1988, pp. 21–22
158. Ramesh Kuntal Megh, 'The Influence of Sufism in the Growth of Hindi Poetry', *Manthan*, Vol. IX No.1, January 1988, p. 29
159. K. R. Malkani, 'How Sufism integrated Perennial Philosophy with the New Faith of Islam', *Manthan*, Vol. IX No. 1, January 1988, pp. 33–36
160. Parvaticharan Bhattacharya, 'Sufism and its Influence in the Growth of Bengali Poetry', *Manthan*, Vol. IX, No. 1, January 1988, p. 44
161. Asghar Ali Engineer quoted in editorial *Manthan*, Vol. VIII, No. 6, June 1988, p. 1
162. K. K. Muhammed, 'What It's Like To Be An Indian Archaeologist Who Refuses To Conform' (Interview by Aravindan Neelakandan), *Swarajya*, 6 December 2017
163. Dilip Awasti, 'HC Allows Acquisition of Land around Disputed Shrine in Ayodhya but Prohibits Construction', *India Today*, 30 November 1991
164. BJP's White Paper on Ayodhya & The Rama Temple Movement, April 1993, pp. 60–61
165. Kalyan Singh interview: *Hindu Vishva*, Vol. 28, Issue 1–3, January–March 1992, p. 41

166. *Junior Vikatan* (Tamil magazine) 28 July 2013
167. *Dinakaran* (Tamil newspaper), 2 July 2013
168. *Dinakaran*, 26 April 2013 (Nagercoil Edition)
169. 'One Held in the Recent Assault on Senior RSS Cadre', *Times of India*, 16 November 2012
170. 'Report on Islamic Terrorism in India', a study conducted by Akhil Bharathiya Vidhyarthi Parishad, Tamil Nadu, 1999
171. '41 years of Imprisonment for Four Al-Umma Activists', *The Hindu*, 10 April 2008
172. 'NDF Received Aid from Foreign Countries', *The Hindu*, 30 Oct. 2005
173. 'ISI, Iran Funded NDF: Rawat', *The Hindu*, 14 May 2005
174. 'Al-Umma Enjoyed AIADMK Support, Alleges BJP Report', *The Indian Express*, 26 April 1998
175. A compilation of localized Tamizh newspaper reports: 'Three Arrested for the Violence (that Killed 5 Persons)', *Dinamani* (Tamil Daily), 9 September 2007; 'Two Muslim Militants Arrested for Hate Posters', *Dinamani*, 13 December 1997; 'A Muslim Militant Arrested for Attack on Police Station', *Dinamani*, 1 January 1998
176. *Malai Murasu*, Evening Tamil daily, 28 January 1997
177. *Sunday* (English magazine) 5–11 May 1995 referred in Srikanta Ghosh, *Pakistan's ISI: Network of Terror in India*, APH Publishing, 2000, p. 59
178. A Ganesh Nadar, 'The Al-Umma has Finally United the Hindus', Rediff Special: accessed on 23 July 2013
179. History of Coimbatore City Police: 90s, http://www.coimbatorecitypolice.com/ccp-history-90s, accessed on 23 July 2013
180. 'Conviction in Blasts Case', *Frontline*, Vol. 20, No. 4, 15–28 February 2003
181. 'Three Held for ABVP Worker's Murder', UNI, 13 April 1998
182. 'All Accused in Paramasivam Murder Case Acquitted', *The Hindu*, 11 July 2002
183. 'All 8 Al-Umma Men Acquitted in Selvaraj Murder Case', *The Hindu*, 27 February 2003
184. 'Five Al-Umma Activists Acquitted', *The Hindu*, 5 April 2003 and 'Eleven Al-Umma Men Acquitted in Bus Burning Case', *The Hindu*, 27 May 2003
185. 'Abdul Nasser Madani: Godfather of Terrorists', *Junior Vikatan* (Tamil Magazine), 8 April 1998
186. 'Syed Munir Hoda: New Home Secretary', *The Hindu*, 13 August 2002
187. 'Jayalalitha Angers Tamil Nadu's Muslims with Remarks on Syed Munir Hoda', 23 September 2006, webIndia.com, accessed on 24 July 2013
188. Thomas P. Joseph, *Commission of Inquiry–Marad Communal Disturbances*, Chapter IV, p. 55
189. 'Marad: Tribunal Examines NIA SP', *The Hindu*, 23 March 2011
190. 'Fundamentalist Outfit Busted at Nellikuppam', *The Hindu*, 29 October 2004
191. 'MHA Confirms Arrest of LeT's Southern Commander Nazeer', *India Today*, 3 December 2009

192. 'Kerala Polls: UDF, LDF Woo Rabble-rousing Abdul Nasser Madani', *India Today*, 17 April 2006
193. 'DMK Turns Jail into Spa for Coimbatore Terror Accused', *The Indian Express*, 23 July 2006
194. 'DMK Bends for MNP, Intelligence Officer Transferred', *The Indian Express*, 8 August 2006
195. 'DMK Govt Ordered Six Cases Dropped against Muslim Hardliners in TN', *The Indian Express*, 8 August 2006
196. 'Melapalayam Attack on Head Constable', *Dinakaran* (Nellai edition), 20 July 2006
197. '6 Imam Ali Aides Shifted out of Madurai Prison', *The New Indian Express*, 26 November 2006
198. 'Attack and Threat to Burn Alive BJP Leader', *Malaimalar* (Tamil, Nagercoil edition), 18 December 2006
199. 'TN: Hindu Munnani Leader Hacked to Death', *Rediff News*, 18 December 2006
200. 'Al-Umma Targets Attractive Women', *Tamizhan Express*, (Tamil), 14 May 2007
201. 'In Tamil Nadu Town, Fundamentalists Play Moral Cops, Even Kill to have Way', *The Indian Express*, 26 March 2007
202. 'Al-Umma Targets Attractive Women', *Tamizhan Express*, (Tamil), 14 May 2007
203. 'Inaugurated: The Malabar Moral Police!', 13 January 2010, www.kafila.org: accessed on 24 July 2013
204. 'I shall Continue to Serve Minority Communities', *The Hindu*, 25 September 2007
205. 'Six Killed in Thenkasi Violence', *Malaimalar*, 14 August 2007. This report filed immediately from the spot clearly states that the Hindu youths were stopped and attacked by Islamists in a pre-planned attack.
206. 'No "Direct" Evidence in Coimbatore Blasts: Judge', IANS, 30 October 2007
207. 'Men Guilty of Coimbatore Blasts Released Early from Jail', NDTV.com, 17 September 2009, accessed on 24 July 2013
208. 'PDP Chief Madani Arrested in Bangalore Blast Case', PTI, 17 August 2010
209. 'Spa Treatment for Madani Costs Govt Rs 8 Lakh', *Times of India*, 8 June 2011
210. 'Congress Win Bades Well for Madani', *Arab News*, 11 May 2013
211. 'Supreme Court Denies Bail to Bangalore Blast Accused Madani', *India Today*, 3 January 2012
212. 'List of Organizations Prohibied from Receiving Foreign Funds', http://mha.nic.in/fcra/NGOS_ProhibitedCategory.pdf (accessed on 23 Jul 2013)
213. 'MH Jawaharullah, 4 Other TMMK Leaders Sentenced in a Cheating Case', *TCN News*, 8 October 2011
214. 'Row Over 'Thuppakki' Ends after Jaya's Intervention', *Deccan Herald*, 28 November 2012
215. 'Protest Turns Violent, City Police Chief Shifted', *The Hindu*, 18 September 2012
216. 'Vishwaroopam may be Released Soon, Compromise on the Cards', *Times of India*, 31

January 2013
217. http://youtu.be/fNa5qI-KLjQ accessed on 24 July 2013
218. 'Ameer Becomes FEFSI President', *IndiaGlitz*, 20 June 2012
219. Sita Ram Goel, 'The Residue of Islamism', *The Hindu Society under siege*, Voice of India, 1989, pp. 7–8.
220. '18 SIMI Activists held with 'Incriminating Documents', *The Indian Express*, 17 August 2006
221. 'Mysore Terrorist got Driving License from Chennai', *The Indian Express*, 4 November 2006
222. 'LeT Men Held with IEDs', *The Times of India*, 1 January 2007
223. 'Suspected Militant Went to Pakistan for Training', *Hindustan Times*, 6 January 2007
224. 'Grenades Seized from Imran Similar to those Used in IISc. Attack', *The Hindu*, 14 January 2007
225. 'Police Patrol Riot-hit Bangalore, IT Firms Operate', *Reuters*, 22 January 2007
226. 'Saddam Execution Condemnation Rally: Police Fires', *Dinadanthi* (Tamil Daily), 20 January 2007
227. 'Boxes of Weapon Seized from a Ship Container from Dubai to Kerala', *Dinakaran* (Tamil), 10 January 2007; also 'More Rifles & Air Guns seized in Cochin, Quran Found in Each Packet', HK Correspondent, 1 September 2007
228. Mohammad Yousaf & Mark Adkin, *Afghanistan: The Bear Trap*, Casemate, 2001, p. 221, 223
229. 'Kochi Arms Haul Tip of Iceberg: Navy Chief', IANS, 16 January 2007
230. 'Concern over One More Outfit', *The New Indian Express*, 17 February 2007
231. 'Kerala "Slip" under Glare', *The Telegraph*, 17 August 2008
232. 'Person Arrested for Giving Fake SIM Card to Kashmir Terrorist', *Dinakaran* (Tamil Daily), January 2008
233. 'Kerala Goes Soft on SIMI, Country Pays', *The Economic Times*, 18 August 2008
234. 'Why Kerala Youth are Part of Fight for Kashmir', Rediff.com, 27 October 2008, accessed on 25 July 2013
235. '*Outfit Involved in 22 Murder Cases*', PTI, 4 August 2010
236. 'Haul Hints at Arms Stockpiling', *The Hindu*, 14July 2010
237. Kerala Chief Minister's Press Conference at New Delhi, 24 July 2010
238. 'Concern in Govt over PFI's Growing Outfits' Spread', *Indian Express*, 5 April 2011
239. 'Dubai: EIFF Holds Grand Reception for SDPI Leader', Media Release 24 October 2011 (Daijiworld.com: accessed on 25 July 2013) and Kuwait India Fraternity Forum organised public program, January 2011
240. V. K. Shashikumar, 'Here Come the Pious', *Tehelka*, 9 October 2010
241. 'Baig was the Mastermind, Recruiter: ATS Chief', *The Hindu*, 10 September 2010
242. 'Kerala: Probing if PFI is Linked to Lashkar', *The Indian Express*, 7 September 2010
243. 'Banning PFI: Government Double Standard Exposed', *The New Indian Express*, 8

September 2010

244. 'Kerala: Accused in Professor's Hand-chopping Case Wins Civic Poll', Rediffmail.com, 28 October 2010

245. 'Dalit Youth Executed "Taliban-style" in Kerala, *The Times of India*, 20 October 2010

246. 'Three Fishermen Stabbed in Azhikkal', *Times of India*,10 December 2011

247. 'PFI is SIMI in Another Form, Kerala Govt Tells HC', *The Indian Express*, 26 July 2012

248. 'ABVP Men's Killing: Call to Ban PFI, Feeder Outfits Intensifies', *Daily Pioneer*, 7 September 2012

249. Vicky Nanjappa, 'PFI, HuJI Helped Spread the Panic!', http://vickynanjapa.wordpress.com, accessed on 25 July 2013

250. Shridseep Biswas, 'In God's Own Country', *Outlook*, 23 November 2010

251. 'Kerala Police Unmasks PFI's Terror Face', *The New Indian Express*, 28 April 2013

252. 'Bengaluru-Narath Links Strengthen', *Deccan Chronicle*, 11 May 2013

253. C. D. Souza, 'SDPI's Emergence in Dakshina Kannada Poses Threat in the Long Run', http://enarada.com/?p=4932, accessed 25 July 2013

254. 'Narath Accused had Links with Dawood, Claims Government', *The New Indian Express*, 2 July 2013

255. 'Police Suspect Use of Foreign Funds', *The Hindu*, 20 May 2013

256. 'Foreign Links of Kerala's Islamist Camp under Lens', *Daily Pioneer*, 1 May 2013

257. 'UDF Govt Playing Game in Narath Case: Kodiyeri', *Mathrubhumi*, 7 May 2013

258. T.S. Subramanian, 'Building New Bases', *Frontline*, Vol. 24, Iss. 24, 21 December 2007

259. 'Two PFI Men Held', *The New Indian Express*, 24 July 2010

260. http://www.popularfrontindia.org/pp/image/mukundan-c-menon-award-presented-dr-udayakumar-nchro, accessed as on 25 July 2013

261. James Lovelock in *Creel Commission Interview with James Lovelock*

262. VCK Supremo Introduces SDPI Candidate for Chennai Mayor election, http://www.popularfrontindia.com/, accessed 25 July 2013

263. 'Sasikumar Murder: NIA Files Supplementary Chargesheet against Two Popular Front of India Members', *New Indian Express*, PTI, 21 June 2018

264. 'Ramalingam Murder Case: NIA Files Chargesheet, Names 18 PFI, SDPI Activists', PTI report dated 3 August 2019

265. Full Text of PM Narendra Modi's Speech at World Sufi Forum, NDTV, 17 March 2016, https://www.ndtv.com/india-news/full-text-of-pm-narendra-modis-speech-at-world-sufi-forum-1288303

266. Fariba Nawa, 'American Sufi: From Texas to the Taliban, and Back', *Foreign Affairs*, 12 October 2016

267. N. P. Shankaranarayaran Rao, *Ashfaqulla Khan*, Rashtrotthana Sahitya Trust, Bangalore, 1974:1996, pp. 6–7

268. Ibid., pp. 32–33

269. Ibid., p. 35

270. Ibid., p. 38
271. Ibid., pp. 40–41
272. 'Muslim Boy from RSS-run School Tops Assam HSLC Examination', PTI Report dated 1 June 2016
273. Harry Oldmeadow, *Journeys East: 20th Century Western Encounters with Eastern Religious Traditions*, World Wisdom, Inc: 2004, p. 219
274. Jules Monchanin, quoted in *Biographical Dictionary of Christian Missions* (Entry author: Daniel O'Connor) Ed. Gerald H. Anderson, Wm. B. Eerdmans Publishing 1999, p. 467, emphasis not in the original
275. J. G. Weber, *In Quest of the Absolute: The Life and Work of Jules Monchanin*, Kalamazoo, Cistercian Publications, p. 73
276. Jules Monchanin quoted in 'An Ashram in India under the Rule of Saint Benedict' by Iona Misquitta, in *Jules Monchanin (1895–1957) as seen from East and West (Vol-II)*, Saccidananda Ashram/ISPCK, Delhi, 2001, p. 76
277. Iona Misquitta:2001, p. 77
278. James Stuart, *Swami Abhishiktananda: His Life Told through his Letters*, ISPCK, Delhi, 2000, p. 35
279. Jules Monchanin, 'Contemplation, The Essential Vocation of the Church and of India', *Swami Parama Arubi Anandam: A Memorial*, Saccidananda Ashram, 2007, p. 125, emphasis not in the original
280. Jules Monchanin quoted in 'Jules Monchanin and Yoga' by Thomas Matus, in *Jules Monchanin (1895–1957) as seen from East and West (Vol-II)*, Saccidananda Ashram / ISPCK, Delhi, 2001, p. 110
281. Jules Monchanin quoted in Thomas Matus:2001, p. 112 (from Jules Monchanin, *Mystique de l'Inde, Mystere chretien*, Paris, Fayrad, 1974, p. 242)
282. Thomas Matus:2001, p. 113
283. Jules Monchanin, quoted in Thomas Matus:2001, p. 113
284. Thomas Matus:2001, p. 113
285. Jules Monchanin, quoted in Thomas Matus:2001, p. 114
286. Jules Monchanin, quoted in *A Christian Pilgrim in India: The Spiritual Journey of Swami Abhishiktananda* by Harry Oldmeadow, World Wisdom Inc:2008, p. 40
287. Jules Monchanin, quoted in Harry Oldmeadow:2008, p. 40
288. Jules Monchanin, J. G. Weber, *In Quest of the Absolute: The Life and Work of Jules Monchanin*, Cistercian Publications:1977, p. 126
289. Harry Oldmeadow:2008, pp. 40–41
290. Bede Griffiths to Swami Devananda letter dated 31.08.1987, in Sita Ram Goel, *Catholic Ashrams: Sannyasins or Swindlers*, Voice of India, 1988:1994, p. 135
291. 'An Indian Christology: The Shanivanam School', *The Golden String*, the bulletin of the Bede Griffiths Trust, Vol. 4, No. 2, Winter 1997–1998, p. 9
292. James Stuart:2000, p. 28

293. Henri Le Saux letter dated 9.11.1949 in James Stuart:2000, p. 33
294. James Stuart:2000, p. 33
295. Henri Le Saux in his letter dated 26.02.1950 in James Stuart:2000, p. 33
296. Henri Le Saux in his letter dated 04.02.1953 in James Stuart:2000, p. 60
297. Henri Le Saux in his letter dated 12.01.1954 in James Stuart:2000, p. 69
298. Henri Le Saux in his letter dated 24.04.1954 in James Stuart:2000, p. 71
299. James Stuart:2000, p. 79
300. James Stuart:2000, p. 81
301. Henri Le Saux in his letter dated 08.11.1955, James Stuart:2000, p. 85
302. John Nicol Farquhar, *The Crown of Hinduism*, Oxford University Press, 1913, pp. 485–486
303. John Nicol Farquhar:1913, p. 51
304. Judson B. Trapnell and Kenneth Cracknell, *Bede Griffiths: A Life in Dialogue*, SUNY Press:2001, p. 102
305. John Nicol Farquhar quoted in Harry Oldmeadow:2008, pp. 229–230
306. Harry Oldmeadow:2008, p. 230
307. James Stuart:2000, p. 146
308. Henri Le Saux, *Sacchindananda: A Christian Approach to Advaitic Experience*, ISPCK Delhi, 1974, p. 47
309. Henri Le Saux:1974, p. 67
310. Henri Le Saux:1974, p. 57
311. Henri Le Saux, *Hindu Christian Meeting Point*, ISPCK, New Delhi, 1983, p. 98
312. Michael Comans, 'Swami Abhisiktananda (Henri Le Saux, O.S.B) and Advaita', in *Religious Traditions in South Asia: Interaction and Change*, Ed, Geoffrey A. Oddie, Routledge:1998, p. 115
313. Henri Le Saux in his letter dated 10.10.1963, James Stuart:2000, p. 154
314. Henri Le Saux in his letter dated 12.04.1965, James Stuart:2000, p. 171
315. James Stuart:2000, p. 159
316. James Stuart:2000, p. 168
317. James Stuart:2000, p. 172
318. Henri Le Saux in his letter dated 29.7.1965 and 28.8.1965, James Stuart:2000, p. 175
319. Henri Le Saux in his letter dated 24.12.1965, James Stuart:2000, p. 175
320. Ringu Tulku and Mullen, *Buddhist Use of Compassionate Imagery, Compassion: Conceptualisations, Research and Use in Psychotherapy* (Ed. Paul Gilbert), Psychology Press:2005, p. 231
321. Ringu Tulku and Mullen:2005. p. 231
322. James Stuart:2000, p. 204
323. Henri Le Saux quoted in Harry Oldmeadow:2008, p. 75
324. Henri Le Saux, Diary entry dated 10.7.1969, *Ascent to the Depth of the Heart: The Spiritual Diary (1948–1973) of Swami Abhishiktananda (Dom Henri Le Saux)*, ISPCK

1998, p. 217

325. Henri Le Saux, Diary entry dated 24.4.1972, ISPCK 1988, p. 346

326. Henri Le Saux, Diary entry dated 28.5.72, ISPCK 1988, p. 352

327. Sita Ram Goel, *Catholic Ashrams: Sannyasins or Swindlers*, Voice of India, 1988:1994:2007, pp. 64–65

328. Bede Griffiths in his letter dated 5.8.1955 from Adrian B Rance, *Falling in love with India: From the letters of Bede Griffiths*, Saccidananda Ashram, 2006

329. Bede Griffiths in his letter dated 25.3.1956 from Adrian B Rance:2006, p. 160

330. Bede Griffiths in his letter dated 8.4.1956 from Adrian B Rance:2006, p. 165

331. Bede Griffiths in his letter dated 27.5.1956 from Adrian B Rance:2006, p. 182

332. Bede Griffiths in his letter dated 23.06.1957 from Adrian B Rance:2006, pp. 272–273

333. Bede Griffiths in his letter dated 22.7.1956 from Adrian B Rance:2006, p. 200

334. Bede Griffiths in his letter dated 12.6.1966 from Adrian B Rance:2006, p. 412

335. Bede Griffiths in his letter dated 22.04.1964 from Adrian B Rance:2006, p. 391

336. Bede Griffiths to Swami Devananda, letter dated 16.10.1987, in Sita Ram Goel, *Catholic Ashrams: Sannyasins or Swindlers*, Voice of India 1988:1994, p. 143

337. Bede Griffiths in his letter dated 04.08.1956 from Adrian B Rance:2006, p. 204

338. Bede Griffiths in his letter dated 06.01.1957 from Adrian B Rance:2006, p. 241

339. Bede Griffiths in his letter dated 22.12.1956 from Adrian B Rance:2006, p. 239

340. Bede Griffiths in his letter dated 22.12.1956 from Adrian B Rance:2006, p. 240

341. Bede Griffiths in his letter dated 06.01.1957 from Adrian B Rance:2006, p. 242

342. Bede Griffiths in his letter dated 19.02.1958 from Adrian B Rance:2006, pp. 300–301

343. Bede Griffiths in his letter dated 10.08.1958 from Adrian B Rance:2006, pp. 323–324

344. Bede Griffiths in his letter dated 10.08.1958 from Adrian B Rance:2006, p. 324

345. Bede Griffiths in his letter dated 03.03.1957 from Adrian B Rance:2006, p. 254

346. Bede Griffiths in his letter dated 23.06.1957 from Adrian B Rance:2006, p. 272

347. Bede Griffiths in his letter dated 21.03.1960 from Adrian B Rance:2006, pp. 350–351

348. Bede Griffiths in his letter dated 19.10.1958 from Adrian B Rance:2006, p. 335

349. Bede Griffiths, *Return to the Centre*, Collins U.K., 1976: pp. 76–77

350. Bede Griffiths in his letter dated 06.06.1959 from Adrian B Rance:2006, pp. 347–348

351. Bede Griffiths in his letter dated 21.03.1960 from Adrian B Rance:2006, p. 350

352. Bede Griffiths in his letter dated 11.12.1960 from Adrian B Rance:2006, p. 358

353. Bede Griffiths in his letter dated 27.08.1960 from Adrian B Rance:2006, pp. 374–375

354. Bede Griffiths in his letter dated 23.07.1960 from Adrian B Rance:2006, pp. 370–373

355. *The Bede Griffiths Sangha Newsletter*, March 2005, Volume 8, Issue 1, pp. 4–6

356. Bede Griffiths in his letter dated 06.04.1990 from Sita Ram Goel 1988:1994, pp. 171–172

357. Bede Griffiths, *The Marriage of East and West*, Templegate Publisher, 1982, p. 8

358. Beatrice Bruteau, 'Film Review: A Human Search: The Life of Father Bede Griffiths', *The Golden String*, Bulletin of the Bede Griffiths Trust, Vol. I, No. I, Spring 1994, p. 7

359. Bede Griffiths in his letter dated 06.06.1959 from Adrian B Rance:2006, pp. 347–348
360. Bede Griffiths in his letter dated 15.10.1961 from Adrian B Rance:2006, pp. 377–378
361. Bede Griffiths quoted in *Self-Surrender and Self-Realization in Bede Griffiths* by Bruno Barnhart, *The Golden String*, Vol. 6, No. 2
362. Bede Griffiths, 'The New Consciousness', p. 70, quoted in 'New Age and New Science in Bede's thought' by Everado Pedraza, *The Golden String*, Vol. 14, No. 1, Summer 2007
363. Wayne Teasdale, 'Bede Griffiths: An Introduction to His Inter-spiritual Thought', pp. 56–57, Everado Pedraza:2007
364. Ibid.
365. Henri Le Saux in his letter dated 18.07.1955, James Stuart:2000, p. 81
366. Bede Griffiths, *Christ in India: Essays Towards a Hindu-Christian Dialogue*, (1967), Bangalore, 1984, p. 20
367. Harry Oldmeadow, *Journeys East: 20th Century Western Encounters with Eastern Religious Traditions*, World Wisdom Inc: 2004, p. 48
368. Bede Griffiths: 1984, p. 100
369. Christ in Meditation, photograph in the *Bede Griffiths Sangha Newsletter*, June 2004, Volume 7, Issue 2
370. 'Sangha plans visit to the sacred sites of Southern India', the *Bede Griffiths Sangha Newsletter*, Volume 2, Issue 2, July 1999
371. Kim Nataraja, 'The Dancing Siva', the *Bede Griffiths Sangha Newsletter*, Volume 2, Issue 3, September 1999
372. Adrian, Editorial, the *Bede Griffiths Sangha Newsletter* , Volume 3, Issue 4, December 2000
373. Russill and Asha D'Silva, 'A Report on Our Third Pilgrimage to South India', *The Golden String*, Bulletin of the Bede Griffiths Trust, Vol. 8, No. 1, Summer 2001
374. Other announcements, the *Bede Griffiths Sangha Newsletter,* Volume 10, Issue 2, Spring 2007
375. Auschwitz cross, http://en.wikipedia.org/wiki/Auschwitz_cross
376. *Sandhya Vandana*, Saccidananda Ashram, Shantivanam, p. 2
377. Ibid., p. 9
378. Rig Veda, Book:7, Hymn LIX..tr. by Ralph T.H. Griffith
(1896) at sacred-texts.com
379. Rolf Sovik, 'Mrityunjaya Mantra, A Mantra for Healing & Comfort', *Yoga International Magazine*, March 2004
380. *Sandhya Vandana*, Saccidananda Ashram, Shantivanam pp. 41–42
381. Ibid., p. 62
382. Bede Griffiths in an interview dated September 1992, from the transcript of 'Exploring the Christian-Hindu Dialogue: A Visit with Bede Griffiths' Inner Explorations USA
383. Rupert Sheldrake, *Prayer: A Challenge for Science*, Noetic Sciences Review, (Summer

1994), 30 4-9

384. John Martin, 'The Spiritual Vision and the Legacy of Fr Bede', the *Bede Griffiths Sangha Newsletter*, September 2006, Volume 10, Issue 1, p. 6

385. John Martin, 'Jesus Christ: A Bridge to Bring Peace to the World', the *Bede Griffiths Sangha Newsletter*, June 2004, Vol 7, Issue 2, pp. 93–94

386. John Martin, 'Jesus Christ: – a Bridge to bring Peace to the World', the *Bede Griffiths Sangha Newsletter*, June 2004, Vol 7 Issue 2

387. Chacko Valiaveetil, 'An Indian Christology: The Shantivanam School', *The Golden String*, Vol. 5, No. 2, Winter 1998–1999, p. 9

388. M.Deivanayagam and D. Devakala, 'Iconography of Hindu Religion', http://www.geocities.com/Athens/Ithaca/1412/iconography.html

389. Catherine A. Robinson, *Interpretations of the Bhagavad-Gita and Images of the Hindu Tradition*, Routledge 2005, p. 81

390. Bede Griffiths with Matthew Fox, in *The Other Half of My Soul: Bede Griffiths and the Hindu-Christian Dialogue*, (compiled by Beatrice Bruteau), Quest Books 1996, p. 328

391. Cyprian Consiglio, 'Awaken and Surrender', *The Golden String*, Bulletin of the Bede Griffiths Trust, Vol. 11, No. 2, Winter 2004–2005. p. 1

392. Jyoti Sahi, 'The Lady and the Cave, Reflections on the Meaning of the Black Madonna', Article available at United Theological College - Women's Studies Department, http://www.womenutc.com/jyotisahi.htm

393. Vincent Wilson, *Christian Folk Traditions: An Introductory Study* (Tamil), Kalari Publications, Bishop House, Nagercoil, 2004, p. 27, quoted research paper: Brigitte Sebastia, Maariyamman–Mariyamman: Catholic practices and image of Virgin in Velankanni, French Institute of Pondicherry, 2000

394. Judson B. Trapnell, *Multireligious Experience and the Study of Mysticism in the Other Half of My Soul: Bede Griffiths and the Hindu-Christian Dialogue*, Compilation: Beatrice Brueau, Quest Books, 1996, p. 204

395. Amaldas, in Preface, *Yoga and Contemplation*, Asian Trading Corporation, India, 1974:2002

396. Bede Griffiths, Foreword, *Yoga and Contemplation*, Asian Trading Corporation, India 1974:2002

397. Amaldas:2002, p. 31

398. Amaldas:2002, p. 71

399. Amaldas:2002, p. 52

400. Amaldas:2002, p. 74

401. Item No: 31, Bharathidasan University, Master Degree Course M.Sc Yoga 2004 Syllabus Annexure No : XXVII p. 21

402. Swami Parama Arubi Anandam (Fr J. Monchanin) A Memorial, Saccidananda Ashram 1959:2007, p. 49

403. Wayne Teasdale, 'Father Bede's Mystical Consciousness: An Adventure in Grace', *The*

Golden String, Vol. 1, No. 2, Winter 1994, p. 2
404. APJ Abdul Kalam, *Wings of Fire: An Autobiography*, Universities Press, 1999, p. 14
405. '16 shot dead by NLFT in Tripura', PTI, 13 January 2002
406. 'Militants Raid Hindu Ashram', *The Telegraph*, 5 December 2000
407. Sandhya Jain, *Evangelical Intrusions, Tripura: A Case Study*, Rupa & Co., 2010, pp. 158–170
408. 'NLFT curb on Hindu institutions', *The Telegraph*, 14 September 2000
409. 'Three Killed by Tripura Rebels', BBC, 14 April 2000
410. Syed Zarir Hussain, 'Tribals Unite against Conversions in Tripura', www.rediff.com/news/2001/aug/02trip.htm
411. Julia Lieblich, 'Southern Baptists target Hindus', *The Associated Press*, 21 October 1999
412. Sheela Raval and Uday Mahurkar, 'Champions of Reconversion Dominate Amid Debate over Gujarat Violence against Christians', *India Today*, 25 January 1999
413. Ghelubhai Naik, fax sent to National Minority Commission, 7 January 1999
414. Ruben Banerjee, 'Backward Areas in Orissa Become Battleground for Religious Zealots and Politicians', *India Today*, 30 March 1998
415. Ruben Banerjee, 'Staines' Killing: Murder of Australian Missionary and His Two Sons in Orissa Shocks India', *India Today*, 8 February 1999
416. Justice D. P. Wadhwa Commission of Inquiry, 21 June 1999 (pdf)
417. *Times of India*, 26 August 2008
418. Basudev Mahapatra, *The Communal Face of Indian Maoists*, 15 October 2008
419. *Life of Sri Ramakrishna: Compiled from Various Authentic Sources: mainly based on Swami Saradananada 'Sri Sri Ramakrishna Lilaprasanga'*, Advaita Ashrama, Mayavati, 1924:1943, pp. 253–254
420. Daniel E. Bassuk, *Incarnation in Hinduism and Christianity: The Myth of the God-Man*, Macmillan, 1987, p. 65
421. Gopal Stavig, *Western Admirers of Ramakrishna and His Disciples* (Ed. Swami Shuddhidananda), Advaita Ashrama, 2010, pp. 33–34
422. Lola Williamson, *Transcendent in America: Hindu-Inspired Meditation Movements as New Religion*, New York University Press, 2010, p. 34
423. Mahendra Nath Gupta, *The Gospel of Sri Ramakrishna* (Trans. Swami Nikhilananda), Sri Ramakrishna Math, 1974, p. 68
424. Ibid., p. 571, 687
425. Ibid., p. 589, 873
426. Ibid., pp. 914–915
427. Mohandas Karamchand Gandhi, 'Letter to Milton Newberry Frantz, 6 April 1926', *Collected Works of Mahatma Gandhi*, Vol. 35, pp. 23–24
428. Sita Ram Goel, *Jesus Christ: an Artifice of Aggression*, Voice of India, 1994:2001, p. v
429. Ibid., p. 85
430. Swami Ranganathananda, 'The Christ We Adore' in *Eternal Values for a Changing*

Society, Bharatiya Vidya Bhavan, 1958, p. 191

431. Ram Swarup, *The Word as Revelation: Names of Gods,* Voice of India, 1980:2001, p. 102

432. Ram Swarup, *Meditations Yogas, Gods, Religions,* Voice of India, 2000, pp. 159–160

433. Arun Shourie quoted in *Arun Shourie and his Christian Critic,* Voice of India, 1995, pp. 45–46

434. Helmut de Terra, *Memories of Teilhard de Chardin* (translated by J. Maxwell Brownjohan), 1969

435. Teilhard de Chardin, *Heart of the Matter,* pp. 60–61

436. Hans Torwesten, *Ramakrishna and Christ or the Paradox of Incarnation,* The Ramakrishna Institute of Culture, 1999, p. 218

437. Amal Kiran (K. D. Sethna), *Teilhard de Chardin and our Time,* The Integral Life Foundation, 2000, p. 343

438. David E. Orberson, *Thomas Merton–Evil and Why We Suffer From Purified Soul Theodicy to Zen,* Cascade Books, 2018, p. 8

439. Thomas Merton, *The Significance of the Bhagavad-Gita in Thoughts on the East,* Burns & Oates, 1996, p. 61

440. Anthony de Mello, SJ, *Sadhana: A way to God: Christian Exercises in Eastern Form: Complete and Unabridged,* Image: Doubleday 1984, pp. 7–8

441. Ibid., pp. 32–33

442. Anthony De Mello, SJ, *The Song of the Bird,* The Crown Publishing Group, Kindle Edition, p. 10

443. Anthony De Mello, SJ, *Wellsprings: A Book of Spiritual Exercises,* Image: Doubleday 1986, pp. 152–153

444. Anthony De Mello, SJ, *The Song of the Bird,* The Crown Publishing Group. Kindle Edition, p. xiii

445. Anthony De Mello, SJ, *One Minute Wisdom,* Gujarat Sahitya Prakash, 1985, p. 2

446. Joseph Card.Ratzinger, *Concerning the Writings of Father Anthony De Mello SJ,* 24 June 1998, https://www.vatican.va/roman_curia/congregations/cfaith/documents/rc_con_cfaith_doc_19980624_demello_en.html

447. Bill de Mello, *Anthony de Mello SJ, The Happy Wanderer,* Gujarat Sahitya Prakash, 2012, pp. 242–243

448. Ibid., p. 247

449. Mark Tully, 'Lives of Jesus', *The Illustrated London News,* Christmas Issue, 1996, p. 33

450. Madav Sadashiv Golwalkar, *Bunch of Thoughts,* Vikram Prakashan, 1968, p. 69

451. Anthony Elenjimittam, *Philosophy and Action of the RSS for the Hind Swaraj,* Laxmi Publications, 1951, p. 1

452. Ibid., pp. 3–4

453. Ibid., p. 8

454. Ibid., p. 15

455. Ibid., p. 18
456. Ibid., p. 20
457. Ibid., p. 22
458. Ibid., p. 30
459. Ibid., p. 47
460. Ibid., p. 33
461. Ibid., p. 70
462. Ibid., p. 122
463. Ibid., p. 145
464. Ibid., p. 150
465. Ibid., p. 179
466. Ibid., p. 186
467. Ibid., pp. 188–189
468. Ibid., p.194

Glossary

Agamas: Literally means 'what was handed down'. There are *agamas* specifically for various schools. They are special sacred texts of Hindu Dharma considered by adherents to various (not all) Saivaite, Tantric and Vaishnavaite schools as texts at par with Vedas. They do not challenge the importance of the Vedas. Adherents to *agamic* schools consider Vedas as common and *agamas* as special texts. They codify the construction of temples, conducting rituals, installation and worship of the deity. There are 77 *agamas* related to Shakti worship; 28 Saiv *agamas* and 108 *agamas* related to Vishnu worship called Pancharatragamas.

Agnihotra: The daily fire ritual that is mandated by Vedic religion. The householder and his wife should perform the fire ritual twice with three fires. The three fires in the domestic fire altars are: the square *ahavaniya fire, the round garhapatya fire and the half-circle dakshinagni fire.*

Ajivika: (Also Ajivakas) This is considered a non-Vedic Indic tradition similar to Buddhism and Jainism. Its founder is considered to be Makkhali Gosala with the worldview centred on *niyati*—a principle of order not very different from Vedic ṛta. According to Indologist A. L. Basham (1914–1986), Ajivikas like 'the other new sects' of their period were 'reviving in one way or other the Vedic concept of ṛta, but incorporating with it an atheistic or impersonal first principle, posited a framework of karmic cause and effect.'

Anti-Semitism: Hatred towards people of Jewish faith and 'ethnicity'. It was extremely institutionalized across Europe and Arabia through a history of at least seven hundred thousand years. Anti-Semitism was also favoured by significant sections of Christianity and Islam. After the Anti-Semitism of Hitler led to Holocaust, the West started purging Anti-Semitism, though it resurfaces in both extreme left and right politics of the West. It is still very much prevalent in Arabian lands.

Arya Marriage Validation Act: In 1937 the Arya Marriage Validation Act recognized the legality of intercaste marriages and marriages with converts to Hinduism among the followers of Arya Samaj. The bill for this legislation was initiated by Dr Narayan Bhaskar Khare (1884–1970). This was instrumental in the Hindu legislature later giving legal sanction to intercaste marriages among Hindus.

Axial Age: The term 'Axial Age' was coined by Karl Jaspers (1883–1969) in 1949. For many anthropologists studying the evolution of ancient civilizations and religions, this is usually the period from the middle of first millennium BCE. This period, according to them, saw across different civilizations then prominent in the planet, radical new ideas arising and becoming dominant, changing the religious history of humanity.

Beef: Refers to bovine meat. It can refer to the meat of cow, ox, buffaloes and bison.

Bhagauti: Guru Gobind Singh uses the term in his works to mean the Divine Sword. In the work the name also means the sword of the Goddess. According to Prof. Surjit Singh Gandhi, Bhagauti was used as 'an attributive name of the Real one in the compositions of Guru Gobind Singh', which in turn 'symbolizes manifestation of Shakti or Divine Power which is to be used in favour of the saints against the demonic powers as a last resort'.

Bhavani: Refers to both the goddesses that Chhatrapati Shivaji, the founder of Hindu Maratha Empire, worshipped. It also refers to his sword, which according to historians he obtained in 1658 CE. He named the sword 'Bhavani' or 'Bhavani ka Talwar', meaning the sword of Goddess Bhavani. To his followers and later in the popular tradition, the sword became that of the Goddess, given to Shivaji to protect Dharma.

Bicameral Mind: Psychologist Julian Jaynes (1920–1997) in his book *The Origin of Consciousness in the Breakdown of the Bicameral Mind* (1976) proposed that humans initially operated in a way that one part of their brain experienced separate inner 'voices' and it was the other part of the brain that acted upon those voices. This is the bicameral model. With the complexity of urbanization, the bicameral mind broke down and unified, thus causing the individual consciousness to evolve. There are researchers who correlate this hypothesis with the view of the Axial Age.

Biogas plants: In India biogas plants are chiefly cow-dung-based, which help generate cooking gas. The Gandhian Joseph Cornelius Kumarappa (1892–1960) was the chief propagator of this green energy technology in the early decades of post-Independent India. The BJP government under Modi launched 'Gobardan', combining the livestock dung and urban waste to produce energy. This project covers 125 districts in India with 324 biogas and compressed biogas plants.

Bionationalism: Herbert Gottweis and Byoung Soo Kim, academicians from the University of Vienna, used the term in 2010 in the context of the fraud committed by the South Korean stem cell scientist, Woo-Suk Hwang. Moving beyond the ethnic and/or racial nationalism that became prevalent during the colonial expansionism of the West, bionationalism uses stem cells and oocytes. This new term with its negative connotations has been used in the completely different context of Hindutva and India by Prof. Banu Subramaniam of the University of Massachusetts Amherst (Feminist Science Studies).

Biotechnic order: A term used by Hindutva ideologue K. R. Malkani (1921–2003) in his 1951 book about the doctrinal need for a new political party. The term used antagonistically to 'mining culture' refers to a proto-ecologically abiding form of living.

Cargo cult: A cult that developed in the Melanesian islands among aboriginal tribes in the aftermath of Second World War. The cult developed as a result of the mix of the phenomenon of World War planes dropping cargoes, aboriginal spiritual beliefs and apocalyptic narratives borrowed from missionaries. According to anthropologist Marvin Harris (1927–2001) belonging to the school of cultural Marxism, the cult also expressed a deeper idea of resistance to colonial subjugation and was creating a response beneath the religious epithelium. According to Harris, Christianity was originally a cargo cult that developed against the Roman rule in Judaea.

Chandi di Var: A work on the heroic demon-slaying battles of Chandi the Goddess written by Guru Gobind Singh (1666–1708), the tenth guru of Sikhs. Though popularly known as *Chandi di Var*, the oldest manuscript title reads *Var Durga Ki*. It is in Punjabi. It has 55 verses. It is part of Dasam Granth. It details the battle of the Goddess with the asuras and their slaying. The work based on Markandeya Purana describes the Goddess killing Mahishasura, Dhumralochana, Chand-Munda, Raktabija, and Shumbha-Nishumbha.

Chandi: A fierce form of the Goddess when She destroys asuras. She is also called Chandika. She is worshipped as the Goddess of the battlefield (Rana Chandi) and Goddess of victory (Jeya Chandi or Joya Chandi). Her worship is prevalent throughout India, cutting across north and south, tribal and non-tribal.

Chaturvarna: The four-fold division of the society into Brahmins (priests, teachers and ritualists), Kshatriyas (warriors), Vaishyas (merchants) and Shudras (manual labourers). While in the pre-modern times the division was mainly based on birth, yet communities moved between the *Varnas* which were more social spaces than rigid categories.

Chilapathikaram (Epic of the ankle bracelet): Tamizh epic variously dated between second century to fifth century CE. Its authorship is attributed to Illango Adigal, a Chera (South Western Tamizh kingdom) prince who became a Jain monk. The epic-drama tells the life of Kannagi, whose husband was wrongly executed by the Pandya king after being accused of the theft of the anklet of the queen. Kannagi not only proves the innocence of her husband but in her fury burns down Madura, the capital of Pandya kingdom.

Commensalism: A symbiotic relationship in which one organism benefits while the other organisms do not get neither benefits nor or they harmed.

Cosmic Dance: In Hindu worldview, the Dance of Siva symbolizes the eternal creation-sustenance-dissolution cycle of existence. It unites the matter, energy, space, time and consciousness. It is at once an expression of spiritual truth and symbolism of scientific worldviews in different domains. The Chola Bronzes' representation of the cosmic dance of Siva are considered one of the finest sculptural expressions of eternity through human creations.

Cow Slaughter: Killing of the cow. Usually this refers to the public killing of the cow and in the Indian context, it usually refers to killing a cow in public with a view to humiliate Hindus, who consider cows to be sacred.

Creationism: The pseudoscience that purports to show evidence for the creation of the earth and the life on it by a creator deity. Creationism in the Biblical context also claims to provide geological evidence for the flood of Nova, anthropological evidence for the re-population of the world by the descendants of Nova. Primarily it tries to establish that species never differentiated from a common ancestor.

Dalit: The term used by certain sections of academia and media to denote the Scheduled Communities in the post-1990 era. However, it was the Hindutvaite Swami Shraddhanand to whom many scholars attribute the first usage of the term 'Dalit'. According to Dr K. B. Saxena, political science scholar and civil servant, Swami was translating the term 'Suppressed Classes' used by Swami Vivekananda.

Devi Yantra: Yantras are ritual diagrams which define sacred spaces. Devi Yantra is the ritual-sacred diagram of the Goddess. It is considered both the presence and manifestation of Herself. Usually an inverted triangle is considered a generic Devi Yantra. This becomes the basis for creating elaborate Mandalas.

Ekatmata Mantra: The Unity Mantra is the official hymn of invocation of theo-diversity, which in the form of prayer brings together the diverse traditions with even their mutually antagonistic conception of ultimate reality and pray for common well being of all existence. It has an interesting parallel with the hymn from *Mahanataka* or *Hanuman Nataka,* which is usually dated to tenth century CE and also found in the inscription of Belur Chenna Kesava temple at Karnataka. This is sung at the place of invocation in the RSS functions.

ESOP: 'Employee Share/Stock Ownership' or ESOP was a concept originally floated in 1967 by Louis Kelso, a San Francisco lawyer and investment banker. It makes labourers partners in private companies and corporations by offering them shares/stocks thus making them owners as well. This system was adopted as part of the strategy of 'labourizing industry' by the Bharatiya Mazdoor Sangh (BMS), the trade union movement of the Sangh Parivar.

Evolution: The theory that a system undergoes changes, usually progressive changes, through time and hence changes from one form into another. Evolution holds that forms are not fixed. Both forms and functions change over the period of time. Most ancient civilizations like Hindus and Greeks had concepts of evolution. Religions with narratives on creation and creator gods have theological problems in dealing with the concept of evolution. Evolution can or cannot be teleological. Again, teleological evolution can also be natural, as in an organ evolving for a specific task, or guided by a supernatural force (like evolution guided by superior intelligence). Thus, there are multiple theories of evolution.

Farz: Mandate by God (in this case Allah of Islam) as duty. The adherent to the religion must obey it. It is a Persian word also found in Urdu language.

Fatwa: An Islamic religious decree on matters both religious and secular. A fatwa can be issued by an Islamic cleric and religious scholar as well as by institutions. Scholar Arun Shourie calls a fatwa 'sharia in action' whereas sharia is the Islamic legal framework and practice derived from Quran, the holy book of Islam, and Hadis, the sayings and events in the life of Muhammad, the last prophet of Muslims.

Free-Thinker: A person who ascribes to free-thinking. A free-thinker places reason above belief and dogma. He or she rejects theological/ideological authority particularly of revealed and organized religion. Free-thinking has a historical and cultural context in the enlightenment era of Europe, particularly in the seventeenth century. In the Indian context mostly, this may apply to individuals who questioned social restrictions and hierarchies based on religious authorities.

Genocide of 1971: The marked and intentional killing of Bengali population of East Bengal by the Pakistani army and its collaborators, mainly comprising Jamat-e-Islami. The period of the genocide was between 26 March—16 December 1971. According to the Bangladesh government, 3 million civilians were killed. According to the Hamoodur Rahman Report commissioned by the Pakistani government, its army officials were given written orders to report how many Hindus they killed every day.

Ghadar Movement: A movement which was started in 1913 in California, United States to free India. It was inspired by revolutionary Lala Har Dayal and hence the name Ghadar, which was the name of the weekly whose founding editor was Har Dayal. Most members of this movement were Sikhs and other Punjabi immigrant workers of Indian origin. Taking advantage of World War I, the Ghadar movement planned an uprising on 19 February 1915, which failed. More than 150 Indians belonging to the movement were either executed or killed. The attempts at a pan-India armed rebellion continued till 1917 but ended in failure. This resulted in the Hindu-German conspiracy trial in the United States.

Gnosticism: The Gnostic traditions existed in Judaea and larger Israeli religious realm just before and soon after the advent of Christianity. Gnostic traditions were not monolithic. From Zoroastrian-like-dualism to Neo-Platonic monism and pantheistic tendencies, the texts show multiple approaches to religion. Many texts centre around the life stories of Jesus and his disciples, including prominence to the female disciple Magdalene. Based on Nag-Hammadi scroll discoveries, the nature of Gnostic traditions throw light on the way Christianity evolved into its modern exclusivist monopolistic religious form.

God-Helmet: An experiment developed by Prof. Michael Persinger, which provides magnetic stimulation to certain parts of the brain, particularly the temporal lobe, and makes the subjects have vivid experiences that are religious or supernatural in the minds of the subjects. Incidentally, Richard Dawkins, the famous evolutionist and atheist, did not have any such experiences when subjected to God-Helmet.

Greenhouse Gas (GHG): A gas that can absorb heat energy and re-emit part of it, leading to warming of the atmosphere (called greenhouse effect). The leading GHGs are carbon dioxide (CO2), Methane (CH4) and Nitrous oxides. The livestock emit methane, which is used as cooking fuel through biogas plants, which in turn reduces this GHG emission into the atmosphere.

Hindavi Swarajya: The concept of a liberated India in proto-modern sense was delineated by Chhatrapati Shivaji. Swarajya means self-rule. Hindavi here refers to the Hindu self-nature of India. According to the traditional narrative of Shivaji's life, in the summer of 1645, Shivaji took a vow before Siva, the presiding deity of Raureshwar temple, to establish Hindavi Swarajya and referred to this in his letter dated 16 May 1645, to Dadaji Naras Prabhu Deshpande.

Hindu Nationalism: Though used generally as a loose English translation of Hindutva, there are qualitative differences between *Hindutva* and the term 'Hindu nationalism', which is understood generally in the West and West-influenced academia. While anchored in the sacred geography of India, Hindutva does not harbour an expansionist or supremacist worldview. It is more a resistance movement aimed at protecting theo-diversity against monopolistic expansionism.

Hindutva: Refers to Hinduness. To its critics Hindutva is an exclusivist ideology. To its upholders it is not an ideology but the essence of Indian reality. In 1901 Rabindranath Tagore (1861–1941) used the term to denote the civilizational process of assimilation of diverse cultures and religions. 'Veer' Vinayak Damodar Savarkar (1883–1966) in his book *Hindutva* (1923) defines it as the national movement and nature of India in all its dimensions—spiritual, cultural, religious, political, ethnic and socioeconomic.

Ijadhist Sufism: A dominant school of Sufism which emphasizes shariat and conversion to Islam. Ijadhist Sufis work in close quarters with the Islamist State. In the aftermath of Islamist invasions they work with people developing syncretic devotional cultures to convert the local populations to Islam mostly with persuasion but when necessary with stern intervention of the Islamist State.

Inculturation: Adaptation of the form of preaching of Christian religious doctrine to imitate the forms of local culture targeted for conversion, or conversely appropriation of the forms and even institutions of the targeted community for religious conversion in order to facilitate proselytization.

Integral Humanism: An indigenous worldview and political philosophy (of the BJP) propounded by Pandit Deendayal Upadhyaya (1916–1968), an ideologue of Bharatiya Jan Sangh (BJS) and a *pracharak* of the RSS. Integral Humanism contextualizes the human being as a holistic individual within the framework of the four *Purusharthas* and places him/her in the web of social, national, ecological and universal contexts. At the national level it emphasizes self-reliance or swadesi. In the context of environmental relations it emphasizes sustainable and decentralized technology. In 1965 BJS adopted Integral Humanism as its official doctrine. Later, after adopting Gandhian socialism as its official doctrine for a few years, the BJP which was formerly BJS, also reaffirmed Integral Humanism as its doctrine.

Intelligent Design: A more sophisticated form of creationism, it advocates the claim that irreducible complexity is proof of intelligent design. Intelligent design is a science-sounding euphemism for creator deity.

Jauhar: Mass self-immolation by Hindu women. The word is said to have derived from the slogan 'Jai Hara'. It had been recorded even by the pre-Islamic non-Indic invaders like the Greeks. But it was not known to have happened in wars between Indic kingdoms. Jauhar took the form of a resistance movement by Hindu women after the Islamist invasions. While in Rajasthan it became a routine form of women's resistance to institutionalized slavery by invaders, in modified forms it manifested during Partition holocaust with Hindu and Sikh women jumping into wells to escape abuse and slavery.

Kafir Tribe: Ancient Hindu tribes which did not convert to Islam and lived in a region called Kafiristan (now in Afghanistan). In 1895 Abdur Rahman Khan, who became Amir of Afghanistan through a British treaty, invaded the region, and through a violent campaign spanning 40 days, he converted most of them to Islam. An order was proclaimed not to spare any males over seven who did not accept Islam and send all the Kafir tribe women to the harem of Amir.

Kafir: In the Islamic doctrine, kafir is a person who denies Allah and His prophet. The linguistic meaning of kafir is one who hides or covers. The term can also be applied to farmers as they hide the seeds (in soil). In the Islamic sense the term refers to one who refuses to accept Islam as he is said to hide the Truth. When the message of Islam is conveyed and a non-Muslim rejects it, then he or she becomes a kafir.

Khalsa Movement: The movement started by Guru Gobind Singh, the tenth Sikh Guru, in the year 1699 CE. The movement aimed to protect the theo-diversity of India against monopolistic aggression and expansionism. Khalsa with emphasis on the Divine and infinite attributes to Divine became an Indic resistance movement. The later Sikh empire of Maharaja Ranjit Singh (1780–1839) was doctrinally anchored in Khalsa.

Kuka Movement: Also known as Kuka rebellion, it refers to the fierce rebellion of Namdhari Sikhs under the supreme spiritual leader of the time Guru Ram Singh

(1816–1885). In 1872 the movement started as a resistance against intentional and institutional cow slaughter initiated by the British, particularly in Amritsar. It soon became a movement against the British. In the end, 65 Namdhari Sikhs were blown to death from canons. Twelve-year-old Bishan Singh was beheaded after refusing to renounce his Dharma.

Kundalini/Muladhar Shakti: According to the Yogic tradition of India, kundalini or Muladhar Shakti (literally primordial fundamental energy) is a spiritual-psychological energy experience involuted in the spinal base of human beings. It is related in the feminine and serpentine form. It is serpentine because of the way it is visualized as coiled like a snake at the spinal base and the way it moves. The kundalini experience is considered universal and resulting in intense divine experiences including feeling oneness with all.

Kuravanchi: A minor literary form in Tamizh where a fortune telling girl from Kuravar—a forest dwelling tribe—visits, and through positive fortune reading, she consoles the heroine, who would be lamenting either the separation from her lover or regarding the uncertain nature of their love.

Madhura Vijayam: Also known as *Conquest of Madhura,* it is a fourteenth century CE Sanskrit minor drama-poetry composed by Ganga Devi, the queen of Kumara Kampanna, the second son of Bukka Raya—one of the founders of the Vijayanagar empire. The work describes the liberation of Madhura or Madurai from the clutches of Sultanate rule, which was both tyrannical and fanatical.

Mandub: A recommended act of faith in Islam. It is a meritorious deed, which will be rewarded by Allah. But omission of the act will not result in divine punishment.

Monism: The concept that all that exists is one and that one may be matter or non-material. There is thus both materialist monism and idealist monism. In monism there is no difference between God or Absolute Being, mind and matter. Famous monists include Adi Sankara (circa seventh century CE) and Baruch Spinoza (1632–1677 CE). Monism is also culturally and philosophically close to pantheism and non-dualism.

Mutualism: A symbiotic relationship in which all the symbionts get benefitted

Namdhari Sikhs: A Sikh section which believes that after the tenth guru, Guru Gobind Singh passed the Guru-ship to Guru Balak Singh (1784/85–1862). Their strong attachment to the Holy Name *(Nam)* became the name of their sect—*Namdhari.*

Natural Selection: The process discovered by Charles Robert Darwin (1809–1882) through the observations he made during his visit to and study of Galapagos islands and from the samples he collected during his voyage in *HMS Beagle* (1831–1836). Basically, it means there is selection when there are variations in a system of self-replicating units and this selection drives evolution. With the publication of his book *The Origin of Species through Natural Selection* in 1859, which announced his discovery of natural selection, Darwin emphatically placed evolution as a science from its place till then as philosophical speculation.

Neurotheology: The study of the neural correlates as well the processes connected with the religious experiences. It is also called the neuroscience of religion. The works of Michael Persinger (1945–2018), Dr Andrew Newberg, V. S. Ramachandran have all contributed to the discipline. Dr Andrew Newberg's book *Principles of Neurotheology (2010)* is considered an important textbook of this newly formed interdisciplinary study.

Nirṛti: A Vedic Goddess. Conventional Western Indologists consider her as a negative Goddess. According to the Vedic scholar Ramachandra Narayan Dandelkar, she signifies the absence of ṛta in the cosmic and ethical context. Prakriti, the benign Earth Goddess, and Nirrti, who manifests when ṛta is disturbed, can both be seen as two extensions of the same Goddess.

Non-Absolutism: The English term used for *anekantavada* and *syadvada* of Jain tradition. The non-absolute stand allows the perception of multiple dimensions of reality. Instead of the simple binary of 'yes' and 'no', the Jain epistemology allows seven states. Four out of these seven states contain the 'indefinable' as a component of the state of reality. With quantum computation, this view of reality gains more relevance today.

Obeidullah Plan: In August 1924, Maulvi Obeidullah (1872–1944), a functionary of the Kabul Congress Committee, revealed a plan to Lala Lajpat Rai (1865–1928), which was to turn India into federal linguistic divisions while at the same time create a strong transnational pan-Islamic unity with the aim of establishing an Indo-Afghan Caliphate with support from other major Islamic nations.

Panchagavya: A traditional mixture of chiefly five *(pancha)* components derived from the cow (gav). The five components are cow dung, cow urine, milk, curd and ghee. It is used in Hindu rituals, worship, traditional medicinal system of Ayurveda and in sustainable agricultural practices in India. Sometimes In addition to the five components derived from cow, other non-cow based components, such as jaggery, tender-coconut, banana and water may be added.

Pegging Act 1943-1946: Colonial South African government legislated an act in 1943 to stop South African Indians from buying real estate in 'white' areas of Durban for residential, occupation or investment purposes. Initially Indians were told that this was for the period of World War II. But in 1946, 'the Asiatic Land Tenure and Indian Representation Act' was introduced by then Prime Minister of South Africa Jan Smuts (1870–1950), which also prevented Indians from purchasing land, forcing them to live in restricted areas much like ghettos.

Pracharak: Life worker of the RSS. Pracharaks are bachelors and work to propagate the Sangh in any given place by increasing the number of shakhas there. They can also be deputed to work on specific functions or projects. They can also be 'loaned' to other Sangh organizations for specific works.

Pratityasamutpada: This is a core Buddhist principle meaning dependent arising or dependent origin. Every manifest phenomenon is an emergence out of the mutual relations of various factors which in turn have emerged of other factors and so on. This has at its core a fractal networked vision of reality, which is in resonance with the insights of modern science in various realms, particularly fractal geometry and ecology.

Pseudoscience: A body of knowledge which is actually based on unscientific assumptions like religious belief or political doctrine being passed on as science. According to philosopher of science Karl Popper (1902–1994), astrology and Marxism are good candidates for the pseudoscience category. Creationism, intelligent design, phrenology and racist eugenics are some more examples of pseudoscience.

Purusharthas: In Hindu tradition the four archetypal and fundamental driving forces for a human being are called the Purusharthas. They are *artha*, or seeking wealth, *kama*, or the force that propels one to fulfil libido and Dharma, the ethnical basis that harmonizes the individual impulse for libido and wealth with social welfare. All these three ultimately move towards individual self-realization and liberation, called Moksha.

Race: A human division based on supposed biological traits. Being a species spread over the entire planet, there exists a lot of variation among human beings in terms of their traits. In the eighteenth and nineteenth century, the emerging sciences of biology, anthropology, etc., started considering these variations in traits as fixed, based on their prevalence in geographical regions and constructed races as fixed biological and scientific categories. However, repeated genetic research has shown that there is not much truth to race as being a fixed biological category.

Racism: A political or social theory and/or a worldview which adapts discrimination based on the categories of race usually to the disadvantage of certain groups of people considered as either inferior and/or dangerous to the dominant racial category in power.

Ranghar (or Rangar): They are a Rajput community mainly comprising Muslims who populate Haryana, Himachal Pradesh, Punjab and Uttar Pradesh. But Hindu Ranghars also exist. The Muslim Ranghars are said to have converted during the reign of Qutub-ud-din and Ala-ud-din mainly in the thirteenth century.

Rashtriyatva: A term proposed by Dattopant Thengadi (1920–2004) as an alternative to 'nationalism', a term which is constantly associated with Hindutva as in 'Hindu nationalism' but which has a negative connotation because of its destructive historic baggage in the West. To Thengadi, *rashtriyatva* is in sync with the universal values of all humanity and hence does not develop supremacist tendencies or have expansionist as well as an exclusivist worldview.

Ṛta: A multidimensional Vedic term, which can primarily mean cosmic natural order, universal harmony and Truth. According to Vedic scholar Vinayak Mahadev Apte, the word means 'primarily … (something) gone over (correctly) or better (the correct order of) going' and secondarily 'the settled Order of Right'. According to Sri Aurobindo, it is the right action of the 'truth of being, … proceeding direct and undeformed out of the Infinite'.

Sacred Animal: An animal that is sacred to a community either religiously or ethnically. The community may have prohibitions against killing the animal for hunting or game. The community may ritually offer the animal meat in special religious rites to the Divinity they may be worshipping. The animal itself may be considered the manifestation of the Divine. Either one or all of these characteristics may make an animal sacred for a community.

Samanvaya: The word occurs in both *Brahma Sutra* of Vyasa and in the Ashokan rock edict (Samanvaya eva sadhu). It essentially means harmony or a harmonizing process among the variety of texts or worldviews. According to the scholar-philosopher and second President of India, Dr S. Radhakrishnan (1888–1975), the author of Brahma Sutra applied this harmonizing process to various schools of thoughts of his time, and this could be extended to various religions of today.

Sangh Parivar: The family of organizations which have come from the RSS or the Sangh. Rashtra Sevika Samiti is an independent women's wing founded in 1936. The organization for the protection of the rights of forest-dwelling communities is Vanvasi Kalyan Ashram (1952).The student organization of the RSS is the Akhil Bharatiya Vidyarthi Parishad (ABVP) founded in 1949. The trade union movement which came from the Sangh is Bharatiya Mazdoor Sangh (BMS) founded in 1955. Yet another organization that is part of the Sangh Parivar is the Viswa Hindu Parishad, an India-based but transnational federation of all traditional as well as modern Hindu institutions and movements; it was founded in 1964. The organization for research and propagation of history is the Akhil Bharatiya Itihas Sankalan Yojana (ABISY, 1973). Vidya Bharati, founded in 1977, is the organization for educational services. Working on the issues of social justice and social harmony is the Samajik Samrasta Manch (1983). The organization for serving economically weaker sections of the society is Seva Bharati (1989). Vijnana Bharati (1991) is the organization for the propagation of science. Bharatiya Jan Sangh (1951–1977) and later the Bharatiya Janata Party (1980) are also considered part of the Sangh Parivar. There is no hierarchical structure, and each is independent in its own domain.

Sanghatan: Literally organization. In the context of Hindutva, the term refers to Hindus coming together and forming an organization in the spirit of unity, transcending and/or obliterating the divisions of caste, language, ethnicity, etc., among themselves without having to shed their diverse traditions. Sanghatan naturally tends more towards egalitarian relations among Hindus and hence in spirit and action opposed to caste system.

Sanghatanist: May refer to a person, organization or movement advocating organized Hindu unity. Usually members of Hindu Mahasabha, Arya Samaj and Rashtriya Swayamsevak Sangh were considered Sanghatanists. Dr Ambedkar considered the Sanghatanist movement essential but impossible without abolishing caste it could not function well.

Sarsanghachalak: The supreme guide of the organization—in this case the RSS. In the RSS the first Sarsanghachalak was Dr Hedgewar, its founder, and then 'Guruji' Madhav Sadashivrao Golwalkar (1906–1973) became the next Sarsanghachalak. He was followed by Madhukar Dattatreya Deoras (1915–1996), Dr Rajendra Singh Tomar (1922–2003), Kuppahalli Sitaramayya Sudarshan (1931–2012) and now Dr Mohan Bhagwat.

Sarva Praharanayuddh: This is the thousandth name in Vishnu Sahasranama the hymn list of the thousand names of Vishnu the Divine, who sustains all existence. It means the one who is adorned with all the tools or weapons. The context in which this name was used by Shivaram Rajguru (1908–1931), the revolutionary of Indian independence, was to justify armed resurrection against British colonial rule. He belonged to the Hindustan Socialist Republican Association. Rajguru along with Bhagat Singh and Sukhdev was executed by the British on 23 March 1931.

Shakha: Literally branch. In the RSS universe, a *shakha* is the basic functional unit, which is the gathering of the local volunteers in a public space where they perform drills, play indigenous games, sing patriotic songs and then enact the national prayer 'Prarthana'.

Soma: A ritual Vedic drink that is also a Vedic deity. It can also refer to the ritual. Soma ritual is considered the central ritual of Vedic religion and culture. According to epigraphist and Harappan-Vedic scholar Iravatham Mahadevan (1930–2018), who was also a Dravidianist scholar, the Harappan society also performed the Soma ritual. He associates the 'cult object' before the famous unicorn seal in Harappan civilization with the Soma ritual.

Swayamsevak: Service volunteer. Member of the Rashtriya Swayamsevak Sangh (RSS), or the Organisation of National Service Volunteers—a *Hindu* sanghatan movement started in 1925 by Dr Keshav Baliram Hedgewar (1889–1940). The RSS is also simply known as the Sangh.

Symbiosis: More than one unrelated organisms coming together and entering into a relationship in which energy and/or nutrients and/or living space are shared or circulated in such a way that one or more than one or all the organisms get benefitted. Symbionts are such organisms which are in relationship.

Theo-diversity: Coined by Buddhist scholar Dr Lokesh Chandra in his paper 'Theo-diversity and Humane Values' (2001), this term is defined as 'the fuzzy wisdom of nature, the light of the Many, and to image the sacrament that enshrines the Multiple'. Theo-diversity is for the spiritual environmental health as important as biodiversity is for the health of the biological ecosystems. According to Prof. Chandra, theo-diversity is essential for human emancipation from what he calls 'the disembodiment of the human at the altar of monocentric theism'.

Thiṇai: An ancient Tamizh literary tradition of the division of land into five biocultural zones. Kurinchi is the hill and forest-related landscape and community, with Murugan (Skanda) as its presiding deity; Mullai is the grazing land and its community of herdsmen with Mayon (Vishnu) as the deity; Marutham contains the farmland and farm-based communities, with Indra as the deity; Neithal is the sea scape, with the coastal community engaged in fishing and pearl harvesting and Varuna as their deity; Palai is the desertified Kurunchi and Mullai, with people engaged in robbery, and Kottravai (Durga) as the deity.

Thirumanthiram: Literally 'auspicious mantra'. A Tamizh Saivaite sacred text assigned to fifth century CE by scholarly consensus. It is a compendium of almost all the Yogic and Tantric traditions presented in a Saivaite framework. Its authorship is attributed to Thirumoolar—a divine saint who is said to have entered the body of a dead cowherd to alleviate the pain of the cows and calves who grieved surrounding his dead body. It forms the tenth section (tenth Thirumurai) of the sacred scriptures of *Siddhanta Saivism*.

Wajib: Arabic term meaning religious obligation or duty. It is an Islamic term which means that a particular deed must be done by the adherents of the faith.

Index

A

Aadhar card, 448
Aadhi, 534
Aandal, 204–205
Aandal Thirumozhi in Tamizh, 157
Abandonment, 235, 507, 572
Abdali, Ahmed Shah, 115, 538
Abducted women, rehabilitation of, 241–245
Abduction of women, 199, 235, 238–239, 241–246
Abdul Kadir Badayuni, 515
Abdullah, Farooq, 314–315
Abhaya Hasta, 605
Abhinash Behera, 336
Abhishiktananda, 578, 580, 607, 631
Abhyankar, D. G., 187
ābhyantarika sārabattā, 21
Abhyudaya, 41
Abiding principle, 349
Abolition, 121, 127, 146, 170, 184–185, 196, 341, 521
Absolute Unitary Being, 39
Abubacker, E., 565–566
Abu Tahir, Syyed, 551
Abuthahir, Syed, 571
ABVP. *see* Akhil Bharatiya Vidyarthi Parishad
Academia, 1, 35, 46, 70, 109, 144, 189, 212, 235, 261–262, 322, 380, 438–439, 460, 484, 496, 537, 543, 624, 628, 716
  humanities, 629
  international, 162
Academicians, 1, 22, 235, 440, 488, 549, 714
Academics, 146–147, 243, 249, 331, 334–335, 338, 373, 417
  left-wing, 318
  modern, 389
Academic Staff College, 163
Achara Kovai, 533
Achara Paddhathi (Protocols for Ritual Purity) (book), 362
Acharyakul Arsh Kanya Gurukul, 200
Acharyas, 176, 206, 239, 257–258, 336, 348–349, 363, 428
Achuthanandan, V. S., 566
Activisms, 205, 347, 389
  green, 387
  social, 369
Activists, 147, 293, 411, 572. *see also* Hindu activists
  animal welfare, 111
  catholic, 598
  environmental, 455
  human rights, 565, 567
  social, 375, 614
Adani, Gautam, 609
Adhikari, G., 81
Adi Brahma Samaj, 85–86
Adigal, llango, 51–52, 101, 204
Adigal, Maraimalai, 72, 201, 203–204
Adi Granth, 494, 543
Adisesha, 63
Aditi, 12, 113
Admiration, 48, 178, 190, 194, 225, 252, 264–265, 270, 395
Adoration, 82, 273, 325, 395, 589, 592
  contemplative, 471
  highest sacred, 365
Adultery, 343
Advaita, 143, 176, 322, 531, 537, 578, 580, 582, 584–585, 587
  Christian, 582, 607
  monistic, 607

qualified visishta, 585
Advaita Vedanta, 319, 430, 523
Advaita Vedantism, 523
Advaitic
basis of equality, 353
experience, 580, 583–584, 586–587, 602–603
humanism of Swami Vivekananda, 335
Advani, Lal Krishna, 315, 376, 493, 511, 559
Adventure, 53, 625, 632
Afak, Abu, 547
Affective dyad, formation of, 635
Afghanistan, 90, 96–98, 274, 282–284, 286–287, 514, 720
Afghan jihad, 97, 564
Africa, 61, 152, 154, 283, 341, 515
African Regional Industrial Property Organization, 438
Aga Khan Palace, 224
Agambagish, Krishnanada, 49
Agarwal, V. S., 397
Agastya, 64, 157
Agehananda Bharati, 190
Aggarwal, Ranjana, 459
Aggi Sutta, 482
Aggressions, 62, 64, 67, 95, 189, 218, 280, 294, 324, 331, 351, 395, 396, 624, 625, 626, 630, 720
civilizational, 67
legitimizing wanton imperialist, 625
religious, 17
Aghnya, 113, 137
Agitations, 136, 170, 306, 309, 312–313, 354, 389, 451
Agni, 55, 114, 137, 481
Agni astra, 421
Agnihotra, 482, 713
Agni missile development, 448
Agra, 167, 325
Agrarian-matriarchal conglomerate, 152–153
Agrarian Reforms Committee of Indian National Congress, 125
Agrawala, Prithvi K., 62
Agrawal, D. P., 69
Agreements, 117, 160, 205, 392, 437
Agriculture, 3, 7, 114, 124, 153–154, 367–368, 402, 446, 458
Agroecosystem, 124
Agwani, Mohammed Shafi, 547
Aham Brahma Asmi, 352, 513, 545, 606
Ahavaniya, 482, 713
Ahilya Bai, 442
Ahir-SC inter-community conflict, 338
A History of Hindu Chemistry, 419
Ahmad, Sheikh Shahabuddin Bin, 520
Ahmedabad, 36, 150, 178, 278, 565
Ahmedabad serial bomb blasts, 565
Ahmed, Ghulam, 570
Ahmed, H. Sayed Nizar, 560
Ahmed, Qazi Hussain, 95
Ahmed, Sayed Nizar H., 560
Ahura Mazda, god, 11–12, 14
AIADMK. *see* All India Anna Dravida Munnetra Kazhagam
AIBEA (All India Bank Employees Association), 389
AICC, 193
AIDWA. *see* All India Democratic Women's Association
AIDWA (All India Democratic Women's Association), 361
AIJC. *see* All India Jihad Council
AIJC (All India Jihad Council), 552–553
Aitareya Brahmana, 58, 419
AIUDF. *see* All India United Democratic Front
AIUDF (All India United Democratic Front), 568–569
Aiyar, Mani Shankar, 212
Aiyar, V. V. S., 217, 222–224
Ajanta cave paintings and Nalanda University, 474
Ajanta Caves, 16
Ajivikas, 482–483, 713
Ajivikism, 4
Ajmal, Badruddin, 568
Akali Dal, 489–491
Akbar, 122, 379, 475, 514–517, 516, 545
biography, 515
brand of religious tolerance, 515
and Dara Shukoh, 511

death, 516
mind, 515
sacking, 514
Akbar, Mughal Emperor, 115, 514
Akbarnama, 516
Akbar Nama, 475
Akhandananda, Swami, 307, 329–330
Akhand Bharat, 46, 78, 89–90, 92–94, 96, 100, 323
Afghanistan as Gandhara, 96–98
as expansionist fantasy, 89–90, 100
image of, 46, 89
Modi and SAARC, 98–100
Mukherjee and Upadhyaya on, 90–93
vision of, 90, 96, 100
vs. pan-Islamic radicalism, 94–96
Akhand Hindustan, 312
Akhil Bharata Desiya Physical Improvement College, 536
Akhil Bharatiya Itihas Sankalan Yojana, 725
Akhil Bharatiya Sanatana Dal, 127
Akhil Bharatiya Vidyarthi Parishad, 301, 360, 555, 725
Akhil Hindu Nama Saptah, 247
Akhil Hindu Tilgul247
Akhil Hindu Yagna, 247
Akhlaq, Mohammad, 109
Alam, Junaid, 316
Ala-ud-din, 724
Alauddin Khilji, 519
Alberuni, 478
Alexander, 234
Alfassa, Mirra, 91, 501, 509
Ali, Aruna Asaf, 309
Aligarh Muslim University, 378, 433, 541, 546
Ali, Hyder, 552
Alipore Bomb, 74
Ali, Salim, 132
Ali, S. Hyder, 560
Allah, 285, 476, 486–488, 522–524, 530–531, 547, 574, 717, 720–721
Allahabad, 125
Allahbadi, Muhibbullah, 521
Allahu Akbar (terror plot code), 555
Allamadevar, 533
Allammadevar, 533
Allauddin Khilji, 236, 240, 515, 545
Alliance, 97, 287, 358–359, 560, 618
anti-Hindu ideological, 157
anti-Hindutva, 358
electoral, 489, 557, 559
extra-territorial, 274
Indic, 197
partner, 157
tactical, 556
All India Anna Dravida Munnetra Kazhagam, 553–558, 560, 571
allergy towards Hindu organizations, 553
electoral alliance with BJP, 557
green signal to Islamist forces, 560–561
tactical alliance with TMMK, 556, 560
tentative steps to curb jihadist terror, 554
All-India Arya Pratinidhi Sabha, 200
All India Catholic University Federation, 609
All-India Congress Committee, 311
All India Democratic Women's Association, 361
All India Hindu Mahasabha, 187, 485
All India Hindu Sabha, 169
All India Jihad Council, 552–553
All India Physical Fitness Improvement Conference, 536
All-India Students' Conference, 389
All India Ulama and Mashaikh Board, 572
All India United Democratic Front, 568–569
All Party Cow Protection Committee, 127
Alpert, Richard, 499
Altaf (Kashmiri terrorist), 565
Altar, 66, 256, 322, 350, 472, 482, 494, 591, 713, 726
alt Movement, 414
Al-Ummah, 552–556, 559
Amaladas, Brahmachari, 606

Amarakosha, 474
Amarasimha, 474
Amar Chitra Katha, 440
Amarnath, 27, 69
Ambaka, 600
Ambani, Mukesh, 609
Ambassadors, 93, 95, 283, 509
Ambedkar, Bhimrao Ramji, 30, 31, 45, 121, 124, 146, 167, 173, 175, 179–182, 186–187, 189, 195–197, 208, 216, 219–220, 224–225, 227, 257–258, 266, 300–301, 311–313, 318, 334, 341, 346–347, 349, 352–353, 357–358, 360, 364–365, 375, 384, 393, 407, 420, 440, 488, 610, 657, 725
  article on caste system, 182–183
  criticism of Gandhi, 224
  critique of caste by, 420
  definition of Hindutva, 29–33
  election agent, 347
  letter, 183
  Mahad Satyagraha of, 180–181
  at Makar Sankranti function of RSS, 300–301
  and Sri Aurobindo, 30
  and Sri Guruji, 361
  and Swami Vivekananda, 353
  on varna system, 181–182
  view of Indian history, 225–226
  views on cow protection, 124
Ambedkarite literature, 352–353
Ambedkarites, 175, 352–353
American diet, 141
American Teilhard Association, 637
Amethi, 287
Ammaiyar, Karaikal, 104
Ammakkadevi, 533
Amma, Lakshmikutty, 457
Ammal, Janaki, 459–460
Ammayaar, Karaikal, 87, 533
Ammunition, 232, 282, 412, 510, 564, 566, 576, 613
Amos, 271
Amrita Bazar Patrika, 281
Amritsar, 309, 488, 490–491, 515, 653, 721
Amritsar massacre, 129
Amritsar Medical College, 491
AMU. *see* Aligarh Muslim University
Ana'al-Haqq, 522
Anal Huq (Aham Brahma Asmi), 545
Ananda Bazar area, 613
Anandamath (novel), 72, 74, 261
Anand, Arun, 351
Anand, Javed, 436
Anand, S., 430–431, 551
Ananthamurthy, U. R., 220
Anantnag riots, 540
Anbukarasu, Swami, 356
Ancient Aliens documentary series, 421
Ancient Aryan "Varnadharma," 170
Ancient Buddhism, 470
Ancient Christian art, 597
Ancient Christianity, 13, 603
Ancient civilizations, 15, 438, 714, 717
Ancient Hindu, 96, 124, 421, 460, 481, 720
  civilization, 412
  Nation, 310
  scriptures, 38
  traditions, 461
  tribes, 720
Ancient India, 7, 41, 47–48, 136, 385, 420, 431–432, 458, 464, 477–479, 483
Ancient Indian, 7, 147, 373
  Catholics, 651
  history, 17, 473–474, 483
  medical texts, 434
  traditions, 606
Ancient Indian art, 62
Ancient Iranians, 11
Ancient Sankhya Darshan, 264
Andaman and Nicobar Islands, 147, 179, 212, 220, 246, 249–251
Andamans jail, 216, 250, 258
Andersen and Damle, 318–323, 371
Andersen, Walter K., 318
Anderson, Warren, 325–326
Andhra cyclone, 323
Andhra Pradesh, 18, 323, 376, 534
Andrews, Charles, 250

Andromeda, 609
Aneja, Ganesh Das, 200–201
Angirasa, Rishi, 71
Anglo-Indian journalists, 278
Anglo-India press, 86
Angra Mainyu, 11
Animism, 627
Aniruddha, 472
Annihilation, 19–20, 293, 364, 413, 475, 477, 479, 512
Ansari, Maulana Iftikhar, 540
Ansari, Ziaur Rahman, 541
Anthem, 47, 84–85, 103
Anti-Brahminism, 164, 610
Anti-Buddhist, 479
  policy, 483
  reputation, 483
Anti-caste movements, 166, 339
Anti-cow slaughter movement, 128, 138
Anti-Dalit Brahminical reactionary movement, 120
Anti-democratic totalitarian supremacist ideological straitjacket, 382
Anti-Hindu, 110, 140, 243, 300, 307, 381, 514, 553, 610
  academics, 138
  attitudes, 243
  bias, 439
  fables, 494
  ideologues, 430
  laws, 514
  polemicists, 342
  propaganda, 439, 622
  rhetoric, 501
  riots, 503
Anti-Hindutva, 140, 152, 246, 339, 360, 458, 485, 498
  forces, 433, 436, 473, 552
  ideologues, 417
  proponents, 498
Anti Hindutvaites, 458
Anti-Hindutva UPA government, 360
Anti-Muslim, 74, 113, 135, 189, 292, 323, 399, 470, 550
Antiscience, 410–411, 457, 465
Anti-Semitism, 141, 153, 270, 495, 505, 610, 713
Anuseelan Samiti, 307
Anwar-al-Sadat government, 510
Anyayogavyavacchedadvatrimsika (text), 472
Apartheid regime, 158–159, 219, 529
A Passage to Infinity (book), 428
Aponaptriya, 58
Apophaticism, radical, 641
Appa, Chimaji, 240
Appeasement, 169, 179, 219, 224, 293, 396, 504, 554–555
Apte, Babasaheb, 309
Apte, Vinayak Mahadev, 724
Arab excesses, 504
Arabia, 57, 286, 544, 571, 713
Arabic supremacism and Maoism Han-racism, 255
Arab League, 510
Arab resistance, 504
Arab violence on Jews, 504
Arab world, in Nehruvian discourse, 510
Archaeological Survey of India, 397, 550
Archaeologists, 7, 15, 62, 69, 103, 114, 397, 549–550, 690
Archaeology, 3–4, 435
Archons, 13
Ardhanarishwara, 62, 86
Aristotelian philosophy, 472
Arjikiya, 59
Arjuna, 61, 341, 536, 575, 636
Arogya Bharati, 443–444
Arta (god), 12
Arthasastra, 137
Arts, 33, 63–64, 414–415, 417, 420–421, 423, 438, 444, 515, 607, 632, 638–639
  calendar, 55, 532
  liberal, 422
Arunachala, 581–583, 585, 598–599
Arupadai Veedu (temple), 500
Arupa-Dvaita, 537
Arvidsson, Stefan, 153
Arya, 156, 168, 200, 489
Aryabhatta, 419, 428–429, 460
Aryabhisaka, 434
Arya Bhoomi, 157–158
Arya Dharma, 32

Arya Kanya Gurukul, 200
Arya Marriage Validation Act, 179, 713
Aryan
  appropriation of non-Aryan genius, 157
  blood, 147–148, 150
  brahminical imposition, 610
  Brahmins, 603, 610
  heritage, 157, 189
  Hinduism, 604
  and Hindutva, 151–156
  home theory, 154
  invasion/migration theory, 30, 56, 114, 151, 154, 155–156
  invasions, 152, 156
  land, 158
  Nazi championship of Hinduism, 189
  race, 25, 30, 33, 148–149, 155, 163, 191, 284
  race theory, 152, 155, 163–165, 225, 254, 604
Aryan-Dravidian race theory, 201, 604
Aryan-non-Aryan theory, 24
Aryapaksha system, 429
Arya Rani, 157
Arya Samaj, 31, 37, 166, 170–171, 197, 250, 253, 255–256, 258–259, 278–282, 356, 488–489, 713
  circles, 171
  connection, 171
  and Hindu Mahasabha, 172
  influence, 175
  and Rashtriya Swayamsevak Sangh, 725
  stream, 167, 197
Arya Samajists, 30, 121, 175, 255, 258–259, 263, 278, 280, 293, 319, 364, 525
Arya Somaj, 166
Arya Somajists, 166
Aryavarta, 522
Asceticism, 4
Ascetics, 5, 7, 261, 262, 270, 483
Aseemanand, Swami, 333
Ashoka Chakra, 313
Ashoka, King, 270, 482–483
Ashokan rock edict, 724
Ashokavadhana, 482–483
Ashraf, Ajaz, 240
Ashtanga Sangraha, 114
Asia, 271, 283–284, 515. *see also* South Asian countries
Asian Games, 490
Asiatic Land Tenure Act, 158
Asiatic Land Tenure and Indian Representation Act, 162, 723
Asiatic lions, 133
Asiatics, 158, 219
Asimov, Isaac, 299
Asma, poetess, 547
Aspirations, 503, 583
Assam, 199, 231, 389, 475, 568–569, 571, 575
Assassination, 77, 81, 84, 94, 171, 179, 197, 200, 217, 222, 303, 491–493, 510, 644
Assisi, Francis, 606
Asthi, 481
Astrobiology, 460–461
Astrochemistry, 460
Astrology, 431–432, 434, 439, 723
Astronomy, 427–429, 431
Asvini Devas, 118
Asylum, 156, 309, 505
Atharva Veda, 7, 41, 53–54, 56, 113–114
Atheist, 152, 202, 271, 293, 351, 498, 573, 601, 642, 718
Atlantic Charter, 218
Atma, 28
Atmabodha, 239
Atmabodha, Swami, 239
Atman, 5, 39, 177, 388, 592
Atmanirbhar Bharat, 462
Atrocities, 117, 240, 251, 254, 283, 316, 355, 363, 479, 515, 564, 613
Attila, 480
AUB. *see* Absolute Unitary Being
Augustine, 584, 607, 629, 636
Auliya, Nizamuddin, 518
Auliya, Nizamuddin Auliya, 519, 520, 572
Aum, 114, 589, 606
Aurangzeb, 65, 115, 250, 378–379, 396,

475, 497, 499, 515, 519–520, 523, 525–528, 545, 576
Aurangzeb Road, renaming, 525
Aurobdino, Sri, 6, 24–27, 35, 37, 47, 71, 73–76, 74, 90–91, 164–165, 338, 377, 397, 403, 501, 509–510, 541, 623, 634–635, 724
and Gandhi influence on Hindutva, 27
influence on Hindutva, 27–29
and Ram Swarup, 44
spiritual collaborator of, 91, 509
time and Sri Aurobindo, 74
Aurora, Jagjit Singh, 490, 491, 493
Auschwitz, 599
Australia, 341, 455
Authentic Hindu search, 578, 581
Authenticity, 638
Authorised Signatories of Coimbatore Muslim Relief Fund, 560
Authoritarian, 317–318, 323
Authoritarianism, 82–83, 145
Authorities, 22–23, 65–66, 82, 88, 134, 153, 184, 189, 204, 213, 215–216, 229, 246, 251, 258, 278, 309, 318, 331, 334, 347, 361, 368, 381, 386, 420–421, 429, 462, 472, 475, 481, 502, 520, 609, 641
birth-based, 362, 534
clerical, 14
colonial, 74, 188
political, 28
religious, 360, 717
scriptural, 22, 25–26, 197, 429
theological/ideological, 717
Avatar, 20, 26, 52, 105, 190–191, 588, 604, 620
Avatarhood, 190–191
Avestan language, 11
Avoda Zara, 495–496
Avvai Kural, 533
Avvaiyaar, the saint poetess, 533
Axial age, 4–7, 12, 714
definition of, 4, 714
developments, indic integration of, 6–9
problem, 6
transition of, 12
Axiomatic inequality, 34, 36
Axis Munda, 53
Ayengar, Indira, 326
Ayodhya, 358, 379, 473, 511, 525, 541, 549–550
Ayodhya Sri Ram Janmabhoomi Movement, 130, 358, 383, 399, 648
as anti-Muslim movement, 399
demolition of domes, 358
intellectual build-up and preparation to, 399
massacre of volunteers, 316
Rath yatra launch, 315
and RSS Samanvaya, 537–551
Ayres, Alyssa, 454
Ayurgenomics, 440
Ayurveda, 431–432, 437–438, 722
Ayyankali, Mahatma, 87
Azad, Chandrasekar, 303, 304
Azad, Ghulam Nabi, 115, 212
Azad Hind Government, 79, 84
Azad Hind Radio, 220, 227
Azad, Maulana Abul Kalam, 171, 306, 311
Azam Educational Trust, 576
Aziz, Abdul, 569

B

Babajan, Hazrat, 532
Babri structure, 396, 541, 549
Babu, Shashi, 262
Backward Caste (BC), 189, 337, 355, 426
Badauni, 515
Badayuni, Abdul Qadir, 516, 517
Badrinath, 69
Badsha, 552, 554, 559
Bagal, Madhavrao, 247
Bagul, Gangadhar, 300
Bahadur, Guru Tegh, 250, 252, 316, 475, 488
Bahishkrit Bharat, 175
Bahmani Kingdom, 513
Bahujan Samaj Party, 109, 112, 358–359
Bahulkar, Rahul, 464

Baig, Himayat, 567
Bail, 322, 558, 560, 565, 570
Bai, Manbhawati, 517
Bai, Mira, 442
Bai, Yamuna, 246–247
Bajaj, Jamnalal, 193
Bajaj, Jitendra, 332
Bajrang Dal, 615, 617, 629
Bakht, Sikander, 553
Bakker, Hans, 479
Bakshi, Sachindra, 574
Balachadi, 508
Baladitya, 17, 474, 480
Balakrishnan, Kodiyeri, 565
Bala Saheb Gurdwara, 493
Balfour declaration, 505
Balkanization of India, 81, 287
Balmukund, Bhai, 250
Bal Shishu Gopal Griha (children's home), 324
Bamiyan Buddha, 609
Ban/banning, 115, 122, 125–126, 129, 132, 134, 208, 245, 298, 301, 308, 357, 441, 556, 561, 567, 641, 647
Banabasi Kalyan Ashram, 616
Bande Mataram cry, 47, 54, 56, 71, 75, 84–85, 274
Bande Mataram magazine, 164, 377
Bandicoot, 461
Banerjee, R. N., 162, 481
Banerjee, Shashipada, 262
Banerjee, Sikata, 261
Bangalore
  bomb blasts, 559–560, 568, 571
  radical Islamist activities in, 562–564
Bangladesh, 90, 93–96, 98, 112, 192, 491, 568
  border, cattle smuggling across, 112–113
  India's exports to, 94
  infiltrators attack on Bodos, 568
  liberation and abducted Hindu women, 243
  terror attack in, 111
'Bangladesh, Bhutan, India and Nepal,' 98
Bangladesh Working Paper (paper), 94
Banu, Rahima, 500
Baptist Church, 611–613
Barbarism, 47, 226, 299
Baroda College, 71
Barot, Ranjit, 76
Bartholomew, Pablo, 327
Basava, 37
Basaveshwara, 346
Basham, A. L., 713
Basheer, Shamnad, 437, 563
Basmati patents, 438
Bass, Garry, 510
Bassuk, Daniel E., 620
Basu, Chandramohan, 21
Basu, Rajnarayan, 21, 42
Batcha, Syed Ahmed, 553
Baucker, S. M., 570
Baumard, Nicolas, 4, 7
Baxter, Craig, 376
Bayazid, Shaikh, 545
BBIN. *see* 'Bangladesh, Bhutan, India and Nepal'
BBINAM framework, 98
Bede, Fr, 598
Bede Griffiths Sangha Newsletter, 594, 598
Bede Griffiths Trust, 581, 599, 603–604, 607
Bedi, Kiran, 433
Beef, 108–111, 113, 115–117, 119–121, 123, 125, 127, 129, 131, 133, 135–137, 139–141, 143, 557, 714
  consumption, 113, 116, 135, 137, 138
  eating festivals, 110, 140
  exporters, 141
  Indian *vs.* international, 138–139
  politics of, 109, 139
  taboo, 138–139, 141
Beef-ranching, 139
Beg, Moazziz Ali, 541, 546
Behera, Abhinash, 336
Behera, Navnita Chadha, 540
Behistun inscription, 12
Belief, 17, 19, 23, 26, 31, 34, 131, 147, 149, 153–154, 174, 176, 190–

191, 254–255, 293, 343, 346, 352, 429, 475, 494, 518, 572, 583, 623, 625, 715, 717, 723
Belur, 485
Belur Chenna Kesava temple, 717
Benedictine monastery, 578
Benedictine Sisters of Perpetual Adoration, 598
Benedict, Saint, 578
Bengal, 103, 185, 192, 231, 241, 265, 389
  Hindu-Muslim riots, 75
  holocaust of 1971, 234
  partition, 47
  population, 718
  revolutionary movement, 47, 49
  Swami Satyananda in, 190
Bengal Hindu Mahasabha, 185, 187
Bengali literature, 48, 75, 545
Bengali Muslim women, systematic abduction and rape of, 243
Bengali renaissance, 21
Bengali revolutionaries, 74, 77, 307
Bengal Medical Mission, 50
Berkeley Political Review, 261
Berry, Thomas, 637–638, 642
Berthelot, Marcellin, 419
Besant, Annie, 148–149, 174, 376
Beveridge, E. J., 309
Bhadrachalam Rama temple, 205
Bhagalpur, 219
Bhaganagar Satyagraha, 306
Bhagavad Gita, 42, 77, 254, 258, 341, 485, 487, 533, 588, 590–592, 625, 632, 635–636, 645
Bhagawa flag, 310–312
Bhagwa dhwaj. *see* Bhagawa flag
Bhagwan Nama Gaumuthi, 239
Bhagwat, B. N., 187, 324, 326, 361
Bhagwat, Mohan, 321, 324, 360–361, 442, 725
Bhairagi, Lal, 521
Bhaiyaji, 375
Bhakti, 37, 71, 329, 394–395, 494, 519, 541–542, 544, 589, 620
  in Buddhist tradition, 395
  cult, 37
  egalitarianism, 35
  movement, 331, 395, 396, 399, 519
  traditions, 395
Bhansali, Sanjay Leela, 234
Bhan, Suraj, 359–360
Bharadwaj, ancient sage, 412
Bharanaiah, R., 348
Bharat, 27, 30, 47, 54, 71, 77, 81–82, 92, 130, 353, 357, 360, 396. *see also* Akhand Bharat; Bharat Mata
Bharata Bhagya Vidhata, 86
Bharata Bharati book series, 574–575
Bharata Lakshmi, 62
Bharata Natya Sastra, 64
Bharat Bala, 76
Bharat Bhumi, 30
Bharat Biotech and ICMR, 463
Bharatheeya Vichara Kendram, 649
Bharathi, Subramania, 73, 76, 79, 157–158
Bharati, 30, 56–57, 59, 610
Bharati Santati, 30
Bharati, Shuddhananda, 201, 202
Bharati, Subramaniya, 105, 367
Bharatiya, 36, 82, 322, 388
Bharatiya culture, 388, 444, 646
Bharatiya Itihasa Sankalana Samiti, 155–156
Bharatiya Janata Party *see* BJP
Bharatiya Jan Sangh, 78, 90–91, 93, 122, 322, 376, 380, 389, 446, 489, 719–720, 725
Bharatiya Kisan Sangh, 391, 393
Bharatiya Mazdoor Sangh, 301, 347, 390–393, 717, 725
Bharatiya model, 388
Bharatiyata, 648
Bharat Mata, 222
  calendar art, 87
  image of, 49, 54
  M. F. Hussain and, 82–83
  Nehru, Nehruvians and, 79–82
  secular exorcism of, 83–87
  temples, 77–79
  tribal, 87
  Vande Mataram, 70, 100
  vedic roots of, 53–56
Bharat Mata ki Jai, 47, 79–80

Bharat Sadhu Samaj, 128
Bharatvarsha/Hindustan, 36
Bhardvaja, Sage, 137
Bhardwaj, Ashutosh, 443
Bhargava, Gopi Chand, 277
Bharoto bhaggo bidhata, identity of, 86
Bhartiya Hindu Shuddhi Sabha, 170
Bhartiya Mazdoor Sangh, 301, 347, 390–393
Bhartiya Shuddhi Sabha, 171
Bhatnagar, Arun, 314
Bhattacharjee, Malini, 331, 334, 337
Bhattacharji, Sukumari, 55, 56
Bhattacharya, Sabyasachi, 74, 85
Bhatt, Chetan, 145–146, 148, 149, 381–383, 382
Bhatty, Zarina, 81
Bhavani, deity, 50, 51, 65–66, 102, 714
Bhavani Mandir, 77
Bhavani worship, 51
Bhave, Vinoba, 400, 593
Bhide, Laxman Rao, 374
Bhikshu Sukta, 332
Bhindranwale, 489–490
Bhishikar, C. P., 349–350
Bhoja, king, 486
Bhoja Prabandhu, 486
Bhoomi sukta, 53–54
Bhoopati, 244
Bhopal gas tragedy, 301, 325–328
Bible, 2, 475, 485, 496, 592, 600, 625, 636, 641
Bicameral mind, 2–3, 5, 6–7, 9, 10, 11, 13, 14, 714
Bigotry, 13, 252, 254, 288, 527, 626
Bihar, 111, 112, 125, 156, 219, 321, 326, 358, 363, 549, 571
Bihar Act, 126
Bihari, Ahmed, 520
Bijapur, 65, 513
Bills, 31, 159, 162, 177–179, 185–186, 558, 713
Binanipuram, 562–563
Binaries, 12, 24, 40, 85, 114, 152, 322, 339, 401–402, 447, 465, 471, 481, 483, 511, 604, 645, 722
Bin Laden, Osama, 97
Biodiversity, 89, 450, 636, 726
Biogas plants, 125, 135, 139, 714, 718
Biology, 145, 269, 373, 723. *see also* Astrobiology
  evolutionary, 147
  modern, 472
Bionationalism, 440, 443, 714, 715
Biosciences, 460
Biotechnic order, 321, 451, 715
Biotechnology, 435, 463
Bipan Chandra Memorial Lecture, 48
Birla, Ghanshyam Das, 172
Birla Mandir, 77
Birth-based discriminations, 339, 362
Bismil, Ram Prasad, 575
Bison, sacred, 116–117, 120–121, 714
BJP, 48, 78, 90, 99–100, 108, 156, 315–316, 320, 324, 359, 361, 364, 376, 380, 393, 402, 412, 442, 446–448, 451, 453, 460, 492, 494, 553, 555–557, 560, 568, 614, 617, 629, 719–720, 725
  government, 338, 361, 364, 393, 439, 451, 453, 549, 560, 609, 714
  led NDA, 436, 460, 613
  negative bias against, 412
  pro-technology narrative, 448
  Shiv Sena government, 433
BJS. *see* Bharatiya Jan Sangh
BKS. *see* Bharatiya Kisan Sangh
Black Madonna, 605
Black Shorts, 432
Blake, William, 424, 449, 636
Blasphemy, 127, 272, 513
Blood Telegram, 510
Bloomfield, Maurice, 8
Blyah river, 517
BMS. *see* Bhartiya Mazdoor Sangh
BNHS. *see* Bombay Natural History Society
Bodas, Mahadev Rajaram, 175
Bodhisattva doctrine, 266
Body-based poetry of Aandal, 204–205
Bohm, David, 596–597
Bole, Rao Bahadur Sitaram Keshav, 185–189
Bole, S. K., 185, 187–189, 311–312

Bolshevism, 191
Bombay, 119, 181, 188–189, 197–198, 218, 265, 280, 290, 312, 327, 380, 554, 597
Bombay Hindu Mahasabha, 175, 188
Bombay Legislative Council, 186, 188
Bombay Natural History Society, 130–133
Bombay Provincial Hindu Sabha, 312
Bomb blasts, 552, 555–556, 563
  Ahmedabad, 565
  Bangalore, 559–560
  Coimbatore, 551–556, 558–560, 565, 571
Boner, Alice, 397
Bonum, Summum, 270
Border Security Force, 112
Border Security Force (BSF), 112
Bose, Jagadish Chandra, 451, 467
Bose, J. C., 267–268
Bose, Nirmal Kumar, 344
Bose, Rash Behari, 218–220
Bose, Sarat Chandra, 225
Bose, Satyendranath, 205, 417, 467
Bose, Subhas Chandra, 21, 79, 84, 218–220, 227, 233, 267, 307, 417, 644, 645
Boudhik, 324
Boyer, Pascal, 4
Brahe, Tycho, 429
Brahma, 118, 352, 359, 415, 534, 604
Brahmachari, Mahanambrata, 636
Brahmachari, Prabhu Dutt, 127
Brahmacharya, 536
Brahmaism, 352
Brahman, 5, 12, 22, 34, 39–40, 61, 154, 166, 176–177, 186, 264, 330, 343, 429, 481, 486–487, 516, 522, 531, 534, 579
Brahmananda, Gurubhai, 262
Brahmananda, Swami, 476
Brahmanas, 8, 15, 164, 177, 256, 332, 482
Brahmanical sects, 478
Brahmanisation, 359
Brahmanism, 17, 34, 174, 258, 478, 481, 526
Brahmans of Mahad, 186
Brahmaputra, 60
Brahmasamaj, 30
Brahma Sangit, 85
Brahma Sutra, 477, 724
Brahminical, 34, 157, 430–431, 481
  Aryan Hinduism, 642
  base, 34
  communism, 358
  contribution, 604
  fire altar tumulus, 472
  gods, 603
  religions, 473, 479, 483
  supremacists, 432
Brahminical Bharat Mata, 87
Brahminical Goddess tradition, 87
Brahminical Hinduism, 369, 484
Brahminism, 33, 36, 182, 226, 257–258, 369, 395, 440, 470
Brahmins, 17, 117, 147, 152, 165, 180, 182, 185–186, 190, 193, 201, 339, 359, 362–363, 371–372, 420, 428, 431, 473, 475, 479, 482, 530, 535, 610, 657, 715
Brahmoism is Hinduism, 86
Brahmo movement, 85
Brahmo Samaj, 163, 281, 620–621
Brahmo-Samajist, 530
Brain, 2, 5, 39, 41, 80, 329, 433, 714, 718
Braliman, 487
Breaking India (book), 577
Breaking India forces, 81
Brethren, 168, 227, 248, 328, 354, 356, 413
Brhadaranyaka, 12
Brihatkatha, 474
Brihat Tantrasara, 49
Brilliant, Larry, 499–500
Brindaban, 258
Brister, Daniel, 117
Britain, 47, 116, 218, 231
Britannia, 46, 48
British, 19, 24, 49–51, 88, 115, 119–120, 122, 125, 138, 143, 157, 160, 163–164, 169, 173, 178, 189, 192, 203–204, 212, 214–216, 220–222, 224–225, 227–228, 232, 248, 250, 252, 260–261,

278–279, 281–282, 284, 286, 288, 291, 303, 305, 308–309, 316, 341, 366, 430, 476, 502–503, 505–508, 574, 593, 627, 721, 726
administration, 72, 75, 278, 293, 368
colonialism, 33, 75, 119, 476
colonization, 49, 278
construction of Hinduism, 19
courts, 177, 283
democratic value system, 369
government, 121–122, 160, 178, 188, 195, 205, 212, 219, 231, 263, 278, 283, 303, 650
hanged Bhai Balmukund, 250
Islamist communal forces and, 75
British Chitral, 283
British disparagement of Indian, 260–261
British East India Company, 20, 50
British Educational System, 265
British Empire, 214, 278, 303, 459
British Imperialism, 195, 398, 503
British-Indian army, 220
British Intelligence, 218, 222, 227, 308
British Labour Party, 380
British Origin of Cow-Slaughter in India (book)), 138
British rule, 34, 49, 113, 119, 223, 368–369, 488
Brookings Institution, 97
Brother Hindus, 75
Brotherhood, 318, 348, 356, 509
Brotherhood in Saffron, The (book), 318
Brown, Emily, 264, 275
Bruteau, Beatrice, 633
Bryant, Edwin, 155–156, 472
BSF. *see* Border Security Force
BSP. *see* Bahujan Samaj Party
Buddha, Bhagwan, 37, 42, 77, 152, 266, 276, 353, 395, 432, 472, 477, 480–482, 486–487, 500, 588, 591, 621, 625, 640, 645–646
Buddha Dharma, 32
Buddha, Gautama, 270
Buddhism, 4, 10, 16, 22, 25, 30, 37, 101, 197, 256, 266, 270, 275, 346, 353, 360, 395, 420, 430, 472, 474, 478–479, 481–483, 488, 521, 526, 589, 592, 596, 604, 631, 645, 650, 713
Zen, 637
Buddhist, 5, 22, 25, 31, 57, 68, 175, 350, 431–432, 464, 473, 478, 480–484, 486–487, 521, 586, 591, 597, 599, 606
doctrine of Pratityasamutpada, 472
hagiography of Ashoka, 482
iconography, 481
inclusivism, 482
literature, 482
monasteries, 479, 483
monks, 16–17, 219, 270, 363, 432, 474, 479
phenomenonalism, 472
stupas, 478, 481
texts, 481
traditsions, 395, 483, 646
Buffaloe, 53, 116–117, 126, 135, 139, 714
Buffalo Field Campaign, 117
Buffalo slaughter, 116–117
Buhari, Kichaan, 558
Bukka Raya, 18, 721
Bullocks, 119–120, 126
Bulls, 15, 114, 118, 120, 137, 479, 603
Bunch of Thoughts, 328, 339, 345–346
Bureaucracy, 173, 266, 314, 453, 615
Bureaucrats, 131, 417, 452
Butchers, 395–396
Butler, Harcourt, 166

C

Calamities, 269, 280, 301, 324–325, 328, 331, 333, 346
human-made, 331
natural, 7, 326
Calcutta, 84–85, 131, 193, 252, 324, 327, 444, 601, 620, 622
Calcutta Dhanna Mandali, 418
Calcutta Session Hindu Mahasabha, 187
Cama, Madam, 150, 227, 261, 263
Campaigns, 50, 66, 84, 99, 108, 126, 130, 189, 249, 280, 282, 358, 434, 436, 566, 568, 571, 623, 654

election, 393
fast-unto-death, 129
genocidal, 283
high voltage smear, 437
Campaign to Stop Funding Hate, 335
Campus Front of India. *see* CFI
Camus, Albert, 638
Canon Law, 651
Cape Comorin, 69, 471
Capitalism, 271–272, 402
crony, 327
monopoly, 647
robber, 153
Capitalist paradigm, 403
Capra, Fritjof, 415, 424, 597
Carcasses, 109, 112
Cargo cult
of colonized left, 430–432
pop socio-psychology, 430
Cargo cult Hindutva, 411, 413, 414, 417, 423, 426, 428, 430, 715
ancient flying machines and atomic weapons, 411–412
Aryabhatta's works and, 428–429
brigade, 427
C. K. Raju and, 427–428, 430
claims of discovery of gravity, 424–426
colours of prism, 424–425
cosmic dance of Siva, 414–417
criticism in Tamil Nadu, 416–417
fundamental ironic paradox of, 417
photomontage of, 415–416
Sagan's views on, 416
symbolism in, 416
traditional interpretation of, 414–415
critique of Newton's worldview, 423–424
cultural illiteracy ailment in, 426
firearms, knowledge of, 421
infinite series of Madhava, 428
Kanada-Newton linkage, 425–426
mantras codified "laws of motion," 425
memes, 411–412
Nataraja statue at CERN, 411, 413
scientific spirit of Nilakantha Somayaji, 429
vs. Hindutva scientific dialogue & duty, 423–430
yantra dedicated to Shani, 411
Carpenter, Edward, 449
Carpenter, Estlin, 646
Carson, Rachel, 386
Cartesian concept of mechanistic tolerance, 477
Cartographic surveying, 68
Casolari, Marzia, 194, 334
Caste-Elimination movement, 253
Caste Hindus, 166, 204–205, 365, 629
Casteism, 228, 350, 378
Caste(s), 23, 30, 33–34, 78, 124, 144–148, 153–154, 163, 165–166, 175, 177, 179–180, 182–186, 193, 200, 203, 207, 245, 247, 256–258, 278, 280, 293, 300, 319, 322, 333–334, 339, 341–342, 344–346, 348, 350–352, 359, 362–363, 371, 376, 382, 386, 420, 439–441, 457, 725
abolishing, 725
annihilation of, 364
arrogance, 165, 182
atrocities, 363
barriers, 179, 356
conflict, 182, 355
consciousness, 301
discrimination, 109, 164, 166, 203
dissentions, 355
divisions, 165, 182–183, 227, 725
essentializing claims of, 440
hegemony, 90, 163–164
identities, 109
landowning, 368
non-upper, 34
prejudices, 164, 178, 193
problems, 192, 366
pro-upper, 189
status, 163, 618
structure, 33
Caste system, 26, 29, 145–147, 154, 165, 179–180, 182–183, 256, 300,

339–342, 344, 346, 420, 725
acial interpretation of, 165, 440
birth-based, 31
supporters of, 300
Cataract, 194
Catholic activists of Shantivanam, 599
Catholic Ashrams, 587
Catholic Ashrams: Sannyasins or Swindlers? (book), 631
Catholic Bishop Council of India, 627–628
Catholic Church, 153, 198, 199, 442, 577, 599, 603, 624, 630, 636, 640–641
Catholic Hindu Mandir, 77
Catholicism, 636, 652
Catholic monk, 636–637
Cattle, 63, 109, 112, 114, 119, 125–126, 130, 132–134, 138, 168, 283, 452
diet, 134
population, 119–120, 125, 130, 133
slaughter of, 120, 125, 132
smuggling mafia, 111–113
unproductive, 133
Cave Temple of Elephanta, 597
CBCI. *see* Catholic Bishop Council of India
CBI. *see* Central Bureau of Investigation
CCRAS. *see* Central Council for Research in Ayurvedic Sciences
Ccult, 11, 114, 413, 424, 446, 607, 633, 715
CDF. *see* Congregation for the Doctrine of the Faith
CDM. *see* Clean Development Mechanism
Cellular Jail, 212–213, 249, 258, 260
Central Bureau of Investigation, 560, 617
Central Council for Research in Ayurvedic Sciences, 115
Central Hindu Yuvak Sabha of Lahore, 253
Central Institute for Medicinal and Aromatic Plants, 135
Central Intelligence Office, 187–188
Central Provinces, 179, 280
Centre for Excellence in Quantum Technology, 464
Centre for the Study of Developing Societies, 90
Centre for West Asian Studies, 502
CEQT. *see* Centre for Excellence in Quantum Technology
CERN, 411, 413, 414
CFI, 566–567
Chabahar port, developing, 98
Chagla, Muhammad Kareem, 93, 538
Chaitanya, 37, 542
Chakras, 41–42, 313
Chakravarty, Nikhil, 451
Chakravarty, Trailokyanath, 307
Chambhars, 180
Chand, Abi, 498
Chandala, 165, 176
Chand Bardai, 18
Chand, Feroz, 277
Chandi Charitra, 66
Chandika, 715
Chandogya Upanishad, 53, 386, 472, 482
Chandra, Lala Ram (Arya Samaj worker), 170
Chandra, Lokesh, 32, 726
Chandran, Raja, 96
Chaos, 52, 63, 86, 91, 128, 242, 288
Chapple, Christopher Key, 637
Chardin, Teilhard de, 417, 633–637, 635–637, 642, 648, 652
Chariot wheels, 86, 118, 142
Charisma, 303, 304, 529
Charity, 256, 271, 280–281, 324, 326–328, 332
Charkha, 313, 463
Charlesworth, 120
Charturvarna, 182
Chatterjee, Angana, 335–336
Chatterjee, Bankim Chandra, 19, 21, 26, 42, 47–48, 51, 54, 56, 68, 71, 73, 85, 103, 261, 417–418, 422, 428
Chatterjee, Nirmal Chandra, 187, 192
Chatterjee, Rajeshwari, 459
Chatterji, Souvik, 111
Chatur Varna, 181–182
Chaturvarnyashram, 300

Chaturvedi, Vinayak, 485
Chatushkoti, 464
Chauhan, Prithviraj, 480
Chaupal, Kameshwar, 358
Chekkutty, N. P., 566
Chenab, 544
Chettiar, Ramanathan, 202
Chetwood Committee, 195
Chhatrasal's movement, 396
Chidambaram, 63, 414, 581–582, 590, 598–599
Chidbhavananda, Swami, 322, 372, 406, 610
Chilapathikaram, 23, 51, 53, 57, 101, 117, 157, 716
Child Marriage Restraint Act, 196
Child marriages, 170, 185, 196–197, 208, 441
Chimur, 309–310
China, 16, 58, 152, 218, 425, 451, 464
Chinese translations of Yasogupta/ Jnanagupta and Yijing, 57
Chinmayananda, Swami, 347
Chintaman temple, 115
Chishti and Naqshbandi Sufi orders, 516
Chishti, Muinuddin, 516
Chishti order of Sufis, 543
Chisti, Anees, 325
Chiti, 381–382, 384–385
Chitod, Akbar's sacking of, 514
Chitpavan Brahmin Sangh, 247
Chitragupta, 216–217
Chitrakoot Gramodaya Vishwavidyalaya, 451
Chokha Mela, 165
Chola Bronzes, 416, 716
Chozha prince, excecution of, 142
Chozha traditions of cow protection, 117–118
Christendom, 270, 341, 616, 632
Christian Al-Qaeda, 611
Christian deity, 590–592, 595, 598, 607
Christian-Democratic movement, 384
Christian doctrine, 631, 642
Christiane Brosius of Ruprecht Karls University, 383
Christian evangelism, 262, 279, 613, 619
Christian faith, 581, 584, 641
Christian-Hindu, 610, 624
Christianity, 19–20, 34, 42, 74, 190, 198–199, 205, 273–275, 284, 324, 331, 352, 362, 388, 397, 410, 485, 528, 546, 620, 622–626, 628, 630–633, 635–636, 641, 643, 649–652, 715, 718
  approaches towards Hinduism
    appropriation through institutional inculturation, 577–608
    political proxy war, 608–611
    violent encounters, 611–619
  Hindutva responses to, 619–638
  Islam, 13, 179, 271, 462, 486, 495, 524, 644, 713
  Pauline, 626
  Western civilization, 262
Christianization, 577, 579–580, 598–600, 605–606, 608, 611
  Advaitic experience, 580
  Hinduism, 582, 603, 607
  India, 579
  Nataraja, 598
  yoga, 579
Christian mantra, 586
Christian mass, 583, 585, 599
Christian missionaries, 279–280, 336, 603, 615, 622, 624
Christian prayer, 598, 600, 606
Christian proselytization, 280, 351, 362, 596, 613, 615, 626
Christian religion, 583, 594, 633
Christian theologians, 39, 261, 580, 628, 631
Christian theology, 14, 472, 587, 620–621, 631, 640
Christian Trinitarian, 603
Christian Unio Mystica, 39
Christian Yoga, 579
Christ in India (book), 597
Christ, Jesus, 14, 38, 283, 476, 486–488, 580, 583–584, 586–592, 594, 597, 598, 602, 606, 608, 613, 616–617, 619–623, 625–626, 630, 636, 639, 641, 643, 649

Christmas, 221, 476, 586, 614
Christu Matha Chethanam (book), 362
Church, 14, 22, 205, 324, 326, 379, 427, 445, 528, 577–581, 584–587, 591, 594, 607–608, 610–612, 614–616, 626–630, 636, 638, 640, 642, 650–651
  Baptist, 611–613
  Christian, 271, 429, 587, 645
Churchill, Winston, 161, 196, 218, 508
CIA, 97, 564
CIMAP. *see* Central Institute for Medicinal and Aromatic Plants
CIO. *see* Central Intelligence Office
Civilization, 2–4, 6, 11, 16, 27, 29, 32, 33, 56, 115, 116, 154, 163, 192, 203, 217, 270–271, 284, 299, 387, 403, 449, 485, 546, 548, 579, 714
  civilizational process, 23–24, 330, 526, 719
  colonized, 370
  Indus valley, 398
  native, 393
  non-Western, 401
  post-bicameral, 11
  pre-Harappan, 398
  urban, 2
Clarion call, 77, 396, 613
Classes, 23, 33, 169, 227, 264, 272, 280, 336, 343, 372, 384, 417, 420, 457, 623
  agricultural, 185
  backward, 185, 312, 363
  depressed, 91, 167, 173, 183, 188, 193
  lower, 200–201
  middle, 221
  new middle, 34
  non-martial, 195
  untouchable, 177, 186
  upper, 262
Clavius, 427
Clean Development Mechanism, 140
Clean India mission, 372
Climate change, 131, 139, 387, 636
Climate politics, 455
Clooney, 495
Code of Gentoo Laws, A (verse), 421
Coimbatore, 551–556, 558–559, 571
Coimbatore bomb blasts, 551–556, 558–560, 565, 571
Coimbatore Central Prison, 557
Coimbatore Muslim Relief Fund, 560
Cold War, 462
Colebrooke's Essays, 419
Collaboration, 74, 136, 217, 463, 554
Collier, Alex, 609
Colonial historiography, 120
Colonialism, 19–20, 33, 75, 119, 187, 211, 263, 341, 384, 423, 476, 622, 647
Colonial period, 35, 68, 72, 82, 120, 488, 627
Colonial regime, 21, 119, 138, 146, 166, 227, 369, 422, 430
Colonies, 150, 301, 390, 422, 506–507
Command, 147, 159, 162, 167, 179–180, 303, 311, 502, 549, 567
Communalism, 125, 195, 378, 557, 645
Communalism Combat (tabloid), 436
Communal riots, 137, 240, 331, 351, 540
Communal violence and conversions, 92, 322, 612–615
Communion, 519, 586, 603
Communism, 125, 358, 400, 647
Communist Party of India, 74, 80, 361, 389
Communist Party of India Marxist, 374, 436, 494, 565, 567
Compassion, 156, 268, 328, 353, 533, 556, 572
Confederacy, 17, 480, 486
Confessions, 636
Confucianism, 637–638
Congregation for the Doctrine of the Faith, 641
Conscience, 62, 263, 281, 355, 379, 389, 609
Consciousness, 2–3, 6, 23, 39, 52, 57–59, 61, 155, 177, 226, 288, 400, 443, 601, 637, 639, 657, 714, 716
  collective, 61
  cosmic, 71
  human, 31

illuminated, 80
individual, 388, 714
national, 53–54, 65, 71, 82
political, 71
unitary, 44
universal, 25
Conservative ideology, 163, 337
Conspiracy, 157, 182, 236, 339, 559–560, 608
Constantine, 12, 14
Constantinople, 273, 379
Constituent Assembly of free India, 84, 91, 178, 202, 312–313
Constitution of India, 29, 649
Consumerism, 397
Controversies, 108, 138, 211, 213, 215, 217, 219, 221, 223, 225, 227, 229, 231, 233, 235, 237, 239, 241, 243, 245, 247, 249, 251, 253, 255, 257, 259, 261, 263, 265, 267, 269, 271, 273, 275, 277, 279, 281, 283, 285, 287, 289, 291, 293, 295, 297, 428, 549, 625, 641
beef-pork, 115
first beef, 109
national, 110
theological, 625
Conversions, 190, 198–199, 205, 213, 225, 234, 235, 237–238, 243–245, 280, 282, 303, 334, 345, 355–356, 365, 365–366, 369, 396, 495, 498, 500, 512, 516, 519, 535, 539, 552, 581, 612–618, 627–628, 631, 643, 649–651, 719
Convictions, 28, 54, 90, 191, 375, 515–516, 523, 524, 539, 621
Cook, Joseph, 620
Coomaraswamy, Ananda, 397, 414
Cooperation, 99–100, 252, 258, 392, 454, 482
Copernican and Darwinian revolutions, 2
Copernican theory, 419
Cornell, Vincent, 513
Coromandel, 60
Cosmic dance of Siva, 411, 414–416, 532, 716
criticism in Tamil Nadu, 416–417
fundamental ironic paradox of, 417
photomontage of, 415–416
Sagan's views on, 416
symbolism in, 416
traditional interpretation of, 414–415
Cosmic unity, 15, 20, 633
Cosmology, 266, 429
Cosmos, 68, 382, 414, 416, 425, 450, 546, 637
Cosmos (book), 416
Council of Scientific and Industrial Research, 115, 136, 435–436, 458–459
Counterterrorism, 511
Covaxin, 463
Covid-19 virus, 462, 463, 464
Cow
as source of greenhouse gases, 139
urine, 115, 135, 456, 722
veneration, 108, 113, 115–116, 119–122, 124
vigilantism, 109–111, 113
worship, 108–143
Cow-based products, Indic tradition of using, 114–115
Cow dung, 114, 125, 140, 714, 722
Cowherd, 52, 727
Cow products, 135, 456
Cow protection, 26, 111, 113, 119–121, 123–125, 127, 130, 135–136, 138, 140–143, 617
Ambedkar's views on, 124
forms, 119
Gandhi's views on, 123–124
holistic, 124, 136
in post-independent India, 124–130
Kumarappa's views, 125
Mohd. Hanif Quareshi case, 125–126
Munshi's views, 124–125
Nehru's views, 125–126
Sangh campaign for, 135–136
Savarkar's views on, 123–124

South Indian traditions of, 117–119
strategies, 138
Cow Protection Committee, 127
Cow protection movement, 121, 129–130, 132, 135, 201
formation of high-level committee of inquiry, 129
Golwalkar's and Kurien's work in, 129–130
Gosevak Samiti, 126
indefinite hunger strikes, 129
Kuka movement, 120–121
of Namdhari Sikhs, 120–121
police firing on rally of sadhus, 127–128
real problems of, 138–141
Sarvadaliya Goraksha Maha-abhiyan Samiti, 127
Cow protection vigilantism, 617
Cow slaughter, 108–138, 716
ban legislation, 125–126
banning, 108, 115, 129
under British rule, 115–116, 119
ecological campaign for, 130–135
institutional, 721
Islamic law concerning, 126
'lynching' incidents related to, 108–110
restricted, 115
as way of asserting Islamist identity, 122
CPI (M), 374, 436, 494, 550, 559, 565, 567
CPI-ML, 550
Craddock, Reginald, 195, 216
Creationism, 267–268, 412, 716, 720, 723
Creative Imagination, 521
Creeds, 78, 254, 379, 624
Cripps Mission, 219
Cripps, Stafford, 219
Cross-breeding, 146–147, 343
Crossing the Threshold of Hope. Here Pope (book), 630
Crown of Hinduism, The (book), 583
CSDS. *see* Centre for the Study of Developing Societies
CSIR. *see* Council of Scientific and Industrial Research
CSIR-National Institute of Science Communication and Information Resources, 459
CSI Synod, 649
Cultural circles, 152–153
Cultural illiteracy, 424, 426
Cultural matrix, 16–17, 87, 484
Cultural nationalism, 26, 29, 81, 164, 225, 376, 379
Cultural unity, 26–27, 80, 100, 197, 223, 225, 334, 548
Culture, 7–8, 28, 32, 37, 41–42, 49, 54, 65, 71, 75, 89, 96, 100, 117, 130, 145, 149–150, 153, 159, 189, 228, 261, 273, 283, 293, 310, 319, 355, 366, 372, 376–377, 386, 388, 409, 412, 422–424, 436, 474, 478, 492, 497, 510–511, 536, 539, 548, 552, 573, 596, 610–613, 620, 625, 627–628, 633, 644–645, 647, 715, 719, 726
Cunningham, Alexander, 69
Cunningham, George, 398
Customs, 23–24, 149, 177, 231, 388, 616, 644
Cyriac Puthenpurakal, 198–199

D

Dabir, Neela, 197
Dabistan-i-Mazahib, 17, 498
Dacoits, 49, 52
Dada Bhai, 150
Dada Naik, 309
Dadri incident, 109–110
Dai-i-Islami (Missionary of Islam) (book), 303
Dakshina Murti, 603
Dalai Lama, 40, 500, 598, 655
Dalit Indian Chamber of Commerce and Industry, 360
Dalitoddhar Mandal, 168
Dalits, 109, 112, 152, 167, 179, 184, 192, 193, 247, 321, 337, 339, 354, 358–360, 363, 365, 368–369,

372, 567, 605, 628, 649–651, 716
converted, 649
oppressed, 366, 369
Damle, Shridhar D., 308, 318–323, 371
Damu Anna, 354
Dandekar, Ramachandra Narayan, 55, 722
Dang region, violence in, 614–615
Danino, Michel, 92
Dar al-Harb to Dar al-Islam, 513
Dara Shikoh, Prince, 475–476, 499, 519–526, 521, 528, 545
Darayavaush, 11
Darbar Sahib, 492
Darius, 12, 14, 18
Darius I, 11–12
Darul Islam, 287
Darwin, Charles Robert, 263, 351, 456, 466, 722
Dasam Granth, 715
Dasaratha, 535
Das, Baba Lal, 521
Das, Deshbandhu C. R., 171, 178, 286–287
Das Kapital, 272
Das, Lal, 521
Dass, Ram, 229, 499–500
Dateline Bhopal (book), 325
Davis, Mike, 119, 368, 484, 509
Davis, Richard H., 484, 508
Dawkins, Richard, 268, 269, 718
Dayal, Lala Har, 211, 227, 263–277, 273, 275, 295, 718
admiration of the West, 264
advocacy of Hindu-Muslim unity, 273
arrest in United States, 273
on British colonial education, 265–266
comparison with Savarkar, 276
criticism of capitalism, 271
criticism of Marxism, 271–272
criticism of mystic notions, 270
criticism of theism, 269–270
criticizing reductionism, 269
in Europe, 263–264
harsh statement on Islamist forces, 274
on Hindutva movement, 275
interest in Buddhism, 266
internationalist secular humanist elements of, 274–275
love for science, 265–269
on oneness of humanity, 276
plunged into national liberation movement, 263
praise for success of Jews, 270–271
in United States, 264
utopian vision of, 272–273
on varna system, 264
view of Dharmavira on, 275
vision and value system, 275
Dayumanavar, 532
D'Costa, Bina, 235, 241–242
Death sentences, 114, 305, 520, 559
Deendayal Research Institute, 311, 394, 396, 399–400, 451, 538, 573
Deepavali, 586, 608
Deep ecology, 123, 143, 424
Defence, 89, 152, 174, 214, 373, 393, 457, 608
Degradation, 234, 236, 256, 518, 535, 643
Dehejia, Vidya, 55
De-Hinduization, 198–199
Dehlvi, Nasiruddin Chiragh, 520
Dehumanizing practice, 449, 461
Deities, 6, 9, 13, 23, 39, 51–52, 58–59, 71, 77, 80, 86, 127, 156, 204, 261, 267, 293, 348, 356, 411, 417, 429, 471, 476, 603, 629, 713, 726–727. *see also* God; Goddess
ancestral, 388
creator, 716, 720
foreign, 495
horned, 6–7
introspective, 6
male, 7, 53
non-Aryan, 604
personal, 471, 518, 602
presiding, 348, 598, 719, 726
sanguinary, 50

territorial, 89
Deivanayakam, 603
Delano, Columbus, 116
Delhi, 48, 91, 97–98, 115, 129, 160, 167, 183, 235–237, 244, 248, 327, 372, 391, 490, 492–493, 499, 508, 513, 527
Delusions, 414, 421, 428
Democracy, 71, 146, 176, 183, 218, 312, 317, 352, 382, 440, 451, 562, 571, 647
Democratic principles, 173, 183, 352
Democratic process, 382
Democratic values, 226, 340
Democratic Youth Federation of India, 559
Demolition, 205, 304, 370, 379, 550, 552–553
Demonization, 444, 629
Denationalization, 86, 265
Dennett, Daniel, 3
de Nobill, Robert, 632
Deoras, Madhukar Dattatreya, 93–94, 351–355, 357–358, 375, 406, 492, 725
  Ambedkarite literature and, 352–353
  on caste-conflicts, 355
  on social justice and social harmony, 353–354
  Vasant Vyakhyanmala lecture series of, 351–353
Desai, Morarji, 83
Desha Droha, 72
Deshmukh, Bhaurao, 306, 309
Deshmukh, Nanaji, 451, 548
Deshpande, Dadaji Naras Prabhu, 18, 719
Deshpande, P. L., 85
Desh Seva, 72
Destiny, 64, 86, 91, 195, 241, 302, 539
Destructive factionalism, 320
Deur Kothar stupa, 483
Deva-Darshan, 184
Devadasi institutions, 535
Devadasis, 535
Devaldevi, Sultana, 237
Devananda, Hindu sannyasin, 581
Devarchana Paddhathi (Protocols for Worshipping the Divine) (book), 362
Devas, 12, 63, 367, 500
Devendra, 367–368
Devendrakula Vellalars, 365–368
Dev, Guru Arjan, 494, 517, 543
Devi, Deval, 236–238
Devi, Ganga, 63–64, 721
Devi, Kamala, 236
Devi Mahatmiya, 58
Devi, Savitri
  association with Hindutva movements, 189–190
  meeting with Swami Satyananda, 190
Devi Yantra, 69, 716
Devotion, 21, 27, 50, 78, 254, 258, 260, 442, 499, 513, 519, 531–532, 582, 588, 604–605, 634, 643
Dev, Shankar, 346
Dhall, Krishan Lal, 489
Dharampal, 138, 338, 456
Dharma, 14, 21, 32–34, 57–58, 63, 74, 101, 118, 165, 172, 204–205, 238, 240, 305, 328, 346, 374, 382–383, 395–396, 403, 481, 488, 499, 508, 512, 644, 721, 723
  protection of, 486, 491, 714
  varnashrama, 26
Dharmacharyas, 347–348, 350, 490
Dharma rajya, 383
Dharmarakshak, 238
Dharmatattva, 21
Dharmavira, 275
Dhar, Sujit, 539
Dhasal, Namdeo, 360
Dhawan, Lal Chand, 253
Dhillon, Chanan Singh, 491
Dhingra, Madan Lal, 222
Dhwajarohana Mandapam of Kapaleeswarar Temple, 87
DICCI. *see* Dalit Indian Chamber of Commerce and Industry
Dignity, 67, 160, 175, 264, 329, 346, 418, 562
Dileepa, 134–135

Dilruba, Shah, 521
Dilruba, Shah Muhammad, 521, 522
Direct Action, 187
Disasters, 280, 324–325, 327, 331, 593
  gas leak, 325–326
  management, 99, 337–338
  man-made, 323
  natural, 280, 301, 327, 331, 335
Discovery of India (book), 80, 480
Dismantling Global Hindutva conference, 444
Disparity, 446, 650
Distortions, 182, 248–249, 333, 344, 379, 381–382, 400, 425, 441, 484, 544, 629
Distress, 279, 328, 331, 491, 506
Distrust, 129, 290
Divide and Rule, 75, 488, 490
Divine, 20–21, 23, 25, 32, 60, 67–69, 258, 330, 362, 411, 476, 484, 488, 496, 522–523, 525, 602, 635, 720, 724–725
  beneficence, 19
  equality, 146
  power, 6, 8, 59, 67, 714
Divine Feminine, 12–14, 23, 52, 54, 57–58, 62, 64, 67–69, 79, 87, 101, 103, 106–107, 262
Divine Mother, 530, 619
Divine Painter, 527
Divine punishment, 326, 721
Divinity, 9, 62, 88–89, 352, 443, 593, 724
Dixit, J. N., 94
Dixit, M.S., 247
DMK. *see* Dravida Munnetra Kazhagam
Dnyaneshwar, 37, 542
Dobzhansky, Theodosius, 147, 344
Doctrine of Trinity, 604
Dogmatism, 268, 383
Doniger, Wendy, 136
Douglas, Col., 251
Drama, 87, 179, 272, 632
Dr Ambedkar: Life and Mission, 313
Dr Ambedkar Memorial Committee, 361
Dravida Munnetra Kazhagam, 157, 366, 550, 554–556, 558–559
Dravidian
  movement, 157, 416, 553, 610
  polity, 552, 610
  racism, 204, 416
Dravidian-Christologist movement, 604
Dravidianist Dravidar Kazhagam, 550
Dravidianists, 152, 157, 203–204, 535, 550–553, 551, 562, 576, 726
Dravidian St Thomas Christianity, 642
DRDO, 458
DRI. *see* Deendayal Research Institute
Duggal, Kartar Singh, 519
Duke, James B., 49
Durand treaty, 282
Durga, Goddess, 46, 56, 58, 61, 66–68, 75, 88–89, 727
Durgavati, 304
Durrany, K. S., 548
Dussehra, 109, 222
Dutta, J. M., 241
Dvaita, 537
Dyer, General, 129
Dying Race, 168

E

East and West, 502, 595, 640
East Asia, 154
East Bengal, 92, 242–243, 307, 718
East India Company, 74, 118, 526
East Pakistan, 92, 225, 241, 243, 510
Eaton, Richard, 513
Eck, Diana, 68–70
Eco-awareness, 449–455
Ecological crisis, 449, 455, 637
Ecological disaster, 130, 141
Ecological thinking, 451, 455
Economic boycott, 120–121
Economics, 250, 264, 387, 417, 449, 647
Economy, 120, 125, 383, 391, 446, 459, 618
Education, 99, 123, 146, 159, 173, 180, 196, 198, 200–202, 231–232, 257–258, 265, 270, 330, 336–337, 344, 378, 432, 441, 498, 590, 618
  female, 119, 166, 171, 200–201, 232, 441

mass hygiene, 397
modern scientific, 433
moral, 198
Educational institutions, 202, 322, 372, 536, 574, 576, 613
Educational Problem (book), 265
Educational services, 336–337, 374, 725
Educational system, 252, 265–266, 417
Eezham, 201
Egalitarian, 127, 226, 470
Egalitarianism, 35, 171, 183, 365
Einstein, Albert, 265, 271
Ekatmata Mantra, 487, 716
Ekatmata Stotra, 322, 487, 538
Ekatmata Yatra, 357, 408
Ekta Yatra, 315–316
Elaine, 500
Elamaram, Nasarudhin, 566
Elenjimittam, Anthony, 476, 644–648
Elenjimittam, Fr, 645–648
Elephanta caves, 597, 604
Eliade, Mircea, 482, 543
Elijah Interfaith Institute, 495
Ellora, 157, 236, 484, 604
Elst, Koenraad, 83, 114, 191, 319, 333, 342, 373, 375, 380, 384, 393, 513, 529
Emancipation, 74, 167–168, 192, 199, 234, 330, 341, 353, 369, 726
Emerson, 621
Emotions, 68, 226, 260, 277, 348–349, 594, 623
Empathy, 40, 124, 292, 325, 401, 496, 542
Employee Share/Stock Ownership Plan, 391, 717
Empower India, 564
Empowerment, 20, 89, 178, 196, 199, 200, 339, 459
Encyclopedia Foundation, 299
Encyclopedia Galactic series, 299
Endorsement, 32, 188, 534
Energy-Matter, 267
Engagements, 181, 231, 285, 334, 374, 399, 501, 577, 621, 633, 635
Engineer, Asghar Ali, 545, 547–548
England, 166, 173, 194–195, 215, 278, 283–284, 504
Environment, 174, 310, 415, 435, 450, 452, 454, 458, 461, 625
Environmentalism, 450–451
EPO. *see* European Patent Office
Equality, 127, 151, 200, 214, 301, 349, 352–353, 356, 386, 528, 573
ESOP. *see* Employee Share/Stock Ownership Plan
Essentials of Hindutva (book), 29
Ethics, 40, 270–271, 423, 482, 547, 595, 645
Ethnic cleansing of Hindus from Kashmir, 314–316
Ethnic conflicts, 85, 145, 398, 577
Ethnicity, 19, 144–145, 151, 713, 725
Eugene G. d'Aquili, 39
Eugenics, 146, 257, 344
Euphemism, 720
Europe, 30, 47–48, 152–153, 163, 190, 194, 196, 198–199, 214, 263, 283, 340, 345, 403, 418–419, 420, 427, 454, 480, 505, 508, 515, 528, 713, 717
European civilization, 116, 251
European Organization for Nuclear Research, 411
European Patent Office, 434
Evangelical onslaught, 88, 617, 630
Evangelical organizations, 440, 628
Evangelism, 189, 262, 263, 279, 617
Evangelists, 74, 205, 263, 555, 603, 616, 618, 621, 624, 629
Evangelization, 612, 630
Even Frontline (tabloid), 137
Evil, 14, 174, 263, 285, 356, 484, 584, 594
Ahriman, 14
developing, 592
empire, 403
Kamsa, 53
primeval, 584
Evolutionary process, 345, 633–634
Evolutionism, 635
Execution, 50, 88, 121, 499, 523, 554–555, 559, 561, 563, 567, 612, 617
Expansionism, 70, 92, 100, 394, 496, 577, 720

Expansionist monotheism, 12–14
Expansionist tendencies, 17, 318, 475
Experience of Saccidananda: Advaitin Experience and its Trinitarian Fulfilment, The (book), 584

F

Facts are Facts: The Untold Story of India's Partition (book), 398
Fahad, Mohammed, 563
Faith, 13, 27, 30, 32, 76, 88, 90, 123, 156, 172, 176, 184, 189, 204, 224, 253–255, 258, 279, 282, 286, 288, 291, 352, 392, 396, 411, 477–478, 513, 517–518, 522, 524, 526, 531, 542, 544, 573–575, 583–584, 586, 593, 623, 626, 635, 640–641, 643, 649, 721, 727
Famine, 49, 74, 118–120, 172, 279–281, 280, 329, 368, 624
Fanaticism, 13, 244, 252, 255, 346, 527, 542, 626, 641
Fanatics, 130, 150, 203, 289, 514, 616, 622
Farid, Baba, 538, 543, 572
Farid Faqir, 519
Farid, Shaikh, 543
Farquhar, John Nicol, 74, 583–584
Fascism, 191–192, 195–196, 335
Fascist, 191, 193, 196, 224, 317–318, 323, 342, 403, 432, 646
  connection of Hindutva movement, 193–196
  elements, 335
  ideology, 334
  nature, 326
  organisation, 323
  totalitarianism, 646
Fasting, 287, 461–462
Fathnama, 516
Fathul Qadir, 285
Fatwas, 285, 547, 611, 613, 717
Faultlines, 186, 188, 301, 339, 357, 495, 562, 577, 628–629
Fazal, Abdul, 545
Fazal, Abul, 475, 516
FEFSI. *see* Film Employees Federation of South India
Feminism and Nationalism in the Third World (book), 441
Feminist Science Studies, 439, 715
Film Employees Federation of South India, 561
Firearms, knowledge of, 421
Firishta, 486
First World War, 71, 214, 251, 263, 287, 393
Fischer, Louis, 507
Flag Committee, 311
Flood, 56, 199, 301, 634, 716
Food, 9, 54, 80, 131, 137, 140–141, 146, 153, 222–223, 245, 322, 329–330, 332, 351, 396, 462, 482, 493, 531, 623, 637
  choice, 141
  culture, 139–140
  fascism, 108, 110
  grains, 200, 279
  habit, 530
  insecurity, 118
  preparing, 371
  producing, 332
  production, 140–141
  security, 136, 142, 332
  staple, 125, 137
  sustainability, 140
  vegetarian Indian, 222
Foot-bagged, 432
Forests, 23, 57, 61, 71, 80, 133–134, 200, 237, 450, 453–454, 474, 522, 572, 617–618
Forward Bloc, 218
Foundation (novel), 299
France, 194–195, 382, 504
Francis of Assisi, St, 589
Francis, Pope, 636
Francis, St., 589
Frantz, Milton Newberry, 623
Frawley, David, 58, 514
Freedom, 56, 71, 82–83, 87, 173, 212, 217, 222–223, 253–254, 264, 271, 275, 279, 284, 290, 304, 310, 338, 369, 386, 403, 429,

450–451, 476, 542, 580, 644–645, 647
absolute, 288
artistic, 83
economic, 87
fighters, 88, 127, 202, 277, 307, 309, 357, 390, 399, 405, 408, 445, 539
movement, 216, 233, 294, 302, 305, 310, 633
political, 197
religious, 87, 125, 292
struggle, 47–48, 57, 76, 150, 157, 212, 230, 234, 605
French, Patrick, 234
Frontline magazine, 193, 212–213, 434
Fulfilment theology, 74, 583–586, 590, 592, 598, 600
Fulsinghji fasting, 172
Futehally, Zafar, 132–133

G

Gadgil, V. N., 433
Gadhadhara, 371
Gadkari, Madhav, 357
Gadre, Anantrao, 312
Gaffar, Kazi Abdul, 72
Gaidinliu, Rani, 88–89
Gaikwad, Bhaurao, 181
Gajendragadkar, P. B., 36, 37
Galactic Empire, 299
Galilei, Galileo, 426–429, 460
Gandhara, 12, 96, 479
Gandharvas, 118
Gandhian Dang Swaraj Ashram, 614
Gandhi: An Illustrated Biography (book), 223
Gandhi, Indira, 83, 93–94, 97, 126–129, 133–135, 134, 212, 366, 378, 445–446, 452, 488, 489–492, 490, 540
assassination of, 493
Machiavellian politics, 489
praised Savarkar, 212
Gandhi, Mahatma, 590
Gandhi, Maneka, 454
Gandhi, Mohandas Karamchand, 26–28, 47, 67, 70, 77–79, 84, 113, 121, 123–124, 140–141, 143, 158, 160, 162, 167, 168, 170, 172, 177–179, 178–180, 190, 193, 196, 203, 215, 220–225, 221, 223, 234–235, 238, 243–244, 250, 252–253, 266, 273, 274, 285, 287–288, 290, 300, 322, 326, 334, 338, 371, 384–385, 389, 395, 397, 449, 451, 463, 502–507, 503–504, 506, 547, 558–559, 610, 623, 627, 638, 644–645, 651
on abduction and conversion of Hindu women, 243–244
on Bhagatji's fast unto death, 172
Hind Swaraj *vs.* Savarkar's Hindutva, 220–224
hunger strike, 224–225
influence on Hindutva, 27–29
on mass suicides of Hindu-Sikh women, 235–236
murder controversy, 217
returns to Hindutva understanding of Jewish homeland, 506–507
Savarkarite criticism of, 224–225
telegram to Ghanshyam Das Birla, 172
and Veer Savarkar, 346
views on cow protection, 123–124
Gandhi, Rahul, 212, 448
Gandhi, Rajiv, 94, 314–316, 452, 490, 492, 525, 540–541
Gandhi, Sonia Maino, 48, 157, 325, 327, 562, 568
Gandhi, Surjit Singh, 66, 714
Ganesha, 83, 368
Ganesh, Veera, 552
Gangadevi, 63
Ganga/Ganges, 27, 59, 60, 118, 329, 357, 585–586, 622, 645
Ganga water, 357, 408
Ganguli, B. N, 401
Ganguly, Kadambini, 459
Ganj-i-Shakar, Farid, 518
Ganpathyar temple, 315

Garbha griha, 591
Garbh Sanskar, 444
Garbhvigyan Anusandhan Kendra, 443
Gaulle, 382–383
Gau Raksha Dal, 138
Gau rakshaks, 111
Gautier, Francois, 372
Gaya, 363, 483
Gayatri Mantra, 600
Geddes, Patrick, 321, 371, 451
Gender, 76, 232–233, 260, 439–441, 443, 465, 533
  barriers, 334
  equality, 197, 321
  supremacist strictures, 382
General Wildlife Conservation Problems (article), 131
Genetic Diversity and Human Equality (book), 344
Genetics, 147, 152, 443
Genocide, 92, 241, 243, 492, 510, 718
Genomic-nationalism, 440
GenRobotics, 461
Geography, 59, 388, 435, 560
  sacred, 14, 27–28, 37, 59, 64, 70–71, 83, 104, 107
George, A. V., 553
George V, King, 84, 85, 86
Germany, 191, 194–195, 251, 271, 444, 504–505, 597
Geruva flag, 312–313
Ghadar Movement, 250, 264, 273, 718
Ghar Vapsi, 404
Ghazni, Mahmud, 240, 486, 538
GHGs. *see* Greenhouse gas
Ghori, Muhammad, 18, 240, 480
Ghose, Hem, 218
Ghosh, Aurobindo, 165, 264, 377, 382, 590
Ghoshitarama monastery, 483
Ghosh, Sailendra Nath, 400–402, 449, 450–454, 453
Ginsberg, Allen, 64
Giri, Chaitanya, 460
Girri, Maheish, 526
Gita. *see* Bhagavad Gita
Gitananda, Swami, 606
Gita Press, 498
Global Environmental Change, 140
Global Hindu Federation, 310
Globalization, 32, 383, 393, 432, 448, 458, 553, 617–618
Gnanananda, Swami Sri, 586
Gnosticism, 589, 718
Gobardan, 714
Göbekli Tepe, 3
God, 2–3, 7–14, 19, 20, 24–25, 30, 38–39, 47, 52, 67, 70, 77, 78, 88, 118, 124, 153, 158, 169, 172, 177, 190, 204, 206, 253, 258–259, 260, 283, 285, 290, 351–353, 395, 411, 462, 476, 487, 494–498, 500, 513, 516, 518–520, 524, 528, 531, 535, 537, 544–546, 572, 574–575, 578, 581–582, 584–585, 588–589, 590–592, 594, 602, 604–605, 622–625, 629–632, 635, 638–639, 641, 645, 717, 721. *see also* Deities
  Bharat Bhagya Vidhata, 86
  Christian, 326
  Helmet, 2
  of infinite justice, 592
  Krishna, 642
  of love, 593
  Particle, 411, 413–414, 417
God Delusion, The (book), 269–270
Goddess, 2, 10–11, 22–23, 46, 49–53, 50–51, 54, 55–58, 56–59, 60–69, 66–68, 72, 74, 76–78, 83, 86–89, 88, 101–104, 106, 158, 261, 308, 371, 603, 607, 621, 714–716, 722
  Amman, 356
  bathing, 67
  Bharati, 57
  Bharat Mata, 69, 76
  Bhavani, 65–66, 102, 714
  Dacoity, 52
  emergence during early Indian colonial resistance, 49–51
  of fertility, 55
  of justice, 61

Lakshmi, 480
Meenakshi, 367
multi-armed fighting, 57–62
Namginai, 88–89
of national historical processes, 71
pan-Indic, 72–77
Parvati, 60, 83, 104–105
Prthivi, 54
Saraswati, 58–59
sword bearing, resurfacing of
Guru Gobind Singh and Bhagavati, 66–68
Kumara Kampana and Meenakshi, 62–65
during national movement, 71–72
sacred geography and divine feminine, 68–70
Shivaji and Bhavani, 65–66
tradition, 49, 51–52, 55–56, 66, 68, 71
tradition of Hindu spirituality, 76
of tribes, 87–89
Uma, 87
Vac and Saraswati, 57
of victory, 715
Godse, Nathuram Vinayak, 306
Goebbels, Joseph, 432
Goel, Sita Ram, 79, 245, 319, 373, 375, 396–397, 431, 513, 515, 529, 538–539, 546–547, 561, 562, 576–577, 581, 587, 595, 608, 622, 624–625, 627–628, 630–631
Gokhale, Baburao, 186
Golden String, 599, 603–604, 607
Golden Temple, 115, 491
Golwalkar, Madhav Sadashivrao, 27, 126–127, 129–130, 135, 140, 156, 191, 307–311, 314, 317, 322, 328–331, 333, 342–351, 353, 355, 357–358, 361, 362, 373–375, 382, 389–390, 401, 405, 489, 622, 643–644, 646–647, 725
dialogue with Indian Christian-Christianity, 643–644
lecture at Gujarat University, 343
non-involvement in national movement, 307–308
pro-Hitler quotes of, 342
support of racist eugenics, 343–345
views on jati and its culmination, 345–351
Go-mutra, 115. *see also* Cow
Goodrick-Clarke, Nicholas, 189, 191
Good Soma, 15
Gopalan, Rama, 398, 552
Gosala, Makkhali, 713
Gosevak Samiti, 127
Goshalas, 128, 135
Goshen-Gottstein, Alon, 495–497, 499
Goshen-Gottstein positions Sarmad, 498
Gospel, 176, 530, 585, 589, 613, 624–626
Christian, 586
neo-nationalistic, 646
of Sri Ramakrishna, 530–531, 589, 621
Goswami, Sharan Bihari, 395
Gothandaraman, 205
Gottweis, Herbert, 440, 714
Gould, Stephen Jay, 456, 593–594, 596, 626
Gour, Hari Singh, 196, 197
Governance, 28, 118, 439
Go Vigyan Anusandhan Kendra, 135, 140
Govindacharya, 128, 359
Gowen, Annie, 443
Granary of Jnana, 533
Grand Mufti, 504
Gratitude, 149, 213, 344, 371–372, 638
Great Calcutta killings, 203
Greenhouse gas, 139–140, 718
Gregory, St, 607
Griffiths, Bede, 581, 587–589, 591–599, 593, 597, 600, 601–602, 604–605, 604–607, 631
GSAT-9, 99
Guha, Ramachandra, 310, 316, 334, 340, 373, 436, 437
Gujarat, 130, 236, 315–316, 354, 454, 484, 613
earthquake, 301, 335, 337

riots, 109
Gujarat Sahitya Prakash, 641
Gujarat State Electricity Corporation, 454
Gunadya, 474
Gupta dynasty, 16, 480
Gupta, Hans Raj, 309, 493
Gupta, Mahendranath, 530
Gupta, Narasimha, 17, 480
Gupta, Samudra, 234
Guru Bhakta Para, 612
Guru Gobind Geeta, 402
Guru Granth Sahib, 493, 572
'Guruji.' *see* Golwalkar, Madhav Sadashivrao
Gurukul system, 182, 200–201, 257, 431
Guru, Narayana, 119, 362, 534
Guru Puja, 310, 492–493
Guruswamy, Siddha Shivalinga, 534
Gurutva, 426–427
GVAK. *see* Go Vigyan Anusandhan Kendra
Gyana Rathams (Wisdom Chariots), 356
Gyan Shaktis, 35

H

Habib, Irfan, 17, 47–48, 82, 432–433, 542
Habib, Muhammad, 542
Habib-ur-Rahman, Maulvi, 284
Hadis, 286, 717
Hagiography, 133, 272, 482
Haider, Syed, 549
Haji Gulam Md. Azam Educational Trust, 576
Haksar, P. N., 133, 510
Halal, 139, 289, 332
Halam, Nagmanlal, 611
Halhed, Nathaniel, 421
Hallaj, 522
Halley, Edmond, 427
Hall of a Thousand Columns, The, 433
Hamoodur Rahman Report, 718
Hansraj, Lala, 171
Hanuman, 156, 486, 500, 614–615, 629
Hanuman Baski, 536
Hanuman Foundation, 499
Hanuman Nataka, 486, 717
Hanuman Poddar Smarak Samiti, 498
Hanuman Prasarak Mandal, 303
Happiness, 11, 59, 71, 213, 271, 276, 450, 578
Hapta Hindu, 11
Haqqani, Husain, 95
Harakatul Mujahidin, 97
Harappan
  civilization, 7, 14–15, 55–56, 64, 69, 89, 114, 151, 398, 726
  culture, 155
  iconography, 6
  seals, 15, 43, 62, 114
  sites of Mohenjodaro and Chanhudaro, 55
  unicorn, 15
Harbouring Cell, 569
Hardiman, David, 368
Hardinge, Lord, 214–215
Haribhadrasuri, 472
Harijan, 78, 172, 178, 184, 204–205, 346, 356, 366, 507, 627, 629
  converting, 651
  welfare, 167, 204
  youth, 346
Harijan magazine, 504
Harijan Sevak, 172
Harisena, Vakataka king, 474
Harkat-ul-Jihad al-Islami, 111–112, 568
Harmandir Saheb, 491
Harmonization, 378, 474–475, 477
Harmony, 10, 23, 53, 65, 67, 89, 172, 176, 225, 252, 351, 354, 356, 359, 361, 363, 384, 449–450, 474, 478, 483, 526, 535, 562, 572, 595, 724
  communal, 115, 379, 551, 554, 600
  cosmic, 14
  destruction of, 562–564
  religious, 478, 528
  spiritual, 535
Harris, Marvin, 120, 413, 715
Harvesting, 367, 453, 616, 629, 727
Harvesting Our Souls: Missionaries, their Design, their Claims (book), 629
Haryana, 109, 171, 200–201, 338, 361,

490, 493, 724
Hassan, Ali, 316
Hassan, Kamal, 561
Hate crimes, 614–615, 629
Hate ideology, 470, 629
Hatha Yoga, 606
Hayat, Perwaiz, 521
Hazrat Mahal, Begum, 248
Hebrews, 271, 475, 496, 511
Hedgewar, Keshav Baliram, 194, 299–307, 309–311, 317–318, 323, 334–335, 355, 358, 371, 373, 404, 646, 725, 726
  death of, 307
  futuristic vision of, 300–302
  mantra of Hindu unification, 300
  on role of saffron flag, 310–311
Hefter, Herzel, 496
Hekmatyar, Gulbuddin, 97
Heliocentric theory, 419, 428–429
Helio-centrism, 460
Hemachandra series, 458, 484–485
Hemu, king, 515
Hephthalite Empire, 479
Heptullah, Najma, 540
Heraka Movement, 88–89
Herman, Phyllis K., 70
Heterodox religions, 478, 480–481, 483
Hierarchies, 153, 629, 717
  birth-based social, 340, 364
  caste-based, 337
  hierarchical structure, 578, 725
  ordained birth-based, 340
  social, 144, 440
Higgs boson, 411, 417
Himalayan mistake, 488–489
Himalayas, 25, 53, 60, 64, 69, 82–83, 419, 480, 573
Hindavi, 572, 719
Hindavi Swaraj, 18, 65–66, 528, 719
Hindoo, 19, 50, 121, 124
Hindoo devotion, 124
Hind Swaraj (book), 26
Hindu, 1, 9, 11–14, 16–23, 26–27, 29–39, 41–42, 45, 48–50, 57, 61, 63, 74–75, 77–78, 82, 92, 115–116, 121–125, 130, 135–137, 140, 144, 148–152, 154, 156, 159, 167–172, 174–176, 180, 182–186, 189–193, 197–198, 202–205, 218, 223–224, 227, 229–231, 234–238, 241–245, 252–257, 259–260, 264–265, 270, 273–276, 280–284, 286–293, 300–303, 306, 312–317, 319, 322, 323, 326–328, 334–335, 338, 340, 342, 345–351, 357, 362–365, 368–369, 372, 377–379, 384, 391, 393, 396–399, 412, 415, 418, 420, 422–424, 429–430, 433, 442, 461, 473, 475–478, 484–485, 487–498, 500, 502–503, 505, 508, 511–512, 514–518, 521, 523–525, 527–533, 535, 537–538, 540, 543–545, 547–548, 554, 559, 562–563, 567, 574–577, 579, 581, 583, 585–591, 594, 597–601, 603–604, 606–607, 612–616, 619, 622–626, 631–634, 636, 644–647, 649–650, 653, 713, 717–718, 725. *see also* Castes
  appellative, 92
  boycott, 75
  consolidation of, 176, 226–227, 549
  definition of, 1, 17, 23, 28, 35, 645
  ethnic cleansing of, 314–316, 525
  high-caste, 190, 321
  high-class, 193
  history, 58, 61, 64, 331, 342, 349, 358, 637
  and Kafirs, 289
  meaning of, 17–18, 29, 31, 93
  and Muslims, 17, 49, 74, 91, 111, 121–122, 167, 172, 284, 292, 396, 535, 546, 549–550, 575–576
  non-Sikh, 489–491
  persecution of, 513, 611
  scriptures, 20, 26, 360, 523–524, 632, 650
  and Sikhs, 231, 235, 241, 285, 288, 307

survival of, 203, 294
untouchable, 183–184
upper caste, 185
Hindu activists, 243, 397, 551–552, 554, 561, 569, 572
Hindu Advaita, 381, 584
Hindu Aikya Vedi, 363
Hindu-Buddhist deities, milk offered to statues of, 433
Hindu-Christian, 577, 613, 642
dialogue, space for, 631–638
encounters, 577, 613, 624, 630, 642
Hindu civilization, 165, 220, 330, 412. *see also* Civilization
Hindu civilizational tryst, 419
Hindu Code Bill, 31
Hindu communalism, 275
Hindu community, 164, 169, 175, 177–178, 231, 241, 280–281, 362, 385, 491
agrarian, 402
forward, 649
fraternal, 549
and Hindu culture, 291
Hindu concept of maya, 521
'Hindu' consciousness emergence, 11–12
Hindu culture, 23, 29, 82, 146, 317, 377, 430, 462, 516, 548, 608, 644
and Hindutva, 261
identity, 26–27
Hindu darshanas, 386
Hindu deities, 6, 9, 23, 39, 51–52, 58–59, 71, 77, 80, 86, 127, 156, 204, 261, 267, 293, 348, 356, 397, 411, 417, 429, 471, 476, 532, 561, 595, 603, 607, 611, 629, 713, 726–727
Hindu Dharma, 1, 21, 32, 39, 183, 202, 238, 245, 253, 322, 340, 396, 403, 410, 439–440, 470, 499, 513, 524, 638, 713
Hindu Dharmera Śreṣṭhatā, 21, 21
Hindudom, 30, 151, 293
Hindu family, 22, 199, 281, 486, 613
arrangements, 174
Brahmin, 358
deity, 50
disputes, 548
life, 390, 634
of religions, 518
of spiritual traditions, 488, 619
structure, 235
Hindu fanatic, 141, 325, 617
Hindu Front, 356, 551–553, 559
Hindu fundamentalism, 113, 156, 412
Hindu-German conspiracy trial, 718
Hindu gods, 204, 261, 531, 590, 603, 607, 609, 621. *see also* Deities; God; Goddess
Hindu guru, 477, 638, 640
Hindu Holocaust Day, 398
Hindu ideals, 431, 515
Hindu identity, 36, 93, 488
Hindu India, 92, 548, 574, 585, 639
Hinduism, 1, 7, 11, 16–20, 19, 22, 24–26, 28–29, 31–36, 74, 83, 86, 114, 116, 119, 122–123, 165, 171, 180, 189, 191, 194, 201–204, 206, 226, 236–237, 239, 245, 261, 264, 270, 274–275, 282–283, 288, 290, 322–323, 326, 339–340, 342, 346, 352, 355, 364–366, 369–370, 384, 395, 397, 412, 415, 417, 429, 440, 462, 481, 485, 495–496, 508, 511–512, 521, 524, 527, 529–530, 548, 577–578, 580–584, 587–590, 592–596, 600, 602–604, 608, 618, 620, 622, 624, 627–628, 631–635, 637–638, 650–651, 713
Christianity approaches towards
appropriation through institutional inculturation, 577–608
political proxy war, 608–611
violent encounters, 611–619
defined, 25, 35, 275
denigrate, 375
destroying, 577, 608, 610
devaluation of, 601, 603
egalitarian, 109
and Hindu society, 262, 594
and Indian roots, 85

missionary portrayal of, 261–262
pre-modern, 33
of secularism, 29
vilification of, 623–624
weakness of, 589
Western 'authoritative' work on, 114
Hinduization, 513, 516, 532, 544, 548
Ashfaqulla Khan, 574
Christianity, 633
moves of Akbar, 516
of Sai Baba tradition, 532
streams, 513
of Sufism of Central Asian type, 544
Hindu Jagran Manch, 614, 616
Hindu-Jewish dialogues, 495, 498–499, 501
Hindu-Judaism dialogues, 495
Hindu Mahasabha, 41, 89, 123, 149–150, 159, 169–170, 175–176, 181, 183–189, 184, 186, 188, 191–192, 197–199, 200, 210, 218, 219, 220, 275, 290, 293, 302, 306–307, 309, 311, 312, 505, 508, 645, 725
1918 annual session, 169
article of faith, 90
Deshmukh's reply to fringe elements in, 306–307
formation of, 169
ideology, 185
national flag of India and, 311–312
resolution, 170
resolution of 1936 Annual Session of, 184
for Satyagraha, 181
on Savarkar, 505–506
social reforms by
Bole resolution, 185–189
Patitpawan Mandir, 185
resolution on untouchability, 183–184
Hindu Mission, 38, 190–191, 193
of Swami Satyananda, 189–191, 193
of universal religion, 38
Hindu movements, 17, 417, 419, 443, 555. *see also* Ayodhya Sri Ram Janmabhoomi Movement
Hindu Munnani, 356
Hindu-Muslim, 241, 525
antagonism, 75
bifurcation, 49
composite, 544
conflict, 525
dialogue, 514, 525–526
differences, 548
interaction, 520, 572
problem, 284, 287, 645
relations, 286–287, 293, 514, 525, 539
riots, 75, 288, 292, 501
unity, 168, 253, 273, 274, 277, 285–286, 292–293, 395, 575
Hindu mysticism, 601
Hindu mystics, 341, 532
Hindu nation, 16, 18, 25, 27–28, 41, 79, 96, 150, 256, 262, 265, 274, 334, 381, 485, 505
Hindu nationalism, 28, 68, 70, 136, 155, 162, 166, 189, 261, 273, 275, 318, 337, 380–381, 393, 439–443, 527, 648, 719, 724
bionationalist, 443
emergence of, 526
exclusive new, 70
militant, 246
resurgent, 527
Hindu Nationalism: A Reader (book), 317–318
Hindu Nationalist Movement, 191–192, 246
Hindu nationalists, 95, 100, 146, 151, 167, 179, 271, 275, 380–381, 393, 412, 433, 440, 442–443, 501
Hinduness, 1, 17–19, 21, 23–24, 26–32, 35–36, 70, 89, 113, 145, 262, 321, 330, 428–430, 485, 719
redefining hindu, 21–26
as resistance term against social stagnation and racism, 35–36
resurfacing of, 17–19
Hindu organizations, 198, 553, 615–616, 626, 651

Hindu Orphan Relief Movement, 279
Hindu Pad Padshahi (book), 65, 228–230, 305
Hindu Paria, 238
Hindu philosophy, 40, 414, 418–419, 428, 601, 631
Hindu population, 18, 30, 514
    of Chittor, 516
    of Jammu and Kashmir, 314
    of Punjab, 494
Hindu race, 197, 266, 274, 344
Hindu 'Race Spirit,' 191
Hindu Raj, 28, 274, 290
Hindu rashtra, 28, 322, 334, 382
Hindu Rashtra Mandir, 77, 78
Hindu Rashtriya Samajik Parishad, 175
Hindu rashtriyatva, 394
Hindu religion, 24, 31, 33, 36–40, 127, 177, 184, 203–204, 238, 274, 282, 366, 369, 471, 488, 519, 524, 547–548, 589, 620, 623
Hindu Religious and Charities Endowment Board, 206
Hindu resistance, 82, 475, 486, 512–513, 613
Hindu revivalism, 164, 258, 423
Hindu Sabha Relief Committee, 199
Hindu Sanghatan, 168, 253, 260, 359, 725
    connections, 186
    female education initiative, 200
    ideologues, 294
    movement, 77, 166–170, 173, 186–187, 189, 192, 201, 206, 249, 252, 254, 257–260, 263, 274–275, 292–293, 319, 356, 361, 445, 725
Hindu Sanghatan (book), 168, 253–254, 258
Hindu Sanghatanists, 170–172, 181, 183–184, 187, 189, 198, 200, 201, 205, 207–208, 260, 263, 289, 311, 341, 365, 725
    Dayal, Lala Har, 263–277
        admiration of the West, 264
        advocacy of Hindu-Muslim unity, 273
        arrest in United States, 273
        on British colonial education, 265–266
        comparison with Savarkar, 276
        criticism of capitalism, 271
        criticism of Marxism, 271–272
        criticism of mystic notions, 270
        criticism of theism, 269–270
        criticizing reductionism, 269
        in Europe, 263–264
        harsh statement on Islamist forces, 274
        on Hindutva movement, 275
        interest in Buddhism, 266
        internationalist secular humanist elements of, 274–275
        love for science, 265–269
        on oneness of humanity, 276
        plunged into national liberation movement, 263
        praise for success of Jews, 270–271
        in United States, 264
        utopian vision of, 272–273
        on varna system, 264
        view of Dharmavira on, 275
        vision and value system, 275
    Parmanand, Bhai, 249–263
        as caste abolitionist, 253
        deported to Andaman, 250
        family condition of, 249–250
        fast unto death, 251–252
        on Hindu Dharma, 253–254
        on inter-caste marriages, 256–257
        on national struggle as people's movement., 253
        observations regarding First World War, 251
        oneness of humanity, 259–260
        on religion, 254–256
        on *samanvaya* process, 258–259
        on Sanghatanist, 260
        Sanghatan views of, 253–260
        on social reforms, 259
        solitary confinement of, 251
        suicidal thoughts in prison,

250–251
teaching work, 252
on varna system, 256–258
Rai, Lala Lajpat, 277–294
appeal for Hindu-Muslim unity, 290, 292
Christian proselytization encountered by, 280–281
communal representation, 291–292
concern for persecution of non-Islamic Kafir tribes, 282–284
death of, 278
deepening fault lines, 291
deported to Mandalay, 278
encounters with Islamist balkanizing strategies, 284–294
famine relief work by, 279–280
fatwas, 284–285
Hindu-Muslim problem, 286–289, 292–293
lathi blows to, 277
letter to C. R. Das, 286
Maulvi Habib-ur-Rahman, 284
Obeidullah, 286–287
pan-Islamist propaganda, 289
Presidential speech, 290–292
protest against Simon Commission, 277
and Shuddhi movement, 281–282
Savarkar, Vinayak Damodar, 212–249
vision of, 361
Hindu Sanghatan—Saviour of the Dying Race (book), 168
Hindu sannyasi, 578
Hindu sannyasin, 581–582, 585, 589
Hindu science, 417–423
Hindu scriptures, 20, 26, 360, 523–524, 632, 650
Hindu-Sikh riots, 493
Hindu society, 23–24, 36, 38, 148, 166, 168–170, 174–175, 177, 181, 183–185, 202–204, 234, 238, 245, 252, 259, 261, 282, 300–301, 319, 322, 339, 344–345, 347–348, 350–352, 354–357, 359, 364, 366, 369, 375, 488, 495, 577, 594, 619, 628, 646, 650–651
casteless, 347
caste-ridden, 227, 346, 369
democratizing, 37
evils of, 384
fragmented, 364
parcel of, 181, 369, 488
reclaim, 282
unity of, 24, 168
Hindu spirituality, 55, 76, 440, 631
and Christian evangelical movement, 631
and Judaism, 499
against social stagnation, 440
Hindustan, 18, 28, 36, 79, 182, 203, 218, 223, 237, 274–275, 286, 289–290, 293, 368, 476, 498, 523, 644
Hindustani Renaissance, 544
Hindustan Revolutionary Army, 303
Hindustan Socialist Republican Army, 303
Hindustan Socialist Republican Association, 230, 726
Hindu Superiority: An Attempt to Determine the Position of the Hindu Race in the Scale of Nations (book), 197
Hindu supremacism, 144, 459
Hindu symbols, 48, 577–578, 603
Hindu temples, 12, 77, 115, 184, 202, 287, 300, 319, 338, 512, 514, 540, 581, 587, 590–592, 597–599, 603
desecration of, 287
destruction of, 512, 514
sectarian, 77
of South India, 603
Hindu traditions, 39, 54, 239, 490, 572, 577, 601–602, 616, 633, 635–636, 723

Hindu tribal resistance, 615
Hindutva
'axial age' developments, 6–9
under colonialism, 19–20
critics of, 84, 220, 393, 412
discourse, 28, 145, 154, 238, 279, 293
divine feminine, 12–14
engagements, 576, 622, 652
expansionist monotheism, 12–14
Gandhi's Hind Swaraj *vs.* Savarkar's, 220–224
'hindu' consciousness emergence, 11–12
hindu cultural identity, 26–27
hindu genesis, 12–14
'hinduness,' resurfacing of, 17–19
ideologues, 78, 100, 128, 145, 236, 333, 403, 423, 538, 561, 651, 715
inner unity and sacred geography, 14–16
masculine portrayal of, 260–261
negative portrayal of, 144
apartheid, 158–162
Arya, 156–158
obscurantism and social emancipation, 163–166
opposition to Aryan invasion/ migration theory, 151–156
racist and ethnic, 145–151
neurocultural emergence of, 2–6
persian schism, 11–12
post-independence stereotype of, 33–35
redefining Hindu, 21–26
responses to Christianity, 619–638
samanvaya to cultural matrix, 16–17
of Savarkar, 220–221, 276
Savarkar–Ambedkar definition of, 29–33
and social emancipation movement, 166
social justice and 'subtle indestructible unity' of, 36–37
Sri Aurobindo–Gandhi influence on, 27–29
Swarup's historical analysis of, 9–11
Hindutva-Hindu Sanghatan movement, 249
Hindutvaites, 27–28, 46, 76, 84, 89–90, 95, 129, 139, 146, 152, 154–155, 159, 162, 174, 178, 184, 245–246, 273, 301, 311, 352, 355, 393–394, 397, 403, 422, 488, 508, 511, 526, 576
Hindutva movement, 20, 28, 46, 49, 122, 130, 145, 156, 169, 173, 189, 193–194, 249, 275, 277, 293, 298, 301–302, 310, 317, 323, 375, 379–383, 393, 399–400, 403, 412, 422, 443, 455, 457, 463, 494, 525, 538, 550, 629, 644, 648, 652. *see also* Hindu Sanghatan
Italian fascist connection of, 193–196
mainstream, 141, 317
modern, 498
post-Independence, 449
and Rajguru, link between, 302–305
Hindutva organizations, 127, 323, 614–615, 619
Hindutva worldview, 68, 211, 249, 293, 411, 447
Hindu Unity, 77, 166, 253, 356, 366, 541, 725
Hindu universalism, 588, 600
Hindu Untouchable Castes Disabilities Removal Bill, 177
Hindu value system, 190, 412, 432
Hindu women, 176, 198, 203, 234–235, 241, 243–244, 720
abduction of, 176, 235, 241–243
destitute, 176
distributed among rioters, 241–242
forced marriages of, 241–243
molested, 240
rehabilitation of abducted, 244–245
rescued, 200
unconverted, 243
Hindu Women's Rescue Home Society, 197–198
Hindu Women's Welfare Society, 198

Hindu youths, 185, 193, 203, 205, 230, 275, 559
Hints for Self Culture (book), 265, 275
Historiography, 189, 229, 524
  colonial, 120
  medieval, 237
  of Vinayak Damodar Savarkar, 225–229, 231–234, 246, 305
History of Hindu-Christian Encounters (book), 630
Hitavadi, India newspaper, 283
Hitchens, Christopher, 325
Hitler, Adolf, 83, 190–192, 217, 224, 261, 382, 503–504, 508, 609, 713
Hitler-Vishnu equivalence, 191
Hizbul Mujahideen, 112
HMS. *see* Hindu Mahasabha
HMS Beagle, 722
Hoda, Syed Munir, 556–558
Holistic environmentalism, 450
Hollande, Frantois, 455
Holocaust, 117, 270, 316, 491–492, 713
Holy Koran, 475–476, 485, 516, 523, 533, 545, 564
Holy Kuran, 528, 540
Holyland, 30, 42, 149
Holy Science: The Biopolitics of Hindu Nationalism (book), 439–444
Holy wars, 477–478
Homelands, 155, 505–507, 511, 612
Homosexuality, 442–443
Hornaday, William T., 117
Housewarming ceremony, 121
HR & CE. *see* Hindu Religious and Charities Endowment Board
HRSP. *see* Hindu Rashtriya Samajik Parishad
HSRA. *see* Hindustan Socialist Republican Association
Hsuan Tsang, 478–479, 483
HuM. *see* Hizbul Mujahideen
Humane Methods of Livestock Slaughter Act, 139
Humanism, 272, 400, 542, 546, 548, 562, 572
Humanity, 2, 4, 10, 13, 20–21, 24, 32, 41, 60, 147–148, 155, 168, 174, 177, 181, 192, 214, 259, 270, 273, 275–276, 283, 288, 290, 293, 328, 330, 353, 357, 386–387, 397, 417, 422, 439–440, 447, 500, 509, 527, 537, 548, 572, 609, 618, 626, 638, 642, 645, 714, 724
Human life, 5, 41, 109, 118, 269, 387, 544
Human mind, 6, 39, 413, 471
Humiliation, 92, 115, 159–160, 177, 231, 235, 245, 293, 365, 490, 518, 536
Husain, Maqbool Fida, 82–83, 104, 115
Hussain, Dilder, 242
Hussain, Sarfaraz, 575
Hussain, Shah, 519, 544
Hussain, Zakir, 458, 552
Hussein, Saddam, 563, 571
Huxley, T. H., 267
Hyafil, Alexander, 4
Hyder, Qazi, 528

I

Ibl al-Arabi, 520–521
Ibn æArabi, 518
Ibn Batutta, 433
IBP. *see* International Biological Programme
Ibrahimbhai, Abha, 337
Ibrahim, Dawood, 569
Ibrahim, Hafiz Mohammed, 383, 545
Idealism, 451, 643, 645
Identity, 29, 63, 86–87, 89, 123, 156, 217, 354, 381, 388, 478, 497–498, 512, 528, 539, 543, 607, 637, 640
  politics, 359, 389, 489
  spiritual, 613
  Tamizh, 72
Ideologies, 1, 90, 111, 113–114, 144, 166, 192, 300, 302, 317, 335, 380, 389, 393, 397, 400, 440, 460, 470, 496, 540, 543, 548, 657, 719
  absolutist, 145
  anti-Christian, 189
  dharmic, 643

Hindu Sanghatanist, 171
Khalistan separatist, 491
pro-beef Hinduphobic, 113
totalitarian, 145
white supremacist, 163
Idolaters, 285–286, 512, 521–522
Idols, 217, 258, 348, 396, 433, 500, 522, 614
idolatry, 24, 80, 261, 495–497
worship, 26, 74, 258, 476, 496, 513, 521–522
IDRF. *see* India Development Relief Fund
IFF. *see* India Fraternity Forum
IGVP. *see* Indian Genome Variation Project
IH. *see* Integral Humanism
Ijadists, 519, 543
Ijadist Sufism, 518–519, 719
Illaiah, Kancha, 610, 629
Illusion, 40, 61, 178, 245, 414, 579, 593, 632
Illustrated Weekly of India, 323, 397, 406
IM. *see* Indian Mujahideen
Immorality, 261, 378, 559, 592
Immortality, 25, 348, 471, 600
Imperialism, 48, 90, 260, 302, 503
INA. *see* Indian National Army
Inamdar, P. A., 576
Incarnation, 88–89, 190, 259, 416, 592, 597, 604, 606–607, 620
Incendiarism, 128
Independence, 39, 47, 65, 75, 78, 83–84, 89, 116, 124–125, 191, 196, 198, 217, 218, 227, 247–248, 250, 253, 263, 271, 277, 283–284, 303, 305–306, 311, 322, 338, 367, 383, 389, 462–463, 488, 726
day of India, 91, 104, 305–306, 434
day of Pakistan, 315, 559
India Development Relief Fund, 336
India Fraternity Forum, 566, 569
India House, 221–222
India Independence League, 218
Indian Army, 195, 220, 230–231, 314, 316, 325, 491, 565
Indian beef *vs.* international beef, 138–139
Indian Bhakti movement, 331, 395, 396, 399, 519, 544
Indian Catholic Jesuit, 642
Indian Christian-Christianity, RSS dialogue with, 643
Elenjimittam, Anthony, 644–648
Golwalkar's views, 643–644
Mathai, M. P., 650–651
Pachpore, Virag, 651–652
Shastri, Shripati, 648–649
Sudarshan, K. S., 650
Indian Christianity, 626, 652
Indian Christology, 603
Indian civilization, 151
Indian Constitution, 29–30, 32–33, 80, 110, 124, 410, 448, 488, 618, 649
Indian culture, 21, 24, 29, 32, 41, 44, 114, 139, 146, 331, 377, 418, 423, 430, 441, 449, 483–484, 646, 648
Indian Genome Variation Project, 440
Indian History, 16, 24, 51, 53, 225, 228, 234, 319, 376, 380, 475, 478, 524, 539, 574
Indianisation, 122, 195, 379
Indian Islam, 524, 577
Indianization, 32, 85, 195, 220, 376, 378–379, 544, 577
Indian languages, 18, 56, 264, 435, 542, 600
Indian Mujahideen, 569
Indian Muslim, 92, 138, 243, 286–287, 289, 538, 543, 562, 577
saintology, 542
syncretic mysticism of, 532–537
Indian National Army, 220, 227, 233–234
Indian National Congress, 48, 75, 79, 81, 84, 85, 86, 127, 129, 157, 159, 162, 167–168, 178–180, 185, 187, 193, 220, 224, 252–253, 278, 284, 287, 293, 302, 305–307, 306, 311, 316, 327, 334, 391, 393, 404, 447–448, 488,

490–493, 491, 493, 502, 504, 506, 511, 540, 558, 560, 568, 617–618, 645
Indian nation-state, 19, 65, 100
Indian patriotism, 59
Indian Peace Keeping Force, 316
Indian Reciprocity Act Amendment Bill, 159
Indian Union Muslim League, 569
Indic Godhead, 602
Indic religions, 5, 22, 114, 488
Indic resistance, 62, 119, 479, 720
Indic systems, 119, 472, 597
Indic traditions, 114, 394, 477, 596, 713
Indic unitary model of consciousness, 39
Indic values to Christianity, 476
Indic vision, 38, 251, 648
Indignation, 121, 530, 582–583
Indira Congress, 315, 397, 446
Indo-Pak war, 316
Indophilia of Geddes, 371
Indra, 52, 57, 118, 367–368, 481, 487, 727
Industrialization, 192, 223, 446, 449, 451
Indus Valley Civilization, 114, 154
Inequalities, 34, 165, 300, 344, 353
Infidelity, 520, 522
Infidels, 284, 515–516, 522
Inner unity and sacred geography, 14–16
Innovation, 11, 139, 459, 461
Instrument of Accession of Kashmir to India, 314
Integral Humanism, 379–381, 383–384, 386–388, 401, 719–720
Intellectual Property and Competitive Strategies in the 21st Century (book), 437
Intellectual Property Rights, 436, 438
Inter-caste marriages, 147, 163, 175, 180, 183, 245, 256, 257, 338, 361, 493
Interim Asiatic Land and Tilling Act, 158
International Biological Programme, 132
International Solar Alliance, 454
International Union for the Conservation of Nature, 133
Internet, 397, 411–413, 417, 576
  based Hindutva, 476
  neo-Hindutvaites, 421
Internet Kshatriyas, 373
Intolerance, 255, 270, 275, 452, 478, 519, 528, 626
  ineradicable, 270, 275
  and violence, 478
Invaders, 17, 62–63, 65, 115, 169, 345, 479–480, 512, 539, 545, 720
  cows slaughtered by, 115
  Indic, 720
  Islamist/Islamic, 12, 18–19, 64–65, 234, 484, 486, 512, 514
  pre-Islamic non-Indic, 720
IPKF. *see* Indian Peace Keeping Force
IPR. *see* Intellectual Property Rights
Iqbal, Muhammad, 259, 289, 501
Iran, 16, 94, 98, 498, 542, 544–545, 553
Iranian monotheism, 13–14
Iraq, 245, 563
Isaiah, 271, 592
Ishavasya Upanishad, 471
Ishq Haqiqi, 545
Ishq Majazi, 545
ISI. *see* Islamic State of Iraq
ISIS, 234, 240, 243
Islam, 14, 42, 122, 236–238, 255, 274–275, 282, 284–286, 288, 303, 331, 343, 355, 366, 388, 396–397, 399, 410, 475–476, 485, 499, 511–514, 516–518, 520–524, 526–531, 537–539, 542, 544–548, 555, 562, 568, 572–574, 576, 589, 717, 719–721
  and Christianity, 20, 189, 270, 397, 496, 529–530
  common sacred civilizational space indigenous, 541
  death or, 512
  egalitarian, 365
  externals of, 522
  and Samanvaya, 572–577
    Dara Shukoh, 520–529
    sufism, 511–520, 573–574
    transformation of Akbar, 514–

517
Islamic Cultural Centre, 366
Islamic form of devotion, 513
Islamic form of sadhana, 530
Islamic fundamentalism and Islamist expansionist politics, 539
Islamic fundamentalist organizations, 95, 561
Islamic invaders, 12, 18–19, 64–65, 234, 484, 486, 512, 514
Islamic law, 126, 286, 547, 559
Islamic-Nazi collaboration, 192
Islamic sadhana, 529–530
Islamic Sevak Sangh, 553
Islamic State, 63, 83, 111, 234, 240, 243
Islamic State of Iraq, 97, 553
Islamic theocracy, 539
Islamic theology, 516, 538
Islamism, 262, 315, 396, 398, 561–562, 572, 577
  of Aurangzeb, 526
  radical, ascedancy of, 562–564
  understanding, 561–562
Islamist, 74, 95, 171–172, 192, 197, 235, 243, 245, 274, 284–285, 289, 292, 316, 365–366, 475, 477, 488, 495, 501, 504, 514, 516–517, 540, 551, 554–559, 561–562, 564, 566–569, 574, 576
  aggression, 224, 294, 395
  attack on Kashmiri Hindus, 316
  attacks on Hindu activists, 552
  Balkanizing strategies, 284
  expansionism, 379, 538, 574
  proselytization, 488, 572
Islamist forces, 274, 552, 555, 560, 568, 645
  foreign, 562
  fundamentalist, 550
  radical, 563, 570
Islamist invasions, 203, 234, 519, 719–720
Islamist opposition to Vande Mataram, 75
Islamist organizations, 234, 557, 561–562, 569–571
Islamist State, 517, 571, 719
Islamist terrorism, 540, 552, 573
Islamization, 562–563, 572
Islam, Shamsul, 148, 343
Israel, 270, 495, 501, 506–507, 509–511
  Judaism and post-independent India, 509–511
ISS. *see* Islamic Sevak Sangh
Italian society, 194–195
IUML. *see* Indian Union Muslim League
Iyengar, V. V. Srinivasa, 205
Iyer, Alladi Krishnaswamy, 202
Iyer, Ramaswami, 201
Iyer, Swaminathan S. Anklesaria, 47–48, 83, 473
Iyya Vazhi movement, 20

J

Jadeja, Digvijaysinhji Ranjitsinhji, 508
Jadhav, G. M., 195
Jadonang, Haipou, 88
Jadu Nath Mallik, garden-house of, 619
Jaffrelot, Christophe, 90, 166, 317–318, 334, 337, 360, 381
Jagadamba, 530–531
Jagannathan, Ki Va, 201
Jagannath temple of Gaya, 363
Jagmohan, Governer, 315, 525
Jai Bajrang Dal, 615, 617
Jail Notebook (book), 229, 297
Jain, Harish, 229–230
Jainism, 4, 22, 30, 37, 360, 470, 473, 478, 481–482, 650, 713
  repudiating, 484
  and Sikh Panth, 488
Jain, Sandhya, 612
Jaish-e-Mohammad, 97
Jakhar, Balram, 511
Jalal, Imran, 563
Jalal ud-Din Ahsan Shah, 62
Jal Jeevan Mission, 452–453
Jamaat-e-Islami, 95, 442, 540, 562–563, 718
Jamatia, Dilip Kumar, 612
Jamatia, Hirendra, 612
Jamatia, Indra Kishore, 612
Jamatia, Joy Kishore, 612

Jamatia, Padma Manik, 612
Jamatia tribals, 612
James, William, 633
Jammu and Kashmir, 313, 376, 452, 540, 557
Jammu and Kashmir Liberation Front, 557
Jammu and Kashmir Panchayati Raj Act, 453
Janata experiment, 94, 355
Janata Party, 93
Jan-i-Jahan, Naqshbandi Sufi Mirza Mazhar, 524
Jan Sangh, 93, 126–127, 129, 372, 376, 488–489
Japan, 58, 218–219, 539
Jaspers, Karl, 4, 714
Jauhar, debate on, 234–240, 245, 720
Jaulushmoni Jamatia community, 612
Jawaharlal Nehru University, 48, 163, 547, 549
Jawahirullah, M. H., 560, 570
Jayakar, Mukund Ramrao, 173–179, 184, 186, 187, 197, 207
  at Bombay Hindu Mahasabha Conference, 175–176
  on removal of caste distinctions, 174
  on resolution on self-government, 173–174
Jayalalithaa, 556, 571
Jayaraman, T., 434
Jayawardena, Kumari, 441
Jaynes, Julian, 2–7, 9–11, 714
Jeebananda, 74
Jeeva Karunya, 533
JeI. *see* Jamaat-e-Islami
Jesuits, 427–428, 635, 641–642, 649
Jesus, 20, 271, 477, 486, 500, 585–588, 591–592, 594, 600, 602–603, 605–607, 619–626, 631, 635, 638, 640–644, 646, 651, 718
Jews, 14, 16, 31, 41, 149–151, 153, 190, 270–271, 276, 285–286, 291–292, 495–497, 499–508, 511–512, 518, 613–614, 616
  Jewish community, 497, 506
  of Khaybar, extermination of, 286
Jeziya/Jizya tax, 396, 512, 514, 518, 521, 527
Jha, Dwijendra Narayan, 136–137, 478, 480, 482–484
Jihad, 235, 274, 282, 284, 292, 478, 511, 513, 515–516, 518, 538, 551, 553, 556–557, 560, 564–565, 573. *see also* Southern jihad
Jihadists, 242–243, 316, 551–552, 554–556, 558, 561, 565, 567–569, 573
Jina images of Kalugumalai, 484
Jinnah, Muhammad Ali, 377, 398, 501–503, 506
Jivakachintamani, 473
Jnana Kalanchiam (book), 533
Jnana Suriyan magazine, 533
Jnana Yoga Rahasyam (book), 533
Jnaneshvarananda, Swami, 487
JNU. *see* Jawaharlal Nehru University
Joga-Vashishta (book), 523
Joglekar, Patange and Sudhir, 357
Johanns, Pierre, 583–584
John Paul, Pope, 630
Joseph, George Gheverghese, 428, 626
Josephson, Brian, 464
Joseph, St, 608
Joseph, Tony, 151–152, 154, 609
Joshi, Anandbai, 459
Joshi, Anandibai, 459
Joshi, G. M., 247
Joshi, Murli Manohar, 315–316, 363, 402, 431, 433–439, 435, 448, 456
  biased critique and negative caricature of, 432–433
  on milk offered to statues of Hindu-Buddhist deities, 432–433
  propaganda against, 432–434
  and Traditional Knowledge Digital Library, 434–436
Joshi, Yadavarao, 350
Joya Chandi, 715
Judaeo-Christian tradition, 189, 602
Judaism, 13–14, 495–496, 501, 511, 546
  and post-independent India, 509
  rejecting, 499

Judgment, 8, 32, 36, 109, 137, 196, 288, 420, 540, 550, 559, 579, 634
Jugantor Patrika, 74
Justice, 53, 58, 61, 67, 110, 118, 123, 129, 161, 181, 292, 321, 328, 393, 395, 504, 556, 574, 649
  moral, 503
  social, 36, 87, 172, 187, 351, 354, 384, 610, 725
Jyotirmeemamsa, 429
Jyotirmeemamsa, 429

K

Kaatupalli, 87
Kabbalah tradition, 496
Kabul Congress Committee, 286, 722
Kadar, Birjis, 248
Kafferistan, 283
Kaffers, 283
Kafir, 36, 282–284, 288–289, 292, 499, 515, 547, 720
  tribe, 720
  women, 282, 720
Kafiristan, 282–284, 720
Kafur, Malik, 236
Kaiyadevanighantau, 434
Kaiyadevanighantau, 434
Kakkan, P., 357, 408
Kakkan, Viswanathan, 357, 408
Kakkarishi Natakam, 87
Kak, Subhash, 41, 429
Kalam, A. P. J. Abdul, 76, 152, 411, 448, 476, 538, 608
Kalanjim, Nalla Mohmed, 560
Kalaram temple, 181, 358
Kalhana (poet), 479
Kalhan, Promilla, 128
Kali, 47, 49–51, 58, 61, 75, 103, 619
Kali, Ayyan, 362
Kalidasa, 134
Kali-Neesa, 20
Kallenbach, Hermann, 503
Kalyana Kalpataru magazine, 498
Kalyan Ashram, 613
Kalyanasundaranar, V., 201
Kamaraj, K., 127–128
Kamba Ramayanam, 157
Kamble, Milind, 360
Kamenetz, Rodger, 500
Kampana, Kumara, 63
Kanakadasa, 348
Kanchi Sankara Mutt, 239, 319
Kanha National Park, 131, 133
Kanjamala, Augustine, 628
Kannan, Srinivasa, 333
Kanta, Shrimati Chander, 242
Kanya Gurukul, 200–201
Kanyakumari, 69, 106, 201, 209, 315, 351, 357, 538, 551
Kapoor, Pramod, 223
Kargil conflict, 96
Karkatha Vellalar, 367
Karma, 4, 118, 216, 341, 426, 494, 601–602
'Karma Kand' courses, 363
Karnataka, 110, 459, 560, 563, 568–569, 717
Karnataka Forum for Dignity, 556, 564
Karnataka Pradesh Vishwa Hindu Parishad, 350
Karpatri, Swami, 126–127
Kar Seva, 492, 550
Karsevaks, 358, 549–550
Karunanidhi, 555, 559
Karuvoorar, 534
Kashani, Sarmad, 497
Kashmir, 91, 96–97, 231, 241, 243, 252, 274, 313–316, 510–511, 525, 538–540, 554, 562, 564, 573
  ethnic cleansing of Hindus from, 314–315
  Hindu women, 252
  jihadists, 316
  jihad of ISI, 97
  negotiations, 314
  problem, 95, 314, 336, 511
Kasi Viswanath Mandir, 127
Kathrada, Ahmad M., 159
Kathri, Maulana Syed Shah Muhammad Inayathullah Kalphatul, 534
Katju, Markandey, 84
Katz, Nathan, 497–498, 511
Kaur, Prabhjot, 544
Kausiki-Vindhyavasini, 58

Kautilya, 81, 137
Kaveri river, 63
Kavirayar, Mahavidwan Kandaswamy, 158, 367
Keer, Dhananjay, 216, 233, 246, 312–313
Kelkar, N. C., 187, 193
Kelly, Bernard, 589
Kelso, Louis, 391, 717
Kempis, Thomas €, 636
Kenoyer, Jonathan Mark, 7
Kepler, Johannes, 419, 427–428
Kerala, 16, 27, 87, 119, 198, 301, 343, 350, 362–364, 389, 400, 428, 456–457, 476, 553, 555, 557, 562–568, 565–567, 566–567, 570–571, 591, 608, 619, 644
Kerala Kummanam Rajesekharan, 363
Kerala Police, 563, 567–568, 571
Ker, James, 72
KFD. *see* Karnataka Forum for Dignity
Khader, Mohammed Abdul, 552
Khalid, Haroon, 123
Khalistan, 491–492
Khalsa, 66–67, 73, 475, 720
Khan, Abdur Rahman, 720
Khan, Afzal, 65
Khan, Amir Abdur Rahman, 282–284, 395, 720
Khan, Arif Muhammad, 540–541
Khan, Ashfaqullah, 152, 303, 476, 538, 574–575, 653
Khan, Ibrahim Ras, 538
Khan, Israil, 59
Khan, Khafi, 528
Khan, Khijra, 236, 237
Khan, Khusro, 236–237
Khan, Maulana Wahiduddin, 546, 548
Khan, Muhammad Ilyas, 546
Khan, Muhammad Israil, 59
Khan, Murtaza, 517
Khanna, Durga Das, 216
Khanna, Madhu, 69
Khan, Saiyid Abdul Qasim, 516
Khan, Shahid Ali, 437
Khan, Tikka, 243
Khan, Wali, 398
Khare, Narayan Bhaskar, 158–162, 179, 219, 309, 713
Khatun, Habba, 545
Khijrakhan, 237
Khilafat movement, 29, 122, 178, 252, 273, 284, 287, 288–289, 503
  and Gandhi's association, 178
  in Istanbul, 286
Khilji, Allauddin, 236–237
Khilji, Jalaluddin, 519
Khomeini, 546, 547
Khusrau, Amir, 48, 82, 475, 517, 545
Kiblinger, Kristin Beise, 482
Kim, Byoung Soo, 440, 714
Kishan, Yuvraj, 481
Kishore, Acharya Girilal, 109
Knowledge, 2, 21, 60, 68, 73, 123, 165, 176, 256, 285, 287, 323, 362, 365, 413–414, 418, 420–422, 424, 427–429, 435–436, 450, 457, 471–472, 477, 487, 522–523, 533, 588, 592–593, 629, 646, 723
  religious, 342
  sacred, 487
  scientific, 49, 319, 456
  systems, 431, 435, 438, 456, 458
  traditional, 434–435, 439
  transmission, 428
Kohli, Atul, 494
Kohli, S. S., 543
Kollywood, 554, 561
  Islamist stranglehold on, 561
  Thupakki (movie), 560–561
Koloi, Jatna, 611
Kongu Vellalar, 367
Koon Pandiyan, 473
Koppers, Wilhelm, 152, 153
Koran, 475–476, 485, 516, 523, 533, 545, 564
Kota, Bilal Ahmed, 563
Kot Diji Phase Button Seal, 103
Kothandaraman, 205
Koumudi, Lahu Siddhanta, 303
Kovalan, 117
Koya, Mohammed, 563
Krishna, 38, 53, 61, 103, 244, 258–260, 341, 348, 357, 544, 588, 592–

593, 604, 618, 622–623, 636, 642
Krishna, Bal, 527–528
Krishna, Nandita, 113
Krishnan, Vidya, 328
Krishnasamy, 369
Krishna slew Kamsa in Mathura, 64
Kshatriyas, 147, 182, 228, 256, 346, 359, 715
Kufr, 512, 520
Kuhn, Thomas, 466
Kuka Movement, 120–121, 720
Kuka, Ram Singh, 120–121, 143
Kulkarni, V. B., 178, 185
Kumara Kampanna, 62, 721
Kumarapala, 485
Kumarappa, J. C., 125, 130
Kumarappa, Joseph Cornelius, 714
Kumaraswamy, P. R., 502
Kumar, Brijesh, 549
Kumari Kandam' Tamils, 610
Kumar, Shiv, 35
Kumar, Vishal, 568
Kumbh Mela, 169, 347, 372, 461
Kundalini/Muladhar Shakti, 41, 312, 537, 721
Kuravanchi, 721
Kuravanji, 158
Kurien, Verghese, 126, 129–130
Kurinchi, 726
Kurunchi, 52, 727
Kutadanta Sutta, 482
Kutrala Kuravanji (literary work), 157
Kuwait India Fraternity Forum, 566

L

Laali, B. S., 112
Lai, Salim, 133
Lakshmibai, Rani, 232–234, 247–248, 249
Lakshmi, goddess, 62, 78, 118, 233
Lakshminarayan Mandir, 77
Lal Chowk of Kashmir, 315
Lalitavistara, 472
Lallan Faqir, 542, 545
Land Acquisition Act, 550
Langa, Saddiq Khan, 76
Lapierre, Dominique, 327
Lashkar-e-Taiba, 97, 557, 563, 567, 573
Latif, Abdul, 545
Latif, Shah Abdul, 542
Latitudinarianism, 518
Laudato Si, 636
Laux, Henri, 607
Laximibai, 247
LDF. *see* Left Democratic Front
Leary, Timothy, 499
Left Democratic Front, 558, 569
Leibniz, 428
Leitner, Dr., 283
Lekhi, Meenakshi, 526
Lenin, 272, 333, 400, 466, 609
Leprosy, 114, 609, 618, 629
Le Saux, Henri, 578, 580–588, 597–599, 607
LeT. *see* Lashkar-e-Taiba
Lewis, Michael, 130–133, 592
LGBTQ community, 442–443
Liberalism, 153, 562
Liberalization, 393, 402, 453, 618
Liberal policies, 215, 516, 528
Liberation, 91, 156, 243, 308, 379, 396, 442, 450, 471, 533, 535, 587, 594, 721, 723
Liberation theology, 262, 618
Liberty, 173, 232, 248, 258, 279, 528, 547
Life of Barrister Savarkar (book), 216–217
Light of the East, The (periodical), 584
Lincoln, Abraham, 353
Lingaitism, 30
Lingayat religion, 31, 37
Linguistic diversity, 377, 474–475
Livestock
  diversity, 136
  domestic, 131–132
  grazing, 131, 133–134
  unproductive, 138
Lohia, Ram Manohar, 92
Loka Samasta Sukhino Bhavantu, 651
Longkumer, Arkotong, 88–89
Lorenzen, David, 18
Louis, Nivedita, 105
Lower castes, 174, 192, 338, 431, 534

Loyalty, 86, 155, 169, 213–214, 243–244, 320, 355, 383, 580
Ludvik, Catherine, 57–59
Lurquin, Paul F., 412
Luther, Martin, 341
Lysenkos, 431

M

Maalism, 610
Macaulay education, 417–418
Mackintosh-Smith, Tim, 433
Madai Kudumar clan, 367
Madani, Abdul Nasser, 553, 554, 556–560
Madhavanji, 362
Madhok, Bal Raj, 122, 313, 376–379, 489, 576
Madhura Vijayam, 721
Madras, 105, 205, 217, 265, 327, 534
Madras film industry, 554
Madurai, 62–63, 367, 473, 570, 721
Maff'ei, Petri, 427
Magdalene, 718
Mahabalipuram, 107, 598, 604
Mahabharata, 10, 14, 54, 61, 69, 77, 82, 96, 276, 398, 421, 476, 500, 515, 517, 536, 610
Mahadevan, Iravatham, 15, 155, 726
Mahadev Yatra, 357
Mahad Satyagraha, 180, 186
Maha Mrityunjaya Mantra, 600
Mahanambrata Brahmachari, 636
Mahan, Paranjothi, 536
Mahapatra, Basudev, 618
Mahaprajna, Acharya, 472
Maharishi, Ramana, 589, 590
Maharishi, Vethathri, 537
Maharshi Patanjali Sanskrit Sansthan, 364
Maharshi, Ramana, 582, 589, 598
Mahasabha Geruwa flag, 312
Mahishasuramardini, 58, 101
Mahomedan fanaticism, 178
Mahomedanism, 531
Mahratta, 281
Mai, Krishan Lal, 489
Maino, Edvige Antonia Albina, 48
Majmua-ul-Baharain, 524
Majoritarianism, 576
Majumdar, Mrittunjoy Guha, 464–465, 515, 526
Majumdar, R. C., 526
Majumdar, Suhas, 515
Makar Sankranti, 300, 330, 349, 611
Malabar, 60, 202, 252
Mala, Shastra Nam, 66
Malaviya, Madan Mohan, 169, 184, 193, 202–203, 210, 296, 445, 447
Malhotra, Rajiv, 577
Malik, Yasin, 557
Malkana Muslims, 171
Malkana Rajputs, 171
Malkangiri, 336
Malkani, Keval Ram, 311, 321, 373, 394, 400, 449, 451, 488, 525, 541, 544, 545–546, 548, 715
Malkani, Sri, 546
Mallars, 366, 368
Mallick, Mani, 530
Mallya, Vijay, 609
Malviya, Madan Mohan, 169, 184, 193, 210, 252, 296, 445
Mamallapuram, 101, 107
Manava Dharma, 648
Mandalas, 71, 332, 600, 716
Mandapam, 87–88, 583, 591
Mangalodan, Sadik, 568
Mangeshkar, Lata, 76
Manimekalai, 332
Manitha Neethi Pasarai, 556–558, 564, 570
Mankind, 25, 41–42, 147, 254, 260, 269–270, 276, 283–284, 353, 449, 477, 487, 546, 584, 588, 620, 623, 646
Manthan, 394, 396, 398–400, 402–403, 449, 452, 454, 538, 541, 544, 546–547
Mantra Sandwich, 586
Manu Murai Kanda Vachagam, 118
Manusmriti, 118, 300, 360, 484
Mao, 609
Maoist China, 81–82, 92
Maoist socialism, 609

Marabala Purana, 367
Marad massacre, 557
Maratha ascendancy, 18
Maratha Empire, 19, 50, 65, 230, 231, 312, 528, 714
 history, 19
 navy, 230–231
 warfare, 230
Maratha Movement, The. see Hindu Pad Padshahi (book)
Maratha Pariah, 165
Marathas, 50, 186, 228, 230–231, 312, 527
Marathawada, 354
Markand Puran, 66
Marriages, 148, 170, 179, 196, 200, 236, 238, 243, 256–257, 361, 441, 545, 595, 713
 forced, 241, 243
 inter-caste, 147, 163, 175, 180, 183, 245, 256, 257, 338, 361, 493, 713
Marshall, John, 483
Martin, John, 602
Marxian internationalism, 403
Marxism, 185, 235, 262, 271–272, 375, 388, 400–401, 403, 423, 451, 723
 cultural, 715
 fundamental deficiency of, 401
Marx, Karl, 116, 263–264, 271–272, 389, 400–403, 466, 609, 645
 doctrine, 400
 humanistic objectives, 402
 observations, 401–402
 parents, 272
Masculine Hinduism, 85, 260–262
Mashelkar, Raghunath Anant, 435–437
Masnavi, 545
Masood, Iqbal, 548
Mass freedom movement and RSS, 305–307
Mass Resistance in Kashmir (book), 562
Mass suicide of women, 234–236
Mastan Sahib, 532
Master-Yogin Jesus, 620
Masud, Fardi-Addin, 543
Mathai, M. P., 650–651
Mathimaran, 157, 610
Mathura Vijayam (book), 63
Mathur, Satish Chandra, 549
Matidas, Bhai, 250
Matilal, Bimal Krishna, 422, 430
Matthews, Stanley, 432
Matus, Thomas, 579
Maurya, 228
Maximiani Portas, 189–190
Maxwell, R. M., 188
Mayawati, 109, 112, 358–359
Mazumdar, Aurobindo, 516
McClain, Ernest G., 15
McKean, Lise, 247–248, 331
McLeod, D. F., 50
Media, 1, 35, 90, 108–110, 141, 161–162, 189, 212, 220, 230, 261–262, 318, 322, 324–325, 327, 365, 379–380, 417, 433, 439, 460, 484, 537, 549, 566, 609, 614, 617–618, 629, 652, 716
 attention, 83, 613
 campaigns, 444
 social, 109, 364, 411–413, 423, 425
Medicine, 114–115, 337, 461–462, 493
 cow-product-based, 114
 herbal, 435
 life-saving, 491
Medieval India, 34, 47–48, 544
Meditation, 7, 329, 395, 461, 580, 605–606, 638
Meenakshi, 62, 64
Meenakshipuram, 355–356, 365
Meerut, 112, 125, 247–248
Meghraj (Arya Samaj leader), 170
Mehta, Sureesh, 564
Mein Kampf (book), 190
Meir, Golda, 510
Melapalayam, 551, 558
Mello, Anthony de, 476–477, 638–639, 641–642, 652
Menon, Achyut, 27
Menon, Gopinath, 54
Menon, K. Gopinath, 53
Menon, Sadanand, 76
Mentality, 6, 10, 203, 255, 292, 531, 646

Mercurous nitrite, 419
Merton, Thomas, 636, 638
Mesopotamia, 152, 286
Middle East, 455, 504, 514, 651
Midnight's Machines: A Political History of Technology in India (book), 439, 444–448
Mihiragula, 17, 480
Mihirakula, 474, 478–479, 479–481
Mihir-o-Sudhakar, 283
Militarization, 192
Military, 92, 95, 117, 227, 231, 233, 242, 244, 247, 306, 334, 491, 513, 647
  aggression, 218
  education, 193–196
  establishments, 95
  expansion, 18, 90, 92
  expansionist agenda, 46
  intelligence officials, 95
  recruitment, 227, 536
  technologies, 465
  training, 194–195, 536
Military Schools of England, 194
Miller, Henry, 374
Milli Gazette (Islamist anti-Sangh magazine), 337
Mindset, 135, 189, 236, 270, 370, 459, 509, 598, 647
Mines and Works Act, 158
Minorities, 42, 92, 158, 292–293, 300, 317–318, 565
  appeasement policy, 555
  institutions, 529
  religious, 108, 336
  rights, 291
Minto, Lord, 166, 278
Mirza, Khur Khusrau, 517
Mishra, Dwaraka Prasad, 389
Mishra, Susan Verma, 484
Misra, Ram Gopal, 486, 512
Missionaries, 19–20, 84, 261–262, 264, 279–281, 283, 331, 589, 598–599, 614, 616, 623–624, 629, 631, 643, 645, 715
  Catholic, 598, 632
  of Charity, 324, 326–327
  Christian, 280–282
  educational, 583
  foreign, 643
  French Catholic, 577
  orphanages, 280
Missionaries in India: Continuities, Changes, Dilemmas (book), 627
Mitra, Ashok, 374
Mittal, Kewal Krishan, 395
MNP. *see* Manitha Neethi Pasarai
Mob attacks, 109–111, 241–242, 491, 493, 554, 558–559, 561, 615
Modern India, 76, 250, 344, 485, 648
Modernization, 263, 635
Modern Review magazine, 264, 272, 272 307, 307
Modern society, 264, 270, 343, 345
Modi, Narendra Damodardas, 98–99, 108–111, 221, 316, 320, 360, 364, 370, 372–373, 393, 439, 445, 447–448, 452, 454, 455, 462, 572–573, 609, 714
  inauguration of global Sufi conference, 572
  statement against vigilantes, 111
  washing feet of sanitary workers, 370
Mohamed Sajjad, Abdul Mohasin, 285
Mohammed, prophet, 547, 640
Mohan, C. Raja, 98
Mohanty, William K., 5
Mohd. Hanif Quareshi case, 125–126
Mojumdar, Kanchanmoy, 307
Molotov-Ribbentrop Pact, 508
Monasteries, 17, 363, 365, 477–479, 578
Monchanin, Jules, 577–584, 581, 588, 607
Mondal, Jati Sankar, 49
Monism, 268, 579, 607, 721
  factitious, 267
  idealist, 721
  materialist, 721
Monoculture, 17, 31, 70, 273, 537, 552
Monopolistic aggression, 720
Monopolistic expansionism, 179, 318, 399, 528, 719
Monopolistic faiths, 275, 495
Monopolistic fanaticism, 516

Monopolistic monocultures, 70, 552
Monotheism, 11, 13–14, 152, 271, 366, 496–497, 524–525, 602
Mookerji, Radhakumud, 332
Moonje, B. S., 184, 189, 193–196, 334
Moplah massacre, 176, 286
Morris, Ian, 4
Morton, Thomas, 636
Morvi dam disaster, 301
Moses, 271, 499, 506, 592, 621
Mosse, David, 368
Mother Goddess, 61, 73, 109, 532, 605
Mother India, 46–47, 54–55, 62, 68, 72, 76–80, 89, 107, 157, 222, 406, 647
Mother of Sri Aurobindo, 509
Mother Tamizh, 107
Moulavi, Ansar, 565
Mubarik, Sultan, 237
Mudaliar, K. N. Shanmuga, 87
Mudaliar, Ramaswamy, 160–162
Mudalif, Abdul, 552
MUDRA scheme of Prime Minister Narendra Modi, 360
Muhammad, Malik, 523
Mukherjee, Jatindranath, 218
Mukherjee, Shyama Prasad, 91, 376, 448, 467, 509, 510
  and Akhand Bharat, 90–93
  on Noakhali riots, 203
  Radhakumud, 71
Mukherjee, Uma, 218
Mukherji, Asit Krishna, 190
Mukhopadhyay, Amartya, 384
Mukhopadhyay, Nilanjan, 246–248, 349, 385
Mukti Bahini, 243
Muladhar Shakti, 41, 721
Mullai, grassland, 52, 726–727
Mulla Sader and Mir Abul Kasem, 498
Muller, Max, 646
Mumbai riots, 554
Mundaka Upanishad, 7
Munde, Gopinath, 433
Mundkur, 247
Muni, Bhoga, 534
Munshat-i-Namak€n, 516
Munshiganj Satyagraha, 192
Munshi, Kanhaiyalal Maneklal, 71, 124, 509
Muradevi, 228
Murugan, deity, 51–52, 368, 500, 609, 611, 726
Musharraf, Pervez, 96
Music and the Making of Modern Science (book), 425
Muslim League, 75, 169, 178, 203, 293, 383, 398, 501–502, 504, 645
  and Gandhi-Nehru, 501–505
  re-Partition, 243
  resolution, 503
Muslim League Pirzada, 502
Muslim women, 238–241, 243, 245, 540, 559
Mussolini, 192–194, 195, 196, 261, 334
Mysticism, 269, 520, 522, 542–543, 573, 579, 607, 626
  advaitic, 607
  bridal, 518, 532
  Hindu, 601
  of Ibn-al-Arabi, 520
  Koranic, 543
  of south Indian Muslims, 532–537
  Sufi, 519, 520, 522
Myth of the Holy Cow (book), 136

N

Naam Tamilar ('We Tamils') party, 608–609
Nafi, Mohammed, 557
Nagaland, 88, 494, 609
Nagarkar, Shridar Waman, 72
Nag Hammadi texts, 13
Nagpur, 161, 167, 299, 304, 312, 314, 369
Naidu, Sarojini, 171, 502
Naidu, Venkitaswamy, 203
Naik, Ghelubhai, 614
Naikkar, Thirumalai, 367
Naik, Zakir, 425
Nair Service Society, 363
Naiyayikas, 487
Nama Japa Meditation, 606
Namboodiripad, Elamkulam Manakkal Sankaran, 399, 400

Namboodri, 343, 362
Namdhari Sikhs, 120, 143
Nampoori, V. P. N., 461
Nanak, Guru, 37, 346
Nanda, Gulzarilal, 127–128
Nanda, Meera, 333
Nandi (Shiva's bull), 125, 479, 532
Nandy, Ashis, 220–221, 321–322, 332–333
Narath, 568–569
Narayana Guru, 346
Nariman, Khurshed Framji, 233
Narlikar, Jayant Vishnu, 460
Narsimha (avtar), 190
NASA, 411, 413–414
Nasir, Tadiyantavide, 567
Nasir-ud-din, emperor, 238
Næss, Arne, 123, 143
Nasser, 509
Nataraja, Kim, 598
Nataraja, statue of, 411, 413, 414, 416, 598
National Botanical Research Institute, 136
National Church for Indian Christians, 651
National Confederation of Human Rights Organisations, 571
National conscience, 17, 48, 131
National Democratic Alliance. *see* NDA
National Development Front, 553, 556, 564, 566
National Environmental Engineering Research Institute, 135
National flag, 61, 189, 306, 310–317, 376
  Ambedkar's views on, 311–313
  Flag Committee recommendations for, 311
  hoisting in Kashmir, 313–316
  Sanghathanists views on, 311–312
  Savarkar's views on, 312–313
National Geographic Society, 140
National Herald, 81, 219
National Investigation Agency, 112, 567, 569, 571–572
Nationalism, 24, 37, 41, 47, 74, 85, 96, 260, 272, 275, 292–293, 334, 345, 382, 384, 393–394, 441, 448, 504, 526–527, 646, 724
  aggressive, 46
  dynamic, 647
  monolithic nation-state, 345
  partial, 527
  racial, 715
  religious, 273, 382, 490
  territorial, 29
Nationality, 26–27, 70, 75, 80, 164, 276, 377, 623
National Liberation Front of Tripura, 611–613
National Security Act, 558
National Thinkers Meet, 398
National unity, 27, 525, 535, 547
National Unity Pilgrimage, 408
National Women Front, 566
Nation-building, 163, 231, 287, 346, 413
Nationhood, 19, 21, 23, 27–28, 42, 78–79, 191, 223, 265, 288, 292, 322, 342, 384
Nation-state, 19, 27, 30, 65, 70, 95, 100, 220–221, 272, 317, 345
Nature-harmonic pursuit of knowledge, 450
Navalar, Arumuga, 201, 209
Navalar magazine, 202
Nawa, Fariba, 573
Nayanar, E. K., 557
Nayar, Kuldip, 337
Nazarene, teachings of, 626
Nazeer, Thadiyantavide, 557
Nazi, 113, 152–153, 162, 189, 191–192, 195, 218, 318, 342, 433, 444, 646
  anti-Semitism, 610
  historiography of, 153
  ideologies, 1, 191, 195, 342
  occupations, 218
  organizations, 298, 317, 323
  racial theory, 152
  racism, 444
  support for Arabs, 503
Nazi Germany, 195, 444, 508
Nazim Jamiat, 285
Nazism, 153, 191, 317

Nazi support for Arabs, 503
NBRI. *see* National Botanical Research Institute
NCHRO. *see* National Confederation of Human Rights Organisations
NCJM. *see* New Central Jute Mills Co. Ltd
NDA, 108, 212, 360, 412, 433, 555, 557
  NDA-I, 138, 363, 433, 456, 460
  NDA-II, 108, 110, 112, 360, 452
NDF. *see* National Development Front
Neela, Dabir, 198–199
Neelakanta, 362
Neem Karoli Baba, 499–500
NEERI. *see* National Environmental Engineering Research Institute
Negative caricature, 373, 433
Negative connotations, 393, 715, 724
Negative stereotype, 190, 261, 380, 444, 575
Nehru, Jawaharlal, 24, 47, 79–80, 79–82, 92, 125–127, 126, 159, 162, 179, 205, 219, 220, 225, 243, 311, 314, 334, 377–378, 410, 445–446, 480, 502–503, 505, 506, 507, 509, 525, 526–527, 529, 645, 647–648
  view of Indian history, 225
Nehru, Motilal, 171
Nehruvian, 81, 152, 366, 373, 377, 447, 501, 510, 526
  appeasement, 396
  and Bharat Mata, 79
  colonial-Marxist, 36
  divide-and-rule, 490
  establishment, 377, 433, 437
  government, 124
  ideology, 47
  polity, 47, 364, 396
  post-Nehru, 377
  prejudices, 146
  regime, 121
  rioters, 493
  secularism, 113, 140
  vision, 378
Nehruvianism, 526, 539
Nehruvian McCarthyism, 436–437
Nehruvian school, 33, 524
Nehruvian State, 490, 495
Neithal, 52, 727
Nene, Rajabhau, 386
Nene, Vasudev, 386
Nene, V. V., 387–388
Neo-Hindu, 34
Neolithic settlements, early, 398
Neurotheology, 38–39, 722
Neutrino project, 608
Newberg, Andrew, 722
Newberg, Andrew B., 38–39, 722
New Central Jute Mills Co. Ltd, 392
Newton, Isaac, 421, 423–428, 460
Newton's worldview, critique of, 423–424
NGOs, 457, 500, 615
NIA. *see* National Investigation Agency
Nicolas, Antonio T. de, 9
Nigam, Aditya, 90
Nilakantha, 427, 429
Niranjandevji, Sri, 348
Nirgrantha Jnatiputra, 482
Nirrti, 55–56, 106, 722
Nirrti-Putra Kapota, 55
Nivedita, Sister, 73, 148–149, 151, 261, 376
Nizami, Hassan, 303–304
Nizami, Khawa Hassan, 303
Nizamuddin, Hazrat, 545, 565
NLFT. *see* National Liberation Front of Tripura
Noakhali massacre, 202–204
Noble, Margaret Elizabeth, 73, 148
Non-absolutism, 472, 722
Non-Brahmin movement, 178, 312, 319
Non-Brahmins, 58, 152, 178, 182, 185, 193, 339, 358, 362, 364, 474, 535
Non-cooperation movement, 178, 284–286, 290
Non-dualism, 520, 537, 580, 602, 721
Non-Hindus, 18, 41, 77, 135, 191, 201, 281, 290–291, 366, 432, 529, 582, 604, 644, 647
Non-Indic religions and Samanvaya
  dialogues with Judaism, 495–497
  Hindu-Jewish religious dialogue,

497–501
Non-Islamic Kafir tribes, concern for persecution of, 282–284
Non-Muslims, 243, 285, 288, 290–291, 512, 518, 538–539, 547, 720
Noorani, A. G., 76, 194
Nooristan, 283
Noosphere, 417, 633, 635
Nowroji, Dadabhai, 150
NSA. *see* National Security Act
NSS. *see* Nair Service Society
Nµss, Arne, 143
Nuh Sipihr, 48
'Nun running,' 198–199
Nussbaum, Martha C., 84, 136

O

OBC. *see* Other Backward Caste
Obeidullah, Maulvi, 286–287, 722
Obeidullah Plan, 287, 722
Obscurantism, 21, 144, 163–166, 203, 342, 345, 351, 433, 460
'Occult Hindu' pseudosciences, 433
Occupation Council Board, 159
October Revolution, 399–400, 402
Odisha, 335–336, 613, 615, 617–618, 629
Odisha Super Cyclone, 335
O'Dwyer, Michael, 251
Ohsumi, Yoshiori, 462
Oldmeadow, Harry, 580, 584, 597
Old Testament, 2, 496, 592, 632
Olsvanger, Immanuel, 502–503
Omar, Mullah, 97
Oneness, 40, 70, 259, 334, 535, 633, 644, 721
  of being, 521
  cultural, 95, 378
  fundamental, 293
One Sun One World One Grid initiative, 455
Operation Blue Star, 492
Orissa Freedom of Religion Act, 616, 1967
Orthodoxy, 4, 146, 175, 179–181, 184–185, 187, 201, 203–205, 209, 259, 288–289, 321, 348, 360, 364, 542
Other Backward Caste, 337, 363
Otto, Rudolph, 597
Our Educational Problem (book), 265
Outcaste, 176–177, 182, 228, 440, 482, 534
Owen, Lisa N., 484

P

Pachpore, Virag, 651–652
Padarthadharmasangrha, 426
Padmavati movie, 234, 240
Pagels, Elaine, 13–14
Paishachic Brihatkatha, 474
Pakistan, 31, 46, 83, 90, 92–100, 217, 224, 231, 235, 241–242, 244, 275, 283, 293, 313–314, 375, 399, 514, 540, 564, 567–568, 573, 645
  flags, 313
  and Islamist terror network, 97
  movement, 122, 501
  of orthodoxy, 205
Pakistan Army, 95, 241–242
Palai, 52, 727
Palani Baba, 552–553
Palaye, Pandurang Bhaskar Shastri, 186, 187, 281
Pal, Bipin Chandra, 222, 377
Pale Blue Dot (book), 276
Palestinian issue, 501–505
Pallavas, 473, 610
Pallus, 367–368
Panchagavya, 114, 722
Panchajanya (magazine), 363, 379
Pancharatra, 471–472
Pancharatragamas, 713
Panchavati, 619
Panchayat board of Thiruchendur, 202
Pandita, Jagannatha, 239
Pandit, Vijayalakshmi, 162
Pandiyan, Kumara, 559
Pandiyan, Sri John, 369
Pandya kingdom, 64, 473, 716
Pan-Hindutva, 197
Panikkar, K. M., 509
Panikkar, Raimundo, 585, 590, 638
Pan-Islamic confederation, 645

Pan-Islamic radicalism *vs.* Akhand Bharat, 94–96
Pan-Islamism, 96, 287, 289, 537
Pannas, scheduled caste, 618
Panter-Brick, Simone, 504
Pantheism, 635, 721
Paramahamsa, 620
Paramahansa, Ramakrishna, 37, 264, 307, 322, 327, 329, 371, 441, 529–531, 530, 581, 589–590, 619–622, 635
 Christ experience, 619
 realisation of, 531
 Vivekananda Vedanta, 329, 370
Paramasivam, 555–556
Parameshwaran, Sri, 649
Paranjothi, Mahan, 537
Paranoia, 99, 400–401
Pardeshi Vyapar, 72
Parivattam, 367, 369
Parliament, 47, 84, 91, 115, 125, 127, 425, 510, 525
Parmanand, Bhai, 211, 249–260, 259, 263, 273, 275, 295
 as caste abolitionist, 253
 deported to Andaman, 250
 family condition of, 249–250
 fast unto death, 251–252
 on national struggle as people's movement., 253
 observations regarding First World War, 251
 on Sanghatanist, 260
 Sanghatan views of, 253–260
  on Hindu Dharma, 253–254
  on inter-caste marriages, 256–257
  oneness of humanity, 259–260
  on religion, 254–256
  on *samanvaya* process, 258–259
  on social reforms, 259
  on varna system, 256–258
 solitary confinement of, 251
 suicidal thoughts in prison, 250–251
 teaching work, 252
Parpola, Asko, 155
Parsees, 22, 148–150, 197
Parsis, 16, 31, 138, 223, 301
Partition, 30, 90–93, 97, 100, 122, 220, 231, 235, 240–241, 307, 389, 501, 511
 holocaust, 720
 riots, 234, 236, 243, 488
Parvati, 58, 60, 83, 87, 365, 368, 479, 599
Paryushan, 110
Pascaline, 598
Pasha, Kamal, 379
Pasteur, Louis, 267
Pastoralism, 449
Pasupati Yogi, 44
Pataliputra, 482
Patange, Ramesh, 300, 354, 357
Patel, Sardar Vallabhbhai, 311, 314, 614, 645
Patel, Vithalbhai, 168, 243
Patents, 115, 135, 434, 436–438, 445
Pathak, Bindheswar, 372
Patil, Nana, 309
Patitpawan Mandir, 185
Patriarchal, 154, 235, 345, 440, 460, 604
Patriarchy, 153, 235, 241, 441
Patriotism, 60, 72, 78, 80, 82, 85, 150, 212, 214, 265, 646, 648
Patwardhana, Achyut, 399
Paul, St, 606
Pawar, Sharad, 357
PDP. *see* People's Democratic Party
Peace, 78, 91, 95–96, 116, 176, 235, 252, 325, 397, 477, 487, 507, 511, 524, 538, 555, 570, 573, 598, 647, 649, 651
Peasants, 75, 120, 329, 341, 400–401, 514
Pedraza, Everardo, 597
Pegging Act, 158–160, 723
Pelagianism, 579
Penance, 64, 110, 118, 287, 534
People's Democratic Party, 553, 558–559
Perception, 1, 48, 97, 132, 149, 169, 174, 225, 333, 393, 397, 403, 503, 594, 617, 620, 722
Perry, John, 510
Persecution, 66, 240–241, 429, 473, 483, 508, 527, 626, 646
Persia, 14, 148

Persian, 14, 35, 48, 271, 435, 542, 545
distortion, 14
lexicons, 36
schism, 11–12
Persinger, Michael, 2, 718, 722
Persuasion, 252, 304, 328, 331, 489, 612, 640, 719
Perur, 365, 368
Perversions, 165, 346, 356
Pesic, Peter, 425
Petitions, 130, 213, 215–216, 529
bail, 560
clemency, 212–213, 216
signed, 434
PFI, 110, 564–572
activists, 568, 572
Assam connection to, 568
Bangalore blast and, 568
camps, 568, 570–571
chopping of hand attack, 566
formation of, 564
frontal organizations of, 565–566
funding of, 566, 569
jihadists, 568, 569, 570
Kerala government statement on, 567–568
and LeT links, 567
media, 569
parade, 570
political considerations determing decisive actions against, 569–570
pro-Dalit voices of, 567
raid on offices of, 566
services provided by, 567
in Tamil Nadu, 570–572
targetted killings by, 567–568
PGAH. *see* Provincial Government of Azad Hind
Pharisaism, 623
Phillip, 615
Philosophy, 3, 5, 25, 36, 179, 267–268, 271, 381–382, 388, 390, 403, 417–418, 425, 430, 449–450, 474–476, 481, 521, 644, 646
eternal, 645
non-materialistic, 384
Phulzele, Sadanand, 361
Pilgrimage centres, 69–70, 452
Pilgrimages, 70, 239, 258, 270, 500, 580–581, 598–599
Pilgrims, 70, 549–550, 599
Pillai, Kavimani Desigavinayagam, 201
Pillai, Manu S., 345–346
Pillai, Sachidanandam, 203
Pillai, Sri Kanagasabapathy, 202
Pillai, Venkatarama Ramalingam, 201–202
Pingle, Moreshwar Nilkanth, 355, 357
Pitha-sthana, 69
Plagiarism, 437
Plofker, Kim, 428, 429
Pluralism, 14, 25, 31, 33, 37, 41, 65, 70, 89, 176, 470, 472, 483–485, 572, 652
Poddar, Hanuman, 498
Poisoning of water wells, 616
Political power, 50, 93, 100, 174, 283, 320, 385, 627, 630, 643
Political proxy war, 577, 608–611
Political representation, 291
Political rivalry, 224, 400, 491
Pollution, 238–239, 241, 322, 371, 637
Popper, Karl, 466, 723
Popular Front of India. *see* PFI
Portas, Maximiani, 189–190
Post-Independent India, 24, 33, 85, 124, 216, 275, 291, 313, 316, 387, 400, 509, 714
Posture, 60
public, 581
yogic, 6–7, 598, 603
Prabhulingaleela, 533
Prabhupada, Bhaktivedanta Swami, 636
Prabodha-Chandrodaya, 523
Pracharaks, 205, 316, 320, 362, 719, 723
initial formative, 389
trained, 320
Prahlad, 190–191
Prajna Bharati, 628
Pran Nath, Sant, 395–396
Prasad, Rajendra, 84, 125, 313, 502
Prasastapada, 426
Pratap, Rana, 480

Pratityasamutpada, 723
Prayag Kumbh Mela, 347
Prayers, 71, 78, 88, 281, 371, 440, 462, 486–487, 510, 527, 574, 585–586, 591, 598–600, 606, 634, 636, 638, 717, 726
Prejudices, 17, 238, 331, 337–338, 349, 353, 355, 370, 375, 401, 432, 444, 531, 575, 652
Pretoria Agreement, 160
Pride, 72, 85, 203, 228, 341, 459, 463, 465, 573, 609, 646
Priesthood, 179, 363, 511
Priests, 8, 75, 319, 321, 332, 339, 358, 362–364, 522, 582, 616, 628, 634, 637, 640, 715
  catholic, 582, 628, 641–642
  certified, 363
  qualified, 362
  SC, 338
  trained, 363
  tribal, 613
Prigogine, Ilya, 416, 466
Principles of Neurotheology (book), 722
Prism, 125, 317, 424, 444, 555
Prison, 129, 212, 216, 218, 251, 305, 561, 574
Prisoners, 213–215, 228, 250–251, 480, 528, 556, 558
Pritam, Amrita, 544
Prithvi, 54–55, 62
Prithviraj Rasa, 18
Proclamation, 13, 136, 202, 204, 237, 304, 356, 436, 440, 600, 605, 630
Pro-Islamism, 76, 567
Project Ganga, 452
Propaganda, 35, 108, 127, 212, 278, 288–289, 349, 412, 432–433, 440, 555, 569, 647
  anti-Hindutva, 439
  battle, 132
  left-wing, 457
  modern Saudi-funded Islamist, 532
  negative, 323, 375
  Pan-Islamist, 289
  political, 192
  posters, 466
  pseudo-rationalist Dravidian, 466
Prophet, 2, 126, 147–148, 271, 285, 520, 524, 545, 586, 645, 648, 717, 720
Proselytization, 20–21, 87, 205–206, 273, 275, 336, 475, 495–496, 501, 513, 518, 526, 551, 579, 622–623, 630, 631, 638, 651, 719
  activity, 616
  agencies, 280
  agenda, 331, 495, 633, 652
  aggression, 357
  charities, 324
  components, 652
  enterprise, 627
  forces, 201
  large-scale, 651
  religions, 283
  work, 171
  zeal, 17
Prosperity, 55, 91, 600
  agricultural, 124
  spiritual, 369
  worldly, 41
Protestant Christian, 34
Protestantism, 624, 652
Protests, 162, 187, 277, 364, 373, 432, 615, 622, 624
  customary, 563
  ignoring, 99
  symbol of, 36, 52
  voices, 13
Proust, Marcel, 638
Provincial Government of Azad Hind, 79
Proxy war, 577, 611
Psalms, 85, 475, 499, 583
Pseudo-rationalism, 416
Pseudoscience, 410–411, 434, 716, 723
  attitude, 465
  eligion-oriented, 456
  motivated, 412
Pseudoscientific, 25, 411–413, 642
Pseudo-scientific creationism, 268
Pseudo-secularism, 315, 399, 476, 552, 564, 648

Psyche, 5, 16, 38, 107, 233, 412, 439, 541, 555
Psychological processes, 37
Psychology, 269, 370, 499, 645
  industrial, 390
  integral, 6
  modern clinical, 196
  modern scientific, 541
  self-righteous, 562
  transpersonal, 6
Public education, revenue from Hindu temples for, 202
Publicity, 83, 320, 323–324, 326
Puja, 362, 397, 582, 599, 637
Pulikunel, Joseph, 649, 655
Punjab crisis, 492, 495
Punjab Hindu Sabha, 169
Punjab Kalyan Forum, 491
Punjab Peedit Sahayata Samiti, 491
Punya Bhumi and Pitru Bhumi definition of Savarkar, 507
Puranas, 26, 50, 54, 244, 257, 332, 367, 420, 429, 471, 487, 533, 574
Puri, 69, 184, 239
Purity, 147, 234–236, 238, 245, 255, 261, 322, 325, 371, 399, 440, 499
Purusharthas, 388, 719, 723
Purusha Sukta, 145, 637
Pushyamitra Shunga, 483

Q

Qadiriyya silsila, 520–521
Qanungo, Kalika-Ranjan, 522–524, 526
Quit India agitation, 220, 307, 309
Quraishi, Shiraz, 112
Quran, 125, 286, 522–524, 717
Qureshi, Mohammad Shafi, 540
Qutb-ad-din, Khwaja, 543, 724
Quwwat-ul-Islam, 115

R

Race, 21, 23–25, 30, 38, 61, 64, 77, 79, 145, 147–155, 163–165, 168, 195, 214, 229, 254, 272, 276, 291, 293, 317–318, 343, 377, 440, 442, 505, 531, 723–724
  biological, 25
  concept, 145–146
  dynamic, 348
  erring, 177
  human, 117, 147, 260, 276, 343–344, 505
  non-martial, 195
  superiority, 162
Racial
  interpretation, 152, 154, 414
  mix-up, 257
  purity, 151–152, 154–155
  selection program, 444
  theory, 152
Racism, 35, 145–148, 151, 162, 166, 204, 255, 257, 444, 593, 724
Racist eugenics, 343, 723
Radhakrishnan, Sarvepalli, 8, 477, 486–487, 644, 724
Radical Islamism, 562–564
Rafeeq, Abdul, 565
Raghuvamsa, 134
Rahalkar, Monali C., 463
Rahim, Mahan Muhammad, 533
Rahman, Abdur, 242
Rai, Baji Nath, 393
Raids, 230, 236, 304, 566, 569, 612
Rai, Govinda, 530–531
Rai, Lakhpat, 498–499
Rai, Lala Lajpat, 197, 211, 229, 252, 277–284, 277–294, 296, 304, 722
  Christian proselytization encountered by, 280–281
  concern for persecution of non-Islamic Kafir tribes, 282–284
  death of, 278
  deported to Mandalay, 278
  encounters with Islamist balkanizing strategies, 284–294
    appeal for Hindu-Muslim unity, 290, 292
    communal representation, 291–292
    deepening fault lines, 291
    fatwas, 284–285
    Hindu-Muslim problem, 286–289, 292–293

Maulvi Habib-ur-Rahman, 284
Obeidullah, 286–287
pan-Islamist propaganda, 289
Presidential speech, 290–292
famine relief work by, 279–280
lathi blows to, 277
letter to C. R. Das, 286
protest against Simon Commission, 277
and Shuddhi movement, 281–282
Rajagopalachari, Chakravarti, 217
Rajah, M. C., 253
Rajan, Tiruvengimalai Sesha Sundara, 217
Rajaraja Chozha, 234
Rajasthan, 50, 114, 234, 240, 264, 279, 346, 565, 720
Rajguru, Shivaram, 230, 302–305, 303, 305, 316, 726
Rajinder Singh and Devki Nandan Rajguru, 316
Rajnikanth, 554
Rajpramukh of Saurashtra government, 508
Rajputs, 23, 50, 166, 508, 515, 526, 724
Raju, C. K., 427–428, 430
Rakesh Singha and Ratan Sharda, 318
Rakhi, Ram, 250
Ramachandran, V. S., 40, 722
Ramakrishna movement, 476
Ramakrishna-Vivekananda Vedanta, 371–372, 476
Ramalingam, killing of, 572
Raman effect, 458
Ramanuja, Acharya, 346
Ramaswamy, Sumathi, 49
Ramayana, 70, 77, 82, 156–157, 517, 610
Ram, Babu Jagjivan, 129, 204, 210
Rambachan, Anantanand, 22
Ramdas, Guru, 515
Ramdev, Acharya, 200
Ramdev, Baba, 442–443
Ramesh, Jairam, 133
Ramesh, killing of, 556
Rameshwaram, 27, 69, 357, 570
Ram, Indrani Jagjivan, 184
Ram, Jagjivan, 184
Rampure, Ramdas, 309
Ram Rajya Parishad, 127
Ram/Rama, 64, 134, 156, 204, 258–259, 371, 494, 499, 500, 523, 535, 544, 622, 629
Ram Temple, 315, 358
Ramzan, 574
Rana Chandi, 715
Ranade, Mahadev Govind, 264
Ranga Iyer and Harbilas Sarda, 177
Ranganathananda, Swami, 16, 476, 625–626
Rao, PV Narshimha, 316, 383, 393, 493
Rao, Shankaranarayana N. P., 574
Rao, Suryanarayana, 28, 349
Rapes, 240–243
Rasappa, Thirikooda, 157
Rashid, Abdul, 171
Rashtradharma press, 379
Rashtra Sevika Samiti, 725
Rashtriya Jagruti, 72
Rashtriya Swayamsevak Sangh. *see* RSS
Rashtriyatva, 394, 724
Rashtrothana Parishat, 398
Rashtrotthana Sahitya, 574
Rath yatra, 315
Rationalism, 113, 261, 275, 288, 397, 416, 562
Ratnam, Mani, 554
Ratnasabapathy, V., 558
Ravana, 20, 156, 244, 302, 371
Ravishankar, Ra., 212
Ravishankar, Sri Sri, 443
Rawat, Neera, 553
Ray, Himanshu Prabha, 484
Ray, Prabha, 484
Ray, Prafulla Chandra, 417, 419–422
Ṛaza, Rahi Mazoom, 476
Reader, John, 115
Realization, 23, 42, 60, 80, 193, 214, 522, 579, 586, 601, 625, 643
Rebellion, 65, 226, 232, 278, 718, 720
Reciprocity Act, 161
Recolonization, 506
Reconciliation, 65, 483, 581
Reconversion, 171, 183, 191
Reddy, Muthulakshmi, 196

Reform movements, 36, 85, 166, 173–175, 180, 183, 186, 196, 203, 259, 281, 319, 342, 347, 350, 384
Refuges, 16, 242, 253, 269, 283, 508, 510, 518, 612, 647
Relief and service works of RSS, 199, 204, 252, 279–280, 301, 328, 331, 337, 481, 491, 560
  academic study of, 331–339
  in Bhopal gas disaster, 325, 327
  Gujarat earthquake, 337
  1996 mid-air collision of Saudi airlineer, 333
  non-discriminatory seva, 333
  Odisha Super Cyclone, 335
  social conflicts, 337–338
  as social welfare strategy, 334–336
  SVM schools, 335–337
  tsunami of 2004, 333
Religion, 1–5, 8, 10, 12, 16, 19–20, 22–33, 35, 37–39, 49, 54, 57, 69, 74–75, 77–78, 89, 132, 144–145, 150–153, 176, 184, 197–199, 202–204, 235, 240, 245, 252–256, 259, 264, 266, 269, 271, 274–275, 280–286, 288, 293, 300, 324, 326, 332–334, 339, 350–351, 397, 411, 418, 423, 441, 443, 457, 462, 474, 476–478, 485–486, 493, 495–496, 498, 500–501, 508, 514–516, 518–521, 526–528, 532, 542, 545, 547, 555, 573, 576, 584, 588, 590, 593, 595, 611, 613, 622–625, 627–628, 630, 633–634, 640–643, 649, 651, 714, 717–719, 722
  monopolistic-expansionist, 642
  monopolistic monotheist, 13
  moralizing, 4
  non-Christian, 630
  prophetic, 431–432
  proselytizing, 254, 282
  scripture-based, 411
  sectarian, 37, 383
  true, 12, 180, 255, 528, 548
  universal, 24, 37–38, 642
Religious boundaries, 112, 642
Religious communities, 29, 193, 288, 511, 538
Religious conversion, 225, 234, 500, 719
Religious identities, 18, 74, 93, 488, 497–498, 512, 608
Religious movements, 146, 359, 411, 487, 596
Religious sect, 19, 33, 263, 281, 485
Religious tolerance, 478, 513, 515
Renaissance, 21, 299, 358, 366, 370–371, 401, 450, 544
Renaming, 212, 526
Renan, Ernest, 23–24, 382, 384–385
Renunciation, 264, 362, 578
Reputation, 168, 436, 483
Rescue operations, 64, 159, 281, 301, 326–327, 333, 337, 349, 359, 411, 558
Reservations, 173, 321, 350, 354, 360, 650
Resistance movement, 49, 88, 231, 719–720
Resolution, 13, 80, 96, 128, 169–170, 173, 175, 183–184, 186–188, 202, 205, 290, 305, 307, 348–350, 354–355, 357–358, 376, 393, 501–502, 558
Revolution, 3, 86, 226, 232–234, 238, 303, 307, 309, 361, 395, 400, 603
Ribeiro, Sidarto, 4
Rig Veda, 7–8, 12, 15, 56–59, 71, 137, 332, 412, 424, 481–482, 600, 635, 637
Riots, 83, 109, 199, 241–243, 245, 252, 273, 288–289, 293, 331, 354, 399, 501, 503, 555, 568, 576, 612
Ripley, 133
Risala-i-Haqnuma, 522
Ritualism, 8, 228, 542
Rituals, 5, 8, 12, 14–15, 34, 49, 114, 151, 154, 176, 212, 300, 356, 363, 370, 431, 471, 482, 509, 543, 642, 713, 726

Rizzolati, Iaccomo, 40
Roja film, 554
Role models, 152, 459, 538
Rolland, Romain, 196
Roman Catholic Church, 578, 618
Roosevelt, Franklin, 217–218
Rose, Sir Hugh, 249
Rosetta Mission, 460
Rowlatt Committee, 251
Roy, Dilip Kumar, 623
Roy, M. N., 235
Roy, Raja Rammohan, 19
Roy, Rammohan, 19
RRP. *see* Ram Rajya Parishad
RSS, 27, 28, 82, 84, 89–90, 93, 94–95, 99–100, 126–129, 127, 130, 135–136, 141, 144, 151, 155, 156, 189, 193–194, 211, 246, 297–302, 298–299, 301–303, 305–335, 342, 357, 363, 373, 423, 432–433, 436, 442–443, 447–448, 451, 456–457, 460, 468–469, 476, 487–495, 491–493, 538, 541–542, 547–549, 572–576, 613, 616, 629–630, 631, 643–651, 646, 651, 653–655, 656, 717, 719, 723, 725–726
  academic attempt to understand, 317–323
  affiliates, 135–136, 301, 321
  Akhil Bharatiya Karyakari Mandal, 355
  appeal to Indian Muslims, 577
  approach to social reformation of traditionalist institutions, 319
  Balraj Madhok and Indianization, 122, 313, 376–379, 489, 576
  branches, 538
  British Intelligence reports on, 308–309
  cadre, 301, 309, 311, 314, 324, 372, 406, 493, 547
  Campaign for Cow Protection, 135
  camps, 300, 308, 322, 324, 372
  challenge of social change, 365–370
  chiefs, 94, 129–130, 305, 306, 350, 361, 374
  children's literature, 574–575
  circles, 325, 327, 355, 375, 386
  conception of Akhand Bharat, 93
  conceptualization of seva, 338
  creation of, 299
  Dattopant Thengadi and, 388–394
  Deendayal Upadhyaya and, 379–388
  under Deoras, 351–358
  Devendrakula Vellalar and, 365–370
  dialogue with Indian Christian-Christianity, 643
    Elenjimittam, Anthony, 644–648
    Golwalkar's views, 643–644
    Mathai, M. P., 650–651
    Pachpore, Virag, 651–652
    Shastri, Shripati, 648–649
    Sudarshan, K. S., 650
  disaster relief, 337
  education services of, 575–576
  engagement with Indian marxists, 399–402
  essentialist *vs.* evolutionary approaches, 339–342
  and freedom movement, 302
  frittering accusation against, 306
  functionary, 347, 551
  functions, 369, 717
  under Golwalkar, 307–310, 342–351
    lecture at Gujarat University, 343
    non-involvement in national movement, 307–308
    pro-Hitler quotes of, 342
    support of racist eugenics, 343–345
    views on jati and its culmination, 345–351
  Guru Puja function, 492
  Hindu nationalism, 317
  ideologues, 321, 381, 399
  ideology, 317
  institution DRI, 451
  intellectual churning process of, 394–399
  intellectualism, 373–379
  labour union, 347, 364

leaders, 342, 350, 363, 374, 456
literature, 325, 333
magazine, 363, 541, 545
Manthan, 394, 396, 398–400, 402–403, 449, 452, 454, 538, 541, 544, 546–547
and mass freedom movement, 305–307
members, 129, 347
and national flag, 310–317
Ambedkar's views on, 311–313
Flag Committee recommendations for, 311
hoisting in Kashmir, 313–316
Sanghathanists views on, 311–312
Savarkar's views on, 312–313
negative stereotyping of, 318–321
organizational dynamics of, 323–324
organizations, 89, 109, 335, 443, 457, 628
organized patrol, 493
post-deoras developments, 358–365
Pracharak, 359, 361
propaganda, 314
Rajguru and Hindutva movement, link between, 302–305
Rashtriya Suraksha Mahashivir, 436
relief and service works of, 280, 301, 328, 331
academic study of, 331–339
in Bhopal gas disaster, 325, 327
Gujarat earthquake, 337
1996 mid-air collision of Saudi airlineer, 333
non-discriminatory seva, 333
Odisha Super Cyclone, 335
social conflicts, 337–338
as social welfare strategy, 334–336
SVM schools, 335–337
tsunami of 2004, 333
resolution, 96, 491
resolutions of, 355–356
response to USSR collapse, 402–403
Samanvaya and Ayodhya movement, 537–551
Sarsanghachalak, 93, 321–322, 539
school, 576
schools runned by, 336, 370, 540, 575–576
and science, 432–434, 456
left-wing propaganda on, 432–434
Nehruvian McCarthyism, 436–437
Science India magazines, 456–465
science popularization culture, 456
Traditional Knowledge Digital Library, 435–439
Vijnana Bharati, 456
service activities of, 324–331, 335–336, 338
shakhas, 28, 372, 436, 494, 726
social emancipation of Hindu society, 339, 362–365
Suruchi Sanstha, 396
training camps, 308
and VHP workers, 337
Vijnana Bharati, 468
vision of Akhand Bharat, 95
volunteers, 300–302, 308, 313, 323
workers, 28, 305, 309–310, 493, 613
worldview, 319, 321, 328–331, 333, 370, 449, 454, 457
RSS: A View to the Inside, The (book), 318
RSS-Christian Perspective Analysis Meet, 649
RSS: The icons of the Indian Right, The (book), 246
Rudras, 57–58, 118, 479
Rupa Dvaita, 537
Rushdie, Salman, 136, 546–547
Ruskin, John, 449

S

SAARC. *see* South Asian Association for Regional Cooperation
Sabarmati Ashram, 178
Saberwal, Vasant, 131
Saccidananda, 578, 584, 586

Saccidananda Ashram, 577–578, 607
Sacred bison, extermination of, 116–117, 121
Sacred forms, 521–522, 525
Sacred geography of India, 14, 16, 30, 54, 61, 69, 719
Sacred spaces, 716
Sacred spots, 576
Sacred texts, 82, 362, 485, 496, 523, 644, 713, 727
Sacrifice, 8, 54, 117–118, 121, 153, 201, 230, 233–235, 240, 245, 249, 252, 254–256, 280, 303, 308, 317, 324, 330, 332, 450, 482, 491, 508, 514, 595, 637, 646
Saddam execution, march condemning, 563–564
Sadhana, 371, 476, 519, 533, 544, 625
Sadhu Jana Paripalana Sangham, 87
Sadhus, 128–129, 580, 724
Saffron colour, 306, 313
Saffron flag, 20, 46, 189, 306, 310–313, 317, 318, 517, 578, 581
Saffronization, 432, 436, 439
Saffron propaganda, 434
Saffron regime, 438
Safiwan-ibn-Umayya, 285–286
Safinat al-Awliya, 521
Sagan, Carl, 276, 416
Sahajananda, 602
Saha, Meghnad, 448, 467
Sahasranama, 494
Sahi, Ajit, 570
Sahi, Jyoti, 605
Sahu, Bhairabi Prasad, 55
Sai Baba of Shirdi, 532
Sai Baba tradition, 532
Saidi Maula, 519
Saivaite, 60, 87, 487, 713
  framework, 727
  text, 60
  and Vaishnavaite figures, 603
Saivaite Nayanmar, 473
Saivas, 486–487
Saiva Siddhanta, 414, 534
Saiva Siddhanta Maha Samajam, 203
Saiva Siddhanta Publishing, 203
Saiva Vellalar, 367
Saivism, 60, 603–604, 610
Sajivini magazine, 283
Sakta Pithas, 70
Salafi-Wahabi forms of political Islamism, 537
Salati, Mohiuddin, 540
Salim, Akbar's son, 115, 517, 563
Salman Rushdie's Satanic Verses, 136
Salu, Sunil K., 489
Salvation, 71, 245, 253, 476, 585, 587, 599, 624, 627
Samajik Samarasta Manch, 338, 357–358, 725
Samajist, 164, 201
Samajwadi Party, 109, 358
Samanvaya, 16–17, 29, 197, 258, 378, 399, 403, 417, 471–472, 474–478, 487–488, 494–495, 497, 511, 526, 529, 531, 572, 724
  brahminical *vs.* heterodox, 481–485
  continuity, 485–488
  to cultural matrix, 16
  holy wars and, 477–478
    Mihirakula, 479–481
  and Islam, 572–577
    Dara Shukoh, 520–529
    sufism, 511–520, 573–574
    transformation of Akbar, 514–517
  movement, 16, 520
  Muslim League and Gandhi-Nehru, 501–505
  and Non-Indic Religions, 495
  and non-Indic religions
    dialogues with Judaism, 495–497
    Hindu-Jewish religious dialogue, 497–501
  process, 115, 259, 475, 499, 511, 537–538
  Ramakrishna-Vivekananda-initiated, 476
  and Sikh Panth, 488–495
  transformation, 652
Sambandar, Jnana, 60, 472, 473, 484
Sambandar, Thirugnana, 473, 484
Sambhaji, 18

Saminana, 71
Sampath, Vikram, 185, 217
Sampurnanand, S., 126
Sampurnanand Sanskrit Vishwavidyalaya, 365
Samskara, 335, 426
Sanatana Dharma, 31, 170, 182, 341, 369, 494
Sanatan Dharm Sabhas, 259
Sanatanism, 30, 175, 258–259
Sanchi Stupa, 483
Sanction, 28, 82, 124, 175, 183, 290, 348, 542, 713
Sandhya Vandana (book), 599–601
Sandwich Mantras, 586
Sane Guruji, 309
Sangha, 395, 482, 646
Sanghism, 90
Sanghi-stereotyping, 374
Sani, Farid, 519
Sanitary workers, washing feet of, 370
Sankaracharya, Adi, 22–23, 27, 60, 176, 474, 580, 645, 721
Sankaracharya, Govardhan, 205
Sankaracharya, Kurtkoti, 187
Sannyasins, 176, 532, 631
Sannyasi rebellion, 49
Sannyasis, 49, 601
Sanskars, 78, 370, 372
Sanskrit, 15, 47, 55, 57, 63, 154, 200, 265, 362, 435, 474–475, 585, 600
  literature, 48, 59, 420–421
  prayers, 487, 591
  texts, 82, 583, 591
  work on Tantric Yoga, 521
  works, 523
Sanskriti Sangam, 656
Sanskrit Sansthan, 363
Sanyasis, 30, 74, 127, 498
Sapru, Bahadur, 225
Saptarshi, 257–258
Saradananda, Swami, 530–531
Sarasvati, 59, 67–68, 118
Saraswathi, Bodhendra, 239
Saraswati, 56–60, 57, 397–398, 533
Saraswati, Dayananda, 37, 166, 168, 207, 346, 397, 495–496
Saraswati, Devanananda, 631
Saraswati, Jayendra, 363
Saraswati, Lakshmanananda, 618–619
Saraswati, Manacharya, 200
Sarda Act, 196
Sarda, Har Bilas, 196, 197, 208
Sardesai, H. S., 66
Sarkar, A. K., 129
Sarkar, Jadunath, 21, 65
Sarmad, 497–499, 545
  in Dara Shukoh, 499
  identity, 498
  love for Abhai Chand, 498
  nudity, 499
  rejection of religious practice, 497
  tomb, 497
Sarsanghachalak, 311, 324, 328, 339, 342, 349, 351, 355, 358, 360, 373–374, 649, 725
SARS-CoV-2 virus, 463–464
Sarvadeshik Hindu Sabha, 169
Sarva Praharanayuddh, 302, 305, 725
Sarvavarma, 474
Sasanka, 483
Sasikumar, 571
Satavalekar, Damodar, 309
Sathe, Shriram, 155
Sathe, Vasanth, 397, 433
Sati, 70, 196, 239, 442, 534
Satpathy, Amar Prasad, 618
Satyagraha, 181, 186, 190, 193, 358, 380, 504
Satyagrahis, 129, 190, 215
Satyananda, Swami, 189–193, 190
Saundarya Lahari, 60
Saunders, John, 304
Saux, Henri Le, 580, 631
Savarkar, Babu Rao, 303
Savarkarite, 33, 220, 224, 254
  approach, 449
  definition of Hindu, 175
  Hindutva, 36, 302
  usage, 21
  worldview, 147
Savarkar, Mai, 247
Savarkar, Vinayak Damodar Veer, 1, 23, 29–31, 37, 41–42, 45, 70, 85,

121, 123, 144, 146–150, 152, 162, 179–183, 185–189, 191–192, 197, 212–234, 236–241, 243–249, 259–261, 273, 275–276, 282, 293, 300, 303, 306, 312–313, 317, 334, 344, 382, 384, 447, 449, 485, 505–507, 514–515, 576, 622, 719
on abduction and conversion of Hindu women, 243–244
in Andamans, 212–217
to Bhagavad Gita, 485
biographer of, 216
book influence on Bhagat Singh, 229–231
clemency petitions of, 212–216
condemnation of caste system and untouchability, 179–181
contacts with revolutionaries overseas, 218
criticism of Gandhi, 224–225
definition of Hindutva, 29–33
double life imprisonment of, 212
Hindu Mahasabha on, 505–506
Hindutva against Gandhi's Hind Swaraj, 24, 220–224
historiography of, 225–229, 231, 234, 246, 305
honouring, 212
influence on Bhagat Singh, 229–231
Jauhar debate, 234–240
juxtaposed Akbar, 514
and Lala Har Dayal, 276, 293
Narayan Damodara, 187
philosophy of social emancipation, 181–183
praise for women of 1857 uprising, 247–248
Presidential address to Hindu Mahasabha, 293
public participation of wife of, 246–247
on rehabilitation of abducted women, 244–245
renaming airport to honour, 212
role in INA, 217–220
role in life of Bose, 218–219
on sexual assault on Muslim women, 240–246
social commentary, 228
and social emancipation, 179–181
sympathy with motives of INC, 219–220
on transformation of Akbar, 514–515
views on cow protection, 123–124
wife of, 246–247
as witness to communal riots, 240–241
women in historiography of, 231–234
work on 1857 rebellion, 232–233
and Yashodabai Bhatt, 198
Savarkar, Yamuna Bai, 246–247
Sawant, Golwalkar, 66
Sayeed, Mufti Mohammad, 540
Sayeed, P. M., 525
SB. *see* Shatapatha Brahmana
Scheduled Caste community, proselytization attempts by evangelists of, 205
Scheduled Castes, 36, 108, 167–168, 173, 179, 185, 195, 205, 300, 360–361, 364, 369
Scheduled Communities, 36, 87, 108, 159, 167, 170, 172, 181, 184, 186–187, 192, 204, 209, 300–301, 322, 348, 355, 358, 363, 567, 628, 657, 716
article on agony of, 204
decision to convert to Islam, 355
Schmidt, Wilhelm, 152–153, 152–154
Scholarship, 190, 263, 317, 448, 629
Schumacher, Ernst F., 423, 445–446
Schuon, 588–589
Science and Hindu movement
Acharya Ray's work on, 419–422
Chatterjee's work on, 418–419
colours of prism, 424–425
divide between theory and practice, 422
eco-awareness, 449–455
Holy Science: The Biopolitics of Hindu Nationalism (book), 439–444

Matilal's work on, 422
Midnight's Machines: A Political History of Technology in India (book), 439, 444–448
'nationalist' school, 420–421
nitrites, 419
social stagnation impact, 420
Vivekananda's work on, 419
Science and RSS, 432–434, 456
left-wing propaganda on, 432–434
Nehruvian McCarthyism, 436–437
Science India magazines, 456–465
science popularization culture, 456
Traditional Knowledge Digital Library, 435–439
Vijnana Bharati, 456
Science India magazines, 456–457, 456–465, 460–462, 464–465, 468
Scindia, Mahadaji, 122
Scott, James, 304
Scriptures, 20, 22–23, 26, 31, 53, 109, 118, 147–148, 348, 360, 412, 417, 487, 498, 513, 727
Sculpture, 87, 157, 458, 590, 603–604
SDPI. *see* Social Democratic Party of India
Second World War, 161, 214, 217, 219, 227, 382, 715
Secularism, 29, 93, 358, 378, 413, 510, 528–529, 648–649
Security, 95, 355–356, 554, 564
Seeman, 608–611
Seethabhai, Rama, 204
Seldon, Hari, 299
Self-immolation, 234, 238
Self-reliance, 120, 266, 457, 719
Self-respect, 203–204, 548
Self-sacrifice, 236, 239, 632
Selvaraj murder case, 554–556
Sen, Indra, 6
Sen, Keshab Chandra, 85, 86, 163, 620–621
Sentier de Gnose (Footpaths of Gnosis - Knowledge), 588
Sentiments, 110, 122, 125–126, 137, 147, 214, 253, 256, 278, 308, 353, 355, 526, 540–541, 544, 549
Separatist Dravidian movement, 553
Sequeira, T. N., 608
Serial bombing, 555, 565
Seshadri, H. V., 384, 423–424
Setalvad, Teesta, 436
Setubandha, 70
SEVA, 500
Seva Bharati, 301, 333, 337–338, 725
Seva Foundation, 500
Seva Mission, 613
Sex slavery, 234
Sexual assault, 240
Sexuality, 440, 443, 593
Shabandri, Sanaulla, 569
Shah Bano case, 539–540
Shah, Bulleh, 519, 538, 542, 544–545, 572
Shah, Firaz, 520
Shah, Gul Mohammad, 540
Shah Jahan, 519–520
Shah, Majnu, 49
Shah, Mubarak, 236
Shah, Mullah, 520–521
Shah, Qutb ud din Mubarak, 237, 571–572
Shah, Sher, shrine of, 122–123
Shah, Syed Ahmed, 305
Shah, Umakant Premanand, 62
Shaikh Abdul Quddus, 545
Shaikh, Anwar, 54
Shaivaite, 483, 485
Shaivism, 473, 604
Shakhas, 298, 300–301, 306, 321, 335, 370, 372, 723, 726
Shaktis, 47, 67, 74, 87, 532, 714
Shalivahana, 474–475
Shame, 73, 199, 235, 237, 241, 283, 371, 396, 495, 533, 615
Shankaracharya, 39, 128–129, 165, 169, 184, 300, 347–348, 350, 360
Shankaracharya of Puri, 128–129
Shankardev, 236
Shankardev Shishu Niketan, 575
Shankar, Gauri, 207
Shankhdhar, M. M., 396
Shantivanam, 581, 583–584, 586–587, 590, 597–603, 605–607, 611

Shantivanam chapel, 603
Shantivanam movement, 581, 594, 604, 607
Shantivanam prayer book, 599, 600–601
Shantivanam products, 601, 605
Shantivanam project, 607, 638
Shantivanam School, 603
Shantivanam worldview, 601
Sharaddhanand, Swami, 77–78, 167–171, 173, 176, 197, 208, 252, 303
Sharda, S. R., 543–544
Sharif, Nawaz, 95, 96
Sharma, Arvind, 17, 28–29, 486–487, 513
Sharma, Jyotirmaya, 221
Sharma, Manmohan, 128
Sharma, Y. D., 550
Shastri, Shripati, 648–649
Shastri, Srinivas, 173
Shastri Yagnapurushdas, 36
Shatapatha Brahmana, 55, 57, 113
Sheikh, Anwar, 54
Sheldrake, Rupert, 597, 601
Shelley, Mary, 449
Shelley, Percy, 449
Sherwani, Ahmed Rashid, 399
Sheshadri, H. V., 27, 375, 423, 449
Shiek, G. M., 560
Shinde, Manohar, 373
Shishu Vidya Mandirs, 335–337
Shiva, 65, 415–416, 478–481, 480, 597–600
  Nataraja, 411, 413–414, 416, 598–599
  trident wielding, 479
Shivaji, Chhatrapati, 18–19, 28, 65–66, 73, 102, 166, 240, 245, 355, 480, 524, 526–528, 714, 719
  administration, 528
  approach to Islam, 527
  attitude towards captured Muslim women, Savarkar's criticism of, 240, 245
  chivalrous behaviour, 245
  failure, 245
  polity, 527
Shiva, Veera, 552
Shivlal, Govindlal Shivlal, 175
Shiv Sena, 357, 494
Shourie, Arun, 110, 627–629, 717
Shraddhanand, Swami, 167–171, 187, 208, 716
Shree Dharmarakshak Nasir-ud-din, 238
Shreema, 611
Shrine, 63, 68, 70, 77, 115, 122–123, 491, 590
Shruti-Smriti-Puranokta Dharma, 31
Shuddhananda Bharati, 201
Shuddhi, 170, 172, 175, 183, 274, 282
  ceremony, 404
  of Moslems, 274
  movement, 171, 281–282
Shuddhi Sabha, 282
Shudras, 182, 256, 343, 715
Shukla, Rajaram, 365
Shura, Nangrarhar, 97
Shvetaketu, 302, 386
Siddhanta Deepika magazine, 414
Siddhanta Saivism, 727
Siddhas, 61, 438, 534, 603
Siddique, N. M., 571
Sikh, 30–31, 33, 42, 66–67, 74, 138, 175, 235, 239, 242, 282, 286, 288, 293, 316, 350, 488, 490–494, 517, 526, 653–654, 715, 718, 721
  history, 66, 492
  riot victims, 493
  terrorism, 489, 494
Sikh Dharma, 32, 74, 654
Sikhism, 30, 37, 282, 360, 492
Sikh Panth, 475, 488, 494, 518
Sikorski, Wladyslaw, 508
SIMI. *see* Students Islamic Movement of India
Simon Commission, 277
Sindhu, 14–15, 54, 59, 148
Singhal, Ashok, 347, 360
Singh, Arjan, 490
Singh, Attar, 492, 542
Singh, Bhagat, 216, 227, 229–230, 252, 297, 302–305, 303, 304, 305, 316, 726
Singh, Bhagat Daryav, 200

Singh, Bhagat Phool, 171–172, 200
Singh, Dara, 617, 629
Singh, Digvijaya, 434
Singh, Durgavati, 304
Singh, Gopal, 494
Singh, Guru Gobind, 51, 66–68, 73–74, 475, 714–715, 720–721
Singh, Guru Ram, 720
Singh, Jai, 524
Singh, Kalyan, 549–550
Singh, Khushwant, 492
Singh, Kirpal, 242
Singh, Kishan, 311
Singh, Lala Sukhbir, 169
Singh, Maharaja Ranjit, 720
Singh, Malwinder Jit, 229–230
Singh, Manmohan, 48, 94, 360, 457
Singh, Mann, 491
Singh, Nikky-Guninder Kaur, 67–68
Singh, Niranjan, 488
Singh, Phool, 171
Singh, Rajendra, 358, 374, 399, 409, 725
Singh, Sardar Uttam, 493
Singh, Satyapal, 425
Singh, Shabeg, 490
Singh, Tara, 489
Singh, Upinder, 12, 479, 483
Sirrs, Owen L., 97
Sitapati, Vinay, 493
Sita Rasois, 70
Siva, 53, 60, 64, 83, 86–87, 104, 118, 158, 359, 365, 367–368, 414–415, 417, 440, 466, 473, 486–487, 532, 535, 583, 590, 592–593, 597–599, 603–604, 609, 611, 716, 719
  consort of, 58, 73, 83
  cosmic dance of, 414–417, 716
  deeds of, 53
  temples, 127, 603
Siva Linga, 27, 509
Sivan, 484
Sivananda, Swami, 589
Sivanism, 610
Siva Raja Yoga, 532
Siva Somanatha, 509
Six Glorious Epochs of Indian History (book), 228, 236, 240, 514
SJPS. *see* Sadhu Jana Paripalana Sangham
Skanda (Murugan), 51, 356, 726
Slaughtering, 62, 64, 109, 111, 115, 117, 122, 126, 132, 137
Slavery, 192, 218, 284, 353, 479, 720
  abolished, 353
  double, 252
  institutionalized, 720
  sexual, 235, 243, 245
Slaves, 35, 228, 284
Sleeman, William, 50
Smith, Adam, 402
Smith, Donald, 321–322
Smith, E. H., 3
Smith, James Dunlop, 166
Smith, Justin E. H., 3, 5
Smith Theory, 194
Smuts, Jan Christian, 158, 162
Snodgrass, Adrian, 481
Social Darwinian, 269, 386
Social Democratic Party of India, 565–569, 571–572
Social emancipation, 35, 163, 166, 170, 173, 178–179, 181, 193, 317, 322, 339–340, 342, 357, 359, 364–365
  and Hindutva, 166
  movement, 146, 166, 197, 201, 294
  Movement and Hindutva, 166–171
  obscurantism and, 163–166
  Savarkar and, 179–181
  Savarkar's philosophy of, 181–183
  schools, 170
Social evils, 185, 201, 346, 651
Social harmony, 252, 354, 356, 359, 361, 363, 643, 725
Socialism, 153, 271–272, 327, 380, 400, 402
Social reforms, 169, 174, 181, 183, 185, 187, 196, 259, 363
Social service, 324, 331, 395, 409
Social stagnation, 20, 35, 144, 146, 183, 188, 206, 211, 224, 226, 228, 245, 340, 345, 361, 363–364, 370, 420, 440

Social structure, 154, 170, 340–341, 345
Social system, 184, 291, 340, 345, 381, 386, 470, 647
Social wmancipation, 163–166
Sohonie, Kamala, 459
Solar Energy Commission in India, 454
Solomos, John, 506
Somayaji, Nilakantha, 429
Somnath, 315, 357, 486
Somnath Sivalinga, 509
Somnath Sivalinga consecration, 509
Songs, 47, 74–76, 79, 84–88, 157, 293, 600, 621, 639–640
  national, 48, 75
  patriotic, 299, 726
  religious, 75
Soundarya Lahari, 23
South Africa, 121, 158–162, 215, 219, 222–223, 438
South African Indians, 158, 162
South Asia, 94, 99, 136, 139, 189, 235, 255, 330, 459, 609
South Asian Association for Regional Cooperation, 93–95, 98–99
South Asian countries, 30, 94, 99, 136, 139, 189, 235, 255, 459, 609
Southern jihad
  AIADMK's steps to curb, 554
  Bangalore bomb blasts, 559–560
  Coimbatore bomb blasts, 553, 555
  globalization attempt of, 553–554
  government green signal to Islamists, 558
  insensitivity towards victims of, 556
  Kerala connection to, 553
  Madras film industry glorifying, 554
  Marad massacre, 557
  MNP and KFD, 556
  police crack down on, 555
  radical Islamist activities, 562–564
  separatist Dravidian movement, 553
  targeted killings, 551–552, 554–555, 558–559
  TMMK, 554, 556
  violent attacks, 558–559
South India, 16–17, 20, 23, 28, 53, 60, 62–64, 87, 118–119, 157, 201, 206, 217, 355, 500, 532, 537, 551, 556–557, 562–564, 590, 599, 604
South Indian Hindu-Sanghatan magazine, 201
South Indian Muslims, syncretic mysticism of, 532–537
South Indian operations, 564
Souza, C. D., 568
Soviet aid arm-twisting India, 448
Soviet-backed regime, 97
Soviet model, 80–81
Soviet occupation of Afghanistan and CIA, 97
Soviet style planning, 446
Soviet Union, 81, 96–97, 400, 402–403, 445, 508
Sovik, Rolf, 600
SP. *see* Samajwadi Party
Spencer, Herbert, 269
Spillett, Juan, 130
Spinoza, Baruch, 721
Spirituality, 16, 38, 265, 289, 377, 415, 417, 484, 498, 500, 503, 514, 516, 524, 530, 534–535, 608, 624, 635, 638, 644, 646, 647
Spiritual traditions, 6, 20, 34, 88, 165, 176, 253, 310, 367, 488, 497, 501, 521, 529, 536–537, 577, 602, 604–605, 607, 618, 637, 652, 656
Spiritual values, 146, 360, 367, 496
Spontaneous generation, 267
Spry, Henry Harpur, 50
Sreenivasan, Rettamalai, 121
Sridhara, Lakshmi, 239
Srinivas, M. D, 332
Sri Ram, 222, 358, 499
Sri Ramakrishna Mission, 16, 203, 327, 529, 625
Sri Ram Janmabhoomi, 396, 541, 549
Sri Rangam, 582, 590
Sri Rangam Nadar, 582
Sri Vaishnavism, 532
Srivastava, Harindra, 221
Srivastava, Harish, 217
Srivastava, K. M., 550

SSM. *see* Samajik Samarasta Manch
SSVM, 335–337
Staal, Frits, 5
Staines, Graham Stewart, 615
Staines murder, 616–618, 629
Stalin, Joseph, 232, 400–401, 508
St Joseph's College, 608–610
Stone, Linda, 412
Stuart, James, 578, 582, 584
Stuart, Kathy, 340
Students Islamic Movement of India, 562–565, 568
Stylites, Simeon, 270
Subair, 571–572
Subash, Arpita, 456
Subrahmanya, 118, 500
Subramaniam, Banu, 439–444, 715
Sudarshan, K. S., 360–361, 363, 396, 539, 649–650, 655
Sudarshan, Kuppahalli Sitaramayya, 725
Sufi Islam, 513
Sufis, 511, 513, 517–521, 541–545, 572
  contribution to Punjabi poetry, 543
  dimension of Islam in India, 513
  heritage, 542, 573
  influence, 514, 516, 520
  movement, 517–518, 544
  mysticism, 477, 519, 573, 640
  orders, 542, 545
Sufi, Shaikh, 523
Sufism, 511, 513–514, 518, 520, 542, 544–545, 572–573, 719
Sufis persecution of, 519
Sugirtharajah, Sharadha, 261
Suicide, 64, 156, 234–235, 270, 517
Sukumar, Arun Mohan, 439, 446–447
Sulabh, 372
Sultan, Ameer, 561
Sundarar episode, 368
Superstition, 5, 37, 116, 124, 266, 269, 413, 415–416
Supreme Court of India, 36, 84, 110, 112, 125, 129, 137, 529–530, 540, 550, 560
Supreme Sacred Congregation, 477, 641
Surjeet, Harkishan Singh, 494
Surya Siddhanta, 428
Sushruta Samhita, 114
Sutta Nipata, 482
Suvarnaprabha Sutra, 57
SVMs. *see* Shishu Vidya Mandirs
Swabhiman, 72
Swachh Rail Mission, 372
Swadeshi, 120, 439, 448
Swadeshi Jagran Manch, 393, 447
Swadeshi Science Movement, 456–457
Swadesi movement, first, 143
Swami ,Chattampi, 362
Swamigal, Vannasarabam Thandabani, 119
Swaminarayan sect, 36
Swaminathan, Venkat, 82
Swami, Praveen, 540
Swami, Sri Malayala, 534
Swamy, Subramanian, 425
Swaraj, 70, 164, 220, 222–223, 249, 252, 274, 284, 308–309, 463, 476, 644
Swaraj Party, 185
Swaraj, Sushma, 438
Swarajya, 111, 167–168, 288, 290, 507, 535–536, 719
Swarup, Devendra, 396
Swarup, Ram, 9–10, 13–14, 396, 446, 449, 496, 529–530, 624–625, 630–631
Swayamsevaks, 84, 299–300, 306, 313, 322, 324–325, 334, 351, 353–354, 361, 371, 403, 436, 491–493, 726
Sword bearing Goddess, resurfacing of
  Guru Gobind Singh and Bhagavati, 66–68
  Kumara Kampana and Meenakshi, 62–65
  during national movement, 71–72
  sacred geography and divine feminine, 68–70
  Shivaji and Bhavani, 65–66
Symbiosis, 726
Symbolism, 15, 55, 64, 72, 80, 83, 316, 416, 425, 482, 509, 532, 543, 590, 716
Symbolization, 68–69, 71, 130, 310, 509,

714
Sympathy, 40, 180, 215, 219–220, 268, 276, 279, 281, 305, 349, 501–506, 558, 622, 644
Syncretic mysticism of South Indian Muslims, 532–537
Syncretism, 12, 412, 605
Syndicated Hinduism, 33–35

T

Tabligh ideologue, 303
Tadikonda, Kalpana K., 481
Tagore, Debendranath, 85–86
Tagore, Rabindranath, 19, 23–24, 80, 83, 84–86, 85, 103, 330, 384–385, 418, 449, 503, 545, 719
  concept of Hinduness, 384
  and Sri Aurobindo, 385
Talageri, Shrikant, 155
Talbot, Cynthia, 18
Taliban, 97–98, 514, 559, 573, 609
  regime in Kabul, 97
  style execution of Dalit youth, 571
  war machine, 97
Talpur, Parveen, 103
Tamil language, 609
Tamil Nadu, 15, 48, 73, 83, 87, 91, 102, 104, 118–119, 121, 127, 157, 201–203, 316, 322, 330, 356, 365–370, 372, 398, 411, 416, 483–484, 532, 537, 551–554, 556–558, 560–561, 563–565, 570–571, 605, 607–608, 609, 610, 654
Tamil Nadu Muslim Munnetra Kazhagam, 554, 556, 558–560, 570–571
Tamil Nadu Towheed Jamat, 561, 570
Tamil nationalism, 609
Tamil nationalist-secessionist movement, 610–611
Tamil Saivism, 60
Tamil separatism, 608
Tamil Women Work Field. *see* Tamizhaga Penkal Seyal Kalam
Tamizh, 56, 73, 716, 721
Tamizhaga Penkal Seyal Kalam, 609–610
Tamizh Buddhist, 332
Tamizh literature, 156, 535
Tamizh mind, 118
Tamizh Pandyas and Chozhas, 65
Tamizh Saivaite, 60, 727
Tamraparni river, 63
Tanthi, Dina, 563
Tantrasangraha, 427
Tao of Physics, The (book), 415
Tarakachironmani, 423
Tarkacudamani, Sasadhar, 418
Tarun Bharat, 357
Tasadruk, 574
'Taylor-series' expansion, 427
TDB. *see* Travancore Devaswom Board
Teasdale, Wayne, 597, 607
Technological development, 422, 445, 463
Technology, 32, 114, 125, 139, 265, 319, 373, 402, 418, 421–422, 433–435, 439, 444–451, 454, 456–463, 465, 511, 541, 714, 720
Tegh Bahadur, Guru, 250, 252, 316, 378, 475, 488
Tehelka magazine, 566
Teilhard, 637
Temple entry, 36, 87, 170, 177, 193, 202, 204–206, 209, 358
  acharyas blessing, 206
  movement, 170, 192, 201, 202, 204
  orthodoxy opposing, 204.205
Teresa of Calcutta, 324–328, 331
Teresa, Saint, 324–325, 325–326, 328
Terror, 112, 231, 494, 540, 546, 555, 558, 592
  camps, 565, 569
  infrastructure, 555
  links, 111
  masterminds, 567
  outfits, 611
  plot code, 555
  radical Islamist, 570
  rumours, 568
  tactics, 615
  victims, 491
  war against, 50

Terrorism, 90, 316, 331, 490, 507, 511, 538, 552, 554, 557, 573
Thadiyantavide, Nazeer, 557
Thanthra Vidya Peedham, 362–363
Thapar, Rajguru, 302–305
Thapar, Romila, 33, 35–36, 76, 163, 164, 331, 332, 473, 483
Thapar, Sukhdev, 216, 229–230, 303–304, 305, 726
Tharoor, Shashi, 319, 547
Thejas publications, 564, 566, 570
Thengadi, Dattopant, 347, 349, 357, 375, 388–391, 388–394, 393–394, 423–424, 449, 724
Thenkasi, 559
Theo-diversity, 11, 19, 23, 32, 66, 89, 246, 275, 399, 498, 513, 524, 528, 551, 642, 644, 652, 656–657, 717, 719–720, 726
Theologians, 322, 597, 607, 636, 638, 649, 655
Theology, 285, 526, 584, 595, 624, 626, 631–632, 642, 652
  catholic, 636
  exclusivist, 626
  of fulfilment, 584, 586
  philosophical, 632
Thevar community, 355, 366
Thevendrakula Vellalar: Spiritual Heritage (book), 367
Thirukural, 157, 533
Thirumaavalavan, Thol, 473
Thirumalai Nayakar, Mahal of, 157
Thirumanthiram, 60, 533, 727
Thirumavalavan, 571
Thirunavukarasu, Marai, 204
Thiruvarur sculpture, 142
Thomas Commission, 557
Thomas, K. T., 649–650
Thomas, Lewis, 268
Thomas, St, 592, 603
Thomas, Wendell, 487
Thondan magazine, 201, 204–206, 209
  article on agony of Scheduled Communities, 204
  article on 'Love of Gothai,' 204–205
  cartoon supporting temple entry, 205–206
  contributors to, 201
  debate on revenue of Hindu temples, 202
  Malaviya's statement on Noakhali riots, 202–203
  Mukerjee's statement on Noakhali riots, 203
  opinion editorial, 203–204
  on orthodoxy opposing temple entry, 204.205
Thoreau, Henry, 449
Throckmorton, James, 116–117
Thupakki (movie), threats of violence against, 560–561
Tikoo, Tej K., 315
Tilak, Bal Gangadhar, 23, 25, 121, 141, 156, 164, 173–174, 264–265, 300, 359, 390, 399, 424
Tipu Sultan, 576
Tiranga jhanda, 310
Tirtha, Rama, 59
Tirtha, Swami Rama, 59
TKDL. *see* Traditional Knowledge Digital Library
TKRC. *see* Traditional Knowledge Resource Classification
TKS. *see* Traditional Knowledge Systems
TMMK. *see* Tamil Nadu Muslim Munnetra Kazhagam
TNTJ. *see* Tamil Nadu Towheed Jamat
Tolerance, 12, 19, 471, 477–478, 497, 514, 528, 548, 631
Trade union movement, 389, 391, 392, 717, 725
Traditionalists, 26, 29, 118, 166, 169–170, 175, 183, 258, 319, 418
Traditional Knowledge Digital Library, 435–439
Traditional Knowledge Resource Classification, 438
Traditional Knowledge Systems, 435, 438, 456, 458
Transformation, 4–6, 53, 124, 135, 164, 171, 257, 268, 273, 289, 359, 387, 452, 514, 541, 586, 607, 617

Trapnell, Judson B., 605
Travancore Devaswom Board, 363–364
Tribal communities, 53, 76, 152, 334, 612–614, 617–619, 643
Tribals, 23, 87, 135, 321, 474, 613–614, 618, 627–628
Tribes, 3, 12, 15, 52, 57, 87, 116–117, 165, 282–283, 341, 352, 613, 618, 657, 715, 721
Tricolour of India, 46, 310–314, 316–317. *see also* National flag
Trinity, 578, 588, 592, 597, 604
Tripura, Shanti Kumar, 612
True God, the, 600, 625
Trust, 9, 150, 177, 286, 508, 575, 588
Tsang, Hieun, 15
Tughlaq, Mohammad Bin, 62, 520, 545
Tukaram, 37, 42, 276, 395
Tukdoji Maharaj, Saint, 310, 405
Tully, Mark, 642
Turkey, 3, 34, 63, 94–95, 178, 264, 286, 545
Turmeric patents, 438
TVP. *see* Thanthra Vidya Peedham
Tyabji, Badruddin, 539
Tyagi, Mansa Ji, 200
Tyranny, 168, 174, 192, 229, 266, 282

U

Ucchedavada, 397
Udayanacarya, 487
UDF. *see* United Democratic Front
Udupi, 348, 350, 356, 365, 372
Udupi Conference, 349–350, 356
Udyogaparava, 421
UGC. *see* University Grants Commission
Unbelief, 179, 518, 521–522
Unification, 69, 300, 330, 363, 385
Union Carbide Plant, 325, 328
Union of Soviet Socialist Republics (USSR), 95, 225, 399
United Democratic Front, 569–570
United Nations, 97, 161–162, 219
United Progressive Alliance, 157, 212, 327, 566
United Provinces, 171
United States, 93, 95, 116, 120, 139, 199, 213, 250, 263–264, 266, 273, 278, 291, 433, 440, 446, 459, 476, 487, 573, 613, 622, 718
United States World Parliament of Religions, 622
Unity, 9–10, 12–13, 17, 21, 24, 27, 47, 60, 81, 91, 123, 147, 170, 192, 203, 248, 269, 271, 274, 276, 285, 291, 293, 330, 337, 343, 377, 386, 388, 397, 486, 494, 496, 505, 509, 521, 538, 596, 602–603, 633, 644, 725
- communal, 84
- conference, 356
- and diversity, 24
- economic, 93, 644
- geo-cultural, 399
- hymn, 487, 538
- Invocation, 487
- mantra, 716
- nation's, 85
- religious, 78, 177, 644
- social, 77, 271, 285

Universal ethics, 40
Universal Feminine, 634–635
Universalism, 384, 516, 542, 562, 588, 606
Universality, 32, 42
Universal Peace Temple, 537
University Grants Commission, 363, 434
Unknown Christ of Hinduism, The (thesis), 585
Unlawful Activities Prevention Act (UAPA), 565
Unnat Bharat Abhyan Campaign, 458
Untouchability, 20, 109, 121, 124, 127, 144, 166, 168, 170, 175–176, 178–180, 183–185, 201, 203, 278, 288, 300, 307, 319, 337, 342, 346–350, 353, 355–356, 358, 365, 370–372, 595, 651
Untouchables, 167–168, 170, 173, 186, 300, 346, 504, 651
UPA. *see* United Progressive Alliance
Upadhyaya, Deendayal, 78, 79, 90–93, 92, 127, 129, 374, 376, 379–380, 379–388, 380–381, 380–385,

382, 384–385, 384–388, 385, 387, 401, 446, 447, 449, 451, 719
Upanishadic thought, 5, 12, 38, 431
Upanishads, 2, 7, 10, 13, 25–26, 35, 38–39, 53, 77, 264–265, 302, 362, 430, 475–476, 482, 523–524, 545, 587, 590, 625, 632, 635, 637
Upper castes, 33–34, 36, 163–164, 180, 185–186, 188, 193, 364, 431, 440, 629
Uprising, 115, 226–227, 247, 307–309, 618, 718
1857 uprising, 226–227
Urbana-Champaign, 213
Urdu, 73, 264, 303, 575, 717
Uttar Pradesh, 109, 111, 346, 360, 548

V

Vac Sukta, 57–58
Vaidicism, 30
Vaidya, Ashok, 436
Vaidya,Vasant Annaji, 379–380
Vaikundar, Iyya, 20
Vaisheshika Darshana, 425–426
Vaishnava, 175, 518
Vaishnavaite, 394, 472, 600
Vaishnavaite-Vedantic Sufism, 519
Vaishnava Samajam, 203
Vaishnavism, 488, 603–604, 610
Vaishya, Muldas, 36
Vaishyas, 180, 256, 264, 343, 359, 715
Vajasaneyi Samhita, 57
Vajpayee, Atal Bihari, 94–95, 97, 108, 109, 136, 138, 376, 380, 393, 433, 459, 492–493, 615
Vajpayee government, 95, 97, 137, 212, 448, 617
Vajpayee-Musharraf Agra Summit meeting, 96
Vakil, A. K., 175
Valiaveetil, Chacko, 603
Vallalar, Chidambaram Ramalingam, 142
Vallalar, Ramalingam, 20, 35, 118, 119, 142
Valmiki, poet, 156
Value system, 275, 372, 424, 440
Vande Mataram, 48
  and Akhand Bharat, 46–47, 49, 51, 53, 55, 57, 59, 61, 63, 65, 67, 69, 71, 73, 75, 77, 79, 81, 83, 85, 87, 89, 91, 93, 95, 97, 99, 101, 103, 105, 107
  and Bharat Mata, 76
  music album titled, 76
  translation of, 72
Vangasena, 434
Vanvasi Kalyan Ashram, 89, 725
Varkey, Mathew, 649
Varnadharma, 170
Varna system, 23, 30, 34, 41, 127, 145, 168, 181–183, 256–258, 264, 339–341, 345, 371–372, 381, 386, 482, 715
  Golwalkar's views on, 343–351
Varna Vyavastha, 345, 386
Var Sri Bhagauti ji ki, 66
Vasant Vyakhyanmala lecture series, 351–353
Vashishtha Dharmasutra, 113
Vasishta, 499, 534–535
Vatican, 199, 627, 651
Vatican Council, 630
Vaughan, Adam, 455
Vedadhikara Nirupanam (book), 362
Vedanta, 26, 35, 40, 73, 323, 464, 476, 487, 519, 525, 542, 548, 580–581, 583–584, 595, 626, 635, 645
Vedanta Baskaran (book), 533
Vedantic humanism, 35
Vedantic monism, 472
Vedas, 7, 9–10, 22–23, 25–26, 30–31, 56, 60–61, 82, 105, 113, 118, 137, 157, 166, 170, 176, 197, 207, 255, 350, 356, 362, 431, 475, 482, 534, 542, 590, 595, 603, 637, 713
Vedic, 5, 15, 25–26, 31, 41, 54, 114, 137, 155, 226, 332, 362, 412, 471–472, 481–482, 484, 507, 603
  age, 114, 420

astrology course, 434
beef eating, myths of, 113
ceremony, 15, 121
conception of rashtri, 62
concept of ṛta, 5, 713
culture, 151, 155
deities, 6, 8, 11, 17, 52, 487, 726
dictum, 528, 645
imagery, 60, 155
literature, 6–7, 53–54, 113, 362, 471, 543, 637
mathematics, 456–457
period, 114, 137, 174, 226, 258, 603
religion, 5, 197, 255, 472, 474, 481, 488, 713, 726
rishis, 425, 522
rituals, 5, 8–9, 14, 56, 175, 201, 481–482
seers, 113, 362, 424
society, 5, 332, 471
tradition, 16, 114, 602–603, 637
veneration of cow, 114
Vedic Astrology, 432, 434
Vedic Authority, 22, 362, 472
Vedic Brahminism, 430, 481
Vedic Goddess, 8, 12, 54–57, 68, 78, 106, 114, 431, 482, 634, 722
Vedic Roots, 53, 57, 89
Vedic Science, 412, 424
Veer Savarkar Hindu Pad Padshahi, 297
Vegetarianism, 110, 140, 221, 535
Vellalars, Puranic forefather of, 367
Vendidad, 11
Venkataswamy, 501
Vernadsky, Vladimir Ivanovitch, 635
Verses, 26, 51, 53–54, 60, 76, 78, 117, 137, 158, 239, 254, 421, 471–472, 474, 486, 499, 520, 523, 533, 544–545, 715
beef-eating, 137
Dirghatmas, 471
divine-intoxicated, 522
emblematical, 66
inscriptional, 486
jihadic, 516
Koranic, 576
Vested interests, 35–36, 100, 188, 226, 318, 335–336, 350, 451, 454
VHP. *see* Vishwa Hindu Parishad
VIBHA (Vijnana Bharati), 456, 458, 725
Victorian holocaust and Indic resistance, 119–121
Victory, 63–65, 158, 184, 193, 196, 204, 219, 319, 359, 370, 480, 483, 516, 544, 552, 715
Vî-Daêvô-Data, 11
Vidhwa Ashram, 199
Vidhwa Viwah Samsthah, 199
Vidiyal Velli, 564
Vidiyal Velli (Dawn Friday) magazine, 564
Viduthalai Chiruthaigal Party (VCK), 571
Vidya Bharati, 301, 575–576, 725
Vigyan Bharati, 301
Vijaya Bharatam magazine, 654
Vijaya, daily paper, 73
Vijayanagara, 18, 64–65
Vijayanagar empire, 63, 486, 721
Vijnana Bharti, 458
Vilayati Mal, 72
Vilification of Hindu religion, 623
Violence, 2, 8, 62, 92, 108–109, 111, 127–128, 136, 166, 193, 223, 229, 235, 240–241, 245, 261, 268, 303, 323, 336, 361, 400, 473, 477–478, 482–484, 489–490, 505, 507, 539–540, 552, 558, 560, 576–577, 611–619, 626, 637, 652, 720
Vishal Hindu Dharma Sammelan, 362, 490
Vishal Hindu Sammelan, 362
Vishnu, 52–53, 78, 87, 104–105, 118, 190–191, 359, 396, 472, 481, 487, 532, 535, 582, 590, 604, 725–726
forms, 86
ncarnation of, 190
Vishnu Sahasranama, 305, 725
Vishnu temples in South India, 590
Vishnu worship, 713
Vishwa Hindu Parishad, 89, 109, 310, 330–331, 337, 347–348,

355–356, 408, 411, 433, 550, 616, 651
Visvakarma, 63
Viswa Hindu Parishad, 109, 310, 405, 725
Viswaroopam (movie), 561
Vivekananda, Swami, 21–23, 22–23, 26, 30, 35, 37, 38–40, 45, 74, 77, 80, 113, 164, 261, 262–264, 329, 334–335, 353, 359, 362, 371, 417, 419, 441–442, 530, 590, 591, 619–622, 620, 621, 625, 635, 716
  and Ambedkar, parallelism between, 353
  critics, 620
  image of masculine Hinduism, 260–261
  Irish disciple of Swami, 73
  lectures on Sri Ramakrishna, 262–263
  'make me a man' call of, 262
  and Sister Nivedita, 371
  and Sri Aurobindo, 164, 386
  and Sri Chattampi Swami, 362
Vivisection, 90, 253
Voice of India (book), 595, 628
Vote bank politics, 339, 351, 355, 364, 365, 366, 539, 564, 572
Vyasa-Ashrama, 534
Vyasa, Parasara, 534

W

Wadhwa Commission of Inquiry, 617
Wagamon SIMI training camp, 565
Wagner, Kim, 50
Wahdat ak-wujud, 521, 525
Wahdat al-wujud, 521
Wakankar, V. S., 397–398
Waqf Board, 550
War, 55, 63, 65, 93–94, 115, 125, 160, 173, 189, 192, 196, 218, 249, 251, 261, 274, 285, 288–289, 308, 323, 411, 608, 626, 636, 720
  chariots, 153
  civil, 398, 501
  communal, 292
  cultural, 624
  evangelical, 619
  fratricidal, 421
  goddess of, 232, 308
  intra-Hindu, 234
  religious, 246
  revolutionary, 227
  sacrifice, 232
  succession, 525
  theo-political, 292
Warmington, Eric Herbert, 61
Water bodies, 118, 185–186, 368, 452
Water management, 367–368
Watson, Jim, 455
Watts, Alan, 39, 632
Wavell, Archibald Percival, 160
Wavell, Lord, 160–161
Wealth, 23, 59, 64, 73, 256, 274, 330, 332, 367, 413, 566, 643, 651–652, 723
Weapons, 58, 61, 63, 66, 68, 241, 284, 411, 421, 564, 573, 611–612, 726
Weber, Edmund, 359
Welfare, 36, 159, 203–204, 254, 256, 288, 374, 390, 535, 614, 618, 723
We or Our Nationhood Defined (academic work), 191, 342
Whitewashing, 156, 235, 342, 378–379
White Yajur Veda, 420
Widows, 119, 176, 179, 185, 198–199, 282, 321, 327, 442, 602
Widows' Home of Baranagore, 262
Widows Remarriage Association, 199
Wiley, Curzon, 222
Williams, Monier, 15, 646
Williamson, Lola, 620
Wings of Fire (book), 608
Wisdom, 20, 32, 40, 53, 60–61, 118, 133, 178, 264–265, 267, 439, 477, 496, 534, 543, 572, 575, 589, 602, 640, 726
Women, 70, 156, 197–198, 231–233, 236, 243, 245, 247, 441, 459
  abduction of, 241, 244–245
  conversion of, 245–246

empowerment, 196–201, 459
abolition of sati, 196
female education, 200–201
great flood of 1934 and, 199
home for helpless women, 197–199
participation in freedom struggle, 196–197
prohibition of child marriage, 196, 197
raising marriage age of girls, 196–197
Vidhwa Ashram, 199
women abducted by Muslims, 199–200
liberation movement, 157
patriotic, 248
role in nation-building, 231–234
scientists, 456, 459–460
self-immolation of, 234, 236
Woo-Suk Hwang, 440, 715
Wordsworth, William, 449
World War, 287, 393, 715, 718
World War I, 71, 214, 251, 263, 287, 393
World War II, 194, 219, 723
Worship, 8–9, 11, 17, 23, 30, 39, 50–51, 57, 66, 70–71, 74–75, 77–78, 80, 122, 124, 129, 175, 184, 193, 258, 260, 284, 308, 328, 330, 334, 355–356, 362, 372, 376, 379, 383, 395, 397, 449, 471, 473, 479–480, 484, 494, 497, 500, 517, 522, 525, 528, 532, 537, 539, 590, 592, 600, 607, 617, 626, 634, 642, 644, 713, 715, 722, 724

Y

Yadav, Akhilesh, 109
Yadav, Hansraj, 605
Yadav, Shankardev, 237
Yajna, 330, 332, 637
Yajur and Sama Vedas, 8
Yajur Veda, 8, 57, 113
Yama, 55, 216, 487
Yameen, Abdullah, 99
Yamini, ruler of Ghazni, 486
Yamuna Bai, 246
Yasodharma, 17, 474, 479–480
YATS. *see* Young Astronomer Talent Search
Yazidis, 234, 240–241, 243, 245
Yoga, 7, 10, 14, 41, 71, 329, 438, 461, 494, 518, 579–580, 591, 605–607, 624, 645
Christianizing, 579–580
of Jnana, 533
karma, 494
Yoga Vasishta, 499, 522, 523
Yogendraji, Sri, 605
Yogi, 44, 532–533, 579, 598
Yogic practices, 536–537
Yogic tradition, 532, 721
Young Astronomer Talent Search, 336
Yugantar Ashram, 264

Z

Zafar, Bahadur Shah, 122, 248
Zarathustra, 477, 640
Zarradi, Sheikh Fakhruddin, 545
Zeal, 122, 173, 175, 585, 643
Zen Roshi, 477, 640
Zia-ur-Rahman, 94
Zilli, Ishtiaq Ahmed, 516
Zinat Mahal, Begum, 248
Zionism, 502–503, 505
zoology, importance of studying, 266–269
Zoroaster, cult of, 11
Zoroastrian monotheism, 11
Zoroastrian religion, 12
Zoroastrians, 16, 148

Books by BluOne Ink

Kali Imprint

Sri Aurobindo & the Literary Renaissance of India
by Pariksith Singh
ISBN: 9788194954781 | ₹995

Sri Aurobindo and Philosophy
by Pariksith Singh
ISBN: 9789392209017 | ₹995

Somewhere Among the Stars
by Adi Varuni
ISBN: 9789392209215 | ₹395

The Eternal Feminine
by Dr. Alok Pandey
ISBN: 9788194954774 | ₹699

Integral Education
by Partho
ISBN: 9788194954705 | ₹499

BluPrint Imprint

Identity's Last Secret
by Makarand R Paranjape
ISBN: 9788194954798 | ₹1495

Swayam Se Parichay (in Hindi)
by Pariksith Singh
ISBN: 9789392209185 | ₹195

Chhutti Ke Din (bilingual in Hindi and Rajasthani)
by Pariksith Singh
ISBN: 9789392209024 | ₹699

Anjali Geetan Ri (in Rajasthani)
by Ikraam Rajasthani
ISBN: 9789392209277 | ₹250

Jana Awjanar Majhe (in Bengali)
by Bimal Chakravartty
ISBN: 9789392209277 | ₹250

The Eternal Gene and Other Tales of Malaise
by Ankush Sam Thorpe
ISBN: 978-93-92209-14-7 | ₹495

Occam Imprint

Confidence Cures
by Lt Gen. S. B. Sehajpal and Mrs Kiran Sehajpal
ISBN: 9789392209260 | ₹395

War Despatches 1971
by Brigadier B. S. Mehta
ISBN: 9789392209123 | ₹899

March to Justice
by Navdeep Singh and Frank Rosenblatt
ISBN: 9788194954712 | ₹995

The Fighting Fourth
by Brigadier Jasbir Singh, SM,
ISBN: 9788194954750 | ₹699

Once Upon a Time in RIMC
by Brigadier Jasbir Singh, SM
ISBN: 9788194954729 | ₹250

Design: A Business Case
by Brigitte Borja de Mozota and Steinar Valade-Amland
ISBN: 9788194954743 | ₹795

MRA Made Simple: Seriously?
by Pariksith Singh, MD and Lynda Dilts-Benson
ISBN: 9781954261006 | $29.99

Compliance Made Simple: Seriously?
by Pariksith Singh, MD and Lynda Dilts-Benson
ISBN: 9781954261013 | $55.99

Snakes in the Ganga: Breaking India 2.0
by Rajiv Mlahotra and Vijaya Viswanathan
ISBN: 978-93-92209-09-3 | ₹895

Bharat ke Janjatiya Krantiveer:
Swatantrata Sangram ki 75 Unsuni Kahaniyaan (in Hindi)
by Dhaval Patel
ISBN: 978-93-92209-16-1

Forthcoming Titles by BluOne Ink

All Stray Dogs Go to Heaven
by Krishna Candeth
ISBN: 978-93-92209-08-6

Life of an Industani: Six Degrees of Separation
by Shiv Kunal Verma
ISBN: 978-93-92209-15-4

Grit to Glory: Raising the 13 Armoured
by Brig. B.S. Mehta
ISBN: 978-93-92209-29-1

Seeing with Hands
by Jinan K.B.
ISBN: 978-93-92209-00-0